About The Nat
Gardens Sche

Welcome to The Yellow Book and to the nearly 4,000 gardens inside, just waiting to be discovered.

The National Gardens Scheme has been opening gardens for charity since 1927, so by visiting an NGS garden this year you will be following in a grand tradition and making a vital contribution to the nursing and caring charities the NGS supports.

Thanks to the generosity and hard work of garden owners, volunteers and visitors, in 2012 the NGS donated £2.6 million to charity. On page 7, our beneficiaries tell us what this consistent funding means to them, and how these 'unrestricted' funds enable them to carry on their invaluable day-to-day work and undertake projects crucial to their future development.

Most of the gardens that open for The National Gardens Scheme are privately owned and offer visitors a unique opportunity to enjoy the garden owners' individual creations. The variety is breathtaking: from village openings to roof gardens, tiny cottage gardens to rolling acres, allotments to barges, you will find gardens to inform and inspire. Your donation, as well as the tea and cake you eat and the lovely plants you buy, will make a real difference to the life of someone who needs care or support at a critical time in their life.

Enjoy your garden visiting in 2013.

Thank you.
Your visit to a garden really counts.

CLARENCE HOUSE

The terrible weather throughout most of the 2012 Summer clearly tested any organization that depends on people visiting gardens for its livelihood and I expected the National Gardens Scheme to be no exception. So I was greatly heartened to hear that, thanks to the stalwart determination of the garden owners and volunteers, and the loyalty of visitors, the charity held up remarkably well in the circumstances.

The sense of well-being that comes from spending time in a garden, the rewards of taking a loved one on such a visit, or the feeling of involvement in one's local community as you admire a neighbour's garden together, are clearly all of great importance to National Gardens Scheme visitors. They will not be deterred by a spot of rain!

I would like to take the opportunity to thank all of those who open their gardens in support of the National Gardens Scheme, or who are involved in organizing the openings, for all that they do to provide so many people with a rich variety of rewards, and to offer my very best wishes for every success in 2013.

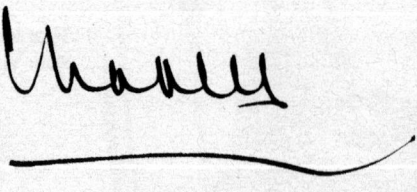

The Old Vicarage, Leics & Rutland by Suzie Gibbons, Midney Gardens, Somerset by Heather Edwards, Hidden Valley Gardens, Cornwall by Marianne Majerus

Contents

ngs gardens open for charity

The National Gardens Scheme
A company limited by guarantee. Registered in England & Wales. Charity No. 1112664. Company No. 5631421

Registered & Head Office: Hatchlands Park, East Clandon, Guildford, Surrey, GU4 7RT

T 01483 211535
Web www.ngs.org.uk

Published by Constable, an imprint of Constable & Robinson Ltd, 55-56 Russell Square, London WC1B 4HP
CONSTABLE
Independent Thinking Since 1895
www.constablerobinson.com

Front cover image: 30 Compton Way, Hampshire
Photographer: Leigh Clapp

Who's who in the NGS

Congratulations to NGS President Joe Swift whose first show garden at Chelsea was awarded an RHS Gold Medal. He is pictured here in his award-winning garden beside one of the huge cedar wood frames which were a feature of the garden. Says Joe:

'My garden was inspired by a lifetime of living in the city. It aimed to provide the home owner with an escape from the man-made surroundings of concrete, glass and steel and connect them with more tactile natural materials.'

Chairman's Message

Having celebrated our 85th birthday last year, we start 2013 optimistically and with nearly 4,000 gardens. Thank you for buying this book which will lead you to gardens of all shapes and sizes – there is something to please everyone. Your visits will enable us to continue to donate substantial sums to the charities we support.

As always we are enormously grateful to the owners who open their gardens and provide pleasure and inspiration, not to mention a great deal of knowledge, to all who attend the open days. What they all have in common is a warm welcome and a desire to foster the community spirit. Many of them also offer home-made teas.

In Her Majesty's Diamond Jubilee year we were honoured to be received at Sandringham to present a commemorative plaque recognising Sandringham as one of our founder gardens. It is a magnificent record that Sandringham has opened every year since 1927.

This year sees the first National Gardens Weekend – the 15 and 16 June. Over 800 gardens will open all around the country and we hope the event will attract significant publicity and spread the word about The National Gardens Scheme, what we do and why we do it. The aim is to reach a wider audience, including those who have never heard of gardens open to the public.

To you, our visitors, our volunteer teams, our garden owners and our staff at Hatchlands my warmest thanks for everything you do to contribute to the continuing success of The National Gardens Scheme.

So, enjoy your garden visits, and thank you for supporting The National Gardens Scheme.

Penny Snell

Above: Penny pictured in her own garden, Moleshill House, Surrey. Image: Nicola Stocken Tomkins
Below: Her Majesty the Queen receives the commemorative plaque from Penny

Our Charitable Heritage

The National Gardens Scheme was founded by the Queen's Nursing Institute to raise funds to support district nurses, for whom the QNI was responsible until the introduction of the National Health Service in 1948. At that time the Scheme had become so successful and popular that the QNI continued it as an annual fundraising project. In 1980 the QNI created an independent charity with the foundation of the National Gardens Scheme Charitable Trust.

Below: Pictured at Help the Hospices Awards 2012, sponsored by the NGS: Lord Howard of Lympne, Chairman of Help the Hospices, Sister Frances Dominica, founder of Helen & Douglas House Hospice, Oxford, and pioneer of palliative care for the young, Recipient of Lifetime Achievement Award and George Plumptre, Chief Executive of the NGS

In addition to supporting the QNI the annual distribution of funds was extended from the 1980s to other particular charities in nursing and caring: Macmillan Cancer Support; the Gardeners' Royal Benevolent Society (now Perennial); the Royal Fund for Gardeners' Children (now merged with Perennial), Marie Curie Cancer Care; Help the Hospices; and Crossroads Care (now Carers Trust).

Since our foundation we have donated some £40 million to nominated beneficiaries, of which nearly £25 million has been given in the last ten years. Our continuing support means that for most of our beneficiaries we are the largest cumulative donor in their histories; this is the case with our two largest beneficiaries, Macmillan Cancer Support and Marie Curie Cancer Care.

The physical and mental health benefits of visiting gardens and, indeed, of actual gardening are very real and form an increasingly significant link between The National Gardens Scheme and its beneficiaries. In a sense it is integral to our charitable heritage. Working together with our beneficiaries for the maximum benefits for all of our audiences is a major priority and we must say thank you to three leading figures who left beneficiary partners in 2012: Tom Hughes-Hallett (since 2012 Sir Tom in recognition of his contribution to palliative care) who retired as Chief Executive of Marie Curie; Rosemary Cook who retired as Director of the Queen's Nursing Institute; and Anne Roberts who retired as Chief Executive of Crossroads Care.

Since 2010 a different annual 'guest' charity has been chosen from recommendations from NGS volunteers. In 2013 the guest charity will be Parkinson's UK. In 2012 the first bursaries from the Elspeth Thompson Memorial Fund (set up by the NGS in 2011) were paid out to small community gardening projects around the country, and the NGS currently provides an annual bursary for a trainee at the Garden Museum in London. The NGS continues to support the National Trust's careership scheme.

The National Gardens Scheme's commitment to nursing and caring remains constant. Every visitor to an NGS garden is making an essential contribution to the care of others, in particular care at home and for those with chronic or life-threatening illness.

Our Beneficiaries

WE ARE MACMILLAN. CANCER SUPPORT

The NGS has been a partner of Macmillan Cancer Support since 1985 and is proud to be the charity's largest single donor. Raising in excess of £13.7 million, this has funded over 143 Macmillan services including clinical nursing specialists, financial advisors, dieticians, physiotherapists and counsellors, helping to make a huge difference to the lives of thousands of people affected by cancer across the UK.

Marie Curie Cancer Care

The NGS has supported Marie Curie Cancer Care for over 15 years, raising a staggering £6 million during this time. This money enables the charity to continue to provide high quality nursing, totally free, to give people with terminal cancer and other illnesses the choice of dying at home, supported by their families.

Help the Hospices

Help the Hospices champions the very best care for everyone facing the end of life. The NGS has supported us, and through our work more than 200 hospices, since 1997. Over the years, generous funding from NGS has supported a variety of programmes including training for hospice staff, equipment for delivering hospice at home, hospice awards and national projects supporting clinical excellence.

carers trust
action · help · advice

Carers Trust works to improve support, services and recognition for anyone living with the challenges of caring, unpaid, for a family member or friend who is ill, frail, disabled or has mental health or addiction problems. Ongoing support from the NGS has meant so much to carers over the years, and countless individuals have benefited as a direct result of its donations.

Qni The Queen's Nursing Institute

The Queen's Nursing Institute campaigns for the best possible nursing care for patients in their own homes. Our community of Queen's Nurses leads by example, and we support practical projects in the community to improve patient care. We believe that skilled, professional and dedicated nursing should be available to everyone, where and when they need it

PERENNIAL
Gardeners' Royal Benevolent Society
Helping Horticulturists In Need Since 1839

Through Perennial, the NGS helps horticulturists who are facing difficulties. The NGS donation is invaluable to the charity's on-going work to help individuals and families. The annual donation to Perennial for gardeners' children also enables on-going support for families when one or both parents have died, and for children who are disadvantaged by other circumstances.

National Trust

Through the donation to the National Trust, the NGS is helping the Trust train new gardeners in the skills and knowledge they need to manage the nation's greatest historic gardens, many of which in turn continue to open for the NGS.

In short, every visitor to an NGS garden is helping to make an essential contribution to someone's life, and especially those who really need care or support through times of personal crisis or chronic and life threatening illness. Thank you!

The Society of Garden Designers

This year The National Gardens Scheme and The Society of Garden Designers have joined forces in an initiative to shine the spotlight on professionally designed gardens. Founded in 1981, the Society is the only professional body for garden designers in the UK and counts some of the leading garden designers among its growing membership. Some of the Society's members have opened for the NGS in previous years but this year introduces many more designers' gardens to the public. This is our first year working with the NGS and I hope that the partnership will gather momentum to become a significant part of the NGS. Of particular interest will be the members' own gardens. It is in our own gardens that we experiment, learn, and develop. Of the gardens that I have visited through the NGS, I have loved most those that show a particular vision either through their focus on a genus or through an unexpected way of forming a garden. The great strength of the Scheme lies in the diversity of work that it encompasses. It is exciting that the gardens that are being opened by members of The Society of Garden Designers demonstrate that there are many ways to design a garden. Some of the highlights are:

Helen Thomas's beautiful romantic garden at **Hill Farm** in Surrey (above) has a looseness and delicacy not often associated with designed gardens. Her understanding of light is shown in her use of grasses punctuated by the weight of the heads of tall Echinacea and Sedum. The style of planting, developed from the German school of naturalistic perennial planting, has a quality reminiscent of the Arts and Crafts movement that complements the Victorian Picturesque style of the house.

While in Berkshire, Virginia von Celsing's own garden at **Pyt House** (left) is a masterpiece of formal elegance and restraint. Strong textures of foliage are interspersed with repeated blocks of flowering bulbs in Spring in formal beds adjacent to the drive. Densely planted beds overflowing over terraces and paths lead the eye out to the fields.

Fiona Cadwallader's garden, **Watergate House** in Kent (above), with its pergola of roses and stone paths, is exuberant in its planting and use of colour.

A classic cruciform design for the walled garden at **The Manor House**, Ayot St Lawrence, (right) Hertfordshire by Julie Toll is gentle in its quiet palette of yellow irises and white allium planted in stone framed beds. At the centre is a square pool with a vortex fountain by Arc Angel. In another part of the garden, the Elizabethan house has inspired the paving in brick and gravel with a parterre of clipped box and topiary set within yew hedges.

In complete contrast is Ian Kitson's remarkable dynamic and fluid design for **Follers Manor** in Sussex. The garden, shown on television in the Landscape Man, is extraordinarily complex

and won three awards in The Society of Garden Designers' 2012 Awards. I was immensely impressed when I visited it this summer. The sinuous flint walls cut into the sloping domed lawn lead from sunken sitting courts to a curvaceous pool traversed by a wooden bridge with a sunset deck. The garden is the foreground to a magnificent valley in the downs behind the coast. Its borrowing of the wider landscape gives it a grandeur of scale and vision that belies its actual size.

Modern classicism is represented by Tom Stuart Smith's fine walled garden at **Broughton Grange**, Oxfordshire. The terraced beds of perennial planting march down the hill to a great formal pool. Here, and in his own garden, **The Barn**, Abbots Langley (see Serge Hill Gardens), Hertfordshire, the use of perennial planting predominates. It is exciting to be able to visit both these gardens and to see the contrast between a garden designed for a client and the garden made for himself and in a state of constant change and experimentation using herbaceous planting set against clipped yew.

One of the great strengths of The National Gardens Scheme is its broadness of scope and scale. At the opposite end of the spectrum are Pamela Johnson's small London garden at **20 Eatonville Road, SW17**, which is exciting in its wonderful combinations of colour and texture in the planting, and Rosemary Coldstream's front garden at **3 St Mary's Walk**, Hertfordshire (above) dominated by box which is baroque in its vigour and boldness. It is exciting to see a front garden which I hope will be an inspiration and manifesto for planting over paving.

Some of the gardens which are opening under the joint scheme are new to it and some have opened many times for The National Gardens Scheme, like Pamela Johnson's which she has opened for 20 years. I too have opened our garden at **51 The Chase, SW4** (left) for the NGS and the RHS for a number of years and found it both rewarding and stimulating. Each year we have had visitors who have come back. A garden is always changing; showing it gives an added incentive to review, revise, and introduce new elements.

I hope that the collaboration will initiate an exciting dialogue between designer and visitor as most designers will be in the gardens for the NGS days.

Charles Rutherfoord
Past Chairman,
Society of Garden Designers

For a list of participating designers, see 715

Carers Trust

Since 1999, funding from The National Gardens Scheme has been instrumental in helping Crossroads Care support carers across England and Wales. In that time NGS has been the charity's largest supporter, giving it more than £1.5m.

So when Crossroads Care merged with The Princess Royal Trust for Carers in Spring 2012, it was delighted that NGS offered to continue with the same support for the newly formed Carers Trust.

Carers Trust is now the UK's largest carers' charity and its Network Partners – Crossroads Care schemes and The Princess Royal Trust for Carers centres – support over 443,000 carers, including more than 34,000 young carers.

With its Network Partners, Carers Trust offers a range of services, support and information to help carers in communities across the UK and Isle of Man.

It also works to raise the profile of carers and the caring role, with all activities geared towards achieving its vision of a world where the role and contribution of unpaid carers is recognised, and where they have access to the quality support and services they need to live their own lives.

NGS's support ties in exactly to this vision, and its donations have been used to develop new services for carers.

In the last two years alone NGS has enabled the charity to launch a fund to establish or extend volunteer-led activities in six locations across its network, as well as the development of three new projects to involve carers of people with dementia.

Examples of these include: an initiative to develop a volunteer befriending service for carers to help them avoid the pitfalls of social isolation; helping carers get online to find quicker ways of accessing the support they need as a carer; and a project to develop a dementia care service that provides respite for the carer and support for the person with dementia.

Each project is producing a series of toolkits and service development models for distribution across the network, enabling all Network Partners to ultimately benefit from NGS's funding.

The learnings will also be used to provide evidence of what works to secure future funding from other sources.

Thea Stein, Chief Executive of Carers Trust, thanked NGS for its continued commitment.

'The concept of opening your garden to raise funds for charity is so simple, yet its impact is huge,' she said.

'NGS's very generous ongoing support has meant so much to carers over the years, and countless individuals have benefited as a direct result of its donations.

'This is such an exciting time for Carers Trust as we look to build on the legacy of both founding charities and use our new voice, strength and reach to support even more carers.

'I would like to express my sincere thanks to all those involved with NGS for the hard work, dedication and generosity they have shown towards carers - either through opening their gardens or by visiting them. You have all made a huge difference to lives of countless carers across the UK.'

carerstrust
action · help · advice

Yellow Book on the Move

Find details of nearly 4,000 gardens to visit with our free iOS app

The app features these shiny features:

- See what's on and share garden opening details with friends via Facebook and Twitter
- Search for and find nearly 4,000 NGS gardens close to your current location or postcode
- View galleries of spectacular images of these gardens
- Latest opening times, prices, contact details and directions
- Save your favourite places – where you've been and where you'd like to go
- Send your friends email invites to visit gardens with you
- Sign-up to receive weekly suggestions of gardens to visit

Our app is suitable for iPhone and iPod Touch running iOS 3.0+.
Screen shot representative of product.

To find out more scan the QR Code.

Also follow The National Gardens Scheme on Twitter and Facebook

YORKSHIRE TEA
TAYLORS OF HARROGATE
YORKSHIRE TEA
For Hard Water
Let's have a proper brew
80 TEA BAGS

National Gardens Weekend

Come rain or shine, the length and breadth of England and Wales, from the earliest snowdrops to the last autumn leaves, there is hardly a weekend when there won't be a yellow 'Garden Open Today' poster to tempt you with the promise of horticultural treasures, and, all the better, tea and home-made cake.

Explore the 2013 Yellow Book and, comfortingly, you will find things just as they should be.

But what's this in the middle of June? **National Gardens Weekend**?

DORSET 181

Sunday 9
Bexington
Butts Cottage
Frankham Farm
Grange Cottage
Manor Farm, Hampreston
Old Down House
Wednesday 12
Broomhill

National Gardens Weekend

Saturday 15
Annalal's Gallery
Chiffchaffs
Chine View
Cottage Row (Evening)
Deans Court
25 Field Barn Drive
Grange Cottage
Holworth Farmhouse
Knitson Old Farmhouse
Mayfield
Mews Cottage
'OLA'
Pilsdon View
Windy Willums
Wolverhollow
Sunday 16
Annalal's Gallery
24 Carlton Road North
Chiffchaffs
Chine View
Cottage Row
Deans Court
Farrs
25 Field Barn Drive
Grange Cottage
Holworth Farmhouse
Knitson Old Farmhouse
Mews Cottage
The Old Vicarage
Q
Windy Willums
Wolverhollow
Monday 17
'OLA'
Tuesday 18
Braddocks
Wednesday 19
Horn Park
Friday 21
Herons Mead (Evening)
Saturday 22
Chideock Manor
Lytchett Minster Gardens
Sunday 23
Chideock Manor
Lytchett Minster Gardens
Manor House, Blandford
The Mill House
The Old Rectory, Manston
2 Pyes Plot
24a Western Avenue

Tuesday 25
Littlebredy Walled Gardens
Pilsdon View
Wednesday 26
Manor House, Blandford
The Old Rectory, Manston
Friday 28
Marren
Saturday 29
The Manor House, Beaminster
Marren
Snape Cottage Plantsman's Garden
Sunday 30
Corfe Barn
4 Noel Road
Snape Cottage Plantsman's Garden

July

Tuesday 2
Littlebredy Walled Gardens
Wednesday 3
Deans Court
Friday 5
Knitson Old Farmhouse
Saturday 6
Kingston Lacy
Knitson Old Farmhouse
Little Bindon
55 Lonnen Road
Sunday 7
Broomhill
Kingston Lacy
Knitson Old Farmhouse
Little Bindon
55 Lonnen Road
4 Noel Road
Tuesday 9
Pilsdon View
Saturday 13
Cranborne Manor Garden
25 Richmond Park Avenue
Sunday 14
Bexington
Corscombe House
Hilltop
The Manor House, Beaminster
25 Richmond Park Avenue
357 Ringwood Road
Thursday 18
25 Richmond Park Avenue
Sunday 21
Annalal's Gallery
Farrs
25 Field Barn Drive
Hilltop
Lakeside
Meadow Views
Wednesday 24
Lakeside

Thursday 25
The Secret Garden and Serles House
Saturday 27
Holy Trinity Environmental Garden
Lakeside
25 Richmond Park Avenue
Snape Cottage Plantsman's Garden
Sunday 28
25 Field Barn Drive
Hilltop
22 Holt Road

Visit a new garden . . .

Holy Trinity Environmental Garden
The Old Rectory, Pulham
25 Richmond Park Avenue
The Secret Garden and Serles House
Snape Cottage Plantsman's Garden
Wednesday 31
The Old Rectory, Pulham
357 Ringwood Road

August

Saturday 3
55 Lonnen Road
Sunday 4
Hilltop
55 Lonnen Road
Manor Farm, Hampreston
Q
The Secret Garden and Serles House
Wednesday 7
Manor Farm, Hampreston
Thursday 8
The Secret Garden and Serles House
Saturday 10
The Secret Garden and Serles House
Sunday 11
Annalal's Gallery
Cottesmore Farm
Domineys
Hilltop
Holworth Farmhouse
24a Western Avenue

Visit a garden on National Gardens Weekend 15 & 16 June

Top: Crawley Gardens, Hampshire
Bottom: Teas at Low Fell, Cumbria by Linda Greening

For the very first time, The National Gardens Scheme has declared a **National Gardens Weekend**, inviting as many gardens as possible to take part in this unique festival of great gardens – large and small – opening for charity.

An astounding 800 gardens have answered the call, making the weekend of the 15th and 16th June the largest garden visiting event in history.

With a fanfare of national publicity, the **National Gardens Weekend** will spread the word to those who are missing out: those who have never heard of the NGS, or, if they have, have only the vaguest notion of what the NGS is and what it stands for: at its heart the remarkable gardens, and beyond, the wider goal of £2.6 million – and more year by year to the beneficiary charities.

Cities, towns, villages and country lanes will be ablaze with yellow, with arrows, posters and balloons pointing the way. Regular visitors will be joined by a throng of new faces, caught up in the excitement.

For 86 years, thanks to the generous spirit of garden owners and hard-working volunteer teams, the NGS has been quietly making a difference to thousands of lives. To those in the know, a flash of yellow in the hedge or on a lamppost means the promise of an excellent garden and home-made refreshments, as well as the knowledge that every garden visit makes a difference to the life of someone needing care or support.

To those **not** in the know, **what** pleasures lie in store!

Who will be able to resist three Manor Houses, including a C19 pinnacled, castellated Rectory Manor House with a fully working kitchen garden, three Old Rectories and four Old Vicarages? The evocative Owl End, or The Miller's Cottage where 'the roses grow like Topsy'? Or the apparently less romantic 11 Park Avenue North, Crouch End, delightfully contradicted by its 'profusion of the exotic and spiky'?

Above: Joshua Kazombo helps put out the signs for Abbotskerswell Gardens in Devon. Joshua is grandson of Jenny & Dave Brook, garden owners at Karibu, one of the gardens opening with the Abbotskerswell group for the National Gardens Weekend.

Come and join the celebration.

Thanks to John Larbalestier for kind permission to use his delightful cartoon which first appeared in the 2004 Yellow Book.

Join the queue, and join the NGS family!

Crabtree & Evelyn®
GARDENERS
Hand Care Collection
Our English passion for gardening inspired the Gardeners Collection; intensive formulas to help restore, soothe and protect hard-working hands.
Free delivery when you spend £20 or more at crabtree-evelyn.co.uk
Enter Code NGSDEL
CRABTREE & EVELYN
GARDENERS
Hand Therapy
CRABTREE & EVELYN
GARDENERS
Hand Therapy
www.crabtree-evelyn.co.uk

Image courtesy of Kiftsgate Court Gardens www.kiftsgate.co.uk

Emma Bridgewater's growing garden

Our growing garden of flowers is more glorious than ever this year. Fittingly, our Sunflower mug continues to be a favourite, as this year Emma and Matthew planted a Sunflower field on the Eastwood Bank land next to our sunny factory in Stoke-on-Trent. For Spring 2013 we're introducing six new mugs into the range including brand new Dahlia and seasonal Snowdrop. Perfect for Valentine's Day and Mother's Day, the Flowers mugs continue to be one of Emma Bridgewater's bestselling patterns and the NGS receives a donation for every piece sold.

Emma Bridgewater®
Some of the nicest things in your kitchen...

Griffin Glasshouses

Griffin Glasshouses is proud to support The National Gardens Scheme as its partner. Griffin Glasshouses creates beautiful bespoke glasshouses, greenhouses and orangeries for discerning gardeners, featuring The National Gardens Scheme (NGS) Collection. This exclusive collection includes five popular designs which can be personalised with a range of accessories and finished in any colour. Griffin's glasshouses are individually designed to be perfect for you, offering many gardener-friendly features, virtually no maintenance and with a lifetime structural guarantee.

GRIFFIN GLASSHOUSES
GLASSHOUSES OF DISTINCTION

Dobies of Devon

By opening their wonderful gardens to the public, the gardeners within The National Gardens Scheme have not only provided great days out and inspiration for millions of visitors but have also raised remarkable sums for many very worthwhile causes. Dobies of Devon, alongside our customers, are proud to support The National Gardens Scheme by raising funds through our plant and seed catalogues and hope to do so for many years to come.

DOBIES of Devon

Buy a Woodmansterne greeting card and spread the word

Woodmansterne's greeting cards have been bringing awareness of the NGS brand to the High Street since 2006 and helping to contribute to the wonderful work of the charities the NGS supports.

Look out for the ever-changing photography being added every year (around 25 designs across different shapes and sizes this year alone). Ever popular are favourite themes such as making fun in the garden, relaxing, admiring flowers and cheeky garden animals. A range of small square cards are the latest innovation.

Cards are available from all good independent card and gift shops, garden centres and WHSmith, Waitrose, and John Lewis.

Woodmansterne

Top-notch British greeting cards for thoughts that count

Quality Garden Tours

Brightwater Holidays support The National Gardens Scheme

Brightwater Holidays are proud to present four holidays for 2013 that directly support The National Gardens Scheme. They will donate a percentage of each booking taken for these four tours to The National Gardens Scheme as well as the donations to the NGS gardens visited.

Experienced tour leaders will lead the four tours in 2013:

Private Gardens of Yorkshire – departs May 31

Lakeland Gardens – departs June 24

London's Secret Gardens – departs July 9

Hidden Gardens of Devon – departs Sept 13

For full details contact Brightwater Holidays 01334 657155 or ngs@brightwaterHolidays.com

brightwater holidays

How to use your Yellow Book

This book lists all gardens opening for the NGS between January 2013 and early 2014. It is divided up into county sections, each including a calendar of opening dates and details of each garden, listed alphabetically.

There are three simple ways to find gardens to visit:

1 **If you are looking for a specific garden**, you can look it up in the index at the back, or if you know which county it is in, you can go straight to the relevant county section.

2 **If you want to find out more about gardens near you or in a specific location**, go to the relevant county map (at the front of each section) and look for the numbered markers. Use those numbers to look up further information in the county listings.

3 **If you are looking to see what is open near you on a specific date**, go straight to the relevant county. There is a calendar of opening dates after each county map.

Images and longer descriptions of the 4,000 gardens that will open this year on behalf of The National Gardens Scheme can be found by visiting: **www.ngs.org.uk**

County name
Gardens in England are listed first, followed by gardens in Wales.

Description
A short description of each garden covers the main features. This is written by the garden owner.

National Gardens Weekend
Garden participating in the NGS National Gardens Weekend on 15 & 16 June 2013.

Group opening information
Showing gardens that open together on the same day or days.

Admission price
The admission price applies to all visitors unless exceptions are noted e.g. child free.

Directions
A simple set of directions to each garden. Most gardens also list postcodes for use with computer or satellite navigation systems.

GWENT 675

in the village of Llanover. Home-made teas. **Adm £5, chd free.** Sat 17 Aug (2-5). **Visitors also welcome by appt Mar to Oct.**
15-acre listed garden and arboretum with well preserved water features and walled gardens. The Rhyd-y-meirch stream tumbles into ponds, down cascades and beneath flagstone bridges suitable for playing poo-sticks. Lawns for children to run around on or play hide and seek. In the circular walled garden the enormous herbaceous borders designed by Mary Payne are full of colour in August. Delicious home-made teas. The House (not open) is the birthplace of Augusta Waddington, Lady Llanover, nineteenth century patriot and supporter of the Welsh Language. The flock of Welsh Black Mountain Sheep which she introduced to Llanover, can still be seen grazing in the park. Gravel and grass paths, lawns.

GROUP OPENING

21 LLANTHONY AND DISTRICT GARDENS
Llanthony NP7 7LB. *5m N of Abergavenny. From Abergavenny r'about take A465 N towards Hereford. After 4.8m turn L onto Old Hereford Rd signed Pantygelli 2m. Mione is ½ m on L. Directions to the other gardens provided from here.* **Combined adm £5.50, chd free (share to Llanthony & District Garden Club).** Sun 30 June (2-6).

CRUCORNEY ALLOTMENTS
Crucorney Allotment Society

MIONE
Yvonne & John O'Neil

PERTHI CRWN
Jim Keates

TRWYN TAL
Mr & Mrs Hart

Three country gardens and a new community allotment site, set in the famously beautiful Llanthony valley of the Black Mountains, around the village of Llanvihangel Crucorney near Abergavenny. The tour incl Mione, a small, modern village garden of unusual plantsman's perennials, sheltered by a rose and clematis-clad pergola underplanted with a fine collection of ferns and a richly planted natural pool with glimpses of the Skirrid mountain beyond; Trwyn Tal, an upland farm cottage with a small modern garden on several levels, pond, a hard-working vegetable patch, and fabulous views down the Llanthony valley; Perthi-Crwn, a garden of broad terraces and stunning views, with a small, walled vegetable garden, teas and plant sales; and a new allotment scheme at Llanvihangel Crucorney, already fully subscribed and thriving (growing advice on offer during NGS openings).

Lawns for children to run around on or play hide and seek . . .

22 LONGHOUSE FARM
Penrhos, Raglan NP15 2DE. Mr & Mrs M H C Anderson. *Midway between Monmouth & Abergavenny. 4m from Raglan. Off Old Raglan/Abergavenny rd signed Clytha. At Bryngwyn/Great Oak Xrds take turn to Great Oak. In Great Oak follow NGS signs from red telephone box down narrow lane.* Home-made teas. **Adm £4, chd free.** Sun 16 June (2-6).
20 yrs, and ongoing, of developing this hidden 2 acre garden with a south facing terrace, millrace wall, pond, spacious lawns. Colourful and unusual plants varying from blossom, irises, summer bulbs, roses, vegetables to asters, grasses and a malus avenue of autumn colour. Unspoilt vistas of Monmouthshire.

THE NEUADD
See Powys

23 THE OLD VICARAGE, PENRHOS
Raglan NP15 2LE. Professor & Mrs Luke Herrmann. *3m N of Raglan. At Raglan turn off A40 for Mitchel Troy. Almost immed turn L for Tregaer. Follow signs for Tregaer, then Penrhos.* **Combined adm £6, chd free.** Sun 28 Apr (2-6). **Combined with Woodlands Farm, Penrhos.**
Traditional garden surrounding beautifully sited Victorian Gothic house (not open) with splendid views over Monmouthshire countryside. Rhododendrons, azaleas and magnolias, early summer roses. Also gazebo, gravel and formal kitchen gardens and ponds. All set in spacious lawns with mature trees. Plant stall.

24 THE PANT
Fforest Coal Pit, Abergavenny NP7 7LT. Dr & Mrs Jeremy Swift & Mr & Mrs Andrew Bruce. *5m N of Abergavenny. From Abergavenny take Hereford rd A465 to Llanvihangel Crucorney. Follow signs to Llanthony Abbey. After 1½ m turn L to Fforest Coal Pit. After further 1½ m, at Fiveways Xrds, turn sharp R uphill following signs.* Home-made teas. **Adm £5, chd free.** Sat 15, Sun 16 June (2-6).
2 adjoining and contrasting gardens set in secluded, spectacular Black Mountains scenery with 25 acres of landscaped woodland, orchard, knot garden, walled garden, Islamic garden and green theatre. Large dry stone turtle, ruined village, curious whale shaped lake, all with wonderful views. Welsh weather permitting, a string quartet will play in the green theatre, both days. Wheelchair users welcome but access is limited to lower gardens only.

25 PENPERGWM LODGE
nr Abergavenny NP7 9AS. Mr & Mrs Simon Boyle, 01873 840208, boyle@penpergwm.co.uk, www.penplants.com. *3m SE of Abergavenny, 5m W of Raglan. On B4598. Turn opp King of Prussia Inn. Entrance 150-yds on L.* **Adm £4, chd free.** Sat 18, Sun 19 May (2-6). **Visitors also welcome by appt Apr to Sept.**
3-acre garden with Jubilee tower overlooking terraced ornamental garden containing canal, cascading water and new loggia at head of canal. S-facing terraces planted with rich profusion and vibrant colours all surrounded by spacious lawns and mature trees. New brick waisted tower in 2011. Some gravel paths.

Spread the word about the NGS: tell your family and friends

Symbols explained

NEW Gardens opening for the first time this year or re-opening after a long break

◆ Garden also opens on non-NGS days. (Gardens which carry this symbol contribute to the NGS either by opening on a specific day(s) and/or by giving a guaranteed contribution.)

♿ Wheelchair access to at least the main features of the garden

Dogs on short leads welcome

Plants usually for sale

NCH Plant Heritage National Collection Holder

Gardens that offer accommodation.

Refreshments are available, normally at a charge

☎ Gardens that welcome visitors by appointment at other times. See the garden entry for details and contact information.

Group Organisers may contact the County Organiser or a garden owner direct to organise a group visit to a particular county or garden. See the end of each county section for County Organiser contact details, or visit www.ngs.org.uk

D Garden designed by a Fellow, Member or Pre-registered Member of The Society of Garden Designers

Children must be accompanied by an adult

Photography is at the discretion of the garden owner; please check first. Photographs must not be used for sale or reproduction without prior permission of the owner.

Share To indicates that a proportion of the money collected will be given to the nominated charity.

Toilets are not usually available at private gardens

Geographical area map

The areas shown on this map are specific to the organisation of The National Gardens Scheme. The Gardens of Wales, listed by area, follow the Gardens of England.

Discover wonderful gardens near you

In 2013 there will be nearly 4,000 gardens across England and Wales opening on behalf of The National Gardens Scheme. In the last 10 years the NGS has donated £26 million to nursing caring and gardening charities.

How you can help support the NGS:

Visit a garden – All our gardens offer something special, and with so many uniquely different gardens to visit you could be spoilt for choice. A visit typically offers the chance to meet the garden owner, with tea and home-made cake in lovely surroundings. Go home inspired with ideas and perhaps a plant from the plant stall - then spread the word to your family and friends!

Open your garden – Joe Swift says: 'It's the sense of community, sharing and fun which makes the gardens which open for the NGS so special'. Opening your garden is a rewarding way to share your passion and hard work while raising money for charity. Size is not critical; many NGS gardens are no larger than typical back gardens. Visitors are looking for interesting design, a good range of plants and gardens which have been tended with love and care. Why not talk to our friendly volunteer team?

Volunteer – **Lend a hand** and join your local team! The NGS is run by volunteers based in each county and over 350 people share the fun and work involved in organising thousands of open garden events. A range of roles is available, so you don't need to be a gardening expert, but should enjoy being part of a team and working with and meeting new people.

Make a donation – support this wonderful tradition by making a donation online at **www.justgiving.com/ngs/donate**

To find out more or to receive our newsletter please visit www.ngs.org.uk or phone 01483 211535.

Image: Offham House, Sussex

BEDFORDSHIRE

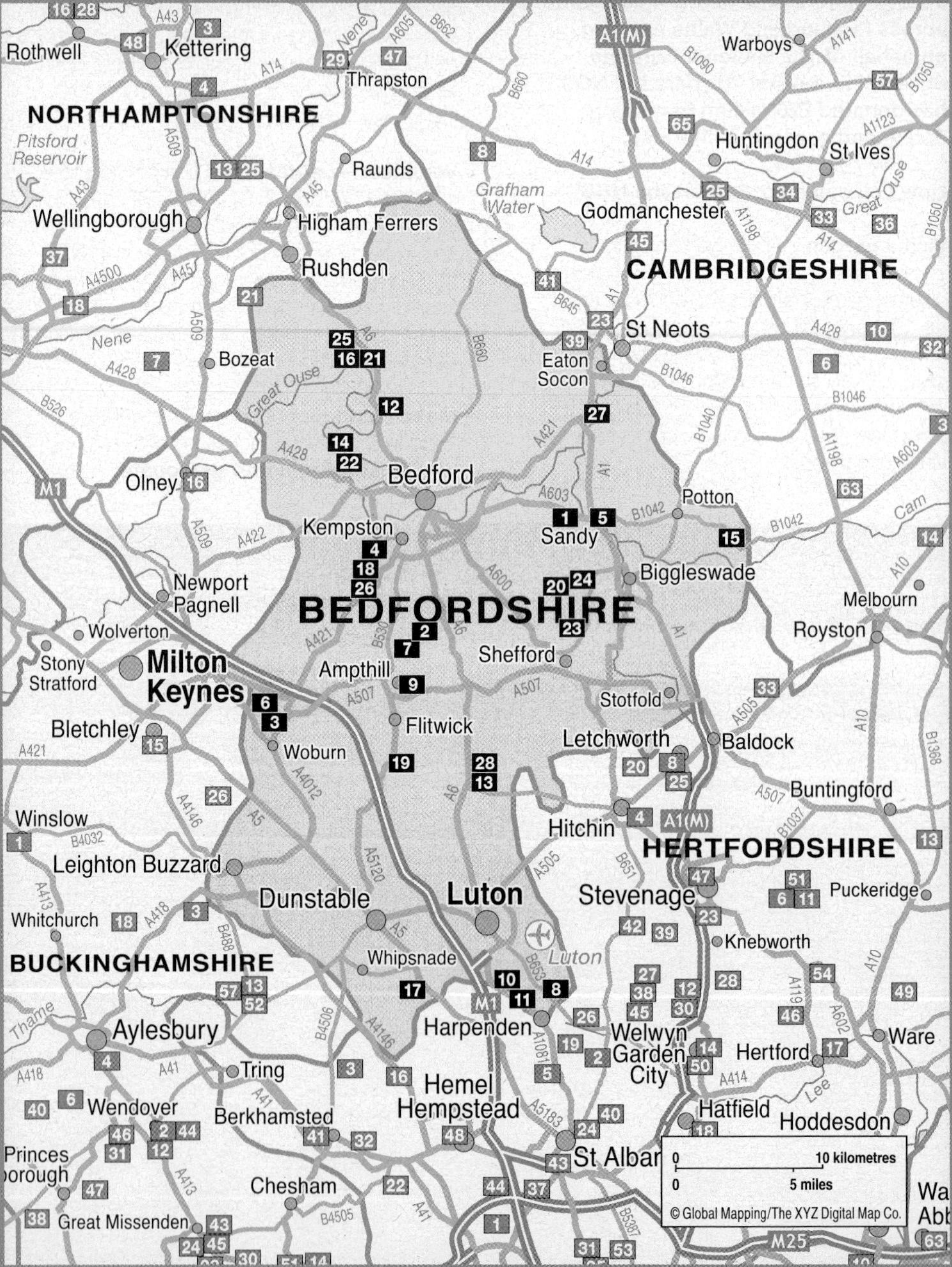

Opening Dates

January

Sunday 27
9 King's Arms Garden

April

Sunday 21
14 The Manor House, Stevington

May

Saturday 11
8 The Hyde Walled Garden
17 Old Farm

Sunday 12
17 Old Farm

Sunday 19
6 Flaxbourne Farm

Sunday 26
22 Park End Thatch

June

Sunday 2
23 Southill Park

National Gardens Weekend

Saturday 15
12 The Manor House, Milton Ernest

Sunday 16
5 The Firs
13 The Manor House, Barton-le-Clay
15 Mill End
22 Park End Thatch
28 Wayside Cottage

Sunday 23
13 The Manor House, Barton-le-Clay
16 The Moat House
21 Ouse Manor
25 Tofte Manor Labyrinth & Garden
28 Wayside Cottage

Saturday 29
4 22 Elmsdale Road
18 The Old Post Office

Sunday 30
4 22 Elmsdale Road
8 The Hyde Walled Garden
18 The Old Post Office

July

Saturday 6
4 22 Elmsdale Road
20 Orchard Grange

Sunday 7
4 22 Elmsdale Road
20 Orchard Grange

Sunday 14
2 31 Broadway
7 How End Cottage
11 Luton Hoo Walled Garden

Saturday 20
27 Walnut Cottage

Sunday 21
27 Walnut Cottage

Saturday 27
1 37 Bedford Road

Sunday 28
1 37 Bedford Road
10 Luton Hoo Hotel Golf & Spa

August

Sunday 11
6 Flaxbourne Farm

October

Sunday 27
9 King's Arms Garden

January 2014

Sunday 26
9 King's Arms Garden

Gardens open to the public

9 King's Arms Garden
11 Luton Hoo Walled Garden
14 The Manor House, Stevington

By appointment only

3 Dawnedge Lodge
19 The Old Vicarage
26 Treize

Also open by Appointment ☎

4 22 Elmsdale Road
5 The Firs
6 Flaxbourne Farm
13 The Manor House, Barton-le-Clay
22 Park End Thatch
27 Walnut Cottage
28 Wayside Cottage

Not an inch of space is wasted in this garden designed for all round interest . . .

The Gardens

ASCOTT
See Buckinghamshire

1 NEW 37 BEDFORD ROAD
Moggerhanger, nr Sandy MK44 3RQ. Ronald Whitlock & Jane Beharrell. *3m W of Sandy on A603. On S-side of Bedford Rd (A603), next to Dynes Place and approx 120metres E of The Guinea. No parking on Bedford Rd, but there should be no problem along St John's Rd or Blunham Rd.* Tea. **Adm £2.50, chd free. Sat 27, Sun 28 July (2-5).**
Established rear garden, about 1/6 acre, divided into 3 areas - lawn with herbaceous borders and specimen trees; 'barbecue area' with wild flower patch, mature trees, small lawns, etc; sizeable vegetable garden with raised beds and fruit trees. Parking on house drive only by prior arrangement. rjwhitlock@aol.com.

38 THE DEERINGS
See Hertfordshire

2 31 BROADWAY
Houghton Conquest, Bedford MK45 3LT. Joan Inwood. *1m N of Ampthill. Turn R off B530 to Houghton Conquest, follow rd through village. 1st turn on L after Royal Oak PH.* Tea at How End Cottage. **Adm £4, chd free. Sun 14 July (2.30-5.30). Combined adm with How End Cottage.**
Small mature cottage style garden packed with perennials, annuals, bulbs, conifers and trees. Lots of pots and containers, small wildlife pond and water features. Ferns, auricula theatre and many other items of interest. Not an inch of space is wasted in this garden designed for all round interest. Wood turning demonstration.

CATWORTH, MOLESWORTH, SPALDWICK & BRINGTON GARDENS
See Cambridgeshire

CHEDDINGTON GARDENS
See Buckinghamshire

ROSE COTTAGE
See Buckinghamshire

3 DAWNEDGE LODGE
Woburn Lane, Aspley Guise MK17 8JH. Phil & Lynne Wallace, 01908 582233, lynnewallace@hotmail.co.uk. *5m W of Ampthill. 3m from J13 M1. In Aspley Guise, turn L in centre of village at Moore Place Hotel.* Home-made teas. **Adm £3, chd free.** **Visitors welcome by appt May to July.**
Victorian walled 1-acre hill top garden with great views to Woburn, with borders described in garden magazine as 'brimming with glorious blooms that are perfect for cutting'. Oak pergola, stone patio with many terracotta pots including 20+ acers, agapanthus aeoniums and agaves. Alliums good.

Beautiful and entertaining fun garden of 3 acres, lovingly developed . . .

4 22 ELMSDALE ROAD
Wootton, Bedford MK43 9JN. Roy & Dianne Richards, 07733 222495, roy.richards60@ntlworld.com. *4m from J13 M1. Join old A421 towards Bedford, follow signs to Wootton. Turn R at The Cock PH follow rd to Elmsdale Rd on R.* Home-made teas. **Adm £3.50, chd free. Sats, Suns 29, 30 June; 6, 7 July (1-5). Also open The Old Post Office 29, 30 June. Visitors also welcome by appt Mar to Sept.**
Topiary garden greets visitors before they enter a genuine Japanese Feng Shui garden incl bonsais, every plant is strictly Japanese, large Koi pond with bamboo bridge and Tea House. The garden was created from scratch by the owners and has many interesting features.

5 THE FIRS
33 Bedford Road, Sandy SG19 1EP. Mr & Mrs D Sutton, 01767 227589, d.sutton7@ntlworld.com. *7m E of Bedford. On B1042 between Sandy town centre and A1. On-road parking.* Home-made teas. **Adm £3.50, chd free. Sun 16 June (2-5). Visitors also welcome by appt June to Sept, adm incl tea and cake.**
¼ -acre town garden with many garden features reflecting the different conditions from full sun to shade. Designed and created from scratch since 2000 this garden is productive in fruit, flowers, vegetables and wildlife. Run organically, this garden has everything from shrubs, trees, alpines, perennials, to water features and railway memorabilia. Some gravel paths.

6 FLAXBOURNE FARM
Salford Road, Aspley Guise MK17 8HZ. Geoff & Davina Barrett, 01908 585329, geoffanddean@gmail.com. *5m W of Ampthill. 1m S of J13 of M1.Turn R in village centre, 1m over railway line.* Home-made teas. **Adm £5, chd free. Sun 19 May, Sun 11 Aug (2-6). Visitors also welcome by appt.**
Beautiful and entertaining fun garden of 3 acres, lovingly developed with numerous water features, windmill, modern arches and bridges, small moated castle, lily pond, herbaceous borders, Greek temple ruin. Recently established three way bridge, planted up with Japanese acers, tree ferns, echiums, bananas and zinnia creating a tropical full of the Wow Factor! New for 2011 Japanese garden with flyover walkway, inspirational woodland setting. Crow's nest, crocodiles, tree house with zip wire for children. Huge Roman stone arched gateway as recently featured in ITV's This Morning programme and BBC One Show. Music by Woburn Sands Band. Featured in Garden News. Wheelchair access is available to all the main parts of the garden.

15 GADE VALLEY COTTAGES
See Hertfordshire

GREAT BRICKHILL GARDENS
See Buckinghamshire

28 POUND HILL
See Buckinghamshire

GREYWALLS
See Northamptonshire

109 HIGH STREET, HAIL WESTON
See Cambridgeshire

7 HOW END COTTAGE
How End Road, Houghton Conquest MK45 3JT. Jeremy & Gill Smith. *1m N of Ampthill. Turn R 1m from Ampthill off B530 towards Houghton Conquest. How End Rd 300yds on RH-side. Garden at end of rd, approx ½ m.* Home-made teas. **Adm £4, chd free. Sun 14 July (2.30-5.30). Combined adm with 31 Broadway.**
Approx 1 acre garden with 2 ponds, large vegetable garden, greenhouse and orchard. Large lawn gives an uninterrupted view of Houghton House. The garden contains mature trees and beds with many types of slow growing fir trees. Flower beds contain home grown bedding plants and roses. 3 acres of paddocks, wood and further pond. Many spring bulbs.

8 THE HYDE WALLED GARDEN
East Hyde, Luton LU2 9PS. D J J Hambro Will Trust. *2m S of Luton. M1 exit J10/10a. A1081 S take 2nd L. At E Hyde turn R then immed L. Junction entrance on R. From A1 exit J4. Follow A3057 N to r'about, 1st L to B653 Wheathamstead/Luton to E Hyde.* Home-made teas. **Adm £3.50, chd free. Sat 11 May; Sun 30 June (2-5).**
Walled garden adjoins the grounds of The Hyde (not open). Extends to approx 1 acre and features rose garden, seasonal beds and herbaceous borders, imaginatively interspersed with hidden areas of formal lawn. An interesting group of Victorian greenhouses, coldframes and cucumber house are serviced from the potting shed in the adjoining vegetable garden. Bluebell walk in season. Gravel paths.

9 ◆ KING'S ARMS GARDEN
1 Brinsmade Road, Ampthill MK45 2PP. Ampthill Town Council, 01525 755648, bryden.k@ntlworld.com. *8m S of Bedford. Free parking in town centre. Entrance opp old Market Place, down King's Arms Yard.* **Adm £2, chd free. For NGS: Sun 27 Jan (2-4); Sun 27 Oct (2-4.30); Sun 26 Jan 2014. For other opening times and information, please phone or email.**
Small woodland garden of about 1½ acres created by plantsman the late William Nourish. Trees, shrubs, bulbs and many interesting

collections throughout the yr. Maintained since 1987 by 'The Friends of the Garden' on behalf of Ampthill Town Council. Whelchair access to most of the garden.

10 LUTON HOO HOTEL GOLF & SPA
The Mansion House, Luton Hoo, Luton LU1 3TQ. Luton Hoo Hotel Golf & Spa, 01582 698806, rbiffen@elitehotels.co.uk, www.lutonhoo.co.uk. *Approx 1m from J10 M1, take London Rd A1081 signed Harpenden for approx 1/2 m - entrance on L for Luton Hoo.* Light refreshments. **Adm £5, chd free.** **Sun 28 July (10-4).**
The gardens and parkland designed by Capability Brown are of national historic significance and lie in a conservation area. Main features - lakes, woodland and pleasure grounds, Victorian grass tennis court and late C19 sunken rockery. Italianate garden with herbaceous borders and topiary garden. Gravel paths.

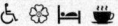

11 ◆ LUTON HOO WALLED GARDEN
Luton Hoo Estate, Luton LU1 4LF. Exors of N H Phillips, 01582 879089, www.lhwg.org.uk. *A1081 between Luton & Harpenden. Take New Mill End turning, turn L after 100m. Follow Walled Garden Project signs. NO entrance from Luton Hoo Hotel. Disabled parking next to garden.* **Adm £3, chd free.** **For NGS: Sun 14 July (10-3).**
For other opening times and information, please phone or see garden website.
The 5 acre Luton Hoo Walled Garden was designed by Capability Brown and established by Lord Bute in the late 1760s. Successive owners of the estate adapted the garden to match changing horticultural fashions, only for it to fall into decline in the 1980s. The garden is now being restored. Exhibition of research material on the history of the garden. Guided tours. Illustrated talks. Exhibition of old tools.

12 NEW THE MANOR HOUSE, MILTON ERNEST
Thurleigh Road, Bedford MK44 1RF. Mrs Deborah Inskip. *Just off the A6 in Milton Ernest, 5m N of Bedford. First house on R (when travelling E on Thurleigh Road) after All Saint's Church, Milton Ernest. Disabled parking available on gravel drive.* **Adm £4, chd free.** **Sat 15 June (2-5).**
3-acre family garden of C17 Manor House next to village church. Mature trees including Hornbeam, Sorbus (Joseph Rock), Cornus contraversa as well as willows around a large wild life pond. Variety of early summer colour. Wheelchair accessible but mostly on grass and not hard paths.

22 Elmsdale Road

13 THE MANOR HOUSE, BARTON-LE-CLAY
87 Manor Road, Barton-le-Clay MK45 4NR. Mrs Veronica Pilcher. *Off A6 between Bedford & Luton. Take old A6 (Bedford Rd) through Barton-le-Clay Village (not the by-pass) and Manor Rd is off Bedford Rd. Parking in paddock.* Home-made teas. **Adm £4, chd free.** **Sun 16, Sun 23 June (2-5). Combined adm with Wayside Cottage (opp). Visitors also welcome by appt May to Sept. Please apply in writing.**
The garden was beautifully landscaped during the 1930s and much interest is created by picturesque stream which incorporates a series of waterfalls. Colourful streamside planting incl an abundance of arum lilies. Sunken garden with lily pond and a magnificent wisteria thrives at the rear of the house. Children under supervision as there is a water hazard. Partial wheelchair access, 2ft wide bridges.

14 ◆ THE MANOR HOUSE, STEVINGTON
Church Road, nr Bedford MK43 7QB. Kathy Brown, 01234 822064, www.kathybrownsgarden.com. *5m NW of Bedford. Off A428 through Bromham.* **Adm £4.50, chd free.** **For NGS: Sun 21 Apr (12-5).**
For other opening times and information, please phone or see garden website.
A modern 4-acre country garden with unusual twists, designed and cared for by owners Simon and Kathy Brown.Tulips and other bulbs bring fantastic colour to the cottage garden, the formal parterres and herbaceous borders. Major container displays, blossoms in the orchard and elsewhere, plus extensive naturalistic planting schemes offer further delights. Featured in House and Garden.

15 MILL END
Potton Road, Wrestlingworth SG19 2EZ. Richard & Liz Whitlock, 01767 631382. *4m E of Biggleswade. On the B1042 out of Wrestlingworth towards Potton.* Home-made teas. **Adm £4, chd free.** **Sun 16 June (2-6).**
2-acre ornamental and vegetable garden planted by present owners since building house 23yrs ago. Extensive mixed borders, large collection euphorbias, rose pergola, arboretum of 100+ unusual and interesting trees. Further into the 13-acre site is an old orchard, woodland of indigenous trees and

wild flower walk through coppiced area harvested for the house wood burner. Musical entertainment from a group of professional and semi-professional singers.

16 NEW THE MOAT HOUSE
High Street, Sharnbrook, Bedford MK44 1PG. Mrs Louise Swallow. *Sharnbrook is approx 9m NE of Bedford off the A6. The entrance to The Moat House is on Kennell Hill which runs into the High Street. Entrances to both Ouse Manor and The Moat House are almost opp each other on this rd.* Teas at The Cake Shop, High Street, 10% to NGS. **Adm £5, chd free. Sun 23 June (2-5). Combined adm with Ouse Manor and Tofte Manor.**
A formal walled garden to the north and east sides of the property with water feature, herbaceous borders and parterre garden. The garden is very much a work in progress and is slowly taking shape.

17 NEW OLD FARM
Clayhall Road, Kensworth LU6 3RF. Murie & Ian Ronald, www.varimus.co.uk. *From M1 J9, take A5 to Dunstable. Turn L off A5 signed Whipsnade Zoo. At top of hill, after 30mph limit, and Kensworth sign, turn L into Clayhall Road. Old Farm is ½ m on R. Parking on verges between garden and village, dangerous corner beyond house.* **Adm £3.50, chd free. Sat 11, Sun 12 May (12-4.30).**
This 1½ -acre garden has been designed and planted from scratch by the current owners. Floriferous cottage style beds with a strong structure of shrubs, wisteria clad pergola, productive organic vegetable garden, soft fruit and fruit trees, grass meadow, specimen trees and dew pond. Year round interest. Gravel drive to negotiate on entrance, slopes and some steps.

OLD FARM COTTAGE
See Cambridgeshire

18 NEW THE OLD POST OFFICE
Church Road, Wootton, Bedford MK43 9EU. Carol Bishop. *From A421 take signs to Wootton. Go along Fields Rd, take a L turn at the end (by the garage) and then immed turn R onto Church Rd. The Old Post Office is half way up Church Rd.* Home-made teas. **Adm £3.50, chd free. Sat 29, Sun 30 June (1-5). Also open 22 Elmsdale Road.**
There are large front and rear gardens, the front primarily a restored Georgian box-edged layout with cottage style planting. The rear garden is totally walled, divided into packed 'rooms' with path terrace and pergola, a well, fruit trees, apple, mulberry, medlar, pear, fig grapevine and peach. Gravel pathway and drive.

Ancient oak and beech trees. River, sweeping views, perennial border, ancient trees . . .

19 THE OLD VICARAGE
Church Road, Westoning MK45 5JW. Ann & Colin Davies, 01525 712721, ann@no1colin.plus.com. *2m S of Flitwick. Off A5120, 2m N of M1 J12. ¼ m up Church Rd, next to church.* Light refreshments. **Adm £5, chd free. Visitors welcome by appt Mar to June, refreshments incl in adm. No parking for coaches.**
A traditional 2-acre vicarage garden on sandy soil with box and laurel hedges, formal lawn, large magnolia grandiflora and numerous other mature shrubs and trees. More recent improvements include many colour co-ordinated herbaceous beds, a romantic cornfield meadow, an English rose garden, a pond, rockery and small vegetable garden. A striking show of hellebores and daffodils in spring. Wheelchair access generally good.

THE OLD VICARAGE
See Cambridgeshire

20 NEW ORCHARD GRANGE
Old Warden, Biggleswade SG18 9HB. Mrs Victoria Diggle. *3m W of Biggleswade. In Old Warden village, just NE of entrance to Shuttleworth College. Parking in garden, or adjacent village hall car park.* **Adm £3, chd free. Sat 6, Sun 7 July (2-5).**
2-acre garden with mature trees and herbaceous borders. Walled kitchen garden with wide selection of vegetables, mature vine and annual wildflower areas. Orchard with perennial wildflowers. Conservatory with collection of pelargoniums. Some parts of the garden may not be wheelchair accessible.

21 NEW OUSE MANOR
High Street, Sharnbrook, Bedford MK44 1PG. Penny Scarisbrick. *In Sharnbrook, at the junction of Kennel Hill and the High Street, go through a wooden farm gate marked Ouse Manor. The property is at the end of the drive. Parking is available in the field parallel to the drive.* **Adm £5, chd free. Sun 23 June (2-5). Combined adm with Tofte Manor and The Moat House.**
Sweeping lawn to River Ouse with far reaching views. Long perennial border and small orchard. Walled garden and ornamental kitchen garden stocked with vegetables, flowers and herbs. Ancient oak and beech trees. River, sweeping views, perennial border, ancient trees.

22 PARK END THATCH
58 Park Road, Stevington, Bedford MK43 7QG. Susan Young, 01234 826430, susankyoung@btconnect.com, www.skygardeninganddesign.com. *5m NW of Bedford. Off A428, through Bromham.* Home-made teas. **Adm £3.50, chd free. Sun 26 May, Sun 16 June (12-5). Visitors also welcome by appt. Parking for 4 cars, no coaches. WC.**
½ -acre cottage garden set within old orchard. View of Stevington windmill. Sunny borders of flowering shrubs with herbaceous planting. Fragrant roses and climber covered pergola. Winding grass paths shaded by trees. Trellis border featuring colour and texture groupings. Fruit production and herbs. Garden cultivated to be drought tolerant. Wildlife friendly. Small plant nursery. Outside WC for use by visitors but cannot be accessed by wheelchair. Main path is gravel on a slight slope, grass paths. Most of the garden is accessible by wheelchair.

PEMBROKE FARM
See Hertfordshire

ROSE COTTAGE
See Buckinghamshire

ST MICHAEL'S CROFT
See Hertfordshire

23 SOUTHILL PARK
Southill, nr Biggleswade SG18 9LL. Mr & Mrs Charles Whitbread. *3m W of Biggleswade. In the village of Southill. 3m from A1 junction at Biggleswade.* Cream teas. **Adm £3.50, chd free.** **Sun 2 June (2-5).**
Large garden, with mature trees and flowering shrubs, herbaceous borders, rose garden and wild garden. Large conservatory with tropical plants. The parkland was designed by Lancelot 'Capability' Brown in 1777.

24 SWISS GARDEN
Old Warden Park, Old Warden, Biggleswade SG18 9ER. Shuttleworth Trust in Partnership with Central Beds Council, 01767 627920, swissgardenoffice@shuttleworth.org, www.shuttleworth.org. *2m W of Biggleswade. Signed from A1 & A600.* **(share to Friends of the Swiss Garden). Closed for restoration during 2013 subject to Lottery Funding.**
This unique Swiss picturesque garden was created for Lord Ongley the 3rd in early C19. Winding paths lead to contrived vistas with the thatched Swiss cottage providing the main focal point, plus beautiful ironwork, the grotto and fernery, ponds and additions made by the Shuttleworth family incl Pulhamite. Gravel paths, some steep slopes, bridges and lawns.

25 TOFTE MANOR LABYRINTH & GARDEN
Souldrop Road, Sharnbrook MK44 1HH. Mrs Suzy Castleman, www.toftemanor.co.uk. *8m N of Bedford. Off A6 between Bedford and Rushden. Exit at r'about signed Sharnbrook, through village towards Souldrop. At Y-Junction take R fork; house is 400yds on L, through large black wrought-iron gates.* **Adm £5, chd free.** **Sun 23 June (2-5). Combined adm with Ouse Manor and The Moat House.**
5 acres of mature and beautifully laid out garden restored and modernised to blend with C17 manor house. Beautiful mature trees, colour themed herbaceous borders. Sunken area with central arbour and crystal ball like water feature. Modern statued parterre garden, unusual swings and crystals throughout garden. Walks and wild areas abound. Grass labyrinth in the design of Chartres Cathedral, France, incorporating crystals and sacred geometry. Water which has travelled the path of the labyrinth can be drunk. This is an unusual spiritual garden for those in search of tranquillity.

26 TREIZE
Cranfield Road, Wootton Green, Bedford MK43 9EA. Roger & Anna Skipper, 01234 768640, roger.skipper@btinternet.com. *5m SW of Bedford. 10m NE of Milton Keynes. C70 Kempston to Cranfield rd, ½ m SW of Wootton. Private Lane on R opp Wootton Green Hamlet sign. Bungalow 125yds along lane on R.* Light refreshments. **Adm £5, chd free. Visitors welcome by appt Mar to Sept. Guided tour of the garden by garden owners.**
1-acre plantsman's garden set out for yr-round interest on heavy clay. Hidden gardens and established herbaceous borders; formal pond; rockery, gravel beds and containers. Around 50 species of established and younger trees, conifers, shrubs, vast collection of perennials, incl over 100 varieties and species of penstemon. The garden continues to evolve. Wheelchair access to majority of garden.

27 WALNUT COTTAGE
8 Great North Road, Chawston MK44 3BD. D G Parker, 0778 4792975. *2m S of St Neots. Between Wyboston & Blackcat r'about on S-bound lane of A1. Turn off at McDonalds, at end of filling station forecourt turn L. Off road parking.* Light refreshments. **Adm £3.50, chd free. Sat 20, Sun 21 July (2-6). Visitors also welcome by appt, refreshments as required.**
Once a land settlement. 4-acre Ass. smallholding. 1 acre cottage garden. Over 2000 species give year round interest. Bulbs, herbaceous, water, bog plants, ferns, grasses, shrubs, trees, coppiced paulownias. Rare, exotic and unusual plants abound. Large pond, level grass paths. 1-acre young trees and shrubs. 2500sq metre glasshouse growing Chinese veg. 1½ -acre picnic and party zone. Level grass paths.

28 WAYSIDE COTTAGE
74 Manor Road, Barton-le-Clay MK45 4NR. Nigel Barrett. *1m off A6. Take old A6 (Bedford Rd) through Barton-le-Clay Village (not the by-pass), Manor Rd is off Bedford Rd. Parking in paddock at the Manor House.* Home-made teas at The Manor House. **Adm £4, chd free. Sun 16, Sun 23 June (2-5). Combined with The Manor House, Barton Le Clay. Visitors also welcome by appt May to Sept. Please apply in writing to The Manor House, Barton Le Clay.**
The garden is sited on a ½ -acre plot. Developed over 50yrs it has mature trees, shrubs and flower borders. A well-stocked pond with fountain and waterfalls. A variety of attractive outbuildings nestle within the old walled garden for a tranquil scene with plenty of hidden corners.

WESTEND HOUSE
See Buckinghamshire

Bedfordshire County Volunteers

County Organiser
Judy Stewart, The Old Vicarage, Melchbourne MK44 1BQ, 01234 708629, jug.stewart@gmail.com

County Treasurer
Colin Davies, The Old Vicarage, Church Road, Westoning MK45 5JW, 01525 712721, colin.davies@which.net

Publicity
David & Susan Sutton, The Firs, 33 Bedford Road, Sandy SG19 1EP 01767 227589, sutton7@ntlworld.com

Assistant County Organisers
Geoff & Davina Barrett, Flaxbourne Farm, Aspley Guise, Milton Keynes MK17 8HZ, 01908 585329, carole@boa.com
Pat Sutcliffe, Valley Forge, 213 Castle Hill Road, Totternhoe, Dunstable LU6 2DA, 01525 221676, sutcliffes@leylandman.co.uk
Victoria Diggle, Orchard Grange, Old Warden, Biggleswade SG18 9HB, 01767 627247, victoria@diggledesign.com

BERKSHIRE

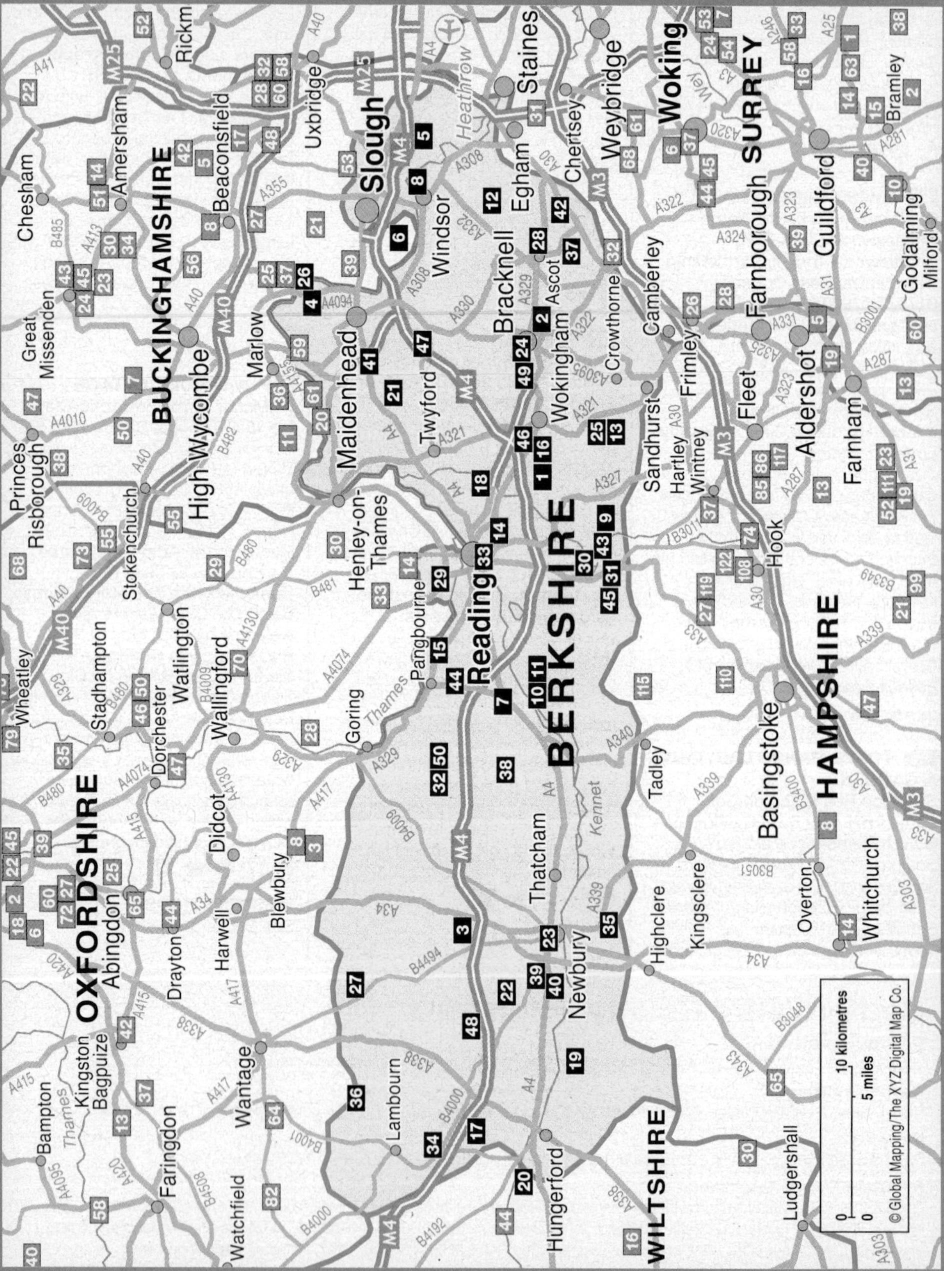
BERKSHIRE
BUCKINGHAMSHIRE
OXFORDSHIRE
HAMPSHIRE
SURREY
WILTSHIRE
Reading
Slough
Maidenhead
Windsor
Bracknell
Wokingham
Newbury
Thatcham
Hungerford
Lambourn
Twyford
Ascot
Egham
Staines
Chertsey
Weybridge
Woking
Guildford
Farnborough
Aldershot
Farnham
Fleet
Camberley
Crowthorne
Sandhurst
Basingstoke
Hook
Tadley
Kingsclere
Highclere
Overton
Whitchurch
Ludgershall
Henley-on-Thames
Pangbourne
Goring
Wallingford
Didcot
Abingdon
Wantage
Faringdon
High Wycombe
Marlow
Beaconsfield
Amersham
Chesham
Uxbridge
Heathrow
Thames
Kennet
10 kilometres
5 miles
© Global Mapping/The XYZ Digital Map Co.

Opening Dates

March

Sunday 24
9 Farley Hill Place Gardens

Friday 29
41 Stubbings House

Saturday 30
17 Inholmes
41 Stubbings House

Sunday 31
41 Stubbings House

April

Monday 1
41 Stubbings House

Sunday 14
27 The Old Rectory Farnborough
43 Swallowfield Horticultural Society

Sunday 21
26 Odney Club

Wednesday 24
34 Rooksnest

It's a lovely place to enjoy afternoon tea . . .

May

Wednesday 1
40 Stockcross House

Saturday 4
41 Stubbings House
45 Trunkwell Garden Project

Sunday 5
2 Bracknell Gardens
17 Inholmes
41 Stubbings House

Monday 6
2 Bracknell Gardens
41 Stubbings House

Saturday 11
33 The RISC Roof Garden, Reading

Sunday 12
27 The Old Rectory Farnborough

Tuesday 14
12 Frogmore House Garden

Sunday 19
1 Bearwood College

Sunday 26
39 Stockcross Gardens

Monday 27
42 Sunningdale Park

June

Saturday 1
4 Cookham Gardens

Sunday 2
40 Stockcross House

Saturday 8
20 Littlecote House Hotel
48 Welford Park

Sunday 9
14 The Harris Garden
20 Littlecote House Hotel

Wednesday 12
34 Rooksnest

National Gardens Weekend

Saturday 15
6 Dorney Court Kitchen Garden
8 Eton College Gardens
17 Inholmes
35 Sandleford Place

Sunday 16
3 Chieveley Manor
6 Dorney Court Kitchen Garden
15 Highveldt
17 Inholmes
24 Moor Close Gardens
27 The Old Rectory Farnborough
35 Sandleford Place
40 Stockcross House
44 The Tithe Barn

Saturday 22
20 Littlecote House Hotel
29 Oxford Cottage

Sunday 23
19 Kintbury Gardens
20 Littlecote House Hotel
29 Oxford Cottage
30 Parklea
43 Swallowfield Horticultural Society
49 Whitehouse Farm Cottage

Saturday 29
32 Pyt House
50 Willow Tree Cottage

Sunday 30
23 The Mill House Donnington
32 Pyt House
36 Sheepdrove Organic Farm
37 Southgate
38 Stanford Dingley Gardens
39 Stockcross Gardens
50 Willow Tree Cottage

July

Wednesday 3
40 Stockcross House

Saturday 6
20 Littlecote House Hotel

Sunday 7
20 Littlecote House Hotel
45 Trunkwell Garden Project

Saturday 13
10 Field Farm Cottage
33 The RISC Roof Garden, Reading

Sunday 14
10 Field Farm Cottage
46 Twigs

Saturday 20
20 Littlecote House Hotel

Sunday 21
20 Littlecote House Hotel
21 Lower Lovetts Farm

Saturday 27
21 Lower Lovetts Farm

Sunday 28
45 Trunkwell Garden Project

August

Saturday 3
20 Littlecote House Hotel

Sunday 4
20 Littlecote House Hotel

Saturday 10
5 Ditton Manor
33 The RISC Roof Garden, Reading

Sunday 25
28 Old Waterfield
30 Parklea

Saturday 31
20 Littlecote House Hotel

September

Sunday 1
20 Littlecote House Hotel

Saturday 14
45 Trunkwell Garden Project

Saturday 21
20 Littlecote House Hotel

Sunday 22
20 Littlecote House Hotel

Gardens open to the public

7 Englefield House
48 Welford Park

By appointment only

11 Folly Farm
13 Glenmere
16 Hostas at 25 Simons Lane
18 Ivydene
22 The Mill House, Boxford
25 Oak Cottage
31 The Priory
47 Waltham Place Gardens

Also open by Appointment ☎

The Gardens

1 BEARWOOD COLLEGE

Winnersh RG41 5BG. Richard Ryall, 0118 974 8300, secondmaster@bearwoodcollege.co.uk. *5m SE of Reading. Off B3030, 1m S of A329/B3030 intersection at Winnersh, midway between Reading and Wokingham. Look for Bearwood Rd & College sign.* Cream teas. **Adm £4, chd free.** **Sun 19 May (2-5).** **Visitors also welcome by appt June, although appts are restricted.**

Late C19 mansion and parkland once owned by the last private owner of The Times newspaper, now an independent school. Azaleas, rhododendrons, walks through mature woodland. Pinetum, lake, natural margins, ice house. Extensive hidden Pulham rock and water garden under restoration. Visits incl access to some of the mansion rooms. Specialist plants, charcoal making (subject to weather).

GROUP OPENING

2 BRACKNELL GARDENS

Bracknell RG12 9BH. *1m S of Bracknell. For Devonia from A322 Horse & Groom r'about take exit into Broad Lane, over 2 r'abouts. 3rd house on L after railway bridge. For Shaftesbury Close at Sports Centre r'about exit to Harmanswater. L on 2 mini r'abouts into Nightingale Crescent, then 2nd on L.* Home-made teas at 10 Shaftesbury Close, plant sale at Devonia. **Combined adm £3.50, chd free.** **Sun 5, Mon 6 May (2-5).**

DEVONIA
Andrew Radgick
Visitors (min 4) also welcome by appt in May, adm £5 incl refreshments.
01344 862683
aradgick@btinternet.com

10 SHAFTESBURY CLOSE
Gill Cheetham

Two interesting town gardens that take into account climatic changes. A must for plantaholics! **Devonia**: 1/3 -acre plantsman's garden designed for all seasons and planted to require minimal watering. Divided into several areas to provide appropriate conditions for over 1300 different shrubs, climbers, perennials, bulbs and alpines, incl many rare and unusual. Hot and dry front garden, shady and sheltered corners to the rear. **10 Shaftesbury Close**: pine woodland garden, with many different ericaceous shrubs and plants. Good spring colour with underplanted trees. Walled garden. Beds planted to reflect climatic changes incl Mediterranean, scree and alpine. Colour themed herbaceous borders planted for yr-round colour.

Curving walkway that weaves through arbours bordered by lush exotic and evergreen planting . . .

3 CHIEVELEY MANOR

Chieveley, nr Newbury RG20 8UT. Mr & Mrs C J Spence, 01635 248208, spence@chieveleymanor.fsworld.co.uk. *5m N of Newbury. Take A34 N, pass under M4, then L to Chieveley. After 1/2 m L up Manor Lane.* Home-made teas. **Adm £4, chd free (share to St Mary's Church Chieveley).** **Sun 16 June (2-5).** **Groups (max 30) also welcome by appt June and July.**

Large garden surrounding listed house (not open) in the heart of Chieveley village. Attractive setting with fine views over stud farm. Walled garden containing lovely borders, shrubs and rose garden, evolving every year. Box parterre, filled with alliums, white geraniums and lavender. Many viticella clematis growing through shrubs. Featured in Amateur Gardening and on BBC Radio Berkshire.

THE COACH HOUSE
See Hampshire

GROUP OPENING

4 COOKHAM GARDENS

Cookham, Maidenhead SL6 9QD. *3 1/2 m N of Maidenhead. On B4447 in Cookham. Car parking is difficult - use NT car park on Cookham Moor or around Cookham rail station. Combined tickets for all 3 gardens available at any garden, follow NGS signs.* Home-made teas at Hunters Lodge. **Combined adm £4, chd free.** **Sat 1 June (2-5).**

2 BELLE VUE COTTAGES
Liz & William Wells

HUNTERS LODGE
Daphne Wardell-Yerburgh

2 VICARAGE CLOSE D
Sue Yerburgh

Three contrasting gardens in the beautiful Thameside village of Cookham, all within 1/2 m walk and close to the Stanley Spencer Gallery. Two showcase innovative use of limited spaces. A small stunning modern garden, **2 Bellevue Cottages** has a curving walkway that weaves through arbours bordered by lush exotic and evergreen planting, punctuated by dabs of intense colour. Sorry not suitable for children. **2 Vicarage Close** is a small contemporary water garden with simplistic planting surrounding a straight sided deep pool with cascading water. An overhanging deck with 'floating' steps over to a small grass area. The third, **Hunters Lodge** is a country style garden with a series of rooms leading to a Victorian summer house. Filled with herbaceous and climbing plants, lawned areas and set behind Victorian house in heart of village, it is a lovely place to enjoy afternoon tea.

DIPLEY MILL
See Hampshire

5 NEW DITTON MANOR

Riding Court Road, Datchet, Slough SL3 9LL. CA Technologies. *Leave M4 J5 & follow signs for Langley. Straight over T-lights (Marriott Hotel on L). After Harvester turn L into Ditton Park Road. Ditton Manor is half way down on R.* Home-made teas. **Adm £3.50, chd free. Sat 10 Aug (11-5).**
Ditton Manor sits on a 14-acre moated island at the centre of a fine 208-acre estate created in the traditional English landscape style, originally designed by Lancelot 'Capability' Brown. The Manor enjoys fine views over parkland, woodland and lakes. Formal lawns, walled garden, kitchen garden and cutting garden.

6 DORNEY COURT KITCHEN GARDEN

Court Lane, Dorney, Windsor SL4 6QP. Ryan & Stretch, www.dckg.co.uk. *3m from M4 J7. Take A4 W. Through T-lights then L at r'about on to B3026 Lake End Rd. Approx 1½ m into Dorney, past Pineapple PH, then R into Court Lane.* Cream teas. **Adm £3, chd free. Sat 15, Sun 16 June (9-5.30).**
Inspirational and educational walled kitchen garden, adjacent to plant nursery, in historic village of Dorney. Sunken garden, water features, herbs, fruit, vegetables, children's tree house and play area. Special family-friendly Open Weekend for the NGS. Will incl children's workshops, music, BBQ and much more. Steps down to sunken garden, otherwise full wheelchair access.

DORNEYWOOD GARDEN

See Buckinghamshire

EASTON ROYAL GARDENS

See Wiltshire

7 ◆ ENGLEFIELD HOUSE

Englefield, Reading RG7 5EN. Mr & Mrs Richard Benyon, 01189 302504, www.englefieldestate.co.uk. *6m W of Reading. 1½ m from J12 M4. 1m from Theale. Entrance on A340 3m S of Pangbourne.* **For opening times and information, please phone or see garden website.**
9-acre woodland garden with interesting variety of trees and shrubs, stream, water garden descending to formal terraces with

2 Belle Vue Cottage

stone balustrades making background for deep borders. Small enclosed gardens of differing character incl children's garden with joke fountains. All enclosed by deer park with lake. Open every Mon throughout yr & Mons-Thurs, Apr-Oct (10-6). Gravel paths.

8 ETON COLLEGE GARDENS

Windsor SL4 6DB. Eton College. *½ m N of Windsor. Parking off B3022 Slough to Eton rd, signed to R, S of junction with Datchet Rd (Pococks Lane), walk across playing fields to entry. Cars with disabled badges will be directed further. Tickets & map at entrance to Head Master's garden.* Home-made teas. **Adm £4, chd free. Sat 15 June (2-5).**
A rare chance to visit a group of central college gardens surrounded by historic school buildings, incl Luxmoore's garden on an island in the Thames reached across an attractive bridge. Also opportunity to explore the fascinating Eton College Natural History Museum. Wheelchair access limited to 3 central gardens and over grass to Luxmoores, with no access to the Museum or further gardens in Eton town.

9 NEW FARLEY HILL PLACE GARDENS

Farley Hill, Reading RG7 1TZ. Mr & Mrs Tony & Margaret Finch, 0118 976 2544, tony.finch7@btinternet.com. *From M4 J11, take A33 towards Basingstoke. At T-lights turn L for Spencers Wood, B3349. After approx 2m turn L for Swallowfield. Follow rd to Farley Hill (approx 2 m). Garden on R ½ m after The George and Dragon PH.* Home-made teas. **Adm £4, chd free. Sun 24 Mar (2-5). Groups (min 20) also welcome by appt 31 Mar to Oct, adm £5.**
A 4-acre, C18 cottage garden, set in the secluded village of Farley Hill. Walled garden full of mixed herbaceous borders, specimen plants, mature trees, colourful shrubs, abundant primroses, daffodils and spring flowering plants.

16 FARM ROAD
See Surrey

10 NEW FIELD FARM COTTAGE
Sulhamstead Hill, Sulhamstead, Reading RG7 4DA. Mrs Anne Froom, www.bandbwestberkshire.co.uk. *From A4 take lane by The Spring Inn for 1m. Garden on L 150yrds past 2 LH turns.* Home-made teas. **Adm £3, chd free. Sat 13, Sun 14 July (2-6).**
A cottage garden in ¾ -acre planted with a wide variety of herbaceous perennials, set in a series of garden rooms. Lovely borders spill over the lawn and there is a large pond which is fed by a natural spring. Wild garden, small white garden and a variety of trees planted by the owner. Small vegetable garden and greenhouse.

11 FOLLY FARM
Sulhamstead Hill, Sulhamstead RG7 4DG. *7m SW of Reading. From A4 between Reading and Newbury (2m W of M4 J12) take rd marked Sulhamstead at The Spring Inn.* Home-made teas. **Adm £25. Private tour for groups of 15 welcome by appt on Weds (pm), 17 July to 28 Aug. Pre booking necessary due to limited availabliity by phoning 01483 211535 or visit www.ngs.org.uk.**
Gardens laid out in 1912 by Sir Edwin Lutyens and Gertrude Jekyll. Garden designs evolved during culmination of their partnership and considered one of their most complex. Extensively restored by current owners and recently re-opened for private group visits. Group organisers are requested to book in advance. Featured in Country Life Magazine.

FRIMLEY GREEN GARDENS
See Surrey

12 ◆ FROGMORE HOUSE GARDEN
Windsor SL4 2HT.
Her Majesty The Queen, www.royalcollection.org.uk. *1m SE of Windsor. Entrance via Park St gate into Long Walk (follow AA signs).* **Tue 14 May. For visitor information please see www.ngs.org.uk or telephone 01483 211535.**
The private royal garden at Frogmore House on the Crown Estate at Windsor. This landscaped garden set in 30 acres with notable trees, lawns, flowering shrubs and C18 lake, is rich in history. It is largely the creation of Queen Charlotte, who in the 1790s introduced over 4,000 trees and shrubs to create a model 'picturesque' landscape.The historic plantings, including tulip trees and redwoods, along with Queen Victoria's Tea House, remain key features of the garden today.

Pass through a secret garden that shows a very small space used to maximum effect . . .

13 GLENMERE
246 Nine Mile Ride, Finchampstead RG40 3PA. Heather Bradly & John Kenney, 01189 733274. *2.5m S of Wokingham. On B3430 E of California Crossroads r'about.* Home-made teas. **Adm £3.50, chd free. Visitors (max 16) welcome by appt all year round.**
Japanese style garden with waiting arbour, raked gravel area, tea house, Torii gate, dry stream bed with bridge and pond. Vegetable garden, greenhouse and soft fruit area. Attractive in all seasons,with added colour during August.

GRANGE DRIVE WOOBURN
See Buckinghamshire

14 THE HARRIS GARDEN
Whiteknights, Reading RG6 6UR. The University of Reading, School of Biological Sciences, www.friendsoftheharrisgarden.org.uk. *1½ m S of Reading. Off A327, Shinfield Rd. Turn R just inside Pepper Lane entrance to campus.* Home-made teas. **Adm £3, chd free. Sun 9 June (2-5.30).**
12-acre amenity, research and teaching garden. Floral meadows, herbaceous borders, stream garden and pond, notable trees and shrubs, some very rare. Plant Heritage Digitalis collection.
NCH

HEARNS HOUSE
See Oxfordshire

HIGHER DENHAM GARDENS
See Buckinghamshire

15 HIGHVELDT
Beech Road, Purley-on-Thames RG8 8DS. Ben & Dorothy Viljoen. *4m NW Reading, off A329. From Pangbourne, Beech Rd is 1st R as you enter Purley. From Reading, across T-lights at Long Lane, across r'about, take 1st L.* Home-made teas. **Adm £3, chd free. Sun 16 June (2-5).**
Attractive ⅓ -acre terraced garden retaining much of original 1930s layout. Down steps through trellis arch to circular lawn with box balls and lavender. Pass through a secret garden that shows a very small space used to maximum effect, then into main terracing incl herbaceous borders, lawns and Chiltern views.

16 HOSTAS AT 25 SIMONS LANE
Wokingham RG41 3HG. Jonathan Hogarth, 0118 977 6879, ahogie25@aol.com. *1m W of Wokingham. Take A329 W towards Reading after Woose Hill r'about. ¼ m take 2nd L. On corner of Walter Rd.* **Adm £2.50, chd free. Visitors (max 20) welcome by appt Apr to Aug.**
This is not a garden but a great opportunity for hosta enthusiasts to view a large private collection of 350 new and old hosta varieties. All specimens displayed in pots and on shelves in a courtyard setting. Owner is active member of all hosta societies and happy to provide information and advice. Ideal visit for gardening clubs. Hostas, hand-made cards and jewellery for sale. Some access over grass.

17 INHOLMES
Woodlands St Mary RG17 7SY. Lady Williams. *3m SE Lambourn. J14 M4 from A338 take B4000 towards Lambourn, Inholmes signed.* Home-made teas. **Adm £4.50, chd free. Sat 30 Mar; Sun 5 May; Sat 15, Sun 16 June (12-4). Visitors and groups (max 30) also welcome by appt 25 Mar to 30 Aug. Please phone Mark Lyons on 07811 381211 to arrange.**
Set in 10 acres with views over parkland. Lots to enjoy with large walled garden, rose beds, cutting and sunken garden. Individual touches include brightly painted gates and

benches and spooky wood. Walks to lake and meadow. Bluebell wood in spring and in summer the inspirational borders burst with colour. Gravel paths.

18 IVYDENE
283 Loddon Bridge Road, Woodley, Reading RG5 4BE. Janet & Bill Bonney, 0118 9697591, janetbonney2003@aol.com. *3½ m E of Reading. A4 from Reading towards Maidenhead. Woodley lies midway between Reading & Maidenhead. Loddon Bridge Rd is main rd through the small town. Garden approx 100yds S of 'Just Tiles' r'about. Parking in adjacent rd.* Home-made teas. **Adm £3.50, chd free. Visitors & groups (max 30) welcome by appt May to Sept.**
Small urban gardeners' garden, with mature tree fern walkway and many unusual hostas, ornamental grasses and plants. Overflowing herbaceous borders and rose bed, using mainly patio roses. The garden also features stained glass and ceramic art to complete the picture. Owner is a previous BBC Gardener of the Year finalist. Featured in Garden News - Garden of the Week.

KAYALAMI
See Buckinghamshire

GROUP OPENING

19 NEW KINTBURY GARDENS
Kintbury, Hungerford RG17 9TR.
From A4 between Hungerford & Newbury take rd signed Kintbury. Over level crossing, river & canal bridges into village centre at shops. Home-made teas at Midsummer House and The Old Vicarage. **Combined adm £5, chd free. Sun 23 June (12-5).**

NEW MIDSUMMER HOUSE
Mr & Mrs Neil & Martine Newport

NEW THE OLD VICARAGE

ROSE COTTAGE
Mr & Mrs D Smith

Three very different gardens in the village of Kintbury. Beyond the garden at **Midsummer House** is a small 'arboretum' planted with a lovely selection of specimen trees. Enjoy identifying them as you follow the tree trail. The ¼ -acre plantswoman's garden at C17 **Rose Cottage** has emphasis on perennials, beautiful cornus, roses and topiary. Attractive C19 church lych gate, gravel areas, water features and shaded area behind gothic facade. The grounds of **The Old Vicarage** extend for 350 yards along the Kennet & Avon Canal. They include terraces, lawns, flower beds, pasture land, herb garden, extensive vegetable garden, rose arch walkway, shrubs and mature trees, including a c200 year-old beech.

20 LITTLECOTE HOUSE HOTEL
Hungerford RG17 0SU. Warner Leisure Hotels, 01488 682509, www.warnerleisurehotels.co.uk.
2m W of Hungerford. From A4 turn R onto B4192 signed Swindon. 1½ m exit L & follow signs. Cream teas. **Adm £4. Sats & Suns 8, 9, 22, 23 June; 6, 7, 20, 21 July; 3, 4, 31 Aug; 1, 21, 22 Sept (11-4).**
Beautiful setting around Grade I listed house with views of the Kennet Valley over lawns and parkland. Formal areas incl herbaceous borders, rose and herb garden, clipped yew and box hedging, fruit trees. Don't miss the stumpery and the courtyard with large planters. Attractive selection of hanging baskets, some on sale at June openings. Sorry, no children. Gravel paths, some slopes.

21 LOWER LOVETTS FARM
Knowl Hill Common, Knowl Hill, Reading RG10 9YE. Mr Richard Sandford, 01628 822051, info@lowerlovettsfarm.com. *Off A4 at Knowl Hill into Knowl Hill Common. Past PH and across Common to T-junction. Turn L down dead end lane.* **Adm £4, chd free. Sun 21, Sat 27 July (12-5). Visitors also welcome by appt 10 July to 20 Aug, adm £5. Groups welcome (lane not suitable for coaches).**
A fascinating large modern organic kitchen garden (60m x 30m). Wide variety of vegetables and fruit grown for home consumption and nutritional value. Flowers grown for eating or herbal teas. Produce is also dried or bottled for yr-round use. Lots of interesting growing techniques and tips. Featured by Monty Don on BBC Gardener's World.

MARYFIELD
See Buckinghamshire

22 THE MILL HOUSE, BOXFORD
Boxford, Newbury RG20 8DP. Mrs Heather Luff, 01488 608385.
5m W of Newbury. From M4 J13, A4 towards Hungerford. Join B4000 & turn R 2m after Stockcross, signed Boxford. Turn L at junction then immed R by The Bell PH. The Mill House is on main rd through village on L after bridge. **Adm £4, chd free. Groups (min 4 - Max 10) welcome by appt 15 Apr to 21 Sept.**
Large mature garden surrounding Grade II listed Mill House with R Lambourn running through. Herbaceous borders, rose garden, espalier fruit trees, lawns and vegetables. Good spring colour with daffodils, tulips and alliums. Riverside walk overlooking water meadows. Lovely autumn garden with sedum, echinacea and clipped box. Featured in Country Homes & Interiors.

Wide variety of vegetables and fruit grown for home consumption and nutritional value . . .

23 THE MILL HOUSE DONNINGTON
Oxford Road, Donnington RG14 2JD. Dr & Mrs Jane Vaidya.
1m N of Newbury on B4494. Mill House on L immed after Donnington Alms Houses. M4 J13, A34 S towards Newbury. Take 1st exit follow signs to Donnington. Approx 2m (B4494 Oxford Rd) pass Castle PH on L. Mill House 50yds on R. Please park with consideration in Donnington village. Home-made teas. **Adm £3.50, chd free. Sun 30 June (2-6).**
2¾ acres of secluded gardens set around the Mill House (not open) and surrounded by the R Lambourn. Small lake, stream and millrace, herbaceous borders, lawns, woodland and bog garden, wild area, lulling sound of water. Art exhibition.

Bearwood College

24 MOOR CLOSE GARDENS
Popeswood Road, Binfield RG42 4AH. Newbold College. *2m W of Bracknell. From M4 take A329M towards Bracknell. Leave at 1st exit (Coppid Beach), take B3408 towards Bracknell at 2nd t-lights turn L & follow signs. From M3 exit at junction, take A322 towards Bracknell, continue onto A329. At A329M exit & take 3rd exit from r'about B3408, at 2nd t-lights turn L & follow signs.* Light refreshments at Newbold Church Centre. **Adm £2.50, chd free. Sun 16 June (2-5).**
Small Grade II listed garden designed 1911-13 by Oliver Hill and a rare example of his early work. Lavender garden, water parterre, remains of Italianate garden. Undergoing long-term restoration, it currently offers most interest in its historical architecture rather than planting. We hope you enjoy learning about its history from our knowledgable volunteers.

25 OAK COTTAGE
99B Kiln Ride, Finchampstead, Wokingham RG40 3PD. Ms Liz Ince, 01189 732238, OakCottage@telchines.co.uk, www.facebook.com/oakcottagegarden. *2½ m S of Wokingham. Off B3430 Nine Mile Ride between A321 Sandhurst Rd and B3016 Finchampstead Rd.* Home-made teas. **Adm £3.50, chd free. Visitors (max 10) welcome by appt, Suns in Feb only. Teas by arrangement.**
¼ -acre garden with woodland feel. Mature trees underplanted with snowdrops and other spring flowering bulbs. Several unusual winter flowering plants including an Edgeworthia chrysantha, Chrysosplenium macrophyllum and many Hellebores. Pine pergola with various climbers, greenhouse, island beds and eclectic planting. Small vegetable patch with fruit trees. Main paths offer wheelchair access, but smaller paths are gravel and bark and unsuitable.

26 ODNEY CLUB
Odney Lane, Cookham SL6 9SR. John Lewis Partnership. *3m N of Maidenhead. Off A4094 S of Cookham Bridge. Signs to car park in grounds.* Light refreshments. **Adm £4, chd free (share to Thames Valley Adventure Playground). Sun 21 Apr (2-6).**
This 120-acre site beside the Thames is continuously developing and, with lovely riverside walks, can take a full afternoon to visit. A favourite with Stanley Spencer who featured our magnolia in his work. Magnificent wisteria, specimen trees, herbaceous borders, side gardens, spring bedding and ornamental lake. Some gravel paths.

27 THE OLD RECTORY FARNBOROUGH
Wantage, Oxon OX12 8NX. Mr & Mrs Michael Todhunter. *4m SE of Wantage. Take B4494 Wantage-Newbury Rd, after 4m turn E at sign for Farnborough.* Home-made teas. **Adm £5, chd free (share to Farnborough PCC). Suns 14 Apr; 12 May; 16 June (2-5.30).**
In a series of immaculately tended garden rooms, incl herbaceous borders, arboretum, boules, rose, pool and vegetables. There is an explosion of rare and interesting plants, beautifully combined for colour and texture. With stunning views across the countryside, it is the perfect setting for the 1749 rectory (not open), once home of John Betjeman, in memory of whom John Piper created a window in the local church. Awarded Finest Parsonage in England by Country Life and the Rectory Society. Some steep slopes and gravel paths.

OLD THATCH & THE MILLENNIUM BARN
See Hampshire

28 OLD WATERFIELD
Winkfield Road, Ascot SL5 7LJ. Hugh & Catherine Stevenson. *6m SW of Windsor. On A330 (Winkfield Rd) midway between A329 & A332 to E of Ascot Racecourse. Parking on practice ground (by kind permission Royal Ascot GC), access by gate adjoining entrance to Golf Club.* Home-made teas. **Adm £3.50, chd free. Sun 25 Aug (2-5).**
Set in 4 acres between Ascot Heath and Windsor Great Park, the original cottage garden has been developed and extended over the past few years. Herbaceous borders, meadow with specimen trees, large productive vegetable garden, orchard, mixed hedging. Plants for sale include unusual varieties grown from seed. Home-made jams and chutneys also for sale.

29 OXFORD COTTAGE
22 Conisboro Avenue, Caversham, Reading RG4 7JB. Louise Farrell. *2m N of Reading. Please park in Grosvenor PH car park - Kidmore Rd (RG4 7NH) From A4074 (Caversham) take Richmond Rd. Straight on at Xrds. L onto Kidmore Rd. PH on L. Walk through back of car park along Kelvedon Way. Turn R into Conisboro Ave. Garden 100 yds on R.* Home-made teas. **Adm £2.50, chd free. Sat 22, Sun 23 June (1-5).**
A long narrow garden (180 x 20ft) designed and planted by owner to deceive in terms of size. A winding path entices the visitor through peaceful rooms encouraging a walk through perennial flowerbeds, shrubs and trees, circular garden, vegetable garden, greenhouse, old apple tree and wildlife pond. Garden design exhibition.

30 NEW PARKLEA
Basingstoke Road, Spencers Wood, Reading RG7 1PH. Miss Erica Marsh. *M4 J11, out of Reading along A33. At 1st T-lights turn L B3349 signed 'Three Mile Cross & Spencers Wood'. Past The Farriers Arms & Warings Bakers on L. On R is long layby, please park here. Garden on same side as Murco garage between garage and Premier Stores. Approaching from Risely on B3349 enter Spencers Wood, garden is 3 properties along from Premier Stores.* Cream teas and cake. **Adm by donation. Suns 23 June; 25 Aug (11-5).**
This beautiful and imaginative garden behind a traditional Victorian semi detached cottage demonstrates just how much interest and beauty can be packed into a tiny space. The owner has created a picture perfect garden bursting with ideas using old and reclaimed materials in an imaginative way. Vintage tool sale.

PONDERS
See Buckinghamshire

31 THE PRIORY
Beech Hill RG7 2BJ. Mr & Mrs C Carter, 0118 9883146, tita@getcarter.org.uk. *5m S of Reading. M4 J11. Follow signs to A33 Basingstoke, turn L at 1st set T-lights signed Spencers Wood & Swallowfield. After 1½ m turn R by Murco garage signed Beech Hill. In village turn opp church into Wood Lane, then R down Priory Dr. House at end of drive.* Home-made teas. **Adm £4, chd free. Visitors welcome by appt June to Aug, groups of 6 - 30.**
Extensive gardens in grounds of former C12 Benedictine Priory (not open), rebuilt 1648. The mature gardens are in an attractive setting beside the R Loddon. Large formal walled garden with espalier fruit trees, lawns, mixed and replanted herbaceous borders, vegetables and roses. Woodland, fine trees, lake and new Italian style water garden.

32 PYT HOUSE
Ashampstead RG8 8RA. Hans & Virginia von Celsing, virginiacelsing@gmail.com. *4m W of Pangbourne. From Yattendon head towards Reading. Rd forks L into a beech wood towards Ashampstead. Keep L and join lower rd. ½ m turn L just before houses.* Home-made teas. **Combined adm £5, chd free. Sat 29, Sun 30 June (2-5). Combined with Willow Tree Cottage. Groups (min 10) also welcome by appt 8 Apr to 12 July, adm £7.**
A 4-acre garden planted over the last 8yrs by designer owner, around C18 house (not open). Mature trees, yew, hornbeam and beech hedges, pleached limes, modern perennial borders, pond, orchard and vegetable garden. New iris beds. Broadly organic, a haven for bees and butterflies. Chickens.

33 THE RISC ROOF GARDEN, READING
35-39 London Street, Reading RG1 4PS. Reading International Solidarity Centre, 01189 470637, mary@risc.org.uk, www.risc.org.uk/garden. *Central Reading. 5 mins walk from Oracle shopping centre. 10 mins from station. Parking in Queens Rd or Oracle car-parks or in top car-park only at back of RISC building (via London St, South St and East St).* Light refreshments at RISC Global Cafe. **Adm £3, chd free (share to RISC). Sat 11 May; Sat 13 July; Sat 10 Aug (12-4). Groups (10 - 20) also welcome by appt for tours.**
Small edible roof forest garden developed to demonstrate sustainability and our dependence on plants. All plants in the garden have an economic use for food, clothing, medicine etc, and come from all over the world. Demonstration of renewable energy, water harvesting and irrigation systems. Garden accessed by external staircase. Regular tours of garden.

A winding path entices the visitor through peaceful rooms . . .

34 ROOKSNEST
Ermin Street, Lambourn Woodlands RG17 7SB. Dame Theresa Sackler, 01488 71678, garden@rooksnest.net. *2m S of Lambourn on B4000. From J14 of M4 take the A338 Wantage rd, turning onto the B4000 (Ermin Street). Rooksnest signposted after 3m.* Home-made teas. **Adm £4.50, chd free. Wed 24 Apr; Wed 12 June (11-4). Visitors also welcome by appt Apr to Aug.**
Approx 10-acre exceptionally fine traditional English garden. Rose and herbaceous garden, newly re-designed and planted pond area, herb garden, vegetables and glasshouses. Many specimen trees and fine shrubs, orchard and terraces renovated and recently replanted. Garden mostly designed by Arabella Lennox-Boyd since 1980. Plants for sale - June only. Mostly grass and hard patio, some gravel. Happy to provide assistance to wheelchair users.

35 SANDLEFORD PLACE
Newtown, Newbury RG20 9AY. Mel Gatward, 01635 40726, melgatward@btinternet.com. *1½ m S of Newbury on A399. House on NW side of Swan r'about at Newtown.* Home-made teas. **Adm £5, chd free. Sat 15, Sun 16 June (2-5.30). Visitors also welcome by appt 19 Jan to 16 Oct. (For groups of less than 10, adm is £7.50).**
A plantswoman's 5 acres, more exuberant than manicured with R. Enborne flowing through. Various areas of shrub and herbaceous borders create a romantic, naturalistic effect. Wonderful old walled garden, potager and herb bed. Yr-round

interest from early carpets of snowdrops, crocus-covered lawn and spring daffodils, to autumn berries and leaf colour. Most areas wheelchair accessible.

36 SHEEPDROVE ORGANIC FARM
Sheepdrove Rd, Lambourn RG17 7UU. Mr & Mrs Peter Kindersley, www.sheepdrove.com. *2m N Lambourn. From Xrds in Lambourn, head N towards Wantage. After ½ m R up Sheepdrove Rd (signed Eco Conference Centre). Continue 2m, through wheelwash, straight on down concrete rd to red barn on L, follow signs. Do not use postcode with Sat Nav, input Sheepdrove Rd.* Light refreshments at Eco-Conference Centre barn. **Adm £4, chd free. Sun 30 June (11-3).**
Four fascinating gardens at the heart of Sheepdrove Farm, home to owners of Neal's Yard Remedies. Juliet's garden at Farmhouse has a potager and gravel garden with herbs, vegetables and flowers. Walled organic vegetable garden with glasshouses nearby. Delightful physic garden designed by Jekka McVicar. Neal's Yard Remedies garden for supplying some of their herbs.

37 NEW SOUTHGATE
Hurstwood, South Ascot SL5 9SP. Mr & Mrs Tony & Judy Bryant, www.jplot.co.uk. *7m SW of Windsor. Off A330 ½ m S of Ascot Racecourse turn R into Coronation Rd, 2nd R into Woodlands Ride, 1st L into Hurstwood. Turn R at T-junction, follow rd to L up slight hill. Garden is on brow of hill.* **Adm £4, chd free. Sun 30 June (11-5).**
Unusual, 1 acre woodland garden on poor acid soil with much dry shade planting under mature trees. Steeply banked and planted rockery water feature and pond, cottage border, woodland walk, vegetable garden and greenhouse. Owner is hosta enthusiast.

GROUP OPENING

38 STANFORD DINGLEY GARDENS
Stanford Dingley RG7 6LS. *5m SW of Pangbourne. From A4 take A340 (Pangbourne Rd), 1st L to Bradfield. After Bradfield L at Xrds, 2½ m, L into village. Car Park will be signposted. Approx 7 mins walk to gardens.* Tea adjacent The Spring. **Combined adm £5, chd free. Sun 30 June (2-5).**

JENNETTS HILL HOUSE
Mr & Mrs Hugh Priestley

THE SPRING
Mr & Mrs Mark Hawkesworth

Enjoy visiting 2 pretty country gardens, then treat yourself to tea and cake in the heart of the village. **Jennetts Hill House** has an attractive small garden with wide variety of roses, shrubs and mixed island beds and borders developed over past 25yrs. **The Spring** is a cottage garden with spring-fed pond and stream, mature specimen trees, fruit and vegetable area, herbaceous and rose borders and a lovely green oak pergola.

Delightful physic garden designed by Jekka McVicar . . .

GROUP OPENING

39 STOCKCROSS GARDENS
Stockcross, Newbury RG20 8JX. *3m W of Newbury. 7m E of Hungerford. Signed off A4. Leave M4 at J13, take A34 (S) towards Winchester. After 3m exit at Bath Rd junction on to A4 (W) towards Hungerford at r'about. After 150yds at next r'about take B4000 signed Stockcross.* Cream teas at Rookwood Farm House. **Combined adm £4, chd free. Sun 26 May; Sun 30 June (11-5).**

ROOKWOOD FARM HOUSE
The Hon Rupert & Charlotte Digby
www.rookwoodfarmhouse.co.uk

SPRINGFIELD COTTAGE
Anne & Ron Cummings

Stockcross is an attractive small village originally developed by the Sutton family as a model village. **Rookwood Farm House**, a 2-acre valley garden with an impressive arrangement of two ponds and connecting cascade whilst **Springfield Cottage** is a delightful thatched cottage with a terraced garden created from a wilderness.

40 STOCKCROSS HOUSE
Stockcross RG20 8LP. Susan & Edward Vandyk, 07765 674863, dragonflygardens@btinternet.com. *3m W of Newbury. 7m E of Hungerford. Signed off A4. From N A34 (S) towards Winchester. 3m S of M4 J13 exit at Bath Rd junction, on to A4 (W) towards Hungerford at r'about. At next r'about take B4000 signed Stockcross. From W join A34 (S) from M4 or use A4. From S take A34 (N) and exit at Bath Rd junction. From W take A4 or leave M4 at J14, take exit towards Wantage and then 1st R on to B4000 to Stockcross (5 m).* **Adm £4, chd free. Wed 1 May (11-4); Sun 2, Sun 16 June (1-5); Wed 3 July (11-4). Groups (10 - 30) also welcome by appt 8 May to 31 July, adm £5. Refreshments by arrangement.**
Two acre garden. Emphasis on plant partnerships, colour combinations and naturalistic planting. Long wisteria and clematis covered pergola, reflecting pool with folly, cascade with pond and duck house, rich variety of roses, vegetable and cutting garden. Sculptural elements by local artists.

STOKE POGES MEMORIAL GARDENS
See Buckinghamshire

41 STUBBINGS HOUSE
Henley Road, Maidenhead SL6 6QL. Mr & Mrs D Good, 01628 825454, info@stubbingsnursery.co.uk, www.stubbingsnursery.co.uk. *2m W of Maidenhead. From A4130 Henley Road follow private access rd (signed) opp Stubbings Church. See website for further directions.* Lunches & refreshments at Nursery Cafe. **Adm £3, chd free. Fri 29, Sat 30, Sun 31 Mar; Mon 1 Apr; Sat 4, Sun 5, Mon 6 May (10.30-4.30). Visitors also welcome by appt Mar to July.**
Parkland garden accessed via adjacent retail nursery. Set around C18 house (not open), home to Queen Wilhelmina of Netherlands in WW2. Large lawn with ha-ha and

Lower Lovetts Farm

woodland walks. Notable trees incl historic cedars and araucaria. March brings an abundance of daffodils, bluebells in April, and in May a 60m wall of wisteria. C18 ice house. Access to adjacent National Trust woodland. Firm, gravel paths. Level site.

42 SUNNINGDALE PARK

Larch Avenue, Ascot SL5 0QE. De Vere Group. *6m S of Windsor. On A30 at Sunningdale take Broomhall Lane. After ½ m, R into Larch Ave. From A329 turn into Silwood Rd towards Sunningdale.* Home-made teas. **Adm £4, chd free. Mon 27 May (2-5).**

Over 20 acres of beautifully landscaped gardens in Capability Brown style. Terrace garden and Victorian rockery designed by Pulham incl cave and water features. Lake area with paved walks, extensive lawns with specimen trees and flower beds, and early rhododendrons. Lovely 1m woodland walk. Grade II listed building (not open). Free garden tour at 3.30pm.

GROUP OPENING

43 SWALLOWFIELD HORTICULTURAL SOCIETY

Swallowfield RG7 1QX. *5m S of Reading. M4 J11 & A33/B3349 signed 'Swallowfield NGS Opening'. Tickets from Russetts, Swallowfield St (April) and Doctors Surgery, The Street (June).* Teas at Lodden Lower Farm (April) and Greenwings (June). Also lunches at Brambles (June only). **Combined adm £4 (April), £6 (June), chd free. Sun 14 Apr (2-5); Sun 23 June (11-5).**

APRIL COTTAGE
Linda & Bill Kirkpatrick.
Open June date only

5 BEEHIVE COTTAGES
Ray Tormey.
Open both dates

BRAMBLES
Sarah & Martyn Dadds.
Open June date only

NEW **5 CURLYS WAY**
Mr & Mrs Carolyn & Gary Clark.
Open June date only

GREENWINGS
Liz & Ray Jones.
Open both dates

LODDON LOWER FARM
Open April date only

NORKETT COTTAGE
Jenny Spencer.
Open June date only

NEW **PRIMROSE COTTAGE**
Mr & Mrs Hilda and Eddie Phillips.
Open June date only

RUSSETTS
Roberta Stewart.
Open both dates

WESSEX HOUSE
Val Payne.
Open June date only

Swallowfield - a real village enhanced by a C12 church, nestled amongst rural countryside, by the Whitewater, Blackwater and Loddon rivers creating an abundance of wildlife and lovely views. We are proud to offer a variety of beautiful well stocked gardens of all shapes and sizes. Most gardens are within walking distance of each other, but transport is required for outlying gardens. You will also see a model train and an Orchid House.

44 THE TITHE BARN

Tidmarsh RG8 8ER. Fran Wakefield. *1m S of Pangbourne, off A340. From J12 M4 take A340 to Pangbourne. Turn R at Greyhound PH in Tidmarsh, over bridge, R into Mill Corner field for parking. Short walk across field to garden.* Home-made teas at adjacent Norman church. **Adm £3.50, chd free. Sun 16 June (2-5).**

This is a delightful village garden (¼ acre) within high brick walls around The Tithe Barn dating from 1760. Formally laid out with parterres of box and yew. There are roses, hostas, topiary and a little fernery as well as interesting vintage pots and containers. Working beehives. Finalist in The Daily Mail National Garden Competition. Plants and pots for sale.

45 TRUNKWELL GARDEN PROJECT

Beech Hill, Reading RG7 2AT, www.thrive.org.uk. *7m S of Reading. From M4 J11, follow signs to A33, Basingstoke. L at 1st set of T-lights onto B3349 signed Spencers Wood & Swallowfield. After 1½ m turn R into Beech Hill Rd then approx 1½ m to Beech Hill, Trunkwell Park on R. Signs in village.* Home-made teas. **Adm £3.50, chd £1. Sat 4 May (11-4); Sun 7, Sun 28 July (2-4.30); Sat 14 Sept (11-4).**

Beautiful 3 acre Victorian walled garden at Thrive, the national charity helping those touched by disability to transform their lives using gardening. Formal and informal interest, pond, butterfly garden, fruit and cut flower areas, potager, glasshouse, sensory and cottage gardens. Award-winning Chelsea garden and now a new gallery of gardens created for people with specific disabilities.

We are proud to offer a variety of beautiful well stocked gardens of all shapes and sizes . . .

46 TWIGS

Old Forest Road, Winnersh, Wokingham RG41 1JA. Jenny & Gerry Winterbourne. *1½ m NW of Wokingham. From A329 Reading-Wokingham rd just S of Sainsbury's T-lights and M4 turn into Old Forest Rd (Forest Rd on some maps); L from Reading, R from Wokingham. Over railway bridge Twigs is 300 metres on L, just past Lowther Rd & just before Commons Rd (both on R).* Home-made teas. **Adm £3, chd free. Sun 14 July (2-5).**

Half acre garden: semi-formal with two lily ponds at the top; gravel paths lead down to less formal woodland area. Planting is mainly trees and shrubs under-planted with drifts of bulbs and perennials; small vegetable garden to one side. Once part of an orchard, the plot was neglected for many years and became partly wooded. The lower half retains a feel of woodland although the planting now includes ordinary garden plants. There are no lawns: except for two ponds and gravel paths the whole garden is given over to plants.

TYLNEY HALL HOTEL
See Hampshire

THE VYNE
See Hampshire

47 ◆ WALTHAM PLACE GARDENS
Church Hill, White Waltham SL6 3JH. Mr & Mrs N Oppenheimer, 01628 825517, www.walthamplace.com. *3½ m W of Maidenhead. From M4 J8/9 take A404. Follow signs for White Waltham. Pass airfield on R. Turn L signed Windsor/Paley St. Pass church, round bend, entrance on L by post box. From Bracknell/Wokingham A3095 to A330 direction Maidenhead. Turn L at Paley St B3024 to White Waltham. Turn R into Church Hill, look for brown Waltham Place signs.* Refreshments in the barn. **Adm £5, chd £1. For NGS: Visitors by appt for tours with a gardener every Weds 22 May to 25 Sept. Please phone to book. For other opening times and information, please phone or see garden website.**
Influenced by Henk Gerritsen, who collaborated with Strilli Oppenheimer to embrace a naturalistic philosophy combining forces with nature. A haven for insects, animals, fungi and indigenous flora. Naturalistic planting, woodland and meadows. Organic and bio-dynamic kitchen garden and farm.

48 ◆ WELFORD PARK
Newbury RG20 8HU. Mrs J H Puxley, www.welfordpark.co.uk. *6m NW of Newbury. On Lambourn Valley Rd. Entrance on Newbury-Lambourn rd.* Home-made teas. **Adm £3.50, chd free. For NGS: Sat 8 June (2-5). For other opening times and information, please see garden website.**
An NGS 1927 pioneer garden with parkland and formal garden with emphasis on wildlife habitat and wild flowers. Naturalistic and healing planting for calm atmosphere and delicious scents. Peony border, rose pergola and large wisteria on south side of Queen Anne house. Gravel paths and uneven surfaces.

Riotously planted with roses, herbs, ferns and other favourites . . .

WEST SILCHESTER HALL
See Hampshire

WHITE GABLES
See Hampshire

THE WHITE HOUSE
See Buckinghamshire

49 WHITEHOUSE FARM COTTAGE
Murrell Hill Lane, Binfield, Bracknell RG42 4BY. Louise Lusby, 01344 423688, garden.cottages@ntlworld.com. *Between Bracknell & Wokingham. From A329 take B3408. At 2nd set of T-lights turn L into St Marks Rd, 2nd L (opp Roebuck PH) into Foxley Lane. L into Murrell Hill Lane. Car parking in lanes. Do not use Sat Nav. Murrell Hill Lane is a No Through Road, only approach from Foxley Lane end.* Home-made teas. **Adm £3.50, chd free (share to Sam Beare Hospice). Sun 23 June (11-5). Groups (10 - 20) also welcome by appt June to 2 Aug, adm £5.**
Atmospheric cottage garden of 'rooms' with brick, china and decorative pebble areas - riotously planted with roses, herbs, ferns and other favourites. The courtyard with pot and lily ponds leads to terrace with circular domed seating area. Pond garden contains a pretty summer house and glasshouse. Featured in The English Garden magazine & on ITV's Love Your Garden.

WHITEWALLS
See Buckinghamshire

50 WILLOW TREE COTTAGE
Ashampstead RG8 8RA. Katy & David Weston, 01635 201356, westonkaty@hotmail.com. *4m W of Pangbourne. From Yattendon head towards Reading. L fork in beech wood to Ashampstead, keep L, join lower rd, ½ m turn L before houses.* Home-made teas. **Combined adm £5, chd free. Sat 29, Sun 30 June (2-5). Combined with Pyt House. Groups (max 20) also welcome by appt 8 Apr to 12 July, adm £3.**
Small pretty cottage garden surrounding the house that was originally built for the gardener of Pyt House. Substantially redesigned and replanted in recent years. Perennial borders, vegetable garden, pond with ducks and chickens.

1 WOGSBARNE COTTAGES
See Hampshire

WOOLSTONE MILL HOUSE
See Oxfordshire

Berkshire County Volunteers

County Organiser
Heather Skinner, 5 Liddell Close, Finchampstead, Wokingham RG40 4NS, 01189 737197, heatheraskinner@aol.com

County Treasurer
Hugh Priestley, Jennetts Hill House, Stanford Dingley, Reading RG7 6JP, 01189 744349, hughpriestley1@aol.com

Assistant County Organisers
Elspeth Ewen, Blossoms, Clay Lane, Beenham RG7 5PA, 01189 712856, elspethewen@btinternet.com
Linda Kirkpatrick, April Cottage, The Street, Swallowfield RG7 1QY, 0118 988 2837, wychwoodint@yahoo.co.uk
Angela O'Connell, 22 The Hatches, Frimley Green GU21 6HE, 01252 668645, angela.oconnell@ntlworld.com
Nikki Sketch, Newlands, Courtlands Hill, Pangbourne RG8 7BE, 07768 934030, nikki@sketch.cc

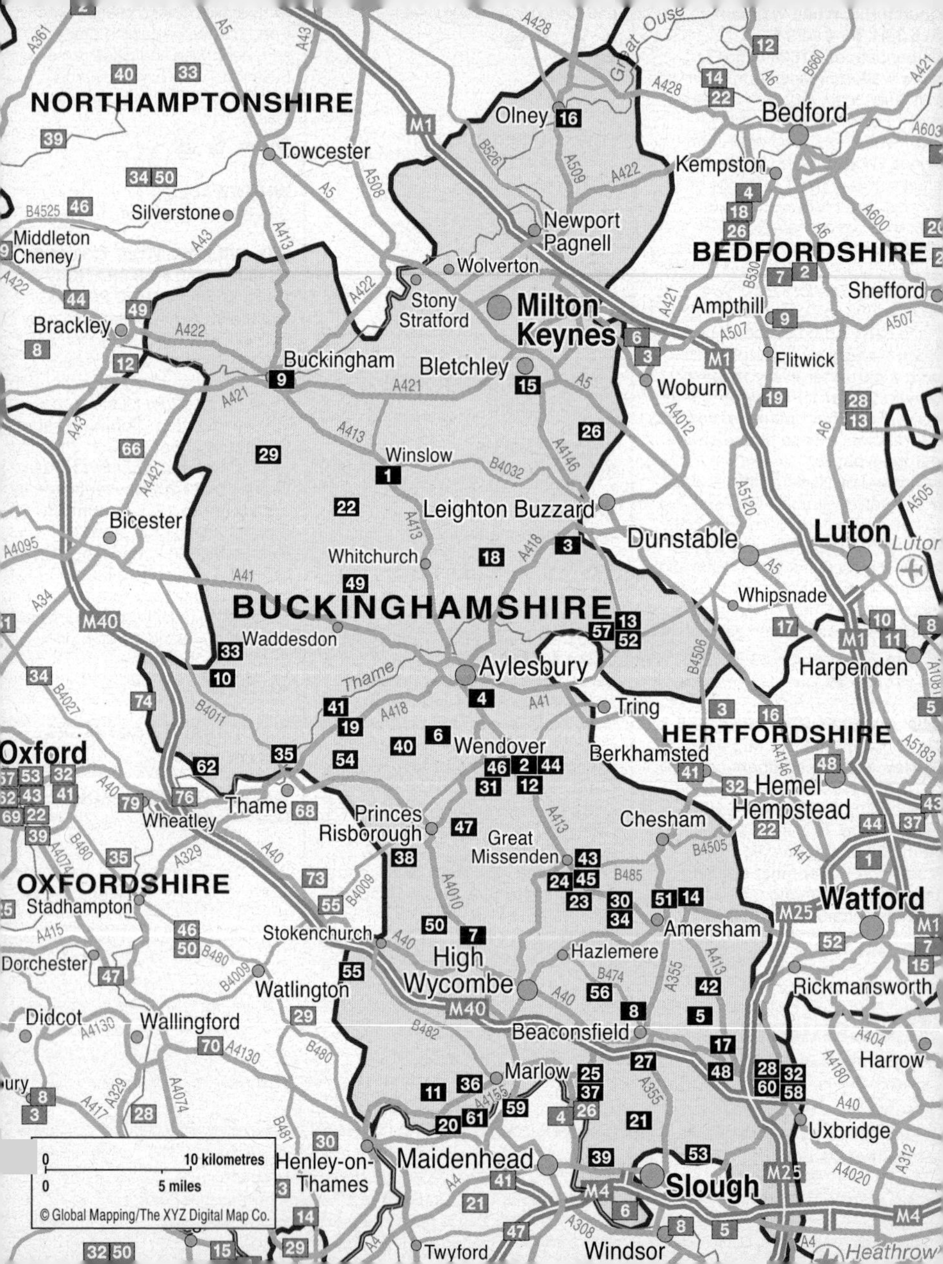
NORTHAMPTONSHIRE
BEDFORDSHIRE
BUCKINGHAMSHIRE
HERTFORDSHIRE
OXFORDSHIRE
Great Ouse
Olney
Bedford
Towcester
Kempston
Silverstone
Newport Pagnell
Middleton Cheney
Wolverton
Stony Stratford
Milton Keynes
Ampthill
Shefford
Brackley
Flitwick
Buckingham
Bletchley
Woburn
Winslow
Leighton Buzzard
Bicester
Dunstable
Luton
Whitchurch
Whipsnade
Waddesdon
Harpenden
Aylesbury
Thame
Tring
Oxford
Wendover
Berkhamsted
Hemel Hempstead
Thame
Wheatley
Princes Risborough
Chesham
Great Missenden
Stadhampton
Watford
Amersham
Stokenchurch
Dorchester
High Wycombe
Hazlemere
Watlington
Rickmansworth
Didcot
Wallingford
Beaconsfield
Harrow
Marlow
Uxbridge
Henley-on-Thames
Maidenhead
Slough
Twyford
Windsor
Heathrow
0 10 kilometres
0 5 miles
© Global Mapping/The XYZ Digital Map Co.

Opening Dates

February

Sunday 24
37 Magnolia House
49 Quainton Gardens

March

Sunday 10
60 Wind in the Willows

Sunday 24
14 Chesham Bois House

Sunday 31
43 Overstroud Cottage

April

Saturday 6
51 Rivendell

Sunday 7
51 Rivendell
57 Westend House

Sunday 14
35 Long Crendon Gardens

Sunday 21
43 Overstroud Cottage
59 Whitewalls

Wednesday 24
21 Dorneywood Garden

Sunday 28
30 Hollydyke House
53 Stoke Poges Memorial Gardens

May

Wednesday 1
24 Gipsy House
45 The Plant Specialist

Sunday 5
38 The Manor House

Monday 6
3 Ascott
41 Nether Winchendon House
54 Turn End

Sunday 12
14 Chesham Bois House
43 Overstroud Cottage
46 The Plough

Sunday 19
58 The White House

Thursday 23
24 Gipsy House
45 The Plant Specialist

Saturday 25
39 Maryfield

Sunday 26
39 Maryfield
53 Stoke Poges Memorial Gardens

Monday 27
23 Fressingwood
41 Nether Winchendon House
46 The Plough

Wednesday 29
21 Dorneywood Garden

Thursday 30
10 Bunyans Cottage
21 Dorneywood Garden
33 Laplands Farm

June

Sunday 2
1 Abbotts House
5 Beech House

Saturday 8
16 Cowper & Newton Museum Gardens

Sunday 9
7 Bradenham Manor
16 Cowper & Newton Museum Gardens
18 Cublington Gardens
28 Higher Denham Gardens
49 Quainton Gardens

Tuesday 11
43 Overstroud Cottage

Home made tea and cakes . . . yummy . . . !

National Gardens Weekend

Saturday 15
8 18 Brownswood Road
11 Burrow Farm
32 Kayalami
44 11 The Paddocks
52 Rose Cottage (Evening)

Sunday 16
8 18 Brownswood Road
11 Burrow Farm
15 Church Green Gardens
22 East and Middle Claydon Gardens
29 Hillesden House
38 The Manor House
42 North Down
44 11 The Paddocks
48 Ponders

Tuesday 18
15 Church Green Gardens

Wednesday 19
24 Gipsy House
45 The Plant Specialist

Thursday 20
36 Lords Wood
40 Moat Farm

Friday 21
8 18 Brownswood Road (Evening)

Saturday 22
2 Acer Corner
25 Grange Drive Wooburn
62 Worminghall Gardens

Sunday 23
2 Acer Corner
6 Bishopstone Gardens
13 Cheddington Gardens
17 Craiglea House
26 Great Brickhill Gardens

Wednesday 26
25 Grange Drive Wooburn

Sunday 30
4 Aylesbury Gardens

July

Friday 5
44 11 The Paddocks (Evening)

Saturday 6
44 11 The Paddocks

Sunday 7
34 Little Missenden Gardens
44 11 The Paddocks

Sunday 14
14 Chesham Bois House
59 Whitewalls

Thursday 18
24 Gipsy House
45 The Plant Specialist

Wednesday 24
21 Dorneywood Garden

Saturday 27
55 The Walled Garden

Sunday 28
19 Cuddington Gardens
47 Pollards

August

Thursday 1
20 Danesfield House

Tuesday 6
20 Danesfield House

Thursday 8
20 Danesfield House

Sunday 11
31 Homelands
57 Westend House

Tuesday 13
20 Danesfield House

Monday 26
3 Ascott
41 Nether Winchendon House

Look out for the NGS yellow arrows...

September

Sunday 1

59 Whitewalls
61 Wittington Estate

Thursday 5

36 Lords Wood

Sunday 8

54 Turn End

October

Saturday 19

2 Acer Corner

Sunday 20

2 Acer Corner

February 2014

Sunday 23

49 Quainton Gardens

A particular feature is the meadow in the back garden with numerous bulbs and flowers . . .

Gardens open to the public

3 Ascott
7 Bradenham Manor
16 Cowper & Newton Museum Gardens
41 Nether Winchendon House
45 The Plant Specialist
53 Stoke Poges Memorial Gardens

By appointment only

9 Buckingham Gardens
12 Cedar House
27 Hall Barn
50 Red Kites
56 Watercroft

Also open by Appointment ☎

1 Abbotts House
2 Acer Corner
4 Tolverne, Aylesbury Gardens
8 18 Brownswood Road
11 Burrow Farm
13 Bridge Cottage, Cheddington Gardens
14 Chesham Bois House
17 Craiglea House
29 Hillesden House
30 Hollydyke House
31 Homelands
32 Kayalami
34 Manor Farm House, Little Missenden Gardens
37 Magnolia House
39 Maryfield
42 North Down
43 Overstroud Cottage
44 11 The Paddocks
49 The Vine, Quainton Gardens
52 Rose Cottage
57 Westend House
59 Whitewalls
60 Wind in the Willows

The Gardens

1 ABBOTTS HOUSE

10 Church Street, Winslow MK18 3AN. Mrs Jane Rennie, 01296 712326, janerennie@connectfree.co.uk. *9m N of Aylesbury. On A413 into Winslow. From town centre take Horn St & R into Church St. Walk up Church Street & take L fork at top. Entrance 20 metres on L through gate in wall. Parking in town centre and adjacent street.* **Adm £3, chd free. Sun 2 June (2-5.30). Visitors also welcome by appt June to Sept.**

Garden on different levels divided into 4. Courtyard near house with arbour and pots, woodland garden (planted 6yrs ago) with rose arbour, swimming pool garden with grasses. Walled Victorian kitchen garden with glass houses, potager, fruit pergola, wall trained fruit and many Mediterranean plants. Limited wheelchair access.

2 ACER CORNER

10 Manor Road, Wendover HP22 6HQ. Jo Naiman, 07958 319234, jo@acercorner.com, www.acercorner.com. *3m S of Aylesbury. Follow A413 into Wendover. L at clock tower r'about into Aylesbury Rd. R at next r'about into Wharf Rd, continue past schools on L, garden on R.* Home-made teas. **Adm £2.50, chd free. Sat 22, Sun 23 June, Sat 19, Sun 20 Oct (2-5). Visitors also welcome by appt May to Nov.**

Garden designer's garden with Japanese influence and large collection of Japanese maples. The enclosed front garden is Japanese in style. Back garden is divided into 3 areas: patio area surrounded by roses; densely planted area with many acers and roses and the corner which incl a productive greenhouse and interesting planting. Featured in Garden News.

3 ◆ ASCOTT

Ascott, Wing, Leighton Buzzard LU7 0PR. Sir Evelyn de Rothschild, National Trust, 01296 688242, www.nationaltrust.org.uk. *2m SW of Leighton Buzzard, 8m NE of Aylesbury. Via A418. Buses: 150 Aylesbury - Milton Keynes, 100 Aylesbury & Milton Keynes.* **Adm £4.80, chd £2.40. For NGS: Mon 6 May, Mon 26 Aug (2-6). For other opening times and information, please phone or see garden website.**

Combining Victorian formality with early C20 natural style and recent plantings to lead it into the C21, with a recently completed garden designed by Jacques and Peter Wirtz who designed the gardens at Alnwick Castle, and also a Richard Long Sculpture. Terraced lawns with specimen and ornamental trees, panoramic views to the Chilterns. Naturalised bulbs, mirror-image herbaceous borders, impressive topiary incl box and yew sundial. Outdoor wheelchairs available from car park. Prior booking advised. Indoor wheelchairs (provided) are used in the House.

ASHRIDGE HOUSE

See Hertfordshire

GROUP OPENING

4 AYLESBURY GARDENS

Aylesbury HP21 7LR. *¾ m SE of Aylesbury Centre. SE of town centre (3 gardens off A413, 1 garden off A41).* Home-made teas 2 Spenser Road. **Combined adm £4, chd free. Sun 30 June (2-6).**

16 MILTON ROAD
Roger & Frances King

2 SPENSER ROAD
Mr & Mrs G A Brown

TOLVERNE
Bill Nuttycombe & Julian Oaten-Wareham
Visitors also welcome by appt (Sats) June to Aug (11-2). Please email for bookings. aylesbury-guy@hotmail.co.uk

NEW **7 WENDOVER WAY**
Ms Jackie Bennett OBE

Four mature town gardens showing a wide range of ideas and designs. Each garden displays the individuality of its owners and their passions, incl tender perennials, herbaceous borders and ponds as well as a new 'wildlife' pond. Other features incl an interesting Victorian greenhouse, vegetable beds and cottage style gardens.

---

5 **NEW** **BEECH HOUSE**

Long Wood Drive, Jordans, Beaconsfield HP9 2SS. Mr & Mrs R Edwards. *Adjoining, but not in, Jordans village. From A40 follow sign for Seer Green & Jordans for approx 1m, turn R into Jordans Way & L into Longwood Drive. Garden 1st on R. From A413 through Chalfont St Giles for approx 1½ m, L into Twitchells & L into Jordans Way.* **Adm £3, chd free. Sun 2 June (2-5.30).**
2 acre plantsman's garden built up over the last 25yrs, with a wide range of plants aimed at providing yr-round interest. Many shrubs, roses, grasses, ferns and trees planted for their ornamental bark and autumnal foliage. A particular feature is the meadow in the back garden with numerous bulbs and flowers. Wheelchair access dependent upon weather conditions.

GROUP OPENING

6 **NEW** **BISHOPSTONE GARDENS**

HP17 8SQ. *2m S of Aylesbury. Between Stoke Mandeville and Stone.* Home-made teas. **Combined adm £4, chd free. Sun 23 June (2-5).**

NEW **BISHOPSTONE FARM COTTAGE**
Mr Martin Clacy

NEW **BISHOPSTONE FARMHOUSE**
Mrs Hetty Taylor

Two gardens adjacent to each other in the rural village of Bishopstone. The Farmhouse is an informal ¾ acre orchard garden with herbaceous borders, vegetable garden and chickens, lovely views from the garden. Farm Cottage has a series of modern landscaped rooms within a traditional cottage garden - a hidden gem. Grass paths. Wheelchair access weather dependent.

100 Church Green Road, Church Green Gardens

---

7 **◆ BRADENHAM MANOR**

Bradenham, High Wycombe HP14 4HF. National Trust, 07989 390940, www.nationaltrust.org.uk. *2½ m NW of High Wycombe, 5m S of Princes Risborough. On A4010, turn by Red Lion PH, car park signed on village green.* Home-made teas Home-made teas in cricket pavillion on village green. **Adm £3.50, chd free. For NGS: Sun 9 June (1-4.30). For other opening times and information, please phone or see garden website.**
Unique opportunity to see this C17 garden with beautiful views over our quintessential Chilterns village and countryside. Reinstated Victorian summer border, yew hedges, restored parterre and orchard. Guided tour of garden by Head gardener - 2pm. Additional charge £1.50. Gravel paths, steep grass slopes.

8 **18 BROWNSWOOD ROAD**

Beaconsfield HP9 2NU. John & Bernadette Thompson, 01494 689959, bthompson018@yahoo.co.uk. *Beaconsfield New Town. From New Town turn R into Ledborough Lane, L into Sandleswood Rd, 2nd R into Brownswood Rd.* **Adm £3, chd free. Sat 15, Sun 16 June (1-5). Evening Opening £3, chd free, wine, Fri 21 June (6-8.30). Visitors also welcome by appt Apr to Sept.**
A plant-filled suburban garden designed by Barbara Hunt. A harmonious arrangement of arcs and circles introduces a rhythm that leads through the garden. Sweeping box curves, gravel beds, brick edging and lush planting. A restrained use of purples and reds dazzle against a grey and green background.

D

GROUP OPENING

9 BUCKINGHAM GARDENS
MK18 1BS, 07860 714758, leonie@pjtassociates.com. *In Buckingham town centre. Start at Hill House, next to the Parish Church (spire visible from most places), gardens all in close proximity. Easy parking - try church yard by Hill House.* **Combined adm £4, chd free. Visitors welcome by appt Apr to Oct.**

NEW GARDEN HOUSE
Mrs Barbara Edmondson

HILL HOUSE
Leonie & Peter Thorogood

WALNUT YARD
Bill & Kathy Robins

Three very different gardener's gardens in Buckingham's leafy conservation area, at the heart of this old market town all within a stone's throw of each other.

Village school sensory garden which is maintained by the pupils' gardening club . . .

10 BUNYANS COTTAGE
5 High Street, Brill HP18 9ST. Peter & Josie Symes. *5m N of Thame. 4m from A41 through Ludgershall. 3m from B4011 Thame/Bicester Rd, signed to Brill. In centre of village.* **Combined adm £3.50, chd free. Thur 30 May (2-5). Combined with Laplands Farm.**
Pretty and colourful, established cottage-style garden in conservation area of village. Constantly evolving, mini orchard and productive areas with lovely view of parish church.

11 BURROW FARM
Hambleden RG9 6LT. David Palmer, 01491 571256. *1m SE of Hambleden. On A4155 between Henley and Marlow, turn N at Mill End. After 300yds, R onto Rotten Row. After ½ m, Burrow Farm entrance on R.* Home-made teas. **Adm £5, chd free (share to Buckinghamshire Community Foundation). Sat 15, Sun 16 June (2-6). Visitors also welcome by appt May to July. Tea & cake £3.00.**
Burrow Farm and the adjacent Cottages (not open) are part Tudor and part Elizabethan, set in the Chilterns above Hambleden Valley where it meets the Thames. Views of pasture and woodlands across the ha-ha greatly enhance the setting. Special features are the parterre, arboretum and C15 barn, where teas are served.

12 CEDAR HOUSE
Bacombe Lane, Wendover HP22 6EQ. Sarah Nicholson, 01296 622131, jeremynicholson@btinternet.com. *5m SE Aylesbury. From Gt Missenden take A413 into Wendover. Take 1st L before row of cottages, house at top of lane.* Light refreshments. **Adm £3.50, chd free. Visitors welcome by appt May to Sept.**
A chalk garden in the Chiltern Hills with a steep sloping lawn leading to a natural swimming pond with aquatic plants. Wildflowers with native orchids. Shaped borders hold a great variety of trees, shrubs and perennials. A lodge greenhouse and a good collection of half hardy plants in pots. Steep, sloping lawn.

CHARLTON GARDENS
See Northamptonshire

GROUP OPENING

13 CHEDDINGTON GARDENS
LU7 0RQ. *11m E of Aylesbury, 7m S of Leighton Buzzard. Turn off B489 at Pitstone. Turn off B488 at Cheddington Station then L at Xrds.* Home-made teas at Methodist Chapel. **Combined adm £6, chd free (share to Methodist Church and St Giles Church). Sun 23 June (1.30-5.30).**

BRIDGE COTTAGE
Mr & Mrs B Hicks
Visitors also welcome by appt Apr to Dec.
01296 660313
georgeous1@gmail.com

CHEDDINGTON ALLOTMENTS
Cheddington Parish Council

CHEDDINGTON COMBINED SCHOOL SENSORY GARDEN

7 HIGH STREET
Irene & Tony Johnson

6 MANOR POUND ROAD
Mrs Cheryl Sibley

THE OLD POST OFFICE
Alan & Wendy Tipple

ROSE COTTAGE
Mrs Margery Jones
(See separate entry)

WOODSTOCK COTTAGE
Mr & Mrs D Bradford

A large village grouping of varied and interesting gardens to view - incl the village school sensory garden which is maintained by the pupil's gardening club and the village allotments which has over 50 plots and benefits from wide views of the Chilterns. Partial wheelchair access.

14 CHESHAM BOIS HOUSE
85 Bois Lane, Chesham Bois HP6 6DF. Julia Plaistowe, 01494 726476, julia@yahoo.co.uk. *1m N of Amersham-on-the-Hill. From Amersham-on-the-Hill follow Sycamore Rd, over double mini r'about which turns into Bois Lane. Past village shops, house is 1/2m on L. Parking in road or on R at school & scout hut.* Home-made teas. **Adm £3.50, chd free. Sun 24 Mar (2-5); Sun 12 May, Sun 14 July (2-5.30). Visitors also welcome by appt.**
3 acre plantswoman's garden with primroses, daffodils and hellebores in early spring. Interesting for most of the yr with lovely herbaceous borders, rill with small ornamental canal, walled garden, old orchard with wildlife pond, handsome trees some of which are toparied. It is a peaceful oasis. Gravel to front of house.

GROUP OPENING

15 NEW CHURCH GREEN GARDENS
Bletchley, Milton Keynes MK3 6BY. *13m E of Buckingham, 11m N of Leighton Buzzard. Off B4034 into Church Green Rd, take L fork.* Home-made teas. **Combined adm £4, chd free. Sun 16 June (2-6); Tue 18 June (2-5).**

NEW **126 CHURCH GREEN ROAD**
David and Janice Hale

100 CHURCH GREEN ROAD
Rosemary & Gordon Farr

Two very diverse gardens situated close to Bletchley Park, the historic site of secret British codebreaking activities during WWII and birthplace of the modern computer: 100 Church Green Road is a very long narrow garden divided into rooms, informally and abundantly planted with a strong cottage garden influence. Awarded Milton Keynes Garden of the Year - Best Large Back Garden and overal winner. 126 Church Green Road, opening for the first time, is a gently sloping mature garden of 1/2 acre. Plant lover's delight that incl a small formal garden, shady areas and mixed borders of shrubs, perennials and roses. Features incl a thatched wendy house, pergola, pond, productive fruit and vegetable garden, greenhouse and patio.

Herb and medicinal plant borders in memory of the garden's original use . . .

COOKHAM GARDENS
See Berkshire

16 ◆ COWPER & NEWTON MUSEUM GARDENS
Market Place, Olney MK46 4AJ. Mrs E Knight, 01234 711516, www.cowperandnewtonmuseum.org.uk. *5m N of Newport Pagnell. 12m S of Wellingborough. On A509. Please park in public car park in East Street.* **Adm £2.50, chd free. For NGS: Sat 8, Sun 9 June (10.30-4.30). For other opening times and information, please phone or see garden website.**
Restored walled flower garden with plants pre-1800, many mentioned by C18 poet, William Cowper, who said of himself 'Gardening was, of all employments, that in which I succeeded best'. Also Summer House Garden in Victorian kitchen style with organic, new and old vegetable varieties. Herb and medicinal plant borders in memory of the garden's original use by an apothecary. Local artist David Purvis will be painting live art - Saturday. Lacemaking demonstration - Sunday.

17 CRAIGLEA HOUSE
Austenwood Lane, Chalfont St Peter, Gerrards Cross SL9 9DA. Jeff & Sue Medlock, 01753 884852, suemedlock@msn.com. *6m SE Amersham. From Gerrards Cross take B416 towards Amersham. Take L fork after 1/2 m into Austenwood Lane, garden 1/3m on right. Park at St Joseph's Church Car Park or Priory Rd.* Home-made teas. **Adm £4, chd free. Sun 23 June (1.30-5). Visitors also welcome by appt Apr to Aug.**
Delightful 1 acre garden complements the Arts and Crafts house which it surrounds. The planting ranges from the formal rose garden, lawns, herbaceous borders and pergola, to the natural planting around wildlife ponds, apple trees and along a fairy inhabited fern walk. Garden contains a wide range of plants, including many hostas, a vegetable garden and many seats affording lovely views of garden.

GROUP OPENING

18 CUBLINGTON GARDENS
Cublington, Leighton Buzzard LU7 0LQ. *5m SE Winslow, 5m NE Aylesbury. From Aylesbury take A413 Buckingham Rd. After 4m, at Whitchurch, turn R to Cublington.* Home-made teas at The Old Rectory. **Combined adm £5, chd free. Sun 9 June (2-5.30).**

LARKSPUR HOUSE
Mr & Mrs S Jenkins

OLD MANOR COTTAGE
Dr J Higgins

THE OLD RECTORY
Mr & Mrs J Naylor

THE OLD STABLES
Mr & Mrs S George

1 STEWKLEY ROAD
Tom & Helen Gadsby

5 very diverse gardens in this small Buckinghamshire village, each garden has its own character. Traditional rectory garden with herbaceous border, shrubbery, mature trees, ponds and hidden garden. Mediterranean patio, moving to a tropical shade garden then to a cottage garden, vegetables, pond and climbing plants. Organic kitchen garden, small orchard and courtyard. Strong focus on home-grown food also part of the Old Stables garden. Partial wheelchair access.

GROUP OPENING

19 CUDDINGTON GARDENS
Cuddington, Nr Thame HP18 0AJ. *3 1/2 m NE Thame, 5m SW Aylesbury. Off A418 Aylesbury/Thame rd. Ample free parking signed within village. Wheelchair visitor parking phone 01844 291 526.* Home-made teas at The Bernard Hall and Tyringham Hall terraces. **Combined adm £5, chd free. Sun 28 July (2-6).**

33 BERNARD CLOSE
Mr & Mrs Tony Orchard

DADBROOK HOUSE
Gerald & Clico Kingsbury
www.dadbrookgallery.co.uk

THE OLD PLACE
Dr & Mrs Michael Straiton

TIBBYS COTTAGE
Anthony & Evelyn Hatch

TYRINGHAM HALL
Mrs Sherry Scott MBE

Picturesque Midsomer Murders village with 5 gardens open, incl this year's re-opening of the ever-popular Dadbrook House garden. All within a pleasant walk taking you past 'chocolate box' cottages, village greens, romantic dell with waterfall, C13 church with attractive churchyard and wildflower reserve. Winners of The Morris Cup and The Wilkinson Sword in Bucks Best Kept Village awards. Access to all gardens except Tibby's Cottage and ajoining dell and waterfal. Gravel fronts.

20 DANESFIELD HOUSE
Henley Road, Marlow SL7 2EY. Danesfield House Hotel, www.danesfieldhouse.co.uk. *3m from Marlow. On the A4155 between Marlow and Henley-on-Thames. Signs on the left hand side - Danesfield House Hotel and Spa.* **Adm £4, chd free. Thur 1, Tue 6, Thur 8, Tue 13 Aug (10-5).**

The gardens at Danesfield were completed in 1901 by Robert Hudson, the Sunlight Soap magnate who built the house. Since the house opened as a hotel in 1991, the gardens have been admired by several thousand guests each year. However, in 2009, it was discovered that the gardens contained outstanding examples of pulhamite in both the formal gardens and the waterfall areas. The 100yr-old topiary is also outstanding. Part of the grounds incl an Iron Age fort. Guided tours welcome on NGS open days. Pre-booking essential. Restricted wheelchair access to the gardens (gravel paths).

♿ 🛏 ☕

DAWNEDGE LODGE
See Bedfordshire

21 DORNEYWOOD GARDEN
Dorneywood Road, Burnham SL1 8PY. National Trust. *1m E of Taplow, 5m S of Beaconsfield. From Burnham village take Dropmore Rd, at end of 30mph limit take R fork into Dorneywood Rd. Entrance is 1m on R. From M40 J2, take A355 to Slough then 1st R to Burnham, 2m then 2nd L after Jolly Woodman, signed Dorneywood Rd. Dorneywood is about 1m on L. Parking in field by entrance to garden reserved for disabled visitors*. Cream teas and cakes made by our resident chef. **Adm £6, chd free. Wed 24 Apr, Wed 29, Thur 30 May, Wed 24 July (2-4.30).**
6-acre 1930's country house garden on several levels with herbaceous borders, greenhouses, orchard, cottage and kitchen gardens providing for the house, lily pond and conservatory. The garden is being renovated over time by our Head Gardener Mark Nelson, with the help of Andrew Ogilby and volunteers. Plants and home-made preserves for sale. Easy level access and parking.

♿ ❀ ☕

GROUP OPENING

22 EAST AND MIDDLE CLAYDON GARDENS
East Claydon MK18 2ND. *1½ m SW Winslow. In Winslow turn R off High St, follow NT signs to Claydon House. The Old Rectory, Middle Claydon is close to the entrance to Claydon House (National Trust).* Home-made teas village hall. **Combined adm £5, chd free. Sun 16 June (2-6).**

9 CHURCH WAY
Ambrose Landon

INGLENOOKS
Mr & Mrs David Polhill

NEW THE OLD RECTORY
Mrs Jane Meisl

THE OLD VICARAGE
Nigel & Esther Turnbull

Two small villages, originally part of the Claydon Estate. Typical N Bucks cottages, 2 C13 churches. Inglenooks is an informal cottage garden with different areas of interest, many roses, surrounding C17 timber-framed thatched cottage (not open). The Old Vicarage, a large garden on clay. Mixed borders, scented garden, dell, shrub roses, vegetables and natural clay pond. Small meadow area and planting to encourage wildlife. Access via gravel drive. 9 Church Way is a small rural garden with outstanding views over the N Bucks countryside. Partial wheelchair access.

♿ ❀ ☕

EVENLEY WOOD GARDEN
See Northamptonshire

FLAXBOURNE FARM
See Bedfordshire

23 FRESSINGWOOD
Hare Lane, Little Kingshill, Great Missenden HP16 0EF. John & Maggie Bateson. *1m S of Gt Missenden, 4m W of Amersham. From A413 Amersham to Aylesbury rd, turn L at Chiltern Hospital, signed Gt & Little Kingshill. Take 1st L into Nags Head Lane. Turn R under railway bridge & 1st L into New Rd. At top, turn into Hare Lane, 1st house on R.* Home-made teas. **Adm £3.50, chd free. Mon 27 May (2-5.30).**
Thoughtfully designed garden with yr-round colour. Shrubbery with ferns, grasses and hellebores. Small formal garden, herb garden, pergolas with wisteria, roses and clematis. Topiary and landscaped terrace. Newly developed area incorporating water with grasses. Herbaceous borders and bonsai collection. Many interesting features.

❀ ☕

The Shades, Grange Drive Wooburn

24 GIPSY HOUSE

Whitefield Lane, Great Missenden HP16 0BP. Mrs Felicity Dahl. *5m NW of Amersham. A413 to Gt Missenden. Take Whitefield Lane, opp Missenden Abbey entrance, under railway bridge. Small Georgian house on R, park in field opp.* Home-made teas. **Adm £4, chd free. Wed 1, Thur 23 May, Wed 19 June, Thur 18 July (2-5). Also opening with The Plant Specialist.**

Late Roald Dahl's garden. York stone terrace, pleached lime walk, with hostas, hellebore and allium. Sunken garden, water feature, sundial garden, topiary oaks, herbaceous perennials, assorted roses. Walled vegetable garden, espalier fruits, herbs, greenhouse with vine, peaches and nectarines. Yew garden with roses and perennials. Wild flower meadow, gypsy caravan. Roald Dahl Museum & Story Centre in village. Very limited wheelchair access. Steps in all parts of garden.

GROUP OPENING

25 GRANGE DRIVE WOOBURN

Wooburn Green HP10 0QD, 01628 525818, alan@lanford.co.uk. *On A4094, 2m SW of A40, between Bourne End & Wooburn. From Wooburn church, direction Maidenhead, Grange Drive is on L before r'dabout, from Bourne End L at 2 mini r'abouts, then 1st R.* Home-made teas. **Combined adm £3.50, chd free. Sat 22, Wed 26 June (2-5).**

MAGNOLIA HOUSE
Alan & Elaine Ford
(See separate entry)

THE SHADES
Pauline & Maurice Kirkpatrick

2 diverse gardens in a private tree-lined drive which formed the entrance to a country house now demolished. Magnolia House is a ½ -acre garden with many mature trees incl magnificent copper beech and magnolia reaching the rooftop, a small cactus bed, fernery, stream leading to pond and greenhouses with 2 small aviaries. 10,000 snowdrops in spring and many hellebores. Front garden now has natural pond and bees. The Shades drive is approached through mature trees and beds of herbaceous plants and 60 various roses. A natural well is surrounded by shrubs and acers. The garden was improved in 2010 to include a natural stone lawn terrace and changes to existing flower beds. A green slate water feature with alpine plants completes the garden. Beehives & aviaries.

Wooded walks around the grove offer respite from the heat on sunny days . . .

GROUP OPENING

26 NEW GREAT BRICKHILL GARDENS

Great Brickhill, Milton Keynes MK17 9AS. *6m S of Milton Keynes. From Milton Keynes stay on main rd through village (Lower Way) until you reach Old Red Lion PH. Turn L into Pound Hill. No. 2 is on corner, opp PH. 28 Pound Hill is further up rd. From Leighton Buzzard or Aylesbury: drive on main rd through village (Ivy Lane). At the PH turn slightly R into the Pound Hill.* Refreshments available at Old Red Lion PH. **Combined adm £4, chd free. Sun 23 June (1-6).**

NEW 2 POUND HILL
Mr Ivan Mears

NEW 28 POUND HILL
Ms Beata Baker

Two village gardens in the picturesque hilltop village of Great Brickhill. 2 Pound Hill is a small terraced cottage garden full of unusual perennials and huge collection of heucheras and hostas. 28 Pound Hill is a mature, ½ acre garden. Extensive deep borders densely filled with shrubs and perennials in contrasting colours and textures. Many unusual plants, 50 different varieties of (mostly) English roses. Other features incl lily and aquatic plants' pond surrounded by naturalistic borders, fruit and vegetable plot and many exotic plants in pots.

27 HALL BARN

Windsor End, Beaconsfield HP9 2SG. The Hon Mrs Farncombe, jenefer@farncombe01.demon.co.uk. *½ m S of Beaconsfield. Lodge gate 300yds S of St Mary & All Saints' Church in Old Town centre. Do not use satnavs.* **Adm £4, chd free. Visitors welcome by appt Jan to Dec.**

Historical landscaped garden laid out between 1680-1730 for the poet Edmund Waller and his descendants. Features 300yr-old 'cloud formation' yew hedges, formal lake and vistas ending with classical buildings and statues. Wooded walks around the grove offer respite from the heat on sunny days. One of the original gardens opening in 1927 for the NGS. Open-air Shakespeare Festival for mid 2 weeks in June. Gravel paths.

GROUP OPENING

28 HIGHER DENHAM GARDENS

Higher Denham UB9 5EA. *6m E of Beaconsfield. From A40 take A412. ¼ m from the junction turn L at part-time T-lights into Old Rectory Lane. 1m on turn into Lower Rd signed Higher Denham. To visit our NEW garden first (recommended) turn off A40 one turning E of A 412 T-lights into Cheapside Lane, Denham Village.* Tea at the community hall. **Combined adm £5, chd free (share to Higher Denham Community Association). Sun 9 June (1-5.30).**

19 MIDDLE ROAD
Sonia Harris

NEW SHILLONG
Mrs Pauline Flack

5 SIDE ROAD
Jane Blythe

WIND IN THE WILLOWS
Ron James
(See separate entry)

Gardens in the delightful chalk stream Misbourne Valley will open in June, 2 weeks later than usual, to catch the last of the usual spring display as well as the early summer flowers (see NGS website for details). Wind-in-the-Willows has over 350 shrubs and trees, informal woodland and wild gardens incl riverside and bog plantings and a collection of 80 hostas. 'Really different' and 'stunning' are typical visitor comments. 19 Middle Rd has a terrace overlooking a garden crowded with as many plants as possible with some fruit bushes and vegetables. 5 Side Rd is a medium sized garden with lawns surrounded by beds of mixed flowering plants and shrubs and a feature for children. Shillong is a long garden owned by a 'plant nut' divided into rooms each with a different character which cannot be seen at a glance and must be explored. Wind in the Willows 'A Water Wonderland' featured in Buckinghamshire Life. Good access. Few steps at 19 Middle Rd. Some lawn and gravel paths at Wind in the Willows but access still good.

29 HILLESDEN HOUSE

Church End, Hillesden MK18 4DB. Mr & Mrs R M Faccenda, 01296 730451, suefaccenda@aol.com. *3m S of Buckingham. Next to church in Hillesden.* Home-made teas. **Adm £4.50 (incl refreshments), chd free. Sun 16 June (2-5). Visitors also welcome by appt June to July.**

By superb church 'Cathedral in the Fields'. Carp lakes, fountains and waterfalls with mature trees. Rose, alpine and herbaceous borders, 5 acres of formal gardens with 80 acres of deer park and parkland. Wild flower areas and extensive lakes developed by the owner. Lovely walks and plenty of wildlife. Also a newly created woodland garden. No wheelchair access to lakes.

30 HOLLYDYKE HOUSE

HP7 0RD. Bob and Sandra Wetherall, 01494 862264, sandra@robertjamespartnership.com. Home-made teas. **Adm £3.50, chd free. Sun 28 Apr (2-5). Visitors also welcome by appt Apr to July.**

3-acre garden, herbaceous borders, shrubs and trees. Old fashioned roses, koi and lily ponds, collection of conifers, kitchen garden. Gravel paths.

31 HOMELANDS

Springs Lane, Ellesborough, Aylesbury HP17 0XD. Jean & Tony Young, 01296 622306, young@ellesborough.fsnet.co.uk. *6m SE of Aylesbury. 4m NE of Princes Risborough. On B4010 2m W of Wendover. Springs Lane is between the village hall at Butlers Cross & St Peter & St Pauls Church. Narrow lane, uneven surface.* Home-made teas. **Adm £3.50, chd free. Sun 11 Aug (2-5). Visitors also welcome by appt June to Aug.**

Secluded $^3/_4$ -acre garden on difficult chalk adjoining open country-side. Designed to be enjoyed from many seating positions. Progress from semi formal to wild flowers meadow and wildlife pond. Deep borders with all season interest and gravel beds with exotic late summer and autumn planting. Featured in WI Life Magazine.

HUNTSMOOR

See Hertfordshire

Designed to be enjoyed from many seating positions . . .

32 KAYALAMI

The Pyghtle, off Village Road, Denham Village UB9 5BD. Hazel de Quervain, 07747 856468, hazel@connexions4africa.com. *3m NW of Uxbridge, 7m E of Beaconsfield. Village Rd is next to Village Green. The Pyghtle is opp Falcon PH and Kayalami is the 3rd house along.* Home-made teas. **Adm £4, chd free. Sat 15 June (2-5). Visitors also welcome by appt June to July. Min group 10, max 40.**

A deep passion for gardening is evident everywhere in this stunning yet secluded 1 acre garden. For 20yrs Hazel and Tony, her gardener and friend, have created what you see today. The garden is a riot of intense but natural planting providing colour, perfume and contrasting foliage. There are beautifully manicured lawns and a wealth of hardy plants,shrubs, trees and luxuriant herbaceous borders. African bead work for sale. Proceeds to HIV Orphans, Natal, S. Africa. Gravel drive, plenty of seats.

33 LAPLANDS FARM

Ludgershall Road, Brill, Aylesbury HP18 9TZ. Roger & Hilary Cope. *Between Brill & Ludgershall. 3m from A41 through Ludgershall towards Brill. 3m from B4011 Thame/Bicester rd, via Oakly through Brill.* Home-made teas. **Combined adm £3.50, chd free. Thur 30 May (2-5). Combined with Bunyans Cottage.**

Self-made country garden of borders dug out of a field incorporating a pond and stream. Majority of plants coming from anywhere but garden centres therefore the garden has evolved rather than planned. Guinea fowl and ducks wander freely while tumbler pigeons fly above. Vegetable area and interesting rare breed fowl.

GROUP OPENING

34 LITTLE MISSENDEN GARDENS

Amersham HP7 0RD. *$2^1/_2$ m NW of Old Amersham. On A413 between Great Missenden & Old Amersham.* Home-made teas. **Combined adm £5, chd free. Sun 7 July (2-6).**

HOLLYDYKE HOUSE
Bob and Sandra Wetherall
(See separate entry)

KINGS BARN
Mr A Playle

NEW **MANOR FARM HOUSE**
Evan Bazzard
Visitors also welcome by appt Aug.
Evan.bazzard@yahoo.co.uk

NEW **MICHAELMAS MEADOW**
Mr & Mrs Mark Ladd

1 MILL END COTTAGES
Philip & Eileen Sharman

MILL HOUSE
Terry & Eleanor Payne

TOWN FARM COTTAGE
Mr & Mrs Tim Garnham

A variety of gardens set in this attractive Chiltern village in an area of outstanding natural beauty. You can start off at one end of the village and wander through stopping off half way for tea at the beautiful Anglo-saxon church built in 975. The gardens vary from a small cottage garden by the R Misbourne to large gardens. The gardens reflect different style houses from several old cottages, a Mill House, more modern houses to a converted barn. There are herbaceous borders, shrubs and trees, old fashioned roses, hostas, topiary, koi and lily ponds, collection of conifers and kitchen gardens. Some gardens are highly colourful, others are just green and peaceful. Limited access to some gardens due to gravel paths and some steps.

GROUP OPENING

35 LONG CRENDON GARDENS

HP18 9AN. *2m N of Thame. Long Crendon village is situated on the B4011 Thame-Bicester Rd. Maps showing the location of the gardens will be available on the day.* Home-made teas at Church House in the High Street. **Combined adm £5, chd free (share to Long Crendon Day Centre/ Local Library). Sun 14 Apr (2-6).**

BAKER'S CLOSE
Mr & Mrs Peter Vaines

BARRY'S CLOSE
Mr & Mrs Richard Salmon

48 CHILTON ROAD
Mr & Mrs M Charnock

25 ELM TREES
Carol & Mike Price

MANOR HOUSE
Mr & Mrs West

MULBERRY HOUSE
Ken Pandolfi & James Anderson

A large variety of gardens to visit during a walk round our lovely village; many old, listed buildings incl St Mary's Church, dating from the C13 and the NT Court House which dates from the early C15. The gardens range from a 2 acre sloping garden with a collection of spring flowering trees and shrubs; 4 acres with 2 ornamental lakes and fine views towards the Chilterns with a mix of planting for sun and shade; two cottage style gardens with bulbs, mixed shrubs and herbaceous plantings; 2 acres on SW slope, partly walled with courtyard, terrace lawns and rockery and a restored vicarage garden with spring bulbs, mature trees and a formal knot garden. Restricted access in some gardens.

36 LORDS WOOD

Frieth Road, Marlow Common SL7 2QS. Mr & Mrs Messum. *1½ m NW Marlow. From Marlow turn off the A4155 at Platts Garage into Oxford Rd, towards Frieth, 1½ m. Garden is 100yds past Marlow Common turn, on L.* Home-made teas. **Adm £4, chd free. Thur 20 June, Thur 5 Sept (11-4.30).**

Lords Wood was built in 1899 and has been the Messums family home since 1974. The 5-acres of garden feature extensive borders in widely varying styles. From vegetable, flower and herb gardens, to large water gardens and rockery, orchard, woodland and meadow with fantastic views over the Chilterns. We are always bringing new ideas to Lords Wood, you will find something different to enjoy with every visit. Partial wheelchair access, gravel paths, steep slopes.

37 MAGNOLIA HOUSE

HP10 0QD. Alan & Elaine Ford, 01628 525818, alan@lanford.co.uk, www.lanford.co.uk/events. *On A9094, 2m SW of A40 between Bourne End & Wooburn.* **Adm £3. Sun 24 Feb (11-2). Visitors also welcome by appt Feb to Aug.**

½ acre, many mature trees incl magnificent copper beech and large magnolia. Wollemi pine, cactus, fernery, stream, beehives, 2 ponds, greenhouses. 2 small aviaries. 10,000 snowdrops and hellebores in spring. Collection of over 60 different hostas. Stay in our self catering accommodation, enjoy the garden. It is constantly being updated and new features added. Large Koi fish, 2 aviaries, 2 beehives.

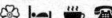

38 THE MANOR HOUSE

Church End, Bledlow, Nr Princes Risborough HP27 9PB. The Lord Carrington. *9m NW of High Wycombe, 3m SW of Princes Risborough. ½ m off B4009 in middle of Bledlow village.* **Adm £5, chd free. Sun 5 May, Sun 16 June (2-6).**

Paved garden, parterres, shrub borders, old roses and walled kitchen garden. Water garden with paths, bridges and walkways, fed by 14 chalk springs. Also 2 acres with sculptures and landscaped planting. Part of gardens have limited access for wheelchairs.

Orchard, woodland and meadow with fantastic views over the Chilterns . . .

39 MARYFIELD

High Street, Taplow SL6 0EX. Jacqueline & Roger Andrews, 01628 667246, japrivate@btinternet.com. *1m S Cliveden, ½ m E Maidenhead. From M4 J7 or M40 J4 follow signs for Taplow. Drive past church & up High St. Maryfield is on L on bend of High St.* Home-made teas. **Adm £4.50, chd free. Sat 25, Sun 26 May (1-4.30). Visitors and groups also welcome by appt. Adm £7.50 (incl refreshments).**

Eclectic mix of gardens wrapped around Victorian home in the heart of Taplow village. Approx 3 acres featuring grasses, white garden, exotic garden and walled vegetable garden. Formal, structured planting with yew topiary and box hedging to prairie-style and ending in a woodland context. Adventurous planting combinations and contemporary designs. Lovely garden to explore or just sit and have tea. Featured in various gardening and home magazines. Limited wheelchair access. Some narrow paths.

40 NEW MOAT FARM

Water Lane, Ford, Aylesbury HP17 8XD. Mr & Mrs P Bergqvist. *Turn up Water Lane by Dinton Hermit in the middle of Ford Village, after approx 200yds turn L over cattle grid between beech hedges into Moat Farm.* Home-made teas. **Adm £4, chd free. Thur 20 June (2-5).**

A country garden with herbaceous borders, roses, trees and water. A moat that flows through the garden and a 'blind' moat through the arboretum. Small walled garden and some vegetables.

11 The Paddocks

41 ◆ **NETHER WINCHENDON HOUSE**

Nether Winchendon, Near Thame, Aylesbury HP18 0DY. Mr Robert Spencer Bernard, 01844 290101, www.netherwinchendonhouse.com. *6m SW of Aylesbury, 6m from Thame. Midway between Thame and Aylesbury on A418 turn to Cuddington. Turn L at Xrds. Follow signs to Nether Winchendon. From Waddesdon turn R signed Upper Winchendon. Turn L to Nether Winchendon. Drive through village and turn R at Church.* **Adm £4, chd free. For NGS: Mon 6, Mon 27 May, Mon 26 Aug (2-5.30). For other opening times and information, please phone or see garden website.**

Nether Winchendon House is set in 7 acres of garden with fine and rare trees and surrounded by parkland. A Founder Garden (1927). Mediaeval and Tudor house set in stunning landscape. The South Lawn runs down to the R Thame. Picturesque village with interesting Church. Wheelchair access to the main features of the garden.

42 **NORTH DOWN**

Dodds Lane, Chalfont St Giles HP8 4EL. Merida Saunders, 01494 872928. *4m SE of Amersham, 4m NE of Beaconsfield. Opp the green in centre of village. At Crown Inn turn into UpCorner, on to Silver Hill. At top of hill fork R into Dodds Lane. N Down is opening on L. Limited parking in Dodds Lane. Car park in village.* Light refreshments. **Adm £3, chd free. Sun 16 June (2-5). Visitors also welcome by appt May to Sept, max group size 30. Sorry no coaches.**

¾ -acre sloping N-facing compartmentalised site with mature trees, described as a 'happy garden'. Designed with scenic effect in mind. Colourful and interesting throughout the yr. Large grassed areas with island beds of mixed perennials, shrubs and some unusual plants. Variety of rhododendrons, azaleas, acers, clematis and a huge Kiftsgate rose up an old apple tree. Displays of sempervivum varieties, alpines, grasses and ferns. Small patio/water feature. Greenhouse. Italianate front patio to owner's design.

ODNEY CLUB
See Berkshire

THE OLD VICARAGE
See Oxfordshire

43 **OVERSTROUD COTTAGE**

The Dell, Frith Hill, Gt Missenden HP16 9QE. Mr & Mrs Jonathan Brooke, 01494 862701, susie@jandsbrooke.co.uk. *½ m E Gt Missenden. Turn E off A413 at Gt Missenden onto B485 Frith Hill to Chesham rd. White Gothic cottage set back in lay-by 100yds up hill on L. Parking on R at church.* Home-made teas (June), Cream Teas at Parish Church (Sundays). **Adm £3.50, chd £0.50. Suns 31 Mar, 21 Apr, 12 May; Tue 11 June (2-5). Visitors also welcome by appt Apr to July. Min group size 20, max 30.**

Artistic chalk garden on 2 levels. Collection of C17/C18 plants. Potager/herb garden, spring bulbs, hellebores, succulents, primulas, pulmonarias, geraniums, species/old fashioned roses and lily pond. Garden studio with painting exhibition. Cottage was once C17 fever house for Missenden Abbey. Share of flower painting proceeds to NGS.

44 **11 THE PADDOCKS**

Wendover HP22 6HE. Mr & Mrs E Rye, 01296 623870, pam.rye@talktalk.net. *5m from Aylesbury, on A413. At Wendover after approx ½ m, turn L at mini-r'about into Wharf Rd. Entrance is 2nd on L. From Gt Missenden, turn L at Clock Tower, then R at next mini r'about.* **Adm £2.50, chd free. Sat 15, Sun 16 June (2-5.30). Evening Opening wine, Fri 5 July (5-8.30); Sat 6, Sun 7 July (2-5.30). Visitors also welcome by appt June to July. Min group size 10, max 30.**

Small peaceful garden with mixed borders of colourful herbaceous perennials and a special show of David Austin roses and a large variety of spectacular named 'Blackmore and Langdon' delphiniums. A tremendous variety of colour in a small area. White garden with peaceful arbour, 'The Magic of Moonlight', created for the BBC. Most of the garden can be viewed from the lawn.

PATCHWORK
See Hertfordshire

45 ◆ **THE PLANT SPECIALIST**
Whitefield Lane, Gt Missenden HP16 0BH. Sean Walter, 01494 866650, www.theplantspecialist.co.uk. *5m NW Amersham. A413 to Gt Missenden. Whitefield Lane opp Missenden Abbey. Under railway bridge on the L.* **Adm £5, chd free. For NGS: Wed 1, Thur 23 May, Wed 19 June, Thur 18 July (2-5). For other opening times and information, please phone or see garden website.**
Plant nursery with herbaceous perennials and grasses, container grown bulbs and half hardy perennials in attractive garden setting and display garden. The Plant Specialist Ltd. maintains the garden at Gypsy House for the Dahl family. On NGS open days the Nursery makes a donation to the charity for plants bought by visitors to the Gypsy House Garden. The nursery is open from 1 Apr to 31 Oct; Wed - Sat (10-5); Sun (10-4). Adm, free. Gravel paths on gentle slope.

46 **THE PLOUGH**
Chalkshire Road, Terrick, Aylesbury HP17 0TJ. John & Sue Stewart. *4m S of Aylesbury. Entrance to garden and car park signed off B4009 Nash Lee Rd. 200yrds E of Terrick r'about. Access to garden from field car park.* Delicious home-made cakes. **Adm £3, chd free. Sun 12, Mon 27 May (1-5).**
Formal garden with open views to the Chiltern countryside and hills. Designed as a series of outdoor rooms around a listed former C18 inn, incl vegetable and fruit gardens, newly planted orchard featuring traditional varieties. Jams made from fruit from the garden.

47 **POLLARDS**
Upper Icknield Way, Whiteleaf, Princes Risborough HP27 0LL. Mr & Mrs George Baker. *3/4m NE Princes Risborough. From A4010; turn up Peters Lane at Monks Risborough.* Home-made teas. **Adm £3.50, chd free. Sun 28 July (2-5).**
1½ acre garden on chalk; formal and informal beds; orchard, vegetables and herb garden; greenhouse and collection of hostas.

48 NEW **PONDERS**
Hedgerley Lane, Gerrards Cross SL9 8SY. Mr & Mrs R Willans. *1½ m S of Gerrards Cross. Take A40 to Gerrards Cross. At the main set of T-lights turn into Windsor Rd (B416). After ½ m, at the next set of T-lights, turn R into Hedgerley Lane. Continue down the hill for ½ m, turn into Ponders which is on the R.* Home-made teas. **Adm £4, chd free. Sun 16 June (2-5).**
The 11 acre garden at Ponders was originally the kitchen garden for nearby Bulstrode Manor. Many original features remain including extensive walls with impressive wrought iron gates, a long pear archway and a vineyard. Today the gardens include a rose garden, long borders, rockery, woodlands with wide selection of mature trees, meadows, orchard, soft fruit and productive vegetable gardens.

GROUP OPENING

49 **QUAINTON GARDENS**
Quainton HP22 4AY. *7m W of Aylesbury, 2m N of Waddesdon A41. Nr Waddesdon turn off A41. Maps given to all visitors.* Teas at Quainton Parish Church (February) and Banner Farm House (June), weather permitting or Parish Church. **Combined adm £4, chd free. Sun 24 Feb (12-4); Sun 9 June (2-6); Sun 23 Feb 2014.**

CAPRICORNER
Mrs Davis

MILL VIEW
Jane & Nigel Jackson
www.millviewquainton.com

THORNGUMBALD
Jane Lydall

THE VINE
Mr & Mrs D A Campbell
Visitors also welcome by appt Feb to July. Max group size 20. 01296 655243
david@dacampbell.com

Four gardens of differing styles. Village lies at foot of Quainton Hills. Fine views over Vale of Aylesbury to Chiltern Hills. C14 church with outstanding monuments, C19 working windmill milling Quainton flour (open Sundays am), steam railway centre. Heavy clay but well-watered from hills. The Vine - many exotic plants largely from Himalayas and China. Winter flowering shrubs and spring bulbs. Open hill grazing above garden. Stream runs through bog garden into pond. Capricorner - small garden planted for yr-round interest with scented plants, winter flowering shrubs and bulbs, small woodland glade. Mill View - themed areas, wild flower meadow, insectivorous plants, scented plants, standard wisteria. Greenhouse with orchids and insectivorous plants with automated environment and rain water harvesting. Thorngumbald - well-planted cottage garden with fine display of spring flowering plants. Sorry, no wheelchair access at The Vine or rear garden at Mill View.

Formal garden with open views to the Chiltern countryside . . .

50 **RED KITES**
46 Haw Lane, Bledlow Ridge HP14 4JJ. Mag & Les Terry, 01494 481474, les.terry@lineone.net. *4m S of Princes Risborough. Off A4010 halfway between Princes Risborough and West Wycombe. At Hearing Dogs sign in Saunderton turn into Haw Lane, then ¾ m on L.* Home-made teas. **Adm £3, chd free. Visitors welcome by appt. Min group 15.**
Chiltern hillside garden with terracing, slopes and superb views. The 1½ acres are planted for yr-round interest and lovingly maintained, with mixed and herbaceous borders, wild flower orchard, established pond, vegetable garden, managed woodland area and hidden garden. Wide use of climbers and clematis throughout.

51 **RIVENDELL**
13 The Leys, Amersham HP6 5NP. Janice & Mike Cross. *Off A416. Take A416 N towards Chesham. The Leys is on L ½ m after Boot & Slipper PH. Park at Beacon School, 100yds N.* Home-made teas. **Adm £3, chd free. Sat 6, Sun 7 Apr (2-5).**
S-facing garden featuring a series of different areas, incl a raised woodland bed under mature trees, bog garden,

gravel area with grasses and pond, vegetable plot, auricula theatre, raised alpine bed, box-edged herbaceous beds surrounding a circular lawn with a rose and clematis arbour and containing a wide variety of shrubs, bulbs and perennials.

52 ROSE COTTAGE

68 High Street, Cheddington, Leighton Buzzard LU7 0RQ. Mrs Margery Jones, 01296 668693. *11m S of Aylesbury. 7m S of Leighton Buzzard. Turn off B489 at Pitstone, turn off B488 at Cheddington Station, turn off Cheddington at Long Marston Rd Xrds.* **Evening Opening £3, chd free, wine, Sat 15 June (6-9). Visitors also welcome by appt Apr to Aug. Max group size 10.**

½ -acre cottage garden with maximum use of space. A balance of evergreens and deciduous resulting in a garden for all seasons, incl a potager, wild life pond, fruit and vegetables. Colour awareness at different levels in many arches covered with roses, clematis and honeysuckles. A painter's garden. Gravel paths.

53 ◆ STOKE POGES MEMORIAL GARDENS

Church Lane, Stoke Poges, Slough SL2 4NZ. South Bucks District Council, 01753 523744, memorial.gardens@southbucks.gov.uk. *1m N of Slough, 4m S of Gerrards Cross. From Gerrards Cross take B416 to Stoke Poges, cont past village from small car show room on R, after passing 5 rds on R, next road on R is Church Lane. Follow Church Lane, go across the Xrds, cont for approx ¼ m, gardens are on R, car park is on L. From Slough, Stoke Poges Lane, leads into Church Lane. St Giles Church is next door.* **Adm £3.50, chd free. For NGS: Sun 28 Apr, Sun 26 May (2-5). For other opening times and information, please phone or see garden website.**

Unique 20-acre Grade I registered garden constructed 1934-9. Rock and water gardens, sunken colonnade, rose garden incl 500 individual gated gardens. Spring garden, bulbs, wisteria, rhododendrons. Recently completed £1m renovation. Guided tours on the hour.

9 TANNSFIELD DRIVE
See Hertfordshire

TREETOPS
See London

54 TURN END

Townside, Haddenham, Aylesbury HP17 8BG. Peter Aldington, www.turnend.org.uk. *3m NE of Thame, 5m SW of Aylesbury. Turn off A418 to Haddenham. Turn at Rising Sun to Townside. Please park at a distance with consideration for neighbours.* Home-made teas. **Adm £3.50, chd £1. Mon 6 May, Sun 8 Sept (2-5.30).**

Intriguing series of garden rooms enveloping architect's own post war 2* listed house (not open). Sunken gardens, raised beds, formal box garden, richly planted borders, curving lawn and glades, framed by ancient walls and mature trees. Spring bulbs, irises, wisteria, roses and climbers. Courtyards with pools, secluded seating and Victorian Coach House. Open studios - displays and demonstrations by creative artists. Gravel and stone paths, narrow archways, some steps.

Courtyards with pools, secluded seating and Victorian Coach House . . .

TURWESTON GARDENS
See Northamptonshire

OATLEYS HALL
See Northamptonshire

UPPER CHALFORD FARM
See Oxfordshire

55 NEW THE WALLED GARDEN

Wormsley, Stokenchurch, High Wycombe HP14 3YE. Wormsley Estate. *Leave M40 at J5. Turn towards Ibstone. Entrance to Estate is ¼ m on R (consisting of iron gates in flint pillars, by a thatched lodge). NB: 20mph speed limit on Estate. Please DO NOT drive on grass verges & only park in spaces provided. Do not deviate off Estate rd until signed R to New Gardens. From Estate entrance, Walled Garden is approx 2m.* Light refreshments. **Adm £6 incl teas, chd free. Sat 27 July (1-5). Advanced booking only, for timed tickets please visit www.ngs.org.uk or phone 01483 211535.**

The Walled Garden at Wormsley Estate is a 2 acre garden providing flowers, vegetables and tranquil contemplative space for the occupiers of the main house. For many years the garden was neglected until Sir Paul Getty purchased the Estate in the mid-1980s. In 1991 the garden was redesigned by the renowned garden designer Penelope Hobhouse. Wheelchair ramp available for garden access. Please ensure the requirement is mentioned upon booking.

56 WATERCROFT

Church Road, Penn HP10 8NX. Mr & Mrs Paul Hunnings, 01494 816535, info@maryberry.co.uk. *3m NW of Beaconsfield, 3m W of Amersham. On B474 from Beaconsfeld, 600yds on L past Holy Trinity Church, Penn.* Home-made teas in garden or glasshouse, some chairs available. **Adm £6.50 (incl home-made tea), chd free. Visitors welcome by appt June to July. Min group size 20.**

Mature 3-acre chalk and clay garden. Large weeping ash. Rose walk with 350 roses. Courtyard with new roses and summer pots and box topiary. Large natural old pond with diving ducks, newly extended pond edge planting and replanted perennial border. Italianate garden with 19yr-old yew hedges and fine view. Wild flower meadow with wild roses. Formal herb garden with culinary herbs, small vegetable garden with hebe hedge. Glasshouse with unusual pelargoniums.

WATERDELL HOUSE
See Hertfordshire

WATERPERRY GARDENS
See Oxfordshire.

57 WESTEND HOUSE

Cheddington, Leighton Buuzzard LU7 0RP. His Honour Judge and Mrs Richard Foster, 01296 661332, westend.house@hotmail.com. *5m N of Tring. From double mini r'about in Cheddington take turn to Long Marston. Take 1st L and Westend House is on your R.* Home-made

teas. **Adm £3, chd free. Sun 7 Apr, Sun 11 Aug (2-6). Visitors also welcome by appt Apr to Oct.**
2-acre garden restored and extended during the last 7yrs featuring herbaceous and shrub borders, formal rose garden, wild flower area adjoining natural pond, vegetable potager and steel bird sculptures. Small orchard and adjoining paddock with rare breed hens, sheep and pigs. Some bespoke bird and butterfly sculptures for sale. Access to wild flower garden and pond limited to one side.

58 THE WHITE HOUSE

Village Road, Denham Village UB9 5BE. Mr & Mrs P G Courtenay-Luck. *3m NW of Uxbridge, 7m E of Beaconsfield. Signed from A40 or A412. Parking in village rd. The White House is in centre of village.* Home-made teas. **Adm £4.50, chd free. Sun 19 May (2-5).**
Well established 6-acre formal garden in picturesque setting. Mature trees and hedges, with R Misbourne meandering through lawns. Shrubberies, flower beds, rockery, rose garden and orchard. Large walled garden with Italian garden and developing laburnum walk. Herb garden, vegetable plot and Victorian greenhouses. Gravel entrance path to gardens.

59 WHITEWALLS

Quarry Wood Road, Marlow SL7 1RE. Mr W H Williams, 01628 482573. *½ m S Marlow. From Marlow cross over bridge. 1st L, 3rd house on L, white garden wall.* **Adm £2.50, chd free. Sun 21 Apr, Sun 14 July, Sun 1 Sept (2-5). Visitors also welcome by appt.**
Thames-side garden approx ½ acre with spectacular view of weir. Large wildlife pond, interesting planting of trees, shrubs, herbaceous perennials and bedding, large conservatory.

60 WIND IN THE WILLOWS

UB9 5EN. Ron James, 07740 177038, r.james@company-doc.co.uk. *Moorhouse Farm Lane, off Lower Road, Higher Denham. Take lane next to the Community Centre & Wind in the Willows is the 1st house.* **Adm £4, chd free. Sun 10 Mar (2-4.30). Visitors also welcome by appt Mar to Sept. 3 weeks notice required please.**
3-acre wildlife-friendly yr-round garden comprising informal, woodland and wild gardens separated by streams lined by iris and primulas. Over 350 shrubs and trees, many variegated or uncommon, marginal and bog plantings incl a collection of 80 hostas. 'Stunning' was the word most often used by visitors last year. Featured in Buckinghamshire Life. Lawn and gravel paths.

61 WITTINGTON ESTATE

Henley Road, Medmenham, Marlow SL7 2EB. SAS Institute, www.sas.com. *The Wittington Estate is located off a r'about approx 1½ m from Marlow on the A4155 Henley Rd.* Light refreshments at the Stables. **Adm £5, chd free. Sun 1 Sept (10-4.30).**
Situated on the banks of the Thames, between Marlow and Henley is SASUK and the Wittington Estate. Built in 1898 for Hudson Ewbank Kearley, later Viscount Devonport. Stunning viewpoints, rose garden, court garden, herbaceous borders, flash-lock capstan wheel, boat house and arboretum (under restoration). Wood tree sculpture. Wheelchair access to main house and surrounding garden.

Paddock with rare breed hens, sheep and pigs . . .

GROUP OPENING

62 WORMINGHALL GARDENS

Worminghall HP18 9LE. *3m NE of Wheatley. 3m NW of Thame. From the A418 follow signs for Worminghall. Turn L into village, follow NGS signs. Follow signs to church parking area at end of the Avenue.* Home-made teas at village hall. **Combined adm £4, chd free. Sat 22 June (2-5.30).**

NEW **55 THE AVENUE**
Ms Sarah Payne

LAPPINGFORD FARM
Mrs Toby Gawith

ROSE TREE COTTAGE
Roger & Penny Rowe

3 gardens open. 2 contrasting gardens either side of C11 church. The large garden at Lappingford Farm offers grass walks and open views over meadowland. Then in complete contrast, Rose Tree Cottage is a small cottage garden enclosed by hedges and country lane. A further simple traditional cottage garden opening off the Avenue set around a Grade II property. Partial wheelchair access at all gardens.

Buckinghamshire County Volunteers

County Organiser
Maggie Bateson, Fressingwood, Hare Lane, Little Kingshill HP16 0EF, 01494 866265, jmbateson@btopenworld.com

County Treasurer
Tim Hart, Kingswood House, The Lee, Great Missenden HP16 9NU, 01494 837328, tim.hart@virgin.net

Publicity
Sandra Wetherall, Holydyke House, Little Missenden, Amersham HP7 0RD, 01494 862264, sandra@robertjamespartnership.com

Assistant County Organisers
Rosemary Brown, 2 Spenser Road, Aylesbury HP21 7LR, 01296 429605, 01494 837328, grahama.brown@virgin.net
Janice Cross, Rivendell, 13 The Leys, Amersham HP6 5NP, 01494 728291, gwendalice@aol.com
Judy Hart, Kingswood House, The Lee, Great Missenden HP16 9NU, 01494 837328, judy.hart@virgin.net
Margaret Higgins, Salway, Crowbrook Road, Askett, Princes Risborough HP27 9LS, 01844 347072, jhiggins816@btinternet.com
Mhairi Sharpley, The Old Sun House, Pednor, Chesham HP5 2SZ, 01494 782870, mhairisharpley@btinternet.com

CAMBRIDGESHIRE

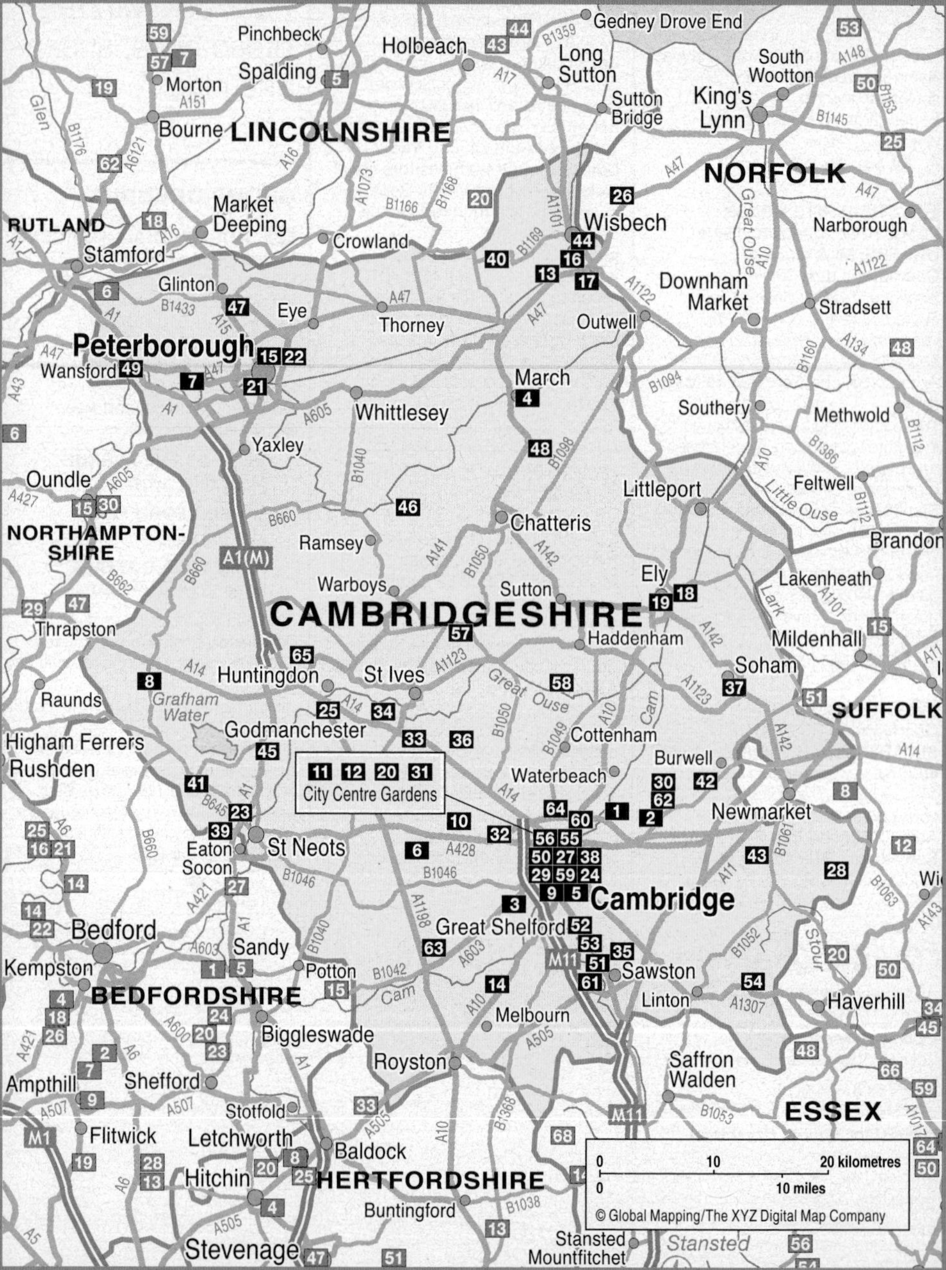

Opening Dates

January

Daily 1 Jan to 21 April

50 Robinson College

March

Sunday 24

28 Kirtling Tower
29 Leckhampton

Sunday 31

37 Netherhall Manor

April

Sunday 7

3 Barton Gardens
28 Kirtling Tower
55 Trinity College, Fellows' Garden

Sunday 14

11 Churchill College
20 Fitzwilliam College

Sunday 28

14 Docwra's Manor
31 Lucy Cavendish College

Varied group of large and small gardens reflecting different approaches to gardening . . .

May

Saturday 4

44 Peckover House

Sunday 5

9 Chaucer Road Gardens
37 Netherhall Manor

Monday 6

9 Chaucer Road Gardens

Sunday 12

30 Lode Gardens

Saturday 18

58 Ty Gwyn

Sunday 19

42 The Paddock
58 Ty Gwyn

Saturday 25

13 Clear View

Sunday 26

13 Clear View
25 Island Hall

June

Sunday 2

18 Ely Gardens 1
26 Kenilworth Smallholding

Saturday 8

23 109 High Street, Hail Weston
39 Old Farm Cottage
40 The Old Rectory
41 The Old Vicarage

Sunday 9

3 Barton Gardens
8 Catworth, Molesworth, Spaldwick & Brington Gardens
10 Childerley Hall
15 289 Dogsthorpe Rd
22 32 Gildenburgh Ave
23 109 High Street, Hail Weston
39 Old Farm Cottage
40 The Old Rectory
41 The Old Vicarage
43 Pavilion House
48 1 Rhonda Park
53 Stapleford Gardens

Thursday 13

2 Anglesey Abbey, Gardens & Lode Mill

National Gardens Weekend

Saturday 15

7 Castor House (Evening)
33 The Manor House
54 Streetly End Gardens
58 Ty Gwyn
59 Upwater Lodge
60 West Chesterton

Sunday 16

19 Ely Gardens 2
30 Lode Gardens
33 The Manor House
54 Streetly End Gardens
58 Ty Gwyn
59 Upwater Lodge
60 West Chesterton
61 Whittlesford Gardens

Saturday 22

65 Wytchwood

Sunday 23

1 Abbots Way
52 Shelford Gardens
65 Wytchwood

Saturday 29

5 Bentley & Newton Road Gardens

Sunday 30

17 Elm Gardens
27 King's College Fellows' Garden
32 Madingley Hall
51 Sawston Gardens

July

Daily 1 July to 31 December

50 Robinson College

Thursday 4

44 Peckover House

Sunday 7

6 Cambourne Gardens
12 Clare College Fellows' Garden
24 Highsett Cambridge

Saturday 13

58 Ty Gwyn

Sunday 14

30 Lode Gardens
35 Mary Challis Garden
46 Ramsey Forty Foot
56 Trinity Hall - Wychfield
58 Ty Gwyn

Saturday 20

4 45 Beaver Lodge

Sunday 21

4 45 Beaver Lodge

Sunday 28

63 Wimpole Estate

August

Sunday 4

16 Elgood's Brewery Gardens
37 Netherhall Manor

Sunday 11

37 Netherhall Manor

Sunday 18

26 Kenilworth Smallholding
38 Norfolk Terrace Garden

Monday 26

7 Castor House

September

Saturday 7

4 45 Beaver Lodge
57 Twin Tarns

Sunday 8

4 45 Beaver Lodge
57 Twin Tarns

Gardens open to the public

2 Anglesey Abbey, Gardens & Lode Mill
14 Docwra's Manor
16 Elgood's Brewery Gardens
34 The Manor, Hemingford Grey
44 Peckover House
63 Wimpole Estate

By appointment only

- 21 39 Foster Road
- 36 5 Moat Way
- 45 23a Perry Road
- 47 11 Redbridge
- 49 6 Robins Wood
- 62 Wild Rose Cottage
- 64 The Windmill

Pergola with large collection of roses, clematis and other climbers . . .

Also open by Appointment ☎

- 4 45 Beaver Lodge
- 8 32 High Street, Catworth, Molesworth, Spaldwick & Brington Gardens
- 8 7 Thrapston Road, Catworth, Molesworth, Spaldwick & Brington Gardens
- 13 Clear View
- 15 289 Dogsthorpe Rd
- 18 12 & 26 Chapel Street, Ely Gardens 1
- 30 21 Lode Road, Lode Gardens
- 37 Netherhall Manor
- 41 The Old Vicarage
- 43 Pavilion House
- 46 The Elms, Ramsey Forty Foot
- 54 Clover Cottage, Streetly End Gardens
- 54 Weaver's Cottage, Streetly End Gardens
- 57 Twin Tarns
- 58 Ty Gwyn
- 59 Upwater Lodge
- 60 35 Orchard Avenue, West Chesterton

The Gardens

1 ABBOTS WAY

Horningsea CB25 9JN. Sally & Don Edwards, 01223 861234. *4m NE of Cambridge. 1/2 m off A14. No access from Abbots Way. Follow signs in Horningsea to garden & car park. If you are a wheelchair user please telephone in advance to arrange alternative access to the garden via the front of the house, as the general entrance from the car park could be difficult for wheelchairs*. Home-made teas. **Adm £4, chd free (share to St Peters Church Horningsea). Sun 23 June (2-5.30).**

1 1/4 -acre sloping garden, with many herbaceous beds. Views to church and over the River Cam and its water meadows. Interesting plants and use of colour. 180ft double herbaceous borders; 116ft pergola with large collection of roses, clematis and other climbers. Natural pond with fish and bridge.

♿ 🐕 ☕

2 ◆ ANGLESEY ABBEY, GARDENS & LODE MILL

Quy Road, Lode, Cambridge CB25 9EJ. National Trust, 01223 810080, www.nationaltrust.org.uk/angleseyabbey. *6m NE of Cambridge. From A14 J35, on B1102 through Stow-cum-Quy*. **Adm £6.55, chd £3.25. For NGS: Thur 13 June (10.30-5). For other opening times and information, please phone or see garden website.**

Anglesey is one of England's great gardens, with captivating views, vibrant colour and delicious fragrance for every season. Delight in the sweeping avenues, classical statuary and beautiful flower borders. June favourites incl the colourful herbaceous borders, rose garden and wildlife rich wildflower meadows. Take a tour with a garden guide and be inspired by the seasonal highlights. Large proportion of gardens fully accessible with hard surfaced paths.

♿ ✿ ☕

GROUP OPENING

3 BARTON GARDENS

Wimpole Road, Barton, Cambridge CB23 7AE. *3 1/2 m SW of Cambridge. M11 J12. Take A603 towards Sandy and either turn R into New Rd after 1/2 m towards centre of village or continue along A603 past Haslingfield Rd (on L) for another 1/2 m looking for signs*. Home-made teas at village hall. **Combined adm £5, chd free. Sun 7 Apr, Sun 9 June (2-5).**

NEW BURWASH COTTAGE
3 School Lane. Alan & Angela Hulme.
Not open 7 Apr

FARM COTTAGE
18 High Street. Dr R M Belbin

GLEBE HOUSE
1 High Street. David & Sue Rapley.
Not open 7 Apr

114 HIGH STREET
Meta & Hugh Greenfield

31 NEW ROAD
Dr & Mrs D Macdonald

THE SIX HOUSES
33-45 Comberton Road. Perennial (GRBS)

247 WIMPOLE ROAD
Ray & Nikki Scrivens.
Not open 7 Apr

WINDY CORNER
245 Wimpole Road. Mike & Jules Webber

Varied group of large and small gardens reflecting different approaches to gardening. Farm Cottage: landscaped cottage garden with herbaceous beds and themed woodland walk. Glebe House: 1-acre mature, partly wooded and walled garden with large duck pond formal fruit/herb garden, Italianate courtyard garden and a secret garden. Burwash Cottage: charming cottage garden in the heart of the village. 114 High Street: small cottage garden with an unusual layout comprising several areas incl vegetables, fruit and a secret garden. 31 New Road: large, wildlife friendly cottage garden with a good show of spring flowers, mature shrubs, trees and a kitchen garden. The Six Houses: recently renovated gardens, including winter and dry gardens, lovely spring bulbs and a small wood. 247 Wimpole Road: evolved over 30yrs, and has several 'outdoor rooms'. A loggia provides cover and a setting for varied climbing plants. Windy Corner: adventurous bustling array of shrubs and perennials in a long, narrow country garden setting.

♿ 🐕 ✿ ☕

4 NEW 45 BEAVER LODGE

Henson Road, March PE15 8BA. Mr & Mrs Maria & Paul Nielsen Bom, 01354 656185, beaverbom@gmail.com. *A141 to Wisbech road into March, turn L into Westwood Ave, follow rd leading to Henson Rd, turn R. Property opposite school playground*. Light refreshments. **Adm £2.50, chd free. Sat 20, Sun 21 July; Sat 7, Sun 8 Sept (10.30-4). Visitors also welcome by appt July to Sept.**

A delightful town garden divided into several rooms. A pergola leads to an ornamental pond with koi carp, surrounded by borders with a large variety of plants and ornamental trees. There is a fern area with ornamental waterfall. The whole garden has an Oriental theme with bonsais and statues. Awarded a distinction in the champion of champions category March in Bloom. No easy access to pond area.

GROUP OPENING

5 BENTLEY & NEWTON ROAD GARDENS

Cambridge CB2 8AW. *1m S of Cambridge city centre. Off Trumpington Rd (A1309) nr St Faiths School & Nuffield Hospital.* Home-made teas at 15 Bentley Road. **Combined adm £5, chd free. Sat 29 June (2-5).**

15 BENTLEY ROAD
Dr & Mrs C Glazebrook

17 BENTLEY ROAD
Mr & Mrs J D Kirk

21 BENTLEY ROAD
Dr Tirza Bleehen

33 NEWTON ROAD
Mr & Mrs Pocock

4 interesting and varied gardens showing the best of planting design, creativity representing classic traditions with a modern twist.
15 Bentley Rd, 1/2 acre low maintenance garden with box hedging topiary shrubs, hostas, alpines and fish pond. 17 Bentley Rd, formal 1/2 acre garden designed by owners over 25 yrs with wide mixed borders, topiary, unusual plants and interesting trees. 21 Bentley Rd, 2/3 acre garden evolved over 30yrs with trees, rockery, herbaceous plants, vegetables and fruit.
33 Newton Rd, 1/3 acre garden, originally natural woodland, all mature trees maintained, magnificent flower containers, rockery and lily ponds. Partial wheelchair access.

BRINKLEY GARDENS
See Suffolk

BURGHLEY HOUSE PRIVATE SOUTH GARDENS
See Lincolnshire

Clare College

© Howard Rice

GROUP OPENING

6 CAMBOURNE GARDENS

Great Cambourne CB23 6AH. *8m W of Cambridge on A428. L at Cambourne junction into Great Cambourne. Follow signs to start at any garden.* **Combined adm £5, chd free. Sun 7 July (11-5).**

NEW **128 GREENHAZE LANE**
Fran and John Panrucker

22 JEAVONS LANE
Mr Sheppard

NEW **5 MAYFIELD WAY**
Debbie & Mike Perry

14 MILLER WAY
Geoff Warmington

43 MONKFIELD LANE
Tony & Penny Miles

NEW **6 ST JOHN'S WAY**
Lower Cambourne. Greg Barnes

7 WATERMEAD CRESCENT
Lower Cambourne. Mr & Mrs Cave

17 WATTLE CLOSE
Jeremy & Linda Carmichael

8 small modern gardens in the new villages of Great and Lower Cambourne, separated by green space and a country park with 2 lakes. No garden is more than 14 years old and many are much younger. They demonstrate how imagination and gardening skill can be combined in a short time to create great effects from what might have seemed unpromising or awkward plots. The grouping includes a garden inspired by the French Riviera complete with a miniature meadow, a foliage garden and three gardens opening for the first time this year, each with its own stunning approach created from scratch. Sunny patios and cool pools abound. 4 Covered on BBC Look East, BBC Radio Cambridgeshire, Cambridge Evening News and Cambridge News.

7 CASTOR HOUSE
Peterborough Road, Castor, Peterborough PE5 7AX. Ian & Claire Winfrey. *4m W of Peterborough. House on main Peterborough rd in Castor. Parking in paddock off Water Lane.* Home-made teas. **Adm £4, chd free. Evening Opening £4, chd free, wine, Sat 15 June (7-10); Mon 26 Aug (2-5.30).**
2 acre garden with mature trees, redesigned 2010/11. Italianate spring fed pond garden and potager, with greenhouse, designed by Bunny Guinness. Stream and woodland gardens. 'Hot' double border. 6 acres of mature woodland with cyclamen. Orchard in old kitchen garden. Late C17 house (not open). WC. Featured in the Cambridgeshire Journal.

GROUP OPENING

8 CATWORTH, MOLESWORTH, SPALDWICK & BRINGTON GARDENS
nr Huntingdon PE28 0PF. *10m W of Huntingdon. A14 W for Catworth, Molesworth & Brington exit at J16 onto B660. For Spaldwick exit A14 at J18.* Tea at Molesworth House, Yew Tree Cottage and 7 Thrapston Road. **Combined adm £4, chd free. Sun 9 June (2-6).**

32 HIGH STREET
Catworth. Colin Small
Visitors also welcome by appt June.
01832 710269
sheila.small@btinternet.com

MOLESWORTH HOUSE
Molesworth. John Prentis.
Next to the church in Molesworth

7 THRAPSTON ROAD
Spaldwick. Stewart & Mary Barnard.
J18 off A14 to centre of village, garden approx 50 metres from George PH
Visitors also welcome by appt June to Aug.
01480 890060
mnbarnard@tiscali.co.uk

YEW TREE COTTAGE
Brington. Mr & Mrs D G Eggleston

4 varied gardens showing the best of planting, design and creativity representing classic tradition but with a modern twist. 32 High Street is a long narrow garden with many rare plants including ferns, herbaceous borders, woodland area and wildlife pond. Molesworth House is a Victorian Rectory garden with a bit of everything, old fashioned and proud of it but with a groovy tropical house. Yew Tree Cottage comprises flower beds, lawn, vegetable patch, boggy area, copse and orchard. Plants in pots and hanging baskets.
7 Thrapston Road comprises mature trees under planted with mixed borders of shrubs, bulbs, herbaceous plants and fish pond. A pleasant outlook to the rear over the village church. Wheelchair access limited.

Stroll these villages for several hours of garden inspiration . . .

GROUP OPENING

9 CHAUCER ROAD GARDENS
16 & 23 Chaucer Road, Cambridge CB2 7EB. *1m S of Cambridge. Off Trumpington Rd (A1309), nr Brooklands Ave junction. Parking available at MRC Psychology Dept on Chaucer Rd.* Home-made teas at Upwater Lodge. **Combined adm £5, chd free. Sun 5, Mon 6 May (2-5).**

16 CHAUCER ROAD
Mrs V Albutt

UPWATER LODGE
Mr & Mrs George Pearson (See separate entry)

16 Chaucer Road, 1/2 -acre garden, divided by arches and hedges into separate areas, each with its own character. The garden is more open this year with some hedges removed. Spring flowering shrubs and trees, bulbs in borders and wildlife area. Waterproof footwear advised.
Upwater Lodge, 6 acres with mature trees, fine lawns, old wisterias, and colourful borders. Small potager and newly planted vineyard. A network of paths through bluebell wood leads down to water meadows, a small flock of rare breed sheep and the River Cam. Enjoy a walk by the river and watch the punts go by. Practice your shots on our top standard lawn tennis court or try your hand at croquet. Cakes made with garden fruit where possible. Swings and climbing ropes. Stalls selling plants, cards, prints and fabric crafts. Some gravel areas and grassy paths with fairly gentle slopes.

10 CHILDERLEY HALL
Dry Drayton CB23 8BB. Mrs Jenkins. *6m W of Cambridge. Between Caldecote r'about and Cambourne on old A428.* Home-made teas. **Adm £4, chd free. Sun 9 June (2-5).**
Romantic 4-acre garden (grade II historic garden) surrounds part Tudor house (not open). Winding paths lead through herbaceous borders to secret areas. Large collection shrub roses and good variety of plants and trees.

11 CHURCHILL COLLEGE
Storey's Way, Cambridge CB3 0DS. University of Cambridge, www.chu.cam.ac.uk. *1m from M11 J13. 1m NW of Cambridge city centre. Turn into Storeys Way from Madingley Rd (A1303), or from Huntingdon Rd (A1307). Parking on site.* Home-made teas. **Combined adm £5, chd free. Sun 14 Apr (2-5). Combined with Fitzwilliam College.**
42-acre site designed in 1960s for foliage and form, to provide year round interest in peaceful and relaxing surrounds with courtyards, large open spaces and specimen trees. Large 75m long parterre, herbaceous plantings. Beautiful grouping of Prunus Tai Haku (great white cherry) trees forming striking canopy and drifts of naturalised bulbs in grass around the site. The planting provides a setting for the impressive collection of modern sculpture. Chapel open (John Piper stained glass windows).

12 CLARE COLLEGE FELLOWS' GARDEN
Trinity Lane, Cambridge CB2 1TL. The Master & Fellows, www.clare.cam.ac.uk. *Central to city. From Queens Rd or city centre via Senate House Passage, Old Court & Clare Bridge.* Light refreshments. **Adm £3.50, chd free. Sun 7 July (2-6).**

2 acres. One of the most famous gardens on the Cambridge Backs. Herbaceous borders; sunken pond garden, fine specimen trees and tropical garden. Gravel paths.

An artist's garden divided into rooms with a focus on layers and visual textures . . .

13 CLEAR VIEW
Cross Lane, Wisbech St Mary PE13 4TX. Margaret & Graham Rickard, 01945 410724, magsrick@hotmail.com. *3m SW of Wisbech. Leave Wisbech on Barton Rd towards Wisbech St Mary. L at Cox Garage Xrds into Bevis Lane. 1st L into Cross Lane. Clear View garden 4th on R with iron gates.* Home-made teas. **Adm £3, chd free. Sat 25, Sun 26 May (11-5). Visitors also welcome by appt Apr to June.**
Approx 1.5-acre with lake incorporating large wildlife area, and wildlife meadow. Secluded cottage garden with many old fashioned plants, herbaceous border, gravel garden with raised bed and pond. Large rose beds, allotments and small orchard. Plenty of secluded seating. John Crocker the well-known clarinettist - formally with Chris Barber - will be playing with The Muddy Boots Jazz Band on Sun 26 May from 11.30am. Gravel paths in cottage garden are too narrow but garden can be viewed from the picket fencing.

DIP-ON-THE-HILL
See Suffolk

14 ◆ DOCWRA'S MANOR
2 Meldreth Road, Shepreth, Royston SG8 6PS. Mrs Faith Raven, 01763 260677, www.docwrasmanorgarden.co.uk. *8m S of Cambridge. ½ m W of A10. Garden is opp the War Memorial in Shepreth. King's Cross-Cambridge train stop 5 min walk.* **Adm £4, chd free. For NGS: Sun 28 Apr (2-5). For other opening times and information, please phone or see garden website.**
2½ acres of choice plants in series of enclosed gardens. Tulips and Judas trees. Opened for NGS for more than 40yrs. Gravel paths. Wheelchair access to most parts of the garden.

15 NEW 289 DOGSTHORPE RD
Peterborough PE1 3PA. Mr & Mrs Michael & Julie Reid, 01733 553784, julie@juliereid.co.uk. *1m N of city centre. S of the city. A1 M exit J17 E onto A1139 Fletton Parkway. Continue approx 9 mins. At sliproad 7 exit towards Eastfield & Dogsthorpe. At T- lights turn L onto Eastfield Rd and R at the next T-lights onto Newark Ave. At end of rd turn R at the T junction onto Elmfield Rd which leads to another T junction and turn L onto Dogsthorpe Rd. House is 300 metres on R.* Home-made teas. **Combined adm £3.50, chd free. Sun 9 June (11-6). Combined with 32 Gildenburgh Avenue. Visitors also welcome by appt June to Sept.**
An artist's garden divided into rooms with a focus on layers and visual textures. Planted with a variety of shrubs, herbaceous perennials, bulbs and trees creating seasonal colour in an array of palettes. Social and intimate seating all around to enjoy delicious home-made refreshments. Open Artists Studio plus Fine Art Exhibition.

16 ◆ ELGOOD'S BREWERY GARDENS
North Brink, Wisbech PE13 1LW. Elgood & Sons Ltd, 01945 583160, www.elgoods-brewery.co.uk. *1m W of town centre. Leave A47 towards Wisbech Centre. Cross river to North Brink. Follow river and brown signs to brewery and car park beyond.* **Adm £3.50, chd free. For NGS: 4 Aug (11.30-4.30). For other opening times and information, please phone or see garden website.**
Approx 4 acres of peaceful garden featuring 250yr old specimen trees providing a framework to lawns, lake, rockery, herb garden, dipping pool and maze. Wheelchair access to Visitor Centre and most areas of the garden.

GROUP OPENING

17 NEW ELM GARDENS
Main Road, Elm, Wisbech PE14 0AB. Mr Martin Gibson. *2m S of Wisbech. From A47 take A1101 towards Downham Market, then B1101 towards March. Wisbech-March bus routes stop at War Memorial. Parking in the paddock of Elm House on Main Road (B1101) opp Halfpenny Ln/Rose Ln junction to N of church.* Light refreshments. **Combined adm £5, chd free. Sun 30 June (2-5.30).**

ELM HOUSE
Mrs Diana Bullard

NEW THE LIMES FARMHOUSE
Robin O'Connor

NEW THE OLD VICARAGE
Mr Martin Gibson

Three large gardens of contrasting character within 250 metres of each other in the picturesque village of Elm. Elm House, C17 (not open), has a walled garden with arboretum, many rare trees and shrubs, mixed perennials and new 3-acre meadow. At The Limes Farmhouse there is over an acre of mature garden with established trees and herbaceous borders with informal planting. Four years ago both garden and 1860's house, The Old Vicarage (not open), were completely derelict. The owner has created a low maintenance, shady garden on the 1-acre plot with lawn, wild flower area and fruit trees. Some gravelled paths.

GROUP OPENING

18 ELY GARDENS 1
CB7 4TX. *14m N of Cambridge. Approaching Ely from A10 S follow signs to the cathedral. Barton Rd car park 10 mins walk to Black Hostelry. OR follow yellow signs on B1382 Prickwillow Rd to Rosewell House. (Ample parking). Maps given at first garden visited.* Home-made teas at Rosewell House. **Combined adm £5, chd free. Sun 2 June (2-6).**

BLACK HOSTELRY
Oyster Lane. Canon & Mrs David Pritchard.
Approach through The Porta and via Oyster lane

12 & 26 CHAPEL STREET
Ken & Linda Ellis
Visitors also welcome by appt June to Sept.01353 664219 ken.ellis1@orangehome.co.uk

50A PRICKWILLOW ROAD
Mr & Mrs J Hunter

ROSEWELL HOUSE
Prickwillow Road. Mr & Mrs A Bullivant.

A delightful and varied group of gardens in an historic Cathedral city. Spend a day in Ely, taking a leisurely circular walk of about 2m from the Cathedral, along the river and Nature Trail to access all gardens, or come by car. Rosewell House has splendid views of the Cathedral and surrounding Fenland. Herbaceous borders, roses, small pond and kitchen garden. Meadow with area of cornfield planting. Trail for children. Exhibition of 'kinetic sculptures', (Rhobiles) by Andrew Jones. Close by is 50A Prickwillow, an enthusiast's small walled garden with shade border, succulents and vegetable plot, the emphasis being on foliage. 12 & 26 Chapel Street: the former a small town garden reflecting the owners' eclectic outlook. From alpines to herbaceous, linked with a model railway. The latter featuring shrubs, an oasis of peace and quiet in the city. The Black Hostelry is an ancient monastic building close to Ely Cathedral, with walls covered in roses and clematis. Lawn with trees. Short trail for children at Rosewell House. Wheelchair access to some areas of most gardens.

GROUP OPENING

19 ELY GARDENS 2

Ely CB7 4HZ. *A10 from Cambridge (14m). From A10 follow yellow signs to Barton Rd car park. All the gardens in the group are within walking distance of Barton Rd car park. Map at first garden visited.* Home-made teas at 36 Barton Rd & Bishop of Huntingdon's Gdn. **Combined adm £5, chd free. Sun 16 June (2-6).**

NEW **40 BARTON ROAD**
Mrs Diana Grove.

NEW **42 BARTON ROAD**
Mrs Grace Bent.

BISHOP OF HUNTINGDON'S GARDEN
Lynn Road. David & Jean Thomson.

BISHOP WOODFORD HOUSE
Barton Road. Miss Michelle Collins.

47 CAMBRIDGE ROAD
Mr & Mrs W N Trotter

HAZELDENE
Barton Road. Mike & Juliette Tuplin.

These are a very disparate group of 6 large and small town gardens all within walking distance of Barton Rd car park. The gardens reflect a wide range of interests and expertise. You will see herbaceous borders, an organic and wildlife garden, a flower arranger's garden, urban chicken coups, ponds and interesting hard landscaping.

20 FITZWILLIAM COLLEGE

Storeys Way, Cambridge CB3 0DG. Master and Fellows, www.fitz.cam.ac.uk. *1m NW of Cambridge city centre. Turn into Storeys Way from Madingley Rd (A1303) or from Huntingdon Rd (A1307). Free parking.* **Combined adm £5, chd free. Sun 14 Apr (2-5). Combined with Churchill College.**
Traditional topiary, borders, woodland walk, lawns from the Edwardian period and specimen trees are complemented by modern planting and wild meadow. The avenue of limes, underplanted with spring

109 High Street, Hail Weston

bulbs, leads to The Grove, the 1813 house once belonging to the Darwin Family (not open). Featured in Cambridgeshire Journal 'A Garden for All Seasons'. Some ramped pathways.

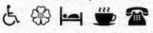

21 39 FOSTER ROAD

off Campaign Ave, Woodston, Peterborough PE2 9RS. Robert Marshall & Richard Handscombe, 01733 555978, robfmarshall@btinternet.com. *1m SW of Peterborough City Centre. From Oundle Rd turn N into Sugar Way at T-lights, L at 2nd r'about onto Campaign Ave, R at next r'about still on Campaign Ave, 2nd R at Foster Rd. Continue to very end of rd, L into final cul-de-sac. Entrance via rear gate in green fence.* Light refreshments. **Adm £3, chd free.** **Visitors welcome by appt Feb to Oct, week days possible.**

Plantsman's garden in small, new estate plot. Informal and formal areas: mixed herbaceous border; woodland/shade; 'vestibule' garden; exotic and ferns; espaliered fruit; pergola; patio; pond; parterre; many pots; octagonal greenhouse; seating and sculpture. Uncommon snowdrops, over 150 hostas, plus daphnes, acers and other choice/unusual cultivars. Trees and hedges in a small garden. 3 British Shorthair cats also seek admiration. Featured in Peterborough Telegraph, Nene Living Magazine, Mail on Saturday. Main garden and WC accessible by wheelchair. 3 very shallow steps to front garden.

22 NEW 32 GILDENBURGH AVENUE

Peterborough PE1 4RF. Mrs Heather Roberts. *1m E of City centre off Eastfield Rd. A1139 on Fletton Parkway. From A47 signed Eastfield & Dogsthorpe. At T-lights turn L onto Eastfield Rd, 2nd L into Gildenburgh Av, opp Newark Hill School, on entering turn R. Ltd parking in Gildenburgh Ave, additional parking in Hill Close shopping area.* Light refreshments. **Combined adm £3.50, chd free. Sun 9 June (11-5). Combined with 289 Dogsthorpe Road.**

Small town garden with a kaleidoscope of planting incl roses, box hostas, rodgersia and much more. Tree planting in 2012 will give a new dimension to this lovely garden.

GUANOCK HOUSE
See Lincolnshire

23 109 HIGH STREET, HAIL WESTON

Hail Weston, St Neots PE19 5JS. Dawn Isaac, www.littlegreenfingers.com. *1m W of St Neots. From A1 take B645 in direction of Kimbolton & High Ferrers, take 1st R signed Hail Weston and follow High St round. 109 is opp church & village hall.* Home-made teas. **Adm £3.50, chd £0.50. Sat 8, Sun 9 June (1-5). Also open Old Farm Cottage & The Old Vicarage.**

Set in 1/3acre, this space has been designed to show that a practical family garden can still be beautiful. There is a large lawn with a sunken trampoline surrounded by mixed borders, ornamental vegetable garden, children's play area and greenhouse. Children's garden trail, garden games on lawn.

GROUP OPENING

24 NEW HIGHSETT, CAMBRIDGE

CB2 1NZ. *Centre of Cambridge. Via Station Rd, Tenison Rd, 1st L Tenison Ave, entrance ahead. Sat nav CB1 2DX.* Home-made teas at 82 & 83 Highsett. **Combined adm £5, chd free. Sun 7 July (2-5).**

NEW 73 HIGHSETT
Mrs P Caldwell

NEW 79 HIGHSETT
Mrs J Evans

NEW 82 HIGHSETT
Mrs A Fleet

NEW 83 HIGHSETT
Ms E Murray

4 small delightful town gardens in central Cambridge to complement the lovely communal gardens also in Highsett. Fine specimen trees and interesting 1950/1960's houses designed by the well-known architect Eric Lyons. 73 Highsett's garden is dominated by a large fatsia japonica and overhanging birch trees creating shade and dappled sun. The fence is covered with evergreen climbers and clematis. A sophisticated and urban feel creating a green and cool oasis in a small space. 79 Highsett is a small town garden landscaped with a variety of herbs. Seating arranged in various places to take advantage of the sun. 82 Highsett is densely planted, colourful small garden to complement the lovely communal gardens of Highsett, one of Cambridge's secret gardens in the middle of the city. 83 Highsett is a contained family garden with raised beds

> Designed to show that a practical family garden can still be beautiful . . .

25 ISLAND HALL

Godmanchester PE29 2BA. Mr Christopher & Lady Linda Vane Percy. *1m S of Huntingdon (A1). 15m NW of Cambridge (A14). In centre of Godmanchester next to free car park.* Home-made teas. **Adm £4, chd free. Sun 26 May (11-5).**

3-acre grounds. Mid C18 mansion (not open). Tranquil riverside setting with mature trees. Chinese bridge over Saxon mill race to an embowered island with wild flowers. Garden restored in 1983 to mid C18 formal design, with box hedging, clipped hornbeams, parterres, topiary and good vistas over borrowed landscape, punctuated with C18 wrought iron and stone urns. The ornamental island has been replanted with Princeton elms (ulmus americana).

JERICHO
See Northamptonshire

26 KENILWORTH SMALLHOLDING

West Drove North, Walton Highway PE14 7DP. John & Marilyn Clarke, 01945 881332, bookings@kenilworthhouse.co.uk, www.kenilworthhouse.co.uk. *6m E of Wisbech. Off A47 through Walton Highway, at E end of village turn N towards Walpole St Peter, on 2nd sharp bend turn R into Farm Ln.* Light refreshments. **Adm £4, chd free. Sun 2 June; Sun 18 Aug (11-5).**

Varied country garden set around 100yr-old Bramleys. Beds, large ponds, fern greenhouse, shade garden and herb bed. Working smallholding with goats and sheep. Tree lined path past paddocks to secluded mixed dessert apple orchard and copse. Teas served in outbuilding housing exhibition of the development of the smallholding and archaeology.

Formal garden with an intricate design formed from box, yew and pleached lime . . .

27 KING'S COLLEGE FELLOWS' GARDEN

Queen's Road, Cambridge CB2 1ST. Provost & Scholars of King's College. *In Cambridge, the Backs. Entry by gate at junction of Queen's Rd & West Rd. Parking at Lion Yard 10mins walk, or some pay & display places in West Rd & Queen's Rd.* Cream teas. **Adm £3.50, chd free. Sun 30 June (2-6).**
Fine example of a Victorian garden with rare specimen trees. With a small woodland walk and a kitchen/allotment garden created in 2011. Gravel paths.

28 KIRTLING TOWER

Newmarket Road, Kirtling, nr Newmarket CB8 9PA. The Lord & Lady Fairhaven. *6m SE of Newmarket. From Newmarket head towards village of Saxon Street, through village to Kirtling, turn L at war memorial, signposted to Upend, entrance is signed on L.* Light refreshments, home-made cakes and cream teas. **Adm £5, chd free. Sun 24 Mar; Sun 7 Apr (11-4).**
Surrounded by a moat, formal gardens and parkland. A recently designed garden with historical features including walnut avenue and Tudor walk. Open for spring interest with grass paths running through swathes of daffodils, narcissus, crocus, muscari, chionodoxa and tulips. Closer to the house; vast lawn areas, walled garden, secret and cutting gardens. Views of surrounding countryside.

29 LECKHAMPTON

37 Grange Road, Cambridge CB3 9BJ. Corpus Christi College. *Runs N to S between Madingley Rd (A1303) & A603. Entrance opp Selwyn College. No parking available on site.* Home-made teas. **Adm £4, chd free. Sun 24 Mar (2-6).**
10 acres comprising formal lawns and extensive wild gardens, featuring walkways and tree-lined avenues, fine specimen trees under-planted with spring bulbs, cowslips, anemones, fritillaries and a large area of lupins. Gravel and grass paths.

GROUP OPENING

30 LODE GARDENS

Cambridgeshire CB25 9FW. *10m NE of Cambridge. Take B1102 from Stow-cum-Quy r'about, NE of Cambridge at junction with A14, Lode is 2m from r'about.* Home-made teas at Carpenters End. **Combined adm £5, chd free. Sun 12 May; Sun 16 June; Sun 14 July (11-5).**

CARPENTERS END
Mr & Mrs Paul Webb

21 LODE ROAD
Mr Richard P Ayres
Visitors also welcome by appt. 01223 811873

THE OLD VICARAGE
Mr & Mrs Hunter.
Not open 16 June

3 varied gardens set in a picturesque village to E of Anglesey Abbey Garden. 21 Lode Road is planted with bold groups of herbaceous plants creating an element of mystery and delight. This contrasts with two recently developed gardens. Carpenters End displays shrubs and trees and a fine lawn. The Old Vicarage is a formal garden with an intricate design formed from box, yew and pleached lime.

31 LUCY CAVENDISH COLLEGE

Lady Margaret Road, Cambridge CB3 0BU. *1m NW of Gt St Mary. College situated on corner of Lady Margaret Rd & Madingley Rd (A1303). Entrance off Lady Margaret Rd.* **Adm £3.50, chd free. Sun 28 Apr (2-5).**
The gardens of 4 late Victorian houses have been combined and developed over past 25yrs into an informal 3 acre garden. Fine mature trees shade densely planted borders. An Anglo Saxon herb garden is situated in one corner. The garden is maintained using organic methods and provides a rich wildlife habitat.

32 MADINGLEY HALL

nr Cambridge CB23 8AQ. University of Cambridge, 01223 746222, reservations@madingleyhall.co.uk, www.madingleyhall.co.uk. *4m W of Cambridge. 1m from M11 J13.* Home-made teas at St Mary Magdalene Church adjcent to Madingley Hall Drive. **Adm £4, chd free. Sun 30 June (2.30-5.30).**
C16 Hall (not open) set in 8 acres of attractive grounds. Features incl landscaped walled garden with hazel walk, alpine bed, medicinal border and rose pergola. Meadow, topiary, mature trees and wide variety of hardy plants. Plant Heritage Cambs Group plant stall. St Mary Magdalene Church open throughout the event.

33 NEW THE MANOR HOUSE

Chequer Street, Fenstanton, Huntingdon PE28 9JQ. Lynda Symonds & Nigel Ferrier. *10 miles NW of Cambridge. Opp chapel and village green, 500 metres E of King William IV PH.* Home-made teas in chapel garden and on village green opp The Manor Hse. **Adm £3.50, chd free. Sat 15, Sun 16 June (1.30-5.30).**
Formal garden with parterre, pleached limes and interesting cottage borders set in just over 1/3 acre surrounding The Manor House, once the home of Capability Brown.

34 ◆ THE MANOR, HEMINGFORD GREY

Hemingford Grey PE28 9BN. Mrs D S Boston, 01480 463134, www.greenknowe.co.uk. *4m E of Huntingdon. Off A14. Entrance to garden by small gate off river towpath. No parking at house except for disabled by arrangement. Park in village.* **For opening times and information, please phone or see garden website.**
Garden designed and planted by author Lucy Boston, surrounds C12 manor house on which Green Knowe books based (house open by appt).

4 acres with topiary; over 200 old roses, extensive collection of irises including Cedric Morris varieties and herbaceous borders with mainly scented plants. Meadow with mown paths. Enclosed by river, moat and wilderness. Care is taken with the planting to extend the flowering season right through to the first frosts. Gravel paths.

35 MARY CHALLIS GARDEN
High Street, Sawston CB22 3BG. A M Challis Trust Ltd. *7m SE of Cambridge. Entrance via lane between 60 High St & 66 High St (Billsons Opticians).* Home-made teas. **Adm £2, chd free.** **Sun 14 July (2-5.30).**
Given to Sawston in 2006 this 2 acre garden is being restored by volunteers: formal flower garden, vegetable beds with vine house, meadow and woodland, with concern for the flora and fauna - and the village children.

MILL END
See Bedfordshire

36 5 MOAT WAY
Swavesey CB24 4TR. Mr & Mrs N Kyberd, 01954 200568, n.kyberd@ntlworld.com. *Off A14, 2m beyond Bar Hill. Look for School Ln/Fen Drayton Rd,at mini r'about turn into Moat Way, no.5 is about 100 metres on L.* **Adm £3, chd free.** **Visitors welcome by appt June to Sept.**
Colourful garden filled with collection of trees, shrubs and perennials. Large patio area displaying many specimen foliage plants in planters, incl pines, hostas and acers.

37 NETHERHALL MANOR
Tanners Lane, Soham CB7 5AB. Timothy Clark Esq, 01353 720269. *6m Ely, 6m Newmarket. Enter Soham from Newmarket, Tanners Lane is 2nd R 100yds after cemetery. Enter Soham from Ely, Tanners Ln is 2nd L after War Memorial.* Home-made teas. **Adm £2, chd free.** **Sun 31 Mar; Sun 5 May; Sun 4, Sun 11 Aug (2-5). Visitors also welcome by appt Mar to Aug. Refreshments by prior arrangement.**
'An elegant garden touched with antiquity' Good Gardens Guide. This is an unusual garden which will appeal to those with an historical interest in the individual collections of genera and plant groups: March - old primroses, daffodils and Victorian double flowered hyacinths. May - old English tulips. Aug - Victorian pelargonium, heliotrope, calceolaria and dahlias. Author of Margery Fish's Country Gardening & Mary McMurtrie's Country Garden Flowers. Owner has written for The Society of Garden Designers on 'Laughter in the Garden' and articles in 'The Garden' on bluebells.

38 NEW NORFOLK TERRACE GARDEN
38 Norfolk Terrace, Cambridge CB1 2NG. John Tordoff & Maurice Reeve. *Central Cambridge. A603 East Rd turn R into St Matthews St to Norfolk St, L into Blossom St and Norfolk Terrace is at the end.* Wine. **Adm £3, chd (under 5) free.**
Sun 18 Aug (12-5).
A small, paved courtyard garden in Moroccan style. Masses of colour in raised beds and pots, backed by oriental arches. An ornamental pool done in patterned tiles offers the soothing splash of water. The owners' previous, London garden, was named by BBC Gardeners' World as 'Best Small Garden in Britain'.

39 NEW OLD FARM COTTAGE
Staploe, St. Neots PE19 5JA. Sir Graham & Lady Fry. *Approx 1m W of St Neots. Leave St Neots on the Duloe Rd. Pass through Duloe. Continue to Staploe and house is last one on L.* Home-made teas. **Adm £3.50, chd £0.50. Sat 8, Sun 9 June (1-5). Also open 109 High Street, Hail Weston & The Old Vicarage.**
Flower garden surrounding thatched house, with 3 acres of orchard, grassland, young woodland and pond maintained for wildlife. Present owners have planted a number of exotic trees as well as extending the area of native woodland. Rough ground and one steep slope.

40 NEW THE OLD RECTORY
Main Road, Parson Drove, Wisbech PE13 4LF. Helen Roberts. *SW of Wisbech. Follow signs to Parson Drove off A47 from Peterborough 1m past Thorney Toll, over Xrds leaving the Swan Inn on R 1.5m to end of village. Garden opp St Johns Church. From Wisbech direction follow B1166 from Leverington 200yds past Five Bells PH on L.* Home-made teas. Pimms tent if sunny. **Adm £3, chd free.**
Sat 8, Sun 9 June (12-5).
Walled Georgian cottage garden of 1 acre, opening into wildflower meadow and paddocks. Long herbaceous border, 2 ponds and unusual weeping ash tree. Terraced areas and outdoor kitchen! No hills but lovely open Fen views.

Ornamental pool done in patterned tiles offers the soothing splash of water . . .

41 THE OLD VICARAGE
Causeway, Great Staughton, St. Neots PE19 5BF. Mr & Mrs Elizabeth & Richard Edmunds, 01480 860397, elizabeth.edmunds4@btinternet.com. *5m off A1, 8m from St Neots. From A1 take B645 to Great Staughton. At end of village main st go straight ahead towards church. Garden before church on R.* Home-made teas. **Adm £3.50, chd £0.50. Sat 8, Sun 9 June (1-5). Also open 109 High Street, Hail Weston & Old Farm Cottage. Visitors also welcome by appt May to Sept.**
A good Old Vicarage garden, redesigned in 2008/9 to enhance original plan. Some gravel paths.

42 THE PADDOCK
43 Lower End, Swaffham Prior CB25 0HT. Judi and Mike Churcher. *10m E of Cambridge off B1102. On entering the village from Cambridge, The Paddock can be found at the far end on L, opp Rogers Rd.* Light refreshments. **Adm £3, chd free. Sun 19 May (2-6).**
Redesigned 7 years ago and still evolving. Gravel paths zig zag between shrub and perennial borders. On the way, relax on the deck; on a bench opposite a raised bed or on a swing seat in the gazebo. Practice golf and explore the playhouse. Round a corner enjoy the colour on the 'flowery mead', where paths snake through herbaceous

perennials and ornamental grasses. We are hoping to have water colours and postcards, with a fenland theme, on sale. The village is famous for its 2 churches and a working windmill (certain dates only). NT Wicken Fen and Anglesey Abbey are nearby.

Free range bluebelle chickens and stunning raised bed organic vegetable potager . . . .

43 PAVILION HOUSE
Station Road, Dullingham, nr Newmarket CB8 9UT. Mrs Gretta Bredin, 01638 508005, gretta@thereliablesauce.co.uk. *4m S of Newmarket. Take turning off A1304, signed Dullingham, Pavilion House is 1m along this rd, 1st house on R. Parking will be signed.* Home-made teas. **Adm £3.50, chd free.** Sun 9 June (2-6). **Visitors & groups max 20, also welcome by appt Apr to July.**
Delightful S-facing 18yr old 1 acre country garden, with traditional colour themed borders. Expansive rural views, wild flower walk, free range bluebelle chickens and stunning raised bed organic vegetable potager. Tombola stall, plants for sale. Gravel driveway.

44 ◆ PECKOVER HOUSE
North Brink, Wisbech PE13 1JR. National Trust, 01945 583463, www.nationaltrust.org.uk. *Centre of Wisbech on N bank of R Nene. Within easy walking distance of town bus stn. Nearest car park in Chapel Rd - no parking on property. Disabled blue badge parking outside property.* **Adm £4.95, chd £2.50.** For NGS: Sat 4 May (12-5); Thur 4 July (11-5).
For other opening times and information, please phone or see garden website.
One of the best Victorian town house gardens, Peckover is a 2-acre site offering many areas of interest. These incl herbaceous borders, bedding, roses, trees, ponds, a propagation glasshouse, lawns, cut flower border, ferns, summerhouses and an orangery with 3 very old fruiting orange trees. Sat 4 May, magnificent wisteria in bloom. Thur 4 July, coincides with Wisbech Rose Fair. Roses in the garden will be labelled and should be at their peak. NGS funded trainee will be on hand to answer questions about the garden and National Trust horticultural training. Gravel paths.

45 23A PERRY ROAD
Buckden, St. Neots PE19 5XG. David & Valerie Bunnage, 01480 810553, d.bunnage@btinternet.com. *5m S of Huntingdon on A1. From A1 Buckden r'about take B661, Perry Rd approx 300yds on L.* **Adm £3.50, chd free.** Visitors welcome by appt **19 Jan to 30 Nov.**
Approx 1 acre garden consisting of many garden designs incl Japanese interlinked by gravel paths. Large selection of acers, pines, rare and unusual shrubs. Also interesting features. Plantsmans garden for all seasons.

GROUP OPENING

46 RAMSEY FORTY FOOT
nr Ramsey PE26 2YA. *3m N of Ramsey. From Ramsey (B1096) travel through Ramsey Forty Foot, just before bridge over drain, turn R, First Cottage 300yds on R, next door to The Elms.* Home-made teas at First Cottage. **Combined adm £3, chd free.** Sun 14 July (2-6).

THE ELMS
Hollow Road. Mr R Shotbolt.
Turn into Hollow Rd at The George PH. The Elms is 200 metres on R
Visitors also welcome by appt May to Aug.
01487 812601
richard@shotbolt.freeserve.co.uk

FIRST COTTAGE
Hollow Road. Mr & Mrs Fort

THE WILLOWS
Jane & Andrew Sills

3 interesting and contrasting gardens in the village of Ramsey Forty Foot. The Elms 1½ -acre water garden around C19 clay pit backed by massive elms. Large collection of shrubs, perennials, bog and aquatic plants. Woodland and arid plantings. First Cottage 150ft x 40ft garden with herbaceous borders, shrub beds, natural pond. Miniature steam railway. The Willows is a cottage garden with riverside location filled with old roses, herbaceous beds; shrubs, ferns, pond and vegetable garden. Some wheelchair access.

47 NEW 11 REDBRIDGE
Peterborough PE4 5DP. Mr & Mrs Mandy & Andy Knowles, 07976 224473, arknowles2@gmail.com. *Werrington, N Peterborough. 4m from city centre on A15. Turn E at Audi/BMW garage onto David's Ln. At traffic lights turn L and Redbridge is 3rd turn on L.* **Adm £2, chd free.** Visitors welcome by appt.
Unusual small walled garden with many tropical plants and ferns. Yellow balau hardwood decking and wall covering with a cobbled brick patio area.

48 NEW 1 RHONDA PARK
Wimblington, March PE15 0QD. Alison & Paul Allen. *From A141 turn off towards Fengrain (grain store), then follow rd past Fengrain and take next L towards Rhonda Park. House 1st on L.* Home-made teas. **Adm £3, chd free.** Sun 9 June (10-4).
A modern contemporary garden, designed by Adam Frost, multi award winning designer incl gold medal at Chelsea Flower show and best in Show at Gardeners' World

49 6 ROBINS WOOD
Wansford, Peterborough PE8 6JQ. Carole & Forbes Smith, 01780 783094, caroleannsmith@tiscali.co.uk. *7m W of Peterborough on A1/A47 junction. From A47 turn towards Wansford. At Xrds by church turn W onto Old Leicester Rd. Approx 500yds turn R into Robins Field, follow on to Robins Wood.* **Adm £2.50, chd free.** Visitors welcome by appt.
Small woodland garden with a collection of 200+ varieties of snowdrops. Various hellebore and corydalis followed by other spring woodland plants and bulbs. Small alpine plant house.

© Howard Rice

50 ◆ **ROBINSON COLLEGE**
Grange Road, Cambridge CB3 9AN. Warden and Fellows, 01223 339100, www.robinson.cam.ac.uk/about/gardens/ngs.php. *Grange Rd runs N to S between Madingley Rd (A1303) & Barton Rd (A603). Turn S on Madingley Rd down Grange Rd, on R. N from Barton Rd on L, opp University Library. Park on st, (parking may be limited). Please report to the Porters Lodge on arrival.* **Adm £2.50, chd free. For NGS: 1 Jan to 21 Apr; 1 July to 31 Dec. Mon-Fri (10-4), Sat & Sun (2-4). For other opening times and information, please phone or see garden website.**
10 original Edwardian gardens are linked to central wild woodland water garden focusing on Bin Brook with small lake at heart of site. This gives a feeling of park and informal woodland, while at the same time keeping the sense of older more formal gardens beyond. Central area has a wide lawn running down to the lake framed by many mature stately trees with much of the original planting intact. More recent planting incl herbaceous borders and commemorative trees. No picnics. Children must be accompanied at all times. Ask at Porters' Lodge for wheelchair access.

GROUP OPENING

51 **SAWSTON GARDENS**
CB22 3HY. *5m SE of Cambridge. 3m from M11 J10. Off junction of A505 & A1301. Sawston village is well signposted. Plenty of parking in the village. Regular buses to/from Cambridge. Nearest railway station Whittlesford (2 m).* Cream teas in the village. **Combined adm £5, chd free. Sun 30 June (1-6).**

DRIFT HOUSE
19a Babraham Road. Mr & Mrs Alan Osborne

35 MILL LANE
Doreen Butler

11 MILL LANE
Tim & Rosie Phillips

THE NEW VICARAGE
Church Lane. Revd Alan Partridge

22 ST MARY'S ROAD
Ann & Mike Redshaw

5 delightful, peaceful and secluded gardens in South Cambridgeshire's largest village set off by houses from the C15 to C20. Excellent value at less than £1 per garden and time to spend a good 40 mins at each. Wide variety of gardening styles and features including: semi-circular striped lawn, wildlife-friendly planting (69 species noted), juniper 'cloud' tree, extensive moving water features, a classic vicarage garden and much, much more to interest and fascinate. Most gardens offer some seating. Shops, pubs and restaurants in the village. Accessible public WC available. Visitors are given an excellent free map of all the gardens and facilities at the first garden they visit.

GROUP OPENING

52 NEW SHELFORD GARDENS
Cambridge CB22 5EG. *3m S of Cambridge. Easy access by train and public transport. Signposted on A1301.* Light refreshments at Malyons, 15 High Green. **Combined adm £5, chd free. Sun 23 June (2-6).**

NEW 44 DAVEY CRESCENT
Lesley & Tony Smith.
Davey Cres off Cambridge Rd. House next to railway bridge and embankment

NEW 23 HIGH STREET
Ruth Morley

MALYONS
15 High Green. Maire & Gilbert Park.
Opp Great Shelford PO. NB High Green not High Street

NEW 7 STONEHILL ROAD
Sara Anstead.
Off Cambridge Rd nr Scotsdales Garden Centre on other side of rd

NEW 30 WESTFIELD ROAD
Rosie Cranmer

NEW 32 WESTFIELD ROAD
Nightingale.
Off Cambridge Rd nr Scotsdales Garden Centre on other side of rd

Delightful and varied new group of gardens. Each garden uses space in a different way and has its own characteristic planting. 23 High Street uses diagonals to emphasise space and is essentially a large open garden with views down the long, colourful herbaceous borders. 44 Davey Crescent has created a winding route through the garden with mature planting which allows views to open before you. 7 Stonehill Road has places to sit and take in the garden's herbaceous planting and mature trees. 30 Westfield Road divides its garden into 3 separate areas each with its own individual character and planting. 32 Westfield Road borrows views across fields echoing this with grasses. Different gardens but sharing the fact that their gardeners are passionate about their space. Photographic exhibition at Malyons, 15 High Green.

GROUP OPENING

53 STAPLEFORD GARDENS
Cambridge CB22 5DG. *4m S of Cambridge on A1301.* Home-made teas at 59-61 London Road. **Combined adm £4, chd free. Sun 9 June (2-6).**

CRISPIN COTTAGE
David & Jean Mann.
Opp The Rose PH

57 LONDON ROAD
Mrs M Spriggs.
Next to Church St

59 - 61 LONDON ROAD
Dr & Mrs S Jones.
Next to Church St

5 PRIAMS WAY
Tony Smith.
Off London Rd, access via 59 - 61 London Rd. There is a gate between the gdns

Contrasting gardens showing a range of size, planting and atmosphere in this village just S of Cambridge. The London Road gardens and Priam's Way form an interlocking series of garden rooms including herbaceous beds, kitchen garden, alpine, pit and summer houses with sculptures set around.

STREET FARM
See Suffolk

Different gardens but sharing the fact that their gardeners are passionate about their space . . .

GROUP OPENING

54 STREETLY END GARDENS
West Wickham CB21 4RP. *3m NW of Haverhill. On A1307 between Linton & Haverhill. Turn N at Horseheath towards West Wickham, from Horseheath turn left at triangle of grass and trees.* Home-made teas at Chequer Cottage. **Combined adm £4, chd free. Sat 15, Sun 16 June (12-5).**

CHEQUER COTTAGE
Mr & Mrs D Sills.
On A1307. Turn N at Horseheath towards W Wickham, at triangle after RH bend, cottage on R
01223 891522
stay@chequercottage.com
www.chequercottage.com

CLOVER COTTAGE
Mrs Shirley Shadford.
On A1307 between Linton and Haverhill. Turn N at Horseheath to West Wickham. From Horseheath turn L at triangle of grass and trees. Next to the old windmill
Visitors also welcome by appt May to June.
01223 893122
shirleyshadford@live.co.uk

WEAVER'S COTTAGE NCH
Sylvia Norton
Visitors also welcome by appt Apr to Sept.
01223 892399

Find arches of roses and clematis at Clover Cottage and many varieties of hardy geraniums, and raised fruit/vegetable beds. Delightful pond and borders of English roses, climbers and herbaceous plants. Also ferns and shade plants and views over open countryside from summerhouse in sunken garden. At Chequer Cottage enjoy mixed cottage and contemporary planting of - Monet style rose arch, perennial beds with many iris, delphiniums, roses. Unusual trees, pond, bog garden, art studio. Long vegetable garden, interesting walls, paths and rockery. In walled garden evergreen shrubs, damp shade and hot dry borders. Weaver's Cottage is a recently rejuvenated plantsman's paradise of many rare and unusual plants. National collection of lathyrus. Also wildlife pond, many new and old 'old' roses, mature shrubs, trees, perennials, bulbous plants. Raised scree bed, fruit and vegetable cage. Art studio open, art work for sale.

Cakes, honey and preserves all home-made at Chequer Cottage. Plants for sale at Clover Cottage.

♿ ❀ NCH ☕

55 TRINITY COLLEGE, FELLOWS' GARDEN
Queens Road, Cambridge CB3 9AQ. Master and Fellows' of Trinity College. *Towards the Northampton St and Madingley Rd end of Queens Rd, between Clare College and St Johns College. Garden Gate is a small metal one set back from rd.* Home-made teas. **Adm £3.50, chd free. Sun 7 Apr (1-4).**
Garden of 8 acres, originally laid out in the 1870s by W B Thomas. Lawns with mixed borders, shrubs and specimen trees. Drifts of spring bulbs. Recent extension of landscaped area among new college buildings to W of main garden. Some gravel paths.

♿ ❀ ☕

Bluebell wood leads down to water meadows and small flock of rare breed sheep by River Cam . . .

56 TRINITY HALL - WYCHFIELD
Storeys Way, Cambridge CB3 0DZ. The Master & Fellows, www.trinhall.cam.ac.uk/about/gardens.asp. *1m NW of city centre. Turn into Storeys Way from Madingley Rd (A1303).* Home-made teas. **Adm £4.50, chd free (share to Parkinson's UK). Sun 14 July (12-4).**
A beautiful garden that complements the interesting and varied architecture. The Edwardian Wychfield House and its associated garden areas contrast with the recent contemporary development located off Storeys Way. Majestic trees, flowering shrubs, roses, herbaceous beds, shady under storey woodland planting and established lawns, work together to provide a picturesque garden. Plant Sale. Some gravel paths.

♿ 🐕 ❀ ☕

57 TWIN TARNS
6 Pinfold Lane, Somersham PE28 3EQ. Michael & Frances Robinson, 01487 843376, mkrobinson12@aol.com. *From A14 take St Ives exit. Take A1096 N until B1040. Continue on B1040 which turns into B1086, turn R into Somersham. Turn R on Church St. Park then walk to Pinfold Ln next to church.* Home-made teas. **Adm £3, chd free. Sat 7, Sun 8 Sept (1-5). Visitors also welcome by appt May to Sept.**
One-acre wildlife garden with formal borders, kitchen garden and ponds, large rockery, mini woodland, wild flower meadow (June/July). Topiary, rose walk, willow sculptures. Character oak bridge. Hammock. Adjacent to C13 village church. Featured in many publications.

❀ ☕ ☎

58 TY GWYN
6 The Borough, Aldreth CB6 3PJ. Sian & Mark Hugo, 01353 740586, sianandmark@artes-mundi.co.uk, www.artes-mundi.co.uk/garden. *7m SW of Ely. 2m S of Haddenham. The Borough is 2nd on L after entering Aldreth Village. Please park in High St, approx 2 mins walk from gdn. Parking for disabled at gdn.* Home-made teas. **Adm £3, chd free. Sat 18, Sun 19 May; Sat 15, Sun 16 June; Sat 13, Sun 14 July (10-5). Visitors also welcome by appt May to July.**
1 acre cottage garden in small fenland hamlet. Grass path walks around mature trees, shrubs, perennials and climbers. Wild flower garden, cactus greenhouse, vegetable patch, orchard, fishpond, animal and bird sculptures. Free range chickens and ducks including rare breeds. Artes Mundi Fair Trade gift shop onsite.

♿ ☕ ☎

59 UPWATER LODGE
23 Chaucer Road, Cambridge CB2 7EB. Mr & Mrs George Pearson, 07890 080303, jmp@pearson.co.uk. *Off Trumpington Rd, near to Brooklands Ave junction.* Home-made teas. **Adm £4, chd free. Sat 15, Sun 16 June (2-5). Visitors also welcome by appt May to Sept.**
6 acres with mature trees, fine lawns, old wisterias, and colourful borders. Small, pretty potager and newly planted vineyard. A network of paths through a bluebell wood leads down to water meadows and small flock of rare breed sheep by river Cam. Enjoy a walk by the river and watch the punts go by. Practice your shots on our top standard lawn tennis court or try your hand at croquet. Cakes made with home grown produce where possible. Some unusual recipes. Swings ropes and plenty of space. Gravel and mown grass paths, some gentle slopes.

♿ ❀ ☕ ☎

WALNUT COTTAGE
See Bedfordshire

GROUP OPENING

60 NEW WEST CHESTERTON
Cambridge CB4 2AQ. *West Chesterton, Cambridge. Accessed from Milton Rd (A10 to Ely) between Gilbert Rd and Elizabeth Way. Some designated parking in Milton Rd; easy parking in nearby side streets.* Home-made teas. **Combined adm £5, chd free. Sat 15, Sun 16 June (2-5).**

NEW 16 CHESTERTON HALL CRESCENT
Eve Corder.
Accessed either from Chesterton Rd or on foot from Milton Rd. Parking limited

NEW 18 CHESTERTON HALL CRESCENT
Hazel & Julian Bland

NEW 10 GURNEY WAY
Gillian Perkins

NEW 60 HURST PARK AVENUE
John & Janet Marshall

NEW 55 MILTON ROAD
Richard & Pauline.
Milton Rd is on A10 toward Ely. No 55 lies approx halfway between Gilbert and Ascham Rds

35 ORCHARD AVENUE
Eunice Fisher.
From Milton Rd turn L into Hurst Park Ave then 1st turn R
Visitors also welcome by appt June to Aug 01223 300744, fisher_eunice@yahoo.co.uk.

6 town gardens of varying size and design reflecting the different interest and aspirations of their owners. 16 Chesterton Hall Crescent is a sculptor's garden with workshop, work area and sculpture set amongst informal planting. 18 Chesterton Hall Crescent next door has herbaceous

border, pond, pergola, climbing roses, shrubs and mature trees. 10 Gurney Way is run by a self-confessed plantaholic with several herbaceous borders and vegetable/ fruit areas. 60 Hurst Park Ave is a newly-created garden with plans showing work-in-progress. 55 Milton Road is divided into 2 areas by a beech hedge, with herbaceous beds and shrubs. 35 Orchard Ave is a long plot subdivided into sections, each offering a different mood and type of planting. Dogs on leads only. No wheelchair access at 18 Chesterton Hall Cres.

Described by one visitor as a garden to write poetry in . . . !

GROUP OPENING

61 WHITTLESFORD GARDENS

CB22 4NR. *7m S of Cambridge. 1m NE of J10 M11 & A505. Parking nr church, additional parking will be signed*. Home-made teas at the church. **Combined adm £4, chd free.** Sun 16 June (2-6).

1 CHURCH CLOSE
Mrs Mary Bulman

11 CHURCH CLOSE
Mrs Val King

4 FARM RISE
Mrs Ann Strange

MARKINGS FARM
32 West End. Mr & Mrs A Jennings.
Parking space

5 PARSONAGE COURT
Mrs L Button.
Please park on rd

RYECROFT
1 Middlemoor Road. Mr & Mrs Paul Goodman

11 SCOTTS GARDENS
Mr & Mrs M Walker

15 SCOTTS GARDENS
Mrs Ann Bayles

There is a sense of going back to older gentler times with this collection of formal and country gardens. Ryecroft is a large elegant garden with trees, shrubs and restful patio area. Markings Farm, a lovely old fashioned country garden with a variety of shrubs and fabulous vegetable patch. Parsonage Court has an arched walkway, shrubs, raised fish pond and delightful seating area around an old tree. Farm Rise, a small cottage garden found via an oak divide has colourful borders and many interesting plants. 15 Scotts Gardens, an immaculate secret walled garden has beautiful clematis and large selection of heuchera. 11 Scotts Gardens, a shady walled cottage garden with chickens and a variety of shrubs and perennials. 1 Church Close, a small modern low maintenance garden with sunny patio. The pride of 11 Church Close is a large selection of begonias in pots and a maturing landscaped garden containing many different plants.

62 NEW WILD ROSE COTTAGE

Church Walk, Lode, Cambridge CB25 9EX. Mrs Joy Martin, joffandjoy@tiscali.co.uk. *From A14 follow signs to Burwell and Lode. After 2m take LH turn in to Lode. As road bends round to L continue straight on down gravel drive between white thatched cottages.* **Adm £3, chd free.** Visitors welcome by appt **Mar to Nov. Please email for appointment.**
A real cottage garden overflowing with plants. Gardens within gardens of abundant vegetation, roses climbing through trees, laburnum tunnel, a daffodil spiral which becomes a daisy spiral in the summer. Circular vegetable garden and wildlife pond. Described by one visitor as a garden to write poetry in! Chickens ducks and dog. Wildlife garden.

63 ◆ WIMPOLE ESTATE

Arrington SG8 0BW. National Trust, 01223 206000, www.nationaltrust.org.uk/wimpole-estate. *7m N of Royston (A1198). 8m SW of Cambridge (A603). J12 off M11, 30 mins from A1(M).* **Adm £4.50, chd £2.90.** For NGS: Sun 28 July (10.30-5). **For other opening times and information, please phone or see garden website.**
New border 2010; a prelude to the walled garden, our showpiece containing fruit, flowers, vegetables. Recreated Sir John Sloane glasshouse, financed with NGS help. Herbaceous borders over 100 metres long with mixed plantings of perennials, roses and choice shrubs. Dutch Garden and Victorian parterres. Expanding collection of fine trees and shrubs. Also National Collection of Juglans (walnuts). New border 2011 to produce cut flowers for the house and restaurant. Electric buggies available, please book before arrival.

NCH

64 THE WINDMILL

Cambridge Road, Impington CB24 9NU. Pippa & Steve Temple, 07775 446443, mill.impington@ntlworld.com, www.impingtonmill.org. *2½ m N of Cambridge. Off A14 at J32, B1049 to Histon and Cottenham, then first L into Cambridge Rd at traffic lights, follow Cambridge Rd round to R and The Windmill is approx 400yds on L.* **Adm £3, chd free.** Visitors welcome by appt **Apr to Oct.**
A previously romantic wilderness of 1½ acres surrounding windmill, now filled with bulbs, perennial beds, pergolas, bog gardens, grass bed and herb bank. Secret paths and wild areas maintain the romance. New - millstone seating area, water features and a hot planting to contrast with the pastel colours of the remainder of the garden. Amazing compost area, plus the start of a vegetable garden. Smock windmill under restoration. Featured in the Daily Mail, local press and on Radio Cambridgeshire.

65 WYTCHWOOD

7 Owl End, Great Stukeley PE28 4AQ. Mr David Cox. *2m N of Huntingdon on B1043. Parking available at Great Stukeley Village Hall in Owl End.* Home-made teas and cream teas. **Adm £3.50, chd free.** Sat 22, Sun 23 June (1.30-5.30).
A 2 acre garden. Brightly planted borders of perennials, annuals and shrubs, lawns and ponds. 1 acre of wild plants, grasses set among rowan, maple and birch trees leading to spinney planted with native trees, bulbs, ferns, hostas and foxgloves. Short gravel drive.

© Val Corbett

Cambridgeshire County Volunteers

County Organiser

George Stevenson, 1a The Village, Orton Longueville, Peterborough, Cambridgeshire PE2 7DN, 01733 391506, chrisgeorge1a@aol.com

County Treasurer

Nicholas Kyberd, 5 Moat Way, Swavesey, Cambridge CB24 4TR, 01954 200568, n.kyberd@ntlworld.com

Booklet Coordinator

Nicole Langstaff, Phantom Cottage, Snailwell Road, Chippenham, Ely CB7 5QZ, 01638 720499, info@fineartmarketing.co.uk

Assistant County Organisers

Pam Bullivant, Rosewell House, 60 Prickwillow Road, Ely CB7 4TX, 01353 667355, pbul@hotmail.com
Patsy Glazebrook, 15 Bentley Road, Cambridge CB2 8AW, 01223 301302, glazebrc@doctors.net.uk
Angie Jones Willow Holt, Willow Hall Lane, Thorney, Peterborough PE6 0QN, 01733 222367 janda.salix@virgin.net
Michael Tuplin, 36 Barton Road, Ely CB7 4HZ 01353 612029 miketuplin@yahoo.co.uk
Annette White, 9 Forestry Cottage, West End, Woodditton, Newmarket CB8 9SW, 01638 730876, annette323@btinternet.com

Plant specialists: look for the Plant Heritage symbol NCH

CHESHIRE & WIRRAL

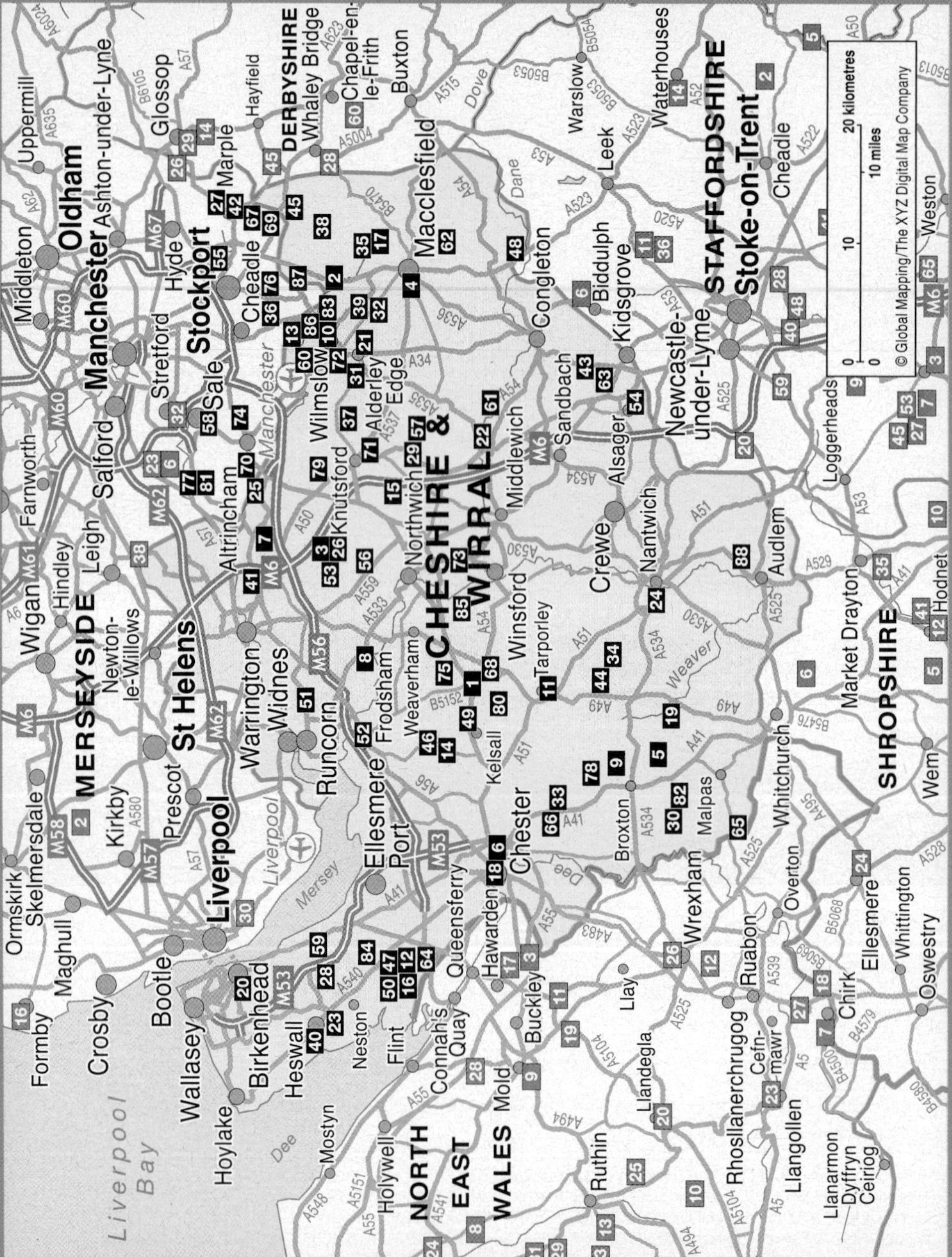

Opening Dates

February

Sunday 17
15 Bucklow Farm
25 Dunham Massey

March

Saturday 2
50 Ness Botanic Gardens

Sunday 24
19 Cholmondeley Castle Garden

April

Sunday 7
56 Parm Place

Saturday 13
59 Poulton Hall

Sunday 14
12 Briarfield
59 Poulton Hall
66 Saighton Grange

Sunday 21
8 Bluebell Cottage Gardens
44 Long Acre

Wednesday 24
79 Tatton Park

Saturday 27
33 Hatton House Gardens

Sunday 28
1 Abbeywood Gardens

May

Saturday 4
60 Quarry Bank House Garden

Sunday 5
34 Haughton Hall
49 Mount Pleasant
60 Quarry Bank House Garden
84 Willaston Village Gardens

Monday 6
49 Mount Pleasant
81 The Vicarage Gardens

Sunday 12
25 Dunham Massey
80 Tirley Garth

Saturday 18
37 Hillside
42 Leawood
58 17 Poplar Grove

Sunday 19
24 Dorfold Hall
37 Hillside
42 Leawood
46 Manley Knoll
58 17 Poplar Grove
78 Tattenhall Hall
80 Tirley Garth

Thursday 23
36 73 Hill Top Avenue (Evening)

Saturday 25
21 34 Congleton Road
67 Sandsend

Sunday 26
21 34 Congleton Road
29 Free Green Farm
67 Sandsend
80 Tirley Garth

June

Saturday 1
53 The Old Parsonage
57 Peover Hall Gardens
74 199 Stockport Road
76 Sun House

Sunday 2
53 The Old Parsonage
57 Peover Hall Gardens
74 199 Stockport Road
76 Sun House
80 Tirley Garth

Saturday 8
47 Medlicott

Sunday 9
20 28 Christchurch Road
47 Medlicott
75 Stonyford Cottage

Wednesday 12
79 Tatton Park

National Gardens Weekend

Saturday 15
14 Brooklands
30 Grafton Lodge
33 Hatton House Gardens
51 Norton Priory Museum & Gardens
52 The Old Cottage
77 Sycamore Cottage
81 The Vicarage Gardens
86 28 Woodlands Road
87 Woodsend

Sunday 16
4 Ashmead
11 Bowmere Cottage
14 Brooklands
23 29 Dee Park Road
30 Grafton Lodge
32 Hare Hill Gardens
44 Long Acre
46 Manley Knoll
52 The Old Cottage
54 Orchard Villa
59 Poulton Hall
70 The School House
77 Sycamore Cottage
86 28 Woodlands Road
87 Woodsend

Saturday 22
6 150 Barrel Well Hill
30 Grafton Lodge

Sunday 23
6 150 Barrel Well Hill
30 Grafton Lodge
78 Tattenhall Hall

Saturday 29
88 Yew Tree House Garden & Special Perennials Nursery

Sunday 30
16 Burton Village Gardens
26 The East Garden
36 73 Hill Top Avenue
56 Parm Place
83 Well House
88 Yew Tree House Garden & Special Perennials Nursery

Uniquely, preferred method of arrival is by leisurely river cruiser from Chester . . .

July

Friday 5
71 Somerford (Evening)

Saturday 6
35 18 Highfield Road
48 Millpool
88 Yew Tree House Garden & Special Perennials Nursery

Sunday 7
27 Edith Terrace Gardens
35 18 Highfield Road
48 Millpool
62 Ridge Hill
88 Yew Tree House Garden & Special Perennials Nursery

Saturday 13
13 Brooke Cottage
31 Greenways
40 Inglewood
65 The Rowans
72 68 South Oak Lane

Sunday 14
13 Brooke Cottage
31 Greenways
40 Inglewood
65 The Rowans
68 Sandymere
71 Somerford
72 68 South Oak Lane

Saturday 20
88 Yew Tree House Garden & Special Perennials Nursery

Sunday 21

1 Abbeywood Gardens
2 Adlington Hall
88 Yew Tree House Garden & Special Perennials Nursery

Saturday 27

22 Dane Mount

Sunday 28

7 Beechwood Cottage
22 Dane Mount
71 Somerford

The grandest chicken shed outside Highgrove . . .

August

Saturday 3

4 Ashmead
69 21 Scafell Close

Sunday 4

3 Arley Hall & Gardens
4 Ashmead
25 Dunham Massey
36 73 Hill Top Avenue
39 Hunters Croft
69 21 Scafell Close

Saturday 10

73 Springbank
88 Yew Tree House Garden & Special Perennials Nursery

Sunday 11

73 Springbank
75 Stonyford Cottage
88 Yew Tree House Garden & Special Perennials Nursery

Saturday 17

41 Laskey Farm
77 Sycamore Cottage

Sunday 18

41 Laskey Farm
77 Sycamore Cottage

Monday 26

8 Bluebell Cottage Gardens
81 The Vicarage Gardens

Saturday 31

18 Chester Cathedral
49 Mount Pleasant

September

Sunday 1

49 Mount Pleasant
88 Yew Tree House Garden & Special Perennials Nursery

Saturday 7

45 Lyme Park
55 39 Osborne Street

Sunday 8

29 Free Green Farm
55 39 Osborne Street
88 Yew Tree House Garden & Special Perennials Nursery

October

Sunday 6

61 The Quinta Arboretum

Gardens open to the public

1 Abbeywood Gardens
2 Adlington Hall
3 Arley Hall & Gardens
8 Bluebell Cottage Gardens
19 Cholmondeley Castle Garden
25 Dunham Massey
32 Hare Hill Gardens
43 Little Moreton Hall
45 Lyme Park
49 Mount Pleasant
50 Ness Botanic Gardens
51 Norton Priory Museum & Gardens
57 Peover Hall Gardens
60 Quarry Bank House Garden
61 The Quinta Arboretum
63 Rode Hall
75 Stonyford Cottage
79 Tatton Park

By appointment only

5 Bank House
9 Bolesworth Castle
10 Bollin House
17 4 Cheshire View
28 Fieldcrest
38 Hillside Cottage
64 Rosewood
82 The Well House
85 Wood End Cottage

Also open by Appointment ☎

11 Bowmere Cottage
12 Briarfield
13 Brooke Cottage
14 Brooklands
16 Lynwood, Burton Village Gardens
18 Chester Cathedral
23 29 Dee Park Road
26 The East Garden
30 Grafton Lodge
31 Greenways
35 18 Highfield Road
40 Inglewood
41 Laskey Farm
44 Long Acre
46 Manley Knoll
47 Medlicott
48 Millpool
52 The Old Cottage
53 The Old Parsonage
54 Orchard Villa
55 39 Osborne Street
56 Parm Place
58 17 Poplar Grove
59 Poulton Hall
62 Ridge Hill
65 The Rowans
66 Saighton Grange
67 Sandsend
69 21 Scafell Close
71 Somerford
72 68 South Oak Lane
73 Springbank
78 Tattenhall Hall
83 Well House

The Gardens

1 ◆ ABBEYWOOD GARDENS

Chester Road, Delamere, Northwich CW8 2HS. The Rowlinson Family, 01606 301374, www.abbeywoodgardenscheshire.co.uk. *11m E of Chester. From the W proceed E from Chester along A51 onto the A54 following onto A556. Before you reach Xrds with B5152 turn R into Abbeywood Gdns opp St Peter's Church. From the E proceed along A556 towards Chester. Cross over B5152, up the hill & turn L into Abbeywood Gdns.* **Adm £5, chd free. For NGS: Sun 28 Apr; Sun 21 July (11-4). For other opening times and information, please phone or see garden website.**
Superb setting near Delamere Forest. Total area 45 acres incl mature woodland, new woodland and new arboretum all with connecting pathways. Approx 4½ acres of gardens surrounding large Edwardian House. Vegetable garden, exotic garden, chapel garden, pool garden, woodland garden, lawned area with beds.

2 ◆ ADLINGTON HALL

Macclesfield SK10 4LF. Mrs Camilla Legh, 01625 829206/ 827595, www.adlingtonhall.com. *4m N of Macclesfield. Well signed off A523 at Adlington.* **Adm £6, chd free. For NGS: Sun 21 July (2-5). For other opening times and information, please phone or see garden website.**

350 Volunteers help run the NGS – why not become one too?

6 acres of formal gardens with herbaceous borders, rose garden, rockeries, yew maze, water garden. Lawns with open views across ha-ha. 32-acre wilderness with mature plantings, various follies incl a 'Temple to Diana', woodland walk. Yew and ancient lime walks. Flower parterre.

3 ◆ ARLEY HALL & GARDENS

Nr Northwich CW9 6NA. The Viscount Ashbrook, 01565 777353, www.arleyhallandgardens.com. *5m from Knutsford, Warrington & Northwich. Well signed from M6 J19 & 20, & M56 J9 & 10.* **Adm £7, chd free.** **For NGS: Sun 4 Aug (11-4.30).** **For other opening times and information, please phone or see garden website.**

One of Britain's finest gardens, Arley has been lovingly created by the same family over 250yrs and is famous for its yew buttressed herbaceous border, avenue of ilex columns, walled garden, pleached lime avenue and Victorian Rootree. A garden of great atmosphere, interest and vitality throughout the seasons. Specialist nursery adjacent.

4 ASHMEAD

2 Bramhall Way, off Gritstone Drive, Macclesfield SK10 3SH. Peter & Penelope McDermott. *1m W of Macclesfield. Along Victoria Rd, 1st L after Macclesfield Hospital complex into Pavilion Way. L onto Gritstone Dr. Turn R into Bramhall Way, corner house. Travelling from Knutsford on the A537 Chelford Rd turn L at the Broken Cross r'about,straight across the next r'about at 'The Villas' down the hill passing the clock tower on your R, Pavilion Way is first R, then Gritstone Dr first L and Ashmead first R on the corner.* Home-made teas. **Adm £3, chd free.** **Sun 16 June; Sat 3, Sun 4 Aug (1-5).**

1/8 acre suburban cottage garden, featuring plant packed mixed borders, rock gardens, kitchen garden, island beds, water feature. The garden demonstrates how small spaces can be planted to maximum effect to create all round interest. Extensive range of plants favoured for colours, texture and scent. Pots used in a creative way to extend and enhance borders.

Hunters Croft

5 BANK HOUSE

Goldford Lane, Bickerton SY14 8LL. Dr & Mrs M A Voisey, 01829 782287, voisey598@btinternet.com. *4m NE of Malpas. 11m S of Chester on A41 turn L at Broxton r'about to Nantwich on A534. Take 5th R (1¾ m) to Bickerton. Take 2nd R into Goldford Lane. Bank House is nearly 1m on L. Field parking.* Home-made teas. **Adm £4, chd free.** **Visitors welcome by appt** **Apr to July, children free if accompanied.**

1¾ -acre garden at the foot of Bickerton Hill, in area of outstanding beauty, with extensive views to Derbyshire and the Marches. Sheltered, terraced borders stocked with a wide range of shrubs, trees and herbaceous plants; established wild garden, Millennium garden with water features and productive vegetable garden. Unfenced swimming pool and ponds. Limited wheelchair access.

6 NEW 150 BARREL WELL HILL

Boughton, Chester CH3 5BR. Dr & Mrs John Browne. *On riverside ¾ m E of Chester off A5115. No parking adj to garden. Preferred access via Bithells Boats, on the hour from 11 - 4, from The Groves central Chester. Cost one way £3.50, child £2. Alternative access on foot from Boughton or bus to St Paul's church. Nearest car parking adj to Bill Smith Motors (100 metres) or at Boughton Retail Centre (250 metres).* Home-made teas. **Adm £3.50, chd £2.** **Sat 22, Sun 23 June (11-5).**

Spectacular terraced garden with views over the R Dee to the Meadows and Clwyd Hills. Uniquely, preferred method of arrival is by leisurely river cruiser from Chester. Informal cottage style garden on historic site by the Martyrs Memorial. Lawns running down to the river, prolific shrub and flower beds, productive vegetable patch and soft and hard fruit areas, springs, stream and lily pond. Not suitable for wheelchairs or children under eight due to unprotected drop into river.

7 BEECHWOOD COTTAGE
64 Crouchley Lane, Lymm WA13 0AT. Ian & Amber Webb. *8m S of Altrincham. 4m from J7 or 2m J21 M6 onto A56 turn into Crouchley Ln past Lymm Rugby Club on R, 300yds on R (opp Crouchley Mews).* Home-made teas, a sumptuous array of delicious home-made cakes. **Adm £4, chd free.** Sun 28 July (11-5).
2½ acre garden looking out to fields. Large lawn with herbaceous borders. Formal walkway with rose arches, topiary garden and orchard. Wild flower meadow - shaded area with tree ferns, hellebores and ferns. The grandest chicken shed outside Highgrove.

Always changing, Liz can't resist a new plant . . . . !

BIDDULPH GRANGE GARDEN
See Staffordshire, Birmingham & West Midlands

8 ◆ BLUEBELL COTTAGE GARDENS
Lodge Lane, Dutton WA4 4HP. Sue & David Beesley, 01928 713718, www.bluebellcottage.co.uk. *5m NW of Northwich. From M56 (J10) take A49 to Whitchurch. After 3m turn R at T-lights towards Runcorn/Dutton. Then 1st turning L.* **Adm £4, chd free.** For NGS: Sun 21 Apr; Mon 26 Aug (10-5). **For other opening times and information, please phone or see garden website.**
1½ -acre south facing garden on a quiet rural lane in the heart of Cheshire. Packed with thousands of rare and familiar hardy herbaceous perennials, shrubs and trees. Unusual plants available at adjacent nursery. April opening co-incides with bluebells flowering in woods - access incl in entry charge. Featured in The Garden. Some gravel paths. Wheelchair access to 90% of garden.

9 BOLESWORTH CASTLE
Tattenhall CH3 9HQ. Mrs Anthony Barbour, 01829 782210, dcb@bolesworth.com. *8m S of Chester on A41. Enter by Lodge on A41.* **Adm £5, chd free.** Visitors welcome by appt **Apr to May.**
One of the finest collections of rhododendrons, camellias and acers in any private garden in the NW. Set on a steep hillside accessed by a gently rising woodland walk and overlooking spectacular view of the Cheshire plain. Formal lawn beside castle with well stocked herbaceous borders. Terraces with lawn, rose gardens and many other plants.

10 NEW BOLLIN HOUSE
Hollies Lane, Wilmslow SK9 2BW. Angela Ferguson & Gerry Lemon, 07828 207492, fergusonang@doctors.org.uk. *From Wilmslow take Station Rd, under Wilmslow Stn railway bridge at end of rd turn L at T-junction onto Adlington Rd. Continue over the bridge up the hill and turn L into Hollies Ln after approx ¼ m just after L turn into One Oak Ln. Down Hollies Ln to turning circle at end. Bollin House is 2nd exit on turning circle. Restricted parking. Up to 5 cars can park in the property and 3 in turning circle.* Light refreshments. **Adm £4, chd free.** Visitors welcome by appt **May to June.**
There are two components to this garden, the formal garden and the wild flower meadow. The garden contains richly planted, deep, herbaceous borders with a wide plant variety.There is also an orchard, wildflower area and vegetable garden. The meadow contains both cornfield annuals and perennial wildflower areas which are easily accessible with meandering mown paths. Ramps to gravel lined paths to most of the garden. Some narrow paths through borders. Mown pathways in the meadow.

11 BOWMERE COTTAGE
Bowmere Road, Tarporley CW6 0BS. Romy & Tom Holmes, 01829 732053, romy@holmes-email.co.uk. *10m E of Chester. From Tarporley High St (old A49) take Eaton Rd signed Eaton. After 100 metres take R fork into Bowmere Rd, Garden 100 metres on LH-side.* Home-made teas. **Adm £4, chd free.** Sun 16 June (1.30-5.30). **Visitors also welcome by appt June to July.**
Mature 1-acre country style garden around a Grade II listed house (not open). Mixed shrub and herbaceous borders, pergolas, 2 plant filled courtyard gardens and small kitchen garden. Shrub and rambling roses, clematis, hardy geraniums and a wide and colourful range of plants make this a very traditional English garden. Cobbled drive and courtyard. Gravel paths. Featured in Concept For Living Magazine.

12 BRIARFIELD
The Rake, Burton, Neston CH64 5TL. Liz Carter, 0151 336 2304, carter.burton@virgin.net. *9m NW of Chester. Turn off A540 at Willaston-Burton Xrds T-lights & follow rd for 1m to Burton village centre.* Home-made teas In St Nicholas' Church, close to gdn. **Adm £4, chd free.** Sun 14 Apr (1.30-5). **Visitors also welcome by appt Apr to Oct.**
Tucked under the S-facing side of Burton Wood the garden is home to many specialist and unusual plants, some available in plant sale. This 2-acre garden is on two sites, a couple of minutes apart along an unmade lane. Shrubs, bulbs, alpines and several water features compete for attention as you wander through four distinctly different gardens. Always changing, Liz can't resist a new plant!

13 BROOKE COTTAGE
Church Road, Handforth SK9 3LT. Barry & Melanie Davy, 01625 536511, barry.davy@ntlworld.com. *1m N of Wilmslow. Centre of Handforth, behind Health Centre. Turn off Wilmslow Rd at St Chads, follow Church Rd round to R. Garden last on L. Parking in Health Centre car park.* Home-made teas. **Adm £3, chd free.** Sat 13, Sun 14 July (12-5). **Visitors also welcome by appt May to Aug.**
Garden designer's plant-filled garden surrounded by trees and shrubs. 3 distinct areas with different planting styles. Woodland garden, circular patio, unusual water feature, many ferns incl tree ferns, astrantias, hydrangeas, foxgloves, other shade-loving plants. Container garden with banana, cannas, ligularias, dahlias, bamboo, daylilies, pond. Colourful naturalistic style borders and island beds, grasses, late flowering plants.

Views over the Cheshire plain to Alderley Edge and Mersey estuary . . .

BROOKFIELD
See Lancashire, Merseyside & Greater Manchester

14 BROOKLANDS
Smithy Lane, Mouldsworth CH3 8AR. Barbara & Brian Russell-Moore, ngsmouldsworth@aol.co.uk. *1½ m N of Tarvin. 5½ m S of Frodsham. Smithy Ln is off B5393 via A54 Tarvin/Kelsall rd or the A56 Frodsham/Helsby rd.* Home-made teas. **Adm £4, chd free. Sat 15, Sun 16 June (2-5). Visitors also welcome by appt 5 May to 7 Sept.**
Lovely country style, ¾ -acre garden with backdrop of mature trees and shrubs. The planting is based around azaleas, rhododendrons, mixed shrub and herbaceous borders. Small vegetable garden, supported by a greenhouse. Modest bonsai collection with some mature specimens. Featured in Gardeners World and Cheshire Life.

BROUGHTON & BRETTON ALLOTMENTS
See North East Wales

15 BUCKLOW FARM
Pinfold Lane, Plumley WA16 9RP. Dawn & Peter Freeman. *2m S of Knutsford. M6 J19, head to Chester A556. L at 2nd set of T-lights by Smoker PH. In 1¼ m L at concealed Xrds, 1st R. From Knutsford A5033, L at Sudlow Ln. Follow rd, becomes Pinfold Ln.* Light refreshments. **Adm £3, chd free (share to Knutsford Methodist Church). Sun 17 Feb (1-3.30).**
Country garden with shrubs, perennial borders, rambling roses, herb garden, vegetable patch, wildlife pond/water feature and alpines. Landscaped and planted over the last 25yrs with recorded changes. Free range hens. Carpet of snowdrops and spring bulbs. Leaf, stem and berries to show colour in autumn and winter. Cobbled yard from car park, but wheelchairs can be dropped off near gate.

GROUP OPENING

16 BURTON VILLAGE GARDENS
Neston, S Wirral CH64 5SJ. *9m NW of Chester. Turn off A540 at Willaston-Burton Xrds T-lights & follow rd for 1m to Burton. Maps given to visitors. Buy your ticket at first garden.* Home-made teas at 4 sites: Village Hall, Burton Manor Walled Garden, The Old Coach House, Woodgates, available throughout the day. **Combined adm £5, chd free. Sun 30 June (11-5).**

BANK COTTAGE
Bunny Beecroft

BRIARFIELD
Liz Carter
(See separate entry)

BURTON MANOR WALLED GARDEN
Friends of Burton Manor
www.burtonmanor.co.uk

LYNWOOD
Neston Road. Pauline Wright. *Burton village centre. Follow main rd round RH bend, signed Ness Gardens. Lynwood on R in dip*
Visitors also welcome by appt May to Sept.
0151 336 2311

MAPLE HOUSE
Ingrid & Neil Sturmey

NEW THE OLD COACH HOUSE
Mr & Mrs Kim & Jan Peters

This year Burton celebrates 25 years with the NGS with an average of 734 visitors a year helping to raise £81,463 so far. Remarkably 2 of our original gardeners are still with us; Bunny Beecroft at Bank Cottage and Pauline Wright at Lynwood. Six gardens are open, more than ever before. Styles range from historic to modern, formal design to natural landscapes; some have productive fruit and vegetable plots. Bank Cottage has a classic cottage garden. Briarfield's sheltered site is home to many unusual plants. Period planting surrounds the restored Edwardian glasshouse in Burton Manor's walled garden. Lynwood, a plantswoman's garden, has views across the Dee to the Clwyd hills. Maple House includes a wildlife pond that merges into the Cheshire countryside. The Old Coach House's well-designed garden surrounds converted stables. Open longer, plant sales at 3 gardens, 4 refreshments sites, convenient car parks. Dovecote Nurseries give 10% sales on the day to the ngs. Join our celebrations.

17 NEW 4 CHESHIRE VIEW
Kerridge, Macclesfield SK10 5AU. Peter & Georgie Everson, 01625 572445, pang@uwclub.net. *3m from Macclesfield. A523 from Macclesfield. A5090 turn 1st R to Kerridge. After 1½ m pass Bull's Head on R and park on rd. Garden is 5min walk over stone stile and 2 fields. Owner will meet you in village by appointment. Ignore sat nav.* Light refreshments. **Adm £3, chd free. Visitors welcome by appt July to Aug. Afternoon and evening openings. Only suitable for active and able visitors.**
A magical ⅔ acre hillside garden at 650ft with W facing views over the Cheshire plain to Alderley Edge and Mersey estuary. Magnificent sunsets. Landscaped on several levels using old railway sleepers with shrubs, late herbaceous perennials and a background of wooded slopes. Visitors must be able bodied and wear stout footwear.

18 NEW CHESTER CATHEDRAL
Chester CH1 2HU. Dean of Chester Cathedral, 01352 840758, philipbhunt@hotmail.co.uk. *Centre of Chester. Admission at SW entrance on St Werburgh St, Chester.* Tea, refreshments and lunches in Norman and C12 monk's refectory. **Adm £3, chd free. Sat 31 Aug (11-4). Visitors also welcome by appt.**
First time opening of new gardens. Cloister Garth 2004 (Cheshire Garden of Distinction), haven of peace and tranquillity surrounded by ancient architecture, sculpture fountain and exotic plants. 2012 Jubilee Garden with abundance of herbaceous and rare trees, fern border and new developments in Abbey Street and Cathedral Green. Gardens designed by botanist and maintained by volunteers. Open day followed by (horticultural) Choral Evensong at 4.15pm in iconic C14 quire, sung by Cathedral Nave Choir.

19 ◆ CHOLMONDELEY CASTLE GARDEN
Cholmondeley, nr Malpas SY14 8AH. Lavinia, Dowager Marchioness of Cholmondeley, 01829 720383, www.cholmondeleycastle.com. *4m NE of Malpas. Signed from A41 Chester-Whitchurch rd & A49 Whitchurch-Tarporley rd.* **Adm £6, chd £3. For NGS: Sun 24 Mar (11-5). For other opening times and information, please phone or see garden website.**
Over 20 acres of romantically landscaped gardens with fine views and eye-catching water features, but still manages to retain its intimacy. Beautiful mature trees form a background to spring bulbs, exotic plants in season incl magnolias, rhododendrons, azaleas and camellias and many other, particularly *Davidia Involucrata* which will be in flower in late May. Magnificent magnolias. Featured in Cheshire Life. Partial wheelchair access.

20 28 CHRISTCHURCH ROAD
Oxton CH43 5SF. **Tom & Ruth Foster.** *1m SW of Birkenhead. From M53 J3 take A552 to Birkenhead. Follow rd passing Sainsbury's cross junction at T-lights (Halfway House PH). Bear L at next T-lights into Woodchurch Rd. Take 2nd L into Heathfield Rd. Christchurch Rd is 1st L after church.* Home-made teas. **Adm £3.50, chd free. Sun 9 June (1-5).**
Grade II listed Victorian Folly with crenellated towers forms a unique feature in this 1/4 -acre plot. The garden is on different levels with gravel areas, water features, herbaceous beds and lawns connected by tunnels, pathways and steps. Planting consists of trees (many acers) shrubs and perennials.

CLOUD COTTAGE
See Derbyshire

Sun House

21 NEW 34 CONGLETON ROAD
Alderley Edge SK9 7AB. Mr Nicholas Clayton. *400 yards S of Alderley Edge on the A34. Park on rd.* **Adm £4, chd free. Sat 25, Sun 26 May (12-6).**
W-facing, 1-acre garden with views on a fine day to the Clwydian Range. Mature rhododendron, magnolias and wisteria with early clematis, hellebores and a range of unusual herbaceous plants and young specimen trees.

THE COTTAGE NURSING HOME
See North East Wales

22 DANE MOUNT
Middlewich Road, Holmes Chapel CW4 7EB. Mr & Mrs D Monks, 01477 532935. *4m E of Middlewich. Approx 1m E of M6 J18.* **Adm £3, chd free. Sat 27, Sun 28 July (1-5).**
1/4 -acre garden, colourful bedding displays, perennials and show gooseberries, interesting layout, with features incl pottery and garden sculptures. Display of artwork in summerhouse.

23 29 DEE PARK ROAD
Gayton CH60 3RG. E Lewis, 0151 342 5893, eileen.lewis29@tiscali.co.uk. *7m S of Birkenhead. From Devon Doorway/Glegg Arms r'about at Heswall, travel SE in Chester direction on A540 for approx 1/4 m. Turn R into Gayton Ln, 5th L into Dee Park Rd. Garden on L after 1/4 m.* Home-made teas. **Adm £3, chd free. Sun 16 June (1.30-5). Visitors also welcome by appt.**
The garden has been created over several yrs and has many shrubs, mature trees and borders filled with cottage garden perennials. A mirror in the secret garden reflects shade-loving plants. Gravel areas have a variety of alpines and thymes. Pergolas are framed with roses, clematis and jasmine. The gated entrance by an arbour leads to a garden room with yet more roses and clematis. A water feature in a renovated border completes this lovely garden.

24 DORFOLD HALL
Nantwich CW5 8LD. Mr & Mrs Richard Roundell. *1m W of Nantwich. On A534 between Nantwich & Acton.* **Adm £6, chd free. Sun 19 May (2-5.30).**
18-acre garden surrounding C17 house (not open) with formal approach; lawns and herbaceous borders; spectacular spring woodland garden with rhododendrons, azaleas, magnolias and bulbs.

DOVE COTTAGE
See North East Wales

25 ◆ DUNHAM MASSEY
Altrincham WA14 4SJ. National Trust, 0161 941 1025, www.nationaltrust.org.uk/dunhammassey. *3m SW of Altrincham. Off A56; M6 exit J19; M56 exit J7. Foot: close to Trans-Pennine Trail & Bridgewater Canal. Bus: Nos 38 & 5.* **Adm £8, chd £4. For NGS: Sun 17 Feb (11-4); Sun 12 May; Sun 4 Aug (11-5.30). For other opening times and information, please phone or see garden website.**
Enjoy the elegance of this vibrant Edwardian garden. Richly planted borders packed with colour and texture, sweeping lawns, majestic trees and shady woodland all await your discovery. Explore the largest Winter Garden in Britain and marvel at the contemporary new Rose Garden opening late May 2013. Water features. C17 Orangery, rare Victorian Bark House. Visitors to the garden, incl NT members, should collect ticket from Ticket Office near Clock Tower.

26 THE EAST GARDEN
Arley Hall, Northwich CW9 6NA. Charles & Jane Foster, 01565 777231, jmefoster@btinternet.com. *6m W of Knutsford. Follow signs for Arley Hall & Gardens signed from M6 J19 & J20 & M56 J9 & J10. Parking in Arley Hall's main car park. Tickets from Arley Hall's Entrance Shop.* **Adm £4.50, chd free. Sun 30 June (11-5.30). Combined with Arley Hall adm £9.00, concession £8.50, chd £2.50. Visitors also welcome by appt July to Aug.**
Two modern, very attractive gardens made since 1992 on the site of the C19 East Garden by the owners of Arley Hall Nursery and the East House, Arley Hall. Old shrub roses, early summer perennials and circular herbaceous borders enclosed by yew hedges. Many varieties of hardy herbaceous perennials - the speciality of the nursery. Refreshments provided in Arley Hall Gardens Tudor Barn restaurant.

Large pergola with sprawling roses and climbers, herbaceous beds, perfumed gazebo, roof terrace with far reaching views . . .

GROUP OPENING

27 EDITH TERRACE GARDENS
Compstall, nr Marple SK6 5JF. *6m E of Stockport. Take Bredbury junction off M60. Follow Romiley-Marple Bridge sign on B6104. Turn into Compstall at Etherow Country Park sign. Take 1st R, situated at end of Montagu St. Parking in village public car parks - short walk to Edith Terrace.* Home-made teas.
Combined adm £4.50, chd free. Sun 7 July (1-5).
Series of gardens in mixed style from cottage to formal, situated to front and rear of Victorian terrace; described by BBC 'Gardeners' World' magazine as 'a colourful and beautiful living space'. Mixed herbaceous perennials, ornamental backyards and back alleyway. In lakeside setting in the conserved mill village of Compstall, adjacent to Etherow Country Park.

10 FERN DENE
See Staffordshire, Birmingham & West Midlands

28 FIELDCREST
Thornton Common Road, Thornton Hough, Wirral CH63 0LT. Paul & Christine Davies, 0151 334 8878, chris@fieldcrest.co.uk, www.fieldcrestgarden.com. *5m S of Birkenhead, 4m SE of Heswall. Exit J 4 M53 Follow B5151 Clatterbridge/Willaston for 1m. Turn L at r'about signed Raby Mere & Wirral RFC. Garden ½ m on R.* Light refreshments. **Adm £3.50, chd free. Visitors welcome by appt, min 10.**
Country garden in 1¼ acres, planted for yr round colour and interest. Cottage garden, shrub borders, potager with fruit, herbs and vegetables. Cut flower beds. Country lane walk, wild flower area with young fruit trees. Wide variety of summer perennials. 'Chocolate' border. Featured in Garden News. 3rd prize winner in the Telegraph's 'Most Imaginatively Mown Lawn' Competition. Some gravel paths and drive.

29 FREE GREEN FARM
Free Green Lane, Lower Peover WA16 9QX. Sir Philip & Lady Haworth. *3m S of Knutsford. Free Green Lane connects A50 with B5081. From Holmes Chapel on A50 turn L after Drovers Arms. From Knutsford on B5081 turn L into Broom Lane, then L into Free Green Lane.* Home-made teas. **Adm £5, chd free. Sun 26 May; Sun 8 Sept (2-6).**
2-acre garden with pleached limes, herbaceous borders, ponds, parterre; garden of the senses and British woodland. Topiary. Wheelchair access not easy in the wood.

30 GRAFTON LODGE
Stretton, Tilston, Malpas SY14 7JE. Simon Carter & Derren Gilhooley, 01829 250670, simoncar@aol.com. *For Sat Nav please use* ***SY14 7JA*** NOT 7JE. 12m S of Chester. *A41 S from Chester turning towards Wrexham onto A534 at Broxton r'about. Past Carden Park Hotel & turn L at Cock-a-Barton PH towards Stretton & Tilston. Through Stretton, garden on R before reaching Tilston.* **Adm £4, chd free. Sat 15, Sun 16, Sat 22, Sun 23 June (1-3). Visitors also welcome by appt June.**
Vibrantly colourful garden of 2 acres crammed with herbaceous plants, shrubs and roses. There are lawns, natural and formal ponds, specimen trees, mixed hedges and garden rooms incl herb garden, standard rose circle, large pergola with sprawling roses and climbers, herbaceous beds, perfumed gazebo, roof terrace with far reaching views.

31 GREENWAYS
82 Knutsford Road, Alderley Edge SK9 7SF. Jenny & Roger Lloyd, 01625 583488, jenny.plants@btinternet.com. *1m W of Alderley Edge. 1m from Alderley Edge & Wilmslow on B5085 to Knutsford. Close to Chorley Village Hall. Parking at Village Hall. Disabled parking at house.* Home-made teas. **Adm £4, chd free. Sat 13, Sun 14 July (2-6). Visitors also welcome by appt May to Aug, max group size - 50.**
Even more plants now in this obsessive collectors garden. Over 400 named varieties and much more. Plant maps available. A personal collection of unusual and familiar perennials and shrubs set in 1½ acres, displaying a diversity of planting styles in a range of growing conditions. Sculpture exhibition and new children's quiz. Unfenced pools. Children's quiz.

32 ◆ HARE HILL GARDENS
Over Alderley SK10 4QB. National Trust, www.nationaltrust.org.uk. *2m E of Alderley Edge. Between Alderley Edge & Prestbury. Turn off N at B5087 at Greyhound Rd.* **Adm £4, chd £2. For NGS: Sun 16 June (10-5). For other opening times and information, please see garden website.**
Attractive spring garden featuring a fine display of rhododendrons and azaleas; good collection of hollies and other specimen trees and shrubs. 10-acre garden incl a walled garden which hosts many wall shrubs incl clematis and vines; borders are planted with agapanthus and geraniums. Partially suitable for wheelchairs.

33 HATTON HOUSE GARDENS
Hatton Heath, Chester CH3 9AP. Judy Halewood. *4m SE of Chester. From Chester on A41 2km past The Black Dog PH. From Whitchurch on A41 7km past the Broxton r'about.* Light refreshments. **Adm £5, chd free. Sat 27 Apr; Sat 15 June (1.30-5).**
Approx 8 acres of beautifully landscaped gardens both formal and natural. Pathways leading through extensive herbaceous borders give way to lawns, azalea rock gardens, waterfalls and wild flowers. The 2 acre lake is rich in wildlife and flanked by woodland, wild flowers, bulbs, bridges and follies. Some areas are still under development. All of the gardens are wheelchair friendly apart from the Sunken Garden.

34 HAUGHTON HALL
Hall Lane, Haughton, Bunbury, Tarporley CW6 9RH. Mr & Mrs Phillip Posnett. *6m SE of Tarporley. Via A49 to Whitchurch & 5m W of Nantwich off A534 Nantwich to Wrexham rd.* Home-made teas. **Adm £5.50, chd free. Sun 5 May (2-5).**
Large garden with interesting collection of trees and recently planted borders leading down to lake. Fantastic display of azaleas and rhododendrons. Gravel paths, some steep slopes.

HAWARDEN CASTLE
See North East Wales

Lake is rich in wildlife and flanked by woodland, wildflowers, bulbs, bridges and follies . . .

HIGH ROOST
See Derbyshire

35 NEW 18 HIGHFIELD ROAD
Bollington, Macclesfield SK10 5LR. Mrs Melita Turner, 01625 260973, david.turner437@ntlworld.com. *3m N of Macclesfield. A523 to Stockport. Turn R at B5090 r'about signed Bollington. Continue along main rd through Bollington. Pass under viaduct, take next R (by Library) up Hurst Ln. Immed after canal bridge turn R into Highfield Rd. Property on L. Park on wider section of rd just past property.* Home-made teas. **Adm £3, chd free. Sat 6, Sun 7 July (11-5). Visitors also welcome by appt July.**
This small terraced garden packed with plants was designed by Melita and has evolved over the past 6 years. This plantswoman is a plantaholic and RHS Certificate holder. An attempt has been made to combine formality through structural planting with a more casual look influenced by the style of Christopher LLoyd.

36 73 HILL TOP AVENUE
Cheadle Hulme SK8 7HZ. Mr & Mrs Martin Land, 0161 486 0055. *4m S of Stockport. Turn off A34 (new bypass) at r'about signed Cheadle Hulme (B5094). Take 2nd turn L into Gillbent Rd, signed Cheadle Hulme Sports Centre. Go to end, small r'about, turn R into Church Rd. 2nd rd on L is Hill Top Ave. From Stockport or Bramhall turn R or L into Church Rd by The Church Inn. Hill Top Ave is 1st rd on R.* **Adm £3.50, chd free (share to Arthritis Research UK). Evening Opening wine, Thur 23 May (5.30-8); Sun 30 June; Sun 4 Aug (2-6).**
1/6 -acre plantswoman's garden. Well stocked with a wide range of sun-loving herbaceous plants, shrub and climbing roses, many clematis varieties, pond and damp area, shade-loving woodland plants and small unusual trees, in an originally designed, long narrow garden.

37 HILLSIDE
Mill Lane, Mobberley WA16 7HY. Paul Hales & Mark Rubery. *2m E of Knutsford. Entrance off Mill Lane, next to Roebuck Inn. Roebuck is sign posted off Mobberley Rd.* Home-made teas. **Adm £5, chd free. Sat 18, Sun 19 May (11-5).**
A magnificent 6-acre garden, home to a huge collection of rare birds incl 90 flamingos. The various ponds are adorned with delightful palm trees, bonsais, agaves and citrus trees. On the opposite side is a woodland setting that features a large, delightful waterfall surrounded by many mature plants and trees.

38 HILLSIDE COTTAGE
Shrigley Road, Pott Shrigley SK10 5SG. Anne & Phil Geoghegan, 01625 572214, annegeoghegan@btinternet.com. *6m N of Macclesfield. On A523. At Legh Arms T-lights turn into Brookledge Ln signed Pott Shrigley. After 1½ m signed Shrigley Hall turn L signed Higher Poynton. After 1m turn R at Methodist Chapel.* Home-made teas. **Adm £6, chd free. Visitors welcome by appt 24 June to 13 Sept, groups 10+. Day or evening. Adm incl refreshments, wine optional for evening openings.**
Set on a hillside, ¼ -acre garden with panoramic vistas over the treetops of the Cheshire Plain and beyond. Filled with colour, texture and the scent of

roses. Landscaped on several levels with a wide variety of shrubs, small trees and 'cottage garden' perennials. Water features and walled patio garden with container planting. Wheelchair access to main areas.

39 HUNTERS CROFT

Wilmslow Road, Mottram St Andrew SK10 4QH. Len & Mary Beth Morris. *3m SE of Wilmslow. Located on A538, Wilmslow Rd, between Wilmslow & Prestbury. 1/2 m from Osteria PH as you drive towards Prestbury. Parking across from house in field.* Home-made teas. **Adm £4, chd free.** Sun 4 Aug (10-4).

1 acre of undulating lawns and ever changing borders from traditional herbaceous to architectural. Rhododendrons and azaleas surrounding a summerhouse. Rockery with mature acers leading to a pond with bog garden. Small woodland, beech and holly hedges with pleached lime trees. Topiary. Greenhouse and vegetable beds. Herb garden. Lovely views.

40 INGLEWOOD

4 Birchmere, Heswall CH60 6TN. Colin & Sandra Fairclough, 0151 3424645, sandra.fairclough@tiscali.co.uk, www.inglewood-birchmere.blogspot.co.uk. *6m S of Birkenhead. From A540 Devon Doorway/Clegg Arms r'about go through Heswall. 1/4 m after Tesco, R into Quarry Rd East, 2nd L into Tower Rd North & L into Birchmere.* Home-made teas. **Adm £4, chd free.** Sat 13, Sun 14 July (2-5). **Visitors also welcome by appt Apr to Aug, min 10, max 25.**

Beautiful 1/2 acre garden with stream, large koi pond, 'beach' with grasses, wildlife pond and bog area. Brimming with shrubs, bulbs, acers, conifers, rhododendrons, azaleas, woodland plants and hostas. Interesting features include hand cart, antique mangle, wood carvings, bug hotel and Indian dog gates leading to secret herbaceous garden. Lots of seating to admire the views.

41 LASKEY FARM

Laskey Lane, Thelwall, Warrington WA4 2TF. Howard & Wendy Platt, 07740 804825, wendy_platt1@excite.com, www.laskeyfarm.com. *3m From M6/M56. From M6/M56 interchange follow signs to Lymm - Cherry Lane, B5158. Turn R on to Elm Tree Rd, B5158. Turn L onto Church Rd A56. Turn R onto B5157. Take 1st R onto Laskey Ln.* Home-made teas. **Adm £4, chd free.** Sat 17, Sun 18 Aug (11-5). **Visitors also welcome by appt 17 June to 9 Aug.**

1-acre garden packed with late summer colour which includes informal borders, rose bed, vegetable garden and parterre. There are a number of pools for wildlife, fish and an unusual terrapin pond.

42 LEAWOOD

off Longhurst Lane, Marple Bridge SK6 5AE. John & Mary Hartley, 0161 427 1882, mary.hartleycat@talktalk.net. *4m E of Stockport. A626 to Marple - Marple Bridge, through village, signed Mellor. 100yds on L from car park in Marple Bridge, down the side of 21 Longhurst Ln.* Light refreshments. **Adm £3, chd free.** Sat 18, Sun 19 May (11-4).

3/4 -acre hidden woodland garden facing E-W surrounded by trout stream. Large lawns and flower beds of mixed planting giving rise to panoramic view of hillside with rhododendrons, azaleas and camellias. Terraced paths pass small spring fed ponds and wildlife areas of bluebells and unusual shade loving plants. Bird box cameras - Owl, Blue Tit, Gt Tit. Ducks, badgers and fox (special wildlife interest).

LEESWOOD GREEN FARM
See North East Wales

43 ◆ LITTLE MORETON HALL

Congleton CW12 4SD. National Trust, 01270 272018, www.nationaltrust.org.uk/littlemortonhall. *4m S of Congleton. On A34.* **For opening times and information, please phone or see garden website.**

1 1/2 -acre garden surrounded by a moat, next to finest example of timber-framed architecture in England. Herb and historic vegetable garden, orchard and borders. Knot garden. Adm incl entry to the Hall with optional free guided tours. Picnic lawn at front of hall. Wheelchairs available, ground floor of hall and garden accessible. Please be aware that courtyard is cobbled.

44 LONG ACRE

Wyche Lane, Bunbury CW6 9PS. Margaret & Michael Bourne, 01829 260944, mjbourne249@tiscali.co.uk. *3 1/2 m SE of Tarporley. On A49. Turn 2nd L after Wild Boar Hotel to Bunbury. L at 1st rd junction then 1st R by Nags Head PH 400yds on L. From A51 turn to Bunbury until Nags Head. Turn into Wyche Ln before PH car park. 400yds to garden. Disabled parking in lane adj to garden.* Home-made teas. **Adm £4, chd free (share to Guide Dogs for the Blind & St Boniface Church Flower Fund).** Sun 21 Apr; Sun 16 June (2-5). **Visitors also welcome by appt Apr to June (14 - 28 Apr and 9 - 23 June preferred), groups 10+.**

Plantswoman's garden of approx 1 acre with unusual plants and trees. Roses, pool gardens, exotic conservatory, herbaceous, specialise in proteas, S African bulbs, clivia, streptocarpus and disa. Spring garden with camellias, magnolias, bulbs.

Indian dog gates leading to secret herbaceous garden . . . lots of seating to admire the views . . .

45 ◆ LYME PARK

Lyme Park, Disley SK12 2NR. National Trust, 01663 762023, www.nationaltrust.org.uk/lyme-park/. *6m SE of Stockport. Just W of Disley on A6. Once you see the brown signs, follow them, not Satnav.* **Adm £7, chd £3.50.** For NGS: Sat 7 Sept (11-5). **For other opening times and information, please phone or see garden website.**

Neglected in the 1940's, and now gloriously restored this 17-acre garden is a relaxed space to enjoy picnics and stroll amongst high Victorian style bedding, the Dutch garden, luxurious Gertrude Jekyll style herbaceous borders, and Edwardian rose garden, An orangery, rare trees, reflection lake, dramatic ravine garden, and mixed borders contrast with sweeping moorland beyond. House and park are also open. Please ask at admissions for wheelchair access. The garden is on many levels, with steps, but an accessible route is available.

46 MANLEY KNOLL
Manley Road, Manley WA6 9DX. Mr & Mrs James Timpson, 01928 752999, james@timpson.com, www.manleyknoll.com. *3m N of Tarvin. On B5393, via Ashton & Mouldsworth. 3m S of Frodsham, via Alvanley.* Home-made teas. **Adm £3.50, chd free. Sun 19 May; Sun 16 June (12-5). Visitors also welcome by appt.**
Arts and Crafts garden created early 1900s. Covering 6 acres, divided into different rooms encompassing parterres, clipped yew hedging and ornamental ponds. Banks of rhododendron and azaleas frame a far-reaching view of the Cheshire Plain. Also a magical quarry/folly garden with waterfall.

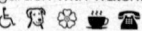

MARLBOROUGH ALLOTMENTS
See Lancashire, Merseyside & Greater Manchester

47 NEW MEDLICOTT
Haddon Lane, Ness, Neston CH64 8TA. Maureen & Jack Aland, 0151 3363386. *Follow sign to Ness Gardens from A540. Opposite Ness Gardens entrance, turn into Haddon Lane & follow signs for parking.* Home-made teas Claire House. **Adm £4, chd free. Sat 8, Sun 9 June (2-6). Visitors also welcome by appt Jan to Dec. Not open July & August.**
Atmospheric garden with relaxed planting and maintenance style. Wide range of mature trees and shrubs planted in a series of garden rooms. Mixed herbaceous and shrub borders, soft fruit, vegetables and natural areas. A garden at ease with nature. Plants of interest throughout the year. Most of garden accessible.

48 MILLPOOL
Smithy Lane, Bosley SK11 0NZ. Joe & Barbara Fray, 01260 226581. *5m S of Macclesfield. Just off A523 at Bosley. Turn L 1m S of A54 T-lights. From Leek, turn R, 2½ m N of The Royal Oak PH at Rushton. Please follow direction to parking areas. No parking at garden.* **Adm £3.50, chd free. Sat 6, Sun 7 July (1-5). Visitors also welcome by appt May to Oct, 40 people max.**
Garden designed to extend the seasons with colour, texture and scent. Lush herbaceous borders and areas of deep shade. Small stream, pond and bog garden. Gravel plantings, containers and a fine collection of bonsai trees. An ever increasing collection of modern ceramics and a most productive vegetable garden in tubs and baskets. Children's interest trail and craft activities and large plant sale.

Productive vegetable garden in tubs and baskets . . . children's interest trail and craft activities and large plant sale . . .

49 ◆ MOUNT PLEASANT
Yeld Lane, Kelsall CW6 0TB. Dave Darlington & Louise Worthington, 01829 751592, www.mountpleasantgardens.co.uk. *8m E of Chester. Off A54 at T-lights into Kelsall. Turn into Yeld Ln opp Farmers Arms PH, 200yds on L. Do not follow Sat Nav directions.* **Adm £5, chd £1. For NGS: Sun 5, Mon 6 May; Sat 31 Aug; Sun 1 Sept (12-5). For other opening times and information, please phone or see garden website.**
10 acres of landscaped garden and woodland started in 1994 with impressive views over the Cheshire countryside. Steeply terraced in places. Specimen trees, rhododendrons, azaleas, conifers, mixed and herbaceous borders; 4 ponds, formal and wildlife. Vegetable garden, stumpery with tree ferns, sculptures, wild flower meadow and Japanese garden. Bog garden, tropical garden. September Sculpture Exhibition. Please ring prior to visit for wheelchair access.

50 ◆ NESS BOTANIC GARDENS
Ness, Neston CH64 4AY. The University of Liverpool, 0151 353 0123, www.nessgardens.org.uk. *10 m NW of Chester. Off A540. M53 J4, follow signs M56 & A5117 (signed N Wales). Turn onto A540 follow signs for Hoylake. Ness Gardens is signposted locally.* **Adm £6.50, chd £3. For NGS: Sat 2 Mar (10-4.30). For other opening times and information, please phone or see garden website.**
Gardens cover some 64 acres, having a distinctly maritime feel and housing The National Collection of Mountain Ash (Sorbus). Among some of the significant specimens that still flourish in the gardens are Pieris Forrestii which was collected for Bulley by George Forrest in Yunnan. Winter garden features, including many varieties of snowdrops. Mobility scooters and wheelchairs available free - advance booking recommended.

51 ◆ NORTON PRIORY MUSEUM & GARDENS
Tudor Road, Manor Park, Runcorn WA7 1SX. Norton Priory Museum Trust, 01928 569895, www.nortonpriory.org. *2m SE of Runcorn. From M56 J11 turn for Warrington & follow signs. From Warrington take A56 for Runcorn & follow signs. From Liverpool, cross Widnes/Runcorn Bridge going S & follow signs.* **Adm £3.50, chd £3.50. Special NGS ticket for Walled Garden Only. For NGS: Sat 15 June (12-4). For other opening times and information, please phone or see garden website.**
40 acres of gardens and grounds, with summerhouses, stream glade and medieval herb garden. 2½ -acre Georgian Walled Garden, with rosewalk, colour borders, soft fruit and cottage garden. Home to the National Collection of Tree Quince (Cydonia Oblonga). Also including historic Pear orchard and wild flower meadow.

52 THE OLD COTTAGE
44 High Street, Frodsham WA6 7HE. John & Lesley Corfield, 01928 735581, corfield@rock44.plus.com. *DO NOT FOLLOW SAT NAV - no parking at gdn. On A56 close to Frodsham town centre. Follow signs from Frodsham*

"Lemon drizzle cake, Victoria sponge ... yummy!"

centre to railway car park, from where the garden will be signed (short walk). Alternatively, park on st in town centre and follow signs N away from town centre, up elevated access rd to the black & white cottage opp the library. Either way, its approx 5mins walk. Home-made teas. **Adm £4, chd free. Sat 15, Sun 16 June (1-6). Visitors also welcome by appt 17 June to 2 Aug.**

At the rear of the Grade II listed C16 cottage (not open) are ²/₃ acre, organic and wildlife friendly garden featuring many aspects that support various forms of wildlife. Steps lead up to a large vegetable and herb garden, with further mixed planting in herbaceous borders. Wildlife pond and bog garden. Further areas of fruit trees and shady woodland borders. Extensive views over Mersey estuary. Partial wheelchair access - please ring for details.

53 THE OLD PARSONAGE

Arley Green, via Arley Hall & Gardens CW9 6LZ. The Viscount & Viscountess Ashbrook, 01565 777277, www.arleyhallandgardens.com. *5m NNE of Northwich. 3m Great Budworth. M6 J19 & 20 & M56 J10. Follow signs to Arley Hall & Gardens. From Arley Hall notices to Old Parsonage which lies across park at Arley Green.* Home-made teas. **Adm £4.50, chd free (share to Save The Children Fund). Sat 1, Sun 2 June (2-3.30). Visitors also welcome by appt June to July, groups 10+.**

2-acre garden in attractive and secretive rural setting in secluded part of Arley Estate, with ancient yew hedges, herbaceous and mixed borders, shrub roses, climbers, leading to woodland garden and unfenced pond with gunnera and water plants. Rhododendrons, azaleas, meconopsis, cardiocrinum, some interesting and unusual trees. Sculpture exhibition at adjoining Arley Hall and Gardens. Wheelchair access over mown grass.

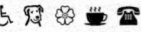

54 ORCHARD VILLA

72 Audley Road, Alsager ST7 2QN. Mr & Mrs J Trinder, 01270 874833, johntrinder@btinternet.com. *6m S of Congleton. 3m W of Kidsgrove. At T-lights in Alsager town centre turn L towards Audley, house is 300yds on R beyond level Xing. Or M6 J16 to North Stoke on A500, 1st L to Alsager, 2m, just beyond Manor House Hotel on L.* Home-made teas. **Adm £4, chd free. Sun 16 June (1.30-5.30). Visitors also welcome by appt Apr to Sept.**

The long narrow garden has a meandering path which leads through a succession of planted rooms reflecting the seasons from spring to autumn and hosting mainly herbaceous plants incl irises, some grasses and supported by alpines, bulbs, ferns and annuals. Always something to interest the plant enthusiast.

55 39 OSBORNE STREET

Bredbury, Stockport SK6 2DA. Geoff & Heather Hoyle, geoff.hoyle@btinternet.com. *1½ m E of Stockport. Osborne St is off Stockport Rd West (B6104), approx 1m from M60. Leave M60 at J27 (from S & W) or J25 (from N & E). Follow signs for Lower Bredbury/Bredbury Hall. Osborne St is adjacent to pelican Xing on B6104. 39 is across from local shops.* Light refreshments. **Adm £3, chd free. Sat 7, Sun 8 Sept (1-5). Visitors also welcome by appt Sept.**

This dahliaholic's garden contains over 300 dahlias in 150+ varieties, mostly of exhibition standard. Shapely lawns are surrounded by deep flower beds that are crammed with dahlias of all shapes, sizes and colours, and complemented by climbers, soft perennials and bedding plants. An absolute riot of early autumn colour. The garden comprises two separate areas, both crammed with very colourful flowers. The dahlias range in height from 18 inches to 8 feet tall, and are in a wide variety of shapes and colours. They are interspersed with salvias, fuchsias, argyranthemums, and bedding plants. Garden on youtube search for A Dahliaholic's Retreat. Featured in Daily Mail and on Gardener's World.

56 PARM PLACE

High Street, Great Budworth CW9 6HF. Peter & Jane Fairclough, 01606 891131, janefair@btinternet.com. *3m N of Northwich. Great Budworth on E side of A559 between Northwich & Warrington, 4m from J10 M56, also 4m from J19 M6. Parm Place is W of village on S side of High Street.* Home-made teas. **Adm £4, chd free (share to Great Ormonde Street Hospital). Sun 7 Apr; Sun 30 June (1-5). Visitors also welcome by appt Apr to July.**

Well-stocked ½ -acre plantswoman's garden with stunning views towards S Cheshire. Curving lawns, shrubs,

Dunham Massey

© Val Corbett

colour co-ordinated herbaceous borders, roses, water features, rockery, gravel bed with grasses. Fruit and vegetable plots. In spring large collection of bulbs and flowers, camellias, hellebores and blossom. Parterre new this year.

57 ◆ PEOVER HALL GARDENS

Over Peover, Knutsford WA16 9HW. Randle Brooks Esq, 01565 724220, www.peoverhall.co.uk. *4m S of Knutsford. Turn off A50 at Whipping Stocks Inn. Drive down Stocks Ln for approx 1¼ m. At sharp L-hand bend, turn R onto Grotto Ln following small white signs to Peover Hall & Church. Turn R after 1½ m onto Blackden Ln following signs. At the next LH bend Peover Hall Entrance is clearly signed on your R.* **Adm £4, chd free.** **For NGS: Sat 1, Sun 2 June (2-5). For other opening times and information, please phone or see garden website.**

Set in 15 acres includes formal gardens designed between 1890-1900 include a series of 'garden rooms' filled with clipped box and topiary, lily ponds, herb and walled gardens, Romanesque loggia, C19 dell, rhododendrons, pleached limes, topiary. Grade II Carolean Stables and C18 park.

58 17 POPLAR GROVE

Sale M33 3AX. Mr Gordon Cooke, 0161 969 9816, gordoncooke.ceramics@gmail.com. *3m N of Altrincham. From the A6144 at Brooklands Stn turn into Hope Rd. Poplar Grove 3rd on R.* Home-made teas. **Adm £3.50, chd free.** **Sat 18, Sun 19 May (2-5). Visitors also welcome by appt.**

This S-facing suburban garden is on many levels. Its strongly diagonal design features a pebble mosaic 'cave', topiary, sculpture garden, living roof and exotic planting. A mix of formality and dense planting in the contemporary 'English' style. Exhibition of Garden Ceramics.

59 POULTON HALL

Poulton Lancelyn, Bebington CH63 9LN. The Lancelyn Green Family, 0151 3342057, jlgpoulton@talktalk.net, www.poultonhall.co.uk. *2m S of Bebington. From M53, J4 towards Bebington; at T-lights R along Poulton Rd; house 1m on R.* Cream teas. **Adm £4, chd free.** **Sat 13, Sun 14 Apr; Sun 16 June (2-5.30). Visitors also welcome by appt 20 Apr to 13 July, groups min 10, max 30.**

3 acres; lawns fronting house, wild flower meadow. A surprising approach to the walled garden, with reminders of Roger Lancelyn Green's retellings, Excalibur, Robin Hood and Jabberwocky. Scented sundial garden for the visually impaired. Memorial sculpture for Richard Lancelyn Green by Sue Sharples. Rose, nursery rhyme, witch. Herb and Oriental gardens. Music at 4pm. New sculpture. Snowdrops daily 2 Feb to 10 March (except Mons) 12-4. Level gravel paths.

Wooden topiary, lots of different areas to explore and enjoy . . .

60 ◆ QUARRY BANK HOUSE GARDEN

Quarry Bank Road, Styal SK9 4LA. National Trust, 0791 755 0425, www.nationaltrust.org.uk. *2m N of Wilmslow. Follow NT signs.* **Adm £5, chd £2.50.** **For NGS: Sat 4, Sun 5 May (10.30-4). For other opening times and information, please phone or see garden website.**

A 'picturesque' valley garden created in the 1790s by cotton mill owner Samuel Greg. The garden is mainly a spring garden, with many fine azaleas and rhododendrons. Some rhododendrons are unique to the garden having been commissioned and introduced by the Greg family during C19. Parts of lower garden are accessible and a map is provided to show the route. Mobility scooter available.

61 ◆ THE QUINTA ARBORETUM

Swettenham CW12 2LD. Tatton Garden Society, 01477 537698, www.tattongardensociety.co.uk. *Turn off A54 N 2m W of Congleton or turn E off A535 at Twemlow Green, NE of Holmes Chapel. Follow signs to Swettenham. Park at Swettenham Arms PH. Entrance at side of PH through picnic area.* **Adm £5, chd free.** **For NGS: Sun 6 Oct (12-4). For other opening times and information, please phone or see garden website.**

The 28-acre arboretum has been established since 1960s and contains around 10,000 trees and shrubs of over 2,000 species, some very rare. Incl National Collections of Pinus and Fraxinus, large collection of oak, a collection of hebes and autumn flowering shrubs. A lake and way-marked walks. A guided tour at 2pm is included. Care required but wheelchairs can access much of the arboretum on the mown paths.

NCH

62 RIDGE HILL

Ridgehill, Sutton, Macclesfield SK11 0LU. Mr & Mrs Martin McMillan, 01260 252353, pat@normanshall.co.uk. *2m SE of Macclesfield. From Macclesfield take A523 to Leek. After Silk Rd look for T-lights signed Langley, Wincle & Sutton. Turn L into Byron's Ln, under canal bridge, 1st L to Langley at junction Church House PH. Ridge Hill Rd is opp turn up Ridge Hill Rd, garden on R.* Home-made teas, wine by donation. **Adm £5, chd free.** **Sun 7 July (10-4.30). Visitors also welcome by appt 5 May to 25 Aug.**

An ever changing garden set in the Cheshire countryside, over 4 acres of shrubs, mixed herbaceous, topiary, water features, old shrub roses, vegetable area, wooden topiary, lots of different areas to explore and enjoy. Raffle. Garden accessories.

63 ◆ RODE HALL

Church Lane, Scholar Green ST7 3QP. Sir Richard & Lady Baker Wilbraham, 01270 873237, www.rodehall.co.uk. *5m SW of Congleton. Between Scholar Green (A34) & Rode Heath (A50).* **Adm £4, chd £1, concessions £3. For opening times and information, please phone or see garden website.**

Nesfield's terrace and rose garden with view over Humphry Repton's landscape is a feature of Rode gardens, as is the woodland garden with terraced rock garden and grotto. Other attractions incl the walk to the lake, restored ice house, working walled kitchen garden and Italian garden. Fine display of snowdrops in February. Daily for snowdrops 2 Feb - 10 March (except Mons) 12-4.

64 ROSEWOOD
Old Hall Lane, Puddington, Neston CH64 5SP. Mr & Mrs C E J Brabin, 0151 353 1193, angela.brabin@btinternet.com. *6m N of Chester. Turn L (W) off Chester to Hoylake A540 to Puddington. Park by village green. Walk to Old Hall Ln, 30yds away then through archway on L to garden. Owner will meet you at green by appt.* Light refreshments. **Adm £3, chd free. Visitors welcome by appt.**
All yr garden; thousands of snowdrops in Feb, camellias in autumn, winter and spring. Rhododendrons in April/May and unusual flowering trees from March to June. Autumn cyclamen in quantity from Aug to Nov. Perhaps the greatest delight to owners is a large Cornus capitata, flowering in June. Bees kept in the garden. Honey sometimes available.

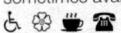

65 THE ROWANS
Oldcastle Lane, Threapwood, nr Malpas SY14 7AY. Paul Philpotts & Alan Bourne, 01948 770522, alanandpaul@btinternet.com. *3m SW of Malpas. Leave Malpas by B5069 for Wrexham, pass church on R, continue for 3m, take 1st L after Threapwood PO into Chapel Ln. L into Oldcastle Ln, garden 1st bungalow on R.* **Adm £4, chd free. Sat 13, Sun 14 July (2-5.30). Visitors also welcome by appt June to Aug, refreshments & coaches by arrangement.**
This 1-acre award winning garden, has an Italianate theme. Divided into numerous formal and natural areas, in which to sit and enjoy the views and feature statuary. Many mature and unusual trees, several ponds, herbaceous borders, vegetable plots, greenhouse, extensive hosta collection, tranquil secret garden. Something of interest for every visitor.

66 SAIGHTON GRANGE
Saighton CH3 6EN. The Governors of Abbey Gate College, 01244 564184, alan.kift@abbeygatecollege.co.uk, www.abbeygatecollege.co.uk. *4m SE of Chester. Take A41 towards Whitchurch. At far end of Waverton turn R to Saighton. Grange is at the end of village.* Home-made teas. **Adm £4, chd free. Sun 14 Apr (1-4). Visitors also welcome by appt Apr to Aug.**
6½ acres of garden designed by Inigo Triggs for the 2nd Duke of Westminster in 1901. Redesigned for the 4th Duchess during the 1960's by Russell, of Castle Howard fame. Now undergoing third development. Present emphasis on a spring garden with magnolias, daffodils and bluebell woodland walk, but development continues to introduce later flowering plants to extend the season. 'First Place' for Best Commercial or Public Premises in Cheshire West and Chester Council's 'Something Blooming Special'.

Tranquil secret garden . . . something of interest for every visitor . . .

67 SANDSEND
126 Hibbert Lane, Marple SK6 7NU. David & Audrey Bomford, 0161 427 5530. *5m SE of Stockport. Leave M60 at J27. A626 to Marple R at Texaco garage, R at mini r'about into Hibbert Ln ½ m on R. Or A6 from Stockport via Hazel Grove to High Ln, L at Horseshoe PH into Windlehurst Rd 1¾ m towards Marple. Hibbert Ln starts at canal bridge on L 200yds past bridge.* Home-made teas. **Adm £3.50, chd free. Sat 25, Sun 26 May (1-5). Visitors also welcome by appt 18 to 26 May. Teas only provided. No plant sales.**
Set back from the road, trees and shrubs give all-yr-round colour to the front garden. Long back garden with raised beds, lawns and winding paths is a journey through varied planting with seats to view all aspects. Small pond, acers, hostas, azaleas, rockeries and herbaceous. Sun and shade and abundant birdsong in surrounding mature trees. African craft sale in aid of Christian Relief Uganda.

68 SANDYMERE
Middlewich Road, Cotebrook CW6 9EH. John & Alex Timpson. *5m N of Tarporley. On A54 about 300yds W of T-lights at Xrds of A49/A54.* Light refreshments. **Adm £5, chd free. Sun 14 July (2-5).**
16 landscaped acres of beautiful Cheshire countryside with terraces, walled garden and amazing hosta garden. Long views, native wildlife and tranquillity of 3 lakes. Elegant planting schemes, shady seats and sun-splashed borders, mature pine woods and rolling lawns accented by graceful wooden structures. Different every year. Kitchen garden with organically grown vegetables, fruit cage and small orchard, also extensive range of penstemon plants. Limited access for wheelchairs.

69 21 SCAFELL CLOSE
High Lane, Stockport SK6 8JA. Lesley & Dean Stafford, 01663 763015, deanstafford@live.co.uk. *On A6 SE of Stockport. On A6 towards Buxton from Stockport 2m past Rising Sun PH. At High Ln turn into Russell Ave opp Dog & Partridge PH, 2nd L to Kirkfell Drive & immed R onto Scafell Close, 21 on R. Parking on L or to the end in turning circle.* Cream teas. **Adm £3, chd free. Sat 3, Sun 4 Aug (1-5). Visitors also welcome by appt 22 July to 9 Aug.**
⅓ acre landscaped suburban garden. Colour themed annuals border the lawn featuring the Kinder Ram statue in a heather garden, passing into vegetables, soft fruits and fruit trees. Returning perennial pathway leads to the fishpond and secret terraced garden with modern water feature and patio planting. Finally visit the blue front garden. Featured in Amateur Gardening magazine. Partial wheelchair access.

70 THE SCHOOL HOUSE
School Lane, Dunham Massey WA14 4SE. Andrew Bushell & Peter White. *1½ m SW of Altrincham. From M56 J7 follow signs for Dunham Massey Hall (NT). Turn into Woodhouse Ln becoming School Ln 100yds after Axe Cleaver PH. Car park available from 1pm.* Home-made teas. **Adm £4, chd free. Sun 16 June (1-5).**
Cottage garden divided into rooms. In picturesque setting attached to village hall and beside the Bridgewater canal. Incl herbaceous borders, rose and bog garden. History of Dunham Massey display in village hall. Walking distance to Dunham Hall (NT). Some gravel paths.

Briarfield

71 NEW SOMERFORD
19 Leycester Road, Knutsford WA16 8QR. Emma Dearman & Joe Morris, 01565 621095, emmadearman1@gmail.com. *1m from centre of Knutsford. From Knutsford town centre, take Toft Rd (A50) direction Holmes Chapel (S). After approx 1m, turn sharp L into Leycester Rd, immed after Esso garage. Cross Legh Rd. Somerford is found on your L opp Leycester Close. Park on Leycester Rd or Legh Rd with consideration to residents.* Home-made teas. **Adm £4, chd free. Evening Opening £5, chd free, wine, Fri 5 July (6-8.30), Sun 14, Sun 28 July (12-5). Visitors also welcome by appt 29 May to 23 Aug. For visits by appointment, cream teas are extra to adm.**
Majestic trees surround this 1½ acre garden which has been completely re-designed and planted. Hard landscaping and sculptures complement lush herbaceous and perennial borders. Croquet and pond lawns are separated by a vast oak pergola. Cube-headed hornbeams lead into the snail-trail walk and informal lawn and fernery. Also: hosta beds, stable courtyard with box parterres and vegetable areas. For evening opening, a glass of wine is included in the Adult Adm cost of £5. Most of the garden is accessible by wheelchair. Ring for further information.

72 68 SOUTH OAK LANE
Wilmslow SK9 6AT. Caroline & David Melliar-Smith, 01625 528147, caroline.ms@btinternet.com. *¾ m SW of Wilmslow. From M56 (J6) take A528 towards Wilmslow, R into Buckingham Rd. From centre of Wilmslow turn R onto B5086 (Knutsford), 1st R into Gravel Ln, 4th R into South Oak Ln. Park by recreation ground.* **Adm £3, chd free. Sat 13, Sun 14 July (11-4.30). Visitors also welcome by appt July to Aug.**
With yr-round colour, scent and interest, this attractive, hedged cottage garden has evolved over the years into 5 natural 'rooms'. These Hardy Plant Society members passion for plants, reflected in shrubs, trees, flower borders and pond, create havens for wildlife. Enjoy tranquillity and peace in this plant-packed garden. Featured in Garden News & Wilmslow Advertiser.

SOUTHLANDS
See Lancashire, Merseyside & Greater Manchester

73 SPRINGBANK
670 London Road, Davenham, Northwich CW9 8LG. Doug & Ann Welch, 01606 43416, doug.and.ann@sky.com. *2½ m S of Northwich. From Peckmill r'about at S end of Davenham Village on A533 Davenham By-pass take rd signed Davenham & Moulton. Garden on L approx 150yds.* Home-made teas. **Adm £3.50, chd free. Sat 10, Sun 11 Aug (2-5). Visitors also welcome by appt June to Aug.**
Lovely interesting garden in ½ acre sheltered hollow with backdrop of mature trees and shrubs. Large colourful herbaceous borders, other mixed borders, roses, pond, bog garden, grasses, hostas and much more. Long pergola with roses, clematis and honeysuckle. High level paths giving views of garden. Chainsaw carvings. Featured in Cheshire Life and Northwich Guardian.

90 ST PETERS PARK
See North East Wales

74 199 STOCKPORT ROAD
Timperley WA15 7SF. Eric & Shirley Robinson, 0161 980 1368, shirley233@sky.com. *1½ m NE of Altrincham. Take A560 out of Altrincham, in 1m take B5165 towards Timperley. B5165 is Stockport Rd.* Home-made teas. **Adm £3, chd free. Sat 1, Sun 2 June (1-5).**
Cottage-style garden full of colourful herbaceous perennials, shrubs and hostas, with a brick-built pond complete with small koi and goldfish. You will not believe how many plants there are in such a small garden. Small front garden with water feature and small shaded plant area.

75 ◆ STONYFORD COTTAGE
Stonyford Lane, Oakmere CW8 2TF. Janet & Tony Overland, 01606 888128, www.stonyfordcottagegardens.co.uk *5m SW of Northwich. From Northwich take A556 towards Chester. ¾ m past A49 junction turn R into Stonyford Ln. Entrance ½ m on L.* **Adm £4, chd free. For NGS: Sun 9 June; Sun 11 Aug (1.30-5). For other opening times and information, please phone or see garden website.**
Set around a tranquil pool this Monet style landscape has a wealth of

moisture loving plants, incl iris and candelabra primulas. Drier areas feature unusual perennials and rarer trees and shrubs. Woodland paths meander through shade and bog plantings with views across the pool to the cottage gardens. Unusual plants available at the adjacent nursery. Open Tues - Sun & BH Mons Apr - Sept 10-5. Featured in Amateur Gardening Magazine. Some gravel paths.

With woodland banking, with a natural spring well and ponds . . .

76 SUN HOUSE
66 Bridge Lane, Bramhall, Stockport SK7 3AW. Peter & Susan Hale. *3½ m S of Stockport. Sun House is on Bridge Ln (A5143) between junction with A5102 at the Bramall Hall r'about and Bramhall Moor Ln.* Home-made teas. **Adm £3.50, chd free. Sat 1, Sun 2 June (1.30-5.30).**
⅓ acre garden enclosed by mature trees, it has a dry acid sandy soil which has been addressed by building numerous ponds and bog areas. A wide range of herbaceous plants, mosaic and ceramic decorations, gravel garden, vegetable plot and chickens plus two life-sized terracotta warriors. Display and sale of ceramics and crafts. Exploration trail for children. Some paths need care, unfenced ponds.

77 NEW SYCAMORE COTTAGE
Manchester Road, Carrington, Manchester M31 4AY. Mrs C Newton. *From M60 J8 take Carrington turn (A6144) through 2 sets of lights past Windmill PH. Garden about 1m past the PH opp Air Products on R. From M6 J20 follow signs for Lymm. In Lymm town centre follow signs for Partington/ Carrington (A6144) follow for 5 or 6m. Garden on L opp Air Products.* Light refreshments. **Adm £3.50, chd free. Sat 15, Sun 16 June; Sat 17, Sun 18 Aug (1-5).**

Approx ⅕ acre Cottage garden split into distinct areas, with woodland banking, with a natural spring well and ponds. Also features decking with two seating areas and a summer house. Was featured on Cupranols TV advert.

78 TATTENHALL HALL
High Street, Tattenhall CH3 9PX. Jen & Nick Benefield, Chris Evered & Jannie Hollins, 01829 770654, janniehollins@gmail.com. *8m S of Chester on A41. Turn L to Tattenhall, through village, turn R at Letters PH, past war memorial on L through Sandstone pillared gates. Park on rd or in village car park.* **Adm £4.50, chd free. Sun 19 May; Sun 23 June (2-5). Visitors also welcome by appt Apr to Aug. Limited parking facilities.**
Plant enthusiasts garden around Jacobean house (not open).
4½ acres, wild flower meadows, interesting trees, large pond, stream, walled garden, colour themed borders, succession planting, spinney walk with shade plants, yew terrace overlooking meadow, views to hills. Glasshouse and vegetable garden. Wildlife friendly sometimes untidy garden, interest throughout the year. Gravel paths, cobbles and some steps.

79 ◆ TATTON PARK
Knutsford WA16 6QN. National Trust, leased to Cheshire East Council, 01625 374400, www.tattonpark.org.uk. *2½ m N of Knutsford. Well signed on M56 J7 & from M6 J19.* **Adm £5.50, chd £3.50. For NGS: Wed 24 Apr; Wed 12 June (10-6). For other opening times and information, please phone or see garden website.**
Features include orangery by Wyatt, fernery by Paxton, restored Japanese garden, Italian and rose gardens. Greek monument and African hut. Hybrid azaleas and rhododendrons; swamp cypresses, tree ferns, tall redwoods, bamboos and pines. Fully restored productive walled gardens.

80 TIRLEY GARTH
Mallows Way, Willington, Nr Tarporley CW6 0RQ. *2m N of Tarporley. 2m S of Kelsall. Entrance 500yds from village of Utkinton. At N of Tarporley take Utkinton rd.* Home-made teas. **Adm £5, chd free.**

Every Sun 12 May to 2 June (1-5).
40-acre garden, terraced and landscaped,designed by Thomas Mawson (considered the leading exponent of garden design in early 20c), it is the only Grade II* Arts & Crafts garden in Cheshire that remains complete and in excellent condition. The gardens are an important example of an early C20 garden laid out in both formal and informal styles. By early May the garden is bursting into flower with almost 3000 Rhododendron and Azalea many 100 years old. Exhibition by local Artists and small marquee selling bric a brac and local crafts.

81 NEW THE VICARAGE GARDENS
Manchester Road, Carrington, Manchester M31 4AG. Christian Community Charity. *From N take M61 join M60 anti clockwise and leave at J8 follow rd for 3½ m to garden entrance on L. From S take M6 leave at J20 take B5158 to join A6144 follow through Partington and on leaving Partington gardens on R.* **Adm £4, chd free. Mon 6 May; Sat 15 June; Mon 26 Aug (9-4.30 all day).**
5 acres of landscaped gardens including 2 acres of woodland crisscrossed with gravel paths. Ponds, streams, shrub and herbaceous beds. Children's swings.

WEEPING ASH
See Lancashire, Merseyside & Greater Manchester

82 THE WELL HOUSE
Wet Lane, Tilston, Malpas SY14 7DP. Mrs S H French-Greenslade, 01829 250332. *3m NW of Malpas. On A41, 1st turn R after Broxton r'about, L on Malpas Rd through Tilston. House & antique shop on L.* **Visitors welcome by appt Jan to Aug. Refreshments by arrangement.**
1-acre cottage garden, bridge over natural stream, spring bulbs, perennials, herbs and shrubs. Triple pond and waterfall feature. Adjoining ¾ -acre field made into wild flower meadow; first seeding late 2003. Large bog area of kingcups and ragged robin. January for snowdrop walk. Antique shop and Victorian parlour. Will be on Antique Road Trip.

83 WELL HOUSE

Dean Row Road, Wilmslow SK9 2BU. Steven & Jill Kimber, 01625 533502, mummykimber@hotmail.com. *2m N of Wilmslow. Via the A34 bypass or Adlington Rd, Well House is on Dean Row Rd (B5358), almost at the junction (r'about) with Adlington Rd (A5102). Parking available at the Unicorn PH 300yds, from the house entrance. Next door to the Shell garage. Less able visitors can drop off then park in Chapel Ln but space is limited.* Home-made teas. **Adm £4.50, chd free. Sun 30 June (12.30-4.30). Visitors also welcome by appt 9 May to 25 July, ideally Thursdays or evenings.**

A richly maturing, 3-acre garden. Offering formal landscaped areas, lush herbaceous borders, rich woodland and an extensive wild flower meadow with naturalised wild orchids continuing to spread. Our great planting success of 2012, a dedicated wildflower room using Olympic style mixes, will be repeated and extended for 2013.

Pergola with clematis and white wisteria . . . borders have unusual small trees, shrubs and herbaceous plants . . .

GROUP OPENING

84 WILLASTON VILLAGE GARDENS

Willaston CH64 1TE. *8m N of Chester. Take A540 Chester to West Kirby rd; turn R on B5151 to Willaston; at village centre turn R into Hooton Rd. Change Lane is ¾ m on R opp garage. All 3 gardens are entered from Change Hey garden. Parking available in field at bottom of Change Lane on RH-side. 15 mins walk from Hooton Stn along B5133 in direction of Willaston. Change Lane on LH-side opp garage. Leave M53 J5. Join A41, travel in direction of Queensferry, N Wales. ¼ m at T- lights turn R B5133. Along Hooton Rd, after ¾ m Hooton Stn on L.* Home-made teas at Change Hey. **Combined adm £4.50, chd free. Sun 5 May (2-5).**

CHANGE HEY
Change Lane. Keith & Joan Butcher

THE DUTCH HOUSE
Michael Ring

SILVERBURN
Prof M P & Dr A M Escudier

3 very different gardens in design and planting. Change Hey: 2 acre garden with mature trees, developing woodland area underplanted with rhododendrons and azaleas. The Dutch House: ⅓ -acre cottage-style garden with some formality. The rear garden vista, terminating with a 1920 Boulton and Paul revolving summerhouse, is surrounded on 2 sides by mature beech, oak and pine trees. Some gravel paths. Silverburn: ½ -acre garden designed by present owners. A plantsperson's garden with varied plantings in the herbaceous beds and mixed borders, species and old-fashioned roses, rhododendrons, azaleas, attractive trees, vegetable garden and small orchard. Bridge linking Silverburn and Change Hey not suitable for wheelchairs. Alternative (separate) access possible. Partial wheelchair access.

85 WOOD END COTTAGE

Grange Lane, Whitegate, Northwich CW8 2BQ. Mr & Mrs M R Everett, 01606 888236, woodendct@supanet.com. *4m SW of Northwich. Turn S off A556 (Northwich bypass) at Sandiway PO T-lights; after 1¾ m, turn L to Whitegate village; opp school follow Grange Ln for 300yds.* Home-made teas. **Adm £4, chd free. Visitors welcome by appt Apr to July.**

Plantsman's ½ acre garden in attractive setting, sloping to a natural stream bordered by shade and moisture-loving plants. Background of mature trees. Well stocked herbaceous borders, trellis with roses and clematis, magnificent delphiniums, many phlox Choice perennials. Interesting shrubs and flowering trees. Vegetable garden. Feature in Cheshire Life.

86 NEW 28 WOODLANDS ROAD

Handforth SK9 3AU. Mrs Toni Fox. *South Manchester. 15 min drive from J5 of M56. Follow signs for Cheadle. Turn R onto Styal Rd (B5166). Continue to follow and turn L onto Station Rd. Take 2nd R onto Stanneylands Rd. Turn L onto Manchester Rd. Turn R onto Station Rd (B5358). Turn L onto Hall Rd. Slight R onto Woodlands Rd. Continue past large green, property on R.* **Adm £3, chd free. Sat 15, Sun 16 June (1.30-5).**

This sloping garden has been developed and landscaped over the last 10 years by the current owner. Paths lead down to a small stream with views over one of the ponds of a local fishing club. Fire pit with seating area and shade sail. Pergola with clematis and white wisteria. Borders have unusual small trees, shrubs and herbaceous plants. Partial wheelchair access.

87 WOODSEND

33 Lostock Hall Road, Poynton SK12 1DP. Ruth & Martin Seabrook. *6m N of Macclesfield. From Macclesfield take A523 towards Stockport. At Poynton Centre turn L onto A5149 Chester Rd, turn L immed after railway bridge to Lostock Hall Rd.* Home-made teas. **Adm £3.50, chd free. Sat 15, Sun 16 June (1-5).**

Small tranquil garden, owner designed, planted and maintained. Features courtyard patio, rose covered pergola and summerhouse, surrounded by deep borders packed with herbaceous plants, roses and shrubs. An informal shady area planted with ferns, hostas and dicentra, and pond. Front garden with a white planting scheme. Local artist Liz Every will be exhibiting and selling her limited edition photo prints and cards. Partial wheelchair access.

88 YEW TREE HOUSE GARDEN & SPECIAL PERENNIALS NURSERY

Hall Lane, Hankelow, nr Audlem CW3 0JB. Janet & Martin Blow, www.specialperennials.com. *Just off A529, 5m S of Nantwich, 1m N of Audlem. Park at village green, follow Hall Lane L along rear of green. Last house on R before junction with A529. Sat Nav will take you down Hall Lane to dead end. We are on*

unsigned section of lane along rear of green. PH, cafes & WC available at nearby Audlem (1m). **Adm £2.50, chd free.** **Sats, Suns 29, 30 June; 6, 7, 20, 21 July; 10, 11 Aug; 1, 8 Sept (2-5).**
Small garden planted in an exuberant cottage style with an abundance of interesting and unusual perennial plants: no lawns just lots of lovely flowers! Specialities include heleniums, day lilies, phlox, centaurea, monarda, grasses plus lots, lots more. The garden is a haven for bees and butterflies. Attached small nursery selling plants grown in the garden. National Collection of Heleniums (100+ varieties - best Aug - Sep). National Collection of Centaurea. For special National Collection weekends and other opening times please see our website. Featured in Mail on Sunday. Gravel paths, some narrow. Wheelchair access is not possible to all of the garden and nursery.
NCH

No lawns just lots of lovely flowers . . . the garden is a haven for bees and butterflies . . .

Grafton Lodge

Cheshire & Wirral County Volunteers

County Organiser
John Hinde, 3 Earle Drive, Parkgate, Neston CH64 6RY, 0151 353 0032, john.hinde@maylands.com

County Treasurer
Andrew Collin, 8 Collingham Green, Little Sutton, Ellesmere Port CH66 4NX, 0151 339 3614, andrewcollin@btinternet.com

Publicity
Graham Beech, 12 Woodlands Road, Pownall Park, Wilmslow SK9 5QB, 01625 402946, gb.ngs@talktalk.net

Booklet Co-ordinator
John Hinde, 3 Earle Drive, Parkgate, Neston CH64 6RY, 0151 353 0032, john.hinde@maylands.com

Assistant County Organisers
Janet Bashforth, Mayfield, The Peppers, Lymm WA13 0JA, 01925 756107, janetbashforth@talktalk.net
Sue Bryant, Hope Cottage, 93 Stamford Road, Bowdon WA14 2JJ, 0161 928 3819, suewestlakebryant@btinternet.com
Jean Davies, Westage Farm, Great Budworth, Northwich CW9 6HJ, 01606 892383, pj@budworth94.fsnet.co.uk
Sandra Fairclough, Inglewood, 4 Birchmere, Heswall, Wirral CH60 6TN, 0151 3424645, sandra.fairclough@tiscali.co.uk
Juliet Hill, The Coach House, Salterswell, Tarporley CW6 0ED, 01829 732804, hill573@btinternet.com
Romy Holmes, Bowmere Cottage, Bowmere Road, Tarporley CW6 0BS, 01829 732053, romy@holmes-email.co.uk
Ros Mahon, Rectory Cottage, Eaton, Congleton CW12 2ND, 01260 274777, ros.mahon@talktalk.net

CORNWALL

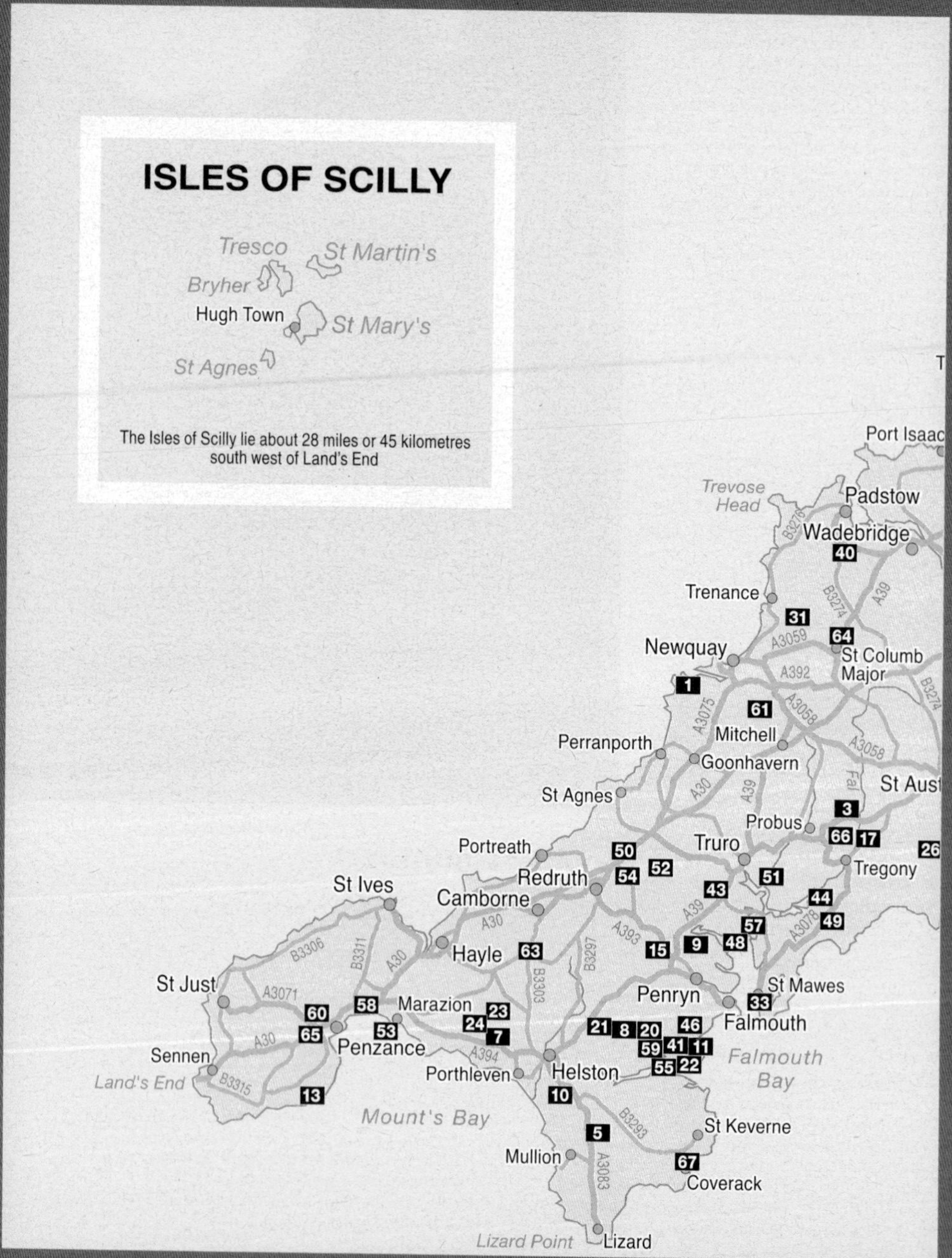
ISLES OF SCILLY
Tresco
St Martin's
Bryher
Hugh Town
St Mary's
St Agnes
The Isles of Scilly lie about 28 miles or 45 kilometres south west of Land's End
Port Isaac
Trevose Head
Padstow
Wadebridge
40
Trenance
31
Newquay
64
St Columb Major
1
61
Perranporth
Mitchell
Goonhavern
St Agnes
St Aust
3
Probus
Portreath
50
52
Truro
66
17
26
Tregony
Redruth
54
51
St Ives
Camborne
43
44
57
49
Hayle
63
15
9
48
St Just
St Mawes
Penryn
33
Marazion
58
60
23
65
53
24
7
21
8
20
46
Falmouth
Penzance
59
41
11
Sennen
Porthleven
Helston
55
22
Falmouth Bay
Land's End
13
10
Mount's Bay
St Keverne
5
Mullion
67
Coverack
Lizard Point
Lizard

CORNWALL
DEVON
Kilkhampton
Bude
Stratton
Bude Bay
Holsworthy
Boscastle
Hallworthy
Camelford
Launceston
Bolventor
Colliford Lake
Callington
Gunnislake
Bodmin
Liskeard
Lostwithiel
Saltash
St Germans
Torpoint
Fowey
Looe
Polperro
Plymouth
Whitsand Bay
Rame Head
St Austell Bay
Mevagissey
Chulmleigh
Winkleigh
Hatherleigh
Highampton
Copplestone
Crediton
Okehampton
Whiddon Down
Dunsford
Lydford
Moretonhampstead
Widecombe in the Moor
Bovey Tracey
Tavistock
Princetown
Dartmeet
Ashburton
Yelverton
Buckfastleigh
Totnes
Plympton
Ivybridge
Halwell
Yealmpton
Modbury
Loddiswell
Kingsbridge
Bigbury-on-Sea
Bigbury Bay
Salcombe
Tamar
Torridge
Teign
Tavy
Dart
Camel
Fowey
Yeo
Taw
0 10 20 kilometres
0 10 miles
© Global Mapping/The XYZ Digital Map Company

Opening Dates

February

Sunday 10
14 Coombegate Cottage

Sunday 17
14 Coombegate Cottage

Sunday 24
14 Coombegate Cottage
30 Ince Castle

March

Sunday 3
14 Coombegate Cottage

Sunday 10
14 Coombegate Cottage

Sunday 17
14 Coombegate Cottage
30 Ince Castle
54 Scorrier House
65 Trewidden Garden

Sunday 24
14 Coombegate Cottage

Monday 25
16 Cotehele

Sunday 31
14 Coombegate Cottage

April

Sunday 7
2 The Barn House

Wednesday 10
45 Pencarrow

Sunday 14
30 Ince Castle
51 Riverside Cottage

Sunday 21
9 Carclew Gardens: Carclew House and Trevorick
10 Carminowe Valley Garden
20 Ethnevas Cottage
46 Penjerrick Garden

Saturday 27
13 Chygurno

Sunday 28
12 Casa Laguna
13 Chygurno
48 Polgwynne

May

Wednesday 1
22 Glendurgan
57 Trelissick
61 Trerice

Thursday 2
25 Headland

Sunday 5
4 Boconnoc
20 Ethnevas Cottage
33 Lamorran House
60 Trengwainton

Monday 6
31 The Japanese Garden & Bonsai Nursery
39 Moyclare

Tuesday 7
34 Lanhydrock House & Gardens

Thursday 9
25 Headland

Saturday 11
47 Pinsla Garden & Nursery

Sunday 12
41 Navas Hill House
43 The Old Vicarage
47 Pinsla Garden & Nursery
56 Trebartha
59 Trenarth (Evening)

Wednesday 15
5 Bonython Manor

Thursday 16
25 Headland

Sunday 19
64 Trewan Hall

Thursday 23
25 Headland

Saturday 35
15 Cosawes Barton

Sunday 26
18 Cutlinwith
51 Riverside Cottage

June

Sunday 9
35 Long Hay
53 St Michael's Mount

National Gardens Weekend

Saturday 15
6 Boscastle Gardens
23 Godolphin
36 Marsh Villa Gardens

Sunday 16
1 Arundell
6 Boscastle Gardens
7 Brea Mor
24 Godolphin Hill Gardens
31 The Japanese Garden & Bonsai Nursery
56 Trebartha
60 Trengwainton
63 Trevoole Farm

Saturday 22
49 Poppy Cottage Garden
50 Primrose Farm

Sunday 23
10 Carminowe Valley Garden
49 Poppy Cottage Garden

Saturday 29
52 Roseland House

Sunday 30
3 Benallack Barn
24 Godolphin Hill Gardens
38 The Mill House
52 Roseland House

July

Sunday 7
2 The Barn House
29 Higher Trenedden

Saturday 13
68 Waye Cottage

Sunday 14
30 Ince Castle
68 Waye Cottage

Thursday 18
34 Lanhydrock House & Gardens

Friday 19
67 Waters Edge

Sunday 21
1 Arundell
67 Waters Edge

Saturday 27
13 Chygurno

Sunday 28
13 Chygurno
67 Waters Edge

Ecologically driven, artistically executed, organically grown . . .

August

Saturday 3
47 Pinsla Garden & Nursery

Sunday 4
7 Brea Mor
28 Highcroft Gardens
47 Pinsla Garden & Nursery
59 Trenarth
62 Trethew Gardens

Saturday 10
36 Marsh Villa Gardens

Sunday 11
36 Marsh Villa Gardens

Monday 12
27 Hidden Valley Gardens

Tuesday 13
27 Hidden Valley Gardens

Wednesday 14
27 Hidden Valley Gardens

Sunday 18
28 Highcroft Gardens

Sunday 25
8 Bucks Head House Garden
21 The 'Garten' Garden

September

Sunday 1
10 Carminowe Valley Garden

Saturday 14
15 Cosawes Barton

Monday 16
16 Cotehele

October

Sunday 13
56 Trebartha
58 Tremenheere Sculpture Garden

February 2014

Sunday 9
14 Coombegate Cottage

Sunday 16
14 Coombegate Cottage

Sunday 23
14 Coombegate Cottage

Gardens open to the public

4 Boconnoc
5 Bonython Manor
11 Carwinion
13 Chygurno
16 Cotehele
17 Creed House
19 Eden Project
22 Glendurgan
23 Godolphin
24 Godolphin Hill Gardens
25 Headland
26 The Lost Gardens of Heligan
27 Hidden Valley Gardens
31 The Japanese Garden & Bonsai Nursery
32 Ken Caro
33 Lamorran House
34 Lanhydrock House & Gardens
36 Marsh Villa Gardens
39 Moyclare
45 Pencarrow
46 Penjerrick Garden
47 Pinsla Garden & Nursery
49 Poppy Cottage Garden
52 Roseland House
53 St Michael's Mount
55 Trebah
57 Trelissick
58 Tremenheere Sculpture Garden
60 Trengwainton
61 Trerice
65 Trewidden Garden
66 Trewithen

Highcroft Gardens
© Rachel Warne

By appointment only

37 Middlewood House
40 Nanfenten
42 The Old Rectory, Trevalga

Also open by Appointment ☎

1 Arundell
7 Brea Mor
8 Bucks Head House Garden
10 Carminowe Valley Garden
14 Coombegate Cottage
20 Ethnevas Cottage
21 The 'Garten' Garden
28 Highcroft Gardens
38 The Mill House
41 Navas Hill House
50 Primrose Farm
51 Riverside Cottage
59 Trenarth
67 Waters Edge
68 Waye Cottage

The Gardens

1 ARUNDELL

West Pentire, Crantock TR8 5SE. Brenda & David Eyles, 01637 831916, david@davideyles.com. *1m W of Crantock. From A3075 take signs to Crantock. At junction in village keep straight on to West Pentire hamlet (1m). Park in field (NGS sign) 300yds or in public car parks at W Pentire.* Cream teas. **Adm £4, chd free. Sun 16 June, Sun 21 July (1-5). Visitors also welcome by appt June to Aug.**

A garden where no garden should be! - on windswept N coast NT headland between 2 fantastic beaches. 1 acre set around original farm cottage. Front: cottage garden. Side: small Mediterranean courtyard. Rear: rockery, shrubbery, more cottage garden leading to pond, stream and bog garden, herbaceous borders, Beth Chatto gravel garden, small pinetum and spectacular exotic garden. Featured in Cornwall Life and Coast magazines. Wheelchair access from public car park with entrance via rear gate. 14 shallow steps in centre of garden useable with care in wheelchair.

2 THE BARN HOUSE

Higher Penhalt, Poundstock, Bude EX23 0DG. Tim & Sandy Dingle, 01288 361365, timdingle237@btinternet.com. *5m S of Bude. 1m off A39 to Widemouth Bay. Take Millook rd by Widemouth Manor Hotel. Follow rd for 1m, signed L at top of hill.* Home-made teas. **Adm £3.50, chd free. Sun 7 Apr, Sun 7 July (11-5).**

Garden that shows you can battle with the elements above dramatic cliffs of N Cornish coast and win. 1/2 -acre garden designed for yr-round interest with many colourful and unusual plants. Divided and enclosed by sheltering hedges. Herbaceous borders, prairie bed, pond, kitchen garden and patio. A walk through fields and wooded valley often gives glimpses of abundant wildlife and wild flowers. April opening - demonstration of willow-weaving by Hilary Workman. July opening - craft demonstration. Partial wheelchair access.

3 NEW BENALLACK BARN
Grampound Road, Truro TR2 4BY. Linda Pelham, 01726 883618, www.benallack.net. *Between Grampound and Grampound Road. From Truro, L to Grampound Road, 1st R. From A30, exit Fraddon to Grampound Road, 1st L after village. From St Austell, R at pet shop in Grampound.* Cream teas. **Adm £3.50, chd free. Sun 30 June (1-5).**
3-acre garden surrounding 400 yr-old converted barn, sloping towards Fal River valley. Gravelled, S-facing courtyard with climbers and planted granite troughs; sculptured cotoneaster hedges and colour-themed herbaceous borders; bog garden; small orchard; vegetable garden, greenhouse; wild meadow leading to small lake with island and summerhouse surrounded by giant gunneras, grasses and perennials.

4 ◆ BOCONNOC
Lostwithiel PL22 0RG. Anthony Fortescue. *Off A390 between Liskeard and Lostwithiel. From East Taphouse follow signs to Boconnoc. (Sat Nav does not work well in this area).* **Adm £4.50, chd free. For NGS: Sun 5 May (2-5). For other opening times and information, please phone 01208 872507 or see garden website www.boconnoc.com.**
20-acre gardens surrounded by parkland and woods with magnificent trees, flowering shrubs and stunning views. The gardens are set amongst mature trees which provide the backcloth for exotic spring flowering shrubs, woodland plants, with newly-planted magnolias and a fine collection of hydrangeas. Featured in Daily Telegraph, Western Morning News, Country Life and Historic House Magazine.

5 ◆ BONYTHON MANOR
Cury Cross Lanes, Helston TR12 7BA. Mr & Mrs Richard Nathan, 01326 240550, sue@bonythonmanor.co.uk, www.bonythonmanor.co.uk. *5m S of Helston. On main A3083 Helston to Lizard Rd. Turn L at Cury Cross Lanes (Wheel Inn). Entrance 300yds on R.* **Adm £6, chd £2. For NGS: Wed 15 May (2-4.30). For other opening times and information, please phone or see garden website.**
Magnificent 20-acre colour garden incl sweeping hydrangea drive to Georgian manor (not open). Herbaceous walled garden, potager with vegetables and picking flowers; 3 lakes in valley planted with ornamental grasses, perennials and South African flowers. A 'must see' for all seasons colour.

Three-acre garden surrounding 400 year-old converted barn . . .

GROUP OPENING

6 BOSCASTLE GARDENS
Boscastle PL35 0BJ. *5m N of Camelford. Park in doctor's surgery car park at top of village (clearly signed). Limited parking for disabled at both gardens. Maps provided.* Home-made teas at Half Acre. **Combined adm £3.50, chd free. Sat 15, Sun 16 June (1.30-5.30).**

HALF ACRE
Mount Pleasant. Carole Vincent Visitors also welcome by appt incl groups. 01840 250263

WILDWOOD
Doctors Hill. Alex Stewart

Boscastle Harbour is well-known to visitors. Both gardens are in older part of village, overlooking cliff, land and sea. Garden paintings exhibition. Half Acre: sculpture in an acre of 3 gardens: Cottage, small wood, the Blue Circle garden, constructed in colour concrete with coastal planting. Studio open. Paintings exhibition. Wildwood: garden of magic deception. Front traditional, rear - lawns leading to wood with pond, tree ferns and shade-loving shrubs.

7 BREA MOR
Tresowes Hill, Ashton, Helston TR13 9TB. Eileen Clarke, 01736 762721, eileenjclarke@gmail.com. *Tresowes Hill, Ashton. 5 m from Helston on A394 towards Penzance. Turn R at Ashton Garage towards Godolphin, Breamor exactly ½ m on R from main Rd.* **Adm £3.50, chd free (share to St Julia's Hospice Appeal). Sun 16 June, Sun 4 Aug (2-5). Visitors also welcome by appt May to Sept.**
Situated on side of Tregonning Hill overlooking Mounts Bay. Wide variety of trees, shrubs and perennial plants. Fern garden, 2 ponds, roses. 2 small vegetable gardens. Developed over 25 years. Designed for bees, birds and butterflies.

8 BUCKS HEAD HOUSE GARDEN
Trengove Cross, Constantine TR11 5QR. Deborah Baker, 01326 340844, deborah.baker@falmouth.ac.uk. *5m SW of Falmouth. From A394 towards Helston, L at Edgcumbe towards Gweek and Constantine. Proceed for 0.8m then L towards Constantine. Further 0.8m, garden on L at Trengove Cross.* Tea. **Adm £3.50, chd free. Sun 25 Aug (1-4.30). Also open The 'Garten' Garden 25 Aug, £6.50 both gardens. Visitors also welcome by appt Aug.**
Enchanting cottage gardens and young woodland of native and rare trees, shrubs and perennials. The site of 1.5 acres is an exposed S-facing Cornish hillside with panoramic views. Nurtured by essential windbreaks, the inspiring collection of plants are chosen to create a calm and tranquil retreat. Local press and radio features. Limited wheelchair access to lower garden and to woodland.

GROUP OPENING

9 CARCLEW GARDENS: CARCLEW HOUSE AND TREVORICK
Carclew, Perranarworthal, Truro TR3 7PB. John & Sally Williams and Mrs. Daphne Neale. *5m SW of Truro, 4m N of Falmouth. Signed Carclew off A39 100m W of Norway Inn, Perranarworthal. At top of hill turn L, then immed L again at Lodge.* Cream teas and home-made teas.

Combined adm £4, chd free. Sun 21 Apr (12-5).
Carclew House: Part of the formal gardens of original Carclew Mansion, former house of the Lemon family. Grade II listed C18 and C19 garden, walls and terraces currently undergoing restoration. Incl Italianate garden, acer glade (40+ varieties), fern dell and woodland walk. Plants of note incl rhododendron Sir Charles Lemon, camellia Captain Rawes and over 40 rhododendron species. Trevorick: Woodland garden developed around romantic ruin of the old Carclew Mansion, dominated by trees and shrubs with many excellent specimens incl Magnolia doltsopa, Rhododendron Cornish red, Liquidambar, Chilean fire bush, over 35 Camellias cultivars and Limes, many of which are 200 yrs+. Featured on Radio Cornwall.

Colourful spring garden . . .

10 CARMINOWE VALLEY GARDEN
Tangies, Gunwalloe TR12 7PU. Mr & Mrs Peter Stanley, 01326 565868, stanley.m2@sky.com. *3m SW of Helston. A3083 Helston-Lizard rd. R opposite main gate to Culdrose. 1m downhill, garden on R.* Home-made teas. **Adm £4, chd free. Suns 21 Apr; 23 June; 1 Sept (1-5). Visitors also welcome by appt Apr to Sept.**
Overlooking the beautiful Carminowe Valley towards Loepool this abundant garden combines native oak woodland, babbling brook and large natural pond with more formal areas. Wildflower meadow, mown pathways, shrubberies, orchard, nectar beds, cutting garden, kitchen garden, summerhouse. Enclosed cottage garden, tulips in spring and roses early summer provide huge contrast. Gravel paths, slopes.

11 ◆ CARWINION
Mawnan Smith TR11 5JA. Anthony & Jane Rogers, 01326 250258, www.carwinion.co.uk. *3m W of Falmouth. 500yds from centre of Mawnan Smith, turn L at Red Lion PH & follow signs.* **For information, please phone or see garden website.**
Stunning 14-acre S-facing Cornish valley garden running down to R Helford. Home of UK's premier bamboo collection. Mixed borders and extensive camellia collection. Wild flowers and ferns abound. A garden of yr-round interest open every day (10-5.30) except Christmas Day, adm £5, chd free. Partial wheelchair access. Disabled entrance free.

12 NEW CASA LAGUNA
School Rd, Lanreath, Looe PL13 2NX. Ivor & Margaret Dungey. *5m SW of East Taphouse. From A390 take B3359 signed Looe Lanreath. Lanreath village 5m. Garden 150yds from Village Hall car park where parking available. Disabled parking at house.* Home-made teas. **Adm £3.50, chd free. Sun 28 Apr (10-5).**
Drive with shrubs leading to colourful spring garden, approx ½ acre. Azaleas, camellias and rhododendrons in arrangement of beds. Assortment of conifers, all intermingled with seasonal bulbs and small plants.

13 ◆ CHYGURNO
Lamorna TR19 6XH. Dr & Mrs Robert Moule, 01736 732153. *4m S of Penzance. Off B3315. Follow signs for The Cove Restaurant. Garden is at top of hill, past Hotel on L.* **Adm £5, chd free. For NGS: Sats, Suns 27, 28 Apr; 27, 28 July (2-5). For other information, please phone.**
Beautiful, unique, 3-acre cliffside garden overlooking Lamorna Cove. Planting started in 1998, mainly S-hemisphere shrubs and exotics with hydrangeas, camellias and rhododendrons. Woodland area with tree ferns set against large granite outcrops. Garden terraced with steep steps and paths. Plenty of benches so you can take a rest and enjoy the wonderful views. Well worth the effort. Also open Weds, Thurs (2-5), Apr - Sept. Featured in The English Garden.

14 COOMBEGATE COTTAGE
St Ive, Liskeard PL14 3LZ. Michael Stephens, 01579 383520, mike@coombegate.wanadoo.co.uk. *4m E of Liskeard. From A390 at St Ive take turning signed Blunts. Then take 2nd L for 400 metres.* Home-made teas in Village Hall. **Adm £3.50, chd free. Every Sun 10 Feb to 31 Mar 2013 (1-4); Suns 9, 16, 23 Feb 2014 (1-4). Visitors also welcome by appt 1 Feb to 30 Mar.**
1-acre garden designed for winter colour and scent, continuing into spring. Witch hazels, daphnes, hellebores, early rhododendrons and interesting collection of more unusual seasonal plants, some for sale. Drifts of snowdrops. Sloping site with steps. Open unless ice/snow - phone to check if in doubt.

15 NEW COSAWES BARTON
Ponsanooth, nr Truro TR3 7EJ. Louise Bishop, 07985 084391, bishop_louise@btinternet.com. *8½ m W of Truro. A39 Truro - Falmouth rd. At Treluswell r'about take A393 Redruth/Ponsanooth rd. After Burnt House 1st L. ¾ m nr 30mph sign, house on R.* Light refreshments. **Adm £4, chd free. Sats 25 May; 14 Sept (10-5).**
An idyllic spot. Gardens surround C18 farmhouse, cottage and courtyard. Inner courtyard garden, a formal, very well-established area and extensive wooded walks covering 14 acres.

16 ◆ COTEHELE
Saltash PL12 6TA. National Trust, 01579 351346, www.nationaltrust.org.uk. *2m E of St Dominick. 4m from Gunnislake. (Turn at St Ann's Chapel); 8m SW of Tavistock; 14m from Plymouth via Tamar Bridge.* **Garden adm £6, chd £3. For NGS: Mon 25 Mar, Mon 16 Sept (11-4). For other opening times and information, please phone or see garden website.**
Formal garden, orchards and meadow. Terrace garden falling to sheltered valley with ponds, stream and unusual shrubs. Historic collection of daffodils. Fine Tudor house (one of the least altered in the country); armour, tapestries, furniture. Gravel paths, some steep slopes in Valley Garden.

17 ◆ CREED HOUSE
Creed, Grampound, Truro TR2 4SL. Jonathon & Annie Croggon, 01872 530372, www.creedhouse.co.uk. *9m W of Truro. From the centre of Grampound on A390, take rd signed to Creed. After 1m turn L opp Creed Church, garden is on L.*

For opening times and information, please phone or see garden website.
5-acre landscaped Georgian rectory garden; tranquil rural setting; spacious lawns. Tree collection; rhododendrons; sunken cobbled yard and formal walled herbaceous garden. Trickle stream to ponds and bog. Natural woodland walk. Restoration began 1974 - continues and incl recent planting.

18 CUTLINWITH

Tideford, Saltash PL12 5HX. Peter & Mary Hamilton. *1½ m N of Tideford, 5m W of Saltash. A38 to Tideford (10m from Plymouth Bridge) then rd N opp butcher's shop to Tideford Cross (1m). R just after sign. Cutlinwith lane entrance ½ m further on R.* **Adm £3.50, chd free. Sun 26 May (2-4.30).**
3-acre garden in small valley. Begun 12yrs ago and now beginning to mature. The design aim is to have all yr round interest. Features trees, borders, water garden incl stream and ponds. Developing acer, magnolia and bluebell walk leading to woodland paths. Music in the garden incl local brass band.

19 ◆ EDEN PROJECT

Bodelva PL24 2SG. The Eden Trust, 01726 811911, www.edenproject.com. *4m E of St Austell. Brown signs from A30 & A390.* **For opening times and information, please phone or see garden website.**
Described as the eighth wonder of the world, the Eden Project is a global garden for the 21st Century. Discover the story of plants that have changed the world and which could change your future. The Eden Project is an exciting attraction where you can explore your relationship with nature, learn new things and get inspiration about the world around you. Year-round programme of talks, events and workshops.

20 ETHNEVAS COTTAGE

Constantine, Falmouth TR11 5PY. Lyn Watson, 01326 340076. *6m SW of Falmouth. Nearest main rds A39, A394. Follow signs to Constantine. At Lower Village sign, at bottom of winding hill, turn off on private lane. Garden ¾ m up hill.* Home-made teas. **Adm £3.50, chd free. Sun 21 Apr; Sun 5 May (12-4). Visitors also welcome by appt Mar to Sept, max 10.**
Isolated granite cottage in 2 acres. Intimate flower and vegetable garden. Bridge over stream to large pond and primrose path through semi-wild bog area. Hillside with grass paths among native and exotic trees (40 different conifers). Many camellias and rhododendrons. Mixed shrub and herbaceous beds, wild flower glade, spring bulbs. Plantaholics' garden.

THE GARDEN HOUSE

See Devon

Lanhydrock House & Gardens

Treat yourself to a plant from the plant stall

21 NEW THE 'GARTEN' GARDEN
Lower Treculliacks, Constantine, Falmouth TR11 5QW. Dr Sara Gadd, 07814 885141, sara@gartendesign.co.uk. *1.5m N of Gweek, 1m NW of Constantine. From Falmouth or Helston take turning to Gweek off A394 at Edgecumb. 2nd L after 1.5m. Only property on R. From Constantine follow signs to Brill, then to Rame. L after 1m to Seworgan. Garden on L.* Home-made teas. **Adm £3.50, chd free. Sun 25 Aug (10-6). Also open Bucks Head House Garden, joint adm £6.50. Visitors also welcome by appt Apr to Sept incl, max 20.**
Ecologically driven, artistically executed, organically grown. Lovingly developed by Drs Sara Gadd & Daro Montag. Embracing ecosystems, home, children, plants, food, wildlife. Enchanting mix of natural materials, enhancing feature plantings in their low carbon life. Hot terrace near fern glades. Olives, bamboos and acers. Creative use of wood and granite, thriving veg garden. Honest yet magical. Partial wheelchair access, uneven ground/boggy areas.

Embracing ecosystems, home, children, plants, food, wildlife . . .

22 ◆ GLENDURGAN
Mawnan Smith, Falmouth TR11 5JZ. National Trust, 01326 252020, www.nationaltrust.org.uk/glendurgan. *5m SW of Falmouth. Follow rd out of Mawnan Smith to Helford Passage. Brown signs to Glendurgan.* **Adm £7.50, chd £3.90. For NGS: Wed 1 May (10.30-5). For other opening times and information, please phone or see garden website.**
Three valleys of natural beauty and amazing plants. Discover lush tender plantings in the jungle-like lower valley and spiky arid plants basking on sunny upper slopes. Wander down to hamlet of Durgan on R Helford. Banks of wildflowers teeming with wildlife - and a 179 yr-old maze! 11am guided tour of the garden to learn about wildflower gardening and making the most out of micro-climates to grow tender plants for exotic effects.

23 ◆ GODOLPHIN
Godolphin Cross, Helston TR13 9RE. National Trust, 01736 763194, www.nationaltrust.org.uk. *5m NW of Helston. From Helston take A394 to Sithney Common, R onto B3302 to Leedstown, turn L, follow signs. From Hayle B3302 to Leedstown, turn R, follow signs. From W, B3280 through Goldsithney, R at Townsend.* **Adm £5, chd £2.50. For NGS: Sat 15 June (10-4). For other opening times and information, please phone or see garden website.**
A near-miraculous survival from C14 and C16, unchanged by fashions through the centuries. The garden is not about flowers and plants but about the surviving remains of a medieval pattern. Acquired by the National Trust in 2007. Limited wheelchair access, gravel paths, steep slopes, uneven surfaces and steps.

24 ◆ GODOLPHIN HILL GARDENS
Trewithen Terrace, Godolphin, Helston TR13 9TQ. John & Vicki Marshall, 07899 803899, vicki@thegardenlady.co.uk, www.thegardenlady.co.uk. *1m S of Godolphin Cross. From Godolphin Cross follow sign for Ashton. R at top of hill, signed Millpool & Trescowe. 300yds down Trewithen Terrace, turn R opp phone box, following signs to car park. No roadside parking, please.* **Adm £3.50, chd free. For NGS: Suns 16, 30 June (2-5). For information, please phone or see garden website.**
Set high on the southern slope of Godolphin Hill, this natural, informal and bio-diverse 3 acre garden has evolved over 20 years, working with nature rather than against it. Long borders containing large variety of species, shrubs and rambling roses along with herbs and herbaceous perennials. Wildlife pond, wildflower meadow, cut flower garden all surrounded by hedgerows which are positively spilling over with rambling roses. Displays of many moths found here in the gardens. These never fail to delight and fascinate visitors who think that only butterflies are colourful. Also open Weds/Thurs 22 May to 18 July (2-5). Featured in Cornwall Today.

HARTLAND ABBEY
See Devon

25 ◆ HEADLAND
Battery Lane, Polruan-by-Fowey PL23 1PW. Jean Hill, 01726 870243, www.headlandgarden.co.uk. *½ m SE of Fowey across estuary. Passenger ferry from Fowey, 10 min walk along West St & up Battery Lane. Or follow signs to Polruan (on E of Fowey Estuary). Ignore first car park, turn L for second car park (overlooking harbour), turn L (on foot) down St Saviour's Hill.* **Adm £3, chd £1. For NGS: Thurs 2, 9, 16, 23 May (2-6).**
1¼ -acre cliff garden with magnificent sea, coastal and estuary views on 3 sides. Planted to withstand salty gales yet includes subtropical plants with intimate places to sit and savour the views. Paths wind through the garden past rocky outcrops down to a secluded swimming cove. Open Thurs May - Aug (2-6). Partial wheelchair access, wheelchair users please phone beforehand.

26 ◆ THE LOST GARDENS OF HELIGAN
Pentewan, St Austell PL26 6EN. Heligan Gardens Ltd, 01726 845100, www.heligan.com. *5m S of St Austell. From St Austell take B3273 signed Mevagissey, follow signs.* **For opening times and information, please phone or see garden website.**
Lose yourself in The Nation's Favourite Garden (BBC poll) and discover the mysterious world of The Lost Gardens. With the finest productive gardens in Britain, a pioneering wildlife project and exotic subtropical jungle just some of the attractions waiting to be explored, you are sure to have a magical day out. Wheelchair access to Northern gardens. Armchair tour shows video of unreachable areas. Wheelchairs available at reception.

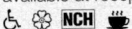

NCH

27 ◆ HIDDEN VALLEY GARDENS
Treesmill, Par PL24 2TU. Tricia Howard, 01208 873225, hiddenvalleygardens@yahoo.co.uk. *2m SW of Lostwithiel. From A390 between St Austell (5m) and Lostwithiel (2m) take B3269 signed Fowey, after 200yds turn R signed Treesmill. After 1m turn L, signed to the gardens (½ m). At end of lane after Colwith Farm. Special parking for unloading wheelchair.* **Adm £4, chd free. For NGS: Mon 12, Tue 13, Wed 14 Aug (10-6). For other opening times and information, please phone or email.**
Award-winning 3-acre colourful garden in 'hidden' valley with nursery. Cottage-style planting with herbaceous beds and borders, grasses, ferns and fruit. Gazebo with country views. Iris fairy well. Fishpond, Japanese garden and vegetable potager. August opening for special displays of agapanthus, dahlias, asters and crocosmia collections. Cream Teas. Children's and Wildlife quiz. Featured in RHS 'The Garden'.

28 HIGHCROFT GARDENS
Cargreen, Saltash PL12 6PA. Mr & Mrs B J Richards, 01752 848048, gardens@bjrichardsflowers.co.uk, www.bjrichardsflowers.co.uk. *5m NW of Saltash. 5m from Callington on A388 take Landulph Cargreen turning. 2m on, turn L at Landulph Xrds. Parking by Methodist Church.* Cream teas in Methodist Church. **Adm £4, chd free. Sun 4, Sun 18 Aug (1.30-5.30). Groups of 10+ also welcome by appt 8 July to 6 Sept.**
3-acre garden in beautiful Tamar Valley. Japanese-style garden, hot border, pastel border, grasses, arboretum with hemerocallis and new blue borders. Prairie planting containing 2,500 plants of herbaceous and grasses. Buddleia and shrub rose bank. Pond. All at their best in July, Aug and Sept.

29 NEW HIGHER TRENEDDEN
Peakswater, nr Pelynt PL13 2QE. Judy & Kevin Channer. *Between Pelynt and Fowey. Off Bodinnick Ferry Rd, from B3359, from East Taphouse or Pelynt. Turn off at 90° corner to follow signs to Valleybrook Cottages. Turn L and follow signs to car park and garden.* Home-made teas. **Adm £3.50, chd free. Sun 7 July (2-5).**
4-acre garden set in quiet valley with countryside views, ranges from established cottage garden to arboretum (planted 2006), with specimen trees, meadow with large pond, and board walk through marshland with an abundance of wild flowers. Gravel paths and several seating areas.

> Board walk through marshland with an abundance of wild flowers . . .

30 INCE CASTLE
Saltash PL12 4RA. Lord and Lady Boyd. *3m SW of Saltash. From A38 at Stoketon Cross take turn signed Trematon, then Elmgate. No large coaches.* Light refreshments Feb, home-made teas other days. **Adm £3.50, chd free. Suns 24 Feb (11-3); 17 Mar; 14 Apr; 14 July (2-5).**
Romantic garden at the end of winding lanes, surrounding C17 pink brick castle on a peninsula in the R Lynher. Old apple trees with bulbs, woodland garden with fritillaries, camellias and rhododendrons. Extraordinary 1960s shell house on edge of formal garden.

31 ◆ THE JAPANESE GARDEN & BONSAI NURSERY
St Mawgan TR8 4ET. Mr & Mrs Hore, 01637 860116, rob@thebonsainursery.com, www.japanesegarden.co.uk. *6m E of Newquay. 1½ m from N coast (Mawgan Porth Beach) Directions by car: (key in Newquay Airport for sat. nav) A30 >A39 > A3059 following signs to Airport & St. Mawgan. 'Japanese Garden' Brown & White Road Signs on A3059 and B3276. St. Mawgan village is directly below Airport.* **Adm £4.50, chd £2, group 10+ £3.50. For NGS: Mon 6 May, Sun 16 June (10-5). For other opening times and information, please phone or see garden website.**
East meets West in unique Garden for All Seasons. Spectacular Japanese maples and azaleas, symbolic teahouse, koi pond, bamboo grove, stroll, woodland, zen and moss gardens. An oasis of tranquillity. Entrance free to adjacent specialist Bonsai and Japanese garden nurseries. Featured in numerous publications. Gravel paths.

32 ◆ KEN CARO
Bicton, nr Liskeard PL14 5RF. Mr & Mrs K R Willcock, 01579 362446. *5m NE of Liskeard. From A390 to Callington turn off N at St Ive. Take Pensilva Rd, follow brown tourist signs, approx 1m off main rd. Plenty of parking*
Connoisseurs garden full of interest all yr round. Lily ponds, panoramic views, plenty of seating, picnic area, in all 10 acres. Garden started in 1970 has been rejuvenated over the last yr. Woodland walk, which has one of the largest beech trees. Good collection of yellow magnolias and herbaceous plants. Daily 10 Mar to 30 Sept (10-5.30), adm £5, chd £2, group visit £4.50. Partial wheelchair access.

33 ◆ LAMORRAN HOUSE
Upper Castle Road, St Mawes, Truro TR2 5BZ. Robert Dudley-Cooke, 01326 270800, info@lamorrangarden.co.uk. *A3078, R past garage at entrance to St Mawes. ¾ m on L. ¼ m from castle if using passenger ferry service.* **Adm £6.50, chd free. For NGS: Sun 5 May (2-5). For other opening times and information, please phone or email.**
4-acre subtropical garden overlooking Falmouth bay. Designed by owner in an Italianate/Cote d'Azur style. Extensive collection of Mediterranean and subtropical plants incl large collection of palms Butia capitata/Butia yatay and tree ferns. Reflects both design and remarkable micro-climate. Beautiful collection of Japanese azaleas and tender rhododendrons. Large collection of S-hemisphere plants.

34 ◆ LANHYDROCK HOUSE & GARDENS
Bodmin PL30 5AD. National Trust, 01208 265950, www.nationaltrust.org.uk. *2½ m SE of Bodmin. 2½ m on B3268. Stn: Bodmin Parkway 1¾ m walk.* **Garden**

adm £7.50, chd £4. For NGS: Tue 7 May, Thur 18 July (10-6). For other opening times and information, please phone or see garden website.
Large formal garden laid out 1857. Good summer colour with herbaceous borders, shrub garden with fine specimens of rhododendrons and magnolias and lovely views. Mainly Victorian country house, though some parts date back to the 17th century, with over 50 rooms open to the public. Garden tours on some days. Wheelchair access route around formal garden. Gravel paths and slopes to higher woodland garden.

35 LONG HAY
Treligga, Delabole PL33 9EE. Bett & Mick Hartley. *10m N of Wadebridge. Take B3314 Pendoggett to Delabole Rd. Turn L at Westdowns from Pendoggett, R from Delabole. Signed Treligga (N). After entering hamlet, follow parking signs.* Morning coffee & cream teas. **Adm £3.50, chd free. Sun 9 June (11-5.30).**
2/3 -acre abundant cottage garden with beautiful vistas of the N coast and sea. Herbaceous beds, shrubs, pond, greenhouse and lawns. Natural meadow of 1 acre overlooking sea with paths leading to copse, vegetable plots, orchard and greenhouse. Cornish coastal garden in beautiful but harsh environment.

36 ◆ MARSH VILLA GARDENS
St Andrew's Road, Par PL24 2LU. Judith Stephens, 01726 815920, www.marshvillagardens.com. *5m E of St Austell. Leave A390 at St Blazey T-lights, by church, into Station Rd, then 1st L, garden 600yds on L.* **Adm £4.50, chd free. For NGS: Sat 15 June; Sat 10, Sun 11 Aug (10-6). For other opening times and information, please phone or see garden website.**
Traditional English garden with mature trees, shrubs, lawns and overflowing flower beds. 100-yd hornbeam avenue divides garden, separating many different planting schemes. Enjoy marshland walks and natural water features. 3 acres full of ideas for budding gardeners. Featured in GGG, The Most Amazing Gardens in Britain, Gardens of Cornwall & The Independent.

37 MIDDLEWOOD HOUSE
Middlewood, North Hill, Launceston PL15 7NN. Brian & Cathy Toole, 01566 782118, brian.toole@btinternet.com. *7m S of Launceston, 7m N of Liskeard. At north end of village on B3254, lay-by directly outside house. Parking for up to 6 cars only and coaches up to 16-seater.* Home-made teas by arrangement. **Adm £3.50, chd free. Visitors welcome by appt 10 Apr to 27 July.**
Beautiful, tranquil 1 1/4 -acre garden nestling in Lynher valley. In a series of semi-formal destinations, spring shrubs and flowers are complemented by extensive herbaceous beds. Fernery, raised beds, water features, wooden and other architectural structures. Garden is sloped but good paths allow wheelchair access to most of it.

38 THE MILL HOUSE
Pendoggett, St Kew, Bodmin PL30 3HN. Trish & Jeremy Gibson, 01208 880308, trishgibson50@gmail.com, www.themillhouse.weebly.com. *2 1/2 m SE of Port Isaac. Take St Teath rd off B3314 at Pendoggett. Parking in adjoining field (disabled drop off nr house).* Cream teas. **Adm £3.50, chd free. Sun 30 June (2-5.30). Visitors also welcome by appt 1-14 July (2-5pm).**
1 1/2 -acre country garden on site of old mill with ponds, stream and bridges and extensive views across farmland. Colourful flower-filled summer and courtyard gardens with mature trees, shrubs, roses and grasses. This year we are working with local sculptors to display examples of their work as focal points in the garden. Partial disabled access.

39 ◆ MOYCLARE
Lodge Hill, Liskeard PL14 4EH. Elizabeth & Philip Henslowe, 01579 343114, elizabethhenslowe@btinternet.com, www.moyclare.co.uk. *1/2 m S of Liskeard centre. Approx 300yds S of Liskeard railway stn on St Keyne-Duloe rd (B3254).* **Adm £3.50, chd free. For NGS: Mon 6 May (2-5). For other opening times and information, please phone or see garden website.**
Gardened by one family for over 80 yrs; mature trees, shrubs and plants (many unusual, many variegated). Once most televised Cornish garden. Now revived and rejuvenated and still a plantsman's delight, still full of character. Camellia, brachyglottis and astrantia (all 'Moira Reid') and cytisus 'Moyclare Pink' originated here. Featured in Western Morning News.

Cornish coastal garden in beautiful but harsh environment . . .

40 NANFENTEN
Little Petherick PL27 7QT. Jackie & Trevor Bould, 01841 540480, nanfentensgarden@hotmail.co.uk, www.nanfentensgarden.com. *3m W of Wadebridge. A389 to Little Petherick. Turn into lane next to white cottage almost opp church, garden 200yds on L. Limited parking. Larger groups please use village hall car park.* Home-made teas. **Adm £3, chd free. Individuals and groups welcome by appt May to Aug.**
2/3 -acre plantsman's garden on side of valley. Views of Petherick Creek to Padstow. Cottage-style planting, rose walk, small pond. Steep sloping aspect to rear garden with many shrubs. Unusual sloping water feature. Pergola and summerhouse. A surprise around every corner with wide variety of plants. Many seating areas.

41 NAVAS HILL HOUSE
Bosanath Valley, Mawnan Smith, Falmouth TR11 5LL. Aline & Richard Turner, 01326 251233, alineturner@btinternet.com. *1 1/2 m from Trebah and Glendurgan Gdns. Follow signs to Trebah Gardens. Pass Trebah on L, follow rd, past Budock Vean Hotel, continue for just under 1m, take rd to R just before sharp L turn at end of creek, gdn 30yds on R. Ignor Sat Nav instructions to turn R just before Mawnan Smith. Plenty of parking.* Home-made teas. **Adm £3.50, chd free. Sun 12 May (2-5.30). Society groups welcome by appointment. Also open 12 May Trenarth (5-7.30).**
8 1/2 -acre garden divided into various

zones; kitchen garden with greenhouses, potting shed, fruit cages, orchard; 2 plantsman areas with specialist trees and shrubs; walled rose garden; ornamental garden with water features and rockery. Seating areas with views across wooded valley, not a car in sight! Walk to Trenarth (approx 15mins). Gravel & grass paths.

42 THE OLD RECTORY, TREVALGA

Trevalga, Boscastle PL35 0EA. Jacqueline M A Jarvis, 01840 250512. *Coastal rd between Tintagel and Boscastle. At Trevalga Xrds turn inland away from hamlet. Garden 1/2 m up narrow, steep hill. Parking limited, minibus/people-carrier only.* **Adm by donation.**

Visitors welcome by appt all yr.

North Cornish coast - challenging, exposed, NW-facing garden with panoramic sea views. 'From Field to Garden' a 25 yr project by artist owner. 1/2 m inland, elevation 500ft, informal incl woodland, perennial borders, sunken and walled areas. Yr-round interest may have appeal to gardening clubs. Has lookout at front of garden (4 stair - spiral stair access) with stunning views across circa 50 miles of the coastline - Hartland Point to Pendeen. Gravel driveways.

43 NEW THE OLD VICARAGE

Kea, Killiow, Truro TR3 6AE. Mrs Jenny Maidwell-Smith. *Take turning for Kea Church signed on A39 between Truro & Playing Place. Follow lane for 1/3 m, garden on R opp church. Park on rd on same side as church.* Home-made teas. **Adm £3.50, chd free. Sun 12 May (2-5).**

2-acre garden within woodland setting. Incl walled vegetable garden and greenhouse, herbaceous garden, shrub borders and courtyard garden. Some steps and gravel.

45 ◆ PENCARROW

Washaway, Bodmin PL30 3AG. Molesworth-St Aubyn family, 01208 841369, info@pencarrow.co.uk, www.pencarrow.co.uk. *4m NW of Bodmin. Signed off A389 & B3266.* **Adm £5.50, chd £2.50. For NGS: Wed 10 Apr (10-5.30). For other opening times and information, please phone or see garden website.**

50 acres of tranquil, family-owned Grade II* listed gardens. Superb specimen conifers, azaleas, magnolias and camellias galore. 700 varieties of rhododendron give a blaze of spring colour; blue hydrangeas line the mile long carriage drive throughout the summer. Discover the Iron Age hill fort, lake, Italian gardens and granite rockery. Free parking, dogs welcome, cafe and children's play area. Gravel paths, some steep slopes.

Year-round interest may have appeal to gardening clubs . . .

46 ◆ PENJERRICK GARDEN

Budock, nr Falmouth TR11 5ED. Mrs Rachel Morin, 01872 870105, www.penjerrickgarden.co.uk. *3m SW of Falmouth. Between Budock-Mawnan Smith, opp. Penmorvah Manor Hotel. Coach parking by arrangement.* **Adm £3, chd £1.50. For NGS: Sun 21 Apr (1.30-4.30). For other opening times and information, please phone or see garden website.**

10-acre subtropical garden, home to important rhododendron hybrids and the C19 Quaker Fox family. The upper garden contains rhododendrons, camellias, magnolias, bamboos, tree ferns and magnificent trees. Across a bridge a luxuriant valley features ponds in a wild primeval setting. Suitable for adventurous fit people wearing gumboots. A jungley experience.

47 ◆ PINSLA GARDEN & NURSERY

Cardinham PL30 4AY. Mark & Claire Woodbine, 01208 821339, cwoodbine@btinternet.com, www.pinslagarden.net. *3 1/2 m E of Bodmin. From A30 or Bodmin take A38 towards Plymouth, 1st L to Cardinham & Fletchers Bridge, 2m on R.* **Adm £3, chd free. For NGS: Sats, Suns 11, 12 May; 3, 4 Aug (9-5.30). For other opening times and information, please phone or see garden website.**

Romantic 1 1/2 acre artist's garden set in tranquil woodland. Naturalistic cottage garden planting surrounds our C18 fairytale cottage. Imaginative design, intense colour and scent, bees & butterflies. Unusual shade plants, acers and ferns. Fantastic range of plants & statues on display and for sale. Friendly advice in nursery. Gravel paths.

48 POLGWYNNE

Feock TR3 6SG. Amanda & Graham Piercy. *5m SW of Truro. Take A39 out of Truro signed Falmouth. At Playing Place turn L onto B3289. After 2m look for NGS signs.* Home-made teas. **Adm £4, chd free. Sun 28 Apr (2-5).**

Wonderful 4-acre garden by the sea, currently being renovated. Walled gardens, unusual planting, formal pond. Vegetable and picking gardens, with greenhouses whose mechanisms were described in The Journal of the RHS in 1852. Terraced lawns and what is believed to be the largest female Ginkgo biloba in Britain. Partial wheelchair access, gravel paths, some slopes.

49 ◆ POPPY COTTAGE GARDEN

Ruan High Lanes, Truro TR2 5JR. Tina & David Primmer, 01872 501411, poppycottagegarden@btinternet.com, www.poppycottagegarden.co.uk. *On the Roseland Peninsula. Turn off the A390 Truro - St Austell road onto the A3078 to St Mawes. Garden 4m out of Tregony.* **Adm £3.50, chd free. For NGS: Sat 22, Sun 23 June (2-5.30). For other opening times and information, please phone or see garden website.**

Situated on the beautiful Roseland peninsula, this 1-acre garden is a plantsman's paradise. Planted for yr-round interest and divided into rooms, its intense planting of shrubs and herbaceous under-planted with bulbs provides colourful and intriguing surprises around every corner. Small orchard with ornamental ducks and chickens. Featured in Land Love, GGG & The Most Amazing Gardens in Britain & Ireland.

Riverside Cottage

See more garden images at www.ngs.org.uk

PORTINGTON
See Devon

50 PRIMROSE FARM
Skinners Bottom, Redruth TR16 5EA. Barbara & Peter Simmons, 01209 890350, babs.simmons@btinternet.com, www.primrosefarmgarden.blogspot.com. *6m N of Truro. At Chiverton Cross r'about on A30 take Blackwater turn. Down hill, R by Red Lion PH up North Hill, 1st L (mini Xrd), garden approx ½ m on L.* Light refreshments. **Adm £3.50, chd free. Sat 22 June (1-5). Visitors also welcome by appt incl groups.**
Rambling informal cottage-style garden with woodland glade. Mature trees and shrubs, herbaceous and mixed borders. Pond with cascades and trickling fountain. Patio area with exotic plants. Gravel path to pergola with scented climbers and summerhouse. Vegetable patch and wildlife pond. New secret garden. A plantsman's garden. Featured on Radio Cornwall.

This 1-acre garden is a plantsman's paradise . . .

51 RIVERSIDE COTTAGE
St. Clement, Truro TR1 1SZ. Billa & Nick Jeans, 01872 263830, billajeans@gmail.com. *1½ m SE of Truro. From Police Station on A39 in Truro, follow signs for St Clement, up St Clement Hill. R at top of hill, continue to car park by river, park as directed.* Home-made teas. **Adm £3.50, chd free. Sun 14 Apr; Sun 26 May (2-5). Visitors also welcome by appt 1 Apr to 9 June, incl groups.**
Small garden on beautiful St Clement Estuary. Cottage garden. Small Victorian orchard and nut walk with wildflower areas, borders and vegetable patch. Steep paths and steps but plenty of seats. Walk through to C13 St Clement Church and 'living churchyard'.

52 ◆ ROSELAND HOUSE
Chacewater TR4 8QB. Mr & Mrs Pridham, 01872 560451, www.roselandhouse.co.uk. *4m W of Truro. At Truro end of main street. Parking in village car park (100yds) or on surrounding roads.* **Adm £4, chd free. For NGS: Sat 29, Sun 30 June (2-5). For other opening times and information, please phone or see garden website.**
The 1-acre garden is a mass of rambling roses and clematis. Ponds and borders alike are filled with plants, many rarely seen in gardens. National Collection of clematis viticella cvs can be seen in garden and display tunnel, along with a huge range of other climbing plants. Some slopes.
NCH

53 ◆ ST MICHAEL'S MOUNT
Marazion TR17 0HT. James & Mary St Aubyn, 01736 710507, clare.sandry@staubynestates.com, www.stmichaelsmount.co.uk. *2½ m E of Penzance. ½ m from shore at Marazion by Causeway; otherwise by motor boat.* **Adm £4, chd £2. For NGS: Sun 9 June (10.30-5). For other opening times and information, please phone or see garden website.**
Walled and terraced gardens are set against a dramatic backdrop of some 200ft from base of castle. The recently replanted wall gardens were built in C18 while many exotic succulents and other semi-tropicals flourish in the terraces.

54 SCORRIER HOUSE
Scorrier, Redruth TR16 5AU. Richard & Caroline Williams. *2½ m E of Redruth. From Truro A390, at 4th r'about slip road A30 to Redruth for 2½ m, A3047 under railway bridge, L at mini r'about to B3287 for ½ m, R on B3207 for 200yds, R by Lodge House. From Falmouth take A393 to Redruth for 7m then B3258, turn at 2nd lodge.* Home-made teas. **Adm £4, chd free. Sun 17 Mar (2-4.30).**
Scorrier House and gardens have been in the Williams family for 7 generations. The gardens are set in parkland with conservatory, knot garden, formal garden with herbaceous borders and walled garden with camellias, magnolias and rare trees, some collected by the famous plant collector William Lobb. Unfenced swimming pool.

55 ◆ TREBAH
Mawnan Smith TR11 5JZ. Trebah Garden Trust, 01326 252200, mail@trebah-garden.co.uk, www.trebah-garden.co.uk. *4m SW of Falmouth. Follow tourist signs from Hillhead r'about on A39 approach to Falmouth or Treliever Cross r'about on junction of A39-A394. Parking for coaches.* **For information, please phone or see garden website.**
26-acre S-facing ravine garden, planted in 1830s. Extensive collection rare/mature trees/shrubs incl glades; huge tree ferns 100yrs old, subtropical exotics. Hydrangea collection covers 2½ acres. Water garden, waterfalls, rock pool stocked with mature koi carp. Enchanted garden for plantsman/artist/family. Play area/trails for children. Use of private beach. March to Oct £8.50, chd £2.50; Nov to Feb £4, chd £1. Steep paths in places. 2 motorised vehicles available, please book in advance.

56 TREBARTHA
nr Launceston PL15 7PE. The Latham Family. *6m SW of Launceston. North Hill, SW of Launceston nr junction of B3254 & B3257. No coaches.* Home-made teas. **Adm £4, chd free. Suns 12 May; 16 June; 13 Oct (2-5).**
Wooded area with lake surrounded by walks of flowering shrubs; woodland trail through fine woods with cascades and waterfalls; American glade with fine trees. Major but exciting renovations are in progress in these fine landscape/woodland gardens which will not interfere with your walk but we do request that visitors keep to the signed paths and other directions.

57 ◆ TRELISSICK
Feock TR3 6QL. National Trust, 01872 862090, www.nationaltrust.org.uk/trelissick. *4m S of Truro. From A39 Truro to Falmouth, turn onto B3289 at Playing Place. Follow signs to Trelissick and King Harry Ferry.* **Adm £8, chd £4. For NGS: Wed 1 May (10.30-5). For other opening times and information, please phone or see garden website.**
Woodland garden with fantastic views out to water on 3 sides. Contrasts between light and shade and inspiration from gardening in a variety

of woodland environments. Mixed borders designed for long term interest with a mixture of popular hardy favourites and tender exotics with foliage interest. Four summerhouses with lovely views. Guided tour of garden to learn about woodland gardening and mixed borders for lasting impact 2.30pm. Partially accessible by wheelchair, map provided. Two manual wheelchairs available and also power mobility vehicles, ring to book these in advance.

58 ◆ TREMENHEERE SCULPTURE GARDEN

Penzance TR20 8YL. Drs Neil Armstrong & Jane Martin, 01736 448089, www.tremenheere.co.uk. *1m E of Penzance. From Gulval church proceed ¾ m due E. L at sign Entrance, gates straight ahead.* Café. **Adult adm £6.50, 11-15 yrs £3, under 11's free. For NGS: Sun 13 Oct (10-5). For other opening times and information, please phone or see garden website.**
Spectacular valley setting overlooking St Michael's Mount provides microclimate for large scale subtropical planting. Habitats from ponds to hot slopes provide wide variety of landscaping styles. High quality contemporary sculpture by internationally-renowned artists. Farmers' Market 13 Oct. Described in Sunday Times as one of the most exciting new gardens in the country. Featured in The Independent and on BBC Gardeners' World.

59 TRENARTH

High Cross, Constantine TR11 5JN. Lucie Nottingham, 01326 340444, lmnottingham@tiscali.co.uk, www.trenarthgardens.co.uk. *6m SW of Falmouth. Nearest main rds A39-A394 Truro to Helston-Falmouth: follow signs for Constantine. At High Cross garage, 1½ m before Constantine, turn L signed Mawnan, then R after 30yds down dead end lane. Garden at end of lane.* Cream teas. **Adm £3.50, chd free. Evening Opening, wine, Sun 12 May (5-7.30); Sun 4 Aug (2-5). Also open Navas Hill House 12 May only (2-5.30). Visitors also welcome by appt Mar to Oct. Guided tours.**
3-acre garden around C17 farmhouse in peaceful pastoral setting. Yr-round interest. Emphasis on tender and unusual plants, structure and form. Courtyard, listed garden walls, yew rooms, vegetable garden, traditional potting shed, orchard, new woodland area and palm and gravel garden. Circular walk down ancient green lane via little lake to Trenarth Bridge, returning through bluebell woods. Abundant wildlife. Bees in tree bole, lesser horseshoe bat colony, swallows and house martins nesting, wildflowers and butterflies. New 'benchmarked' walk, and 'wolery'.

Farmers' Market 13 October . . .

60 ◆ TRENGWAINTON

Madron, Penzance TR20 8RZ. National Trust, 01736 363148, www.nationaltrust.org.uk/trengwainton-garden. *2m NW of Penzance. ½ m W of Heamoor. On Penzance-Morvah rd (B3312), ½ m off St Just rd (A3071). Signed from A30.* **Adm £7, chd £3.50. For NGS: Sun 5 May; Sun 16 June (10.30-5). For other opening times and information, please phone or see garden website.**
Glorious spring displays of magnolias, rhododendrons, azaleas and camellias; walled kitchen garden built to dimensions of Noahs Ark and breathtaking views across Mounts Bay. Lose yourself amongst winding, wooded paths, picnic by the stream or simply find a quiet corner to sit within Trengwainton's peaceful 25 acres. WW2 'Dig for Victory' allotment, complete with reproduction Anderson shelter. Free guided tour 11.30am. Main drive tarmac, other paths gravel. Slope, wheelchair assistance may be needed. 2 manual wheelchairs available, booking essential.

61 ◆ TRERICE

Kestle Mill, Newquay TR8 4PG. National Trust, 01637 875404, www.nationaltrust.org.uk/trerice. *3m SE of Newquay. From Newquay via A392 & A3058; turn R at Kestle Mill (NT signs) or signed from A30 at Summercourt via A3058.* **Adm £8, chd £4. For NGS: Wed 1 May (10.30-4.30). For other opening times and information, please phone or see garden website.**
Summer/autumn-flowering garden unusual in content and layout and for neutral alkaline soil varieties. Orchard planted with old varieties of fruit trees. Experimental Tudor garden developed in partnership with local primary school. Guided tour of the garden at 11am to learn about archeology and plans to recreate lost gardens.

GROUP OPENING

62 TRETHEW GARDENS

Lanlivery, Bodmin PL30 5BZ. *3m W of Lostwithiel. On rd between Lanlivery and Luxulyan. Signed from these 2 villages and from the A390.* Home-made teas. **Combined adm £5, chd free. Sun 4 Aug (12-6).**

TRETHEW
Ginnie & Giles Clotworthy

TRETHEW MILL
Becky Martin

2 adjacent gardens in markedly different styles on secluded hillside with magnificent and far-reaching views. Lichen and moss-covered granite abounds. Trethew: Series of profusely planted and colourful rooms surrounding an ancient Cornish farmhouse. Features incl terracing with pergola, parterre, gazebo and herbaceous borders within yew hedges, all overlooking orchard and pond. Trethew Mill: Garden has developed around mill stream which flows into the garden over water wheel and through series of ponds. Strong, natural features, especially granite, complement bold, informal planting. Grasses, ferns and exotic plants are used to create areas of distinctly different moods.

63 TREVOOLE FARM

Trevoole, Praze-an-Beeble, Camborne TR14 0RN. Mr & Mrs Stevens, 01209 831243, beth@trevoolefarm.co.uk, www.trevoolefarm.co.uk. *3m SSW of Camborne. From Camborne on B3303 towards Helston. Past*

Pendarves Nature Reserve, L into lane just after 2 mine chimneys. Home-made teas. **Adm £3, chd free. Sun 16 June (2-5).**
The gardens are nestled around C18 smallholding. Old farmhouse and shade garden, charming courtyard of restored granite buildings. Old orchard and herb garden. Patchwork potager. New bog garden, Victorian greenhouse, shepherd's hut cottage garden and rose walk. Featured in Cornwall Today and Country Living magazine. Gravel paths.

64 TREWAN HALL

St Columb TR9 6DB. Mrs Jo Davies, www.trewan-hall.co.uk. *6m E of Newquay. N of St Columb Major, off A39 to Wadebridge. 1st turning on L signed to St Eval & Talskiddy. Entrance ¾ m on L in woodland. Map on website.* Tea. **Adm £3.50, chd free. Sun 19 May (2-5).**
Set within 36 acres of parkland, fields and broadleaved woodland, with features incl flower borders, rose beds, kitchen garden enclosed by recently-restored cob wall and traditional orchard with beehive. Driveway bordered by mature rhododendron and hydrangea leading to Grade II star listed C17 manor house (not open). Children's play area. 156 solar panels in back paddock. Long standing David Bellamy Gold Conservation Award. Disabled WC.

65 ◆ TREWIDDEN GARDEN

Buryas Bridge, Penzance TR20 8TT. Mr A R Bolitho, 01736 363021/351979, www.trewiddengarden.co.uk. *2m W of Penzance. Entry on A30 just before Buryas Bridge. Sat nav*

Cotehele

Recycle – bring a bag for your plant purchases

TR19 6AU. **Adm £6, chd free. For NGS: Sun 17 Mar (10.30-5.30, last adm 4.30). For other opening times and information, please phone or see garden website.**
Historic Victorian garden with magnolias, camellias and magnificent tree ferns planted within ancient tin workings. Tender, rare and unusual exotic plantings create a riot of colour thoughout the season. Water features, specimen trees and artefacts from Cornwall's tin industry provide a wide range of interest for all.

66 ◆ TREWITHEN

Truro TR2 4DD. Mr & Mrs Michael Galsworthy, 01726 883647, info@trewithengardens.co.uk, www.trewithengardens.co.uk. *1/2 m East of Probus. Entrance on A390 Truro-St Austell road. Sign posted*. **For opening times and information, please phone or see garden website.**
Internationally renowned and historic garden of 30 acres laid out between 1912 and 1960 with much of original seed and plant material collected by Ward Forrest. Towering magnolias and rhododendrons and very large collection of camellias. Flattish ground amidst original woodland park and magnificent landscaped lawn vistas. Rose garden currently in development. Garden is now responding to the challenge of climate change with many new introductions. As part of Cornwall Red Squirrel Project aiming to reintroduce red squirrels to the Lizard & Penwith peninsulas, Trewithen is proud to be part of this breeding programme and currently has 3 squirrels on view to the public. In 2012 the gardens were awarded the prestigious honour of becoming an International Camellia Garden of Excellence - one of thirty worldwide. Gravel paths.

Lush and blue in July with swathes of agapanthus . . .

67 WATERS EDGE

North Corner, Coverack TR12 6TG. Lizzie Cartwright, lizzie@lizziebrownart.co.uk, www.lizziebrownart.co.uk. *10m from Helston. From Helston take B3293. Park in Coverack car parks, follow yellow signs, garden next to Porthgwarra Nursing Home*. Home-made teas. **Adm £3, chd free. Fri 19, Sun 21, Sun 28 July (2-5). Visitors also welcome by appt July to Aug.**
Coverack, on the unique Lizard Peninsula, is a Conservation Area and SSSI. Small, narrow, sheltered garden, lush and blue in July with swathes of agapanthus. Hidden seating, stream, pond and artist's studio to enjoy. Homemade cakes on terrace with stunning views of harbour, beach and sea. Artist's studio open Children's Creature Trail and painting. Featured in Cornwall Life.

68 WAYE COTTAGE

Lerryn, nr Lostwithiel PL22 0QQ. Malcolm & Jennifer Bell, 01208 872119. *4m S of Lostwithiel. Village parking, garden 10min, level stroll along riverbank/stepping stones*. Cream teas. **Adm £3.50, chd free. Sat 13, Sun 14 July (2-5). Visitors also welcome by appt 27 Apr to 7 Sept, max 30.**
Never immaculate but abundantly-planted, this 1-acre cottage garden has large and interesting collection of plants, some rare and unusual. Wander along the meandering paths, sit on the many benches and enjoy stunning river views. Steep and sadly only for those sound in wind and limb. Attractive riverside village with pub and shop which supplies picnics to eat on trestle tables on the village green.

WICK FARM GARDENS
See Devon

Cornwall County Volunteers

County Organiser
William Croggon, Creed Lodge, Creed, Grampound, Truro TR2 4SL, 01872 530499, wrcroggon@btinternet.com

County Treasurer
Andrew Flint, Wheal Eliza, Boscundle, St.Austell PL25 3RJ, 01726 879336, flints@elizaholidays.co.uk

Booklet Coordinator
Peter Stanley, Mazey Cottage, Tangies, Gunwalloe, Helston TR12 7PU, 01326 565868, stanley.m2@sky.com

Publicity
Nutty Lim, Kilmarth, Par PL24 2TL, 01726 815247, christianne.gf.lim@gmail.com

Assistant County Organisers
Barry Champion, Lillys Cottage, Dicky Lane, Trelissick, Feock, Truro TR3 6QL, 01872 870750, wbchampion2003@yahoo.co.uk
Ginnie Clotworthy, Trethew, Lanlivery, Bodmin PL30 5BZ, 01208 872612, giles.clotworthy@btopenworld.com
Bryan Coode, Carwinnick, Grampound, Truro TR2 4RJ, 01726 882488, bhcoode@btconnect.com
Lally Croggon, Creed Lodge, Creed, Grampound, Truro TR2 4SL, 01872 530499
Sar Gordon, Hillburn Cottage, Henwood, Liskeard PL14 5BP, 01579 362076, sar.gordon@virgin.net
Caroline Latham, Stonaford Manor, North Hill, Launceston PL15 7PE, 01566 782970
Alison O'Connor, Tregoose, Grampound, Truro TR2 4DB, 01726 882460, tregoose@tregoose.co.uk
Marion Stanley, Mazey Cottage, Tangies, Gunwalloe, Helston TR12 7PU, 01326 565868, stanley.m2@sky.com
Virginia Vyvyan-Robinson, Mellingey Mill House, St Issey, Wadebridge PL27 7QU, 01841 540511

CUMBRIA

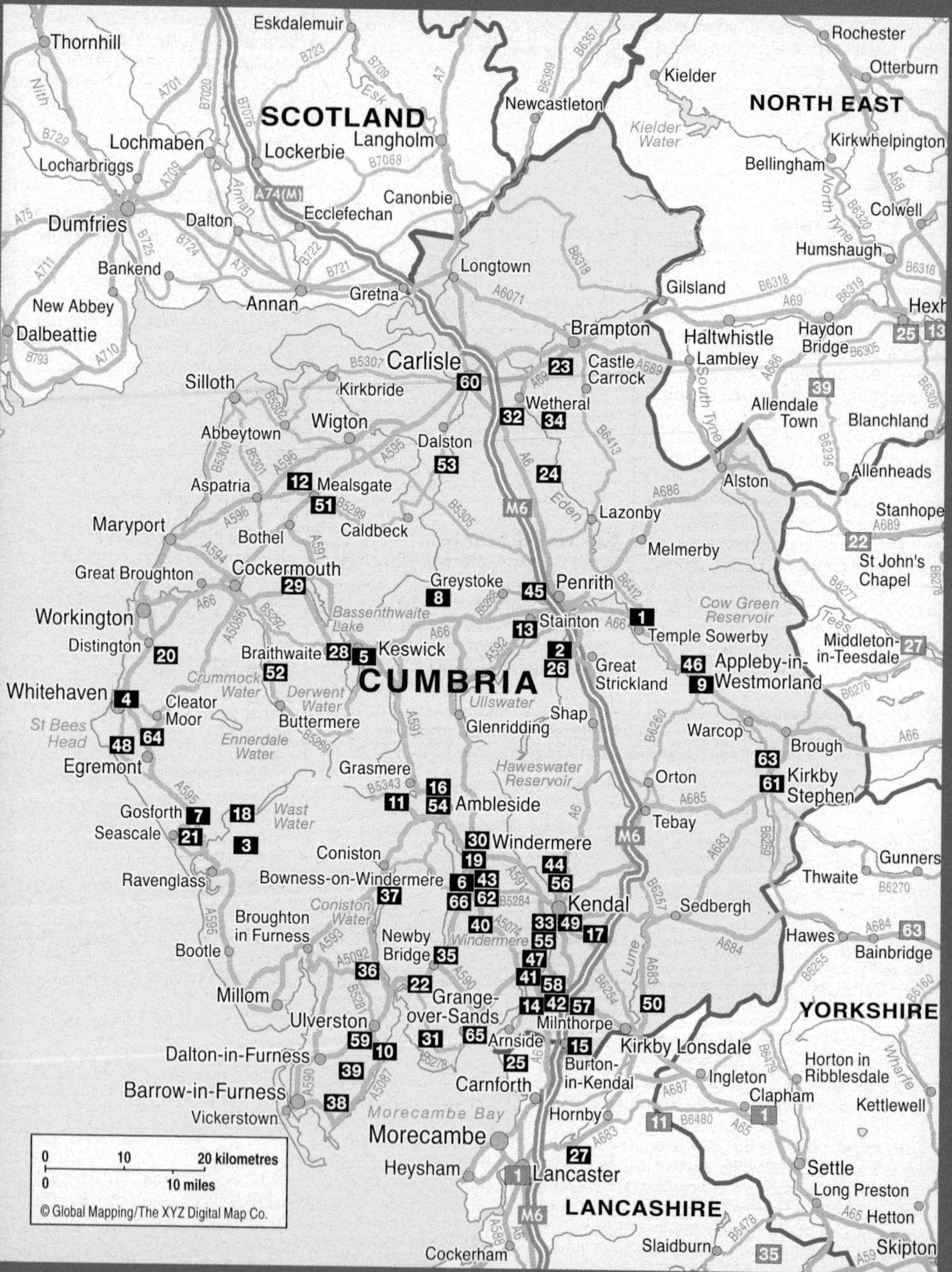
SCOTLAND
NORTH EAST
CUMBRIA
YORKSHIRE
LANCASHIRE
Thornhill
Eskdalemuir
Lochmaben
Lockerbie
Langholm
Locharbriggs
Dumfries
Dalton
Ecclefechan
Canonbie
Bankend
New Abbey
Dalbeattie
Annan
Gretna
Longtown
Newcastleton
Kielder
Kielder Water
Rochester
Otterburn
Kirkwhelpington
Bellingham
Colwell
Humshaugh
Gilsland
Haltwhistle
Haydon Bridge
Brampton
Lambley
Allendale Town
Blanchland
Carlisle
Silloth
Kirkbride
Castle Carrock
Wetheral
Wigton
Abbeytown
Dalston
Aspatria
Mealsgate
Alston
Allenheads
Stanhope
Lazonby
Caldbeck
Maryport
Bothel
Melmerby
St John's Chapel
Great Broughton
Cockermouth
Greystoke
Penrith
Workington
Bassenthwaite Lake
Stainton
Temple Sowerby
Cow Green Reservoir
Middleton-in-Teesdale
Distington
Braithwaite
Keswick
Great Strickland
Appleby-in-Westmorland
Whitehaven
Cleator Moor
Crummock Water
Derwent Water
Buttermere
Ullswater
Glenridding
Shap
Warcop
Brough
St Bees Head
Egremont
Ennerdale Water
Grasmere
Haweswater Reservoir
Orton
Kirkby Stephen
Gosforth
Seascale
Wast Water
Ambleside
Tebay
Windermere
Coniston
Ravenglass
Bowness-on-Windermere
Thwaite
Gunnerside
Kendal
Sedbergh
Broughton in Furness
Coniston Water
Newby Bridge
Windermere
Hawes
Bainbridge
Bootle
Millom
Grange-over-Sands
Ulverston
Milnthorpe
Arnside
Kirkby Lonsdale
Dalton-in-Furness
Burton-in-Kendal
Ingleton
Horton in Ribblesdale
Clapham
Barrow-in-Furness
Carnforth
Vickerstown
Morecambe Bay
Hornby
Kettlewell
Morecambe
Heysham
Lancaster
Settle
Long Preston
Hetton
Slaidburn
Skipton
Cockerham
0 10 20 kilometres
0 10 miles
© Global Mapping/The XYZ Digital Map Co.

Opening Dates

February

Sunday 17
42 Lower Rowell Farm & Cottage
57 Summerdale House

Friday 22
59 Swarthmoor Hall

Saturday 23
59 Swarthmoor Hall

Sunday 24
57 Summerdale House
59 Swarthmoor Hall

Monday 25
59 Swarthmoor Hall

Tuesday 26
59 Swarthmoor Hall

Wednesday 27
59 Swarthmoor Hall

March

Friday 1
59 Swarthmoor Hall

Saturday 2
59 Swarthmoor Hall

Sunday 3
59 Swarthmoor Hall

Sunday 24
1 Acorn Bank
16 Dora's Field
28 High Moss
30 Holehird Gardens
45 Newton Rigg College Gardens
53 Rose Castle (by appointment only)
54 Rydal Hall

Sunday 31
57 Summerdale House

April

Friday 5
11 Copt Howe
57 Summerdale House

Sunday 7
64 Woodend House

Tuesday 9
11 Copt Howe

Friday 12
11 Copt Howe
57 Summerdale House

Friday 19
11 Copt Howe
57 Summerdale House

Tuesday 23
11 Copt Howe

Friday 26
57 Summerdale House

Saturday 27
5 Bishop's House
10 Conishead Priory & Buddhist Temple

Sunday 28
10 Conishead Priory & Buddhist Temple

From spring bulbs; through summer roses and herbaceous plants galore; to the late perennials and graceful grasses well into late autumn . . .

May

Wednesday 1
11 Copt Howe

Friday 3
8 Chapelside
57 Summerdale House

Saturday 4
8 Chapelside

Sunday 5
3 Beckstones
6 Brackenrigg Lodge
8 Chapelside
57 Summerdale House
62 Windy Hall

Wednesday 8
11 Copt Howe

Friday 10
57 Summerdale House

Saturday 11
5 Bishop's House
19 Gatesbield

Sunday 12
14 Dallam Tower

Tuesday 14
11 Copt Howe

Friday 17
8 Chapelside
11 Copt Howe
57 Summerdale House

Saturday 18
8 Chapelside

Sunday 19
1 Acorn Bank
8 Chapelside
43 Matson Ground

Friday 24
11 Copt Howe
57 Summerdale House

Sunday 26
7 Buckbarrow House
18 Galesyke
24 Hazel Cottage
28 High Moss
29 Higham Hall

Monday 27
7 Buckbarrow House
18 Galesyke
26 Helton Village Gardens

Friday 31
8 Chapelside
57 Summerdale House

June

Saturday 1
8 Chapelside

Sunday 2
6 Brackenrigg Lodge
8 Chapelside
20 Gilgarran Gardens
62 Windy Hall
65 Yewbarrow House

Wednesday 5
11 Copt Howe

Friday 7
57 Summerdale House

Sunday 9
12 Crookdake Farm
25 Hazelwood Farm

Wednesday 12
11 Copt Howe

Friday 14
8 Chapelside
57 Summerdale House

National Gardens Weekend

Saturday 15
4 Berriedale
8 Chapelside
52 Rannerdale Cottage

Sunday 16
1 Acorn Bank
8 Chapelside
40 Low Fell West
51 Quarry Hill House
52 Rannerdale Cottage
56 Sprint Mill

Wednesday 19
9 Church View
22 Haverthwaite Lodge
35 Lakeside Hotel & Rocky Bank

Thursday 20
11 Copt Howe
38 Leece & Dendron Village Gardens (Evening by appointment only)

Friday 21
57 Summerdale House

Saturday 22
50 Park House

Sunday 23
24 Hazel Cottage
27 Heywood House
38 Leece & Dendron Village Gardens
47 Orchard Cottage
50 Park House
66 Yews

Wednesday 26
45 Newton Rigg College Gardens

Friday 28
8 Chapelside
57 Summerdale House

Saturday 29
5 Bishop's House
8 Chapelside
42 Lower Rowell Farm & Cottage

Sunday 30
2 Askham Hall
8 Chapelside
15 Dalton Hamlet Gardens
17 Ewebank Farm
34 Ivy House
42 Lower Rowell Farm & Cottage

July

Friday 5
57 Summerdale House

Sunday 7
23 Hayton Village Gardens
27 Heywood House
39 Little Urswick Village Gardens
57 Summerdale House
65 Yewbarrow House

Friday 12
8 Chapelside
57 Summerdale House

Saturday 13
8 Chapelside

Sunday 14
8 Chapelside
48 Orchard House
61 Westview
63 Winton Park

Wednesday 17
9 Church View

Thursday 18
30 Holehird Gardens
54 Rydal Hall

Friday 19
57 Summerdale House

Saturday 20
55 Sizergh Castle

Sunday 21
33 Horticare
56 Sprint Mill
64 Woodend House

Friday 26
57 Summerdale House

Sunday 28
21 Hall Senna
32 Holme Meadow

August

Friday 2
57 Summerdale House

Sunday 4
25 Hazelwood Farm
65 Yewbarrow House

Thursday 8
54 Rydal Hall

Friday 9
57 Summerdale House

Sunday 11
39 Little Urswick Village Gardens
44 Meadow House

Friday 16
57 Summerdale House

Saturday 17
58 Sunnyside

Sunday 18
58 Sunnyside

Wednesday 21
9 Church View

Friday 23
57 Summerdale House

Sunday 25
4 Berriedale

Wednesday 28
22 Haverthwaite Lodge
35 Lakeside Hotel & Rocky Bank

Friday 30
31 Holker Hall Gardens
57 Summerdale House

September

Sunday 1
49 8 Oxenholme Road
65 Yewbarrow House

Wednesday 18
9 Church View

October

Wednesday 2
45 Newton Rigg College Gardens

Wildlife sanctuary, red squirrels, badgers, slow-worms, lizards, hotel for wild birds . . .

Wednesday 16
9 Church View

Sunday 20
40 Low Fell West

February 2014

Sunday 16
42 Lower Rowell Farm & Cottage
57 Summerdale House

Gardens open to the public

1 Acorn Bank
10 Conishead Priory & Buddhist Temple
11 Copt Howe
16 Dora's Field
30 Holehird Gardens
31 Holker Hall Gardens
54 Rydal Hall
55 Sizergh Castle
59 Swarthmoor Hall
60 Tullie House

By appointment only

36 Langholme Mill
37 Lawson Park
41 4 Low Pastures
46 Olde Oaks

Also open by Appointment ☎

3 Beckstones
4 Berriedale
5 Bishop's House
7 Buckbarrow House
8 Chapelside
9 Church View
12 Crookdake Farm
15 Pear Tree Cottage, Dalton Hamlet Gardens
21 Hall Senna
22 Haverthwaite Lodge
28 High Moss
32 Holme Meadow
33 Horticare
35 Lakeside Hotel & Rocky Bank
40 Low Fell West
42 Lower Rowell Farm & Cottage
43 Matson Ground
47 Orchard Cottage
49 8 Oxenholme Road
50 Park House
51 Quarry Hill House
56 Sprint Mill
57 Summerdale House
62 Windy Hall
64 Woodend House
65 Yewbarrow House

The Gardens

1 ◆ ACORN BANK
Temple Sowerby CA10 1SP. National Trust, 017683 61893, www.nationaltrust.org.uk. *6m E of Penrith. Off A66; ½ m N of Temple Sowerby. Bus: Penrith-Appleby or Carlisle-Darlington; alight Culgaith Rd end.* **Adm £5.50, chd £2.75. For NGS: Suns 24 Mar; 19 May; 16 June (10-5). For other opening times and information, please phone or see garden website.**
Sheltered and tranquil walled gardens contain a herb garden with more than 250 medicinal and culinary plants. Traditional apple orchards and mixed borders. Beyond the walls lie woodland walks with a wonderful display of snowdrops, daffodils and wild flowers in spring. Dogs welcome on leads on woodland walks. 24 March, Cartmel to Carlisle: Wordsworth's Daffodil Legacy. Access map and information available.

2 ASKHAM HALL
Askham, Penrith CA10 2PF. Countess of Lonsdale, 01931 712348, www.askhamhall.co.uk. *5m S of Penrith. Turn off A6 for Lowther and Askham.* Home-made teas. **Adm £5.50, chd free (share to Askham and Lowther Churches). Sun 30 June (2-5).**
Askham Hall is a pele tower, incorporating C14, C16 and early C18 elements in courtyard plan (opening this year as luxury accommodation). Splendid formal outlines of garden with terraces of herbaceous borders and topiary, dating back to C17. Meadow area with trees and pond.

3 BECKSTONES
Eskdale CA19 1TN. Ron & Audrey Postlethwaite, 019467 23372, a.postlethwaite37@btinternet.com. *17m S of Whitehaven. Situated in Eskdale 500yds from The Bower House Inn. Follow A595 Turn towards Eskdale, follow NGS signs to Beckstones to rear of Fell View garage.* Home-made teas. **Adm £3, chd free. Sun 5 May (10-5). Visitors also welcome by appt.**
A mature garden of 1½ acres. A large selection of specimen trees and shrubs. Mixed borders with many interesting and unusual perennials. Wildlife pond and waterfall. Vegetable garden. Marvellous views of The Eskdale Fells. Featured in Cumbria Life.

4 BERRIEDALE
15 Loop Road South, Whitehaven CA28 7TN. Enid & John Stanborough, 01946 695467. *From S, A595 through T-lights onto Loop Rd approx 150yds on R. From N, A595 onto Loop Rd at Pelican Garage, garden approx 1½ m on L.* Home-made teas. **Adm £3, chd free. Sat 15 June; Sun 25 Aug (2-5). Visitors also welcome by appt Mar to Dec.**
Large cottage style garden divided into several areas including Japanese style, wildlife, patio, large vegetable garden with fruit trees, show class vegetables and flowers. Large front garden, 2 lawns surrounded by flower borders and small pond. Large pond with seating area leading to greenhouse of fuchsias and plants for sale. Oil paintings by local artist. Featured in Cumbria Life, local papers and on Radio Cumbria. Limited wheelchair access.

5 NEW BISHOP'S HOUSE

Ambleside Road, Keswick CA12 4DD. Mrs Alison Newcome, 01768 773430/07530 572480. *Turn off A66 at Keswick onto A591 to Windermere. At t-junction tn L up steep hill. After ½ m tn R signed Castlerigg Manor. Continue to St John's Church on L. Driveway marked with slate plaque.* Home-made teas. **Adm £3, chd free. Sats 27 Apr; 11 May; 29 June (2-6). Visitors also welcome by appt.**

The garden is approx 1 acre and comprises a mixture of woodland garden, small rockery, herbaceous bed, pond, orchard area, trees and shrubs. A Garden 'in the making' only having been recreated in the last three years, so a lot of the structures and plantings are new amidst the mature beech and yew trees which provided the starting point of this development. Gravel paths.

6 BRACKENRIGG LODGE

Windy Hall Road, Bowness-on-Windermere LA23 3HY. Lynne Bush, www.brackenriggs.co.uk. *½ m S of Bowness. Just off B5284 on Windy Hall Rd, opp Linthwaite House Hotel entrance.* **Adm £4, chd free. Suns 5 May; 2 June (10-5). Combined with Windy Hall adm £6.**

3 acres of wildlife garden run on organic lines with a combination of native and cultivated plants, shrubs and trees. Water features created from a diverted culvert giving streams, waterfall and pond. Woodland area, bog garden, wild flower meadows. The new deer fence works a treat. Stout footwear needed.

7 BUCKBARROW HOUSE

Denton Park Court, Gosforth CA20 1BN. John Maddison, 019467 25431, jhnmaddison@gmail.com. *13m S of Whitehaven. Turn off A595. Through centre of Gosforth Village. At 'Y' junction take L fork towards Wasdale. After 150yds turn L (before church) into Denton Park. Keep bearing R. House is last on R in Denton Park Court.* Light refreshments. **Adm £3, chd free. Sun 26, Mon 27 May (11-5). Also open Galesyke. Visitors also welcome by appt May to Sept.**

Small densely-planted garden with a number of compartments incl wildlife pond, shrub area, cottage garden borders, and natural stream. Larger area taken over by Japanese style garden including small gravel garden. Decking area. Decorative stone front garden. Favourite plant acers. A visitor said 'A small garden which appears to be much larger than it is!' Grass taken over by green slate. Increasing Japanese Garden influence.

A visitor said 'A small garden which appears to be much larger than it is . . . !'

8 CHAPELSIDE

Mungrisdale, Penrith CA11 0XR. Tricia & Robin Acland, 017687 79672. *12m W of Penrith. On A66 take unclassified rd N, signed Mungrisdale. After 2 miles, house is far end of scattered village on L immed after tiny church on R. Use parish church room parking at foot of our short drive.* **Adm £3, chd free (share to Mungrisdale Parish Church). Fri 3, Sat 4, Sun 5, Fri 17, Sat 18, Sun 19, Fri 31 May; Sat 1, Sun 2, Fri 14, Sat 15, Sun 16, Fri 28, Sat 29, Sun 30 June; Fri 12, Sat 13, Sun 14 July (1-5). Visitors also welcome by appt, refreshments for groups by arrangement.**

1-acre mature organic garden below fell, around C18 farmhouse and outbuildings, latter mainly open. Tiny stream, large pond. Alpine, herbaceous, raised, gravel, damp and shade beds, bulbs in grass. Extensive range of plants, many unusual. art constructions in and out, local stone used creatively. Fine views, so unkind winds. Shown on BBC Look North.

9 CHURCH VIEW

Bongate, Appleby-in-Westmorland CA16 6UN. Mrs H Holmes, 017683 51397, engcougars@btinternet.com, www.engcougars.co.uk/church-view. *Northbound on A66 take B6542 to Appleby. After 2m St Michael's Church on L garden opp. Southbound on A66 take Appleby slip rd, B6542 under railway bridge, pass R Eden on R and continue up hill to Royal Oak Inn. Garden next door opp church.* **Adm £3.50, chd free. Weds 19 June; 17 July; 21 Aug; 18 Sept; 16 Oct (12-4). Visitors also welcome by appt.**

A modern cottage garden with coherent layers of colour, texture and interest. From spring bulbs; through the lushness of summer roses and herbaceous plants galore; to the inherent richness of late perennials and graceful grasses well into late autumn. New, a vegetable production area! All providing joy for humans, birds, bees and butterflies. Approx ⅖ acre. Featured in 'Cumbria Life'. The main garden is on a sloping site, gravel paths.

CLEARBECK HOUSE

See Lancashire, Merseyside & Greater Manchester

10 ◆ CONISHEAD PRIORY & BUDDHIST TEMPLE

A5087 Coast Road, Ulverston LA12 9QQ. Manjushri Kadampa Meditation Centre, 01229 584029, visits@manjushri.org. *2m S of Ulverston on A5087 Coast Road. 30 mins from M6 J36, follow A590 to Ulverston then L onto A5087 Coast Road signed Bardsea & coastal route to Barrow.* **Adm £3.50, chd free. For NGS: Sat 27, Sun 28 Apr (11-7). For other opening times and information, please phone or email.**

40 acres of gardens and woodland surrounding Gothic mansion. Temple garden an oasis of peace, wildlife garden, arboretum, cottage gardens. Free map with 3 woodland walks. 6 minute woodland walk to Morecambe Bay. 'It is an amazing house, one of the most spectacular in Cumbria', Hunter Davies in 'Best of Lakeland'. Free guided tours of Temple and part of house. Cafe and gift shop. Disabled WC near Temple.

11 ◆ COPT HOWE

Chapel Stile, Great Langdale LA22 9JR. Professor R N Haszeldine, Please tel 015394 37685 for weekly recorded message. *5m W of Ambleside. On B5343, ¼ m past Chapel Stile. Park by side of road, not up the drive to the house. Please tel for info re*

special needs transprt provided up the drive. **Adm £4, chd free. For NGS: Fri 5, Tue 9, Fri 12, Fri 19, Tue 23 Apr; Wed 1, Wed 8, Tue 14, Fri 17, Fri 24 May; Wed 5, Wed 12, Thur 20 June (12.30-4.30). For other opening times and information, please phone.**
2-acre plantsman's mountain paradise garden. Superb views Langdale Pikes. Extensive collections of acers, camellias, azaleas, rhododendrons, oaks, beeches, rare shrubs, trees, unusual perennials; herbaceous and bulbous species; alpines, trough gardens; rare conifers; expedition plants from worldwide mountainous regions. Outstanding spring and autumn colour. Wildlife sanctuary, red squirrels, badgers, slow-worms, lizards, hotel for wild birds. Major new garden extensions and features. 24yr of opening for NGS. Featured in GGG and many papers, magazines, radio and TV programmes.

12 CROOKDAKE FARM

Aspatria, Wigton CA7 3SH. Kirk & Alannah Rylands, 016973 20413, alannah.rylands@me.com. *3m NE of Aspatria. Between A595 & A596. From A595 take B5299 at Mealsgate signed Aspatria. After 2m turn sharp R in Watch Hill signed Crookdake. House 1m on L.* Home-made teas. **Adm £3.50, chd free. Sun 9 June (1-5). Visitors also welcome by appt June to July.**
Windswept informal farmhouse (not open) garden with a careful colour combination of planting sympathetic to the landscape incl various different areas with densely planted herbaceous borders, vegetable patch, wild meadow and large pond area home to moisture-loving plants, tame hens and wild moorhens. Opening supported by old vehicle enthusiasts. All types of old vehicles encouraged to attend.

14 DALLAM TOWER

Milnthorpe LA7 7AG. Mr & Mrs R T Villiers-Smith. *7m S of Kendal. 7m N of Carnforth. Nr junction 36 off the M6. A6 & B5282. Stn: Arnside, 4m; Lancaster, 15m.* Cream teas. **Adm £3.50, chd free. Sun 12 May (2-5).**
Large garden; natural rock garden, water garden; wood walks, lawns, shrubs. C19 cast iron orangery.

GROUP OPENING

15 DALTON HAMLET GARDENS

Burton-in-Kendal LA6 1NN. *4m W of Kirkby Lonsdale. 10m S of Kendal. From village of Burton-in-Kendal (A6070) follow Vicarage Lane for 1m. Parking at Russell Farm (signed).* Home-made teas Refreshments at Crow Trees Barn. **Combined adm £4.50, chd free. Sun 30 June (12-5).**

CROW TREES BARN
Carole Bentham

2 FORESTRY HOUSES
David & Carol Haigh

PEAR TREE COTTAGE
Burton-in-Kendal. Linda & Alec Greening
Visitors also welcome by appt June to July, refreshments available by arrangement.
01524 781624
linda.greening@virgin.net
www.peartreecottagecumbria.co.uk

3 gardens set in a peaceful rural hamlet near Burton-in-Kendal, overlooking the remains of a probable Bronze Age settlement and with lovely country views. Each garden has its own distinctive character: one garden making innovative use of its steeply sloping site; another a plantsperson's garden with a wildlife friendly approach; the third a country garden set on different levels, with beautiful open views, which can be reached by a short road walk or a stroll through the woods. Well stocked herbaceous borders, mature shrubs and trees, gravel beds, ponds, rare and unusual plants, and a collection of more than 200 different ferns, all within a short stroll of each other. Wide range of home-grown plants available.

16 ◆ DORA'S FIELD

Rydal, Ambleside LA22 9LX. National Trust, www.nationaltrust.org.uk. *1½ m N of Ambleside. Follow A591 from Ambleside to Rydal. Dora's Field is next to St Mary's Church.* **Adm £3, chd free. For NGS: Sun 24 Mar (11-4). For other opening times and information, please phone or see garden website.**
Named for Dora, the daughter of the poet William Wordsworth. Wordsworth planned to build a house for Dora on the land but, after her early death, he planted the area with daffodils in her memory. Now known as Dora's field the area is renowned for its spring display of daffodils. 24th March 2013; Wordsworth's Daffodil Legacy.

> Wild meadow and large pond area home to moisture-loving plants, tame hens and wild moorhens . . .

17 EWEBANK FARM

Old Hutton, Kendal LA8 0NS. Sue & Barry Sharkey. *3m NE of Kendal. From Oxenholme Stn continue along B6254, towards Old Hutton, taking 3rd turning on the L. R turnings at next 2 junctions. From M6. Leave at J37, take A684 to Sedbergh. Take 1st R & immediately R again. Follow lane back over motorway, continue approx 3m before turning L to Ewebank.* Home-made teas. **Adm £3, chd free. Sun 30 June (1-5).**
Relaxing, rural, flower arrangers garden, friendly hens and suggestions of music. Large lawn sloping down to a steam where curved decking follows the gentle contours of the land. Planting mostly formal with areas of shade for ferns, hostas and other moisture-loving plants. Mixed borders, statues, topiary, orchard and espaliered apples.

18 GALESYKE

Wasdale CA20 1ET. Christine & Mike McKinley. *From N follow signs to Nether Wasdale, through village take rd to The Lake & Wasdale Head. After approx ¾ m Galesyke on R on sharp R-hand bend with wooden fence. From S turn R at Santon Bridge, follow signs to Wasdale Head, Galesyke 2½ m on R.* Cream teas. **Adm £3, chd free. Sun 26, Mon 27 May (11-5). Also open Buckbarrow House.**

Partially landscaped garden of several acres on banks of R Irt with views of Wasdale Fells, noted for its display of rhododendrons and azaleas. During the November 2009 floods the garden suffered some damage; the beds immediately adjacent to the river were completely washed away; and further downstream, several trees were lost. This damage will not have been made good in time for the garden opening'.

19 GATESBIELD

New Road, Windermere LA23 2LA. Gatesbield Quaker Housing Assoc, 015394 45578 enquiries@gatesbield.org.uk, www.gatesbield.org.uk. *½ m from Windermere Rail/Bus stn. From Windermere take New Road southward (direction Bowness). Gatesbield is on the right shortly after the Ellerthwaite Hotel.* Home-made teas. **Adm £3.50, chd free. Sat 11 May (2-5).**

Extensive gardens with fine collection of rhododendrons, azaleas, and specimen trees in rocky dells. Former home of Stanley, distinguished Arts and Crafts furniture maker, and Emily Davies, now sheltered housing. Exhibition. Teas served in Gatesbield House. Some gravel paths and steep slopes.

GROUP OPENING

20 GILGARRAN GARDENS

Gilgarran CA14 4RD. *5m N of Whitehaven, 5m E of Workington. Turn off A595 towards Distington Crematorium. After 1m turn L for Gilgarran for The Avenue & Pinewoods. The Avenue 1st rd on R, Pinewoods 2nd rd on R. To visit Gilgarran Park 1st, ignore 1st turn for Gilgarran, carry on for 1m, turn L into Gilgarran Park. All gardens within easy stroll of each other. Sturdy footwear recommended in wet weather.* **Combined adm £3, chd free. Sun 2 June (12-5).**

STILEFIELD
13 Pinewoods. Brian & Alice Middleton

6 THE AVENUE
Brian & Avril Dixon

WOODSIDE HOUSE
17 Gilgarran Park. David & Brenda Forster

Three contrasting gardens in this peaceful rural hamlet overlooking the Cumbrian coast and fells, each with their own distinctive character, using colour, texture and foliage to best advantage. Well-stocked gardens vary from formal landscaping to woodland and wildlife gardens, and a variety of tranquil water features. Plant Sale at Stilefield. Featured in Cumbria Life.

Pear Tree Cottage

© Linda Greening

21 HALL SENNA
Hallsenna, Gosforth, Holmrook CA19 1YB. Chris & Helen Steele, 01946 725436, helen.steele5@btinternet.com. *2m SW of Gosforth. Follow main A595 either N or S. 1m S of Gosforth turn down lane opp Seven Acres Caravan Park, proceed for approx 1m.* Home-made teas. **Adm £3, chd free. Sun 28 July (10.30-5). Visitors also welcome by appt May to Aug. Access is via a public bridleway no coaches.**
Tucked away within the hamlet of Hallsenna close to the West Cumbrian coast this garden provides the visitor with many different aspects of gardening. The 1 acre site includes borders fully planted for year round colour and many delightful structures built to provide interest, and punctuate your journey through the garden. New water feature completed during 2011. Garden tombola, plant sales, home made teas. Featured in Cumbria Life magazine and local village publications. Wheelchair access is limited due to steep slopes on entry into the garden.

22 HAVERTHWAITE LODGE
Haverthwaite LA12 8AJ. David Snowdon, 015395 39841, sheena.taylforth@lakesidehotel.co.uk. *100yds off A590 at Haverthwaite. Turn E off A590 opp Haverthwaite railway stn.* **Adm £3, chd free. Weds 19 June; 28 Aug (11-4). Combined with Lakeside & Rocky Bank adm £6. Visitors also welcome by appt.**
Traditional Lake District garden that has been redesigned and replanted. Gardens on a series of terraces leading down to the R Leven and incl: rose garden, cutting garden, dell area, rock terrace, herbaceous borders and many interesting mature shrubs. In a stunning setting the garden is surrounded by oak woodland and was once a place of C18 and C19 industry.

GROUP OPENING

23 HAYTON VILLAGE GARDENS
Hayton, Brampton CA8 9HR. *7m E of Carlisle. 3m W of Brampton. From W./J43 M6, A69 E. towards Hexham/Newcastle. 5m turn R signed Hayton. From E./Brampton, A69 W towards Carlisle. 1m turn L at Lane End PH signed Hayton. Maps of garden locations available to visitors. Parking along road on one side only please. One central ticket sales point for 2013 in middle of village.* Home-made teas at Hayton Village Primary School. **Combined adm £3, chd free (share to Hayton Village Primary School). Sun 7 July (1-5).**

BRACKENHOW
Susan & Jonny Tranter

THE CEDARS
Mrs Lynda Hayward

CURLEW COTTAGE
Frances & David Scales

HAYTON C OF E PRIMARY SCHOOL

KINRARA
Tim & Alison Brown

LITTLE GARTH
Dugald Campbell

NEW **MEADOW VIEW**
Mr Andrew Welsh

MILLBROOK
Emily & Angus Dawson

THE NOOK
Marion Beveridge

PEAR TREE HOUSE
John & Charlotte Noble

Easily accessible village of many characterful old sandstone properties, green with ancient walnut tree, church and Inn (weekend meals and WCs). Not far from Hadrian's Wall, Talkin Tarn, North Pennine fells, Eden Valley and small market town of Brampton with particular attractions such as a Philip Webb church (Burne Jones stained glass). Gardens of varied size and styles all within ½ m, mostly of old stone cottages. Smaller and larger cottage gardens, courtyards and containers, steep wooded slopes, sweeping lawns, sheep dip pond, exuberant borders, frogs, pools and poultry, colour and texture throughout. Homemade Teas at the school. Pimms or similar, depending on weather! Informal treasure hunt for children young and old. Gardens additional to those listed also generally open and views into numerous others. Plants for sale. Varying degrees of access from full to minimal.

24 HAZEL COTTAGE
Armathwaite CA4 9PG. Mr D Ryland & Mr J Thexton. *8m SE of Carlisle. Turn off A6 just S of High Hesket signed Armathwaite, after 2m house facing you at T-junction.* Home-made teas. **Adm £3.50, chd free. Suns 26 May; 23 June (12-5).**
Developing flower arrangers and plantsmans garden. Extending to approx 5 acres. Incls herbaceous borders, pergola, ponds and planting of disused railway siding providing home to wildlife. Many variegated and unusual plants. Varied areas, planted for all seasons, S-facing, some gentle slopes. Featured in spring edition of' the flower arranger' magazine.

Informal treasure hunt for children young and old . . .

25 HAZELWOOD FARM
Hollins Lane, Silverdale, Carnforth LA5 0UB. Glenn & Dan Shapiro, www.hazelwoodfarm.co.uk. *4m NW of M6 J35. From Carnforth follow signs to Silverdale, after 1m turn L signed Silverdale, after level xing turn L then 1st L into Hollins Lane. Farm on R.* Home-made teas. **Adm £3.50, chd free. Suns 9 June; 4 Aug (11-5).**
A theatre of light curtained by backdrops of woodland. Steep paths winding up and through natural limestone cliff, intersected by a tumbling rill joining ponds, provide staging for alpine gems and drifts of herbaceous, prairie and woodland planting. Old and English roses, bulbs and the National Collection of Hepatica. Wildlife friendly garden surrounded by NT access land. New bird, bee and butterfly garden. Featured in Amateur Gardening, Lakeland Gardener.

NCH

GROUP OPENING

26 HELTON VILLAGE GARDENS

Helton, Penrith CA10 2QA. *6m S of Penrith. A6 S from Penrith. After Eamont Bridge, turn R on B5320. After 1m fork L to Askham. Through Askham, 1m to Helton. Follow signs.* Home-made teas at The Nook. **Combined adm £3, chd free. Mon 27 May (10-4).**

CASTLE VILLA
Linda Challis.
Up the rd to Helton Fell, the entrance is on L, 50m beyond the prominent oak tree

CHAPEL YAT
Val & Tony Corbett.
Briefly up the rd to Helton Fell, Chapel Yat on R, high above the village green. Either walk up the steep grass bank of the village green opp Castle Villa or take one of the two tracks on R above Castle Villa

HOLLY COTTAGE
Mr and Mrs G. Emerson.
Holly Cottage is the next to last house on R as you head S out of the village

NEW LONSDALE HOUSE
Mr & Mrs E and R Edwards.
Heading S, Lonsdale House is immed after 2 modern-ish bungalows

THE NOOK
Brenda & Philip Freedman.
As for Castle Villa but follow the track past the front of Castle Villa

Five walled gardens attached to C18 cottages spread around a compact picturesque hamlet. Helton is a spring-line settlement, sitting on limestone, facing east above the R Lowther and at eight hundred feet above sea level - a fairly challenging environment. Three of the gardens are traditional cottage gardens with lawn, borders and vegetables whilst the other two merely lack lawn. Each garden has something different or unusual to offer. In addition, a well-known local farmer who manufacturers highly regarded composts will have his produce for sale. In 2013, we also propose to offer some musical entertainment. Sale of local-made composts (Lakeland Gold, etc) by noted produces (Simon) Bland and (Dr Jane) Barker. Steps limit wheelchair access and only one of the gardens can be completely accessed by wheelchair. Varying access is available at the others.

Woodland walks with many wild birds and a chance to see red squirrels . . .

27 HEYWOOD HOUSE

Littledale Road, Brookhouse LA2 9PW. Mike & Lorraine Cave. *4m E of Lancaster. From J34 M6, follow A683 to Caton/Kirkby Lonsdale. At mini island turn R to Brookhouse. At Black Bull PH turn R, garden 3/4 m on LH-side.* Home-made teas. **Adm £3.50, chd free. Suns 23 June; 7 July (11-5).**
Secluded 2-acre garden with many unusual trees and shrubs, sweeping lawns with beautiful herbaceous borders leading to large natural wildlife pond, gravel garden, pergolas with an abundance of roses and climbers, rockery, folly, woodland garden with natural stream, under development. Garden railway train rides for adults and children.

28 HIGH MOSS

Portinscale, Keswick CA12 5TX. Christine & Peter Hughes, christine_hug25@hotmail.com. *1m W of Keswick. Enter village off A66, take 1st turning R through white gates, on R of rd after 1/3 m.* Home-made teas. **Adm £4, chd free (share to Keswick Mountain Rescue). Sun 24 Mar (11-4); Sun 26 May (2-5.30). Visitors also welcome by appt Apr to Sept.**
Lakeland Arts and Craft house (mentioned in Pevsner, not open) and garden under restoration with help from Tom Attwood of Halecat Nurseries. Returned to the Scheme in 2010 after many years' absence. 4 1/2 acres of formal and informal S-facing terraced gardens with magnificent views of the fells. Many fine trees, rhododendrons and azaleas. Old tennis court has been converted into vegetable/flower parterre to mark the Diamond Jubilee. Open as part of Cumbria Daffodil Day on 24th March. Featured in article by Tom Longville and Val Corbett in Cumbria Life.

29 NEW HIGHAM HALL

Bassenthwaite Lake, Cockermouth CA13 9SH. Higham Hall College, www.highamhall.com. *Northern edge of Lake District, between Cockermouth and Keswick, 1m from Bassenthwaite Lake. From Penrith (M6 J40) or Keswick, follow the A66 along the side of Bassenthwaite Lake take 1st turning R at the end of the lake - signed Dubwath & Castle Inn. Follow brown tourist signs for Higham Hall. Travelling from Carlisle take A595 towards Cockermouth, turn L at Bothel onto A591. Continue to the Castle Inn Hotel. Turn R at the hotel onto B5291, bear R after Ouse Bridge then follow brown sign for Higham Hall.* Home-made teas. **Adm £3.50, chd free. Sun 26 May (11-5).**
19th Century Gothic mansion set in approximately 6 acres of mature garden with wonderful open views of Skiddaw and surrounding fells. Many interesting trees and perennials, stream with wildlife pond, large lawn, putting green and croquet lawn, raised bed vegetable area. Woodland walks with many wild birds and a chance to see red squirrels. Plant sales and the opportunity to cut your own flowers. Garden Tours available on NGS day. 12 and 3.

30 ◆ HOLEHIRD GARDENS

Patterdale Road, Windermere LA23 1NP. Lakeland Horticultural Society, 015394 46008, www.holehirdgardens.org.uk. *1m N of Windermere. On A592, Windermere to Ullswater road.* **Adm £3, chd free. For NGS: Sun 24 Mar; Thur 18 July (10-5). For other opening times and information, please phone or see garden website.**
The garden is run by volunteers with the aim of promoting knowledge of the cultivation of alpine and herbaceous plants, shrubs and trees, especially those suited to Lakeland conditions. One of the best labelled gardens in the UK. National Collections of *Astilbe* and *Polystichum* (ferns). Set on the fellside with stunning views over Windermere the walled garden gives protection to

"Lemon drizzle cake, Victoria sponge ... yummy!"

mixed borders whilst alpine houses protect an always colourful array of tiny gems. Consistently voted among the top gardens in Britain and Europe.

♿ ✿ NCH

31 ◆ HOLKER HALL GARDENS

Cark-in-Cartmel, Grange-over-Sands LA11 7PL. Lord & Lady Cavendish, 015395 58328, www.holker.co.uk. *4m W of Grange-over-Sands. 12m W of M6 (J36) Follow brown tourist signs.* **Adm £7.50, chd free. For NGS: Fri 30 Aug (10.30-5.30). For other opening times and information, please phone or see garden website.**

25 acres of romantic gardens, with peaceful arboretum, inspirational formal gardens, flowering meadow and Labyrinth. Spring sees thousands of bulbs and flowers. Summer brings voluptuous mixed borders and bedding. Discover unusually large rhododendrons, magnolias and azaleas, and the National Collection of Stryracaceae. Discover our latest garden feature - The Pagan Grove, designed by Kim Wilkie. Guided tour of the gardens, take the opportunity to tour the gardens with our experienced guide. Donation required.

♿ ✿ NCH ☕

32 HOLME MEADOW

1 Holme Meadow, Cumwhinton, Carlisle CA4 8DR. John & Anne Mallinson, 01228 560330, jwai.mallinson@btinternet.com. *2m S of Carlisle. From M6 J42 take B6263 to Cumwhinton, in village take 1st L then bear R at Lowther Arms, Holme Meadow is immediately on R.* Tea. **Adm £3, chd free. Sun 28 July (11-5). Visitors also welcome by appt June to July.**

Village garden developed and landscaped from scratch by owners. Incl shrubbery, perennial beds supplemented by annuals, pergola and trellis with climbers, slate beds and water feature, ornamental copse, wild flower meadow and kitchen garden. Designed, planted and maintained to be wildlife friendly.

✿ ☕ ☎

33 HORTICARE

54 Wattsfield Road, Kendal LA9 5JN. Mr John Taylor, 1539773518, horticare@cumbria.gov.uk. *From Milnthorpe Rd (A6) turn onto Wattsfield Rd. Take 2nd L onto Wattsfield Avenue. Horticare is across the rd at the end.* Home-made teas. **Adm £3, chd free. Sun 21 July (12-4). Visitors also welcome by appt.**

Horticare is a Horticultural Day Service providing a therapeutic and supportive environment for people with learning disabilities. It is a working nursery growing shrubs, perennials and ornamental bedding as well as providing a garden maintenance service. It is run with a strong emphasis on recycling and sustainability; much of the potting compost is made from waste sawdust provided by a local business mixed with grass mowings from the garden maintenance service. A small therapy garden, made mainly with reclaimed and recycled materials, offers both tranquillity and a feast for the senses. Information on horticulture as therapy.

♿ 🐕 ✿ ☕ ☎

34 IVY HOUSE

Cumwhitton, Brampton CA8 9EX. Martin Johns & Ian Forrest. *6m E of Carlisle. At the bridge at Warwick Bridge on A69 take turning to Great Corby & Cumwhitton. Through Great Corby & woodland until you reach a T-junction. Turn R to Cumwhitton (approx 4m from A69).* Home-made teas. **Adm £3.50, chd free. Sun 30 June (1-5).**

Approx 2 acres of sloping fell-side garden with meandering paths leading to a series of 'rooms': pond, fern garden, gravel garden with assorted grasses, vegetable and herb garden. Copse with meadow leading down to beck. Trees, shrubs, bamboos and herbaceous perennials planted with emphasis on variety of texture and colour. Featured in Cumbria Life. Steep slopes.

♿ 🐕 ☕

35 LAKESIDE HOTEL & ROCKY BANK

Lake Windermere, Newby Bridge, Ulverston LA12 8AT. Mr N Talbot, 015395 30001, sheena.taylforth@lakesidehotel.co.uk, www.lakesidehotel.co.uk. *1m N of Newby Bridge. On S shore of Lake Windermere. From A590 at Newby Bridge, cross the bridge which leads onto Hawkshed rd. Follow this rd for 1m, hotel on R. Rocky Bank is just past the hotel on L. Complimentary parking available.* Light refreshments at Lakeside Hotel. **Combined adm £5, chd free, also combined with Haverthwaite Lodge, adm £6.00. Weds 19 June; 28 Aug (11-4). Visitors also welcome by appt May to Sept.**

Two diverse gardens on the shores of Lake Windermere. Lakeside has been created for year round interest, packed with choice plants, incl some unusual varieties. Main garden area with herbaceous borders and foliage shrubs, scented and winter interest plants and seasonal bedding. Roof garden with lawn, espaliered local heritage apple varieties and culinary herbs. Lawn art on front lawn. New Rocky Bank is a traditional garden with rock outcrops. Planted with unusual specimen alpines. Herbaceous borders, shrubs and ornamental trees. Woodland area with species rhododendrons. Working greenhouse and polytunnels. Wild flower garden and cut flower garden. Cumbria Tourism Large Hotel of the Year, Cumbria in Bloom, Cumbria Tourism Trophy, Jackie Sanderson Trophy - Hotel Category. Wheelchair access not available at Rocky Bank.

✿ 🛏 ☕ ☎

Copse with meadow leading down to beck . . .

36 LANGHOLME MILL

Woodgate, Lowick Green LA12 8ES. Judith & Graham Sanderson, 01229 885215, judith@themill.bizz. *7m NW of Ulverston. Take A5092 at Greenodd towards Broughton for 3¾ m on L ½ m after River Deep & Mountain High Outward Bound Centre (formerly Lowick School). Parking in front of property.* **Visitors welcome by appt. Please phone Judith on 01229 885215.**

Approx 1 acre of mature woodland garden with meandering lakeland stone paths surrounding the mill race stream which can be crossed by a variety of bridges. The garden hosts well established bamboo, rhododendrons, hostas, acers and astilbes and a large variety of country flowers. Featured in Cumbria Life and also the Westmorland Gazette.

🐕 🛏 ☎

37 LAWSON PARK
East of Lake, Coniston LA21 8AD. Karen Guthrie & Grizedale Arts, 015394 41242, karen@somewhere.org.uk, www.lawsonpark.org. *5m East of Coniston village. Follow signs to East of Lake or brown signs to Brantwood. Turning to garden track 1 mile South of Brantwood, past two semi-detached houses (Forestry Commission sign-post at junction). Please note 2 mile forestry track to garden can be rough. Garden car park provided but please bring as few cars as possible. Alternatively use Machell's Coppice car park 200m S of Brantwood and access garden on foot via 20 mins brisk walk up forest footpath from rear of car park or from Brantwood garden.* Tea. **Adm £4, chd free. Visitors welcome by appt June to Sept, by prior arrangement only.**
Ambitious garden and small-holding created over the last decade on fellside in a spectacular setting overlooking Coniston Water. Sinuous drystone terraces overflow with many unusual herbaceous plants. Sensitive stone and timber hard landscaping. Great late summer colour and texture. Woodland and water gardens, meadow, orchard, bees, poultry and kitchen gardens. 'This garden is a triumph' (Eric Robson, broadcaster). Poultry, apiary, water gardens, wildflower meadow, wildlife. Featured in Cumbria Life.

GROUP OPENING

38 LEECE & DENDRON VILLAGE GARDENS
Cumbria LA12 0QP, winander@aol.com. *2m E of Barrow-in-Furness. 6m SW of Ulverston. J36 M6 onto A590 to Ulverston. A5087 coast rd to Barrow. Approx 8m turn R for Leece Village, and a further ¼ m for Dendron (signed, look for concrete sea wall on L). Village parking for gardens. Maps supplied to visitors.* Light refreshments at Leece Village Hall. **Combined adm £3.50, chd free. Sun 23 June (11-5). Evening Opening Thur 20 June (6.30-8); by appointment only.**

BRIAR HOUSE
Jeff & Gill Lowden

NEW ◆ **THE DIN DRUM, DENDRON**
Mr & Mrs Adrian & Julie Newnham

LANE END HOUSE
Lisa & Alan Sharp

3 PEAR TREE COTTAGE
Jane & Rob Phizacklea

NEW ◆ **ST MARGARETS, LEECE**
Mr & Mrs Lyn & Sabine Dixon

WINANDER
Mrs Enid Cockshott

Two small close villages on the Furness Peninsula 1½ m from Morecombe Bay, rural but not remote, with working farms centred around a small tarn. Gardens of varying size and individual styles, all of which enjoy wonderful views. Features incl a willow yurt, green roof, a white garden, hay meadow with maze, mature trees, herbaceous borders, wildlife ponds and streams, bees, cottage garden, alpines, perennials, shrubs, water features, climbers ... and much much more! No wheelchair access.

Alpines, perennials, shrubs, water features, climbers . . . and much much more . . . !

GROUP OPENING

39 LITTLE URSWICK VILLAGE GARDENS
nr Ulverston LA12 0PL. *4m W of Ulverston. A590 from Ulverston approx 2m to Little Urswick.* Home-made teas at Redmayne Hall. **Combined adm £3.50, chd free. Suns 7 July; 11 Aug (11-5).**

BECKSIDE FARM
Anna Thomason

BURNSMEAD FARM
Richard & Anne Kenyon.
In centre of Little Urswick, above the village green

CORNAA
Ulverston. Mike & Bev Williams.
Behind the green, up short drive

HILL COTTAGE
Mrs Christine Winder

REDMAYNE HALL
Jennie Werry

A small quiet village on the Furness Peninsula with houses set around small village green. Five very diverse gardens varying in size with individual attractions and interests.

40 LOW FELL WEST
Crosthwaite, Kendal LA8 8JG. Barbie & John Handley, 015395 68297, barbie@handleyfamily.co.uk. *4.6m S of Bowness. Off A5074, turn W just S of Damson Dene Hotel. Follow lane for ½ m.* Home-made teas. **Adm £3.50, chd free. Suns 16 June; 20 Oct (10-5). Visitors also welcome by appt Mar to Oct.**
This 2 acre woodland garden in the tranquil Winster Valley has extensive views to the Pennines. The garden, restored over the last 8yrs, incl expanses of rock planted sympathetically with grasses, unusual trees and shrubs, climaxing for autumn colour. There are areas of plant rich meadows and native hedges. A woodland area houses a gypsy caravan and there is direct access to Cumbria Wildlife Trust's Barkbooth Reserve of Oak woodland and open fellside. Limited wheelchair access, rough paths, steep slopes.

41 4 LOW PASTURES
Lowgate, Levens, Kendal LA8 8QH. Peter & Pam Martin, 015395 60441, pammartin47@gmail.com. *5m S of Kendal. From A590 take 3rd R going west from Brettargh Holt r'about - signed to Levens Village & Brigsteer. Continue up the hill passing the Hare & Hounds on RH-side. 4 Low Pastures is 600yds on LH-side.* Home-made teas. **Adm £3, chd free. Visitors welcome by appt May to Aug, groups 10 to 30.**
A sustainable garden for wildlife, totally renovated in the last 4-5 years. Single, perennial flowers and mixed, preferably flowering evergreens provide food and cover for insects and birds. Totally organic and peat free. Wildlife pond. Ornamental kitchen garden. File of articles on wildlife / sustainable gardening available to read. Featured inMember's garden in the Journal of the Lakeland Horticultural Society.

'Me and My Garden': Westmorland Gazette. No wheelchair access. Ornamental garden may be viewed from a balcony on request. Kitchen garden may be viewed from bottom path.

42 LOWER ROWELL FARM & COTTAGE

Milnthorpe LA7 7LU. John & Mavis Robinson & Julie & Andy Welton, 015395 62270. *2m NE of Milnthorpe. Signed to Rowell off B6385. Garden ½ m up lane on L.* Light refreshments. **Adm £3.50, chd free.**
Sun 17 Feb (1-4.30); Sat 29, Sun 30 June (1-5); Sun 16 Feb 2014. Visitors also welcome by appt June to July, groups 20+, refreshments available by arrangement.
Approx ¾ -acre garden. Borders and beds with shrubs and interesting herbaceous perennials. Retro greenhouse and vegetable plots. Very peaceful with open views to Farleton Knott, Pennines and Lakeland hills. Adjacent cottage garden also open.

43 MATSON GROUND

Windermere LA23 2NH. Matson Ground Estate Co Ltd, 015394 47892, info@matsonground.co.uk. *⅔ m E of Bowness. From Kendal turn R off B5284 signed Heathwaite, 100yds after Windermere Golf Club. Garden on L after ⅓ m. From Bowness turn L onto B5284 from A5074. After ½ m turn L at Xrds. Garden on L ½ m along lane.* Home-made teas. **Adm £3.50, chd free.**
Sun 19 May (1-5). Visitors also welcome by appt.
2 acre formal garden with a mix of established borders, wildflower areas and a stream leading to a large pond and developing aboretum. New rose garden and newly planted topairy terrace borders; white garden. Walled kitchen garden with raised beds, fruit trees and greenhouse. The garden is constantly developing and regular visitors will see changes each year.

44 MEADOW HOUSE

Garnett Bridge Road, Burneside, Kendal LA8 9AY. Paul Burrill. *4m N of Kendal. Leave A591 2m N of Kendal signed R towards Burneside. Cross railway and turn R at T junction. Take 1st L past Premier Store. After ½ m take 2nd L towards Longsleddale (opp Burneside Hall). After ¾ m turn L signed Meadow House. Go immed R over cattle grid. Park as directed, majority of parking in field.* Home-made teas. **Adm £4, chd free.**
Sun 11 Aug (1-5).
2-acre rural garden in tranquil setting with superb countryside views. Provides a range of garden interest, surprise and enjoyment. Plenty of seats. Of special interest are the water features with ponds and streams; large, attractive and productive vegetable and fruit garden with glasshouses and polytunnel; hot border; agapanthus, pot plants and other ornamental plantings. The garden 'centre piece' is the vegetable garden - a very special place. The garden blends ornamental beauty with food production. Honey bees. New for 2013 is a woodland trail with stream side paths. Superb rural views. Several water features and streams. Ornamental beds and vegetable garden.

45 NEWTON RIGG COLLEGE GARDENS
Newton Rigg, Penrith CA11 0AH. Newton Rigg College, 01768 893640, shelagh.todd@newtonrigg.ac.uk, www.askham-bryan.ac.uk. *1m W of Penrith. 3m W from J40 & J41 off M6. ½ m off the B5288 W of Penrith.* Tea. **Adm £4, chd free. Sun 24 Mar (11-4); Wed 26 June (3-8.30); Wed 2 Oct (3-6).**
The gardens and campus grounds have much of horticultural interest incl herbaceous borders, ponds, organic garden with fruit cage and display of composting techniques, woodland walk, scented garden, 2 arboretums, annual meadows, pleached hornbeam walkway and extensive range of ornamental trees and shrubs. Guided tour of the gardens by the horticultural team at Newton Rigg, incl the organic garden, ornamental garden, the aboretum and herbaceous borders. Expert staff available for information on courses in horticulture, garden design and floristry as well as an extensive range of long based subjects.

46 OLDE OAKS
Croft Ends, Appleby CA16 6JW. Chantal Knight, 07966 226447, chantalknight@midwife.plus.com. *1½ m N of Appleby. Heading N out of Appleby take rd to Long Marton for 1m. 1st L, continue on ½ m, garden last on R.* Home-made teas. **Adm £3.50, chd free. Visitors welcome by appt** June to Aug.
A secret ½ -acre cottage garden. Big sweeping borders filled with interesting and colourful herbaceous perennial planting. Fabulous views of the Pennines and Lakeland fells. Lovely relaxing garden to sit and relax. 2-acre woodland walk with free range hens. Koi carp pond and wildlife pond. Tree house.

47 ORCHARD COTTAGE
Hutton Lane, Levens, Kendal LA8 8PB. Shirley & Chris Band, 015395 61005, chrisband67@gmail.com. *6m S of Kendal. Turn N off A590 or A6 signed Levens. From Xrds by Methodist Church, 300 metres down Hutton Lane. Park near this Xrds. Garden access via 'The Orchard'.* Light refreshments at Levens Village Institute. **Adm £3.50, chd free. Sun 23 June (1-5). Visitors also welcome by appt Mar to Oct, groups max 30.**
¾ acre sloping garden in old orchard. Plantsperson's paradise with winding paths, diverse habitats, secret vistas, hidden places. All yr round interest and colour. Collections of ferns (100+), hellebores (70+), grasses, cottage plants, geraniums. Auricula theatres, 'imaginary' stream, bog garden. Trees support clematis, roses and honeysuckle. Wildlife friendly. Featured in Westmorland Gazette 'Me and My Garden'.

Cottage borders with hues of soft pinks and purples . . .

48 NEW ORCHARD HOUSE
Main Street, St. Bees CA27 0AA. Dr Juliet Rhodes. *From Main Street, wooden gates onto gravelled driveway. Approx 500yds walk up hill (Egremont direction) from railway station. Very limited on street parking. Free parking available at station car park.* Home-made teas & refreshments at village hall. **Adm £3, chd free. Sun 14 July (10-5).**
Surprisingly generous secluded cottage style garden behind Georgian house on village main street sheltered from coastal winds by tall trees. Designed and developed by owner since 2005 it's varied planting is enhanced by local red sandstone in walls and paving. Features incl a well, woodland area, greenhouse, vegetable plot, espaliered fruit trees gravel garden, wild flower area, bees and hens.

49 NEW 8 OXENHOLME ROAD
Kendal LA9 7NJ. Mr & Mrs John & Frances Davenport, 01539 720934, frandav8@btinternet.com. *From Kendal, take A65 (Burton Rd) towards Oxenholme. At T- lights past leisure centre, veer L into Oxenholme Road. Our house is first entry on L after red post box.* Tea. **Adm £3.50, chd free. Sun 1 Sept (10-5). Visitors also welcome by appt May to Sept.**
Approx ½ acre of mixed planting designed for year-round interest, including two small ponds. The garden runs all round the house with a gravel garden at the front, as well as a number of woodland plant areas.

50 PARK HOUSE
Barbon, Kirkby Lonsdale LA6 2LG. Mr & Mrs P Pattison, 015242 76346, philip@ppattison.co.uk. *2½ m N of Kirkby Lonsdale. A65 to Kirkby Lonsdale. Turn at Devil's Bridge onto A683 towards Sedburgh, 3m turn R Barbon village, R at memorial, pass church up hill, follow signs. N.B please note at busy periods parking will be at the village hall, therefore creating a short walk to the event.* Cream teas. **Adm £4.50, chd free. Sat 22 June (10.30-4.30); Sun 23 June (11-4). Visitors also welcome by appt June to Aug, groups 10 to 30.**
Romantic Manor house. Extensive vistas. Formal tranquil pond encased in yew hedging. Meadow with meandering pathways, water garden filled with bulbs and ferns. Formal lawn gravel pathways, cottage borders with hues of soft pinks and purples. shady border, kitchen garden. An evolving garden to follow. New terraced border.

51 QUARRY HILL HOUSE
Mealsgate, Boltongate, Wigton CA7 1AE. Mr & Mrs Charles Woodhouse, 016973 71225, cfwoodhouse@btinternet.com. *1m E of Mealsgate, ½ m W of Boltongate. Between Boltongate & Mealsgate on B5299. ½ m W of Boltongate(8m SSW of Wigton). At Mealsgate, on A595 Cockermouth to Carlisle rd, turn E onto B5299 for Boltongate, Ireby & Caldbeck. Approx 1m along rd, entrance gates to Quarry Hill House on L.* Home-made teas. **Adm £4, chd free (share to Hospice at Home Carlisle & N Lakeland). Sun 16 June (1.30-5). Visitors also welcome by appt Mar to Oct.**
3 acre parkland setting country house (not open) woodland garden with good views. Herbaceous borders, trees, shrubs, potager vegetable garden. Extensively planted arboreta with many specimen trees, especially varieties of sorbus with lovely woodland walks. Much tree planting

and many regeneration projects since 2000 incl recreation for wildlife of former shooting ponds. Featured in Cumbria Life.

52 RANNERDALE COTTAGE
Buttermere CA13 9UY. The McElney Family. *8m S of Cockermouth. 10m W of Keswick. B5289 on Crummock Water, in the Buttermere Valley.* Home-made teas. **Adm £3.50, chd free. Sat 15, Sun 16 June (12-5).**
½ -acre garden with beck and woodland walk overlooking Crummock Water with splendid mountain views. Herbaceous, shrubs, roses, perennial geraniums, tree peonies, pond with fish. The house and garden were badly damaged during flash flooding in 2012.

53 NEW ROSE CASTLE
Dalston CA5 7BZ. Claire Hexter, marketing@dalmain.com. *3m S of Dalston off the B5299. Follow signs.* **Adm £3, chd free. Sun 24 Mar (11-4). Visits need to be booked in advance by tel 01228 710947.**
Rose Castle was the palace of the Bishops of Carlisle from 1230 until 2009. The grounds are of historic interest and incl a C13 fish pond, walled gardens and a disused moat. The landscaping of the terraces and rosary was done for Bishop Percy (1826-56) by the noted horticulturist Sir Joseph Paxton.

54 ◆ RYDAL HALL
Ambleside LA22 9LX. Diocese of Carlisle, 01539 432050, www.rydalhall.org. *2m N of Ambleside. E from A591 at Rydal signed Rydal Hall.* **Adm £3, chd free. For NGS: Sun 24 Mar; Thur 18 July; Thur 8 Aug (11-4). For other opening times and information, please phone or see garden website.**
Formal Italianate gardens designed by Thomas Mawson in 1911 set in 34 acres. The gardens have recently been restored over a 2yr period returning to their former glory. Informal woodland garden, leading to C17 viewing station/ summerhouse, fine herbaceous planting, community vegetable garden, orchard and apiary. Opening for Wordsworth's Daffodil Legacy - 24th March.

55 ◆ SIZERGH CASTLE
nr Kendal LA8 8AE. National Trust, 015395 69811, www.nationaltrust.org.uk. *3m S of Kendal. Approach rd leaves A590 close to & S of A590/A591 interchange.* **Adm £5.85, chd £2.93. For NGS: Sat 20 July (11-5). For other opening times and information, please phone or see garden website.**
⅔ -acre limestone rock garden, largest owned by National Trust; collection of Japanese maples, dwarf conifers, hardy ferns; hot wall border with fruiting trees. Wild flower areas, herbaceous borders, 'Dutch' garden. Terraced garden and lake; kitchen garden; fruit orchard with spring bulbs. National Collection of Asplenium scolopendrium, Cystopteris,Dryopteris, Osmunda. Open for Wordsworth Daffodil legacy 24 March.

NCH

Beautiful setting with fine views across to Farleton Fell . . .

56 SPRINT MILL
Burneside LA8 9AQ. Edward & Romola Acland, 01539 725168, edwardacland@freeuk.com. *2m N of Kendal. From Burneside follow signs to Skelsmergh for ½ m then L into drive of Sprint Mill.* Light lunches & home-made teas. **Adm £3, chd free. Suns 16 June; 21 July (11-5). Visitors also welcome by appt May to Sept.**
Unorthodox organic garden (atypical NGS) combining the wild and natural alongside provision of owners' wood, fruit and vegetables. 5 acres to explore, riverside setting, hand-crafted seats. Large vegetable and soft fruit area, following no-dig and permaculture principles. Hand-tools prevail. Historic water mill with original turbine, housing owner's art studio and personal museum, incl collection of many old hand tools associated with rural crafts. Green woodworking demonstrations. Grass slopes.

57 SUMMERDALE HOUSE
Nook, nr Lupton LA6 1PE. David & Gail Sheals, 015395 67210, sheals@btinternet.com, www.summerdalegardenplants.co.uk. *7m S of Kendal, 5m W of Kirkby Lonsdale. From J36 M6 take A65 towards Kirkby Lonsdale, at Nook take R turn Farleton.* Home-made teas Suns only. Home -made soups and bread February, March. **Adm £3.50, chd free. Suns 17, 24 Feb; 31 Mar (11-4.30); Every Fri 5 Apr to 30 Aug; Suns 5 May; 7 July (11-4.30); Sun 16 Feb 2014. Visitors also welcome by appt Feb to Aug, groups 10 to 30.**
1½ -acre part-walled country garden set around 18c former vicarage. Several defined areas have been created by hedges, each with its own theme and linked by intricate cobbled pathways. Beautiful setting with fine views across to Farleton Fell. Traditional herbaceous borders, ponds, woodland and meadow planting provide year round interest. Large collections of auricula, primulas and snowdrops. Adjoining nursery features in RHS 'Britain's Favourite Plants'. Home made jams and chutneys for sale. Featured in The English Garden, Cumbria Life.

58 SUNNYSIDE
Woodhouse Lane, Heversham, Milnthorpe LA7 7EW. Bill & Anita Gott. *1½ m N of Milnthorpe. From A6 turn into Heversham, then R at church signed Crooklands in ½ m turn L down lane.* Home-made teas. **Adm £3.50, chd free. Sat 17, Sun 18 Aug (1-5).**
½ -acre country cottage garden with his and hers areas, incl pond and mixed borders and a stunning display of prize winning dahlias. Large immaculate vegetable garden. Sit on one of our many seats and watch birds, butterflies and free range hens. New area to attract bees and insects. Voted Best Garden in local competition.

59 ◆ SWARTHMOOR HALL
Ulverston LA12 0JQ. Jane Pearson, 01229 583204, www.swarthmoorhall.co.uk. *1½ m SW of Ulverston. A590 to Ulverston. Turn off to Ulverston railway station. Brown tourist signs to hall, R into Urswick Rd, then R into Swarthmoor Hall Lane.* Tea, coffee and cake available - honesty box provided for

donations. **Adm by donation. For NGS: Fri 22, Sat 23, Sun 24, Mon 25, Tue 26, Wed 27 Feb, Fri 1, Sat 2, Sun 3 Mar (10.30-4.30). For other opening times and information, please phone or see garden website.**
Wild purple crocus late February early March depending on weather, earlier if mild winter later if cold and frosty.

60 ◆ TULLIE HOUSE
Castle Street, Carlisle CA3 8TP. Tullie House Museum and Art Gallery Trust, 01228 618718, www.tulliehouse.co.uk. *City Centre. Signed as Museum on brown signs, see website for map.* **For opening times and information, please phone or see garden website.**
Open all year this tranquil garden in city centre setting incl new area developed during 2012 to reflect a Roman peristyle garden with Roman influenced planting incl figs, vines, myrtle, acanthus, herbs. Delightful garden to front of Jacobean house with mature Arbutus unedo and Cornus kousa growing alongside Fatsia japonica variegata and Eucryphia glutinosa. The garden surrounds the Jacobean building of the museum which displays a fine collection of Pre-raphelite artworks and porcelain, well worth a visit as is the rest of the museum displaying Roman, Natural and Social History objects. Interactive and fun the museum has something for everyone.

61 WESTVIEW
Fletcher Hill, Kirkby Stephen CA17 4QQ. Reg & Irene Metcalfe. *Kirkby Stephen town centre, T-lights opp Pine Design.* **Adm £5, chd free. Sun 14 July (11-5). Combined admission with Winton Park.**
Tucked away behind the town centre, this secret walled cottage garden is a little haven. The main garden is filled with perennials, shrubs and large collection of hostas, with small wildlife pond. The adjacent prairie-style nursery beds are at their best in July.

62 WINDY HALL
Crook Road, Windermere LA23 3JA. Diane & David Kinsman, 015394 46238, dhewitt.kinsman@gmail.com. *½ m S of Bowness-on-Windermere. On western end of B5284 (Crook Road) up Linthwaite House Hotel driveway.* Home-made teas. **Adm £4.50, chd free. Suns 5 May; 2 June (10-5). Combined with Brackenrigg Lodge adm £6. Visitors also welcome by appt Apr to Sept.**
2 people, 4-acres, 6ft rain & 30+ years. Fellside woodland with rhododendrons, camellias, magnolias, hydrangeas, bluebells and foxgloves. Pond, kitchen, 'privy' and 'Best' gardens, Japanese influenced quarry garden. Waterfowl garden with stewartias and large gunneras, alpine area with very small gunneras. Moss path & wildflower meadow. Abundant wildlife with many native birds nesting in the garden. National Collections of *Aruncus* & *Filipendula*. Exotic waterfowl and pheasants. Black, multi-horned Hebridean sheep.

NCH

63 WINTON PARK
Appleby Road, Kirkby Stephen CA17 4PG. Mr Anthony Kilvington. *2m N of Kirkby Stephen. On A685 turn L signed Gt Musgrave/Warcop (B6259). After approx 1m turn L as signed.* Light refreshments. **Adm £5, chd free. Sun 14 July (11-5). Combined adm with Westview.**
3-acre country garden bordered by the Banks of the R Eden with stunning views. Many fine conifers, acers and rhododendrons, herbaceous borders, hostas, ferns, grasses and several hundred roses. Four formal ponds plus rock pool.

64 NEW WOODEND HOUSE
Woodend, Egremont CA22 2TA. Grainne & Richard Jakobson, 01946 813017, gmjakobson@sky.com. *2m S of Whitehaven. Take the A595 from Whitehaven towards Egremont. On leaving Bigrigg take first turn L. Go down hill, garden is at bottom on R opp Woodend Farm.* Home-made teas. **Adm £3, chd free. Suns 7 Apr; 21 July (10.30-5). Visitors also welcome by appt.**
Secluded garden in quiet location set against background of mature trees. Relaxed style of planting, colour themed with unusual plants. Main garden slopes away from attractive Georgian house with meandering gravel paths. A wildlife friendly garden includes small wildlife pond, summer wildflower meadow and mini native woodland and shady walk. Interested in plants for shade and Vit Clematis.

65 YEWBARROW HOUSE
Hampsfell Road, Grange-over-Sands LA11 6BE. Jonathan & Margaret Denby, 015395 32469, jonathan@bestlakesbreaks.co.uk, www.yewbarrowhouse.co.uk. *¼ m from town centre. Follow signs in centre of Grange. Turn R at HSBC Bank into Pig Lane, 1st L into Hampsfell Rd. Garden 200yds on left-follow sign to Yewbarrow Wood at brow of hill.* Cream teas. **Adm £4, chd free. Suns 2 June; 7 July; 4 Aug; 1 Sept (11-4). Visitors also welcome by appt May to Sept.**
Mediterranean style garden on 4½ -acre elevated site with magnificent views over Morecambe Bay. The garden features a restored walled Victorian kitchen garden; Italianate terrace garden; exotic gravel garden; fern garden, Japanese Hot Spring pool. Dahlia trial beds, Orangery, Sculpture and Sensory gardens.

66 YEWS
Middle Entrance Drive, Storrs Park, Bowness-on-Windermere LA23 3JR. Sir Oliver & Lady Scott. *1m S of Bowness-on-Windermere. A5074. Middle Entrance Drive, 50yds.* Home-made teas. **Adm £3.50, chd free. Sun 23 June (2-5.30).**
Medium-sized formal Edwardian garden; fine trees, ha-ha, herbaceous borders; greenhouse. Bog area being developed, bamboo, primula, hosta. Young yew maze and vegetable garden.

A wildlife friendly garden includes small wildlife pond, summer wild flower meadow and mini native woodland and shady walk . . .

Stilefield, Gilgarran Gardens

Cumbria County Volunteers

County Organiser

Diane Hewitt, Windy Hall, Crook Road, Windermere LA23 3JA, 015394 46238, dhewitt.kinsman@googlemail.com

County Treasurer

Derek Farman, Mill House, Winster, Windermere, Cumbria LA23 3NW, 015394 44893, derek@derejam.myzen.co.uk

Publicity

(Web) Tony Connor, 01524 781119, tonconnor@aol.com

Assistant County Organisers

Central (Gardens & Special Interest) Carole Berryman, 1 Cragwood Cottages, Ecclerigg, Windermere LA23 1LQ, 01539 443649, carole.berryman@student.sac.ac.uk

North Alannah Rylands, Crookdake Farm, Aspatria, Wigton CA7 3SH, 016973 20413, alannah.rylands@me.com

East Alec & Linda Greening, Pear Tree Cottage, Dalton, Burton-in-Kendal, Carnforth LA6 1NN, 01524 781624, linda.greening@virgin.net

West Chris & Helen Steele, Hall Senna, Gosforth, Holmbrook CA19 1YB, 019467 25436, helen.steele5@btinternet.com

Borders Liaison Sue Clapperton, 01387 381004, charlieclapperton@hotmail.com

DERBYSHIRE

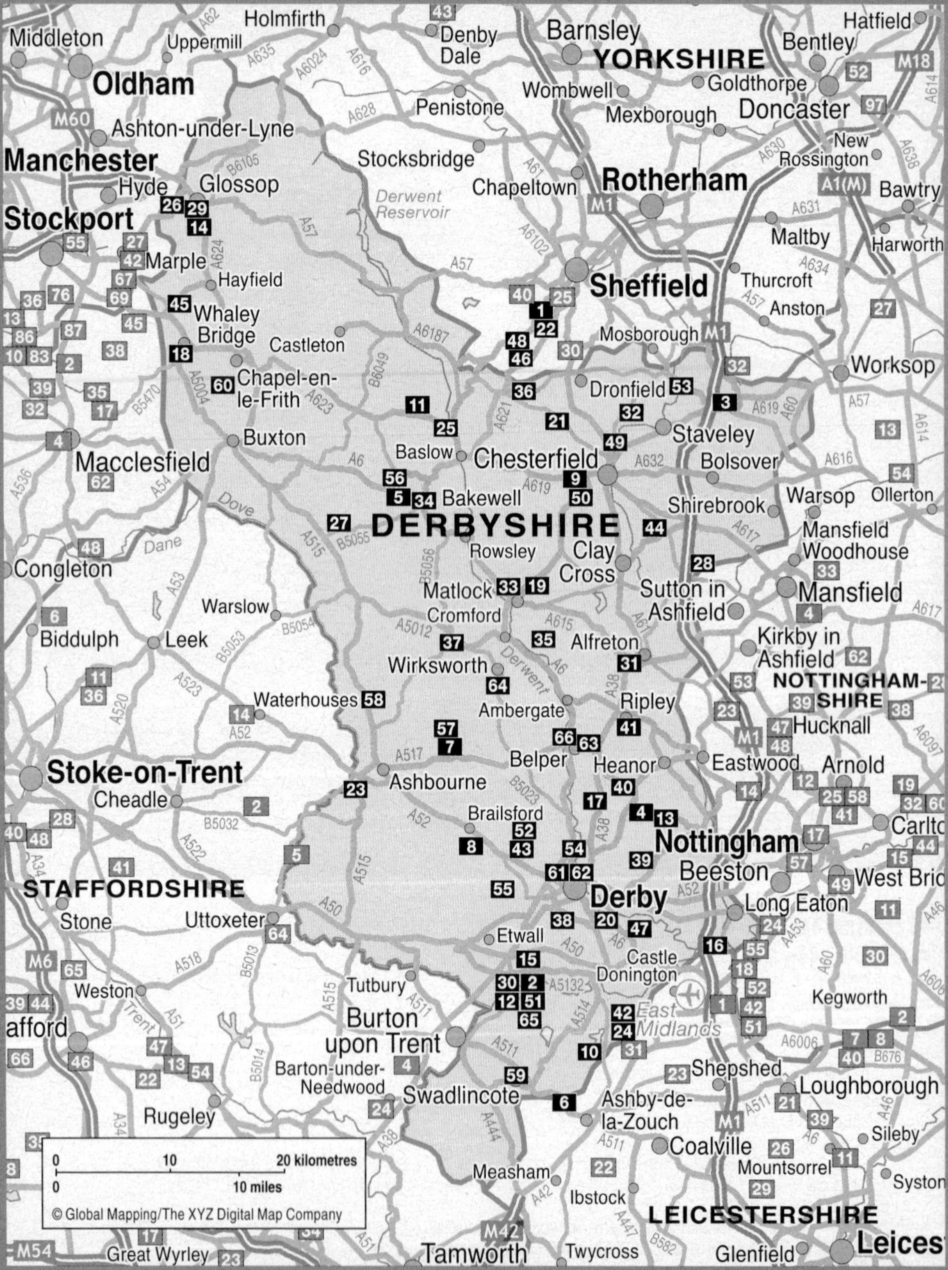
Middleton
Uppermill
Holmfirth
Denby Dale
Barnsley
YORKSHIRE
Hatfield
Bentley
Oldham
Wombwell
Goldthorpe
Penistone
Mexborough
Doncaster
Ashton-under-Lyne
Manchester
Stocksbridge
New Rossington
Hyde
Glossop
Chapeltown
Rotherham
Bawtry
Derwent Reservoir
Stockport
Maltby
Harworth
Marple
Hayfield
Sheffield
Thurcroft
Whaley Bridge
Anston
Castleton
Mosborough
Worksop
Chapel-en-le-Frith
Dronfield
Staveley
Buxton
Baslow
Chesterfield
Bolsover
Macclesfield
Bakewell
Shirebrook
Warsop
Ollerton
DERBYSHIRE
Mansfield Woodhouse
Rowsley
Clay Cross
Congleton
Matlock
Sutton in Ashfield
Mansfield
Warslow
Cromford
Biddulph
Leek
Alfreton
Kirkby in Ashfield
Wirksworth
NOTTINGHAMSHIRE
Waterhouses
Ripley
Ambergate
Hucknall
Stoke-on-Trent
Belper
Heanor
Eastwood
Arnold
Cheadle
Ashbourne
Brailsford
Nottingham
Beeston
West Bridgford
STAFFORDSHIRE
Derby
Long Eaton
Stone
Uttoxeter
Etwall
Castle Donington
East Midlands
Tutbury
Weston
Kegworth
Burton upon Trent
Barton-under-Needwood
Shepshed
Swadlincote
Loughborough
Rugeley
Ashby-de-la-Zouch
Coalville
Sileby
Mountsorrel
Measham
Syston
Ibstock
LEICESTERSHIRE
Great Wyrley
Tamworth
Twycross
Glenfield
0 10 20 kilometres
0 10 miles
© Global Mapping/The XYZ Digital Map Company

Opening Dates

February

Saturday 9
6 Bluebell Arboretum and Nursery

Saturday 23
6 Bluebell Arboretum and Nursery

March

Wednesday 13
6 Bluebell Arboretum and Nursery

Sunday 24
64 Windward

Thursday 28
6 Bluebell Arboretum and Nursery

April

Monday 1
8 The Burrows Gardens

Friday 5
1 12 Ansell Road

Wednesday 10
6 Bluebell Arboretum and Nursery

Sunday 14
4 334 Belper Road

Saturday 20
47 Old English Walled Garden, Elvaston Castle Country Park

Sunday 21
12 10 Chestnut Way
30 37 High Street

Sunday 28
6 Bluebell Arboretum and Nursery
66 35 Wyver Lane

May

Sunday 5
17 Coxbench Hall

Monday 6
1 12 Ansell Road
8 The Burrows Gardens
57 Tilford House

Wednesday 8
6 Bluebell Arboretum and Nursery

Sunday 12
14 Cloud Cottage
39 Locko Park

Sunday 19
2 Askew Cottage
4 334 Belper Road
12 10 Chestnut Way
14 Cloud Cottage
25 Fir Croft
49 The Paddock

Friday 24
52 Rectory House

Saturday 25
23 Dove Cottage

Sunday 26
6 Bluebell Arboretum and Nursery
13 13 Chiltern Drive
14 Cloud Cottage
23 Dove Cottage
26 Gamesley Fold Cottage
31 Highfield House
43 Meynell Langley Trials Garden

Monday 27
8 The Burrows Gardens

Thursday 30
36 The Leylands

June

Saturday 1
42 Melbourne Hall Gardens

Sunday 2
1 12 Ansell Road
25 Fir Croft
42 Melbourne Hall Gardens

Saturday 8
22 122 Dobcroft Road
33 The Holly Tree

Sunday 9
4 334 Belper Road
22 122 Dobcroft Road

Meet a pair of passionate, practical, compost loving gardeners . . .

26 Gamesley Fold Cottage
33 The Holly Tree

Wednesday 12
4 334 Belper Road

National Gardens Weekend

Saturday 15
1 12 Ansell Road
15 Clovermead
24 The Dower House
36 The Leylands
46 9 Newfield Crescent
48 Owl End
51 22 Pinfold Close
54 Rosebank

Sunday 16
6 Bluebell Arboretum and Nursery
8 The Burrows Gardens
11 Cherry Hill
15 Clovermead
20 8 Curzon Lane
24 The Dower House
28 Hardwick Estate
36 The Leylands
40 9 Main Street
43 Meynell Langley Trials Garden
46 9 Newfield Crescent
48 Owl End
50 Park Hall
51 22 Pinfold Close
61 24 Wheeldon Avenue
62 26 Wheeldon Avenue
63 26 Windmill Rise
64 Windward
66 35 Wyver Lane

Monday 17
8 The Burrows Gardens

Saturday 22
18 Craigside

Sunday 23
15 Clovermead
18 Craigside
25 Fir Croft
29 High Roost

Monday 24
18 Craigside

Saturday 29
34 Holme Grange
60 Westgate

Sunday 30
6 Bluebell Arboretum and Nursery
23 Dove Cottage
30 37 High Street
37 The Lilies
44 Moorfields

July

Saturday 6
27 Green Meadows
45 New Mills School Business & Enterprise College

Sunday 7
12 10 Chestnut Way
31 Highfield House
45 New Mills School Business & Enterprise College
65 Woodend Cottage

Wednesday 10
6 Bluebell Arboretum and Nursery

Saturday 13
10 Calke Abbey
20 8 Curzon Lane

Sunday 14
20 8 Curzon Lane
59 13 Westfield Road
64 Windward

Monday 15
8 The Burrows Gardens

Saturday 20
3 Barlborough Gardens
27 Green Meadows
41 2 Manvers Street

Sunday 21
3 Barlborough Gardens
9 Byways
22 122 Dobcroft Road

You are always welcome at an NGS garden!

12 Ansell Road

41 2 Manvers Street
43 Meynell Langley Trials Garden

Thursday 25
36 The Leylands

Saturday 27
63 26 Windmill Rise

Sunday 28
6 Bluebell Arboretum and Nursery
15 Clovermead
63 26 Windmill Rise

Tuesday 30
36 The Leylands

August

Sunday 4
17 Coxbench Hall
40 9 Main Street

Wednesday 7
1 12 Ansell Road
6 Bluebell Arboretum and Nursery
57 Tilford House

Sunday 11
49 The Paddock

Monday 12
10 Calke Abbey

Wednesday 14
1 12 Ansell Road

Saturday 17
34 Holme Grange
47 Old English Walled Garden, Elvaston Castle Country Park

Sunday 18
12 10 Chestnut Way
51 22 Pinfold Close
56 Thornbridge Hall
65 Woodend Cottage

Saturday 24
16 The Cottage

Sunday 25
6 Bluebell Arboretum and Nursery
16 The Cottage
43 Meynell Langley Trials Garden
59 13 Westfield Road

Monday 26
8 The Burrows Gardens
58 Tissington Hall

September

Sunday 1
37 The Lilies
38 Littleover Lane Allotments

Wednesday 11
6 Bluebell Arboretum and Nursery

Sunday 15
2 Askew Cottage
64 Windward

Monday 16
8 The Burrows Gardens

Sunday 22
43 Meynell Langley Trials Garden

Sunday 29
6 Bluebell Arboretum and Nursery

October

Wednesday 9
6 Bluebell Arboretum and Nursery

Sunday 13
43 Meynell Langley Trials Garden

Wednesday 30
6 Bluebell Arboretum and Nursery

November

Wednesday 13
6 Bluebell Arboretum and Nursery

Saturday 30
6 Bluebell Arboretum and Nursery

December

Wednesday 11
6 Bluebell Arboretum and Nursery

Gardens open to the public

6 Bluebell Arboretum and Nursery
8 The Burrows Gardens
10 Calke Abbey
28 Hardwick Estate
35 Lea Gardens
42 Melbourne Hall Gardens
43 Meynell Langley Trials Garden
47 Old English Walled Garden, Elvaston Castle Country Park
53 Renishaw Hall & Gardens
58 Tissington Hall

By appointment only

5 Birchfield
7 Brick Kiln Farm
19 Cuckoostone Cottage
21 Dam Stead
32 Hillside
55 Thatched Farm

Also open by Appointment

1 12 Ansell Road
2 Askew Cottage
4 334 Belper Road
9 Byways
11 Cherry Hill
12 10 Chestnut Way
14 Cloud Cottage
15 Clovermead
16 The Cottage
18 Craigside
20 8 Curzon Lane

The Gardens

ADLINGTON HALL
See Cheshire & Wirral

1 12 ANSELL ROAD
Ecclesall, Sheffield S11 7PE. Dave Darwent, 01142 665881, dave@poptasticdave.co.uk, www.poptasticdave.co.uk/_/Horticulture.html. *Approx 3m SW of City Centre. Travel to Ringinglow Rd (88 or 83 bus), then Edale Rd (opp Ecclesall C of E Primary School). 3rd R - Ansell. 12 on L 3/4 way down, solar panel on roof.* Home-made teas. **Adm £2.50, chd free. Fri 5 Apr (12-5); Mon 6 May, Sun 2, Sat 15 June (11-5); Weds 7, 14 Aug (3-8.30). Visitors also welcome by appt Mar to Aug.**
Established 1930s, the garden contains many original plants maintained in the original style. Traditional rustic pergola and dwarf-wall greenhouse. Owner (grandson of first owner) aims to keep the garden as a living example of how inter-war gardens were cultivated to provide decoration and produce. More detail online. Featured in Dronfield Eye and Telegraph Gardening.

2 NEW ASKEW COTTAGE
Milton Road, Repton, Derby DE65 6FZ. Louise Hardwick, 01283 701608, louise.hardwick@hotmail.co.uk. *6m S of Derby. From A38/A50 junction S of Derby follow signs to Willington then Repton on B5008. In Repton turn L at r'about into Boot Hill, bear sharp R into Milton Rd. Askew Cottage is on the next LH bend.* Light refreshments. **Adm £3, chd free. Sun 19 May, Sun 15 Sept (2-6). Visitors also welcome by appt May to Nov.**
The rear garden encompasses several different areas, all connected with flowing curved paths. Formal hedges give structure and features in the garden incl a box-edged herb garden, a small wildlife pool and bog garden, a kitchen garden with raised beds, a circle of meadow grass set within a 'cloud' box hedge, apples trained as a 'Belgian Fence' and plenty of interesting shrubs and perennials. Featured in The Derbyshire magazine.
D

BANKCROFT FARM
See Staffordshire, Birmingham & West Midlands

GROUP OPENING

3 BARLBOROUGH GARDENS
Barlborough, Chesterfield S43 4ER. *7m NE of Chesterfield. Off A619 midway between Chesterfield & Worksop. 1/2 m E M1 J30. Follow signs for Barlborough then NGS signs.* Light refreshments at Stone Croft and Church Institute. **Combined adm £5, chd free. Sat 20, Sun 21 July (1-6).**

NEW CLARENDON
Neil & Lorraine Jones

NEW GOOSE COTTAGE
Mick & Barbara Housley

THE HOLLIES
Vernon Sanderson

LINDWAY
Thomas & Margaret Pettinger

ROSE COTTAGE
Kathy & Steve Thomson

STONE CROFT
Mrs June Widdowson

Barlborough is an attractive historic village and a range of interesting buildings can be seen all around the village centre. Enjoy 6 lovely gardens which are entirely different from each other. Rose Cottage is a mature 1/3 acre cottage garden, a well established garden can be found at Stone Croft with mature trees and planting together with a fruit and vegetable section. At Lindway there are lawns with integral planting of shrubs, perennials and annual flowers. The Hollies maximises the unusual garden layout, Clarendon has several water features, a large patio and a short tennis court and Goose Cottage is a small walled garden with a pond, lawn, a selection of hostas, annual flowers and acers. Opening coincides with the village well dressing and St James's Church Flower Festival. Partial wheelchair access at Rose Cottage & The Hollies. Access to the rear of Clarendon via stone slabs.

THE BEECHES
See Staffordshire, Birmingham & West Midlands

Plenty of seating to enjoy our highly recommended home-made cakes . . .

4 334 BELPER ROAD
Stanley Common DE7 6FY. Gill & Colin Hancock, 01159 301061, www.hamescovert.com. *7m N of Derby. 3m W of Ilkeston. On A609, 3/4 m from Rose & Crown Xrds (A608). Please park in field up farm drive or Working Men's Club rear car park if wet.* **Adm £3, chd free. Sun 14 Apr (12-5); Sun 19 May, Sun 9 June (1-5); Wed 12 June (2-8). Visitors also welcome by appt Apr to Sept. Adm £6 incl tea, coffee and cake and our personal attention.**
Relax in our constantly evolving country garden with informal planting and features with plenty of seating to enjoy our highly recommended home-made cakes. Take a stroll across the field into the young 10-acre wood with wild flower glades to a 1/2 -acre lake. In April see our hellebores, cowslips and try our home-made soups. As featured in The Derbyshire magazine. Paths round wood and lake not suitable for wheelchairs.

5 BIRCHFIELD
Dukes Drive, Ashford in the Water, Bakewell DE45 1QQ. Brian Parker, 01629 813800. *2m NW of Bakewell. On A6 to Buxton between New Bridge & Sheepwash Bridge.* **Visitors welcome by appt. April - Sept £3, Oct - March £2, chd free (share to Thornhill Memorial Trust).**
Beautifully situated 3/4 -acre part terraced garden with pond and a 1 1/4 -acre arboretum and wild flower meadow. An extremely varied selection of trees, shrubs, climbers, perennials, bulbs, grasses and bamboos, all designed to give yr-round colour.

Interest throughout the year with spring flowers, cool leafy areas in summer and sensational autumn colour . . .

6 ◆ BLUEBELL ARBORETUM AND NURSERY
Annwell Lane, Smisby, Ashby de la Zouch LE65 2TA. Robert & Suzette Vernon, 01530 413700, www.bluebellnursery.com. *1m NW of Ashby-de-la-Zouch. Arboretum is clearly signed in Annwell Lane, 1/4 m S, through village of Smisby off B5006, between Ticknall & Ashby-de-la-Zouch.* **Adm £2.50, chd free. For NGS: Sats 9, 23 Feb, Wed 13, Thur 28 Mar, Wed 10 Apr (9-4.30); Sun 28 Apr (10.30-4); Wed 8 May (9-4.30); Suns 26 May, 16, 30 June (10.30-4); Wed 10 July (9-4.30); Sun 28 July (10.30-4); Wed 7 Aug (9-4.30); Sun 25 Aug (10.30-4); Wed 11 Sept (9-4.30); Sun 29 Sept (10.30-4); Weds 9, 30 Oct, 13 Nov (9-4.30); Sat 30 Nov, Wed 11 Dec (9-4). For other opening times and information, please phone or see garden website.**
Beautiful 9-acre woodland garden with a large collection of rare trees and shrubs. Interest throughout the year with spring flowers, cool leafy areas in summer and sensational autumn colour. Many information posters describing the more obscure plants. Bring wellingtons in wet weather. Adjacent specialist tree and shrub nursery. Please be aware this is not a wood full of bluebells, despite the name. The woodland garden is fully labelled and the staff can answer questions or talk at length about any of the trees or shrubs on display. Full access in dry, warm weather however grass paths in garden can become wet and inaccessible in snow or after rain.

7 BRICK KILN FARM
Hulland Ward, Ashbourne DE6 3EJ. Mrs Jan Hutchinson, 01335 370440, robert.hutchinson123@btinternet.com. *4m E of Ashbourne (A517). 1m S of Carsington Water. From Hulland Ward, take Dog Lane, past church, take 2nd L 100yds on R. From Ashbourne A517, Bradley Corner, turn L, follow sign for Carsington Water. Approx 1m up on L.* Cream teas. **Adm £3.50, chd free (share to Great Dane Adoption Society). Visitors welcome by appt.**
A small country garden created out of a field over 20 yrs ago. Courtyard with original well. Pond made using reclaimed stone, ironwork, leads to lawned area, well filled herbaceous borders, a duck pond, pets memorial garden. Can be viewed online on Peak District TV. Level garden, some uneven flagstones, gravel drive.

8 ◆ THE BURROWS GARDENS
Burrows Lane, Brailsford DE6 3BU. Mr B C Dalton, 01335 360745, www.burrowsgardens.com. *5m SE of Ashbourne; 5m NW of Derby. From Ashbourne: A52 towards Derby 5m to Brailsford. Turn R after Rose & Crown PH, then 1st L. Cont 1/2 m, garden on R. From Derby: A52 towards Ashbourne, until 1 1/2 m after Kirk Langley.Turn L at Xrds, Burrows Lane. After 1/2 m R at grass triangle, garden in front.* **Adm £4, chd free. For NGS: Mons 1 Apr, 6, 27 May, Sun 16, Mon 17 June, Mons 15 July, 26 Aug, 16 Sept (10.30-4.30). For other opening times and information, please phone or see garden website.**
5 acres of stunning garden set in beautiful countryside where immaculate lawns show off exotic rare plants and trees, mixing with old favourites in this fabulous garden. A vast variety of styles from temple to Cornish, Italian and English, gloriously designed and displayed. This is a must-see garden. Open every Tues, Fri, and Sun from April - September inclusive.

9 BYWAYS
7A Brookfield Avenue, Brookside, Chesterfield S40 3NX. Terry & Eileen Kelly, 01246 566376, telkel1@aol.com. *1 1/2 m W of Chesterfield. Follow A619 from Chesterfield towards Baslow. Brookfield Av is 2nd R after Brookfield Sch. Please park on Chatsworth Rd (A619).* Home-made teas. **Adm £2.50, chd free (share to Ashgate Hospice). Sun 21 July (12.30-5.30). Visitors also welcome by appt July to Aug.**
The rear garden has been developed over the last 5yrs and now has well stocked, colourful perennial borders featuring many plant varieties incl helenium, monardas, phlox, grasses. Large collection of acers (30+), rock garden, alpine garden and many planters containing hostas, ferns, roses, fuchsias and geraniums. Enjoy the view from any of the 5 seating areas around the garden. Awarded Best Back Garden - Chesterfield in Bloom.

10 ◆ CALKE ABBEY
Ticknall DE73 7LE. National Trust, 01332 865587, www.nationaltrust.org.uk. *10m S of Derby. On A514 at Ticknall between Swadlincote & Melbourne.* **Adm £4.70, chd £2.40. For NGS: Sat 13 July, Mon 12 Aug (10-5). For other opening times and information, please phone or see garden website.**
Late C18 walled gardens gradually repaired over the last 24yrs. Flower garden with summer bedding, herbaceous borders and the unique auricula theatre. Georgian orangery, impressive collection of glasshouses and garden buildings. Icehouse and recently repaired grotto. Vegetable garden growing heirloom varieties of fruit and vegetables, often on sale to visitors. Electric buggy available.

11 CHERRY HILL

The Nook, Eyam, Derbyshire S32 5QP. June Elizabeth Skinner, 01433 631036, juneliza.s@btinternet.com, www.peakdistrictart.com. *6m NW of Chatsworth in the Peak National Park. Off A623. In Eyam past church on R take 1st R up Hawkhill Rd. Car Park opp. museum. 200yds up hill walk on to The Nook, entrance drive on R.* Wonderful cakes baked by husband. **Adm £3, chd free. Sun 16 June (1-5). Visitors also welcome by appt Feb to June.**

One-acre naturally planted artists' garden. The S-facing aspect is a delightful blend of herbaceous borders, secret areas, and a geranium carpeted orchard. Sculptures hidden amongst the foliage reflect the quirky and different style, which the present owner has brought to this garden. Artist's Studio open with a display of ceramics for sale. Garden sculptures made by the owner to be found around the garden.

12 10 CHESTNUT WAY

Repton DE65 6FQ. Robert & Pauline Little, 01283 702267, rlittleq@gmail.com, www.littlegarden.org.uk. *6m S of Derby. From A38, S of Derby, follow signs to Willington, then Repton. In Repton turn R at r'about. Chestnut Way is ¼ m up hill, on L.* Home-made teas. **Adm £3, chd free. Sun 21 Apr (1-6); Sun 19 May, Sun 7 July (11-6); Sun 18 Aug (1-6). Combined with Woodend Cottage & 22 Pinfold Close. Adm £6, (18 Aug only). Visitors also welcome by appt Apr to Sept. Adm £6 incl home-made teas and guided tour.**

Lose yourself in an acre of sweeping mixed borders, spring bulbs, mature trees to a stunning butterfly bed, young arboretum, established prairie and annual meadow. Meet a pair of passionate, practical, compost loving gardeners who gently manage this plantsman's garden. Designed and maintained by the owners. Expect a colourful display throughout the year. Plenty of seats, conservatory if wet. Excellent plant stall. Special interest in viticella clematis and organic vegetables. All in all a happy garden. Radio Derby outside broadcast (in thunderstorm). Featured in Garden News. Level garden, good solid paths to main areas. Some grass/bark paths.

13 13 CHILTERN DRIVE

West Hallam, Ilkeston DE7 6PA. Jacqueline & Keith Holness. *Approx 7m NE of Derby. 2m W of Ilkeston and 7m NE Derby on A609, 1.5m from Rose and Crown Xrds (A608). Take St Wilfred's Rd to West Hallam, 1st R Derbyshire Ave, 3rd L is Chiltern Drive.* A warm welcome and delicious cakes (some gluten-free) awaits all visitors. **Adm £3, chd free (share to Teenage Cancer Trust). Sun 26 May (11-5).**

Small, secret walled suburban garden, every corner packed with plants, many rare and unusual. Pretty summerhouse, two small ponds and fernery, together with 75 acers and some well-hidden lizards! Garden on 2 levels separated by steps.

14 CLOUD COTTAGE

Simmondley SK13 6JN. Mr R G Lomas, 01457 862033. *1m SW of Glossop. On High Lane between Simmondley & Charlesworth. From M67 take A57, turn R at Mottram (1st T-lights) through Broadbottom & Charlesworth. In Charlesworth up Town Lane by Grey Mare. Cloud Cottage ½ m on R. From Glossop, A57 towards Manchester, turn L at 2nd of two mini r'abouts up Simmondley Lane, Cloud Cottage on L after Hare & Hounds.* Home-made teas. **Adm £3, chd free. Sun 12, Sun 19, Sun 26 May (2-5). Visitors also welcome by appt.**

1¼ -acre arboretum and rhododendron garden. Altitude 750ft on side of hill in Peak District National Park. Collections of conifers, most over 40yrs old. Species and hybrid rhododendrons and a wide variety of shrubs. We have extended the Japanese inspired garden by diverting a stream to make 6 ponds. Listed in Journal of the Japanese Garden Society.

15 CLOVERMEAD

Commonpiece Lane, Findern DE65 6AF. David & Rosemary Noblet, 01283 702237, daverose1221@btinternet.com. *4m S of Derby. From Findern village green, turn R at church into Lower Green, R turn into Commonpiece Lane, approx 500yds on R.* Home-made teas. **Adm £3, chd free. Sat 15, Sun 16, Suns 23 June, 28 July (1-5). Visitors also welcome by appt June to Aug.**

Cottage garden set in approx 1-acre. Garden rooms packed full of perennial flowers. Honeysuckle, roses, jasmine and sweet peas scent the air. Clematis ramble everywhere over 100 varieties. Pergolas and archways give height to the garden. Fishponds and bandstand with seating. Greenhouses, large vegetable plot, wildlife orchard. New long rose walk. Pathway to village nature park and canal. Featured in Derbyshire life.

7 COLLYGATE
See Nottinghamshire

COLOUR MILL
See Staffordshire, Birmingham & West Midlands

> Sculptures hidden amongst the foliage reflect the quirky and different style . . .

16 THE COTTAGE

25 Plant Lane, Old Sawley, Long Eaton NG10 3BJ. Ernie & Averil Carver, 01158 491960. *2m SW of Long Eaton. From Long Eaton green take sign for town centre. Onto B6540 through to Old Sawley, take R at Nags Head PH into Wiln Rd. 400yds take R turn into Plant Lane at the Railway Inn. Garden 200yds on R.* Light refreshments at Sawley Church Flower Festival. **Adm £2.50, chd free (share to Canaan Trust). Sat 24 Aug (11-5); Sun 25 Aug (12-5). Visitors also welcome by appt July to Aug.**

Cottage garden full of colour, steeped in herbaceous borders. Annual plants raised from the greenhouse. Number of surprising features. Summerhouse in a walled sheltered garden, providing a charming environment.

17 COXBENCH HALL

Alfreton Road, Coxbench, Derby DE21 5BB. Mr Brian Ballin. *4m N of Derby close to A38. After passing through Little Eaton, turn L onto the old coaching rd. After 1 m Coxbench Hall is located on the L next to The Fox & Hounds PH between Little Eaton and Holbrook.* Home-made teas. **Adm £3, chd free. Sun 5 May, Sun 4 Aug (2.30-4.30).**

Formerly the ancestral home of the Meynell family, the gardens reflect the Georgian house standing in 4½ -acres of grounds most of which is accessible and wheelchair friendly. The garden has 2 fishponds connected by a stream, a sensory garden for the sight impaired, a short woodland walk through shrubbery, a vegetable plot and seasonal displays in the mainly lawned areas.

18 CRAIGSIDE

Reservoir Road, Whaley Bridge SK23 7BW. Jane & Gerard Lennox, 01663 732381, jane@lennoxonline.net. *11m SE of Stockport. 11m NNW of Buxton. Turn off A6 on to A5004 to Whaley Bridge. Turn at Jodrell Arms/train stn, under railway bridge, immed bear L along Reservoir Rd ½ m. Rd narrows to single track with passing places. Park on roadside or ½ m walk from village.* Home-made teas. **Adm £3.50, chd free. Sat 22, Sun 23, Mon 24 June (1-5). Visitors also welcome by appt May to Sept.**

1 acre rising steeply for magnificent views across Todbrook reservoir into Peak District. Gravel paths, stone steps with stopping places. Many mature trees incl 400yr old oak. Spring bulbs, summer fuchsias, herbaceous borders, alpine bed, steep mature rockery, wild flower meadow. Herbs, vegetables and fruit trees.

19 CUCKOOSTONE COTTAGE

Chesterfield Road, Matlock Moor, Matlock DE4 5LZ. Barrie & Pauline Wild, 07960 708415, paulinewild@sky.com. *2½ m N of Matlock on A632. Past Matlock Golf Course look for Cuckoostone Lane on L. Turn here & follow for ¼ m. 1st cottage on bend.* Light refreshments. **Adm £4, chd free. Visitors welcome by appt May to Sept.**

Situated on a sloping, SW-facing rural hillside at 850ft, this ½ -acre is a plantsman's garden. Developed from a field in 9yrs it incorporates colour-themed borders, several ponds, bog garden and conservatory. Large collection of unusual trees, shrubs and perennials make this a yr-round garden but best from late May to late summer. In total over 1200 different species of plants, shrubs, trees.

A sensory garden for the sight impaired . . .

20 8 CURZON LANE

Alvaston, Derby DE24 8QS. Mrs Marian Gray, 01332 601596, maz@cvnation.com, www.curzongarden.com. *2m SE of Derby city centre. From city centre take A6 (London Rd) towards Alvaston. Curzon Lane on L, approx ½ m before Alvaston shops.* **Adm £2.50, chd free. Sun 16 June, Sat 13, Sun 14 July (2-6). Visitors also welcome by appt July.**

Mature garden with lawns, borders packed full with perennials, shrubs and small trees, tropical planting. Ornamental and wildlife ponds, greenhouse, gravel area, large patio with container planting. Also recently added extra mixed borders and potager garden.

21 DAM STEAD

3 Crowhole, Barlow, Dronfield S18 7TJ. Derek & Barbara Saveall, 01142 890802, barbarasaveall@hotmail.co.uk. *3½ m NW of Chesterfield. From A61 Sheffield/Derby take B6051 Barlow at Chesterfield North. Through Barlow, pass Tickled Trout PH on L. Pass Springfield Rd on L then R (unamed rd). Last house on R.* Light refreshments. **Adm £2.50, chd free. Visitors welcome by appt.**

Approx 1 acre with stream, weir, fragrant garden, rose tunnel (new), orchard garden and dam with an island. Long woodland path, alpine troughs, rockeries and mixed planting. A natural wildlife garden-large summerhouse with seating inside and out. 3 village well-dressings and carnival over one week mid-August.

DAVRYL

See Nottinghamshire

22 122 DOBCROFT ROAD

Millhouses, Sheffield S7 2LU. Hedley & Margaret Harper, 01142 962394, hedley.j.harper@gmail.com. *3m SW of city centre. From city centre take A625 signed Bakewell (Ecclesall Rd S) pass Prince of Wales PH on L. Dobcroft Rd is 5th on L after PH. Follow rd for ⅔ m, garden on L.* Home-made teas. **Adm £3, chd free (share to Hounds for Heroes). Sat 8, Sun 9 June, Sun 21 July (11-5). Visitors also welcome by appt May to Sept.**

Attractive long (250ft) garden, with colourful herbaceous borders, 2 wildlife ponds, productive vegetable garden with raised beds and greenhouse. Fine old oak tree. Summerhouse and various secluded sitting areas.

23 DOVE COTTAGE

off Watery Lane, Clifton, Ashbourne DE6 2JQ. Stephen & Anne Liverman, 01335 343545, astrantiamajor@hotmail.co.uk. *1½ m SW of Ashbourne. Enter Clifton village. Turn R at Xrds by church. After 100yds turn L, Dove Cottage 1st house on L. Always well signed on open days.* Home-made teas. **Adm £3.50, chd free (share to British Heart Foundation). Sat 25, Suns 26 May, 30 June (11-4). Visitors also welcome by appt Mar to July.**

Much admired, long standing NGS ¾ -acre cottage garden by the R Dove, with fine collections of new and traditional hardy plants and shrubs, notably astrantias, alchemillas, alliums, berberis, geraniums, euphorbias, hostas, variegated and silver foliage plants. This plantsman's garden is noted for the number of separate areas, incl a ribbon border of purple flowering plants and foliage, woodland glade planted with daffodils and shade loving plants. Of interest is an existing wall of 60 year old cordon pears. Featured in Derbyshire Life. Limited access.

Cherry Hill

24 THE DOWER HOUSE
Church Square, Melbourne DE73 8JH. William & Griselda Kerr, 01332 864756, griseldakerr@btinternet.com. *6m S of Derby. 5m W of exit 23A M1. 4m N of exit 13 M42. Church Sq is off Church St. On entering square, turn R before church and immed after war memorial. Dower House is at W end of Norman church. Parking on nearby streets & in Church Square.*
Adm £3.50, chd free. Sat 15, Sun 16 June (10-5). Visitors also welcome by appt. Advance booking essential.
Beautiful view of Melbourne Pool from balustraded terrace running length of 1838 house. Garden drops steeply by way of paths and steps to lawn with 70ft herbaceous border and late summer beds. A rose tunnel, glade, orchard, small area of woodland, hellebore bed, peony bed, rockery, herb garden, other small lawns and also cottage garden with roses and vegetables. Featured in Derbyshire Life. Wheelchair access is limited to the top level terrace, woodland, rockery, herb garden, rose garden and cottage garden.

EDITH TERRACE GARDENS
See Cheshire & Wirral

FELLEY PRIORY
See Nottinghamshire

25 FIR CROFT
Froggatt Road, Calver S32 3ZD. Dr S B Furness, www.alpineplantcentre.co.uk. *4m N of Bakewell. At junction of B6001 with A625 (formerly B6054), adjacent to Power Garage.* **Adm by donation. Sun 19 May, Suns 2, 23 June (2-5).**
Massive scree with many varieties. Plantsman's garden; rockeries; water garden and nursery; extensive collection (over 3000 varieties) of alpines; conifers; over 800 sempervivums, 500 saxifrages and 350 primulas. Tufa and scree beds.

26 GAMESLEY FOLD COTTAGE
Gamesley Fold, Glossop SK13 6JJ. Mrs G Carr, 01457 867856, www.gamesleyfold.co.uk. *2m W of Glossop. Off A626 Glossop to Marple rd, nr Charlesworth. Turn down lane directly opp St Margaret's School. White cottage at bottom. Car parking in adjacent field.* Home-made teas.
Adm £2.50, chd free. Sun 26 May, Sun 9 June (1-4). Visitors also welcome by appt May to June.
Old-fashioned cottage garden. Spring garden with herbaceous borders, shrubs and rhododendrons, wild flowers and herbs in profusion to attract butterflies and wildlife. Good selection of herbs and cottage garden plants for sale. Featured in local press.

GRAFTON COTTAGE
See Staffordshire, Birmingham & West Midlands

27 GREEN MEADOWS
Cross Lane, Monyash, Bakewell DE45 1JN. Mr & Mrs Mike Cullen. *5m West of Bakewell. From centre Bakewell take B5055 to Monyash. At Xrds by village green go straight onto Tagg Lane. At the 2nd bend turn R into Cross Lane.* Home-made teas. **Adm £2.50, chd free. Sat 6, Sat 20 July (12-5).**
Compact cottage garden surrounded by enclosures, in superb countryside with far reaching views of the Dales. Herbaceous borders, shrubs, wild flowers, lavender hedges and kit parterre in daily use filled with a profusion of herbs to attract butterflies and wildlife. Water features and limestone garden. Large greenhouse and raised beds. Featured in The Derbyshire magazine, Garden News, Amateur Gardening Weekly and Reflections Magazine.

28 ◆ HARDWICK ESTATE
Doe Lea, Chesterfield S44 5QJ. National Trust, 01246 858400, www.nationaltrust.org.uk. *8m SE of Chesterfield. S of A617. Signed from J29 M1.* **Adm £6, chd free. For NGS: Sun 16 June (9-6). For other opening times and information, please phone or see garden website.**
The gardens are beautifully presented in a series of courtyards, where you can move from one garden 'room' to the next to explore the herb garden, orchards and colourful borders. Tours and Talks throughout the day will bring the garden to life with stories of its history to vegetable growing tips. Themed garden talks & family fun activities. The Gardens are wheelchair accessible. An electric shuttle bus is provided from the Visitor Centre to the Hall for those who have difficulties walking.

29 HIGH ROOST
27 Storthmeadow Road, Simmondley, Glossop SK13 6UZ. Peter & Christina Harris, 01457 863888, peter-harris9@sky.com. *¾ m SW of Glossop. From M67 take A57, turn R at Mottram (1st T-lights), through Broadbottom & Charlesworth. In Charlesworth turn R up Town Lane by side of Grey Mare PH, cont up High Lane, past Hare & Hounds PH, Storthmeadow Rd is 2nd turn on L. From Glossop, A57 towards Manchester, L at 2nd mini r'about, up Simmondley Lane, turn R into Storthmeadow Rd, nr top, no 27 last house on L. On rd parking nearby, please take care not to block drives.* Light refreshments. **Adm £2.50, chd free (share to Manchester Dogs Home). Sun 23 June (12-5). Visitors also welcome by appt June to July.**
Garden on terraced slopes, views over fields and hills. Winding paths, archways and steps explore different garden rooms packed with plants, designed to attract wildlife. Alpine bed, vegetable garden, water features, statuary, troughs and planters. A garden which needs exploring to discover its secrets tucked away in hidden corners. Craft stall, fancy goods sale, childrens garden quiz and lucky dip.

30 37 HIGH STREET
Repton DE65 6GD. David & Jan Roberts. *6m S of Derby. From A38, A50 junction S of Derby follow signs to Willington, then Repton. In Repton continue past island and shops. Garden on L.* Home-made teas. **Adm £3, chd free. Sun 21 Apr, Sun 30 June (2-5.30).**
Over 1 acre of gardens with bridge over Repton Brook which meanders through. Formal and wildlife ponds, mixed borders of herbaceous, shrubs and trees. Rhododendrons and woodland, grasses, ferns and bamboos. Vegetable garden and greenhouses, container planting for spring and summer colour and alpine troughs. A surprising garden for all seasons with interest for everyone. Brook flows through the garden. Partial access for wheelchairs.

31 HIGHFIELD HOUSE
Wingfield Road, Oakerthorpe, Alfreton DE55 7AP. Paul & Ruth Peat and Janet & Brian Costall, 01773 521342, highfieldhouseopengardens @hotmail.co.uk, www.highfieldhouse.weebly.com. *Approx 1m from Alfreton town centre on A615 Alfreton-Matlock Rd. From Matlock: A615 to Alfreton. Turn R into Alfreton Golf Club. From Derby: A38 to Alfreton. A615 to Matlock. After houses on L of Wingfield Rd, turn L into Alfreton Golf Club.* **Adm £3, chd free. Sun 26 May, Sun 7 July (11-5.30). Visitors also welcome by appt May to July.**
Lovely country garden of approx 1 acre, incorporating a shady garden, woodland, tree house, laburnum tunnel, orchard, parterre, herbaceous borders and productive vegetable garden. Pleasant level walk to Derbyshire Wildlife Trust Nature reserve, where there is a pond and boardwalk and beautiful spotted orchids. A lovely afternoon out and you must try our AGA baked cakes and light lunches too. Featured in Reflections, Derbyshire Magazine and Gardeners Weekly. Some steps, slopes and gravel areas.

HIGHFIELD HOUSE
See Leicestershire & Rutland

18 HIGHFIELD ROAD
See Cheshire & Wirral

HILL PARK FARM
See Leicestershire & Rutland

Winding paths, archways and steps explore different garden rooms . . .

32 HILLSIDE
286 Handley Road, New Whittington, Chesterfield S43 2ET. Mr E J Lee, 01246 454960, eric.lee5@btinternet.com. *3m N of Chesterfield. From A6135, take B6052 through Eckington & Marsh Lane 3m. Turn L at Xrds signed Whittington, then 1m. From Coal Aston (Sheffield), take B6056 towards Chesterfield to give way sign, then 1m. From Chesterfield, take B6052.* Tea. **Adm £2.50, chd free. Visitors welcome by appt.**
⅓ -acre sloping site. Herbaceous borders, rock garden, alpines, streams, pools, bog gardens, asiatic primula bed, and alpine house. Acers, bamboos, collection of approx 150 varieties of ferns, eucalypts, euphorbias, grasses, conifers, Himalayan bed. 1000+ plants permanently labelled. Yr-round interest.

HILLSIDE COTTAGE
See Cheshire & Wirral

33 NEW THE HOLLY TREE
21 Hackney Road, Hackney, Matlock DE4 2PX. Carl Hodgkinson. *1/2 m NW of Matlock, off A6. Take the A6 NW in the direction of Bakewell, past bus station on your R & take the 1st R up Dimple Rd. Follow this road to a T-junction, turn R and then immed L, signed Farley & Hackney (you are going uphill almost constantly from leaving the A6). Take the 1st L onto Hackney Rd, the Laburnum Inn is on the corner. We are approximately 1/4 m along Hackney Rd on LHS.* **Adm £2.50, chd free. Sat 8, Sun 9 June (11-5).**
The garden is in excess of 1 1/2 acres and set on a steeply sloping S-facing site, sheltering behind a high retaining wall and incl a small arboretum, bog garden, herbaceous borders, pond, vegetables, fruits, apiary and chickens. Extensively terraced with many paths and steps and with spectacular views across the Derwent valley to Snitterton and Oker.

34 NEW HOLME GRANGE
Holme Lane, Bakewell DE45 1GF. Mrs Shirley Stubbs, 01629 814728, shirleystubbs@hotmail.co.uk. *Close to centre of Bakewell. From Bakewell centre, take A619 towards Baslow, over river bridge, 1st L into Holme Lane. Follow the lane which runs between meadows. Holme Grange is on the R, bounded by a stone wall. For parking, go past entrance, and take track to R.* Home-made teas. **Adm £3, chd free. Sat 29 June, Sat 17 Aug (11-4). Visitors also welcome by appt May to Sept.**
Holme Grange has a garden of about an acre, and offers a range of mixed borders, large lawned area and woodland offering some unusual trees, shrubs and plants.

35 ◆ LEA GARDENS
Lea, nr Matlock DE4 5GH. Mr & Mrs J Tye, 01629 534380, www.leagarden.co.uk. *5m SE of Matlock. Off A6 & A615.* **Adm £4.50, chd 50p. For opening times and information, please phone or see garden website.**
Rare collection of rhododendrons, azaleas, kalmias, alpines and conifers in delightful woodland setting. Gardens are sited on remains of medieval quarry and cover about 4 acres. Specialised plant nursery of rhododendrons and azaleas on site. Open daily 20 March to 31 July (9-5). Gravel paths, steep slopes. Free access for wheelchair users.

36 THE LEYLANDS
Moorwood Lane, Owler Bar (Holmesfield), Nr Sheffield S17 3BS. Richard & Chris Hibberd, 01142 890833, hibberd3@btinternet.com. *2m W of Dronfield. Situated on the edge of the Peak District National Park, adjacent to the B6054. Moorwood Lane is 1m from the Owler Bar junction with the A621 (Sheffield-Bakewell) or 2nd turn on R after leaving Holmesfield village if travelling W towards Owler Bar.* **Adm £3, chd free (share to Water Aid). Thur 30 May (1-5); Sat 15 June (2-5); Sun 16 June (10.30-5.30); Thur 25, Tue 30 July (1-5). Visitors also welcome by appt Apr to Aug.**
A 2-acre country garden, set on a sloping site at the edge of the Peak District. The site has family ties from 1947, the garden being developed by the current owners over recent decades, as a means of accommodating the wide variety of plants, habitats and water systems. Paths winding through the plantings provide further interest. Exhibition of watercolour paintings 'Looking at nature' (May/June openings). Childrens trails and play equipment.

37 THE LILIES
Griffe Grange Valley, Grangemill, Matlock DE4 4BW. Chris & Bridget Sheppard, www.thelilies.com. *4m N Cromford. On A5012 Via Gellia Rd 4m N Cromford. 1st house on R after junction with B5023 to Middleton. From S Grangemill 1st house on L after Stancliffe Quarry.* Home-made teas. **Adm £3, chd free. Sun 30 June, Sun 1 Sept (11.30-5).**
1-acre garden being restored after some neglect. Area adjacent to house with seasonal planting and containers, mixed shrubs and perennial borders many raised from seed. 3 ponds, vegetable plot, barn conversion with separate cottage style garden. Natural garden with stream developed from old mill pound. Walks in large wild flower meadow and ash woodland both SSSI's. Handspinning and natural dyeing demonstration using materials from the garden and wool from sheep in the meadow. Featured on BBC TV East Midlands Today. Steep slope from car park, limestone chippings at entrance, some boggy areas if wet.

ALLOTMENTS

38 LITTLEOVER LANE ALLOTMENTS
19 Littleover Lane, Derby DE23 6JH. Littleover Lane Allotments Assoc, www.littleoverlaneallotments.org.uk. *3m SW of Derby. Off Derby ring rd A5111 into Stenson Rd. R into Littleover Lane. Garden on L. On street parking opp Foremark Ave.* Light refreshments. **Adm £3, chd free. Sun 1 Sept (11-5).**
Allotment site with over 180 plots cultivated in a variety of styles. A museum collection of heritage gardening equipment. Range of heritage and unusual vegetable varieties grown. Annual produce show.

Exhibition of watercolour paintings 'Looking at nature' . . .

39 LOCKO PARK
Spondon, Derby DE21 7BW. Mrs Lucy Palmer, www.lockopark.co.uk. *6m NE of Derby. From A52 Borrowash bypass, 2m N via B6001, turn to Spondon (more directions on www.lockopark.co.uk. NB. Satnav input 'via Locko Rd').* Home-made teas. **Adm £3, chd free. Sun 12 May (2-5).**
An original 1927 open garden for the NGS. Large garden; pleasure gardens; rose gardens designed by William Eames. House (not open) by Smith of Warwick with Victorian additions. Chapel (open) Charles II, with original ceiling. Featured in Derby Telegraph and on BBC Radio Derby. Limited wheelchair access, steps to main garden.

40 9 MAIN STREET
Horsley Woodhouse DE7 6AU. Ms Alison Napier, 01332 881629, ibhillib@btinternet.com. *3m SW of Heanor. 6m N of Derby. Turn off A608 Derby to Heanor rd at Smalley, towards Belper, (A609). Garden on A609, 1m from Smalley turning.* Cream teas. **Adm £2.50, chd free.** **Sun 16 June, Sun 4 Aug (2-5). Visitors also welcome by appt Mar to Sept. Teas available by prior arrangement for groups 16 or less.**
1/3 -acre hilltop garden overlooking lovely farmland view. Terracing, borders, lawns and pergola create space for an informal layout with planting for colour effect. Features incl large wildlife pond with water lilies, bog garden and small formal pool. Emphasis on carefully selected herbaceous perennials mixed with shrubs and old-fashioned roses. Additions incl gravel garden for sun-loving plants and scree garden, both developed from former drive. Featured in Garden News - Garden of the week. Wheelchair-adapted WC.

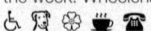

41 2 MANVERS STREET
Ripley DE5 3EQ. Mrs D Wood & Mr D Hawkins, 01773 743962, davidshawkins@tiscali.co.uk. *Ripley Town centre to Derby rd turn L opp Leisure Centre onto Heath Rd. 1st turn R onto Meadow Rd, 1st L onto Manvers St.* Home-made teas. **Adm £2.50, chd free. Sat 20, Sun 21 July (2-5). Visitors also welcome by appt July to Aug.**
Summer garden with backdrop of neighbouring trees, 10 borders bursting with colour surrounded by immaculate shaped lawn. Perennials incl 26 clematis, annuals, baskets, tubs and pots. Ornamental fish pond. Water features, arbour and summerhouse. Plenty of seating areas to take in this awe-inspiring oasis.

42 ◆ MELBOURNE HALL GARDENS
Church Square, Melbourne, Derby DE73 8EN. The Melbourne Trust, 01332 862502, www.melbournehall.com. *6m S of Derby. 5m W of exit 21A off M1, 4M N of exit 13 off M42. In Melbourne turn off main rd at Market Place on to Church St. Church Square is off Church St. Garden entrance is via the Visitor Centre next to the tea room.* **Adm £4.50, chd £3.50. For NGS: Sat 1, Sun 2 June (1.30-5.30). For other opening times and information, please phone or see garden website.**
A 17 acre historic garden with an abundance of rare trees and shrubs, woodland and waterside planting with extensive herbaceous borders. Meconopsis, candelabra primulas, styrax japonica, cornus kousa 'Eddies white wonder'. The other garden features incl Bakewells wrought iron arbour, a yew tunnel and fine C18 statuary and water features. Gravel paths, uneven surface in places, some steep slopes.

43 ◆ MEYNELL LANGLEY TRIALS GARDEN
Lodge Lane (off Flagshaw Lane), Nr Kirk Langley, Derby DE6 4NT. Robert & Karen Walker, 01332 824358, www.meynell-langley-gardens.co.uk. *4m W of Derby, nr Kedleston Hall. Head W out of Derby on A52. At Kirk Langley turn R onto Flagshaw Lane (signed to Kedleston Hall) then R onto Lodge Lane. Follow Meynell Langley Gdns sign for 1 1/2 m. From A38 follow signs for Kedleston Hall (past 1st entrance).* **Adm £2.50, chd free. For NGS: Sun 26 May, Sun 16 June, Sun 21 July, Sun 25 Aug, Sun 22 Sept, Sun 13 Oct (10-4.30). For other opening times and information, please phone or see garden website.**
Formal 3/4 -acre Victorian-style garden established 19yrs, displaying and trialling new and existing varieties of bedding plants, herbaceous

perennials and vegetable plants grown at the adjacent nursery. Over 180 hanging baskets and floral displays. 85 varieties of apple, pear and other fruit. Summer fruit pruning demonstrations late summer and apple tasting in October. Level ground and firm grass.

MILLPOOL
See Cheshire & Wirral

44 MOORFIELDS
257/261 Chesterfield Road, Temple Normanton, Chesterfield S42 5DE. Peter, Janet & Stephen Wright, 01246 852306, peterwright100@hotmail.com. *4m SE of Chesterfield. From Chesterfield take A617 for 2m, turn on to B6039 through Temple Normanton, taking R fork signed Tibshelf. Garden 1/4 m on R. Limited parking on site.* **Adm £3, chd free.** **Sun 30 June (1-5). Visitors also welcome by appt Apr to July.**
Two adjacent gardens, the larger developed from field over last few yrs and has newly extended gravel garden, herbaceous island beds, small wild flower area, large wildlife pond, orchard and soft fruit, vegetable patch. Show of late flowering tulips. Smaller back and front gardens of No.257 feature herbaceous borders. Views across to mid-Derbyshire. Free-range eggs for sale.

45 NEW NEW MILLS SCHOOL BUSINESS & ENTERPRISE COLLEGE
Church Lane, New Mills, High Peak SK22 4NR. New Mills School Business & Enterprise College, 07833 373 593, www.newmills11-18.derbyshire.sch.uk. *New Mills School Business & Enterprise College. Approx 9m SE of Stockport and 12m NNW of Buxton. Turn off A6 onto the A6015 signed New Mills, Hayfield. At St George's CE Church, on LHS of the rd, turn L onto Church Lane. School is on LHS of the rd, opp the Primary School.* Light refreshments School Library. **Adm £3, chd free. Sat 6 July (10-5); Sun 7 July (1-5).**
Approx 3 acres of informally designed, colourful, mixed herbaceous perennials and shrub borders, with mature trees and lawns and a gravel border situated in the semi rural setting of the High Peak. The site incl a Grade II listed stone building with 4 themed individual quads, 2 greenhouses and small developing wild life garden and Plant Nursery. African Key Hole and Bag Garden, Bible and Monastic Garden, Vegetable and Cuttings Garden. Students are actively involved in the garden and community work. Featured in local press. Ramps allow access to most of the outside, flower beds and into the building and library, Quads viewed from the windows only.

46 9 NEWFIELD CRESCENT
Dore, Sheffield S17 3DE. Mike & Norma Jackson, 01142 366198, mandnjackson@googlemail.com. *Dore - SW Sheffield. Turn off Causeway Head Rd on Heather Lea Avenue. 2nd L into Newfield Crescent. Parking on roadside.* Light refreshments. **Adm £2.50, chd free. Sat 15, Sun 16 June (2-6). Visitors also welcome by appt.**
Mature, wildlife friendly garden planted to provide all-yr interest. Upper terrace with alpines in troughs and bowls. Lower terrace featuring 1 of 2 ponds with connecting stream and cascade. Bog garden, rock gardens, lawn alpine bed, wilder areas, mixed borders with trees, shrubs and perennials. Featuring azaleas, rhododendrons, primulas. Wheelchair access to top terrace offering full view of garden.

THE OLD CHAPEL
See Leicestershire & Rutland

47 ◆ OLD ENGLISH WALLED GARDEN, ELVASTON CASTLE COUNTRY PARK
Borrowash Road, Elvaston, Derby DE72 3EP. Derbyshire County Council, 01332 571342, www.derbyshire.gov.uk/elvaston. *4m E of Derby. Signed from A52 & A50. Car parking charge applies.* **Adm £2.50, chd free. For NGS: Sat 20 Apr, Sat 17 Aug (12-4). For other opening times and information, please phone or see garden website.**
Visit Elvaston Castle and discover the beauty of the Old English walled garden. Take in the peaceful atmosphere and enjoy the scents and colours of all the varieties of trees, shrubs and plants. Spring bulbs, summer bedding, large herbaceous borders and herb garden. Estate gardeners on hand during the day.

48 OWL END
Newfield Lane, Dore, Sheffield S17 3DB. Sue & Roger Thompson. *5m SW Sheffield City Centre. On A625 to Hathersage, turn L at Dore Moor Inn, 1st R into Newfield Lane. 200yds on R. Please park considerately on Newfield Lane & surrounding rds. Blue Badges only down drive.* Home-made teas. **Adm £3.50, chd free. Sat 15, Sun 16 June (2-6).**
Large garden of 1 1/2 -acres with additional woodlands and meadow. Herbaceous and mixed borders. Vegetables, soft fruit, greenhouse and polytunnel. Views towards Blackamoor. Two-storey Wendy House. Wheelchair access to main part of garden, but care is needed beyond this due to some sloping areas.

Take in the peaceful atmosphere and enjoy the scents and colours . . .

49 THE PADDOCK
12 Mankell Road, Whittington Moor, Chesterfield S41 8LZ. Mel & Wendy Taylor, 01246 451001. *2m N of Chesterfield. Whittington Moor just off A61 between Sheffield & Chesterfield. Parking available at Lidl supermarket, garden signed from here.* Cream teas. **Adm £3, chd free. Sun 19 May, Sun 11 Aug (11-5). Visitors also welcome by appt May to Aug.**
1/2 -acre garden incorporating small formal garden, stream and koi filled pond. Stone path over bridge, up some steps, past small copse, across the stream at the top and back down again. Past herbaceous border towards a pergola where cream teas can be enjoyed.

50 PARK HALL
Walton Back Lane, Walton, Chesterfield S42 7LT. Kim & Margaret Staniforth, 01246 567412, kim.staniforth@btinternet.com. *2m SW of Chesterfield centre. From Chesterfield take A632 for Matlock. After start of 40mph section take 1st R into Acorn Ridge & then L into Walton Back Lane. 300yds on R, at end of high stone wall. Park on field side of Walton Back Lane only.* Cream teas. **Adm £3.50, chd free (share to Bluebell Wood Childrens Hospice). Sun 16 June (2-5.30). Visitors also welcome by appt Apr to July.**
Romantic 2-acre plantsmans garden, in a stunningly beautiful setting surrounding C17 house (not open) 4 main rooms-terraced garden, parkland area with forest trees, croquet lawn, sunken garden with arbours, pergolas, pleached hedge, topiary, statuary, roses, rhododendrons, camellias, several water features. Newly planted driveside.

51 22 PINFOLD CLOSE
Repton DE65 6FR. Mr O Jowett, 01283 701964, owenjowett@btinternet.com. *6m S of Derby. From A38, A50 J, S of Derby follow signs to Willington then Repton. Off Repton High Street find Pinfold Lane, Pinfold Close 1st L.* Sun 18 Aug - home-made teas at 10 Chestnut Way and Woodend Cottage. **Adm £2.50, chd free. Sat 15, Sun 16 June (2-5); Sun 18 Aug (1-6). Combined with Woodend Cottage & 10 Chestnut Way. Adm £6, (18 Aug only). Visitors also welcome by appt June to Aug.**
Small garden with an interest in tropical plants. Palms, gingers, tree ferns, cannas, bananas. Mainly foliage plants.

52 RECTORY HOUSE
Kedleston, Derby DE22 5JJ. Helene Viscountess Scarsdale. *5m NW Derby. A52 from Derby turn R Kedleston sign. Drive to village turn R. Brick house standing back from rd on sharp corner.* Home-made teas. **Adm £3.50, chd free. Fri 24 May (2-5).**
Garden re-established 6yrs ago. The 3 acres now has shrub border with rare varieties, grasses, rhododendrons, azaleas and shrub roses. Large pond with candelabra primulas, gunneras, good collection of willows. Part of garden wild but atmospheric with winding paths. Small potager and orchard. Summerhouse to sit in and plenty of seats. Limited wheelchair access. Some uneven grass paths.

53 ◆ RENISHAW HALL & GARDENS
Renishaw, nr Sheffield S21 3WB. Alexandra Haywood, 01246 432310, www.renishaw-hall.co.uk. *10m from Sheffield city centre. Situated on the A6135 between Eckington & Renishaw Villages. J30 of M1 follow A6135 through Renishaw Village, turn off where signed between the villages of Renishaw & Eckington.* **For opening times and information, please phone or see garden website.**
Renishaw Hall and Gardens boasts 7 acres of stunning gardens created by Sir George Sitwell in 1885. The Italianate gardens feature various 'rooms' with extravagant herbaceous borders. Rose gardens, rare trees and shrubs, national collection of Yuccas, sculptures, woodland walks and lakes create a magical and engaging garden experience. Open Wed to Sun, BH Mons, 30 March to 29 Sept. Wheelchair route around garden.

RIDGE HILL
See Cheshire & Wirral

Clovermead

See more garden images at www.ngs.org.uk

54 ROSEBANK
303 Duffield Road, Allestree, Derby DE22 2DF. Patrick & Carol Smith. *2m N of Derby. Follow A6 from Derby towards Matlock. On crossing A38 island cont for 150 metres turning L into Gisborne Crescent then R into service rd.* Cream teas. **Adm £2.50, chd free. Sat 15 June (2-6).**
Interesting garden of variety on a gentle, upward sloping site. Access by steps and paths. Incl colourful borders with imaginative planting and a water feature in a natural setting. Small orchard and soft fruit garden, lawns, rockery, shrubs, trees and greenhouse. Wildlife friendly. Children welcomed. The garden has an Auricula Theatre which houses a vivid display of Streptocarpus during the Summer. A running computer display in the summerhouse features the garden in different seasons together with photographs and wildlife information such as a checklist of birds observed in the garden. Featured in Derbyshire magazine.

SANDSEND
See Cheshire & Wirral

SYCAMORES HOUSE
See Nottinghamshire

Romantic 2-acre plantsmans' garden, in a stunningly beautiful setting . . .

55 THATCHED FARM
Radbourne, Ashbourne, Derby DE6 4LY. Mrs J Pegram, 01332 824507, jenniepegramuk@aol.com. *2m N of Derby ring rd. From Derby. Exit A52 Derby-Ashbourne Rd at Brun Lane not Radbourne Lane. Turn L at 1st junction & then R at the 2nd & next L. We are 2nd group of buildings on L. From Etwall. Exit at the island following the Radbourne sign. Straight over Xrds to T-junction, turn L. Garden is 1st group of buildings on the R. Maps sent to groups of visitors. Parking in field & courtyard. Coaches welcome.* Home-made teas. **Adm £3, chd free. Visitors welcome by appt 15 June to 15 July. Parking in field and courtyard. Coaches welcome.**
The wild garden has been fenced off to reduce maintenance. The other changes have been the introduction of a long scree bed, a white garden and the creation of a woodland garden. These changes have allowed the introduction of more rare and unusual plants. Plantings incl bulbs, trees, shrubs, alpines, roses and hardy perennials. Vegetable and fruit garden. Ramp from courtyard onto lawns.

56 THORNBRIDGE HALL
Ashford in the Water DE45 1NZ. Jim & Emma Harrison. *2m NW of Bakewell. From Bakewell take A6, signed Buxton. After 2m, R onto A6020. ½ m turn L, signed Thornbridge Hall.* Light refreshments. **Adm £4.50, chd free. Sun 18 Aug (10-4).**
A stunning 10-acre garden overlooking rolling Derbyshire countryside. This C19, rarely opened garden has many distinct areas incl Italian garden with statuary, knot garden, water garden, 100ft herbaceous border, working potager, scented terrace, koi lake, thatched summer house and glasshouses. Gravel paths, steep slopes, steps.

THRUMPTON HALL
See Nottinghamshire

57 TILFORD HOUSE
Hognaston, Ashbourne DE6 1PW. Mr & Mrs P R Gardner, 01335 372001, peter.rgardner@mypostoffice.co.uk. *5m NE of Ashbourne. A517 Belper to Ashbourne. At Hulland Ward follow signs to Hognaston. Down hill (2m) to bridge. Roadside parking 100 metres.* Home-made teas. **Adm £3, chd free. Mon 6 May, Wed 7 Aug (2-5). Visitors also welcome by appt May to Aug.**
A 1½ - acre streamside plantlovers country garden. Mixed borders containing some unusual plants lie sympathetically beside untamed areas Raised vegetable beds, fruit trees, collections of hostas, irises, clematis and primulas. Wander through this magical setting, admire the unusual trees or just sit and listen to the sounds of the countryside.

58 ◆ TISSINGTON HALL
nr Ashbourne DE6 1RA. Sir Richard & Lady FitzHerbert, 01335 352200, www.tissingtonhall.co.uk. *4m N of Ashbourne. E of A515 on Ashbourne to Buxton rd.* **Adm £5, chd £1. For NGS: Mon 26 Aug (12-3). For other opening times and information, please phone or see garden website.**
Large garden celebrating over 70yrs in the NGS, with stunning Rose garden on West Terrace, herbaceous borders and 5 acres of grounds. Wheelchair access advice from ticket seller.

59 13 WESTFIELD ROAD
Swadlincote DE11 0BG. Val & Dave Booth, 01283 221167, valerie.booth@sky.com. *5m E of Burton-on-Trent, off A511. From Burton on Trent take A511 follow signs for Swadlincote. Turn R into Springfield Rd. Take 3rd turn on R into Westfield Rd. Garden is situated 200 yds on L.* Home-made teas. **Adm £2.50, chd free. Sun 14 July, Sun 25 Aug (1-5). Visitors also welcome by appt June to Sept.**
A garden on 2 levels of approx ½ an acre, developed over the last 9yrs. Packed herbaceous borders designed for colour. Roses and clematis scrambling over pergolas. Shrubs, baskets and tubs. Greenhouses, raised bed vegetable area, fruit trees and bushes. Free range chicken area. Plenty of seating. Featured in Derbyshire Evening Telegraph, Derbyshire Magazine and Garden News.

60 NEW WESTGATE
Combs Road, Combs, Chapel-en-le-Frith, High Peak SK23 9UP. Maurice & Christine Lomas. *N of Chapel-en-le-Frith off B5470. Turn L immed before Hanging Gate PH, signed Combs Village. ¾ m on L by railway bridge.* **Adm £3, chd free. Sat 29 June (12-5).**
Large sloping garden in quiet village with beautiful views. Features incl mixed borders and beds containing many hosta and heuchera. Vegetable and fruit beds. Natural pond and stream with bog area and two formal ponds.

61 24 WHEELDON AVENUE
Derby DE22 1HN. Laura Burnett, 01332 384893 or 01332 342204. *1m N Derby city centre. Approached directly from Kedleston Rd or from A6, Duffield Rd via West Bank Ave. Limited on street parking. Good bus services on Kedleston Rd or Duffield Rd.* Home-made teas at 28 Wheeldon Avenue. **Combined adm £4, chd free.** Sun 16 June (2-5). **Combined with 26 Wheeldon Avenue. Visitors also welcome by appt June & July. Combined adm with 26 Wheeldon Av (Jun/July).**
Small Victorian garden, with original walling supporting many shrubs and climbers with contrasting colour and texture. Circular lawn surrounded by herbaceous border with main colour scheme of blue, purple, black, yellow and orange tones. This leads to a small area at rear of garden given to more natural planting to suit shade and natural habitat. This is a garden produced on a low income budget, with varied tones and textures throughout the planting. Photo of garden used on front cover of a book on designing small gardens by Ian Cook. Selection of fruit trees planted for this year.

62 26 WHEELDON AVENUE
Derby DE22 1HN. Ian Griffiths, 01332 342204, ig@moodyandwoolley.co.uk. *1m N of Derby. 1m from city centre & approached directly off the Kedleston Rd or from A6 Duffield Rd via West Bank Ave. Limited on-street parking.* Home-made teas. **Combined adm £4.00, chd free.** Sun 16 June (2-5). **Combined with 24 Wheeldon Avenue. Visitors also welcome by appt May to July. Adm £2 (May), combined adm with 24 Wheeldon Av (Jun/July).**
Tiny Victorian walled garden near to city centre. Lawn and herbaceous borders with newly expanded old rose collection, lupins, delphiniums and foxgloves. Small terrace with topiary, herb garden and lion fountain. Garden available for filming and photo-shoots. Also horticultural and design students welcome to photograph. BBC TV feature.

63 26 WINDMILL RISE
Belper DE56 1GQ. Kathy Fairweather. *½ m from Belper market place. From Belper Market Place take Chesterfield Rd towards Heage. Top of hill 1st R, Marsh Lane. 1st R Windmill Lane, 1st R Windmill Rise. Please do not park on Windmill Rise.* Home-made teas. **Adm £3, chd free (share to local charities).** Sun 16 June, Sat 27, Sun 28 July (11-4).
An original and unusual plant lovers' organic garden full of surprises impossible to glimpse from the road. Large variety of plants, some unusual and rare. Garden divided into sections: woodland, Japanese, secret garden, cottage, edible, patio gardens. Fish and wildlife ponds, small running stream. Specimen fir tree. Lush, restful atmosphere, with paths meandering to many seating areas. Featured in Derby Telegraph, Belper News and on BBC Radio Derby.

64 WINDWARD
62 Summer Lane, Wirksworth, Matlock DE4 4EB. Audrey & Andrew Winkler, 01629 822681, audrey.winkler@w3z.co.uk, www.grandmafrogsgarden.co.uk. *5m S of Matlock. From Wirksworth Market Place take the B5023 towards Duffield. After 300 yds turn R onto Summer Lane at mini r'about. Windward is approx 500yds on R.* **Adm £3, chd free (share to Ruddington Framework Knitters Museum).** Suns 24 Mar, 16 June, 14 July, 15 Sept (1-4). **Visitors also welcome by appt Mar to Aug.**
An informal green garden of 1 acre, with pockets of colour throughout the year. Wildlife friendly, with flowers, shrubs and trees, catering for allcomers - from the smallest insect to the bigger birds - incl the occasional peregrine falcon. Paths wind around the garden, making sure you don't miss anything, with interesting details tucked away to surprise you. A garden for all seasons. Visit our Art Gallery.

65 WOODEND COTTAGE
134 Main Street, Repton DE65 6FB. Wendy & Stephen Longden, 01283 703259, wendylongden@btinternet.com. *6m S of Derby. From A38, S of Derby, follow signs to Willington, then Repton. In Repton, straight on at r'bout through village. Woodend Cottage is 1m on R before Woodend Children's Nursery.* Home-made teas. **Adm £3, chd free.** Sun 7 July, Sun 18 Aug (1.30-6). **Combined with 22 Pinfold Close & 10 Chestnut Way . Adm £6, (18 Aug only). Visitors also welcome by appt June to Aug.**
Plant lover's garden with glorious views on a sloping 2½ -acre site developed organically for yr-round interest. On lower levels herbaceous borders are arranged informally and connected via lawns, thyme bed, pond and pergolas. Mixed woodland and grassed labyrinth lead naturally into fruit, vegetable and herb potager with meadows beyond. Especially colourful in July and Aug. Small specialist nursery selling perennials and grasses. Also visit St Wystans Church, Repton. Wheelchair access on lower levels only.

An original and unusual plant lovers' organic garden full of surprises . . .

WOODLEIGHTON GROVE GARDENS
See Staffordshire, Birmingham & West Midlands

APOLLONIA
See Staffordshire, Birmingham & West Midlands

KARIBU
See Staffordshire, Birmingham & West Midlands

66 35 WYVER LANE
Belper DE56 2UB. Jim & Brenda Stannering, 01773 824280, Wyver35@gmail.com. *8m N of Derby. Take A6 from Derby through Belper to T-lights at triangle. Turn L for A517 to Ashbourne, over river bridge, 1st R onto Wyver Lane. Parking in River Gardens, entrance on A6. No parking in Wyver Lane.* Home-made teas. **Adm £2.50, chd free.** Sun 28 Apr, Sun 16 June (1-5). **Visitors also welcome by appt Apr to Oct.**
Cottage garden of approx 500sq yds on side of R Derwent opp Belper River Gardens. Full of hardy perennial plants with pergola, troughs, greenhouse, small pond. Demonstration of patchwork, embroidery, doll making etc by garden owner on request.

The Dower House

© Louise Jolley

Derbyshire County Volunteers

County Organiser

Irene Dougan, Field Farm, Field Lane, Kirk Ireton, Ashbourne DE6 3JU, 07791 525706, irene.dougan@btinternet.com

County Treasurer

Robert Little, 10 Chestnut Way, Repton DE65 6FQ, 01283 702267, rlittleq@gmail.com

Publicity

Christine Morris, 9 Langdale Avenue, Ravenshead NG15 9EA, 01623 793827, christine@ravenshead.demon.co.uk

Booklet Distribution

Kathy Fairweather, 26 Windmill Rise, Belper DE56 1GQ, 01773 825255, kathyf100@hotmail.com

Booklet Coordinator

Pauline Little, 10 Chestnut Way, Repton DE65 6FQ, 01283 702267, plittle@hotmail.com

Assistant County Organisers

Jane Lennox, Craigside, Reservoir Road, Whaley Bridge SK23 7BW, 01663 732381, jane@lennoxonline.net

Gill & Colin Hancock, 334 Belper Road, Stanley Common, nr Ilkeston DE7 6FY, 01159 301061

Pauline Little, 10 Chestnut Way, Repton DE65 6FQ, 01283 702267, rlittleq@gmail.com

Christine Sanderson, The Hollies, 87 Clowne Road, Barlborough, Chesterfield S43 4EH, 01246 570830, christine.r.sanderson@uwclub.net

Kate & Peter Spencer, Merle Close, 41 Summer Lane, Wirksworth, Matlock DE4 4EB, 01629 822499

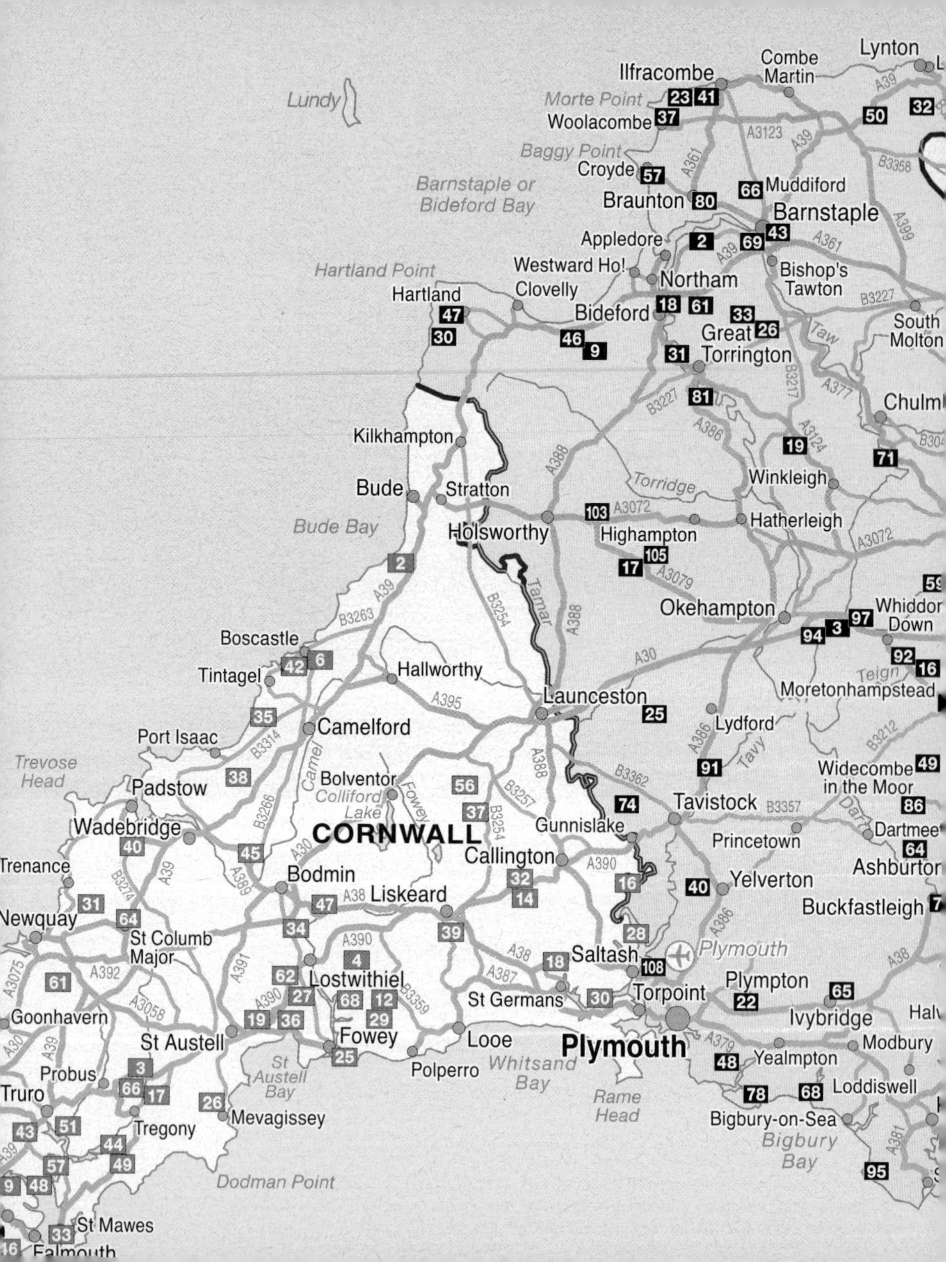

Lundy
Ilfracombe
Combe Martin
Lynton
Morte Point
Woolacombe
Baggy Point
Croyde
Barnstaple or Bideford Bay
Braunton
Muddiford
Barnstaple
Appledore
Westward Ho!
Northam
Bishop's Tawton
Hartland Point
Hartland
Clovelly
Bideford
South Molton
Great Torrington
Taw
Kilkhampton
Bude
Stratton
Torridge
Winkleigh
Bude Bay
Holsworthy
Highampton
Hatherleigh
Tamar
Okehampton
Whiddon Down
Boscastle
Tintagel
Hallworthy
Teign
Moretonhampstead
Launceston
Lydford
Camelford
Port Isaac
Tavy
Trevose Head
Padstow
Bolventor
Camel
Colliford Lake
Fowey
Widecombe in the Moor
Tavistock
Wadebridge
CORNWALL
Gunnislake
Princetown
Dart
Dartmeet
Trenance
Callington
Ashburton
Bodmin
Liskeard
Yelverton
Buckfastleigh
Newquay
St Columb Major
Plymouth
Saltash
Lostwithiel
Plympton
Torpoint
St Germans
Ivybridge
Goonhavern
Looe
Fowey
St Austell
Plymouth
Modbury
Whitsand Bay
Polperro
St Austell Bay
Yealmpton
Probus
Truro
Rame Head
Loddiswell
Mevagissey
Tregony
Bigbury-on-Sea
Bigbury Bay
Dodman Point
St Mawes
Falmouth
A39
A3123
A361
B3358
A399
B3227
A377
B3217
A3124
A386
A388
A3072
A3079
B3254
B3263
A30
A395
B3314
B3266
B3257
B3362
B3357
B3212
A389
A38
A390
A3075
A392
A3058
B3274
A391
A387
B3359
A379
A381

Bridgwater Bay
Foreland Point
Porlock
Minehead
Dunster
Watchet
Wheddon Cross
Williton
Exford
Burnham-on-Sea
Highbridge
Cheddar
Wedmore
Wells
Shepton Mallet
Bridgwater
Westonzoyland
Street
Glastonbury
SOMERSET, BRISTOL AREA & S. GLOS
Bruton
Castle Cary
Bishop's Lydeard
Dulverton
Wiveliscombe
Milverton
Taunton
Langport
Somerton
Wellington
Bampton
Ilchester
Yeovil
Sherborne
Ilminster
South Petherton
Witheridge
Hemyock
Chard
Crewkerne
Middlemarsh
DEVON
Tiverton
Bickleigh
Cullompton
Yarcombe
Copplestone
Honiton
Beaminster
DORSET
Crediton
Axminster
Maiden Newton
Ottery St Mary
Exeter
Lyme Regis
Bridport
Dorchester
Topsham
Sidford
Seaton
Abbotsbury
Broad
Bovey Tracey
Exmouth
Sidmouth
Budleigh Salterton
Weymouth
Dawlish
Teignmouth
Lyme Bay
Fortuneswell
Newton Abbot
Torquay
Bill of Portland
Paignton
Brixham
Dartmouth
Start Bay
Start Point
0 10 20 kilometres
0 10 miles
© Global Mapping/The XYZ Digital Map Co.

Opening Dates

February

Sunday 3
19 Cherubeer Gardens

Sunday 10
35 1 Feebers Cottage
62 Littleham House Cottage

Monday 11
35 1 Feebers Cottage

Friday 15
19 Cherubeer Gardens

Sunday 17
62 Littleham House Cottage

Sunday 24
34 East Worlington House

Jungle area with bamboo tree house . . .

March

Sunday 3
34 East Worlington House

Sunday 10
31 The Downes

Monday 11
31 The Downes

Tuesday 12
31 The Downes

Wednesday 13
31 The Downes

Thursday 14
31 The Downes

Friday 15
31 The Downes

Saturday 16
31 The Downes

Sunday 17
31 The Downes
108 Woodvale Cottage

Monday 18
31 The Downes

Tuesday 19
31 The Downes

Wednesday 20
31 The Downes

Thursday 21
31 The Downes

Friday 22
31 The Downes

Saturday 23
17 Chapel Farm House

Sunday 24
43 Gorwell House
93 Summers Place

Friday 29
48 The Haven

Saturday 30
48 The Haven

Sunday 31
48 The Haven
55 Kia-Ora Farm & Gardens

April

Monday 1
41 The Gate House
55 Kia-Ora Farm & Gardens

Tuesday 2
41 The Gate House

Wednesday 3
41 The Gate House

Thursday 4
41 The Gate House

Friday 5
41 The Gate House

Saturday 6
41 The Gate House
78 Rowden House

Sunday 7
41 The Gate House
49 Heathercombe
107 Wood Barton

Monday 8
41 The Gate House

Tuesday 9
41 The Gate House

Wednesday 10
41 The Gate House

Thursday 11
41 The Gate House

Friday 12
41 The Gate House

Saturday 13
41 The Gate House
44 Haldon Grange

Sunday 14
3 Andrew's Corner
7 Bickham Gardens
20 Chevithorne Barton
41 The Gate House
44 Haldon Grange
55 Kia-Ora Farm & Gardens
80 St Merryn
82 Shapcott Barton Estate
94 Taikoo
107 Wood Barton

Monday 15
41 The Gate House

Tuesday 16
7 Bickham Gardens
41 The Gate House

Wednesday 17
7 Bickham Gardens
41 The Gate House

Thursday 18
41 The Gate House

Friday 19
41 The Gate House

Saturday 20
17 Chapel Farm House
41 The Gate House
44 Haldon Grange
84 Sidbury Manor

Sunday 21
41 The Gate House
44 Haldon Grange
84 Sidbury Manor
107 Wood Barton

Monday 22
41 The Gate House

Tuesday 23
41 The Gate House

Wednesday 24
41 The Gate House

Thursday 25
41 The Gate House

Friday 26
41 The Gate House

Saturday 27
17 Chapel Farm House
41 The Gate House
44 Haldon Grange
52 Hillrise

Sunday 28
41 The Gate House
43 Gorwell House
44 Haldon Grange
52 Hillrise
109 Yonder Hill

Monday 29
41 The Gate House

Tuesday 30
41 The Gate House

May

Wednesday 1
41 The Gate House

Thursday 2
41 The Gate House

Friday 3
41 The Gate House

Saturday 4
28 Dicot
41 The Gate House
44 Haldon Grange
68 Mothecombe House

Sunday 5
3 Andrew's Corner
5 Ash Tree Farm
28 Dicot
41 The Gate House
44 Haldon Grange

55 Kia-Ora Farm & Gardens
62 Littleham House Cottage
68 Mothecombe House
102 Whitstone Farm
109 Yonder Hill

Monday 6
3 Andrew's Corner
5 Ash Tree Farm
18 Cherry Trees Wildlife Garden
28 Dicot
39 Fursdon
41 The Gate House
44 Haldon Grange
55 Kia-Ora Farm & Gardens
109 Yonder Hill

Tuesday 7
41 The Gate House

Wednesday 8
41 The Gate House
44 Haldon Grange

Thursday 9
41 The Gate House

Friday 10
41 The Gate House

Saturday 11
15 Carpenter's Cottage
17 Chapel Farm House
41 The Gate House
44 Haldon Grange
57 Langtrees
71 The Old Glebe
72 The Old Vicarage

Sunday 12
3 Andrew's Corner
7 Bickham Gardens
15 Carpenter's Cottage
16 Castle Drogo
41 The Gate House
44 Haldon Grange
49 Heathercombe
62 Littleham House Cottage
71 The Old Glebe
72 The Old Vicarage
80 St Merryn
109 Yonder Hill

Monday 13
41 The Gate House

Tuesday 14
7 Bickham Gardens
41 The Gate House

Wednesday 15
7 Bickham Gardens
41 The Gate House
44 Haldon Grange

Thursday 16
41 The Gate House

Friday 17
14 Cadhay
41 The Gate House

Saturday 18
17 Chapel Farm House
41 The Gate House
44 Haldon Grange
59 Lewis Cottage
67 Moretonhampstead Gardens
71 The Old Glebe

Sunday 19
20 Chevithorne Barton
32 Durcombe Water
37 Foamlea
41 The Gate House
43 Gorwell House
44 Haldon Grange
49 Heathercombe
50 Heddon Hall
55 Kia-Ora Farm & Gardens
59 Lewis Cottage
67 Moretonhampstead Gardens
71 The Old Glebe
77 Ridgehill
109 Yonder Hill

Much new planting at Fossleigh this year . . .

Monday 20
32 Durcombe Water
41 The Gate House
67 Moretonhampstead Gardens

Tuesday 21
41 The Gate House

Wednesday 22
41 The Gate House
44 Haldon Grange

Thursday 23
41 The Gate House

Friday 24
41 The Gate House

Saturday 25
41 The Gate House
44 Haldon Grange
49 Heathercombe

Sunday 26
3 Andrew's Corner
19 Cherubeer Gardens
32 Durcombe Water
41 The Gate House
44 Haldon Grange
49 Heathercombe
55 Kia-Ora Farm & Gardens
86 Southcombe Gardens
88 Sowton Mill
109 Yonder Hill

Monday 27
3 Andrew's Corner
32 Durcombe Water
41 The Gate House
44 Haldon Grange
55 Kia-Ora Farm & Gardens
86 Southcombe Gardens
109 Yonder Hill

Tuesday 28
41 The Gate House

Wednesday 29
24 Collepardo
41 The Gate House

Thursday 30
24 Collepardo
41 The Gate House

Friday 31
41 The Gate House
54 Idestone Barton
83 Shutelake

June

Saturday 1
10 Bovey Tracey Gardens
17 Chapel Farm House
41 The Gate House
42 Goren Farm (Evening)
51 High Garden
54 Idestone Barton
83 Shutelake

Sunday 2
10 Bovey Tracey Gardens
41 The Gate House
42 Goren Farm (Evening)
49 Heathercombe
60 Little Ash Bungalow
83 Shutelake
86 Southcombe Gardens
109 Yonder Hill

Monday 3
41 The Gate House
42 Goren Farm (Evening)

Tuesday 4
41 The Gate House
42 Goren Farm (Evening)

Wednesday 5
41 The Gate House
42 Goren Farm (Evening)

Thursday 6
41 The Gate House
42 Goren Farm (Evening)

Friday 7
41 The Gate House
42 Goren Farm (Evening)
63 The Lookout

Saturday 8
33 East Woodlands Farmhouse
41 The Gate House
42 Goren Farm (Day & Evening)
52 Hillrise

Sunday 9
7 Bickham Gardens
30 Docton Mill
33 East Woodlands Farmhouse
36 Feebers Gardens
41 The Gate House
42 Goren Farm (Day & Evening)
52 Hillrise

55 Kia-Ora Farm & Gardens
63 The Lookout
74 Portington
86 Southcombe Gardens
94 Taikoo
97 2 Town Barton
109 Yonder Hill

Monday 10
41 The Gate House
42 Goren Farm (Evening)

Tuesday 11
7 Bickham Gardens
41 The Gate House
42 Goren Farm (Evening)

Wednesday 12
7 Bickham Gardens
41 The Gate House
42 Goren Farm (Evening)

Thursday 13
41 The Gate House
42 Goren Farm (Evening)

Friday 14
41 The Gate House
42 Goren Farm (Evening)
76 Regency House

National Gardens Weekend

Saturday 15
1 Abbotskerswell Gardens
3 Andrew's Corner (Evening)
6 12A Baring Crescent and Crescent Garden
9 Bocombe Mill Cottage
11 Bramble Torre
17 Chapel Farm House
18 Cherry Trees Wildlife Garden
28 Dicot
41 The Gate House
42 Goren Farm (Day & Evening)
56 Kilmington (Shute Road) Gardens
59 Lewis Cottage
66 Marwood Hill
70 The Old Dairy
76 Regency House
79 Runnymede
89 Springdale
98 Venn Cross Railway Gardens
104 Willand Old Village Gardens
105 Winsford Walled Garden

Sunday 16
1 Abbotskerswell Gardens
3 Andrew's Corner (Evening)
9 Bocombe Mill Cottage
11 Bramble Torre
17 Chapel Farm House
18 Cherry Trees Wildlife Garden
25 Coombe Trenchard
26 The Croft
27 Dartington Hall Gardens
28 Dicot
37 Foamlea
39 Fursdon
41 The Gate House
42 Goren Farm (Day & Evening)
43 Gorwell House
50 Heddon Hall
53 Hollycombe House
56 Kilmington (Shute Road) Gardens
57 Langtrees
59 Lewis Cottage
70 The Old Dairy
74 Portington
76 Regency House
79 Runnymede
81 School House
86 Southcombe Gardens
89 Springdale
98 Venn Cross Railway Gardens
104 Willand Old Village Gardens
109 Yonder Hill

Abbotskerswell Gardens adds two new offerings . . .

Monday 17
41 The Gate House
42 Goren Farm (Evening)
76 Regency House

Tuesday 18
41 The Gate House
42 Goren Farm (Evening)

Wednesday 19
41 The Gate House
42 Goren Farm (Evening)

Thursday 20
41 The Gate House
42 Goren Farm (Evening)

Friday 21
14 Cadhay
41 The Gate House
42 Goren Farm (Evening)

Saturday 22
24 Collepardo
41 The Gate House
42 Goren Farm (Evening)
46 Harbour Lights
64 Lower Spitchwick Gardens
80 St Merryn
85 Sidmouth Gardens

Sunday 23
4 Ash Gardens
5 Ash Tree Farm
24 Collepardo
41 The Gate House
42 Goren Farm (Evening)
46 Harbour Lights
49 Heathercombe
55 Kia-Ora Farm & Gardens
64 Lower Spitchwick Gardens
80 St Merryn
85 Sidmouth Gardens
86 Southcombe Gardens
109 Yonder Hill

Monday 24
24 Collepardo
41 The Gate House
42 Goren Farm (Evening)

Tuesday 25
24 Collepardo
41 The Gate House
42 Goren Farm (Evening)

Wednesday 26
24 Collepardo
41 The Gate House
42 Goren Farm (Evening)

Thursday 27
24 Collepardo
41 The Gate House
42 Goren Farm (Evening)

Friday 28
24 Collepardo
41 The Gate House
42 Goren Farm (Evening)

Saturday 29
9 Bocombe Mill Cottage
21 Cleave Hill
24 Collepardo
41 The Gate House
42 Goren Farm (Evening)
51 High Garden

Sunday 30
9 Bocombe Mill Cottage
21 Cleave Hill
24 Collepardo
25 Coombe Trenchard
41 The Gate House
42 Goren Farm (Evening)
49 Heathercombe
51 High Garden
86 Southcombe Gardens
109 Yonder Hill

July

Monday 1
23 Cliffe
41 The Gate House
42 Goren Farm (Evening)

Tuesday 2
23 Cliffe
41 The Gate House
42 Goren Farm (Evening)

Wednesday 3
23 Cliffe
41 The Gate House
42 Goren Farm (Evening)

Thursday 4
23 Cliffe
41 The Gate House
42 Goren Farm (Evening)

Friday 5
- 23 Cliffe
- 41 The Gate House
- 42 Goren Farm (Evening)

Saturday 6
- 23 Cliffe
- 41 The Gate House
- 42 Goren Farm (Day & Evening)

Sunday 7
- 19 Cherubeer Gardens
- 22 Cliff Cottage
- 23 Cliffe
- 41 The Gate House
- 42 Goren Farm (Day & Evening)
- 103 Wick Farm Gardens
- 109 Yonder Hill

Monday 8
- 23 Cliffe
- 41 The Gate House
- 42 Goren Farm (Evening)
- 103 Wick Farm Gardens

Tuesday 9
- 23 Cliffe
- 41 The Gate House
- 42 Goren Farm (Evening)

Wednesday 10
- 23 Cliffe
- 41 The Gate House
- 42 Goren Farm (Evening)

Thursday 11
- 23 Cliffe
- 41 The Gate House
- 42 Goren Farm (Evening)

Friday 12
- 23 Cliffe
- 41 The Gate House
- 42 Goren Farm (Evening)

Saturday 13
- 23 Cliffe
- 41 The Gate House
- 42 Goren Farm (Day & Evening)
- 61 Little Webbery
- 75 Prospect House
- 96 Teignmouth Gardens
- 98 Venn Cross Railway Gardens
- 99 Weirfield Meadows Allotment Gardens

Sunday 14
- 7 Bickham Gardens
- 23 Cliffe
- 25 Coombe Trenchard
- 37 Foamlea
- 41 The Gate House
- 42 Goren Farm (Day & Evening)
- 53 Hollycombe House
- 55 Kia-Ora Farm & Gardens
- 61 Little Webbery
- 75 Prospect House
- 77 Ridgehill
- 82 Shapcott Barton Estate
- 96 Teignmouth Gardens
- 98 Venn Cross Railway Gardens
- 99 Weirfield Meadows Allotment Gardens
- 109 Yonder Hill

Bickham House, Bickham Gardens

Monday 15
- 23 Cliffe
- 41 The Gate House
- 42 Goren Farm (Evening)

Tuesday 16
- 7 Bickham Gardens
- 23 Cliffe
- 41 The Gate House
- 42 Goren Farm (Evening)

Wednesday 17
- 7 Bickham Gardens
- 23 Cliffe
- 41 The Gate House
- 42 Goren Farm (Evening)

Thursday 18
- 23 Cliffe
- 41 The Gate House
- 42 Goren Farm (Evening)

Friday 19
- 14 Cadhay
- 23 Cliffe
- 41 The Gate House
- 42 Goren Farm (Evening)

Saturday 20
- 12 Brendon Gardens
- 17 Chapel Farm House
- 23 Cliffe
- 29 Dittisham Gardens
- 38 Fossleigh
- 41 The Gate House
- 42 Goren Farm (Evening)
- 72 The Old Vicarage

Sunday 21
- 12 Brendon Gardens
- 23 Cliffe
- 26 The Croft
- 29 Dittisham Gardens
- 38 Fossleigh
- 39 Fursdon
- 41 The Gate House
- 42 Goren Farm (Evening)
- 43 Gorwell House
- 69 20 Old Bideford Road
- 72 The Old Vicarage
- 80 St Merryn
- 109 Yonder Hill

Monday 22
- 23 Cliffe
- 41 The Gate House
- 42 Goren Farm (Evening)

Tuesday 23
- 23 Cliffe
- 41 The Gate House
- 42 Goren Farm (Evening)

Wednesday 24
- 23 Cliffe
- 41 The Gate House
- 42 Goren Farm (Evening)

Thursday 25
- 23 Cliffe
- 41 The Gate House
- 42 Goren Farm (Evening)

Friday 26
- 23 Cliffe
- 41 The Gate House
- 42 Goren Farm (Evening)

Saturday 27
- 23 Cliffe
- 28 Dicot
- 41 The Gate House
- 42 Goren Farm (Evening)
- 87 Southern Comfort
- 98 Venn Cross Railway Gardens
- 100 4 Wellswood Heights

Sunday 28
- 23 Cliffe
- 25 Coombe Trenchard
- 28 Dicot
- 41 The Gate House
- 42 Goren Farm (Evening)
- 55 Kia-Ora Farm & Gardens
- 81 School House
- 82 Shapcott Barton Estate
- 87 Southern Comfort
- 90 Squirrels
- 98 Venn Cross Railway Gardens
- 100 4 Wellswood Heights
- 103 Wick Farm Gardens
- 109 Yonder Hill

Chickens roam . . . all organic . . .

Monday 29
- 23 Cliffe
- 41 The Gate House
- 42 Goren Farm (Evening)
- 103 Wick Farm Gardens

Tuesday 30
- 23 Cliffe
- 41 The Gate House
- 42 Goren Farm (Evening)

Wednesday 31
- 23 Cliffe
- 41 The Gate House
- 42 Goren Farm (Evening)

August

Thursday 1
- 23 Cliffe
- 41 The Gate House
- 42 Goren Farm (Evening)

Friday 2
- 23 Cliffe
- 41 The Gate House
- 42 Goren Farm (Evening)

Saturday 3
- 23 Cliffe
- 41 The Gate House
- 42 Goren Farm (Evening)
- 78 Rowden House
- 90 Squirrels
- 99 Weirfield Meadows Allotment Gardens

Sunday 4
- 23 Cliffe
- 41 The Gate House
- 42 Goren Farm (Evening)
- 57 Langtrees
- 82 Shapcott Barton Estate
- 90 Squirrels
- 99 Weirfield Meadows Allotment Gardens
- 102 Whitstone Farm
- 109 Yonder Hill

Monday 5
- 23 Cliffe
- 41 The Gate House
- 42 Goren Farm (Evening)

Tuesday 6
- 23 Cliffe
- 41 The Gate House
- 42 Goren Farm (Evening)

Wednesday 7
- 23 Cliffe
- 41 The Gate House
- 42 Goren Farm (Evening)

Thursday 8
- 23 Cliffe
- 41 The Gate House
- 42 Goren Farm (Evening)

Friday 9
- 23 Cliffe
- 41 The Gate House
- 42 Goren Farm (Evening)

Saturday 10
- 6 12A Baring Crescent and Crescent Garden
- 23 Cliffe
- 41 The Gate House
- 42 Goren Farm (Evening)
- 97 2 Town Barton

Sunday 11
- 6 12A Baring Crescent and Crescent Garden
- 7 Bickham Gardens
- 23 Cliffe
- 41 The Gate House
- 42 Goren Farm (Evening)
- 55 Kia-Ora Farm & Gardens
- 97 2 Town Barton
- 109 Yonder Hill

Monday 12
- 23 Cliffe
- 41 The Gate House
- 42 Goren Farm (Evening)

Tuesday 13
- 7 Bickham Gardens
- 23 Cliffe
- 41 The Gate House
- 42 Goren Farm (Evening)

Wednesday 14
- 7 Bickham Gardens
- 23 Cliffe
- 41 The Gate House
- 42 Goren Farm (Evening)

Thursday 15
- 23 Cliffe
- 41 The Gate House
- 42 Goren Farm (Evening)

Friday 16
- 23 Cliffe
- 41 The Gate House
- 42 Goren Farm (Evening)

Saturday 17
- 12 Brendon Gardens
- 17 Chapel Farm House
- 23 Cliffe
- 38 Fossleigh
- 41 The Gate House
- 42 Goren Farm (Evening)
- 105 Winsford Walled Garden

Sunday 18
- 12 Brendon Gardens
- 23 Cliffe
- 26 The Croft
- 38 Fossleigh
- 39 Fursdon
- 41 The Gate House
- 42 Goren Farm (Evening)
- 60 Little Ash Bungalow
- 109 Yonder Hill

Monday 19
- 23 Cliffe
- 41 The Gate House
- 42 Goren Farm (Evening)

Tuesday 20
- 23 Cliffe
- 41 The Gate House
- 42 Goren Farm (Evening)

Wednesday 21
- 23 Cliffe
- 41 The Gate House
- 42 Goren Farm (Evening)

Thursday 22
- 23 Cliffe
- 41 The Gate House
- 42 Goren Farm (Evening)

Friday 23
- 23 Cliffe
- 41 The Gate House
- 42 Goren Farm (Evening)

Saturday 24
- 14 Cadhay
- 23 Cliffe
- 41 The Gate House
- 42 Goren Farm (Evening)
- 64 Lower Spitchwick Gardens
- 85 Sidmouth Gardens

Sunday 25
- 2 32 Allenstyle Drive
- 14 Cadhay
- 23 Cliffe
- 41 The Gate House
- 42 Goren Farm (Evening)
- 55 Kia-Ora Farm & Gardens
- 64 Lower Spitchwick Gardens
- 85 Sidmouth Gardens
- 91 The Stannary
- 109 Yonder Hill

Monday 26
- 2 32 Allenstyle Drive
- 23 Cliffe
- 41 The Gate House
- 42 Goren Farm (Evening)
- 55 Kia-Ora Farm & Gardens
- 85 Sidmouth Gardens
- 91 The Stannary
- 109 Yonder Hill

Tuesday 27
- 23 Cliffe
- 41 The Gate House
- 42 Goren Farm (Evening)

Wednesday 28
- 23 Cliffe
- 41 The Gate House
- 42 Goren Farm (Evening)

Thursday 29
- 23 Cliffe
- 41 The Gate House
- 42 Goren Farm (Evening)

Friday 30
- 23 Cliffe
- 41 The Gate House
- 42 Goren Farm (Evening)

Saturday 31
- 23 Cliffe
- 41 The Gate House

Romantic woodland of rare trees and shrubs . . .

September

Sunday 1
- 2 32 Allenstyle Drive
- 7 Bickham Gardens
- 23 Cliffe
- 41 The Gate House
- 93 Summers Place
- 109 Yonder Hill

Monday 2
- 23 Cliffe
- 41 The Gate House

Tuesday 3
- 7 Bickham Gardens
- 23 Cliffe
- 41 The Gate House

Wednesday 4
- 7 Bickham Gardens
- 23 Cliffe
- 41 The Gate House

Thursday 5
- 23 Cliffe
- 41 The Gate House

Friday 6
- 23 Cliffe
- 41 The Gate House

Saturday 7
- 23 Cliffe
- 41 The Gate House
- 75 Prospect House

Sunday 8
- 2 32 Allenstyle Drive
- 23 Cliffe
- 41 The Gate House
- 43 Gorwell House
- 55 Kia-Ora Farm & Gardens
- 75 Prospect House
- 109 Yonder Hill

Monday 9
- 23 Cliffe
- 41 The Gate House

Tuesday 10
- 23 Cliffe
- 41 The Gate House

Wednesday 11
- 23 Cliffe
- 41 The Gate House

Thursday 12
- 23 Cliffe
- 41 The Gate House

Friday 13
- 23 Cliffe
- 41 The Gate House

Saturday 14
- 41 The Gate House
- 57 Langtrees
- 67 Moretonhampstead Gardens

Sunday 15
- 5 Ash Tree Farm (Evening)
- 16 Castle Drogo
- 41 The Gate House
- 53 Hollycombe House
- 67 Moretonhampstead Gardens
- 92 Stone Lane Gardens
- 109 Yonder Hill

Monday 16
- 41 The Gate House

Tuesday 17
- 41 The Gate House

Wednesday 18
- 41 The Gate House
- 104 Willand Old Village Gardens

Thursday 19
- 41 The Gate House

Friday 20
- 41 The Gate House

Saturday 21
- 17 Chapel Farm House
- 41 The Gate House

Sunday 22
- 41 The Gate House
- 109 Yonder Hill

Monday 23
- 41 The Gate House

Tuesday 24
- 41 The Gate House

Wednesday 25
- 41 The Gate House

Thursday 26
- 41 The Gate House

Friday 27
- 41 The Gate House

Saturday 28
- 41 The Gate House
- 59 Lewis Cottage

Sunday 29
- 41 The Gate House
- 59 Lewis Cottage
- 109 Yonder Hill

Monday 30
- 41 The Gate House

October

Tuesday 1
- 41 The Gate House

Wednesday 2
- 41 The Gate House

Thursday 3
- 41 The Gate House

Friday 4
- 41 The Gate House

Saturday 5
- 41 The Gate House

Sunday 6
- 7 Bickham Gardens
- 41 The Gate House
- 109 Yonder Hill

Monday 7
- 41 The Gate House

Tuesday 8
- 41 The Gate House

Wednesday 9
- 41 The Gate House

Thursday 10
- 41 The Gate House

Friday 11
- 41 The Gate House

Saturday 12
- 31 The Downes
- 41 The Gate House

Sunday 13
- 3 Andrew's Corner

31 The Downes
41 The Gate House
76 Regency House

Monday 14
31 The Downes
41 The Gate House

Tuesday 15
31 The Downes
41 The Gate House

Wednesday 16
31 The Downes
41 The Gate House

Thursday 17
31 The Downes
41 The Gate House

Friday 18
31 The Downes
41 The Gate House

Saturday 19
17 Chapel Farm House
41 The Gate House

Sunday 20
41 The Gate House

Monday 21
41 The Gate House

Tuesday 22
41 The Gate House

Wednesday 23
41 The Gate House

Thursday 24
41 The Gate House

Friday 25
41 The Gate House

Saturday 26
41 The Gate House

Sunday 27
41 The Gate House

Monday 28
41 The Gate House

Tuesday 29
41 The Gate House

Wednesday 30
41 The Gate House

Thursday 31
41 The Gate House

February 2014

Sunday 2
19 Cherubeer Gardens

Sunday 9
62 Littleham House Cottage

Friday 14
19 Cherubeer Gardens

Saturday 15
35 1 Feebers Cottage

Sunday 16
35 1 Feebers Cottage
62 Littleham House Cottage

Gardens open to the public

8 Blackpool Gardens
13 Burrow Farm Gardens
14 Cadhay
16 Castle Drogo
27 Dartington Hall Gardens
30 Docton Mill
39 Fursdon
40 The Garden House
47 Hartland Abbey
50 Heddon Hall
65 Lukesland
66 Marwood Hill
73 Plant World
82 Shapcott Barton Estate
92 Stone Lane Gardens
103 Wick Farm Gardens
105 Winsford Walled Garden

By appointment only

45 Hamblyn's Coombe
58 Lee Ford
95 Tamarisks
106 Withleigh Farm

Also open by Appointment ☎

1 Abbotskerswell Gardens
2 32 Allenstyle Drive
3 Andrew's Corner
5 Ash Tree Farm
7 Bickham Cottage, Bickham Gardens
7 Bickham Gardens
9 Bocombe Mill Cottage
11 Bramble Torre
17 Chapel Farm House
19 Cherubeer Gardens
19 Higher Cherubeer, Cherubeer Gardens
20 Chevithorne Barton
21 Cleave Hill
23 Cliffe
24 Collepardo
25 Coombe Trenchard
26 The Croft
31 The Downes
33 East Woodlands Farmhouse
35 1 Feebers Cottage
37 Foamlea
38 Fossleigh
41 The Gate House
42 Goren Farm
43 Gorwell House
44 Haldon Grange
46 Harbour Lights
48 The Haven
49 Heathercombe
51 High Garden
53 Hollycombe House
55 Kia-Ora Farm & Gardens
57 Langtrees
59 Lewis Cottage
60 Little Ash Bungalow
61 Little Webbery
62 Littleham House Cottage
67 Moretonhampstead Gardens
67 Sutton Mead, Moretonhampstead Gardens
68 Mothecombe House
72 The Old Vicarage
74 Portington
75 Prospect House
76 Regency House
80 St Merryn
81 School House
83 Shutelake

Abbotsford, Abbotskerswell Gardens

Follow NGS Twitter at @NGSOpenGardens

86 Southcombe House, Southcombe Gardens
87 Southern Comfort
88 Sowton Mill
89 Springdale
90 Squirrels
91 The Stannary
93 Summers Place
94 Taikoo
98 The Engine House, Venn Cross Railway Gardens
98 Venn Cross Railway Gardens
100 4 Wellswood Heights
102 Whitstone Farm
107 Wood Barton
109 Yonder Hill

The Gardens

ABBOTSBURY GARDENS
See Dorset

GROUP OPENING

1 ABBOTSKERSWELL GARDENS

Abbotskerswell TQ12 5PN, 01626 356004, christinemack@clara.co.uk. *2m SW of Newton Abbot town centre. Take A381 Newton Abbot/Totnes, sharp L turn into village or R turn if coming from Totnes. Field car parking at Fairfield or in village. Maps available at all gardens, in Model Stores & Church House.* Home-made teas at Church House. **Combined adm £5, chd free (share to Friends of St Marys). Sat 15, Sun 16 June (1-5). Visitors also welcome by appt Apr to Sept, number of gardens available agreed on request.**

ABBOTSFORD
Mrs W Grierson.
Maps at all locations

NEW **ABBOTSKERSWELL ALLOTMENTS**
Margaret Crompton

NEW **1 ABBOTSWELL COTTAGES**
Ford Rd. Jane Taylor

BRIAR COTTAGE
1 Monk's Orchard. Peggy & David Munden

COURT COTTAGE
Mr & Mrs A R W Rooth

8 COURT FARM BARNS
Wilton Way. Pat Mackness

FAIRFIELD
Vicarage Rd. Christine & Brian Mackness

KARIBU
35 Wilton Way. Jenny & Dave Brook

PRIORS
Brenda & Brian Gilbert

In 2013 popular Abbotskerswell Gardens adds two new offerings. The Allotments have 22 plots, many nurtured over years, showing a wide range of skills and production methods. 1 Abbotswell Cottages is a delightful garden which hides its charms - until you enter the back garden! Backing onto a stream with woodland and bog gardens, a lawned area with pergola and herbaceous borders, gravel garden and productive vegetable area. A further 7 gardens in this pretty village display beautiful cottage planting, wild flower areas, specialist plants, dry shillet gardening, dramatic terracing, redevelopment areas incorporating imaginative hard landscaping, and a garden which specialises in foliage and topiary. We welcome people to picnic in the field or arboretum at Fairfield if the weather is good. Children will enjoy the miniature Shetland ponies, plus finding their way through winding paths among high grasses. See You Tube Abbotskerswell Gardens 2011 for a taster. Featured on Radio Devon The Potting Shed. Disabled access to 4 gardens.

2 32 ALLENSTYLE DRIVE

Yelland, Barnstaple EX31 3DZ. Steve & Dawn Morgan, 01271 861433, fourhungrycats@aol.com, www.devonsubtropicalgarden.co.uk. *5m W of Barnstaple. Take B3233 towards Instow. Through Bickington & Fremington. L at Yelland sign into Allenstyle Rd. 1st R into Allenstyle Dr. Light blue bungalow.* Light refreshments. **Adm £3.50, chd free. Sun 25, Mon 26 Aug, Sun 1, Sun 8 Sept (11-5.30). Visitors also warmly welcomed by appt Aug to Sept.**
Subtropical planting in small (50x100ft) garden in mild estuary location. Bananas, hedychiums (gingers), palms, colocasia, aroids, brugmansias, exotic collection of passionflowers, prairie planting and much more. Lots of seating so you can take your time and enjoy our late summer burst of scent, colour and high impact planting.

3 ANDREW'S CORNER

Belstone EX20 1RD. Robin & Edwina Hill, 01837 840332, edwinarobinhill@btinternet.com, www.belstonevillage.net. *3m E of Okehampton. Signed to Belstone. In village signed Skaigh. Parking restricted but cars may be left on nearby common.* Home-made teas. **Adm £3.50, chd free. Sun 14 Apr; Sun 5, Mon 6, Suns 12, 26, Mon 27 May (2.30-5.30). Candlelit evening openings £5, chd £2, wine, Sat 15, Sun 16 June (7-10); Sun 13 Oct (2.30-5.30). Also open 14 Apr Taikoo. Visitors also welcome by appt.**
Well-established, wildlife-friendly, well-labelled plantsman's garden in stunning high moorland setting. Variety of garden habitats incl woodland areas, bog garden, pond; wide range of unusual trees, shrubs, herbaceous plants for yr-round effect incl alpines, rhododendrons, bulbs and maples; spectacular autumn colour. Organic kitchen garden, greenhouses and chickens. Family quiz sheet. Featured on Radio Devon and in Grow Your Own Magazine. Wheelchair access difficult when wet.

2 delightful gardens of contrasting styles . . .

GROUP OPENING

4 NEW ASH GARDENS

Ash, Dartmouth TQ6 0LR. *2m SW of Dartmouth. Leave A3122 (Halwell to Dartmouth rd) at R turn beside white house just before Sportsman's Arms. Follow signs to Ash. After 1½ m at 2nd X-rds, park at Ash Tree Farm.* Home-made teas. **Combined adm £4, chd free. Sun 23 June (2-5).**

ASH TREE FARM
Ms Stevie Rogers
(See separate entry)

NEW **BAY TREE COTTAGE**
Jenny Goffe

2 delightful gardens of contrasting styles in the tiny hamlet of Ash. Ash

Tree Farm: see separate entry. The beautiful intimate little garden at Bay Tree Cottage sits in a quiet secluded valley with wonderful sunlit views across open farmland. The perfect curved lawn leads the eye to small 'rooms' filled with surprise and clever planting. Ornamental trees punctuate the boundary and a tiny vegetable garden of raised beds overflows with produce. Bring photos or drawings of your garden and discuss your ideas or problems with a member of the Society of Garden Designers and a previous judge at Chelsea Flower Show.

5 ASH TREE FARM
Ash Cross, Dartmouth TQ6 0LR. Ms Stevie Rogers, 01803 712437, stevie@ashtreefarm.com, www.ashtreefarm.com. *2m SW of Dartmouth. (see Ash Gardens for directions).* Home-made teas. **Adm £3.50, chd free. Sun 5, Mon 6 May (2-5). Evening Opening £3.50, chd free, wine, Sun 15 Sept (5-9). Also open with Ash Gardens 23 June. Visitors also welcome by appt incl groups.**
Our rainbow garden is an interesting, informative and unconventional new garden, full of original ideas. Colour-themed, cottage garden style plantings. Whole garden planted for the benefit of wildlife. Wildflower banks and orchard, kitchen garden and wildlife pond. Level pathways, plenty of seating. Nursery growing wildflowers, cottage garden and vegetable plants. Access to farm walks. The farm is also home to the 'Hoofbeats' Horse Sanctuary for rescued and retired horses. Featured in Devon Life. All pathways are level and accessible to wheelchairs unless very wet. Plenty of seating around the garden for the less mobile.

6 NEW 12A BARING CRESCENT AND CRESCENT GARDEN
Exeter EX1 1TL. Liz & Trevor Philpott. *15mins walk from Exeter City Centre. From M5 exit J29, take B3183 towards City Centre. After approx 2.5 miles fork L into Magdalen road. After 700yds turn R into Baring Crescent. Parking available, follow signs. Also on D bus route from city centre.* Home-made teas. **Adm £3.50, chd free. Sat 15 June; Sat 10, Sun 11 Aug (1-6).**
Set in a Conservation area, walled garden at 12A is a charming example of a cherished city garden. With its Georgian property as the backdrop, relax and enjoy many aspects of this pollen and nectar rich garden with its colourful herbaceous borders, hostas, shrubs, roses, grasses, rockery, lawn and ornamental trees. A peaceful woodland space nurtures a small pond teeming with wildlife. Continue your visit into the Georgian Crescent Garden with grand lawn, expanse of hedging, large trees and mature shrubs.

A charming example of a cherished city garden . . .

THE BARN HOUSE
See Cornwall

GROUP OPENING

7 BICKHAM GARDENS
Kenn EX6 7XL, 01392 832671, jandjtremlett@hotmail.com. *6m S of Exeter. 1m off A38. Leave A38 at Kennford Services, follow signs to Kenn. 1st R in village, follow lane for ¾ m to end of no through rd.* Cream teas. **Combined adm £4.50, chd free.**
Suns, Tues, Weds (2-5pm)
14, 16, 17 Apr;
12, 14, 15 May;
9, 11, 12 June;
14, 16, 17 July;
11, 13, 14 Aug;
1, 3, 4 Sept;
Sun 6 Oct.
Visitors also welcome by appt Apr to Oct, coaches by arrangement.

BICKHAM COTTAGE
Steve Eyre

BICKHAM HOUSE
John & Julia Tremlett

Adj gardens in private valley under Haldon Hills. Bickham House: 7-acre garden with much recent replanting. Colour co-ordinated borders, mature trees incl massive tulip tree. Croquet lawn. Fernery and water garden. Formal parterre with lily pond. 1-acre walled garden with profusion of vegetables and flowers. Palm tree avenue leading to summerhouse. Spring garden incl cowslips, bluebells. Alpine house with over 100 immaculately displayed plants. Wide selection of well-grown plants for sale. Bickham Cottage: small cottage garden divided into separate areas by old stone walls and hedge banks. Front garden with mainly South African bulbs and plants. Lawn surrounded by borders incl agapanthus, eucomis, crocosmia, dierama. Stream garden with primulas, and glasshouses with collections of nerines and tulbaghias. Pond with large koi carp. October opening for nerines, 450 varieties. Featured in Independent Magazine, Devon Life, Western Morning News, Amateur Gardener, Country Living and on Radio Devon.

8 ◆ BLACKPOOL GARDENS
Dartmouth TQ6 0RG. Sir Geoffrey Newman, 01803 771801, www.blackpoolsands.co.uk. *3m SW of Dartmouth. From Dartmouth follow brown signs to Blackpool Sands on A379. Entrance to gardens via Blackpool Sands car park.* **For information, please phone or see garden website.**
Tenderly restored C19 subtropical plantsman's garden with collection of mature and newly-planted tender and unusual trees, shrubs and carpet of spring flowers. Paths and steps lead gradually uphill and above the Captain's seat offering spectacular coastal views. Recent plantings follow the S hemisphere theme with callistemons, pittosporums, acacias and buddlejas. Open 1 Apr - Sept (10-4) weather permitting.

9 BOCOMBE MILL COTTAGE
Bocombe, Parkham EX39 5PH. Mr Chris Butler & Mr David Burrows, 01237 451293, www.bocombe.co.uk. *6m E of Clovelly, 9m SW of Bideford. From A39 just outside Horns Cross village, turn to Foxdown. At Xrds follow signs for parking.* Home-made teas/Devon cream teas. **Adm £4, chd £1. Sats, Suns 15, 16, 29, 30 June (12-5). Groups of 10+ also welcome by appt Mar to Sept.**
Not so much a garden, more a landscape punctuated with gardens. Short flower gardens walk, and circular walk approx 1m (boots suggested). Streams, bog gardens, pools plus a dozen water features.

white pergola. Surprise grotto and hermitage. Orchard. Soft fruit & kitchen gardens. Wild meadow, a wildlife haven. All organic, in 5 acres. Garden Plan available. Goats on hillside.

BOSCASTLE GARDENS
See Cornwall

GROUP OPENING

10 BOVEY TRACEY GARDENS
Bovey Tracey TQ13 9NA. *6m N of Newton Abbot. Gateway to Dartmoor. Take A382 to Bovey Tracey. Car parking available at Mary St, Station Rd, library. Car parks at Whitstone, Pottery Road and Parke.* Home-made teas at Gleam Tor. **Combined adm £4.50, chd free. Sat 1, Sun 2 June (2-6).**

BOVEY COMMUNITY GARDEN
Chapple Rd. NT and Bovey Tracey Climate Action.
Follow signs to Parke, parking in visitors' car park
http://boveycommunitygarden.org.uk

NEW 5 BRIDGE COTTAGES
Cath Valentine.
Down lane at base of Pottery Rd, near r'about, opp Mike Harding Landrover dealership

NEW FOOTLANDS
Chapple Road. Mrs Moira Squire.
close to Gleam Tor

GLEAM TOR
Gillian & Colin Liddy.
Last house on L at end of Brimley Rd before rd narrows

PENNY PARK
3 Devon House Dr. John & Angela Tibbs.
Near entrance to Coombe Cross Hotel

11 ST PETER'S CLOSE
Mr & Mrs Gregory.
Parking available in surrounding roads

23 STORRS CLOSE
Mr Roger Clark & Ms Chie Nakatani.
From town centre pass Library on L, school on R. Turn up hill into Priory L then L again into Storrs Close. No 23 is 3rd on R. Please park with consideration

WHITSTONE HOUSE
Laura Barclay.
Park in Whitstone Quarry at top of Whitstone Lane

Pretty cob and Dartmoor granite built town by R Bovey. 8 enormously varied gardens in or close to the town. Whitstone House's mature garden with undulating heather feature, woodland walk, granite tor and panoramic views looks down to Storrs Close, plantsman's paradise with plants grown from seed from around the world. St Peter's Close: small town garden packed with interesting plants and model railway. Penny Park: bursting with colour in a relaxed planting style and circular lawn. Gleam Tor: abundance of herbaceous colour and new curved wall garden with prairie planting. Footlands: low maintenance with interesting shapes and colours.
5 Bridge Cottages: productive and quirky cottage garden. In the walled garden at the NT's Parke, a successful community garden, with productive fruit trees, and many vegetables (inc. heritage varieties). Limited wheelchair access at some gardens.

Quirky cottage garden . . .

11 BRAMBLE TORRE
Dittisham, nr Dartmouth TQ6 0HZ. Paul & Sally Vincent, 01803 722227, salv@hotmail.co.uk, www.rainingsideways.com. *3/4 m from Dittisham. Leave A3122 Halwell to Dartmouth rd at Sportsmans Arms and head towards Dittisham. In village turn hard L towards Cornworthy. Garden 3/4 m straight ahead - L turn by gates to park.* Cream teas. **Adm £4, chd free. Sat 15, Sun 16 June (2-6). Visitors also welcome by appt May to July.**
Set in 20 acres of farmland, the 3-acre garden follows rambling stream through steep valley. Lily pond, herbaceous borders, camellias, shrubs and roses are dominated by huge embothrium, scarlet in late spring against a sometimes blue sky! Formal herb and vegetable garden runs along one side of stream while chickens scratch in an orchard of ditsum plums and cider apples on other side. Well behaved dogs on leads welcome. Limited wheelchair access, parts of garden very steep and uneven. Tea area with wheelchair access and excellent garden view.

GROUP OPENING

12 NEW BRENDON GARDENS
Brendon, Lynton EX35 6PU. *1m S of A39 North Devon coast rd, between Porlock and Lynton.* Light lunches and homemade teas. **Combined adm £3.50, chd free. Sats, Suns 20, 21 July; 17, 18 Aug (11-5).**

NEW 1 DEERCOMBE COTTAGES
Valerie and Stephen Exley.
From village green in Brendon. Drive into village and park in Village hall car park. Garden 250 yds on L. Set down possible directly outside garden

HIGHER TIPPACOTT FARM
Angela & Malcolm Percival.
From X-rds at Brendon village green follow signs to Tippacott, 1m to T-junction fronting moor. Turn R, proceed 200 yds. Parking on R

Within a stunningly beautiful part of Exmoor Nat. Park, Brendon nestles in the E Lyn river valley surrounded by heather moorland and with dramatic coastline close by. An area of excellent walking; level walk along N bank of the dramatically beautiful river between Brendon and Rockford, also moorland walk and SW coastpath. 1 Deercombe Cottages: delightful small garden situated in this steeply wooded valley overlooking lane and river, created using ditched stone to provide a variety of levels and spaces enabling appreciation of the planting at close quarters. Rich in contrasting foliage and variety of perennials. Higher Tippacott Farm: on open moor high above Brendon alt. 950ft. Garden faces S overlooking its own pretty valley pasture and stream and has sunny levels of interesting herbaceous planting, stone walls and old barns. Vegetables and soft fruit areas perched high up with distant sea view. Chickens roam. All organic.

13 ◆ BURROW FARM GARDENS

Dalwood, Axminster EX13 7ET. Mary & John Benger, 01404 831285, enquiries@burrowfarmgardens.co.uk, www.burrowfarmgardens.co.uk. *3½ m W of Axminster. From A35 turn N at Taunton Xrds then follow brown signs*

Beautiful 10-acre garden with unusual trees, shrubs and herbaceous plants. Traditional summerhouse looks towards lake and ancient oak woodland with rhododendrons and azaleas. Early spring interest and superb autumn colour. The more formal Millennium garden features a rill. Anniversary Garden featuring late summer perennials and grasses. A photographers dream. Café and Gift Shop 1st April - 31st October (10-7). Featured in Devon Life magazine.

14 ◆ CADHAY

Ottery St Mary EX11 1QT. Rupert Thistlethwayte, 01404 813511, www.cadhay.org.uk. *1m NW of Ottery St Mary. On B3176 between Ottery St Mary and Fairmile. From E exit A30 at Iron Bridge. From W exit A30 at Patteson's Cross.* **Adm £3, chd free. For NGS: Fris 17 May, 21 June, 19 July; Sat 24, Sun 25 Aug (2-5). For other opening times and information, please phone or see garden website.**

Tranquil 2-acre setting for Elizabethan manor house. 2 medieval fish ponds surrounded by rhododendrons, gunnera, hostas and flag iris. Roses, clematis, lilies and hellebores surround walled water garden. 120ft herbaceous border walk informally planted with cottage garden perennials and annuals. Walled kitchen gardens have been turned into allotments and old garden store is now tearoom. Gravel paths.

15 NEW CARPENTER'S COTTAGE

Knowle, Crediton EX17 5BX. Mrs Joan Tolley. *4 m W Crediton. From Crediton A377 W, after 4 m L to Knowle From Copplestone A377 E after 1 m turn R to Knowle.* Home-made teas. **Adm £3, chd free. Sat 11, Sun 12 May (2-5).**

1 acre plantaholic's cottage garden. Winding paths throughout densely planted areas take you through exotic planting, Acer glade, white garden, wildlife ponds and many shady areas with unusual woodland planting and late spring bulbs. Park in Church car park.

Densely planted areas take you through exotic planting . . .

16 ◆ CASTLE DROGO

Drewsteignton EX6 6PB. National Trust, 01822 820320, www.nationaltrust.org.uk. *12m W of Exeter. 5m S of A30. Follow brown signs.* **Adm £5.50 garden only, chd £3. For NGS: Suns 12 May; 15 Sept (9.30-5.30). For other opening times and information, please phone or see garden website.**

Medium-sized Grade II* listed garden with formal structures designed by Edwin Lutyens and George Dillistone during the late 1920s. These consist of formal rose beds, herbaceous borders, shrubbery and circular croquet lawn surrounded by mature yew hedges. Rhododendron garden overlooks spectacular views of Teign valley gorge and Dartmoor. Garden tours. **Stone Lane Garden** (a few miles away) open on same day September. Partial wheelchair access, purpose-built access path to main terrace.

17 CHAPEL FARM HOUSE

Halwill Junction, Beaworthy EX21 5UF. Robin & Toshie Hull, 01409 221594. *12m NW of Okehampton. On A3079. At W end of village.* Cream teas. **Adm £3.50, chd free. Sats 23 Mar; 20, 27 Apr; 11, 18 May; Sat 1, Sat 15, Sun 16 June; Sats 20 July, 17 Aug, 21 Sept, 19 Oct (11-5). Visitors also welcome by appt.**

Approx ½ -acre garden started in 1992 by present owners, landscaped with shrub borders, heathers, rhododendrons and azaleas. Alpine bed. Kitchen garden. 2 small greenhouses for mixed use. Small bonsai collection. 3 acres of mixed young woodland with wildlife and flowers. Japanese garden and stone lantern. Gravel car park and paths.

18 CHERRY TREES WILDLIFE GARDEN

5 Sentry Corner, East the Water, Bideford EX39 4BW. Henry and Evelyn Butterfield, cherrytrees.weebly.com. *East The Water. From Bideford Old Bridge, follow up hill past The Royal Hotel. Follow signs to Sentry Corner (approx ¾ m), parking at Pollyfield Centre.* Light refreshments. **Adm £3, chd free. Mon 6 May; Sat 15, Sun 16 June (2-5).**

Small demonstration garden showing what can be done to bring wildlife into the town. Incl courtyard garden, summer cornfield, summer wildflower meadow, cottage garden border, mini copse, and 2 small ponds. Newly-constructed folly and stumpery. Enjoy a friendly chat about wildlife gardening over tea and biscuits with the owners. Photo collection of garden's wildlife visitors. Small natural history collection. Featured in garden column of The Bideford Post.

GROUP OPENING

19 CHERUBEER GARDENS

Dolton EX19 8PP, 01805 804265, hynesjo@gmail.com, https://sites.google.com/site/cherubeergardens/the-gardens. *8m SE of Great Torrington. 2m E of Dolton. From A3124 turn S towards Stafford Moor Fisheries, take 1st R, gardens 500m on L.* Home-made teas Higher Cherubeer. **Combined adm £4, chd free. Sun 3, Fri 15 Feb (2-5); Suns 26 May; 7 July (2.30-5.30); Sun 2, Fri 14 Feb 2014 (2-5). Visitors also welcome by appt Feb to July.**

CHERUBEER NCH
Janet Brown

HIGHER CHERUBEER
Jo & Tom Hynes
Visitors also welcome by appt Feb to Sept.
01805 804265
hynesjo@gmail.com

MIDDLE CHERUBEER
Heather Hynes.
not open in the summer, 26/5/13 & 7/7/13

The 3 Cherubeers, a family affair, form a small hamlet in rolling farmland at

500 ft at the top of a SW facing valley. Despite the exposed location and stony acid clay soil, the gardens provide a wealth of colour right through the season. Cherubeer: cottage garden set around a C15 thatched house (not open). Ponds, paths, and steps filled with colourful perennials and herbs set off by mature shrubs and trees. Higher Cherubeer: 1-acre country garden with gravelled courtyard, raised beds and alpine house, large herbaceous border, shady woodland beds with over 200 varieties of snowdrops, colourful collection of basketry willows, vegetable garden and National Collection of hardy cyclamen. Middle Cherubeer: colourful small garden. 3 separate areas with bog garden, pond and massed herbaceous perennials interlinked with paths. Many cyclamen and snowdrop bank. Partial wheelchair access due to slopes and gravel. Very little access at Cherubeer.

NCH

20 CHEVITHORNE BARTON
Tiverton EX16 7QB. Michael & Arabella Heathcoat Amory, pottinger985@btinternet.com. *3m NE of Tiverton. M5, J27, leave A361 by 1st exit after 300 yds, through Sampford Peverell and Halberton towards Tiverton. Immed past golf course, R then R at next T-junction. Over bridge, L through Craze Lowman, carry on through lanes to T-junction, R then 1st L.* Home-made teas. **Adm £3.50, chd free. Suns 14 Apr, 19 May (2-5.30). Visitors also welcome by appt.**
Terraced walled garden, summer borders and romantic woodland of rare trees and shrubs. In spring, garden features large collection of magnolias, camellias, rhododendrons and azaleas. Also incl one of only two NCCPG oak collections situated in 12 hectares of parkland and comprising over 200 different species.

NCH

CHIDEOCK MANOR
See Dorset

21 CLEAVE HILL
Membury, Axminster EX13 7AJ. Andy & Penny Pritchard, 01404 881437, penny@tonybengerlandscaping.co.uk. *4m NW of Axminster. From Membury Village, follow rd down valley. 1st R after Lea Hill B&B, last house on drive, approx 1m.* Cream teas. **Adm £3.50, chd free. Sat 29, Sun 30 June (11-5). Visitors also welcome by appt, not enough room for coaches.**
Artistic garden in pretty village situated on edge of Blackdown Hills. Cottage-style garden, planted to provide all-season structure, texture and colour. Designed around pretty thatched house and old stone barns. Wonderful views, attractive vegetable garden and orchard, wild flower meadow.

Burrow Farm Gardens

22 CLIFF COTTAGE
Colebrook Road, Plympton, Plymouth PL7 4AG. Mrs Marie Kay. *4m E of Plymouth. From Marsh Mill r'about, follow signs to Plympton B3416. Glen Rd for 1.5m. L at mini r'abouts over bridge, R onto Boringdon Rd, through village. House/garden on L. Small car park on R.* Home-made teas. **Adm £3.50, chd free. Sun 7 July (11.30-4.30).**
Be transported back in time by this charming intimate garden. Fragrant roses and sweetpeas mingle with fennel fronds in this oasis of country charm. Rest awhile among the flower beds of this delightful cottage and enjoy the gentle clucking of chickens as you take tea and home-made cakes. Local preserve tasting.

23 CLIFFE
Lee, Ilfracombe EX34 8LR. Dr & Mrs Humphreys, 07854 131935, gill.heavens@virgin.net. *3m W of Ilfracombe. Garden is past sea front at Lee, towards top of steep hill on coast rd. Entrance through black wrought iron gates on L. Lee Bay car park at bottom of hill (no parking on approach rd).* **Adm £3, chd free. Mon 1 July to Fri 13 Sept incl (10-4). Visitors also welcome by appt Apr to Sept.**
Cliff-side terraced garden with spectacular coastal views. Diverse range of habitats from Mediterranean to woodland. Colourful herbaceous borders throughout summer and exotic hedychiums, canna and salvias flowering into autumn. Featured in Coast Magazine and Hardy Plant Journal and on Radio Devon.

Look out for the NGS yellow arrows...

24 COLLEPARDO
3 Keyberry Park, Newton Abbot TQ12 1BZ. Betty & Don Frampton, 01626 354580 collepardo@btinternet.com. *Take A380 Newton Abbot. From Newton Abbot (Penn Inn) r'about follow sign for town centre. 1st L slip rd before T-lights, then 1st R, 2nd L.* Home-made teas. **Adm £3, chd free. Wed 29, Thur 30 May; Sat 22 - Sun 30 June incl (11-5). Groups also welcome by appt.**
1/3-acre garden laid out in series of interlinked colour-themed garden rooms, explored via 400 metres of meandering paths. Circular rockery of 30 metres enclosing new lawn. Herbaceous and shrub borders, pond, raised walkway, and gazebo allow the visitor every opportunity to view 1,500 varieties of hardy plants, shrubs and trees. First prize for landscape section of Newton In Bloom 2012.

Large collection of rare and unusual plants . . .

25 COOMBE TRENCHARD
Lewtrenchard EX20 4PW. Philip & Sarah Marsh, 01566 783179, Sarah@coombetrenchard.co.uk, www.coombetrenchard.co.uk. *14m N of Tavistock and W of Okehampton. In Lewdown take turning for Lewtrenchard, at bottom of hill turn R opposite Lewtrenchard Manor Hotel. Garden 100yds on R up unmarked lane.* Light refreshments. **Adm £5, chd free. Suns 16, 30 June; 14, 28 July (10-5). Visitors also welcome by appt Apr to July.**
Coombe Trenchard's 8-acre Arts & Crafts garden was designed in 1906 by architect Walter Sarel, with terraces, garden buildings, paths and bridges. Still a work in progress, forgotten paths, woodland garden, water gardens and the pattern of long forgotten Edwardian planting schemes are being discovered and restored. Sculpture exhibition. Featured in Devon Life. Mostly wheelchair access. Gravel paths in woodland.

COOMBEGATE COTTAGE
See Cornwall

COTEHELE
See Cornwall

COTHAY MANOR & GARDENS
See Somerset, Bristol & South Gloucestershire

26 THE CROFT
Yarnscombe, Barnstaple EX31 3LW. Sam & Margaret Jewell, 01769 560535. *8m S of Barnstaple, 10m SE of Bideford, 12m W of South Molton, 4m NE of Torrington. From A377, turn W opp Chapelton railway stn. Follow Yarnscombe signs, after 3m parking in village hall car park L of village sign. From B3232, 1/4 m N of Huntshaw X TV mast, turn E follow Yarnscombe signs for 2m, parking in village hall car park nearby.* Cream teas. **Adm £3.50, chd free (share to N Devon Animal Ambulance). Suns 16 June; 21 July; 18 Aug (2-6). Visitors also welcome by appt Feb to Oct, min 3 days notice required.**
1-acre plantswoman's garden featuring exotic Japanese garden with tea house, koi carp pond and cascading stream, tropical garden with exotic shrubs and perennials, herbaceous borders with unusual plants and shrubs,bog garden with collection of irises, astilbes and moisture-loving plants, duck pond. Exotic borders, new beds around duck pond and bog area, large collection of rare and unusual plants. Featured in Amateur Gardening Magazine.

CUTLINWITH
See Cornwall

27 ◆ DARTINGTON HALL GARDENS
Dartington TQ9 6EL. Dartington Hall Trust, 01803 847058, gardens@dartington.org, www.dartington.org. *1 1/2 m NW of Totnes. From Totnes take A384, turn R at Dartington Parish Church. Proceed up hill for 1m. Hall & Gardens on R. Car parking on L.* **Adm £5, chd free. For NGS: Sun 16 June (10-4). For other opening times and information, please phone or see garden website.**
28-acre modern garden, created since 1925 around C14 medieval hall (not open). Courtyard and Tournament Ground. Dry landscape Japanese garden. Extensive wild flower meadows and mixed shrub and herbaceous border. Stylish access bridge, designed by Peter Randall-Page. Guided tour available at 2pm. Recently voted 1 of the UK's top 50 gardens to visit, by the Independant newspaper. Mostly wheelchair access, phone for details.

28 DICOT
Chardstock EX13 7DF. Mr & Mrs F Clarkson, www.dicot.co.uk. *5m N of Axminster. Axminster to Chard A358 at Tytherleigh to Chardstock. R at George Inn, L fork to Hook, R to Burridge, 2nd house on L.* Home-made teas. **Adm £3, chd free. Sat 4, Sun 5, Mon 6 May; Sats, Suns 15, 16 June; 27, 28 July (2-5.30).**
Secret garden hidden in East Devon valley. 3 acres of unusual and exotic plants - some rare. Rhododendrons, azaleas and camellias in profusion. Meandering stream, fish pool, Japanese-style garden and interesting vegetable garden with fruit cage, tunnel and greenhouses. Surprises round every corner. Featured in Country Gardener and on BBC Radio Devon.

GROUP OPENING

29 DITTISHAM GARDENS
Dittisham, nr Dartmouth TQ6 0ES, www.dittisham.org.uk. *On R Dart between Totnes and Dartmouth. Leave A281 (Totnes - Kingsbridge Rd) at Halwell - A3122 to Dartmouth. At Hemborough post straight on to village of Dittisham (PH on corner Sportsman's Arms) down steep hill, views of river ahead.* Cream teas at Dittisham Village Hall. **Combined adm £5, chd free. Sat 20, Sun 21 July (2-6).**

CAMELOT
Lower St. Stella Stothart

DEEDAS COTTAGE
Manor St. Mrs Gail Mosley

DOVE COTTAGE
The Level. Mrs M Pusey

FERRY VIEW
The Lane. Mr & Mrs J Young

NEW **LOW DOLPHIN**
Lower Street. Ms Colette Charsley

SHEARWATER
Riverside Rd. Mr & Mrs Smith. *Enter village leaving church on L. Follow wide rd (Riverside Rd)*

passing field on R. Shearwater 1st house after small lane to The Ham on R

Dittisham overlooks the widest stretch of the beautiful R Dart just 3 miles up river from Dartmouth. The village, protected from the worst weather by rolling hills and the temperance of the Gulf Stream, is a gardener's paradise! Thatched cottages with gardens filled with all the old fashioned favourites, look out across the water towards Dartmoor in the distance. There are modern gardens too with contemporary planting, one even under construction. Terraced gardens cling to the hillside, the famous Dit'sum Plum orchards flourish still and cream teas can be had in the Village Hall overlooking the river. Read more about the village on www.dittisham.org.uk. Beautiful village on steep slopes overlooking R Dart opp Greenway (Agatha Christie). Limited wheelchair access; the village is very steep.

30 ◆ DOCTON MILL

Lymebridge, Hartland EX39 6EA. Lana & John Borrett, 01237 441369, doctonmill@tiscali.co.uk, www.doctonmill.co.uk. *8m W of Clovelly. Follow brown tourist signs on A39 nr Clovelly.* **Adm £4.50, chd free. For NGS: Sun 9 June (10-5). For other opening times and information, please phone or see garden website.**

Situated in stunning valley location. Garden surrounds original mill pond and the microclimate created within the wooded valley enables tender species to flourish. Recent planting of herbaceous, stream and summer garden give variety through the season. Scrummy cream teas all day.

31 THE DOWNES

Monkleigh, Bideford EX39 5LB. Richard Stanley-Baker, 07729 511671, downes.gardens@gmail.com, downes-gardens.com. *3m NW of Great Torrington. On A386 between Bideford & Torrington. Drive leads off A386 4½ m from Bideford, 2½ m from Torrington. Do not go to Monkleigh.* Cream teas. **Adm £5, chd free. Sun 10 to Fri 22 Mar incl; Sat 12 to Fri 18 Oct incl (12-4). Visitors also welcome by appt, notice required preferably email.**

15 acres of landscaped lawns with spectacular views over Torridge Valley. Arboretum with woodland walk, narcissi, bluebells. Unusual trees and shrubs sourced by two generations of Stanley-Bakers, from all over the world. Energetic programme of new plantings and border restoration initiated by new Head Gardener, Nigel Alford. Lovely garden environment, open to the public for some 30 yrs, and features many specimen shrubs and trees. It borders on the Tarka Trail, and itself offers a lovely woodland walks - especially good at bluebell time, and is delightfully secluded, rich in wild life. The garden has some steep slopes however, with due care, wheelchair access should be manageable, preferably when accompanied by friend.

32 DURCOMBE WATER

Furzehill, Barbrook, Lynton EX35 6LN. Pam & David Sydenham, 01598 753658, pam.sydenham@virgin.net. *3m S of Lynton. From Barnstaple take A39 towards Lynton. On entering Barbrook go past Total garage (do not turn to Lynton) take the next turn R (about 100yds). Follow this single track rd for 2m, gates on L.* Home-made teas. **Adm £4, chd free. Suns, Mons 19, 20, 26, 27 May (11-5).**

Stunning views across Exmoor. A silent relaxing 2½ acres, enlivened with streams, ponds and waterfalls falling 40ft through 8 tiered ponds. Different types of garden - cottage, landscaped terraces, oriental and art gallery, each with colour, scents and beauty. A feast of colour with rhododendrons, azaleas, perennials and shrubs. Lots of seats to enjoy the peace, views and beauty. The garden has been created single-handedly by the owner over the last 12 years since his retirement, and is maintained solely by him. Featured in The Exmoor Magazine and the North Devon Journal.

33 EAST WOODLANDS FARMHOUSE

Newton Tracey, Barnstaple EX31 3PP. Ann & Richard Harding, 01271 858776, hardingfarmhouse@aol.com, www.the-farmhouse.co.uk. *5m NE of Great Torrington, 5m S of Barnstaple, off B3232. From Great Torrington, turn R into single track rd before Alverdiscott; from Barnstaple turn L after leaving Alverdiscott into single track lane. 1m down lane, R fork at Y junction.* Home-made teas. **Adm £3.50, chd free. Sat 8, Sun 9 June (2-5). Visitors also welcome by appt May to Sept, phone or email at least 1 month prior to visit.**

From 1-acre blank landscape, East Woodlands has been transformed into a hidden oasis of swaying grasses, spectacular bamboos and cool to hot terraces. Little havens have been created where you can sit and enjoy the garden with its rolling, tireless views. Pond (unfenced) and bog garden. A potager's delight. Featured in North Devon Journal and Torrington Crier. Partial wheelchair access.

Thousands of crocuses . . . in 2-acre garden . . .

34 NEW EAST WORLINGTON HOUSE

East Worlington, Crediton EX17 4TS. Mr & Mrs Barnabas Hurst-Bannister. *In the centre of East Worlington, 2m W of Witheridge. In Witheridge (B3137 Tiverton/South Molton) into the square and R at small sign to East Worlington. Along West Street to Drayford Lane, 1.4 miles R at T-junction in Drayford, over bridge and L to Worlington. 0.3 miles enter East Worlington and L at the T-junction. East Worlington House after parish hall on L.* **Adm £3, chd free. Suns 24 Feb, 3 Mar (1.30-5.30).**

Thousands of Crocuses. In 2-acre garden, set in lovely position with views down the valley to Little Dart river, these spectacular crocuses have spread over many years through the garden and into the neighbouring churchyard. Cream teas in the parish hall (in aid of its thatch fund) next door. Disabled parking at the house. Parking nearby. Dogs on leads please.

35 1 FEEBERS COTTAGE
Broadclyst. EX5 3DQ. Mr & Mrs M J Squires, 01404 822118, feebers@onetel.com. *8m NE of Exeter. From B3181 Exeter to Taunton bear E at Dog Village towards Whimple. After 1½ m fork L for Westwood.* Light refreshments In garden of no 2 Feebers. **Adm £3, chd free. Sun 10, Mon 11 Feb; Sat 15, Sun 16 Feb 2014 (12-3). Visitors also welcome by appt.**
Mature but evolving cottage garden of 1 acre, with a maze of pathways, alpine area, herbaceous plants, trees, shrubs and vegetable garden. Many varieties of snowdrops in spring, in autumn colchicums and cyclamen. Wheelchair access if dry.

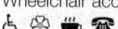

GROUP OPENING

36 FEEBERS GARDENS
Westwood, nr Broadclyst EX5 3DQ. *8m NE of Exeter. From B3181 Exeter to Taunton bear E at Dog Village towards Whimple. After 1½ m fork L for Westwood.* Home-made teas Teas at No2. **Combined adm £3, chd free. Sun 9 June (2-6).**

1 FEEBERS COTTAGE
Mr & Mrs M J Squires
(See separate entry)

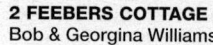

2 FEEBERS COTTAGE
Bob & Georgina Williams

2 pretty gardens in a Devon hamlet. 1 Feebers Cottage: evolving cottage garden of 1 acre - a maze of pathways, alpine area, herbaceous, trees, shrubs and vegetable garden. In spring, 60 different snowdrops; in autumn, colchicums and cyclamen. 2 Feebers Cottage: colourful, formal garden contrasting the cottage garden. Delightful flower beds, small alpine house and gravel area with variety of potted shrubs and plants. Wheelchair access if dry.

FERNHILL
See Somerset, Bristol & South Gloucestershire

37 FOAMLEA
Chapel Hill, Mortehoe EX34 7DZ. Beth Smith, 01271 871182, bethmortepoint@fmail.co.uk. *¼ m S of Mortehoe village. A361 N from Barnstaple. L at Mullacott Cross onto B3343 to Mortehoe. No parking near or at house. Use village car park, L past church, down steep hill, garden further 200yds.* Home-made teas. **Adm £3, chd free. Suns 19 May; 16 June; 14 July (2-5). Visitors also welcome by appt May to Sept, minibus access to gate only.**
10 yr old collection of plants thriving in open cliff top site with uninterrupted view to Morte Point (NT). The mild climate and a gradient providing natural drainage favour many temperate and semi-tropical species. Drystone walling, slate steps and shillet paths feature throughout. Colour-schemed areas, rockery and mixed plantings. Featured in Coast magazine.
NCH

The Engine House, Venn Cross Railway Gardens

38 FOSSLEIGH
Burlescombe EX16 7JH. David & Glenis Beard, 01823 672907, d.beard@virgin.net. *3m from M5, J27. From J27 take A38 to Wellington, pass over M5, 1st L to Burlescombe. 1m, L just before canal bridge. Limited parking, public car park 150m from garden, over bridge then immed L.* Cream teas. **Adm £3, chd free. Sats, Suns 20, 21 July; 17, 18 Aug (2-5). Visitors also welcome by appt June to Sept.**
The garden borders the Grand Western Canal near Devon Somerset border. Imaginative use of space, many surprises: Water garden, bog garden, herbaceous borders, Japanese garden, miniature bowling green, sundial vegetable plot, fruit cage, sunken walkways surrounded by flowers and foliage. Fernery. Much new planting this yr. Enjoy a stroll by canal after your visit.

39 ◆ FURSDON
Cadbury, Thorverton, Exeter EX5 5JS. David & Catriona Fursdon, 01392 860860, admin@fursdon.co.uk, www.fursdon.co.uk. *2m N of Thorverton. L (after Xrds by Blue Cross rescue centre) on A3072 travelling from Bickleigh towards Crediton. Fursdon approx 1m from turning. Or go to Thorverton signed on A396 and follow Fursdon signs for approx 2m from village.* **Adm £4, chd free. For NGS: Mon 6 May; Suns 16 June, 21 July, 18 Aug (12-5). For other opening times and information, please phone or see garden website.**
The garden surrounds Fursdon, home of same family for 7 centuries. Hillside setting with extensive views S over parkland and beyond. Sheltered by house, hedges and cob walls, there are terraces of roses, herbs and perennials in mixed traditional and contemporary planting. Woodland walk and pond in meadow garden.

Fursdon House open for guided tours on NGS days. Some steep slopes and gravel paths.

40 ◆ **THE GARDEN HOUSE**
Buckland Monachorum, Yelverton PL20 7LQ. The Fortescue Garden Trust, 01822 854769, office@thegardenhouse.org.uk, www.thegardenhouse.org.uk. *10m N of Plymouth. Signed off A386 at Yelverton*
8 acres, incl romantic walled garden surrounding ruins of medieval vicarage. Other areas pioneering 'new naturalism' style, inspired by great natural landscapes. South African garden, quarry garden, cottage garden, acer glade. Stunning views and more than 6000 plant varieties. Famous for spring bulb meadow, rhododendrons, camellias, innovative planting and yr-round colour and interest. Open Mar to Oct (10.30-5). Partial wheelchair access.

41 **THE GATE HOUSE**
Lee EX34 8LR. Mr & Mrs D Booker, 01271 862409, booker@loveleebay.co.uk. *3m W of Ilfracombe. Park in Lee village car park. Take lane alongside The Grampus PH. Garden approx 30 metres past inn buildings.* **Adm by donation. Mon 1 Apr to Thur 31 Oct incl (10-4) by appt. (open most days but wise to check by tel/email).**
Described by many visitors as a peaceful paradise, this streamside garden incl collection of over 100 rodgersia (at their best in June), interesting herbaceous areas, patio gardens with semi-hardy exotics, many unusual mature trees and shrubs and large organic vegetable garden. The Grampus Inn is well recommended for home-made meals (organic and local produce), excellent wine list and delicious cream teas! Level gravel paths.

42 **GOREN FARM**
Broadhayes, Stockland, Honiton EX14 9EN. Julian Pady, 01404 881335, gorenfarm@hotmail.com, www.goren.co.uk. *6m E of Honiton, 6m W of Axminster. From A35 or A30 along Stockland Hill (between Axminster and Honiton) to TV mast. Follow signs from Ridge Cross, (100 metres N of TV mast). Do not go into Stockland itself.* Light refreshments. **Adm £2.50, chd free. Evening Openings Sat 1 June to Fri 30 Aug incl (5-9); Sats, Suns 8, 9, 15, 16 June; 6, 7, 13, 14 July (10-5). Visitors also welcome by appt May to Aug.**
Wander through 50 acres of natural species rich wild flower meadows. Dozens of varieties of wild flowers and grasses. Orchids early June, butterflies July. Stunning views of Blackdown Hills. Georgian house and gardens, guided walks 10.30 and 2.30 on open weekends, evenings, or by appointment. Local and national press coverage incl Daily Mail, Coast and Country and Country Living. Partial wheelchair access to meadows.

Orchids early June, butterflies July . . .

43 **GORWELL HOUSE**
Goodleigh Rd, Barnstaple EX32 7JP. Dr J A Marston, 01271 323202, artavianjohn@gmail.com, gorwellhousegarden.co.uk. *3/4m E of Barnstaple centre on Bratton Fleming rd. Drive entrance between two lodges on L.* Cream teas. **Adm £4, chd free. Suns 24 Mar, 28 Apr, 19 May, 16 June, 21 July, 8 Sept (2-6). Visitors also welcome by appt Mar to Nov.**
Created mostly since 1979, this 4-acre garden overlooking the Taw estuary has a benign microclimate which allows many rare and tender plants to grow and thrive, both in the open and in the walled garden. Several strategically-placed follies complement the enclosures and vistas within the garden. Opening on 24 March for magnolias. Featured in N Devon Journal, The English Garden and Devon Life magazines and on BBC Radio Devon. Almost all the garden is accessible but some steep slopes.

44 **HALDON GRANGE**
Dunchideock EX6 7YE. Ted Phythian, 01392 832349. *5m SW of Exeter. From A30 (N) at Exeter pass through Ide village to Dunchideock 5m. In centre of village turn L to Lord Haldon Hotel, Haldon Grange is just past hotel drive. From A38 (S) turn L on top of Haldon Hill follow Dunchideock signs, R at village centre (at thatched house) to Lord Haldon Hotel.* Home-made teas. **Adm £3.50, chd free. Sats, Suns 13, 14, 20, 21, 27, 28 Apr (1-5): Sats, Suns, Mons, Weds 4, 5, 6, 8, 11, 12, 15, 18, 19, 22, 25, 26, 27 May (1-5). Visitors also welcome by appt 13 Apr to 2 June.**
12-acre well-established garden with camellias, magnolias, azaleas, various shrubs and rhododendrons; rare and mature trees; small lake and ponds with river and water cascades. 5-acre arboretum planted 2011 with wide range of trees and shrubs. Wheelchair access to main features.

45 **HAMBLYN'S COOMBE**
Dittisham, Dartmouth TQ6 0HE. Bridget McCrum, 01803 722228. *3m N of Dartmouth. From Red Lion Inn follow The Level until it forks & go straight up steep private rd and through 'River Farm' gate. Continue straight on to end of farm track as signed.* **Adm by donation. Visitors welcome by appt.**
7-acre garden with stunning views across the river to Greenway House and sloping steeply to R Dart at bottom of garden. Extensive planting of trees and shrubs with unusual design features accompanying Bridget McCrum's stone carvings and bronzes. Wild flower meadow and woods. Good rhododendrons and camellias, ferns and bamboos, acers and hydrangeas. Exceptional autumn colour.

HANGERIDGE FARMHOUSE
See Somerset, Bristol & South Gloucestershire

46 **HARBOUR LIGHTS**
Horns Cross, Bideford EX39 5DW. Brian & Faith Butler, 01237 451627, brian.nfu@gmail.com. *7m W of Bideford, 3m E of Clovelly. On the main A39 between Bideford and Clovelly, half way between Hoops Inn and Bucks Cross.* Light lunches & cream teas. **Adm £3.50, chd free. Sat 22, Sun 23 June (11-6). Visitors**

also welcome by appt June to Aug.
½-acre colourful garden with Lundy Views. A garden of wit, humour, unusual ideas and surprises. Water features, shrubs, harbaceous, foliage area, grasses in an unusual setting, fernery, bonsai and polytunnel. Interesting time saving ideas.You will never have seen a garden like this! Superb conservatory for cream teas. Free leaflet. We like our visitors to leave with a smile! Child friendly. Photovoltaic cells to be seen and discussed. Intriguing artwork of various kinds. Child-friendly garden. Featured in Amateur Gardening.

A garden of wit, humour, unusual ideas and surprises . . .

47 ◆ HARTLAND ABBEY

Hartland, nr Bideford EX39 6DT. Sir Hugh & Lady Stucley, 01237 441496, ha_admin@btconnect.com, www.hartlandabbey.com. *15m W of Bideford, 15m N of Bude. Turn off A39 W of Clovelly Cross on B3248 to Hartland. Abbey between Hartland & Hartland Quay.* **For opening times and information, please phone or see garden website.**
Much in this enchanting valley leading to the Atlantic had been lost since 1914 but lately ongoing restoration has resulted in beautiful plants flowering again, the bog garden and fernery discovered, paths reopened and the gazebo and summerhouse rebuilt. Fascinating house, woodland walks to beach and C18 walled gardens. Stunning wild flowers. Peacocks, black sheep, donkeys.

48 THE HAVEN

Wembury Road, Hollacombe, Wembury, South Hams PL9 0DQ. Mrs S Norton & Mr J Norton, 01752 862149, suenorton1@hotmail.co.uk. *20 minutes from Plymouth city centre. Use A379 Plymouth to Kingsbridge Rd. At Elburton r'about follow signs to Wembury. Parking on roadside. Bus stop outside, route 48 from Plymouth.* Cream teas. **Adm £3.50, chd free. Fri 29, Sat 30, Sun 31 Mar (10-4.30). Visitors also welcome by appt.**
½-acre sloping plantsman's garden in the South Hams AONB. Views of South Hams countryside. Tea room and seating areas. 2 ponds. Substantial collection of large flowering Asiatic and hybrid tree magnolias. Large collection of camellias including camellia reticulata. Rare dwarf, weeping and slow growing conifers. Daphnes, early azaleas and rhododendrons, spring bulbs, fritillaria and hellebores. Large flowering tree magnolias, michelias, manglietias, camellia, camellia reticulata, weeping conifers, rare conifers, early azaleas, bulbs, fritillaria, daphnes, hellebores. Wheelchair access to top part of garden only.

49 HEATHERCOMBE

Manaton, Nr Bovey Tracey TQ13 9XE. Claude & Margaret Pike Woodlands Trust, 01626 354404, gardens@pike.me.uk, www.heathercombe.com. *7m NW of Bovey Tracey. From Bovey Tracey take rd to Becky Falls and Manaton. Continue on same rd for 2m beyond village to Heatree Cross then follow signs to Heathercombe. (From Widecombe take rd past Natsworthy).* Cream teas. **Adm £4.50, chd free (share to Rowcroft Hospice). Suns 7 Apr; 12, 19 May; Sat 25, Sun 26 May; Suns 2, 23, 30 June (1.30-5.30). Visitors also welcome by appt Feb to Oct.**
Tranquil valley with tumbling streams and quiet ponds, setting for 30 acres of spring and summer interest - daffodils, extensive bluebells complementing large displays of rhododendrons, lovely cottage gardens, interesting herbaceous planting, woodland walks, many specimen trees, bog and fern gardens, orchard and wild flower meadow. Fine sculptures, seats and mainly level sandy paths.

50 ◆ HEDDON HALL

Parracombe EX31 4QL. Mr & Mrs de Falbe, 01598 763541, www.heddonhall.co.uk. *10m NE of Barnstaple. Follow A39 towards Lynton around Parracombe (avoiding village centre), then L towards village; entrance 200 yds on L.* **Adm £4, chd free. For NGS: Sun 19 May, Sun 16 June (11-4). For other opening times and information, please phone or see garden website.**
Stunning walled garden laid out by Penelope Hobhouse with clipped box and cordoned apple trees, herbaceous secret garden and natural rockery leading to a bog garden and three stew ponds. Very much a gardeners' garden, beautifully maintained, with many rare species, ferns, mature shrubs and trees all thriving in 4 acres of this sheltered Exmoor valley. Wheelchair access to walled garden only.

HIDDEN VALLEY GARDENS
See Cornwall

51 HIGH GARDEN

Chiverstone Lane, Kenton EX6 8NJ. Chris & Sharon Britton, 01626 899106, highgarden@highgarden.co.uk. *5m S of Exeter on A379 Dawlish Rd. Leaving Kenton towards Exeter, L into Chiverstone Lane, 50yds along lane. Entrance clearly marked.* Home-made teas. **Adm £3, chd free. Sat 1, Sat 29, Sun 30 June (2-5.30). Groups of 10+ also welcome by appt Apr to Sept.**
Stunning recently developed garden of over 4 acres with huge range of interesting, rare and exciting plants. 70m double herbaceous border for high summer colour. Tropical border, large vegetable and fruit garden. Adjoining plantsman's nursery open on NGS days and all year Tuesday to Friday.

HIGHCROFT GARDENS
See Cornwall

HIGHER TIPPACOTT FARM
(see Brendon Gardens)

52 HILLRISE

24 Windsor Mead, Sidford EX10 9SJ. Mr & Mrs D Robertshaw. *1m N of Sidmouth. Off A3052 approx ¼ m W of Sidford T-lights (towards Exeter) signed R to Windsor Mead. R at top of hill, last on R.* Home-made teas. **Adm £3.50, chd £1.50. Sat 27, Sun 28 Apr, Sat 8, Sun 9 June (1.30-5.30).**
Plant enthusiasts' garden on S-facing slope. Fine countryside and sea views. Yr-round colour and interest from wide variety of plants. Borders for New Zealand plants, penstemons, cannas, dahlias, grasses with

kniphofias and hemerocalis, kaleidoscope border. Fern garden, shaded area for woodland plants. Greenhouse with pelargoniums, streptocarpus, cacti and succulents. Troughs, hostas, colourful shrubs and trees.

53 HOLLYCOMBE HOUSE
Manor Rd, Bishopsteignton TQ14 9SU. Jenny Charlton & Graham Jelley, 01626 870838, hollycombealpacas@live.co.uk, www.hollycombealpacas.co.uk. *From Newton Abbot A381, L after Jack's Patch GC, or from Teignmouth R at sign Old Walls Vineyard - Church Rd - R at PH, Radway Hill, L Manor Rd, R at Rock.* Cream teas. **Adm £3.50, chd free. Suns 16 June, 14 July, 15 Sept (2-5). Visitors also welcome by appt May to Sept.**
Nearly 5 acres of stunning garden with views over Teign Estuary. Some say the best view Devon. Stylish borders, shrubs for every day of the year. Organic vegetables in raised beds - compost from alpacas! Attractive large pond, water lilies, koi carp, call ducks, alpacas with their babies and free range chickens all create an area of individuality: also we have Harley the Harris Hawk! Limited wheelchair access to view pond, white silkie chickens, ducks, fish & alpacas.

54 NEW IDESTONE BARTON
Dunchideock, Exeter EX2 9UE. Mr & Mrs James Studholme. *At Ide, drive through village and continue straight on at the mini r'about at Poachers Inn. After approx 1/2 m, turn R, signed Idestone. After 1m turn L and continue over mini X-rds and down steep banked S bend. Idestone Barton on L with Cottage opp.* Light refreshments. **Adm £4, chd free. Fri 31 May, Sat 1 June (11.30-5.30).**
Romantic 6-acre country garden in unspoilt countryside only 3m from Exeter. Built on 5 different levels, with several distinctive rooms, garden features yew-hedged kitchen garden, croquet lawn, rose terrace, orchard and arboretum. Picturesque kitchen garden. Garden still in development.

INCE CASTLE
See Cornwall

KEN CARO
See Cornwall

55 KIA-ORA FARM & GARDENS
Knowle Lane, Cullompton EX15 1PZ. Mrs M B Disney, 01884 32347, rosie@kia-orafarm.co.uk, www.kia-orafarm.co.uk. *6m SE of Tiverton. J28 of M5. Straight through Cullompton town centre to r'about, take 3rd exit into Swallow Way, follow rd through houses up to sharp R-hand bend. On bend turn L into Knowle Lane, garden beside Rugby Club with ample parking sufficient for coaches also.* Cream teas/wide selection of homemade cakes to be enjoyed inside or out. **Adm £3, chd free. Sun 31 Mar; Mon 1, Sun 14 Apr; Sun 5, Mon 6, Sun 19, Sun 26, Mon 27 May; Suns 9, 23 June; Suns 14, 28 July; Suns 11, 25, Mon 26 Aug; Sun 8 Sept (2-5.30). Visitors also welcome by appt.**
Charming, peaceful 10-acre garden with lawns, lakes, & ponds. Water features with swans, ducks & other wildlife. Mature trees, shrubs, rhododendrons, azaleas, heathers, roses, herbaceous borders and rockeries. Nursery avenue, novelty crazy golf and something new to see every year. Surprises everywhere!

Novelty crazy golf . . .

GROUP OPENING

56 KILMINGTON (SHUTE ROAD) GARDENS
Kilmington, Axminster EX13 7ST, www.Kilmingtonvillage.com. *Signed off A35 1 1/2 m W of Axminster. Signed off A35 1 1/2 m W of Axminster.* Home-made teas at Bywood. **Combined adm £5, chd free. Sat 15, Sun 16 June (1.30-5).**

BREACH
J A Chapman & B J Lewis.
Off Shute Rd

NEW BYWOOD
David and Sandra Ingles

SPINNEY TWO
Paul & Celia Dunsford

WAYSFIELD
Mrs Sydie Bones

Set in rural E Devon in AONB yet easily accessed from A35. 4 gardens within 1/4 m circle. Spinney Two: 1/2 acre on a southerly slope with yr-round colour, foliage and texture. Spring flowering bulbs, shrubs, climbers and trees. Breach: set in over 3 acres with majestic woodland partially underplanted with rhododendrons, also extensive areas of grass, colourful beds, ponds, orchard and vegetable garden. Waysfield: 1/2 -acre country garden beautifully designed with interesting planting, mixed borders, small pond, elegant terrace and expansive views across Axe valley. Bywood: Adjoining Waysfield. 1 1/2 acres of well kept grounds with excellent views. An ideal setting for teas.

57 LANGTREES
10 Cott Lane, Croyde, Braunton EX33 1ND. Paul & Helena Petrides, 01271 890202, angelrest@lineone.net, www.langtrees.info. *10m W of Barnstaple. From Barnstaple A361 to Braunton, L on B3231 to Croyde, past Croyde Bay Holidays on L. Cott Lane on R as rd narrows towards village centre. No parking in lane, park in village car park 200yds L by village hall.* Home-made teas. **Adm £3.50, chd free. Sat 11 May, Sun 16 June, Sun 4 Aug, Sat 14 Sept (12-5). Visitors also welcome by appt.**
1-acre plantsman's garden with eclectic selection of plants. Many S hemisphere shrubs and other tender species. Yr-round interest with landscaping and design features. Flowers all seasons from rhododendrons, viburnums and magnolias in spring to salvias, cannas and ginger lilies in autumn. Interesting selection of trees.

58 LEE FORD
Knowle, Budleigh Salterton EX9 7AJ. Mr & Mrs N Lindsay-Fynn, 01395 445894, crescent@leeford.co.uk. *3 1/2 m East of Exmouth. After Exeter/Exmouth/ Budleigh Salterton roundabout, turn left into village of Knowle. Entry to Lee Ford is the first entrance on the left through a stone wall.* Light refreshments. **Adm £5, chd £5 (share to Lindsay-Fynn Trust). Visitors welcome by appt Apr to Sept.**

Extensive, formal and woodland garden, largely developed in 1950s, but recently much extended with mass displays of camellias, rhododendrons and azaleas, incl many rare varieties. Traditional walled garden filled with fruit and vegetables, herb garden, bog garden, rose garden, hydrangea collection, greenhouses. Ornamental conservatory with collection of pot plants. Moderately steep slopes to woodland garden.

59 LEWIS COTTAGE

Spreyton, nr Crediton EX17 5AA. Mr & Mrs M Pell and Mr R Orton, 07773 785939, richard@yaxleyhall.com. *5 miles NE of Spreyton, 8 miles W of Crediton. From Spreyton: (village junction at Bowbeer Lane) drive N 1.2m then turn R onto Bowbeer Lane signed Hillerton. Drive straight across staggered Xrds, keeping Stone Cross to your R. Drive approx 1.5m, Lewis Cottage on L, proceed across cattle grid.* Home-made teas. **Adm £4, chd free. Sats, Suns 18, 19 May; 15, 16 June; 28, 29 Sept (12-5). Visitors also welcome by appt May to Sept.**

Deep in the Mid Devon countryside, surrounded by 4 acres of wild, informal but beautiful gardens and woods lies Lewis Cottage, a hidden gem of a garden. The wonderful combination of relaxed planting schemes and formal borders affords the garden a long season of interest from April to October and exemplifies how to garden on heavy clay using a wide and diverse range of plants. Not suitable for wheelchair access.

60 LITTLE ASH BUNGALOW

Fenny Bridges, Honiton EX14 3BL. Helen & Brian Brown, 01404 850941, helenlittleash@hotmail.com. *3m W of Honiton. Leave A30 at Iron Bridge from Honiton 1m, Patteson's Cross from Exeter ½ m and follow NGS signs.* Tea. **Adm £3.50, chd free. Suns 2 June, 18 Aug (1.30-5.30). Visitors also welcome by appt June to Sept.**

Plantswoman's 1½ acre garden packed with different and unusual perennials, shrubs, bamboos. Designed for yr-round interest and owners' pleasure. Inspirational colour co-ordinated mixed long borders provide interest in late spring, summer and autumn. Natural stream and damp woodland area, mini wildlife meadows and gravel/alpine garden. Featured in local press and on BBC Radio Devon 'Potting Shed'. Grass paths.

Winding paths lead you to horticultural surprises round every corner . . .

61 LITTLE WEBBERY

Webbery, Bideford EX39 4PS. Mr & Mrs J A Yewdall, 01271 858206, jyewdall1@gmail.com. *2m E of Bideford. Either from Bideford (East the Water) along Alverdiscott Rd, or from Barnstaple to Torrington on B3232, take rd to Bideford at Alverdiscott and pass through Stoney Cross.* Home-made teas. **Adm £4, chd free. Sat 13, Sun 14 July (2-6). Visitors also welcome by appt Apr to Oct.**

Approx 3 acres in valley setting with pond, lake, mature trees, 2 ha-has and large mature raised border. Large walled kitchen garden with yew and box hedging incl rose garden, lawns with shrubs and rose and clematis trellises. Vegetables and greenhouse and adjacent traditional cottage garden.

LITTLEBREDY WALLED GARDENS

See Dorset

62 LITTLEHAM HOUSE COTTAGE

11 Douglas Avenue, Exmouth EX8 2EY. Pat & Phil Attard, 01395 266750, patricia.attard@sky.com. *¼ m from Exmouth seafront. E along seafront, L into Maer Rd by Fortes Kiosk, L again. Public car park on R. Short 250yd walk to garden, follow NGS arrows. A little unrestricted parking in Douglas Ave.* Light refreshments. **Adm £3.50, chd free. Suns 10, 17 Feb (12-3.30); Suns 5, 12 May (2-5); Suns 9, 16 Feb 2014 (12-3.30). Visitors also welcome by appt Feb to Sept.**

This secret spring garden is full of colour, foliage and flair. Winding paths lead you to horticultural surprises round every corner; spring bulbs, flowering shrubs and other treasures abound in this cottage garden. Organically-grown vegetables, herbs and a variety of fruit trees - something for everyone. Featured on Radio Devon and local press and BBC2 Open Gardens. Limited wheelchair access - gravel paths.

LONG HAY

See Cornwall

63 THE LOOKOUT

Sowden Lane, Lympstone EX8 5HE. Will & Jackie Michelmore, www.lympstone.org/businesses/lookout-landscapes/. *9m SE of Exeter, 2m N of Exmouth. A376 to Exmouth. 1st R after Marine Camp signed Lower Lympstone, 1st R in village into The Strand, past Londis shop into Sowden Lane. PARKING - none on site or on road. If dry, nearby field parking will be signed. Otherwise please use village car park at Underhill between Londis & Globe Inn - 8 min walk. New Exe Estuary Cycle Trail adjacent - pleanty of bike parking!* Cream teas. **Adm £4, chd free. Fri 7 June (2-5); Sun 9 June (2-6).**

2 wildlife-friendly acres on edge of Exe Estuary. Lovingly created from derelict site over last 8yrs to harmonise with coast and countryside location and maximise on views. Flotsam and jetsam finds sit amongst naturalistic seaside planting. Circular walk through wild flower meadow to pond, through copse and along riverbank. Walled mediterranean courtyard, small jungley area. Giant sandpit with buckets and spades for children. Photographic display showing how the site has evolved from 1920s to present day. Limited wheelchair access, some gravel paths, steps, steep slopes.

GROUP OPENING

64 NEW LOWER SPITCHWICK GARDENS
Poundsgate, Newton Abbot TQ13 7NU. *By Spitchwick Common, near New Bridge, Dartmoor. B3357 from Pear Tree Cross (A38) proceed 4m to New Bridge. First turning on R after bridge - drive slowly as it's easy to miss the turning which is on steep L-hand bend. Lower Lodge is ½ m on L. Limited parking at the gardens, further car parks 300m along lane. Pleasant walk along the R Dart.* Home-made teas. **Combined adm £4, chd free. Sat 22, Sun 23 June, Sat 24, Sun 25 Aug (1.30-5.30).**

NEW EAST LOWER LODGE
Pauline Lee

NEW RIVERSIDE COTTAGE
Maggie Baty

Two adjoining gardens set in woodland valley alongside the R Dart. East Lower Lodge: atmospheric woodland garden with imaginative planting in natural setting. Contains jungle area with bamboo tea-house, meandering grass pathways, lawns, borders with stream, potager and vegetable garden. Ceramic sculpture inspired by plant forms, and artist's studio. Riverside Cottage: small hidden woodland garden set in beautiful Dart River valley. Narrow paths wind through densely-planted trees, shrubs, old roses, mixed wild and herbaceous planting. Iris, sweet rocket and candelabra primulas surround wildlife-friendly ponds and stream. Partial wheelchair access.

65 ◆ LUKESLAND
Harford, Ivybridge PL21 0JF. Mrs R Howell & Mr & Mrs J Howell, 01752 691749, lorna.lukesland@gmail.com, www.lukesland.co.uk. *10m E of Plymouth. Turn off A38 at Ivybridge. 1½ m N on Harford rd, E side of Erme valley*
24 acres of flowering shrubs, wild flowers and rare trees with pinetum in Dartmoor National Park. Beautiful setting of small valley around Addicombe Brook with lakes, numerous waterfalls and pools. Extensive and unusual collection of rhododendrons, a champion Magnolia campbellii and a huge Davidia involucrata. Superb spring and autumn colour. Impressive

Plant World

recovery from a severe flood in July 2012. Open Suns, Weds and BH 14 Apr - 19 May (2-6); autumn Suns and Weds 13 Oct - 10 Nov (11-4). Adm £5. chd free. Children's trail. Partial wheelchair access.

66 ◆ MARWOOD HILL
Marwood EX31 4EB. Dr J A Snowdon, 01271 342528, info@marwoodhillgarden.co.uk, www.marwoodhillgarden.co.uk. *4m N of Barnstaple. Signed from A361 & B3230. Look out for Brown Signs. See website for map. New Coach and Car Park.* **Adm £6, chd free. For NGS: Sat 15 June (10-5). For other opening times and information, please phone or see garden website.**
20 acres with 3 small lakes. Extensive collection of camellias under glass and in open; daffodils, rhododendrons, rare flowering shrubs, rock and alpine scree; waterside planting; bog garden; many clematis; Australian native plants and many eucalypts. National Collections of Astilbe, *Iris ensata*, Tulbaghia. Winner of MacLaren Cup at Rhododendron and Camellia Show RHS Rosemoor. Featured in North Devon Journal, Country Gardener and Devon Life. Partial wheelchair access.

NCH

MIDDLEWOOD HOUSE
See Cornwall

GROUP OPENING

67 MORETONHAMPSTEAD GARDENS
Moretonhampstead TQ13 8PW, 01647 440296, miranda@allhusen.co.uk. *12m W of Exeter & N of Newton Abbot. On E slopes of Dartmoor National Park. Parking at both gardens.* Home-made teas. **Combined adm £4.50, chd free. Sat 18, Sun 19, Mon 20 May; Sat 14, Sun 15 Sept (2-6). Visitors also welcome by appt.**

MARDON
Graham & Mary Wilson.
From centre of village, head towards church, turn L into Lime St. Bottom of hill on R

SUTTON MEAD
Edward & Miranda Allhusen.
½ m N of village on A382. R at de-restriction sign
Visitors also welcome by appt, mini bus possible. 01647 440296 miranda@allhusen.co.uk

2 large gardens close to moorland town. One in a wooded valley, the other higher up with magnificent views of Dartmoor. Dogs on leads welcome. Plant sale, teas are a must.

Both have mature orchards and year round vegetable gardens. Substantial rhododendron, azalea and tree planting, croquet lawns, summer colour and woodland walks through hydrangeas and acers. Something for all the family. Mardon: 4 acres based on its original Edwardian design. Long herbaceous border, rose garden and formal granite terraces supporting 2 borders of agapanthus. Fernery beside stream-fed pond with its thatched boathouse. New arboretum with 60 specimen trees. Sutton Mead: Paths wander through tranquil woodland, unusual planting. Lawns surrounding granite-lined pond with seat at water's edge. Elsewhere dahlias, grasses, bog garden, rill- fed round pond, secluded seating and unusual concrete greenhouse. A garden of variety. Scrummy teas at both gardens.

---

68 MOTHECOMBE HOUSE

Holbeton, nr Plymouth PL8 1LB. Mr & Mrs A Mildmay-White, 01752 830444, annemildmaywhite@hotmail.com, www.flete.co.uk. *12miles east of Plymouth Devon. From A379 between Yealmpton & Modbury turn S for Holbeton. Continue 2m to Mothecombe.* Cream teas. **Adm £4, chd free. Sat 4, Sun 5 May (2-5). Visitors also welcome by appt.**
Queen Anne house (not open) with Lutyens additions and terraces set in private estate hamlet. Walled pleasure gardens, borders and Lutyens courtyard. Orchard with spring bulbs, unusual shrubs and trees, camellia walk. Autumn garden, streams, bog garden and pond. Bluebell woods leading to private beach. Yr-round interest. Sandy beach at bottom of garden, unusual shaped large liriodendron tulipifera. Gravel paths, one slight slope.

MOYCLARE

See Cornwall

69 NEW 20 OLD BIDEFORD ROAD

Sticklepath, Barnstaple EX31 2DE. Ian Allen. *1m W of Barnstaple town centre. From Stones r'about by new bridge take B3233 (sp Petroc) to top of Sticklepath Hill. L at r'about into Old Torrington Rd, over small r'about then R into Old Bideford Rd (approx 100 yards). 200 yards on R. Parking in road.* Home-made teas. **Adm £3, chd free. Sun 21 July (2-5).**
Approx 1/4 -acre plantsman's garden. Colourful borders surround 3 lawns and are packed with hundreds of perennials, grasses and shrubs plus ornamental trees; a tapestry of colour and texture - secluded and restful. Wheelchair access for small/average size chair.

70 THE OLD DAIRY

Sidbury, Sidmouth EX10 0QR. Alison Carnwath & Peter Thomson. *1/2 m from Sidbury. Off A3052, follow signs to Sidbury. In village, R at church into Church St, over humpback bridge to T-junction then L and then 1st R up Hatway Hill (no rd signs). Proceed 1/2 m, Old Dairy on L down small lane. Ample parking.* Light refreshments. **Adm £4, chd free. Sat 15, Sun 16 June (1-5).**
Extensive woodland and semi-formal areas providing short or longer walks. Roses, herbaceous borders, late rhododendrons, bog garden and greenhouse. Care needed in boggy areas. Panoramic views over Sid and Roncombe valleys.

71 THE OLD GLEBE

Eggesford EX18 7QU. Mr & Mrs Nigel Wright. *20m NW of Exeter. Turn S off A377 at Eggesford Stn (halfway between Exeter & Barnstaple), cross railway & R Taw, drive straight uphill (signed Brushford) for 3/4 m; turn R into bridleway.* Home-made teas. **Adm £3, chd £1 (share to Friends of Eggesford All Saints Trust). Sat 11, Sun 12, Sat 18, Sun 19 May (2-5).**
7-acre garden of former Georgian rectory (not open) with mature trees and several lawns, courtyard, walled herbaceous borders, bog garden and small lake; emphasis on species and hybrid rhododendrons and azaleas, 750 varieties. Adjacent rhododendron nursery open by appt.
Rhododendrons magnificent in May.

THE OLD RECTORY, TREVALGA

See Cornwall

72 THE OLD VICARAGE

West Anstey, South Molton EX36 3PE. Tuck & Juliet Moss, 01398 341604. *9m E of South Molton. From South Molton 9m E on B3227 to Jubilee Inn. Sign to West Anstey. Turn L for 1/4 m then dog-leg L then R following signs. Through Yeomill to T-junction. R following sign. Garden 1st house on L. From Tiverton r'about take A396 7m to B3227 (L). Continue to Jubliee Inn. Then as above.* Cream teas. **Adm £3, chd £2. Sats, Suns 11, 12 May; 20, 21 July (2-5). Visitors also welcome by appt Apr to Sept.**
Croquet lawn leads to multi-level garden overlooking three large ponds with winding paths, climbing roses and overviews. Brook with waterfall flows through garden past fascinating summerhouse built by owner. Benched deck overhangs first pond. Features rhododendrons, azaleas and primulas in spring and large collection of Japanese iris in summer. Limited wheelchair access. No stairs, but often moderately steep grass paths that can be slippery when wet. Gravel driveway makes progress difficult.

Scrummy teas at both gardens . . .

PILSDON VIEW

See Dorset.

73 ◆ PLANT WORLD

St Marychurch Road, Newton Abbot TQ12 4SE. Ray Brown, 01803 872939, raybrown@plant-world-seeds.com, www.plant-world-gardens.com. *2m SE of Newton Abbot. 1 1/2 m from Penn Inn r'about. Follow brown tourist signs at end of A380 dual carriageway from Exeter*
The 4 acres of landscape gardens with fabulous views have been called Devon's 'Little Outdoor Eden'. Representing each of the five continents, they offer an extensive collection of rare and exotic plants from around the world. Superb mature cottage garden and Mediterranean garden will delight the visitor. Attractive new viewpoint café and shop. Open 29 Mar - mid Oct (9.30-5). Wheelchair access to the cafe and nursery only.

74 PORTINGTON
nr Lamerton PL19 8QY. Mr & Mrs I A Dingle, 01822 870364. *3m NW of Tavistock. From Tavistock B3362 to Launceston. 1/4 m beyond Blacksmiths Arms, Lamerton, fork L (signed Chipshop). Over Xrds (signed Horsebridge) first L, L again (signed Portington). From Launceston turn R at Carrs Garage and R again (signed Horsebridge), then as above.* Home-made teas. **Adm £3, chd free (share to Operation Sunshine). Sun 9, Sun 16 June (2-5.30). Visitors also welcome by appt June.**
Garden in peaceful rural setting with fine views over surrounding countryside. Mixed planting with shrubs and borders. Walk to small lake through woodland and fields, which have been designated a county wildlife site.

A pond and stream complete the bucolic picture . . .

75 PROSPECT HOUSE
Lyme Road, Axminster EX13 5BH. Peter Wadeley, 01297 631210, wadeley@btinternet.com. *From Axminster town centre (Trinity Square) proceed uphill past George Hotel into Lyme St & Lyme Rd. Garden approx 1/2 m up rd on R, just before petrol stn.* Home-made teas. **Adm £3.50, chd free. Sat 13, Sun 14 July, Sat 7, Sun 8 Sept (1.30-5).Visitors also welcome by appt.**
1-acre plantsman's garden hidden behind high stone walls with Axe Valley views. Well-stocked borders with rare shrubs, many reckoned to be borderline tender. 200 varieties of salvia, and other late summer perennials including rudbeckia, helenium, echinacea, helianthus, crocosmia and grasses. A gem, not to be missed.

76 REGENCY HOUSE
Hemyock EX15 3RQ. Mrs Jenny Parsons, 01823 680238, jenny.parsons@btinternet.com, www.regencyhousehemyock.co.uk. *8m N of Honiton. M5 J26. From Hemyock take Dunkeswell-Honiton Rd. Entrance 1/2 m on R from Catherine Wheel PH and church. Disabled parking (only) at house.* Home-made teas. **Adm £4.50, chd free. Fri 14, Sat 15, Sun 16, Mon 17 June, Sun 13 Oct (2-6). Visitors also welcome by appt May to Oct.**
5-acre plantsman's garden approached across private ford. Many interesting and unusual trees and shrubs. Visitors can try their hand at identifying plants with the plant list. Plenty of space to eat your own picnic. Walled vegetable and fruit garden, lake, ponds, bog plantings and sweeping lawns. Horses, Dexter cattle and Jacob sheep.

77 NEW RIDGEHILL
5 Dart Bridge Road, Buckfastleigh TQ11 0DY. Paul & Pip Wadsworth, www.facebook.com/ridgehillgarden.devon. *On the Eastern edge of Buckfastleigh, Devon. Approach on A38, either direction. Dart Bridge exit to Buckfastleigh/Buckfast/Totnes. Turn to Buckfastleigh/Buckfast. At T-junction over R Dart turn L into Dart Bridge Rd. Ridgehill is 400yds on R.* Home-made teas. **Adm £3.50, chd free. Suns 19 May; 14 July (1-5).**
Compact, 0.4 acre, mature garden in Dart valley. Several distinct, heavily-planted beds, many uncommon plants, alpine/rockery, wildlife pond, herbaceous and ferns, copse, grasses & bamboo, small orchard, fruit and veg, work area, shrubbery, roses. Several DIY projects using fencing poles, footer boards and old tools! Child's Find The Animal Quiz and other surprises.

78 NEW ROWDEN HOUSE
Stoke Road, Noss Mayo, Plymouth PL8 1JG. Mr & Mrs Andrew Kingsnorth. *1/2 m from village of Noss Mayo. From Plymouth or Modbury take A379 to Yealmpton. Opp The Volunteer turn off on B3186 to Noss Mayo. After 3m take L turn signed Bridgend and Noss Mayo. At bottom cross creek and travel up through village to church. Bear L and after 1/2 m arrive at Rowden House (last house on R).* Home-made teas. **Adm £3 (share to Operation Hernia), chd free. Sats 6 Apr, 3 Aug (1-5).**
Beautiful 1-acre sloping S-facing garden in rural setting with views across adjacent fields. Landscaped with drystone walls, steps and grassy paths, mature trees and shrubs provide a framework for underplanted bulbs and perennial beds, giving yr-round interest. A pond and stream complete the bucolic picture.

79 RUNNYMEDE
2 Orchard Close, Manor Road, Sidmouth EX10 8RS. Veronica Wood. *12m SE of Exeter. A3052 to Sidmouth. 1st R, B3176. 1 1/2 m, R at Manor Pavilion Theatre. 1/2 m to Manor Rd car park (advised). Alternatively if using Google maps arrive lower end of Witheby (road at rear of Runnymede) and follow NGS pedestrian directions on rear fence. Disabled parking only Orchard Close.* Home-made teas. **Adm £3, chd free. Sat 15 June (1.30-5.30); Sun 16 June (3.30-5.30).**
On western edge of Sidmouth. Beautiful tranquil garden about 1/4 acre artistically landscaped with circles, pool and rill designed by Naila Green RHS Chelsea medallist. Abundance of colourful and unusual plants. Woodland and gravel areas. Microclimate, tender plants, plentiful seating, level paths. Raised vegetable beds and greeenhouse with vines. Featured in Amateur Gardening and Sidmouth Herald.

80 ST MERRYN
Higher Park Road, Braunton EX33 2LG. Dr W & Mrs Ros Bradford, 01271 813805, ros@st-merryn.co.uk. *5m W of Barnstaple. From Barnstaple, at 30 MPH sign R (following sign to Elliott Gallery). After 400yds, R at mini-r'about into Lower Park Rd. Continue to Tyspane Nursing Home on L then L into unmarked lane, R at top. Pink house 200yds on R. Parking in drive or where available. Sat Nav unreliable.* Home-made teas. **Adm £3.50, chd free. Sun 14 Apr; Sun 12 May; Sat 22, Sun 23 June; Sun 21 July (2-6). Visitors also welcome by appt Apr to Aug.**
Very sheltered, peaceful, gently sloping, artist's garden, emphasis on shape, colour, scent and all-year round interest. A garden for pleasure with thatched summerhouse leading down to herbaceous borders. Winding crazy paving paths, many seating areas. Shrubs, mature trees, fish ponds, grassy knoll, gravel areas, hens. Many environmental features. Open gallery (arts & crafts). Extended open gallery (art and crafts).

Cliffe

Cross a bridge and discover an S-facing, tiered garden surrounding C17 farmhouse (not open). Varied planting, herbaceous borders, lawns, ponds and lakes, romantic arbours to rest awhile and a sculpture collection. Woodland escape to wander through beside the stream.

84 SIDBURY MANOR
Sidbury, Sidmouth EX10 0QE. Sir John & Lady Cave, www.sidburymanor.co.uk. *1m NW of Sidbury. Signed in Sidbury Village off A375 between Honiton and Sidmouth.* Tea. **Adm £4.50, chd free. Sat 20, Sun 21 Apr (2-5).**
Built in the 1870s this Victorian manor house built by owner's family and set within East Devon AONB comes complete with 20 acres of garden incl substantial walled gardens, an extensive arboretum containing many fine trees and shrubs, a number of champion trees, and areas devoted to magnolias, rhododendrons and camellias. Partial wheelchair access.

81 SCHOOL HOUSE
Little Torrington. EX38 8PS. Michael & Jo Sampson, 01805 623445, jo.sampson@rocketmail.com. *2m S of Torrington. Situated by A386. Signed Little Torrington, follow rd to village green near Church. Park here. Garden 50yds along bridle path.* Home-made teas in village hall. **Adm £3.50, chd free. Sun 16 June, Sun 28 July (2-5). Visitors also welcome by appt 1 June to 25 Aug.**
2/3 -acre informally planted garden enclosed by native hedging with rambling roses and honeysuckle. Winding paths through mixed planting areas, some shady, some colour-themed. Mature wildlife pond and 2 other water features. Mature trees. Arbour and pergola with a variety of climbers. Small raised alpine bed.

82 ◆ SHAPCOTT BARTON ESTATE
(East Knowstone Manor), East Knowstone, South Molton EX36 4EE. Anita Allen, 01398 341664. *13m NW of Tiverton. J27 M5 take Tiverton exit. 6 1/2 m to r'about, take exit South Molton 10m, on A361. Turn R signed Knowstone (picnic area). Leave A361 at this point, travel 1 1/4 m to Roachhill, through hamlet, turn L at Wiston Cross, entrance on L 1/4 m.* **Adm £3.50, chd free (share to Cats' Protection). For NGS: Suns 14 Apr; 14, 28 July; 4 Aug (10-4.30).**
Large, ever developing garden of 200-acre estate around ancient historic manor house. Wildlife garden. Restored old fish ponds, stream and woodland rich in birdlife. Exotic breeds of poultry. Unusual fruit orchard. Scented bulbs in Apr. Flowering burst July/Aug of National Plant Collections *Leucanthemum superbum* (shasta daisies) and Buddleja davidii. Many butterfly plants incl over 40 varieties of phlox. Kitchen garden and standard orchard.

NCH

83 SHUTELAKE
Butterleigh. EX15 1PR. Jill & Nigel Hall, 01884 38812, jhall22@btinternet.com. *3m W of Cullompton; 3m S of Tiverton. Follow signs for Silverton from Butterleigh village. Take L fork 100yds after entrance to Pound Farm. Car park sign on L after 150yds.* Home-made teas in barn conversion. **Adm £4, chd free. Fri 31 May (2-6); Sat 1 June (11-5.30); Sun 2 June (2-6). Visitors also welcome by appt Mar to Oct, no coaches.**

GROUP OPENING

85 SIDMOUTH GARDENS
Sidmouth, EX10 9JP & EX10 8XQ. *Road plan provided at each Garden.* Home-made teas. **Combined adm £4, chd free. Sat 22, Sun 23 June; Sat 24, Sun 25, Mon 26 Aug (1.30-5.30).**

BYES REACH
26 Coulsdon Rd. EX10 9JP. Lynette Talbot & Peter Endersby.
On A3052. R at Sidford T-lights. In 3/4 m turn L

44 WOOLBROOK PARK
Sidmouth. Barbara & Alan Mence.
A3052. 10 m from Exeter turn R at bottom of hill beyond Bowd Inn into Woolbrook Rd. After 1/2 m turn R beside St Francis Church. Garden on L

Situated on Jurassic Coast World Heritage Site, Sidmouth. It has fine beaches, beautiful gardens and magnificent coastal views.
2 contrasting gardens about 1 mile apart. Byes Reach: edible garden of 1/5 acre. Potager style, raised beds, espalier fruit trees on arched walkway, designed for those with mobility problems. Herbaceous borders, colour-themed flower beds combining

perennials, herbs, ferns and hostas. Pond, rockery, greenhouse and studio. Backing onto The Byes nature reserve and R Sid, offering an opportunity for a short walk from the garden gate. 44 Woolbrook Park: approx ¼ acre on steep NW- facing slope, generously planted with trees, shrubs, perennials and bulbs for yr-round interest. Steps lead to wide zigzag path rising gently to woodland edge of birch and rowan, with shady seat under Mexican pine. Benches at every corner and summerhouse looking towards wooded hills. Wheelchair access to Byes Reach, regret none to 44 Woolbrook Rd.

GROUP OPENING

86 SOUTHCOMBE GARDENS

Dartmoor, Widecombe-in-the-Moor TQ13 7TU. *6m W of Bovey Tracey. Take B3387 from Bovey Tracey. After village church take rd SW for 400yds then sharp R, signed Southcombe, up steep hill. After 200yds, pass C17 farmhouse & park on L.* Home-made teas at Southcombe Barn. **Combined adm £4, chd free. Sun 26, Mon 27 May (2-5); Every Sun 2 June to 30 June (2-5).**

SOUTHCOMBE BARN
Amanda Sabin & Stephen Hobson

SOUTHCOMBE HOUSE
Dr & Mrs J R Seale
Visitors also welcome by appt. 01364 621365

Village famous for its Fair, Uncle Tom Cobley and its C14 church - the 'Cathedral of the Moor'. Featured in RHS 'The Garden'. Southcombe Barn is the woodland end of Southcombe Gardens. In May and June it is dazzlingly colourful. Grass paths wind through 3 acres of flowering and exotic trees with shade patches and sunny clearings full of wild and garden flowers. Sit on a bench, feast on colour and listen to bees. Southcombe House: 5 acres, SE-facing garden, arboretum and orchid-rich restored wild flower meadow with bulbs in spring and four orchid species (early purple, southern marsh, common spotted and greater butterfly). On steep slope at 900ft above sea level with fine views to nearby tors.

87 SOUTHERN COMFORT

Meadfoot Sea Road, Torquay TQ1 2LQ. Dr Maciej Pomian-Srzednicki & Mrs Ewa Pomian-Srzednicka, 01803 201813, maciej@pomian.co.uk, www.pomian.co.uk/garden. *½ m from Torquay Harbour. From harbourside clock tower take rd uphill towards Babbacombe. 1st R at T-lights, follow main rd up hill. Garden 200yds on L after brow of hill.* **Adm £2.50, chd free. Sat 27, Sun 28 July (2-5). Also open 4 Wellswood Heights, combined adm £4, chd free. Visitors also welcome by appt Mar to Oct except July/Aug.**

¼ -acre S-facing town plot, part-naturalistic planting of trees, shrubs and perennials, many exotic/tender species. Exceptional microclimate, shelter and variety of microhabitats in Meadfoot Valley allows palms, tree ferns, agaves, aloes, bromeliads, aroids, bananas and other individualistic plants to thrive. Emphasis on foliage. Spring-fed pond and rill. Recommended for exotica enthusiasts. Featured in Coast magazine.

Small town garden with waterfall . . .

88 SOWTON MILL

Dunsford EX6 7JN. S Newton, 01647 252263, sonianewton@sowtonmill.eclipse.co.uk. *7m W of Exeter. From Dunsford take B3193 S for ½ m. Entrance straight ahead off sharp R bend by bridge. From A38 N along Teign valley for 8m. Sharp R after humpback bridge.* Home-made teas. **Adm £4, chd free (share to Cygnet Training Theatre). Sun 26 May (2-6). Visitors also welcome by appt Mar to Oct.**

4 acres laid out around former mill (not open), leat and river. Part woodland with multitudes of wild flowers in spring, ornamental trees and shrubs, mixed borders. Yr-round interest. Partial wheelchair access, some steep slopes.

89 SPRINGDALE

Smeatharpe, Honiton EX14 9RF. Graham & Ann Salmon, 01823 601182, gkalsalmon@btinternet.com. *8m N of Honiton. Parking at Village Hall.* Home-made teas. **Adm £4, chd free. Sat 15, Sun 16 June (2-5). Visitors also welcome by appt 1 May to 15 Sept.**

Astride Devon/Somerset border, set high in the magnificent Blackdown Hills, is a developing 2-acre plantsman's garden with adjoining 16 acres of SSSI. Hundreds of wild orchids in flower early summer. Extensive planting of choice trees, shrubs and perennials, waterside and alpine beds complemented by cacti and auricula collections. Damp, acid garden designed for plants, wildlife and people to enjoy.

90 SQUIRRELS

98 Barton Road, Torquay TQ2 7NS. Graham & Carol Starkie, 01803 329241, calgra@talktalk.net. *5m S of Newton Abbot. From Newton Abbot take A380 to Torquay. After ASDA store on L, turn L at T-lights up Old Woods Hill. 1st L into Barton Rd. Bungalow 200yds on L.* Tea. **Adm £3.50, chd free. Sun 28 July, Sat 3, Sun 4 Aug (2-5). Visitors also welcome by appt Aug.**

Plantsman's small town environmental garden, landscaped with small ponds and 7ft waterfall. Interlinked areas incl Japanese, Italianate, Tropical. Specialising in fruit incl peaches, figs, kiwi. Tender plants incl bananas, tree fern, brugmansia, lantanas, oleanders. Collections of fuchsia, abutilons, bougainvilleas. Colourful pergolas, many clematis. Perennial borders. Many nesting boxes, ducks on slug patrol. Environmentally friendly water features. 21 cleverly hidden water storage containers. Advice on free electric from solar (p.v.) panels. Featured on BBC Radio 4 'Gardeners Question Time', in local newspapers and BBC radio Devon.

91 THE STANNARY

Mary Tavy, Tavistock PL19 9QB. Michael & Ali, 01822 810897, garden@stannary.co.uk, www.stannary.co.uk. *4m N of Tavistock. On A386 Tavistock-Okehampton rd, towards the north of the village.* Light refreshments incl vegetarian lunches. **Adm £3.50, chd**

free. Sun 25, Mon 26 Aug (11-5). Groups of 10 to 30 also welcome by appt, £4.50 incl light refreshments.**

Informal 2-acre country garden with views of Dartmoor as a backdrop. Originally a field, the planting is naturalistic and abundant, with areas for wildlife, ponds and meadow. Polytunnel and vegetable growing areas. Being 900ft above sea level, and having deer and rabbits, gardening here is a challenge. Garden Room available for wet weather. The owners previously ran The Stannary as a vegetarian restaurant and vegetarian lunches are available on open days. Gravel or grass paths, only slight slopes. There are steps to get into the Garden Room but help can be provided.

♿ ✿ 🛏 ☕ ☎

92 ◆ STONE LANE GARDENS

Stone Farm, Chagford TQ13 8JU. June Ashburner, 01647 231311, paul.bartlett@stonelanegardens.com, www.stonelanegardens.com. *Halfway between Chagford and Whiddon Down, E of A382. 2m from Castle Drogo.* **Adm £5, chd £2.50. For NGS: Sun 15 Sept (2-6). For other opening times and information, please phone or see garden website.**

Beautiful and unusual 5-acre woodland and water garden on edge of Dartmoor National Park. National collections of birch and alder trees. Summer sculpture exhibition. Many rare and unusual trees. Our birch have lovely colourful peeling bark, from dark brown, reds, orange, pink and white. Interesting under-planting. **Castle Drogo** open on same day. Featured in several magazines/newspapers and on BBC Radio Devon. Partial wheelchair access. No disabled toilets.

🐕 ✿ NCH ☕

93 SUMMERS PLACE

Little Bowlish, Whitestone EX4 2HS. Mr & Mrs Stafford Charles, 01647 61786. *6m NW of Exeter. From M5, A30 Okehampton. After 7m, R to Tedburn St Mary, immed R at r'about past golf course. 1st L after ½ m signed Whitestone, straight ahead at Xrd, follow signs. From Exeter on Whitestone rd 1m beyond Whitestone, follow signs from Heath Cross. From Crediton, follow Whitestone rd through Fordton.* Home-made teas. **Adm £3, chd free. Sun 24 Mar, Sun 1 Sept (2-5). Visitors also welcome by appt Mar to Oct, 48 hrs notice required, refreshments by arrangement.**

Original shady sloping garden of trees/shrubs over native/cultivated ground cover. Criss-crossed by rustic paths, walkways and bridges leading to secluded seats, sculptures, follies and ponds. Divided house area (climbers). Now extended with streamside stroll, grass steps to dewpond, sunnier white orchard (shrub roses etc). Larger, more colour, views and adventure. Sculptures. Chickens and ducks. Children's prize trail. Dogs especially welcome. Featured in local press.

🐕 ✿ ☕ ☎

94 TAIKOO

Belstone EX20 1QZ. Richard & Rosamund Bernays, 01837 840217, richard@bernays.net. *3m SE of Okehampton. Fork L at stocks in middle of village. Keep left. Entrance to Car Park 300yds on R.* Cream teas. **Adm £3.50, chd free. Sun 14 Apr, Sun 9 June (2-5). Also open 14 Apr Andrew's Corner. Visitors also welcome by appt.**

3-acre hillside moorland garden, recently extended to include heathers, grasses and moorland plants. Interesting collections of rhododendrons, acers, fuchsias, hydrangeas, magnolias, camellias, Chinese and Himalayan roses and other shrubs and trees. Herb garden. Sculptures and water features. Magnificent views over Dartmoor from terraces of Taipan's house (not open).

☕ ☎

95 TAMARISKS

Inner Hope Cove, Kingsbridge TQ7 3HH. Barbara Anderson, 01548 561745, bba@talktalk.net. *6m SW of Kingsbridge. On entering Hope Cove, turn L at sign to Inner Hope. After ¼ m, turn R into lane beneath Sun Bay Hotel. Tamarisks is next house. Park opp hotel or in lane (larger car park in Outer Hope, follow path leading to Inner Hope into lane).* **Adm £3.50, chd free (share to Butterfly Conservation). Visitors welcome by appt.**

Sloping ⅓ acre directly above sea with magnificent view. Garden is exciting with rustic steps, extensive stonework, ponds, rockeries, feature corners, patios, 'wild' terrace overlooking sea. Very colourful. Demonstrates what can flourish at seaside - notably hydrangeas, mallows, crocosmia, achillea, sea holly, convolvulus, lavender, sedum, roses, grasses, ferns, conifers, fruit trees. Bird and butterfly haven. Butterfly Conservation and BTO Birdwatch. Craft exhibition and sale of enamel work, bowls, jewellery and photos of local area.

🐕 ✿ ☕ ☎

A lovely secluded wildlife haven . . .

GROUP OPENING

96 NEW TEIGNMOUTH GARDENS

TQ14 8TW. *1m from Teignmouth town centre. From Teignmouth, take A379 towards Dawlish. At top of hill R into Cliff Rd. Park in Cliff Rd, take footpath on R signed To the Seafront. Berry Cottage few yds on R. Limited parking in garden.* Home-made teas at High Tor. **Combined adm £4, chd free. Sat 13, Sun 14 July (2-5).**

NEW BERRY COTTAGE
Cliffe Rd. Maureen Fayle

NEW HIGH TOR
Cliff Rd. Gill Treweek

NEW PINEWOOD
52 Woodland Ave. Pam & Ron Martin.
1 m up hill on road from Teignmouth to Dawlish. 3rd road from brow of hill

The artist owner of Berry Cottage has developed a lovely secluded wildlife haven and will have a display of her stunning artwork. At Pinewood a variety of colourful plants are divided into several rooms with panoramic views over Lyme Bay. High Tor is a large sunny garden with sea views and abundant cottage garden style planting.

✿ ☕

97 NEW 2 TOWN BARTON
South Tawton, Okehampton EX20 2LP. Susan & Mark Freeman. *4km W of Okehampton. From Exeter, take A30 West. Turn off at Whiddon Down junction and take rd towards Sticklepath. After 4m, turn R at Ford Cross towards South Tawton. At the X-rds, straight across, village is 1/2 m. On L is stone monument with village oak tree, Church and Church House. Park in village square, follow signs to garden at rear of 2 Town Barton*. Home-made teas and guided tours at The Church House. **Adm £3, chd free. Sun 9 June; Sat 10, Sun 11 Aug (10-6).**
Small, diverse garden, hidden in heart of S Tawton, that makes every inch edible, useful and beautiful. Developed as sustainable forest garden with numerous fruit and nut trees underplanted with unusual soft fruit and spice bushes, many of Scandinavian and high-altitude origin, with ground cover of perennial vegetables, herbs, wild flowers and plants for dyeing and basket-making.

TREBARTHA
See Cornwall

GROUP OPENING

98 VENN CROSS RAILWAY GARDENS
Venn Cross, Waterrow, Taunton TA4 2BE. *Devon/Somerset border. 4m W of Wiveliscombe, 6m E of Bampton on B3227. Easy access. Ample tarmac parking*. Home-made teas. **Combined adm £4, chd free. Sats, Suns 15, 16 June; 13, 14, 27, 28 July (2-6). Groups also welcome by appt.**

THE ENGINE HOUSE
Kevin & Samantha Anning.
Groups also welcome by appt.
01398 361392
venncross@gmail.com

STATION HOUSE
Pat & Bill Wilson
Groups also welcome by appt.
01398 361665,
bill_wilson.daveneer@btinternet.com

Set in beautiful countryside straddling Devon/Somerset border between Bampton and Wiveliscombe. 2 large adjoining gardens covering site of former station and goods yard on GWR line between Taunton and Barnstaple. The Engine House: 4 acres with colour from trees, shrubs and bulbs in spring to the wildflower meadow, bog gardens and sweeping herbaceous borders as summer progresses. Streams, ponds (incl koi), vegetable plot, hornbeam walkway and woodland paths. Railway and sculptural features add interest throughout. Station House: 2-acre sheltered garden in deep cutting. Site of old station. Steep banks featuring hostas and other plants. Deep herbaceous beds packed with flowers. Vegetable beds. Tunnel (no entry permitted) at end forming part of dell garden. Access to top of tunnel with view of garden. Woodland walk. Featured in Somerset Country Gardener. Wheelchair access to main areas. Some gravel paths, gentle grass slopes.

Every inch edible, useful and beautiful . . .

ALLOTMENTS

99 NEW WEIRFIELD MEADOWS ALLOTMENT GARDENS
Near Trews Weir, Exeter EX2 4DJ. Mrs Beverley Langley, www.weirfieldmeadows.co.uk. *Metered parking available in Trews Weir Reach (off the A3015, Topsham Rd) from which access to the allotments is on foot. From Trews Weir Reach, short walk to end of Belle Isle Drive then follow footpath to Trews Weir Suspension Bridge. Cross bridge and entrance to allotment gardens is on L. Nearest bus stop from City Centre is County Hall (Topsham Road). See website for alternative directions and parking*. Home-made teas. **Adm £3, chd free. Sats, Suns 13, 14 July; 3, 4 Aug (11-4).**
In an enviable setting with almost 1/4 m of river frontage on the Exe, these working allotments provide a tranquil oasis in the City of Exeter. Each allotment has its own unique style, with an abundance of fruits, vegetables and flowers. Together with hedgerows, mature trees and riverbank, this unique mix of nature and nurture has created a quiet haven for gardeners and wildlife alike. Limited wheelchair access.

100 4 WELLSWOOD HEIGHTS
Higher Erith Rd, Wellswood, Torquay TQ1 2NH. Mr & Mrs S W Tiller, 01803 296387, sue.tiller@tiscali.co.uk. *1m from Torquay town centre. From Torquay harbourside towards Babbacombe, Burlington Hotel on R. R after red post box on R into Lincombe Hill Rd then R at top, garden immed on L.* Home-made teas. **Adm £2.50, chd free. Sat 27, Sun 28 July (2-5). Also open Southern Comfort combined adm £4, chd free. Visitors also welcome by appt.**
Small exotic garden. Large variety of exotics incl palms, tree ferns, aloes and other unusual trees, shrubs and succulents mainly from S hemisphere. Side jungle border, succulent bank at bottom of garden. Unusual plants for shady areas. Rear courtyard area with mature bamboos, palm trees and lots of plants in pots.

101 NEW WHITSTONE BLUEBELLS
Bovey Tracey, Newton Abbot TQ13 9NA. *Whitstone Lane. From A382 turn towards hospital (sign opp golf range) after 1/3 m turn L at swinging sign 'Private road leading to Whitstone'. Follow lane uphill & bend to left follow signs to car parking in Whitstone Quarry*. **Combined adm £4, chd free. Open day to be advised.**
3 stunning spring gardens each with its own character and far reaching views over Dartmoor. Whitstone House: clouds of bluebells throughout woodland walk area. Old Whitstone: wander amongst the bluebells and spring shrubs in the old orchard. Whitstone Farm: bluebells intermingle amongst camellias, azaleas, rhododendrums and magnolias. Please see NGS website for update information on open days or phone 01626 832258 or email katie@whitstonefarm.co.

102 WHITSTONE FARM

Whitstone Lane, Bovey Tracey TQ13 9NA. Katie & Alan Bunn, 01626 832258, katie@whitstonefarm.co.uk. *1/2 m N of Bovey Tracey. From A382 turn toward hospital (signed opp golf range) after 1/3 m turn L at swinging sign 'Private road leading to Whitstone'. Follow lane uphill & bend to L. Whitstone Farm on R at end of long barn. Limited parking*. Tea. **Adm £3.50, chd free. Suns 5 May, 4 Aug (2-5). Visitors also welcome by appt May to Sept, group/society tours by arrangement.**

Nearly 4 acres of steep hillside garden with stunning views of Haytor and Dartmoor. Arboretum planted 40yrs ago of over 200 trees from all over the world, incl magnolias, camellias, acers, alders, betula, davidias and sorbus. Major plantings of rhododendron and cornus. Late summer opening for flowering eucryphias. National Collection of Eucryphias. Beautiful all-yr round garden. Featured in Plant Heritage Devon magazine.

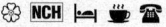

NCH

103 ◆ WICK FARM GARDENS

Cookbury, Holsworthy EX22 6NU. Martin & Jenny Sexton, 01409 253760, www.wickfarmgardens.co.uk. *3m E of Holsworthy. From Holsworthy take Hatherleigh Rd for 2m, L at Anvil Corner, 1/4 m then R to Cookbury, garden 1 1/2 m on L*. Home-made teas. **Adm £3.50, chd free. For NGS: Sun 7, Mon 8, Sun 28, Mon 29 July (2-6).**

8-acre pleasure garden with many attractive features, arranged around house into rooms. Fernery, small ornamental pond, borders, sculptures, long border around lake with large variety of plants to attract butterflies and bees. Arboretum with over 300 varieties of trees. Ample seating, tropical oasis, croquet lawn. Open Easter to Oct. Mon, Tues and Wed 2-5 p.m. Some gravel paths, motor wheelchair friendly.

GROUP OPENING

104 NEW WILLAND OLD VILLAGE GARDENS

Willand Old Village, Cullompton EX15 2RH. *From J27 or J28 of M5 follow signs B3181 to Willand. Turn at PO sign, gardens approx 200 yds, follow yellow signs. Parking in village.* **Combined adm £3.50, chd free. Sat 15, Sun 16 June, Wed 18 Sept (2-5.30).**

NEW CHURCH LEA
Mrs D Anderson

NEW NONSUCH, DYE HOUSE LANE
E. Whiteley

Plus 3 more gardens

Five gardens in close proximity to attractive old village centre and church (also open). Particularly welcoming environment for anyone in a wheelchair. Nonsuch: imaginative use of space in village garden for all seasons. Yr-round colour, established shrubs, camelias, rhododendrons, hostas, roses, hydrangeas, herbaceous, summer bedding. Church Lea: full of ideas to use limited space for the enjoyment of able persons and wheelchair users. Garden all around bungalow sends visitors on an unexpected series of discoveries - pond, rockery with alpines, pots, vegetables and areas to sit and enjoy views. Colour and interest at the heart of this evolving new garden design. These gardens, the village and church have good accessibility for wheelchair users with modest slopes and few changes of level.

105 NEW ◆ WINSFORD WALLED GARDEN

Halwill Junction EX21 5XT. Dugald and Adel Stark, 01409 221477, dugald@dugaldstark.co.uk, www.winsfordwalledgarden.info. *10m NW of Okehampton. On A3079 follow brown tourism signs from centre of Halwill Junction (1m). Straight on through Anglers Paradise.* **Adm £4, chd free. For NGS: Sats 15 June; 17 Aug (10-5).**

Under new ownership of the landscape painter, Dugald Stark. Historic walled gardens, redesigned and brimming with colourful and interesting planting. Large restored Victorian glasshouses and extensive mature bamboo grove. Studio open. Garden open April - Sept, Wed - Sun (10-5).

Fairfield, Abbotskerswell Gardens

106 WITHLEIGH FARM
Withleigh, Tiverton EX16 8JG. T Matheson, 01884 253853. *3m W of Tiverton. On B3137, 10yds W of 1st small 30mph sign on L, entrance to drive by white gate.* Light refreshments. **Adm £4, chd free. Visitors welcome by appt.**
Peaceful undisturbed rural setting with valley garden, 28yrs in making; stream, pond and waterside plantings; bluebell walk under canopy of mature oak and beech; wild flower meadow, primroses and daffodils in spring: wild orchids in June. Dogs on leads please.

107 WOOD BARTON
Kentisbeare EX15 2AT. Mrs Richard Horton, 01884 266285. *8m SE of Tiverton, 3m E of Cullompton. 3m from M5 J28. Take A373 Cullompton to Honiton rd. After 2m turn L signed Bradfield & Willand on Horn Rd for 1m, turn R at Xrds. Farm drive 1/2 m on L. Bull on sign.* Home-made teas. **Adm £4, chd free. Sun 7, Sun 14, Sun 21 Apr (2-6). Visitors also welcome by appt Mar to Dec, refreshments by arrangement.**
Established 2-acre arboretum with species trees on S-facing slope. Magnolias, 2 davidia, azaleas, camellias, rhododendrons, acers; several ponds and water feature. Autumn colour. New planting of woodland trees and bluebells opp house (this part not suitable for wheelchairs but dogs are welcome here). Sculptures.

Beautiful waterside garden in wooded valley . . .

108 NEW WOODVALE COTTAGE
Truro Drive, Plymouth PL5 4LA. Mr & Mrs Graham Lindsay. *NW side of Plymouth. From A38 Plymouth Parkway take the St Budeaux exit and follow signs for Crownhill. At T- lights, L into Budshead Rd, at mini r'about last exit, again Budshead Rd. 1st L into Milford Lane, then 1st L into Truro Dr. Continue past post box, up hill and turn very sharp L after white garage. Coaches or larger vehicles should park on Truro Drive.* Light refreshments. **Adm £4, chd free. Sun 17 Mar (11-4).**
Surprising and beautiful waterside garden in wooded valley. The garden is being developed but already contains large variety of trees, shrubs, bulbs and flowers. Water features, small orchard, vegetable and fruit gardens along with network of winding pathways, some steep. Craft stalls. Wheelchair access to main garden only, some pathways are rustic and steep.

109 YONDER HILL
Shepherds Lane, Colaton Raleigh EX10 0LP. Judy McKay, Eddie Stevenson, Sharon Attrell, Bob Chambers, 07864 055532, judy@yonderhill.me.uk, www.facebook.com/groups/YonderHIllGarden www.yonderhill.me.uk. *4m N of Budleigh Salterton. On B3178 between Newton Poppleford and Colaton Raleigh, take turning signed to Dotton, then immed R into small lane. 1/4 m, 1st house on R. Large car park.* Cream teas. **Adm £3, chd £1. Every Sun 28 Apr to 6 Oct (1.30-5); Mon 6, Mon 27 May, Mon 26 Aug (1.30-5). Visitors also welcome by appt Apr to Oct, morning coffee/tea.**
3 1/2 -acre unconventional garden paradise. After major alterations last year, reopening with new tea room. Wildflower meadow, woodland tunnel path and other new features. Discover wildlife-friendly mixed borders, shady paths, sunny glades, ponds, woodland. Seating throughout. A garden with 'Soul', must experience to appreciate. Garden attracts great variety of wildlife. Wheelchair available, phone to book.

Devon County Volunteers

County Organisers and Central Devon area
Edward & Miranda Allhusen, Sutton Mead, Moretonhampstead TQ13 8PW, 01647 440296, miranda@allhusen.co.uk

County Treasurer
Julia Tremlett, Bickham House, Kenn, Nr Exeter EX6 7XL, 01392 832671, jandjtremlett@hotmail.com

Publicity
Brian Mackness, Fairfield, Vicarage Road, Abbotskerswell TQ12 5PN, 01626 356004, brianmackness@btinternet.com
Cath Pettyfer, Mill Cottage, Bondleigh, North Tawton EX20 2AH, 01837 89024, cathpettyfer@tiscali.co.uk

Show Gardens
Dorothy Anderson, Church Lea, Willand Old Village, Cullompton EX15 2RH, 01884 33415, dorothyanderson321@btinternet.com

Assistant County Organisers
North East Devon Jill Hall, Shutelake Farm, Butterleigh, Cullompton EX15 1PR, 01884 38812, jhall22@btinternet.com
Plymouth Maria Ashurst, 57 Fegen Road, Plymouth PL5 1HY, 01752 351396, maria.ashurst@sky.com
North Devon Jo Hynes, Higher Cherubeer, Dolton, Winkleigh EX19 8PP, 01805 804265, hynesjo@gmail.com
Exeter Jenny Phillips, 25 Rosebarn Avenue, Exeter EX4 6DY, 01392 254076, jennypips25@hotmail.co.uk
Exmoor Juliet Moss, The Old Vicarage, West Anstey EX36 3PE, 01398 341604, julietm@onetel.com
South Devon Sally Vincent, Bramble Torre, Dittisham, Dartmouth TQ6 0HZ, 01803 722227, salv@hotmail.co.uk
South West Devon Ali Fife & Michael Cook, The Stannary, Mary Tavy, Tavistock PL19 9QB, 01822 810897, garden@stannary.co.uk
East Devon Peter Wadeley, Prospect House, Lyme Road, Axminster EX13 5BH, 01297 631210, wadeley@btinternet.com
Torbay Christine Mackness, Fairfield, Vicarage Road, Abbotskerswell TQ12 5PN, 01626 356004, christinemack@clara.co.uk

DORSET

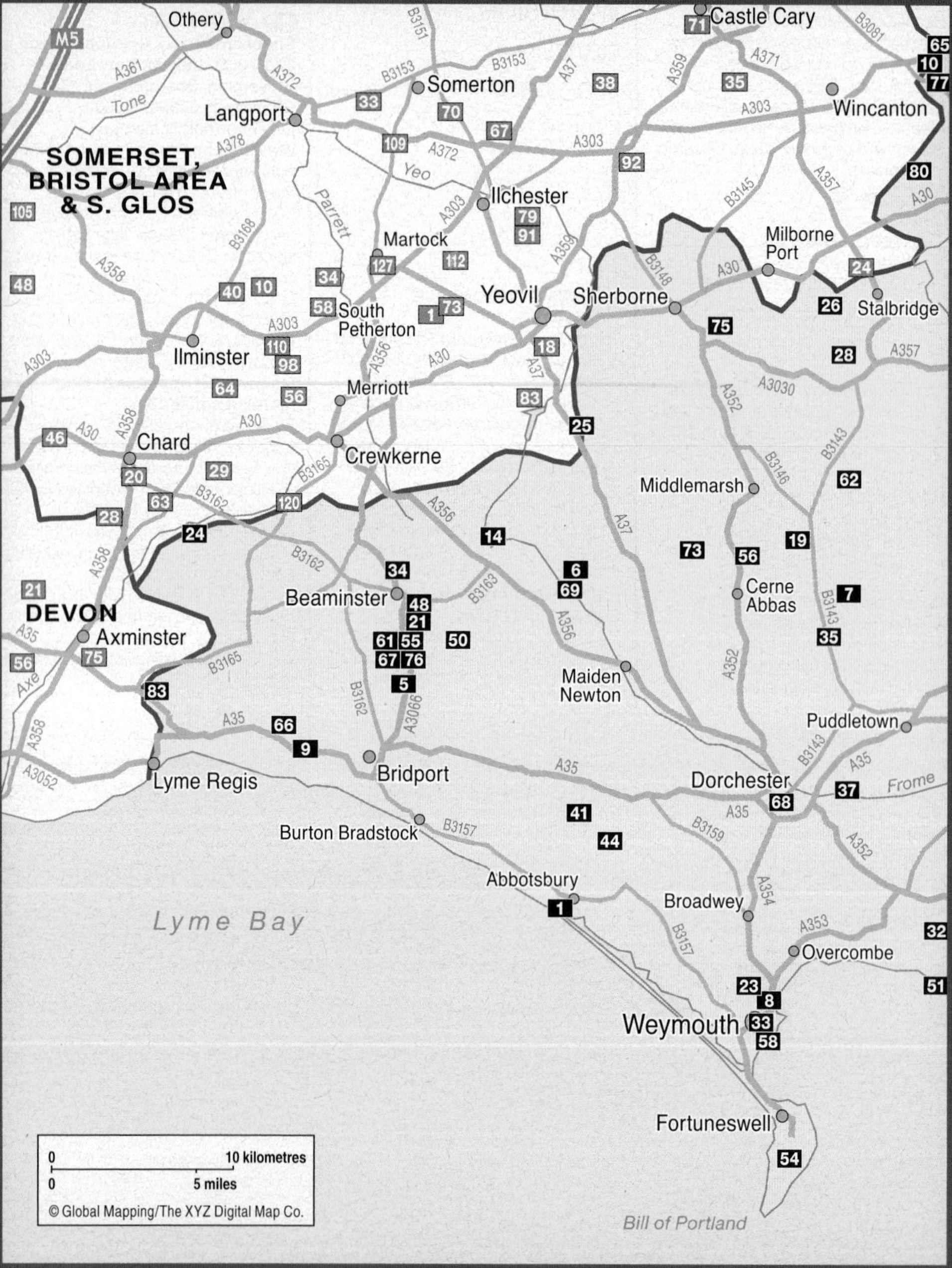
SOMERSET, BRISTOL AREA & S. GLOS
DEVON
Othery
Castle Cary
Somerton
Langport
Wincanton
Ilchester
Martock
Milborne Port
Yeovil
Sherborne
Stalbridge
South Petherton
Ilminster
Merriott
Chard
Crewkerne
Middlemarsh
Beaminster
Cerne Abbas
Axminster
Maiden Newton
Puddletown
Lyme Regis
Bridport
Dorchester
Burton Bradstock
Abbotsbury
Broadwey
Overcombe
Weymouth
Fortuneswell
Bill of Portland
Lyme Bay
Tone
Yeo
Parrett
Axe
Frome
M5
A361
A372
A378
A303
A358
A30
A37
A359
A371
A357
A356
A3030
A352
A35
A3066
A3052
A354
A353
B3151
B3153
B3081
B3145
B3148
B3146
B3143
B3168
B3165
B3162
B3163
B3157
B3159
0
10 kilometres
0
5 miles
© Global Mapping/The XYZ Digital Map Co.

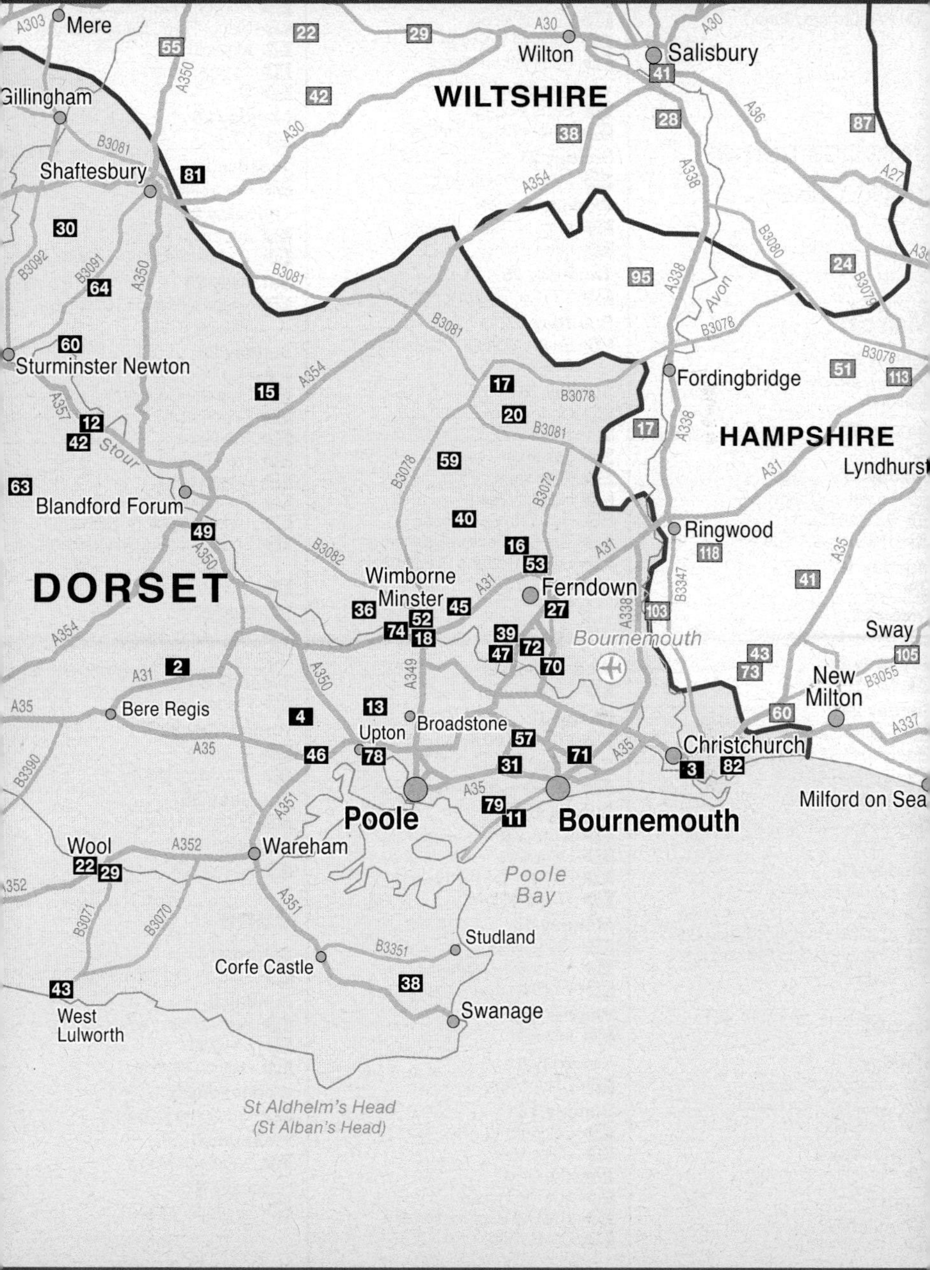
Mere
Gillingham
Shaftesbury
Sturminster Newton
Blandford Forum
DORSET
WILTSHIRE
HAMPSHIRE
Wilton
Salisbury
Fordingbridge
Lyndhurst
Ringwood
Wimborne Minster
Ferndown
Bournemouth
Sway
New Milton
Christchurch
Milford on Sea
Bere Regis
Upton
Broadstone
Poole
Bournemouth
Wool
Wareham
Poole Bay
Studland
Corfe Castle
Swanage
West Lulworth
St Aldhelm's Head
(St Alban's Head)
Stour
Avon

Opening Dates
Dorset

February

Sunday 24
47 Manor Farm, Hampreston
69 Rampisham Manor

Delicious home-made cakes . . .

March

Sunday 3
42 Lawsbrook
68 Q

Sunday 10
68 Q

Sunday 17
25 Frankham Farm
31 22 Holt Road
64 The Old Vicarage

Monday 18
58 'OLA'

Friday 22
51 Marren

Saturday 23
51 Marren

Sunday 24
10 Chiffchaffs
26 Frith House
29 Herons Mead

Saturday 30
77 Snape Cottage Plantsman's Garden

Sunday 31
9 Chideock Manor
29 Herons Mead
61 The Old Rectory, Netherbury
77 Snape Cottage Plantsman's Garden

April

Monday 1
9 Chideock Manor
20 Edmondsham House
63 Old Smithy

Wednesday 3
20 Edmondsham House

Sunday 7
19 Domineys
55 The Mill House

Wednesday 10
17 Cranborne Manor Garden
20 Edmondsham House
35 Ivy House Garden

Sunday 14
6 Broomhill
8 24 Carlton Road North
27 The Glade
31 22 Holt Road
64 The Old Vicarage
69 Rampisham Manor

Wednesday 17
7 Butts Cottage
20 Edmondsham House

Sunday 21
35 Ivy House Garden

Wednesday 24
20 Edmondsham House
34 Horn Park

Thursday 25
61 The Old Rectory, Netherbury

Saturday 27
77 Snape Cottage Plantsman's Garden

Sunday 28
13 Corfe Barn
22 The Ferns
25 Frankham Farm
27 The Glade
29 Herons Mead
32 Holworth Farmhouse
61 The Old Rectory, Netherbury
77 Snape Cottage Plantsman's Garden

May

Wednesday 1
18 Deans Court

Friday 3
38 Knitson Old Farmhouse

Saturday 4
38 Knitson Old Farmhouse

Sunday 5
11 Chine View
19 Domineys
38 Knitson Old Farmhouse
83 Wolverhollow

Monday 6
11 Chine View
35 Ivy House Garden
83 Wolverhollow

Wednesday 8
52 Mayfield

Saturday 11
11 Chine View

Sunday 12
4 Bexington
11 Chine View
27 The Glade
55 The Mill House
62 The Old Rectory, Pulham
63 Old Smithy
67 2 Pyes Plot
76 Slape Manor
81 Wincombe Park

Thursday 16
81 Wincombe Park

Sunday 19
31 22 Holt Road
32 Holworth Farmhouse
47 Manor Farm, Hampreston
52 Mayfield
64 The Old Vicarage
68 Q

Monday 20
58 'OLA'

Tuesday 21
5 Braddocks

Thursday 23
2 Anderson Manor
61 The Old Rectory, Netherbury

Saturday 25
77 Snape Cottage Plantsman's Garden

Sunday 26
7 Butts Cottage
12 Coombe Cottage
13 Corfe Barn
22 The Ferns
27 The Glade
42 Lawsbrook
48 The Manor House, Beaminster
61 The Old Rectory, Netherbury
77 Snape Cottage Plantsman's Garden
83 Wolverhollow

Monday 27
48 The Manor House, Beaminster
83 Wolverhollow

Tuesday 28
66 Pilsdon View

Wednesday 29
52 Mayfield
59 Old Down House

Thursday 30
2 Anderson Manor

Friday 31
38 Knitson Old Farmhouse

June

Saturday 1
38 Knitson Old Farmhouse

Sunday 2
38 Knitson Old Farmhouse
52 Mayfield
70 Resting Laurels

Wednesday 5
59 Old Down House

Thursday 6
2 Anderson Manor

Saturday 8
28 Grange Cottage

Sunday 9
- 4 Bexington
- 7 Butts Cottage
- 25 Frankham Farm
- 28 Grange Cottage
- 47 Manor Farm, Hampreston
- 59 Old Down House

Wednesday 12
- 6 Broomhill

National Gardens Weekend

Saturday 15
- 3 Annalal's Gallery
- 10 Chiffchaffs
- 11 Chine View
- 15 Cottage Row (Evening)
- 18 Deans Court
- 23 25 Field Barn Drive
- 28 Grange Cottage
- 32 Holworth Farmhouse
- 38 Knitson Old Farmhouse
- 52 Mayfield
- 54 Mews Cottage
- 58 'OLA'
- 66 Pilsdon View
- 82 Windy Willums
- 83 Wolverhollow

Sunday 16
- 3 Annalal's Gallery
- 8 24 Carlton Road North
- 10 Chiffchaffs
- 11 Chine View
- 15 Cottage Row
- 18 Deans Court
- 21 Farrs
- 23 25 Field Barn Drive
- 28 Grange Cottage
- 32 Holworth Farmhouse
- 38 Knitson Old Farmhouse
- 54 Mews Cottage
- 64 The Old Vicarage
- 68 Q
- 82 Windy Willums
- 83 Wolverhollow

Monday 17
- 58 'OLA'

Tuesday 18
- 5 Braddocks

Wednesday 19
- 34 Horn Park

Friday 21
- 29 Herons Mead (Evening)

Saturday 22
- 9 Chideock Manor
- 46 Lytchett Minster Gardens

Sunday 23
- 9 Chideock Manor
- 46 Lytchett Minster Gardens
- 49 Manor House, Blandford
- 55 The Mill House
- 60 The Old Rectory, Manston
- 67 2 Pyes Plot
- 79 24a Western Avenue

Tuesday 25
- 44 Littlebredy Walled Gardens
- 66 Pilsdon View

Wednesday 26
- 49 Manor House, Blandford
- 60 The Old Rectory, Manston

Friday 28
- 51 Marren

Saturday 29
- 48 The Manor House, Beaminster
- 51 Marren
- 77 Snape Cottage Plantsman's Garden

Sunday 30
- 13 Corfe Barn
- 57 4 Noel Road
- 77 Snape Cottage Plantsman's Garden

July

Tuesday 2
- 44 Littlebredy Walled Gardens

Wednesday 3
- 18 Deans Court

Friday 5
- 38 Knitson Old Farmhouse

Saturday 6
- 36 Kingston Lacy
- 38 Knitson Old Farmhouse
- 43 Little Bindon
- 45 55 Lonnen Road

Sunday 7
- 6 Broomhill
- 36 Kingston Lacy
- 38 Knitson Old Farmhouse
- 43 Little Bindon
- 45 55 Lonnen Road
- 57 4 Noel Road

Tuesday 9
- 66 Pilsdon View

Saturday 13
- 17 Cranborne Manor Garden
- 71 25 Richmond Park Avenue

Sunday 14
- 4 Bexington
- 14 Corscombe House
- 30 Hilltop
- 48 The Manor House, Beaminster
- 71 25 Richmond Park Avenue
- 72 357 Ringwood Road

Thursday 18
- 71 25 Richmond Park Avenue

Sunday 21
- 3 Annalal's Gallery
- 21 Farrs
- 23 25 Field Barn Drive
- 30 Hilltop
- 40 Lakeside
- 53 Meadow Views

Wednesday 24
- 40 Lakeside

Thursday 25
- 74 The Secret Garden and Serles House

Saturday 27
- 33 Holy Trinity Environmental Garden
- 40 Lakeside
- 71 25 Richmond Park Avenue
- 77 Snape Cottage Plantsman's Garden

Sunday 28
- 23 25 Field Barn Drive
- 30 Hilltop
- 31 22 Holt Road

Visit a new garden . . .

- 33 Holy Trinity Environmental Garden
- 62 The Old Rectory, Pulham
- 71 25 Richmond Park Avenue
- 74 The Secret Garden and Serles House
- 77 Snape Cottage Plantsman's Garden

Wednesday 31
- 62 The Old Rectory, Pulham
- 72 357 Ringwood Road

August

Saturday 3
- 45 55 Lonnen Road

Sunday 4
- 30 Hilltop
- 45 55 Lonnen Road
- 47 Manor Farm, Hampreston
- 68 Q
- 74 The Secret Garden and Serles House

Wednesday 7
- 47 Manor Farm, Hampreston

Thursday 8
- 74 The Secret Garden and Serles House

Saturday 10
- 74 The Secret Garden and Serles House

Sunday 11
- 3 Annalal's Gallery
- 16 Cottesmore Farm
- 19 Domineys
- 30 Hilltop
- 32 Holworth Farmhouse
- 79 24a Western Avenue

Tuesday 13
5 Braddocks

Sunday 18
6 Broomhill
16 Cottesmore Farm
30 Hilltop
53 Meadow Views
72 357 Ringwood Road

Saturday 24
77 Snape Cottage Plantsman's Garden

Sunday 25
3 Annalal's Gallery
12 Coombe Cottage
21 Farrs
74 The Secret Garden and Serles House
77 Snape Cottage Plantsman's Garden

Monday 26
74 The Secret Garden and Serles House

September

Sunday 1
74 The Secret Garden and Serles House

Saturday 7
74 The Secret Garden and Serles House

Sunday 8
16 Cottesmore Farm
74 The Secret Garden and Serles House

Sunday 15
10 Chiffchaffs
21 Farrs
29 Herons Mead
31 22 Holt Road
65 Pen Mill Farm
74 The Secret Garden and Serles House

Sunday 22
74 The Secret Garden and Serles House

October

Wednesday 2
20 Edmondsham House

Wednesday 9
20 Edmondsham House

Sunday 13
25 Frankham Farm

Wednesday 16
20 Edmondsham House

Wednesday 23
20 Edmondsham House

November

Sunday 3
42 Lawsbrook

Gardens open to the public

1 Abbotsbury Gardens
10 Chiffchaffs
17 Cranborne Manor Garden
20 Edmondsham House
24 Forde Abbey Gardens
30 Hilltop
32 Holworth Farmhouse
36 Kingston Lacy
37 Kingston Maurward Gardens
39 Knoll Gardens
44 Littlebredy Walled Gardens
50 Mapperton Gardens
56 Minterne House
75 Sherborne Castle
77 Snape Cottage Plantsman's Garden
78 Upton Country Park

'A feast of a garden at all times of the year . . .'

By appointment only

41 Langebride House
73 The Secret Garden
80 Weston House

Also open by Appointment ☎

3 Annalal's Gallery
4 Bexington
5 Braddocks
6 Broomhill
11 Chine View
12 Coombe Cottage
13 Corfe Barn
15 Cottage Row
18 Deans Court
19 Domineys
23 25 Field Barn Drive
25 Frankham Farm
26 Frith House
27 The Glade
28 Grange Cottage
29 Herons Mead
31 22 Holt Road
34 Horn Park
35 Ivy House Garden
42 Lawsbrook
45 55 Lonnen Road
51 Marren
52 Mayfield
54 Mews Cottage
55 The Mill House
60 The Old Rectory, Manston
65 Pen Mill Farm
66 Pilsdon View
68 Q
71 25 Richmond Park Avenue
72 357 Ringwood Road
74 The Secret Garden and Serles House
76 Slape Manor
79 24a Western Avenue
82 Windy Willums
83 Wolverhollow

The Gardens

1 ◆ ABBOTSBURY GARDENS
nr Weymouth DT3 4LA. Ilchester Estates, 01305 871412, www.abbotsburygardens.co.uk.
8m W of Weymouth. From B3157 Weymouth-Bridport, 200yds W of Abbotsbury village. **For opening times and information, please phone or see garden website.**
30 acres, started in 1760 and considerably extended in C19. Much recent replanting. The maritime micro-climate enables Mediterranean and southern hemisphere garden to grow rare and tender plants. National collection of Hoherias (flowering Aug in NZ garden). Woodland valley with ponds, stream and hillside walk to view the Jurassic Coast. Open all yr except Christmas week. Featured on Countrywise and Gardeners' World. Limited wheelchair access, some very steep paths and rolled gravel.
♿ 🐕 ✿ NCH ☕

6 ALFRED CLOSE
See Hampshire

2 NEW ANDERSON MANOR
Anderson, Blandford Forum DT11 9HD. Jeremy & Rosemary Isaac, www.andersonmanor.co.uk.
3m E Bere Regis, 12m W Wimborne, 8m SW Blandford. From Wimborne W on A31 approx 12m to Red Post Xrds, turn R signed Anderson. From Bere Regis E on A31 approx 3m to Red Post turn L. From Blandford via Winterborne Kingston, L at end of village, 1m to Anderson. Home-made teas (in the Great Hall if wet). **Adm £4, chd free. Thurs 23, 30 May, 6 June (2-5).**
Approx 3 acres of mature topiary, old roses and herbaceous borders surrounding Elizabethan/Jacobean manor house (Grade 1 listed, not open). Formal garden, gazebos,

The Old Rectory, Netherbury

bowling green, walled garden, parterre and orchard. Yew and box hedges, pleached lime walk, old rose walk by R Winterborne and avenue of walnut trees. Wildlife photography exhibition 30th May C12 church open next to house 23rd May, 30th May & 6th June. Separate car parking via Church Lane. All gardens accessible. No gravel, mainly grass.

3 ANNALAL'S GALLERY

25 Millhams Street, Christchurch BH23 1DN. Anna & Lal Sims, 01202 567585, anna.sims@ntlworld.com, www.annasims.co.uk. *Town centre. Park in Saxon Square PCP - exit to Millham St via alley at side of church.* **Adm £3, chd free. Sat 15, Suns 16 June; 21 July; 11, 25 Aug (2-4). Visitors also welcome by appt June to Aug.**

Enchanting 100 yr-old cottage, home of two Royal Academy artists. 32ft x 12½ ft garden on 3 patio levels. Pencil gate leads to colourful scented Victorian walled garden. Sculptures and paintings hide among the flowers and shrubs. Paintings and sculptures also on display. Talk on artwork.

ATHELING VILLAS
See Hampshire

AVIEMORE
See Hampshire

BARHI
See Hampshire

4 BEXINGTON

Lime Kiln Road, Lytchett Matravers BH16 6EL. Mrs Doreen Crumpler, 01202 622068. *5m SW of Wimborne Minster. Opp old school at W end of village.* Cream teas. **Adm £3, chd free. Suns 12 May; 9 June; 14 July (2-5.30). Visitors also welcome by appt.**

½ acre colourful garden of interest maintained by owner, with spring bulbs to autumn colour. Mixed borders of many interesting and unusual plants, shrubs and trees. Bog garden incl primulas, collection of grasses and ferns, with walkways over bog area connecting two lawns.

5 NEW BRADDOCKS

Oxbridge, Bridport DT6 3TZ. Dr & Mrs Roger Newton, 01308 488441, rogernewton329@btinternet.com. *3m N of Bridport. From Bridport, A3066 to Beaminster.3m, just before Melplash, L into Camesworth Lane signed Oxbridge. This single track rd with passing places descends down steep hill with 90 degree turn to R. Garden 90 degrees to L, 100m on R.* Home-made teas. **Adm £4, chd free. Tues 21 May; 18 June; 13 Aug (2-5). Visitors also welcome by appt Apr to Sept.**

3 acres of plant-packed sloping gardens, conceived, planted and looked after by owner. 'A feast of a garden at all times of the year'. Wild flower meadows and water. Herbaceous, underplanted shrubs and roses of all types and hues. Shady woodland garden and fine mature specimen trees. The steep slopes and gravel paths make the garden unsuitable for wheelchairs.

BRAEMOOR
See Hampshire

6 BROOMHILL

Rampisham DT2 0PU. Mr & Mrs D Parry, 01935 83266, carol.parry2@btopenworld.com. *11m NW of Dorchester. From Yeovil take A37 towards Dorchester, 7m turn R signed Evershot. From Dorchester take A37 to Yeovil, 4m turn L A356 signed Crewkerne; at start of wireless masts R to Rampisham. From Crewkerne A356, at end of wireless masts L to Rampisham - follow signs.* Home-made teas 14th April in Rampisham Village Hall, at Broomhill other days. **Adm £4, chd free. Sun 14 Apr (2-6); Wed 12 June; Sun 7 July; Sun 18 Aug (2-5). Also open Rampisham Manor on April 14th £7.00 joint or £4 single entry. Visitors also welcome by appt 20 May to 28 Aug.**

Once a farmyard now a delightful, tranquil garden set in 1½ acres. Island beds and borders are planted with shrubs, roses, perennials and choice annuals to give vibrancy and colour from Spring to Autumn. Lawns and paths lead to a less formal area with a large wildlife pond, bog garden and late summer border. Featured in The Gardens of Dorset.

7 BUTTS COTTAGE

Plush DT2 7RJ. John & Jane Preston. *9m N Dorchester. At Piddletrenthide (on B3143) take turning E to Plush; after 1½ m follow 'no through rd' sign then 1st R.* **Adm £3, chd free. Wed 17 Apr, Sun 26 May, Sun 9 June (2-5).**

Tranquil village garden of ¾ acre sheltered by mature beech trees around C18 cottage in fold of N Dorset Downs. Stream, pond, wild flowers and marsh orchids. Pleasant place to sit or wander amongst wide variety of flowers, vegetables, shrubs and trees. Partial wheelchair access.

8 NEW 24 CARLTON ROAD NORTH

Weymouth DT4 7PY. Anne Mellars and Rob Tracey, 01305 786121, mellie_52@hotmail.com. *8m S of Dorchester. New ring rd from Dorchester, L at Morrisons r'about onto A354 then R into Carlton Rd N just before Rembrandt Hotel on L. Garden on R after Alexandra Rd turning. From town centre follow esplanade towards Dorchester, L into Carlton Rd S which leads to Carlton Rd N. House on L.* Home-made teas. **Adm £3, chd free. Sun 14 Apr, Sun 16 June (2-5).**

Long garden on several levels. Steps and narrow sloping paths lead to beds and borders overflowing with trees, shrubs and herbaceous plants. Unusual plants including exotics in interesting combinations merit a second look. A garden of discovery reflecting an interest in texture, shape, colour, wildlife and above all plants.

CHERRY BOLBERRY FARM

See Somerset, Bristol & South Gloucestershire

21 CHESTNUT ROAD

See Hampshire

9 CHIDEOCK MANOR

Chideock, nr Bridport DT6 6LF. Mr & Mrs Howard Coates. *2m W of Bridport on A35. In centre of village turn N at church. The Manor is ¼ m along this rd on R.* Home-made teas. **Adm £5, chd free. Sun 31 Mar; Mon 1 Apr; Sat 22, Sun 23 June (2-5).**

6/7 acres of formal and informal gardens. Bog garden beside stream and series of ponds. Yew hedges and mature trees. Lime and crab apple walks, herbaceous borders, colourful rose and clematis arches, fernery and nuttery. Walled vegetable garden and orchard. Woodland and lakeside walks. Fine views. Featured in Country Life. Partial wheelchair access.

10 ◆ CHIFFCHAFFS

Chaffeymoor, Bourton, Gillingham SP8 5BY. Mr K R Potts, 01747 840841. *3m E of Wincanton. W end of Bourton. N of A303 On border of Somerset and Wiltshire.* Refreshments at Pen Mill Farm 15 Sept only. **Adm £3.50, chd free. For NGS: Sun 24 Mar; Sat 15, Sun 16 June; Sun 15 Sept (2-5). Also open 15 Sept Pen Mill Farm. For other opening times and information, please phone.**

A well known mature garden for all seasons planted round stone cottage with many interesting plants, bulbs, shrubs, herbaceous border and shrub roses. Attractive walk to woodland garden with far-reaching views across Blackmore Vale. New stream and waterfall feature.

11 CHINE VIEW

15a Cassel Avenue, Poole BH13 6JD. John & Jeannie Blay, 01202 760751, jblay2@tiscali.co.uk. *2m W of Bournemouth. From centre of Westbourne turn S into Alumhurst Rd, take 8th turning on R into Mountbatten Rd then 1st L into Cassel Ave.* **Adm £3, chd free. Sun 5, Mon 6, Sat 11, Sun 12 May; Sat 15, Sun 16 June (2-5). Visitors also welcome by appt Apr to June.**

Unique Chine garden adjacent to public footpath leading to beach. Features incl extensive terraced rockery incorporating 330 tons of Purbeck stone, palladian rotunda, water features, sculptural pieces, subtropical plants and profusion of azaleas and rhododendrons. Steep steps and uneven paths make it unsuitable for the less mobile.

12 COOMBE COTTAGE

Shillingstone DT11 0SF. Mike & Jennie Adams, 01258 860220, mikeadams611@gmail.com. *5m NW of Blandford. On main rd (A357) in middle of village between Gunn Lane and Old Ox PH. Parking advised in Gunn Lane.* **Adm £3, chd free. Suns 26 May; 25 Aug (2-6). Also open 26 May Lawsbrook. Visitors also welcome by appt 1 May to 15 Sept.**

0.4-acre profusely-planted mixed garden with broad borders edged by walls, hedges, fences and arbours. Cottage favourites jostle with more unusual herbaceous and bulbous perennials, shrubs, trees and climbers, and self-seeders rub shoulders with late-flowering and bold-leaved subtropicals. Large glasshouse and some non-botanical surprises. Licensed tea-room, The Willows, 3 mins walk away, is open when Coombe Cottage is open.

Interesting combinations merit a second look . . .

13 CORFE BARN

Corfe Lodge Road, Broadstone BH18 9NQ. Mr & Mrs John McDavid, 01202 694179. *1m W of Broadstone centre. From main r'about in Broadstone, W along Clarendon Rd ¾ m, N into Roman Rd, after 50yds W into Corfe Lodge Rd.* Tea. **Adm £2.50, chd free. Suns 28 Apr; 26 May; 30 June (2-5). Visitors also welcome by appt May to June incl.**

⅔ acre on three levels on site of C19 lavender farm. Informal country garden with much to interest both gardeners and flower arrangers. Parts of the original farm buildings and walls have been incorporated into the design. Very wildlife friendly.

14 CORSCOMBE HOUSE

Corscombe DT2 0NU. Jim Bartos. *3½ m N of Beaminster. On the Dorchester to Crewkerne rd, A356, take the Southern turning of two signed to Corscombe then R signed Church. Or A37 Yeovil to Dorchester, turn W signed Sutton Bingham/ Halstock/ Corscombe. Straight past Fox Inn, up hill then L signed Church.* Cream teas in vicarage garden. **Adm £4, chd free. Sun 14 July (2-5.30).**

Garden in grounds of former rectory with view of Church. Garden rooms with colour-themed cool and hot borders, sunny and shady beds, parterre, reflecting pool, part-walled vegetable garden, orchard and wild flower meadow. Secret garden with Mediterranean planting.

15 COTTAGE ROW

School Lane, Tarrant Gunville, nr Blandford Forum DT11 8JJ. Carolyn & Michael Pawson, 01258 830212, michaelpawson637@btinternet.com. *6m NE of Blandford Forum. From Blandford take A354 towards Salisbury, L at Tarrant Hinton. After 1½ m R in Tarrant Gunville into School Lane*. Cream teas. **Adm £4, chd free. Evening Opening Sat 15 June (5-8), wine; Sun 16 June (2-5), cream teas. Visitors also welcome by appt.**

Young (2005), ½ -acre, hidden, partly-walled garden. Pergola, arbour, brick paths, Yorkstone terrace, tree house, well, kitchen garden. White wisteria, clematis, shrub and climbing roses, tulips, alliums. This sophisticated cottage garden reflects the owners' love of unusual plants, structure and an artist's eye for sympathetic colour.

16 COTTESMORE FARM

Newmans Lane, West Moors BH22 0LW. Paul & Valerie Guppy. *Newmans Lane, 1m N of West Moors. Off B3072 Bournemouth to Verwood rd. Car parking in owner's field*. Home-made teas. **Adm £4, chd free. Suns 11, 18 Aug; 8 Sept (2-5).**

His and hers gardens of over an acre. His-luxuriant tropical planting with many rare plants,including bamboos, bananas, and over 100 palm trees. Hers-stunning herbaceous colour, with plenty of seating to admire the garden whilst enjoying delicious home made teas. Featured in Gardens of Dorset.

17 ◆ CRANBORNE MANOR GARDEN

Cranborne BH21 5PP. Viscount Cranborne, 01725 517248, www.cranborne.co.uk. *10m N of Wimborne on B3078. Enter garden via Cranborne Manor Garden Centre, on L as you enter top of village of Cranborne*. **Adm £5, chd £1. For NGS: Wed 10 Apr (9-4), Sat 13 July (10-4). For other opening times and information, please phone or see garden website.**

Beautiful and historic garden laid out in C17 by John Tradescant and enlarged in C20, featuring several gardens surrounded by walls and yew hedges: blue and white garden, cottage-style and mount gardens, water and wild garden. Many interesting plants, with fine trees and avenues. Mostly wheelchair access.

18 DEANS COURT

Deans Court Lane, Wimborne Minster BH21 1EE. Sir William Hanham, 01202 849314, jonathan@deanscourt.org, www.deanscourt.org. *¼ m SE of Minster. Cars: Entrance on Poole Rd (A349); heading S, 300m on R after Rodways r'about (BH21 1QF). Pedestrians: From Deans Court Lane, continuation of High St, over Xrds at Holmans shop*. Cream teas. **Adm £4, chd free (share to Friends of Victoria Hospital). Wed 1 May, Sat 15, Sun 16 June, Wed 3 July (11-6). Also open 15 June Mayfield, Wimborne. Visitors also welcome by appt, preferably 15+.**

13 acres of peaceful, partly wild gardens in ancient setting with mature specimen trees, Saxon fish pond, herb garden and apiary beside R Allen close to town centre of Wimborne Minster. Apple orchard with wild flowers. 1st Soil Association accredited kitchen garden within C18 serpentine walls. Lunches and teas served in the garden and tea room, using estate produce (also for sale). Tours of the house by the owner available, pre-booking essential. Follow signs for parking closer to the gardens.

19 DOMINEYS

Buckland Newton, nr Dorchester DT2 7BS. Mr & Mrs W Gueterbock, 01300 345295, cottages@domineys.com, www.domineys.com. *11m N of Dorchester, 11m S of Sherborne. 2m E A352 or take B3143. Take 'no through rd' between Church & Gaggle of Geese. Entrance 100 metres on L. Park & picnic in arboretum on R, 10 metres before garden entrance. Coaches can drop off and return for picking up, but not stay*. Home-made teas. **Adm £4, chd free. Suns 7 Apr; 5 May, 11 Aug (2-6). Visitors also welcome by appt, adm £5.**

Garden started 1961, surrounds attractive cottages. Small arboretum dates from 1996. Starting ignorant, with growing learning curve, we have a garden for all seasons. May be the antithesis of instant gardening. Rarities, mix with old favourites. Trees, shrubs, herbaceous, bulbs, annuals and pots, with a kitchen garden. Experience has brought changes to give a place to relate to, enjoy and share. Ideas for the small garden and choosing trees and shrubs. Articles in West Country media and on local radio. Wheelchair access excludes arboretum.

DURMAST HOUSE

See Hampshire

EDGEWOOD

See Hampshire

His and hers gardens of over an acre . . .

20 ◆ EDMONDSHAM HOUSE

Edmondsham, Nr Cranborne, Wimborne BH21 5RE. Mrs Julia Smith, 01725 517207, Julia.edmondsham@yahoo.co.uk. *9m NE of Wimborne. 9m W of Ringwood. Between Cranborne & Verwood. Edmondsham off B3081*. Tea. **Adm £2.50, chd £0.50. For NGS: Mon 1, Weds 3, 10, 17, 24 Apr (2-5); Weds 2, 9, 16, 23 Oct (2-5). For other opening times and information, please phone or see garden website.**

6 acres of mature gardens, grounds, views, trees and shaped hedges surrounding C16 house, giving much to explore incl Church. Large Victorian walled garden is productive and managed organically (since 1984) using 'No Dig' vegetable beds. Wide herbaceous borders planted for seasonal colour. Traditional potting shed and working areas.

FAIRWEATHER'S NURSERY

See Hampshire

21 FARRS
Whitcombe Rd, Beaminster DT8 3NB. Mr & Mrs John Makepeace, www.johnmakepeacefurniture.com. *Southern edge of Beaminster. On B3163. Car parking on site only for those in wheelchairs. Enter through garden door in wall adjacent to museum Park in square area.* Light refreshments. **Adm £5, chd free. Suns 16 June; 21 July; 25 Aug; 15 Sept (11-5).**
At Farrs, enjoy several distinctive walled gardens, gallery of art and furniture by John Makepeace in historic house. Rolling lawns, sculpture and giant topiary around the house; John's inspirational 'grasses' garden; Jennie's riotous potager with cleft-oak fruit-cage. Glasshouse, straw-bale studio; geese in orchard contrasting with elegant courtyard. House open on NGS days with selection of furniture by John Makepeace, and paintings, sculpture and applied arts by living artists. Plants for sale. Featured on Gardeners World and in Telegraph, Mail on Sunday and Gardens Illustrated. Some gravel paths, but with alternative route through the orchard.

22 THE FERNS
East Burton, Wool BH20 6HE. John & Jill Redfern. *Approaching Wool from Wareham, turn R just before level crossing into East Burton Rd. Garden on R, just under a mile down this rd.* Home-made teas. **Adm £2.50, chd free. Sun 28 Apr, Sun 26 May (2-5).**
Profusely planted with varied herbaceous borders and shrubs. Interesting use of hard landscaping. Fruit and vegetable garden leads to small woodland garden and stream and a scene from Dorset clay-mining history. 'A lovely, secret garden' (Dorset Life & Country Gardener). New planted areas.

23 25 FIELD BARN DRIVE
Southill, Weymouth DT4 0ED. Paul & Julie Smith, 07813 901677/07929 533458, sky4369julie@sky.com. *From clock tower on esplanade, down King St and straight across junction to Westham Xrds. R onto A354 signed Dorchester. At Chafeys r'about take 3rd exit (Southill) into Field Barn Dr. Just round bend on L (look for large palm tree). Please park considerately.* Home-made teas. **Adm £3, chd free. Sat 15, Suns 16 June; 21, 28 July (2-4.30). Groups (max 20) also welcome by appt June to Aug, notice required.**
Previous owners of NGS garden at Lanehouse Rocks Rd, we have created a brand new garden at our new address. Featuring towering echiums and huge-leafed ricepaper plants, palms and gravel paths lead to sunny mixed borders, encouraging butterflies and bees. A warm welcome is guaranteed! Featured in Amateur Gardening Magazine.

24 ◆ FORDE ABBEY GARDENS
Chard TA20 4LU. Mr & Mrs Julian Kennard, 01460 221290, www.fordeabbey.co.uk. *4m SE of Chard. Signed off A30 Chard-Crewkerne & A358 Chard-Axminster. Also from Broadwindsor B3164.* **For information, please phone or see garden website.**
30 acres, fine shrubs, magnificent specimen trees, ponds, herbaceous borders, rockery, bog garden containing superb collection of Asiatic primulas, Ionic temple, working kitchen garden supplying the Tea Room. Centenary fountain, England's highest powered fountain. Gardens open daily (10-6, last adm 4.30pm). Please ask at reception for best wheelchair route.

FOREST COTTAGE
See Hampshire

THE FOUNTAINS
See Hampshire

25 FRANKHAM FARM
Ryme Intrinseca, Sherborne DT9 6JT. Richard Earle, 01935 872819. *3m S of Yeovil. A37 Yeovil-Dorchester; turn E; drive 1/4 m on L.* Home-made teas. **Adm £3, chd free. Sun 17 Mar, Sun 28 Apr, Sun 9 June, Sun 13 Oct (2-5). Groups welcome by appt.**
3 1/2 -acre garden, created since 1960 by the late Jo Earle for year-round interest. This large and lovely garden is filled with a wide variety of well grown plants, roses, unusual shrubs and trees from around the world. Productive vegetable garden and climbers cover the walls. Spring bulbs through to autumn colour, particularly oaks. Sorry, no dogs. Ramp for the 2 steps to main garden.

Pen Mill Farm

26 FRITH HOUSE
Stalbridge DT10 2SD. Mr & Mrs Patrick Sclater, 01963 250809, rosalynsclater@btinternet.com. *5m E of Sherborne. Between Milborne Port and Stalbridge. From A30 1m, follow sign to Stalbridge. From Stalbridge 2m and turn W by PO.* Home-made teas. **Adm £4, chd free. Sun 24 Mar (2-5). Groups welcome by appt May-July incl Mon-Fri only.**
Approached down long drive with fine views. 4 acres of garden around Edwardian house and self-contained hamlet. Range of mature trees, lakes and flower borders. House terrace edged by rose border and featuring Lutyensesque wall fountain and game larder. Well-stocked kitchen gardens.

27 THE GLADE
Woodland Walk, Ferndown BH22 9LP. Mary & Roger Angus, 01202 872789, mary@gladestock.co.uk. *3/4 m NE of Ferndown centre. N off Wimborne Rd East, nr Tricketts Cross r'about, Woodland Walk is a metalled but single carriageway lane with no parking bays; please park on main rd and access on foot (5 mins/330yds). Drop-off/pick-up for those with restricted mobility by arrangement only, please phone.* Home-made and cream teas. **Adm £3.50, chd free. Suns 14, 28 Apr; 12, 26 May (1-5). Groups of 20+ also welcome by appt 8 Apr to 9 June, refreshments by arrangement, £6 pp incl refreshments, chd free.**
The name captures the setting. Award-winning 1¾ -acre spring garden. Terraced lawns for lingering over tea. Woodland walks through blossom trees, wild anemones, primroses and bluebells. Extensive shrubbery with camellias, azaleas and rhododendrons. Stream and large wildlife pond with primulas, marginals and waterlilies. Bog garden, wet meadow, spring bulbs and herbaceous and mixed borders. Featured in Gardens of Dorset.

28 GRANGE COTTAGE
Golden Hill, Stourton Caundle DT10 2JP. Fleur Miles, 01963 364651, fleurmiles@ekit.com. *6m SE of Sherborne. Park near The Trooper Inn or close to Grange Cottage.* Cream teas. **Adm £3.50, chd free. Sats, Suns 8, 9, 15, 16 June (2-5). Visitors also welcome by appt May to Sept.**
Come and discover the peace and tranquillity of a real cottage garden. Follow the meandering paths and find many flower borders, box and yew hedging, two ponds, topiary creatures and much more to delight you. Hellebores and spring bulbs a particular feature.

Waterfall cascading into a pebble beach . . .

29 HERONS MEAD
East Burton Road, East Burton, Wool BH20 6HF. Ron & Angela Millington, 01929 463872, ronamillington@btinternet.com. *6m W of Wareham on A352. Approaching Wool from Wareham, turn R just before level crossing into East Burton Rd. Herons Mead 3/4 m on L.* Home-made teas. **Adm £3, chd free. Suns 24, 31 Mar; 28 Apr (2-5). Evening Opening £4.50, chd free, wine, Fri 21 June (6-8); Sun 15 Sept (2-5). Groups of 10+ welcome by appt Mar to Sept.**
½ -acre plantlover's garden full of interest from spring (bulbs, 200 hellebores, pulmonaria, fritillaries) through abundant summer perennials, old roses scrambling through trees and late-seasonal exuberant plants amongst swathes of tall grasses. Wildlife attractive, especially bees and butterflies. Tiny woodland. Cacti. 'Out of the ordinary' (WI Life). 'Interesting and Unique' (Dorset Life). Local community choir singing 21st June. Featured in WI Life, Dorset Life, Country Gardener and Amateur Gardening.

30 ◆ HILLTOP
Woodville, Stour Provost SP8 5LY. Josse & Brian Emerson, 01747 838512, the.emersons@tiscali.co.uk, www.hilltopgarden.co.uk. *7m N of Sturminster Newton, 5m W of Shaftesbury. On B3092 turn E at Stour Provost Xrds, signed Woodville. After 1¼ m thatched cottage on R.* **Adm £2.50, chd free. For NGS: Every Sun 14 July to 18 Aug (2-6). For other opening times and information, please phone or see garden website.**
Summer at Hilltop is a gorgeous riot of colour and scent, the old thatched cottage barely visible amongst the flowers. Unusual annuals and perennials grow alongside the traditional and familiar, boldly combining to make a spectacular display, which attracts an abundance of wildlife. Always something new, the unique, gothic garden loo a great success. Nursery.

HINTON ADMIRAL
See Hampshire

31 NEW 22 HOLT ROAD
Branksome, Poole BH12 1JQ. Mr & Mrs Alan & Sylvia Lloyd, 01202 387509, alan.lloyd22@ntlworld.com. *2.5 m W of Bournemouth Square 3 m E of Poole Civic Centre. From Alder Rd turn into Winston Ave, 3rd R into Guest Ave 2nd R into Holt Rd at end of cul de sac. Park in Holt Rd or alternatively in Guest Ave.* Home-made teas. **Adm £3.50, chd free. Suns 17 Mar; 14 Apr; 19 May; 28 July; 15 Sept (2-5.30). Visitors also welcome by appt Apr to Sept.**
3/4 acre walled garden for all seasons. Garden seating throughout the diverse planting areas, comprising Mediterranean courtyard garden, wisteria pergola. Walk up slope beside rill and bog garden to raised bed vegetable garden. Return through shrubbery and rockery back to waterfall cascading into a pebble beach. Partial wheelchair access.

32 ◆ HOLWORTH FARMHOUSE
Holworth, Nr Dorchester DT2 8NH. Anthony & Philippa Bush, 01305 852242, bushinarcadia@yahoo.co.uk, www.inarcadia-gardendesign.co.uk. *7m E of Dorchester. 1m S of A352. Follow signs to Holworth. Through farmyard with duckpond on R. 1st L after 200yds. Ignore 'no access' signs.* **Adm £3.50, chd free. For NGS: Sun 28 Apr, Sun 19 May, Sat 15, Sun 16 June, Sun 11 Aug (2-6).**
This garden is not of the normal run. It is tucked away without being isolated and has an atmosphere of

extraordinary peace and tranquility. At no point do visitors perceive any idea of the whole, but have to discover, by degrees and at every turn, its element of surprise, its variety of features and its appreciation of space. At all times you are invited to look back, to look round and to look up. Birds and Butterflies. Also open Weds (2-6) 22 May to 4 Sept. Limited wheelchair access.

33 HOLY TRINITY ENVIRONMENTAL GARDEN
Cross Rd, Weymouth DT4 9QX. Holy Trinity C E Primary School & Nursery, holytrinityenvironmentalgarden.blogspot.co.uk. *1m W of Weymouth centre. Follow A354 from Weymouth harbour junction by Asda. R at top of hill into Wyke Rd. 3rd L into Cross Rd. 200yds on R school car park.* Home-made teas. **Adm £3.50, chd free. Sat 27, Sun 28 July (1-5).**
This award winning wildlife garden is home to the Hampton Court 2008 Best in Show garden. There are also children's raised beds, a large wildlife pond, a quiet memory corner, a small orchard area and a bird garden with a hide. In 2011 a WWII garden was created with a genuine Anderson shelter. There is also a large living willow classroom which seats 30 and new for 2013 a composting eco toilet. Butterfly hunt for children. Featured in The Dorset Magazine and Dorset Life Magazine. Wheelchair access to most of garden and WC.

HORDLE WALHAMPTON SCHOOL
See Hampshire

34 HORN PARK
Tunnel Rd, Beaminster DT8 3HB. Mr & Mrs David Ashcroft, 01308 862212, angieashcroft@btinternet.com. *1½ m N of Beaminster. On A3066 from Beaminster, L before tunnel (see signs).* Home-made teas. **Adm £4.50, chd free. Wed 24 Apr, Wed 19 June (2-4.30). Visitors also welcome by appt Apr to Oct, Tues to Thurs only.**
Large, plantsman's garden with magnificent view to sea. Many rare and mature plants and shrubs in terraced, herbaceous, rock and water gardens. Woodland garden and walks in bluebell woods. Good autumn colouring. Wild flower meadow with 164 varieties incl orchids. Some parts may be inaccessible to wheelchairs due to steep inclines.

THE HOUSE IN THE WOOD
See Hampshire

This garden is not of the normal run . . .

35 IVY HOUSE GARDEN
Piddletrenthide DT2 7QF. Bridget Bowen, 01300 348255, bridgetpbowen@hotmail.com. *9m N of Dorchester. On B3143. In middle of Piddletrenthide village, opp PO/village stores near Piddle Inn.* Home-made teas. **Adm £4, chd free. Wed 10, Sun 21 Apr, Mon 6 May (2-5). Groups of 10+ welcome by appt 11 Apr to 25 May.**
Unusual and challenging ½ -acre garden set on steep hillside, with fine views. A wildlife-friendly garden with mixed borders, ponds, propagating area, vegetable garden, fruit cage, greenhouses and polytunnel, chickens and bees, nearby allotment. Daffodils, tulips and hellebores in quantity for spring openings. Come prepared for steep terrain and a warm welcome! Wildlife-friendly, run on organic lines with plants to attract bees and other insects.

36 ◆ KINGSTON LACY
Wimborne Minster BH21 4EA. National Trust, 01202 883402, www.nationaltrust.org.uk. *1½ m W of Wimborne Minster. On the Wimborne-Blandford rd B3082.* **Adm £7, chd £3.50. For NGS: Sat 6, Sun 7 July (10.30-6). For information, please phone or email.**
35 acres of formal garden, incorporating a Parterre and Sunk Garden planted with Edwardian schemes during the spring and summer. 5 acre Kitchen Garden and Allotments, Victorian fernery containing over 35 varieties. Rose garden, mixed Herbaceous borders, vast formal lawns and a Japanese garden restored to Henrietta Bankes' creation of 1910. 2 National Collections: Convallaria and Anemone nemorosa. Deep gravel on some paths but lawns suitable for wheelchairs. Slope to Visitor Reception & S lawn.

NCH

37 ◆ KINGSTON MAURWARD GARDENS
Dorchester DT2 8PY. Kingston Maurward College, 01305 215003, events@kmc.ac.uk, www.kmc.ac.uk/gardens. *1m E of Dorchester. Off A35. Follow brown Tourist Information signs.* **For information, please phone or see garden website.**
35 acres of gardens laid out in C18 and C20 with 5-acre lake. Generous terraces and gardens divided by hedges and stone balustrades. Stone features and interesting plants. Elizabethan walled garden laid out as demonstration. National Collections of penstemons and salvias. Open 2 Jan to 20 Dec (10-5.30). Partial wheelchair access, gravel paths, steep slope to lake.

NCH

38 KNITSON OLD FARMHOUSE
Corfe Castle, Wareham BH20 5JB. Rachel Helfer, 01929 421681, rachel@knitson.co.uk. *1m NW of Swanage. 3m E of Corfe Castle. Signed L off A351 to Knitson. Very narrow rds for 1m. Ample parking in yard or in adjacent field.* Cream teas. **Adm £3, chd free. Fri 3, Sat 4, Sun 5, Fri 31 May; Sat 1, Sun 2, Sat 15, Sun 16 June; Fri 5, Sat 6, Sun 7 July (1-5). Visitors also welcome by appt.**
Mature cottage garden nestled at base of chalk downland in dry coastal conditions. Herbaceous borders, rockeries, climbers and shrubs. Evolved and designed over 50yrs for yr-round colour and interest. Large organic kitchen garden for self-sufficiency. Rachel is delighted to welcome visitors and discuss gardening. Exceptional views. Following in her Father's footsteps, Rachel is a passionate follower of Permaculture methods and believing in the importance of replacing nutrients, using home raised plants and mixing plants together for mutual benefit. This results in a reward of joyful exuberant plants and vegetables. Uneven, sloping paths.

39 ◆ KNOLL GARDENS
Hampreston BH21 7ND. Mr Neil Lucas, 01202 873931, enquiries@knollgardens.co.uk, www.knollgardens.co.uk. *2½ m W of Ferndown. ETB brown signs from A31. Large car park.* **For opening times and information, please phone or see garden website.**
Exciting collection of grasses and perennials thrive within an informal setting of shrubs, mature and unusual trees. Mediterranean-style gravel garden, Dragon Garden and Decennium border planted in the naturalistic style. National Collection of Pennisetum. Some slopes. Various surfaces including gravel, paving, grass and bark.
NCH

Garden activities for all the family . . .

40 LAKESIDE
12 Queens Copse Lane, Holtwood BH21 7EF. Stan & Margaret Mernagh. *5m N of Wimborne. 1m from Wimborne take 2nd R off B3078 (signed Furzehill and Holt). Follow rd through Holt Village then 2nd R at Pondhead. After 1m, R onto gravel track just after white stones. From the N: from B3078, L at Horton Inn, 1st R in Horton Village and stay on same rd through Chalbury Common. L at Xrds, through Holtwood and L onto gravel track on leaving hamlet. Queens Copse Lane immed on L.* Home-made teas. **Adm £3, chd free. Sun 21, Wed 24, Sat 27 July (2-5).**
½ -acre village garden. S-facing Mediterranean rear garden divided by arcading with open swimming pool, cascading water feature and lush lawn. Raised beds with mixed planting backed by Cypresses and native trees. Shaded garden, rose garden and covered arches with views of lakes and Horton Tower. Mixed borders at front. Wheelchair access only if weather is and has been dry.

41 LANGEBRIDE HOUSE
Long Bredy DT2 9HU. Mrs J Greener, 01308 482257. *8m W of Dorchester. S off A35, midway between Dorchester and Bridport. Well signed. 1st gateway on L in village.* **Adm £5, chd free. Visitors welcome by appt Feb to July.**
Substantial old Rectory garden. Mature trees, pleached limes, herbaceous borders, flowering trees and shrubs and extensive carpets of spring bulbs, snowdrops, crocus cyclamen and daffodils en masse. Some steep slopes.

42 LAWSBROOK
Brodham Way, Shillingstone, Dorset DT11 0TE. Clive, Faith & Gina Nelson, 01258 860148, cne70bl@aol.com, on Facebook ... search for Lawsbrook Garden. *5m NW of Blandford. Follow signs to Shillingstone on A357. Turn off A357 at old PO, continue up Gunn Lane, 2nd junction on R, 1st house on R (200yds).* Home-made teas; locally made lunches available on 26 May. **Adm £3, chd free. Suns 3 Mar; 26 May; 3 Nov (10-4). Also open 26 May Coombe Cottage. Visitors also welcome by appt 21 Feb to 10 Nov.**
6 acres. Over 200 trees incl the mature and unusual. Formal borders, wildflower and wildlife areas, vegetable garden. Relaxed and friendly, lovely opportunity for family walks in all areas including wildlife, stream, meadow. Children and dogs welcome. Year-round interest incl extensive snowdrops, hellebores and bulbs in early spring through full summer colour to intense autumn hues. Large and unusual labelled tree collection. Garden activities for all the family. Gravel path at entrance, grass paths over whole garden.

43 LITTLE BINDON
West Lulworth BH20 5PS. The Weld Estate/Mr Richard Wilkin. *Park in W Lulworth BH20 5RJ. Walk to Cove, around it (shingle) to far side. Ascend steps (steep, no hand rail, signed), follow path signed Little Bindon, Range Walks and Mupes Bay. Wooded area, wicket gate to garden on R just before Range flag. 20mins from car park.* Light refreshments. **Adm £3, chd free. Sat 6, Sun 7 July (12-4.30).**
Remote and romantic C11 monastic chapel. Wild, secret garden. Bluebells and spring bulbs. Exuberant rose growth, sculptured vegetation, winding paths and vistas to adjacent cliffs and hills. Complete tranquillity. Slightly challenging access as on far side of Lulworth Cove, repaid by this special and unusual place, dramatic coastal scenery en route and beyond. Featured in Country Life.

44 ◆ LITTLEBREDY WALLED GARDENS
Littlebredy DT2 9HL. The Walled Garden Workshop, 01305 898055, secretary@wgw.org.uk, www.littlebredy.com. *8m W of Dorchester. 10m E of Bridport. 1½ m S of A35. On NGS Days park on Littlebredy village green by round bus shelter then walk 300yd to garden. For the less mobile (and on regular open days) drive down lane to garden car park.* **Adm £4, chd free. For NGS: Tue 25 June, Tue 2 July (2-7). For other information, please phone or see garden website.**
1-acre walled garden on S-facing slopes of Bride River Valley. Herbaceous borders, riverside rose walk, lavender parterre and potager vegetable and cut flower gardens. Original Victorian glasshouses, one under renovation. Gardens also open Easter to end-Sept, Wed, Sun & BHs (2-5) in dry weather. Featured in Dorset Magazine and Dorset Gardens Trust journal. Partial wheelchair access, some steep grass slopes. For disabled parking please follow signs to main entrance.

45 55 LONNEN ROAD
Colehill, Wimborne BH21 7AT. Malcolm Case & Jenny Parr, 01202 883549. *1½ m N of Wimborne. From Canford Bottom r'about where A31 meets B3073, exit N marked Colehill for 1¼ m, R into Lonnen Rd.* Home-made teas. **Adm £3, chd free. Sats, Suns 6, 7 July; 3, 4 Aug (2-5). Visitors also welcome by appt July to Aug.**
Perfectionist's garden on 3 levels, with colour co-ordinated planting using wide range of plants, with borrowed view over adjacent fields. Circular box parterre infilled with vegetables. Watering cans hang in a row behind tool shed, by bridge over little stream. Lots for the eye and senses to enjoy. Featured in Dorset Life.

GROUP OPENING

46 LYTCHETT MINSTER GARDENS

Lytchett Minster BH16 6JF. *3m W of Wimborne. From A35 Bakers Arms PH r'about (junction with A351), follow signs to Lytchett MInster B3067. L opp St Peters Finger PH, follow parking signs. Garden guide/adm at car park.* Home-made teas at The Old Bakehouse, 55 Dorchester Rd. **Combined adm £5, chd free. Sat 22, Sun 23 June (2-5).**

15 ASHBROOK WALK
Sue Allison

54 DORCHESTER ROAD
Ayla Hill

HERON HOUSE
Geraldine Stevens

OLD BUTTON COTTAGE
Thelma Johns

4 OLD FORGE CLOSE
Liz Allen

10 ORCHARD CLOSE
Daphne Turner

Lytchett Minster, 'The Gateway to the Purbecks', is W of Poole on the old Dorchester rd. Mixture of old and new houses, 2 churches, 2 PHs and an ancient pound. The 6 small to medium-sized gardens offer variation in cottage-style planting with many varieties of herbaceous perennials and hardy geraniums, some lush waterside planting, magnificent displays of climbing roses, small fruit and vegetable plots and many other interesting features. Dogs on leads in 3 gardens.

MACPENNYS WOODLAND GARDEN & NURSERIES
See Hampshire

47 MANOR FARM, HAMPRESTON

Wimborne BH21 7LX. Guy & Anne Trehane. *2½ m E of Wimborne, 2½ m W of Ferndown. From Canford Bottom r'about on A31, take exit B3073 Ham Lane. ½ m turn R at Hampreston Xrds. House at bottom of village.* Home-made teas. **Adm £3.50, chd free. Sun 24 Feb (12-4); Suns 19 May, 9 June, 4 Aug (1-5); Wed 7 Aug (2-5).**
Traditional farmhouse garden designed and cared for by 3 generations of the Trehane family. This year marks the celebration of 100 years of farming and gardening at Hampreston. Garden is noted for its herbaceous borders and rose beds within box and yew hedges. Mature shrubbery, water and bog garden. Opening for hellebores in February for the first time in conjunction with the Hardy Plant Society. Dorset Hardy Plant Society plant sale.

MANOR HOUSE
See Wiltshire

Garden with Mediterranean feel, tamed in a naturalistic way . . .

48 THE MANOR HOUSE, BEAMINSTER

North St, Beaminster DT8 3DZ. Christine Wood. *200yds N of town square. From Square - up North St (by Red Lion). Entrance signed on L. Parking in Square or central car park. Disabled parking available on site for limited number of cars.* Home-made teas. **Adm £5, chd free. Sun 26, Mon 27 May, Sat 29 June, Sun 14 July (11-5).**
Set in heart of Beaminster, 16½ acres of stunning parkland with mature specimen trees, lake and waterfall. Recently restored walled garden - serendipity. Designed and planted over last 5 yrs as a formal garden. Entire garden is an ongoing project with woodland walk and wild flower meadow recently introduced. Featured in Country Life and Dorset Magazines.

49 MANOR HOUSE, BLANDFORD

Church Lane, Lower Blandford St Mary, Blandford DT11 9ND. Mr & Mrs Jeremy Mains. *¼ m E of Blandford. Signed off A350 to Poole from Blandford Forum Ring Road (Tesco r'about).* Home-made teas. **Adm £4, chd free. Sun 23, Wed 26 June (2-5).**
Traditional 3-acre walled garden surrounding Jacobean House (not open). Formal rose beds with mixed herbaceous borders. Working fruit and vegetable garden. Large shrub borders with varied collections, climbing roses along walls. Present owners continue to develop and make changes to garden.

50 ◆ MAPPERTON GARDENS

nr Beaminster DT8 3NR. The Earl & Countess of Sandwich, 01308 862645, www.mapperton.com. *6m N of Bridport. Off A356/A3066. 2m SE of Beaminster off B3163*
Terraced valley gardens surrounding Tudor/Jacobean manor house. On upper levels, walled croquet lawn, orangery and Italianate formal garden with fountains, topiary and grottos. Below, C17 summerhouse and fishponds. Lower garden with shrubs and rare trees, leading to woodland and spring gardens. Garden open 1 Mar to 31 Oct (except Sats) (11-5); café open 28 Mar to 30 Sept. Partial wheelchair access (lawn and upper levels).

51 NEW MARREN

Holworth, Dorchester DT2 8NJ. Mr & Mrs Peter Cartwright, 01305 851503, wcartwright@tiscali.co.uk, www.wendycartwright.net. *SE of Dorchester. Do not use SAT NAV. From Warmwell r'about A353 towards Weymouth. After Poxwell on sharp L bend, L to Ringstead. Go straight at turn to Ringstead. Continue up hill into NT Car Park, park near gate marked 'No Cars' on far side and walk through. Follow signed footpath to garden returning via track.* Home-made teas. **Adm £3.50, chd free. Fris, Sats 22, 23 Mar; 28, 29 June (1.30-5). Visitors also welcome by appt 22 Mar to 29 June, refreshments by arrangement, £5 adults.**
4 acres of gardening on steep slopes looking across to Portland and Weymouth. Garden with Mediterranean feel, tamed in a naturalistic way. On terrace, pots, pergola and topiary give more structure closer to house. Butterfly-friendly nectar sources, unusual and tender plants grow in heavy clay despite the SW prevailing sea gales. Garden is on a series of different levels. The top one was made by weaving a 'fedge' from willow. Italianate courtyard with fountain and

water trough at front, hornbeam arbour on terrace. Not suitable for the unfit, many steps.

52 MAYFIELD

4 Walford Close, Wimborne Minster BH21 1PH. Mr & Mrs Terry Wheeler, 01202 849838, terry.wheeler@tesco.net. *½m N of Wimborne. B3078 out of Wimborne, R into Burts Hill, 1st L into Walford Close*. Home-made teas. **Adm £3, chd free (share to The Friends of Victoria Hospital, Wimborne). Wed 8, Sun 19, Wed 29 May, Sun 2, Sat 15 June (2-5). Also open 29 May Old Down House; 15th June, Dean's Court. Visitors also welcome by appt 6 May to 21 June.**

Town garden of approx ¼ acre. Front: formal hard landscaping planted with drought-resistant shrubs and perennials. Shady area has wide variety of hostas. Back: winding beds separated by grass paths and arches. Pond, vegetable beds and greenhouses containing succulents. Display of artwork by local sculptor & craftsman Chris Davies. www.recyclart.co.uk.

53 NEW MEADOW VIEWS

32 Riverside Road, West Moors, Ferndown BH22 0LQ. Sue & Norman Lynch. *2m from Ferndown on Station Rd towards Verwood. From main rd through West Moors (B3072) going N turn L. Last house on R. Parking in rd, avoiding driveways*. Home-made teas. **Adm £2.50, chd free. Suns 21 July; 18 Aug (2-5).**

Discover peace and tranquillity at this small, informal garden overlooking Mannington Brook and open farmland. Island beds with colourful herbaceous mixed planting and two themed areas. Damselflies dance in the sunshine and the lobster pot sits near the water's edge with the latest catch! Some steps and gravel paths/driveway.

54 MEWS COTTAGE

34 Easton Street, Portland DT5 1BT. Peter & Jill Pitman, 01305 820377, penstemon@waitrose.com. *3m S of Weymouth. Situated on top of the Island, 50yds past Punchbowl Inn, small lane on L. Park in main street & follow signs*. Light refreshments 15

357 Ringwood Road

June, home-made teas 16 June. **Adm £2, chd free. Sat 15 June (11-5); Sun 16 June (2-5). Visitors also welcome by appt June to Aug.**

New waterfall with stepped alpine bed behind pond should be completed for 2013, also reorganisation of National Collection of cultivar Penstemon, and crevice bed for species penstemon grown from APS seed. Well established agapanthus. Raised beds of wild orchids, roscoea and bletilla with several new stunning dierama provide colour late in the season. Ceramics by Tiffany. 2 small steps to WC.

NCH

THE MILL AT GORDLETON

See Hampshire

55 THE MILL HOUSE

Crook Hill, Netherbury DT6 5LX. Michael & Giustina Ryan, 01308 488267, themillhouse@dsl.pipex.com. *1m S of Beaminster. Turn R off A3066 Beaminster to Bridport rd at signpost to Netherbury. Car park at Xrds at bottom of hill*. Home-made teas. **Adm £4, chd free. Suns 7 Apr, 12 May, 23 June (2-6). Combined with 2 Pyes Plot 12 May, 23 June, 2 gardens £6, teas at Mill House. Additional combined openings to be announced. Groups of 6+ also welcome by appt Apr to Sept.**

6½ acres of garden around R Brit, mill stream and mill pond. Formal walled, terraced and vegetable gardens. Bog garden. Emphasis on Spring bulbs, scented flowers, hardy geraniums, lilies, clematis and water irises. Wander through the wild garden planted with interesting trees including conifers, magnolias, fruit trees and oaks underplanted with bulbs. Partial wheelchair access.

56 ◆ MINTERNE HOUSE
Minterne Magna DT2 7AU. The Hon Henry & Mrs Digby, 01300 341370, www.minterne.co.uk. *2m N of Cerne Abbas. On A352 Dorchester-Sherborne road.* **For information, please phone or see garden website.**
20 acres wild woodland gardens landscaped in C18, laid out in a horseshoe over 1m round. Home to the Churchill and Digby families for 350yrs. From spring to autumn the magnificent mature and newly-planted specimen shrubs and trees create surprises and superb vistas around the lake, ending with sensational autumn colouring. Open 1 March - 9 Nov (10-6). Regret unsuitable for wheelchairs.

MOORE BLATCH
See Hampshire

57 4 NOEL ROAD
Wallisdown BH10 4DP. Lesley & Ivor Pond. *4m NE of Poole. From Wallisdown Xrds enter Kinson Rd. Take 5th rd on R, Kingsbere Ave. Noel Rd is first on R.* Home-made teas. **Adm £3, chd free. Sun 30 June, Sun 7 July (2-5).**
Exciting small garden, 100ft x 30ft, with big ideas. On sloping ground many Roman features incl water and impressive temple. Most planting is in containers. Several new features. Camera is a must. Come and give us your opinion 'Is this garden over the top?'. Steps to upper part of the garden.

NORTH COTTAGE & WOODVIEW COTTAGE
See Wiltshire

58 'OLA'
47 Old Castle Road, Rodwell, Weymouth DT4 8QE. Jane Uff & Elaine Smith. *1m from Weymouth centre. Follow signs to Portland. Off Buxton Rd, proceed to lower end of Old Castle Rd. Bungalow just past Sandsfoot Castle ruins/gardens. Easy access by foot off Rodwell Trail at Sandsfoot Castle.* Home-made teas. **Adm £3.50, chd free. Mon 18 Mar, Mon 20 May, Sat 15, Mon 17 June (2-5).**
Seaside garden with stunning views overlooking Portland Harbour. 1930s-designed garden, once part of Sandsfoot Castle estate. Mixed herbaceous borders, shrubs and roses. Rockeries, fish pond, vegetables, orchard and 7 dwarfs bank. Circular sunken stone walled area with box bushes and statuary. Lovingly restored from neglected overgrown jungle. Featured in Dorset Life.

'Is this garden over the top? . . .'

59 OLD DOWN HOUSE
Horton, Wimborne BH21 7HL. Dr & Mrs Colin Davidson. *7½ m N of Wimborne. From Wimborne take B3078 Wimborne to Cranborne rd. At Horton Inn, R to Horton Village. 1st L to North Farm and follow track. 5 min walk to garden down farm track. Drop off/pick-up for those with restricted mobility by prior arrangement, please phone 01258 840969.* Home-made teas. **Adm £3, chd free. Wed 29 May, Wed 5, Sun 9 June (2-5). Also open 29 May Mayfield.**
Nestled down a farm track, this ¾ -acre garden on chalk surrounds C18 farmhouse. Stunning views over Horton Tower and farmland. Cottage garden planting with formal elements, climbing roses clothe pergola and house walls along with stunning wisteria sinensis and banksia rose. Part-walled potager. Featured in Dorset Life.

60 THE OLD RECTORY, MANSTON
Manston, Sturminster Newton DT10 1EX. Andrew & Judith Hussey, 01258 474673, judithhussey@hotmail.com. *6m S of Shaftesbury, 2½ m N of Sturminster Newton. From Shaftesbury, take B3091. On reaching Manston, past Plough Inn, L for Child Okeford on R-hand bend. Old Rectory last house on L.* Home-made teas. **Adm £4, chd free. Sun 23, Wed 26 June (2-5). Visitors also welcome by appt 15 May to 12 Sept.**
Beautifully restored 5-acre garden. S-facing wall with 120ft herbaceous border edged by old brick path. Enclosed yew hedge flower garden. Wildflower meadow marked with mown paths and young plantation of mixed hardwoods. Well-maintained walled Victorian kitchen garden. New walnut tree knot garden. Featured in Dorset Life.

61 THE OLD RECTORY, NETHERBURY
nr Beaminster DT6 5NB. Simon & Amanda Mehigan, oldrectorynetherbury.tumblr.com. *2m SW of Beaminster. Turn off A3066 Beaminster/Bridport rd & go over R Brit, into centre of village & up hill. The Old Rectory is on L opp church. Please park considerately in village.* Home-made teas after 2pm. **Adm £5, chd free. Sun 31 Mar; Thur 25, Sun 28 Apr; Thur 23, Sun 26 May (11-5).**
5-acre garden surrounding C16 house. Formal areas with topiary near house, natural planting elsewhere. Extensive bog garden with pond and stream planted with drifts of irises, primulas and other moisture lovers. Woodland areas with magnolias, cornus, species peonies, wood anemones. Orchards with naturalised bulbs. Starred entry in Good Gardens Guide.

62 THE OLD RECTORY, PULHAM
Dorchester DT2 7EA. Mr & Mrs N Elliott. *13m N of Dorchester. 8m SE of Sherborne. On B3143 turn E at Xrds in Pulham. Signed Cannings Court.* Home-made teas. **Adm £5, chd free. Sun 12 May, Sun 28, Wed 31 July (2-6).**
4 acres formal and informal gardens surround C18 rectory with splendid views. Yew hedges enclose circular herbaceous borders with late summer colour. Exuberantly planted terrace with purple and white beds. Box parterres, mature trees, pond, waterfall, fernery, ha-ha, pleached hornbeams. 10 acres woodland walks. Flourishing and newly extended bog garden with islands; awash with primulas and irises in May. Home made teas and cakes, interesting plants for sale. Featured in Country Life, Homes and Gardens, Country Homes and Interiors. Mostly wheelchair access.

63 OLD SMITHY

Ibberton DT11 0EN. Carol & Clive Carsley. *9m NW of Blandford Forum. From Blandford A357 to Sturminster Newton. After 6.5m L to Okeford Fitzpaine. Follow signs to Ibberton, park by village hall, 5 min walk to garden.* Home-made teas in Village Hall. **Adm £3, chd free. Mon 1 Apr, Sun 12 May (2-5).**

Worth driving twisty narrow lanes to reach rural 2½ -acre streamside garden framing thatched cottage. Back of beyond setting which inspired international best seller Mr Rosenblum's List. Succession of ponds. Mown paths. Spring bulbs, aquilegia and hellebores. Sit beneath rustling trees. Views of Bulbarrow and church. Featured in Dorset Life.

64 THE OLD VICARAGE

East Orchard, Shaftesbury SP7 0BA. Miss Tina Wright. *4½ m S of Shaftesbury, 3½ m N of Sturminster Newton. On B3091, Shaftesbury side of 90° bend. Drop passengers at lay-by with telephone box and park in narrow rd to East Orchard nr church.* Home-made teas. **Adm £4, chd free. Suns 17 Mar (2-4); 14 Apr; 19 May; 16 June (2-5).**

Winner of the best large Dorset Wildlife Friendly garden 2012. This garden of 1.7 acres has been described as inspiring with ideas to take away. It has a number of wetland areas which have been called impressive. Rockery, bog gardens, shrub and herbaceous borders. Colour and interest all year with early spring bulbs, winter flowering plants, berrying shrubs and mature trees. Children and dogs welcome. Pond dipping available, swing and tree platform overlooking Duncliffe woods. Teas indoors and various shelters around the garden if wet. Featured in Country Gardener. Not suitable for wheelchairs if very wet.

PATRICK'S PATCH
See Hampshire

65 PEN MILL FARM

Pen Selwood, Wincanton BA9 8NF. Mr & Mrs Peter FitzGerald, 01747 840895, fitzgeraldatpen@aol.com, www.penmillcottage.co.uk. *1m from Stourhead, off A303 between Mere and Wincanton. Turn off A303 at B3081 junction (Gillingham/Bruton). Take turning to Penselwood from old A303. 2nd L fork up narrow unsignposted hill. At grass triangle with bench, R to Zeals out of village down steep hill. Garden on R, metal railings and white gate. On border of Somerset and Wiltshire.* Ploughman's lunches/home-made teas. **Adm £3.50, chd free. Sun 15 Sept (12-5). Also open Chiffchaffs. Visitors also welcome by appt Sept.**

Romantic garden with acid-loving mature trees and shrubs in secluded valley on Dorset, Somerset and Wiltshire border where tributary of R Stour cascades into the lake and onwards. Late summer herbaceous borders with abundant colour and over 40 salvias. Enjoy the peace and quiet of this lovely setting. Ploughman's lunches,and delicious teas prepared by members of St. Michael's Church, Penselwood Plant stall, especially salvia and penstemon plants. Featured in Dorset Country Gardener and Garden Questions and Answers. Mostly wheelchair access.

Winner Best Large Dorset Wildlife Friendly Garden . . .

PENNINGTON HOUSE
See Hampshire

PILLEY HILL COTTAGE
See Hampshire

66 PILSDON VIEW

Junction Butts Lane & Pitman's Lane, Ryall, Bridport DT6 6EH. D Lloyd, 01297 489377, davidlloyd001@hotmail.com. *5m W of Bridport. From Bridport follow A35 W through Chideock. Up hill, R at Ryall sign (opp Felicity's Farm Shop). Garden ¾ m on L at junction Butts Lane and Pitmans Lane. Large hedge, PO box in wall. From Axminster follow A35 E to Morecombelake. L at sign Ryall then as above.* **Adm £4, chd free. Tue 28 May, Sat 15, Tue 25 June, Tue 9 July (12-4). Visitors also welcome by appt 4 June to 9 July.**

Started over 25 yrs ago, the hard landscaping provides different levels with breathtaking views over the Marshwood Vale towards Pilson Pen. A mature copper beech and evolving garden gives all yr round interest. Water features with wildlife add to the essence of the garden. Bring your own picnic. Mostly wheelchair access.

PROSPECT HOUSE
See Devon

67 2 PYES PLOT

St. James Road, Netherbury, Bridport DT6 5LP. Ms Sarah Porter. *2m SW of Beaminster. Turn off A3066 Beaminster/Bridport road. Go over R Brit into centre of village. L into St James Rd, signed to Way Town, R corner Hingsdon Lane. Please park considerately in village.* **Adm £3, chd free. Sun 12 May, Sun 23 June (2-5.30). Combined with Mill House both days, 2 gardens £6, teas at Mill House.**

Small but perfectly formed front and back courtyard garden, created from new in 2007. Cream walls and black paintwork make a striking framework for softer planting. Climbing plants, foliage and running water feature enhance the tranquil feel to this space, which uses every inch creatively.

PYLEWELL PARK
See Hampshire

68 Q

113 Bridport Road, Dorchester DT1 2NH. Heather & Chris Robinson, 01305 263088, hev.robinson@talktalk.net. *Approx 300m W of Dorset County Hospital. From Top o' Town roundabout head west towards Dorset County Hospital and Q is 300 metres further on.* Home-made teas. **Adm £3, chd free. Suns 3 Mar (2-4.30); 10 Mar, 19 May, 16 June, 4 Aug (2-5). Visitors also welcome by appt Feb to Aug, parties up to 40 1wks notice please.**

A town garden for all seasons where every inch counts. Themed rooms transport you from the hustle and bustle of town life. Garden reflects the owners many interests, featuring unusual spring bulbs, 100+ clematis plus other climbers, trees herbaceous, shrubs and bedding plants, water, gravel, veg and fruit trees. 3 Mar- talks on Butterflies in the Garden & Herbs & the Sensory

Garden; 10 Mar celebrating Mothering Sunday + Talk by Dorset Wildlife Trust. 19 May Herbs & Their Usage + talk by Dorset Beekeepers. 16 June celebrating Fathers day & talk on Climbers. 4 Aug wood turning demo. Featured on Gardeners World and in local press. Small number of paths available for wheelchair users.

69 RAMPISHAM MANOR

Rampisham Manor, Rampisham DT2 0PT. Robert Boileau. *11m NW of Dorchester. From Yeovil take A37 towards Dorchester, 7m turn R signed Evershot. From Dorchester take A37 to Yeovil, 4m turn L A356 signed Crewkerne; at start of wireless masts R to Rampisham. Follow signs.* Feb home made soup and ploughmans in village hall; Apr home-made teas in village hall. **Adm £3 Feb, £4 Apr, chd free. Sun 24 Feb (12-3); Sun 14 Apr (2-6). Also open 14 Apr Broomhill, joint adm £7.**
Beech and yew hedges are strong features in this mature sloping garden. The spacious grounds are effectively planted and well filled herbaceous and shrub beds around oval pond give the visitor much to enjoy. The top garden (flat), borrows the surrounding landscape and offers more surprises. Woodland walk, vegetables. February Snowdrops. April Spring bulbs and blossom. Accessed over gravel drive. Some steep slopes and steps.

70 RESTING LAURELS

14 Chine Walk, Ferndown BH22 8PU. Paul Jefferies. *2m SE of Bournemouth International Airport. From Parley Cross T-lights, off Christchurch Rd B3073, 1st R turn.* Home-made teas. **Adm £3, chd free. Sun 2 June (11-4).**
The immaculate lawns set off the planting in this ¾ -acre green oasis. The difficult sandy soil supports many mature trees and shrubs with good focal points and an exciting pond area. Organic kitchen garden. Spring and autumn colour. Featured in Amateur Gardener.

71 NEW 25 RICHMOND PARK AVENUE

Bournemouth BH8 9DL. Barbara Hutchinson and Mike Roberts, 01202 531072, barbarahutchinson@tiscali.co.uk. *2.5 miles NE Bournemouth Town Centre. From T-lights at junction with Alma Rd and Richmond Park Rd, head N on B3063 Charminster Rd,*

Little Bindon

© Val Corbett

take 2nd turning on R into Richmond Park Ave. Home-made teas. **Adm £3, chd free. Sat 13, Sun 14, Thur 18, Sat 27, Sun 28 July (2-6). Visitors also welcome by appt July.**
65 sq ft beautifully designed town garden. Pergola leading to raised decking, with ivy canopy, over wildlife pond with waterfall. Herbaceous border imaginatively planted to attract bees and butterflies. Small S-facing courtyard garden, at front of property, sparkling with vibrant colour and Mediterranean planting incl brugmansias, fig and lemon trees. Partial wheelchair access.

72 357 RINGWOOD ROAD
Ferndown BH22 9AE. Lyn & Malcolm Ovens, 01202 896071, malcolm@mgovens.freeserve.co.uk, www.lynandmalc.co.uk. *3/4 m S of Ferndown. On A348 towards Longham. Parking in Glenmoor Rd or other side rds. Avoid parking on main rd*. Home-made teas. **Adm £3, chd free. Sun 14 July (11-5); Wed 31 July (2-5); Sun 18 Aug (11-5). Visitors also welcome by appt 1 July to 8 Sept.**
Plantaholics' prize-winning His and Hers garden. Hers is in cottage style with clematis, phlox, lilies, roses, monarda, encouraging butterflies and bees, providing a riot of colour and perfume into late summer.Walk through a Moorish keyhole doorway into His exotic garden with brugmansias, canna, oleander, banana, dahlia and bougainvillea. Ferndown Common nearby. Featured on German TV with 5 English gardens incl Great Dixter.

ROOKES COTTAGE
See Hampshire

ST CHRISTOPHER'S
See Hampshire

73 THE SECRET GARDEN
The Friary, Hilfield DT2 7BE. The Society of St Francis, 01300 341345, hilfieldssf@franciscans.org.uk, www.hilfieldfriary.org.uk. *10m N of Dorchester, on A352 between Sherbourne & Dorchester. 1st L after Minterne Magna, 1st turning on R signed The Friary. From Yeovil turn off A37 signed Batcombe, 3rd turning on L*. Light refreshments. **Adm £3.50, chd free. Visitors welcome by appt Mar to Sept.**
Ongoing reclamation of neglected woodland garden. Vegetables and courtyard garden. New plantings from modern day plant hunters. Mature trees, bamboo, rhododendrons, azaleas, magnolias, camellias, other choice shrubs with a stream on all sides crossed by bridges, and in spring a growing collection of Loderi hybrids with other choice shrubs. Stout shoes recommended for woodland garden. Friary grounds open where meadows, woods and livestock can be viewed.

Courtyard garden with vibrant colour and Mediterranean planting . . .

74 THE SECRET GARDEN AND SERLES HOUSE
47 Victoria Road, Wimborne BH21 1EN. Ian Willis, 01202 880430. *Centre of Wimborne. On B3082 W of town, very near hospital, Westfield car park 300yds. Off-road parking close by*. Home-made teas. **Adm £3, chd free (share to Wimborne Civic Society and NADFAS). Thur 25, Sun 28 July; Sun 4, Thur 8, Sat 10, Sun 25, Mon 26 Aug; Sun 1, Sat 7, Sun 8, Sun 15, Sun 22 Sept (2.30-5). Visitors also welcome by appt July to Sept.**
Alan Titchmarsh described this amusingly creative garden as 'one of the best 10 private gardens in Britain'. The ingenious use of unusual plants complements the imaginative treasure trove of garden objects d'art. The enchanting house is also open. Gentle live music accompanies your tour as you step into a world of whimsical fantasy that is theatrical and unique. Live piano music at each opening. Wheelchair access to garden only. Narrow steps may prohibit wide wheelchairs.

75 ◆ SHERBORNE CASTLE
New Rd, Sherborne DT9 5NR. Mr J K Wingfield Digby, 01935 813182, enquiries@sherbornecastle.com, www.sherbornecastle.com. *1/2 m E of Sherborne. On New Road B3145. Follow brown signs to 'Sherborne Castles' from A30 & A352.* **For opening times and information, please phone or see garden website.**
40+ acres. A Capability Brown garden with magnificent vistas across the surrounding landscape, incl lake and views to ruined castle. Herbaceous planting, notable trees, mixed ornamental planting and managed wilderness are linked together with lawn and pathways. 'Dry Grounds Walk'. Partial wheelchair access, gravel paths, steep slopes, steps.

76 SLAPE MANOR
Netherbury DT6 5LH. Mr & Mrs Antony Hichens, 01308 488232, antony.hichens@virgin.net. *1m S of Beaminster. Turn W off A3066 to village of Netherbury. House 1/3 m S of Netherbury on back rd to Bridport signed Waytown*. Home-made teas. **Adm £4, chd free. Sun 12 May (2-6). Visitors also welcome by appt.**
River valley garden with spacious lawns and primula fringed streams down to lake. Magnificent hostas and gunneras, horizontal cryptomeria Japonica 'Elegans'. Wellingtonias, ancient wisterias and rhododendrons. Slightly sloping lawns/grass paths and gravel paths, unfenced water features.

77 ◆ SNAPE COTTAGE PLANTSMAN'S GARDEN
Chaffeymoor, Bourton, Nr Gillingham SP8 5BZ. Ian & Angela Whinfield, 01747 840330 (evenings), www.snapecottagegarden.co.uk. *5m NW of Gillingham. On border of Somerset & Wiltshire, At W end of Bourton, N of A303. Opp Chiffchaffs*. **Adm £3.50, chd free. For NGS: Sats, Suns 30, 31 Mar; 27, 28 Apr; 25, 26 May; 29, 30 June; 27, 28 July; 24, 25 Aug (2-5). For other opening times and information, please phone or see garden website.**
Mature country garden containing exceptional collection of hardy plants and bulbs, artistically arranged in

informal cottage garden style, organically managed and clearly labelled. Specialities incl snowdrops, hellebores, 'old' daffodils, pulmonarias, auriculas, herbs, irises and geraniums. Wildlife pond, beautiful views, tranquil atmosphere. The home of Snape Stakes plant supports.

SPINNERS GARDEN
See Hampshire

THE STABLE FAMILY HOME TRUST GARDEN
See Hampshire

SWAY VILLAGE GARDENS
See Hampshire

78 ◆ UPTON COUNTRY PARK
Upton, Poole BH17 7BJ, 01202 262753, www.uptoncountrypark.com. *3m W of Poole town centre. On S side of A35/A3049. Follow brown signs.* **For information incl activities and events, please phone or see garden website.**
Over 100 acres of award-winning parkland incl formal gardens, walled garden, woodland and shoreline. Maritime micro-climate offers a wonderful collection of unusual trees, vintage camellias and stunning roses. Home to Upton House, Grade II* listed Georgian mansion. Regular special events. Plant centre, art gallery and tea rooms. Winter (8-6); summer (8-9).

WAYFORD MANOR
See Somerset, Bristol & South Gloucestershire

79 24A WESTERN AVENUE
Branksome Park, Poole BH13 7AN. Mr Peter Jackson, 01202 708388, peter@branpark.wanadoo.co.uk. *3m W of Bournemouth. ½ m inland from Branksome Chine beach. From S end Wessex Way (A338) take The Avenue. At T-lights turn R into Western Rd. At church turn R into Western Ave.* Home-made teas. **Adm £3.50, chd free. Sun 23 June, Sun 11 Aug (2-5.30). Groups of 12+ also welcome by appt June to Sept, refreshments by arrangement.**
'This secluded and magical 1-acre garden captures the spirit of warmer climes and begs for repeated visits' (Gardening Which?) Rose, wall, courtyard, woodland and herbaceous gardens. Topiary/wood sculptures. June sees rose garden at its best; herbaceous borders and lush tropical planting flourish with 2nd flush of roses in August. Wheelchair access to ¾ garden.

This magical garden begs for repeated visits . . .

80 WESTON HOUSE
Buckhorn Weston, Gillingham SP8 5HG. Mr & Mrs E A W Bullock, 01963 371005, mrsjbullock@gmail.com. *4m W of Gillingham, 3m SE of Wincanton. From A30 turn N to Kington Magna, continue towards Buckhorn Weston & after railway bridge take L turn towards Wincanton. 2nd on L is Weston House.* Home-made teas. **Adm £4, chd free. Visitors welcome by appt 15 Mar to 15 Sept, home-made teas by arrangement.**
Delightful colourful, scented garden of spring flowers, summer borders, old-fashioned roses and interesting trees. 1½ acres of beauty and peace with views of Blackmore Vale. Beyond the lawn, grass paths lead to wild flower meadows attracting butterflies and other insects. Natural pond shelters newts and dragonflies. Gravel yard and gentle slope to patio.

WHITE BARN
See Hampshire

WILLOWS
See Hampshire

81 WINCOMBE PARK
Shaftesbury SP7 9AB. John & Phoebe Fortescue. *2m N of Shaftesbury. A350 Shaftesbury to Warminster, past Wincombe Business Park, 1st R signed Wincombe & Donhead St Mary. ¾ m on R.* Home-made teas. **Adm £3.50, chd free. Sun 12, Thur 16 May (2-5).**
Extensive mature garden with sweeping panoramic views over lake and woods. Regeneration in progress. Azaleas, rhododendrons and camellias in flower amongst shrubs and unusual trees. Beautiful walled kitchen garden. Stalls and fun for the family. Partial wheelchair access, slopes and gravel paths.

82 WINDY WILLUMS
38 Island View Avenue, Christchurch BH23 4DS. Julie King, 01425 277046, enquiries@windywillums.co.uk, www.windywillums.co.uk. *6m E of Bournemouth. From A35 Somerford r'about, take A337 for Highcliffe. At next roundabout take last exit (Runway). 2nd L after Sandpiper PH. Car park 100yds past garden.* **Adm £3.50, chd free. Sat 15, Sun 16 June (2-5). Visitors also welcome by appt Apr to June, refreshments by arrangement.**
A peaceful haven close to the sea. ⅓ -acre garden divided into 3 rooms, each with its own colour theme and naturalistic planting. Large collection of roses and clematis, unusual and scented perennials and shrubs within formal boundaries of yew hedging. Folly in gravel garden, where plants are left to self-seed. Wild but tamed. Places to sit and ponder.

83 WOLVERHOLLOW
Elsdons Lane, Monkton Wyld DT6 6DA. Mr & Mrs D Wiscombe, 01297 560610. *4m N of Lyme Regis. 4m NW of Charmouth. Monkton Wyld is signed from A35 approx 4m NW of Charmouth off dual carriageway. Wolverhollow is next to the church.* Home-made teas. **Adm £3.50, chd free. Sun 5, Mon 6, Sun 26, Mon 27 May, Sat 15, Sun 16 June (11-5). Visitors also welcome by appt.**
Over 1 acre of informal garden. Lawns, with unusual summerhouse, lead past borders and rockeries to shady valley with babbling brook. Numerous paths pass wide variety of colourful and uncommon plants. An area, once field, sympathetically extends the garden with meadow and streamside planting with abundance of primulas! Must be seen.

© Val Corbett

Dorset County Volunteers

County Organiser
Harriet Boileau, Witcham Farm, Rampisham, Dorchester DT2 0PX, 01935 83612, h.boileau@btinternet.com

County Treasurer
Richard Smedley, 60 Huntly Road, Bournemouth BH3 7HJ, 01202 528286, richard@carter-coley.co.uk

Publicity Officer
Gillian Ford, Rosemary Cottage, Rampisham DT2 0PX, 01935 83645, gillianford33@btinternet.com

Booklet Editor
Judith Hussey, The Old Rectory, Manston, Sturminster Newton DT10 1EX, 01258 474673, judithhussey@hotmail.com

Website
Oonagh Stewart, West Compton Manor, West Compton, Dorchester DT2 0EY, 01300 320400, info@westcomptonmanor.co.uk

Assistant County Organisers
North Central Caroline Renner, Croft Farm, Fontmell Magna, Shaftesbury SP7 0NR, 01747 811140, croftfarm@talktalk.net
North East/Ferndown Mary Angus, The Glade, Woodland Walk, Ferndown BH22 9LP, 01202 872789, mary@gladestock.co.uk
North West Victoria Baxter, Longburton House, Longburton, Sherborne DT9 5NU, 01935 815992, victoria@lborchard.co.uk
Central East Trish Neale, Badbury View, 3 Witchampton Mill, Witchampton, Wimborne BH21 5DE, 01258 840345, trishneale1@yahoo.co.uk
Central Wendy Jackson, Vine Cottage, Melcombe Bingham, Dorchester DT2 7PE, 01258 880720, wendyjacks@fsmail.net
West Central Paul & Susie Stopford Adams, Steppes Farm, Frampton, Dorchester DT2 9NJ, 01300 320283, psa@stopford-adams.com
South Caroline Edwards, Westbrook House, Upwey, Weymouth DT3 5QB, 01305 812929, caroline@westbrookhousedorset.co.uk
South West Christine Corson, Stoke Knapp Cottage, Norway Lane, Stoke Abbott, Beaminster DT8 3JZ, 01308 868203, christinecorson612@btinternet.com
Bournemouth, Poole and Christchurch Penny Slade, Flat 1, Portadene, 6 Portarlington Road, Bournemouth BH4 8BT, 01202 763984

Essex

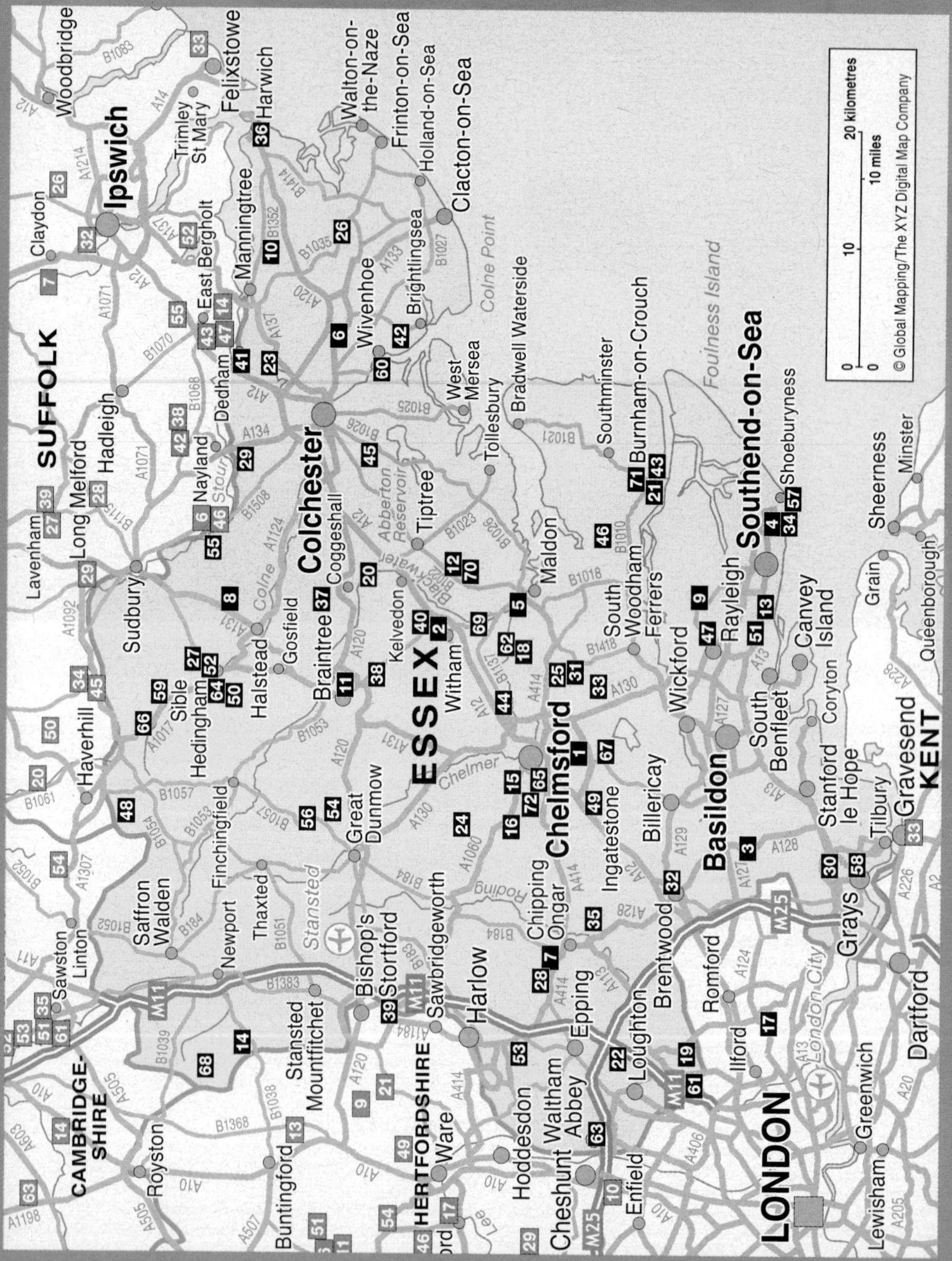
SUFFOLK
Ipswich
Woodbridge
Felixstowe
Trimley St Mary
Claydon
Hadleigh
Long Melford
Lavenham
Sudbury
Haverhill
East Bergholt
Manningtree
Harwich
Dedham
Nayland
Colchester
Wivenhoe
Brightlingsea
Walton-on-the-Naze
Frinton-on-Sea
Holland-on-Sea
Clacton-on-Sea
Colne Point
West Mersea
Tollesbury
Bradwell Waterside
Tiptree
Coggeshall
Abberton Reservoir
Kelvedon
Witham
Maldon
Halstead
Gosfield
Braintree
Sible Hedingham
Finchingfield
Thaxted
Great Dunmow
ESSEX
Chelmsford
Southminster
Burnham-on-Crouch
Foulness Island
Southend-on-Sea
Shoeburyness
South Woodham Ferrers
Wickford
Rayleigh
Basildon
South Benfleet
Canvey Island
Billericay
Ingatestone
Chipping Ongar
Brentwood
Romford
Ilford
Grays
Stanford le Hope
Coryton
Tilbury
Gravesend
KENT
Dartford
Greenwich
Lewisham
LONDON
London City
Enfield
Cheshunt
Waltham Abbey
Loughton
Epping
Harlow
Sawbridgeworth
Bishop's Stortford
Stansted
Stansted Mountfitchet
Newport
Saffron Walden
Linton
Sawston
CAMBRIDGE-SHIRE
Royston
Buntingford
HERTFORDSHIRE
Ware
Hoddesdon
Sheerness
Minster
Grain
Queenborough
0 10 20 kilometres
0 10 miles
© Global Mapping/The XYZ Digital Map Company

Opening Dates

February

Sunday 10
72 Writtle College

Tuesday 12
27 Hedingham Castle

Saturday 16
44 The Old Rectory

Sunday 17
44 The Old Rectory

March

Sunday 31
60 Tudor Roost
70 Wood View

April

Monday 1
60 Tudor Roost

Tuesday 2
70 Wood View

Thursday 4
20 Feeringbury Manor

Friday 5
20 Feeringbury Manor

Thursday 11
20 Feeringbury Manor
49 Peacocks

Friday 12
12 60 Colchester Road
20 Feeringbury Manor

Saturday 13
12 60 Colchester Road

Sunday 14
4 102 Barnstaple Road
57 South Shoebury Hall

Tuesday 16
16 Dragons

Thursday 18
3 Barnards Farm
20 Feeringbury Manor

Friday 19
20 Feeringbury Manor
29 Horkesley Hall

Saturday 20
60 Tudor Roost

Sunday 21
60 Tudor Roost

Wednesday 24
25 Furzelea

Thursday 25
3 Barnards Farm
20 Feeringbury Manor

Friday 26
5 Beeleigh Abbey Gardens
20 Feeringbury Manor
69 Wickham Place Farm

Sunday 28
62 Ulting Wick

May

Thursday 2
3 Barnards Farm
20 Feeringbury Manor

Friday 3
20 Feeringbury Manor
69 Wickham Place Farm

Sunday 5
12 60 Colchester Road
28 Hobbans Farm
68 Wickets

Monday 6
12 60 Colchester Road
70 Wood View

Tuesday 7
41 Monks Cottage

Thursday 9
3 Barnards Farm
20 Feeringbury Manor

Friday 10
20 Feeringbury Manor
69 Wickham Place Farm

A tiny fairy glen and hidden 'pixie walk' . . . hidden quirky objects such as a family of meerkats, and fairies . . .

Sunday 12
48 Parsonage House
56 Snares Hill Cottage

Thursday 16
3 Barnards Farm
20 Feeringbury Manor
46 One Brook Hall Cottages

Friday 17
20 Feeringbury Manor
69 Wickham Place Farm

Saturday 18
26 Hannams Hall

Sunday 19
26 Hannams Hall
28 Hobbans Farm

Tuesday 21
16 Dragons

Thursday 23
3 Barnards Farm
20 Feeringbury Manor

Friday 24
20 Feeringbury Manor
69 Wickham Place Farm

Saturday 25
42 Moverons
54 St Helens

Sunday 26
32 The Lembic
42 Moverons
44 The Old Rectory

Thursday 30
3 Barnards Farm
20 Feeringbury Manor

Friday 31
20 Feeringbury Manor
33 The Limes (Evening)
69 Wickham Place Farm

June

Saturday 1
33 The Limes

Sunday 2
25 Furzelea
27 Hedingham Castle
28 Hobbans Farm
32 The Lembic
40 Miraflores
52 Rookwoods

Tuesday 4
15 8 Dene Court
16 Dragons

Thursday 6
3 Barnards Farm
20 Feeringbury Manor

Friday 7
20 Feeringbury Manor
69 Wickham Place Farm

Saturday 8
2 Barnardiston House

Sunday 9
23 Fountain Farm
50 Peppers Farm

Thursday 13
3 Barnards Farm
20 Feeringbury Manor

Friday 14
20 Feeringbury Manor
69 Wickham Place Farm

National Gardens Weekend

Saturday 15
10 Chippins
15 8 Dene Court
39 The Millers Cottage
54 St Helens

Sunday 16
2 Barnardiston House
7 Blake Hall
10 Chippins
11 352 Coggeshall Road
13 Court View
14 Deers
19 Fairwinds

22 56 Forest Drive
28 Hobbans Farm
30 Julie's Garden
39 The Millers Cottage
40 Miraflores
48 Parsonage House
49 Peacocks
50 Peppers Farm
51 Reprise
59 Spencers
61 37 Turpins Lane
63 Waltham Abbey
64 Washlands
66 West End Cottage
70 Wood View
72 Writtle College

Thursday 20
3 Barnards Farm
20 Feeringbury Manor

Friday 21
20 Feeringbury Manor
69 Wickham Place Farm

Saturday 22
2 Barnardiston House (Afternoon & Evening)

Large collection of heucheras create foliage interest. . . .

Sunday 23
2 Barnardiston House
21 4 Fernlea Road
40 Miraflores
43 Mulberry House Boat
64 Washlands

Tuesday 25
15 8 Dene Court

Thursday 27
3 Barnards Farm
20 Feeringbury Manor

Friday 28
20 Feeringbury Manor
69 Wickham Place Farm

Saturday 29
11 352 Coggeshall Road
21 4 Fernlea Road
43 Mulberry House Boat

Sunday 30
3 Barnards Farm
11 352 Coggeshall Road
28 Hobbans Farm
40 Miraflores
58 Southview

July

Tuesday 2
41 Monks Cottage

Thursday 4
3 Barnards Farm
20 Feeringbury Manor

Friday 5
20 Feeringbury Manor
69 Wickham Place Farm

Saturday 6
68 Wickets

Sunday 7
24 Fudlers Hall
35 Little Myles
38 60 Mill Lane

Wednesday 10
18 Elwy Lodge

Thursday 11
3 Barnards Farm
20 Feeringbury Manor
29 Horkesley Hall

Friday 12
20 Feeringbury Manor
69 Wickham Place Farm

Saturday 13
53 69 Rundells

Sunday 14
10 Chippins
13 Court View
28 Hobbans Farm
51 Reprise
57 South Shoebury Hall

Tuesday 16
15 8 Dene Court
16 Dragons
18 Elwy Lodge

Thursday 18
3 Barnards Farm
18 Elwy Lodge
20 Feeringbury Manor
31 Kingsteps

Friday 19
20 Feeringbury Manor
69 Wickham Place Farm

Saturday 20
12 60 Colchester Road

Sunday 21
12 60 Colchester Road
18 Elwy Lodge
22 56 Forest Drive
61 37 Turpins Lane

Tuesday 23
15 8 Dene Court

Thursday 25
3 Barnards Farm
20 Feeringbury Manor

Friday 26
20 Feeringbury Manor
69 Wickham Place Farm

Saturday 27
60 Tudor Roost

Sunday 28
1 24 Attwoods Close
48 Parsonage House
58 Southview
60 Tudor Roost
65 45 Waterhouse Lane
70 Wood View

August

Thursday 1
3 Barnards Farm

Saturday 3
36 447 Main Road

Sunday 4
24 Fudlers Hall
36 447 Main Road
51 Reprise
58 Southview
65 45 Waterhouse Lane

Tuesday 6
15 8 Dene Court
16 Dragons

Thursday 8
3 Barnards Farm

Sunday 11
13 Court View
38 60 Mill Lane

Thursday 15
3 Barnards Farm
46 One Brook Hall Cottages

Saturday 17
34 Little Foxes

Sunday 18
17 6 Elms Gardens
34 Little Foxes
66 West End Cottage

Tuesday 20
16 Dragons

Thursday 22
3 Barnards Farm

Saturday 24
54 St Helens

Sunday 25
14 Deers
60 Tudor Roost
65 45 Waterhouse Lane (Evening)

Monday 26
60 Tudor Roost

Thursday 29
3 Barnards Farm
31 Kingsteps

September

Sunday 1
3 Barnards Farm
28 Hobbans Farm
65 45 Waterhouse Lane (Evening)

Thursday 5
20 Feeringbury Manor

Friday 6
20 Feeringbury Manor
69 Wickham Place Farm

Sunday 8
- 13 Court View
- 42 Moverons
- 63 Waltham Abbey

Wednesday 11
- 25 Furzelea

Thursday 12
- 20 Feeringbury Manor

Friday 13
- 20 Feeringbury Manor
- 69 Wickham Place Farm

Saturday 14
- 71 Woodpeckers

Sunday 15
- 28 Hobbans Farm
- 59 Spencers
- 62 Ulting Wick

Tuesday 17
- 16 Dragons

Thursday 19
- 20 Feeringbury Manor

Friday 20
- 20 Feeringbury Manor
- 69 Wickham Place Farm

Saturday 21
- 71 Woodpeckers

Thursday 26
- 20 Feeringbury Manor

Friday 27
- 20 Feeringbury Manor
- 69 Wickham Place Farm

Saturday 28
- 71 Woodpeckers

October

Sunday 13
- 72 Writtle College

Sunday 20
- 32 The Lembic

Thursday 24
- 3 Barnards Farm

December

Sunday 1
- 70 Wood View

February 2014

Sunday 9
- 72 Writtle College

Gardens open to the public

- 5 Beeleigh Abbey Gardens
- 6 Beth Chatto Gardens
- 27 Hedingham Castle
- 37 Marks Hall Gardens & Arboretum
- 59 Spencers

Dragons

By appointment only

- 8 Byndes Cottage
- 9 Canonteign
- 45 Olivers
- 47 Orchard Cottage
- 55 Shrubs Farm
- 67 West Hanningfield Hall

Also open by Appointment ☎

- 2 Barnardiston House
- 3 Barnards Farm
- 4 102 Barnstaple Road
- 10 Chippins
- 11 352 Coggeshall Road
- 13 Court View
- 15 8 Dene Court
- 16 Dragons
- 19 Fairwinds
- 20 Feeringbury Manor
- 22 56 Forest Drive
- 25 Furzelea
- 26 Hannams Hall
- 28 Hobbans Farm
- 29 Horkesley Hall
- 30 Julie's Garden
- 38 60 Mill Lane
- 40 Miraflores
- 41 Monks Cottage
- 42 Moverons
- 44 The Old Rectory
- 46 One Brook Hall Cottages
- 49 Peacocks
- 51 Reprise
- 52 Rookwoods
- 53 69 Rundells
- 54 St Helens
- 56 Snares Hill Cottage
- 58 Southview
- 60 Tudor Roost
- 61 37 Turpins Lane
- 62 Ulting Wick
- 65 45 Waterhouse Lane
- 66 West End Cottage
- 68 Wickets
- 69 Wickham Place Farm
- 70 Wood View
- 71 Woodpeckers

The Gardens

1 24 ATTWOODS CLOSE

Galleywood, Chelmsford CM2 8QJ. Mrs Wendy Cummin. *3m S of Chelmsford. Exit J16 A12. B1007 to Eagle PH. Turn R at T-lights then 2nd R Well Lane, 1st L Attwoods Close.* Light refreshments. **Adm £3, chd free.** Sun 28 July (2-6). **Also open 45 Waterhouse Lane.**

Small and secluded 'jungle' packed with colour and mixed foliage. Tall planting includes bamboos, cordyline, Indian bean tree and large bottle brush. Masses of pots contain a variety of plants including brugmansia, nandina and eucomis. A photographer's dream. Also a tiny fairy glen and hidden 'pixie walk', newly developed for 2013. All this in a 40ft square space! Hidden quirky objects such as a family of meerkats, fairies, and assorted small statues. Small decking area to enjoy tea and cake, with gentle background music.

2 BARNARDISTON HOUSE

35 Chipping Hill, Witham CM8 2DE. Ruth & Eric Teverson, 01376 502266, ruthteverson@yahoo.co.uk. *10m NE of Chelmsford. A12 S-bound J22 to town centre. At George PH turn R then L at mini r'abouts. Garden opp White Horse PH. A12 N-bound J21, L at r'about to town centre, L at T-lights beyond White Hart Hotel. L at mini r'abouts as above. For Sat Nav use CM8 2JU. Parking on rd outside house.* Light refreshments. **Adm £3, chd free.** Sat 8, Sun 16, Sat 22, Sun 23 June (Sats 2.30-9) (Suns 11-5). **Combined with Miraflores, adm £5, 16, 23 June. Visitors also welcome by appt June to July.**

A medium-sized town garden, designed and created over last 15yrs by the owners. The garden has two lawns, deep borders, raised beds, seating areas and bee hives. A wide range of unusual and insect friendly plants as well as fruit, heritage vegetables and succulents, all of which must enjoy hot and dry conditions. Evening openings. Partial wheelchair access.

3 BARNARDS FARM

Brentwood Road, West Horndon, Brentwood CM13 3LX. Bernard & Sylvia Holmes & The Christabella Charitable Trust, 01277 811262, sylvia@barnardsfarm.eu, www.barnardsfarm.eu. *5m S of Brentwood. On A128 $1\frac{1}{2}$ m S of A127 Halfway House flyover. From junction continue on A128 under the railway bridge. Garden on R just past bridge.* Light refreshments & light lunches on Thurs, home-made teas on Suns. **Adm £6, chd free (Thurs), adm £7.50, chd free (Suns) (share to St Francis Church).** Every Thur 18 Apr to 29 Aug (11-4.30); Suns 30 June; 1 Sept (2-5.30); Thur 24 Oct (11-4). **Visitors also welcome by appt May to Sept. Group visits by arrangement on non open days.**

17 hectare, yr-round interest garden and woodland. Landscaped ponds, Japanese garden, living wall, major sculpture collection and national Malus collection (blossom April-May). Golf buggy tours for less able walkers. Bernard's Sunday sculpture tour (3pm), veteran and vintage vehicle collection, 1920s cycle shop (Suns only). Rides through the woodland on a miniature railway. Collect loyalty points on Thur visits and earn a free Sun or Thur visit. Aviators welcome (PPO), see website for details. Wheelchair accessible WC.

Wide range of unusual and insect friendly plants as well as fruit . . .

4 102 BARNSTAPLE ROAD

Thorpe Bay SS1 3PW. Ann Safwat, 01702 586615, annstripe@hotmail.com. *2m E of Southend. From A127 follow signs to Shoebury (A1159). At end of Royal Artillery Way take RH lane, straight over r'about into Thorpe Hall Ave. Barnstaple Rd 3rd on L. From A13 follow signs to seafront, past Kursall towards Shoebury. At mini r'about L into Thorpe Hall Ave, then R into Barnstaple Rd. Nr Thorpe Bay Stn.* Home-made teas. **Adm £3, chd free.** Sun 14 Apr (1-5). **Visitors also welcome by appt Jun to Aug.**

An ordinary façade belies a plantaholic's secret garden with appeal for everyone. A veritable paradise with woodland, herbaceous mixed borders, dry stream and gravel beds, formal topiary and lawns. Productive area of fruit and vegetables plus greenhouses with stunning cacti. Massed floral display in April. Considered a 'favourite' garden by many visitors. Original art. Featured on Essex radio.

5 ◆ BEELEIGH ABBEY GARDENS

Abbey Turning, Beeleigh, Maldon CM9 6LL. Christopher & Catherine Foyle, 07779 223321, www.visitmaldon.co.uk/beeleigh-abbey. *1m NW of Maldon. From central Maldon take London Rd. Up past cemetery (on L). 1st R into Abbey Turning. Continue straight down hill 700yds - 1st R into private rd. Consult before arranging coach travel - difficult narrow access.* **Adm £4, chd £2.** For NGS: Fri 26 Apr (10.30-3.30). **For other opening times and information, please phone or see garden website.**

3 acres of secluded gardens in rural historic setting. Mature trees surround variety of planting and water features, woodland walks underplanted with bulbs leading to tidal river, cottage garden, kitchen garden, orchard, wild flower meadow, rose garden, wisteria walk, magnolia trees, lawn with 85yd long herbaceous border. Scenic backdrop of remains of C12 abbey incorporated into private house (not open). Features in BBC4 history series and radio and TV coverage of launch for Christopher Foyle's book on Beeleigh Abbey. Gravel paths, some gentle slopes. Large WC with ramp and handlebars.

6 ◆ BETH CHATTO GARDENS

Elmstead Market, Colchester CO7 7DB. Mrs Beth Chatto, 01206 822007, www.bethchatto.co.uk. *$\frac{1}{4}$ m E of Elmstead Market. On A133 Colchester to Clacton Rd in village of Elmstead Market.* **Adm £6.95, chd free. For opening times and information, please phone or see garden website.**

Internationally famous gardens, including dry, damp and woodland areas. The result of over fifty years of hard work and application of the huge body of plant knowledge possessed by Beth Chatto and her late husband Andrew. Visitors cannot fail to be affected by the peace and beauty of the garden. Large plant nursery and modern Tea Room. Featured in Daily

Telegraph - top 20 British Garden makers, The English Garden, Gardens Illustrated, RHS Magazine, House and Garden and BBC TV Chelsea preview. Disabled WC and parking.

16 BEVERLEY ROAD, E4
See London

BEVILLS
See Suffolk

7 BLAKE HALL

Bobbingworth CM5 0DG. Mr & Mrs H Capel Cure, www.blakehall.co.uk. *10m W of Chelmsford. Just off A414 between Four Wantz r'about in Ongar & Talbot r'about in North Weald. Signed on A414.* Teas served in C17 barn. **Adm £4, chd free. Sun 16 June (11-4).**
25 acres of mature gardens within the historic setting of Blake Hall (not open). Arboretum with broad variety of specimen trees. Spectacular rambling roses clamber up ancient trees. Traditional formal rose garden and herbaceous border. Sweeping lawns. Some gravel paths.

5 BRODIE ROAD, E4
See London

BROMLEY HALL
See Hertfordshire

8 BYNDES COTTAGE

Pebmarsh, nr Halstead CO9 2LZ. David & Margaret MacLennan, 01787 269500, byndes2@btinternet.com. *2m N of Halstead. On A131 from Halstead to Sudbury, take R turning signed Pebmarsh & Bures. 3rd house on L before Pebmarsh village round sharp bend.* Light refreshments. **Adm £5 incl refreshments, chd free. Groups welcome by appt all year round incl snowdrop time (late Jan to early March).**
7-acre garden planted and maintained by enthusiastic owners who enjoy giving a conducted tour to groups. Extensive mix of borders, trees and shrubs with diverse and interesting plantings. Practical ideas for maintenance and conservation. National collection of Galanthus. Featured in Countryside and Essex Life magazines. Radio Essex interview on snowdrop collection. Mostly grass with some paving and gravel.

NCH

9 CANONTEIGN

47a Hill Lane, Hawkwell SS5 4HW. Margaret Taylor, 01702 206387. *4m NE of Rayleigh. Leave A127 at Rayleigh Weir, take B1013 towards Rayleigh. Pass through Rayleigh towards Hockley, then through Hockley by Spa PH over hill turn L at White Hart Garage into Hill Lane.* Home-made teas. **Adm £3, chd free. Visitors welcome by appt June to Sept.**
Divided into a series of rooms, this town garden's delights unfold as you wander through. From a courtyard, with vertically striking planting, through 'grassed' suntrap to a climber covered trellis walkway with views across the ornamental pond. Beyond are raised beds with colourful perennials and evergreens surrounding raised sculpture. Featured in Southend on Sea Evening Echo. Wheelchair access in patio area only.

111 CAPEL ROAD, E7
See London

12 CEDAR AVENUE
See London

10 CHIPPINS

Heath Road, Bradfield CO11 2UZ. Kit & Ceri Leese, 01255 870730, ceriandkit@john-lewis.com. *3m E of Manningtree. On B1352, take main rd through village. Bungalow is directly opp primary school.* Home-made teas. **Adm £3.50, chd free. Sat 15, Sun 16 June, Sun 14 July (11-4). Visitors also welcome by appt May to Aug.**
Artist's garden and plantaholics paradise packed with interest. Springtime heralds irises, hostas and alliums. Stream and wildlife pond brimming with bog plants. Summer hosts an explosion of colour-abundance of tubs and hanging baskets. Wide borders feature hemerocallis with swathes of lilies, later dahlias and exotics (South African streptocarpus, aeonium and unusual agaves). Art and photographic display. Featured in Garden News.

11 352 COGGESHALL ROAD

Braintree CM7 9EH. Sau Lin Goss, 01376 329753, Richard.goss@talktalk.net. *15m W of Colchester. 10m N of Chelmsford. From M11 J8 take A120 Colchester. Follow A120 to Braintree r'about (McDonalds). 1st exit into Cressing Rd follow to T-lights. R into Coggeshall Rd. 500yds on R opp bus company.* Light refreshments. **Adm £3, chd free. Sun 16, Sat 29, Sun 30 June (1-5). Also open Miraflores 16, 30 June. Visitors also welcome by appt June to Aug.**
Sau Lin arrived from Hong Kong to become enthralled with English gardening. 'My little heaven', she says of her garden which has themed areas, perennials, roses and many other plants. Japanese mixed border, fruit trees and shrubs. Seating and relaxing areas, fish pond with plants and wildlife. Mediterranean patio with water feature and wide array of pots. Featured in Essex Style magazine, Amateur Gardening and Garden Answers. Partial wheelchair access, ramp from patio to main garden.

Divided into a series of rooms, this town garden's delights unfold as you wander through . . .

12 60 COLCHESTER ROAD

Great Totham, Maldon CM9 8DG. Mrs Sue Jackman. *5m NE of Maldon. On B1022 Maldon to Colchester rd.* **Adm £3, chd free. Fri 12, Sat 13 Apr; Sun 5, Mon 6 May; Sat 20, Sun 21 July (11-5).**
¾ acre plantwoman's garden with large colour-themed borders, in both sun and shade, planted for a long season of interest with many unusual species. Rock garden full of alpines, rill leading to watersteps, and circular pool overlooked by a summerhouse. Small vegetable garden.

13 COURT VIEW

276 Manchester Drive, Leigh-on-Sea SS9 3ES. Ray Spencer & Richard Steers, 01702 713221, arjeyeski@courtview.demon.co.uk, www.facebook.com/courtview.ngs essex. *4m W of Southend. From A127 London: Under A129 to*

T-lights. R to Leigh-on-Sea. R at T-lights. At r'about straight on. 3rd rd on R into Kingswood Ch. Over Bonchurch Ave, L to Manchester Dr. From A13: 3rd rd W from Waitrose turn N into Kingswood Ch, R into Manchester Dr. Home-made teas. **Adm £3.50, chd free.** Suns 16 June; 14 July; 11 Aug; 8 Sept (1-5). **Also open Reprise 16 June, 14 July, South Shoebury Hall 14 July. Visitors also welcome by appt June to Sept, weekdays only. Homemade lunch or cream tea.**
Front garden densely planted with shrubs and perennials. Exuberant rear garden reached beyond a clematis and fern walk. Bold planting, fiery colours and scented plants surround many seating areas. Water and sculpture add to the sensory experience. Completely redesigned and planted for 2013 is the old deck and swimming pool area. Come and see what we have done.

DASSELS BURY
See Hertfordshire

14 DEERS

Clavering CB11 4PX. Mr S H Cooke. *7m N of Bishop's Stortford. On B1038. Turn W off B1383 (old A11) at Newport and follow signs to Langley and Ford End.* Home-made teas. **Adm £5, chd free (share to Clavering Jubilee Field).** Sun 16 June, Sun 25 Aug (2-5).
9 acres. Judged by visitors to be a very romantic garden. Shrub and herbaceous borders, 3 ponds with water lilies, old roses in formal garden, pool garden, walled vegetable garden, moon gate, field and woodland walks. Plenty of seats to enjoy the tranquility of the garden. Dogs on leads.

15 8 DENE COURT

Chignall Road, Chelmsford CM1 2JQ. Mrs Sheila Chapman, 01245 266156. *W of Chelmsford (Parkway). Take A1060 Roxwell Rd for 1m. Turn R at T-lights into Chignall Rd. Dene Court 3rd exit on R. Parking in Chignall Rd.* **Adm £3, chd free.** Tue 4, Sat 15, Tue 25 June; Tues 16, 23 July; 6 Aug (2-5). **Also open Dragons 4 June, 16 July, 6 Aug. Visitors also welcome by appt, refreshments by arrangement.**
Beautifully maintained and designed compact garden (250sq yds). Owner is well-known RHS gold medal-winning exhibitor (now retired). Circular lawn, long pergola and walls festooned with roses and climbers. Large selection of unusual clematis. Densely-planted colour co-ordinated perennials add interest from May to Sept.

16 DRAGONS

Boyton Cross, Chelmsford CM1 4LS. Mrs Margot Grice, 01245 248651, mandmdragons@tiscali.co.uk. *5m W of Chelmsford. On A1060. ½ m W of The Hare PH or ½ m E of India Lounge.* Home-made teas. **Adm £3.50, chd free.** Tues 16 Apr; 21 May; 4 June; 16 July; 6, 20 Aug; 17 Sept (11-5). **Also open 8 Dene Court 4 June,16 July, 6 Aug. Visitors also welcome by appt.**
A plantswoman's ?-acre garden, planted to encourage wildlife. Sumptuous colour-themed borders with striking plant combinations, featuring specimen plants, fernery, clematis, mature dwarf conifers and grasses. Meandering paths lead to ponds, patio, scree garden and small vegetable garden. 2 summerhouses, one overlooking stream and farmland.

EAST BERGHOLT PLACE - THE PLACE FOR PLANTS
See Suffolk

17 NEW 6 ELMS GARDENS

Dagenham RM9 5TX. Peter & Kathy Railton. *1m from Becontree Heath. A124 Wood Ln towards Barking. Elms Gdns located off Five Elms Rd/Halbutt St.* Home-made teas. **Adm £3, chd free.** Sun 18 Aug (2-5).
Plant lovers garden (approx 80ft x 60ft) featuring wide range of herbaceous plants and shrubs with yr round interest. Colourful begonias in baskets and containers. Large collection of heucheras create foliage interest. Magnificent magnolia grandifloras. Winding paths lead to quiet seating, Koi fishpond and small woodland shade area.

One Brook Hall Cottages

18 NEW ELWY LODGE

West Bowers Rd, Woodham Walter, Maldon CM9 6RZ. David & Laura Cox. *Just outside Woodham Walter village. From Chelmsford, A414 towards Danbury, L at 2nd mini r'about into Little Baddow Rd. Turn R after The Generals Arms into Spring Elms Ln. Follow NGS signs. From Colchester, A12 to Hatfield Peverel, L onto B1019, R towards Woodham Walter. Follow NGS signs.* Light refreshments. **Adm £3.50, chd free.** Wed 10, Tue 16, Thur 18, Sun 21 July (11-6). **Also open Kingsteps 18 July.**

Rural location offering peace, tranquility and lovely countryside views. Scented roses in front garden leading to flowing lawns, herbaceous/ shrub borders, trees, wildlife pond and meadow area. The garden then slopes down to a secluded chamomile-scented lower garden with raised vegetable beds, soft fruits and fruit trees. This is an ever-changing garden being developed to blend with the rural setting.

This is an ever-changing garden being developed to blend with the rural setting . . .

19 FAIRWINDS

Chapel Lane, Chigwell Row IG7 6JJ. Sue & David Coates, 07731 796467, scoates@forest.org.uk. *2m SE of Chigwell. Tube: Turn R at exit. 10 mins walk up hill from Grange Hill Car: nr M25 J26 & North Circular. Signed Chigwell. Turning off Lambourne Rd. Please park in Lodge Close Car Park. Visitors must not park in Chapel Lane. (Space for 2 disabled cars to park by the house).* Home-made teas. **Adm £3.50, chd free.** Sun 16 June (2-5). **Also open 37 Turpins Lane. Visitors also welcome by appt Mar to Oct. Refreshments by arrangement. Groups preferred.**

Country garden with a rich variety of planting styles. Gravelled front garden. Side entrance leads to an area with themed large mixed borders and an ornamental greenhouse. Central area includes a patio, fire pit, woodland, bug house and 'Eglu'. Beware dragons and chickens! Rustic fence separates wildlife pond and vegetable plot. Wood chip paths in woodland area may require assistance.

20 FEERINGBURY MANOR

Coggeshall Road, Feering, Colchester CO5 9RB. Mr & Mrs Giles Coode-Adams, 01376 561946, seca@btinternet.com. *12m SW of Colchester. Between Coggeshall & Feering on Coggeshall Rd, 1m from Feering village.* **Adm £5, chd free (share to Firstsite).** Every Thur & Fri 4 Apr to 26 July; 5 Sept to 27 Sept (10-4). **Visitors also welcome by appt.**

There is always plenty to see in this 10 acre garden leading down to the R Blackwater. Spectacular tulips in April and May lead on to a huge number of different and colourful plants, many unusual, culminating in a purple explosion of michaelmas daisies in Sept. A small arboretum is planted with rare trees collected on Japanese expedition with Kew Gardens. Sculpture by Ben Coode-Adams. Featured in The English Garden. No wheelchair access to arboretum, steep slope.

21 4 FERNLEA ROAD

Burnham-on-Crouch CM0 8EJ. Frances & Andrew Franklin, www.franklins.f2s.com. *On the edge of Millfields Country Park, Burnham-on-Crouch. Take B1010 to Burnham-on-Crouch. Cross the railway bridge then take 4th turn on R, Hillside Rd. Fernlea Rd 2nd L, no.4 nr end of cul de sac on L.* Home-made teas. Wine and nibbles on board Mulberry Houseboat. **Adm £5, chd free.** Sun 23, Sat 29 June (2-7). **Combined with Mulberry Houseboat.**

Mediterranean/Moroccan oasis on edge of riverside park. Small (50ft x 50ft) back garden with vine-covered pergola, tranquil water features, mosaics, sculptures, dense planting featuring some unusual varieties. Climate-tolerant, low maintenance and with various seating areas incl a Moroccan style tent! This garden is for relaxing in. Opening coincides with Burnham Art Trail www.burnhamarttrail.co.uk. Various publications and books, incl Dream Gardens of England: 100 Inspirational Gardens and Gardening in a Changing Climate.

22 56 FOREST DRIVE

Theydon Bois CM16 7EZ. John & Barbara, 01992 814459, john.vale@live.co.uk. *2m S of Epping. J26 M25 onto A121 to Wake Arms r'about. 2nd exit B172 to Theydon Bois. Turn L at Bull PH, 1st L into Forest Drive. In the centre of the village of Theydon Bois and only a 5min walk from the underground station.* Self service cream teas in summerhouse. **Adm £3, chd free.** Sun 16 June, Sun 21 July (12-6). **Also open 37 Turpins Lane. Visitors also welcome by appt June to July, viewing after noon.**

Elegant, tranquil garden set on a sloping site, developed by us since 1996, featuring specimen trees and plants. Shaded seating areas in this surprisingly secluded natural garden allow visitors to sit and watch the birds and admire Gladys in her reflective pool. 2nd place in The Garden News' Gardener of the Year, container category.

23 NEW FOUNTAIN FARM

Wick Lane, Ardleigh, Colchester CO7 7RG. Mr & Mrs C P Tootal. *4m NE of Colchester. At A12/A120 junction (Crown R'about) take exit towards Harwich/Clacton and immediately turn L following signs to 'Gnome Magic'. Past Crown PH, Wick Ln next turning R, house 1m on L. From Colchester take A137 towards Manningtree, bear L after Wooden Fender PH, then L at X-roads, house is 1st on R over causeway.* Home-made teas. **Adm £3.50, chd free.** Sun 9 June (2-5.30).

5 acres on the bank of Ardleigh Reservoir, surrounding listed farmhouse and 2 Essex barns (one listed). The garden has evolved over 40 yrs and is divided into small 'rooms' arising from the old farmyards. Two 10-yr-old areas of wildflowers, vegetable garden and more formal area of grass from the front of the house down to the reservoir. Trees and shrubs, many planted soon after our arrival in 1971. Gravel drive but access possible.

24 FUDLERS HALL
Fox Road, Mashbury, Chelmsford CM1 4TJ. Mr & Mrs A J Meacock. *7m NW of Chelmsford. From Chelmsford A1114, R into Chignal Rd, ½ m L towards Chignal St James (Tin Chapel on corner) approx 5m 2nd turning R into Fox Rd signed Gt Waltham - 2nd house on L. Alternatively from Gt Waltham take Barrack Lane opp church- house 2½ m on R.* **Adm £4, chd free.** **Suns 7 July; 4 Aug (2-6). Also open Little Myles 7 July, 45 Waterhouse Lane 4 Aug.**
An award winning, romantic 2 acre garden surrounding C17 farmhouse with lovely pastoral views. Old walls divide garden into many rooms, each having a different character, featuring long herbaceous borders, ropes and pergolas festooned with rambling old fashioned roses. Enjoy the vibrant hot border in late summer. Yew hedged kitchen garden. Ample seating.

25 FURZELEA
Bicknacre Road, Danbury CM3 4JR. Avril & Roger Cole-Jones, 01245 225726, randacj@gmail.com. *4m E of Chelmsford, 4m W of Maldon. A414 to Danbury. In village centre (Eves Corner) turn S into Mayes Lane. Take first R, go past Cricketers PH, then L onto Bicknacre Rd. Parking in NT car park on L. Garden further along on R.* Home-made teas. **Adm £3.50, chd free.** **Wed 24 Apr, Sun 2 June, Wed 11 Sept (11-5). Visitors also welcome by appt Apr to Sept, adm £5.50 incl tea and cake.**
A country garden planted for scent and colour in ⅔ acre. Sumptuous mixed borders overflowing with bulbs, perennials, and old-fashioned roses. Archways clad in climbers, roses, and clematis, chamomile steps to lily pond, black and white garden, courtyard with tropical and tender plants. Many unusual plants. Opp Danbury Common (NT), short walk to Danbury Country Park and Lakes and short drive to RHS Hyde Hall. Featured in Essex Life. Limited wheelchair access, some steps and gravel paths.

20 GOLDHAZE CLOSE
See London

GREAT THURLOW HALL
See Suffolk

17 GREENSTONE MEWS, E11
See London

26 HANNAMS HALL
Thorpe Road, Tendring CO16 9AR. Mr & Mrs W Gibbon, 01255 830292, w.gibbon331@btinternet.com. *10m E of Colchester. From A120 take B1035 at Horsley Cross, through Tendring Village (approx 3m) pass Cherry Tree PH on R, after ⅓ m over small bridge 1st house L.* **Adm £3.50, chd free.** **Sat 18, Sun 19 May (2-6). Visitors also welcome by appt Mar to Dec. Spring bulbs and autumn colour.**
C17 house (not open) set in 6 acres of formal and informal gardens and grounds with extensive views over open countryside. Herbaceous borders and shrubberies, many interesting trees incl flowering paulownias. Lawns and mown walks through wild grass and flower meadows, woodland walks, ponds and stream. Walled vegetable potager and orchard. Lovely autumn colour for visitors by appt.

Sweeping lawns to wild woodland . . . a timeless garden . . . wonderful bird life . . .

27 ◆ HEDINGHAM CASTLE
Bayley Street, Castle Hedingham, Halstead CO9 3DJ. Mr & Mrs Lindsay, 01787 460261, www.hedinghamcastle.co.uk. *Centrally located within the East Anglian region. From M11 take exit 8 (A120 Colchester) to Braintree bypass and follow the castle signs. On the edge of the village of Castle Hedingham, within the castle grounds.* **Adm £6.50, chd £4, concessions £4.90.** **For NGS: Tue 12 Feb, Sun 2 June (11-3). For other opening times and information, please phone or see garden website.**
Walk around the C18 formal parkland landscape, with stunning mature lime trees, a huge sweet chestnut tree, all surrounding the lake, with dovecote, bog pond and formal pond, set amongst C12 ramparts, dominated by the spectacular Norman keep. Carpets of snowdrops in Feb and young rhododendrons in May. Keep interior can only be accessed by ancient, uneven steps but the keep itself can be viewed from level ground.

28 HOBBANS FARM
Stoney Lane, Bobbingworth, Ongar CM5 0LZ. John & Anne Webster, 01277 890245. *10m W of Chelmsford. N of A414 between Ongar Four Wantz r'about & N Weald 'Talbot' r'about, turn R past Blake Hall. 1st farm entrance on R after St Germain's Church.* Cream teas. **Adm £3.50, chd free.** **Suns 5, 19 May; 2, 16, 30 June; 14 July; 1, 15 Sept (2-5). Visitors also welcome by appt Apr to Sept. Tea/coffee, biscuits and cake.**
From the beautiful blossoms of May to the riot of roses in June and July and the glowing colours of September, there is much to see and surprise in this romantic garden. Bees, butterflies, wonderful scents. Plenty of places to sit. Come and explore, linger awhile, and enjoy a delicious cream tea. Some narrow paths.

29 NEW HORKESLEY HALL
Little Horkesley, Colchester CO6 4DB. Mr & Mrs Johnny Eddis, 01206 271371, pollyeddis@hotmail.com. *3m N of Colchester. W of A134. Access is via church car park.* Home-made teas. **Adm £4, chd free.** **Fri 19 Apr, Thur 11 July (11-5.30). Visitors also welcome by appt Apr to Oct, adm £6 incl refreshments.**
8 acres of romantic garden surrounding classical house (not open) in mature parkland setting. Stream feeds 2 lakes. Wonderful trees some very rare. Largest ginkgo tree outside Kew. Walled garden, pear avenue, acer walk. Blossom, bluebells and spring bulbs, topiary. Formal terrace overlooking sweeping lawns to wild woodland. A timeless garden. Wonderful bird life, vast plane trees and stunning tree barks. Ponies, mare and foal. Limited wheelchair access, gravel paths and slopes.

30 JULIE'S GARDEN
163 Whitmore Avenue, Stifford Clays, Grays RM16 2HT. Julie Sadgrove & Harry Edwards, 01375 377780, juliesadgrove@hotmail.co.uk. *2m E of Lakeside shopping centre. Exit A13 at Grays, take Orsett turn off r'about, follow Stifford Clays Rd for a few hundred metres, turn R into Kingsman Drive, then L into Prince Phillip Ave. At T-junction L into Whitmore Ave. 100 metres on L.* Home-made teas. **Adm £3, chd free.** **Sun 16 June (12-4). Visitors also welcome by appt July.**
Now for something different. Quirky, unusual small garden (100ft x 30ft) where art and plants combine to bring colour, life and interest. A personal constantly-evolving space which reflects the owners' numerous, varied interests and talents, made using recycled resources. A surprise around every corner, incl African, Australian, Indian and beach artefacts and themes.

31 NEW KINGSTEPS
Moor Hall Lane, Danbury, Chelmsford CM3 4ER. Mr David Greenwood. *5m E of Chelmsford. S of Danbury in Bicknacre. A414 to Danbury to Eves Corner, Turn S into Mayes Lane. At T-junction. L towards Bicknacre approx ½ m past common. Turn R by post box. ¼ m on LH-side. Parking in rd opp. Disabled parking on drive.* Home-made teas. **Adm £3, chd free. Thurs 18 July; 29 Aug (1-5). Also open Elwy Lodge 18 July.**
Country garden in ½ acre plot. Gardens front and rear with good selection of herbaceous plants and shrubs, roses, fuchsias, dahlias, begonias, bedding plants, tubs and hanging baskets. Fish pond with Koi carp and others. Well kept lawns and plenty of colour, especially late summer. Large horse chestnut tree in rear. Many seating areas.

42 LATIMER ROAD, E7
See London

32 THE LEMBIC
Hallwood Crescent, Shenfield, Brentwood CM15 9AA. Charmaine & Fred Cox. *½ m NE of Brentwood. From London take A12 then A1023 through Brentwood. Take 3rd L after crossing A128. From Chelmsford take A12 then A1023, continue through T-lights and take 2nd R.* Home-made teas. **Adm £3, chd free. Suns 26 May; 2 June; 20 Oct (2-5).**
½ acre garden in quiet cul-de-sac. Fully grown forest trees and mature shrubs featuring rhododendron, azalea and acer. Perennial border and interesting walkways between shrubs. Large sculpture incorporating an analemma and garden seats designed for contemplation while enjoying your tea and home-made cake. Wheelchair access, main garden accessible.

A surprise around every corner, including African, Australian, Indian and beach artefacts and themes . . .

33 THE LIMES
The Tye, East Hanningfield CM3 8AA. Stan & Gil Gordon. *6m SE of Chelmsford. In centre of East Hanningfield across village green from The Windmill PH.* Home-made teas. **Adm £3.50, chd free. Evening Opening wine, Fri 31 May (6-9); Sat 1 June (2-6).**
Plant lovers' 1-acre well-established 'garden of many rooms' surrounding Victorian house (not open). Owner-designed to lure you round this tranquil garden with its mature trees, interesting planting of shrubs, perennials, grasses, roses and clematis. Also orchard, soft fruit and vegetable area, formal garden and courtyard pots. Lots to enjoy, several seats and easy parking nearby. Approx 1m from RHS garden Hyde Hall. Gravel drive and grass paths.

34 LITTLE FOXES
Marcus Gardens, Thorpe Bay, Southend-on-Sea SS1 3LF. Mrs Dorothy Goode. *2½ m E of Southend. From Thorpe Bay Stn (S-side) proceed E, take 4th on R into Marcus Ave then 2nd L into Marcus Gdns.* Home-made teas. **Adm £3, chd free. Sat 17, Sun 18 Aug (2-5).**
A ⅓ -acre garden offering relaxing afternoon in beautiful surroundings. Island beds packed with flowers and foliage. 400ft of herbaceous and shrub borders. Ornamental trees and conifers provide seclusion. Salvias, agapanthus, dahlias, alstromerias and rarely seen burgundy eucomis. Pretty water feature and containers incl 25 hostas. A seaside stroll is only minutes away. Featured on BBC Essex Radio.

35 LITTLE MYLES
Ongar Road, Stondon Massey, nr Brentwood CM15 0LD. Judy & Adrian Cowan. *1½ m SE of Chipping Ongar. Turn off A128 at Stag PH, Marden Ash, (Ongar) towards Stondon Massey. Over bridge, 1st house on R after S bend. (400yds the Ongar side of Stondon Massey Church).* Home-made teas. **Adm £3.50, chd £1. Sun 7 July (11-4). Also open Fudlers Hall.**
Romantic garden surrounded by wild flowers and grasses, set in 3 acres. Full borders, hidden features, meandering paths, pond, hornbeam pergola and fountains. Herb garden, full of nectar-rich and scented herbs, used for handmade herbal cosmetics. Asian garden with pots, statues and bamboo, ornamental vegetable patch, woven willow Gothic window feature and wire elephant. Crafts and handmade herbal cosmetics for sale. Gravel paths.

LONG MELFORD GROUP
See Suffolk

CONDUIT HOUSE
See Suffolk

SUN HOUSE
See Suffolk

36 447 MAIN ROAD
Harwich CO12 4HB. J Shrive & S McGarry. *1m out of Dovercourt town centre. Follow A120 from Colchester to Harwich. Straight over Churchill r'about at Ramsey onto bypass. Turn R at next r'about up Parkeston Hill, turn R at mini r'about. 300yds on LH-side.* Home-made teas. **Adm £3, chd free. Sat 3 Aug (11-5); Sun 4 Aug (11-3).**
Family town garden with interest for young and old alike, colourful perennial borders with immaculate lawn leading to a tropical oasis complete with Treasure Island. Cannas, bamboo and specimen

palms abound lending dramatic height and structure. The decked dining area encompasses a huge stand of banana amidst which nestles a water feature.

37 ◆ MARKS HALL GARDENS & ARBORETUM

Coggeshall CO6 1TG. Marks Hall Estate, 01376 563796, www.markshall.org.uk. *1½ m N of Coggeshall. Follow brown & white tourism signs from A120 Coggeshall bypass.* **Adm £4.50, chd £1.50, concessions £4. For opening times and information, please phone or see garden website.**

The walled garden is a unique blend of traditional long borders within C17 walls and 5 contemporary gardens. Inventive landscaping, grass sculpture and stunningly colourful mass plantings. On opp lake bank is millennium walk designed for winter shape, scent and colour surrounded by over 100 acres of arboretum, incl species from all continents. New bridge across the brook making central area usable whatever the weather, from snowdrops to autumn colour. Hard paths now lead to all key areas of interest.

MICHAELS FOLLY

See Hertfordshire

38 60 MILL LANE

Tye Green, Cressing CM77 8HW. Pauline & Arthur Childs, 01376 325904. *2m S of Braintree. 15m W of Colchester, 5m N of Witham. From M11 J8 take A120 Colchester, follow A120 to Braintree r'about, then take B1018 to Witham approx ¾ m (Tye Green), turn R into Mill Lane 400yds. From Witham follow the Braintree sign.* Home-made teas. **Adm £2.50, chd free. Sun 7 July; 11 Aug (2-5). Visitors also welcome by appt June to Aug. Tea and cake.**

A hidden little gem. Plantaholic's paradise packed with interesting flowers and ferns. Very colourful garden with hostas, penstemons, fuchsias and clematis in profusion, some rather unusual. 3 water features add a sense of calm. Relax on patio with delicious home-made cakes while admiring our beautiful containers, topiary and hanging baskets. Cressing Temple Barns nearby. Featured in Colchester Daily Gazette.

39 NEW THE MILLERS COTTAGE

Pig Lane, Bishop's Stortford CM22 7PA. Mandy & Marcus Scarlett. *1m S of Bishop's Stortford. Leave Bishop's Stortford on the A1060 towards Hallingbury, after approx 1m turn R into Pig Lane. The Miller's Cottage is the first track on the L - after about 300yds. Car Parking available.* Home-made teas. **Adm £4, chd free. Sat 15, Sun 16 June (11-4).**

Essentially a romantic cottage garden with hundreds of roses that - like Topsy - just growed. Now nearly four acres the garden embraces many themes from the woodland brook side walk, through formal parterre and kitchen gardens, an architectural pool garden to the wide vistas of the open fields. Most of all it is a garden in development with much still to do. Some steps but largely accessible by wheelchair.

Essentially a romantic cottage garden with hundreds of roses that - like Topsy - just growed . . .

40 MIRAFLORES

5 Rowan Way, Witham CM8 2LJ. Yvonne & Danny Owen, 01376 515187, danny@dannyowen.co.uk. *A12 S-bound J22 to town centre. At George PH turn R onto Braintree Rd B1018. Just past Morrisons Store, over railway bridge, turn R at 1st mini r'about into Cypress Rd. Bear L into Forest Rd. Access via Forest Rd Community Centre car park CM8 2PF. Enter garden through rear gate. Any problems on arrival please call.* Home-made teas. **Adm £3, chd free. Suns 2, 16, 23, 30 June (11-5). Combined with Barnardiston House, adm £5, 16, 23 June. Also open 352 Coggeshall Road 16, 30 June. Visitors also welcome by appt May to June, min 15 for groups.**

An award-winning, medium-sized garden described by one visitor as a 'little bit of heaven'. A blaze of colour with roses and clematis. Triple fountain with crystal clear water attracts many birds. Clematis and poppies galore. Tranquil seating areas. Exuberant, cascading hanging baskets, as featured in Garden Answers. Gentle background music. Camera enthusiasts welcome. Owner is a professional who can advise on flower photography, especially macro.

41 NEW MONKS COTTAGE

Monks Lane, Dedham, Colchester CO7 6DP. Nicola Baker, 01206 322210, nicola_baker@tiscali.co.uk. *6m NE of Colchester. Leave A12 from Ipswich at Dedham exit. Follow rd into Dedham turn R at T-junction. Follow rd out of village, take 2nd turning on R (post box on corner). After ¾ m turn L into Monks Lane (no-through road). Monks Cottage is 3rd house down. From the Colchester/ Chelmsford, exit A12 at Dedham/ Stratford St Mary turning. After ½ m take 1st R, ¾ m turn R into Monks Lane.* Home-made teas. **Adm £3.50, chd free. Tues 7 May; 2 July (11-5). Visitors and small groups also welcome by appt May to July.**

½ acre cottage garden on sloping site in the heart of Constable country. Colour-themed borders filled with shrubs and perennials. Mature trees and pond. Highlights include roses, clematis and box-edged beds filled with tulips. Features boggy area with strong foliage shapes and mini meadow. Gin-and-tonic balcony with views of the garden.

42 MOVERONS

Brightlingsea CO7 0SB. Lesley Orrock & Payne Gunfield, 01206 305498, lesleyorrock@me.com, www.moverons.co.uk. *7m SE of Colchester. B1027. Turn R in Thorrington onto B1029 signed Brightlingsea. At old church turn R signed Moverons Farm, follow lane & garden signs for approx 1m. Beware some sat navs take you the wrong side of the river.* Home-made teas. **Adm £4, chd free. Sat 25, Sun 26 May, Sun 8 Sept (11-5). Visitors also welcome by appt May to Sept.**

Beautiful, peaceful 4 acre country

"Lemon drizzle cake, Victoria sponge ... yummy!"

garden with stunning estuary views. A wide variety of planting to suit different growing conditions including a small courtyard, reflection pool garden, mixed borders, dry stream and large natural ponds. Magnificent mature native trees give this garden real presence. A growing collection of metal sculptures and practical metalwork.

43 NEW MULBERRY HOUSE BOAT

West Quay, Burnham-On-Crouch CM0 8AS. David & Melanie Lewin, mulberry1@fastmail.fm. *Take B1010 to Burham-on-Crouch. Cross the railway bridge and take 5th turning on R by library, follow signs to public car park and walk to the quay. House boat on R moored by the playing fields*. Wine. Teas at 4 Fernlea Road. **Adm £5, chd free.** Sun 23, Sat 29 June (2-7). **Combined with 4 Fernlea Road, an easy and pleasant 5 min walk across the playing fields.**

This houseboat overlooking the R Crouch is bedecked with a plethora of vegetation, both decorative and edible. Facing west you will find packed to the gunnels an assortment of flowers and shrubs mingling with the chains and ropes. To the east, hard landscaping is softened by a large vegetable trough. There is a sitting area looking out over the water surrounded by more shrubs and vegetables. Additional 'pop up' openings when weather and state of the tide permit. Please see NGS website or email for information. Featured in Essex Chronicle and Burnham and Dengie Review, Burnham in Bloom prize winner. Maritime environment; appropriate shoes and care needed, not suitable for young children or people with walking difficulties.

OLD FELIXSTOWE GARDENS
See Suffolk

44 THE OLD RECTORY

Church Road, Boreham CM3 3EP. Sir Jeffery & Lady Bowman, 01245 467233, bowmansuzy@btinternet.com. *4m NE of Chelmsford. Take B1137 Boreham Village, turn into Church Rd at the Lion PH. ½ m along on R opp church*. Home-made teas. **Adm £4, chd free.** Sat 16, Sun 17 Feb (12-3); Sun 26 May (2-5). **Visitors also welcome by appt Feb to June. Evening visits with wine possible.**

2½ -acre garden surrounding C15 house (not open). Ponds, stream, with bridges and primulas, small wildflower meadow and wood with interesting trees and shrubs, herbaceous borders with emphasis on complementary colours. Vegetable garden. February opening for crocus, snowdrops and cyclamen. Possibly largest gunnera in Essex. Lovely views over Chelmer/Blackwater canal. Featured in Country Homes and Interiors. Gravel drive but large part of garden accessible.

Fudlers Hall

45 OLIVERS

Olivers Lane, Colchester CO2 0HJ. Mrs G Edwards, 01206 330575, gay.edwards@virgin.net. *3m SW of Colchester. Between B1022 & B1026. From zoo continue 1m towards Colchester. Turn R at r'about (Cunobelin Way) & R into Olivers Lane. From Colchester via Maldon Rd turn L at r'about, R into Olivers Lane.* **Adm £5, chd free.** Visitors welcome by appt**, guided tours & refreshments provided for groups of 15+.**

Four acres of peaceful south-sloping garden. Yew backed borders and beds have dense to overflowing plantings for all seasons. Teas on the terrace of mellow red brick C18 house (not open) overlooking lawn, meadow and water. Bridges cross to woodland with fine trees, underplanted with rhododendrons, with paths through a mass of spring bulbs and bluebells. Featured in Country Life and Gardens Illustrated. Electric buggy available.

46 ONE BROOK HALL COTTAGES

Steeple Road, Latchingdon CM3 6LB. John & Corinne Layton, 01621 741680, corinne@arrow250.fsnet.co.uk. *1m from Latchingdon Church. From Maldon drive through Latchingdon to mini r'about at church taking exit towards Steeple & Bradwell. Approx 1m turn R at bungalow onto gravel drive*. Home-made teas, light refreshments & home-made soup. **Adm £3.50.** Thurs 16 May; 15 Aug (11-5). **Visitors also welcome by appt July to Aug.**

Uniquely designed terraced garden on 3 levels planted with a wide range of perennials in a naturalistic style to encourage wildlife. The garden rises up from the back of the house to a large deck with boardwalk leading to a 'natural' pond. Lawn edged with pleached limes and box hedges. Narrow paths and steep steps not suitable for children and visitors with walking difficulties. Footpath walk to R Blackwater. Featured in Woman and Home & Essex Life magazines.

47 ORCHARD COTTAGE

219 Hockley Road, Rayleigh SS6 8BH. Heather & Harry Brickwood, 01268 743838, henry.brickwood@homecall.co.uk. *1m NE from Rayleigh town centre. Leave A127 at Rayleigh Weir and take B1013 towards Rayleigh. Pass through Rayleigh and proceed towards Hockley. Please park opp on grass verge.* Home-made teas. **Adm £4, chd free.** Visitors welcome by appt **May to Aug.**

Award winning 3/4 -acre garden. Central bed in the front is a mass of colour; June's main feature will be the 500+ aquilegias, backed up by roses, lilies and numerous other herbaceous perennials; July will see exuberant lilies, hemerocallis, agapanthus and rudbeckia. There is a pond, stream and many flowering shrubs.

48 PARSONAGE HOUSE

Wiggens Green, Helions Bumpstead, Haverhill CB9 7AD. The Hon & Mrs Nigel Turner. *3m S of Haverhill. 8m NE of Saffron Walden. From Xrds in village centre turn up Church Hill, follow rd for 1m. Park in orchards opp. 3m from Haverhill follow signs 'To Village Only' from by-pass. After approx 2½ m garden is on R. Parking on L 200yds on in orchards.* Home-made teas. **Adm £3.50, chd free.** Suns 12 May; 16 June; 28 July (2-5).

C15 house (not open) surrounded by 3 acres of formal gardens with mixed borders, topiary, pond, potager and greenhouse. Further 3-acre wild flower meadow with rare trees and further 3 acre orchard of old East Anglian apple varieties. Featured in Country Life, The English Garden and Hortus magazines. Gravel drive and small step into WC.

49 PEACOCKS

Roman Road, Margaretting CM4 9HY. Phil Torr, 07802 472382, phil.torr@btinternet.com. *50 yards from Margaretting Village Centre. Situated on the B1002 near Margaretting Xroads (towards Ingatestone). From A12 N bound take Margaretting exit and turn R at top of slip rd. From S bound A12 follow signs for Margaretting/Ingatestone.* Light refreshments. **Adm £4, chd free (share to St Francis Hospice).** Thur 11 Apr (2-5); Sun 16 June (2-6). **Visitors also welcome by appt Apr to June. Adm £6 incl refreshments.**

5-acre natural garden surrounding regency house with mature native and specimen trees. Restored horticultural buildings. Formal walled garden (2nd under construction), long herbaceous/mixed border. Restored temple and 'wildlife lake'. Woodland walk and orchard/flower meadow.

50 PEPPERS FARM

Forry Green, Sible Hedingham, Halstead CO9 3RP. Mrs Pam Turtle. *1m SW of Sible Hedingham. From Braintree after Gosfield L for Southey Gn - L for Forry Gn. From N for Sible Hedingham R at Sugar Loaves PH, Rectory Rd L at White Horse (past school) until Forry Gn.* Home-made teas. **Adm £3.50, chd free.** Suns 9, 16 June (2-5). **Combined adm £6.50 with Washlands, 16 June. Also open Spencers.**

½ acre country garden set high on quiet rural green with farmland views. Hedges divide informal borders featuring flowering shrubs, fruit and specimen trees, many grown from seed. Beautiful alpine scree and sinks overlook spring fed pond. Garden owner has been a 'seedaholic' since small enough to seek fairies in tulips. Partial wheelchair access, large pond with steep sides. Some gravel.

THE PRIORY
See Suffolk

RAVENSCROFT
See Suffolk

51 REPRISE

5 Mornington Crescent, Hadleigh, Benfleet SS7 2HW. David & Rosemary King, 01702 557632, david.rosie@talktalk.net. *5m W of Southend-on-Sea. A13 E, through Hadleigh town, farmland on R. Woodfield Rd on L, signed St Barnabas Church/ Nature Reserve. A13 W, pass Hadleigh boundary sign then 2nd R Woodfield Rd. In Woodfield Rd take 3rd L to Chandos Parade, re becomes Mornington Crescent. Garden on R near end of crescent.* Home-made teas. **Adm £3, chd free.** Suns 16 June; 14 July; 4 Aug (2-5). **Also open Court View 16 June, 14 July. Visitors also welcome by appt June to Aug, private viewings, adm £6 incl cream teas.**

A 250 sq-metre garden, created over 5yrs. Patio, with flower-filled containers, gives garden views. The gravel path winds through colourful perennials to a secluded seating area beneath an apple tree and climbers. Beyond the lawn is a pond, backed by shrubs and trees. Vegetable plot and greenhouse tucked away completes the scene.

Garden owner has been a 'seedaholic' since small enough to seek fairies in tulips . . .

52 ROOKWOODS

Yeldham Road, Sible Hedingham CO9 3QG. Peter & Sandra Robinson, 01787 460224, sandy1989@btinternet.com. *8m NW of Halstead. Sible Hedingham on A1017 between Braintree & Haverhill. From Haverhill, on entering Sible Hedingham take 1st R almost immed after 30mph sign, turn L by gate lodge through white gates.* Home-made teas. **Adm £3.50, chd free.** Sun 2 June (11-4.30). **Visitors also welcome by appt May to Sept.**

Tranquil garden with mature and young trees and shrubs. Simple herbaceous borders with columns of tumbling roses. Pleached hornbeam leading to wild flower bed all being warmed by Victorian red brick wall enhanced with clematis and vitis coignetiae. Wander through meadow of buttercups to ancient oak wood. Enjoy tea relaxing under dreamy wisteria. Beehive with glass lid available to those who would like to take a peep at the busy honey bee. Gravel drive.

ROSEDALE
See Suffolk

ROSEMARY
See Suffolk

53 69 RUNDELLS
Harlow CM18 7HD. Mr & Mrs K Naunton, 01279 303471, nauntonkeith@gmail.com. *Harlow. 1m from J7 M11 & A414. From M11 J7 take A414 Harlow at r'about 1st exit Southern Way, at 2nd mini r'about L Trotters Rd over 2 speed humps, follow rd round bend 2nd L into Rundells. past R turn to Latton Green School/Hillyfield. Garden is situated at top of path ahead as the rd bears to the L.* Home-made teas. **Adm £2.50, chd free. Sat 13 July (2-5). Visitors also welcome by appt July to Sept. Please give plenty of notice.**
As featured on Alan Tichmarsh's 'Love Your Garden' programme (entitled the 'Secret Garden') 69 Rundells is a vibrant, colourful, small town garden packed with a wide variety of shrubs, perennials, herbaceous and bedding plants in over 200 assorted containers. Hard landscaping on different levels incls summer house, various seating areas and water features. Steep steps Access to adjacent allotment, open to view. Honey and other produce for sale (conditions permitting). Full size hot tub/jacuzzi.

54 ST HELENS
High Street, Stebbing CM6 3SE. Stephen & Joan Bazlinton, 01371 856495, revbaz@care4free.net. *3m E of Great Dunmow. Leave Gt Dunmow on B1256. Take 1st L to Stebbing, at T-junction turn L into High St, garden 2nd house on R.* Home-made teas. **Adm £3.50, chd free (share to Dentaid). Sats 25 May; 15 June; 24 Aug (11-5). Visitors also welcome by appt.**
A garden of contrasts due to moist and dry conditions, laid out on a gentle Essex slope from a former willow plantation. These contours give rise to changing vistas and unanticipated areas of seclusion framed with hedging and generous planting. Walkways and paths alongside natural springs and still waters. Limited wheelchair access. Featured in Amateur Gardening.

87 ST JOHNS ROAD, E17
See London

55 SHRUBS FARM
Lamarsh, Bures CO8 5EA. Mr & Mrs Robert Erith, 01787 227520, bob@shrubsfarm.co.uk, www.shrubsfarm.co.uk. *1¼ m from Bures. On rd to Lamarsh, the drive is signed to Shrubs Farm.* Home-made teas. Barn closed for thatching until September 2013. Refreshments in garden or conservatory by agreement with tour leader. **Adm £5, chd free. Visitors welcome by appt Apr to Oct.**
2 acres with shrub borders, lawns, roses and trees. 50 acres parkland and meadow with wild flower paths and woodland trails. Over 60 species of oak. Superb 10m views over Stour valley. Ancient coppice and pollards incl largest goat (pussy) willow (*Salix caprea*) in England. Wollemi and Norfolk pines, and banana trees. Full size black rhinoceros. Display of Bronze age burial urns. Guided Tour. Some ground maybe boggy in wet weather.

56 SNARES HILL COTTAGE
Duck End, Stebbing CM6 3RY. Pete & Liz Stabler, 01371 856565, lizstabler@hotmail.com. *Between Dunmow & Bardfield. 1½ m past Stebbing turning past B&T auto salvage yard on B1057.* Home-made teas. **Adm £4, chd free. Sun 12 May (11-4). Visitors also welcome by appt Apr to Sept.**
A 'quintessential English Garden' - Gardeners World. Our quirky 1½ acre garden has surprises round every corner and many interesting sculptures. A natural swimming pool is bordered by romantic flower beds, herb garden and Victorian folly. A bog garden borders woods and leads to silver birch copse, beach garden and 'Roman' temple.

57 SOUTH SHOEBURY HALL
Church Road, Shoeburyness SS3 9DN. Mr & Mrs M Dedman. *4m E of Southend-on-Sea. Enter Southend on A127 to Eastern Ave A1159 signed Shoebury. R at r'about to join A13. Proceed S to Ness Rd. R into Church Rd. Garden on L 50 metres.* Home-made teas. **Adm £3.50, chd free. Suns 14 Apr; 14 July (2-5). Also open 102 Barnstaple Road 14 April, Court View and Reprise 14 July.**
Delightful, 1-acre established walled garden surrounding Grade II listed house (not open) and bee house. New agapanthus and hydrangea beds. April is ablaze with 3000 tulips and fritillaria. July shows 120+ varieties of agapanthus. Unusual trees, shrubs, rose borders, with 40yr old plus geraniums, Mediterranean and Southern Hemisphere planting in dry garden. St Andrews Church open to visitors. Garden close to sea.

SOUTHLEIGH
See Suffolk

Mirrors are used to create illusion of depth and to allow a view of summerhouse roof. 'Secret garden' is designed as a tranquil area for contemplation . . .

58 NEW SOUTHVIEW
11 Palmers Avenue, Grays RM17 5TX. Mrs Juliana Baker, 01375 375881, juliebaker28@googlemail.com. *½ m E of Grays Town Centre. Follow Orsett Rd E which runs into Palmers Ave (A1013). Or from Lodge Ln (A1013) follow Southend Rd into Palmers Ave. Both options can be accessed from Grays exit from the A13.* Home-made teas. **Adm £3, chd free. Suns 30 June; 28 July; 4 Aug (12-4.30). Visitors also welcome by appt July to Sept.**
A delightful traditionally designed town garden, with a cottage style front garden. Side access with pots at different levels, our take on vertical gardening! Patio and plenty of seating. Lawn surrounded with densely planted borders. Beyond the pond is a secret garden and the summerhouse with a 'living roof'. Mirrors are used to create illusion of depth and to allow a view of summerhouse roof. 'Secret garden' is designed as a tranquil area for contemplation. Wheelchair access does not incl 'secret garden'.

Tudor Roost

59 ◆ SPENCERS
Tilbury Road, Great Yeldham CO9 4JG. Mr & Mrs Colin Bogie, 01787 238175, www.spencersgarden.net. *Just N of Gt Yeldham on Tilbury Road. Turn off A1017 in Gt Yeldham at Domesday Oak. Keep L (signed Clare, Belchamp St Paul). Pass 1st entrance to Spencers and 1/4 m later turn L at Spencers Lodge.* **Adm £5, chd free. For NGS: Suns 16 June; 15 Sept (2-5). For other opening times and information, please phone or see garden website.**
Romantic C18 walled garden laid out by Lady Anne Spencer, now overflowing with blooms following Tom Stuart-Smith's renovation. Huge tumbling wisteria, armies of Lord Butler delphiniums ('Rab' lived at Spencers 1970s-80s). Many varieties of roses, spectacular herbaceous borders, vibrant clover lawn, oldest greenhouse in Essex. Set in mature grounds with many ancient trees. Victorian woodland garden. Opens Thurs May to Oct 2-5.

4 STRADBROKE GROVE
See London

STREETLY END GARDENS
See Cambridgeshire

TATTINGSTONE PLACE
See Suffolk

60 TUDOR ROOST
18 Frere Way, Fingringhoe, Colchester CO5 7BP. Chris & Linda Pegden, 01206 729831, pegdenc@gmail.com. *5m S of Colchester. In centre of village by Whalebone PH, follow sign to Ballast Quay, after 1/2 m turn R into Brook Hall Rd, then 1st L into Frere Way.* Home-made teas. **Adm £3.50, chd free. PLEASE CONFIRM OPENING DATES ON NGS WEBSITE OR TEL. Sun 31 Mar; Mon 1, Sat 20, Sun 21 Apr; Sat 27, Sun 28 July; Sun 25, Mon 26 Aug (2-5). Visitors also welcome by appt Apr to Aug. Min 10 people.**
An unexpected hidden colourful § 1/4 -acre garden. Well manicured grassy paths wind round island beds and ponds. Densely planted subtropical area with architectural and exotic plants - cannas, bananas, palms, agapanthus, agaves and tree ferns surround a colourful gazebo. Garden planted to provide yr-round colour and encourage wildlife. Many peaceful seating areas. Within 1m of Fingringhoe Wick Nature Reserve. Local pub that serves meals. Featured in Colchester Gazette and on Radio Essex.

61 37 TURPINS LANE
Chigwell, Woodford Green IG8 8AZ. Fabrice Aru & Martin Thurston, 0208 5050 739, martin.thurston@talktalk.net. *Between Woodford & Epping. Tube: Chigwell, 15 mins walk. 2m from North Circular Rd at Woodford, follow the signs for Chigwell (A113) through Woodford Bridge into Manor Rd & turn L after Essex county sign. Bus 275 from Walthamstow or Barkingside.* Light refreshments. **Adm £3, chd free. Suns 16 June; 21 July (11-6). Also open Fairwinds, 16 June; 56 Forest Drive, 16 June; 21 July. Visitors also welcome by appt May to July.**
An unexpected hidden, magical, small part-walled garden showing how much can be achieved in a small space. An oasis of calm with densely planted rich, lush foliage, tree ferns, hostas, topiary and an abundance of well maintained shrubs complemented by a small pond and 3 water features designed for yr round interest. Awarded 2nd place by Gardening News for Best Small Garden.

62 ULTING WICK
Crouchmans Farm Road, Maldon CM9 6QX. Mr & Mrs B Burrough, 01245 380216, philippa.burrough@btinternet.com, www.ultingwickgarden.co.uk. *3m NW of Maldon. Take turning to Ulting off B1019 as you exit Hatfield Peverel. Garden on R after 2m.* Tea.

Adm £5, chd free (share to All Saints Ulting Church). Suns 28 Apr (11-5); 15 Sept (2-5). Visitors also welcome by appt Apr to Oct. Coaches welcome.
Listed black barns provide backdrop for colourful, exuberant and dramatic planting in 8 acres. Thousand of tulips, herbaceous borders, pond, mature weeping willows, productive vegetable garden, late hot summer displays of dahlias, grasses and annuals. Newly planted drought tolerant wild flower meadow and front border. Woodland. Many plants propagated in-house. All Saints Ulting will be open in conjunction with the garden for talks on its history. Featured in RHS 'The Garden', Country Life and Essex Life. Some gravel around the house but main areas of interest are accessible for wheelchairs.

GROUP OPENING

63 WALTHAM ABBEY

Waltham Abbey EN9 1LG. *8m W of Epping Town. From the M25, J26 follow signs (A121) to Waltham Abbey. At T-lights by MacDonalds, turn R to r'about. Take 2nd exit off (town bypass) to the next r'about. Take 3rd exit (A112) to T-lights. Turn L into Monkswood Avenue (signs to open gardens).* Home-made teas at Silver Birches, Quendon Drive. **Combined adm £5, chd free. Suns 16 June; 8 Sept (12-6).**

39 HALFHIDES
Chris Hamer

76 MONKSWOOD AVENUE
Cathy & Dan Gallagher

SILVER BIRCHES
Linda & Frank Jewson

Historic Waltham Abbey is a market town on the edge of Epping Forest. The Abbey is purported to be last resting place of King Harold. Lee Valley Regional Park which runs alongside the leafy banks of the R Lee, incl an SSSI where visitors could see 23 different types of dragonflies. Silver Birches boasts 3 lawns on 2 levels. This surprisingly secluded garden has many mixed borders packed with early autumnal colour. Mature shrubs and trees create a short woodland walk. Crystal clear water flows through a shady area of the garden. At 39 Halfhides the garden has evolved over 45yrs. It features mixed shrubs and perennial borders on 2 levels. Waterfall linking two ponds leads to small shade garden with ferns and shade loving plants. Alpines thrive on scree and in troughs. Beautiful autumn colour. 76 Monkswood Ave is a plantswoman's garden simply designed for all yr colour. Mixed borders filled with specimen trees, shrubs and perennials incl asters, dahlias and late-flowering anemones. Wildlife pond and attractive seating areas. The White Water rafting centre built specially for the Olympics of 2012 is just a short walk away (approx 35 mins) and is open to the public.

64 WASHLANDS

Prayors Hill, Sible Hedingham, Halstead CO9 3LE. Tony & Sarah Frost. *$^1/_4$ m NW of Sible Hedingham Church. At Sugar Loaves PH on A1017 turn SW into Rectory Rd, R at White Horse PH, pass St Peters Church on RH-side, $^1/_4$ m NW on Prayors Hill.* Home-made teas. **Adm £3.50, chd free. Suns 16, 23 June (2-5). Combined adm £6.50 with Peppers Farm, 16 June. Also open 16 June Spencers.**
Informal, tranquil garden approx 1 acre with good views over rolling countryside. Features incl a recently restored horse pond. Wide herbaceous, shrub and woodland borders incl roses and peonies. Many young and mature trees enhance the garden. A developing retirement project. Pond has steep banks. Woodland walk unsuitable for wheelchairs.

65 45 WATERHOUSE LANE

Chelmsford CM1 2TE. Peter & Julie Richmond, 01245 269277, richmond876@btinternet.com. *W side of Chelmsford between Widford & Chelmsford. Waterhouse Ln is on A1016 between Rainsford Lane & Westway. Parking in Bilton Rd opp & between 2 car showrooms. No restriction in Bilton Rd on Sundays.* Home-made teas. **Adm £3.50, chd free. Suns 28 July; 4 Aug (2-5). Evening Openings £12.50, wine, canapes, Suns 25 Aug; 1 Sept (7-9.30). Also open 24 Attwoods Close 28 July, Fudlers Hall 4 Aug. Visitors also welcome by appt June to Sept.**
A big surprise behind a busy road! Plantsman's town garden with artistic and creative ideas. Subtropical seating area with architectural and exotic plants - dry and shade areas. Display of old garden tools, spring-fed crystal clear pond and stream with ornamental fish. The evening opening will be an illuminated garden visit with wine and canapés. Numbers will be strictly limited to 30. Tickets £12.50 per head must be booked in advance (tel and email above). Featured in Amateur Gardening magazine.

Described by visitors as stunning and inspirational and 'oh those cakes' . . .

66 WEST END COTTAGE

Drury Lane, Ridgewell, nr Halstead CO9 4SL. Joy & Harry Crane, 01440 788336, crane@cutlersgreen.orangehome.co.uk. *On A1017 Ridgewell is 3m S of Haverhill or 2m N of Gt Yeldham. In village follow sign for village hall. Cottage on L a little way past hall.* **Adm £3.50, chd free. Suns 16 June; 18 Aug (11-5). Also open Spencers 16 June. Visitors also welcome by appt June to Aug (2-5).**
Pretty thatched cottage (not open) and quintessential front garden. Go through the five bar gate to a plantaholic's paradise. Approx $^1/_3$ acre, the garden is divided into areas. Woodland walk, gravel knot and alpine gardens, island beds, shrub borders, archways, fences and pergolas dripping with roses, wisteria and clematis. Described by visitors as stunning and inspirational and 'oh those cakes'. Short gravel drive.

67 WEST HANNINGFIELD HALL

Hall Lane, West Hanningfield CM2 8FN. Michael & Diana Iles, 01277 841818, iles6777@gmail.com. *5m S of Chelmsford. Leave A12 J16 onto B1007 (S), at Ship PH turn L into Ship Rd, after $^3/_4$ m turn L into Hall Ln. Or leave A130 onto A132, 1st L at r'about, 1st exit signed Rettendon & the Hanningfields. After $3^1/_2$ m turn L*

signed West Hanningfield. At Compasses PH bear R, L at bottom of hill, 2nd R into Hall Ln. Home-made teas. **Adm £3, chd free.** **Visitors welcome by appt** **May to Sept.**
Stunning large country garden surrounded by farmland originally developed over 30yrs ago on a sloping site and considerably extended, altered and restocked during last 10yrs. Lawns with large borders containing shrubs, shrub roses and wide variety of perennials. Features incl formal rose garden, 2 ponds, pergola, vegetable area and collection of young trees. Close to RHS Hyde Hall and Hanningfield Reservoir Visitor Centre. Gravel areas, 2 steep slopes.

12 WESTERN ROAD, E13
See London

68 WICKETS
Langley Upper Green CB11 4RY. Susan & Doug Copeland, 01799 550553, susan.copeland2@btinternet.com. *7m W of Saffron Walden, 10m N of Bishops Stortford. Turn W off B1383 at Newport. After 5m turn R off B1038 at Clavering, signed Langley. Drive adj to river. Upper Green 3m further on. At cricket green turn R signed Duddenhoe End. Last house on R. Park opp at village hall.* Home-made teas in village hall opp garden. **Adm £4, chd free. Sun 5 May, Sat 6 July (1-5). Visitors also welcome by appt May to July.**
Romantic country garden. Wide, informal mixed borders include camassia, shrub roses and alliums. Landscaped meadows with fine pastoral views framed by specimen trees. Large lily pond sheltered by groups of silver birch. Curvilinear design links themed planting areas. Espalier apples enclose parterre featuring sweet peas. Lots of places to sit, unwind and relax. Featured in Essex Life and on BBC Radio Essex. Gravel drive.

69 WICKHAM PLACE FARM
Station Road, Wickham Bishops, Witham CM8 3JB. Mrs J Wilson, 01621 891282, judith@wickhamplacefarm.co.uk, www.wickhamplacefarm.co.uk. *2½ m SE of Witham. Take B1018 from Witham to Maldon. After going under A12 take 3rd L (Station Rd). 1st house on L.* Teas. **Adm £4, chd free (share to Farleigh Hospice). Every Fri 26 Apr to 26 July; 6 Sept to 27 Sept (11-4). Visitors also welcome by appt Apr to Sept. Coaches and groups welcome anytime.**
14 acres for all seasons. Includes ponds, intricate knot garden and lovely woodland walks with rabbit resistant plants. The walled garden is home to climbers, shrubs, perennials and bulbs with many varieties available to buy in our nursery. Renowned for enormous wisterias in May (one over 250ft long) with further flowering in July. In September cyclamen carpet the woodland, replacing earlier bluebells. Adjacent to unique wooden trestle railway viaduct. 2013 will be our last year of regular Friday openings.

September's stronger colours and nectar-rich varieties encourage bees and butterflies . . .

WINDMILL COTTAGE
See Suffolk

70 WOOD VIEW
24 Chapel Road, Great Totham, nr Maldon CM9 8DA. Edwin Parsons & Ian Roxburgh, 07540 798135, www.woodviewgardenessex.co.uk. *5m NE of Maldon. Situated in Great Totham North. Chapel Rd is off the B1022 Maldon/Colchester Road.* Home-made teas at URC Hall (opp). **Adm £3.50, chd free. Sun 31 Mar; Tue 2 Apr; Mon 6 May; Suns 16 June; 28 July (1-5); Sun 1 Dec (3-6). Sun 1 Dec adm £6, chd £4. Visitors also welcome by appt Feb to July. Pre booked groups - adm £6 incl refreshments.**
Plantsman's contemporary garden containing unusual species. Pergolas and terraces create seating areas in this haven for wildlife. In spring, bulbs and primroses. Summer has herbaceous perennials and shrubs. Display of dahlias and grape covered walkway for autumn. 2 allotments nearby where refreshments, car parking and WC are available. Christmas illuminated evening. Please check garden owners' website for more details from 1 Nov.

71 WOODPECKERS
Mangapp Chase, Burnham-on-Crouch CM0 8QQ. Neil & Linda Holdaway, & Lilian Burton, 01621 782137, lindaholdaway@btinternet.com, www.essexgardens.co.uk. *1m N of Burnham-on-Crouch. B1010 to Burnham-on-Crouch. Just beyond town sign turn L into Green Lane. Turn L after ½ m. Garden 200yds on R.* Light refreshments, home-made soup, bread and cake available all day. **Adm £3.50, chd free. Sats 14, 21, 28 Sept (11-5). Visitors also welcome by appt Sept to Oct, adm £6 incl refreshments.**
Hedges divide and add structure to exuberant planting in this 1½ -acre country garden. Spring brings blossom in the orchard, wild flowers and drifts of bulbs, later there's summer abundance in the kitchen garden and wide densely-planted borders. September's stronger colours and nectar-rich varieties encourage foraging bees and clouds of butterflies. Featured in The English Garden and Essex Life magazines.

72 WRITTLE COLLEGE
Writtle CM1 3RR. Writtle College, www.writtle.ac.uk. *4m W of Chelmsford. On A414, nr Writtle village, clearly signed.* Light refreshments in The Garden Room (main campus) and The Lordship tea room (Lordship campus). **Adm £4, chd free. Suns 10 Feb; 16 June; 13 Oct (10-3). Sun 9 Feb 2014.**
15 acres; informal lawns with naturalised bulbs and wild flowers. Large tree collection, mixed shrubs, herbaceous borders. Landscaped gardens designed and built by students. Development of 13-acre parkland. Orchard meadow started. Landscaped glasshouses and wide range of seasonal bedding. NEW tropical 'HOT' bedding area added to quadrant garden. Herbaceous perennial borders under renovation autumn 2012 in readiness for summer colour 2013. Extended naturalised bulb areas on front campus lawns. Some gravel, however majority of areas accessible to all.

60 Colchester Road

Essex County Volunteers

County Organiser

Susan Copeland, Wickets, Langley Upper Green, Saffron Walden CB11 4RY, 01799 550553, susan.copeland2@btinternet.com

County Treasurer

Neil Holdaway, Woodpeckers, Mangapp Chase, Burnham-on-Crouch CM0 8QQ, 01621 782137, mail@neilholdaway.com

Publicity & Assistant County Organisers

Doug Copeland, Wickets, Langley Upper Green, Saffron Walden CB11 4RY, 01799 550553, dougcopeland@btinternet.com

Linda Holdaway, Woodpeckers, Mangapp Chase, Burnham-on-Crouch CM0 8QQ, 01621 782137, lindaholdaway@btinternet.com

Ray Spencer, Court View, 276 Manchester Drive, Leigh-on-Sea SS9 3ES, 01702 713221, arjeyeski@courtview.demon.co.uk

Booklet Coordinator

Doug Copeland, Wickets, Langley Upper Green, Saffron Walden CB11 4RY, 01799 550553, dougcopeland@btinternet.com

Groups and Talks Coordinator

Linda Holdaway, Woodpeckers, Mangapp Chase, Burnham-on-Crouch CM0 8QQ, 01621 782137, lindaholdaway@btinternet.com

Assistant County Organiser

Richard Steers, Court View, 276 Manchester Drive, Leigh-on-Sea SS9 3ES, 01702 713221, arjeyeski@courtview.demon.co.uk

GLOUCESTERSHIRE

(for South Gloucestershire see Somerset, Bristol Area & S Glos)

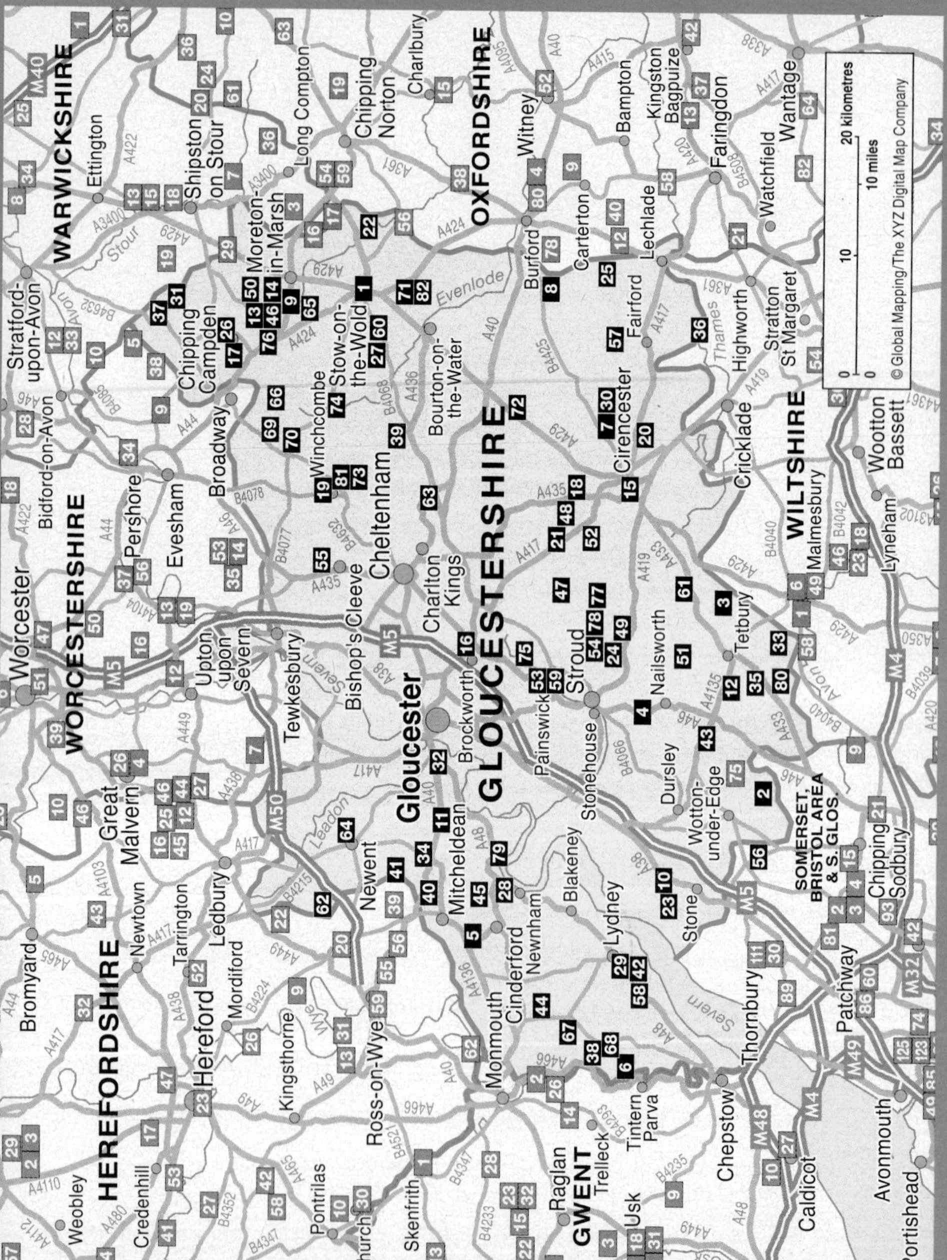

Opening Dates

January

Sunday 27
34 Home Farm
38 Lindors Country House

February

Sunday 10
34 Home Farm
36 Kempsford Manor

Monday 11
52 The Old Rectory, Duntisbourne Rous

Sunday 17
36 Kempsford Manor
75 Trench Hill

Sunday 24
23 Dr Jenner's House & Garden
75 Trench Hill

March

Sunday 3
9 Batsford Arboretum

Sunday 10
34 Home Farm

Monday 18
52 The Old Rectory, Duntisbourne Rous

Sunday 31
12 Beverston Castle
38 Lindors Country House
47 Misarden Park
75 Trench Hill

April

Monday 1
5 Aunt Martha's
12 Beverston Castle
75 Trench Hill

Sunday 7
1 Abbotswood
32 Highnam Court
50 The Old Chequer
67 South Lodge

Monday 8
37 Kiftsgate Court

Sunday 14
34 Home Farm
55 Pear Tree Cottage
71 Stone House

Sunday 21
36 Kempsford Manor
46 Mill Dene Garden
76 Upton Wold

Monday 22
52 The Old Rectory, Duntisbourne Rous

Sunday 28
18 Cerney House Gardens
20 The Coach House Garden
34 Home Farm

May

Sunday 5
24 Eastcombe, Bussage and Brownshill Gardens
32 Highnam Court
58 Ramblers
70 Stanway Fountain & Water Garden

Monday 6
5 Aunt Martha's
24 Eastcombe, Bussage and Brownshill Gardens

Wednesday 8
22 Daylesford House
42 Lydney Park Spring Garden

Sunday 12
36 Kempsford Manor
51 The Old Rectory, Avening
67 South Lodge

Wednesday 15
38 Lindors Country House

Saturday 18
19 Charingworth Court

Sunday 19
13 Blockley Gardens
19 Charingworth Court
29 Green Cottage
61 Rodmarton Manor
72 Stowell Park

Wednesday 22
41 Lower Farm House

Glimpse a graceful giraffe . . .

Saturday 25
35 Hookshouse Pottery

Sunday 26
29 Green Cottage
35 Hookshouse Pottery
44 Meadow Cottage
63 Sandywell Barn House

Monday 27
3 Ashley Grange
5 Aunt Martha's
35 Hookshouse Pottery
63 Sandywell Barn House

Tuesday 28
35 Hookshouse Pottery

Wednesday 29
35 Hookshouse Pottery
41 Lower Farm House

Thursday 30
35 Hookshouse Pottery

Friday 31
35 Hookshouse Pottery

June

Saturday 1
35 Hookshouse Pottery
40 Longhope Gardens

Sunday 2
29 Green Cottage
32 Highnam Court
35 Hookshouse Pottery
40 Longhope Gardens

Wednesday 5
17 Campden House
26 Ernest Wilson Memorial Garden
75 Trench Hill

Saturday 8
4 Atcombe Court
67 South Lodge

Sunday 9
21 Cotswold Farm
29 Green Cottage
33 Hodges Barn
63 Sandywell Barn House
74 Temple Guiting Manor
77 Waterlane Gardens

Monday 10
33 Hodges Barn

Wednesday 12
17 Campden House
21 Cotswold Farm
26 Ernest Wilson Memorial Garden
60 Rockcliffe House
75 Trench Hill

National Gardens Weekend

Saturday 15
14 Bourton House Garden
38 Lindors Country House
40 Longhope Gardens
62 Rose Cottage
75 Trench Hill
81 Winchcombe Gardens

Sunday 16
10 Berkeley Castle
15 25 Bowling Green Road
16 Brockworth Court
29 Green Cottage
36 Kempsford Manor
38 Lindors Country House
40 Longhope Gardens
43 Matara Gardens of Wellbeing
47 Misarden Park
49 Oakridge Lynch Open Gardens
58 Ramblers
62 Rose Cottage
69 Stanton Village Gardens
70 Stanway Fountain & Water Garden
72 Stowell Park
75 Trench Hill

Wednesday 19
75 Trench Hill

Saturday 22
11 Berrys Place Farm

Sunday 23
11 Berrys Place Farm
13 Blockley Gardens
15 25 Bowling Green Road
29 Green Cottage
54 Paulmead
57 Quenington Gardens
63 Sandywell Barn House
65 Sezincote
68 St Briavels Gardens
78 Wells Cottage

Wednesday 26
11 Berrys Place Farm
27 Eyford House
60 Rockcliffe House
75 Trench Hill

Thursday 27
11 Berrys Place Farm

Friday 28
66 Snowshill Manor & Garden

Sunday 30
15 25 Bowling Green Road
28 The Gables
30 Herbs for Healing
39 Littlefield Garden
48 Moor Wood
67 South Lodge

Home-made teas, how yummy . . . !

July

Monday 1
15 25 Bowling Green Road

Saturday 6
31 Hidcote Manor Garden

Sunday 7
15 25 Bowling Green Road
32 Highnam Court

Monday 8
15 25 Bowling Green Road

Sunday 14
15 25 Bowling Green Road
16 Brockworth Court
36 Kempsford Manor

Monday 15
15 25 Bowling Green Road
52 The Old Rectory, Duntisbourne Rous

Sunday 21
6 Barn House
59 Richmond Village
75 Trench Hill

Wednesday 24
44 Meadow Cottage

Sunday 28
8 Barrington Downs
38 Lindors Country House
80 Westonbirt School Gardens

August

Sunday 4
32 Highnam Court

Sunday 11
36 Kempsford Manor

Monday 12
37 Kiftsgate Court

Tuesday 13
7 Barnsley House

Sunday 18
30 Herbs for Healing
59 Richmond Village

Sunday 25
38 Lindors Country House
75 Trench Hill

Monday 26
5 Aunt Martha's

September

Sunday 1
32 Highnam Court

Sunday 8
28 The Gables
79 Westbury Court Garden
82 Wyck Rissington Gardens

Sunday 15
6 Barn House

Saturday 28
38 Lindors Country House

October

Friday 11
73 Sudeley Castle Gardens & Exhibitions

Sunday 27
1 Abbotswood

November

Sunday 3
38 Lindors Country House

January 2014

Sunday 26
38 Lindors Country House

February 2014

Sunday 2
34 Home Farm

Sunday 9
36 Kempsford Manor

Sunday 16
34 Home Farm
36 Kempsford Manor
75 Trench Hill

Sunday 23
23 Dr Jenner's House & Garden
75 Trench Hill

Gardens open to the public

9 Batsford Arboretum
14 Bourton House Garden
18 Cerney House Gardens
20 The Coach House Garden
23 Dr Jenner's House & Garden
30 Herbs for Healing
31 Hidcote Manor Garden
36 Kempsford Manor
37 Kiftsgate Court
42 Lydney Park Spring Garden
43 Matara Gardens of Wellbeing
46 Mill Dene Garden
47 Misarden Park
53 Painswick Rococo Garden
61 Rodmarton Manor
65 Sezincote
66 Snowshill Manor & Garden
70 Stanway Fountain & Water Garden
71 Stone House
73 Sudeley Castle Gardens & Exhibitions
79 Westbury Court Garden
80 Westonbirt School Gardens

By appointment only

2 Alderley Grange
25 Eastleach House
45 The Meeting House
56 Pemberley Lodge
64 Schofields

Also open by Appointment ☎

5 Aunt Martha's
8 Barrington Downs
12 Beverston Castle
15 25 Bowling Green Road
16 Brockworth Court
19 Charingworth Court
21 Cotswold Farm
34 Home Farm
38 Lindors Country House
44 Meadow Cottage
48 Moor Wood
50 The Old Chequer
51 The Old Rectory, Avening
55 Pear Tree Cottage
63 Sandywell Barn House
67 South Lodge
75 Trench Hill
81 The Gate, Winchcombe Gardens

The Gardens

1 ABBOTSWOOD

Stow-on-the-Wold GL54 1EN. Mr R Scully. *1m W of Stow-on-the-Wold. On B4068 nr Lower Swell or B4077 nr Upper Swell.* **Adm £5, chd free. Sun 7 Apr (1.30-6); Sun 27 Oct (1-5).**

Massed plantings of spring bulbs, heathers, flowering shrubs and rhododendrons in dramatic, landscaped hillside stream gardens; fine herbaceous planting in elegant formal gardens with lily pond, terraced lawn and fountain created by Sir Edwin Lutyens Acers giving good autumn colour later in year. Wheelchair access to main parts of garden.

2 ALDERLEY GRANGE

Alderley GL12 7QT. The Hon Mrs Acloque, 01453 842161. *2m S of Wotton-under-Edge. Turn NW off A46 Bath to Stroud rd, at Dunkirk. L signed Hawkesbury Upton & Hillesley. In Hillesley follow sign to Alderley.* **Adm £4, chd free. Visitors welcome by appt June only. Please phone for bookings. Refreshments available by prior arrangement.**

Walled garden with fine trees, old fashioned roses, herb garden and aromatic plants. A garden of character, charm and historical interest. A phased replanting programme is in progress, which started in 2011. Some gravel paths.

3 NEW ASHLEY GRANGE

Ashley, Tetbury GL8 8SX. Mr & Mrs Richard Atkinson. *Centre of hamlet of Ashley. Ashley has no signage. Ashley Grange is opp entrance to XII century church (indicated).* Home-made teas. **Adm £4.50, chd free. Mon 27 May (2-6).**

The original garden was designed by the late Miss Avice Pearson and was opened in the 1990s through the NGS. The current owners have extended the garden and added a number of new borders. The peonies and iris borders are a feature of the garden in late May. Wheelchair access to refreshment areas will require some assistance.

ASTHALL MANOR
See Oxfordshire

Atcombe Court

4 ATCOMBE COURT

South Woodchester GL5 5ER. John & Josephine Peach. *2m S of Stroud. Take turning off A46 signed South Woodchester, Frogmarsh Mill (NOT turning signed South Woodchester, The Ram).* Home-made teas. **Adm £3.50, chd free. Sat 8 June (2-6).**

12-acre grounds around C17 house (not open) with later Regency front. Delightful views over valley with lakes, mature trees and paddocks. Terraced herbaceous borders, lawns, extensive shrubberies, cutting garden mostly annuals. Long peony border. Woodland walk through beechwood.

5 AUNT MARTHA'S

The Branch, Drybrook GL17 9DB. Philip & Nadine Carr, 01594 824514, auntmartha@hotmail.co.uk, www.auntmartha.co.uk. *1m N of Cinderford. Signed off A4151 near junction with A4136. Adjacent to Steam Mills Primary School.* Light refreshments at Aunt Martha's Victorian Tea-rooms. **Adm £3, chd free. Mons 1 Apr, 6, 27 May, Mon 26 Aug (12-4.30). Visitors also welcome by appt Mar to Sept.**

Created to complement the authentic Victorian tea-rooms, the surrounding 1/4 acre garden has many elements that might inspire the visitor. From the simple log-garden entrance, one can wander through the courtyard, orchard, kitchen garden, and back yard, then into a series of small 'rooms' representing an easy maintenance garden, classical garden, cottage garden, herb garden, oriental garden, castle keep and finally the new 'Secret Garden'.

BADMINTON HOUSE
See Somerset, Bristol & South Gloucestershire

6 NEW BARN HOUSE

Brockweir Common, Chepstow NP16 7PH. Mrs Kate Patel. *10m S of Monmouth, 8m N of Chepstow. From Chepstow take A466 towards Monmouth, continue past Tintern Abbey. 2m from Abbey turn R across Brockweir Bridge, over R Wye, Brockweir Inn on R. Drive out of village, up Mill Hill for ½ m, turn L at 'The Rock', signed to Cold Harbour. Follow rd for 1m as it twists & turns. Look for Woodbine Cottage on L, Wye Valley Barns on L, sharp R at The Paddock (pink bunglow), Two Springs on R, Lymington House on R, Barn House on L.* Home-made teas. **Adm £3.50, chd free. Suns 21 July, 15 Sept (2-5.30).**

Gently sloping 1 acre garden in secluded, rural setting. Informally landscaped providing different areas of interest. Wide variety of ornamental grasses, incl 70 metre miscanthus hedge. Attractive late summer, many species long flowering. Hardy geraniums complement the usual prairie favourites. Exuberantly planted vegetable area screened by bamboos. Small orchard, pleasant view across the valley.

7 BARNSLEY HOUSE

Barnsley, Cirencester GL7 5EE. Calcot Health & Leisure Ltd, www.barnsleyhouse.com. *4m NE of Cirencester. From Cirencester, take B4425 to Barnsley. House entrance on R as you enter village.* **Adm £6, chd free. Tue 13 Aug (12.30-4.30).**

The beautiful garden at Barnsley House, created by Rosemary Verey, is one of England's finest and most famous gardens incl knot garden, potager garden and mixed borders in Rosemary Verey's successional planting style. The House also has an extensive kitchen garden which will be open with plants and vegetables available for purchase. Narrow paths mean restricted access but happy to provide assistance.

8 BARRINGTON DOWNS

Aldsworth, Nr Cheltenham GL54 3PT. Sir Jeremy & Lady Morse, 0207 302265 or 01451 844382, belindamorse@btinternet.com. *2m E of Aldsworth on B4425. Entrance marked on rd.* Home-made teas. **Adm £3, chd free. Sun 28 July (2-5.30). Visitors also welcome by appt June and July. Min. 2 weeks advance notice required.**

Barrington Downs is a charming rural garden surrounded by farmland. It has a wide selection of herbaceous plants, shrubs and borders designed to look their best in high summer. Vegetable and herb garden. Sculpture by William Pye and others. Children's play area. Several improvements since last opening.

BARTON HOUSE

See Warwickshire

Wander through 56 acres of wild gardens, paths and streams, enjoy breathtaking views . . .

9 NEW ◆ BATSFORD ARBORETUM

Batsford, Moreton-In-Marsh GL56 9AB. Batsford Foundation Trust, 01386 701441, www.batsarb.co.uk. *1½ m W of Moreton-in-Marsh on A44. From Moreton-in-Marsh take A44 towards Bourton on the Hill. Batsford Arboretum & Garden Centre is clearly signed on R, just before entering Bourton on the Hill. For satnav use GL56 9AB.* **Adm £7, chd £3. For NGS: Sun 3 Mar (10-5). For other opening times and information, please phone or see garden website.**

Batsford is home to one of the country's largest private tree collections providing yr-round colour. Wander through 56 acres of wild gardens, paths and streams, enjoy breathtaking views across the Evenlode Valley and discover the oriental-inspired statues. Famous for autumn colour, Batsford is equally beautiful in spring thanks to snowdrops and aconites, daffodils and flowering cherries. Light refreshments at The Garden Terrace Cafe. Featured in gardening magazines and local media. Visitor Centre accessible by wheelchair. 2 trampers available in advance by members of SW Countryside Mobility scheme.

NCH

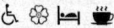

THE BELL AT SKENFRITH

See Gwent

10 BERKELEY CASTLE

Berkeley GL13 9PJ. Mr & Mrs J R G Berkeley, www.berkeley-castle.com. *Half-way between Bristol & Gloucester 10 mins from J14 of M5. From M5 follow signs to Berkeley on A38 & B4066. Visitors' entrance is on L of Canonbury St, just before town centre.* Light refreshments. **Adm £5, chd £2. Sun 16 June (12-6).**

Unique terraced garden of a plantsman, with far-reaching views across the R Severn. Designed with the advice of Gertrude Jekyll, the gardens contain many rare plants which thrive in the warm micro-climate against the stone walls of the mediaeval castle. Woodland, historic trees and stunning summer borders. Butterfly House open: walk amongst free-flying butterflies. Cakes for sale in yurt near butterfly house and kitchen garden.

11 BERRYS PLACE FARM

Bulley Lane, Churcham GL2 8AS. Anne Thomas. *6m W of Gloucester. A40 towards Ross. Turning R into Bulley Lane at Birdwood.* Refreshments incl Anne's special cream teas & home made sponges. **Adm £3, chd free. Sat 22, Sun 23, Wed 26, Thur 27 June (11-5).**

Country garden, approx 1 acre, surrounded by farmland and old orcharding. Lawns and large sweeping mixed herbaceous borders with over 100 roses. Formal kitchen garden and beautiful rose arbour leading to lake and summerhouse with a variety of water lilies and carp. All shared with peacocks and ducks. Featured on radio Gloucestershire and in Gloucester Citizen & Echo.

12 BEVERSTON CASTLE

nr Tetbury GL8 8TU. Mrs A L Rook, 01666 502219, ejarook1@btinternet.com. *2m W of Tetbury. On A4135 to Dursley between Tetbury & Calcot X'rds.* Home-made teas. **Adm £4, chd £2.50. Sun 31 Mar, Mon 1 Apr (2.30-5). Visitors also welcome by appt Mar to May.**

Overlooked by romantic C12-C17 castle ruin (not open), overflowingly planted paved terrace leads from C18 house (not open) across moat to sloping lawn with spring bulbs in abundance, and full herbaceous and shrub borders. Large walled kitchen garden and greenhouses. Partial wheelchair access.

BIRCH TREE WELL
See Gwent

BLICKS HILL HOUSE
See Wiltshire

GROUP OPENING

13 BLOCKLEY GARDENS

Blockley GL56 9DB. *3m NW of Moreton-in-Marsh. Take A44 either from Moreton or Broadway & follow signs to Blockley. Parking & entry tickets available at St George's Hall. Shuttle coach service connecting gardens.* Home-made teas at Mill Dene (May) and St George's Hall, 23 Little Village Hall and The Manor House (June). **Combined adm £6, chd free. Suns 19 May, 23 June (2-6).**

BELL BANK
Mr & Mrs C D Walters.
Open June date only

COLEBROOK HOUSE
Richard & Melanie Slimmon.
Open May date only

HOLLYROSE HOUSE
Mr & Mrs Peter Saunders.
Open May date only

MALVERN MILL
Mr & Mrs J Bourne

THE MANOR HOUSE
George & Zoe Thompson

◆ MILL DENE GARDEN
Mr & Mrs B S Dare.
Open May date only
(See separate entry)

THE OLD CHEQUER
Mr & Mrs H Linley
(See separate entry)

THE OLD SILK MILL
Mr & Mrs A Goodrick-Clarke.
Open May date only

NEW **SNUGBOROUGH MILL**
Mr Rupert Williams-Ellis

WOODRUFF
Mr Paul & Mrs Maggie Adams.
Open June date only

This popular hillside village has a great variety of high quality, well-stocked gardens - large and small, old and new. Blockley Brook, an attractive stream which flows right through the village, graces some of the gardens; these incl gardens of former water mills, with millponds attached. From some gardens there are wonderful rural views. Small children welcome but close supervision required. Access to some gardens quite steep and allowances should be made.

The unusual, rare and exotic make this garden a plantsman's delight . . .

14 ◆ BOURTON HOUSE GARDEN

Bourton-on-the-Hill GL56 9AE. Mr & Mrs R Quintus, www.bourtonhouse.com. *2m W of Moreton-in-Marsh. On A44.* **Adm £6, chd free. For NGS: Sat 15 June (10-5). For other opening times and information, please phone or see garden website.**

Award-winning 3 acre garden featuring wide herbaceous borders with stunning plant, texture and colour combinations. Imaginative topiary incl knot garden and parterre, water features, unique shadehouse and creatively planted pots. The unusual, rare and exotic make this garden a plantsman's delight. Home-made teas served in Grade I listed 16th century Tithe Barn. Cards and gifts available. 70% access for wheelchairs.

15 25 BOWLING GREEN ROAD

Cirencester GL7 2HD. Fr John & Susan Beck, 01285 653778, sjb@beck-hems.org.uk. *On NW edge of Cirencester. Take A435 to Spitalgate/Whiteway T-lights, turn into The Whiteway (Chedworth turn) then 1st L into Bowling Green Rd. Please respect neighbours' driveways, no pavement parking.* **Adm £3, chd free. Every Sun 16 June to 14 July (2-5); Mons 1, 8, 15 July (11-4). Visitors also welcome by appt June and July. Maximum groups size 35-40. Light refreshments can be provided for groups.**

Wander at will through our civilised jungle of colour, described by visitors as a wonderful hidden gem and even as 'cool' by the young, to glimpse a graceful giraffe and friendly frogs sharing their space with hosts of hemerocallis and hostas, precious perennials, romantic roses and curvaceous clematis in the biggest small garden ever. Featured in Cotswold Essence and Amateur Gardening.

BRETFORTON MANOR
See Worcestershire

BRIZE NORTON GARDENS
See Oxfordshire

16 BROCKWORTH COURT

Court Road, Brockworth GL3 4QU. Tim & Bridget Wiltshire, 01452 862938, timwiltshire@hotmail.co.uk. *6m E of Gloucester. 6m W of Cheltenham. From A46 Stroud/Cheltenham, turn into Mill Lane by Brockworth House. At T-junction turn R, L, R. Garden next to St George's Church. From Ermin Rd, follow signs to Churchdown.* Home-made teas served in Tithe Barn. **Adm £5, chd free. Suns 16 June, 14 July (1-5). Visitors also welcome by appt Apr to Sept.**

This intense, yet informal and relaxed garden surrounds an Historic Manor House (not open) which once belonged to Llanthony Secunda Priory. Organic, with distinct cottage-style planting areas that seamlessly blend together. Natural pond with Monet bridge leading to island with thatched fiji house. Water lilies and koi carp. Secret walled kitchen garden once cultivated by the monks. CPRE award winning Tithe barn restored 2000. Adjacent Norman Church (open). Featured in Cotswold Life, The Gloucestershire Citizen and on Cotswold TV.

BROUGHTON POGGS & FILKINS GARDENS
See Oxfordshire

BURMINGTON GRANGE
See Warwickshire

17 CAMPDEN HOUSE
Chipping Campden GL55 6UP. The Hon Philip & Mrs Smith. *Entrance on Chipping Campden to Weston Subedge Rd (Dyer's Lane), approx ¼ m SW of Campden, 1¼ m drive.* Home-made teas. **Combined adm £5, chd free. (Tickets available at Campden House only for entry to both gardens. Ernest Wilson Garden may be viewed individually by donation).** Weds 5, 12 June (2-6). **Combined with The Ernest Wilson Garden.**
2 acres featuring mixed borders of plant and colour interest around house and C17 tithe barn (neither open). Set in fine parkland in hidden valley with lakes and ponds. Woodland walk, vegetable garden. Gravel paths, steep slopes.

18 ◆ CERNEY HOUSE GARDENS
North Cerney GL7 7BX. Lady Angus, 01285 831300, www.cerneygardens.com. *4m NW of Cirencester. On A435 Cheltenham rd. Turn L opp Bathurst Arms, past church up hill, pillared gates on R.* **Adm £5, chd free.** For NGS: Sun 28 Apr (10-5). **For other opening times and information, please phone or see garden website.**
Romantic walled garden filled with old-fashioned roses and herbaceous borders. Working kitchen garden, scented garden, well-labelled herb garden, Who's Who beds and genera borders. Spring bulbs in abundance all around the wooded grounds. Bothy pottery.

19 NEW CHARINGWORTH COURT
Broadway Road, Winchcombe GL54 5JN. Susan & Richard Wakeford, 01242 603033, susanwakeford@googlemail.com, http://charingworthcourtcotswoldsgarden.com/. *In Winchcombe, 8m NE of Cheltenham. 400 metres N of Winchcombe town centre car park in Bull Lane; walk down Chandos St, L onto Broadway Rd. Garden is on L.* **Adm £4, chd free.** Sat 18 May (11-7); Sun 19 May (2-6). **Combined with Winchcombe Gardens Sat 15 June. Combined adm £6.50, chd free. Visitors also welcome by appt between Mon 20 & Sun 26 May. Evening opening from 6pm - please call for details.**
Artistically and lovingly created 1½ -acre gardens surrounding restored Georgian/Tudor house (not open). Relaxed country style, with Japanese influences, lily pond and productive walled vegetable garden. Mature copper beech trees, Cedar of Lebanon and Wellingtonia; and younger trees replacing an earlier excess of cupressus leylandii. The garden will be the backdrop for a garden sculpture selling exhibition on 18 and 19 May.

20 NEW ◆ THE COACH HOUSE GARDEN
Ampney Crucis, Cirencester GL7 5RY. Mr & Mrs Nicholas Tanner, 01285 850256, www.thecoachhousegarden.co.uk. *3m E of Cirencester. Turn into village from A417, immed next to Crown of Crucis Inn. Over hump-back bridge, parking immed to R on cricket field.* **Adm £5, chd free.** For NGS: Sun 28 Apr (2-5.30). **For other opening times and information, please phone or see garden website.**
Approximately 1½ acres and full of structure and design. This garden is divided into rooms which incl gravel garden, rose garden, herbaceous borders, green garden with pleached lime allee, potager and rill. Created over the last 25yrs by the present owners. Rare plant sales. Featured in Cotswold Life.

CONDERTON MANOR
See Worcestershire

21 COTSWOLD FARM
Duntisbourne Abbots, Cirencester GL7 7JS. Mrs Mark Birchall, 01285 821857, ionacotswoldfarm@uwclub.net, www.cotswoldfarmgardens.org.uk. *5m NW of Cirencester. Off old A417. From Cirencester turn L signed Duntisbourne Abbots Services, then immed R & R again into underpass. Private drive straight ahead. From Gloucester turn L signed Duntisbourne Abbots Services. Pass services, private drive on L.* Cream teas. **Adm £5, chd free (share to A Rocha).** Sun 9, Wed 12 June (2-6). **Visitors also welcome by appt anytime.**
Arts and Crafts garden in lovely position overlooking quiet valley on

Highnam Court

Treat yourself to a plant from the plant stall

descending levels with terrace designed by Norman Jewson in 1930s. White border overflowing with flowers, texture and scent. Shrubs, trees, shrub roses, bog garden, snowdrops named and naturalised. Allotments in Old Walled garden, 8 native orchids, 100's of wild flowers and Roman Snails. Family day out. Croquet and toys on lawn. Picnics welcome.

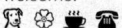

Snowdrops and wild garlic guide you around, past the herb garden . . .

22 DAYLESFORD HOUSE
Daylesford GL56 0YG. Sir Anthony & Lady Bamford. *5m W of Chipping Norton. Off A436. Between Stow-on-the-Wold & Chipping Norton.* Light refreshments. **Adm £5, chd free.** **Wed 8 May (1-5).**
Magnificent C18 landscape grounds created 1790 for Warren Hastings, greatly restored and enhanced by present owners. Lakeside and woodland walks within natural wild flower meadows. Large walled garden planted formally, centered around orchid, peach and working glasshouses. Trellised rose garden. Collection of citrus within period orangery. Secret Garden with pavilion and formal pools. Very large garden with substantial distances to be walked.

DORSINGTON GARDENS
See Warwickshire

23 ◆ DR JENNER'S HOUSE & GARDEN
Church Lane, Berkeley GL13 9BN. Helen Jeffrey, 01453 810631, www.jennermuseum.com. *Midway between Bristol & Gloucester just off A38. Follow signs to Berkeley, then brown tourist signs to Jenner Museum.* **For NGS: Sun 24 Feb (11-4); Sun 23 Feb 2014. For other opening times and information, please phone or see garden website.**
Informal woodland garden at the former home of Dr Edward Jenner. Snowdrops and wild garlic guide you around, past the herb garden and site of the archaeological dig, to the Grade II* listed Temple of Vaccinia, the 200yr old plane tree and into the vinery where Jenner's Hampton Court Palace vine grows. Children's trail. Gravel paths.

GROUP OPENING

24 EASTCOMBE, BUSSAGE AND BROWNSHILL GARDENS
Eastcombe GL6 7DS. *3m E of Stroud. 2m N of A419 Stroud to Cirencester rd on turning signed to Bisley & Eastcombe. Please park considerately in villages.* Home-made teas at Eastcombe Village Hall. **Combined adm (covering both open days) £5, chd free (share to Cotswold Care Hospice; Acorns Children's Hospice; Hope for Tomorrow). Sun 5, Mon 6 May (2-6).**

12 HIDCOTE CLOSE
Mr & Mrs K Walker

HIGHLANDS
Helen & Bob Watkinson

1 THE LAURELS
Andrew & Ruth Fraser

MARYFIELD AND MARYFIELD COTTAGE
Mrs M. Brown

MIDDLEGARTH
Helen & Peter Walker

ROSE COTTAGE
Mrs Juliet Shipman

WOODVIEW COTTAGE
Julian & Eileen Horn-Smith

YEW TREE COTTAGE
Andy & Sue Green

A group of gardens, medium and small, set in a picturesque hilltop location. Some approachable only by foot. (Exhibitions may be on view in village hall). Gloucestershire Plant Heritage plant sale (5 May only). Wheelchair access not available at all gardens.

25 EASTLEACH HOUSE
Eastleach Martin, Cirencester GL7 3NW. Mrs David Richards, garden@eastleachhouse.com, www.eastleachhouse.com. *5m NE of Fairford. From Fairford on A417, signed to Eastleach on L. 4m to village, turn R down hill towards bridge. Entrance to garden by church gates. No access for coaches - drop visitors at gate & park outside village at lay-by on A361 outside Lechlade. Limited parking at house for individual visitors.* Refreshments at The Victoria Inn, 01367 850277. **Adm £8, chd free. Visitors welcome by appt May to Sept. Please write or email for bookings.**
Large traditional all-yr-round garden. Wooded hilltop position with long views S and W. New parkland, lime avenue and arboretum. Wild flower walk, wildlife pond, lawns, walled and rill gardens, with modern herbaceous borders, yew and box hedges, iris and paeony borders, lily ponds, formal herb garden and topiary. Rambling roses into trees. Featured in Cheltenham Echo and Country Life. Gravel paths and some steep slopes.

26 NEW ERNEST WILSON MEMORIAL GARDEN
Leysbourne, Chipping Campden GL55 6DL. EWMG Trust. *High St. Chipping Campden, at Leysbourne below church.* **Combined adm £5, chd free. (Tickets available at Campden House only for entry to both gardens. Ernest Wilson Garden may be viewed individually by donation). Weds 5, 12 June (7am-8pm). Combined with Campden House.**
The Ernest Wilson Memorial Garden was created in 1984 in memory of Ernest Wilson the celebrated plant hunter who was born in Chipping Campden in 1816. This small tranquil walled garden in the centre of the town features entirely plants, shrubs and trees introduced by Ernest Wilson.

NCH

27 EYFORD HOUSE
Upper Slaughter, Nr Cheltenham GL54 2JN. Mrs C Heber-Percy. *2½ m from Stow on the Wold on the B4068 Stow to Andoversford Rd.* Cream teas. **Adm £4, chd free. Wed 26 June (2-6). Also open Rockliffe House.**
1½ -acre sloping N facing garden, ornamental shrubs and trees. Laid out originally by Graham Stuart Thomas, 1976. West garden and terrace, red border, walled kitchen garden, two lakes with pleasant walks and views, boots recommended! Holy well. Walled garden not open in 2013 due to reconstruction.

28 NEW THE GABLES
Riverside Lane, Broadoak, Newnham on Severn GL14 1JE. Bryan Bamber. *1m NE of Newnham on Severn. Park in the White Hart PH unsurfaced car park, to R when facing river. Walk 250 metres along rd past PH to The Gables. Access through marked field gate.* Home-made teas. **Adm £3, chd free. Suns 30 June, 8 Sept (11-5).**
The garden was started in 2006 from a blank canvas. It is a large flat garden with formal lawns, herbaceous borders and shrubberies. It incl a wild flower meadow incorporating soft fruits and fruit trees and an allotment size vegetable plot.

29 GREEN COTTAGE
Watery Lane, Lydney GL15 6BS. Mrs M Baber, www.peony-ukgardeners.co.uk. *1/4 m SW of Lydney. Approaching Lydney from Gloucester on A48, turn R, signed Lydney, Bream, Whitecroft on brow of hill. Follow main rd through town. Leaving Lydney turn R into Watery Lane at de-limit sign. From Chepstow take A48 approx 8m through Aylburton village. At traffic island, take 1st. exit towards Lydney. Watery Lane 2nd Left.* **Adm £3, chd free. Every Sun 19 May to 23 June (2-5).**
1 1/2 acre country garden planted for seasonal interest and wildlife. Mature trees, natural stream with bridges leading to woodland paths and plantings of hellebores, ferns and pulmonarias. Duck pond, few ducks, hens, bog plants. Cottage garden. Wide range herbaceous peonies from Europe and USA (May). National collection of rare Victorian and Edwardian cultivars (June). Unsuitable for wheelchairs in March due to location of hellebores.
NCH

HELLENS
See Herefordshire

30 ◆ HERBS FOR HEALING
Claptons Lane (behind Barnsley House Hotel), Barnsley GL7 5EE. Davina Wynne-Jones, 07773 687493, www.herbsforhealing.net. *4m NE of Cirencester. Turn R after Barnsley House Hotel and R again at the dairy barn. Follow sign.* **Adm £4, chd free. For NGS: Suns 30 June, 18 Aug (2-5). For other opening times and information, please phone or see garden website.**
Not a typical NGS garden, rural and naturalistic. Davina, the daughter of Rosemary Verey, has created a unique nursery, specialising in medicinal herbs and a tranquil organic garden in a secluded field where visitors can enjoy the beauty of the plants and learn more about the properties and uses of medicinal herbs. Tours of the garden explaining current and historical uses of the plants. Access to WC is difficult for wheelchair users.

Walk through woods and fields to show carpets of spring flowers . . .

31 ◆ HIDCOTE MANOR GARDEN
Hidcote Bartrim, Chipping Campden, nr Mickleton GL55 6LR. National Trust, 01386 438333, www.nationaltrust.org.uk. *4m NE of Chipping Campden. Off B4081, close to the village of Mickleton.* **Adm £10, chd £5. For NGS: Sat 6 July (11-6). For other opening times and information, please phone or see garden website.**
One of England's great gardens, 10 1/2 -acre Arts and Crafts masterpiece created by Major Lawrence Johnston. Series of outdoor rooms, each with a different character and separated by walls and hedges of many different species. Many rare trees and shrubs, outstanding herbaceous borders and unusual plant species from all over the world.

HIGH GLANAU MANOR
See Gwent

32 HIGHNAM COURT
Highnam, Gloucester GL2 8DP. Mr and Mrs R J Head, www.HighnamCourt.co.uk. *2m W of Gloucester. Leave Gloucester on A40 towards Ross-on-Wye. DO NOT take Newent turning, proceed to next big r'about. Take R exit for Highnam Court, entrance directly off r'about.* Home-made teas in The Orangery. **Adm £5, chd free. Suns 7 Apr, 5 May, 2 June, 7 July, 4 Aug, 1 Sept (11-5).**
40 acres of Victorian landscaped gardens surrounding magnificent Grade I house (not open), set out by the artist Thomas Gambier Parry. Lakes, shrubberies and listed Pulhamite water gardens with grottos and fernery. Exciting ornamental lakes, and woodland areas. Extensive 1-acre rose garden and many features, incl numerous wood carvings around the site. Some gravel paths and steps to refreshment area. Disabled WC.

33 HODGES BARN
Shipton Moyne, Tetbury GL8 8PR. Mr & Mrs N Hornby. *3m S of Tetbury. On Malmesbury side of village.* **Adm £5, chd free. Sun 9, Mon 10 June (2-6).**
Very unusual C15 dovecote converted into family home. Cotswold stone walls host climbing and rambling roses, clematis, vines, hydrangeas and together with yew, rose and tapestry hedges create formality around house. Mixed shrub and herbaceous borders, shrub roses, water garden, woodland garden planted with cherries, magnolia and spring bulbs.

34 HOME FARM
Newent Lane, Huntley GL19 3HQ. Mrs T Freeman, 01452 830210, torill@ukgateway.net. *4m S of Newent. On B4216 1/2 m off A40 in Huntley travelling towards Newent.* **Adm £3, chd free. Suns 27 Jan, 10 Feb, 10 Mar, 14, 28 Apr (2-5.30); Suns 2, 16 Feb 2014. Visitors also welcome by appt.**
Set in elevated position with exceptional views. 1m walk through woods and fields to show carpets of spring flowers. Enclosed garden with fern border, sundial and heather bed. White and mixed shrub borders. Stout footwear advisable in winter.

35 HOOKSHOUSE POTTERY
Hookshouse Lane, Tetbury GL8 8TZ. Lise & Christopher White, hookshousepottery.co.uk. *2 1/2 m SW of Tetbury. From Tetbury take A4135 towards Dursley, then take 2nd L, should be signed Leighterton. Pottery 1 1/2 m on R.* Home-made teas. **Adm £3, chd free. Sat 25 May to Sun 2 June incl (11-6).**

A combination of dramatic open perspectives and intimate corners. Borders, shrubs, woodland glade, water garden containing treatment ponds (unfenced) and flowform cascades. Kitchen garden with raised beds, orchard. Sculptural features. Run on organic principles. Pottery showroom with hand-thrown wood-fired pots incl. frostproof garden pots. Art & craft exhibition incl. garden sculptures (25 May - 2 June).

ILMINGTON GARDENS
See Warwickshire

36 ◆ KEMPSFORD MANOR
High Street, Kempsford GL7 4EQ. Mrs Z I Williamson, 01285 810131, www.kempsfordmanor.com. *3m S of Fairford. Take A419 from Cirencester or Swindon. Kempsford is signed 10m (approx) from each. The Manor is in the centre of village.* **Adm £4, chd free. For NGS: Suns 10, 17 Feb, 21 Apr, 12 May, 16 June, 14 July, 11 Aug (2-5); Suns 9, 16 Feb 2014. For other opening times and information, please phone or see garden website.**
Early spring garden with variety of bulbs incl snowdrop walk along old canal. Peaceful, expansive summer garden for relaxation, regular cricket matches in adjacent cricket field, croquet and outdoor games and quizzes for children. Occasional musical events, art exhibitions, occasional talks on gardening. Canal path unsuitable for wheelchairs. Disabled parking at garden entrance.

KENCOT GARDENS
See Oxfordshire

37 ◆ KIFTSGATE COURT
Nr Chipping Campden GL55 6LN. Mr & Mrs J G Chambers, 01386 438777, www.kiftsgate.co.uk. *4m NE of Chipping Campden. Adjacent to Hidcote NT Garden. 3m NE of Chipping Campden.* **Adm £7.50, chd £2.50. For NGS: Mons 8 Apr, 12 Aug (2-6). For other opening times and information, please phone or see garden website.**
Magnificent situation and views, many unusual plants and shrubs, tree peonies, hydrangeas, abutilons, species and old-fashioned roses incl largest rose in England, Rosa filipes 'Kiftsgate'. Steep slopes.

Peaceful, expansive summer garden for relaxation . . .

38 LINDORS COUNTRY HOUSE
The Fence, St. Briavels, Lydney GL15 6RB. Christian Guild, 01594 530283, neil.lindors@christianguild.co.uk, www.lindors.co.uk. *From M4 & the S, take M48 across Severn Bridge, immed leave the M48 taking the A466 signed Chepstow & Monmouth. Cont on this rd around outskirts of Chepstow, through Tintern & Llandogo, across Bigsweir Bridge (controlled by T-lights). Immed after crossing bear R up hill following signs for Coleford. Entrance to Lindors approx ¾ m along rd on R.* Light refreshments. **Adm £4, chd free. Suns 27 Jan, 31 Mar, Wed 15 May, Sat 15, Suns 16 June, 28 July, 25 Aug, Sat 28 Sept, Sun 3 Nov (11-4); Sun 26 Jan 2014. Visitors also welcome by appt Feb to Dec.**
Lindors is a garden for all seasons. Mature 9 acres of woodland gardens incl trees over 200 yrs old set amongst streams and ponds. Recently opened woodland way with waterfalls and spring flowers. Bible garden with flowers and shrubs mentioned in the bible and outdoor recreational features. Some gravel paths.

39 LITTLEFIELD GARDEN
Hawling, Cheltenham GL54 5SZ. Mr & Mrs George Wilk. *From A40 Cheltenham to Oxford Rd at Andoversford turn onto the A436 towards Stow-On-The-Wold. Take 2nd signed Rd to Hawling & follow through to Methodist Chapel in the village.* Home-made teas. **Adm £4, chd free. Sun 30 June (11-5).**
Surrounded by idyllic countryside with fine views over a small valley, site of the old medieval village of Hawling, Littlefield Garden was originally designed by Jane Fearnley-Whittingstall. More recently the planting in the yew walk was created by Sherborne Gardens. It offers a rose garden, mixed borders, a lily pond, a wildflower meadow and lavender borders. Visitors can stroll down some 200yds across the meadow to a natural pond or have tea and relax under the pergola. Featured in Gloucestershire Echo. Most of garden accessible for wheelchair users. Gravel path and paved terraces.

GROUP OPENING

40 LONGHOPE GARDENS
Longhope GL17 0LL. *10m W of Gloucester. 6m E of Ross on Wye. Take Longhope turn off A40 into Church Rd. Parking on Church Rd for Court Leet, 3 Church Rd & West View. Limited parking at Springfield House, otherwise short walk from Church Rd.* Home-made teas. **Combined adm £5, chd free. Sat 1 June (11-5); Sun 2 June (2-6); Sat 15 June (11-5); Sun 16 June (2-6).**

3 CHURCH ROAD
Rev Clive & Mrs Linda Edmonds

COURT LEET
Annie & Gary Frost

SPRINGFIELD HOUSE
Sally & Martin Gibson

WEST VIEW
Don Vallance

Small village in a valley with wonderful views and C12 church offering 4 well-planted gardens open to view. 3 Church Road is a long garden divided into 'rooms' with a large collection of hardy geraniums, many of them unusual varieties. Court Leet is a densely planted cottage garden around a C17 house (not open) with wonderful blooms and perfume. Springfield House is a large enclosed garden abundantly planted with shrubs, herbaceous borders and vegetables. West View is a large garden with a wide variety of plants and shrubs, a pond and lovely planting leading to a stream. A good variety of gardens for all tastes.

41 LOWER FARM HOUSE
Cliffords Mesne GL18 1JT. Gareth & Sarah Williams. *2m S of Newent. From Newent follow signs to Cliffords Mesne & Birds of Prey Centre (1½ m). Approx ½ m beyond 'Centre', turn L at Xrds, signed Kents Green. Garden 150yds down hill on bend. Car park (limited if wet). Beware, Sat Nav directions locally misleading.* Home-made teas. **Adm £3.50, chd free. Weds 22, 29 May (2-6).**

2-acre garden, incl woodland, stream and large natural lily pond with rockery and bog garden. Herbaceous borders, pergola walk, terrace with ornamental fishpond, kitchen and herb garden; many interesting and unusual trees and shrubs incl collections of magnolia and cornus. Some gravel paths.

42 ◆ LYDNEY PARK SPRING GARDEN

Lydney GL15 6BU. The Viscount Bledisloe, 01594 842844/842922, www.lydneyparkestate.co.uk. *½ m SW of Lydney. On A48 Gloucester to Chepstow rd between Lydney & Aylburton. Drive is directly off A48.* **Adm £4, chd £0.50. For NGS: Wed 8 May (10-5). For other opening times and information, please phone or see garden website.**

Spring garden in 8-acre woodland valley with lakes, profusion of rhododendrons, azaleas and other flowering shrubs. Formal garden; magnolias and daffodils (April). Picnics in deer park which has fine trees. Important Roman Temple site and museum.

43 ◆ MATARA GARDENS OF WELLBEING

Kingscote, Tetbury GL8 8YA. Herons Mead Ltd, 01453 861050, www.mataragardensofwellbeing.com. *5½ m NW of Tetbury. On A4135 towards Dursley. From Tetbury direction, at Hunter's Hall Inn turn R into Kingscote village. Enter Park at first gate on R. Additional parking at Hunter's Hall Inn across rd.* Home-made teas. **Adm £5, chd free. For NGS: Sun 16 June (1-5). For other opening times and information, please phone or see garden website.**

Trees of life - enjoy the tranquil beauty of Matara's Gardens of Wellbeing and its dedication to the symbolic, spiritual and cultural role of trees. What makes us special are our Chinese Scholar Garden, Japanese Tea Garden, Shinto Woodland, a Celtic wishing tree, labyrinth, healing spiral, Field of Dreams and ornamental herb and flower gardens. Featured in The Cotswolds' Finest Gardens. Limited wheelchair access. Some steps around house area. Some grass paths.

44 MEADOW COTTAGE

59 Coalway Road, Coalway, nr Coleford GL16 7HL. Mrs Pamela Buckland, 01594 833444. *1m SE of Coleford. From Coleford take Lydney & Chepstow Rd at T-lights in town. Turn L after police stn, signed Coalway & Parkend. Garden on L ½ m up hill opp layby.* Light refreshments. **Adm £3, chd free. Sun 26 May, Wed 24 July (2-6). Visitors also welcome by appt Apr to Sept.**

½ -acre cottage garden, a plantaholic craftworker's creation with shrubs, perennials, spring bulbs in colourful borders and interlinking garden rooms. Lawned area. Gravel paths leading to small pond with waterfall and bog garden. Vegetable garden in raised beds. Gravel garden with grasses, bamboos and pots and containers in abundance.

If you search, you will find a tiny cricket lawn and pavilion, a rose walk and a 'scratch n' sniff' herb garden . . .

45 NEW THE MEETING HOUSE

New Road, Flaxley, Newnham GL14 1JS. Chris & Sally Parsons, 01452 760733. *Off A48, close to Westbury-on -Severn. Take A48 S from Westbury-on-Severn. Turn R signed Flaxley. Take 2nd L. The Meeting House is 1st house on L. Parking for coaches 500yds away (drop-off at garden).* **Adm £5, chd free. Visitors welcome by appt Apr to Oct. Please leave clear message on answering machine.**

Cottage with 2 acres developed by owners over the last 18yrs. Hedges, lawns, herbaceous borders, organic fruit trees, soft fruit and vegetables, greenhouse, orchard with wild flowers, reed bed sewage system and Japanese Shingon Buddhist dojo. Also open, are the surrounding 17 acres of wild flower meadows, old and new orchards and ponds, managed for conservation.

46 ◆ MILL DENE GARDEN

School Lane, Blockley, Moreton-in-Marsh GL56 9HU. Mr & Mrs B S Dare, 01386 700457, www.milldenegarden.co.uk. *3m NW of Moreton-in-Marsh. From A44, follow brown signs from Bourton-on-the-Hill, to Blockley. Approx 1¼ m down hill turn L behind village gates. Parking for 8 cars. Coaches by appointment.* Home-made teas. **Adm £5.50, chd £3. For NGS: Sun 21 Apr (2-5). For other opening times and information, please phone or see garden website.**

RHS partner garden, Mill Dene is hidden in the Cotswolds. It surrounds a water-mill and stream. If you search, you will find a tiny cricket lawn and pavilion, a rose walk and a 'scratch n' sniff' herb garden with rills. Masses of tulips and bulbs in the Spring. Come and see how the Dares are trying to make the garden easier to work. Birman cats live here! Many water features. Historic site: wheel pit under the water mill will be on show. Half of garden wheelchair accessible. Please ring in advance for reserved parking and ramps.

47 ◆ MISARDEN PARK

Miserden, Stroud GL6 7JA. Major M T N H Wills, 01285 821303, www.miserdenpark.co.uk. *6m NW of Cirencester. Follow signs off A417 or B4070 from Stroud.* **Adm £5, chd free. For NGS: Suns 31 Mar, 16 June (2-6). For other opening times and information, please phone or see garden website.**

Essentially formal, dating from C17, magnificent position overlooking the Golden Valley. Walled garden with just over 300ft long mixed borders, yew walk leading to a lower lawn with rill and summerhouse. Arboretum with spring bulbs and blossom. Climbing roses and rose walk linking parterre. Silver and grey border, blue border and scented border. Blue/gold walkway below house. Featured in Gloucestershire Echo.

48 MOOR WOOD

Woodmancote GL7 7EB. Mr & Mrs Henry Robinson, 01285 831692, susie@moorwoodhouse.co.uk. *3½ m NW of Cirencester. Turn L off A435 to Cheltenham at North Cerney, signed Woodmancote 1¼ m; entrance in village on L beside lodge with white gates.* Home-made teas.

Adm £4, chd free. Sun 30 June (2-6). Visitors also welcome by appt.
2 acres of shrub, orchard and wild flower gardens in isolated valley setting. Holder of the National Collection of rambler roses.
NCH

NEWARK PARK
See Somerset, Bristol & South Gloucestershire

GROUP OPENING

49 NEW OAKRIDGE LYNCH OPEN GARDENS
Oakridge Lynch, Stroud GL6 7NS. Peter & Gillian Wimperis. *2m S of Bisley, off Bisley to Eastcombe rd. From Bisley, turn L on leaving village. From Stroud, A419, turn L to Chalford Hill & follow signs to Bisley. Turn R before entering Bisley*. Home-made teas at Little Cleeve (not open). **Combined adm £4, chd free. Sun 16 June (2-6).**

NEW HILLSIDE COTTAGE
Mrs Elizabeth White

NEW HOPE COTTAGE
Peter & Gillian Wimperis

NEW OLD COTTAGE
Richard & Judy Mackie

NEW OLD POST OFFICE COTTAGE
Eileen Herbert

NEW SWEETBRIAR COTTAGE
David & Caroline Cook

Beautiful hillside village of pretty cottages and stunning views. Selection of small to medium sized lovely gardens packed with interesting plants: herbaceous borders, roses, herbs, climbers, vines, fruit and vegetables, chickens etc. Limited wheelchair access at most gardens.

50 THE OLD CHEQUER
GL56 9LB. Mr & Mrs H Linley, 01386 700647, g.f.linley1@btinternet.com. *2m NE of Moreton-in-Marsh. From Blockley turn R by cemetery & continue for approx 1m in easterly direction. From Moreton-in-Marsh take L turn by supermarket to Batsford, then R, then L. This takes you down steep hill into the village*. Home-made teas.

Rockcliffe House

Adm £3, chd free. Sun 7 Apr (1-5). Visitors also welcome by appt Apr to July.
A cottage garden, created by owner, set in 2 acres of old orchard with original ridge and furrow. Emphasis on spring planting but still maintaining yr-round interest. Kitchen garden/soft fruit, herbaceous, shrubs, Croquet lawn, unusual plants, alpines and dry gravel borders.

THE OLD CORN MILL
See Herefordshire

51 THE OLD RECTORY, AVENING
60 High Street, Avening GL8 8NF. Mrs Anthea Beszant, anthea@avening.eclipse.co.uk. *3m W of Tetbury. 2m N of Nailsworth. On B4014 in High St close to Avening Church. Opp Woodstock Lane. On corner of Rectory Lane*. Home-made teas. **Adm £4, chd free. Sun 12 May (2-6). Visitors also welcome by appt Feb to Oct. Please email for bookings.**
3 acre garden around C17 Cotswold Rectory (not open). Walks through mature woodland. Paddock with stream and Japanese Bridge. Italianate terrace, steep steps and banks. Supported in places by stone age megaliths transported here in the 1800s. Shady planting, rose and mixed borders, wild garden, sculptures by Darren Yeadon. Limited wheelchair access, gravel paths, steep slopes & steps.

52 THE OLD RECTORY, DUNTISBOURNE ROUS
Cirencester GL7 7AP. Charles & Mary Keen, mary@keengardener.com. *4m NW of Cirencester. From Daglingworth take rd to Duntisbournes. Or from A417 from Gloucester take Duntisbourne Leer turning & follow signs for Daglingworth*. **Adm £5, chd free. Mons 11 Feb, 18 Mar (2-5); 22 Apr (12-5); 15 July (12-6).**
Garden in an exceptional setting made by designer and writer Mary Keen. Subject of many articles and Telegraph column. Designed for atmosphere, but collections of galanthus, hellebores, auriculas and half hardies - especially dahlias - are all features in their season. Sheffield meadow now a regular feature. Plants for sale Feb and April.

THE OLD VICARAGE, BLEDINGTON
See Oxfordshire

OVERBURY COURT
See Worcestershire

53 ◆ PAINSWICK ROCOCO GARDEN
Painswick GL6 6TH. Painswick Rococo Garden Trust, 01452 813204, www.rococogarden.org.uk. *¼ m N of Painswick. ½ m outside village on B4073.* **For opening times and information, please phone or see garden website.**
Unique C18 garden from the brief Rococo period, combining contemporary buildings, vistas, ponds, kitchen garden and winding woodland walks. Anniversary maze, plant nursery. Snowdrop display late winter. Art in the Garden - August.

Peaceful country garden with hedge 'windows' onto wild flower meadow . . .

54 PAULMEAD
Bisley GL6 7AG. Judy & Philip Howard. *5m E of Stroud. On S edge of Bisley at head of Toadsmoor Valley on top of Cotswolds. Garden & car park well signed in Bisley village. Disabled visitors can be dropped off at garden prior to parking car.* **Combined adm £6, single garden adm £4, chd free.** Sun 23 June (2-6). **Combined with Wells Cottage.**
Approx 1-acre landscaped garden constructed in stages over last 25yrs. Terraced in 3 main levels: natural stream garden; formal herbaceous and shrub borders; yew and beech hedges; formal vegetable garden; lawns; summerhouse with exterior wooden decking by pond and thatched roof over well head. Unusual tree house.

55 PEAR TREE COTTAGE
58 Malleson Road, Gotherington GL52 9EX. Mr & Mrs E Manders-Trett, 01242 674592, edandmary@talktalk.net. *4m N of Cheltenham. From A435, travelling N, turn R into Gotherington 1m after end of Bishop's Cleeve bypass at garage. Garden on L approx 100yds past Shutter Inn.* Light refreshments. **Adm £3.50, chd free.** Sun 14 Apr (2-5). **Visitors also welcome by appt Mar to June.**
Mainly informal country garden of approx ½ acre with pond and gravel garden, grasses and herbaceous borders, trees and shrubs surrounding lawns. Wild garden and orchard lead to greenhouses, herb and vegetable gardens. Spring bulbs, early summer perennials and shrubs particularly colourful.

56 PEMBERLEY LODGE
Churchend Lane, Old Charfield GL12 8LJ. Rob & Yvette Andrewartha, 01454 260885, www.gryfindor.info. *3m S of Wotton-under-Edge. From M5 take J14 towards Wotton-under-Edge. At r'about take 2nd exit on to Churchend Lane. Garden is approx 600 metres on R.* Light refreshments. **Adm £5, chd free.** Visitors welcome by appt **Jan to Dec. Advance notice required.**
Small private garden designed and planted in 2002 by Lesley Rosser. Densely planted for yr-round interest and low maintenance. Incorporates trees, shrubs, perennials, grasses, water, gravel and hard landscaping to give an informal and peaceful feel. Roof garden added in 2006. New garden area added in 2010/11.

PENTWYN FARM
See Gwent

GROUP OPENING

57 QUENINGTON GARDENS
nr Fairford GL7 5BW. *8m NE of Cirencester. Gardens well signed once in Village.* Home-made teas at The Old Rectory. **Combined adm £5, chd free.** Sun 23 June (2-5.30).

BANK VIEW
Mrs J A Moulden

BEECH HOUSE
Mr & Mrs A H Bradley

THE OLD POST HOUSE
Mrs D Blackwood

THE OLD RECTORY, QUENINGTON
Mr & Mrs David Abel Smith

POOL HAY
Mrs E A Morris

YEW TREE COTTAGES
Mr J Lindon

A rarely visited Coln Valley village delighting its infrequent visitors with C12 Norman church and C17 stone cottages (not open). An opportunity to discover the horticultural treasures behind those Cotswold stone walls and visit 6 very different but charming gardens incorporating everything from the exotic and the organic to the simple cottage garden; a range of vistas from riverside to seclusion. Fresh Air 2013 Contemporary Sculpture show held in The Old Rectory. Featured in local and national press.

58 RAMBLERS
Lower Common, Aylburton, nr Lydney GL15 6DS. Jane & Leslie Hale. *1½ m W of Lydney. Off A48 Gloucester to Chepstow Rd. From Lydney through Aylburton, out of de-limit turn R signed Aylburton Common, ¾ m along lane.* Home-made teas. **Adm £3.50, chd free.** Suns 5 May, 16 June (2-6).
Peaceful medium-sized country garden with informal cottage planting, herbaceous borders and small pond looking through hedge 'windows' onto wild flower meadow. Front woodland garden with shade-loving plants and topiary. Large productive vegetable garden. Apple orchard.

59 NEW RICHMOND VILLAGE
Stroud Road, Painswick GL6 6UL. *From N, take A46 signed Stroud. Travel through village of Painswick, after 500yds turn R into the rugby club car park. Follow signs to Richmond Village by foot. From S, take A419 follow signs for Stroud & A46 to Cheltenham. On entering Painswick turn L into rugby club car park. Follow signs to Richmond village by foot. Disabled parking at Richmond Village Painswick. Please follow signs.* Home-made teas. **Adm £3.50, chd free.** Suns 21 July, 18 Aug (11-4.30).
Award winning garden situated on the

southern slopes of the beautiful village of Painswick. Richmond Painswick is a purpose built retirement community set in 4 acres of meticulously maintained landscaped gardens. Incl are creatively planted herbaceous borders, a thriving wildflower meadow with stunning views of the 5 valleys and a selection of roof top gardens. Gentle slopes in wild flower meadow.

60 ROCKCLIFFE HOUSE

Upper Slaughter, Cheltenham GL54 2JW. Mr & Mrs Simon Keswick. *2m SW of Stow-on-the-Wold. 1½ m from Lower Swell on B4068. From Stow-on-the-Wold to Cheltenham go through Lower Swell. Climb hill staying on B4068. Converted barn on L. Round corner & start dropping down hill. Rockcliffe halfway down on R, ½ m from Lower Swell.* Home-made teas. **Adm £5, chd free (share to Kates Home Nursing). Weds 12 June (11-6); 26 June (11-4). Also open Eyford House Wed 26 June.**

Large traditional English garden of 8 acres incl pink, white and blue gardens, herbaceous border, rose terrace, walled kitchen garden and orchard. Greenhouses and stone dovecot with pathway of topiary birds leading up through orchard to it. Pond with 6 large cornus contraversa variegata around it. 2 wide stone steps through gate, otherwise good wheelchair access.

61 ◆ RODMARTON MANOR

Cirencester GL7 6PF. Mr Simon Biddulph, 01285 841442, www.rodmarton-manor.co.uk. *5m NE of Tetbury. Off A433. Between Cirencester & Tetbury.* **Adm £5, chd £1. For NGS: Sun 19 May (2-5). For other opening times and information, please phone or see garden website.**

The 8-acre garden of this fine Arts and Crafts house (not open on NGS day) is a series of outdoor rooms each with its own distinctive character. Leisure garden, winter garden, troughery, topiary, hedges, lawns, rockery, containers, wild garden, kitchen garden, magnificent herbaceous borders. Snowdrop collection. Featured on BBC2 and in Daily Telegraph. Wheelchair access to most of garden.

62 NEW ROSE COTTAGE

Kempley, Nr Dymock GL18 2BN. Naomi Cryer. *3m from Newent towards Dymock. From Xrds/T-lights at Newent take turning just after PH, on R from Gloucester direction, signed Kempley. Follow rd for approx 3m, over motorway and through wood. On entering Kempley, Rose Cottage is 2nd house on L.* Home-made teas. **Adm £3.50, chd free. Sat 15, Sun 16 June (11-5).**

About 1 acre of flat garden, put mostly to herbaceous borders. There is a hot bed and a long border leading to a borrowed view, a small parterre in the orchard area, a grass bed and a pond. To the side of that is a small wild flower pasture which is at its best in June. There is also a rose garden, a vegetable plot, a nursery bed and cutting garden. Although quite flat, access is mostly across lawn and grass which may make wheelchair use difficult.

SALFORD GARDENS

See Oxfordshire

63 SANDYWELL BARN HOUSE

Sandywell Park, Whittington, Cheltenham GL54 4HF. Shirley & Gordon Sills, 01242 820606, shirleysills@btinternet.com. *4m E of Cheltenham on A40. 1m from Andoversford, 300 yds from & opp turning to Whittington village.* Home-made teas. **Adm £4, chd free. Sun 26, Mon 27 May, Suns 9, 23 June (11-5). Visitors also welcome by appt end May to mid July.**

2½ -acre plantaholic's garden inside the weathered walls of a former Victorian kitchen garden. Designed, created and maintained by the owners as a series of exhuberantly planted enclosures both formal and informal, sometimes quirky. Herbaceous, climbers, roses, shrubs, trees, lawns, hedges, structures, vistas, water features, spring-fed stream and small pond.

64 SCHOFIELDS

30 Ford House Road, Newent GL18 1LQ. John & Linda Schofield, 01531 820370, linda@hazelschofield.co.uk. *1½ m NE of Newent. At T-lights on Newent by-pass, take B4215 N signed Dymock. Pass fire station & turn R into Tewkesbury Rd. Continue for approx 1m. Ford House Rd is signed to L. Take L turn then L onto concrete rd between 2 caravan fields. Continue to 4th house on L. Parking for cars & 20 seat coach.* Home-made teas. **Adm £3.75. Visitors welcome by appt Mar to Sept Morning, afternoon or evenings.**

Tranquil 5 acres developed from 1970s providing 2½ -acre spring woodland garden, plantsman's ¾ -acres mature trees and shrubs, bulb, herbaceous and hot borders, autumn colour, berries, lavender walk, knot garden and lily ponds. Adjacent 1000sq.m exotic glasshouse garden planted with palms, tender and fruiting trees, shrubs, bulbs, climbers and succulents. Seating areas throughout garden. Please note: we regret the garden is not suitable for children. Enquiries from artists and photography groups welcome, with indoor facilities. Retired Professional Horticulturists own garden. Gravel paths, moderate slopes in woodland.

A series of outdoor rooms each with its own distinctive character . . .

65 ◆ SEZINCOTE

nr Moreton-in-Marsh GL56 9AW. Mr & Mrs D Peake, 01386 700444, enquiries@sezincote.com, www.sezincote.co.uk. *3m SW of Moreton-in-Marsh. From Moreton-in-Marsh turn W along A44 towards Evesham; after 1½ m (just before Bourton-on-the-Hill) take turn L, by stone lodge with white gate.* **Adm £5, chd free. For NGS: Sun 23 June (2-6). For other opening times and information, please phone or see garden website.**

Exotic oriental water garden by Repton and Daniell with lake, pools and meandering stream, banked with massed perennials. Large semi-circular orangery, formal Indian garden, fountain, temple and unusual trees of vast size in lawn and wooded park setting. House in Indian manner designed by Samuel Pepys Cockerell.

Lower Farm House

66 ◆ SNOWSHILL MANOR & GARDEN

Snowshill, nr Broadway WR12 7JU. National Trust, 01386 852410, www.nationaltrust.org.uk. *2½ m SW of Broadway. Off A44 bypass into Broadway village.* **Adm £5.50, chd £2.90. For NGS: Fri 28 June (11-5). For other opening times and information, please phone or see garden website.**

A delightful hillside garden surrounding a beautiful Cotswold manor, designed in the Arts & Crafts style. The garden consists of a series of contrasting 'outdoor rooms'. Simple, colourful plantings tumble and scramble down the terraces and around byres and ponds. Enjoy produce from the kitchen garden in the restaurant. Garden produce and plants for sale (when available).

67 SOUTH LODGE

Church Road, Clearwell, Coleford GL16 8LG. Andrew & Jane MacBean, 01594 837769, southlodgegarden@btinternet.com, www.southlodgegarden.co.uk. *2m S of Coleford. Off B4228. Follow signs to Clearwell. Garden on L of castle driveway. Please park on the road in front of the church or in the village.* Home-made teas. **Adm £3, chd free. Sun 7 Apr, Sun 12 May, Sat 8, Sun 30 June (1-5). Visitors also welcome by appt Apr to June Tea and cake included.**

Peaceful country garden in 2 acres with stunning views of surrounding countryside. High walls provide a backdrop for rambling roses, clematis, and honeysuckles. An organic garden with a large variety of perennials, annuals, grasses, shrubs and specimen trees with yr-round colour. Vegetable garden, wildlife and formal ponds. Rustic pergola planted with English climbing roses and willow arbour amongst wildflowers. Gravel paths and steep slopes.

SPECIAL PLANTS

See Somerset, Bristol & South Gloucestershire

GROUP OPENING

68 ST BRIAVELS GARDENS

Coleford Road, St. Briavels, St Briavels GL15 6TW. *7 m N of Chepstow. Directions to start point & parking - Take B4228 from Chepstow to St Briavels (approx 5m). On entering St Briavels village, after approx ⅓ m, take the 2nd L (at Xrds) into East St Continue for 50yds and take the 1st R through the Memorial Gates onto playing field. Parking & admission maps for all gardens will be available here. For Sat Nav use GL15 6TW.* Home-made teas at The Green House. **Combined adm £5, chd free. Sun 23 June (12-6).**

THE GREEN HOUSE
Jean & Jasper Saunders

NEW HIGH VIEW
Ms Beuschel & Stringfellow

NEW LEIGH GARDENS
Mr & Mrs J Billingsley

NEW POOL COTTAGE
Prof & Mrs A Bensted

NEW SUNNYCROFT
Mr & Mrs E Stubbs

NEW TAFFRAIL
Mr & Mrs S Harris

NEW WYEHOLME LODGE
Mr & Mrs John Porter-Davison

A large variety of gardens to visit whilst walking round this pretty, historic village set high above the Wye Valley. Most of the gardens are a short level walk from the start point. You may wish to drive onto Pool Cottage and Wyeholme Lodge (parking available) as these two gardens are approx 1 mile out of the village, but are an easy, level, 20 mins walk for the more able.

69 STANTON VILLAGE GARDENS

Stanton, nr Broadway WR12 7NE. *3m SW of Broadway. Off B4632, between Broadway (3m) & Winchcombe (6m).* Home-made teas in Burland Hall in village centre. **Adm £5, chd free (share to local charities). Sun 16 June (2-6).**

An extensive group of over 20 gardens set in this picturesque C17 Cotswold village. Many houses border the street with gardens stretching out behind, hidden from general view. Gardens range from large houses with colourful herbaceous borders, established trees, shrubs and formal vegetable gardens, to tiny cottage gardens packed with interest. Popular plant stall and legendary homemade teas. Regret not all gardens suitable for wheelchair users.

70 ◆ STANWAY FOUNTAIN & WATER GARDEN
nr Winchcombe GL54 5PQ. The Earl of Wemyss & March, 01386 584528, www.stanwayfountain.co.uk. *9m NE of Cheltenham. 1m E of B4632 Cheltenham to Broadway rd or B4077 Toddington to Stow-on-the-Wold rd.* **Adm £4.50, chd £1.50. For NGS: Sun 5 May (2-5); Sun 16 June (2-5.30). For other opening times and information, please phone or see garden website.**
20 acres of planted landscape in early C18 formal setting. The restored canal, upper pond and 165ft high fountain have re-created one of the most interesting Baroque water gardens in Britain. Striking C16 manor with gatehouse, tithe barn and church. Britain's highest fountain at 300ft, the world's highest gravity fountain.

71 ◆ STONE HOUSE
Wyck Rissington GL54 2PN. Mr & Mrs Andrew Lukas, 01451 810337, www.stonehousegarden.co.uk. *3m S of Stow-on-the-Wold. Off A429 between Bourton-on-the-Water & Stow-on-the-Wold. Last house in village behind high bank on R.* **Adm £5, chd free. For NGS: Sun 14 Apr (2-6). Combined with Wyck Rissington Gardens,** Sun 8 Sept. **For other opening times and information, please phone or see garden website.**
2½ acres full of unusual bulbs, shrubs and herbaceous plants. Crab apple walk, rose borders, herb and water garden, meadow walk. Plantswoman's garden with yr-round interest. Hellebores and early spring bulbs a speciality in March. Private visits also welcome March to Sept by prior arrangement. Featured in several Magazines and in books by Ursula Buchan and Andrew Lawson. The English Garden Noel Kingsbury. Garden Designers at Home. Wheelchair access to most of garden.

72 STOWELL PARK
Yanworth, Northleach, Cheltenham GL54 3LE. The Lord & Lady Vestey, www.stowellpark.co.uk. *8m NE of Cirencester. Off Fosseway A429 2m SW of Northleach.* Home-made teas. **Adm £6, chd free. Sun 19 May, Sun 16 June (2-5).**
Magnificent lawned terraces with stunning views over Coln Valley. Fine collection of old-fashioned roses and herbaceous plants, with pleached lime approach to C14 house (not open). Two large walled gardens containing vegetables, fruit, cut flowers and range of greenhouses. Long rose pergola and wide, plant-filled borders divided into colour sections. New water features and hazel arch at the bottom of the garden. Open continuously for 50 years. Plant Sale 19 May only.

STRETTON-ON-FOSSE GARDENS
See Warwickshire

Look out for *by appointment gardens* and visit at a time to suit you . . .

73 ◆ SUDELEY CASTLE GARDENS & EXHIBITIONS
Winchcombe GL54 5JD. Lady Ashcombe, 01242 602308, www.sudeleycastle.co.uk. *8m NE of Cheltenham. From Cheltenham take B4632 (A46) into Winchcombe. Follow brown signs to castle. Or J9 off M5 A46 to Teddington r'about, follow signs to Winchcombe then follow brown signs to castle.* **Adm £11, chd £6.50. For NGS: Fri 11 Oct (10.30-5). For other opening times and information, please phone or see garden website.**
Surrounded by stunning views of this Cotswold Hills, the setting of Sudeley Castle is breathtaking in itself. The gardens have been restored and redesigned to compliment the beauty of the castle and its ruins and to echo the elegant gardens which have grown here in years gone by. Exhibitions, pheasantry including owls, adventure playground, private rooms and garden tours, award winning gardens. Gravel paths, limited wheelchair access to exhibitions.

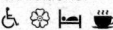

SUNNYSIDE
See Gwent

74 TEMPLE GUITING MANOR
Temple Guiting, nr Stow on the Wold GL54 5RP. Mr & Mrs S Collins, www.templeguitingmanor.co.uk. *7m from Stow-on-the-Wold. From Stow-on-the-Wold take B4077 towards Tewkesbury. On descending hill bear L to village (signed) ½ m. Garden in centre of village on R.* Home-made teas. **Adm £4, chd free. Sun 9 June (2-6).**
Five acres of formal contemporary gardens with a newly designed kitchen garden, to a Grade I listed historic manor house (not open) in Windrush Valley. Designed by Jinny Blom, gold medal winner Chelsea Flower Show. Gravel pathways.

75 TRENCH HILL
Sheepscombe GL6 6TZ. Celia & Dave Hargrave, 01452 814306, celia.hargrave@btconnect.com. *1½ m E of Painswick. On A46 to Cheltenham after Painswick, turn R to Sheepscombe. Approx 1½ m (before reaching village) turn L by telegraph poles, Trench Hill at top of lane.* Home-made teas. **Adm £3, chd free. Suns 17, 24 Feb (11-5); Sun 31 Mar, Mon 1 Apr (11-6); Every Wed 5 June to 26 June (2-6); Sat 15, Sun 16 June, Suns 21 July, 25 Aug (11-6); Suns 16, 23 Feb 2014. Visitors also welcome by appt Feb to Sept. Not suitable for large coaches (max 42 seater).**
Approx 3 acres set in small woodland with panoramic views. Variety of herbaceous and mixed borders, rose garden, extensive vegetable plots, wild flower areas, plantings of spring bulbs with thousands of snowdrops and hellebores, woodland walk, 2 small ponds, waterfall and larger conservation pond. Interesting wooden sculptures. Run on organic principles. Many wooden sculptures within the garden. Much of the garden is accessible but there are parts which are not wheelchair user friendly because of steps and slopes.

76 UPTON WOLD
Moreton-in-Marsh GL56 9TR. Mr & Mrs I R S Bond, www.uptonwoldgarden.co.uk. *4½ m W of Moreton-in-Marsh. On A44 1m past A424 junction at Troopers Lodge Garage, on R. look out for marker posts.* Home-made teas. **Adm £7.50, chd free. Sun 21 Apr (11-5).**

Ever-developing and changing garden, architecturally and imaginatively laid out around C17 house (not open) with commanding views. Yew hedges; herbaceous walk; some unusual plants and trees; vegetables; pond and woodland gardens. National Collections of Juglans and Pterocarya. 2 Star award from GGG.

NCH

Three gardens in this historic Cotswolds town, each with its own distinct feel . . .

GROUP OPENING

77 WATERLANE GARDENS

Waterlane, nr Bisley GL6 7PN. *5m E of Stroud. Between Sapperton & Bisley. Turn down No Through rd in Waterlane, then follow signs.* **Combined adm £4, chd free. Sun 9 June (12-5).**

LIMBRICK COTTAGE
Suzanne Barr

WATERCOMBE HOUSE
Mr Alastair Matchett

Waterlane is a small hamlet hidden near the top of the Cotswolds hills. The gardens feature dramatic views across unspoiled valleys. There are several excellent walks in the immediate area.

78 WELLS COTTAGE

Wells Road, Bisley GL6 7AG. Mr & Mrs Michael Flint, 01452 770289, flint_bisley@talktalk.net. *5m E of Stroud. Garden & car park well signed in Bisley village. Garden lies on S edge of village at head of Toadsmoor Valley, N of A419.* **Combined adm £6, single garden adm £4, chd free. Sun 23 June (2-6). Combined with Paulmead.**
Just under an acre. Terraced on several levels with beautiful views over valley. Much informal planting of trees and shrubs to give colour and texture. Lawns and herbaceous borders. Collection of grasses. Formal pond area. Rambling roses on rope pergola. Vegetable garden with raised beds. No access to upper terraces for wheelchair users.

79 ◆ WESTBURY COURT GARDEN

Westbury-on-Severn GL14 1PD. National Trust, 01452 760461, www.nationaltrust.org.uk. *11m SW of Gloucester. on A48.* **Adm £5, chd £2.50. For NGS: Sun 8 Sept (10-5.30). For other opening times and information, please phone or see garden website.**
The finest example of a Dutch water garden in the country. Wheelchair access to most of garden.

WESTON HALL
See Herefordshire

WESTON MEWS
See Herefordshire

80 ◆ WESTONBIRT SCHOOL GARDENS

Tetbury GL8 8QG. Holfords of Westonbirt Trust, 01666 880333, www.holfordtrust.com. *3m SW of Tetbury. Opp Westonbirt Arboretum, on A433 (follow brown tourist information signs).* **Adm £5, chd free. For NGS: Sun 28 July (11-5). For other opening times and information, please phone or see garden website.**
22 acres. Former private garden of Robert Holford, founder of Westonbirt Arboretum. Formal Victorian gardens incl walled Italian garden now restored with early herbaceous borders and exotic border. Rustic walks, lake, statuary and grotto. Rare, exotic trees and shrubs. Beautiful views of Westonbirt House open with guided tours on designated days of the year. Guided tours of Westonbirt House to see fascinating Victorian interior. Tea, coffee and refreshments available in the restored Camellia House of the walled Italianate gardens.

WESTWELL MANOR
See Oxfordshire

WHATLEY MANOR
See Wiltshire

WHITCOMBE HOUSE
See Worcestershire

WHITEHILL FARM
See Oxfordshire

GROUP OPENING

81 NEW WINCHCOMBE GARDENS

Winchcombe, Cheltenham GL54 5JE. *The Gate is on North St, nr town centre. Charingworth Court is on Broadway Rd, Woodlands Farm is on Rushley Lane. Both on N edge of town nr The Footbridge. Please park in town centre car parks.* **Combined adm £6.50, chd free. Sat 15 June (10-4.30).**

NEW CHARINGWORTH COURT
Susan & Richard Wakeford
(See separate entry)

NEW THE GATE
Mrs Sue Paine.
North St is one of two main shopping streets in centre of Winchcombe. 'The Gate' is on same side as Co-op, approx 300yrds from town centre
Visitors also welcome by appt 1 June to 7 Sept.
01242 602798
sue.newton@btinternet.com

NEW WOODLANDS FARM
Mrs Morag Dobbin.
From Winchcombe town centre go down hill on Hailes St heading towards Broadway. Turn R into Rushley Lane just after footbridge. Garden entrance behind sign for Stancombe Lane, on bend of Rushley Lane. From Broadway & Toddington, Rushley Lane is 2nd on L just after entering 30mph limit

Three gardens in the historic Cotswolds town of Winchcombe, each with its own distinct feel. The Gate is a cottage garden within the courtyard of an historic coaching inn, with a separate walled kitchen garden. Charingworth Court is a 2 acre garden surrounding an impressive Tudor/Georgian house, with mature trees, perennial and shrub borders, roses and a large Japanese inspired pond. Woodlands Farm has distinct garden rooms, incl formal double borders either side of a long contemporary pond, herbaceous planting and an unusual monolith surrounded by hornbeam hedging. Beautiful views of the Cotswolds.

WOODVIEW
See Herefordshire

GROUP OPENING

82 WYCK RISSINGTON GARDENS
Cheltenham GL54 2PN. *Nr Stow-on-the-Wold & Bourton-on-the-Water. 1m from Fosse Way A429.* Home-made teas in village hall. **Combined adm £6, chd free (share to Friends of St Laurence).** **Sun 8 Sept (1-5).**

CHESTNUT COURT
Mr & Mrs N Hampton

GREENFIELDS FARM
Andrew & Elizabeth Ransom

MACES COTTAGE
Tim & Pippa Simon

◆ STONE HOUSE
Mr & Mrs Andrew Lukas
(See separate entry)

Wyck Rissington is an unspoilt Cotswold village and is unusual because of its wide village green planted with fine horse chestnuts. The gardens open are within easy reach of the convenient parking and of contrasting styles. If you need inspiration for autumn planting or just delight in the mellow hues of September, this is for you. There is a different mix of gardens in this popular group opening this year. Specialist plant sale, garden produce for sale. Wheelchair access available at all gardens.

Temple Guiting Manor
© Andrew Lawson

Gloucestershire County Volunteers

County Organiser
Norman Jeffery, 28 Shrivenham Road, Highworth, Swindon SN6 7BZ, 01793 762805, normjeffery28@btinternet.com

County Treasurer
Graham Baber, 11 Corinium Gate, Cirencester GL7 2PX, 01285 650961, grayanjen@onetel.com

Booklet Coordinator
Nick Kane, Church Farm, Goosey, Faringdon SN7 8PA, nick@kanes.org, 07768 478668.

Assistant County Organisers
Sue Hunt, 5 Oatground, Synwell, Wotton-under-Edge GL12 7HX, 01453 521263, suehunt2@btinternet.com
Trish Jeffery, 28 Shrivenham Road, Highworth, Swindon SN6 7BZ, 01793 762805, trishjeffery@btinternet.com
Valerie Kent, 9 Acer Close, Bradwell Grove, Nr Burford, Oxon OX18 4XE, 01993 823294
Shirley & Gordon Sills, Barn House, Sandywell Park, Whittington, Cheltenham GL54 4HF, 01242 820606, shirleysills@btinternet.com
Pat Willey, Orchard Cottage, Lynch Road, France Lynch, Stroud, GL6 8LP, 01453 883736, willey800@talktalk.net
Gareth & Sarah Williams, Lower Farm House, Cliffords Mesne, Newent GL18 1JT, 01531 821654, dgwilliams84@hotmail.com

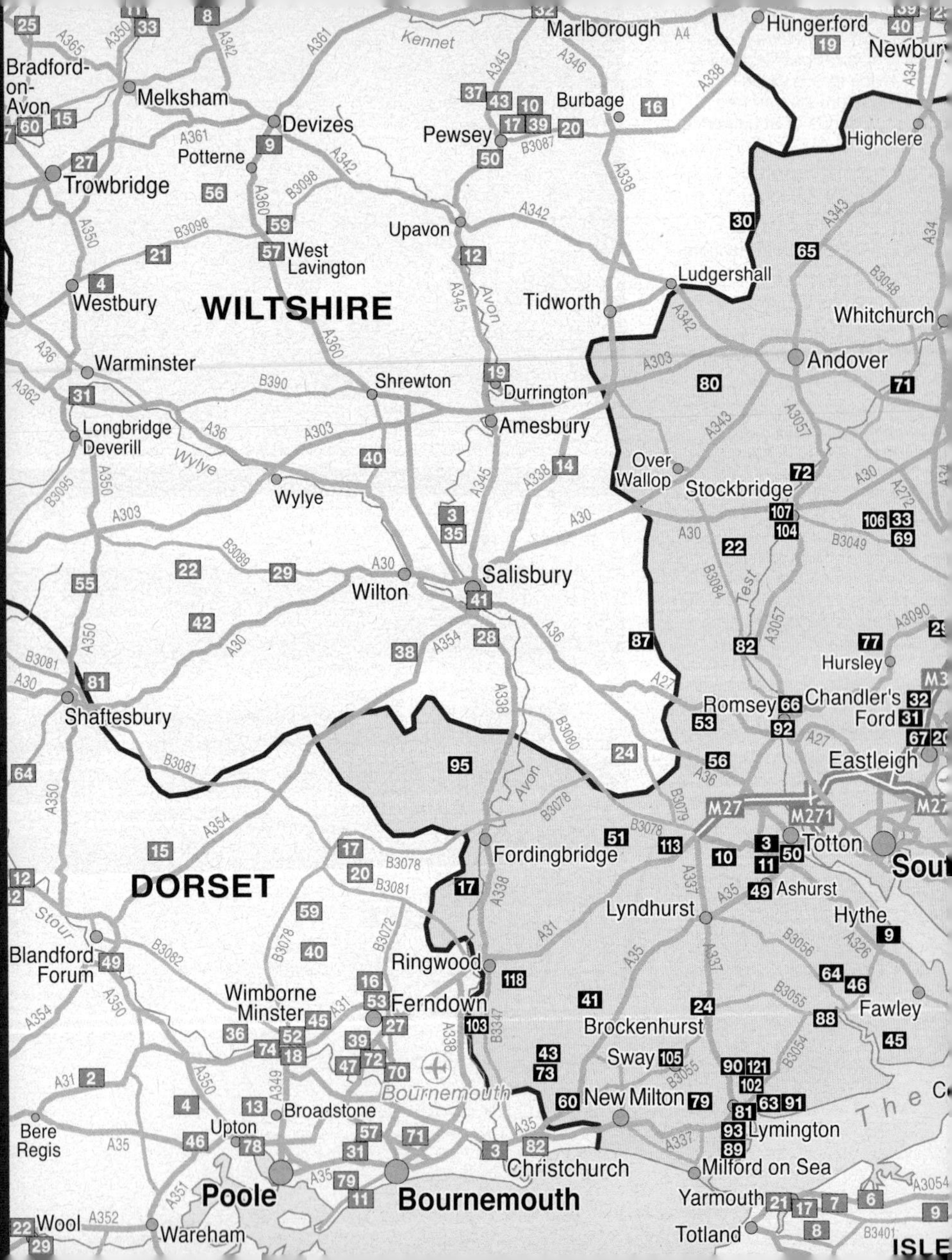
WILTSHIRE
DORSET
Marlborough
Hungerford
Newbury
Bradford-on-Avon
Melksham
Devizes
Potterne
Pewsey
Burbage
Highclere
Trowbridge
Upavon
West Lavington
Westbury
Tidworth
Ludgershall
Whitchurch
Andover
Warminster
Shrewton
Durrington
Amesbury
Longbridge Deverill
Wylye
Over Wallop
Stockbridge
Salisbury
Wilton
Hursley
Romsey
Chandler's Ford
Eastleigh
Shaftesbury
Fordingbridge
Totton
Ashurst
Lyndhurst
Hythe
Blandford Forum
Ringwood
Wimborne Minster
Ferndown
Fawley
Brockenhurst
Sway
New Milton
Bournemouth
Broadstone
Bere Regis
Upton
Lymington
Christchurch
Milford on Sea
Poole
Yarmouth
Wool
Wareham
Totland
Kennet
Avon
Test
Stour
Wylye

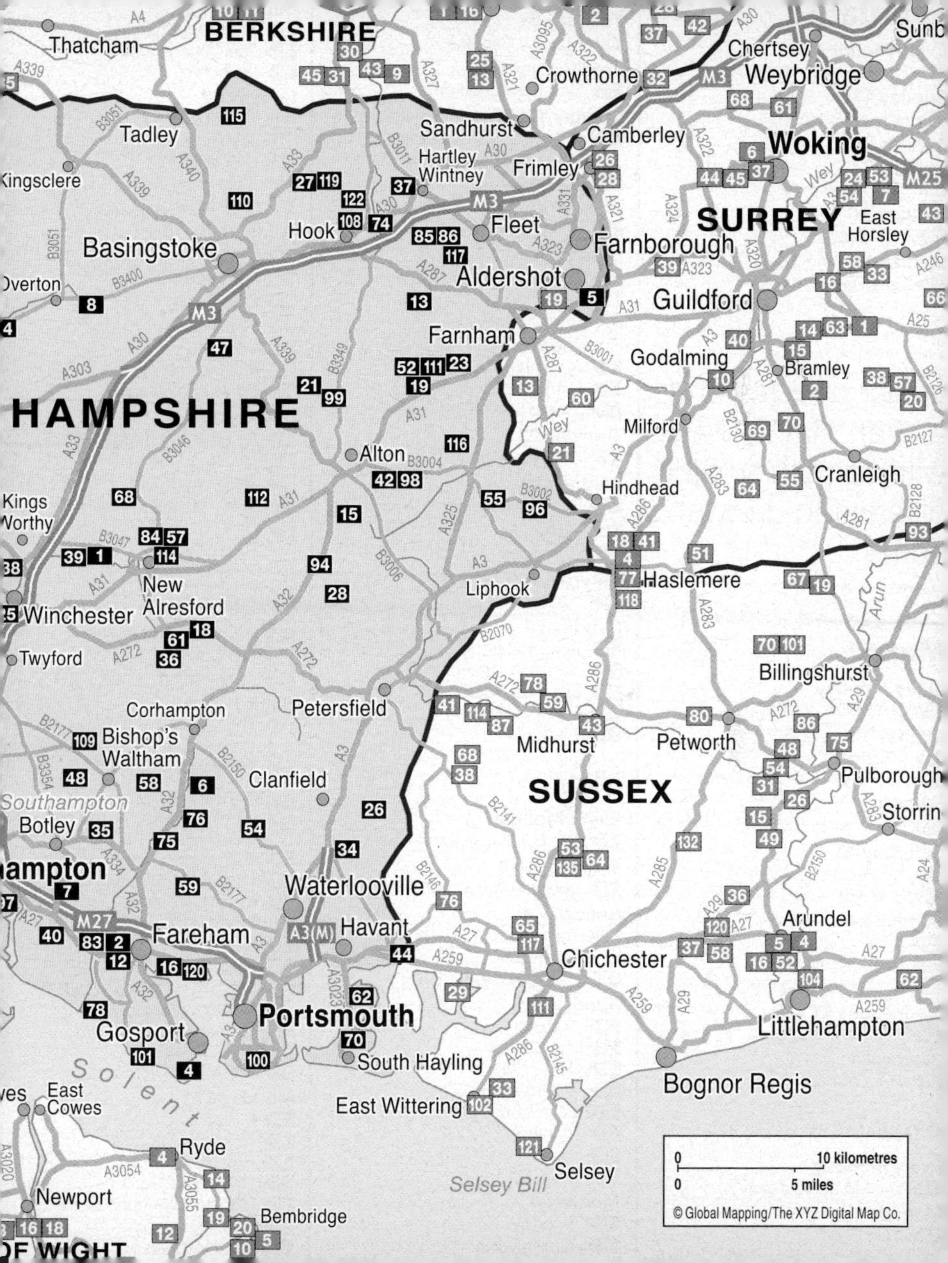

BERKSHIRE
HAMPSHIRE
SURREY
SUSSEX
Thatcham
Tadley
Kingsclere
Basingstoke
Overton
Sandhurst
Hartley Wintney
Hook
Crowthorne
Camberley
Frimley
Fleet
Farnborough
Aldershot
Farnham
Chertsey
Weybridge
Woking
East Horsley
Guildford
Godalming
Bramley
Milford
Cranleigh
Hindhead
Haslemere
Liphook
Alton
Kings Worthy
New Alresford
Winchester
Twyford
Corhampton
Bishop's Waltham
Petersfield
Clanfield
Southampton
Botley
Waterlooville
Havant
Fareham
Portsmouth
Gosport
South Hayling
East Wittering
Solent
East Cowes
Ryde
Newport
Bembridge
Selsey
Selsey Bill
Chichester
Bognor Regis
Littlehampton
Arundel
Midhurst
Petworth
Billingshurst
Pulborough
Storrin
Sunb
Wey
Arun
0 10 kilometres
0 5 miles
© Global Mapping/The XYZ Digital Map Co.

Opening Dates

January

Every Monday
79 The Mill at Gordleton

February

Every Monday
79 The Mill at Gordleton

Sunday 17
18 Bramdean House
39 The Down House

Friday 22
69 Little Court

Sunday 24
69 Little Court

Monday 25
69 Little Court

Linger over tea and a chat, maybe leave with something a bit different to grow at home . . .

March

Every Monday
79 The Mill at Gordleton

Sunday 10
48 Flintstones
66 The Island

Friday 22
25 12 Christchurch Road

Saturday 23
9 Atheling Villas
14 Bere Mill

Sunday 24
9 Atheling Villas
25 12 Christchurch Road
95 St Christopher's

Wednesday 27
13 Beechenwood Farm

Sunday 31
91 Pylewell Park

April

Every Monday
79 The Mill at Gordleton

Monday 1
69 Little Court

Wednesday 3
13 Beechenwood Farm

Sunday 7
33 Crawley Gardens
37 Dipley Mill
38 The Dower House
41 Durmast House
95 St Christopher's

Tuesday 9
33 Crawley Gardens

Wednesday 10
13 Beechenwood Farm

Sunday 14
86 Old Thatch & The Millennium Barn
95 St Christopher's

Wednesday 17
13 Beechenwood Farm

Saturday 20
9 Atheling Villas
61 Hinton Ampner
98 'Selborne'

Sunday 21
9 Atheling Villas
18 Bramdean House
98 'Selborne'

Tuesday 23
5 23 Anglesey Road

Wednesday 24
13 Beechenwood Farm

Thursday 25
110 The Vyne

Saturday 27
111 Walbury

Sunday 28
15 Berry Cottage
63 Hordle Walhampton School
102 Spinners Garden
108 Tylney Hall Hotel
111 Walbury

May

Every Monday
79 The Mill at Gordleton

Wednesday 1
13 Beechenwood Farm

Saturday 4
66 The Island
70 Littlewood
105 Sway Village Gardens

Sunday 5
9 Atheling Villas
31 The Cottage
37 Dipley Mill
66 The Island
70 Littlewood
94 Rotherfield Park
105 Sway Village Gardens
119 White Gables

Monday 6
8 Ashe Park
9 Atheling Villas
31 The Cottage
96 Sandy Slopes
119 White Gables

Wednesday 8
13 Beechenwood Farm

Thursday 9
54 Hambledon House

Saturday 11
21 Brick Kiln Cottage
31 The Cottage
98 'Selborne'

Sunday 12
2 80 Abbey Road
31 The Cottage
34 Crookley Pool
64 The House in the Wood
98 'Selborne'

Wednesday 15
13 Beechenwood Farm

Thursday 16
69 Little Court
106 Tanglefoot

Saturday 18
24 21 Chestnut Road
89 Pennington House

Sunday 19
24 21 Chestnut Road
60 Hinton Admiral
69 Little Court
85 The Old Rectory, Winchfield
89 Pennington House
91 Pylewell Park
106 Tanglefoot
107 Terstan

Wednesday 22
13 Beechenwood Farm
20 6 Breamore Close
36 Dean House

Saturday 25
103 The Stable Family Home Trust Garden
105 Sway Village Gardens

Sunday 26
20 6 Breamore Close
37 Dipley Mill
40 7 Downland Close
71 Longparish Gardens
75 Meon Orchard
80 Monxton & Amport Gardens
87 Ordnance House
92 Romsey Gardens
103 The Stable Family Home Trust Garden
105 Sway Village Gardens
114 Weir House
115 West Silchester Hall

Monday 27
20 6 Breamore Close
40 7 Downland Close
54 Hambledon House
71 Longparish Gardens
80 Monxton & Amport Gardens
92 Romsey Gardens
96 Sandy Slopes

115 West Silchester Hall

Wednesday 29

13 Beechenwood Farm
15 Berry Cottage

Definitely one for plantaholics . . . !

June

Every Monday

79 The Mill at Gordleton

Saturday 1

11 Barhi
40 7 Downland Close

Sunday 2

10 Aviemore
11 Barhi
40 7 Downland Close
48 Flintstones
99 Shalden Park House

Monday 3

48 Flintstones

Wednesday 5

6 Appletree House
13 Beechenwood Farm
74 1 Maple Cottage

Thursday 6

74 1 Maple Cottage
104 Stockbridge Gardens

Saturday 8

9 Atheling Villas

Sunday 9

3 6 Alfred Close
9 Atheling Villas
30 Conholt Park
67 53 Ladywood
101 Spindles
104 Stockbridge Gardens
108 Tylney Hall Hotel
109 Upham Farm

Monday 10

67 53 Ladywood

Wednesday 12

74 1 Maple Cottage

Thursday 13

33 Crawley Gardens
68 Lake House
74 1 Maple Cottage
76 Meon Place

National Gardens Weekend

Saturday 15

7 Appletrees
12 19 Barnwood Road
14 Bere Mill
26 Clibdens
35 Curdridge Grange
40 7 Downland Close
43 Edgewood
52 Froyle Gardens
61 Hinton Ampner
76 Meon Place
85 The Old Rectory, Winchfield
107 Terstan

Sunday 16

3 6 Alfred Close
7 Appletrees
12 19 Barnwood Road
14 Bere Mill
18 Bramdean House
20 6 Breamore Close
24 21 Chestnut Road
26 Clibdens
28 Colemore House Gardens
32 Cranbury Park
33 Crawley Gardens
35 Curdridge Grange
40 7 Downland Close
43 Edgewood
47 Farleigh House
50 The Fountains
52 Froyle Gardens
58 Hill Top
68 Lake House
72 Longstock Park
77 Merdon Manor
84 Old Alresford House
96 Sandy Slopes

Monday 17

24 21 Chestnut Road
28 Colemore House Gardens
43 Edgewood

Tuesday 18

5 23 Anglesey Road
84 Old Alresford House

Wednesday 19

6 Appletree House
15 Berry Cottage
36 Dean House
48 Flintstones (Evening)

Thursday 20

43 Edgewood

Friday 21

43 Edgewood
112 Walden

Saturday 22

43 Edgewood
89 Pennington House

Sunday 23

37 Dipley Mill
38 The Dower House
39 The Down House
89 Pennington House
93 Rookes Cottage
97 The Secret Garden Nature Reserve
112 Walden
120 Wicor Primary School Community Garden

Wednesday 26

39 The Down House

Saturday 29

42 East Worldham Gardens
83 Oakfields
86 Old Thatch & The Millennium Barn (Evening)
90 Pilley Hill Cottage

Sunday 30

15 Berry Cottage
41 Durmast House
42 East Worldham Gardens
51 Fritham Lodge
83 Oakfields
87 Ordnance House
90 Pilley Hill Cottage

July

Every Monday

79 The Mill at Gordleton

Wednesday 3

8 Ashe Park
36 Dean House

Thursday 4

19 Bramlins
44 Emsworth Gardens
111 Walbury

Friday 5

17 Braemoor

Saturday 6

17 Braemoor
27 The Coach House

Sunday 7

8 Ashe Park
17 Braemoor
101 Spindles
120 Wicor Primary School Community Garden

Thursday 11

33 Crawley Gardens

Saturday 13

21 Brick Kiln Cottage
61 Hinton Ampner
100 Southsea Gardens (Evening)

Sunday 14

30 Conholt Park
33 Crawley Gardens
36 Dean House
93 Rookes Cottage
107 Terstan
115 West Silchester Hall
117 Whispers
122 1 Wogsbarne Cottages

Monday 15
122 1 Wogsbarne Cottages

Wednesday 17
6 Appletree House
15 Berry Cottage

Friday 19
17 Braemoor

Saturday 20
16 8 Birdwood Grove
17 Braemoor
46 Fairweather's Nursery
90 Pilley Hill Cottage

Sunday 21
16 8 Birdwood Grove
17 Braemoor
18 Bramdean House
20 6 Breamore Close
37 Dipley Mill
78 Michaelmas
90 Pilley Hill Cottage

Monday 22
78 Michaelmas

Thursday 25
106 Tanglefoot

Saturday 27
16 8 Birdwood Grove
29 30 Compton Way
42 East Worldham Gardens
121 Willows

Sunday 28
29 30 Compton Way
42 East Worldham Gardens
56 Hideaway
75 Meon Orchard
106 Tanglefoot
121 Willows

Wednesday 31
29 30 Compton Way

August

Every Monday
79 The Mill at Gordleton

Thursday 1
57 Hill House

Friday 2
17 Braemoor

Saturday 3
17 Braemoor
46 Fairweather's Nursery
66 The Island

Sunday 4
10 Aviemore
17 Braemoor
36 Dean House
56 Hideaway
57 Hill House
62 The Homestead
66 The Island
97 The Secret Garden Nature Reserve
98 'Selborne'

Monday 5
98 'Selborne'

Tuesday 6
57 Hill House

Wednesday 7
23 Bury Court

Friday 9
65 Ibthorpe Tower

Saturday 10
22 The Buildings
24 21 Chestnut Road
65 Ibthorpe Tower
121 Willows

Sunday 11
22 The Buildings
24 21 Chestnut Road
115 West Silchester Hall
121 Willows

Wednesday 14
36 Dean House

Saturday 17
53 Gilberts Nursery
81 Moore Blatch
107 Terstan
116 Wheatley House

Sunday 18
15 Berry Cottage
18 Bramdean House
81 Moore Blatch
116 Wheatley House

Saturday 24
53 Gilberts Nursery

Sunday 25
53 Gilberts Nursery
121 Willows

Monday 26
54 Hambledon House
121 Willows

Saturday 31
90 Pilley Hill Cottage

September

Every Monday
79 The Mill at Gordleton

Sunday 1
75 Meon Orchard
86 Old Thatch & The Millennium Barn
90 Pilley Hill Cottage

Saturday 7
22 The Buildings

Sunday 8
22 The Buildings
34 Crookley Pool

Saturday 14
27 The Coach House
61 Hinton Ampner

Sunday 15
14 Bere Mill
18 Bramdean House
47 Farleigh House
54 Hambledon House
58 Hill Top
114 Weir House

Tuesday 17
5 23 Anglesey Road

Sunday 22
37 Dipley Mill

October

Every Monday
79 The Mill at Gordleton

Sunday 6
108 Tylney Hall Hotel

Sunday 13
84 Old Alresford House

Tuesday 15
84 Old Alresford House

November

Every Monday
79 The Mill at Gordleton

December

Mondays 2 & 9
79 The Mill at Gordleton

February 2014

Sunday 16
18 Bramdean House
39 The Down House

Friday 21
69 Little Court

Sunday 23
69 Little Court

Monday 24
69 Little Court

Gardens open to the public

4 Alverstoke Crescent Garden
45 Exbury Gardens & Steam Railway
61 Hinton Ampner
73 Macpennys Woodland Garden & Nurseries
82 Mottisfont Abbey & Garden
88 Patrick's Patch
102 Spinners Garden
110 The Vyne

Bring a bag for plants – help us give more to charity

30 Compton Way

By appointment only

- 1 Abbey Cottage
- 55 Hanging Hosta Garden
- 59 2 Hillside Cottages
- 113 Waldrons
- 118 White Barn

Also open by Appointment ☎

- 2 80 Abbey Road
- 3 6 Alfred Close
- 5 23 Anglesey Road
- 6 Appletree House
- 9 Atheling Villas
- 10 Aviemore
- 11 Barhi
- 12 19 Barnwood Road
- 13 Beechenwood Farm
- 14 Bere Mill
- 15 Berry Cottage
- 16 8 Birdwood Grove
- 17 Braemoor
- 20 6 Breamore Close
- 21 Brick Kiln Cottage
- 22 The Buildings
- 24 21 Chestnut Road
- 25 12 Christchurch Road
- 27 The Coach House
- 30 Conholt Park
- 31 The Cottage
- 34 Crookley Pool
- 35 Curdridge Grange
- 37 Dipley Mill
- 39 The Down House
- 40 7 Downland Close
- 41 Durmast House
- 44 23 New Brighton Road, Emsworth Gardens
- 48 Flintstones
- 50 The Fountains
- 51 Fritham Lodge
- 54 Hambledon House
- 57 Hill House
- 58 Hill Top
- 62 The Homestead
- 66 The Island
- 67 53 Ladywood
- 68 Lake House
- 69 Little Court
- 76 Meon Place
- 77 Merdon Manor
- 78 Michaelmas
- 87 Ordnance House
- 90 Pilley Hill Cottage
- 92 4 Mill Lane, Romsey Gardens
- 95 St Christopher's
- 97 The Secret Garden Nature Reserve
- 98 'Selborne'
- 101 Spindles
- 106 Tanglefoot
- 107 Terstan
- 108 Tylney Hall Hotel
- 111 Walbury
- 114 Weir House
- 115 West Silchester Hall
- 116 Wheatley House
- 119 White Gables
- 121 Willows

Take your Group to an NGS garden ☎

The Gardens

1 ABBEY COTTAGE

Rectory Lane, Itchen Abbas SO21 1BN. Patrick Daniell, 01962 779575, patrickdaniell@talktalk.net, www.abbeycottage.org.uk. *2½ m W of Alresford. On B3047 between Kings Worthy and Alresford, ½ m E of the Trout Inn at Itchen Abbas.* **Adm £4, chd free. Visitors welcome by appt 24 Apr to 23 Aug.**

This 1½ -acre organic garden, on alkaline soil, is a fine garden by any standards. Inside the C18 walls of an old kitchen garden there are enclosures, on different levels, which together make an inspirational garden, designed, created and now maintained by the owner. The adjoining meadow contains specimen trees, an orchard, spring bulbs, summer wild flowers and a plantation of native trees. Late summer wild-flower meadow in early August.

2 80 ABBEY ROAD

Fareham PO15 5HW. Brian & Vivienne Garford, 01329 843939, vgarford@aol.com. *1m W of Fareham. From M27 J9 take A27 E to Fareham for approx 2m. At top of hill, turn L at lights into Highlands Rd. Turn 4th R into Blackbrook Rd. Abbey Rd is 4th L.* Home-made teas. **Adm £3, chd free. Sun 12 May (11-5). Visitors also welcome by appt Apr to Aug.**

Unusual small garden with large collection of herbs and plants of botanical and historical interest, many for sale. Box hedging provides structure for relaxed planting. Interesting use of containers, and ideas for small gardens. 2 ponds and tiny meadow for wildlife. New summerhouse for 2013. Trails for children. Living willow seat, trained grapevine. Art exhibition and sale by local artist.

3 6 ALFRED CLOSE

West Totton. SO40 8TD. Josephine Bond, 07401 001201, jbond1127@yahoo.co.uk. *3m W of Southampton. From M27 J2 take A326 to Fawley. At 1st r'about L into Michigan Way. After Morrisons on L, take 1st L into Stonechat Drive. 3rd L into Goldcrest Lane. At T-junction turn L on Alfred Close and follow signs.* Home-made teas. **Adm £2.50, chd free. Suns 9, 16 June (1-5.30).** Also open 16 June **The Fountains, Forest Cottage & 21 Chestnut Road. Visitors also welcome by appt May to June.**

Hold your breath as you squeeze past the water-butts and be thrilled with a spectacle of colour and sparkle at all levels, from the mushroom fountain to the dovecote and pretty painted summerhouse. All this is achieved in a small garden dominated by a large protected oak, to the south.

4 ◆ ALVERSTOKE CRESCENT GARDEN

Crescent Road, Gosport PO12 2DH. Gosport Borough Council, 02392 422467, www.angleseyville.co.uk. *1m S of Gosport. From A32 & Gosport follow signs for Stokes Bay. Continue alongside bay to small r'about, turn L into Anglesey Rd. Crescent Garden signed 50yds on R.* **For opening times and information, please phone or see garden website.**

Restored Regency ornamental garden, designed to enhance fine crescent (Thomas Ellis Owen 1828). Trees, walks and flowers lovingly maintained by community/Council partnership. Garden's considerable local historic interest highlighted by impressive restoration and creative planting of adjacent St Mark's churchyard. Worth seeing together. Heritage, history and horticulture: a fascinating package. Plant Sale & refreshments Sat 18 May (10-4). Green Flag Award.

5 23 ANGLESEY ROAD

Aldershot GU12 4RF. Adrian & Elizabeth Whiteley, 01252 677623. *On E edge of Aldershot. From A331 take A323 towards Aldershot. Keep in RH lane, turn R at T-lights into North Lane, then immed L into Lower Newport Rd. Round bend turn immed R into Newport Rd, 1st R into Wilson Rd. Round L-hand bend turn immed R into Roberts Rd, Anglesey Rd 1st on L. Please park considerately in local roads.* Home-made teas. **Adm £2.50, chd free. Tues 23 Apr; 18 June; 17 Sept (2-5). Visitors also welcome by appt.**

This very small plot holds much to intrigue the curious visitor, richly rewarding leisurely close inspection. A strong geometric design is abundantly softened with rare and interesting flowering and foliage plants in pleasing harmony with cottage-garden stalwarts. Linger over tea and a chat, maybe leave with something a bit different to grow at home.

Hold your breath as you squeeze past the water-butts and be thrilled with a spectacle of colour and sparkle at all levels . . .

6 APPLETREE HOUSE

Station Road, Soberton SO32 3QU. Mrs J Dover, 01489 877333, jennie.dover@yahoo.co.uk. *10m N of Fareham. A32 N to Droxford, at Xrds turn R B2150. Turn R under bridge into Station Rd, garden 1m. Parking in lay-by 300yds or in rd.* Light refreshments. **Adm £2.50, chd free. Weds 5, 19 June; 17 July (12-4). Visitors also welcome by appt. Light lunches by arrangement.**

'A gardener's garden with the wow factor' - a comment made by a visiting group on a cold, wet afternoon in 2012. Designed to look larger than its 40ft x 90ft, this garden has both shady and sunny areas allowing a variety of planting, including a large collection of clematis viticella.

7 APPLETREES

267 Botley Rd, Burridge SO31 1BS. Kath & Ray Butcher. *2m S of Botley. From A27 take A3051 Park Gate to Botley, on L after 1½ m. From Botley take A3051, Appletrees is 2m on R.* Home-made teas. **Adm £3, chd free. Sat 15, Sun 16 June (11-5).**

A garden to explore, down narrow winding paths edged with subtle and original plant associations, leading to secluded seats. Created by flower-arranger owner, with good use of contrasting foliage and flowers. No lawn, just a crown of clipped box contrasting with the relaxed and exuberant planting elsewhere. Sinks and container planting, small pond and waterfall.

8 ASHE PARK
nr Ashe, Overton RG25 3AF. Graham & Laura Hazell. *2m E of Overton. Entrance on B3400, approx 500yds W of Deane Gate Inn.* Home-made teas. **Adm £5, chd free. Mon 6 May, Wed 3, Sun 7 July (2-6).**
Extensive new gardens within the grounds of a Georgian country house and estate, with further development in progress. Parkland and specimen trees, woodland and bluebell walks, large contemporary potager, lime avenue and several newly planted areas.

9 ATHELING VILLAS
16 Atheling Road, Hythe, Southampton SO45 6BR. Mary & Peter York, 02380 849349, athelingvillas@gmail.com. *At M27 J2, take A326 for Hythe/Fawley. Cross all r'abouts until Dibden r'about (1/2 m after Marchwood Priory Hospital) L to Hythe. After Shell garage, Atheling Road is 2nd L.* Home-made teas. **Adm £3, chd free (share to The Children's Society). Sat 23, Sun 24 Mar; Sat 20, Sun 21 Apr; Sun 5, Mon 6 May; Sat 8, Sun 9 June (2-5). Visitors also welcome by appt Mar to Aug max group size 50.**
Inspirational, imaginatively designed and comprehensively planted 1/3 -acre Victorian villa garden with many rare plants. In spring enjoy bulbs, hellebores and pulmonarias as you explore meandering paths set amongst structural planting. At later openings delight in the flowering trees, shrubs, bulbs and herbaceous planting of this tranquil and welcoming garden. Several seating areas throughout garden. Teas in Old Laundry (log fire at early openings). Self-guide leaflet and children's quiz. Display of original art in Garden Room.

10 AVIEMORE
Chinham Road, Bartley, Southampton SO40 2LF. Sandy & Alex Robinson, 02380 813651. *3m N of Lyndhurst, 7m W of Southampton. From M27 J1 go towards Lyndhurst on A337. After 3/4 m turn L to Bartley and follow NGS signs.* Home-made teas. **Adm £3, chd free. Suns 2 June; 4 Aug (2-5). Also open 2 June Barhi. Visitors also welcome by appt May to Aug, refreshments by arrangement.**
Richly planted, small garden in north New Forest. Our aim is to please the plant connoisseur and introduce enthusiasts to new plants and ideas for smaller plots. Every plant must play its part within a seasonal symphony of shrubs, climbers, perennials and grasses. Oak bridges criss-cross a small stream. Old alpine troughs and quirky artifacts add texture, structure and colour to this 'all yr garden'. Featured in Country Homes and Interiors. Some gravel and stream areas inaccessible to wheelchairs.

Step through the gate to an enchanting garden with an abundance of floral colour and delightful features . . .

11 BARHI
27 Reynolds Dale, Ashurst SO40 7PS. Mrs Finuala Barnes, www.barhi.net/garden. *3m W of Southampton. From M27 J2 take A326 to Fawley. At 4th r'about, L into Cocklydown Lane. At mini r'about, L into Ibbotson Way. 1st L into Reynolds Dale & follow signs.* **Adm £2.50, chd free. Sat 1, Sun 2 June (2-5). Also open 2 June Aviemore.**
Small, compact 'modern cottage' garden shared with lively Springer Spaniels, designed around a chambered nautilus spiral. No lawn, so lots of space for plants. The dense planting, meandering paths, secluded pergola, raised formal pond and feature patio have led visitors to describe the garden as 'Tardis-like'.

12 19 BARNWOOD ROAD
Fareham PO15 5LA. Jill & Michael Hill, 07814 811956, thegarden19@gmail.com. *1m W of Fareham. From M27 J9 take A27 towards Fareham. At top of hill past Titchfield Mill PH turn L at T-lights into Highlands Rd. Take 4th R into Blackbrook Rd, Meadow Bank 4th turn on R. Barnwood Rd is off Meadow Bank. Please consider the neighbours when parking.* Home-made teas. **Adm £3, chd free. Sat 15, Sun 16 June (11-4.30). Groups of 10+ also welcome by appt May to Aug.**
Step through the gate to an enchanting garden designed for peace with an abundance of floral colour and delightful features. Greek-style courtyard leads to natural pond with bridge and bog garden, complemented by a thatched summerhouse and jetty, designed and built by owners. Secret pathways, hexagonal greenhouse and new mosaic seating area. Featured in Real Homes and Woman and Home magazine.

13 BEECHENWOOD FARM
Hillside, Odiham RG29 1JA. Mr & Mrs M Heber-Percy, 01256 702300, beechenwood@totalise.co.uk. *5m SE of Hook. Turn S into King St from Odiham High St. Turn L after cricket ground for Hillside. Take 2nd turn R after 1 1/2 m, modern house 1/2 m.* Home-made teas. **Adm £3.50, chd free. Every Wed 27 Mar to 5 June (2-5). Visitors also welcome by appt Mar to June.**
2-acre garden in many parts. Lawn meandering through woodland with drifts of spring bulbs. Rose pergola with steps, pots with spring bulbs and later aeoniums. Fritillary and cowslip meadow. Walled herb garden with pool and exuberant planting. Orchard incl white garden and hot border. Greenhouse and vegetable garden. Rock garden extending to grasses, ferns and bamboos. Shady walk to belvedere. 8-acre copse of native species with grassed rides. Gravel drive and some shallow steps (avoidable).

14 BERE MILL
London Road, Whitchurch RG28 7NH. Rupert & Elizabeth Nabarro, 01256 892210, rnabarro@aol.com. *9m E of Andover, 12m N of Winchester. In centre of Whitchurch, take London Rd at r'about. Up hill 1m, turn R 50yds beyond The Gables on R. Drop-off point for disabled at garden.* **Adm £5, chd free (share to Smile Train). Sat 23 Mar; Sat 15, Sun 16 June; Sun 15 Sept (1.30-5). Groups of 10+ also welcome by appt Feb to Nov.**
In a beautiful setting beside the River Test, with carriers and large lake next to restored SSSI water meadow,

grazed by Welsh Mountain sheep, lambs and Belted Galloway cattle. Riverside walks, species tulips, Japanese prunus, peonies, wisteria collection, roses, bog garden at its best in autumn. Double perennial beds and swamp cypress avenue. Eastern influence incl Japanese Tea House, many different riverside irises and unique bridges. The working mill was where Portals first made paper for the Bank of England. Unfenced and unguarded rivers and streams. Restricted wheelchair access if very wet.

15 BERRY COTTAGE

Church Road, Upper Farringdon, nr Alton GU34 3EG. Mrs P Watts, 01420 588318. *3m S of Alton off A32. Turn L at Xrds, Ist L into Church Rd. Follow rd past Massey's Folly, 2nd house on R opp church.* Home-made teas. **Adm £2.50, chd free. Sun 28 Apr; Wed 29 May; Wed 19, Sun 30 June, Wed 17 July, Sun 18 Aug (2.30-5). Visitors also welcome by appt.**

Small organic cottage garden with all-yr interest. Spring bulbs, roses, clematis and herbaceous borders. Pond and bog garden. Shrubbery and small kitchen garden. The owner-designed and maintained garden surrounds C16 house. The borders are colour-themed and contain many unusual plants. Close to Massey's Folly built by the Victorian rector incl 80ft tower with unique handmade floral bricks, C11 church and some of the oldest yew trees in the county.

16 8 BIRDWOOD GROVE

Downend, Fareham PO16 8AF. Jayne & Eddie McBride, 01329 280838, jayne.mcbride@ntlworld.com. *½ m E of Fareham. M27, J11: take L lane slip to Delme r'about. Turn L towards Portchester (A27) over 2 sets of T-lights, completely around small r'about & Birdwood Grove is 1st L.* Home-made teas. **Adm £2.50, chd free. Sat 20, Sun 21, Sat 27 July (2-6). Visitors also welcome by appt July to Sept.**

The sub-tropics in Fareham! This small garden is influenced by the flora of Australia and New Zealand and includes many rare and unusual indigenous species. The 4 climate zones - arid, medium, lush fertile and a shady fernery - are all densely planted to make the most of dramatic foliage. Definitely one for plantaholics! Fareham in Bloom, gold award plantsman's small back garden. South & South East in Bloom, certificate of excellence. One step, wheelchair assistance supplied.

Aviemore

17 BRAEMOOR

Bleak Hill, Harbridge, Ringwood BH24 3PX. Tracy & John Netherway & Judy Spratt, 01425 652983, jnetherway@btinternet.com. *2½ m S of Fordingbridge. Turn off A338 at Ibsley. Go through Harbridge village to T-junction at top of hill, turn R for ¼ m.* Home-made teas. **Adm £3, chd free. Fris, Sats, Suns 5, 6, 7, 19, 20, 21 July, 2, 3, 4 Aug (2-5.30). Visitors also welcome by appt July.**

¾ -acre garden brimming with bold, colourful planting and interest. One of our moongates leads to a seaside haven of painted beach huts and driftwood gems. Another enters the cottage garden with overflowing herbaceous borders, stream and pond. Greenhouse with cacti and carnivorous plants. Vegetable area with bantam chickens. Small adjacent nursery. Some gravel paths.

18 BRAMDEAN HOUSE

Bramdean SO24 0JU. Mr & Mrs H Wakefield, victoria@bramdeanhouse.com. *4m S of Alresford. In centre of village on A272.* **Adm £4, chd free. Suns 17 Feb (2-4); 21 Apr; 16 June; 21 July; 18 Aug; 15 Sept (2-4.30); 16 Feb 2014 (2-4).**

Beautiful 5-acre garden famous for its mirror-image herbaceous borders. Carpets of spring bulbs especially snowdrops. A large and unusual collection of plants and shrubs giving yr-round interest incl. over 40 varieties of sweet pea. 1-acre walled garden featuring prize-winning vegetables, fruit and flowers. Small arboretum. Boxwood castle. Wild-flower meadow and small arboretum.

19 BRAMLINS

Lower Froyle GU34 4LG. Mrs Anne Blunt. *5m NE of Alton. Access to Lower Froyle from A31 between Alton and Farnham at Bentley. Bramlins is almost opp the village hall where parking is available.* Home-made teas. **Combined adm £4, chd free.**

Thur 4 July (2-5). Combined with Walbury. Also open 15 & 16 June with Froyle Gardens.

A flower arranger's garden, informally planted to harmonise with surrounding countryside. The house is surrounded by several garden rooms including a conservatory with tender plants, secret scented garden, kitchen garden and small orchard with flowers. Gravel drive.

20 6 BREAMORE CLOSE

Eastleigh SO50 4QB. Mr & Mrs R Trenchard, 02380 611230, dawndavina6@yahoo.co.uk. *1m N of Eastleigh. M3 J12, follow signs to Eastleigh. Turn R at r'about into Woodside Ave, then 1st L into Broadlands Ave (park here). Breamore Close 3rd on L.* Home-made teas. **Adm £3, chd free. Wed 22, Sun 26, Mon 27 May, Sun 16 June, Sun 21 July (1-5.30). Visitors also welcome by appt May to July.**

Delightful plant lover's garden with coloured foliage and unusual plants, giving a tapestry effect of texture and colour. Many hostas displayed in pots. The garden is laid out in distinctive planting themes with seating areas to sit and contemplate. In May, magnificent wisteria over a pergola with flowers 3ft-4ft long; in June many clematis scramble through roses followed by phlox in July. Small gravel area wheelchairs may find hard to negotiate.

21 BRICK KILN COTTAGE

The Avenue, Herriard, Basingstoke RG25 2PR. Barbara Jeremiah, 01256 381301, barbara@klca.co.uk. *4m NE of Alton. A339 from Basingstoke to Alton. Turn L following signs to Lasham Gliding Club onto The Avenue. Past Back Lane on L & after 1 field turn L into Brick Kiln Cottage drive.* Home-made teas. **Adm £3.50, chd free. Sat 11 May, Sat 13 July (1.30-5). Groups also welcome by appt May to Sept.**

Cottage garden in a bluebell wood. Woodland garden in 2 acres incl natural water feature, billabong, stumpery and ferny hollow. Tree house (children must be accompanied by an adult). Woodland walk. Tea pavilion. Croquet and boules, weather permitting.

22 THE BUILDINGS

Broughton, Stockbridge SO20 8BH. Dick & Gillian Pugh, 01794 301424, dickandgillianpugh@ukf.net. *3m W of Stockbridge. NGS yellow signs 2m W of Stockbridge off A30, or 6m N of Romsey off B3084.* Home-made teas. **Adm £3.50, chd free (share to Friends of St Mary's Broughton and St James's Bossington). Sats & Suns 10, 11 Aug; 7, 8 Sept (2-5). Visitors & groups also welcome by appt June to Sept.**

In a renovated farmstead, high on the Hampshire Downs, we offer modern planting in gravel gardens, borders, and an exuberant pergola, all on our thin chalk soil. Often described as 'inspirational', the planting and layout are widely admired. Many unusual plants and varieties especially in the salvia, viticella clematis and pelargonium families. Featured in Salisbury Life and Period Homes and Interiors.

23 BURY COURT

Bentley GU10 5LZ. John Coke, www.burycourtbarn.com. *5m NE of Alton. 1m N of Bentley. Take Hole Lane, then follow signs towards Crondall.* Home-made teas. **Adm £5, chd free. Wed 7 Aug (2-5.30).**

Designed in cooperation with Piet Oudolf, created from old farmyard, in the continental 'naturalistic' style, making heavy use of grasses in association with perennials selected for an extended season of interest. Area designed by Christopher Bradley-Hole in minimalist style, featuring grid of gravel paths bisecting chequerboard of naturalistically planted raised squares edged in rusted steel.

24 21 CHESTNUT ROAD

Brockenhurst SO42 7RF. Iain & Mary Hayter, 01590 622009, iain@hayter.fsnet.co.uk. *4m S of Lyndhurst. S on A337 to Brockenhurst, take R fork B3055, Grigg Lane, opp Careys Manor Hotel. Garden 500yds from junction via 2nd L Chestnut Rd and 2nd L again for no 21. Parking limited; please use village car park nearby. To avoid delays in Lyndhurst, leave M27 J2, follow 'Heavy Lorry Route'.* Home-made teas. **Adm £3, chd free. Sat 18 May (11-5); Sun 19 May (1-5); Sun 16 (11-5), Mon 17 June (2-5); Sat 10 Aug (11-5); Sun 11 Aug (1-5). Also open 15 & 16 June The Fountains, 16 June 6 Alfred Close & 10 & 11 Aug Willows. Visitors also welcome by appt Apr to Oct min of 10.**

A plant lover's dream, where colour, form and scent dictate. Many ideas for wet and dry, sun or shady areas. Naturalistic and formal planting, with wildlife areas and a pond. Here sits a summerhouse, where home-made teas may be enjoyed. New for 2013, the 'Shy Maiden' border. Photo and painting exhibition in summerhouse. Visit Brockenhurst village and enjoy seeing the ponies and cattle roaming freely around the village. Lots of ideas to copy in this ⅓ -acre garden with many plants available to purchase. Featured in Hampshire Country Gardener. No wheelchair access to raised deck or some parts of the garden if wet.

Magnificent wisteria over a pergola with flowers 3ft-4ft long . . .

25 12 CHRISTCHURCH ROAD

Winchester SO23 9SR. Iain & Penny Patton, 01962 854272, pjspatton@yahoo.co.uk, For B&B info visit www.visitwinchester.com. *S side of city. Leave centre of Winchester by Southgate St, 1st R into St James Lane, 3rd L into Christchurch Rd.* Home-made teas. **Adm £2.50, chd free. Fri 22, Sun 24 Mar (2-6). Visitors and groups of up to 20 also welcome by appt Feb to Nov.**

Small town garden with strong design enhanced by exuberant and vertical planting. All-yr interest incl winter-flowering shrubs,bulbs and hellebores. 2 water features, including slate-edged rill, and pergolas provide structure. Small front garden designed to be viewed from the house with bulbs, roses and herbaceous planting. Featured in The English Garden and in Amateur Gardener.

"Lemon drizzle cake, Victoria sponge ... yummy!"

26 CLIBDENS
Chalton PO8 0BG. Michael & Jacqueline Budden. *6m S of Petersfield. Turn L off A3M N of Horndean then directly R over motorway to Chalton. Clibdens is 1st turning on L in village, directly before Chalton village sign.* Home-made teas. **Adm £4, chd free. Sat 15, Sun 16 June (11-5.30).**
1-acre chalk garden comprising 5 separate rooms. Terrace set with stone urns, agapanthus and succulents. New blue-toned herbaceous border fringing drive. Stunning natural yew sculpture, wildlife pond and sunken bog garden. Self-seeded gravel garden. Oak posts with rope and roses. Yew and box topiary animals. All beautifully gardened and maintained.

27 THE COACH HOUSE
Reading Road, Sherfield on Loddon RG27 0EX. Jane & Peter Jordan, 01256 880852, jane@janejordangarden-design.com. *5m N of Basingstoke. A33 to main Sherfield on Loddon r'about. Turn into village & follow signs to free car parks. Short walk to garden, situated in centre of village opp village hall. Drop-off only at house.* Home-made teas. **Adm £3.50, chd free. Sat 6 July, Sat 14 Sept (2-5). Visitors also welcome by appt May to Sept.**
A hidden gem, this 510sq metre walled garden has been replanted extensively over the past 5yrs. Includes mature trees, a wide range of plants and grasses chosen for texture and colour, herb garden, formal pond and sunken brick terrace. The style is relaxed, the content stimulating and the tea fresh, so come enjoy!
D

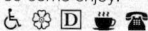

28 COLEMORE HOUSE GARDENS
Colemore, Alton GU34 3RX. Mr & Mrs Simon de Zoete. *4m S of Alton (off A32). Approach from N on A32, take L turn (Shell Lane), 1/4 m S of East Tisted. Go under bridge, keep L until you see Colemore Church. Park on verge of church.* **Adm £3.50, chd free. Sun 16, Mon 17 June (2-6).**
4 acres in lovely unspoilt country, featuring masses of unusual plants and different aspects - a spectacular arched rose walk, water rill, mirror pond, herbaceous and shrub borders and a new woodland walk. Many admire the lawns, new grass gardens and thatched pavilion. A small arboretum is being planted. Change and development is ongoing, and increasing the diversity of interesting plants is a prime motivation. Thatched pavilion built by students from the Prince's Trust. Grass gardens, lawns, hedges and rooms containing many unusual plants.

A spectacular arched rose walk . . .

29 NEW 30 COMPTON WAY
Winchester SO22 4HS. Susan Summers, www.summersgd.co.uk. *2m SW of Winchester. From M3 J11, follow A3090 Badger Farm Road uphill. Turn L into Oliver's Battery Road South. Take 2nd L into Compton Way. House on R before Austen Ave.* Home-made teas. **Adm £3, chd free. Sat 27, Sun 28, Wed 31 July (2-5).**
Contemporary garden owned by local garden designer on the outskirts of Winchester. Sunny hilltop 1/4 -acre plot. Themed borders of colourful mixed planting on chalky soil, including dahlias and agapanthus. Kitchen and herb gardens, and pond. Image on the cover of The Yellow Book.
D

30 CONHOLT PARK
Hungerford Lane, nr Chute SP11 9HA. Conholt Park Estate, 07917 796826, conholt.garden@hotmail.com. *7m N of Andover. Turn N off A342 Andover to Devizes rd at Weyhill Church. Go 5m N through Clanville. Turn L at T-junction, Conholt 1/2 m on R, just off Chute causeway. A343 to Hurstbourne Tarrant, turn to and go through Vernham Dean, next turn L signed Conholt.* Home-made teas. **Adm £5, chd free. Suns 9 June; 14 July (11-5). Visitors also welcome by appt Apr to Nov.**
10 acres surrounding Regency house (not open), with mature cedars. Rose, sensory, winter and secret gardens, fern dell and poppy garden. Glasshouses, flower cartwheel, berry wall and orchard occupy the walled garden. New summer border and gravel garden. Ladies Walk and large laurel maze with viewing platform. Visitors welcome to picnic. Working dog display on open days. Deep gravel and steps.

COOKSCROFT
See Sussex

31 THE COTTAGE
16 Lakewood Road, Chandler's Ford SO53 1ES. Hugh & Barbara Sykes, 02380 254521, barandhugh@aol.com. *2m NW of Eastleigh. Leave M3 J12, follow signs to Chandler's Ford. At King Rufus on Winchester Rd, turn R into Merdon Ave, then 3rd rd on L.* Home-made teas. **Adm £3, chd free. Sun 5, Mon 6, Sat 11, Sun 12 May (2-6). Visitors also welcome by appt Apr to May.**
3/4 acre. Azaleas, bog garden, camellias, dogwoods, erythroniums, free-range bantams, geraniums, hostas, irises, jasmines, kitchen garden, landscaping began in 1950, maintained by owners. New planting, osmunda, ponds, quiz for children, rhododendrons, sun and shade, trilliums, unusual plants, viburnums, wildlife areas, eXuberant foliage, yr-round interest, zantedeschia. 'A lovely tranquil garden' - Anne Swithinbank. Honey from our garden hives for sale. Hampshire Wildlife Trust Wildlife Garden Award.

32 CRANBURY PARK
Otterbourne, nr Winchester SO21 2HL. Mr & Mrs Chamberlayne-Macdonald. *3m NW of Eastleigh. Main entrance on old A33 between Winchester and Southampton, by bus stop at top of Otterbourne Hill. Entrances also in Hocombe Rd, Chandler's Ford & next to church in Otterbourne.* Home-made teas. **Adm £4, chd free (share to St Deny's church Chilworth). Sun 16 June (2-6).**
Extensive pleasure grounds laid out in late C18 and early C19 by Papworth; fountains, rose garden, specimen trees and pinetum, lakeside walk and fern walk. Family carriages and collection of prams will be on view, also photos of King George VI, Eisenhower and Montgomery reviewing Canadian troops at Cranbury before D-Day. Disabled WC.

GROUP OPENING

33 CRAWLEY GARDENS
nr Winchester SO21 2PU. *5m NW of Winchester. From M3 J9 take A34 N, exit after 3m & at r'about take 4th exit (A272). After 1.7m turn L to Crawley. From Winchester or Stockbridge take B3049. Parking throughout village, best nr Church.* Home-made teas in the Village Hall. **Combined adm £6, chd free. Sun 7, Tue 9 Apr (2-5.30); Thur 13, Sun 16 June; Thur 11, Sun 14 July (2-6).**

BAY TREE HOUSE D
Julia & Charles Whiteaway.
Open June & July dates

GABLE COTTAGE
Patrick Hendra & Ken Jones.
Open April dates only

LITTLE COURT
Prof & Mrs A R Elkington.
Open April & June dates
(See separate entry)

PAIGE COTTAGE
Mr & Mrs T W Parker.
Open April & July dates

TANGLEFOOT
Mr & Mrs F J Fratter.
Open June & July dates
(See separate entry)

Crawley is an exceptionally pretty village nestling in chalk downland with thatched houses, C14 church and delightful village pond with ducks. A different combination of gardens opens each month providing seasonal interest with varied character, and with traditional and contemporary approaches to landscape and planting. Most of the gardens have beautiful country views and there are other excellent gardens to be seen from the road. The spring gardens are Paige Cottage, Gable Cottage and the 3-acre traditional English country garden at Little Court with carpets of spring bulbs. In summer, other gardens open. At Bay Tree House there are pleached limes, a rill and contemporary borders; while at Tanglefoot there are colour-themed borders, herb wheel, exceptional kitchen garden and a traditional Victorian boundary wall supporting trained fruit incl apricots. Also in the summer, Little Court has a mass of colourful herbaceous planting while Paige Cottage is a typical mixed cottage garden.

34 CROOKLEY POOL
Blendworth Lane, Horndean PO8 0AB. Mr & Mrs Simon Privett, 02392 592662, simon.privett123@btinternet.com. *5m S of Petersfield. 2m E of Waterlooville, off A3. From Horndean village go up Blendworth Lane between bakery and hairdresser. Entrance 200yds before church on L with white railings.* Home-made teas. **Adm £3.50, chd free. Sun 12 May, Sun 8 Sept (2-5.30). Visitors also welcome by appt, teas by arrangement.**
Here the plants decide where to grow. Californian tree poppies elbow valerian aside to crowd round the pool. Evening primroses obstruct the way to the door and the steps to wisteria-shaded terraces. Hellebores bloom under the trees. Salvias, pandorea jasminoides, justicia, pachystachys lutea and passion flowers riot quietly with tomatoes in the greenhouse. Not a garden for the neat or tidy minded, although this is a plantsman's garden full of unusual plants and a lot of tender perennials. Bantams stroll throughout. Display of watercolour paintings of flowers found in the garden.

Magical areas, the Rust garden, the pill-box grotto or the ornamental courtyard . . .

35 CURDRIDGE GRANGE
Curdridge Lane, Curdridge, Southampton SO32 2BH. Joanne & David Furby, 01489 782454, joanne@furby.me.uk. *5m N of Fareham. From Fareham, N on A32, then A334 towards Botley. Turn R at top of hill (after 2m) in Curdridge. R into Lockhams Lane. At end of Lockhams Lane turn R. Gate 1st R.* Home-made teas. **Adm £4, chd free. Sat 15, Sun 16 June (11-5). Visitors also welcome by appt Apr to Oct.**
A Victorian country-house garden of 2½ acres, with uninterrupted views over surrounding farmland. Sunken garden with lily pond and formal beds planted with a bright mix of traditional and modern plants. Habitat pond with toads, newts and house martins. Restored Victorian greenhouses and woodland walk. Plenty to interest all the family. Limited wheelchair access, some gravel paths and steps.

36 DEAN HOUSE
Kilmeston SO24 0NL. Mr P H R Gwyn, (Julian Blackwell, Head Gardener), www.deanhousegardens.co.uk. *5m S of Alresford. Via village of Cheriton or off A272 signed at Cheriton Xrds. Follow signs for Kilmeston, through village and turn L at Dean House sign.* Home-made teas. **Adm £5, chd free. Weds 22 May, 19 June, 3 July (10-4.30); Suns 14 July, 4 Aug (11.30-4.30); Wed 14 Aug (10-4.30).**
The 7 acres have been described as 'a well-kept secret hidden behind the elegant facade of its Georgian centrepiece'. Sweeping lawns, York stone paths, gravel pathways, many young and mature trees and hedges, mixed and herbaceous borders, symmetrical rose garden, pond garden, working walled garden, with 125 different varieties of vegetable, and glasshouses all help to create a diverse and compact sliver of Eden. Over 1700 individually documented plant species and cultivars in our collection. Featured in Country Life. Gravel paths.

37 DIPLEY MILL
Dipley Road, Hartley Wintney, Hook RG27 8JP. Miss Rose McMonigall, 07885 745904, rose@rosemcm.demon.co.uk, www.dipleymill.org.uk. *2m NE of Hook. Turn E off B3349 at Mattingley (1½ m N of Hook) signed Hartley Wintney, West Green and Dipley. Dipley Mill ½ m on L just over bridge.* Home-made teas. **Adm £5, chd free. Suns 7 Apr (1-4); 5, 26 May (1-5); 23 June; 21 July (1-5.30); 22 Sept (1-4). Visitors also welcome by appt Apr to Sept.**
A romantic adventure awaits as you wander by the meandering streams surrounding this Domesday Book listed mill! Explore many magical areas, such as the Rust garden, the pill-box grotto or the ornamental courtyard. Or just escape into wild meadows. 'One of the most beautiful gardens in Hampshire' according to Alan Titchmarsh in his TV programme 'Love Your Garden'. Animals, local fruit stalls (depending on availability). Featured on ITV 'Love Your Garden'.

38 THE DOWER HOUSE
Springvale Road, Headbourne Worthy, Winchester SO23 7LD. Mrs Judith Lywood, www.thedowerhouse.net. *2m N of Winchester. From M3, J9, take A34 N, keep in RH lane to A33 towards Kingsworthy. Turn L (B3047). After bridge 1st R into Bedfield Lane. Follow signs for wheelchair access parking.* Home-made teas. **Adm £3.50, chd free. Sun 7 Apr, Sun 23 June (2.30-5.30).**
5½ acres with easy paths, numerous seats, good views, colourful perennials, shrubs and mature trees (incl large Indian bean tree and cercis 'Forest Pansy'). Bog garden, good pond with fish and water lilies. Small secret courtyard garden and excellent container planting on residents' patios. Parking at main entrance to house, following path to garden.

39 THE DOWN HOUSE
Itchen Abbas SO21 1AX. Jackie & Mark Porter, 01962 791054, markstephenporter@gmail.com, www.thedownhouse.co.uk. *6m E of Winchester on B3047. 5th house on R after Itchen Abbas village sign.* Home-made teas. **Adm £4, chd free (share to PCaSo, Prostate Cancer Support). Sun 17 Feb (12-4); Sun 23, Wed 26 June (2-6); Sun 16 Feb 2014 (12-4). Groups of 10+ also welcome by appt Feb to July.**
3-acre garden developed by owners since 2001, laid out in rooms overlooking Itchen Valley, adjoining the Pilgrim's Way, with walks through a large meadow to the river. Carpet of snowdrops and crocus, plus borders of coloured stems in winter. Roped rose garden, hot borders, wildlife pond and shady places in summer. Pleached hornbeams, yew-lined avenues, woodland nut and orchard walk. Working vineyard and potager. **Live jazz on 23 June**. The garden in winter was featured in Country Homes and Interiors magazine, and the potager in Countryside magazine.

DOWN PLACE
See Sussex

40 7 DOWNLAND CLOSE
Locks Heath, nr Fareham SO31 6WB. Roy Dorland, 07768 107779, roydorland@hotmail.co.uk. *3m W of Fareham. Leave M27 J9 (Whitely). Follow A27 on Southampton Rd to Park Gate. Past Kams Palace restaurant, L into Locks Rd, 3rd R into Meadow Ave, 2nd L into Downland Close.* Home-made teas. **Adm £2.50, chd free. Sun 26, Mon 27 May, Sat 1, Sun 2, Sat 15, Sun 16 June (12-5). Visitors also welcome by appt May to July.**
Visit this prizewinning, beautiful, restful and inspirational 50ft x 45ft plantsman's garden, packed with ideas for the 'modest-sized' plot. Many varieties of hardy geraniums, hostas, heucheras, shrubs, ferns and other unusual perennials, weaving a tapestry of harmonious colour. Attractive water feature, plenty of seating areas and charming summerhouse. A garden to fall in love with! Runner up in Hampshire Gardener of the Year.

DURFORD MILL HOUSE
See Sussex

Carpet of snowdrops and crocus, plus borders of coloured stems . . .

41 DURMAST HOUSE
Bennetts Lane, Burley BH24 4AT. Mr & Mrs P E G Daubeney, 01425 402132, philip@daubeney.co.uk, www.durmasthouse.co.uk. *5m SE of Ringwood. Off Burley to Lyndhurst rd, nr White Buck Hotel.* Cream teas. **Adm £4, chd free (share to Delhi Commonwealth Women's Assn Medical Clinic). Sun 7 Apr, Sun 30 June (2-5). Visitors also welcome by appt, admission includes talk and teas.**
Designed by Gertrude Jekyll, Durmast has contrasting hot and cool colour borders, formal rose garden edged with lavender and a long herbaceous border. Many old trees, Victorian rockery and orchard with beautiful spring bulbs. Rare azaleas: Fama, Princeps and Gloria Mundi from Ghent. New rose bowers with rare French roses Eleanor Berkeley and Euphrosyne. New Jekyll border, blue, yellow & white scheme. Featured in Gardeners' World. Listed in Hampshire Register of Historic Gardens. Many stone paths, some gravel paths.

GROUP OPENING

42 NEW EAST WORLDHAM GARDENS
East Worldham, Alton GU34 3AE, www.worldham.org.uk. *2m SE of Alton on B3004. Gardens & car parking signed in village.* Home-made and cream teas in East Worldham Village Hall. **Combined adm £5, chd free. Sats & Suns 29, 30 June; 27, 28 July (2-6).**

EAST WORLDHAM MANOR
Worldham Hill. Mrs H V Wood.
Open June dates only. East Worldham Manor is down driveway on R immediately after Village Hall

NEW THE OLD HOP KILN
Blanket Street. John & Kate Denyer.
Open July dates only. Turn R at Three Horseshoes PH signed Blanket Street. The Old Hop Kiln's entrance is up gravel track 100yds on L opp farm entrance

'SELBORNE'
Caker Lane. Brian & Mary Jones.
Open June and July dates
(See separate entry)

NEW SILVER BIRCHES
Old House Gardens. Jenny & Roger Bateman.
Open July dates only. Past Three Horseshoes PH, take 2nd turning L, signed Wyck and Binsted. Silver Birches is on R in Old House Gardens (signed)

NEW WYCK HOUSE
Wyck Lane. Chris & Penny Kehoe.
Open June dates only. Take 2nd turning L after Three Horseshoes PH, signed Wyck and Binsted. Wyck House is 100yds on R

Described as a honey-pot of gardens, East Worldham Gardens returns to the Yellow Book. A different combination of gardens with varied characters and styles and far-reaching views is offered on each of the two openings. East Worldham Manor is a walled Victorian garden with restored greenhouses and rose garden. Gravel paths, some naturalised, wind through the garden. Wyck House's mature garden contains interesting shrubs and trees, roses and perennials and a shady area. A large collection of clematis is a major feature. 'Selborne' has a very old orchard, metal and stone sculptures and mixed borders with a wide range of hardy geraniums. The garden at 'Silver Birches', recently redesigned from an overgrown jungle, offers mixed borders, fishpond, stream, rockery and rose garden. Sitting areas provide opportunities for contemplation. The Old Hop Kiln's terraced garden has free-flowing planting which complements the hard landscaping. A waterfall links the upper and lower levels. C14 church. Garden quizzes, sandpit and bookstall at 'Selborne'. Very limited access for wheelchairs to the Old Hop Kiln.

43 EDGEWOOD

175 Burley Road, Bransgore, Christchurch BH23 8DE. Teresa Knight. *3m S of Burley. From Bransgore village take Burley Rd towards Burley for 1m. Edgewood is approx ¼ m past Macpenny's Garden Centre.* Cream teas. **Adm £3, chd free (share to Southampton Hospital Charity). Sat 15, Sun 16 June (2-5); Mon 17, Thur 20, Fri 21 June (12-3); Sat 22 June (2-5).**
Welcome to Edgewood, a garden we treasure, come in and enjoy, sit at your leisure. We have roses and arches, chickens and bees, all scattered around our many fruit trees. The greenhouse and veg plot are next to the flowers with benches to sit on and while away hours. The paths are all winding and take you around, then back for a cream tea that's now quite renowned. Some gravel paths.

GROUP OPENING

44 EMSWORTH GARDENS

Emsworth PO10 7PR. Lucy Watson & Mike Rogers. *7m W of Chichester, 2m E of Havant. Take A259 W of Chichester, follow signs to Emsworth r'about N of town centre.* Home-made teas at 23 New Brighton Rd. **Combined adm £5, chd free. Sun 16 June (1.30-5.30); Thur 4 July (12-4).**

MEADOWLARK, 4 ELDERFIELD CLOSE
Miss M Morelle.
From main Emsworth r'about go N for ½ m (signed Rowlands Castle). Turn R into Wickor Way, L into Westbourne Ave, L into Elderfield Close

Dean House
© Leigh Clapp

23 NEW BRIGHTON ROAD
Lucy Watson & Mike Rogers.
From main Emsworth r'about go N for ½ m (signed Rowlands Castle) under railway bridge and flyover, immediately on L up slope. If no parking available on road, use local recreation ground
Visitors also welcome by appt June and July.
01243 699669
lucywatson100@hotmail.com

Two contrasting 'Mother & Daughter' gardens close to the centre of Emsworth, an historic fishing and sailing village on Chichester Harbour with numerous pubs, small local museum and walks along the foreshore and around mill pond. Mum: Meadowlark is a small Mediterranean-style garden densely planted with a large range of small shrubs, ornamental trees, perennials and climbers. Full of inspiration for those with a limited space plus innovative ideas for container planting. Winner Emsworth Horticultural Society small garden competition. Daughter: With its eclectic mix of plants and ornaments, 23 New Brighton Road features a narrow 250ft-long garden which ranges from full sun to full shade where informal planting maximises the available space. A large number of containers, a wildlife pond, greenhouse, summerhouse, shady reading area and mixed borders. Unusual plants and an unusual garden for the plantsperson. Display of old garden tools at 23 New Brighton Road.

45 ◆ EXBURY GARDENS & STEAM RAILWAY

New Forest, Southampton SO45 1AZ. The Rothschild Family, 02380 891203, www.exbury.co.uk. *16m S of Southampton. 4m Beaulieu. Exbury 20mins M27 J2.* **For opening times and information, please phone or see garden website.**
Created by Lionel de Rothschild in the 1920s, the gardens are a stunning vision of his inspiration offering 200 acres of natural beauty and horticultural variety. Woodland garden with world-famous displays of rhododendrons, azaleas, camellias and magnolias. Rock garden, exotic garden, herbaceous gardens, ponds, cascades, river walk and seasonal trails. Superb autumn colour, incl National Collection of Nyssa and Oxydendrum. Steam railway (wheelchair accessible). Buggy tours available. Hudson's Heritage Awards Best Garden.

NCH

46 NEW **FAIRWEATHER'S NURSERY**
Hilltop, Beaulieu, Brockenhurst SO42 7YR. Patrick & Aline Fairweather. *1½ m NE of Beaulieu village. Signed Beacon Gate on B3054 between Heather r'bout (A326) & Beaulieu village.* **Adm £2.50, chd free. Sats 20 July; 3 Aug (11-5).**
Fairweather's holds a specialist collection of 300 Agapanthus grown in pots and display beds. The collection should be looking at its best. Visitors can join a demonstration of how to get the best from Agapanthus and there will be nursery tours during the day. Aline Fairweather's garden (adjacent to the nursery) will also be open; it has mixed shrub & perennial borders containing many unusual plants. Agapanthus and a range of other traditional and new perennials for sale.

47 **FARLEIGH HOUSE**
Farleigh Wallop, nr Basingstoke RG25 2HT. The Earl & Countess of Portsmouth. *3m SE of Basingstoke. Off B3046 Basingstoke to Preston Candover rd.* Home-made teas in a nearby barn. **Adm £5, chd free. Suns 16 June; 15 Sept (2-5).**
Contemporary garden of great tranquillity designed by Georgia Langton, surrounded by wonderful views. 3-acre walled garden in 3 sections: ornamental potager, formal rose garden and wild rose garden. Greenhouse full of exotics, serpentine yew walk, contemplative pond garden and lake with planting for wildlife. Approx 10 acres and 1 hour to walk around.

48 **FLINTSTONES**
Sciviers Lane, Durley SO32 2AG. June & Bill Butler, 01489 860880, j.b.butler@hotmail.co.uk. *5m E of Eastleigh. From M3 J11 follow signs for Marwell Zoo. From B2177 turn R opp Woodman PH. From M27 J7 follow signs for Fair Oak then Durley, turn L at Robin Hood PH.* Home-made teas (teas March). **Adm £3, chd free. Sun 10 Mar (2-5); Sun 2, Mon 3 June (2-6). Evening Opening £4.50, chd free, wine, Wed 19 June (6.30-8.30). Visitors also welcome by appt Apr to Sept.**
Garden of great tranquillity. All yr pleasing tapestry effect of contrasting and blending foliage and flowers. Plantswoman's garden developed from a field on fertile acid clay. Large perennial plant collections, especially hardy geraniums. Interesting island beds to wander round and explore. Plants for sale (not March). Wheelchair access only when dry, recommend checking by telephone prior to visit.

Trellis covered in rambling roses, with flowers for every season . . .

50 **THE FOUNTAINS**
34 Frampton Way, Totton SO40 9AE. Jean Abel, 02380 865939. *1m from Southampton West. From Southampton, A35 toward Lyndhurst. 1 m to r'about. U-turn and return towards Southampton on A35. Immed L into Rushington Ave, then follow signs.* Home-made teas. **Adm £2.50, chd free. Sun 16 June (1-5.30). Also open 16 June, 6 Alfred Close, 21 Chestnut Road. Visitors also welcome by appt June to Aug.**
A garden of several 'rooms', each with hedges and connecting rose-covered arches. Filled with a variety of fruit trees, soft fruit cordons and espaliers. Trellis covered in rambling roses, with flowers for every season. Plantswoman's garden designed for all yr interest with vegetable plot, wildlife ponds and chickens. 'Cottage garden meets the Good Life' - a garden to relax in and enjoy.

51 **FRITHAM LODGE**
Fritham SO43 7HH. Sir Chris & Lady Rosie Powell, 02380 812650, chris.powell@adamandeveddb.com. *6m N of Lyndhurst. 3m NW of M27 J1 (Cadnam). Follow signs to Fritham.* Home-made teas. **Adm £3.50, chd free. Sun 30 June (2-5). Visitors also welcome by appt June to Sept.**
Set in heart of New Forest in 18 acres; with 1-acre old walled garden round Grade II listed C17 house (not open) originally one of Charles II hunting lodges. Parterre of old roses, potager with wide variety of vegetables, herbs and fruit trees, pergola, herbaceous and blue and white mixed borders, ponds, walk across hay meadows to woodland and stream, with ponies, donkeys, sheep and rare breed hens. Featured in Country Life.

GROUP OPENING

52 **FROYLE GARDENS**
Walbury, Lower Froyle, Froyle GU34 4LJ. Ernie & Brenda Milam. *5m NE of Alton. Access to Lower Froyle from A31 between Alton & Farnham, at Bentley. Follow signs from Lower Froyle to Upper Froyle. Maps given to all visitors.* Home-made teas at Froyle Village Hall. **Combined adm £5, chd free. Sat 15, Sun 16 June (2-6).**

BRAMLINS
Mrs Anne Blunt
(See separate entry)

DAY COTTAGE
Mr Nick Whines & Ms Corinna Furse
www.daycottage.co.uk

FORDS COTTAGE
Mr & Mrs M Carr

NEW **GLEBE COTTAGE**
Barbara & Michael Starbuck

LONG BARLANDS
Maureen Allan

THE OLD SCHOOL
Nigel & Linda Bulpitt

WALBURY
Ernie & Brenda Milam
(See separate entry)

WARREN COTTAGE
Mrs A A Robertson

Visitors have been returning to Froyle (The Village of Saints) for 14yrs to enjoy the wonderful variety of gardens on offer, the warm welcome and the excellent home-made teas in the village hall. The gardens harmonise gently with their surroundings, many with lovely views of beautiful countryside. Eight gardens will open their gates this year, not only providing plant interest, colour and scent, but animals frequently associated with a true cottage garden - as well as vegetables, orchards, greenhouses and wild-flower meadows. Large display of richly decorated C18 church vestments in St Mary's Church Upper Froyle, separate donation.

53 GILBERTS NURSERY
Dandysford Lane, Sherfield English, nr Romsey SO51 6DT. Nick & Helen Gilbert, gilbertsdahlias.co.uk. *Midway between Romsey and Whiteparish on A27, in Sherfield English village. From Romsey 4th turn on L, just before small petrol stn on R, visible from main rd.* Light refreshments. **Adm £2.50, chd free. Sat 17, Sat 24, Sun 25 Aug (11-4).**
This may not be a garden but do come and be amazed by the sight of over 300 varieties of dahlias in our dedicated 1½ -acre field. The blooms are in all colours, shapes and sizes and can be closely inspected from wheelchair-friendly hard grass paths. An inspiration for all gardeners.

54 HAMBLEDON HOUSE
Hambledon PO7 4RU. Capt & Mrs David Hart Dyke, 02392 632380, dhartdyke@tiscali.co.uk. *8m SW of Petersfield, 5m NW of Waterlooville. In village centre, driveway leading to house in East St. Do not go up Speltham Hill even if advised by SatNav.* Home-made teas. **Adm £3.50, chd free. Thur 9, Mon 27 May, Mon 26 Aug, Sun 15 Sept (2-5). Visitors and groups of up to 30 also welcome by appt Mar to Oct, refreshments by arrangement.**
2-acre partly walled plantsman's garden for all seasons. Large border filled with a wide variety of unusual shrubs and perennials with imaginative plant combinations culminating in a profusion of colour in late summer. Hidden, secluded areas reveal surprise views of garden and village rooftops. Exciting new planting started in 2011. Exhibition of watercolours.

HAMPTWORTH ESTATE
See Wiltshire

55 HANGING HOSTA GARDEN
Narra, Frensham Lane, Lindford, Bordon GU35 0QJ. June Colley & John Baker, 01420 489186, hanginghostas@btinternet.com. *Approx 1m E of Bordon. From the A325 at Bordon take the B3002, then B3004 to Lindford. Turn L into Frensham Lane at Xrds, 3rd house on L.* **Adm £3.50, chd free. Visitors and groups of up to 30 welcome by appt 8 - 20 July.**
This garden is packed with almost 2000 plants. The collection of over 1300 hosta cultivars is one of the largest in England. Hostas are displayed at eye level to give a wonderful tapestry of foliage and colour. Islamic garden, waterfall and stream garden, cottage garden. Talks given to garden clubs.

56 NEW HIDEAWAY
Hamdown Crescent, East Wellow, Romsey SO51 6BJ. Caroline & Colin Hart. *3m W of Romsey. From M27 J2 take A36 NW towards Salisbury. After 2m, turn R by speed camera into Whinwhistle Rd. Hamdown Crescent is 3rd L.* Home-made teas. **Adm £3, chd free. Suns 28 July; 4 Aug (2-5.30).**
A treasure trove of exciting plants with mid-summer interest. Different habitats within ½ acre - some dazzling areas, some more gentle: grass gardens, ferns, perennials, cutting garden of annuals, woodland area, pond, fountains, vegetable areas, fruit cage, variety of pots. Developed in 5 yrs from a basic framework by current owners. A peaceful garden. Some gravel at entrance.

57 HILL HOUSE
Old Alresford SO24 9DY. Mrs W F Richardson, 01962 732720, hillhouseolda@yahoo.co.uk. *1m W of Alresford. From Alresford 1m along B3046 towards Basingstoke, then R by church.* Home-made teas. **Adm £3.50, chd free. Thur 1, Sun 4, Tue 6 Aug (1.30-5). Groups of 10+ also welcome by appt July to Aug.**
Traditional English 2-acre garden, established 1938, divided by yew hedge. Large croquet lawn framing the star of the garden, the huge multi-coloured herbaceous border. Impressive dahlia bed and butterfly-attracting sunken garden in lavender shades. Prolific old-fashioned kitchen garden with hens and bantams both fluffy and large. Small Dexter cows, possibly with calves. Dried flowers.

58 HILL TOP
Damson Hill, Upper Swanmore SO32 2QR. David Green, 01489 892653, tricia1960@btinternet.com. *1m NE of Swanmore. Junction of Swanmore Rd and Church Rd, turn N up Hampton Hill into Park Lane. Sharp L-hand bend. After 300yds, junction with Damson Hill, house on L. Disabled parking by house.* Home-made teas. **Adm £3.50, chd free. Suns 16 June; 15 Sept (2-5). Visitors also welcome by appt.**
2 acres with extensive colourful borders and wide lawns, this garden has stunning views to the Isle of Wight. The glasshouses produce unusual fruit and vegetables from around the world. The outdoor vegetable plots bulge with well-grown produce. Many potted specimen plants. Colour and interest are maintained throughout the season.

A treasure trove of exciting plants . . . some dazzling areas, some more gentle . . .

59 2 HILLSIDE COTTAGES
Trampers Lane, North Boarhunt PO17 6DA. John & Lynsey Pink, 01329 832786, landjpink@tiscali.co.uk. *5m N of Fareham. 3m E of Wickham. From A32 at Wickham take B2177 E. Trampers Lane 2nd on L (approx 2m). Hillside Cottages approx ½ m on L.* **Adm £2.50, chd free. Visitors welcome by appt.**
This 1-acre garden, on gently rising ground, contains so much of interest for plantspeople. Many rare and unusual specimens are shown off in sweeping borders in a tranquil setting. The National Collection of salvias is well displayed, all colours, sizes and growing habits. Something for everyone and an ideal venue for a group visit from spring through to autumn.
NCH

60 HINTON ADMIRAL
Christchurch BH23 7DY. MEM Ltd, www.hintonadmiral.myzen.co.uk. *4m NE of Christchurch. On N side of A35, ¾ m E of Cat & Fiddle PH.* **Adm £5, chd free. Sun 19 May (1-4.30).**
Magnificent 20-acre garden (within a much larger estate) now being restored and developed. Mature plantings of deciduous azaleas and rhododendrons amidst a sea of bluebells. Wandering paths lead through rockeries and beside ponds

and a stream with many cascades. Orchids appear in the large lawns. The 2 walled gardens are devoted to herbs and wild flowers and a very large greenhouse. The terrace and rock garden were designed by Harold Peto. No refreshments, but picnics may be taken in the orchard. Some gravel paths.

♿ 🐕

61 ◆ HINTON AMPNER

Alresford SO24 0LA. National Trust, 01962 771305, www.nationaltrust.org.uk. *3½ m S of Alresford. S on A272 Petersfield to Winchester rd.* **Adm £7, chd £3.50 (share to Julia's House Children's Hospice). For NGS: Sats 20 Apr; 15 June; 13 July; 14 Sept (10-6). For other opening times and information, please phone or see garden website.**

12 acres. C20 garden created by Ralph Dutton. Manicured lawns and topiary combine with unusual shrubs, climbers and herbaceous plants. Vibrant dahlias alternate in spring with tulips. Rose border incorporates over 45 old and new rose varieties. Dramatic foliage planting in the Dell; orchard with spring bulbs; magnolia and philadelphus walks; restored walled garden.

♿ ❀ ☕

62 THE HOMESTEAD

Northney Road, Hayling Island PO11 0NF. Stan & Mary Pike, 02392 464888, jhomestead@aol.com, www.homesteadhayling.co.uk. *3m S of Havant. From A27 Havant/Hayling Island r'about, travel S over Langstone Bridge & turn immed L into Northney Rd. 1st house on R after Langstone Hotel.* Home-made teas. **Adm £3, chd free. Sun 4 Aug (2-5.30). Groups of 10+ also welcome by appt June to Aug.**

1¼ -acre garden surrounded by working farmland with views to Butser Hill and boats in Chichester Harbour. Very colourful herbaceous borders, rock garden beside tennis court and kitchen garden with trained apples and peaches. A quiet and peaceful atmosphere with plenty of seats to enjoy the vistas within the garden and beyond.

♿ 🐕 ❀ ☕ ☎

63 HORDLE WALHAMPTON SCHOOL

Beaulieu Road, Walhampton, Lymington SO41 5ZG. Hordle Walhampton School Trust Ltd. *1m E of Lymington. From Lymington follow signs to Beaulieu (B3054) for 1m & turn R into main entrance at 1st school sign 200yds after top of hill.* **Adm £4.50, chd free (share to St John's Church, Boldre). Sun 28 Apr (2.30-5). Also open Spinners Garden.**

Glorious walks through large C18 landscape garden surrounding magnificent mansion (not open). Visitors discover 3 lakes, serpentine canal, climbable prospect mount, period former banana house/orangery, shell grotto, glade and terrace by Peto (c1907) and terrace, drives and colonnade by Mawson (c1914). Seating, guided tours with garden history. Gravel paths, can be muddy when wet, some slopes.

♿ 🐕 ☕

Whispers

© Leigh Clapp

THE HOUSE IN THE WOOD
Beaulieu SO42 7YN. Victoria Roberts. *8m NE of Lymington. Leaving the entrance to Beaulieu motor museum on R (B3056) take next R turn signed Ipley Cross. Take 2nd gravel drive on RH-bend, approx ½ m.* Cream teas. **Adm £4, chd free. Sun 12 May (2-6).**
Peaceful 12-acre woodland garden with continuing progress and improvement. New areas and streams have been developed and good acers planted among mature azaleas and rhododendrons. Used in the war to train the Special Operations Executive. 'A magical garden to get lost in' and popular with bird-watchers.

65 IBTHORPE TOWER
Windmill Hill, Hurstbourne Tarrant, Andover SP11 0DQ. Mr & Mrs P Gregory. *5m N of Andover. Off A343 at top of Hurstbourne Hill, signed The Chutes and Tangley. 1st turning on R.* Home-made teas. **Adm £4, chd free. Fri 9, Sat 10 Aug (2-5.30).**
3½ acres of garden planted in contemporary style, focusing on colour and texture, in tranquil spot, elevated and with glorious views. Large wildlife pond, woodland garden, potager and long banks and large borders planted with hardy perennials in imaginative drifts. Allow plenty of time to visit our plant stall, a real feature with many unusual perennials, particularly salvias.

66 THE ISLAND
Greatbridge, Romsey SO51 0HP. Mr & Mrs Christopher Saunders-Davies, 01794 512100, ssd@testvalleytrout.co.uk. *1m N of Romsey on A3057. Entrance alongside Greatbridge (1st bridge Xing the R Test), flanked by row of cottages on roadside.* **Adm £4, chd free. Sun 10 Mar, Sat 4, Sun 5 May, Sat 3, Sun 4 Aug (2-5.30). Groups of 10+ also welcome by appt.**
6 acres either side of the R Test. Fine display of daffodils and spring-flowering trees. Main garden has herbaceous and annual borders, fruit trees, rose pergola, lavender walk and extensive lawns. An arboretum planted in the 1930s by Sir Harold Hillier contains trees and shrubs providing interest throughout the yr. Bring your own picnic. Featured in Salisbury Life.

KENT HOUSE
See Sussex

67 53 LADYWOOD
Eastleigh SO50 4RW. Mr & Mrs D Ward, 02380 615389, sueatladywood@btinternet.com. *1m N of Eastleigh. Leave M3 J12. Follow signs to Eastleigh. Turn R at r'about into Woodside Ave, then 2nd R into Bosville. Ladywood 5th on R. Please park in Bosville.* Home-made teas at 52 Ladywood (Sun only). **Adm £3.50, chd free. Sun 9 June (11-5); Mon 10 June (2-5). Groups of 10+ also welcome by appt May to July.**
Celebrating its 20th year of NGS opening, this lovely garden, only 45ft x 45ft, is full of ideas and creative ways of using every available space to grow over 2000 different plants. Clever use of numerous unusual foliage plants enhance the flower borders throughout the seasons. Pond garden and tiny shade garden are created using trellis onto which many climbers are grown.

68 LAKE HOUSE
Northington SO24 9TG. Lord Ashburton, 07795 364539, lukeroeder@hotmail.com. *4m N of Alresford. Off B3046. Follow English Heritage signs to The Grange, then directions.* Home-made teas. **Adm £4, chd free. Thur 13, Sun 16 June (12.30-5). Groups of 10+ also welcome by appt.**
2 large lakes in Candover Valley set off by mature woodland with waterfalls, abundant bird life, long landscaped vistas and folly. 1½-acre walled garden, with rose parterre, mixed borders, long herbaceous border, rose pergola leading to moon gate. Formal kitchen garden, flowering pots, conservatory and greenhouses. Picnicking by lakes. Grass paths.

69 LITTLE COURT
Crawley, nr Winchester SO21 2PU. Prof & Mrs A R Elkington, 01962 776365, elkslc@tiscali.co.uk. *5m NW of Winchester. From M3 J9 take A34 N, exit after 3m & at r'about take 4th exit (A272); after 1.7 m turn L to Crawley. From Winchester or Stockbridge take B3049. Garden 300yds from either village pond or church.* Home-made teas in the village hall. **Adm £4, chd free. Fri 22, Sun 24, Mon 25 Feb (2-5); Mon 1 Apr, Thur 16, Sun 19 May (2-5.30); Fri 21, Sun 23, Mon 24 Feb 2014 (2-5). Also open 16, 19 May Tanglefoot & opening with Crawley Gardens 7, 9 Apr; 15, 16 June. Visitors also welcome by appt Feb to July.**
A tranquil country garden spectacular in spring, with carpets of bulbs, hellebores and snowdrops. Cowslips and butterflies and emphasis on wildlife. Prolific perennials all summer especially hardy geraniums. 3 acres incl paddock; fun for children with tree house, swings and alpacas. Garden is sheltered, many seats and beautiful views. Traditional kitchen garden.

2½-acre bluebell wood and spring-flowering garden surrounded by fields and near sea . . .

70 LITTLEWOOD
West Lane, Hayling Island PO11 0JW. Mr & Mrs Steven Schrier. *3m S of Havant. From A27 Havant/Hayling Island junction, travel S for 2m, turn R into West Lane and continue 1m. House set back from rd in wood. Disabled come to very top of drive.* Home-made teas. **Adm £3, chd free. Sat 4, Sun 5 May (11-5).**
2½-acre bluebell wood and spring-flowering garden surrounded by fields and near sea, protected from sea winds by multi-barrier hedge. Rhododendrons, azaleas, camellias and many other shrubs. Woodland walk to full-size tree house. Features incl pond, bog garden, house plants, summerhouse, conservatory and many places to sit outside and under cover. Dogs on leads and picnickers welcome. Close to Hayling Billy coastal trail.

GROUP OPENING

71 LONGPARISH GARDENS
nr Andover SP11 6PS. *7m E of Andover. Off A303. To village centre on B3048. Parking at Lower Mill only, except for disabled.* Home-made teas at Longmead House. **Combined adm £6, chd free. Sun 26, Mon 27 May (2-6).**

LONGMEAD HOUSE
John & Wendy Ellicock

LOWER MILL
Mill Lane. Mrs K-M Dinesen

Longparish is a small beautiful village on River Test with many thatched cottages. Two gardens offer a wide variety of interest. The 2-acre organic and wildlife garden at Longmead House is full of interest with a large, hedged vegetable garden with deep beds, polytunnel, greenhouse, fruit cage and composting area. There are also fish and wildlife ponds and a wild-flower meadow, as well as herbaceous and shrub borders and a woodland walk. Magnificent trees and water are the keys at Lower Mill, a mainly informally planted 15-acre garden on the Test which delights at every turn. Teardrop-shaped beds are boldly planted with shrubs and underplanted with swathes of grasses and perennials. Harmonious borders around the house lead to a hidden sunken garden and an immaculate water garden. Riverside walks, vegetable garden and wildlife lake await your discovery. Limited wheelchair access at Lower Mill.

72 LONGSTOCK PARK
Leckford, Stockbridge SO20 6EH. Leckford Estate Ltd, part of John Lewis Partnership, www.longstockpark.co.uk. *4m S of Andover. From A30 turn N on to A3057; follow signs to Longstock.* Home-made teas at Longstock Park Nursery. **Adm £5, chd £1. Sun 16 June (2-5).**
Famous water garden with extensive collection of aquatic and bog plants set in 7 acres of woodland with rhododendrons and azaleas. A walk through park leads to National Collections of *Buddleja* and *Clematis viticella*; arboretum, herbaceous border. Assistance dogs only.
NCH

73 ◆ MACPENNYS WOODLAND GARDEN & NURSERIES
Burley Road, Bransgore, Christchurch BH23 8DB. Mr & Mrs T M Lowndes, 01425 672348, www.macpennys.co.uk. *6m S of Ringwood, 5m NE of Christchurch. Midway between Christchurch & Burley. From A35, at Xrds by The Crown PH turn R & proceed 1/4 m. From A31 (towards Bournemouth) L at Picket Post, signed Burley, then R at Burley Cross. Garden on L after 3m.* **For opening times and information, please phone or see garden website.**
12 acres of nursery with 4-acre gravel pit converted into woodland garden planted with many unusual plants. Offering interest all yr but particularly in spring and autumn. Large Nursery displaying a wide selection of trees, shrubs, conifers, perennials, hedging plants, fruit trees and bushes. Partial wheelchair access.

MALT HOUSE
See Sussex

Riverside walks, vegetable garden and wildlife lake await your discovery . . .

74 NEW 1 MAPLE COTTAGE
Searles Lane, off London Road (A30), Hook RG27 9EQ. John & Pat Beagley. *Nr Hook House (Hotel). A30: Hartley Wintney side of Hook, turn into Searles Lane opp Hampshire Prestige Cars. Parking courtesy of Hook House in overflow car park immediately on L. 1/4 m up Searles Lane to Maple Cottage. Entrance and disabled parking at rear of property.* Home-made teas. **Adm £3, chd free. Wed 5, Thur 6, Wed 12, Thur 13 June (1.30-5).**
1/3 -acre; views over farmland towards River Whitewater. Mature apple trees and shrubs, vegetable plots, cottage-style herbaceous borders, courtyard garden, small wildlife pond with named hostas. 'Tree cave' for children. Relax with tea and home-made cakes, whilst listening for call of buzzards as they soar overhead. Good selection of birds, including nest box with camera - residents may be home. Some paved paths, mainly grassed areas. Avoidable steps.

75 MEON ORCHARD
Kingsmead, N of Wickham PO17 5AU. Doug & Linda Smith. *5m N of Fareham. From Wickham take A32 N for 1 1/2 m. Turn L at Roebuck Inn. Continue 1/2 m.* Home-made teas. **Adm £3.50, chd free. Sun 26 May, Sun 28 July, Sun 1 Sept (2-6).**
1 1/2 -acre garden designed and constructed by current owners. An exceptional range of rare, unusual and architectural plants incl National Collections of Eucalyptus, Podocarpaceae and Araliaceae. Much use made of dramatic foliage plants from around the world, both hardy and tender, big bananas, huge taros, tree ferns, cannas, hedychiums and palms. Streams and ponds, combined with an extensive range of planters, complete the display. See plants you have never seen before. Plant sale of the exotic and rare Sun 1 Sept. Garden fully accessible by wheelchair, reserved parking.
NCH

76 NEW MEON PLACE
Selworth Lane, Soberton SO32 3PX. Mrs Sarah Paul, 01489 877925, sa.paul@virgin.net. *By War Memorial on Selworth Lane. Between Droxford and Wickham, turn E off A32 opp Cott Street, follow rd over 1 bridge and under another. Selworth Lane is around L bend.* Home-made teas. **Adm £4, chd free. Thur 13, Sat 15 June (2-6). Visitors also welcome by appt Apr to Oct.**
Picturesque 2-acre garden with formal parterres containing a mix of perennials, roses and clematis. A contemporary naturally heated swimming pool, croquet lawn, small meadow, knot garden, herb bed, new organic kitchen garden and orchard. The whole scene is bound together by elegant, towering Italian cypresses. A beautiful setting. Possible wheelchair access to main features. Reserved parking in gravel drive.

77 MERDON MANOR
Merdon Castle Lane, Hursley SO21 2JJ. Mr & Mrs J C Smith, 01962 775215/775281, vronk@bluebottle.com. *5m SW of Winchester. From A3090 Winchester to Romsey rd, turn R at Standon, Merdon Castle Lane, proceed 1½ m.* Home-made teas. **Adm £3.50, chd free. Sun 16 June (2-6). Visitors also welcome by appt Mar to Oct.**
A country garden surrounded by spectacular views all round, with a ha-ha to keep out the black sheep. 5 acres. Roses, shrub walk, container plants, wild pond, with special secret walled garden. Wonderfully tranquil and quiet.

78 MICHAELMAS
2 Old Street, Hill Head, Fareham PO14 3HU. Ros & Jack Wilson, 01329 662593, jazzjack00@gmail.com. *4½ m S of Fareham. From M27, J9 take A27 signed Fareham. After approx 3m at gyratory follow B3334 to Gosport. After 2¼ m at 2nd r'about in Stubbington go straight over, signed Hill Head. Approx 500yds turn R into Bells Lane. 1m pass Osborne View PH, next R is Old St.* Home-made teas. **Adm £3, chd free. Sun 21, Mon 22 July (2-5). Groups of 10-20 also welcome by appt July to Aug.**
Very cheerful, colourful small garden with the 'wow' factor. A variety of tall plants for a tall lady! Many are grown from seed or cuttings. Small vegetable garden, greenhouse, garden room, pot-grown vegetables and flowers. Styled in the fashion of a country garden with a wide range of plants with the emphasis on perennials. 1-min walk from beach, 5-mins walk from Titchfield Haven Nature Reserve.

79 NEW THE MILL AT GORDLETON
Silver Street, Sway, Lymington SO41 6DJ. Mrs Liz Cottingham, www.themillatgordleton.co.uk. *2m W of Lymington. From Lymington town centre head N on A337, in 500yds turn L after The Toll House PH, for Sway & Hordle. Garden is 2m.* Light refreshments. **Adm £3, chd free. Every Mon 7 Jan to 9 Dec (11-4).**
A meandering stream bisects this old mill garden, with areas of different character. Recently opened is the new 'Secret Garden' - a tranquil space to wander through. The Mill Art Walk is a fascinating display of metal, glass and wooden sculptures. Salmon, trout and perch are abundant in the river, and we have a family of ducks. Garden Sculpture Walk. Featured in Hampshire Society magazine.

Enjoy the long vista across the croquet lawn to mature gardens beyond . . .

THE MILL HOUSE DONNINGTON
See Berkshire

GROUP OPENING

80 MONXTON & AMPORT GARDENS
Amport SP11 8AY. *3m SW of Andover. Turn off A303 signed to E Cholderton from E or Thruxton village from the W. Follow signs to Amport. Parking in field next to Amport village green. NOTE: Follow NGS signs.* **Combined adm £5, chd free. Sun 26, Mon 27 May (2-5.30).**

AMPORT HOUSE
Ministry of Defence

AMPORT PARK MEWS
Amport Park Mews Ltd

BRIDGE COTTAGE
Jenny Burroughs

WHITE GABLES
Mr & Mrs D Eaglesham

Monxton and Amport are two pretty villages linked by Pill Hill Brook. Visitors have four gardens to enjoy. Amport House is a listed garden, designed by Gertrude Jekyll and Edwin Lutyens, with superb hard landscaping, vistas, pleached limes and parterre, and fine view. Bridge Cottage is a 2-acre haven for wildlife, with the banks of the trout stream and lake planted informally with drifts of colour, a large vegetable garden (not suitable for wheelchairs), fruit cage, small mixed orchard and arboretum with specimen trees. Amport Park Mews has 11 borders arranged around a communal space surrounded by converted stable/carriage blocks in historic mews. White Gables has a collection of interesting trees, incl a young giant redwood - an unexpected feature in a cottage-style garden - along with old roses and herbaceous plants. The ⅙-acre garden leads down to Pill Hill Brook. No wheelchair access to White Gables.

81 NEW MOORE BLATCH
48 High Street, Lymington SO41 9ZQ. *Top end of Lymington High St, on S side. Follow signs for Lymington Town Centre and use High Street car parks.* Home-made teas. **Adm £3.50, chd free. Sat 17 Aug (10.30-4.30); Sun 18 Aug (2-5).**
Situated behind this elegant Georgian town house lies a surprising S-facing walled garden of 1 acre. From the raised terrace, enjoy the long vista across the croquet lawn to mature gardens beyond and then over to the Isle of Wight. Amusing and varied topiary among established, herbaceous borders. Lymington Saturday Market and lively waterfront at bottom of High St.

82 ◆ MOTTISFONT ABBEY & GARDEN
Romsey SO51 0LP. National Trust, 01794 340757, www.nationaltrust.org.uk. *4½ m NW of Romsey. From A3057 Romsey to Stockbridge rd turn W at sign to Mottisfont.* **For opening times and information, please phone or see garden website.**
Built C12 as Augustinian priory, now house of some note. 30-acre landscaped garden incl spring or 'font', from which house derives its name, magnificent ancient trees and walled gardens with National Collection of over 300 varieties of old roses. Tranquil walks in grounds, along the R Test and in the glorious countryside of the estate. Large developing Winter Garden, and thousands more spring bulbs.
NCH

83 OAKFIELDS

45 Segensworth Road East, Titchfield, Fareham PO15 5EA. Denise & Dudley McGowan. *2m W of Fareham. From M27 J9 take A27 towards Fareham. At Titchfield Mill PH turn L into Mill Lane. 1st L after Titchfield Abbey into Segensworth Rd East. Garden 200yds on L. Parking at Abbey Croft Nursery, 200yds on L past garden.* Home-made teas. **Adm £3.50, chd free. Sat 29, Sun 30 June (1-5).**

A peaceful and naturalistic 1-acre garden that evokes nostalgic childhood memories. Organic and wildlife friendly, featuring many facets, fruit and vegetable potager, orchard, wildflower meadow, woodland, ponds and many herbaceous beds. Alluring combinations of planting, all complemented by artistic sculptures. Resident honey bees and chickens complete the garden. Fareham in Bloom large plantsman's garden gold winner, wildlife garden gold and overall winner. Big wildlife garden competition Highly Commended. Featured in Hampshire & Isle of Wight Wildlife Magazine.

84 OLD ALRESFORD HOUSE

Colden Lane, Old Alresford SO24 9DY. Mike Hall & Shuna MacKillop, www.oldalresfordhouse.com. *7m E of Winchester. A31 to (New) Alresford; turn into Broad St at top of town (B3046). After 1/2 m arrive at Old Alresford. Car park on L opp church, garden adjacent. Disabled may park by house.* Home-made teas and wine. **Adm £5, chd free. Sun 16, Tue 18 June, Sun 13, Tue 15 Oct (10-5).**

C18 landscape garden (Grade II listed) restored from original plans. 22-acre parkland with rare breeds surrounded by 13-acre gardens and perimeter woodland walk (30 mins) featuring ha-ha, immaculate lawns, shrubberies, wildlife pond, chalk stream with bog garden, boardwalk and medieval coach road. Views and vistas. Also, contemporary Mediterranean walled garden. Illustrated talk by owner at 11am & 2pm (40 mins). Perimeter walk bumpy in places. Chalk stream not wheelchair accessible but beautiful views from coach road above. **n.b. Dogs welcome Tues only.**

85 NEW THE OLD RECTORY, WINCHFIELD

Bagwell Lane, Winchfield, Hook RG27 8DB. George & Sarah Adams. *4m S of M3 J5. From M3 exit J5 take A287 in direction of Farnham. On reaching dual carriageway turn L into London Rd signed Winchfield. Take 1st R signed Winchfield Church into Bagwell Lane, continue to St Mary's Church, driveway entrance on R. House not visible from lane, drive to house approx 500yds.* Home-made teas. **Adm £3.50, chd free. Sun 19 May, Sat 15 June (2-6).**

The Old Rectory Winchfield is adjacent to Grade I Norman church. 3 acres plus extensive woodland walks. Formal topiary with areas of different character to explore. Wild flowers with formal close-mown paths in grid pattern. Swimming pool is now a handsome pond. Broad views to surrounding fields with lambs and woodland.

GROUP OPENING

86 OLD THATCH & THE MILLENNIUM BARN

Sprats Hatch Lane, Winchfield, Hook RG27 8DD, www.old-thatch.co.uk. *3m W of Fleet. From A287 Odiham to Farnham rd turn N to Dogmersfield. L by Queens Head PH and L opp Barley Mow PH. From Winchfield stn car park turn R towards Dogmersfield and after 1.3m R opp Barley Mow. Follow signs for parking in adjacent field. Limited disabled parking on site (ask at car park entrance).* Home-made teas. **Combined adm £3, chd free. Sun 14 Apr (2-6). Evening Opening £5, chd free, wine, Sat 29 June (7-10); Sun 1 Sept (2-6).**

THE MILLENNIUM BARN
Mr & Mrs S White

OLD THATCH
Jill Ede
www.old-thatch.co.uk

Two gardens in one! A small secluded haven sits under the old oak tree next to the pond, surrounded by yr-round colour and seasonal fragrance from roses and honeysuckle. You can listen to birdsong, wind-chimes and the trickling of a small waterfall whilst enjoying views of Old Thatch and the cottage garden beyond. Who could resist visiting Old Thatch, a 'chocolate box' thatched cottage, featured on film and TV, and evolving smallholding alongside the Basingstoke Canal (unfenced). A succession of spring bulbs, a profusion of wild flowers, perennials and home-grown annuals pollinated by our own bees and fertilised by the donkeys, who await your visit. Over 30 named clematis and rose cultivars. Lambs in April, donkey foals in summer. Children: enjoy our quiz on Sundays and look-out in a tree (supervised, please). Dads love the cakes. Mums enjoy the music and candlelight in the evening. Arrive by boat! Slipway opp Barley Mow PH. Surrey & Hants Canal Society may have boat trips to coincide with Sunday openings. **For boat enquiries only** please contact Marian Gough on 01962 713564. Featured in numourous publications. DVD for sale. Wheelchair access by grass slopes & paths.

Wild flowers with formal close-mown paths in grid pattern . . .

87 NEW ORDNANCE HOUSE

West Dean, Salisbury SP5 1JE. Terry & Vanessa Winters, 01794 341797, terry.winters@ordnancehouse.com, www.ordnancehouse.com. *7m W of Romsey. On Moody's Hill heading toward Salisbury. From Romsey take B3084 to Lockerley Rd, follow signs to West Dean. From Stockbridge take A30, follow signs to W.Tytherley, take Dean Rd to West Dean. Limited parking; additional parking in village, 250yds.* Light refreshments. **Adm £3, chd free. Sun 26 May (1-5); Sun 30 June (11-5). Visitors also welcome by appt May to Aug.**

New garden designed and planted by owners. Herbaceous beds, orchard, soft fruit and vegetable gardens, formal parterre. Use of unusual varieties of lavender. Seating areas with garden views of surrounding countryside and walks to Dean Hill. Owners previously created NGS garden at Linden Barn.

88 ◆ PATRICK'S PATCH
Fairweather's Garden Centre, High Street, Beaulieu SO42 7YB. Mr P Fairweather, 01590 612307, www.fairweathers.co.uk. *SE New Forest at head of Beaulieu River. Leave M27 at J2 & follow signs for Beaulieu Motor Museum. Go up High St & park in Fairweathers on LHS.* Refreshments at Steff's Kitchen in garden centre opp. **For opening times and information, please phone or see garden website.**
Model kitchen garden with a full range of vegetables, trained top and soft fruit and herbs. Salads in succession used as an educational project for all ages. Maintained by volunteers, primary school children and a part-time gardener. A very productive garden enclosed by walls built from New Forest heather bales and local softwood.

89 PENNINGTON HOUSE
Ridgeway Lane, Lower Woodside, Lymington SO41 8AA. Sue Stowell & John Leach. *1½ m S of Lymington. S on A337 from Lymington approx ⅓ m to Pennington r'about. Turn L into Ridgeway Lane. At L bend, fork R to continue along Ridgeway Lane for ⅓ m until Chequers PH. Turn R immed by post box into private drive. Car parking at the house.* Home-made teas. **Adm £4, chd free. Sat 18, Sun 19 May, Sat 22, Sun 23 June (2-4.30). Also open 23 June Rookes Cottage.**
7-acre garden created around 1910 by Frederick Grotian, featuring expansive lawns, an Italian sunken garden, rose garden, rockeries, ponds, stream and a large Victorian walled garden in full use. Entirely organic for 20 years. All set in a rural, tranquil setting. Some gravel paths.

90 PILLEY HILL COTTAGE
Pilley Hill, Pilley, Lymington SO41 5QF. Steph & Sandy Glen, 01590 677844, stephglen@hotmail.co.uk, www.pilleyhillcottage.com. *Off A337 Lymington to Brockenhurst rd. 2m N of Lymington, 2½ m S of Brockenhurst, turn into Rope Hill for Pilley, Boldre and Spinners. Go 1m via Boldre Bridge, up Pilley Hill. Also signed from B3054 Beaulieu to Lymington rd. Leave M27 at J2 and follow 'Heavy Lorry Route' to avoid traffic delays at Lyndhurst.* Cream teas. **Adm £3, chd free. Sats & Suns 29, 30 June; 20, 21 July; 31 Aug; 1 Sept (2-5). Visitors also welcome by appt Mar to Sept.**
Naturalistic, wildlife-friendly garden of surprises around every corner. Enter through the rose-covered lych-gate, to a spectacle of colour. Wild flowers rub shoulders with perennials among quaint objects and oak structures. Meander through the old orchard through willow walks and oak archways, on to the shady pond garden. Take tea on the front lawn surrounded by herbaceous borders. Raffle and a children's quiz.

Braemoor
© Leigh Clapp

THE PRIORY
See Berkshire

91 PYLEWELL PARK
South Baddesley, Lymington SO41 5SJ. Lord Teynham. *2m E of Lymington. From Lymington follow signs for Car Ferry to IOW, continue for 2m to S Baddesley.* Home-made teas. **Adm £3.50, chd free (share to St Mary's Church). Suns 31 Mar; 19 May (2-5.30).**
A large parkland garden, laid out in 1890. Enjoy a walk along the extensive grass paths, bordered by rhododendrons, magnolias, embothriums and cornus. Wild daffodils should be in bloom at Easter leading you to the large lakes bordered by giant gunnera - and on to views of the Solent. Lovely for families and dogs.

GROUP OPENING

92 ROMSEY GARDENS

Romsey SO51 8EU. *Town centre, all gardens within walking distance of Romsey Abbey, clearly signed. Car parking by King John's Garden.* Home-made teas at King John's House. **Combined adm £6, chd free. Sun 26, Mon 27 May (11-5.30).**

KING JOHN'S GARDEN
Friends of King John's Garden & Test Valley Borough

THE LAKE HOUSE
64 Mill Lane. David & Lorraine Henley

4 MILL LANE
Miss J Flindall
Visitors & coaches also welcome by appt. 01794 513926

Romsey is a small unspoilt historic market town with the majestic C12 Norman Abbey as a backdrop to 4 Mill Lane, a garden described by Joe Swift as 'the best solution for a long thin garden with a view'. King John's Garden, with its fascinating listed C13 house, has all period plants that were available before 1700. It also has an award-winning Victorian garden with a courtyard where tea is served (no dogs here, please). Lake House has 4½ acres and a large meadow, lake to walk round and a pastoral view. It is a very tranquil place, yet is only 5 mins from the centre of Romsey. Spot the kingfishers if you're lucky! No wheelchair access at 4 Mill Lane.

Discover a hidden water garden using recycled and natural materials . . .

93 ROOKES COTTAGE

35 Rookes Lane, Lymington SO41 8FP. Andrew & Barbara Hunt. *SW Lymington. From centre of Lymington take A337 towards Christchurch. After ½ m turn L at Pennington Cross r'about into Ridgeway Lane, signed 'Marinas'. After 200yds bear L into Rookes Lane.* Home-made teas. **Adm £3, chd free. Suns 23 June; 14 July (2-5). Also open 23 June Pennington House.**

Out of town garden with differently themed areas incl azaleas and rhododendrons and roses. Abundant planting of shrubs, herbaceous and annuals. Rose garden featuring over 100 plants - many David Austin. Unusual walled courtyard with interesting architectural features and some tender planting. Some gravel paths.

94 ROTHERFIELD PARK

East Tisted, Alton GU34 3QE. Sir James & Lady Scott. *4m S of Alton on A32.* Home-made teas. **Adm £4, chd free. Sun 5 May (2-5).**

Take some ancient ingredients: ice house, ha-ha, lime avenue; add a walled garden, fruit and vegetables, trees and hedges; set this 12-acre plot in an early C19 park (picnic here from noon) with views to coin clichés about. Mix in a bluebell wood and Kim Wilkie's modern take on an amphitheatre by the stable block. Good disabled access to walled garden.

95 ST CHRISTOPHER'S

Whitsbury, Fordingbridge SP6 3PZ. Christine Southey & David Mussell, 01725 518404, chrismarysouthey@gmail.com. *3½ m NW of Fordingbridge. In village centre, 200yds down from Cartwheel PH.* Home-made teas in village hall 120yds away. **Adm £3.50, chd free. Sun 24 Mar, Sun 7, Sun 14 Apr (2-5). Groups of 20+ also welcome by appt Mar to June.**

Tranquil, ¾ -acre, long sloping garden with superb views. Alpines in S-facing scree bed with unusual beds, incl dwarf iris, tulips and narcissi, and alpine troughs. In spring, wild banks of bluebells and primroses, fern bed with erythroniums, hellebores, anemone blanda and many shrubs. Pond and bog gardens full of primula. In summer, 25ft rambling roses, beds of delphiniums, eremurus and many herbaceous treasures. Fruit and vegetable garden.

SANDHILL FARM HOUSE
See Sussex

SANDLEFORD PLACE
See Berkshire

96 SANDY SLOPES

Honeysuckle Lane, Headley Down GU35 8EH. Mr & Mrs R Thornton. *6m S of Farnham. From A3 take B3002 through Grayshott, on to Headley Down. Turn L at mini r'about by garage, down hill to 2nd turning L, bungalow 3rd drive on R. From Headley village take B3002 towards Grayshott, after S bend on to sharp L bend up hill to Honeysuckle Lane on R. Parking very limited.* **Adm £3, chd free. Mon 6, Mon 27 May, Sun 16 June (2-5).**

Sloping and partly terraced plantsman's and garden lecturer's garden with many special features incl woodland with rhododendrons, camellias, magnolias, rare meconopsis, primulas, trilliums, lilies and other seasonal plants. Stream and pool, herbaceous mixed shrub borders. Rock gardens. Many trees and unusual plants within about ¼ acre incl davidia, cornus, paulownia, lomatia and koelreuteria. Steep slopes and steps, regret no wheelchair access, and unsuitable for pushchairs and very young children.

97 NEW THE SECRET GARDEN NATURE RESERVE

High Street, Bursledon, Southampton SO31 8DL. John & Alison Horne, 02380 616262, horneja@btinternet.com. *4m E of Southampton. From M27 J8 follow A27 to Bursledon, R into Long Lane, L into School Rd, R into Church Lane, L into High St, garden 50yds on R.* Home-made teas. **Adm £2.50, chd free. Suns 23 June; 4 Aug (12-6.30). Visitors also welcome by appt June to Sept.**

Situated in the middle of a small nature reserve, with views to the Isle of Wight, discover a hidden water garden being continuously developed using recycled and natural materials. Many ponds with magnificent water lilies dominate the formal garden which merges into the reserve's native ecosystem. Organic management ensures an astonishing variety of wildlife.

98 'SELBORNE'

Caker Lane, East Worldham GU34 3AE. Brian & Mary Jones, 01420 83389, mary.trigwell-jones@virgin.net. *2m SE of Alton. On B3004 at Alton end of East Worldham opp The Three Horseshoes PH (please note, NOT in*

the village of Selborne). Parking signed. Home-made teas. **Adm £3, chd free (share to Tafara Mission Zimbabwe in April). Sats & Suns 20, 21 Apr; 11, 12 May; Sun 4, Mon 5 Aug (2-5). Also open 29, 30 June & 27, 28 July with East Worldham Gardens. Visitors and groups also welcome by appt Apr to Aug.**
A garden of surprises. 1/2 -acre mature garden with old established orchard of named varieties. Meandering paths provide changing vistas across farmland. Mixed borders feature a large collection of hardy geraniums and other herbaceous plants and shrubs. Soft fruit garden, containers, metal and stone sculpture and summerhouses. Relax and take tea in the dappled shade of the orchard, or in the conservatory. Book stall, garden quizzes for children, sandpit. Some gravel paths.

SENNICOTTS
See Sussex

99 SHALDEN PARK HOUSE
The Avenue, Shalden, Alton GU34 4DS. Mr & Mrs Michael Campbell. *4 1/2 m NW of Alton. B3349 from Alton or J5 M3 onto B3349. Turn W at Golden Pot PH marked Herriard, Lasham, Shalden. Entrance 1/4 m on L*. Home-made teas. **Adm £3, chd free. Sun 2 June (2-5).**
Large 4-acre garden to stroll round, with beautiful views. Herbaceous borders incl kitchen walk and rose garden, all with large-scale planting and foliage interest. Pond, pool, arboretum, perfect kitchen garden and new garden statuary.

GROUP OPENING

100 SOUTHSEA GARDENS
Southsea PO4 0QE. *Turn into St Ronan's Rd from Albert Rd at junction opp Trinity Methodist Church. Alternatively follow signs from seafront and then follow yellow NGS signs from Canoe Lake and Eastern Parade. Park at Craneswater School in St Ronan's Rd. Entrance to all gardens from St Ronan's Ave*. **Evening Opening £6, chd free, wine, Sat 13 July (4-8).**

27 ST RONAN'S AVENUE
Mr & Mrs S C Johns

28 ST RONAN'S AVENUE
Ian Craig & Liz Jones
www.28stronansavenue.co.uk

85 ST RONAN'S ROAD
Mr Mike Hodges

87 ST RONAN'S ROAD
Miss Judy Walker

Four town gardens conveniently within 100m of each other. Each has a distinctive style, with different designs showing what can be achieved in an urban setting. 85 St Ronan's Road is a city garden with a classical twist, featuring a Neptune water feature in a pool of smoke. There is exceptional design at 27 St Ronan's Avenue where landscaping has been used to create a modern family concept with exuberant planting. The 'inside-out' garden at 87 St Ronan's Road captures busy urban living at its best, with an impressive dining area and sitting room with a permanent outside fireplace. 28 St Ronan's Avenue showcases a mixture of tender, exotic and dry-loving plants along with more traditional incl king protea, bananas, ferns, agave, echeveria and echiums.

A city garden with a classical twist, featuring a Neptune water feature in a pool of smoke . . .

101 SPINDLES
24 Wootton Road, Lee-on-the-Solent, Portsmouth, Hants PO13 9HB. Peter & Angela Arnold, 02392 550490, ah.arnold@ntlworld.com. *Approx 6m S of Fareham. Exit A27, turn L Gosport Rd A32. At r'about 2nd exit Gosport Rd Newgate Lane B3385. Through 3 r'abouts staying on B3385, turn L Marine Parade B3333 onto Wootton Rd*. Home-made teas. **Adm £2.50, chd free. Sun 9 June, Sun 7 July (11-5). Visitors and groups of up to 30 also welcome by appt May to Aug.**
Plantswoman's delightful small garden with all-yr interest. Ferns, grasses, shrubs, succulent collection, scented rose-covered pergolas, hostas and clematis. Unusual trees and palms, bananas, ginger lilies and exuberant herbaceous borders. Mini bog garden, soft fruit and herbs. Interest to new and experienced gardeners.

102 ◆ SPINNERS GARDEN
School Lane, Boldre, Lymington SO41 5QE. Andrew & Victoria Roberts, 01590 612196, www.spinnersgarden.co.uk. *1 1/2 m N of Lymington. Follow the brown signs off the A337 between Lymington and Brockenhurst. Also signed off the B3054 Beaulieu to Lymington rd. Map on website*. Cream teas. **Adm £4.50, chd free. For NGS: Sun 28 Apr (2-6). For other opening times and information, please phone or see garden website.**
Peaceful woodland garden on a slope overlooking the Lymington valley. Azaleas, rhododendrons, magnolias, acers and other rare shrubs interplanted with a wide variety of choice woodland and ground-cover plants. The garden is under development and new paths have been opened in the woodland garden while the lower garden has been extended and encompasses a new pond. Limited wheelchair access.

103 THE STABLE FAMILY HOME TRUST GARDEN
Bisterne, Ringwood BH24 3BN. Mr David Mowinski, www.sfht.org.uk. *3 1/2 m S of Ringwood. Follow B3347 through Bisterne village from Ringwood. Past Manor House, entrance on L*. Home-made teas. **Adm £3, chd free (share to SFHT). Sat 25, Sun 26 May (2-5.30).**
3 walled gardens lovingly tended by our head gardener and some of the 100 adults with learning difficulties in our care. Gravel garden a riot of colour with flowers, shrubs and herbs and adorned with pottery objects made here. Kitchen garden with polytunnels, greenhouse and raised vegetable beds. The small rose garden is a place of peace, leading to main lawn with pond and dragon-head fountain, also made in our pottery.

GROUP OPENING

104 STOCKBRIDGE GARDENS
Stockbridge SO20 6EX. *9m W of Winchester. On A30, at junction of A3057 & B3049. Parking on High St. All gardens on High St/Winton Hill.* Home-made teas on St Peter's Church Lawn. **Combined adm £5, chd free (share to St Peter's Church & Town Hall). Thur 6, Sun 9 June (2-5.30).**

LITTLE WYKE
High Street. Mrs Mary Matthews

NEW **THE OLD RECTORY**
High Street. Mr Robin Colenso

SHEPHERDS HOUSE
Winton Hill. Kim & Frances Candler

TROUT COTTAGE
High Street. Mrs Sally Milligan

Stockbridge with its many listed houses, excellent shops and pubs is on the famous River Test. Four gardens are open this year offering a variety of styles and character. Tucked in behind the High Street, Trout Cottage's small walled garden flowers for almost 10 months of the year. Little Wyke, also on the High Street next to the Town Hall, has a long mature town garden with curved mixed borders and fruit trees New for 2013, the Old Rectory is a mature garden with formal pond and planting near the house and woodland and bog areas bounded by a carrier stream of the River Test. Shepherds House, 50yds east of the White Hart roundabout, is a south-facing 3/4 acre garden on rising ground around a Georgian house. Continuing renovation includes lawns and terraces, mixed borders, ponds, small orchard and viewpoint overlooking the village.

♿ ✿ ☕

SWALLOWFIELD HORTICULTURAL SOCIETY
See Berkshire

Atheling Villas 10

© Louise Jolley

GROUP OPENING

105 SWAY VILLAGE GARDENS
Sway, SO41 6DT, 01590 681014, ashenbank@yahoo.co.uk. *7m S of Lyndhurst, 3m N of Lymington. From A337 take B3055 at Brockenhurst & turn R into Sway village. Follow NGS signs.* Home-made teas at Ashen Bank and 12 Gilpin Hill only. **Combined adm £5, chd free. Sats & Suns 4, 5, 25, 26 May (12-5).**

ASHEN BANK
SO41 6EG. Richard & Deborah Walker
01590 681014
ashenbank@yahoo.co.uk
www.ashenbank.com

12 GILPIN HILL
SO41 6DT. Jack & Sonia McPhie

NEW **HIGH FOREST**
SO41 6AS. David & Karen Ball

Sway Village lies deep in the heart of the New Forest National Park, with its roaming cattle and New Forest ponies along with miles of lowland heath. Three complementary gardens are located close to the village centre. Ashen Bank is a mature haven of trees and shrubs set in a 1/2 -acre tranquil setting. Beautiful old apple trees are underplanted with azaleas, hellebores and spring bulbs. Mature shrubs provide a wonderful background for the spring flowers. 12 Gilpin Hill is a small garden packed with a wide variety of unusual plants and trees. A wooded area and bog area planted with candelabra primulas surround a pond, a haven for dragonflies, frogs and newts. High Forest is a 1 1/2 -acre mature woodland garden with a mind of its own. Colourful rhododendrons, camellias, shrubs, perennials, roses, lawns and pools are contained within a peaceful setting. Large terrace with space for picnics with partial wheelchair access. All three gardens in the group have good wheelchair access but with some areas restricted.

♿ ✿ ☕

106 TANGLEFOOT
Crawley, Winchester SO21 2QB. Mr & Mrs F J Fratter, 01962 776243, fred@tanglefoot-house.demon.co.uk. *5m NW of Winchester. From M3 J9 take A34 N, exit after 3m & at r'about take 4th exit*

(A272); after 1.7m turn L to Crawley. From Winchester or Stockbridge take B3049. Private lane beside entrance to Crawley Court (Arqiva). Drop-off & disabled parking only at house, parking in field 50yds. **Adm £3.50, chd free. Thur 16, Sun 19 May; Thur 25, Sun 28 July (2-5.30). Also open 16, 19 May Little Court & opening with Crawley Gardens 13, 16 June; 11, 14 July. Visitors also welcome by appt May to July.**
Designed and developed by owners since 1976, Tanglefoot's ½-acre garden is a blend of influences, from Monet-inspired rose arch and small wildlife pond to Victorian boundary wall with trained fruit trees. Highlights include a raised lily pond, wild-flower meadow, herbaceous bed (a riot of colour later in the summer), herb wheel, large productive kitchen garden and unusual flowering plants. Plants from the garden for sale.

107 TERSTAN

Longstock, Stockbridge SO20 6DW. Alexander & Penny Burnfield, penny.burnfield@andover.co.uk, pennyburnfield.wordpress.com. *½ m N of Stockbridge. From Stockbridge (A30) turn N to Longstock at bridge. Garden ½ m on R.* Home-made teas. **Adm £3.50, chd free. Sun 19 May, Sat 15 June, Sun 14 July, Sat 17 Aug (2-6). Visitors also welcome by appt May to Aug.**
A country garden for the C21. Unusual plants, an ever-changing display of half-hardy specimens in pots, and an artist's eye for colour. Secluded and peaceful, with views to the River Test and the Hampshire Downs. Explore contrasting areas, linked by vistas, with a theme of circles and ovals. Featured in Amateur Gardening and Salisbury Life. Some gravel paths and steps.

TRUNKWELL GARDEN PROJECT

See Berkshire

108 TYLNEY HALL HOTEL

Ridge Lane, Rotherwick RG27 9AZ. Elite Hotels, 01256 764881, sales@tylneyhall.com, www.tylneyhall.com. *3m NW of Hook. From M3 J5 via A287 & Newnham, M4 J11 via B3349 & Rotherwick.* Cream teas. **Adm £4, chd free. Suns 28 Apr; 9 June; 6 Oct (10-5). Visitors also welcome by appt. Must be pre-booked and arranged in advance.**
Large garden of 66 acres with extensive woodlands and fine vista being restored with new planting. Fine avenues of wellingtonias; rhododendrons and azaleas, Italian garden, lakes, large water and rock garden, dry-stone walls originally designed with assistance of Gertrude Jekyll. Parts of the garden close to the main house are accessible by wheelchairs but not the full grounds due to uneven paths and steps.

109 UPHAM FARM

Upham SO32 1JD. Penny Walker. *2m NW of Bishop's Waltham. Turn into Upham St from B2177, then ½ m on R just past post box on R.* Home-made teas. **Adm £3, chd free. Sun 9 June (2-5).**
Established 1½ -acre garden with mature trees and shrubs. Borders recently renovated with new plantings of perennials. Features include a 'hot' border, a new woodland garden and an exciting extension to the wild-flower meadow with mass plantings of ornamental grasses leading down to a lake. Together with a traditional orchard, rose garden and productive kitchen garden, Upham Farm is well worth a visit. Gravel drive and path to garden.

110 ◆ THE VYNE

Sherborne St John RG24 9HL. National Trust, 01256 883858, www.nationaltrust.org.uk. *4m N of Basingstoke. Between Sherborne St John & Bramley. From A340 turn E at NT signs.* **Adm £7.50, chd £3. For NGS: Thur 25 Apr (11-5). For other opening times and information, please phone or see garden website.**
A good mix of garden areas including C18 landscape, Edwardian-style summerhouse garden, and a walled garden which incl glasshouse and vegetable plots. Vegetables grown by gardeners from the charity Thrive.

111 WALBURY

Lower Froyle, Alton GU34 4LJ. Ernie & Brenda Milam, 01420 22216, walbury@uwclub.net. *5m NE of Alton. Access to Lower Froyle from A31 between Alton and Farnham at Bentley. Parking available nr Walbury village hall.* Home-made teas. **Adm £4, chd free. Sat 27, Sun 28 Apr, Thur 4 July (2-5). Combined opening 4 July with Bramlins. Also opening 15, 16 June with Froyle Gardens. Visitors also welcome by appt Apr to July.**
3 gardens in one. All gardens have a cottage-garden atmosphere in different styles. Each one is packed with plants in colour-themed borders including many unusual plants. There are water features, an alpine house and fern walk.

Fine avenues of wellingtonias; rhododendrons and azaleas . . .

112 WALDEN

Common Hill, Medstead, nr Alton GU34 5LZ. Terri & Neil. *5m S of Alton. From A31 take rd to Medstead and into village centre. L at High St then L into Common Hill after church. From A339 take rd to Beech. Follow road through village centre. L after church into Common Hill. Walden ½ m down hill.* Home-made teas. **Adm £2.50, chd free. Fri 21, Sun 23 June (1.30-5).**
2-acre sloping garden on chalk, designed by the owners, with panoramic views towards Winchester. Restored 60ft rockery with many alpine species. Early summer colour with hardy perennials, peonies, roses, mature shrubs and fruit trees. Interesting sculptures enhance the garden whilst recycled objects add interest and humour.

113 WALDRONS

Brook, Bramshaw SO43 7HE. Major & Mrs J Robinson, 02380 813367, robinson08@btinternet.com. *4m N of Lyndhurst. On B3079 1m W from J1 M27. 1st house L past Green Dragon PH & directly opp Bell PH.* Home-made teas. **Adm £3, chd free. Visitors welcome by appt May to July.**
Come and be surprised by our tranquil 1-acre garden hiding behind a high hedge. First opened for the NGS in 1994, it features raised vegetable beds, a fruit cage, alpine

garden, hosta area and herbaceous borders. Enjoy the peaceful sitting areas for tea whilst watching the wildlife in the garden.

♿ ☕ ☎

114 WEIR HOUSE

Abbotstone Road, Old Alresford SO24 9DG. Mr & Mrs G Hollingbery, 01962 735549, jhollingbery@me.com. *½ m N of Alresford. From Alresford down Broad St (B3046) past Globe PH. Take 1st L, signed Abbotstone. Park in signed field.* **Adm £5, chd free. Sun 26 May, Sun 15 Sept (2-5). Groups of 10+ also welcome by appt Apr to Sept.**

Spectacular riverside garden with sweeping lawn backed by old walls, yew buttresses and mixed perennial beds. Contemporary vegetable and cut flower garden at its height in September. Also includes newly designed garden around pool area, bog garden (at best in May) and wilder walkways through wooded areas. Children can use the playground at their own risk. Covered by many magazines and TV programmes over the last 15 yrs. Wheelchair access to most, but not all, of garden.

♿ 🐕 ☕ ☎

A raised vegetable garden, rhododendron, azalea and conifer beds await you . . . !

115 WEST SILCHESTER HALL

Silchester RG7 2LX. Mrs Jenny Jowett, 0118 970 0278, www.jennyjowett.com. *9m N of Basingstoke. 9m S of Reading, off A340 (signed from centre of village).* Home-made teas. **Adm £3.50, chd free. Sun 26, Mon 27 May, Sun 14 July, Sun 11 Aug (2-6). Visitors also welcome by appt May to Sept for groups of 10+, coaches possible.**

This much loved 2-acre garden has fascinating colour combinations, inspired by the artist owners. Herbaceous borders crammed with rare and unusual plants, very good clematis, pots full of half hardies, wild pond garden and self-supporting kitchen garden with lovely view across to field of grazing cattle. Nr Roman site of Silchester. Studio with exhibition of botanical, landscape and portrait paintings. Archaelogical dig on Roman site in August. Gravel drive.

♿ ❀ ☕ ☎

116 WHEATLEY HOUSE

between Binsted and Kingsley GU35 9PA. Mr & Mrs Michael Adlington, 01420 23113, mikeadlington36@tiscali.co.uk. *4m E of Alton, 5m SW of Farnham. From Alton follow signs to Holybourne & Binsted. At end of Binsted turn R signed Wheatley. ¾ m down lane on L. From Farnham/Bordon on A325 take turn signed Binsted at Bucks Horn Oak. 1½ m turn L signed Wheatley.* Home-made teas. **Adm £4, chd free. Sat 17, Sun 18 Aug (1.30-5.30). Visitors also welcome by appt Mar to Oct.**

Magnificent setting with panoramic views over fields and forests. Sweeping mixed borders, shrubberies and grasses. 1½ acres, designed by artist-owner. The colours are spectacular. 'White & black' border. Local crafts and paintings in Old Barn. Wheelchair access with care on lawns.

♿ ❀ ☕ ☎

117 WHISPERS

Chatter Alley, Dogmersfield RG27 8SS. Mr & Mrs John Selfe. *3m W of Fleet. Turn N to Dogmersfield off A287 Odiham to Farnham rd. Turn L by Queen's Head PH.* Home-made teas. **Adm £4, chd free (share to Samantha Dickson Brain Tumour Trust). Sun 14 July (12-5).**

Visitors say you could spend all day discovering new plants in these 2 acres of manicured lawns surrounded by large borders of colourful shrubs, trees and long-flowering perennials. Alstromerias and salvias a speciality. Wild flower area, water storage system, greenhouse, kitchen garden and living sculptures. Spectacular waterfall cascades over large rock slabs and magically disappears below the terrace. A garden not to be missed. Assistance available on request over gravel entrance.

♿ ❀ ☕

118 WHITE BARN

Woodend Road, Crow Hill, Ringwood BH24 3DG. Marilyn & Barrie Knight, 01425 473527, bandmknight@btinternet.com. *2m SE of Ringwood. From Ringwood take B3347 towards Winkton and Sopley. After 1m turn L immed after petrol stn into Moortown Lane, proceed 1m, Woodend Rd, gravel rd on L.* **Adm £3.50, chd free. Groups up to 30 welcome by appt May to July, coaches can be accommodated by arrangement.**

A romantic and tranquil ¾ -acre garden in the New Forest National Park. Over 200 clematis, roses, hollyhocks, poppies and many unusual plants provide successional harmonious flowering from spring to summer. Birds, butterflies and bees abound. Paths lead to new views and surprises. Arches, pots and topiary give structural interest and complement the house and its surroundings. Featured in Hampshire Life. Some narrow paths.

♿ ☕ ☎

119 WHITE GABLES

Breach Lane, Sherfield-on-Loddon RG27 0EU. Terry & Brian Raisborough, 01256 882269, brianraisborough@aol.com, www.white_gables.net. *5m N of Basingstoke. From Basingstoke follow A33 towards Reading for approx 5m. Breach Lane is unmade lane immed on R before Sherfield-on-Loddon r'about. Limited parking for disabled by house. Main parking in 2 free signed car parks in main village. Short walk to garden.* Home-made teas. **Adm £3.50, chd free. Sun 5, Mon 6 May (1-5). Visitors also welcome by appt May to June.**

Come and meet Willemena, one of 4 life-sized statues as you meander through our plantaholics paradise. Follow the path as it takes you through various themed areas including large hosta collection, cacti and succulents. Greet Jemima, watching over the pond as your journey takes you past the raised banana bed, the tropical and oriental borders containing many unusual plants. A raised vegetable garden, rhododendron, azalea and conifer beds await you!

❀ ☕ ☎

120 NEW **WICOR PRIMARY SCHOOL COMMUNITY GARDEN**
Portchester, Fareham PO16 9DL. Louise Bryant. *Half way between Portsmouth and Fareham on A27. Turn S at Seagull PH r'about into Cornaway Lane, 1st R into Hatherley Drive. Entrance to School is almost opp.* Home-made teas. **Adm £3.50, chd free. Sun 23 June, Sun 7 July (10.30-4).**
Beautiful school gardens tended by pupils, staff and community gardeners. Lush orchard, courtyard, stumpery, wildlife areas and allotment featuring our Camera Obscura, one of only 12 in the south of England, and sculpture made by pupils. The gardens are situated in historic Portchester with views of Portsdown Hill and vistas of shoreline. The planting has been chosen to provide nectar and habitat for Wicor's rich wildlife. Featured in 'Popular Astronomy', The News and The Echo. Flat ground, wheelchair access to all areas.

121 **WILLOWS**
Pilley Hill, Boldre, nr Lymington SO41 5QF. Elizabeth & Martin Walker, 01590 677415, elizabethwalker13@gmail.com, www.willowsgarden.co.uk. *2m N Lymington off A337. 2½ m S of Brockenhurst, turn into Rope Hill for Pilley, Boldre and Spinners. Go 1m via Boldre Bridge, up Pilley Hill. Garden at school sign. Also signed from B3054 Beaulieu to Lymington rd. Leave M27 at J2 and follow 'Heavy Lorry Route' to avoid traffic delays at Lyndhurst. Park in school.* Cream teas. **Adm £3.50, chd free. Sat 27, Sun 28 July, Sat 10, Sun 11, Sun 25, Mon 26 Aug (2-5). Also open 10 & 11 Aug with 21 Chestnut Rd. Groups 20+ also welcome by appt July to Sept.**
A boat containing a golden Indian Bean Tree stands at the entrance to this country garden with a tropical twist. Pond, bog garden, fernery and deep borders brimming with late-summer colour plus towering bamboos at the front. Drought-tolerant plants and clever water-saving techniques at the back. Tranquil courtyards to enjoy cream-teas. Come to us via the picturesque historic village of Beaulieu - and enjoy the peaceful scenery of the New Forest.

122 **1 WOGSBARNE COTTAGES**
Rotherwick RG27 9BL. Mr R & Miss S Whistler. *2½ m N of Hook. M3 J5, M4 J11, A30 or A33 via B3349.* Home-made teas. **Adm £3, chd free. Sun 14, Mon 15 July (2-5).**
Small traditional cottage garden with a 'roses around the door' look, much photographed, seen on calendars, jigsaws and in magazines. Mixed flower beds and borders. Vegetables grown in abundance. Ornamental pond and alpine garden. Views over open countryside to be enjoyed whilst you take afternoon tea on the lawn. Small vintage motorcycle display (weather permitting). Some gravel paths.

YARMOUTH TOWN GARDENS
See Isle of Wight

Ashen Bank

Hampshire County Volunteers

County Organiser
Publicity and Central West area Patricia Elkington, Little Court, Crawley, Winchester SO21 2PU, 01962 776365, elkslc@tiscali.co.uk

County Treasurer
Fred Fratter, Tanglefoot, Crawley, Winchester SO21 2QB, 01962 776243, fred@tanglefoot-house.demon.co.uk

Assistant County Organisers
Central East Sue Alexander, The Hyde, Old Alresford, Alresford SO24 9DH, 01962 732043, suegreenhouse@hotmail.co.uk
North & North East Cynthia Oldale, Yew Tree Cottage, School Lane, Bentley, Farnham GU10 5JP, 01420 520438, c.k.oldale@btinternet.com
Central Winchester Mark Porter, The Down House, Main Road, Itchen Abbas, Winchester SO21 1AX, 01962 791054, markstephenporter@gmail.com
North & North East Mary Trigwell-Jones, 'Selborne', Caker Lane, East Worldham, Alton GU34 3AE, 01420 83389, mary.trigwell-jones@virgin.net
North West Carol Pratt, 10 Catherine's Walk, Abbotts Ann, Andover SP11 7AS, 01264 710305, carolacap@yahoo.co.uk
East Linda Smith, Meon Orchard, Kingsmead, Wickham PO17 5AU, 01329 833253, linda.ngs@btinternet.com
West Christopher Stanford, Oakdene, Sandleheath, Fordingbridge SP6 1TD, 01425 652133, christopher.stanford@homecall.co.uk
South area Barbara Sykes, The Cottage, 16 Lakewood Road, Chandler's Ford SO53 1ES, 02380 254521, barandhugh@aol.com
South West Elizabeth Walker, Willows, Pilley Hill, Boldre, Lymington SO41 5QF, 01590 677415, elizabethwalker13@gmail.com

HEREFORDSHIRE

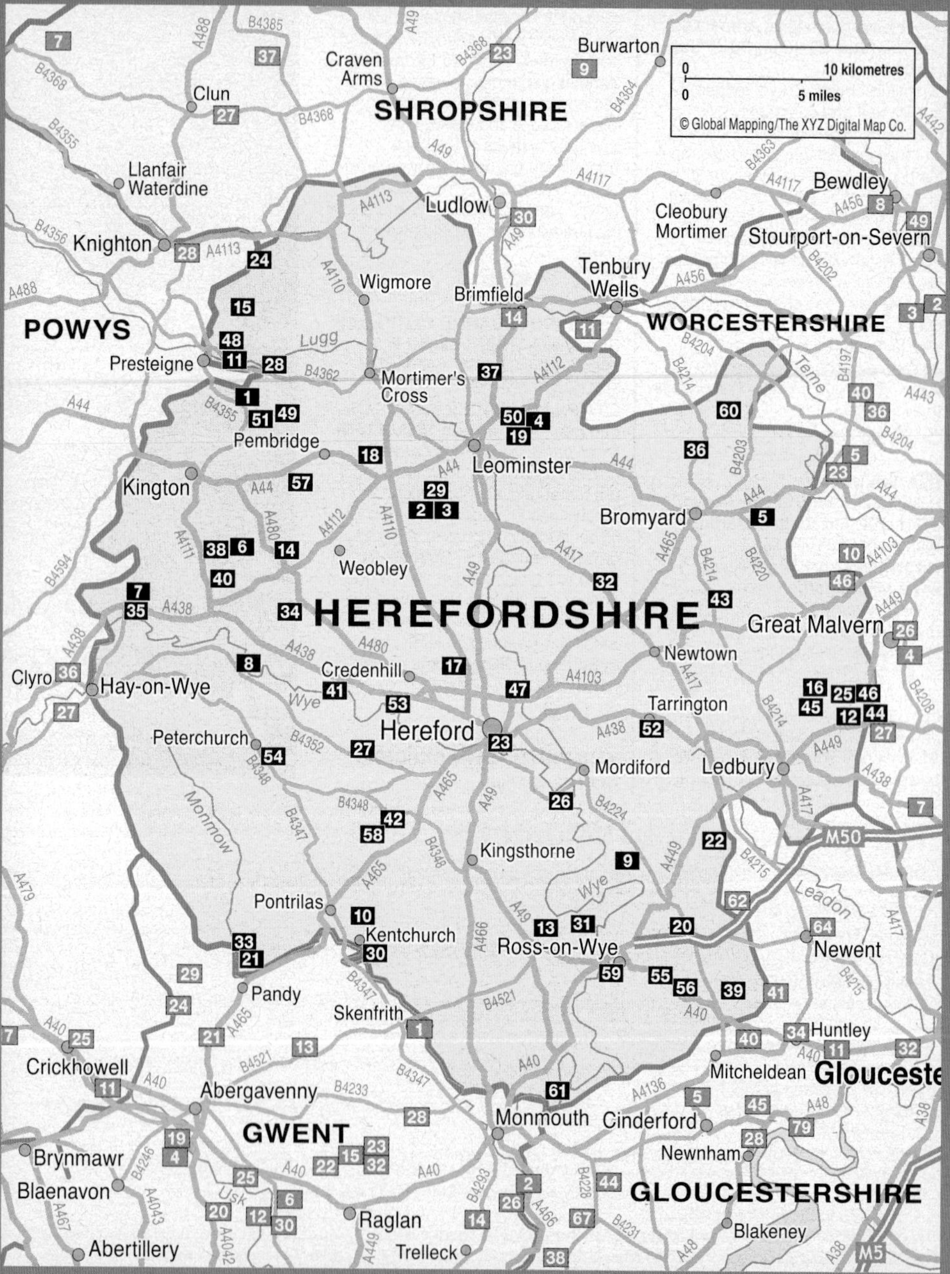

Opening Dates

February

Every Thursday
29 Ivy Croft

Wednesday 20
53 The Weir

March

Sunday 10
39 The Old Corn Mill

April

Monday 1
39 The Old Corn Mill
50 Stockton Bury Gardens Ltd

Sunday 7
6 Batch Cottage
32 Lower Hope
58 Whitfield

Monday 8
36 Moors Meadow Gardens & Nursery

Sunday 14
3 Aulden Farm
29 Ivy Croft

Wednesday 17
8 Brobury House Gardens

Sunday 28
7 Brilley Court

May

Sunday 5
39 The Old Corn Mill

Sunday 12
4 Bachefield House
15 Cloister Garden
24 Hill House Farm

Monday 13
11 Bryan's Ground
36 Moors Meadow Gardens & Nursery

Wednesday 15
27 Inglewood
42 The Old Rectory, Thruxton

Thursday 16
49 Staunton Park

Saturday 18
45 Phelps Cottage Garden

Sunday 19
3 Aulden Farm
29 Ivy Croft
32 Lower Hope
42 The Old Rectory, Thruxton
45 Phelps Cottage Garden

Thursday 23
49 Staunton Park

Friday 24
22 Hellens

Saturday 25
22 Hellens

Sunday 26
18 Glan Arrow
37 The Nest

Monday 27
37 The Nest
39 The Old Corn Mill

Tuesday 28
13 Church Cottage

Wednesday 29
13 Church Cottage

Thursday 30
49 Staunton Park

There are shady areas, places to sit . . . the garden feels mature but is still evolving . . .

June

Sunday 2
55 Weston Hall

Tuesday 4
13 Church Cottage

Wednesday 5
13 Church Cottage

Thursday 6
49 Staunton Park

Friday 7
17 Daimor

Saturday 8
17 Daimor
21 Grove Farm (cellar gallery)
33 Middle Hunt House

Sunday 9
6 Batch Cottage
9 Brockhampton Cottage
20 Grendon Court
21 Grove Farm (cellar gallery)
33 Middle Hunt House
48 Stapleton Castle Court Garden

Monday 10
36 Moors Meadow Gardens & Nursery
38 Newport House
48 Stapleton Castle Court Garden

Tuesday 11
13 Church Cottage
38 Newport House
47 The Rambles

Wednesday 12
13 Church Cottage
38 Newport House

Thursday 13
38 Newport House
49 Staunton Park

Friday 14
38 Newport House

National Gardens Weekend

Saturday 15
2 Aulden Arts and Gardens (Evening)
16 The Cross
21 Grove Farm (cellar gallery)
25 The Hollies
39 The Old Corn Mill
41 The Old Rectory, Byford
56 Weston Mews

Sunday 16
2 Aulden Arts and Gardens
5 The Bannut
10 The Brooks
12 Caves Folly Nurseries
16 The Cross
21 Grove Farm (cellar gallery)
25 The Hollies
26 Holme Lacy House Hotel
30 Kentchurch Gardens
39 The Old Corn Mill
43 The Orchards
56 Weston Mews
58 Whitfield
59 Wilton Castle on the Wye

Tuesday 18
13 Church Cottage

Wednesday 19
13 Church Cottage
27 Inglewood
28 Ivy Cottage
42 The Old Rectory, Thruxton

Thursday 20
49 Staunton Park

Friday 21
23 Hereford Cathedral Gardens

Sunday 23
35 Montpelier Cottage
42 The Old Rectory, Thruxton
44 Perrycroft

Tuesday 25
13 Church Cottage
47 The Rambles

Wednesday 26
13 Church Cottage

Thursday 27
49 Staunton Park

Saturday 29
1 Ashley Farm
52 The Vine
54 Wellbrook Manor

You are always welcome at an NGS garden!

Sunday 30
- 1 Ashley Farm
- 4 Bachefield House
- 8 Brobury House Gardens
- 54 Wellbrook Manor
- 57 Westonbury Mill Water Garden

July

Tuesday 2
- 13 Church Cottage

Wednesday 3
- 13 Church Cottage

Thursday 4
- 49 Staunton Park

Saturday 6
- 41 The Old Rectory, Byford

Sunday 7
- 41 The Old Rectory, Byford
- 60 Wolferlow House

Monday 8
- 36 Moors Meadow Gardens & Nursery

Tuesday 9
- 13 Church Cottage

Wednesday 10
- 13 Church Cottage

Thursday 11
- 49 Staunton Park

Sunday 14
- 15 Cloister Garden
- 24 Hill House Farm
- 32 Lower Hope
- 59 Wilton Castle on the Wye
- 61 Woodview

Tuesday 16
- 13 Church Cottage

Wednesday 17
- 13 Church Cottage
- 27 Inglewood
- 42 The Old Rectory, Thruxton

Thursday 18
- 49 Staunton Park

Sunday 21
- 5 The Bannut
- 14 Clarkesfield
- 26 Holme Lacy House Hotel
- 42 The Old Rectory, Thruxton
- 61 Woodview

Tuesday 23
- 13 Church Cottage

Wednesday 24
- 13 Church Cottage

Thursday 25
- 49 Staunton Park

Sunday 28
- 43 The Orchards

Tuesday 30
- 13 Church Cottage
- 47 The Rambles

Wednesday 31
- 13 Church Cottage

August

Thursday 1
- 49 Staunton Park

Sunday 4
- 3 Aulden Farm
- 29 Ivy Croft
- 46 The Picton Garden

Tuesday 6
- 13 Church Cottage

Wednesday 7
- 13 Church Cottage
- 28 Ivy Cottage

Thursday 8
- 49 Staunton Park

Saturday 10
- 46 The Picton Garden

Sunday 11
- 30 Kentchurch Gardens

Monday 12
- 36 Moors Meadow Gardens & Nursery

Tuesday 13
- 13 Church Cottage

Wednesday 14
- 13 Church Cottage

Thursday 15
- 49 Staunton Park

Sunday 18
- 5 The Bannut
- 26 Holme Lacy House Hotel
- 46 The Picton Garden

Thursday 22
- 46 The Picton Garden
- 49 Staunton Park

Sunday 25
- 48 Stapleton Castle Court Garden

Monday 26
- 46 The Picton Garden
- 48 Stapleton Castle Court Garden

Thursday 29
- 49 Staunton Park

Bring a picnic, your paint brushes, binoculars and linger awhile . . .

September

Sunday 1
- 34 Midland Farm

Wednesday 4
- 46 The Picton Garden
- 53 The Weir

Thursday 5
- 49 Staunton Park

Sunday 8
- 3 Aulden Farm
- 29 Ivy Croft
- 42 The Old Rectory, Thruxton

Thursday 12
- 49 Staunton Park

Sunday 15
- 10 The Brooks
- 46 The Picton Garden

Wednesday 25
- 8 Brobury House Gardens

Sunday 29
- 32 Lower Hope

October

Sunday 6
- 44 Perrycroft

Thursday 10
- 46 The Picton Garden

Saturday 12
- 38 Newport House

Sunday 13
- 38 Newport House

Monday 14
- 38 Newport House

Tuesday 15
- 38 Newport House

Wednesday 16
- 38 Newport House

Thursday 17
- 38 Newport House

Friday 18
- 38 Newport House

Saturday 19
- 38 Newport House

Sunday 20
- 38 Newport House
- 46 The Picton Garden

February 2014

Thursday 6
- 29 Ivy Croft

Thursday 13
- 29 Ivy Croft

Wednesday 19
- 53 The Weir

Thursday 20
- 29 Ivy Croft

Thursday 27
- 29 Ivy Croft

Gardens open to the public

- 3 Aulden Farm
- 5 The Bannut
- 8 Brobury House Gardens
- 11 Bryan's Ground
- 12 Caves Folly Nurseries
- 22 Hellens

23 Hereford Cathedral Gardens
29 Ivy Croft
33 Middle Hunt House
36 Moors Meadow Gardens & Nursery
46 The Picton Garden
49 Staunton Park
50 Stockton Bury Gardens Ltd
53 The Weir
57 Westonbury Mill Water Garden

By appointment only

19 Grantsfield
31 Lawless Hill
40 The Old Quarry
51 Upper Tan House

Also open by Appointment ☎

1 Ashley Farm
6 Batch Cottage
7 Brilley Court
9 Brockhampton Cottage
13 Church Cottage
18 Glan Arrow
21 Grove Farm (cellar gallery)
24 Hill House Farm
25 The Hollies
28 Ivy Cottage
32 Lower Hope
38 Newport House
39 The Old Corn Mill
41 The Old Rectory, Byford
42 The Old Rectory, Thruxton
44 Perrycroft
45 Phelps Cottage Garden
47 The Rambles
48 Stapleton Castle Court Garden
55 Weston Hall
56 Weston Mews
58 Whitfield
60 Wolferlow House
61 Woodview

The Gardens

1 ASHLEY FARM

Stansbatch HR6 9LN. Roger & Jackie Pietroni, 01544 267405, jackiepietroni@gmail.com, www.ashleyfarm.net. *2m S of Presteigne. 1m N of Titley. On B4355.* Home-made teas. **Adm £4, chd free.** **Sat 29, Sun 30 June (2-5). Visitors & groups also welcome by appt June to Sept.**
5-acre garden started in 2005. Designed as a series of formal rooms surrounding the house becoming more informal further away. Many places to sit and contemplate. Wonderful views. Colour-themed borders, roses plentiful, orchards enchanting in blossom time. Squirrels love the nuttery, bees and butterflies think they're in heaven in the decorative and productive kitchen garden. Much more besides. Featured in The English Garden.
✿ ☕ ☎

GROUP OPENING

2 NEW AULDEN ARTS AND GARDENS

Aulden, Leominster HR6 0JT, www.auldenfarm.co.uk. *4m SW of Leominster. From Leominster take Ivington/Upper Hill Road, ¾ m after Ivington Church turn R signed Aulden. From A4110 signed Ivington, take 2nd R signed Aulden.* Home-made teas & home-made ice cream (Sun). **Combined adm £6, chd free.** **Evening Opening, wine, Sat 15 June (5-8); Sun 16 June (2-6).**

◆ AULDEN FARM NCH
Alun & Jill Whitehead
(See separate entry)
For other opening times and information, please phone or see garden website.

NEW HILL VIEW
Tricia and Andy Mitchell.
On L opp Aulden farm

NEW HONEYLAKE COTTAGE
Jennie and Jack Hughes

Is gardening an art form? We are a group of neighbours who share an active interest in art and gardens, and believe that gardens give ever-changing colour and composition in 3 dimensions. Art, in many forms, including print, mixed media, oil and sculpture will be displayed, and also the etching press and equipment. So why not come and decide for yourself, see the gardens, the related paintings, sculpture and other works. The 3-acre garden at Aulden Farm is planted with wildlife in mind, with emphasis on structure and form, with a hint of quirkiness. It is a garden to explore. Irises thrive around the natural pond, Hemerocallis intermingle with sculpture and grasses and kniphofias give added zing. There are shady areas, places to sit; the garden feels mature but is still evolving. At Hill View the sweeping lawn makes a green space for the display of sculpture, whilst the mature trees, wildflowers and hardscape provide further interest. Honeylake Cottage has views over the wonderful Herefordshire countryside. The garden emphasis on traditional cottage flowers is reflected in the art work. The garden also includes a productive vegetable patch.
✿ NCH ☕

The Orchards

3 ◆ AULDEN FARM
Aulden, Leominster HR6 0JT. Alun & Jill Whitehead, 01568 720129, www.auldenfarm.co.uk. *4m SW of Leominster. From Leominster take Ivington/Upper Hill Rd. ¾ m after Ivington Church, turn R (signed Aulden), garden 1m on R. From A4110 signed Ivington, take 2nd R (approx ¾ m), garden ¾ m on L.* **Adm £3.50. For NGS: Suns 14 Apr; 19 May; 4 Aug; 8 Sept (2-5.30). For other opening times and information, please phone or see garden website.**
Informal country garden surrounding old farmhouse. 3 acres planted with wildlife in mind. Emphasis on structure and form with hint of quirkiness, a garden to explore. Irises thrive around the natural pond, hemerocallis intermingle with sculpture, grasses and kniphofias for added zing. Shady areas, places to sit, feels mature but still evolving. National Collection of Siberian Iris & plant nursery. Featured in Country Living, Herefordshire Life and The English Garden.
NCH

4 BACHEFIELD HOUSE
Kimbolton HR6 0EP. Jim & Rowena Gale. *3m E of Leominster. Take A4112 off A49 (signed Leysters), after 10yds 1st R (signed Stretford/ Hamnish). 1st L to Grantsfield over Xrds (signed Bache), continue for approx 1m, garden on R past rd to Gorsty Hill.* Home-made teas. **Adm £3.50, chd free. Suns 12 May; 30 June (2-5.30).**
Charming traditional cottage-style garden of 1 acre. On gentle hill slope, the beds and borders bulge with beautiful blooms and foliage. Part-walled kitchen and cutting garden, gravel beds, pond and summerhouse with fine views; particular emphasis on roses, peonies and irises.

5 ◆ THE BANNUT
Bringsty, Bromyard WR6 5TA. Daphne & Maurice Everett, 01885 482206, www.bannut.co.uk. *2½ m E of Bromyard. On A44 Worcester Rd, ½ m E of entrance to National Trust, Brockhampton.* **Adm £4.50, chd £2. For NGS: Suns 16 June; 21 July; 18 Aug (12.30-5). For other opening times and information, please phone or see garden website.**
3 acres of enchanting gardens with much to enjoy throughout the seasons - colourful herbaceous plants, heather gardens, interesting trees and shrubs. Garden rooms, unusual knot garden, 'secret' garden, water features, lovely views to the Malvern Hills. Many seats around the garden. Home-made lunches and teas.

BARNARD'S GREEN HOUSE
See Worcestershire

THE BARTON
See Worcestershire

6 BATCH COTTAGE
Almeley HR3 6PT. Jeremy & Elizabeth Russell, 01544 327469. *16m NW of Hereford. 2m off A438-A4111 to Kington, turn R at Eardisley.* Cream teas. **Adm £4, chd free. Suns 7 Apr; 9 June (2-5). Visitors & groups also welcome by appt Mar to Oct.**
Established unregimented, conservation-oriented garden of some 2½ acres with streams and large pond, set in a natural valley, surrounded by woodland and orchard. Over 360 labelled trees and shrubs, mixed borders, fern and bog beds, wild flower bank, stumpery, woodland walk. Fritillaries and spotted orchids abound in season. Some gravel paths and steep slopes.

BIRTSMORTON COURT
See Worcestershire

BRIDGES STONE MILL
See Worcestershire

7 BRILLEY COURT
Whitney-on-Wye HR3 6JF. Mr & Mrs David Bulmer, 01497 831467, rosebulmer@hotmail.com. *6m NE of Hay-on-Wye. 5m SW of Kington. 1½ m off A438 Hereford to Brecon rd signed to Brilley.* Home-made teas. **Adm £4, chd free. Sun 28 Apr (1.30-6). Visitors & groups always welcome by appt.**
3-acre garden, walled ornamental kitchen garden. Spring tulip collection, summer rose and herbaceous borders. 7-acre arboretum/wild stream garden, wild flowers and rhododendron collection. Featured in Homes & Gardens, The English Garden & Gardens Illustrated. Limited wheelchair access.

8 ◆ BROBURY HOUSE GARDENS
Brobury by Bredwardine HR3 6BS. Keith & Pru Cartwright, 01981 500229, www.broburyhouse.co.uk. *10m W of Hereford. S off A438 signed Bredwardine & Brobury. Garden 1m on L (before bridge).* **Adm £4, chd free. For NGS: Wed 17 Apr (2-5); Sun 30 June (11-5); Wed 25 Sept (2-5.30). For other opening times and information, please phone or see garden website.**
9 acres of gardens, set on the banks of an exquisitely beautiful section of the R Wye, offer the visitor a delightful combination of Victorian terraces with mature specimen trees, inspiring water features, architectural planting and woodland areas. Redesign and development is ongoing. Bring a picnic, your paint brushes, binoculars and linger awhile. Wheelchair users, strong able-bodied assistant advisable.

Is gardening an art form? . . . we are a group of neighbours who share an active interest in art and gardens . . .

9 BROCKHAMPTON COTTAGE
Brockhampton HR1 4TQ. Peter & Ravida Clay, 07974 569037, peter.clay@crocus.co.uk. *8m SW of Hereford. 5m N of Ross-on-Wye off B4224. In Brockhampton take rd signed Brockhampton Church, continue up hill for ½ m, after set of farm buildings, driveway on L over cattle grid. Car park 500yds from garden.* **Adm £5, chd free. Sun 9 June (10.30-2). Combined with Grendon Court (2-5) adm £8. Groups of 20+ also welcome by appt May to Sept.**
Created from scratch in 1999 by the owners and Tom Stuart-Smith, this beautiful hilltop garden looks S and W over miles of unspoilt countryside. On one side a woodland garden and wild flower meadow, on the other side a

Perry pear orchard and in valley below: lake, stream and arboretum. Picnic parties welcome by lake until 2pm. Visit Grendon Court (2-5) after your visit to us. Featured in House and Garden, Gardens Illustrated, The English Garden, The Observer and Country Living.

10 THE BROOKS

Pontrilas HR2 0BL. Marion & Clive Stainton, www.marionet.co.uk/the_brooks. *12m SW of Hereford. From the A465 Hereford to Abergavenny rd, turn L at Pontrilas onto B4347, take 2nd L signed Orcop & Garway Hill. Garden 1¾ m on L.* Home-made teas. **Adm £3.50, chd free. Suns 16 June; 15 Sept (2-5.30).**

This 2½ -acre Golden Valley garden incl part-walled enclosed vegetable garden and greenhouse (wind/solar-powered), orchard, ornamental, perennial, shade and shrub borders, wildlife pond, evolving arboretum cum coppice, and meadow with stunning views. Surrounding a stone 1684 farmhouse (not open), the garden has mature elements, but much has been created since 2006, with future development plans.

11 ◆ BRYAN'S GROUND

Letchmoor Lane, nr Stapleton, Presteigne LD8 2LP. David Wheeler & Simon Dorrell, 01544 260001, www.bryansground.co.uk. *12m NW of Leominster. Between Kinsham & Stapleton. At Mortimer's Cross take B4362 signed Presteigne. At Combe, follow signs. SATNAV is misleading.* **Adm £6, chd £2. For NGS: Mon 13 May (2-5). For other opening times and information, please phone or see garden website.**

8-acre internationally renowned contemporary reinterpretation of Arts & Crafts garden dating from 1912, conceived as series of rooms with yew & box topiary, parterres, colour-themed flower & shrub borders, reflecting pools, potager, Edwardian greenhouse, heritage apple orchard, follies. Arboretum planted mainly for autumn colour with wildlife pool beside River Lugg. Home of Hortus, garden journal. Featured in Period Living and Telegraph magazine. The majority of the garden is accessible by wheelchair, though there are some steps adjoining the terrace.

12 ◆ CAVES FOLLY NURSERIES

Evendine Lane, Colwall WR13 6DX. Wil Leaper & Bridget Evans, 01684 540631, www.cavesfolly.com. *1¼ m NE of Ledbury. B4218. Between Malvern & Ledbury. Evendine Lane, off Colwall Green.* **Adm £3, chd free. For NGS: Sun 16 June (2-5). For other opening times and information, please phone or see garden website.**

Organic nursery and display gardens. Specialist growers of herbaceous, alpines, grasses, vegetable and herb plants, all grown organically. This is not a manicured garden! It is full of drifts of colour and wild flowers and a haven for wildlife.

13 NEW CHURCH COTTAGE

Hentland, Ross-on-Wye HR9 6LP. Sue Emms and Pete Weller, 01989 730222, sue.emms@mac.com. *6m from Ross-on-Wye. A49 to Hereford R to Hentland. At bottom of hill take sharp R to St Dubricious Church. Follow narrow lane, please take care - single track with few passing places. Unsuitable for motor homes and caravans. Church Cottage on L.* Tea. **Adm £3, chd free. Every Tue, Wed 28 May to 14 Aug (2-5). Visitors also welcome by appt May to Sept.**

Garden designer and plantswoman's new ½ -acre evolving garden packed with plants, many unusual varieties mixed with old favourites providing interest over a long period. Wildlife pond, rose garden, potager, mixed borders, white terrace, gravel garden. Interesting plant combinations and design ideas to inspire.

14 CLARKESFIELD

Meer, Woonton, Hereford HR3 6QP. Christopher & Marion Scott. *13m NW of Hereford. Follow signs to Kington (A480), turn R (signed) Meer/Broxwood. ½ m LH-side.* Cream teas. **Adm £3, chd free. Sun 21 July (2-5.30).**

The garden has been redeveloped since 2006 by present owners. Contemporary herbaceous borders for lasting interest and colour, incorporating grasses, small formal pond and Japanese area. Kitchen garden and cutting flower garden now completed. Wildlife pond now being planted with walks through meadowland. Stunning views towards Black Mountains.

15 NEW CLOISTER GARDEN

Pant Hall, Willey, Presteigne LD8 2LY. Malcolm Temple & Karen Roberts. *3m N of Presteigne. 3m from Presteigne Bridge follow rd from bridge, signed to Willey. Past Stapleton Castle on R. Pant Hall on L.* Home-made teas. **Adm £3.50, chd free. Suns 12 May; 14 July (2-6). Also open Hill House Farm.**

The ½ -acre garden incl terraced lawns, flower beds and shrubberies leading down to a wildlife pond and bog garden. Bordering one side is a tumbling stream over which a bridge leads to a pasture containing remnants of an ancient orchard.

A tumbling stream where a bridge leads to a pasture containing remnants of an ancient orchard . . .

16 THE CROSS

Coddington, Ledbury HR8 1JL. Brian & Megan Taylor. *4m N of Ledbury. From Colwall turn into Mill Lane and follow signs to Coddington. After 3m, parking for garden is L 50yds after L turn to Coddington. From Bosbury, take B4220 to Cradley. Pass through Bosbury village, take R turn sign Colwall & Coddington. After 2m parking for garden is on L just before R turn to Coddington.* Home-made teas. **Adm £3, chd free. Sat 15, Sun 16 June (2-5).**

1-acre informal country garden. Generous mixed borders lavishly planted with shrubs, roses, perennials and bulbs. Wildlife pond and native flower patch. Gravel area and kitchen garden. Pleasant walk through paddock leads to a tranquil path through 5 acres of mature woodland. Lovely views of the Malvern Hills. All paths are gravel.

The Hollies

17 DAIMOR
Burghill, Hereford HR4 7RN. Mr & Mrs R M Jenman. *3m NE of Hereford. From Hereford turn off A4103 to Burghill, after 1m fork R, garden in centre of village on L.* Cream teas. **Adm £3, chd free.** **Fri 7, Sat 8 June (2-6).**
This delightful 4yr-old garden, has been created to form a modern space catering for four generations of family, incl a games lawn with cottage-style planting, lavender walk with rose swags, raised-bed vegetable and fruit gardens, tree house and greenhouse, new large pond surrounded by a wild flower meadow attracting many species of insect and bird life. The front garden is being redeveloped.

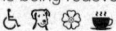

18 GLAN ARROW
Eardisland HR6 9BW. Christopher & Lotty James, 01544 388207, lotty@glanarrow.com. *5m W of Leominster on B4529. Cross bridge & immed turn sharp L up driveway. Recommend parking in car park opposite the dovecote and walking up drive.* Home-made teas. **Adm £3.50, chd free. Sun 26 May (2-6). Visitors & groups max 30 also welcome by appt.**
4-acre English riverside garden with herbaceous borders, roses, bog garden leading to small lake, white garden, herringbone ha-ha and potager.

19 GRANTSFIELD
nr Kimbolton, Leominster HR6 0ET. Colonel & Mrs J G T Polley, 01568 613338. *3m NE of Leominster. A49 N from Leominster, A4112 turn R & follow signs.* **Adm £3.50, chd free. Visitors welcome by appt Apr to Sept.**
Contrasting styles in gardens of old stone farmhouse; wide variety of unusual plants, trees and shrubs, old roses, climbers, herbaceous borders, superb views. 1½ -acre orchard and kitchen garden with flowering and specimen trees and shrubs. Spring bulbs. Comma butterfly saved from extinction here by Emma Hutchinson in 1890s.

20 GRENDON COURT
Upton Bishop HR9 7QP. Mark & Kate Edwards. *3m NE of Ross-on-Wye. M50 J3 towards Hereford. Follow B4224 to Hereford past Moody Cow PH, down hill, up other side, 1st gate on R. From Ross A40, B449, at Xrds, R to Upton Bishop, 100yds on L.* Home-made teas (as the barn is being renovated tea will be outdoors, weather permitting). **Adm £4, chd free. Sun 9 June (2-5). Combined with Brockhampton Cottage (morning opening) adm £8.**
A contemporary garden designed by Tom Stuart-Smith. Planted on 2 levels, a clever collection of mass-planted perennials and grasses of different heights, textures and colour give all-yr round interest. The upper walled garden with a sea of flowering grasses makes a highlight. Views of pond and valley walk. Visit Brockhampton Cottage (10.30-2) before you visit us (picnic by the lake).

21 GROVE FARM (CELLAR GALLERY)
Walterstone HR2 0DX. David & Christine Hunt, 01873 890293, davidbhunt@tiscali.co.uk. *A465 Abergavenny to Hereford, at Pandy turn L at the Pandy Inn, follow signs to Cellar Gallery, turn R at Carpenters Arms, our drive is L at bottom of the hill.* **Adm £3.50, chd free. Sats, Suns 8, 9, 15, 16 June (11-5). Visitors & groups max 10 also welcome by appt May to July.**
Large tranquil courtyard with ponds, shrubs, specimen trees, greenhouse and gallery created from the old cattle yard and parlour. Banks of herbaceous borders, shrubberies and rose-covered pergolas leading to vegetable and herb garden, wild pond and orchard. Christine's art gallery (Cellar Gallery) is also open.

22 ◆ HELLENS
Much Marcle, Ledbury HR8 2LY. PMMCT, 01531 660504, www.hellensmanor.com. *6m from Ross-on-Wye. 4m SW of Ledbury, off A449.* **Adm £2.50, chd free. For NGS: Fri 24, Sat 25 May (10-4). For other opening times and information, please phone or see garden website.**
In the grounds of Hellens manor house, the gardens are being gently redeveloped to reflect the C17 ambience of the house. Incl a rare octagonal dovecote, 2 knot gardens and yew labyrinth, lawns, herb and kitchen gardens, short woodlands and pond walk. Longer walk to Hall Wood, SSSI. Gardens are fairly level but pathways are gravel.

23 ◆ HEREFORD CATHEDRAL GARDENS
Hereford HR1 2NG. Dean of Hereford Cathedral, 01432 374202, www.herefordcathedral.org. *Centre of Hereford. Approach roads to the Cathedral are signed. Tours leave from information desk in the cathedral building.* **Adm £5 (share to homeless charity). For NGS: Fri 21 June (10.30-4). For other opening times and information, please phone or see garden website.**
Guided tours of historic gardens which won 2 top awards in 'It's Your Neighbourhood 2012'. The tour includes: a courtyard garden; an atmospheric cloisters garden enclosed by C15 buildings; the Vicar's Choral garden; the Dean's own garden; and the Bishop's garden with fine trees, vegetable and cutting garden, outdoor chapel for meditation in a floral setting, all sloping to the Wye. Featured in the 'Give & Grow' section of The English Garden. Limited wheelchair access.

HIGH VIEW
See Worcestershire

24 HILL HOUSE FARM
Knighton LD7 1NA. Simon & Caroline Gourlay, 01547 528542, simongourlay@btinternet.com. *4m SE of Knighton. S of A4113 via Knighton (Llanshay Lane, 3m) or Bucknell (Reeves Lane, 3m).* Home-made teas. **Adm £4, chd free. Suns 12 May; 14 July (2-5.30). Also open Cloister Garden. Visitors & groups max 30 also welcome by appt May to Aug.**
S-facing 5-acre hillside garden developed over past 40yrs with magnificent views over unspoilt countryside. Herbaceous area amongst magnificent mature oak trees, extensive lawns and paths surrounded by roses, shrubs and specimen trees. Sloping paths to Oak Pool 200ft below house. Transport available from bottom of garden if needed.

25 THE HOLLIES
Old Church Road, Colwall WR13 6EZ. Margaret & Graham White, 01684 540931, whites@mandgwhite.co.uk. *3m SW of Malvern. Take B4218 past Old Court Nursery (Picton Gardens), turn R into Old Church Rd. Hollies 400yds on R.* Home-made teas. **Adm £3, chd free. Sat 15, Sun 16 June (2-5.30). Individuals and groups also welcome by appt Feb to Nov.**
Intensively planted 1/2 acre with views of the Malvern Hills, which has been developed by a hardy plants enthusiast. The continually evolving beds and borders contain a wide range of shrubs, bulbs and herbaceous perennials. These have been chosen to provide interest throughout the year, with emphasis on leaf form and colour. Views towards the Malvern Hills. Some areas in full sun, some in deep shade. Vegetable plot with raised beds. Featured in Amateur Gardening, Country Gardener & on Radio Hereford and Worcester. Some gravel paths suitable for wheelchairs.

HOLMCROFT
See Shropshire

Medieval 'hortus conclusus' including quadrant design, arbour, central 'tree of life' and early Christian symbols . . .

26 HOLME LACY HOUSE HOTEL
Holme Lacy HR2 6LP. Warner Leisure Hotels, 01432 870870, www.holmelacyhouse.co.uk. *5m SE of Hereford. From Hereford B4399, from Gloucester B4215, then B4224, from Ledbury A438 signed from Holme Lacy village.* Light refreshments. **Adm £3, chd free. Suns 16 June; 21 July; 18 Aug (10-4).**
The gardens were conceived on a very bold scale in 'The Grand Manner' and is Herefordshire's only surviving example of such gardens. Battlement gardens, ancient yew hedging, formal Italian gardens with ponds. Herbaceous borders, walled garden and orchard with historic pear trees. The gardens are going through phases of renovation and replanting, in keeping with the historical period of the house and existing garden features. Gravel paths, some steep slopes, unfenced pond.

27 NEW INGLEWOOD
Madley, Hereford HR2 9NR. Alice Vale. *6m SW of Hereford. From A465 towards Abergavenny turn R on to B4349/B4352 to Madley. Pass through village. After Tinglebrook estate on R, take first L (signed Archenfield leading to Patterson Close) and park on L along fencing opp Inglewood (2nd drive on R).* Home-made teas. **Adm £2.50, chd £1. Weds 15 May; 19 June; 17 July (11-5).**
Small village garden richly planted and full of interest. Enclosed rear garden incorporates features of the Medieval 'hortus conclusus' incl quadrant design, arbour, central 'tree of life' and early Christian symbols evoking earthly paradise. Gravelled front garden with raised shrub, herb and vegetable beds. Attractive containers and 'objets trouvés'. Sale of brick sculptures by Chiselbrick, suitable for garden use.

28 IVY COTTAGE
Kinsham LD8 2HN. Jane & Richard Barton, 01544 267154, rjjebarton@btinternet.com. *12m NW of Leominster. From Mortimer's Cross take B4362 towards Presteigne. Turn R at Combe towards Lingen for 1m. Easy parking.* Home-made teas. **Adm £3.50, chd free. Weds 19 June; 7 Aug (2-5.30). Visitors & groups also welcome by appt May to Aug, refreshments by arrangement.**
A mature 1/2 -acre garden 'divided' into distinct areas for long season interest and colour co-ordination. Mixed borders with roses, shrubs, clematis, hardy and half-hardy perennials. Ancient apple trees create a tranquil, shady area with bulbs and foliage plants. Small areas of wild flower meadow. Vegetable and fruit area with raised beds. A true cottage garden for the traditionalist and the plantaholic.

29 ◆ IVY CROFT
Ivington Green, Leominster HR6 0JN. Sue & Roger Norman, 01568 720344, www.ivycroftgarden.co.uk. *3m SW of Leominster. From Leominster take Ryelands Rd to Ivington. Turn R at church, garden 3/4 m on R. From A4110 signed Ivington, garden 1 3/4 m on L.* **Adm £3.50, chd free. For NGS: Every Thur 7 Feb to 28 Feb (9-4); Suns 14 Apr; 19 May; 4 Aug;**

8 Sept (2-5.30); Every Thur 6 to 27 Feb 2014. **For other opening times and information, please phone or see garden website.**
Garden created since 1997 surrounds C17 cottage (not open) in 4 acres of rich grassland. Plant lovers' garden designed for all-yr interest. Raised beds, mixed borders, trees, alpines, troughs, formal vegetable garden framed by trained fruit trees; collections of ferns, willows and snowdrops. Partial wheelchair access.

Modernist, Japanese-influenced garden with dramatic views over River Wye . . .

GROUP OPENING

30 KENTCHURCH GARDENS
Kentchurch Court, Pontrilas HR2 0DB. *12m SW of Hereford. From Hereford A465 to Abergavanny, at Pontrilas turn L signed Kentchurch. After 2m fork L, after Bridge Inn. Drive opp church.* Home-made teas. **Combined adm £5, chd free.** Suns 16 June; 11 Aug (11-5).

KENTCHURCH COURT
Mrs Jan Lucas-Scudamore. 01981 240228 jan@kentchurchcourt.co.uk www.kentchurchcourt.co.uk

UPPER LODGE
Jo Gregory.

Kentchurch Court is sited close to the Welsh border. The large stately home dates to C11 and has been in the Scudamore family for over 1000yrs The deer-park surrounding the house dates back to the Knights Hospitallers of Dinmore and lies at the heart of an estate of over 5000 acres. Historical characters associated with the house incl Welsh hero Owain Glendower, whose daughter married Sir John Scudamore. The house was modernised by John Nash in 1795. First opened for NGS in 1927. Formal rose garden, traditional vegetable garden redesigned with colour, scent and easy access. Walled garden and herbaceous borders, rhododendrons and wild flower walk. Deer-park and ancient woodland. Extensive collection of mature trees and shrubs. Stream with habitat for spawning trout. Upper Lodge is a tranquil and well-established walled cottage garden situated at the centre of the main garden. Incl a wide variety of herbaceous plants, bulbs and shrubs ranging from traditional favourites to the rare and unusual. Kentchurch Court featured in Herefordshire and Wye Valley Life. Most of the garden can be accessed by wheelchairs.

31 NEW LAWLESS HILL
Sellack, Ross-on-Wye HR9 6QP. Keith Meehan and Katalin Andras, 07595 678837, info@lawlesshill.com, www.lawlesshill.com. *4m NW of Ross-on-Wye/western end of M50. On A49 towards Hereford: take 2nd R turn signed to Sellack. Follow lane for approx 2m until junction (white house on R), turn R following Sellack Church sign. Follow lane and turn L onto narrow lane at next Sellack Church sign. Garden on L, halfway down lane before church.* Light refreshments, selection of teas, home made cakes and soup. **Adm £3, chd free.** Visitors welcome by appt.
Modernist, Japanese-influenced garden with dramatic views over River Wye. Collection of 'rooms' sculpted from the steep hillside using network of natural stone walls and huge rocks. Among exotic and unusual plantings, natural ponds are held within the terracing forming waterfalls between them. Due to steep steps and stepping stones by open water, the garden is unsuitable for the less mobile and young children. Tea and cake in the round house and magical views overlooking waterfall and the river valley. Featured in The Historic Gardens of England series.

LITTLE MALVERN COURT
See Worcestershire

TRWYN TAL
See Gwent

LOWER FARM HOUSE
See Gloucestershire

32 LOWER HOPE
Ullingswick HR1 3JF. Mr & Mrs Clive Richards, 01432 820557, cliverichards@crco.co.uk. *5m S of Bromyard. From Hereford take A465 N to Bromyard. After 6m turn L at Burley Gate on A417 signed Leominster. Approx 2m take 3rd turning on R signed Lower Hope & Pencombe, ½ m on LH-side.* Home-made teas. **Adm £5, chd £1.** Suns 7 Apr; 19 May; 14 July; 29 Sept (2-5). **Groups of 20+ also welcome by appt visits within 5 days after each open day.**
5-acre garden facing S and W. Herbaceous borders, rose walks and gardens, laburnum tunnel, Mediterranean garden, new Italian garden, bog gardens. Lime tree walk, lake landscaped with wild flowers, streams, ponds. Conservatories and large glasshouse with exotic species incl orchids, colourful butterflies, bougainvilleas. Prizewinning herd of pedigree Hereford cattle, flock of pedigree Suffolk sheep.

33 ◆ MIDDLE HUNT HOUSE
Walterstone, Hereford HR2 0DY. Trustees of Monnow Valley Arts & Rupert & Antoinetta Otten, 01873 860529, www.monnowvalleyarts.org. *4m W of Pandy, 17m S of Hereford, 10m N of Abergavenny. A465 to Pandy, L towards Longtown, turn R at Clodock Church, 1m on R. Disabled parking available.* **Adm £5, chd free.** For NGS: Sat 8, Sun 9 June (2-5). **For other opening times and information, please phone or see garden website.**
4-acre modern garden with outstanding views, surrounding stone-built farmhouse, converted gallery barn and artist's studio. A Dutch-concept garden using swathes of herbaceous plants and grasses. Sensory, vegetable and Japanese gardens, and hornbeam alley. Special features: birches underplanted with irises, rose borders, William Pye water features, Art and Memory collection of contemporary carved lettering in the Memory Field and sculpture. See website for details of exhibitions that will be held during NGS opening weekend. Partial wheelchair access.

34 MIDLAND FARM

Pig Street, Norton Wood HR4 7BP. Sarah & Charles Smith. *10m NW of Hereford. From Hereford take the A480 towards Kington. 1/2 m after Norton Canon turn L towards Calver Hill. At bottom of the hill turn R into Pig St, garden 1/4 m on L.* Home-made teas. **Adm £3, chd free. Sun 1 Sept (11-4).**

A new 1.2-acre cottage garden begun in 2008 and ongoing. Designed as a series of rooms incl flower, spring and kitchen gardens; a cutting garden. Perennials and old shrub roses a speciality. Small plant nursery.

Quirky garden sculpture . . . children's trail . . . plentiful birds and butterflies . . . peace and tranquility . . .

35 MONTPELIER COTTAGE

Brilley, Whitney-on-Wye, Hereford HR3 6HF. Dr Noel Kingsbury & Ms Jo Eliot, www.noelkingsbury.com. *Between Hay-on-Wye and Kington. From A438 1/2 m E of Rhydspence Inn, take road signed Brilley, then 0.9m. From Kington, follow road to Brilley, then 0.6m from Brilley Church.* Home-made teas. **Adm £5, chd free. Sun 23 June (2-6).**

Exuberant wild-style garden created by well-known garden writer. Approx 1 acre of garden and trial beds where English cottage style meets German parks and American prairie. Wide range of perennials, plus ponds, vegetable garden and fruit. A further 3 acres incl hay meadow habitat and unusual wild flower-rich wet meadow. Children's playground. Featured in Gardens Illustrated.

36 ◆ MOORS MEADOW GARDENS & NURSERY

Collington, Bromyard HR7 4LZ. Ros Bissell, 01885 410318, www.moorsmeadow.co.uk. *4m N of Bromyard, on B4214. 1/2 m up lane follow yellow arrows.* **Adm £5, chd £1. For NGS: Mons 8 Apr; 13 May; 10 June; 8 July; 12 Aug (11-5). For other opening times and information, please phone or see garden website.**

Gaining international recognition for its phenomenal range of wildlife and rarely seen plant species, this inspirational 7-acre organic hillside garden is a 'must see'. Full of peace, secret corners and intriguing features and sculptures with fernery, grass garden, extensive shrubberies, herbaceous beds, meadow, dingle, pools and kitchen garden. Artist blacksmith. Featured in The English Garden and Country Homes & Interiors.

37 THE NEST

Moreton, Eye HR6 0DP. Sue Evans & Guy Poulton. *5 miles north of Leominster. 1m W of A49 at Ashton, 4m N of Leominster, last driveway on L.* Home-made teas. **Adm £4, chd free. Sun 26, Mon 27 May (2-5).**

Classic cottage garden, 1 acre surrounding 1530s timber-framed house (not open). Summer garden with water features, pond, waterfall, Mediterranean plants, ferns, potager, scree and gravel gardens. Canal remnant and wild-flower meadow with rare orchids. Some gravel, assistance available, otherwise good wheelchair access.

38 NEWPORT HOUSE

Almeley HR3 6LL. David & Jenny Watt, 07754 234903, david.gray510@btinternet.com. *5m S of Kington. 1m from Almeley Church, on rd to Kington. From Kington take A4111 to Hereford. After 4m turn L to Almeley, continue 2m, garden on L.* Cream teas. **Adm £4, chd free. Mon 10 to Fri 14 June (11-7); Sat 12 to Sun 20 Oct incl (11-6). Visitors & groups also welcome by appt May to Oct.**

20 acres of garden, woods and lake (with walks). Formal garden set on 3 terraces with large mixed borders framed by formal hedges, in front of Georgian House (not open). 2 1/2 -acre walled organic garden in restoration since 2009. October: sculpture exhibiton. Featured in Hereford and Wye Valley Life.

39 THE OLD CORN MILL

Aston Crews, Ross-on-Wye HR9 7LW. Mrs Jill Hunter, 01989 750059. *5m E of Ross-on-Wye. A40 Ross to Gloucester. Turn L at T-lights at Lea Xrds onto B4222 signed Newent. Garden 1/2 m on L. Parking for disabled down drive. DO NOT USE THE ABOVE POSTCODE IN YOUR SAT NAV as this will take you to the wrong address. You can try HR9 7LA.* Home-made teas. **Adm £2.50, chd free. Suns, Mons 10 Mar; 1 Apr; 5, 27 May; Sat 15, Sun 16 June (11-5). Visitors & groups max 55 also welcome by appt Jan to Dec.**

Surrounding the award-winning converted C18 Mill (not open), this valley garden has been designed to merge into the surrounding fields. Massed banks and borders provide colour all yr while streams, ponds, meadows and native trees support a variety of wildlife. Wild daffodils, common spotted orchids and primulas are spring highlights. Quirky garden sculpture. Children's trail. Plentiful birds and butterflies. Peace and tranquility. Featured in Herefordshire & Wye Valley Life and on BBC Hereford & Worester.

40 THE OLD QUARRY

Almeley Road, Eardisley HR3 6PR. John & Anne Davis, 01544 327264, old.quarry@virgin.net. *16m NW of Hereford. 3/4 m off A438 - A4111 to Kington, turn R at Eardisley.* Home-made teas. **Adm £3.50, chd free. Visitors welcome by appt Apr to Oct.**

Gently-sloping garden of 2 1/2 acres, laid out in the 1930s now being renovated and developed for yr-round interest. Terraces and old quarry gardens with rhododendrons and mature trees, parterre, vegetable garden and herbaceous beds. Far-reaching views of Black Mountains and Hay Bluff. Limited wheelchair access in some parts of the gardens.

41 NEW THE OLD RECTORY, BYFORD
Hereford HR4 7LD. Mr & Mrs Charles Mayson, 01981 590218, audreymayson@gmail.com. *8m W of Hereford. Take the A438 Brecon rd from Hereford, 6m from Wyevale Garden Centre look for the bright green sign for Byford turn on L, take 1st drive on R. Disabled parking at house otherwise outside the property on the wide verge.* Home-made teas. **Adm £3, chd free. Sat 15 June; Sat 6, Sun 7 July (1-5). Visitors & groups max 30 also welcome by appt May to Oct.**
A magnificent cedar of Lebanon dominates our 1-acre garden. Herbaceous borders are seen from all aspects of the house whilst further borders are planted with shrubs, clematis, bulbs and ground cover. Beyond the lawn are 3 copper beeches underplanted with bluebells and foxgloves. Nearby is a rose bed for cutting, a vegetable plot and lots of sitting areas.

42 THE OLD RECTORY, THRUXTON
Thruxton HR2 9AX. Mr & Mrs Andrew Hallett, 01981 570401, ar.hallett@gmail.com. *6m SW of Hereford. A465 to Allensmore. At Locks (Shell) garage take B4348 towards Hay-on-Wye. After 1½ m turn L towards Abbey Dore & Cockyard. Car park 150yds on L.* Home-made teas. **Adm £3.50, chd free. Weds, Suns 15, 19 May; 19, 23 June; 17, 21 July; 8 Sept (2-5.30). Visitors & groups also welcome by appt May to Sept.**
2-acre plantsman's garden with outstanding panoramic views. Extensive borders stocked with shrubs, unusual perennials and old shrub roses,formal gazebo and vegetable parterre. Most of our plants are labelled. Additional 2-acre paddock with collection of young ornamental trees, old varieties of fruit trees and rare breed bantams. Newly established wildlife pond. Featured on Hereford and Worcester radio. Some level gravel paths.

43 THE ORCHARDS
Golden Valley, Bishops Frome, nr Bromyard WR6 5BN. Mr & Mrs Robert Humphries. *14m E of Hereford. A4103 turn L at bottom of Fromes Hill, through village of Bishops Frome on B4214. Turn R immed after de-regulation signs along narrow track for 250yds. Park in field by garden.* Home-made teas. **Adm £3, chd free. Suns 16 June; 28 July (2-6).**
1-acre garden designed in areas on various levels. 15 water features incl Japanese water garden and tea house, Mediterranean area, rose garden with rill, aviary. Large rose, clematis, fuchsia and dahlia collections. Seating areas on all levels. New projects every yr.

PEN-Y-MAES
See Powys

Copper beeches underplanted with bluebells and foxgloves . . .

44 PERRYCROFT
Jubilee Drive, Upper Colwall, Malvern WR13 6DN. Gillian & Mark Archer, 07858 393767, gillianarcher@live.co.uk. *Between Malvern & Ledbury. From A449 Malvern to Ledbury rd, take B4232 at British Camp (Jubilee Drive). Garden 1m on L. Park in Gardiners Quarry car park on R (pay & display), short walk to garden. No parking at house.* Home-made teas. **Adm £4, chd free. Sun 23 June, Sun 6 Oct (2-5). Visitors & groups also welcome by appt all year, adm £5.**
10-acre garden and woodland on upper slopes of Malvern Hills with magnificent views. Arts and Crafts house (not open), garden partly designed by CFA Voysey. Ongoing restoration, walled garden, yew hedges, old roses, natural wild flower meadows, ponds (unfenced), bog garden, gravel and grass walks. Some steep and uneven paths. Featured in House and Garden, Country Life, Gardens Illustrated.

45 PHELPS COTTAGE GARDEN
Coddington, Ledbury HR8 1JH. David & Diane Hodgson, 01531 640622, hodgson@ukf.net. *From Ledbury take Bromyard Rd. 1st R for Wellington Heath on to T junction. Turn R then first L for Coddington follow signs from Worcester to Colwall signed for Coddington.* Home-made teas. **Adm £3.50, chd free. Sat 18, Sun 19 May (2-5.30). Visitors & groups max 20 also welcome by appt May to Aug.**
Plantsmans ¾ -acre cottage garden on different levels (some steps), mixed borders, terrace, wild areas, stream and bog garden, large fruit and vegetable potager with poly tunnel. Featured in Herefordshire and Wye Valley Life and on BBC Hereford and Worcester.

46 ◆ THE PICTON GARDEN
Old Court Nurseries, Colwall WR13 6QE. Mr & Mrs Paul Picton, 01684 540416, www.autumnasters.co.uk. *3m W of Malvern. On B4218 (Walwyn Rd) N of Colwall Stone. Turn off A449 from Ledbury or Malvern onto the B4218 for Colwall.* **Adm £3.50, chd free. For NGS: Sun 4, Sat 10, Sun 18, Thur 22, Mon 26 Aug; Wed 4, Sun 15 Sept; Thur 10, Sun 20 Oct (11-5). For other opening times and information, please phone or see garden website.**
1½ acres W of Malvern Hills. Interesting perennials and shrubs in Aug. In Sept and Oct colourful borders display the National Plant Collection of Michaelmas daisies, backed by autumn colouring trees and shrubs. Many unusual plants to be seen, incl bamboos, ferns and acers. Features raised beds and silver garden. National Plant Collection of autumn-flowering asters and an extensive nursery that has been growing them since 1906. Featured in Gardens Illustrated.

NCH

SHUTTIFIELD COTTAGE
See Worcestershire

48 STAPLETON CASTLE COURT GARDEN
Stapleton, Presteigne LD8 2LS. Margaret & Trefor Griffiths, 01544 267327. *2m N of Presteigne. From Presteigne travel down Broad St. Crossing the Lugg Bridge follow this*

The Nest

© Julia Stanley

rd to Stapleton, do not take the RH-turn signed Stapleton, pass a red-brick bungalow on L after approx 100 yds turn R into drive. **Adm £4, chd free.** **Suns, Mons 9, 10 June; 25, 26 Aug (2-6).** **Visitors & groups also welcome by appt May to Sept.** Situated on a gentle slope overlooked by the ruins of Stapleton Castle. The garden developed over the past 6 yrs by an enthusiastic plantswoman and benefits from considered and colour-themed borders. Guided tour of the castle ruins at 3pm each day. Wheelchairs not suitable for castle tour.

49 ◆ STAUNTON PARK

Staunton-on-Arrow, Leominster HR6 9LE. Susan Fode, 01544 388556, www.stauntonpark.co.uk. *3m N of Pembridge. From Pembridge (on A44) take rd signed Presteigne, Shobdon. After 3m look out for red phone box on R. Staunton Park is 150yds on L. Do not go to Staunton-on-Arrow.* **Adm £4, chd free.** **For NGS: Every Thur 16 May to 12 Sept (11-5).** **For other opening times and information, please phone or see garden website.** 10-acre garden and grounds incl drive with stately wellingtonias, informal box and lavender knot garden, separate kitchen garden, large, very colourful mixed borders flowering well into September, Victorian rock garden, lake and lakeside walk with views. Specimen trees incl mature monkey puzzle, gigantic liriodendron, *Davidia involucrata*, *Ginkgo bilobas* and several ancient oaks. 2 steps to WC.

50 ◆ STOCKTON BURY GARDENS LTD

Kimbolton HR6 0HB. Raymond G Treasure Esq, 01568 613432, www.stocktonbury.co.uk. *2m NE of Leominster. On A49 turn R onto A4112 Kimbolton rd. Gardens 300yds on R.* **Adm £5, chd £3.** **For NGS: Mon 1 Apr (12-5).** **For other opening times and**

Support the NGS – eat more cake!

information, please phone or see garden website.
Superb, sheltered 4-acre garden with a very long growing season giving colour and interest all yr. Extensive collection of plants, many rare and unusual set amongst medieval buildings, a real kitchen garden. Pigeon house, tithe barn, grotto, cider press, pools, ruined chapel and rill, all surrounded by unspoilt countryside. Unsuitable for children. (This is no ordinary garden). Wheelchair access 80%.

TAWRYN
See Powys

51 UPPER TAN HOUSE
Stansbatch, Leominster HR6 9LJ. James & Caroline Weymouth, 01544 260574, james@uppertanhouse.com, www.uppertanhouse.com. *4m W of Pembridge. From A44 in Pembridge, take turn signed Shobdon & Presteigne by telephone box. After exactly 4m and at Stansbatch Nursery take lane down hill. Upper Tan House is on L 100 yds after Chapel.* **Adm £4, chd free. Visitors & groups welcome by appt May to Sept.**
S-facing garden sloping down to Stansbatch brook in idyllic spot. Deep herbaceous borders with informal and unusual planting, pond and bog garden, formal vegetable garden framed by yew hedges and espaliered pears. Reed beds, wild-flower meadow with orchids in June. Good late summer colour and diverse wildlife.

52 THE VINE
Tarrington HR1 4EX. Richard Price. *Between Hereford & Ledbury on A438. Follow signs from Tarrington Arms on A438. Park as directed. Disabled parking only at house.* Cream teas. **Adm £4, chd free. Sat 29 June (2.30-6).**
Mature, traditional garden in peaceful setting with stunning views of the surrounding countryside. Consisting of various rooms with mixed and herbaceous borders. Secret garden in blue/yellow/white, croquet lawn with C18 summer house, temple garden with ponds, herb and nosegay garden, vegetable/cutting/soft fruit garden around greenhouse on the paddock.

53 ◆ THE WEIR
Swainshill, Hereford HR4 7QF. National Trust, 01981 590509, www.nationaltrust.org.uk. *5m W of Hereford. On A438, signed The Weir Garden.* **Adm £5, chd free. For NGS: Wed 20 Feb (11-4); Wed 4 Sept (11-5); Wed 19 Feb 2014. For other opening times and information, please phone or see garden website.**
A stunning riverside garden with sweeping views along the R Wye and Herefordshire countryside. Drifts of snowdrops and spring bulbs give way to wild flowers. Walled garden for summer interest. Riverside and wooded walk, snowdrops in full bloom in February. Limited wheelchair access.

Croquet lawn with C18 summer house, temple garden with ponds, herb and nosegay garden . . .

54 WELLBROOK MANOR
Peterchurch, Hereford HR2 0SS. The Vivat Trust, 01981 550753, bronwn@vivat-trust.org. *11m W of Hereford. Going towards Hay on Wye on the B4348 turn R when entering Peterchurch (signed Stockley Hill). Wellbrook Manor is on L before you leave the village.* Home-made teas. **Adm £4, chd free. Sat 29, Sun 30 June (1-5).**
The garden was created by the late Mrs Joan Griffith. Noted for its structural topiary, potager garden, rare variety orchard and soft succulent atmosphere. Over the weekend the roses will thrill and, weather permitting, the fragrant peonies will delight. Works are in progress to lay out the paddock area. The Grade I-listed Wellbrook Manor (not open) sits in the centre of the garden.

55 WESTON HALL
Weston-under-Penyard, Ross-on-Wye HR9 7NS. Mr P & Miss L Aldrich-Blake, 01989 562597, aldrich-blake.weston@lineone.net. *1m E of Ross-on-Wye. On A40 towards Gloucester.* Light refreshments. **Adm £4, chd free. Sun 2 June (11-5). Groups of 10+ also welcome by appt May to July.**
6 acres surrounding Elizabethan house (not open). Large walled garden with herbaceous borders, vegetables and fruit, overlooked by Millennium folly. Lawns with both mature and recently planted trees, shrubs with many unusual varieties. Ornamental ponds and lake. 4 generations in the family, but still evolving year on year. Opened for NGS in 1927.

56 WESTON MEWS
Weston-under-Penyard HR9 7NZ. Ann Rothwell & John Hercock, 01989 563823. *2m E of Ross-on-Wye. Going towards Gloucester on A40, continue approx 100yds past the Weston Cross PH and turn R into grey brick-paved courtyard.* **Adm £3, chd free. Sat 15, Sun 16 June (11-5). Visitors & groups also welcome by appt June to Aug, wine.**
Walled ex-kitchen garden divided by yew and box hedges. Traditional in style and planting with large herbaceous beds and borders at different levels. Broad range of plants incl roses. Enclosed garden with sundial. Large vine house.

57 ◆ WESTONBURY MILL WATER GARDEN
Pembridge HR6 9HZ. Mr & Mrs Richard Pim, 01544 388650, www.westonburymillwatergardens.com. *8m W of Leominster. On A44 1½ m W of Pembridge, L into signed drive.* **Adm £4.50, chd £1. For NGS: Sun 30 June (11-5). For other opening times and information, please phone or see garden website.**
3½ -acre water-mill garden situated amid fields and orchards. Colourful waterside plantings of bog and moisture-loving plants around a tangle of streams and ponds, together with a natural bog garden in the area of the Old Mill pond. Adjacent wild-flower meadow with stream-side walk. Enjoy the series of dotty and delightful follies, incl giant

water-powered cuckoo clock. Featured in Gardens Illustrated. Wheelchair access to 80% of garden. Disabled WC.

58 WHITFIELD

Wormbridge HR2 9BA. Mr & Mrs Edward Clive, 01981 570202, tclive@whitfield-hereford.com, www.whitfield-hereford.com. *8m SW of Hereford. The entrance gates are off the A465 Hereford to Abergavenny rd, ½ m N of Wormbridge.* Home-made teas. **Adm £4, chd free.** Sun 7 Apr (2-5); Sun 16 June (2-5.30). **Visitors also welcome by appt Mar to Nov. Tour & refreshments available for groups 15+.**

Parkland, wild flowers, ponds, walled garden, many flowering magnolias (species and hybrids), 1780 ginkgo tree, 1½ m woodland walk with 1851 redwood grove. Picnic parties welcome. Gravel paths and some steep slopes mean that the garden is only partially accessible to wheelchair users.

59 WILTON CASTLE ON THE WYE

Wilton, Ross-on-Wye HR9 6AD. Alan & Suzie Parslow, www.wiltoncastle.co.uk. *½ m NW of Ross on R Wye. Signed at Wilton r'about on M50/A40/A449 trunk rd. Immed turn L opp garage, down lane. Castle entrance behind Castle Lodge Hotel. DO NOT go over river bridge into Ross.* Home-made teas. **Adm £4, chd £2.** Suns 16 June; 14 July (12-5).

The romantic ruins of a restored C12 castle and C16 manor house (ruin) form the perfect backdrop for herbaceous borders, roses entwined around mullioned windows, an abundance of sweetly scented old-fashioned roses, gravel gardens and shrubberies. The 2-acre gardens are surrounded by a dry moat which leads down to the R Wye with swans, ducks, kingfishers etc. No disabled access into dry moat area, or inside towers; disabled WC.

Dry moat which leads down to the River Wye with swans, ducks, kingfishers . . .

60 WOLFERLOW HOUSE

Wolferlow, nr Upper Sapey HR7 4QA. Stuart & Jill Smith, 01886 853311, hillheadfm@aol.com, www.theretreatholidaylettings.co.uk. *5m N of Bromyard. Off B4203 or B4214 between Upper Sapey & Stoke Bliss. Disabled parking at the house.* Home-made teas. **Adm £3.50, chd free.** Sun 7 July (10.30-5). **Visitors and groups (max 25) welcome by app one week either side of NGS day.**

Surrounded by farmland this former Victorian rectory is set within formal and informal gardens with planting to attract wildlife. Walks through the old orchard and ponds to sit by, space to relax and reflect taking in the views of borrowed landscape. Fruit, vegetable and cutting garden and wild-flower meadow. Gravel paths.

61 WOODVIEW

Great Doward, Whitchurch, Ross-on-Wye HR9 6DZ. Janet & Clive Townsend, 01600 890477, clive.townsend5@homecall.co.uk. *6m SW of Ross-on-Wye, 4m NE of Monmouth. A40 Ross/Monmouth. At Whitchurch follow signs to Symonds Yat West. Then signs to Dowards Park Campsite. Take Forestry Rd, 1st L, garden 2nd on L. Or follow NGS signs from Whitchurch. Parking at house.* **Adm £3.50, chd free.** Suns 14, 21 July (1-6). **Visitors & groups also welcome by appt Apr to Sept, please telephone for details.**

Formal and informal gardens approx 2 acres in woodland setting. Herbaceous borders, hosta collection, mature trees, shrubs and seasonal bedding. Gently sloping lawns. Statuary and found sculpture, local limestone, rockwork and pools. Woodland garden, wild-flower meadow and indigenous orchids. Collection of vintage tools and memorabilia. Croquet, clock golf and garden games. Featured in local press.

Herefordshire County Volunteers

County Organiser

Rowena Gale, Bachefield House, Kimbolton, Leominster HR6 0EP, 01568 615855, rowena.jimgale@btinternet.com

County Treasurer

Michael Robins, Newsholme, 77 Bridge Street, Ledbury HR8 2AN, 01531 632232

Publicity

Sue Evans, The Nest, Moreton, Eye, nr Leominster HR6 0DP, 01568 614501, s.evans.gp@btinternet.com

Gill Mullin, The White House, Lea, Ross-on-Wye HR9 7LQ, 01989 750593, gill@longorchard.plus.com

County Booklet

Chris Meakins, Yew Tree Cottage, Huntington, Kington HR5 3PF, 01544 370215, christine.meakins@btinternet.com

Assistant County Organisers

Andy Hallett, The Old Rectory, Thruxton HR2 9AX, 01981 570401, ar.hallett@gmail.com

David Hodgson, Phelps Cottage, Coddington, nr Ledbury HR8 1JH, 01531 640622, hodgson@ukf.net

Sue Londesborough, Brighton House, Newton St Margarets, Vowchurch HR2 0JU, 01981 510148, slondesborough138@btinternet.com

Penny Usher, Old Chapel House, Kimbolton, Leominster HR6 0HF, 01568 611688, pennyusher@btinternet.com

Recycle – bring a bag for your plant purchases

HERTFORDSHIRE

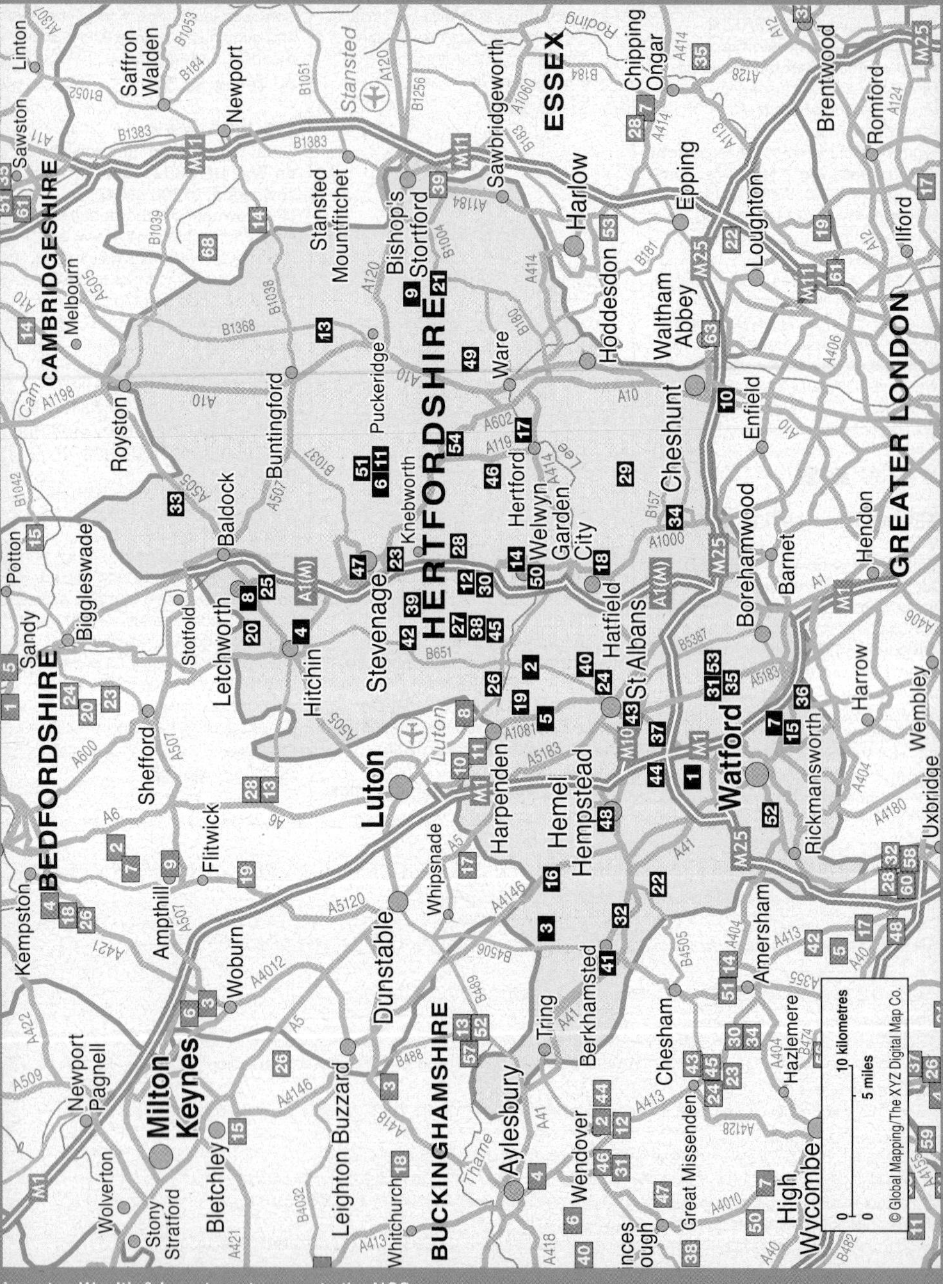

Opening Dates

February

Saturday 9
51 Walkern Hall

Sunday 10
51 Walkern Hall

March

Saturday 9
10 Capel Manor Gardens

Sunday 10
10 Capel Manor Gardens

Saturday 23
18 Hatfield House West Garden

April

Sunday 7
42 St Paul's Walden Bury

Sunday 21
2 Amwell Cottage
22 Huntsmoor
33 Pembroke Farm

Friday 26
30 The Mill House (Evening)

Sunday 28
30 The Mill House

May

Sunday 5
32 Patchwork

Sunday 12
24 19 Lancaster Road
42 St Paul's Walden Bury

Sunday 19
27 The Manor House, Ayot St Lawrence
28 43 Mardley Hill

Sunday 26
34 Queenswood School
49 Thundridge Hill House

Monday 27
1 The Abbots House

Friday 31
26 Mackerye End House (Evening)

June

Sunday 2
16 15 Gade Valley Cottages

Saturday 8
38 2 Ruins Cottage

Sunday 9
3 Ashridge House
38 2 Ruins Cottage
42 St Paul's Walden Bury
45 Shaw's Corner

Wednesday 12
20 Hitchin Lavender (Evening)

Friday 14
39 Rustling End Cottage (Evening)

National Gardens Weekend

Saturday 15
9 Bromley Hall

Sunday 16
9 Bromley Hall
24 19 Lancaster Road
39 Rustling End Cottage (All day & evening)
44 Serge Hill Gardens

Friday 21
37 The Royal National Rose Society (Evening)

Sunday 23
11 Croft Cottage
12 17 Danesbury Park Mews
41 St Michael's Croft
54 Woodhall Park

Friday 28
46 South Wing (Evening)

Sunday 30
6 Benington Lordship
26 Mackerye End House
29 Michaels Folly
43 St Stephens Avenue Gardens
46 South Wing

A stylish town garden with a contemporary feel, combining elegant design with knowledgeable plantsmanship . . .

July

Sunday 7
24 19 Lancaster Road

Friday 12
20 Hitchin Lavender (Evening)

Sunday 14
13 Dassels Bury
19 3 Highfield Avenue
25 Letchworth Garden City - Two gardens

Sunday 21
5 Beesonend Gardens
48 9 Tannsfield Drive
50 84 Valley Road

Wednesday 24
17 8 Gosselin Road

Friday 26
4 22a The Avenue (Evening)
50 84 Valley Road (Evening)

Saturday 27
15 42 Falconer Road

Sunday 28
14 35 Digswell Road
15 42 Falconer Road
31 Oakridge Avenue Gardens

August

Friday 2
8 44 Broadwater Avenue

Saturday 3
15 42 Falconer Road

Sunday 4
8 44 Broadwater Avenue
15 42 Falconer Road
16 15 Gade Valley Cottages

Sunday 11
28 43 Mardley Hill
35 Radlett Allotments
47 Southend Farm

Monday 12
20 Hitchin Lavender (Evening)

Sunday 18
32 Patchwork
36 Reveley Lodge
48 9 Tannsfield Drive

Monday 26
11 Croft Cottage

Friday 30
40 3 St Marys Walk

September

Sunday 1
40 3 St Marys Walk
53 3 Watford Road

Thursday 12
20 Hitchin Lavender (Evening)

Sunday 15
22 Huntsmoor

October

Sunday 13
17 8 Gosselin Road

Saturday 19
10 Capel Manor Gardens

Sunday 20
10 Capel Manor Gardens
14 35 Digswell Road

November

Saturday 9
15 42 Falconer Road (Evening)

Gardens open to the public

- 3 Ashridge House
- 6 Benington Lordship
- 10 Capel Manor Gardens
- 18 Hatfield House West Garden
- 20 Hitchin Lavender
- 21 Hopleys
- 23 Knebworth House Gardens
- 33 Pembroke Farm
- 37 The Royal National Rose Society
- 42 St Paul's Walden Bury
- 45 Shaw's Corner

By appointment only

- 7 47 Bournehall Avenue
- 52 Waterdell House

Also open by Appointment ☎

- 1 The Abbots House
- 9 Bromley Hall
- 11 Croft Cottage
- 13 Dassels Bury
- 14 35 Digswell Road
- 31 45 Oakridge Avenue, Oakridge Avenue Gardens
- 32 Patchwork
- 43 20 St Stephens Avenue, St Stephens Avenue Gardens
- 48 9 Tannsfield Drive
- 49 Thundridge Hill House

The Gardens

1 THE ABBOTS HOUSE

10 High Street, Abbots Langley WD5 0AR. Peter & Sue Tomson, 01923 264946, peter.tomson@btinternet.com. *5m NW of Watford. Exit J20 on M25. Take A4251 signed Kings Langley. R at 1st r'about (Home Park Industrial Estate). R at T-junction. Follow rd, under railway bridge and the yellow signs will become apparent. Free parking in village car park.* Home-made teas. **Adm £4, chd free (share to Friends of St Lawrence Church).** Mon 27 May (2-5). **Visitors also welcome by appt Apr to Sept.**

1¾ -acre garden with unusual trees, shrubs, mixed borders with interesting colour combinations, scented garden, sunken garden, pond, conservatory and a bed with many Himalayan plants. A garden of 'rooms' with different styles and moods. Many half-hardy plants. Some plants propagated from the garden are for sale. Pea shingle path.

♿ ❀ ☕ ☎

2 AMWELL COTTAGE

Amwell Lane, Wheathampstead AL4 8EA. Colin & Kate Birss. *½ m S of Wheathampstead. From St Helen's Church, Wheathampstead turn up Brewhouse Hill. At top L fork (Amwell Lane), 300yds down lane, park in field opp.* Home-made teas. **Adm £3.50, chd free.** Sun 21 Apr (2-5).

Informal garden of approx 2½ acres around C17 cottage (not open). Large orchard of mature apples, plums and pear laid out with paths. Extensive lawns with borders, framed by tall yew hedges and old brick walls. A large variety of roses, stone seats with views, woodland pond, greenhouse and recently designed fire-pit area. Gravel drive.

♿ 🐕 ❀ ☕

3 ◆ ASHRIDGE HOUSE

Berkhamsted HP4 1NS. Ashridge (Bonar Law Memorial) Trust, 01442 843491, www.ashridge.org.uk. *3m N of Berkhamsted. A4251, 1m S of Little Gaddesden.* **Adm £4.50, chd £2.50.** For NGS: Sun 9 June (9-6). **For other opening times and information please phone or see garden website.**

The gardens cover 190-acres forming part of the Grade II Registered Landscape of Ashridge Park. Based on designs by Humphry Repton in 1813 modified by Jeffry Wyatville. Small secluded gardens, as well as a large lawn area leading to avenues of trees. 2013 marks the 200th anniversary of Repton presenting Ashridge with the Red Book, detailing his designs for the estate. The Gardens are open 2-6 every weekend between Easter and the end of Sept. The House and Gardens are open for guided tours for five weeks in July-Aug. Please visit website for details.

♿ 🐕 ☕

4 22A THE AVENUE

Hitchin SG4 9RL. Martin Woods. *½ m E of town centre. Opp St Mary's Church take Windmill Hill, continue to top into Wymondley Rd. The Avenue is 1st turning on L.* **Adm £4, chd free** Evening Opening, wine, Fri 26 July (6-9).

A stylish town garden with a contemporary feel, combining elegant design with knowledgeable plantsmanship. A patio area is bordered by a formal raised pond. Steps up to the garden are lined with pots of unusual and interesting succulents, alpines, species pelargoniums and other tender plants. The borders contain mainly herbaceous perennials and grasses planted in imaginative groupings.

☕

BARNET GARDENS
See London

8 Gosselin Road

190 BARNET ROAD
See London

GROUP OPENING

5 BEESONEND GARDENS
Harpenden AL5 2AN. *1m S of Harpenden. Take A1081 S from Harpenden, after 1m turn R into Beesonend Lane, bear R into Burywick to T-junction. Follow signs to Barlings Road & The Deerings.* Home-made teas at 17 The Deerings. **Combined adm £5, chd free.** **Sun 21 July (2-5.30).**

2 BARLINGS ROAD
Liz & Jim Machin

17 THE DEERINGS
Mr & Mrs Phillip Thompson. *Access from A1081, 1m S of Harpenden via Beesonend Lane*

38 THE DEERINGS
Christine Viollet

Set in a mature development these gardens reflect their owners individual interests and needs. 2 Barlings Road is packed with unusual plants, shrubs and climbers to provide yr-round structure. The colourful courtyard garden with water feature and secluded shade garden add extra interest. 17 The Deerings offers specimen trees, architectural plants, ornamental grasses, herbaceous borders as well as a compact kitchen garden and herb bed. 38 The Deerings is a generous 1/2 acre of mature enclosed formal and informal garden rooms. A sunny sunken garden with ornamental fish pond, colour themed herbaceous borders and a large wildlife pond all invite closer inspection.

6 ◆ BENINGTON LORDSHIP
nr Stevenage SG2 7BS. Mr & Mrs R R A Bott, 01438 869668, www.beningtonlordship.co.uk. *5m E of Stevenage. In Benington Village, signs off A602. Next to church.* **Adm £5, chd free. For NGS: Sun 30 June (12-5). For other opening times and information, please phone or see garden website.**
7-acre garden incl historic buildings, kitchen garden, lakes, roses. Spectacular herbaceous borders, unspoilt panoramic views.

7 47 BOURNEHALL AVENUE
Bushey WD23 3AU. Caroline & Jim Fox, 0208 950 0727, carolinefox@f2s.com. *1m S of Watford. Bushey Village A411, Falconer Rd, Herkomer Rd, 2nd on L is Bournehall Ave. Map on* www.jamespfox.co.uk. Home-made teas. **Adm £3.50, chd free. Visitors welcome by appt June to Aug.**
Medium sized village garden on 3 levels, designed by owners. Garlanded planters overlook sunken garden with acers and pond. Wisteria and vine covered pergola leads to fruited potager. Step up to sculpted lawn edged with small trees, shrubs and sumptuous perennials.

8 44 BROADWATER AVENUE
Letchworth Garden City SG6 3HJ. Karen & Ian Smith. *1/2 m SW Letchworth town centre. A1(M) J9 signed Letchworth. Straight on at 1st three r'abouts, 4th r'about take 4th exit then R into Broadwater Ave.* Home-made teas. **Adm £4, chd free. Evening Opening Fri 2 Aug (6-9); Sun 4 Aug (1-5).**
Town garden in the Letchworth Garden City conservation area that successfully combines a family garden with a plantswoman's garden. Out of the ordinary, unusual herbaceous plants and shrubs. Attractive front garden designed for yr-round interest. Featured in Amateur Gardening. Winner Letchworth in Bloom Best Front Garden.

9 BROMLEY HALL
Standon, Ware SG11 1NY. Julian & Edwina Robarts, 01279 842 422, edwina.robarts@btinternet.com, www.bromley-hall.co.uk. *6m W of Bishop's Stortford. From A120 turn into Standon High St. Follow rd for 1 1/2 m towards Much Hadham.* Home-made teas. **Adm £4.50, chd free. Sat 15, Sun 16 June (2-5.30). Visitors also welcome by appt. Home made teas & or wine available on request.**
4 1/2 acres surrounding C16 farmhouse. Some elements are traditional - formal hedging, Irish yews, and mixed borders, vegetables, mown paths through long grass. Others are modern, a grove of white poplars surrounding cranes and a modern formal garden on the site of the old tennis court. Everywhere there are places to sit, view and contemplate.

33A BROOKHILL ROAD
See London

7 BYNG ROAD
See London

A grove of white poplars surrounding cranes and a modern formal garden on the site of the old tennis court . . . everywhere there are places to sit, view and contemplate. . . .

10 ◆ CAPEL MANOR GARDENS
Bullsmoor Lane, Enfield, Middlesex EN1 4RQ. Capel Manor Charitable Corporation, 08456 122 122, www.capelmanorgardens.co.uk. *2m from Cheshunt. 3 mins from J25 of M25/A10. Nearest train station is Turkey Street, then 20 mins walk.* **Adm £5.50, chd £2.50. For NGS: Sat 9, Sun 10 Mar (10-5); Sat 19, Sun 20 Oct (10-5.30). For other opening times and information, please phone or see garden website.**
A beautiful 30-acre estate providing a colourful and scented oasis surrounding a Georgian Manor House and Victorian Stables. Be inspired by prize winning themed, model and historical gardens incl the latest additions the Old Manor House Garden and the Australian Garden (Chelsea Gold Medal winner). Wheelchair loan available and free with advanced booking.

11 CROFT COTTAGE
9 Church Green, Benington SG2 7LH. Richard Arnold-Roberts & Julie Haire, 01438 869688, richard@richardar.plus.com. *4m E of Stevenage. From A1 J7. Take A602 to Ware and Hertford. Go straight across 4 r'abouts. Road becomes single c'way. At the next*

r'about turn L on to Gresley Way, down hill to mini r'about. Go straight across - caution - narrow road, up hill and through Aston village. After 1½ m go straight across Xrds and continue 1½ m into Benington. Croft Cottage on R soon after the sign for Benington. Park opp where the road widens. Home-made teas. **Adm £3, chd free. Sun 23 June (1-5); Mon 26 Aug (10-5). Visitors also welcome by appt May to Aug.**
C16 cottage with small, extensively planted garden divided into several areas. Many variegated and colourful-leafed shrubs and perennials. Mixed border in pastel shades. Euphorbia and hosta collection. Pool with fish, waterspout and seat. Rose and clematis shaded arbour with view over fields. Japanese maple garden with pool overlooking C13 church. Gravel paths.

12 17 DANESBURY PARK MEWS

North Ride, Welwyn AL6 9SA. Francoise Austin. *Danesbury Estate. From South, leave A1(M) J6, cross 2 r'abouts, turn L on to B656 towards Codicote. Follow yellow NGS arrows.* Home-made teas. **Adm £3, chd free. Sun 23 June (2-5.30).**
Beautiful long mixed borders featuring roses, peonies and a plethora of unusual and traditional plants within the grounds of the former Danesbury Estate.

13 DASSELS BURY

Dassels, Braughing SG11 2RW. Martin & Kate Slack, 07775 884714, dasselsburykate@btinternet.com. *2m SE of Buntingford; 1m N of Braughing on B1368. B1368 runs to the E of the A10. Parking in field on E of the B1368 at S end of Dassels.* Home-made teas. **Adm £5, chd free. Sun 14 July (1.30-5). Visitors also welcome by appt.**
Not just a garden! Walk through wild flower meadows and woodland. 20 acres in total with alpacas and rare breed chickens. Terracing creates stunning views. Double herbaceous border with inspired planting and fountain; kitchen garden with raised beds, soft fruit and asparagus. Wildlife pond, fine glass house, croquet lawn and borders. Gravel and steep paths.

14 35 DIGSWELL ROAD

Welwyn Garden City AL8 7PB. Adrian & Clare de Baat, 01707 324074, adrian.debaat@ntlworld.com. *½ m N of Welwyn Garden City centre. From the Campus r'about in centre of City take N exit just past public library into Digswell Rd. Over the White Bridge, 200yds on L.* Home-made teas. **Adm £3.50, chd free. Sun 28 July (2-5.30); Sun 20 Oct (2-5). Visitors also welcome by appt June to Oct, adm incl home-made tea.**
Town garden of around ⅓ -acre Piet Oudolf-inspired naturalistic borders with herbaceous plants and grasses surround the lawn. Beyond are island beds packed with perennials, linked by grass paths. The contemporary planting gives way to the exotic, incl succulent bed and lush jungle garden with bamboos, bananas and tree ferns. Plants for sale at July opening. Featured in RHS The Garden. Grass paths, gentle slopes.

DOCWRA'S MANOR
See Cambridgeshire

207 EAST BARNET ROAD
See London

ELM COURT GARDENS, EAST BARNET EN4
See London

15 NEW 42 FALCONER ROAD

Bushey Herts, Watford WD23 3AD. Mrs Suzette Fuller. *Bushey. M1 J 5 follow signs for Bushey. From London A40 via Stanmore towards Watford. From Watford via Bushey Arches, through to Bushey High St turn L into Falconer Rd, opp St James church.* Light refreshments. **Adm £3, chd free. Sats, Suns 27, 28 July, 3, 4 Aug (11-7.30). Evening Opening wine, Sat 9 Nov (5-9).**
Enchanting magical unusual Victorian style space. Children so very welcome. Winter viewing for fairyland lighting, for all ages, bring a torch. Bird cages and chimneys a feature, plus a walk through conservatory with orchids.

54 FERNDOWN
See London

16 15 GADE VALLEY COTTAGES

Dagnall Road, Great Gaddesden, Hemel Hempstead HP1 3BW. Bryan Trueman. *3m N of Hemel Hempstead. Follow A4146 N from Hemel Hempstead. Past Water End. Go past turning for Great Gaddesden. Gade Valley Cottages on R. Park in village hall car park.* **Adm £3, chd free. Suns 2 June; 4 Aug (1.30-5).**
165ft x 30ft sloping rural garden. Patio, lawn, borders and pond. Paths lead through a woodland area emerging by wildlife pond and sunny border. A choice of seating offers sunny rural views or quiet shady contemplation with sounds of rustling bamboos and bubbling water. Gravel paths and some steps.

Enchanting magical unusual Victorian style space. Children so very welcome. Winter viewing for fairyland . . .

17 8 GOSSELIN ROAD

Bengeo, Hertford SG14 3LG. Annie Godfrey & Steve Machin, www.daisyroots.com. *Take B158 from Hertford signed to Bengeo. Gosselin Rd 2nd R after White Lion PH (phone box on corner).* **Adm £3.50, chd free. Wed 24 July (2-5); Sun 13 Oct (12-5).**
Owner of Daisy Roots nursery, garden has been redesigned and completely replanted since it last opened in 2006. Lawn replaced by a wide gravel path, flanked by deep borders packed with perennials and grasses. Pelargonium collection in pots. New sunken area surrounded by plants chosen for scent. Small front garden with lots of foliage interest. Featured on BBC Gardeners' World, Mail on Sunday, Gardens Illustrated and RHS The Garden.

18 ◆ HATFIELD HOUSE WEST GARDEN

Hatfield House, Hatfield AL9 5NQ. The Marquess of Salisbury, 01707 287010, www.hatfield-house.co.uk. *Opp Hatfield Stn, 21m N of London, M25 J23. 7m A1(M) J4 signed off A414 & A1000. Free parking.* **Adm £6, chd free. For NGS: Sat 23 Mar (11-5). For other opening times and information, please phone or see garden website.**

Visitors can enjoy the spring bulbs in the lime walk, sundial garden and view the famous Old Palace garden, childhood home of Queen Elizabeth I. The adjoining woodland garden is at its best in spring with masses of naturalised daffodils and bluebells. Restaurant open. Exclusive shopping in Stable Yard.

19 NEW 3 HIGHFIELD AVENUE

Harpenden AL5 5UB. Val Fsadni, 01582 768540, val.fsadni@virginmedia.com. *2/3 m from Harpenden Railway Stn. From Harpenden village drive up Station Rd, under the bridge turn R into Milton Rd. Proceed for 1/2 m into Topstreet Way. Take 1st L into Fairmead, which becomes Highfield Ave after 200yds. Street parking with no restrictions.* Cream teas, light refreshments and cakes for sale. **Adm £3, chd free. Sun 14 July (2-5.30).**

Romantic, peaceful, organic garden (80' x 30', N-facing), designed over 10yrs for all-year colour. Informal garden rooms interlinked by winding grass paths and wide traditional borders creating seating areas with different atmospheres. Arches with wisteria, rose and lonicera. Trees incl silver birch, ash, rowan and acers. Small raised vegetable patch, sedum roof on garden shed. Wormery.

20 ◆ HITCHIN LAVENDER

Cadwell Farm, Ickleford, Hitchin SG5 3UA. Mr Nick Hunter, 01462 434343, www.hitchinlavender.com. *2m N of Hitchin. From Hitchin take A600 N. At r'about R into Turnpike Lane. Continue into Arley Rd, garden on R after railway Xing.* **For NGS: Evening Openings £4, chd £1, Light refreshments, Wed 12 June, Fri 12 July, Mon 12 Aug, Thur 12 Sept (5-9). For other opening times and information, please phone or see garden website.**

Visitors are encouraged to walk through the miles of lavender rows at Hitchin Lavender. As well as taking home some great photos you can also pick a bunch of lavender. The fields are a great spot for photographers, artists or those just wanting to take life a little slower. Entrance incl pick your own bunch of lavender - please bring your own scissors!. Featured in Enjoy Hertfordshire, Hertfordshire Life, Countryside Magazine, The Daily Telegraph, Daily Mail. Also presented HM The Queen with a bouquet on her visit to Hitchin during Jubilee celebrations. Limited wheelchair access.

21 ◆ HOPLEYS

High Street, Much Hadham SG10 6BU. Aubrey & Jan Barker, 01279 842509, www.hopleys.co.uk. *5m W of Bishop's Stortford. On B1004. M11 (J8) 7m or A10 (Puckeridge) 5m via A120. 50yds N of Bull PH in centre of Much Hadham.* **For opening times and information, please phone or see garden website.**

4 acres laid out in informal style with island beds. The garden has become a useful collection of stock plants and trial ground for many new plants collected over the years, and features a wide selection of trees, shrubs, perennials and grasses. The nursery production area is hidden by an avenue of fastigiate hornbeams.

22 NEW HUNTSMOOR

Stoney Lane, Bovingdon, Hemel Hempstead HP3 0DP. Mr Brian Bradnock. *Between Bovingdon and Hemel Hempstead. You must come up Bushfield Road. Sat Navs try to take you along Stoney Lane: not a good route, pot holes two feet deep. Huntsmoor is the house looking down Bushfield Road. Car parking in field nearby off B4505.* Home-made teas. **Adm £4, chd free. Suns 21 Apr; 15 Sept (2-6).**

Rose garden, rhododendron border, arboretum, Koi pond, nature pond, shrub and herbaceous borders. Also has a 'cave', chickens and lots of places to sit. Full access to garden including easy access to WC.

THE HYDE WALLED GARDEN
See Bedfordshire

23 ◆ KNEBWORTH HOUSE GARDENS

Knebworth SG1 2AX. The Hon Henry Lytton Cobbold, 01438 812661, www.knebworthhouse.com. *28m N of London. Direct access from A1(M) J7 at Stevenage. Stn, Stevenage 3m.* **For opening times and information, please phone or see garden website.**

Knebworth's magnificent gardens were laid out by Lutyens in 1910. Lutyens' pollarded lime avenues, Gertrude Jekyll's herb garden, the restored maze, yew hedges, roses and herbaceous borders are key features of the formal gardens with peaceful woodland walks beyond. Gold garden, green garden, brick garden and walled kitchen garden.

Winding grass paths and wide traditional borders creating seating areas with different atmospheres . . .

24 19 LANCASTER ROAD

St Albans AL1 4EP. Pauline & Michael Foers. *1/2 m N of St Albans city centre. From city centre take A1081 towards Harpenden then B651 towards Sandridge, after 100yds turn R into Sand Pit Lane, take 5th on L into Lancaster Rd.* Home-made teas. **Adm £3, chd free. Suns 12 May, 16 June; 7 July (2-5.30).**

Unusual trees and shrubs together with richly-planted herbaceous borders give year-round colour in our medium-sized garden. From May, azaleas and rhododendrons give way to a tulip tree and a Judas tree, lilac and callicallicanthus before lobelia tupa, carpentaria and phlox compete with heuchera and salvias. Small terrace with pots.

GROUP OPENING

25 LETCHWORTH GARDEN CITY - TWO GARDENS

Letchworth Garden City SG6 3LB. *½ m E of city centre. A1(M) J9 signed to Letchworth on A505. At 2nd r'about turn L towards Hitchin still on A505. At T-lights turn R into Norton Way South for 324 Norton Way. Alternatively continue straight over T-lights for further ⅓ m along A505 for Scudamore which is on L between Muddy Lane & Letchworth Lane.* Home-made teas served at Scudamore, Ploughman's lunches at 324 Norton Way South. **Combined adm £5, chd free. Sun 14 July (10-5).**

324 NORTON WAY SOUTH
Roger & Jill Thomson

SCUDAMORE, 1 BALDOCK ROAD
Michael & Sheryl Hann

Two contrasting gardens within easy walking distance. Scudamore (SG6 3LB): ½ -acre family garden of mature trees, mixed borders, pond and stream, wet bed, wild garden and orchard/vegetable area. Many sculptures add interest to the garden. 324 Norton Way South (SG6 1TA): a mature ⅕ -acre organic garden with David Harbur armillary as the lawn focal point surrounded by rockery, scree beds, flower borders and summerhouse. Structural tree planting, a productive kitchen garden and greenhouse increase the interest. Family quiz at Scudamore.

♿ 🐕 ✿ ☕

LUTON HOO HOTEL GOLF & SPA

See Bedfordshire

LUTON HOO WALLED GARDEN

See Bedfordshire

26 MACKERYE END HOUSE

Mackerye End, Harpenden AL5 5DR. Mr & Mrs G Penn. *3m E of Harpenden. A1 J4 follow signs Wheathampstead then Luton. Turn R at Cherry Trees Restaurant. Follow signs. M1 J10 follow Lower Luton Rd (B653) To Cherry Trees Restaurant. Turn L follow signs Mackerye End.* Home-made teas. **Adm £5, chd free. Evening Opening wine, Fri 31 May (6-9); Sun 30 June (2-5).**
C16 (Grade 1 listed) Manor House (not open) set in 15 acres of formal gardens, parkland and woodland, front garden set in framework of formal yew hedges. Victorian walled garden with extensive box hedging and box maze, cutting garden, kitchen garden and lily pond. Courtyard garden with extensive yew and box borders. West garden enclosed by pergola walk of old English roses. Plants for sale (Sun). Walled garden access by gravel paths.

♿ ✿ ☕

THE MANOR HOUSE, BARTON-LE-CLAY

See Bedfordshire

27 THE MANOR HOUSE, AYOT ST LAWRENCE

Welwyn AL6 9BP. Rob & Sara Lucas. *4m W of Welwyn. 20 mins from J4 A1(M). Take B653 to Wheathampstead. Turn into Codicote Road follow signs to Shaw's Corner. Parking on village field, short walk from the garden.* Home-made teas. **Adm £5, chd free. Sun 19 May (11-5).**
A 6-acre garden set in mature landscape around Elizabethan Manor House (not open). 1-acre walled garden incl glasshouses, fruit and vegetables, double herbaceous borders, rose and herb beds. Herbaceous perennial island beds, topiary specimens. Parterre and temple pond garden surround the house. Gates and water features by Arc Angel. Garden designed by Julie Toll.

D ☕

28 NEW 43 MARDLEY HILL

Welwyn AL6 0TT. Kerrie & Pete. *5m N of Welwyn Garden City. On B197 between Welwyn & Woolmer Green, on crest of Mardley Hill by bus stop for Arriva 300/301.* Cream teas, wine. **Adm £3, chd free. Suns 19 May; 11 Aug (12-5).**
Rear garden on varied levels transformed in 4 years by plantaholics and filled with many unusual plants. Mature trees and shrubs are framework for perennials and bulbs for a long season of interest. Open-plan design with aspects from full sun to shady banks. Incl outdoor lounge, pond fed by naturalistic rock cascade, bog area, alpine slate bed and free-range bantams. Plant sales in May.

✿ ☕

Romantic garden has ancient apple trees underplanted with an abundant display of tulips and white narcissi. . . .

29 MICHAELS FOLLY

Henderson Place, Epping Green SG1 38NE. Fabrizia Verrecchia, Tessa Verrecchia & Tim Metcalfe, www.bitzia.co.uk. *4m SW of Hertford. From A414 follow signs to Little Berkhamsted. Turn L at war memorial. At Epping Green past Beehive Pub, turn R into Henderson Place. Garden 100yds on L.* Home-made teas. **Adm £3.50, chd free. Sun 30 June (2-5).**
Something different! For those who are interested in a simple lifestyle. An atmospheric naturalistic garden. Meander the woodland walk to sit and reflect by the large natural swimming pond. An abundant organic kitchen garden festooned with roses. Interesting structures abound a straw bale studio for yoga and dance and a Mongolian Yurt where tea will be served. Don't forget to meet the goats. Sensory solutions herbalist remedy stall and herb info walk- sensory solutions.co.uk Also visit. Artist Tessa Verrechia's Stained glass studio fusingglass.co.uk. Featured in Hertfordshire Life and St Albans Life. Wheelchair access to most of garden.

♿ ✿ ☕

30 NEW THE MILL HOUSE

31 Mill Lane, Welwyn AL6 9EU. Sarah & Ian. *Old Welwyn. J6 A1M approx ¾ m to garden, follow yellow arrows to Welwyn Village.* Home-made teas. **Adm £3.50, chd free. Evening Opening wine, Fri 26 Apr (6-8.30); Sun 28 Apr (2-6).**
Listed millhouse (not open) with semi-walled garden bordered by a Venetian bridged millstream and mill race. This romantic garden has ancient apple trees underplanted with an abundant display of tulips and white narcissi. These set off a garden full of perennial promise, within nestles a stylish summerhouse, a hidden parterre and productive potager.

♿ ✿ ☕

© Rosalind Simon

THE MILLERS COTTAGE
See Essex

GROUP OPENING

31 OAKRIDGE AVENUE GARDENS

Radlett WD7 8EW. *Radlett. 1m N of Radlett off A5183, Watling St. From S, through Radlett Village last turning on L.* Cream teas. **Combined adm £3.50, chd free.** Sun 28 July (2-5.30).

45 OAKRIDGE AVENUE
Leonora & Edgar Vaughan. Visitors also welcome by appt Apr to Sept. 01923 854650 ekvaughan@btinternet.com

47 OAKRIDGE AVENUE
Scott Vincent

Two varied interconnecting gardens in attractive village near St Albans. Both have lovely views over open countryside. The main features of no. 45 are the plants carefully chosen to combine the use of colour throughout the year. The garden is in two halves approx 150ft x 60ft on 3 levels of terracing, looping around to a garden of vegetables and soft fruit. The owner propagates plants with passion and can advise on the right place for the right plant. No. 47 is a spacious and mature garden, approx 1 acre with a large pond with goldfish. There is a small orchard and a local brook runs alongside the garden which edges a working farm.

32 PATCHWORK

22 Hall Park Gate, Berkhamsted HP4 2NJ. Jean & Peter Block, 01442 864731. *3m W of Hemel Hempstead. Entering E side of Berkhamsted on A4251, turn L 200yds after 40mph sign.* Light refreshments. **Adm £3, chd free.** Suns 5 May; 18 Aug (2-5). **Visitors also welcome by appt Mar to Oct.**

¼ -acre garden with lots of yr-round colour, interest and perfume, particularly on opening days. Sloping site with background of colourful trees, rockeries, two small ponds, patios, shrubs and trees, spring bulbs, herbaceous border, roses, bedding, fuchsias, dahlias, patio pots and tubs galore and hanging baskets. Seating and cover from the elements.

33 NEW ◆ PEMBROKE FARM

Slip End, nr Ashwell, Baldock SG7 6SQ. Krysia Selwyn-Gotha, 01462 743100, pembrokefarmgarden.co.uk. *½ m S of Ashwell. Off A505 take Ashwell turn opp Wallington junction at bottom of hill. Pass under railway bridge, Pembroke Farm Garden is ⅛ m on R. From Ashwell High St turn up Kingsland Way, by PO. After approx ¾ m garden on L at the bottom of hill.* **Adm £3.50, chd free.** For NGS: Sun 21 Apr (12-5). **For other opening times and information, please phone or see garden website.**

A country house garden with a wildlife walk and formal surprises. You are invited to meander through changing spaces creating a palimpsest of nature and structure.

34 QUEENSWOOD SCHOOL
Shepherds Way, Brookmans Park, Hatfield AL9 6NS. *3m N of Potters Bar. From S: M25 J24 signed Potters Bar. In ½ m at lights turn R onto A1000 signed Hatfield. In 2m turn R onto B157. School is ½ m on R. From N: A1000 from Hatfield. In 5m turn L onto B157.* Light refreshments. **Adm £4, chd free.** Sun 26 May (11-6).
120 acres of informal gardens and woodlands. Rhododendrons, fine specimen trees, shrubs and herbaceous borders. Glasshouses. Fine views to Chiltern Hills. Picnic area. Full Sunday Roast served alongside Scampi and Chips, also a vegetarian option. Muffins, strawberries and cream teas. Some gravel areas.

ALLOTMENTS

35 RADLETT ALLOTMENTS
Gills Hill, Radlett WD7 8DA. Aldenham Parish Council. *½ m W of Radlett centre. From Radlett on A5183 drive W up Station Rd, via Upper Station Rd into Gills Hill. At top of Gills Hill turn L into car park. Allotments a short walk across recreation ground. If car park full, park in nearby streets. Parking for disabled badge holders on allotments. Entrance in Gills Hill Lane opp St John's Church (WD7 8DF).* Home-made teas. **Adm £2.50, chd free.** Sun 11 Aug (12-5.30).
84 well established allotments cultivated in a variety of styles in a peaceful environment. Wide selection of fruit, vegetables and flowers incl dahlias, giant onions and giant pumpkins (hopefully). Some plots divided into mini allotments. Many plot holders will be present. Fresh vegetables and plants for sale. Barbeque, fun quiz, herb stall and welly throwing. Main paths are accessible by wheelchair but paths between allotments are too narrow. Access to teas will be difficult.

36 NEW REVELEY LODGE
88 Elstree Road, Bushey Heath, Bushey WD23 4GL. Bushey Museum Property Trust. *3½ m E of Watford and 1½ m E of Bushey Village. From A41 take A411 signed Bushey & Harrow. At mini-r'about 2nd exit into Elstree Rd. Garden ½ m on L.* Home-made teas. **Adm £3.50, chd free.** Sun 18 Aug (2-6).
2½ -acre garden surrounding a Victorian house bequeathed to Bushey Museum in 2003 and in process of re-planting and renovation. Featuring colourful annual, tender perennial and medicinal planting in beds surrounding a mulberry tree. Conservatory, lean-to greenhouse, vegetable garden and beehive. Analemmatic (human) sundial constructed in stone believed unique to Hertfordshire.

Analemmatic (human) sundial constructed in stone believed unique to Hertfordshire . . .

37 ◆ THE ROYAL NATIONAL ROSE SOCIETY
Chiswell Green Lane, St Albans AL2 3NR. The Secretary, 0845 833 4344, www.rnrs.org.uk. *Follow brown signs, access off Chiswell Green Lane.* **For NGS: Evening Opening £6, chd free, light refreshments, Fri 21 June (6-8.30).**
For other opening times and information, please phone or see garden website.
The gardens were completely rebuilt to a design by Michael Balston & Co in 2007, in the winter of 2009 the garden design was further enhanced by the introduction of additional grass paths enabling visitors more access to the roses. Also at this time a decision was taken to support general gardening trends by the introduction of many more companion plants. The garden showcases over 15,000 roses old and new, fragrant and colourful, displaying the stunning heritage of our favorite flower in a beautiful setting.

38 2 RUINS COTTAGE
Ayot St Lawrence AL6 9BU. Sally Trendell. *4m W of Welwyn. A1(M) J6 follow signs to Welwyn, Codicote (B656) then Ayot St Lawrence (Shaws Corner NT).* **Adm £3.50, chd free (share to Ayot St Lawrence Old Church Preservation Trust).** Sat 8, Sun 9 June (2-6).
Enter through adjacent romantic church ruins, this cottage garden has an eccentric twist with unusual architectural pieces and featuring a unique tree deck with stunning views and an impressive summerhouse. Natural pond, koi pond, rose garden and luscious fernery, reflecting owner's eclectic taste. 'A hidden gem! surreal! incredibly beautiful'. Ayot St Lawrence annual Art Show in nearby Palladian Church 8, 9 & 10 June (serving teas). Wheelchair access only to lower levels, gravel paths.

39 RUSTLING END COTTAGE
Rustling End, nr Codicote SG4 8TD. Julie & Tim Wise, www.rustlingend.com. *1m N of Codicote. From B656 turn L into '3 Houses Lane' then R to Rustling End. House 2nd on L.* Light refreshments. **Adm £4, chd free.** Evening opening, wine, Fri 14 June (4-9); Sun 16 June (all day & evening 7am-9pm).
Meander through our wild flower meadow to a cottage garden with contemporary planting. Behind lumpy hedges explore a simple box parterre, topiary and reflecting pool. Late flowering borders feature blue Camassia in the spring. Naturalistic planting includes the use of wildflowers with perennials and grasses. Hens and vegetables abound. Featured in Garden Answers magazine.

40 NEW 3 ST MARYS WALK
St. Albans AL4 9PD. Mrs Rosemary Coldstream, www.rosemarycoldstream.com. *Marshalswick, North St Albans. Located off Pondfield Crescent or via walkway from The Ridgeway, follow yellow NGS signs.* Home-made teas. **Adm £3, chd free.** Evening Opening wine, Fri 30 Aug (6-9); Sun 1 Sept (2-5.30).
This contemporary and late-summer garden features an unusual collection of antipodean and English plants. A garden designer's own family garden, pathways lead off in all directions from a central oval-shaped lawn. The borders are packed with grasses, perennials, ferns, tree ferns, exotic trees and shrubs and some quirky topiary. The garden also houses Rosemary's design studio. Some parts of the garden have steps and pebble paths.
D

41 ST MICHAEL'S CROFT
Woodcock Hill, Durrants Lane, Berkhamsted HP4 3TR. Sue & Alan O'Neill. *1.3m W of Berkhamsted town centre. Leave A41 at A416 Chesham turn. Follow sign to Berkhamsted. After 500 metres go straight on to Shootersway (not sharp R), 1m further turn R into Durrants Lane. Garden 1st on L.* Home-made teas. **Adm £3.50, chd free. Sun 23 June (2-6).**
1-acre S-facing garden with variety of densely planted borders surrounded by mature trees. Rhododendrons, azaleas, hostas, ferns, alliums, palms and bananas. Water features and waterfall from lock gate. Pergolas with clematis and climbers, vegetable beds, 2 greenhouses. Working beehives. Seating and cover. Home produced honey and plants for sale. Easy access for wheelchairs.

Rose garden and luscious fernery, reflecting owner's eclectic taste . . . hidden gem! surreal! incredibly beautiful . . .

42 ◆ ST PAUL'S WALDEN BURY
Whitwell, Hitchin SG4 8BP. Simon & Caroline Bowes Lyon, 01438 871218, www.stpaulswaldenbury.co.uk. *5m S of Hitchin. On B651; 1/2 m N of Whitwell village. From London leave A1(M) J6 for Welwyn (not Welwyn Garden City). Pick up signs to Codicote, then Whitwell.* **Adm £5, chd £1. For NGS: Suns 7 Apr; 12 May; 9 June (2-7). For other opening times and information, please phone or see garden website.**
Open for NGS since 1927. Spectacular formal woodland garden, Grade 1 listed, laid out 1720. Long rides lined with clipped beech hedges lead to temples, statues, lake and a green terraced theatre. Seasonal displays of snowdrops, daffodils, cowslips, irises, magnolias, rhododendrons, lilies. Wild flowers are encouraged. Birthplace and childhood home of the late Queen Mother. Though ephemeral plantings grow and decline the architecture of the garden remains unchanged. Open Garden combined with Open Farm Sunday 9 June. Suitable for wheel chairs in part of the garden. Steep grass slopes in places.

GROUP OPENING

43 ST STEPHENS AVENUE GARDENS
St Albans AL3 4AD. *1 1/2 m S of St Albans City Centre. From A414 former M10 r'about take A5183 Watling St. At double mini-r'about by St Stephens Church/King Harry PH take B4630 Watford Rd. St Stephens Ave is 1st R.* Home-made teas at no. 20. **Combined adm £4, chd free. Sun 30 June (2-6).**

20 ST STEPHENS AVENUE
Heather & Peter Osborne
Visitors also welcome by appt Apr to Oct, adm £5 incl tea and home-made cake.
01727 856354
heather.osborne20@btinternet.com

30 ST STEPHENS AVENUE
Carol & Roger Harlow

Two gardens of similar size and aspect, developed in different styles.The front of number 20 is planted in blue and yellow, the St Albans colours. Hostas, ferns and seasonal containers surround the patio. Colour-themed mixed borders encircle a wildlife pond. Specimen trees, and fences clothed with honeysuckle, clematis and roses ensure privacy. Winding paths lead to a new white border, a gravel area with grasses and architectural plants and through the arch to the 'hot' beds. Number 30 has an informal gravel front garden; the Mediterranean style planting is tolerant of very dry conditions and poor soil. Clipped box, beech and hornbeam provide a framework for herbaceous planting and lawns in the back garden. Different sections incl a sunken garden, black garden and productive greenhouse.

GROUP OPENING

44 SERGE HILL GARDENS
Sergehill Lane, Bedmond, Watford WD5 0RT. *1/2 m E of Bedmond. Set Sat Nav for WD5 0RT. From Bedmond, turn into Serge Hill Lane by white tin church. Follow signs to take you down drive to Serge Hill (avoid the lane which can become congested). From Chiswell Green, take Chiswell Green Lane by Three Hammers PH. Follow signs to Bedmond.* Home-made teas at Serge Hill. **Combined adm £7, chd free. Sun 16 June (2-5).**

THE BARN D
Sue & Tom Stuart-Smith

SERGE HILL
Kate Stuart-Smith

Two very diverse gardens. At its entrance the Barn has an enclosed courtyard, with tanks of water, herbaceous perennials and shrubs tolerant of generally dry conditions. To the N there are views over the 5-acre wild flower meadow, and the West Garden is a series of different gardens overflowing with bulbs, herbaceous perennials and shrubs. Serge Hill is originally a Queen Anne House (not open), beautifully remodelled by Busby (architect of Brighton and Hove) in 1811. It has wonderful views over the ha-ha to the park; a walled vegetable garden with a large greenhouse, roses, shrubs and perennials leading to a long mixed border. At the front of the house there is an outside stage used for family plays, and a ship.

45 ◆ SHAW'S CORNER
Ayot St Lawrence, nr Welwyn AL6 9BX. National Trust, 01438 820307, www.nationaltrust.org.uk/shawscorner. *2m NE of Wheathampstead. At SW end of village, approx 2m from B653 (A1 J4, M1 J10). Signed from B653 (Shaw's Corner/The Ayots).* **Adm £6.50, chd £3.25. For NGS: Sun 9 June (12-5.30). For other opening times and information, please phone or see garden website.**
Approx 3 1/2 acres with richly planted borders, orchard, small meadow, wooded areas and views over the Hertfordshire countryside. Historical garden, belonging to George Bernard Shaw from 1906 until his death in

1950. Hidden among the trees is the revolving writing hut where Shaw retreated. Ionian Singers will perform in the garden on NGS open day. No wheelchair accessible WC.

♿ ✿ ☕

46 NEW SOUTH WING
Bramfield House, Bramfield, Hertford SG14 2QT. Mr Keith Henderson. *3m NE of Hertford. From Hertford take A119 towards Watton-at-Stone. Turn L to Bramfield. In Bramfield turn R into Well Green.* Home-made teas. **Adm £4, chd free. Evening Opening wine, Fri 28 June (6-9); Sun 30 June (2-6).**
Just under 5 acres, and situated to the S of a wing of a Victorian villa. Perennial herbaceous beds follow the view to the lake. Summer beds planted fully and to succeed from spring to late autumn. Prairie-style beds near the lake, and more large perennial beds lead to a large meadow. Only in its 3rd year since planting, the garden is one of long vistas with large flowering beds.

✿ ☕

47 SOUTHEND FARM
Stevenage SG1 3HS. Janet Tyndale & Peter Craig. *Approx 1½ m from J8 A1(M). From S A1(M) J7, from N A1(M) J8, take A602, follow signs to Old Town. 15 mins walk Stevenage railway stn. Garden on corner of Church Lane.* Home-made teas. **Adm £3.50, chd free. Sun 11 Aug (1.30-5).**
An oasis in the heart of Stevenage Old Town. Informal garden surrounding a Grade 2* Listed Medieval Wealden Farmhouse. Approx ⅓ -acre with mixed borders, traditional cottage garden style planting, colour-themed borders, dry shade border. Continually evolving garden. Belgian mechanical organs providing musical entertainment. Small garden railway. Featured in Garden News. Wheelchair access to all areas except patio.

♿ ☕

Dassels Bury

48 9 TANNSFIELD DRIVE
Hemel Hempstead HP2 5LG. Peter & Gaynor Barrett, 01442 393508, tterrabjp@ntlworld.com. *1m NE of Hemel Hempstead town centre. Approx 2m W of J8 on M1. From J8 straight across r'about onto A414 dual carriageway to Hemel Hemstead. Pass under footbridge and straight across r'about, then 1st R across the dual carriageway into Leverstock Green Rd. Continue straight on into High St Green, then L into Ellingham Rd. R into Orchard Close, L into Tannsmore Close which leads into Tannsfield Drive.* Home-made teas. **Adm £3, chd free. Suns 21 July; 18 Aug (1.30-5). Visitors also welcome by appt mid May to mid Sept, adm £3.50 chd free, tea and coffee available.**
This small, town garden is decorated with over 400 plants creating a welcoming oasis of calm. The owners love to experiment with the garden planting schemes which ensures the look of the garden alters from year to year. Narrow paths divide, leading the visitor on a discovery of the garden's many features. The sound of water is ever-present. Water features, metal sculptures, wall art and mirrors run throughout the garden. As a time and cost saving experiment all hanging baskets are planted with hardy perennials most of which are normally used for ground cover.

✿ ☕ ☎

49 THUNDRIDGE HILL HOUSE
Cold Christmas Lane, Ware SG12 0UE. Mr & Mrs Christopher Melluish, 01920 462500, c.melluish@btopenworld.com. *2m NE of Ware. ¾ m from The Sow & Pigs PH off the A10 down Cold Christmas Lane, crossing new bypass.* Cream teas. **Adm £4, chd free. Sun 26 May (2-5.30). Visitors also welcome by appt.**
Well-established garden of approx 2½ acres; good variety of plants, shrubs and roses, attractive hedges. We are at present creating an unusual yellow-only bed. Several delightful places to sit. Wonderful views in and out of the garden especially down to the Rib Valley. 'A most popular garden to visit'.

♿ 🐕 ☕ ☎

50 84 VALLEY ROAD
Welwyn Garden City AL8 7DP. Marion Jay. *W side of Welwyn Garden City. Turn R off Great North Rd at Lemsford r'about, go under the bridge then 2nd turning next r'about. 200 yds on L.* Cream teas & home-made cakes. **Adm £3, chd free. Sun 21 July (2-5.30). Evening Opening wine, Fri 26 July (7-9).**
A dramatic garden rising steeply from the back of the house, using an 'amphitheatre' of stone wall terracing to accommodate the slope. Planting is largely in the modern perennial style, mixing drifts of drought-tolerant herbaceous plants with a variety of grasses. Three ponds and new front garden prairie planting. Plants for sale. Featured in Garden News. Difficult for those walking with sticks.

This medieval hunting park is known for its trees, tulip and a London plane tree . . .

51 NEW WALKERN HALL
Stevenage SG2 7JA. Mrs Kate de Boinville. *Walkern. Turn L at War Memorial as you leave Walkern, heading for Benington (immed after small bridge). Garden 1m up hill on R.* Home-made teas. **Adm £3.50, chd free. Sat 9, Sun 10 Feb (12-4).**
Walkern Hall is essentially a winter woodland garden. Set in 8 acres, the carpet of snowdrops and aconites is a constant source of wonder in Jan/Feb. This medieval hunting park is known more for its established trees such as the tulip trees and a magnificent London plane tree which dominates the garden.

52 WATERDELL HOUSE
Little Green Lane, Croxley Green, Rickmansworth WD3 3JH. Mr & Mrs Peter Ward, 01923 772775, peterward31@yahoo.com. *1½ m NE of Rickmansworth. M25, J18, direction Rickmansworth to join A412 towards Watford. From A412 turn L signed Sarratt, along Croxley Green, fork R past Coach & Horses, cross Baldwins Lane into Little Green Lane, then L at top.* Light refreshments. **Adm £4, chd free. Visitors welcome by appt Mar to Sept, afternoon & evenings.**
1½ -acre walled garden systematically developed over 60yrs by present owner/gardener. Mature and young trees, topiary holly hedge, herbaceous borders, modern island beds of shrubs, old-fashioned roses, grasses and pond garden.

53 NEW 3 WATFORD ROAD
Radlett WD7 8LA. Mrs Alison Wisenfeld. *5m S of St Albans. Situated W of Watling Street, Follow yellow signs. Watford Rd is continuation of Aldenham Rd off A5183 Watling St. Main garden entrance in Barn Close.* Cream teas. **Adm £4, chd free. Sun 1 Sept (9-6).**
An Edwardian Arts and Crafts house (not open) with a garden on several levels. Specimen trees and steep weathered limestone rockery, hidden paths and grottoes forming a natural amphitheatre. This garden has architectural features and a wide range of plants and trees. The flint walled, stone flagged upper Italian garden has tree ferns, olive trees and herbs in formal beds and terracotta pots.

WAYSIDE COTTAGE
See Bedfordshire

WEST LODGE PARK
See London

WICKETS
See Essex

WIMPOLE ESTATE
See Cambridgeshire

54 WOODHALL PARK
Watton-at-Stone, Hertford SG14 3NF. Mr & Mrs Ralph Abel Smith, www.woodhallestate.co.uk. *4m N of Hertford. 6m S of Stevenage, 4m NW of Ware. Main lodge entrance to Woodhall Park on A119, Hertford to Stevenage, between villages of Stapleford & Watton-at-Stone.* Home-made teas. **Adm £5, chd free. Sun 23 June (12-5).**
Mature 4-acre garden created out of surrounding park in 1957 when C18 stable block was converted into a dwelling house (not open). Special features: courtyard, rose borders, rose arbours, herbaceous and mixed borders, kitchen garden and areas to sit with unspoilt views. Grassland park full of mature and ancient trees traversed by the River Beane and lake. Visitors welcome to walk and picnic in the Park. Featured in Hertfordshire Mercury.

Hertfordshire County Volunteers

County Organiser
Julie Wise, Rustling End Cottage, Rustling End, Nr Hitchin SG4 8TD, 01438 821509, juliewise@f2s.com

County Treasurer
Peter Barrett, 9 Tannsfield Drive, Hemel Hempstead HP2 5LG, 01442 393508, tterrabjp@ntworld.com

Publicity
Julie Knight, 27 Glenferrie Road, St Albans AL1 4JT, 01727 752375, jknight21@gmail.com
Chris Roper 12 Twynham Road, Maidenhead SL6 5AS, 01628 636893, chris.roper@talktalk.net

Booklet co-ordinator
Edwina Robarts, Bromley Hall, Standon, Ware SG11 1NY, 01279 842422, edwina.robarts@btinternet.com

Assistant County Organisers
Sarah Marsh, The Mill House, 31 Mill Lane, Welwyn AL6 9EU, 078130 83126, sarahkmarsh@hotmail.co.uk
Christopher Melluish, Thundridge Hill House, Cold Christmas Lane, Ware SG12 0UF, 01920 462500, c.melluish@btinternet.com
Virginia Newton, South Barn, Kettle Green, Much Hadham SG10 6AE, 01279 843232, vnewton@southbarn.net
Karen Smith, 44 Broadwater Avenue, Letchworth Garden City SG6 3HJ, 01462 673133, hertsgardeningangel@googlemail.com

ISLE OF WIGHT

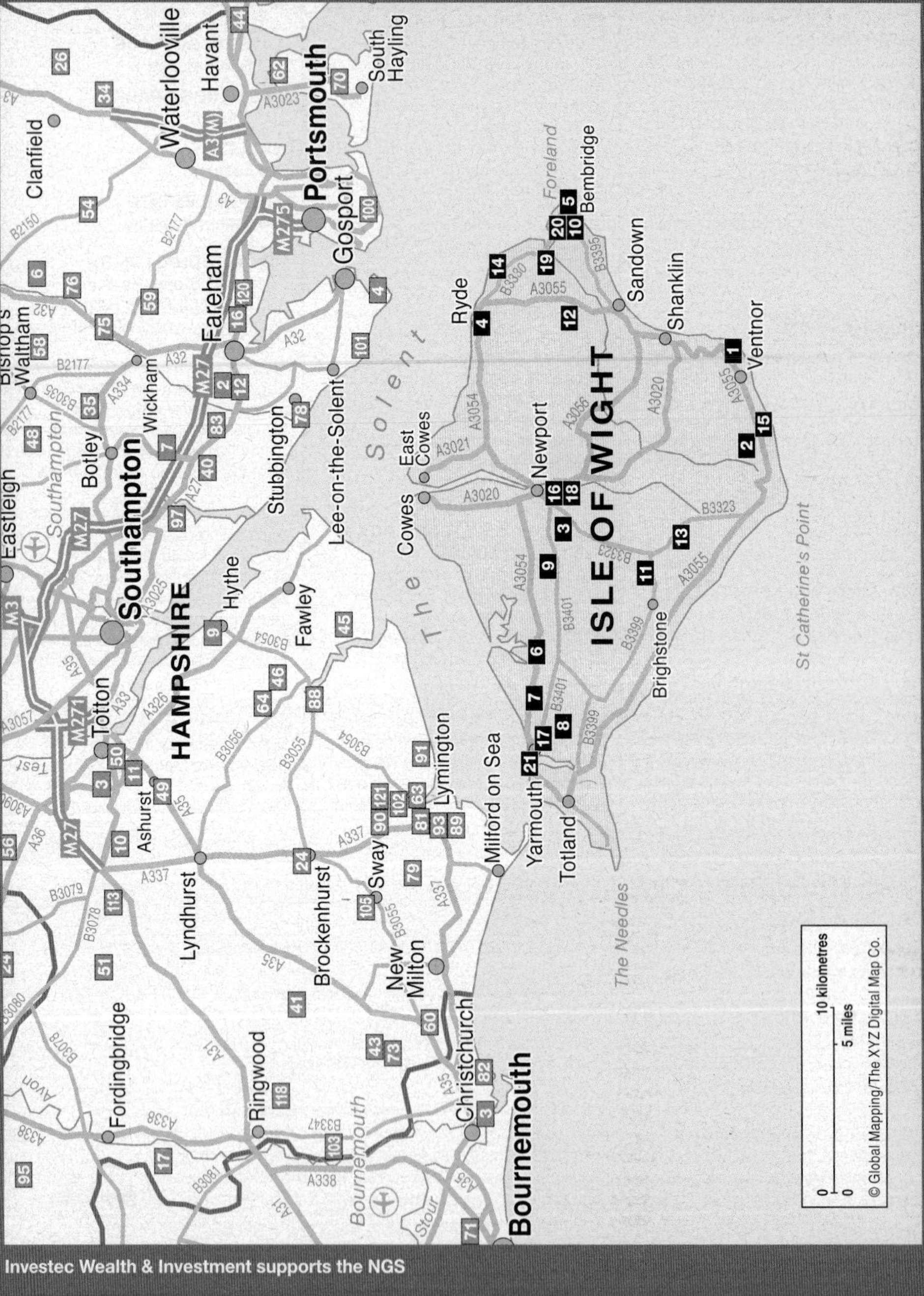

Opening Dates

May

Sunday 19
3 Badminton

Sunday 26
9 Meadowsweet
11 Northcourt Garden

Friday 31
5 Blue Haze
20 1 White Cottages

June

Sunday 9
14 Salterns Cottage

National Gardens Weekend

Saturday 15
4 Blenheim House

Sunday 16
4 Blenheim House
10 Mill Farm
12 Nunwell House
13 The Old Rectory

Thursday 20
19 Wayside

Saturday 22
1 Ashcliff

Sunday 23
1 Ashcliff
8 Dog Kennel Cottage

Sunday 30
5 Blue Haze
20 1 White Cottages
21 Yarmouth Town Gardens

July

Saturday 6
2 Ashknowle House

Sunday 7
2 Ashknowle House

Sunday 14
17 Thorley Manor

August

Sunday 11
15 The Shute
16 The Spinney
18 39 Watergate Road

Thursday 15
7 Cranmore Avenue Gardens

Sunday 18
6 Crab Cottage

Saturday 31
5 Blue Haze
20 1 White Cottages

Gardens open to the public

12 Nunwell House

Also open by Appointment ☎

4 Blenheim House
7 Highwood
11 Northcourt Garden
13 The Old Rectory

The Gardens

1 ASHCLIFF

The Pitts, Bonchurch, nr Ventnor PO38 1NT. Judi & Sid Lines. *From A3055 follow directions for Bonchurch. Follow signs for Bonchurch pond and park in village or continue, following signs for parking in Bonchurch Shute.* Home-made teas. **Adm £3, chd free. Sat 22, Sun 23 June (11-5).**
The garden was started from a blank canvas 9yrs ago and now contains many diverse areas of interest including areas of sun and shade. Plantings are of interesting and unusual perennials, shrubs and trees over approx 1 acre blending into the natural landscape part of which is a cliff.

2 ASHKNOWLE HOUSE

Ashknowle Lane, Whitwell, Ventnor PO38 2PP. Mr & Mrs K Fradgley. *4m W of Ventnor. Take the Whitwell Road from Ventnor or Godshill. Turn into unmade lane next to Old Rectory. Field Parking. Disabled parking at house.* Home-made teas. **Adm £4, chd free. Sat 6, Sun 7 July (11.30-4.30).**
A variety of features to explore in the grounds of this Victorian house. Informative woodland walks, borders, wildlife pond and other water features. Ongoing development of ornamental areas. The well-maintained kitchen garden is highly productive and boasts a wide range of fruit and vegetables grown in cages, tunnels, glasshouses and raised beds. New orchard site. Display and video of red squirrel living on site. Article in The Kitchen Garden.

Ashcliff

© Heather Edwards

3 BADMINTON
Clatterford Shute, Carisbrooke, Newport PO30 1PD. Mr & Mrs G S Montrose. *1½ m SW of Newport. Free parking in Carisbrooke Castle car park. Public footpath to Millers Lane in corner of car park leads down to garden, approx 200yds. Parking for disabled can be arranged; please phone prior to opening.* Home-made teas. **Adm £3, chd free. Sun 19 May (2-5).**
One-acre garden on sheltered S- and W-facing site with good vistas. Planted for all-yr interest with many different shrubs, trees and perennials to give variety, structure and colour. Natural stream and pond being developed alongside kitchen garden.

4 BLENHEIM HOUSE
Spencer Road (use Market St entrance), Ryde PO33 2NY. David Rosewarne & Magie Gray, 01983 614675, dwrosewarne@homecall.co.uk. *Market St entrance behind Ryde Town Hall/Theatre.* Home-made teas. **Adm £3, chd free. Sat 15, Sun 16 June (1-5). Visitors also welcome by appt.**
A garden developed over 9yrs, exploring the decorative qualities and long term effects of pattern making, colour and texture, This terraced 116ft x 30ft sloping site is centred on a twisting red brick path that both reveals and hides interesting and contrasting areas of planting, creating intimate and secluded spaces that belie it's town centre location.

5 NEW BLUE HAZE
24 Beachfield Road, Bembridge PO35 5TN. Gerry Price, www.thecoastalgardener.co.uk. *Take B3395 for Bembridge. At Windmill Inn turn into Lane End, 2nd R into Egerton Rd, L into Howgate Rd, then 1st R. Unmade road.* Home-made teas. **Combined adm £3, chd free. Fri 31 May, Sun 30 June, Sat 31 Aug (10-4). Combined with 1 White Cottages.**
A passion for plants, art and the coast inspired the creation of this small coastal garden which wraps around Blue Haze. Native coastal plants thrive alongside more cultivated species whilst sculptures made from objects washed ashore augment the theme. Fruit, vegetables and a small nursery are integrated into the garden making it productive as well as attractive.

6 CRAB COTTAGE
Mill Road, Shalfleet PO30 4NE. Mr & Mrs Peter Scott. *4½ m E of Yarmouth. Turn past New Inn into Mill Rd. Please park before going through NT gates. Entrance 1st on L, less than 5 mins walk.* Home-made teas. **Adm £3, chd free. Sun 18 Aug (11.30-5).**
1¼ acres on gravelly soil. Part glorious views across croquet lawn over Newtown Creek and Solent leading to wild flower meadow, woodland walk and hidden water lily pond. Part walled garden protected from westerlies, with mixed borders, leading to terraced sunken garden with ornamental pool and pavilion, planted with exotics, tender shrubs and herbaceous perennials. Gravel path, uneven grass paths.

Northcourt Garden
© Heather Edwards

GROUP OPENING

7 NEW CRANMORE AVENUE GARDENS
PO41 0XR. *A3054 from Yarmouth. Approx 2m E of Yarmouth on Yarmouth to Newport Rd. Bus shelter opp entrance to Cranmore Ave.* Home-made teas at Oakwood. **Combined adm £5, chd free. Thur 15 Aug (11-4).**

NEW FUNAKASHI
Mrs Helen Mount

HIGHWOOD
Cranmore. Mr & Mrs Cooper. *Approx 2m E of Yarmouth on Yarmouth to Newport Rd. Bus shelter opp entrance to Cranmore Ave*
Visitors also welcome by appt. 01983 760550

NEW OAKWOOD
D M Chesterton

3 gardens in an area of outstanding natural beauty. All different in character, reflecting their location along this S-facing, heavy clay hillside, the owner's individuality and variety of plants that can be grown

successfully in sometimes hostile conditions. Highwood - A garden for all seasons. In spring, snowdrops, hepaticas and hellebores. In summer, perennials, grasses, ferns, wild flowers, orchids particularly. In autumn, asters, berries and much colour. S-facing slope leads to an oak copse. Clay soil, so good footwear needed if inclement weather. Oakwood - A woodland edge garden, approx 1 acre, incl orchard area, vegetables and glasshouse. Large number of mature oaks. Borders and beds are mixed shrubs and herbaceous. Funakashi - Recently developed from semi-derelict plant nursery. A blend of perennials and annuals provide all-yr interest and nectar for pollinating insects. Small woodland, with bee hives, where cultivated and native plants grow together. Herbaceous borders, mainly 'hot' colours, a raised water feature reclaimed from part of the house plus a fruit and vegetable patch. Partial wheelchair access at Oakwood & Funakoshi on pathways and lawns, grassed areas depending on weather. No wheelchair access at Highwood.

♿ ❀ ☕

8 DOG KENNEL COTTAGE

Broad Lane, Thorley, Yarmouth PO41 0UH. Malcolm & Helen Peplow. *2m SE of Yarmouth. On B3401. Turn R at Thorley Xrds 100yds before Thorley Church into Broad Lane. 8m W of Newport on B3401 via Calbourne, Newbridge and Wellow to Thorley. Turn L 100yds after Thorley Church, and proceed 800yds up Broad Lane.* Home-made teas. **Adm £3, chd free. Sun 23 June (11.30-5).**

3-acre garden with a panoramic view of Yarmouth and the Western Solent. Featuring a gravel garden, large rockery, climbing old roses, clematis, small stream, copse and kitchen garden. Some gravel paths.

♿ 🐕 ❀ ☕

9 MEADOWSWEET

5 Great Park Cottages, off Betty-Haunt Lane, Carisbrooke PO30 4HR. Gunda Cross. *4m SW of Newport. From A3054 Newport to Yarmouth rd turn L at crossroads Porchfield-Calbourne into Betty-Haunt Lane, over bridge and into lane on R. Parking along L side on grass verge, past Meadowsweet.* Home-made teas. **Adm £3, chd free. Sun 26 May (11-4.30).**

From windswept barren 2-acre cattle field to developing tranquil country garden. Natural, mainly native, planting and wild flowers. Cottagey front garden, herb garden, orchard, fruit cage and large pond. The good life and haven for wildlife! Flat level garden with grass paths.

♿ ❀ ☕

10 MILL FARM

Mill Road, Bembridge PO35 5PD. Peter, Alice & Kirsty Summerhayes. *Follow brown signs to Bembridge Windmill, come through NT gate, past windmill to the R. Limited parking on roadside.* Light refreshments. **Adm £3, chd free. Sun 16 June (12-4).**

Delightful informal cottage garden surrounding C17 farmhouse (not open) in windswept location with wonderful views. The garden is set out in a number of areas incl a gravel garden and vegetable patch and orchard. Main drive gravel.

♿ ❀ ☕

The good life and haven for wildlife . . . !

11 NORTHCOURT GARDEN

Main Road, Shorwell PO30 3JG. Mr & Mrs J Harrison, 01983 740415, john@northcourt.info, www.northcourt.info. *4m SW of Newport. Entering Shorwell from Carisbrooke, entrance on R, immed after rustic footbridge, opp thatched cottages. From Chale or Brighstone take Newport rd, turn L on bend shortly after PO.* Home-made teas. **Adm £4.50, chd free. Sun 26 May (11.30-5). Groups of 8+ also welcome by appt Apr to Oct.**

15-acre garden surrounding large C17 Manor House (not open), incl walled kitchen garden, chalk stream, terraces, magnolias and camellias. Subtropical planting. Boardwalk along jungle garden. Very large range of plants enjoying the different microclimates. Late summer beds of dahlias, cannas, grasses and bananas. The terraces rise 80ft behind the house with collection of hydrangeas. Picturesque wooded valley around the stone manor house. Bath house and snail mount leading to terraces. 200yd chalk stream bordered with primulas. Wheelchair access only on main paths.

♿ 🐕 ❀ 🛏 ☕ ☎

12 ◆ NUNWELL HOUSE

West Lane, Brading PO36 0JQ. Steven & Rose Bonsey, 01983 407240, info@nunwellhouse.co.uk. *3m S of Ryde. Sign posted off A3055 into Coach Lane.* **Adm £3, chd free. For NGS: Sun 16 June (1-5). For other opening times and information, please phone or email.**

5-acres of beautifully set formal and shrub gardens and old-fashioned shrub roses prominent. Exceptional Solent views from the terraces. Small arboretum and walled garden with herbaceous borders. House (not open) developed over 5 centuries and full of architectural interest.

❀ ☕

13 THE OLD RECTORY

Kingston Road, Kingston PO38 2JZ. Derek & Louise Ness, 01983 551701, louiseness@gmail.com, www.kingstonrectorygarden.co.uk. *8m S of Newport. Entering Shorwell from Carisbrooke, take L turn at mini r'about towards Chale (B3399). Follow rd until Kingston sign, house 2nd on L after this. Park in adjacent field.* Home-made teas. **Adm £3.50, chd free. Sun 16 June (2-5). Visitors also welcome by appt June, refreshments by arrangement.**

Constantly evolving romantic country garden. Areas of interest include the walled kitchen garden, orchard, formal and wildlife ponds and a wonderfully scented collection of old and English roses. Featured in Period Living and Country Homes and Interiors.

🐕 ❀ ☕ ☎

14 SALTERNS COTTAGE

Salterns Road, Seaview PO34 5AH. Susan & Noël Dobbs. *Enter Seaview from W via Springvale, Salterns Rd links the Duver Rd with Bluett Ave.* Light refreshments. **Adm £4, chd free. Sun 9 June (12-4).**

A glasshouse, a potager, exotic borders & fruit trees are some of the many attractions in this 33ft x 131ft garden behind Salterns Cottage built in 1640 and listed. Enjoy the garden created by Susan in 2005, add a light lunch or home made tea and learn about the Dracula connection. Bram Stoker was Noel's great grandfather. Featured in the English Garden magazine & IOW County Press.

15 THE SHUTE
Seven Sisters Road, St. Lawrence, Ventnor, Isle of Wight PO38 1UZ. Mr & Mrs C Russell. *Half way along Seven Sisters Rd, opp bottom of St Lawrence Shute. Parking in Fishers or Twining Rd (two minute walk) or in Undercliff Drive (a steep but pleasant walk 10 minute walk).Sorry but no parking in the shared drive.* Home-made teas. **Adm £3, chd free. Sun 11 Aug (11.30-4.30).**
About ½ acre, formerly part of a large Victorian garden. Views from the terrace across the lawn and newly planted white border to the sea. In the lower area we mix herbaceous planting with fruit and vegetables. Annuals complement the dahlias, agapanthus etc for a show of late summer colour.

16 NEW THE SPINNEY
74 Watergate Road, Newport PO30 1XP. Mrs Patricia Minns. *Shide area, S of Newport. Head out of Newport on the Sandown Rd (A3020). Turn R at the National Tyre Garage into Shide Rd (B3401). At mini r'about turn L. 400yds on R.* Home-made teas. **Combined adm £3.50, chd free. Sun 11 Aug (10-5). Combined with 39 Watergate Road.**
½ -acre country garden on the edge of town, planted on a slope with views over the Medina Valley to St Georges down beyond. Colourful borders in sun and shade, extensive lawns, small vegetable garden and greenhouse. A passion for clematis and colour and the acquisitive nature of the head gardener make this developing garden on chalk, interesting.

17 THORLEY MANOR
Thorley, Yarmouth PO41 0SJ. Mr & Mrs Anthony Blest. *1m E of Yarmouth. From Bouldnor take Wilmingham Lane. House ½ m on L.* Home-made teas. **Adm £3, chd free. Sun 14 July (2.30-5).**
Delightful informal gardens of over 3 acres surrounding Manor House (not open). Garden set out in a number of walled rooms incl herb garden, colourful perennial and self seeding borders, sweeping lawn and shrub borders, plus unusual island croquet lawn. Venue renowned for excellent home-made teas and the eccentric head gardener.

18 NEW 39 WATERGATE ROAD
Newport PO30 1XP. Ms Alexandra Muir-Mackenzie. *Shide area, S of Newport. Head out of Newport on the Sandown Rd (A3020). Turn R at the National Tyre Garage into Shide Rd (B3401). At mini r'about turn L.* Home-made teas at The Spinney. **Combined adm £3.50, chd free. Sun 11 Aug (10-5). Combined with The Spinney.**
Stunningly imaginative gravel gardens at the front and back of this property show how different a suburban garden can be. Created from a blank canvas 6yrs ago the gardens are planted with an exciting range of grasses and perennials for a long season of interest. A shallow wildlife pond and sculpture add points of interest.

19 WAYSIDE
Carpenters Road, St Helens, Ryde PO33 1YG. Mr & Mrs B M Cole. *Take the B3330 for St Helens and park on St Helens Green.* Home-made teas. **Adm £3, chd free. Thur 20 June (11-5).**
Well-established informal cottage garden with a mixture of trees, shrubs, climbing roses and clematis and densely planted with many unusual plants (propagated by the owner). S-facing with stunning views across to Culver Downs. Some uneven paving stones, but area of lawn for wheelchairs.

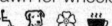

20 NEW 1 WHITE COTTAGES
109 High Street, Bembridge PO35 5SF. Mr Nik Inigo Peirce. *B3395 for Bembridge. The 'Old' High St is straight on through village or past Windmill PH if coming from Sandown or Brading.* Home-made teas. **Combined adm £3, chd free. Fri 31 May, Sun 30 June, Sat 31 Aug (10-4). Combined with Blue Haze.**
A dry gravel garden. Mainly used to grow and breed day lilies (Hemerocallis) and these are in full bloom end June and beginning July. The garden is predominantly herbaceous mixed with grasses and thus the garden changes dramatically over the year. Spring flowers provide interest before the day lilies and grasses and late perennials after. The garden is long and narrow with narrow winding paths. Daylilies, 100 registered varieties and seedlings in garden setting and seedling borders.

Stunningly imaginative gravel gardens . . .

GROUP OPENING

21 YARMOUTH TOWN GARDENS
Yarmouth, Isle Of Wight PO41 0NU. *8m W of Newport on A3054. Ferry from Lymington comes into the centre of Yarmouth. Parking in main town car park and in town. Yellow signs for NGS will be displayed and a map provided. Individual gardens are within easy walking distance of each other.* Home-made teas at Mill Creek House. **Combined adm £5, chd free. Sun 30 June (11.30-4).**

NEW CLEMATIS COTTAGE
St James Street. N Hawkes.
At the end of gravel footpath off St James St, opp Yarmouth Institute

NEW FERNLEA
Norton. Mr Tom Symes

NEW HOPE COTTAGE
St James Street. Ms Biddy O'Grady.
Along gravel footpath off St James St, opp the Yarmouth Institute

MILL CREEK HOUSE
Mill Lane. Richard & Sue Price

Four very different gardens providing a diversity of styles and planting including cottage plants, exotics and mediterranean influences. Planting in all gardens has to tolerate and thrive in a coastal location with all the accompanying difficulties that presents. On the plus side, there is little or no frost.

Meadowsweet

© Heather Edwards

Isle of Wight County Volunteers

County Organiser

Jennie Fradgley, Ashknowle House, Ashknowle Lane, Whitwell, Ventnor, Isle of Wight PO38 2PP, 01983 730805, jenniemf805@yahoo.co.uk

Assistant County Organisers

Sukie Hillyard, Spithead House, Seaview Lane, Seaview, Isle of Wight PO34 5DG, 01983 565093 robin@robinandsukie.plus.com

Sally Parker, Beach House, The Duver, Seaview, Isle of Wight PO34 5AJ, 01983 612495, sallyparkeriow@btinternet.com

KENT

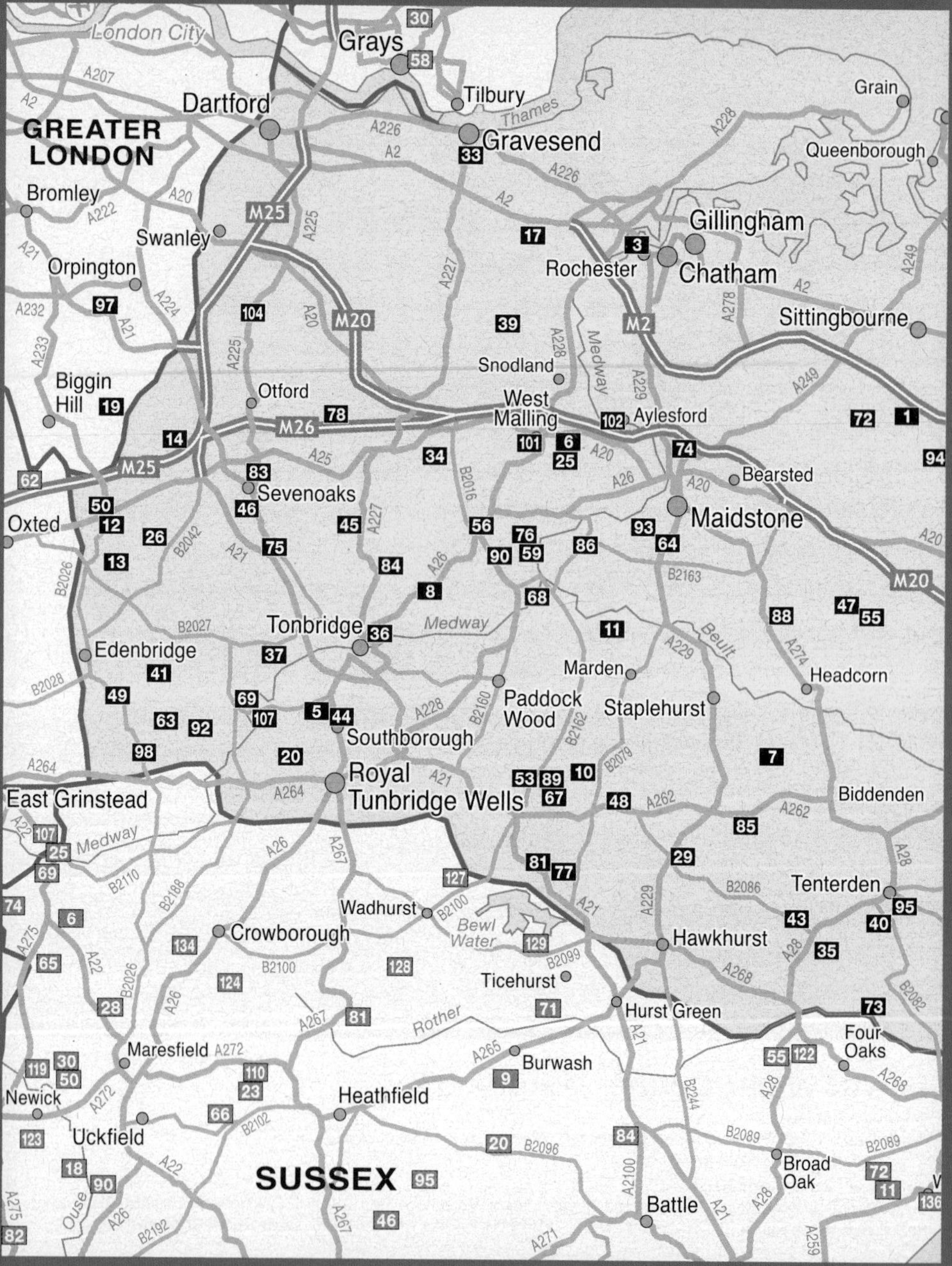
London City
Grays
Tilbury
Thames
Dartford
GREATER LONDON
Gravesend
Grain
Queenborough
Bromley
Swanley
Gillingham
Rochester
Chatham
Orpington
Sittingbourne
Snodland
Medway
Biggin Hill
Otford
West Malling
Aylesford
Bearsted
Sevenoaks
Maidstone
Oxted
Tonbridge
Medway
Beult
Edenbridge
Marden
Headcorn
Paddock Wood
Staplehurst
Southborough
Royal Tunbridge Wells
Biddenden
East Grinstead
Medway
Tenterden
Wadhurst
Crowborough
Bewl Water
Hawkhurst
Ticehurst
Hurst Green
Rother
Four Oaks
Maresfield
Burwash
Newick
Heathfield
Uckfield
Broad Oak
SUSSEX
Ouse
Battle

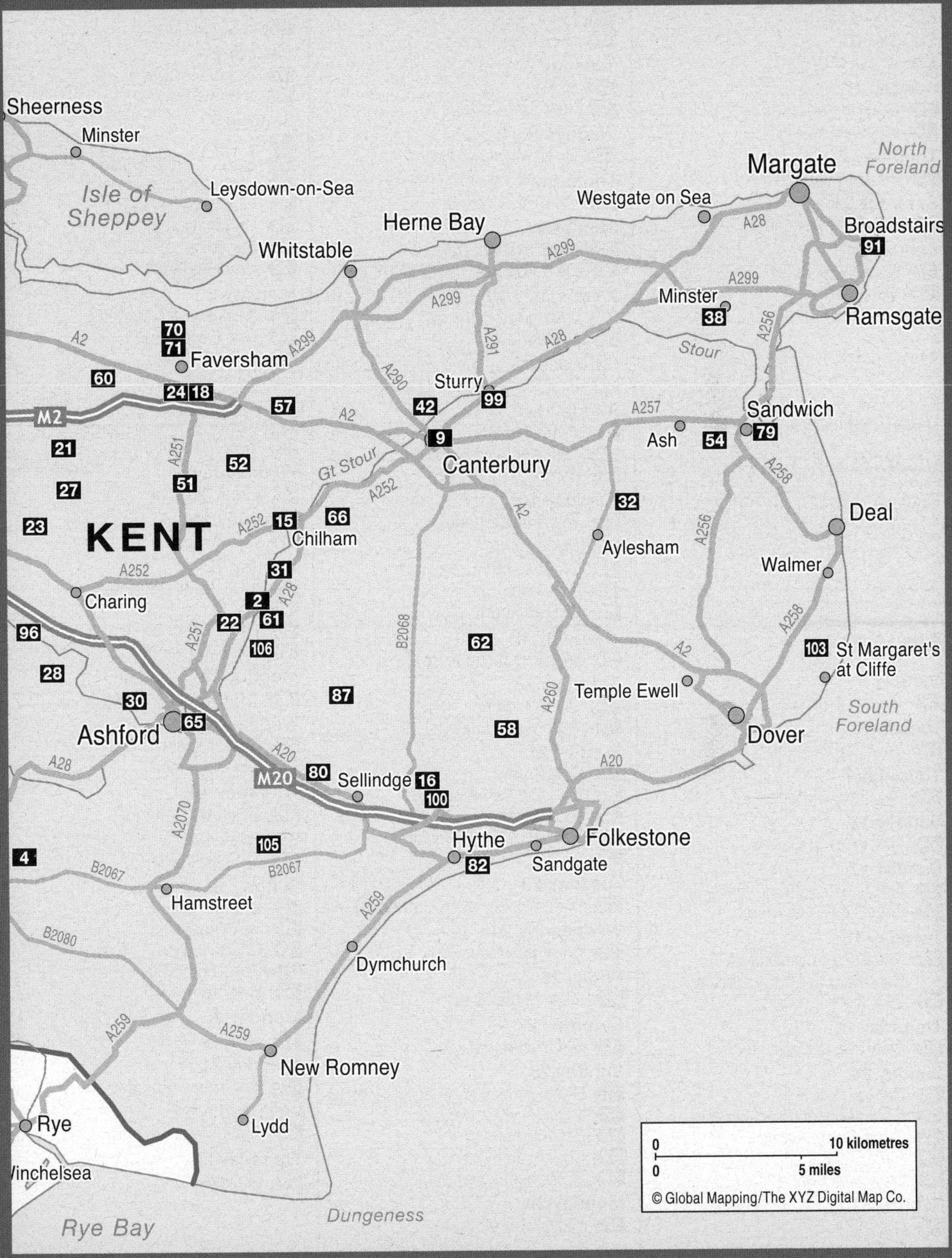
Sheerness
Minster
Isle of Sheppey
Leysdown-on-Sea
Whitstable
Herne Bay
Westgate on Sea
Margate
North Foreland
Broadstairs
91
Ramsgate
Minster
38
A28
A299
A256
Stour
A2
70
71
Faversham
A299
60
24
18
M2
57
A2
A290
A291
Sturry
99
42
9
A257
Sandwich
79
Ash
54
Canterbury
A258
21
A251
52
51
Gt Stour
A252
27
66
15
Chilham
A2
32
Aylesham
A256
Deal
Walmer
23
KENT
A252
31
Charing
2
A28
22
61
A251
106
B2068
62
A258
96
28
30
87
A260
A2
Temple Ewell
103
St Margaret's at Cliffe
South Foreland
Ashford
65
58
Dover
A28
A20
A20
M20
80
Sellindge
16
100
A2070
105
Hythe
82
Folkestone
Sandgate
4
B2067
B2067
Hamstreet
A259
B2080
Dymchurch
A259
A259
New Romney
Rye
Lydd
Winchelsea
Rye Bay
Dungeness
0
10 kilometres
0
5 miles
© Global Mapping/The XYZ Digital Map Co.

Opening Dates

February

Saturday 2
88 Spring Platt

Sunday 3
88 Spring Platt

Sunday 10
47 Knowle Hill Farm

Sunday 17
18 Copton Ash
56 Mere House

Thursday 21
8 Broadview Gardens

Saturday 23
107 Yew Tree Cottage

Sunday 24
47 Knowle Hill Farm
56 Mere House
107 Yew Tree Cottage

We will welcome you to explore, have a gardening chat . . .

March

Sunday 3
34 Great Comp Garden

Tuesday 5
107 Yew Tree Cottage

Thursday 7
107 Yew Tree Cottage

Sunday 10
34 Great Comp Garden

Sunday 17
32 Goodnestone Park Gardens
34 Great Comp Garden

Tuesday 19
79 The Secret Gardens of Sandwich at The Salutation
107 Yew Tree Cottage

Thursday 21
107 Yew Tree Cottage

Sunday 24
18 Copton Ash
30 Godinton House & Gardens
34 Great Comp Garden
56 Mere House
92 Stonewall Park

Sunday 31
18 Copton Ash
30 Godinton House & Gardens
34 Great Comp Garden
52 Luton House

April

Monday 1
18 Copton Ash
56 Mere House
68 Parsonage Oasts

Tuesday 2
46 Knole
107 Yew Tree Cottage

Wednesday 3
35 Great Maytham Hall

Thursday 4
107 Yew Tree Cottage

Sunday 7
31 Godmersham Park
67 Orchard End

Wednesday 10
35 Great Maytham Hall
53 Marle Place

Saturday 13
24 East Kent Weekend Group

Sunday 14
2 Bilting House
24 East Kent Weekend Group
68 Parsonage Oasts

Tuesday 16
107 Yew Tree Cottage

Wednesday 17
35 Great Maytham Hall
43 Hole Park
63 Old Buckhurst

Thursday 18
107 Yew Tree Cottage

Saturday 20
63 Old Buckhurst
99 Watergate House

Sunday 21
4 Boldshaves
27 Frith Old Farmhouse
63 Old Buckhurst
73 Potmans Heath House
74 11 Raymer Road

Tuesday 23
75 Riverhill Himalayan Gardens

Wednesday 24
35 Great Maytham Hall

Friday 26
85 Sissinghurst Castle

Saturday 27
63 Old Buckhurst

Sunday 28
6 Bradbourne House and Gardens
7 1 Brickwall Cottages
18 Copton Ash
44 Honnington Farm
90 St Michael's Gardens

Monday 29
7 1 Brickwall Cottages

May

Wednesday 1
35 Great Maytham Hall
63 Old Buckhurst

Thursday 2
107 Yew Tree Cottage

Friday 3
91 3 Stone Road

Saturday 4
77 Rogers Rough
91 3 Stone Road

Sunday 5
7 1 Brickwall Cottages
27 Frith Old Farmhouse
63 Old Buckhurst
65 One Dering Road
77 Rogers Rough
80 Sandown
92 Stonewall Park

Monday 6
7 1 Brickwall Cottages
65 One Dering Road
77 Rogers Rough
80 Sandown

Tuesday 7
46 Knole
107 Yew Tree Cottage

Wednesday 8
35 Great Maytham Hall

Saturday 11
63 Old Buckhurst

Sunday 12
7 1 Brickwall Cottages
37 Hall Place
48 Ladham House
94 Torry Hill

Monday 13
7 1 Brickwall Cottages

Wednesday 15
35 Great Maytham Hall
63 Old Buckhurst

Thursday 16
107 Yew Tree Cottage

Saturday 18
63 Old Buckhurst

Sunday 19
2 Bilting House
4 Boldshaves
12 Charts Edge
21 Doddington Place
43 Hole Park

Monday 20
81 Scotney Castle

Tuesday 21
107 Yew Tree Cottage

Wednesday 22
35 Great Maytham Hall

Thursday 23
89 Sprivers

Saturday 25
9 Canterbury Cathedral Gardens
76 Rock Farm
77 Rogers Rough

Sunday 26
7 1 Brickwall Cottages
9 Canterbury Cathedral Gardens
18 Copton Ash
19 Cottage Farm
23 Eagleswood
37 Hall Place
62 Old Bladbean Stud
65 One Dering Road
77 Rogers Rough
80 Sandown

Monday 27
7 1 Brickwall Cottages
18 Copton Ash
19 Cottage Farm
65 One Dering Road
77 Rogers Rough
80 Sandown

Wednesday 29
35 Great Maytham Hall
76 Rock Farm

June

Saturday 1
16 Churchfield
19 Cottage Farm
100 West Court Lodge
105 Wyckhurst

Sunday 2
16 Churchfield
19 Cottage Farm
44 Honnington Farm
61 Olantigh
62 Old Bladbean Stud
65 One Dering Road
86 Smiths Hall
90 St Michael's Gardens
100 West Court Lodge
105 Wyckhurst

Monday 3
60 Norton Court

Tuesday 4
19 Cottage Farm
46 Knole
60 Norton Court
107 Yew Tree Cottage

Wednesday 5
35 Great Maytham Hall
63 Old Buckhurst

Thursday 6
107 Yew Tree Cottage

Saturday 8
13 Chartwell
63 Old Buckhurst
70 Pheasant Barn
71 Pheasant Farm
105 Wyckhurst

Sunday 9
19 Cottage Farm
25 East Malling Gardens
70 Pheasant Barn
71 Pheasant Farm
96 Tram Hatch

Wednesday 12
10 Capel Manor Estate Gardens
35 Great Maytham Hall
63 Old Buckhurst
75 Riverhill Himalayan Gardens

National Gardens Weekend

Saturday 15
3 Bishopscourt
4 Boldshaves (Evening)
7 1 Brickwall Cottages
15 Chilham Castle
19 Cottage Farm
52 Luton House
58 Mounts Court Farmhouse
65 One Dering Road
76 Rock Farm
80 Sandown
99 Watergate House
102 Wickham Lodge
105 Wyckhurst

Sunday 16
2 Bilting House
3 Bishopscourt
4 Boldshaves
7 1 Brickwall Cottages
10 Capel Manor Estate Gardens
18 Copton Ash (Evening)
19 Cottage Farm
21 Doddington Place (Dawn opening)
27 Frith Old Farmhouse
31 Godmersham Park
37 Hall Place
52 Luton House
58 Mounts Court Farmhouse
59 Nettlestead Place
62 Old Bladbean Stud
65 One Dering Road
66 The Orangery
68 Parsonage Oasts
73 Potmans Heath House
78 St Clere
80 Sandown
94 Torry Hill
95 Townland
97 223 Tubbenden Lane
101 West Malling June Gardens
104 The World Garden at Lullingstone Castle
105 Wyckhurst

Monday 17
26 Emmetts Garden
60 Norton Court

Tuesday 18
60 Norton Court
107 Yew Tree Cottage

Wednesday 19
19 Cottage Farm
35 Great Maytham Hall
43 Hole Park
76 Rock Farm
98 Upper Pryors

Thursday 20
107 Yew Tree Cottage

Friday 21
30 Godinton House & Gardens

Saturday 22
19 Cottage Farm
47 Knowle Hill Farm (Evening)
50 Little Gables
55 Masons Farm (Evening)
63 Old Buckhurst
67 Orchard End
76 Rock Farm
77 Rogers Rough
84 Shipbourne Gardens

Wild flowers grown specially to attract bees . . .

Sunday 23
14 Chevening
19 Cottage Farm
29 Goddards Green
50 Little Gables
55 Masons Farm
62 Old Bladbean Stud
63 Old Buckhurst
67 Orchard End
77 Rogers Rough
84 Shipbourne Gardens
103 Windy Ridge
106 Wye Gardens

Wednesday 26
35 Great Maytham Hall
76 Rock Farm

Thursday 27
51 Lords
57 Mount Ephraim

Friday 28
79 The Secret Gardens of Sandwich at The Salutation

Saturday 29
19 Cottage Farm
28 Garden House
76 Rock Farm

Sunday 30
5 Boundes End
19 Cottage Farm
28 Garden House
36 115 Hadlow Road
51 Lords
83 Sevenoaks Allotments

July

Tuesday 2
46 Knole
107 Yew Tree Cottage

Wednesday 3
35 Great Maytham Hall
76 Rock Farm

Thursday 4
19 Cottage Farm
107 Yew Tree Cottage

Friday 5
85 Sissinghurst Castle

Saturday 6
76 Rock Farm
80 Sandown

Sunday 7
19 Cottage Farm
22 Downs Court
62 Old Bladbean Stud
65 One Dering Road
80 Sandown
86 Smiths Hall

Wednesday 10
21 Doddington Place
35 Great Maytham Hall
63 Old Buckhurst
76 Rock Farm

Endless surprises are here in abundance . . .

Thursday 11
45 Ightham Mote

Saturday 13
63 Old Buckhurst
70 Pheasant Barn
77 Rogers Rough

Sunday 14
77 Rogers Rough
94 Torry Hill
95 Townland
96 Tram Hatch

Tuesday 16
107 Yew Tree Cottage

Wednesday 17
35 Great Maytham Hall

Thursday 18
89 Sprivers
107 Yew Tree Cottage

Saturday 20
33 Gravesend Gardens Group
63 Old Buckhurst
67 Orchard End

Sunday 21
1 Bexon Manor
33 Gravesend Gardens Group
42 Highlands
58 Mounts Court Farmhouse
63 Old Buckhurst
65 One Dering Road
67 Orchard End
95 Townland

Wednesday 24
35 Great Maytham Hall
63 Old Buckhurst

Sunday 28
1 Bexon Manor
29 Goddards Green
47 Knowle Hill Farm
62 Old Bladbean Stud
66 The Orangery

Wednesday 31
35 Great Maytham Hall

August

Thursday 1
107 Yew Tree Cottage

Sunday 4
1 Bexon Manor
49 Leydens
63 Old Buckhurst

Tuesday 6
46 Knole
107 Yew Tree Cottage

Wednesday 7
35 Great Maytham Hall

Saturday 10
80 Sandown
91 3 Stone Road

Sunday 11
20 Cutlass Cottage
65 One Dering Road
80 Sandown
91 3 Stone Road
96 Tram Hatch

Wednesday 14
35 Great Maytham Hall
53 Marle Place

Thursday 15
107 Yew Tree Cottage

Friday 16
15 Chilham Castle (Evening)

Saturday 17
15 Chilham Castle

Sunday 18
20 Cutlass Cottage
89 Sprivers

Tuesday 20
107 Yew Tree Cottage

Wednesday 21
35 Great Maytham Hall

Sunday 25
36 115 Hadlow Road
62 Old Bladbean Stud
65 One Dering Road

Monday 26
65 One Dering Road

Wednesday 28
35 Great Maytham Hall

Saturday 31
67 Orchard End
80 Sandown

September

Sunday 1
67 Orchard End
80 Sandown

Tuesday 3
107 Yew Tree Cottage

Wednesday 4
63 Old Buckhurst

Thursday 5
107 Yew Tree Cottage

Saturday 7
3 Bishopscourt
63 Old Buckhurst
80 Sandown

Sunday 8
3 Bishopscourt
12 Charts Edge
59 Nettlestead Place
62 Old Bladbean Stud
63 Old Buckhurst
80 Sandown
103 Windy Ridge

Wednesday 11
69 Penshurst Place

Saturday 14
40 Heronden
63 Old Buckhurst

Sunday 15
40 Heronden

Sunday 22
32 Goodnestone Park Gardens
62 Old Bladbean Stud

Friday 27
85 Sissinghurst Castle

Sunday 29
57 Mount Ephraim

October

Friday 4
79 The Secret Gardens of Sandwich at The Salutation

Sunday 6
43 Hole Park
62 Old Bladbean Stud

Sunday 20
23 Eagleswood
56 Mere House

Sunday 27
21 Doddington Place

February 2014

Saturday 8

- 88 Spring Platt

Sunday 9

- 88 Spring Platt

Sunday 16

- 18 Copton Ash
- 56 Mere House

Sunday 23

- 56 Mere House

Gardens open to the public

- 8 Broadview Gardens
- 12 Charts Edge
- 13 Chartwell
- 15 Chilham Castle
- 17 Cobham Hall
- 21 Doddington Place
- 26 Emmetts Garden
- 30 Godinton House & Gardens
- 32 Goodnestone Park Gardens
- 34 Great Comp Garden
- 41 Hever Castle & Gardens
- 43 Hole Park
- 45 Ightham Mote
- 46 Knole
- 53 Marle Place
- 57 Mount Ephraim
- 63 Old Buckhurst
- 69 Penshurst Place
- 75 Riverhill Himalayan Gardens
- 79 The Secret Gardens of Sandwich at The Salutation
- 81 Scotney Castle
- 85 Sissinghurst Castle
- 89 Sprivers
- 104 The World Garden at Lullingstone Castle

By appointment only

- 11 3 Chainhurst Cottages
- 38 Haven
- 39 Haydown
- 54 Marshborough Farmhouse
- 64 Old Orchard
- 72 Placketts Hole
- 82 Sea Close
- 87 South Hill Farm
- 93 Timbers

Also open by Appointment ☎

- 2 Bilting House
- 5 Boundes End
- 7 1 Brickwall Cottages
- 10 Church View, Capel Manor Estate Gardens
- 10 The Courtyard, Capel Manor Estate Gardens
- 16 Churchfield
- 18 Copton Ash
- 22 Downs Court
- 23 Eagleswood
- 24 Bayfield Farm, East Kent Weekend Group
- 27 Frith Old Farmhouse
- 29 Goddards Green
- 31 Godmersham Park
- 35 Great Maytham Hall
- 36 115 Hadlow Road
- 42 Highlands
- 44 Honnington Farm
- 47 Knowle Hill Farm
- 51 Lords
- 52 Luton House
- 58 Mounts Court Farmhouse
- 60 Norton Court
- 65 One Dering Road
- 66 The Orangery
- 67 Orchard End
- 68 Parsonage Oasts
- 70 Pheasant Barn
- 73 Potmans Heath House
- 76 Rock Farm
- 77 Rogers Rough
- 80 Sandown
- 88 Spring Platt
- 94 Torry Hill
- 100 West Court Lodge
- 105 Wyckhurst
- 106 Mistral, Wye Gardens

Garden House

The Gardens

109 ADDINGTON ROAD
See London

BARNARDS FARM
See Essex

BATEMAN'S
See Sussex

1 BEXON MANOR

Hawks Hill Lane, Bredgar ME9 8HE. Mr & Mrs Robert Reeves. *3m S of Sittingbourne. B2163 at Bredgar, turn into Bexon Lane at church. Approx 1m turn R into Hawks Hill Lane.* Home-made & Cream teas. **Adm £4, chd free.** **Suns 21, 28 July; 4 Aug (1.30-5).**
2 acres of garden, divided into a series of rooms. Clipped yew hedges, topiary, borders with a wide variety of unusual annuals grown from seed, perennials, roses, many colourful shrubs. Terrace (for delicious home-made teas) overlooking walled kitchen garden with dwarf yew squares filled with organic vegetables, flowers, roses, herbs and bamboo. Rose-covered gazebo, water feature. 5-acre woodland walk. Paths slippery when wet.

2 BILTING HOUSE

nr Ashford TN25 4HA. Mr John Erle-Drax, 020 7629 5161, jdrax@marlboroughfineart.com. *5m NE of Ashford. A28, 9m from Canterbury. Wye 1½ m.* Home-made teas. **Adm £4, chd free. Suns 14 Apr; 19 May; 16 June (2-6). Visitors also welcome by appt 10 Apr to 30 June.**

6-acre garden with ha-ha set in beautiful part of Stour Valley. Wide variety of rhododendrons, azaleas and ornamental shrubs. Woodland walk with spring bulbs. Mature arboretum with recent planting of specimen trees. Rose garden and herbaceous borders. Conservatory.

3 NEW BISHOPSCOURT

24 St Margarets Street, Rochester ME1 1TS. Mrs Bridget Langstaff. *Central Rochester, nr castle & cathedral. House is on St Margarets St at junction with The Vines. Rochester rail station 10 mins walk. Disabled parking only at Bishopscourt, many car parks within 5-7 mins walk.* Home-made teas. **Adm £3, chd free. Sat 15 June (11-4); Sun 16 June (1-5); Sat 7 Sept (11-4); Sun 8 Sept (1-5).**

The residence of the Bishop of Rochester, this is a peaceful 1-acre garden in the heart of Rochester with views of the castle from a raised 'lookout'. Clipped yew hedges, rose garden, gravel garden, wild flowers and mixed borders with a variety of shrubs perennials and grasses. Greenhouse and small vegetable garden. Most of garden is accessible by wheelchair.

4 BOLDSHAVES

Woodchurch, nr Ashford, Kent TN26 3RA. Mr & Mrs Peregrine Massey, 01233 860302, masseypd@hotmail.co.uk, www.boldshaves.co.uk. *Between Woodchurch & High Halden off Redbrook St. From A28 towards Ashford, turn R at village green in High Halden. 2nd R, Redbrook St, towards Woodchurch, before R on unmarked lane after ½ m. After ½ m, R through brick entrance. Ignore oast house on L, follow signs to car park. If approaching through Woodchurch, past church, L on Susan's Hill, next R, then L through brick entrance (as above).* Home-made teas in C18 barn. **Adm £5, chd free (share to Kent Minds). Suns 21 Apr; 19 May (2-6). Evening Opening, wine, Sat 15 June (6-9); Sun 16 June (2-6). For other opening times and information, please phone or see garden website.**

7-acre garden with a number of new features being developed. Partly terraced, S-facing, with ornamental trees and shrubs, walled garden, Italian Garden, Diamond Jubilee Garden, herbaceous borders (including flame bed and red borders), bluebell walks in April, woodland and ponds. Featured in Good Gardens Guide. Grass paths.

With views of the castle from a raised 'lookout' . . .

5 BOUNDES END

2 St Lawrence Avenue, Bidborough, Tunbridge Wells TN4 0XB. Carole & Mike Marks, 01892 542233, carole.marks@btinternet.com, www.boundesendgarden.co.uk. *Between Tonbridge and Tunbridge Wells off A26. Take B2176 Bidborough Ridge signed to Penshurst. Take 1st L into Darnley Drive, then 1st R into St Lawrence Ave.* Home-made teas. **Adm £2.50, chd free (share to Hospice in the Weald). Sun 30 June (11-5). Visitors and groups of up to 20 also welcome by appt July to Aug.**

Garden, designed by owners, on an unusually-shaped ⅓ acre plot formed from 2 triangles of land. Front garden features raised beds, and the main garden divided into a formal area with terrace, pebble bed and 2 pergolas, an informal area in woodland setting with interesting features and specimen trees. Plenty of places to sit and enjoy the garden. Some uneven ground in lower garden.

6 BRADBOURNE HOUSE AND GARDENS

New Road, East Malling ME19 6DZ. East Malling Trust, www.bradbournehouse.org.uk. *4m NW of Maidstone. Entrance is E of New Rd, which runs from Larkfield on A20 S to E Malling.* **Adm £3.50, chd free. Sun 28 Apr (2-5).**

Demonstration fruit plantings within a walled former kitchen garden. Apple and pear trees pruned into 25 different forms incl pyramid, goblet, le bateau, fan, arch, arcure, espalier, table, vase etc. Examples of 47 varieties of apple, 28 varieties of pear and individuals of medlar, nectarine, peach and fig. Queen Anne period house, science exhibits, music, beekeeping exhibits, produce and plant sales. Featured on 'Sunday Gardening', BBC Radio Kent's popular weekly gardening programme.

7 1 BRICKWALL COTTAGES

Frittenden, Cranbrook TN17 2DH. Mrs Sue Martin, 01580 852425, sue.martin@talktalk.net, www.geumcollection.co.uk. *6m NW of Tenterden. E of A229 between Cranbrook & Staplehurst & W of A274 between Biddenden & Headcorn. Park in village & walk along footpath opp school.* Home-made teas. **Adm £3.50, chd free. Suns, Mons: 28, 29 Apr; 5, 6, 12, 13, 26, 27 May; Sat 15, Sun 16 June (2-5.30). Visitors & groups of up to 30 also welcome by appt from 21 Apr to 2 June.**

Although less than ¼ acre, the garden gives the impression of being much larger as it is made up of several 'rooms' all intensively planted with a wide range of hardy perennials, bulbs and shrubs, with about 100 geums which comprise the National Collection planted throughout the garden. Pergolas provide supports for climbing plants and there is a small formal pond. Featured in RHS The Garden, Country Life, Gardens Illustrated and The English Garden.

NCH

8 ◆ BROADVIEW GARDENS

Hadlow College, Hadlow TN11 0AL, www.broadviewgardens.co.uk. *4m NE of Tonbridge. On A26 9m SW of Maidstone.* **Adm £3, chd free. For NGS: Thur 21 Feb (10-5). For other opening times and information, please phone or see garden website.**

10 acres of ornamental planting in attractive landscape setting; 100m double mixed border, island beds with mixed plantings, lakes and water gardens; series of demonstration gardens incl Italian, Oriental and Sutton's vegetable garden. National Collections of *Anemone japonica* and hellebores. Wheelchair access limited in wet weather.

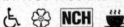

NCH

GROUP OPENING

9 CANTERBURY CATHEDRAL GARDENS

Canterbury CT1 2EP, www.canterbury-cathedral.org. *Canterbury Cathedral Precincts. Enter Precincts by main Christchurch gate.* ***No access for cars: please use park & ride and public car parks.*** Gardens will be signed within Precincts. Home-made teas at 15 The Precincts. **Combined adm £5, chd free. Sat 25 May (11-5); Sun 26 May (2-5).**

ARCHDEACONRY
The Archdeacon, Sheila Watson

THE DEANERY
The Dean

15 THE PRECINCTS
Canon Treasurer

19 THE PRECINCTS
Canon Irvine

22 THE PRECINCTS
Canon Clare Edwards

A unique opportunity to visit five Canonical gardens within the historic Precincts of Canterbury Cathedral. Enjoy the Deanery Garden with its small wild meadow and orchard, unusual medlar tree, vegetable garden and wild fowl enclosure. The Archdeaconry incl the ancient mulberry tree, contrasting traditional and new ongoing modern planting. The three further Precinct gardens, varied in style, offer sweeping herbaceous banks, delightful enclosed spaces, and areas planted to attract and support birds, insects and wildlife. All the gardens now incl vegetable plots personal to each house. Step back in time and see the monastic dormitory ruins and see the herb garden, which reflects the use of herbs for medicinal purposes in the Middle Ages. The walled memorial garden has wonderful wisteria, formal roses, mixed border and the stone war memorial at its centre. Gardeners' plant stall. Wheelchair access to all gardens but Archdeaconry has separate wheelchair access.

Stunning Mediterranean courtyard garden using tranquil-coloured planting . . .

GROUP OPENING

10 CAPEL MANOR ESTATE GARDENS

Grovehurst Lane, Horsmonden TN12 8BG. *Approx 8m SE of Tonbridge. Follow yellow NGS signs in Horsmonden village, head out of village towards Goudhurst, leaving Gun and Spitroast PH on your R. Tickets available at both gardens.* Home-made teas at The Courtyard. **Combined adm £5, chd free. Wed 12, Sun 16 June (12-5).**

NEW **CHURCH VIEW**
Mr & Mrs H Tangen
Groups of 10+ also welcome by appt June to Sept, one weeks notice required.
01892 722465
christinatangen01@gmail.com

THE COURTYARD
Mr & Mrs Iain Stewart
Groups of 10+ also welcome by appt June to Aug, one week's notice required.
01892 722769
georgina.stewart@btinternet.com

Horsmonden is a lively, picturesque village which has been shaped by three main industries: weaving, hop growing and gun-founding. The Courtyard is a mid C19 Italianate garden, forming a substantial part of the Capel Manor Estate built for the Austen family (relatives of the renowned Jane Austen) of Horsmonden. The Courtyard gardens cover several acres of formal gardens and woodland including a stunning Mediterranean courtyard garden using tranquil-coloured planting with a fountain at its centre. In addition there is a small formal raised-bed garden set within wrought iron gates at the entrance to the courtyard, beautiful borders surrounding the courtyard with a lovely selection of viburnum and hydrangea, a vivacious herbaceous border, a swimming pool garden, a rose garden, a vegetable garden and a large area of formal woodland garden with a lovely mixture of trees and shrubs. There are many seating areas. The Courtyard is opening in conjunction with Church View next door. Amazing tea-room situated in the Courtyard with plenty of seating and a delicious selection of cakes and scones. Most of the gardens can be seen by wheelchair users but the paths are gravel and therefore not ideal.

11 3 CHAINHURST COTTAGES

Dairy Lane, Marden, Tonbridge TN12 9SU. Heather & Richard Scott, 01622 820483, heatherscott@waitrose.com. *6m S of Maidstone, 3m N of Marden. From Maidstone take A229. At Stile Bridge Inn fork R, then 1st R where NGS signs appear.* **Adm £5, chd free. Visitors welcome by appt.**

The garden surrounding this Kent peg tiled cottage is formally designed with relaxed cottage style planting in shades of soft purple, pink and burgundy. Low box hedging, brick paths, hornbeam and beech hedging divide the garden into small areas making the whole feel larger than it is. Raised vegetable beds contain cutting flowers as well as vegetables and step over apples. An informal gravelled area surrounded by a brick wall marks the end of the garden.

THE CHALET
See Surrey

12 ◆ CHARTS EDGE

Westerham TN16 1PL. Mr & Mrs J Bigwood, 07833 385169, www.chartsedgegardens.co.uk. *½ m S of Westerham, 4m N of Edenbridge. On B2026 towards Chartwell.* **Adm £4.50, chd free. For NGS: Suns 19 May; 8 Sept (2-5). For other opening times and information, please phone or see garden website.**

8-acre hillside garden being updated by present owners. Large collection of rhododendrons, azaleas and magnolias; among specimen trees, 2 copper beech recorded as the tallest in UK. Majority of plants labelled, rock garden, water gardens, rainbow borders and rill. The origin of plants from around the world. Fine views over N Downs. Partial access for wheelchair users.

♿ 🐕 ✿ ☕

13 ◆ CHARTWELL
Mapleton Road, nr Westerham TN16 1PS. National Trust, www.nationaltrust.org.uk. *4m N of Edenbridge. 2m S of Westerham. Fork L off B2026 after 1½ m.* **Adm £6.80, chd £3.30. For NGS: Sat 8 June (10-4). For other opening times and information, please see garden website.**
Informal gardens on hillside with glorious views over Weald of Kent. Water garden and lakes together with red-brick wall built by Sir Winston Churchill, former owner of Chartwell. Avenue of golden roses runs down the centre of a productive kitchen garden. Hard paths to Lady Churchill's rose garden and the terrace. Some steep slopes and steps.

♿ 🐕 ✿ ☕

CHAUFFEUR'S FLAT
See Surrey

14 CHEVENING
Chevening nr Sevenoaks TN14 6HG. The Board of Trustees of the Chevening Estate, www.cheveninghouse.com. *4m NW of Sevenoaks. Turn N off A25 at Sundridge T-lights on to B2211; at Chevening Xrds 1½ m turn L.* Home-made teas. **Adm £4, chd £1. Sun 23 June (2-5).**
27 acres with lawns and woodland garden, lake, maze, formal rides, parterre. Gentle slopes, gravel paths throughout.

♿ 🐕 ✿ ☕

15 ◆ CHILHAM CASTLE
Chilham CT4 8DB. Mr & Mrs Wheeler, 01227 733100, www.chilham-castle.co.uk. *6m SW of Canterbury, 7 m NE of Ashford, centre of Chilham Village. Follow signs for garden open day from A 28 or A252 up to Chilham village square, and through main gates of Chilham Castle.* **Adm £5, chd free. For NGS: Sat 15 June (2-5). Evening Opening, light refreshments, Fri 16 Aug (5-8); Sat 17 Aug (2-5). For other opening times and information, please phone or see garden website.**
The garden surrounds Jacobean house 1616 (not open). C17 terraces with herbaceous borders. Topiary frames the magnificent views with lake walk below. Extensive kitchen and cutting garden beyond spring bulb filled Quiet Garden. Established trees and ha-ha lead onto park. Featured in Country Life and Independent. Restricted wheelchair access.

♿ 🐕 ✿ ☕

Knowle Hill Farm

16 CHURCHFIELD
Pilgrims Way, Postling, Hythe CT21 4EY. Mr & Mrs C Clark, 01303 863558, coulclark@hotmail.com. *2m NW of Hythe. From M20 J11 turn S onto A20. 1st L after ½ m on bend take rd signed Lyminge. 1st L into Postling.* Home-made teas in the Village hall. **Adm £3, chd free. Sat 1, Sun 2 June (1-5). Combined adm with West Court Lodge £5, chd free. Visitors also welcome by appt Apr to Aug.**
At the base of the Downs springs rising in this garden form the source of the East Stour. Two large areas are home to wildfowl and fish and the banks have been planted with drifts of primula and large leaved herbaceous. The rest of the 5-acre garden is a Kent cobnut platt and vegetable garden, large grass areas and naturally planted borders with an area under development as a prairie garden. Postling Church open for visitors. Areas around water may be slippery. Children must be carefully supervised.

🐕 ✿ ☕ ☎

17 ◆ COBHAM HALL
Cobham DA12 3BL. Mr D Standen (Bursar), 01474 823371, www.cobhamhall.com. *5m W of Rochester. 8m E of M25 J2. Take A2 to exit signed Cobham, Shorne, Higham. Disregard Sat Nav directions to Lodge Lane; entrance to Cobham Hall on Brewers Rd 100m S of A2.* **For opening times, dates and information, please phone or see www.ngs.org.uk.**
c1584 brick mansion and gardens of historical importance, now a boarding and day school for girls. Herbaceous borders, formal parterres, C17 garden walls, yew hedges and lime avenue. Humphry Repton design parkland, veteran trees with many wild flowers. Organic woodland areas returned to glades with parkland vistas, garden follies restored. Pleasure Grounds around Main Hall. Gravel and slab paths through gardens. Land uneven and many slopes to contend with.

♿ 🐕 ☕

18 COPTON ASH
105 Ashford Road, Faversham ME13 8XW. Drs Tim & Gillian Ingram, 01795 535919, coptonash@yahoo.co.uk, www.coptonash.plus.com. *1/2 m S of Faversham. On A251 Faversham to Ashford rd, opp E-bound J6 with M2.* Home-made teas. **Adm £3, chd free. Sun 17 Feb (12-4); Suns, Mons: 24, 31 Mar; 1, 28 Apr; 26, 27 May (2-5.30). Evening Opening Sun 16 June (5-8); Special snowdrop and hellebore opening Sun 16 Feb 2014. Also open 13, 14 April with East Kent Group. Visitors also welcome by appt Mar to Oct.**
Garden grown out of a love and fascination with plants from an early age. Contains very wide collection incl many rarities and newly introduced species raised from wild seed. Special interest in woodland flowers, snowdrops and hellebores with flowering trees and shrubs of spring. Wide range of drought-tolerant plants. Raised beds with choice alpines and bulbs. Article on Yucca whipplei in RHS 'The Garden'. Gravel drive and some narrow grass paths.

19 COTTAGE FARM
Cackets Lane, Cudham TN14 7QG. Phil Baxter, www.cottagefarmgardens.com. *5m NW of Sevenoaks, 4m SW of Orpington. Sign for Cudham from Green-Street-Green r'about on A21. 3m into village, turn L past garage. 2nd block cottages on R. Entrance through working farmyard.* Cream teas. **Adm £5, chd free (share to Harris Hospiscare). Sun 26, Mon 27 May, Sat 1, Sun 2, Tue 4, Sun 9, Sat 15*, Sun 16, Wed 19, Sat 22, Sun 23, Sat 29, Sun 30 June, Thur 4, Sun 7 July (1.30-5). *Sat 15 June opening with BBQ, extra £5.**
Cottage garden of approx 1-acre. No lawns! Self-sufficient vegetable and fruit gardens, with raised beds growing vegetables for exhibition. Tropical garden, cut flower garden, fernery, greenhouses with tender and tropical fruits and flowers; rose-covered pergolas and wildlife ponds. Large rockery, grass borders and National collection of rhipsalis cactus. Created and maintained by owner. Massive sale of plants. Fit pusher required for wheelchair.
NCH

20 NEW CUTLASS COTTAGE
Langton Road, Speldhurst, Tunbridge Wells TN3 0NR. Mr & Mrs Stephen & Christine Lee, www.speldhurstnurseries.co.uk. *3m W of Tunbridge Wells. Cutlass Cottage is set within Speldhurst Nurseries in Speldhurst village. Take A264 from Tunbridge Wells to Langton Green. Turn R by Hare PH into Speldhurst Rd (leads into Langton Rd). Cutlass Cottage 1.2m on R.* Home-made teas. **Adm £4, chd free. Suns 11, 18 Aug (11-5).**
Garden created and maintained solely by resident owners of adjacent plant nursery over the past 13 years from what was pastureland. The challenge was to sympathetically link their new cottage with surrounding area of outstanding natural beauty. Its design reflects a passion for outdoor entertaining and includes formal pond, mixed borders, picking garden and a romantic 'cosy-up' sunken terrace. Access for wheelchairs to most parts of garden.

Its design reflects a passion for outdoor entertaining . . . a romantic 'cosy-up' sunken terrace . . .

21 ◆ DODDINGTON PLACE
nr Sittingbourne ME9 0BB. Mr & Mrs Richard Oldfield, 01795 886101, www.doddingtonplacegardens.co.uk. *6m SE of Sittingbourne. From A20 turn N opp Lenham or from A2 turn S at Teynham or Ospringe (Faversham), all 4m.* **Adm £5.50, chd £1. For NGS: Sun 19 May (11-5); Early Opening Sun 16 June (6am-5pm); Wed 10 July, Sun 27 Oct (11-5). For other opening times and information, please phone or see garden website.**
10-acre garden, landscaped with wide views; trees and clipped yew hedges; woodland garden with azaleas and rhododendrons; Edwardian rock garden recently renovated (not wheelchair accessible); formal garden with mixed borders. Gothic folly. **Dawn opening for photographers and birdwatchers 16 June from 6am.**

22 DOWNS COURT
Church Lane, Boughton Aluph, Ashford TN25 4EU. Mr & Mrs Bay Green, 07984 558945, bay@baygee.com. *4m NE of Ashford. From A28 Ashford or Canterbury, after Wye Xrds take next turn NW to Boughton Aluph Church. Fork R at pillar box, garden only drive on R.* **Adm £4.50, chd free. Sun 7 July (2-5). Visitors also welcome by appt May to July.**
Three-acre downland garden on alkaline soil with fine trees, mature yew and box hedges, mixed borders with many unusual plants. Shrub roses and rose arch pathway, small parterre. Sweeping lawns and lovely views over surrounding countryside. Opening on Sun 7 July in association with Hardy Plant Society. There will be a Plant Fair.

36 DOWNS HILL
See London

23 EAGLESWOOD
Slade Road, Warren Street, Lenham, Maidstone ME17 2EG. Mike & Edith Darvill, 01622 858702, mike.darvill@btinternet.com. *Going E on A20 nr Lenham, L into Hubbards Hill for approx 1m then 2nd L into Slade Rd. Garden 150yds on R.* Light refreshments. **Adm £3.50, chd free (share to Demelza House Hospice). Suns 26 May; 20 Oct (11-5). Visitors also welcome by appt.**
1½-acre plantsman's garden situated high on N Downs, developed over the past 25yrs. Wide range of trees and shrubs (many unusual), herbaceous material and woodland plants grown to give yr-round interest, particularly in spring and for autumn colour. Some gravel areas, grass paths may be slippery when wet.

"Lemon drizzle cake, Victoria sponge ... yummy!"

GROUP OPENING

24 NEW ▶ EAST KENT WEEKEND GROUP
ME13 8XW, www.alpinegardensociety.net. *1/2 m S of Faversham. On A251, opp E-bound exit of M2 J6.* Home-made teas. **Combined adm £6, chd free (share to Alpine Garden Society Kent). Sat 13, Sun 14 Apr (2-5).**

BAYFIELD FARM
Painters Forstal. Mr & Mrs John Moor.
S on Brogdale Rd from A2 at Faversham signed Painters Forstal
Visitors also welcome by appt May.
01795 532367

NEW ▶ 16 CHERRY ORCHARD
Canterbury, CT4 8BQ. Mr Paul Powis.
From A28 take Shalmsford Rd to Old Wives Lees, L down Cobb's Hill, 1st R into Cherry Orchard

COPTON ASH
Drs Tim & Gillian Ingram
(See separate entry)

NEW ▶ 34 CROSS ROAD
Deal, CT14 9LB. Mr Peter Jacob & Mrs Margaret Wilson.
Take A258 from Dover to Deal. In Upper Walmer turn L into Station Rd. Under railway bridge, Cross Rd is 2nd R

MOUNTS COURT FARMHOUSE
Graham & Geraldine Fish
(See separate entry)

NEW ▶ 43 THE RIDINGS
Whitstable, CT5 3QE. David & Sylvie Sayers.
From r'about on A2990 at Chestfield, turn onto Chestfield Rd, 5th turning on L onto Polo Way which leads into The Ridings

6 gardens owned by Alpine Garden Society members, spread from Faversham/Whitstable to the east coast. Bayfield Farm, 3/4 -acre garden developed over 50yrs from an open site to densely planted woodland, informal, romantic garden! Mix of trees, shrubs, herbaceous, annuals & grasses. 16 Cherry Orchard, charming small garden artistically planted with perennials and bulbs. Rock garden. Copton Ash, features alpines grown in sand, raised beds & woodland plants under fruit trees, incl rare species raised from seed. 34 Cross Road, combines artistic sensibility with an extensive variety of plants. 1/3 -acre plantsman's garden. Daphnes, hardy geraniums, herbaceous beds, unusual trees, shrubs & alpines. Mounts Court Farm, developed from 1 1/2 -acre paddock over 30yrs in an Area of Outstanding Natural Beauty at a height of 150 metres. Trees, shrubs & grasses. Winding paths through densely planted borders varying from herbaceous to woodland. Pond and bog garden. 43 The Ridings, delightful small garden brimming with interesting plants. Gravel garden, raised alpine beds, bulbs & borders with unusual perennials and shrubs. Gravel drive and some narrow grass paths.

♿ ✿ ☕

Delightful small garden brimming with interesting plants . . .

GROUP OPENING

25 ▶ EAST MALLING GARDENS
ME19 6AJ. *4m NW of Maidstone. S of A20 at Larkfield. Court Lodge is next to St James the Great in Church Walk, 1st L after entering village. Other three gardens are all in Chapel St. Parking at Institute car park, behind King and Queen PH.* Home-made teas at Ivy House Farm. **Combined adm £4.50, chd free (share to Heart of Kent Hospice & Blackthorn Trust). Sun 9 June (2-5).**

COURT LODGE
Church Walk. Mr & Mrs Gordon

IVY HOUSE FARM
42 Chapel Street. Jonathan & Mary Ann Colvile

THE LIMES
32 Chapel Street. Mr & Mrs R Butler

ORCHARD HOUSE
10 Chapel Street. Mr & Mrs J Dowling

Four gardens around the centre of the village show the varied interests of their gardeners. Opening for the first time in 2013, Court Lodge, Church Walk is a 2/3 -acre garden round a Queen Anne Grade II listed house with an C18 feel, specimen trees, vegetable garden, herbaceous borders and small pond. 10 Chapel Street is a 1/2 -acre family garden with lawns, herbaceous and shrub borders, herb and vegetable garden, small pond and orchard. Also opening for the first time The Limes, a 1 1/2 -acre private family garden surrounding a Grade II listed Georgian house. Traditional English cottage garden, walled herbaceous border, woodland garden, white bed, vegetable/kitchen garden. Lawns, rose and lavender border. Ivy House Farm, a half-timbered Grade II listed Tudor house, surrounded by a 2-acre formal garden, with a range of interest such as a courtyard garden, lawns, herbaceous borders, mature trees and shrubs, vegetable garden, water features and walled swimming pool garden. Limited wheelchair access at all gardens.

✿ ☕

26 ▶ ◆ EMMETTS GARDEN
Ide Hill, Sevenoaks TN14 6BA. National Trust, www.nationaltrust.org.uk. *5m SW of Sevenoaks. 1 1/2 m S of A25 on Sundridge-Ide Hill Rd. 1 1/2 m N of Ide Hill off B2042.* **Adm £7.30, chd £3. For NGS: Mon 17 June (10-4). For other opening times and information, please see garden website.**
5-acre hillside garden, with the highest tree top in Kent, noted for its fine collection of rare trees and flowering shrubs. The garden is particularly fine in spring, while a rose garden, rock garden and extensive planting of acers for autumn colour extend the interest throughout the season. Hard paths to the stable tea room and toilets. Some steep slopes.

♿ 🐕 ✿ ☕

FAIRLIGHT HALL
See Sussex

27 ▶ FRITH OLD FARMHOUSE
Frith Road, Otterden, Faversham ME13 0DD. Drs Gillian & Peter Regan, 01795 890556, peter.regan@virgin.net. *1/2 m off Lenham to Faversham rd. From A20 E of Lenham turn up Hubbards Hill, follow signs to Eastling. After 4m turn L signed Newnham, Doddington. From A2 in Faversham, turn S towards Brogdale and continue through Painters Forstal and Eastling. Turn R 1 1/2 m beyond Eastling.*

Home-made teas. **Adm £3.50, chd free. Suns 21 Apr; 5 May; 16 June (11-5). Visitors also welcome by appt Apr to Sept, please contact owners well in advance.**
A riot of plants growing together as if in the wild, developed over 30 years. No neat edges or formal beds, but a very wide range of unusual & interesting plants, together with trees and shrubs chosen for year-round appeal. Special interest in bulbs and woodland plants. Visitor comments - 'a plethora of plants', 'inspirational', 'a hidden gem'. Featured in Kent Life and RHS 'The Garden'.

28 GARDEN HOUSE

off Swan Lane, Surrenden, Pluckley TN27 0PR. Michael & Gillian Bushell. *7m W of Ashford. A20 between Ashford & Maidstone. Take turn to Pluckley at Charing Xrds. Proceed 3m and immed after sign for Pluckley and 30mph, L into Swan Lane. 1/2 m down hill, 1st entrance on R through high wall. SatNav not reliable, please follow yellow NGS signs.* Home-made teas. **Adm £4.50, chd free. Sat 29, Sun 30 June (12-6).**
Originally the kitchen garden to the Surrenden Dering Estate containing a 2-acre walled garden. Collection of magnolia, unusual specimen trees, yew topiary and an avenue of tulip trees. Recently planted parterre leads onto a cobnut walk underplanted with spring bulbs. Deep herbaceous beds and productive potager. Plenty of seating to enjoy the tranquillity of this garden.

29 GODDARDS GREEN

Angley Road, Cranbrook TN17 3LR. John & Linde Wotton, 01580 715507, jpwotton@gmail.com. *1/2 m SW of Cranbrook. On W of Angley Rd. (A229) at junction with High St, opposite War Memorial.* Home-made teas. **Adm £5, chd free. Suns: 23 June; 28 July (12-4.30). Visitors & groups of up to 30 also welcome by appt May to Sept.**
Garden of about 2 acres, surrounding beautiful 500yr-old clothier's hall (not open), laid out in 1920s and redesigned over past 18yrs to combine traditional and modern planting schemes. Fountain, rill and water garden, borders with bulbs, herbaceous plants, flowering shrubs and exotics, birch grove, grass border, pond, kitchen garden and mature mixed orchard. Also open 23 June Cranbrook Garden Safari.

30 ◆ GODINTON HOUSE & GARDENS

Godinton Lane, Ashford TN23 3BP. Godinton House Preservation Trust, 01233 643854, www.godinton-house-gardens.co.uk. *1 1/2 m W of Ashford. M20 J9 to Ashford. Take A20 towards Charing and Lenham, then follow brown tourist signs.* **Adm £5, chd free. For NGS: Suns: 24, 31 Mar; Fri 21 June (2-5.30). For other opening times and information, please phone or see garden website.**
13 acres complement the magnificent Jacobean house. Terraced lawns lead through herbaceous borders, rose garden and formal lily pond to intimate Italian Garden and large walled garden with delphiniums, potager, cut flowers and iris border. March/April the Wild Garden is a mass of daffodils, fritillaries, other spring flowers. June 21 NGS day during Delphinium Festival Week. Partial wheelchair access to the ground floor of house and most of the gardens.

31 GODMERSHAM PARK

Godmersham CT4 7DT. Mrs Fiona Sunley, 01227 730293. *5m NE of Ashford. Off A28, midway between Canterbury & Ashford.* Home-made teas. **Adm £5, chd free (share to Godmersham Church). Suns 7 Apr; 16 June (1-5). Visitors also welcome by appt.**
24 acres restored wilderness and formal gardens set around C18 mansion (not open). Topiary, rose garden, herbaceous borders, walled kitchen garden and recently restored Italian garden. Superb daffodils in spring and roses in June. Historical association with Jane Austen. Also visit the Heritage Centre. Deep gravel paths in walled garden.

32 ◆ GOODNESTONE PARK GARDENS

Wingham, Canterbury CT3 1PL. Margaret, Lady FitzWalter, 01304 840107, www.goodnestoneparkgardens.co.uk. *6m SE of Canterbury. Village lies S of B2046 from A2 to Wingham. Brown tourist signs off B2046.* **Adm £6, chd £2. For NGS: Suns 17 Mar; 22 Sept (12-5). For other opening times and information, please phone or see garden website.**
10-12 acres with good trees, woodland garden, snowdrops, spring bulbs and walled garden with old-fashioned roses. Connections with Jane Austen who stayed here.
2 arboretums planted in 1984 and 2001, gravel garden. Picnics allowed.

> Luscious planting along the rocky banks, fascinating water features . . .

GROUP OPENING

33 GRAVESEND GARDENS GROUP

DA12 1JZ. *From A2 (Gravesend Central exit) take A227 towards Gravesend. At T-lights turn R into Cross Lane W. At next T-lights turn L, straight over T-lights before Old Prince of Orange PH. 1st R into Leith Park Rd. L at Xrds into Sandy Bank Rd. (closest for parking). 68 South Hill Rd is at top of Sandy Bank Rd. For 58A Parrock Rd walk up Leith Park Rd. At T-junction, turn R and cross over. Garden is 70 yds on L. Additional parking 300yds on at Echo Square. Gardens 5 mins walk apart.* **Combined adm £3.50, chd free. Sat 20, Sun 21 July (12-5).**

58A PARROCK ROAD
Mr Barry Bowen

68 SOUTH HILL ROAD
Judith Hathrill

Enjoy two lovely gardens, very different in character, close to Windmill Hill which has extensive views over the Thames estuary. 58A Parrock Road is a beautiful, well-established town garden, approx 120ft x 40ft, nurtured by owner for 50yrs. There is a stream running down to a pond, luscious planting along the rocky banks, fascinating water features, mature trees and shrubs, magnificent display of hostas and succulents. 68 South Hill Road is an award-winning wildlife garden, showing that wildlife friendly gardens need not be 'wild'. Colourful herbaceous borders, flowers, herbs and salads in the potager, raised vegetable and herb beds, ferns, grasses and colourful containers. Mediterranean vegetables thrive in the greenhouse, two ponds planted with native species. Plants for sale and teas at both gardens. Jazz Trio at 58A Parrock Road. Regret neither garden has wheelchair access due to steps.

34 ◆ GREAT COMP GARDEN

Comp Lane, Platt, nr Borough Green, Sevenoaks TN15 8QS. Great Comp Charitable Trust, 01732 885094, www.greatcompgarden.co.uk. *7m E of Sevenoaks. A20 at Wrotham Heath, take Seven Mile Lane, B2016; at 1st Xrds turn R; garden on L ½ m.* **Adm £6, chd £2.50. For NGS: Suns 3, 10, 17, 24, 31 Mar (11-5). For other opening times and information, please phone or see garden website.**

Skilfully designed 7-acre garden of exceptional beauty. Spacious setting of well-maintained lawns and paths lead visitors through plantsman's collection of trees, shrubs, heathers and herbaceous plants. Good autumn colour. Early C17 house (not open). Magnolias, hellebores and snowflakes (leucojum), hamamellis and winter flowering heathers are great feature in spring. A great variety of perennials in summer incl salvias, dahlias and crocosmias.

GREAT DIXTER HOUSE, GARDENS & NURSERIES

See Sussex

35 GREAT MAYTHAM HALL

Maytham Road, Rolvenden, Tenterden TN17 4NE. The Sunley Group, 01580 241346, great.maytham@sunley.co.uk. *3m from Tenterden. Maytham Rd off A28 at Rolvenden Church, ½ m from village on R.* Home-made teas. **Adm £5, chd free. Every Wed 1 Apr to 31 Aug (1-4). Visitors also welcome by appt Apr to Oct.**

Lutyens-designed gardens famous for having inspired Frances Hodgson Burnett to write 'The Secret Garden' (pre-Lutyens). Parkland, woodland with bluebells. Walled garden with herbaceous beds and rose pergola. Pond garden with mixed shrubbery and herbaceous borders. Interesting specimen trees. Large lawned area, rose terrace with far-reaching views.

36 115 HADLOW ROAD

Tonbridge TN9 1QE. Mr & Mrs Richard Esdale. *1½ m N of Tonbridge stn. Take A26 from N end of High St signed Maidstone, house 1m on L in service rd.* **Adm £3.50, chd free. Suns 30 June; 25 Aug (2-5).**

Almost ½ -acre unusual terraced garden with large collection of modern roses, island herbaceous border, many clematis, hardy fuchsias, heathers, grasses, hostas, phormiums, and ferns, shrub borders, alpines, annuals, kitchen garden and pond; well labelled.

Densely planted in a natural style with meandering stepping stone paths . . .

37 HALL PLACE

Leigh TN11 8HH. The Lady Hollenden. *4m W of Tonbridge. From A21 Sevenoaks to Tonbridge, B245 to Hildenborough, then R onto B2027 through Leigh & on R.* Home-made teas. **Adm £6, chd £3. Suns 12, 26 May; 16 June (2-6).**

Large outstanding garden with 11-acre lake, lakeside walk crossing over picturesque bridges. Many rare and interesting trees and shrubs.

HARCOURT HOUSE

See London

38 NEW HAVEN

22 Station Road, Minster, Ramsgate CT12 4BZ. Robin Roose-Beresford, 01843 822594, robin.roose@hotmail.co.uk. *Off A299 Ramsgate Rd, take Minster exit from Manston r-bout, straight rd, R fork at church is Station Rd.* **Adm £3, chd free. Visitors welcome by appt Feb to Oct, reasonable notice. Small groups only.**

A smallish (300ft x 30ft) garden, designed with wildlife in mind, devised and maintained by the owner, densely planted in a natural style with meandering stepping stone paths. Two ponds (one for wildlife), gravel garden, rock garden, bog areas, fernery, Japanese garden, hostas and carnivorous plant beds, many exotic and unusual trees, shrubs and plants, colourful in leaf and flower. All yr interest.

39 HAYDOWN

Great Buckland, nr Cobham DA13 0XF. Dr & Mrs I D Edeleanu, 01474 814329. *6m W of Rochester. 4m S of A2. Take turning for Cobham, at war memorial straight ahead down hill, under railway bridge to T-junction. Turn R, after 200yds take L fork, follow narrow lane for 1½ m. Entrance on L.* Home-made teas, light refreshments & wine (Haydown wine available). **Adm £7, chd free. Visitors welcome by appt Apr to Oct.**

9-acre garden on North Downs created over nearly 40yrs. Formerly scrubland, it now incl woodland of indigenous and unusual trees, orchard, ponds and vineyard (wine available). Meadowland with many varieties of wild orchids in June, and abundant wild flowers in August. A haven for wildlife, incl badgers. Conducted tours of the garden.

40 HERONDEN

Smallhythe Road, Tenterden TN30 7LR. Peter & Vicky Costain. *From Tenterden High St, take B2082 Rye rd. Leave Tesco on L and take next R, lane marked to potato shop, Morghew. Entrance 1st R in lane.* Cream teas. **Adm £4, chd free (share to Tenterden & District Day Centre). Sat 14, Sun 15 Sept (2-5).**

Old walled garden consisting of spring, summer herbaceous and autumn borders. Centre of walled garden redesigned and prairie planted in April 2009 with mixed grasses and flowers. Remaining garden mixed shrubs incl hydrangeas. House and garden set in park. Featured in Kent Life. Grass paths, ramp to walled garden.

41 ◆ HEVER CASTLE & GARDENS

nr Edenbridge TN8 7NG. Broadland Properties Ltd, 01732 865224, www.hevercastle.co.uk. *3m SE of Edenbridge. Between Sevenoaks & East Grinstead off B2026. Signed from J5 & J6 of M25,*

A21, A264. **For opening times and information, please phone or see garden website.**
Romantic double moated castle, the childhood home of Anne Boleyn, set in 125 acres of formal and natural landscape. Topiary, Tudor herb garden, magnificent Italian gardens with classical statuary, sculpture and fountains. 38-acre lake, yew and water mazes. Walled rose garden with over 4000 roses, 110 metre-long herbaceous border. Partial wheelchair access.

42 HIGHLANDS
Hackington Close, St Stephen's, Canterbury CT2 7BB. Dr & Mrs B T Grayson, 01227 765066, terrygrayson@supanet.com. *1m N of Canterbury. At the foot of St Stephen's Hill, 200yds N of Archbishops School, on rd to Tyler Hill & Chestfield. Car parking on St Stephen's Hill Rd or Downs Rd, opp Hackington Close, or nearby side streets*. Home-made teas. **Adm £5, chd free. Sun 21 July (1-5). Visitors also welcome by appt.**
2-acre peaceful garden, set in S-facing bowl, with sweeps of narcissus in spring and island beds of herbaceous perennials, roses, azaleas, acers, hydrangeas, hebes and other shrubs. Many conifer and broad-leafed trees, incl plantation of ornamental trees. Two ponds, small alpine bed and hanging gardens feature. Also includes carved features from trees.

43 ◆ HOLE PARK
Rolvenden, Cranbrook TN17 4JB. Mr & Mrs E G Barham, 01580 241344, www.holepark.com. *4m SW of Tenterden. Midway between Rolvenden & Benenden on B2086*. **Adm £6, chd £1. For NGS: Wed 17 Apr, Sun 19 May, Wed 19 June, Sun 6 Oct (11-6). For other opening times and information, please phone or see garden website.**
Hole Park is proud to stand amongst the group of gardens which first opened in 1927 soon after it was laid out by my great grandfather, so we have grown with the NGS and seen many changes over the intervening period. Our 15-acre garden is surrounded by parkland with beautiful views and contains yew hedges, large lawns and specimen trees. Walled gardens, pools and mixed borders combine with bulbs, rhododendrons and azaleas. Massed bluebells in woodland walk, standard wisterias, orchids in flower meadow and glorious autumn colours make this a garden for all seasons. The Sundial Garden is redesigned and newly planted for 2013.

Rock Farm

44 HONNINGTON FARM
Vauxhall Lane, Southborough, Tunbridge Wells TN4 0XD. Mrs Ann Tyler, 01892 536990, ann.honnington@btinternet.com, www.honningtonfarmgardens.co.uk. *Between Tonbridge and Tunbridge Wells. A21 to A26. Signed Honnington Equestrian Centre. Enter at Honnington and cottages*. Cream teas & lunches. **Adm £5, chd free. Suns 28 Apr; 2 June (11-4). Groups of 10+ also welcome by appt May to Sept.**
6-acre garden, with heavy clay soil enriched yearly and producing a wide range of habitats, incl water and bog gardens, primrose and bluebell walks. Wildlife promotion a priority. Natural pool in wild flower meadow. Rose walkways, rockery, lakes and water features. Large herbaceous beds, some with New Zealand influence. Wonderful views. Sculptures exhibited by our local sculptor. Large plant sale. Newly renovated Kent Barn which holds 60 for teas/lunches. Featured in Period Homes and Gardens. Steep slopes and gravel drives.

45 ◆ IGHTHAM MOTE
Ivy Hatch, Sevenoaks TN15 0NT. National Trust, 01732 810378, www.nationaltrust.org.uk. *6m E of Sevenoaks. Off A25, 2½ m S of Ightham. Buses from rail stns Sevenoaks or Borough Green to Ivy Hatch, ½ m walk to Ightham Mote.* **Adm £11.50, chd £5.75. For NGS: Thur 11 July (10.30-5). For other opening times and information, please phone or see garden website.**
14-acre garden and moated medieval manor c1320, first opened for NGS in 1927. North lake and pleasure gardens, ornamental pond and cascade created in early C18. Orchard, enclosed, formal, vegetable and cutting gardens all contribute to the famous sense of tranquillity. Free guided tours of garden (donations to NGS welcome). Garden team on hand for tips and advice.

22 KELSEY WAY
See London

KNELLSTONE HOUSE
See Sussex

46 ◆ KNOLE
Sevenoaks TN13 1HU. The Lord Sackville & The National Trust, 01732 462100, www.nationaltrust.org.uk. *½ m SE of Sevenoaks. Foot: Park entrance at S end of Sevenoaks town centre, opposite St. Nicholas's Church. Road: M25 J5 (A21). Train: Sevenoaks 1½ m.* **Adm £5, chd £2.50. For NGS: Tues 2 Apr; 7 May; 4 June; 2 July; 6 Aug (11-4). For other opening times and information, please phone or see garden website.**
Lord Sackville's private garden at Knole commands the most beautiful view of the house. An impressive display of bluebells can be seen in Apr and May. Towards the end of May and throughout June, the magnificent wisteria wall provides the most glorious and delicately scented backdrop to the garden. Wheelchair access limited in wet weather.

47 KNOWLE HILL FARM
Ulcombe, Maidstone ME17 1ES. The Hon Andrew & Mrs Cairns, 01622 850240, elizabeth.cairns@btinternet.com. *7m SE of Maidstone. From M20 J8 follow A20 towards Lenham for 2m. Turn R to Ulcombe. After 1½ m, 1st L, ½ m 2nd R Windmill Hill. Past Pepper Box PH, ½ m 1st L.* Home-made teas. **Adm £4, chd free. Suns 10, 24 Feb (11.30-3.30). Evening Opening, wine, Sat 22 June (5-7.30); Sun 28 July (2-6). Visitors also welcome by appt May to Sept.**
1½ -acre garden, created over nearly 30yrs, on S-facing slope of N Downs with spectacular views. Mixed borders: Mediterranean and tender plants, roses, agapanthus, verbenas, salvias and grasses, flourish on the light soil. Many unusual plants. Evolving topiary. Lavender ribbons are magnets for bees. Pool and rill enclosed in small walled garden planted mainly with white flowers. New green garden should be complete in 2013. Kent Life Amateur Gardener of the Year Winner.

48 LADHAM HOUSE
Goudhurst TN17 1DB. Mr Guy Johnson. *8m E of Tunbridge Wells. On NE of village, off A262. Through village towards Cranbrook, turn L at The Chequers PH. 2nd R into Ladham Rd, main gates approx 500yds on L.* Light refreshments. **Adm £4, chd £1. Sun 12 May (2-5).**
Large garden and parkland with rhododendrons, camellias, azaleas and magnolias. Spectacular twin borders, a rose garden and an arboretum containing some fine specimens. Also, an Edwardian sunken rockery (inaccessible to wheelchairs), woodland walk, ha-ha and vegetable garden.

212 LANGLEY WAY
See London

49 LEYDENS
Hartfield Road, Edenbridge TN8 5NH. Roger Platts, www.rogerplatts.com. *1m S of Edenbridge. On B2026 towards Hartfield (use Nursery entrance & car park).* **Adm £4, chd free. Sun 4 Aug (12-5). Also open Old Buckhurst.**
Small private garden of garden designer, nursery owner and author who created NGS Garden at Chelsea in 2002, winning Gold and Best in Show, and in 2010 Gold and People's Choice for the M&G Garden. Constant development with wide range of shrubs and perennials incl late summer flowering perennial border adjoining wild flower hay meadow. Kitchen garden. Plants clearly labelled and fact sheet available.

50 LITTLE GABLES
Holcombe Close, Westerham TN16 1HA. Peter & Elizabeth James. *Centre of Westerham. Off E side of London Rd A233, 200yds from The Green. Please park in public car park, no parking available at house.* Home-made teas. **Adm £3.50, chd free. Sat 22, Sun 23 June (2-5).**
¾ -acre plant lover's garden extensively planted with a wide range of trees, shrubs, perennials etc, incl many rare ones. Collection of climbing and bush roses. Large pond with fish, water lilies and bog garden. Fruit and vegetable garden. Large greenhouse. Featured in Kent Life.

51 LORDS
Sheldwich, Faversham ME13 0NJ. Jane Wade, 01795 536900, jane@sellwade.co.uk. *4m S of Faversham. From A2 or M2 take A251 towards Ashford. ½ m S of Sheldwich church find entrance lane on R side adjacent to wood. (3½ m N of Challock Xrds).* Light refreshments. **Adm £4, chd free. Thur 27, Sun 30 June (2-5.30). Visitors also welcome by appt July.**
C18 canted walled garden and greenhouse. A herb terrace overlooks a citrus standing and beyond is a flowery mead beneath medlar and quince trees. Across a grass tennis court is a cherry orchard grazed by Jacob sheep. A shady fernery leads to lawns, ponds and wild area. Old specimen trees include redwoods, planes, copper beech, yew hedges and 120ft tulip tree. Some gravel paths.

Across a grass tennis court is a cherry orchard grazed by Jacob sheep . . .

52 LUTON HOUSE
Selling ME13 9RQ. Sir John & Lady Swire. *4m SE of Faversham. From A2 (M2) or A251 make for White Lion, entrance 30yds E on same side of rd.* **Adm £3.50, chd free. Sun 31 Mar, Sat 15, Sun 16 June (2-5). Visitors also welcome by appt.**
6 acres; C19 landscaped garden; ornamental ponds; trees underplanted with azaleas, camellias, woodland plants. Hellebores, spring bulbs, magnolias, cherries, daphnes, halesias, maples, Judas trees and cyclamen. Depending on the weather, those interested in camellias, early trees and bulbs may like to visit in late Mar/early April.

53 ◆ MARLE PLACE
Marle Place Road, Brenchley, nr Tonbridge TN12 7HS. Mr & Mrs Gerald Williams, 01892 722304, www.marleplace.co.uk. *8m SE of Tonbridge. From A21 Lamberhurst bypass, at Forstal Farm r'about follow*

brown tourism signs B2162 Horsmonden direction. From A21 Kippings Cross r'about B2160 to Matfield. R at Xrds to Brenchley, and follow brown tourist signs. **Adm £6, chd £2. For NGS: Wed 10 Apr, Wed 14 Aug (10-6). For other opening times and information, please phone or see garden website.**
Victorian gazebo, plantsman's shrub borders, walled scented garden, Edwardian rockery, herbaceous borders, bog and kitchen gardens. Woodland walks, mosaic terrace, artists' studios and gallery with contemporary art. Autumn colour. Restored Victorian 40ft greenhouse with orchids. C17 listed house (not open). Collection of interesting chickens. Nature trail.

54 MARSHBOROUGH FARMHOUSE

Farm Lane, Marshborough, Sandwich CT13 0PJ. David & Sarah Ash, 01304 813679. *$1\frac{1}{2}$ m W of Sandwich, $\frac{1}{2}$ m S of Ash. From Canterbury take A257 to Sandwich. After Wingham turn R to Ash. Through Ash, take R fork approx 200yds after War Memorial to Woodnesborough. After 1m, sign to Marshborough, take 1st L at white thatched cottage on unmade rd. Garden 100yds on L.* Home-made teas. **Adm £4, chd free. Visitors welcome by appt May, June & between 19 Aug - 30 Sept.**
Fascinating $2\frac{1}{2}$-acre plantsman's garden, developed enthusiastically over 14yrs. Original lawns are rapidly shrinking, giving way to meandering paths around informal island beds with many unusual shrubs, trees and perennials creating yr-round colour and interest. Herbaceous borders, pond, rockery, raised dry garden, vegetables and tender pot plants. WC nearby.

55 MASONS FARM

Headcorn Road, Grafty Green, Maidstone ME17 2AP. Paul & Sharon Jennings. *3.8m E of Headcorn. From Headcorn follow A274 towards Maidstone. On leaving village turn R at the green into Lenham Rd. Follow for approx 3.8m to Grafty Green. Masons Farm approx 300yds on R.* Home-made teas. **Adm £4, chd free (share to St Nicholas Church). Evening Opening, wine, Sat 22 June (5-8.30); Sun 23 June (12-5).**
1-acre garden designed by local landscape architect, Tom La Dell. Constructed and extensively planted over past 3yrs around C16 farmhouse. Shrubs, grasses and perennials hedged with box and yew. Rose garden, herb parterre, Mediterranean courtyard. Beautiful views in an AONB. Please take care around swimming pool.

> Winding paths flow through deep, densely planted mixed borders . . .

56 MERE HOUSE

Mereworth ME18 5NB. Mr & Mrs Andrew Wells, www.mere-house.co.uk. *7m E of Tonbridge. From A26 turn N on to B2016 & then into Mereworth village. $3\frac{1}{2}$ m S of M20/M26 J, take A20, then B2016 to Mereworth.* Home-made teas. **Adm £4, chd free. Sun 17, Sun 24 Feb, Sun 24 Mar, Mon 1 Apr, Sun 20 Oct, Sun 16, Sun 23 Feb 2014 (2-5).**
6-acre garden with C18 lake. Snowdrops, daffodils, lawns, herbaceous borders, ornamental shrubs and trees with foliage contrast and striking autumn colour. Woodland walk and major tree planting and landscaping. Park and lake walks.

57 ◆ MOUNT EPHRAIM

Hernhill, Faversham ME13 9TX. Mr & Mrs E S Dawes & Mr W Dawes, 01227 751496, www.mountephraimgardens.co.uk. *3m E of Faversham. From end of M2, then A299 take slip rd 1st L to Hernhill, signed to gardens.* **Adm £6, chd £2.50 (under 4's free). For NGS: Thur 27 June, Sun 29 Sept (11-5). For other opening times and information, please phone or see garden website.**
Herbaceous border; topiary; daffodils and rhododendrons; rose terraces leading to small lake. Rock garden with pools; water garden; young arboretum. Rose garden with arches and pergola planted to celebrate the Millennium. Magnificent trees. Grass maze. Superb views over fruit farms to Swale estuary. Village craft centre.

58 MOUNTS COURT FARMHOUSE

Acrise, nr Folkestone CT18 8LQ. Graham & Geraldine Fish, 01303 840598, graham.s.fish@btinternet.com. *6m NW of Folkestone. From A260 Folkestone to Canterbury rd, turn L at Swingfield (Densole) opp Black Horse Inn, $1\frac{1}{2}$ m towards Elham & Lyminge, on N side.* Home-made teas. **Adm £5, chd free. Sat 15, Sun 16 June; Sun 21 July (1-5). Also open 13, 14 April with East Kent Group. Visitors also welcome by appt May to Sept.**
Developed from a $1\frac{1}{2}$-acre horse paddock over 30yrs in surroundings designated as an Area of Outstanding Natural Beauty at a height of 150 metres. Variety of trees, shrubs and grasses. Wide winding paths flow through deep, densely planted mixed borders varying from herbaceous to woodland in character, with an eye to foliage pattern and changing colour mixes. Pond and bog garden.

59 NETTLESTEAD PLACE

Nettlestead ME18 5HA. Mr & Mrs Roy Tucker, www.nettlesteadplace.co.uk. *6m W/SW of Maidstone. Turn S off A26 onto B2015 then 1m on L, next to Nettlestead Church.* Home-made teas. **Adm £5, chd free. Suns 16 June; 8 Sept (2-5).**
C13 manor house in 10-acre plantsman's garden. Large formal rose garden. Large herbaceous garden of island beds with rose and clematis walkway leading to garden of China roses. Fine collection of trees and shrubs; sunken pond garden, terraces, bamboos, glen garden, acer lawn. Young pinetum adjacent to garden. Sculptures. Wonderful open country views. New, large, steep bank in course of development. Gravel paths. Sunken pond garden and new lower area in development, not wheelchair accessible.

One Dering Road

60 NORTON COURT
Teynham, Sittingbourne ME9 9JU. Tim & Sophia Steel, 01795 522941, sophia@nortoncourt.net. *Off A2 between Teynham & Faversham. J6 M2 onto A251 Faversham, L onto A2 direction Sittingbourne. Through Ospringe, over small r'about, approx 1½ m turn L at Texaco garage into Norton Lane. 1st L into Provender Lane, then L signed to Church for car park.* Home-made teas. **Adm £5, chd free. Mons, Tues: 3, 4, 17, 18 June (2-5). Visitors also welcome by appt May to July.**
10-acre garden within parkland setting. Mature trees, topiary, wide lawns and clipped yew hedges. Orchard with mown paths through wild flowers. Walled garden with mixed borders and climbing roses. Pine tree walk. Formal box and lavender parterre. Tree house in the Sequoia. Church open, adjacent to garden. Gravel paths.

61 OLANTIGH
Olantigh Road, Wye TN25 5EW. Mr & Mrs J R H Loudon. *10m SW of Canterbury, 6m NE of Ashford. Turn off A28 to Wye. 1m from Wye on Olantigh rd towards Godmersham.* **Adm £3.50, chd free. Sun 2 June (2-5).**
Edwardian garden in beautiful 20-acre setting; wide variety of trees; river garden; rockery; shrubbery; herbaceous border; extensive lawns; tree sculpture and woodland walks. This is, quite simply, a beautiful garden. Sorry, no teas, but available in Wye. Uneven ground and gravel paths.

62 OLD BLADBEAN STUD
Bladbean, Canterbury CT4 6NA. Carol Bruce, www.oldbladbeanstud.co.uk. *6m S of Canterbury. From B2068, follow signs into Stelling Minnis, turn R onto Bossingham Rd, then follow yellow NGS signs.* Cream teas. **Adm £5.50, chd free. Suns 26 May; 2, 16, 23 June; 7, 28 July; 25 Aug; 8, 22 Sept; 6 Oct (2-6).**
Three acres of interlinked gardens designed and created by the owners from scratch between 2003 and 2011. Romantic walled old rose garden, tranquil yellow and white garden, blended pastels square garden, 300ft-long colour-schemed symmetrical double borders and an organic fruit and vegetable self-sufficiency project. Featured in The Mail on Sunday.

63 ◆ OLD BUCKHURST
Markbeech, nr Edenbridge TN8 5PH. Mr & Mrs J Gladstone, 01342 850825, www.oldbuckhurst.co.uk. *4m SE of Edenbridge. B2026, at Queens Arms PH turn E to Markbeech. In approx 1½ m, 1st house on R after leaving Markbeech. Parking in paddock if dry.* **Adm £4, chd free. For NGS: Wed 17, Sat 20, Sun 21, Sat 27 Apr; Wed 1, Sun 5, Sat 11, Wed 15, Sat 18 May, Wed 5, Sat 8, Wed 12, Sat 22, Sun 23 June; Wed 10, Sat 13, Sat 20, Sun 21, Wed 24 July; Sun 4 Aug; Wed 4, Sat 7, Sun 8, Sat 14 Sept (11-5). For other opening times and information, please phone or see garden website.**
1-acre partly-walled cottage garden around C15 Grade II Listed farmhouse with catslip roof (not open). Comments from Visitors' Book: 'perfect harmony of vistas, contrasts and proportions. Everything that makes an English garden the envy of the world'. 'The design and planting is sublime, a garden I doubt anyone could forget'. Mixed borders with roses, clematis, wisteria, poppies, iris, peonies, lavender, July/Aug a wide range of day lilies. Parking and picnics in paddock if dry, on roadside if wet. Groups welcome by arrangement. WC. Featured in Kent Life and photographed for Japanese TV and BBC Gardeners' World.

64 OLD ORCHARD
56 Valley Drive, Loose, Maidstone ME15 9TL. Mike & Hazel Brett, 01622 746941, mandh.brett@tiscali.co.uk. *2½ m S of Maidstone. From Maidstone on A229, turn R into Lancet Lane, 1st L into Waldron Drive then 1st R into Valley Drive. Garden at end of cul-de-sac. Access also from Old Loose Hill via footpath between bus stop and allotments.* **Adm £2.50, chd free. Visitors welcome by appt Mar to June.**
Secluded garden with S-facing rear acre overlooking conservation area. Meandering grass paths around informal island beds containing usual and unusual trees, shrubs and perennials. Numerous alpines, bulbs, dwarf irises, and dwarf shrubs in extensive rockeries, screes, raised beds and troughs with woodland plants in shadier areas. Small arboretum for foliage, form and colour.

65 ONE DERING ROAD

Ashford TN24 8DB. Mrs Claire de Sousa Barry, 07979 816104, nazgulnota-bene@ntlworld.com. *Town centre. Just off Hythe Rd nr Henwood roundabout. Short walk from pay and display car park located just past fire stn in Henwood Rd. Please do not park in Dering Rd.* Home-made teas. **Adm £3.50, regret children not admitted. Sun 5, Mon 6, Sun 26, Mon 27 May, Sun 2, Sat 15, Sun 16 June; Sun 7, Sun 21 July; Sun 11, Sun 25, Mon 26 Aug (2-5). Groups of 10-20 also welcome by appt mid-May to Aug, refreshments by arrangement.**

Plantsperson's romantic small town garden. Optimum use of space with yr-round interest. Successional planting. Vitex, crinodendron, acer, cardiocrinum, buddlia, roses, honeysuckle, lilies, delphiniums, clematis, dahlias, fuchsias, azaleas, trillium, arisaema, rhododendrons plus a host of other plants, trees and shrubs. Ever-changing canvas of colour, scent and form 'wonderful, inspirational'. Regret no WC. Featured in numerous publications and on BBC, ITV, Radio Kent and Chelsea (Secret Gardens).

66 THE ORANGERY

Mystole, Chartham, Canterbury CT4 7DB. Rex Stickland & Anne Prasse, 01227 738348, rex@mystole.fsnet.co.uk. *5m SW of Canterbury. Turn off A28 through Shalmsford Street. After 1½ m at Xrds turn R down hill. Keep straight on, ignoring rds on L (Pennypot Lane) & R. Ignore drive on L signed 'Mystole House only' & at sharp bend in 600yds turn L into private drive signed Mystole Farm.* Home-made teas. **Adm £3.50, chd free. Suns 16 June; 28 July (1-6). Visitors also welcome by appt Apr to Oct.**

1½ -acre gardens around C18 orangery, now a house (not open). Front gardens, established well-stocked herbaceous border and large walled garden with a wide variety of shrubs and mixed borders. Splendid views from terraces over ha-ha and paddocks to the lovely Chartham Downs. Water features and very interesting collection of modern sculptures set in natural surroundings.

67 ORCHARD END

Cock Lane, Spelmonden Road, Horsmonden TN12 8EQ. Mr Hugh Nye, 01892 723118, hughnye@aol.com. *8m E of Tunbridge Wells. From A21 going S turn L at r'about towards Horsmonden on B2162. After 2m turn R into Spelmonden Rd, ½ m to top of hill, R into Cock Lane. Garden 50yds on R.* Home-made teas. **Adm £3.50, chd free (share to Amyloidosis). Sun 7 Apr; Sats, Suns: 22, 23 June; 20, 21 July; 31 Aug; 1 Sept (11-5). Groups of 10+ also welcome by appt June to Sept.**

Contemporary classical garden within a 4-acre site. Made over 15yrs by resident landscape designer. Divided into rooms with linking vistas. Incl hot borders, white garden, exotics, oak and glass summerhouse amongst magnolias. Dramatic changes in level. Formal pool with damp garden, ornamental vegetable potager. Wildlife orchards and woodland walks.

68 PARSONAGE OASTS

Hampstead Lane, Yalding ME18 6HG. Edward & Jennifer Raikes, 01622 814272. *6m SW of Maidstone. On B2162 between Yalding village & stn, turn off at Anchor PH over canal bridge, continue 150yds up lane. House and car park on L.* Cream teas. **Adm £3, chd free. Mon 1, Sun 14 Apr, Sun 16 June (2-5.30). Visitors also welcome by appt Feb to Oct.**

Our garden has a lovely position on the bank of the river Medway. Typical Oast House (not open) often featured on calendars and picture books of Kent. Sixty year old garden now looked after by grandchildren of its creator. 3/4 acre garden with walls, daffodils, crown imperials, shrubs and a spectacular magnolia. Exhibition and sale of pottery in barn. Unfenced river bank. Gravel paths.

PENGE GARDENS, SE20

See London

69 ◆ PENSHURST PLACE

Penshurst TN11 8DG. Viscount De L'Isle, 01892 870307, www.penshurstplace.com. *6m NW of Tunbridge Wells. SW of Tonbridge on B2176, signed from A26 N of Tunbridge Wells.* **Adm £7.80, chd £5.80. For NGS: Wed 11 Sept (10.30-6). For other opening times and information, please phone or see garden website.**

11 acres of garden dating back to C14; garden divided into series of rooms by over a mile of yew hedge; profusion of spring bulbs. Official re-opening of Jubilee border in 2012; formal rose garden; famous peony border. Woodland trail and arboretum. All-yr interest. Toy museum.

Romantic small town garden . . . ever-changing canvas of colour, scent and form 'wonderful, inspirational' . . .

70 PHEASANT BARN

Church Road, Oare ME13 0QB. Paul & Su Vaight, 01795 591654, paul.vaight@btinternet.com. *2m NW of Faversham. Entering Oare from Faversham, turn R at Three Mariners PH towards Harty Ferry. Garden 400yds on R, before church. Parking on roadside.* Home-made teas at Pheasant Farm 9 June. **Adm £4, chd free. Sat 8, Sun 9 June, Sat 13 July (1-5). Combined adm £6 with Pheasant Farm 8, 9 June. Visitors also welcome by appt Apr to July, refreshments by arrangement.**

Series of smallish gardens around award-winning converted farm buildings in beautiful situation overlooking Oare Creek. Main area is nectar-rich planting in formal design with a contemporary twist inspired by local landscape. Also vegetable garden, parterre, water features, wild flower meadow and labyrinth. July optimum for wild flowers. Spring blossom. Kent Wildlife Trust Oare Marshes Bird Reserve within 1m. Two village inns serving lunches/dinners.

71 NEW PHEASANT FARM
Church Road, Oare, Faversham ME13 0QB. Jonathan & Lucie Neame. *2m NW of Faversham. On entering Oare from Faversham, turn R at Three Mariners PH towards Harty Ferry. Entrance to garden 450yds on R, beyond Pheasant Barn, before church. Parking on roadside.* Home-made teas at Pheasant Barn 8 June & at Pheasant Farm 9 June. **Adm £3.50, chd free. Combined adm £6 with Pheasant Barn. Sat 8, Sun 9 June (1-5).**
A recently redesigned walled garden surrounding C17 farmhouse with outstanding views over Oare marshes and creek. Kent Wildlife Trust Oare Marshes Bird Reserve within 1m and Oare Gunpowder Works Country Park. Two village inns serving lunches/dinners. Wheelchair access to main garden.

72 PLACKETTS HOLE
Bicknor, nr Sittingbourne ME9 8BA. Allison & David Wainman, 01622 884258, aj@aj-wainman.demon.co.uk. *5m S of Sittingbourne. W of B2163. Bicknor is signed from Hollingbourne Hill & from A249 at Stockbury Valley. Placketts Hole is midway between Bicknor & Deans Hill.* Light refreshments. **Adm £5, chd free. Visitors and groups of up to 30 welcome by appt May to Sept.**
Mature 3-acre garden in Kent Downland valley incl herbaceous borders, rose and formal herb garden, small, walled kitchen garden and informal pond intersected by walls, hedges and paths. Many unusual plants, trees and shrubs provide colour and interest from spring to autumn. Most of garden is accessible by wheelchair users.

73 POTMANS HEATH HOUSE
Wittersham TN30 7PU. Dr Alan & Dr Wilma Lloyd Smith, 01797 270221, potmansheath@hotmail.com. *1½ m W of Wittersham. Between Wittersham and Rolvenden, 1m from junction with B2082. 200yds E of bridge over Potmans Heath Channel.* **Adm £5, chd free (share to St John the Baptist Church). Sun 21 Apr, Sun 16 June (2-6). Visitors also welcome by appt for Autumn and Winter visits.**
Large, colourful and easily explored compartmentalised country garden. Large collection of climbing roses. Specimen trees, apple and cherry orchards, part-walled vegetable garden. Adjoins open farmland (meadows) with views over Wittersham Levels which encourages a rich variety of wild birds. Widespread naturalised bulbs and spectacular blossom in spring. Duck ponds. Current new development of managed parkland. Public WC at Wittersham Church.

Secret woodland garden created under the canopy of a strawberry tree . . .

74 11 RAYMER ROAD
Penenden Heath, Maidstone ME14 2JQ. Mrs Barbara Badham. *From M20 J6 at Running Horse r'about take Penenden Heath exit along Sandling Lane, direction Boxley, Bearsted. At T-lights turn into Downsview Rd and follow signs.* Home-made teas. **Adm £3, chd free. Sun 21 Apr (11-4).**
Barbara's garden has lovely views of the Downs. Divided into different areas and intensely planted for maximum use of an average-sized plot. Cottage garden border, oriental themed pond, secret woodland garden created under the canopy of a strawberry tree. Organic fruit and veg in raised beds and containers minarette fruit trees underplanted with wild flowers. Featured as Garden of the Month in Kent Life. Finalist Kent Life Garden of the Year.

75 ◆ RIVERHILL HIMALAYAN GARDENS
Riverhill, Sevenoaks TN15 0RR. The Rogers Family, 01732 459777, www.riverhillgardens.co.uk. *2m S of Sevenoaks on A225.* **Adm £7.25, chd £4.95, concessions £6.50. For NGS: Tue 23 Apr, Wed 12 June (10.30-5). For other opening times and information, please phone or see garden website.**
Beautiful hillside garden, privately owned by the Rogers family since 1840. Extensive views across the Weald of Kent. Spectacular rhododendrons, azaleas and fine specimen trees. Bluebell and natural woodland walks. Walled Garden open for 2013 - extensive new planting, terracing and water feature. Children's adventure playground, den-building trail, hedge maze and 'Yeti Spotting'. Featured on Channel 4's Country House Rescue & Country House Rescue Revisited. Wheelchair access only to New Walled Garden, free access to cafe, shop & tea terrace.

76 ROCK FARM
Gibbs Hill, Nettlestead ME18 5HT. Mrs S E Corfe, 01622 812244. *6m SW of Maidstone. Turn S off A26 onto B2015, then 1m S of Wateringbury turn R up Gibbs Hill.* **Adm £4, chd free (share to Nettlestead Church). Sat 25, Wed 29 May (11-6); Every Wed & Sat 15 June to 10 July (11-6). Visitors also welcome by appt May to July.**
2-acre garden set around old Kentish farmhouse (not open) in beautiful setting; created with emphasis on all-yr interest and ease of maintenance. Plantsman's collection of shrubs, trees and perennials for alkaline soil; extensive herbaceous border, vegetable area, bog garden and plantings around two large natural ponds.

77 ROGERS ROUGH
Chicks Lane, Kilndown TN17 2RP. Richard & Hilary Bird, 01892 890554, rb3042@gmail.com. *10m SE of Tonbridge. From A21 2m S of Lamberhurst turn E into Kilndown; take 1st R down Chicks Lane until rd divides.* Home-made teas. **Adm £4, chd free. Sats, Suns: 4, 5, 6, 25, 26, 27 May; 22, 23 June; 13, 14 July (11-5.30). Visitors also welcome by appt May to July.**
Garden writer's 1½ -acre garden, divided into many smaller gardens containing mainly herbaceous borders, but also rock gardens, shrubs, small wood and pond. Very wide range of plants, incl many unusual or rare ones. Very wide range of herbaceous plants. Some steps but these can be bypassed.

78 ST CLERE

Kemsing, Sevenoaks TN15 6NL. Mr & Mrs Simon & Eliza Ecclestone, www.stclere.com. *6m NE of Sevenoaks. Take A25 from Sevenoaks toward Maidstone; 1m past Seal turn L signed Heaverham & Kemsing. In Heaverham take rd to R signed Wrotham & W Kingsdown; in 75yds straight ahead marked private rd; 1st L & follow rd to house.* **Adm £5, chd £1. Sun 16 June (2-5).**
4-acre garden, full of interest. Formal terraces surrounding C17 mansion (not open), with beautiful views of the Kent countryside. Herbaceous and shrub borders, productive kitchen and herb gardens, lawns and rare trees. Garden tours with Head Gardener at 2.30, 3.30 & 4.30 (£1 per head). Some gravel paths and small steps.

79 ◆ THE SECRET GARDENS OF SANDWICH AT THE SALUTATION

Knightrider Street, Sandwich CT13 9EW. Mr & Mrs Dominic Parker, 01304 619919, www.the-secretgardens.co.uk. *In the heart of Sandwich. Turn L at Bell Hotel and into Quayside car park. Entrance on far R-hand corner of car park.* **Adm £6.50, chd £3. For NGS: Tue 19 Mar, Fri 28 June (10-5); Fri 4 Oct (10-4). For other opening times and information, please phone or see garden website.**
3½ acres of ornamental and formal gardens designed by Sir Edwin Lutyens and Gertrude Jekyll in 1911 surrounding Grade I listed house. Designated historic park and garden, lake, white, yellow, spring, woodland, rose, kitchen, vegetable and herbaceous gardens. Designed to provide yr-round changing colour. Unusual plants for sale. Gardens, tearoom and shop are wheelchair friendly.

80 SANDOWN

Plain Road, Smeeth, nr Ashford TN25 6QX. Malcolm & Pamela Woodcock, 01303 813478, pmw@woodcock.mail1.co.uk. *4m SE of Ashford. Exit M20 J10 onto A20 and take the 3rd left at Smeeth Xrds. At Woolpack PH turn R, past garage on L, past next L, garden on L. Park in lay-by on R up hill.* Light refreshments. **Adm £3, regret no children. Suns, Mons: 5, 6, 26, 27 May; Sats, Suns: 15, 16 June; 6, 7 July; 10, 11, 31 Aug; 1, 7, 8 Sept (1-5). Visitors also welcome by appt May to 1st week of Sept.**
Our small and compact Japanese-style garden and Koi pond has a Japanese arbour, tea house/veranda, waterfall and stream. Acers, bamboos, ilex crenata, ginkgo, gunnera magellanica, fatsia japonica, equisetum, ferns, akebia quinatas, clerodendrum trichotomum, pinus mugos, wisterias, hostas, daturas, agapanthus and 'mind your own business' for ground cover. WC available. Regret no children owing to deep pond.

Allotment owners grow a massive variety of flowers, fruit and vegetables . . .

81 ◆ SCOTNEY CASTLE

Lamberhurst TN3 8JN. National Trust, 01892 893819, www.nationaltrust.org.uk. *6m SE of Tunbridge Wells. On A21 London-Hastings, brown tourist signs. Bus: (Mon to Sat) Tunbridge Wells-Wadhurst, alight Lamberhurst Green.* **Adm £8.20, chd £4.10. For NGS: Mon 20 May (11-4.30). For other opening times and information, please phone or see garden website.**
Scotney Castle's garden has seen many changes since the 1920s when it first opened as part of the NGS open days. You could say it has been a true survivor - from bombs in WW2 to the great storm of 1987 which brought down over 90 substantial trees. Its doors however are still proudly open and the full glory of this romantic setting still encapsulates the original picturesque inspiration. March is all about atmosphere, with low mists across the moat and the first signs of spring to come. With over 20 acres of garden to explore it is a great time to get back out into the garden after the winter. Wheelchairs available for loan.

82 SEA CLOSE

Cannongate Road, Hythe CT21 5PX. Major & Mrs R H Blizard, 01303 266093. *½ m from Hythe. Towards Folkestone (A259), on L, signed.* **Adm £3, chd free (share to The Royal Signals). Visitors welcome by appt Apr to Dec, opening times between 10-5.**
With sea views, a 1-acre garden on steep hill, the marine climate allows growing of tender and semi-tender plants and shrubs collected over the years by the partnership of 90 year old knowledgeable owner and his supportive wife. No more open days but we will welcome you to explore, have a gardening chat, sit peacefully, have your own picnic (extra £3) on the lower lawn. Give us a ring. Featured in Roots. Steep hill and steps to reach the top.

ALLOTMENTS

83 SEVENOAKS ALLOTMENTS

Allotment Lane, off Quakers Hall Lane, Sevenoaks TN13 3UZ. Sevenoaks Allotment Holders Assn, www.sevenoaksallotments.co.uk. *Quakers Hall Lane off A225, St John's Hill. Site directly behind St John's Church.* Light refreshments. **Adm £3, chd free. Sun 30 June (10-5).**
The Association self-manages 11½ acres of productive allotment gardens situated in the heart of the town. A wide cross-section of allotment owners grow a massive variety of flowers, fruit and vegetables using a number of different techniques. Gardeners cite healthy produce, exercise and relaxation in a beautiful open space as reasons to rent a plot. Main paths concrete with some steep slopes.

GROUP OPENING

84 SHIPBOURNE GARDENS

Puttenden Road, Shipbourne, Shipbourne, nr Tonbridge TN11 9RJ. *Off A227 between Tonbridge and Borough Green. Gardens and car parking signed. See below for detailed directions to each garden. Combined group ticket and map available at each garden.* Coffee & Home-made teas at Village Hall.

Recycle – bring a bag for your plant purchases

Combined adm £5, chd free. **Sat 22, Sun 23 June (11-5).**

GREAT OAKS HOUSE
Puttenden Road. Mr & Mrs M Cohen.
Turn R on leaving Plantation House (see directions below). After 200yds turn R into Claygate Lane. At end of lane, turn L for Great Oaks House
01732 810739
oldstablescottage@btinternet.com

HOOKWOOD HOUSE
Puttenden Road. Mr & Mrs Nicholas Ward.
Turn R on leaving Plantation House (see directions below). After 200yds turn R into Claygate Lane. At end of lane, turn R for Hookwood House

PLANTATION HOUSE
Reeds Lane. Viv Packer & Don Williamson.
From A227 turn across Green into Upper Green Rd opp The Chaser PH. Straight on for ¾ m, garden on R

Contrasting gardens around the parish will include Hookwood House, with herbaceous borders, herb garden, topiary, nut plat, vegetable garden; Great Oaks House, a romantic garden with herbaceous borders, roses, wild garden with pond and mature trees; Plantation House, an informal garden with roses, perennials, organic vegetable garden, sculptures. Teas in our pretty village hall on the village green which in June is a mass of wild flowers. Limited wheelchair access.

Lose yourself in numerous themed rooms: sunken water garden, iris beds, scented old fashioned rose walk . . .

85 ◆ SISSINGHURST CASTLE
Sissinghurst TN17 2AB. National Trust, 01580 710700, www.nationaltrust.org.uk. *On A262 1m E of Sissinghurst. Bus: Arriva Maidstone-Hastings, alight Sissinghurst 1¼ m. Approx 30 mins walk from village.* **Adm £11.90, chd £5.80. For NGS: Fris 26 Apr; 5 July; 27 Sept (11-5.30). For other opening times and information, please phone or see garden website.**
Garden created by Vita Sackville-West and Sir Harold Nicolson. Spring garden, herb garden, cottage garden, white garden, rose garden. Tudor building and tower, partly open to public. Moat. Vegetable garden and estate walks. Free welcome talks and estate walks leaflets.

86 SMITHS HALL
Lower Road, West Farleigh ME15 0PE. Mr S Norman, www.smithshall.com. *3m W of Maidstone. A26 towards Tonbridge, turn L into Teston Lane B2163. At T-junction turn R onto Lower Rd B2010. Opp Tickled Trout PH.* Home-made teas. **Adm £4.50, chd free (share to Dandelion Time). Suns 2 June; 7 July (11-5).**
Delightful 3-acre gardens surrounding a beautiful 1719 Queen Anne House (not open). Lose yourself in numerous themed rooms: sunken water garden, iris beds, scented old fashioned rose walk, formal rose garden, intense wild flowers, peonies, deep herbaceous borders and specimen trees. Walk, 9 acres of park & woodland with great variety of young native and American trees and fine views of the Medway valley. Gravel paths.

SOUTH GRANGE
See Sussex

87 SOUTH HILL FARM
Tamley Lane, Hastingleigh, Ashford TN25 5HL. Sir Charles Jessel, 01233 750325, sircjj@btinternet.com. *4½ m E of Ashford. Turn off A28 to Wye, go through village & ascend Wye Downs. In 2m turn R at Xrds marked Brabourne & South Hill, then 1st L. From Stone St (B2068) turn W opp Stelling Minnis, follow signs to Hastingleigh. Continue towards Wye & turn L at Xrds marked Brabourne & South Hill, then 1st L.* **Adm £4.50, chd free. Visitors welcome by appt mid-end June.**
2 acres high up on N Downs, C17/18 house (not open). Old walls, ha-ha, formal water garden; old and new roses, unusual shrubs, perennials and coloured foliage plants.

41 SOUTHBROOK ROAD, SE12
See London

88 SPRING PLATT
Boyton Court Road, Sutton Valence, Maidstone ME17 3BY. Mr & Mrs John Millen, carolyn.millen@virginmedia.com, www.kentsnowdrops.com. *5m SE of Maidstone. From Maidstone on A274 turn L into Chartway Street: take 1st R, then straight over next Xrds, house 1st on R. From S on A274 turn R into Heniker Lane, bear L into Boyton Court Road, house on L after double bend.* Soups, bread and teas, all home-made. **Adm £3.50, chd free. Sat 2, Sun 3 Feb (10.30-3). Sat 8, Sun 9 Feb 2014. Groups of 10-20 also welcome by appt Feb to Mar.**
1-acre garden under continual development with panoramic views of the Weald. Over 350 varieties of snowdrop grown in tiered display beds with spring flowers in borders. An extensive collection of alpine plants in rockeries and a large greenhouse. Vegetable garden. Featured in Kent Life and Amateur Gardening. Slopes and gravel paths.

89 ◆ SPRIVERS
Lamberhurst Road, Horsmonden, Tonbridge TN12 8DR. National Trust, 01892 893820, www.nationaltrust.org.uk. *From Horsmonden Village Xrds take Lamberhurst Rd B2162. House approx 1m on R.* **Adm £3, chd £1.50. For NGS: Thurs 23 May; 8 July; Sun 18 Aug (11-3). For other opening times and information, please phone or see garden website.**
3-acre garden to wisteria-clad Georgian house with Tudor origins (not open). Yew hedges surround rhododendron garden and shrubbery. Two newly planted herbaceous borders and walled rose garden. Lawns to the rear of house lead to a wild flower meadow bordering ponds. Kitchen garden under restoration. Most areas are accessible, lawn and brick paths.

© Leigh Clapp

GROUP OPENING

90 ST MICHAEL'S GARDENS

Roydon Hall Road, East Peckham TN12 5NH. *5m NE of Tonbridge, 5m SW of Maidstone. On A26 at Mereworth r'about take S exit (A228 Paddock Wood). After 1½ m turn L into Roydon Hall Rd. Gardens ½ m up hill on L. From Paddock Wood A228 towards West Malling. 1m after r'about with wheelbarrow turn R into Roydon Hall Rd.* Home-made teas. **Combined adm £4.50, chd free (share to Friends of St Michael's Church, Roydon). Sun 28 Apr, Sun 2 June (2-5).**

ST MICHAEL'S COTTAGE
Mr Peter & Mrs Pauline Fox

ST MICHAEL'S HOUSE
Mrs W Magan

A Victorian house and cottage garden come together to provide colour, scent and inspiration in April and June in this rural village. The year unfolds at the grey stone old vicarage with a lovely display of tulips in spring, followed by irises, then a mass of roses from red hot to old soft colours, all complemented by yew topiary hedges and wonderful views from the meadow. The traditional cottage garden, with a wildlife area, was designed so it cannot be seen all at once. Explore and enjoy the collection of lavenders, hostas, clematis, ferns and heathers. Southdown sheep and lambs, chickens.

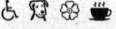

91 NEW 3 STONE ROAD

Broadstairs CT10 1DY. Mrs Sandra Holloway. *Close to Broadstairs town centre on rd heading towards North Foreland Lighthouse.* **Adm £3.50, chd free. Fri 3, Sat 4 May; Sat 10, Sun 11 Aug (11-5).**

Adjoining a fine Regency House built in 1827 in a lovely conservation area of charming Broadstairs is this small walled Italianate garden. Created and maintained by the owner, it is an English adaptation of an Italian garden featuring box hedging topiary, olive trees, tulips in the spring and lots of colour courtesy of bedding plants and hydrangeas in the summer. Plenty of seating with interesting vantage points.

92 STONEWALL PARK

Chiddingstone Hoath, nr Edenbridge TN8 7DG. The Fleming Family. *4m SE of Edenbridge. Via B2026. Halfway between Markbeech & Penshurst.* Home-made teas. **Adm £4.50, chd free (share to Sarah Matheson Trust & St Mary's Church). Suns 24 Mar; 5 May (2-5.30).**

Romantic woodland garden in historic setting featuring species rhododendrons, magnolias, azaleas, a range of interesting trees and shrubs, wandering paths and lakes. Historic parkland with cricket ground, Victorian walled garden with herbaceous borders and vegetable garden backed by 100 yr-old espalier pear trees. Sea of wild daffodils in March.

THREE CHIMNEYS
See Sussex

93 TIMBERS

Dean Street, East Farleigh, nr Maidstone ME15 0HS. Mrs Sue Robinson, 01622 729568, suerobinson.timbers@gmail.com. *2m S of Maidstone. From Maidstone take B2010 to East Farleigh. Opp The Bull turn into Vicarage Lane, then L into Forge Lane and L into Dean St. Garden 50yds on R, park through gates in front of house.* Home-made teas & light lunches available on request. **Adm £4.50, chd free. Visitors welcome by appt Apr to July. Evening openings.**

5-acre garden, well stocked with unusual hardy plants, annuals and shrubs designed with flower arranger's eye. Formal areas comprising parterre, pergola, herbaceous, vegetables, fruit, lawns and mature specimen trees surrounded by 100 yr-old Kentish cobnut plat, wild flower meadows and woodland. Natural rock pool with waterfalls. Valley views. Plant list. Most of garden is flat, some steep slopes to the rear.

TITSEY PLACE GARDENS
See Surrey

94 TORRY HILL

Frinsted/Milstead, Sittingbourne ME9 0SP. The Lord & Lady Kingsdown, 01795 830258, lady.kingsdown@btinternet.com. *5m S of Sittingbourne. From M20 J8 take A20 (Lenham). At r'about by Ramada Inn turn L Hollingbourne (B2163). Turn R at Xrds at top of hill (Ringlestone Rd). Thereafter Frinsted-Doddington (not suitable for coaches), then Torry Hill/NGS signs. From M2 J5 take A249 towards Maidstone then 1st L (Bredgar) L again (follow Bredgar signs) R at War Memorial (T-junction) in Bredgar, 1st L (Milstead) then Torry Hill/NGS signs from Milstead.* Home-made teas. **Adm £4, chd free (share to St Dunstans Church Apr/June, Kent Minds July). Suns 12 May; 16 June; 14 July (2-5). Groups of 10-30 also welcome by appt April - Aug weekdays only. Tea/coffee & biscuits.**

8 acres; large lawns, specimen trees, flowering cherries, rhododendrons, azaleas and naturalised daffodils; walled gardens with lawns, shrubs, herbaceous borders, rose garden incl shrub roses, wild flower areas and vegetables. Extensive views to Medway and Thames estuaries. Some shallow steps. No wheelchair access to rose garden but can be viewed from pathway.

English adaptation of an Italian garden featuring box hedging topiary, olive trees . . .

95 TOWNLAND

Sixfields, Tenterden TN30 6EX. Alan & Lindy Bates. *From centre of Tenterden High St, turn into Jackson's Lane next to Webbs Ironmongers. Follow the lane to end (400m). Townland at end on R.* Home-made teas. **Adm £4, chd free. Suns: 16 June; 14, 21 July (2-5.30).**

A 1.8 acre family garden in a unique position. Landscaped features incl a rose garden, Mediterranean gravel garden and shrubbery. Wander around and discover the meadow areas, stunning mixed borders and herbaceous beds providing a riot of colours and textures, wide range of fruit and vegetables. Also wild flowers grown specially to attract bees.

96 TRAM HATCH

Charing Heath, Ashford TN27 0BN. Mrs P Scrivens, www.tramhatchgardens.co.uk. *10m NW of Ashford. A20 turn towards Charing railway stn. Continue on Pluckley Rd over motorway, 1st R signed Barnfield to end. Turn L, follow lane past Barnfield, Tram Hatch on L.* Home-made teas. **Adm £4, chd free. Suns 9 June; 14 July; 11 Aug (12.30-5.30).**
Meander your way off the beaten track to a mature and extensive garden changing through the seasons. You will enjoy a garden laid out in rooms - what surprises are round the corner: large selection of trees (some unusual), vegetable, rose and gravel gardens, colourful containers. The Great River Stour and the Angel of the South enhance your visit. Please come and enjoy. Featured in Kent Life. The garden is totally flat, apart from a very small area which can be viewed from the lane.

97 NEW 223 TUBBENDEN LANE

Orpington BR6 9NN. Dr & Mrs Disha Sehmi. *1m SW of Orpington. Off A21 into Tubbenden Lane. Turn 1st R into Beechcroft Rd, entrance is through garage between 1A & 3 Beechcroft Rd.* Home-made teas. **Adm £5, chd free. Sun 16 June (2-5).**
A small plantsman's garden with lots of interest created by exotic planting. The emphasis is on foliage provided by ferns, bamboos and hostas. These are set off by topiary, sculpture and water features.

98 UPPER PRYORS

Butterwell Hill, Cowden TN8 7HB. Mr & Mrs S G Smith. *4½ m SE of Edenbridge. From B2026 Edenbridge-Hartfield, turn R at Cowden Xrds & take 1st drive on R.* Home-made teas. **Adm £5, chd free. Wed 19 June (1-9).**
Ten acres of English country garden surrounding C16 house - a garden of many parts; colourful profusion, interesting planting arrangements, immaculate lawns, mature woodland, water and a terrace on which to appreciate the view, and tea!

99 NEW WATERGATE HOUSE

King Street, Fordwich, Canterbury CT2 0DB. Fiona Cadwallader. *From Canterbury follow signs to Sandwich A257. 2m beyond Canterbury turn L after Canterbury Golf Course (signed Fordwich). Take next L into Moat Lane which leads down into Fordwich High St. Watergate House is straight ahead at bottom of hill. Turn R in front of house, follow signs to parking area.* Home-made teas. **Adm £4, chd free. Sats 20 Apr; 15 June (2-6).**
Magical walled garden by the River Stour: defined areas of formal, spring, woodland, vegetable and secret garden reveal themselves in a naturally harmonious flow, each with its own colour combinations. Ancient walls provide the garden's basic structure, while a green oak pergola echoes a monastic cloister.

Magical walled garden . . . vegetable and secret garden reveal themselves in a naturally harmonious flow . . .

100 WEST COURT LODGE

Postling Court, The Street, Postling, nr Hythe CT21 4EX. Mr & Mrs John Pattrick, 01303 863285, malliet@hotmail.co.uk. *2m NW of Hythe. From M20 J11 turn S onto A20. Immed 1st L. After ½ m on bend take rd signed Lyminge. 1st L into Postling.* Home-made teas in village hall. **Adm £3, chd free. Sat 1, Sun 2 June (1-5). Combined adm with Churchfield £5, chd free. Visitors and groups of up to 20 also welcome by appt Apr to Aug.**
S-facing 1-acre walled garden at the foot of the N Downs, designed in 2 parts: main lawn with large sunny borders and a romantic woodland glade planted with shadow loving plants and spring bulbs. Lovely C11 church will be open next to the gardens.

GROUP OPENING

101 WEST MALLING JUNE GARDENS

West Malling ME19 6LW. *On A20, nr J4 of M20. Park in West Malling for Little Went & Went House. Follow directions to New Barns Cottages & 2 New Barns Oast. Maps and combined ticket at each garden.* Home-made teas at New Barns Cottages and 2 New Barns Oast. **Combined adm £5, chd free (share to St Mary's Church). Sun 16 June (12-5).**

LITTLE WENT
106 High Street. Anne Baring.
In middle of West Malling, opp car park

NEW BARNS COTTAGES
Lavenders Road. Mr & Mrs Anthony Drake.
From West Malling High St, past shops, 1st L after car park into Water Lane. To far end, then R up Lavenders Rd. At top bear L over bypass, garden on L after sharp R bend

2 NEW BARNS OAST
Lavenders Road. Nick Robinson & Becky Robinson Hugill.
Limited disabled parking. Otherwise visitors may park at New Barns Cottages, 2 mins walk

WENT HOUSE
83 Swan Street. Alan & Mary Gibbins.
Opp Abbey and cascade

West Malling is an attractive small market town with some fine buildings. Enjoy four lovely gardens that are entirely different from each other and cannot be seen from the road. In the middle of the town, Little Went's long narrow secret garden has fish ponds, an aviary with love birds, conservatory, gravel garden and parterre, lavender garden and statues, as well as an exhibition of paintings. Went House is a Queen Anne house surrounded by a secret garden with a stream, specimen trees, old roses, mixed borders, attractive large kitchen garden, fountain and parterre. Approx ½ m S of the town, New Barns Cottages, developed over 30yrs from a blank site, is a 2½ -acre garden and paddock surrounded by orchards and woodland. From the parking area, the garden is approached via a meadowed pathway leading to a romantic roomed garden explored via serpentine paths inviting surprise and discovery. 2 New Barns Oast is a child-friendly garden with interesting hard landscaping features and raised vegetable garden. All gardens have wheelchair access. Little Went has no disabled parking.

Discover the origins of some 6,000 different plants - you'll be amazed where they come from . . . !

102 WICKHAM LODGE
The Quay, High Street, Aylesford ME20 7AY. Cherith & Richard Bourne, 01622 717267, wickhamlodge@aol.com, www.wickhamlodge.co.uk. *3m NW of Maidstone. Off High St on riverbank, turning into The Quay by Chequers PH. Park in village car park.* Light refreshments, Cream Teas & fresh Cornish Pasties. **Adm £4.50, chd free (share to St Peter and St Paul Church Aylesford). Sat 15 June (11-5).**
There is a sense of romance, peace and tranquillity in these 14 small and varied inspirational gardens. Every corner of this walled and terraced ½ -acre plot has been used to create gardens that could be picked up and recreated anywhere. Journey from productive kitchen garden to formal Tudor, from Japanese to funky banana foliage. Endless surprises are here in abundance. Featured on French TV.

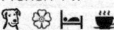

103 WINDY RIDGE
Victory Road, St Margarets-at-Cliffe CT15 6HF. Mr & Mrs D Ryder, 01304 853225, www.gardenplants-nursery.co.uk. *4½ m NE of Dover. From Duke of York r'about on A2 N of Dover follow A258 signed Deal. Take 3rd rd on R (Station Rd), then 3rd rd on L (Collingwood Rd). Continue onto unmade track & follow signs (approx ½ m). Telephone for map.* Home-made teas. **Adm £3.50, chd free. Sun 23 June, Sun 8 Sept (2-6).**
Plantsman's garden on top of chalk hill accessed via unmade tracks. Extensive views over open country and sea. Island beds of shrubs and perennials (many rare). Large collection of penstemon and salvia. Wildlife pond. New boardwalk garden leading to raised seating area and viewpoint. New colour themed herbaceous borders, kitchen garden and trees and shrubs on former nursery site. Plants for sale. Extensively remodelled during 2012 to extend the garden onto the former nursery site after the owners retirement.

104 ◆ THE WORLD GARDEN AT LULLINGSTONE CASTLE
Eynsford DA4 0JA. Guy Hart Dyke, 01322 862114, www.lullingstonecastle.co.uk. *1m from Eynsford. M25 J3, signs to Brands Hatch then Eynsford. In Eynsford turn R at church over ford bridge. Follow lane under viaduct, with Lullingstone Roman Villa on R, to private rd sign, follow signs for World Garden via Gatehouse. Also an entrance via A225 which has more parking.* **Adm £7, chd £4. For NGS: Sun 16 June (12-5). For other opening times and information, please phone or see garden website.**
Interactive world map of plants laid out as a map of the world within a walled garden. The oceans are your pathways as you navigate the world in 1 acre. You can see Ayers Rock and walk alongside the Andes whilst reading intrepid tales of plant hunters. Discover the origins of some 6,000 different plants - you'll be amazed where they come from! Plant nursery and Lullingstone World Garden seeds for sale. Wheelchairs available upon request.
NCH

105 WYCKHURST
Mill Road, Aldington, Ashford, Kent TN25 7AJ. Mr & Mrs Chris Older, 01233 720395, cdo@rmfarms.co.uk. *4m SE of Ashford. Leave M20 at J10, onto A20 travel east 2m to Aldington turning; turn R at Xrds; proceed 1½ m to Aldington village hall. Turn R and immed L by Walnut Tree Inn. Take rd down Forge Hill signed to Dymchurch, after ¼ m take first turn R into Mill Rd.* Home-made teas. **Adm £4, chd free. Sats, Suns: 1, 2, 8, 15, 16 June (12-6). Visitors also welcome by appt June.**
C16 cottage (not open) nestles in romantic seclusion at the end of a drive. This enchanting garden is a mixture of small mixed herbaceous borders and unusual topiary, with extensive views across Romney Marsh towards the sea. Some gentle slopes.

GROUP OPENING

106 WYE GARDENS
Wye TN25 5BJ. *3m NE of Ashford. From A28 take turning signed Wye. Bus: Ashford to Canterbury via Wye. Train: Wye. Collect map at the Church.* Home-made teas at Wye Church. **Combined adm £4.50, chd free. Sun 23 June (2-6).**

3 BRAMBLE CLOSE
Bramble Lane. Dr M Copland

CUMBERLAND COURT D
Church Street. Mr & Mrs F Huntington

MISTRAL
Oxenturn Road. Dr & Mrs G Chapman
Visitors also welcome by appt May to July, adm £2. 01233 813011 geoff@chapman.invictanet.co.uk

YEW TREES
Scotton Street. Ian & Elizabeth Coulson

Start at the centre of this historic village to visit four unusual gardens. 3 Bramble Close is a unique experience, a very wild garden with meadow, pond and ditches, mown paths and hedges buzzing with wildlife. A water feature and unusual artefacts complement the exciting courtyard garden at Cumberland Court, once an asphalt car park now densely planted with a wide range of unusual plants and many pots. Look out for the recently added secret garden too. 250 species of botanical interest (all labelled) flourish at Mistral, once part of an old hard tennis court, incl white and alpine gardens. Also centre stage, see a mini outdoor theatre! Yew Trees is a large traditional garden divided into 3 distinct and secluded areas with lawns, a naturalised wildlife area with a pond, mature trees and wide borders planted with shrubs, grasses and herbaceous perennials and an enclosed potager. Wye Gardens opening coincides with Stour Music Festival.

---

107 YEW TREE COTTAGE
Penshurst TN11 8AD. Mrs Pam Tuppen, 01892 870689. *4m SW of Tonbridge. From A26 Tonbridge to Tunbridge Wells, join B2176 Bidborough to Penshurst rd. 2m W of Bidborough, 1m before Penshurst. Unsuitable for coaches. Please phone if needing advice for directions*. Light refreshments. **Adm £2.50, chd free. Sat 23, Sun 24 Feb; Tues, Thurs: 5, 7, 19, 21 Mar; 2, 4, 16, 18 Apr; 2, 7, 16, 21 May; 4, 6, 18, 20 June; 2, 4, 16, 18 July; 1, 6, 15, 20 Aug; 3, 5 Sept (12-5).**
Small, romantic, hillside cottage garden with steep entrance. Lots of seats and secret corners, many unusual plants - hellebores, spring bulbs, old roses, many special perennials. Small pond; something to see in all seasons. Created and maintained by owner, a natural garden full of plants.

Mere House

Kent County Volunteers

Joint County Organisers
Jacqueline Anthony, 44 Cambridge Street, Tunbridge Wells TN2 4SJ, 01892 518879, jacquelineanthony7@googlemail.com
Jane Streatfeild, The Bungalow, Hoath House, Chiddingstone Hoath, Edenbridge TN8 7DB, 01342 850362/07531 001277, jane@hoath-house.freeserve.co.uk

County Treasurer
Richard Stileman, Arnold Yoke, Back Street, Leeds ME17 1TF, 01622 863002, richstileman@btinternet.com

Publicity
Liz Moore, Mereworth Cottage, Laddingford, Maidstone ME18 6BU, 01622 871269, liz_m30@yahoo.co.uk

Radio
Jane Streatfeild (as above)

Advertising
Marylyn Bacon, Ramsden Farm, Stone-cum-Ebony, Tenterden TN30 7JB, 01797 270300, ngsbacon@ramsdenfarm.co.uk

Booklet distribution
Diana Morrish, Cacketts Farmhouse, Haymans Hill, Horsmonden, Tonbridge TN12 8BX, 01892 723905, diana.morrish@hotmail.co.uk

Assistant County Organisers
Marylyn Bacon (as above)
Clare Barham, Hole Park, Rolvenden, Cranbrook TN17 4JB, 01580 241386, clarebarham@holepark.com
Virginia Latham, Stowting Hill House, Ashford TN25 6BE, 01303 862881, lathamvj@gmail.com
Caroline Loder-Symonds, Denne Hill Farm, Womenswold, Canterbury CT4 6HD, 01227 831203, cloder_symonds@hotmail.co.uk
Ingrid Morgan Hitchcock, 6 Brookhurst Gardens, Southborough, Tunbridge Wells TN4 0UA, 01892 528341, ingrid@morganhitchcock.co.uk
Diana Morrish (as above)
Julia Stanton, Mill House Farm, Waltham, Canterbury CT4 5SL, 01227 700421, familystanton@hotmail.com
Felicity Ward, Hookwood House, Shipbourne TN11 9RJ, 01732 810525, hookwood1@yahoo.co.uk

LANCASHIRE

Merseyside & Greater Manchester

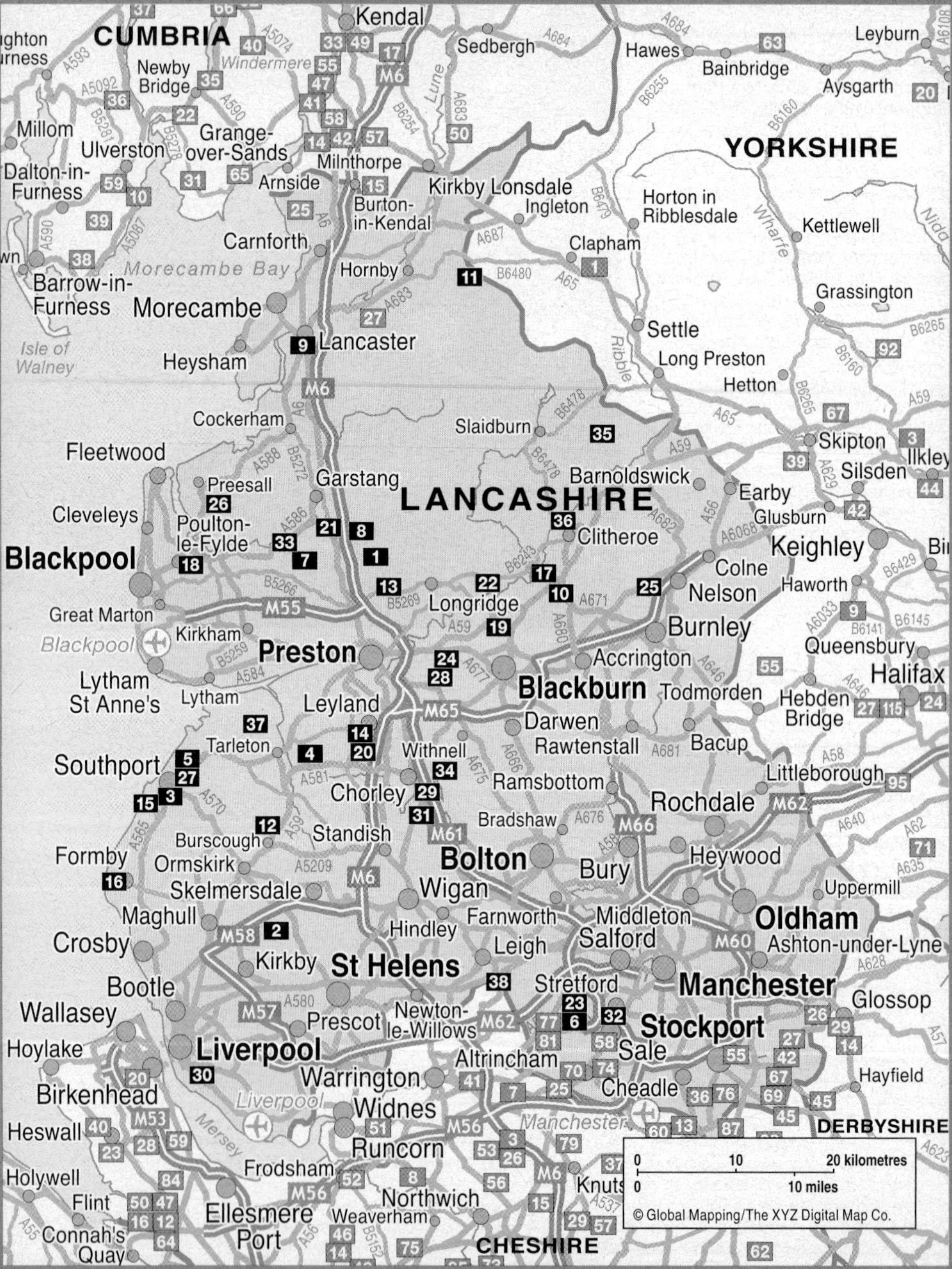

Opening Dates

February

Sunday 3
38 Weeping Ash

Sunday 10
38 Weeping Ash

Sunday 17
38 Weeping Ash

Sunday 24
38 Weeping Ash

March

Sunday 31
26 Moss Side House

April

Monday 1
26 Moss Side House

Saturday 13
13 Dale House Gardens

Sunday 14
13 Dale House Gardens
38 Weeping Ash

Sunday 28
27 15 Preston Road

May

Monday 6
29 The Ridges

Saturday 18
20 Le Jardin

Sunday 19
4 Bretherton Gardens
12 Crabtree Lane Gardens
20 Le Jardin

Sunday 26
3 Birkdale Village Gardens
11 Clearbeck House
36 Waddow Lodge Garden

Monday 27
11 Clearbeck House

June

Saturday 1
25 Montford Cottage

Sunday 2
21 Little Stubbins
25 Montford Cottage

Monday 3
21 Little Stubbins

Saturday 8
1 The Barn on the Green
24 Mill Barn
33 St Michael's Gardens

Sunday 9
4 Bretherton Gardens
10 Casa Lago
24 Mill Barn
33 St Michael's Gardens

National Gardens Weekend

Saturday 15
3 Birkdale Village Gardens
9 Carr House Farm
17 Great Mitton Hall
26 Moss Side House

Sunday 16
3 Birkdale Village Gardens
9 Carr House Farm
12 Crabtree Lane Gardens
17 Great Mitton Hall
26 Moss Side House

Saturday 22
2 Barrow Nook Gardens
7 Brookvale Court Gardens
24 Mill Barn

Sunday 23
2 Barrow Nook Gardens
7 Brookvale Court Gardens
11 Clearbeck House
18 Green Farm Cottage
24 Mill Barn
37 Wedgwood

Sunday 30
11 Clearbeck House
30 Sefton Park Gardens

An expanding group of gardens encircling the attactive, bustling Victorian village of Birkdale . . .

July

Saturday 6
8 Carr Cottage & Hill House Gardens

Sunday 7
8 Carr Cottage & Hill House Gardens
15 Foxbury
16 Freshfield Gardens

Saturday 13
32 Southlands
34 The Stones & Roses Garden

Sunday 14
4 Bretherton Gardens
32 Southlands
34 The Stones & Roses Garden

Sunday 21
6 Brookfield
14 Deerhurst
23 Marlborough Allotments
34 The Stones & Roses Garden
36 Waddow Lodge Garden

Saturday 27
31 Silver Birches

Sunday 28
31 Silver Birches

August

Saturday 10
22 Lower Dutton Farm

Sunday 11
3 Birkdale Village Gardens
22 Lower Dutton Farm

Monday 26
29 The Ridges

September

Saturday 7
24 Mill Barn
28 Primrose Hill

Sunday 8
24 Mill Barn
28 Primrose Hill

February 2014

Sunday 2
38 Weeping Ash

Sunday 9
38 Weeping Ash

Sunday 16
38 Weeping Ash

Sunday 23
38 Weeping Ash

Gardens open to the public

29 The Ridges

By appointment only

5 4 Brocklebank Road
19 Greenacre
35 Varley Farm

Also open by Appointment ☎

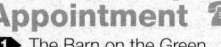

1 The Barn on the Green
3 71 Dunbar Crescent, Birkdale Village Gardens
3 Maple Tree Cottage, Birkdale Village Gardens
3 14 Saxon Road, Birkdale Village Gardens
4 Hazel Cottage, Bretherton Gardens

- 4 Pear Tree Cottage, Bretherton Gardens
- 6 Brookfield
- 7 Brookvale Court Gardens
- 9 Carr House Farm
- 10 Casa Lago
- 12 79 Crabtree Lane, Crabtree Lane Gardens
- 12 Crabtree Lane Gardens
- 13 Dale House Gardens
- 14 Deerhurst
- 15 Foxbury
- 16 37 Brewery Lane, Freshfield Gardens
- 20 Le Jardin
- 21 Little Stubbins
- 24 Mill Barn
- 26 Moss Side House
- 31 Silver Birches
- 32 Southlands
- 34 The Stones & Roses Garden
- 37 Wedgwood

Low maintenance garden for people with limited time and budget . . .

The Gardens

1 THE BARN ON THE GREEN

Silk Mill Lane, Inglewhite PR3 2LP. Arthur & Vivienne Massey-Fairhurst, 01995 641008, vivs@live.co.uk, www.thebarnonthegreen.co.uk. *9m N of Preston, 6.2m E of Garstang. From M55, take A6 towards Garstang for 2½ m. At the Roebuck PH turn R into Bilsborrow Lane for 2½ m to the hamlet of Inglewhite. 1st R just before The Green. Garden on immed R next to Green Man PH where you can park, parking also available at Inglewhite Chapel just past PH & garden.* **Adm £4.50, chd free (share to Rotary). Sat 8 June (11-4). Visitors also welcome by appt, please contact Vivienne & Arthur.**
This delightful 1¼ -acre garden, overlooking stunning scenery, guides the visitor through a series of rooms, some secluded and secretive others allowing panoramic views. A vast array of plants, trees, bushes, bulbs, roses, hostas, water lilies, vegetables, pond, river bed and much more. Too much for you to miss. Featured in Lancashire Life. Wheelchair access, please see a steward.

GROUP OPENING

2 BARROW NOOK GARDENS

Bickerstaffe L39 0ET. *5m SW of Ormskirk. From M58, J3 to Southport (A570) to T-lights at Stanley Gate PH, turn L into Liverpool Rd, then 1st L into Church Rd, then Hall Lane, approx 1m into Barrow Nook Lane.* Cream teas at Barrow Nook Farm. **Combined adm £3.50, chd free. Sat 22, Sun 23 June (1-5).**

BARROW NOOK FARM
Cynthia & Keith Moakes

18 BARROW NOOK LANE
Paul & Sheila Davies

26 BARROW NOOK LANE
Gary Jones

Barrow Nook Gardens are 3 neighbouring gardens of very different styles within a short walking distance, set in rural surroundings. Barrow Nook Farm is a peaceful country garden planted in cottage garden style to attract birds, bees, butterflies and much more. The large wildlife pond is an attractive feature. Pergola leads to orchard with soft and stoned fruit. Home-made jams for sale. 18 Barrow Nook Lane is a small diverse garden with herbaceous borders, pergola, gravel paths, rockery, herbs, island beds, fruit trees and raised vegetable beds. 26 Barrow Nook Lane is a low maintenance garden for people with limited time and budget who appreciate outdoor living, dining and relaxing.

GROUP OPENING

3 BIRKDALE VILLAGE GARDENS

Birkdale, Southport PR8 2AX. *1m S of Southport. Off A565 Southport to Liverpool rd. 4th on L after r'about, opp St James Church. Maps available at each location.* Home-made teas at Saxon Rd, bacon sandwiches at Maple Tree Cottage. **Combined adm £4.50, chd free (share to CLIC Sargent (for children with cancer)). Sun 26 May; Sat 15, Suns 16 June; 11 Aug (11-5).**

23 ASHTON ROAD
PR8 4QE. John & Jennifer Mawdsley.
Open all 4 dates. ¾ m S from village along Liverpool Rd, turn R into Sandon Rd (church on corner) 2nd L Ashton Rd

NEW 71 DUNBAR CRESCENT
PR8 3AA. Mrs Kimberley Gittins.
Open 15 June. S along A565 from the town centre, over the railway bridge at Hillside. Dunbar Crescent is 3rd rd on L
Visitors also welcome by appt May to June.
01704 579325
kgo611@ymail.com

FOXBURY
Pam & Richard James.
Open 16 June
(See separate entry)

MAPLE TREE COTTAGE
22 Hartley Crescent, SPR8 4SG. Sandra & Keith Birks.
Open 26 May, 11 August. ½ m from village, S along Liverpool Rd, turn R into Richmond Rd, 1st R Hartley Rd, then 1st R Hartley Crescent
Visitors also welcome by appt May to July.
01704 567182
sandie.b@talktalk.net

10 MEADOW AVENUE
PR8 5HF. John & Jenny Smith.
Open 26 May, 15 & 16 June. S on A5267 through Birkdale Village, L at T-lights, continue past zebra Xing, just before next turn R into Warwick St, then 2nd L

14 SAXON ROAD
PR8 2AX. Margaret & Geoff Fletcher.
Open all 4 dates
Visitors also welcome by appt May to July, homemade teas incl in adm.
01704 567742
geoffwfletcher@hotmail.co.uk

An expanding group of gardens encircling the attractive, bustling Victorian village of Birkdale, some within easy walking distance, others reached by a short car journey. 2 gardens opening on all 4 dates, others less. Gardens feature a ½ -acre inspirational cottage garden, a quirky large family garden full of reclaimed materials and surprises, a low lying suburban garden inland

The Barn on the Green

© Julia Stanley

from the dunes with mixed beds and mature shrubs, a walled garden with an array of tender plants amongst informal island beds, a garden of different rooms with a wonderful fruit and vegetable plot. New this year a developing family garden with pond, mini orchard, reclaimed materials and lots of good ideas. Maps are available at all gardens and refreshments available at 2 gardens.

♿ ❀ ☕

GROUP OPENING

4 BRETHERTON GARDENS

Near Leyland PR26 9AN. *8m SW of Preston. Between Southport & Preston, from A59, take B5247 towards Chorley for 1m. Gardens off North Rd (B5248) & South Rd (B5247).* Home-made teas at Bretherton Congregational Church. **Combined adm £5, chd free (share to St Catherine's Hospice). Suns 19 May; 9 June; 14 July (12-5).**

GLYNWOOD HOUSE
Eyes Lane, PR26 9AS. Terry & Sue Riding

HAZEL COTTAGE
6 South View, PR26 9AN. John & Kris Jolley
Visitors also welcome by appt.
01772 600896
jolley@johnjolley.plus.com

◆ HAZELWOOD
North Road, PR26 9AY. Jacqueline Iddon & Thompson Dagnall
01772 601433.
www.jacquelineiddon hardyplants.co.uk
For other opening times and information, please phone or see garden website.

OWL BARN
Flag Lane, PR26 9AD. Richard & Barbara Farbon

PEAR TREE COTTAGE
Eyes Lane, PR26 9AS. John & Gwenifer Jackson.
In Bretherton turn into Eyes Lane at the War Memorial
Visitors also welcome by appt June to Sept.
01772 601212
gweniferjackson@gmail.com

Five contrasting gardens spaced across 2m in an attractive village with conservation area. Glynwood House has $^3/_4$ -acre mixed borders, pond with drystone-wall water feature, woodland walk, patio garden with pergola and raised beds, all in a peaceful location with spectacular open aspects. Pear Tree Cottage garden blends seamlessly into its rural setting with informal displays of ornamental and edible crops, water and mature trees, against a backdrop of open views to the West Pennine Moors. Owl Barn has a model kitchen garden, fountains and harmonious formal borders with exuberant planting to complement an historic C18 listed building (not open). Hazelwood Garden, Nursery and Sculpture Gallery cover $1^1/_2$ acres of mature orchard, with a beautifully integrated range of habitats showing the finest plants for every situation, from moist shade to well-drained sun. Hazel Cottage garden has evolved from $^1/_3$ acre Victorian subsistence plot to encompass a series of themed spaces packed with plants to engage the senses and the mind. Sculpture demonstration at 2pm at Hazelwood, live music at Hazelwood and Glynwood House. Home-made preserves for sale at Pear Tree Cottage.

♿ ❀ ☕ ☎

5 4 BROCKLEBANK ROAD

Southport PR9 9LP. Alan & Heather Sidebotham, 01704 543389, alansidebotham@yahoo.co.uk. *$1\frac{1}{4}$ m N of Southport. Off A565 Southport to Preston Rd, opp North entrance to Hesketh Park.* Home-made teas. **Adm £3.50, chd free. Visitors welcome by appt May to Aug.**

The garden consists of a series of separate areas and water features, each with different planting. Whenever possible the landscaping materials used are from reclamation materials from historic sites in the Southport area, thus creating a garden of interest to complement the planting schemes.

6 BROOKFIELD

11 Irlam Road, Flixton M41 6JR. Bob & Beryl Wheeler, 0161 748 6985, rcpwheeler@aol.com. *$2\frac{1}{2}$ m SW of Urmston. From J10 on M60 go S through 2 r'abouts to T-lights, turn R into Moorside Rd. At next r'about take 2nd rd signed Lymm, after next T-lights take 5th rd on R Irlam Rd.* Home-made teas. **Adm £3, chd free. Sun 21 July (1-5). Combined with Marlborough Allotments. Visitors also welcome by appt June to Aug.**

$\frac{1}{3}$-acre suburban garden on a triangular plot divided into sections with several pathways. Large selection of plants in herbaceous beds and borders with mature trees and shrubs planned for year round effect. Raised beds, rockery, pond and water features, shade areas, patio with troughs and containers. Greenhouse and cold frames. Featured in Lancashire Life.

GROUP OPENING

7 BROOKVALE COURT GARDENS

Sowerby Road, Sowerby, Nr Preston PR3 0TT, 01995 679317, karen@lavender2.plus.com. *3m W of A6 at Myerscough. Heading N up A6, turn L at Myerscough turn, 2nd L into Pinfold Lane after approx $2\frac{1}{2}$ m, L into Sowerby Rd and Gardens situated on LH-side. Parking at Swan Farm (LH-side).* Home-made teas. **Combined adm £4, chd free (share to St John's Hospice). Sat 22, Sun 23 June (11-5). Visitors also welcome by appt June to Sept to all four gardens.**

COBBLE BARN
Mimi Walder

NEW FOXGLOVE BARN
Ms Sarah Turner

LAVENDER BARN
Karen Sienkiewicz

MEADOW BARN
Debbie Meadows

Created following the conversion of old barns in 1993, four contrasting gardens positioned next to each other with far reaching views of Bowland Fells. Cobble Barn offers an interesting blend of hard landscaping using some of the original farmyard materials. Lavender Barn offers full cottage garden planting incl raised vegetable beds, natural pond plus arbour with roses, clematis and delphiniums. Meadow Barn has an eclectic mix of farmyard paraphernalia incorporating many unusual galvanised items sourced from near and far and planted imaginatively. Foxglove Barn provides a calm and tranquil environment for the visitor with mixed borders and well stocked vegetable plot. The gardens will also incl a visiting artist, hand made jewellery stall, plus stall offering unique planted containers and garden art to complement the overall visit. Children's garden treasure hunt with free entry.

GROUP OPENING

8 CARR COTTAGE & HILL HOUSE GARDENS

Smithy Lane, Claughton-on-Brock, Preston PR3 0PN. *8m N of Preston. 5m N of J32 (M6) r'about, turn E off A6 into New Lane by Shell Garage. This junction is $\frac{1}{2}$ m N of Barton Grange Garden Centre r'about. Follow signs for Carr Cottage for 2m. Park & Ride at Carr Cottage for Hill House.* Home-made teas. **Combined adm £4, chd free. Sat 6, Sun 7 July (11-5).**

1 CARR COTTAGE
Smithy Lane, PR3 0PN. Mr Jim Cross

HILL HOUSE
May Lane, PR3 0PD. Michael & Elizabeth Giles

1 Carr Cottage a small cottage garden in the hamlet of Claughton set in open countryside. Packed with plants in mixed borders incl many small conifers, herbaceous plants and shrubs. Summerhouse, greenhouse, tiny vegetable plot and small scree garden. Hill House is an elevated $1\frac{1}{2}$-acre garden surrounding converted stone barn. Set in open countryside near the lovely Brock Valley. The garden has been designed for variation and interest incl a natural stream with rhododendrons, conifers and moisture-loving plants, pretty rear garden, wild wooded area, paddock with trees and shrub roses, conservatory.

A hidden gem in historic City of Lancaster . . .

9 CARR HOUSE FARM

Carr House Lane, Lancaster LA1 1SW. Robin & Helen Loxam, 01524 60646. *SW of Lancaster City. From A6 Lancaster city centre turn at hospital, past B&Q and 1st R, straight under railway bridge into farm.* Home-made teas. **Adm £4, chd free (share to Fairfield Flora & Fauna Association). Sat 15, Sun 16 June (10.30-4). Visitors also welcome by appt May to Sept.**

A hidden gem in historic City of Lancaster. Farmhouse gardens incl Mediterranean, rustic and cottage flowers and trees intertwined beautifully with 2 ponds fed naturally by 'Lucy Brook' attracting all manner of wildlife. Apple, pear, plum, lemon and orange trees mix well within the scene. See rare breed cattle and enjoy nature walk in adjoining fields. Slope towards pond.

10 CASA LAGO
1 Woodlands Park, Whalley BB7 9UG. Carole Ann & Stephen Powers, 01254 824903, powers@carolepowers6.orangehome.co.uk. *2½ m S of Clitheroe. From M6 J31, take A59 to Clitheroe. 9m take 2nd exit at r'about for Whalley. After 2m reach village and follow yellow signs. Parking in village car parks or nearby.* Light refreshments. **Adm £3, chd free. Sun 9 June (1-5). Visitors also welcome by appt June to Sept.**
Casa Lago has two koi ponds, ferns from around the world, acers, bamboos, grasses, bananas and a succulent garden. Interesting features include black limestone wall, oak pergolas and fruit patio. Consistent visitor comments: 'Fantastic inspiring ideas' 'Wish I had a garden like yours', 'excellent, great diversity in the space'... 'and very welcoming hosts'.

11 CLEARBECK HOUSE
Mewith Lane, Higher Tatham via Lancaster LA2 8PJ. Peter & Bronwen Osborne, www.clearbeckgarden.org.uk. *13m NE of Lancaster. Signed from Wray (M6 J34, A683, B6480) & Low Bentham.* Light refreshments. **Adm £3, chd free. Sun 26, Mon 27 May; Suns 23, 30 June (11-5).**
'A surprise round every corner' is the most common response as visitors encounter fountains, streams, ponds, sculptures, boathouses and follies: Rapunzel's tower, temple, turf maze, giant fish made of CDs, walk-through pyramid. 2-acre wildlife lake attracts many species of insects and birds. Planting incl herbaceous borders, grasses, bog plants and many roses. Vegetable and fruit garden. Painting studio open. Children- friendly incl quiz. Artists and photographers welcome by arrangement. Awarded Good Garden Guide Star. Many grass paths, some sloped. Tramper disability electric chair available by prior arrangement.

GROUP OPENING

12 CRABTREE LANE GARDENS
Burscough L40 0RW. *3m NE of Ormskirk. Follow A59 Preston - Liverpool Rd to Burscough. From N before 1st bridge turn R into Redcat Lane - brown sign Martin Mere. From S pass through village over 2nd bridge, then L into Redcat Lane, after ¾ m turn L into Crabtree Lane. Gardens by level Xing.* Home-made teas at no.79. **Combined adm £3.50, chd free. Suns 19 May; 16 June (11-4). Visitors also welcome by appt May to July.**

79 CRABTREE LANE
Sandra & Peter Curl
Visitors also welcome by appt May to July.
01704 893713
peter.curl@btinternet.com

81 CRABTREE LANE
Prue & Barry Cooper

2 very diverse gardens looked after by avid plants persons 79 Crabtree Lane is a ¾ -acre garden that over recent yrs has been changed and replanted but still has many established and contrasting hidden areas. Colour themed herbaceous beds. Rose garden recently replanted, fishpond surrounded by a large rockery and a koi pond with waterfall and shallow area for wildlife. Spring and woodland garden, pergola, alpine garden and late summer hot bed. Hosta and fern walk. A derelict, dry stone bothy and stone potting shed with a Mediterranean garden surrounded by stone walls. 81 Crabtree Lane has water features, old fashioned rockery, vine and rose covered pergola, trompe l'oeils. Central gazebo with climbers. Herbaceous plants. Arches with clematis and roses. Art studio at no. 81. Wheelchair access at no. 79.

CRAIGSIDE
See Derbyshire

13 DALE HOUSE GARDENS
off Church Lane, Goosnargh, Preston PR3 2BE. Caroline & Tom Luke, 01772 862464, tomlukebudgerigars@hotmail.com. *2½ m E of Broughton. M6 J32 signed Garstang Broughton, T-lights turn R onto Whittingham Lane, 2½ m to Whittingham & Goosnargh at r'about turn L onto Church Lane, garden between nos 17 & 19.* Home-made teas. **Adm £3.50, chd free (share to Goosnargh Scout Group). Sat 13, Sun 14 Apr (10-4). Visitors also welcome by appt Mar to Oct.**
½ -acre tastefully landscaped gardens comprising of limestone rockeries, well stocked herbaceous borders, raised alpine beds, well stocked koi pond, lawn areas, greenhouse and polytunnel, patio areas, specialising in alpines rare shrubs and trees, large collection unusual bulbs. All year round interest. Large indoor budgerigar aviary. 300+ budgies to view. Gravel path, lawn areas.

'Wish I had a garden like yours, excellent, great diversity in the space . . . and very welcoming hosts . . .'

14 DEERHURST
10 Forestway, Leyland PR25 1HL. Julia Harwood-Geall & Fred Bell, 01772 452094, jharwoodgeall@aol.co.uk. *6m S of Preston. Leave M6 J28, turn R to T-lights, then R onto A49, next T-lights turn R into B5248, down to Fox & Lion PH. Turn R into Fox Lane. Forestway 1st R.* Cream teas. **Adm £3, chd free. Sun 21 July (1-5). Visitors also welcome by appt July to Aug.**
This garden, which sits squarely in the medium-sized range, will appeal to the plantaholic, with its vast array of hardy perennial plants, documented for reference. Created over 16yrs, it has colourful borders surrounding a well-tended lawn. Also a vegetable plot.

15 FOXBURY
47 Westbourne Road, Birkdale, Southport PR8 2HY. Pam & Richard James, 01704 569251, richjame@aol.com. *2m S of Southport. Off A565 Southport to Liverpool Rd. After r'about at end of Lord St, proceed towards Liverpool, at 2nd T-lights turn R into Grosvenor Rd. Turn L at end.* **Adm £2.50, chd free. Sun 7 July (11-5). Visitors also welcome by appt May to Sept.**
½ -acre suburban garden just inland from dunes and famous golf course of Birkdale. Very low lying. Mature

pine tree shelters water feature. Mixed beds and newly planted trees are interspersed through a well maintained lawn. Mature shrubs and hedges shelter this developing garden from off-shore winds, giving a peaceful atmosphere. Featured in Lancashire and Lancashire Life magazines.

GROUP OPENING

16 FRESHFIELD GARDENS
Freshfield L37 1PB. *6m S of Southport. From A565 (Crosby to Southport rd) take B5424 signed Formby. At Grapes PH mini r'about turn R into Green Lane, Turn R into West Lane & Brewery Lane. For Victoria Rd & Gorse Way (off Larkhill Lane), drive over Freshfield level Xing towards beach*. Home-made teas.
Combined adm £4, chd free.
Sun 7 July (10.30-4.30).

37 BREWERY LANE
L37 7DY. Mr & Mrs P Thornton
Visitors also welcome by appt July to Aug.
01704 873107

2 GORSE WAY
L37 1PB. Brenda & Ray Doldon

THE SQUIRRELS
67 Victoria Road, L37 1LN. Kathleen & Andrew Train

6 WEST LANE
L37 7BA. Laurie & Sue Lissett.

WOODLANDS
46 Green Lane, L37 7BH. Ken & Rita Carlin

5 suburban gardens on sandy soil near to Formby sand dunes and NT nature reserve, home to the red squirrel. 2 Gorse Way completely redesigned by the present owners. This split-level garden features a sunken garden, pergola, pond, beach area and colour themed beds. The Squirrels is a plant collector's well-stocked garden, primarily to attract wildlife. Unusual tender plants in containers and interesting collection of cacti. 37 Brewery Lane. A compact garden with grasses, pergola, dry-stone wall and interesting conifers. 'Twenty shades of green' contrast with bright summer bedding and architectural plants. 6 West Lane is a child friendly garden with pergola and arches, mixed planting and rockery. Baskets and containers. Woodlands a leafy suburban, shady front garden with mature trees under preservation leading to oblong rear garden, with cottage style colourful borders, small pond and plenty of seating areas to relax and view.

GAMESLEY FOLD COTTAGE
See Derbyshire

2 Gorse Way

© Fiona Lea

Spread the word about the NGS: tell your family and friends

17 GREAT MITTON HALL

Mitton Road, Mitton, nr Clitheroe BB7 9PQ. Jean & Ken Kay. *2m W of Whalley. Take Mitton Rd out of Whalley pass Mitton Hall on L, Aspinall Arms on R over bridge. Hall is on R next to Hillcrest tearooms.* Home-made teas. **Adm £3.50, chd free (share to Help the Heroes). Sat 15, Sun 16 June (1-5).**

Overlooked by C12 Allhallows Church, with stunning views to the river and Pendle Hill the terraced gardens with herbaceous borders, lawn, topiary and raised lily pond, sympathetically surround the medieval hall (not open). Stalls on village green at side of hall.

18 GREEN FARM COTTAGE

42 Lower Green, Poulton-le-Fylde FY6 7EJ. Sharon McDonnell & Eric Rawcliffe. *500yds from Poulton-le-Fylde Village. M55 J3 follow A585 Fleetwood. T- lights turn L. Next lights bear L A586. Poulton 2nd set of lights turn R Lower Green. Cottage on L.* Light refreshments. **Adm £3, chd free. Sun 23 June (10-4).**

⅓ -acre well-established formal cottage gardens. Feature koi pond, paths leading to different areas. Lots of climbers and rose beds. Packed with plants of all kinds. Many shrubs and trees. Themed colour borders. Well laid out lawns. Said by visitors to be 'a real hidden jewel'.

19 GREENACRE

157 Ribchester Road, Clayton-le Dale, Blackburn BB1 9EE. Dorothy & Andrew Richards, 01254 249694, andrewfrichards@talk21.com. *3m N of Blackburn, near junction of A59 and B6245. Leave M6 J31 take A59 towards Clitheroe. In 7m at T-lights turn R towards Blackburn on B6245. Greenacre is ½ m on RHS.* Home-made teas. **Adm £4.50, chd free. Visitors welcome by appt, refreshments variable by arrangement.**

A lived in 1-acre garden on edge of the Ribble Valley. Many beds, profusely planted, have unusual trees, perennials and tender plants. Always colourful with our signature yellow foliage. Brimming potager set in a mature orchard with some heritage apple varieties. A continually evolving plant collector's garden with stunning views, many areas to explore and loads of ideas to take home. Interesting and entertaining guided garden tours. Home-made cakes a speciality and refreshments and plants for sale indoors in poor weather. Rare pelargoniums in greenhouse.The garden features different kinds of hedges and a large composting system.

HAZELWOOD FARM
See Cumbria

HEYWOOD HOUSE
See Cumbria

Themed colour borders . . . well laid out lawns . . . said by visitors to be 'a real hidden jewel' . . .

20 LE JARDIN

12 Crocus Field, Leyland PR25 3DY. Margaret Moore, 01772 456616. *7m S of Preston. From M6, J28 take B5256 towards Leyland, 1st r'about take 1st exit, next r'about 2nd exit (B5248) in 600yds L into Beech Avenue, T-junction turn R. From W, Fox Lane to Leyland Cross (Tesco store). T-lights straight on 150yds, R into Beech Ave.* Home-made teas. **Adm £3.50, chd free. Sat 18, Sun 19 May (1-5). Visitors also welcome by appt.**

A background of mature trees surrounds this well-established garden. Features include herbaceous borders, gravel area which supports artifacts and a patio which contains many pots of seasonal plants. The garden houses unusual plants and shrubs which are evident throughout the year, areas are continually evolving. A natural harmonious ambience is felt in this garden.

21 LITTLE STUBBINS

Stubbins Lane, Claughton-on-Brock, Preston PR3 0PL. Margaret & Mick Richardson, 01995 640376, marg254@btinternet.com, www.littlestubbins.co.uk. *2m S of Garstang. Leave M6 at J32. Follow signs for Garstang 6m, turn R onto B6340, 2nd on R, Stubbins Lane ½ m on R.* Home-made teas. **Adm £3, chd free. Sun 2 June (1-5); Mon 3 June (11-4.30). Visitors also welcome by appt.**

Plantaholic's delightful country garden, providing lots of colour with stunning planting combinations. ¾ acre garden packed full with shrubs, perennials, bulbs, climbers and old English roses to provide long season of interest. Beautiful professional hard landscaping. Hostas a speciality, over 90 varieties on show, mostly in pots and some amongst the planting. 4 x Gold awards North West in Bloom. Featured in Lancashire Life. Gravel drive.

22 LOWER DUTTON FARM

Gallows Lane, Ribchester PR3 3XX. Mr R Robinson. *1½ m NE of Ribchester. Leave M6 J31. Take A59 towards Clitheroe, turn L at T-lights towards Ribchester. Signed from B6243 & B6245. Ample car parking.* Teas & wine. **Adm £3.50, chd free. Sat 10, Sun 11 Aug (1-5).**

Traditional long Lancashire farmhouse and barn (not open), with 1½ acre garden. Formal gardens nr house with mixed herbaceous beds, wild flower beds and shrubs, sweeping lawns leading to wildlife area and established large pond and small woodland with mix of trees and plants. Ample parking on adjacent field. Lawns may be difficult in very wet weather.

ALLOTMENTS

23 NEW MARLBOROUGH ALLOTMENTS

Marlborough Road, Flixton, Manchester M41 5QP. Lesley Pye. *2.5 m SW of Urmston. From J10 M60 go S through 2 r'abouts to T-lights, turn R into Moorside Rd. At next r'about take 2nd exit signed Lymm. After next T-lights take 5th road on R into Irlam Rd then 1st R into Marlborough Rd.* Home-made teas. **Adm £3, chd free. Sun 21 July (1-5). Combined with Brookfield.**

4 acres with 109 plots. Large variety of fruit and veg. Mini orchard and 500yds of grassed walkways with colourful perennial and annual flower borders. Borough of Trafford award-winning allotments. Many places to sit and relax with a wide range of plants, baskets, containers and other garden items for sale.

24 MILL BARN

Goosefoot Close, Samlesbury, Preston PR5 0SS. Chris Mortimer, 01254 853300, chris@millbarn.net. *6m E of Preston. From M6 J31 $2\frac{1}{2}$ m on A59/A677 B/burn. Turn S. Nabs Head Lane, then Goosefoot Lane.* Cream teas. **Adm £3, chd free. Sats, Suns 8, 9, 22, 23 June; 7, 8 Sept (1-5). Combined opening, adm £4 with Primrose Hill, 7, 8 Sept. Visitors also welcome by appt May to Sept. Min group donation £40.**

Tranquil terraced garden along the banks of R Darwen. A garden on many levels, both physical and psychological. A sense of fun and mystique is present and an adventurous spirit may be needed to negotiate the various parts. Flowers, follies and sculptures engage the senses, moving up from the semi formal to the semi wild where nature is only just under control. A grotto dedicated to alchemy, a suspension bridge over the R Darwen 20m wide at this point, and a tower on the far bank above the 'Lorelei' rocks where a princess might wait for her lover. Partial wheelchair access, visitors have not been disappointed in the past. The synthesis between cottage garden planting, garden buildings, statuary and follies evokes atmosphere which you are encouraged to soak up - by relaxing and using the plentiful seating areas in the garden. Visitors comment that they lost all sense of time and place - is it the magic of the witch country that casts its spell over this $1\frac{1}{2}$ -acre plot?

Visitors comment that they lost all sense of time and place - is it the magic of the witch country . . . ?

25 MONTFORD COTTAGE

Cuckstool Lane, Fence-in-Pendle BB12 9NZ. Craig Bullock & Tony Morris, www.craigbullock.net/garden.html. *4m N of Burnley. From J13 M65, take A6068 (signed Fence), in 2m turn L onto B6248 (signed Brierfield). Proceed down hill for $\frac{1}{2}$ m (past pub/restaurant). Entrance to garden on L, with limited car park further down hill on L.* Light refreshments. **Adm £3.50, chd free. Sat 1, Sun 2 June (11-5).**

Artist's garden in Pendle Hill country.

26 MOSS SIDE HOUSE

Moss Side Lane, Stalmine, Poulton-le-Fylde FY6 0JW. Mrs Muriel Bradshaw, 01253 700408. *3m N of Poulton-Le-Fylde. M55 J3 follow A585 to Fleetwood T-lights turn L next lights bear R still on A585, T-lights turn R Shard Lane A588 through Hambleton to Stalmine, 4th turning R onto Moss Side Lane. 3rd on R.* Cream teas. **Adm £4, chd free. Sun 31 Mar; Mon 1 Apr; Sat 15; Sun 16 June (11-4). Visitors also welcome by appt May to July.**

Delightful country garden with something new at every turn. Wildlife ponds with bridge, waterwall, boat, mini gravel beach with deck chairs. Colourful selection of trees, shrubs, annuals, roses, unusual plants, water features, large display of spring flowers, hidden areas and lawns with gazebos and tables for picnics. Also opening **Barndale** (family's adjoining garden) well planted mixed garden, small orchard and vegetable garden. Family garden that has matured with four children!!

27 NEW 15 PRESTON ROAD

Southport PR9 9EG. Michèle Martin, www.outsideinfluence.co.uk. *1m N of Southport. Take A565 Southport to Preston Rd turn R at T-lights at Hesketh Park into Park Rd, turn L into Park Crescent, take 3rd exit at r'about into Park Ave, Preston Rd 2nd on R.* Home-made teas. **Adm £3, chd free (share to Queenscourt Hospice & Cancer Research UK). Sun 28 Apr (1-5).**

A walled town garden developed by a garden designer with a passion for Chinese gardens. Some unusual plants grown from seed e.g. a black mulberry, artichokes and Eucryphia nymansensis 'Nymansay'. Plus heritage varieties of vegetables. Most of the garden is accessible.

28 PRIMROSE HILL

Goose Foot Lane, Samlesbury Bottoms, Preston PR5 0RQ. Mrs S Childs. *4m E of Preston. From M6 J31, $2\frac{1}{2}$ m on A59 then A677 towards Blackburn. Turn R into Nabs Head Lane, then R into Goosefoot Lane, go down hill round very sharp bend into Samlesbury Bottoms.* Cream teas at Mill Barn. **Adm £4, chd free. Sat 7, Sun 8 Sept (1-5). Combined opening with Mill Barn.**

After the drama of summer come to my garden as it dissolves into autumn. The apple trees should be bearing fruit and the grasses will be at their best. Enjoy the drowsy, comfy, last flowering of the borders and take a moment to relax in a quiet country garden.

29 ◆ THE RIDGES

Weavers Brow (cont. of Cowling Rd), Limbrick, Chorley PR6 9EB. Mr & Mrs J M Barlow, 01257 279981, www.bedbreakfast-gardenvisits.com. *2m SE of Chorley town centre. M6 J27, M61 J8 follow signs for Chorley A6, then Cowling & Rivington. At Morrison's up Brook St. to mini r'about. Take Cowling Brow, garden on RH-side after Spinners Arms.* **Adm £3.50, chd free. For NGS: Mon 6 May; Mon 26 Aug (11-5). For other opening times and information, please phone or see garden website.**

3 acres, incl old walled orchard garden, cottage-style herbaceous borders, and perfumed rambling roses through the trees. Arch leads to formal lawn, surrounded by natural woodland, shrub borders and trees with contrasting foliage. Woodland walks and dell. Natural looking stream, wildlife ponds. Walled water feature with Italian influence, and walled herb garden. Classical music played. Home made cakes, baked and served by ladies of St James Church, Chorley. Some gravel paths and woodland walks not accessible.

GROUP OPENING

30 SEFTON PARK GARDENS

Liverpool L8 3SL. *3m S of Liverpool city centre. From end of M62 take A5058 Queens Drive ring rd S through Allerton to Sefton Park and follow signs. Parking roadside in Sefton Park. Maps and tickets at all gardens.* Light refreshments, home-made teas, ice cream, strawberries and cream, Pimms. **Combined adm £5, chd free.** Sun 30 June (12-5).

PARKMOUNT
38 Ullet Road, L17 3BP. Jeremy Nicholls.

SEFTON PARK ALLOTMENTS
Greenbank Drive, L8 3SA. Sefton Park Allotments Society.
Next door to Sefton Park cricket club

SEFTON VILLA
14 Sefton Drive, L8 3SD. Patricia Williams. 0151 281 3687 seftonvilla@live.co.uk

VICE CHANCELLOR'S GARDEN
12 Sefton Park Road, L8 3SL. Liverpool. University of Liverpool, Vice-Chancellor Sir Howard & Lady Sheila Newby.

YORK HOUSE GARDENS
Croxteth Drive, L17 3AQ. Jean Niblock & Arena Homes.

A varied and interesting group of gardens showing the wide range of gardening opportunities existing in the city of Liverpool. From manicured lawns and shrub roses of the 1-acre Vice-Chancellor's lodge garden, to the 6 acres of vegetables and flowers of the allotments in Sefton Park, there is something to please every gardening enthusiast. York House Gardens is an inspirational garden surrounding a tower block with herbaceous borders and colourful containers and large greenhouse. There are some surprises and rare and unusual plants at Parkmount - one of Liverpool's old merchant house gardens - as well as Paddy Christian's special plants for sale and refreshments. The small walled garden at Victorian Sefton Villa is secluded and tranquil, with rare plants and interesting features, incl an enclosed Japanese garden. There will be musical entertainment and plants from Ness Gardens at the Vice Chancellor's lodge, and Sefton Park Allotments will have full afternoon teas. Old shrub roses at Vice Chancellor's Lodge. Stunning colour themed perennial planting at Parkmount. String Quartet playing and Ness Gardens experts at the Vice Chancellor's Lodge. Wheelchair access at York House and Sefton Park Allotments. Limited access at the Vice-Chancellor's Lodge. Wheelchair access WC at the allotments.

31 NEW SILVER BIRCHES
Rawlinson Lane, Heath Charnock, Chorley PR7 4DE. Margaret and John Hobbiss, 01257 480411. *2½ m S of Chorley. From either N or S directions, travel along the A6 (Chorley-Bolton rd). Turn into Wigan Lane A5106. After 0.4m turn L into Rawlinson Lane. Silver Birches is approx 0.2m on L. Please park on road. Disabled parking (with prior arrangement) may be available by the house.* Home-made teas. **Adm £2.50, chd free (share to St George's Church & Bolton Lads & Girls Club).** Sat 27, Sun 28 July (1-5). **Visitors also welcome by appt July to Aug.**
The garden has evolved from a family garden into one of variety with herbaceous borders, sunken shaded dell, an African hut with surrounding flowers, lawns, 2 ponds, polytunnel, vegetable, soft fruit areas and orchard. The embankment of a disused railway has been turned into rockeries with a wood of native trees. There are paths for exploring which lead to the nearby Leeds-Liverpool canal. Access is possible to many areas of the garden and the woodland path, although uneven.

The embankment of a disused railway has been turned into rockeries . . .

32 SOUTHLANDS
12 Sandy Lane, Stretford M32 9DA. Maureen Sawyer & Duncan Watmough, 0161 283 9425, moe@southlands12.com, www.southlands12.com. *3m S of Manchester. Sandy Lane (B5213) is situated off A5181 (A56) ¼ m from M60 J7.* Home-made teas. 'Cake Away' service (take a slice of your favourite cake home). **Adm £3.50, chd free.** Sat 13, Sun 14 July (1-6). **Visitors also welcome by appt June to Aug. Guided tours for groups over 10.**
Artist's multi-award winning, inspirational S facing garden unfolding into a series of beautiful garden 'rooms' each with its own theme incl courtyard, Mediterranean, ornamental and woodland garden. Organic kitchen garden with large glasshouse containing vines and tomatoes. Extensive herbaceous borders, stunning containers of exotics, succulents and annuals, 2 ponds and water feature. Live jazz. Exhibition of art work derived from the garden. Featured in the Open Gardens Exhibition at the Museum of Garden History, Finalist Lambeth for CGS and in Daily Mail competition. Featured in 'Weekend' Daily Mail magazine and Manchester Evening News.

GROUP OPENING

33 NEW ST MICHAEL'S GARDENS
St Michael's, Preston PR3 0UE. *9m N of Preston. Head N on the A6. Turn L onto the A586 for 2½ m into St Michael's village.* Home-made teas at Catteralls Farm. **Combined adm £4, chd free.** Sat 8, Sun 9 June (10.30-4.30).

NEW 1 ASH GROVE
PR3 0TP. Mrs Dawn Gerrard.
From St Michaels village, turn into Rawcliffe Rd, take the 1st turning on L, house is 2nd corner house on the L

NEW CATTERALLS FARM
PR3 0UE. Anika & Andy Gibbons.
Turn R onto Rawcliffe Rd 0.3m Catteralls Farm is on the R

NEW THE CROFT
PR3 0TE. Mr Bill Patterson.
The Croft is on the R as you drive into the village

NEW MALLARD COTTAGE
PR3 0TE. Ms Jeanette Martin.
Garden to rear of Post Office Row on A586 Garstang Rd. Pedestrian access only via driveway between terraced cottages and The Coach House

NEW 11 RAWCLIFFE ROAD
PR3 0UD. John & Christine Holmes.
Next Door to St Kilda's garden

NEW ST. KILDA
PR3 0UD. Mrs Pat Kaylor.
Turn R on to Rawcliffe Rd & St Kilda is on the LH side 0.1m. No parking at the property

St Michael's is a small village on the R Wyre surrounded by farmland and woods.The village flower beds and churchyard are looked after by a group of volunteers and in North West In Bloom last year were awarded a Gold. The 6 gardens in the group are of varying sizes. 1 Ash Grove is a corner site with a pond, greenhouse and well planted borders. Catteralls Farm is a working dairy farm with an inspiring range of planting and structures incl parterre, rill and archways, watched over by a family of Pygmy goats. The Croft is a mature garden in which a display of acers and ferns lead into a secret area. Mallard Cottage is a compact garden which boasts a variety of shrubs, plants and attractive planting of clipped box. 11 Rawcliffe Road has a colourful display in well filled borders leading to a bespoke patio. Finally St Kilda, a large cottage garden planted in different styles with a glorious continuous tapestry of colour through all seasons. Disabled parking at Catteralls Farm.

34 THE STONES & ROSES GARDEN

White Coppice Farm, White Coppice, Chorley PR6 9DF. Raymond & Linda Smith, 01257 277633, stonesandroses@btinternet.com, www.stonesandroses.org. *3m NE of Chorley. J8 M61 (next to the Mormon Temple & Botany Bay) take A674 to Blackburn, 3rd R to Heapey & White Coppice. Parking up hill next to the garden.* Home-made teas. **Adm £3, chd free. Sat 13, Sun 14, Sun 21 July (2-5). Visitors also welcome by appt July. Individuals may be added to group bookings.**

The garden where the cows used to live set in the beautiful hamlet of White Coppice with wonderful views. Sunken rose garden, fountains, waterfalls, herbaceous borders, all with colour themed planting. Fruit tree walk to small lake with wild flower planting, formal kitchen garden. Wonderful walking area with beautiful cricket field. Gravel paths 3/4 of garden accessible by wheelchair.

35 VARLEY FARM

Anna Lane, Forest Becks, Bolton-by-Bowland, Clitheroe BB7 4NZ. Mr & Mrs B Farmer, 07887 638436, varleyforestbecks@btinternet.com. *7m N of Clitheroe. 9m S of Settle. 7 m E of Clitheroe. Leave A59 at Sawley & follow signs to Settle, take the 2nd L after the Copy Nook PH onto Settle Rd, turn L onto Anna Lane at the black & white road sign (Settle 9m Clitheroe 7m). If you go down a dip and over a bridge you have gone too far! Follow the lane to a sharp R turn. Varley Farm on L. Do not follow the Sat.Nav. to Wittons Farm.* Home-made teas. **Adm £4, chd free. Visitors welcome by appt May to Sept.**

1½ -acre garden that's been developing from 2004. Varley Farm is 700ft above sea level with views across the Forest of Bowland and Pendle. Herbaceous lawned cottage garden, flagged herb garden and walled gravel garden, steps to orchard and organic kitchen garden. Stream and pond area planted in 2009 still maturing with a grassed walk through natural meadow.

Parterre, rill and archways, watched over by a family of Pygmy goats . . . a glorious continuous tapestry of colour through all seasons . . .

36 WADDOW LODGE GARDEN

Clitheroe Road, Waddington, Clitheroe BB7 3HQ. Liz Dean & Peter Foley, www.gardentalks.co.uk. *1½ m N of Clitheroe. From M6 J31 take A59 (Preston-Skipton). A671 to Clitheroe then B6478. 1st house on L in village. Parking available on rd; blue badges in drive parking area on gravel.* Home-made teas. **Adm £3.50, chd free. Suns 26 May; 21 July (1-5).**

Inspirational 2-acre organic garden for all seasons surrounding Georgian house (not open) with views to Pendle and Bowland. An enthusiast's collection of many unusual plants with herbaceous borders, large island beds, shrubs, heathers, rhododendrons, small mature wooded area, old fashioned and hybrid roses. Extensive kitchen garden of vegetables and soft fruit, interesting heritage apple orchard, herbs, alpines and greenhouse plus developing wildlife meadow. Many colourful containers. Featured in Lancashire Magazine, Northern Life and on BBC Radio Lancashire. Euoparc Partner and Gold Green Tourism Award. Some gravel/bark paths, otherwise level surfaces.

37 WEDGWOOD

Shore Road, Hesketh Bank, Preston PR4 6XP. Denis & Susan Watson, 01772 816509, heskethbank@aol.com, www.wedgwoodgarden.com. *10m SW of Preston and 8m E of Southport. From Preston take A59 towards Liverpool. Turn R at T-lights for Tarleton. Through Tarleton & Hesketh Bank, 2½ m straight down Hesketh Lane/Station Rd. Bear L onto Shore Rd. Garden 1.3m. Parking on road.* Home-made teas. **Adm £3, chd free. Sun 23 June (11-5). Visitors also welcome by appt June to July.**

1-acre country garden containing gravel garden with pots, formal pond, 2 lawns surrounded by extensive herbaceous borders in sun or shade, with mature trees, 50ft square glasshouse, 50ft x 30ft walled patio (new for 2013) leading to 90ft parterre with colour themed beds, archways, pergolas and rose covered gazebo, wild flower meadow, fruit trees. Featured in Lancashire Life. Wood chip paths in parterre.

38 WEEPING ASH

Bents Garden & Home, Warrington Road, Glazebury WA3 5NS. John Bent, www.bents.co.uk. *15m W of Manchester. Located next to Bents Garden & Home, just off the East Lancs Rd A580 at Greyhound r'about near Leigh. Follow brown 'Garden Centre' signs.* Refreshments at Bents Garden & Home, located adjacent to Weeping Ash Garden. **Adm by donation. Suns 3, 10, 17, 24 Feb; 14 Apr (10-2); Suns 2, 9, 16, 23 Feb 2014.**

Created by retired nurseryman and photographer John Bent, Weeping Ash is a garden of all-yr interest with beautiful display of early snowdrops. Broad sweeps of colour lend elegance to this beautiful garden, which is currently undergoing an extensive re-design. Awarded the Garden Centre Association's Best Garden Centre.

The Stones & Roses Garden

Lancashire, Merseyside & Greater Manchester County Volunteers

County Organisers

Brenda Doldon, 2 Gorse Way, Formby, Merseyside L37 1PB, 01704 834253, rayandbrenda@o2.co.uk

Margaret Fletcher, 14 Saxon Road, Birkdale, Southport, Merseyside PR8 2AX, 01704 567742, geoffwfletcher@hotmail.co.uk

County Treasurer

Geoff Fletcher, 14 Saxon Road, Birkdale, Southport, Merseyside PR8 2AX, 01704 567742, geoffwfletcher@hotmail.co.uk

Publicity

Christine Ruth, 15 Princes Park Mansions, Croxteth Road, Liverpool L8 3SA, 0151 727 4877, caruthchris@aol.com

Lynn Kelly, 48 Bedford Road, Birkdale PR8 4HJ, 01704 563740, lynn-kelly@hotmail.co.uk

Assistant County Organisers

Ray Doldon, 2 Gorse Way, Formby, Merseyside L37 1PB, 01704 834253, rayandbrenda@o2.co.uk

Phil & Mel Gibbs 12 Bowers Avenue, Davyhulme, Urmston M41 5TG, 016174 79243, melphil@freeuk.com

Dorothy & Andrew Richards, Greenacre, 157 Ribchester Rd, Clayton-Le-Dale, Blackburn BB1 9EE, 01254 249694, andrewfrichards@talk21.com

LEICESTERSHIRE & RUTLAND

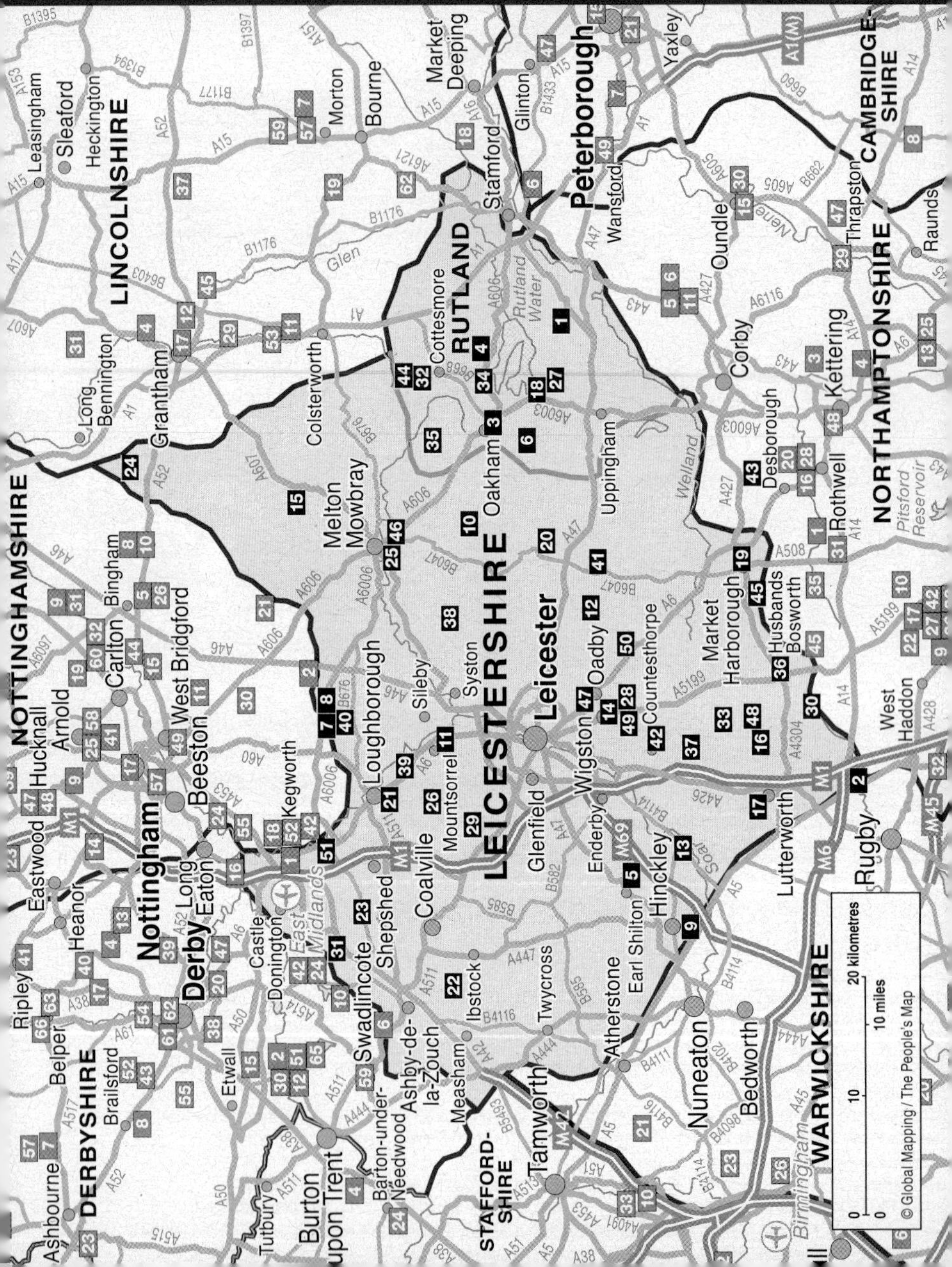

Opening Dates

February

Sunday 24
9 Burbage Gardens

March

Sunday 3
4 Barnsdale Gardens
24 The Homestead
50 Westview

Sunday 17
19 Hammond Arboretum

Sunday 31
18 Gunthorpe Hall

April

Open every day in April
26 Long Close

Sunday 28
32 The Old Hall

May

Open every day in May
26 Long Close

Sunday 5
3 Barleythorpe Gardens
20 Hedgehog Hall
46 Tresillian House

Monday 6
20 Hedgehog Hall

Saturday 11
15 Goadby Marwood Hall

Sunday 12
35 The Old Vicarage, Whissendine

Wednesday 15
45 Thorpe Lubenham Hall

Sunday 19
13 Dairy Cottage
27 Manton Gardens
50 Westview

Sunday 26
28 Mill House
34 The Old Vicarage, Burley

June

Open every day in June
26 Long Close

Sunday 2
10 Burrough Hall
39 Quorn Orchard Gardens

Wednesday 5
43 Stoke Albany House

Sunday 9
6 Braunston Gardens
7 88 Brook Street
8 109 Brook Street
33 The Old Stables

Wednesday 12
34 The Old Vicarage, Burley (Evening)
43 Stoke Albany House

National Gardens Weekend

Saturday 15
14 28 Gladstone Street
21 134 Herrick Road
23 Hill Park Farm
25 1 Leicester Road
28 Mill House
36 Orchard House
40 Ridgewold Farm
46 Tresillian House
49 1 Wellhouse Close

Sunday 16
5 Barracca
13 Dairy Cottage
14 28 Gladstone Street
21 134 Herrick Road
22 Highfield House
23 Hill Park Farm
25 1 Leicester Road
28 Mill House
36 Orchard House
40 Ridgewold Farm
44 59 Thistleton Road
46 Tresillian House
49 1 Wellhouse Close
51 Whatton Gardens

Wednesday 19
43 Stoke Albany House

Friday 21
21 134 Herrick Road (Evening)

Saturday 22
16 The Grange
30 Oak Tree House
31 The Old Chapel

Sunday 23
16 The Grange
20 Hedgehog Hall
30 Oak Tree House
31 The Old Chapel

Wednesday 26
43 Stoke Albany House

Saturday 29
49 1 Wellhouse Close

Sunday 30
22 Highfield House
48 Walton Gardens
49 1 Wellhouse Close

Whether your interest is in plants, fruit and vegetables or garden design, we have it all . . .

July

Open every day in July
26 Long Close

Wednesday 3
43 Stoke Albany House
48 Walton Gardens

Sunday 7
5 Barracca
37 Peatling & Willoughby Gardens

Monday 8
6 Braunston Gardens (Evening)

Wednesday 10
43 Stoke Albany House

Thursday 11
41 Rolleston Hall

Saturday 13
14 28 Gladstone Street
28 Mill House

Sunday 14
1 Acre End
14 28 Gladstone Street
28 Mill House
50 Westview

Saturday 20
12 Cupplesfield
42 70 Station Road

Sunday 21
12 Cupplesfield
37 Peatling & Willoughby Gardens
42 70 Station Road

Wednesday 24
17 Green Wicket Farm

Sunday 28
23 Hill Park Farm
29 Mountain Ash
33 The Old Stables

August

Open every day in August
26 Long Close

Sunday 4
29 Mountain Ash
37 Peatling & Willoughby Gardens
46 Tresillian House

Wednesday 7
17 Green Wicket Farm

Sunday 11
36 Orchard House
47 University of Leicester Botanic Garden

Sunday 25
2 Avon House

September

Open every day in September
26 Long Close

Sunday 8
50 Westview

October

Open every day in October

26 Long Close

Sunday 6

19 Hammond Arboretum

Sunday 13

46 Tresillian House

Sunday 20

4 Barnsdale Gardens

Gardens open to the public

4 Barnsdale Gardens
51 Whatton Gardens

By appointment only

11 7 The Crescent
38 Pine House

Water garden with a stream and 'champagne' pond . . .

Also open by Appointment ☎

1 Acre End
2 Avon House
5 Barracca
7 88 Brook Street
8 109 Brook Street
14 28 Gladstone Street
15 Goadby Marwood Hall
18 Gunthorpe Hall
20 Hedgehog Hall
21 134 Herrick Road
22 Highfield House
23 Hill Park Farm
24 The Homestead
26 Long Close
28 Mill House
30 Oak Tree House
31 The Old Chapel
32 The Old Hall
33 The Old Stables
34 The Old Vicarage, Burley
35 The Old Vicarage, Whissendine
37 Peatling & Willoughby Gardens
40 Ridgewold Farm
42 70 Station Road
43 Stoke Albany House
46 Tresillian House
48 Orchards, Walton Gardens
49 1 Wellhouse Close
50 Westview

The Gardens

1 ACRE END

The Jetties, North Luffenham LE15 8JX. Jim & Mima Bolton, 01780 720906, mmkb@mac.com. *7m SE of Oakham via Manton & Edith Weston, 7m SW of Stamford via Ketton. 2m off A47 through Morcott village.* Light refreshments at North Luffenham Community Centre. **Adm £5, chd free. Sun 14 July (11-6). Visitors also welcome by appt June to Aug. Guided tours available on request.**

1-acre garden, imaginatively designed, intensively planted, incl knot garden, oriental courtyard garden, mixed borders, circular lawn with island beds, herb and scented garden. Working fruit and vegetable garden, long herbaceous borders, woodland garden. Many unusual trees, shrubs, herbaceous perennials, tender exotics in containers. All organically managed to encourage wildlife. Paintings, cards, crafts (share to NGS). Wildlife wood carvings display. Challenging Quiz. Featured in GGG. Mainly grass paths and lawns, some gravel.

♿ ✿ ☕ ☎

ARTHINGWORTH OPEN GARDENS
See Northamptonshire

25 ASHBY ROAD
See Nottinghamshire

2 AVON HOUSE

4 Rugby Road, Catthorpe, Lutterworth LE17 6DA. David & Julia King, 01788 860346, avonhouse4@btinternet.com. *3m NE Rugby 3m S Lutterworth. 1m SW M1 J19, A14, M6 Junctions. ½ m NE A5.* Parking and Refreshments at Manor Farm Shop, 200yds. **Adm £2.50, chd free.**
Sun 25 Aug (11-5). Visitors also welcome by appt May to Aug, max 20.

A surprising ½ -acre garden in the heart of the village with varied interest. Large vegetable plot, mixed borders of late season interest, fruit trees, hens, bees and garden ponds all tucked away behind a country cottage. Some gravelled areas.

♿ 🐕 ✿ ☕ ☎

GROUP OPENING

3 BARLEYTHORPE GARDENS

Barleythorpe, nr Oakham LE15 7EQ. *1m from Oakham on A6006 towards Melton Mowbray. Car park in Pasture Lane 1st turn L in Barleythorpe by post box. Please park in field on L not on lane.* Home-made teas at Dairy Cottage. **Combined adm £5, chd free (share to East Midlands Immediate Care Scheme). Sun 5 May (2-5).**

DAIRY COTTAGE
Mr & Mrs W Smith

THE LODGE
Dr & Mrs T J Gray

8 MANOR LANE
Richard Turner

Visit 3 beautiful gardens in this Rutland village. Dairy Cottage (opp car park), is a cottage-style garden at rear with interesting and unusual shrubs and spring bulbs. Paved/walled garden to front (with pond) and lime hedge. Orchard with spring bulbs and unusual shrubs and trees. The Lodge (next door), with mixed flowers within walled garden, ½ lawn and part-walled kitchen garden small stretch of gravel path between lawned area and vegetable garden. Follow path alongside Dairy Cottage, turn left into Barleythorpe House, 8 Manor Lane - offering both water and woodland. Flowering shrubs, large weeping trees, small lake and woodland walk.

♿ 🐕 ✿ ☕

4 ◆ BARNSDALE GARDENS

The Avenue, Exton, Oakham LE15 8AH. Nick Hamilton, 01572 813200, www.barnsdalegardens.co.uk. *3m E of Oakham. Turn off A606, between Oakham & Stamford, at Barnsdale Lodge Hotel then 1m on L.* **Adm £6.50, chd £2.50. For NGS: Sun 3 Mar, Sun 20 Oct (9-5). For other opening times and information, please phone or see garden website.**

Consisting of 39 individual gardens and features, the Barnsdale television garden has a wealth of ideas for your garden. Whether your interest is in plants, fruit and vegetables or garden design, we have it all. A garden enjoyed by gardeners and non-gardeners alike. Featured on BBC's RHS Chelsea Flower Show programme. Wheelchairs and mobility scooter available for use free of charge. Please book in advance.

♿ ✿ ☕

5 BARRACCA
Ivydene Close, Earl Shilton LE9 7NR. Mr & Mrs John & Sue Osborn, 01455 842609, susan.osborn1@btinternet.com. *10m W of Leicester. From A47 after entering Earl Shilton, Ivydene Close is 4th on L from Leicester side of A47.* Cream teas. **Adm £3, chd free. Sun 16 June, Sun 7 July (11-5). Visitors also welcome by appt May to July, 10+.**

1-acre garden with lots of different areas, a silver birch walk, wildlife pond with seating, apple tree garden, Mediterranean planted area and lawns surrounded with herbaceous plants and shrubs. Patio area with climbing roses and wisteria. There is also a utility garden with greenhouse, vegetables in beds, herbs and perennial flower beds, lawn and fruit cage. Part of the old gardens owned by the Cotton family who used to open approx 9 acres to the public in the 1920's. Partial wheelchair access.

♿ ✿ ☕ ☎

BAXTER FARM
See Nottinghamshire

BLUEBELL ARBORETUM AND NURSERY
See Derbyshire

GROUP OPENING

6 NEW BRAUNSTON GARDENS
Oakham LE15 8QS. *Village of Braunston, nr Oakham. Hill Top Farm is 1/2 m from Oakham on Braunston Rd on R (driving from Oakham) on brow of hill. Parking available. Quaintree Hall is 1st house on L in Cedar St off High St past village green with red telephone box in centre of village. Parking in Cedar St & around church.* Home-made teas. **Combined adm £5, chd free (share to Royal Agricultural Benevolent Institution). Sun 9 June (2-6). Evening Opening, wine, Mon 8 July (6-9).**

The Old Vicarage, Burley

© Suzie Gibbons

NEW HILL TOP FARM 🛏
Oakham. Jane & William Cross 01572 755744 janecross49@yahoo.co.uk www.cross-in-rutland.co.uk

QUAINTREE HALL
Mrs Caroline Lomas

Two 1½ acre gardens belonging to keen gardening friends (spot the matching greenhouses) with different styles. Hill Top Farm - Fabulous views of the surrounding countryside from this aptly named garden. The terrace surrounding the house is host to containers and beds packed with sun-loving plants. Paths invite the visitor to stroll amongst borders filled with interesting shrubs and perennials, over treed lawns and through wildflower areas. Quaintree Hall - An established garden surrounding the medieval hall house (not open) incl a formal box parterre to the front of the house, a woodland walk, formal walled garden with yew hedges, a small picking garden and terraced courtyard garden with conservatory. A wide selection of interesting plants can be enjoyed, each carefully selected for its specific site by the knowledgeable garden owner. Some gravel and steps.

♿ 🐕 ✿ 🛏 ☕

7 88 BROOK STREET
Wymeswold LE12 6TU. Adrian & Ita Cooke, 01509 880155, itacooke@btinternet.com. *4m NE of Loughborough. From A6006 Wymeswold turn S by church onto Stockwell, then E along Brook St. Roadside parking on Brook St.* Light refreshments. **Combined adm £3, chd free. Sun 9 June (11-5). Combined with 109 Brook Street. Visitors also welcome by appt May to June, max 20.**

The ½ acre garden is set on a hillside, which provides lovely views across the village, and comprises 3 distinct areas: firstly, a 'cottage-style' garden; then a water garden with a stream and 'champagne' pond; and finally at the top there is a vegetable plot, small orchard and wild flower meadow.

🐕 ✿ ☕ ☎

8 109 BROOK STREET

Wymeswold LE12 6TT. Maggie & Steve Johnson, 01509 880866, sameuk@tiscali.co.uk. *4m NE of Loughborough. From A6006 Wymeswold turn S onto Stockwell, then E along Brook Street. Road side parking along Brook Street. Steep drive with limited disabled parking at house.* Home-made teas. **Combined adm £3, chd free. Sun 9 June (11.30-5). Combined with 88 Brook Street. Visitors also welcome by appt May to June 10+. Min 2 weeks notice required please.**

S-facing ¾ -acre gently sloping garden with views to open country. Mature garden much improved. Patio with roses and clematis, wildlife and fish ponds, mixed borders, vegetable garden, orchard, hot garden, woodland garden plus more. David Austin roses and wide selection of shrubs and perennials.

Demonstration of rain water harvesting on limited budget. Some gravel paths.

Come and see how many plants you can get into a small garden . . .

GROUP OPENING

9 BURBAGE GARDENS

Sketchley Manor Estate. LE10 2LR. *1m S of Hinckley. From M69 J1, take B4109 signed Hinckley. 1st L after 2nd r'about into Sketchley Manor Estate then 1st R, 1st L. Both gardens within walking distance.* Light refreshments at 7 Hall Road. **Combined adm £3.50, chd free. Sun 24 Feb (11-4).**

6 DENIS ROAD
Mr & Mrs D A Dawkins

7 HALL ROAD
Don & Mary Baker

A pleasant West Leicestershire village. **6 Denis Road,** small garden designed to look much larger. Wide range of plants incl ferns, hostas and special clematis. Alpines in sinks and large collection of snowdrops. **7 Hall Road,** medium-sized garden with mixed borders and a good mix of shrubs. Foliage plants, hellebores, spring bulbs, hardy geraniums and unusual perennials.

10 BURROUGH HALL

Somerby Road, Burrough-on-the-Hill, Melton Mowbray LE14 2QZ. Richard & Alice Cunningham. *Close to B6047. 10 mins from A606. 20 mins from Melton Mowbray.* Home-made teas. **Adm £3.50, chd free. Sun 2 June (2-5).**

A developing garden redesigned in 2008 and offering magnificent views. Surrounded by mature trees and shrubs, the garden consists of developing borders, vegetable garden, fruit trees and woodland walks. Every year has seen new planting which will continue. In essence a family garden to be enjoyed by all generations. Gravel paths & lawn.

CALKE ABBEY
See Derbyshire

THE COTTAGE
See Derbyshire

11 7 THE CRESCENT

Rothley LE7 7RW. Mrs Fiona Dunkley, 01162 376301, fiona.dunkley@btinternet.com. *Off Montsorrel Lane, Rothley. Parking available in Montsorrel Lane.* Home-made teas. **Adm £2, chd free. Visitors welcome by appt May to Oct, min 10, max 30.**

Small, well designed garden with interesting and unusual plants. Good display of bulbs in spring, especially alliums. Many diverse grasses and bamboos combined with verbena bonariensis create a very special effect in late summer and autumn.

12 NEW CUPPLESFIELD

2 Stoughton Road, Gaulby LE7 9BB. Roger & Ruth Harris. *The village of Gaulby lies between Leicester & Market Harborough close to main A47. Garden is on outskirts of Gaulby & is 1st property on L on entering the village from the direction of Stoughton & Leicester.* **Adm £3.50, chd free. Sat 20, Sun 21 July (1.30-5.30).**

One acre garden packed full of surprises! Themes range from a contemporary Japanese style area to a long informal herbaceous border and Piet Oudolf inspired prairie beds. Interesting borders incl a hidden 'jungle', a small wild life pond and low walled potager. The garden is alive with sculptures and 'hedge art' which add that extra interest. Such a lot in so little. Most parts accessible by wheelchair in dry conditions. Reduced when wet due to grass paths.

13 DAIRY COTTAGE

15 Sharnford Road, Sapcote LE9 4JN. Mrs Norah Robinson-Smith. *9m SW of Leicester. Follow NGS signs from centre of Sapcote.* Home-made teas. **Adm £3, chd free. Sun 19 May, Sun 16 June (11-4).**

Old cottage garden set in ¾ acre, extensively planted with a wide range of bulbs, shrubs and perennials. With over 70 varieties of clematis and many roses climbing over arches, ropes and trees. Walled garden with pergola. Garden extends into a potager.

THE DOWER HOUSE
See Derbyshire

ELM HOUSE
See Nottinghamshire

FROGGERY COTTAGE
See Northamptonshire

14 28 GLADSTONE STREET

Wigston Magna LE18 1AE. Chris & Janet Huscroft, 01162 886014, chris.huscroft@tiscali.co.uk. *4m S of Leicester. Off Wigston by-pass (A5199) follow signs off r'about.* Home-made teas. **Adm £2, chd free. Sat 15 June (11-5); Sun 16 June (12-5); Sat 13 July (11-5); Sun 14 July (12-5). Combined with Westview, 14 July, adm £3. Visitors also welcome by appt June to July, max 20.**

Our small town garden is divided into rooms and bisected by a pond with a bridge. It is brimming with unusual hardy perennials, incl collections of ferns and hostas. David Austin roses chosen for their scent feature throughout, incl a 30' rose arch. An unusual shade house with rare plants, incl hardy orchids and arisaemas. Come and see how many plants you can get into a small garden. Frameworks Knitters Museum nearby - open Sundays.

15 GOADBY MARWOOD HALL

Goadby Marwood LE14 4LN. Mr & Mrs Westropp, 01664 464202. *4 miles NW of Melton Mowbray. Between Waltham on the Wolds & Eastwell.* Home-made teas at Village Hall. **Adm £5, chd free. Sat 11 May (11-4). Visitors also welcome by appt. Coaches welcome.**

Redesigned in 2000 by the owner based on C18 plans. A chain of 5 lakes and several walled gardens all interconnected. Lakeside woodland walk. Yr-round interest. Landscaper trained under plantswoman Rosemary Verey at Barnsley House. Beautiful C13 church open. Swans on lake. Featured in episode of Castles in Country. Gravel and grass paths.

16 THE GRANGE

Kimcote, Lutterworth LE17 5RU. Shaun & Mary Mackaness, www.thegrangekimcote.co.uk. *12m S of Leicester. 4m from J20 of M1. From Lutterworth town centre follow signs to Kimcote. From Leicester turn L at Dunton Bassett towards Gilmorton & Kimcote. From A5199 towards Bruntingthorpe then via Walton.* Teas at All Saints Church. **Combined adm £3.50, chd free (share to LOROS). Sat 22, Sun 23 June (1-5). Combined with Oak Tree House.**

Newly designed and renovated English country garden hidden behind original brick walls of beautiful Grade II listed Queen Anne house. ¾-acre garden with immaculate expanses of lawn, parterre, pond, croquet lawn and stone terraces. Herbaceous borders with collection of Old English roses. Green oak structures and hand-forged gazebo and rose arches. Walkways with mature trees, pleached hornbeams and naturalised bulbs.

17 NEW GREEN WICKET FARM

Ullesthorpe Road, Bitteswell, Lutterworth LE17 4LR. Mrs Anna Smith. *2m NW of Lutterworth J20 M1. From Lutterworth follow signs for Bitteswell, drive through village towards Ullesthorpe. After approx ¾ m Green Wicket Farm is situated behind Bitteswell Cricket Club. Field parking signposted on the day.* Home-made teas. **Adm £3, chd free. Wed 24 July, Wed 7 Aug (2-5.30).**

A developing garden created in 2008 on a working farm. Clay soil and very exposed but beginning to look established. Many unusual hardy plants along with a lot of old favourites have been used to provide a long season of colour and interest. Formal pond and water features. Some gravel paths.

GREENWAY

See Northamptonshire

18 GUNTHORPE HALL

Gunthorpe, nr Oakham LE15 8BE. Tim Haywood, 01572 737203, timhaywood20@gmail.com. *1m S of Oakham. A6003, up drive between lodges. Proceed over railway bridge to gardens, 400 yards ahead. Please follow the signs for parking.* Light refreshments. **Adm £4, chd free. Sun 31 Mar (2-5). Visitors also welcome by appt Mar to Sept.**

Large garden in a most beautiful country setting with extensive views across the Rutland landscape. A great deal of recent re-design and new plantings have transformed this garden. The new spring bulbs and shrubs are once again spectacular.

19 HAMMOND ARBORETUM

Burnmill Road, Market Harborough LE16 7JG. The Robert Smyth Academy. *From High St, follow signs to The Robert Smyth Academy via Bowden Lane to Burnmill Rd. Park in 1st entrance on L.* Home-made teas. **Adm £3, chd free. Sun 17 Mar, Sun 6 Oct (2-5).**

A site of just under 2½-acres containing an unusual collection of trees and shrubs, many from Francis Hammond's original planting dating from 1913 to 1936 whilst headmaster of the school. Species from America, China and Japan with malus and philadelphus walks and a moat. Proud owners of 4 'champion' trees identified by national specialist. Guided walks and walk plans available. Some steep slopes.

20 HEDGEHOG HALL

Loddington Road, Tilton on the Hill LE7 9DE. Janet & Andrew Rowe, 01162 597339, janetnandrew@btinternet.com. *8m W of Oakham. 2m N of A47 on B6047 between Melton & Market Harborough. Turn between church & PH in Tilton towards Loddington & follow signs.* Cream teas. **Adm £3, chd free. Sun 5, Mon 6 May, Sun 23 June (11-5). Visitors also welcome by appt June to July, 10+.**

½-acre organically managed plant lover's garden. Steps leading to three stone-walled terraced borders filled with shrubs, perennials and bulbs. Lavender walk, herb border, spring garden, colour themed long border and serpentine island bed packed with campanulas, astrantias, sanguisorbas, roses, clematis and many more. Sheltered walled courtyard filled with hostas, ferns and wisteria. Hot terraced borders. Cake stall.

Secluded town garden brimming with texture, colour and creative care . . .

21 NEW 134 HERRICK ROAD

Loughborough LE11 2BU. Janet Currie & Pete Mosley, 01509 212191, janet.currie@me.com, www.thesecateur.com. *1m SW of Loughborough. From M1 J23 - take A512 Ashby Rd towards Loughborough. At r'about turn R onto A6004 Epinal Way. At Beacon Rd r'about turn L, Herrick Rd is 200ft on R. 134 is approx 200ft on the R. From town centre - take B5350 towards Nanpanton. At r'about turn L onto A6004 Epinal Way. At Beacon Rd r'about turn L, next R onto Herrick Rd. Directions as above.* Light refreshments. **Adm £2, chd free. Sat 15, Sun 16 June (12-4). Evening Opening, wine, Fri 21 June (5-9). Visitors also welcome by appt June to Sept.**

Pass through the wooden gate of our Victorian terrace into a part-walled haven. Designed for tranquillity, wildlife and produce, this small, secluded town garden is brimming with texture, colour and creative flair. We're holding a Secret Craft Fair on the 15/16th June as part of National Gardens Day. Specially selected high quality crafts with a garden theme will be on sale and displayed amongst the plants.

Rolleston Hall

sempervivums. National Collection of heliotropes. A garden where plants (incl vegetables) come first to produce a peaceful and relaxed overall effect.

25 NEW 1 LEICESTER ROAD
Melton Mowbray LE13 0DB. Mrs Jane Cooper. *1m W Melton Mowbray on A607. Opposite Melton Mowbray Building Society offices & Baptist church*. Home-made teas. **Combined adm £3.50, chd free. Sat 15, Sun 16 June (2-5.30). Combined with Tresillian House.**
A surprisingly large and private garden on the edge of a housing estate overlooking open countryside. Originally a large area of grass, hawthorn and fir trees - interest has been added by planting a variety of trees, mixed borders, gravel border and railway sleeper stepped beds. Ponds, a vegetable plot and hen enclosure aim to create interest around each corner of this developing garden. Wheelchair access via double gates. Boards will be provided to gain access to raised patio area with awning offering general overview of garden.

22 HIGHFIELD HOUSE
1 Highfield Close, Normanton Le Heath, Coalville LE67 2TN. Mr & Mrs T Ikin, 01530 260375, maryikin@aol.com. *3m E of A42 at Ashby-de-la-Zouch. On minor rd midway between Ashby de la Zouch & Ibstock. Highfield Close is off Main Street, opp church*. Home-made teas. **Adm £3, chd free. Sun 16, Sun 30 June (2-6). Visitors also welcome by appt June to Aug.**
This garden was established in 2004 on a farmyard site. SW facing with views over the Mease Valley, it comprises of gardens within a garden. The courtyard is a cottage garden with trellises, roses, water feature and tubs with small raised bed. Vegetable patch. Terraced lawns with herbaceous borders. A wild area with shrubs and trees, and two large ponds. Koi carp are fed late afternoon.

23 HILL PARK FARM
Dodgeford Lane, Belton LE12 9TE. John & Jean Adkin, 01530 222208. *6m W of Loughborough. Dodgeford Lane off B5324 between Belton & Osgathorpe*. Home-made teas. **Adm £3, chd free. Sat 15, Sun 16 June, Sun 28 July (2-6). Visitors also welcome by appt May to Sept, max 30.**
Beautiful medium sized garden to a working farm. Shrubs, fruit trees and vegetable garden. Rock garden and herbaceous borders brimming with colour. Pergola with clematis and roses, water features, and many planted stone troughs and window boxes.

24 THE HOMESTEAD
Normanton-by-Bottesford NG13 0EP. John & Shirley Palmer, 01949 842745. *8m W of Grantham. From A52. In Bottesford turn N, signed Normanton; last house on R before disused airfield. From A1, in Long Bennington follow signs S to Normanton, 1st house on L*. Home-made teas. **Adm £2, chd free. Sun 3 Mar (2-5). Visitors also welcome by appt Feb to June, max 30.**
3/4 -acre informal plant lover's garden. Vegetable garden, small orchard, woodland area, many hellebores, growing collection (over 100) of snowdrops and some single peonies and salvias. Collections of hostas and

26 LONG CLOSE
Main St, Woodhouse Eaves LE12 8RZ. John Oakland, 01509 890376, longclosegardens@talktalk.net. *4m S of Loughborough. Nr M1 J23. From A6, W in Quorn*. Home-made teas (19 May only). **Adm £4, chd £0.50. For NGS: Open daily April to Oct incl Bank Hols (10-5). Also special open day Sun 19 May (11-4). Visitors also welcome by appt Apr to Oct. Coaches permitted.**
5 acres spring bulbs, rhododendrons, azaleas, camellias, magnolias, many rare shrubs, mature trees, lily ponds; terraced lawns, herbaceous borders, potager in walled kitchen garden, penstemon collection, wild flower meadow walk. Winter, spring, summer and autumn colour, a garden for all seasons. Orchid Meadow guided walks from 10th June to mid July. Slopes and some uneven paths.

THE MALTINGS
See Northamptonshire

GROUP OPENING

27 MANTON GARDENS
Oakham LE15 8SR. *3m N of Uppingham. 3m S of Oakham. Manton is on S shore of Rutland Water 1/4 m off A6003. Please park carefully in village.* Home-made teas in Village Hall. **Combined adm £5, chd free. Sun 19 May (2-6).**

FRYERS COTTAGE
Martin & Tricia Lawrence

HALL COTTAGE
Mike & Mary Stenson

MANTON GRANGE
Anne & Mark Taylor

NEW **SHAPINSAY**
Mr & Mrs Tony & Jane Bews

4 varied gardens in small village on S shore of Rutland Water. Fryers Cottage - 3/4 -acre garden with beautiful views of Rutland Water. Interesting and varied areas of planting including wild areas, gravel garden and small fruit and vegetable potager. Hall Cottage - Small walled country cottage garden with extremely clever planting, incl roses, shrubs and perennials, with beautiful secret areas. A little gem! Manton Grange - 2 1/2 -acre garden with interesting trees, shrubs and herbaceous borders. Kitchen garden. Rose garden. Water features; lime tree walk and pergola walk with many clematis. Shapinsay - 2/3 - acre garden with mature trees framing views over the Chater Valley. The garden has a variety of features including a woodland walk, perennial borders, island shrub borders and a stream linking numerous ponds constructed in November 2011 by a local RHS gold medal garden designer.

28 MILL HOUSE
118 Welford Road, Wigston LE18 3SN. Mr & Mrs P Measures, 01162 885409, petemeasures@hotmail.co.uk. *4m S of Leicester. From Leicester take A5199 around r'about & continue on Bull Head St. At 2nd set of main T-lights (excl. Pedestrian) continue across to Welford Rd A5199 & pass Mercers Newsagents on L & 100 yds further on at brow of the hill, Mill House is on L.* Home-made teas. **Adm £2.50, chd free. Sun 26 May, Sat 15, Sun 16 June, Sat 13, Sun 14 July (11-5). Visitors also welcome by appt May to Aug.**
Walled town garden with extensive plant variety, many rare and unusual. A plant lovers garden, with interesting designs incorporated with the borders, rockery and scree. It is full of surprises with memorabilia and bygones a reminder of our past. Featured in Leicester Mercury, Fleckney Cummunici, BBCTV.

Several places to sit and relax around the garden . . .

29 NEW **MOUNTAIN ASH**
140 Ulverscroft Lane, Newtown Linford LE6 0AJ. Mike & Liz Newcombe. *7m SW of Loughborough, 7m NW of Leicester, 1m NW of Newtown Linford. From Newtown Linford 1/2 m N along Main Street towards Sharpley Hill, fork L into Ulverscroft Lane. Mountain Ash is 1/2 m on L.* Light refreshments. **Adm £3.50, chd free. Sun 28 July, Sun 4 Aug (11-5).**
2-acre SW facing garden with stunning views across Charnwood countryside. Near the house are patios, lawns, water features, flower and shrub beds, fruit trees, greenhouses and vegetable gardens. Lawns then slope down to a gravel garden, a large wildlife pond with waterfall and three areas of woodland, with pleasant walks though many species of trees. Several places to sit and relax around the garden.

30 OAK TREE HOUSE
North Road, South Kilworth, Lutterworth LE17 6DU. Pam & Martin Shave, 01858 575481, pamelashave@btconnect.com. *15m S of Leicester. From M1 J20, take A4304 towards Market Harborough. At North Kilworth turn R, signed South Kilworth.* Home-made teas. **Combined adm £3.50, chd free with The Grange. Sat 22, Sun 23 June (1-5). Visitors also welcome by appt June to Sept. Coaches permitted.**
2/3 acre garden. Formal design, softened by cottage style planting. Upper lawn with stone circle and sculpture. Large, colourful herbaceous borders, ornamental vegetable plots, pond with waterfall and greenhouse. Collection of perennial violas. Trees chosen for attractive bark. Arched pergola with roses and clematis. Many benches to sit on and admire the views! Surrounded by mature trees.

31 THE OLD CHAPEL
Main Street, Breedon-on-the-Hill DE73 8AN. Mr & Mrs S Jones, 01332 865460, vanessajjones@hotmail.co.uk. *2m W of E Mids Airport. 5m E of Ashby-de-la-Zouch, on the rd to Castle Donington. Rd is unclassified but runs between the B587 and A453. Parking & light refreshments at Priory Garden Centre approx 100yrds from garden.* Home-made teas. **Adm £3, chd free. Sat 22, Sun 23 June (11-5). Visitors also welcome by appt June to Sept.**
In the shadows of Breedon Hill lies The Old Chapel garden. With the brook running through the centre, two bridges lead to the other side which rises steeply through terraces to a high level pond and patios. The garden, more cottage than formal, is young with mixed shrubs and small trees. There is a formal lawn surrounded by borders consisting of herbaceous plants, roses and perennials.

32 THE OLD HALL
Main Street, Market Overton LE15 7PL. Mr & Mrs Timothy Hart, 01572 767276, stefahart@hambletondecorating.co.uk. *6m N of Oakham. Beyond Cottesmore; 5m from A1 via Thistleton. 10m E from Melton Mowbray via Wymondham.* Home-made teas. **Adm £4, chd free (share to Rutland Macmillan Cancer Support). Sun 28 Apr (2-6). Visitors also welcome by appt Apr to Sept. Refreshments available (extra cost).**
Set on a southerly ridge overlooking Catmose Vale, the garden is now on

4 levels. Stone walls and yew hedges divide the garden into enclosed areas with herbaceous borders, shrubs, and young and mature trees. In 2006 the lower part of garden was planted with new shrubs to create a walk with mown paths. Terrace and lawn give a great sense of space, enhancing the view. Neil Hewertson has been involved in the gardens design since 1990s.

33 THE OLD STABLES
Bruntingthorpe LE17 5QL. Gordon & Hilary Roberts, 0116 2478713, gordon.hilary.1943@btinternet.com. *10m S of Leicester. From Leicester A5199, R at Arnesby, follow signs for Bruntingthorpe. At end of village R towards Peatling Parva, 200 yds on R. From M1, J20 for Lutterworth A426. In town R front of police station, follow signs for Bruntingthorpe. Additional parking in village and approach through churchyard.* Home-made teas. **Adm £3, chd free. Sun 9 June, Sun 28 July (11-5). Visitors also welcome by appt June to July, 10+.**
Plant-lovers' delightful 1-acre country garden. A range of individual but interconnecting areas give a feeling of spaciousness and tranquillity. Wide grass walks set off the large herbaceous borders packed with a collection of interesting perennials, shrubs and climbers. Many mature trees, wild-life area with pond; striking views to Leicester. Rockery and raised alpine beds, tender plants in containers.

34 THE OLD VICARAGE, BURLEY
Church Road, Burley, Oakham LE15 7SU. Jonathan & Sandra Blaza, 01572 770588, sandra.blaza@btinternet.com. *1m NE of Oakham. In Burley just off B668 between Oakham and Cottesmore. Church Rd is opposite the village green, the Old Vicarage first left off Church Rd.* Home-made teas. **Adm £4, chd free (share to Eden Valley Hospice). Sun 26 May (1.30-5). Evening Opening, wine, Wed 12 June (6-9). Visitors also welcome by appt late May to June.**
3-acre country garden, planted for year-round interest, incl walled garden (with vine-house) producing fruit, herbs, vegetables and cut flowers. Formal lawns and borders, lime walk, rose gardens and a rill through an avenue of standard wisteria. Wildlife garden with pond, 2 orchards and beech woodland. Winner - Country Living Kitchen Table Talent Awards. Some gravel and steps.

Raised beds backed by small gothic orangery burgeoning with tender plants . . .

35 THE OLD VICARAGE, WHISSENDINE
LE15 7HG. Prof Peter & Dr Sarah Furness, 01664 474549, shfdesign@pathology.plus.com. *5m N of Oakham. Whissendine village is signed from A606 between Melton Mowbray & Oakham. Head for church - very visible tower. The Old Vicarage is adjacent, higher up the hill. Main entrance on opp side, 1st L on Station Rd; alternative entrance from churchyard. Maps available on website.* Home-made teas at local church. **Adm £3.50, chd free. Sun 12 May (2-5). Visitors also welcome by appt Apr to July. Refreshments available incl Pimms at evening visits (extra cost).**
2/3 -acre packed with variety. Terrace with topiary, a formal fountain courtyard and raised beds backed by small gothic orangery burgeoning with tender plants. Herbaceous borders surround main lawn. Wisteria tunnel leads to orchard filled with naturalised bulbs, home to four beehives, Gothic hen house plus six rare breed hens. Hidden 'white walk', unusual plants and much, much more! Featured in GGG. Partial access due to gravel paths, slopes and steps.

36 ORCHARD HOUSE
Husbands Bosworth, Lutterworth LE17 6LR. David & Ros Dunmore. *6m W of Market Harborough. A4304 from Market Harborough enter village. Mowsley Rd is 3rd R. A4304 from Lutterworth/ M1, enter village. Mowsley Rd is 3rd L.* Home-made teas. **Adm £2.50, chd free (share to Brook House Residential Care Home). Sat 15, Sun 16 June, Sun 11 Aug (11-5).**
A hidden gem. Small enclosed cottage garden with elements of surprise around each corner. Five 'garden rooms' shaded by mature trees and linked by Victorian gravel paths. Patio area with summer planting, small pond and other water features. Alpine bed and varied use of container planting. Wheelchair access to main features of the garden. Some additional gravel paths.

GROUP OPENING

37 PEATLING & WILLOUGHBY GARDENS
Willoughby Waterleys LE8 6UD. Eileen Spencer, 0116 2478321, eileenfarmway9@msn.com. *9m S of Leicester. Peatling Magna 2m W of Arnesby on A5199. For Willoughby take A426 to Dunton Bassett X'rds and follow signs to Willoughby.* Light refreshments at Willoughby Village Hall (7 July), Willoughby Church (21 July), Coldor (4 Aug). **Combined adm £3.50, chd free. Sun 7 July (11-5). Combined adm £3, chd free, Suns 21 July; 4 Aug (11-5). Visitors also welcome by appt July to Aug.**

COLDOR
Mr & Mrs C Shepherd.
Open 7 July, 4 Aug only

FARMWAY
Eileen Spencer.
Open all dates

JOHN'S WOOD
John & Jill Harris.
Open 7, 21 July only

Separated by a mile, the small villages of Peatling Magna and Willoughby Waterleys lie in the South Leicestershire countryside. Willoughby's name comes from springs which are near the surface. The church dates from Norman times. Peatling is thought to be the oldest village in Leicestershire. The church here dates from 1120, the windows from 1154. **Coldor** in Peatling is a 1/4 -acre garden with immaculate lawns, mixed herbaceous and shrub borders, pond, water features, alpine rockery and many containers. **Farmway** in Willoughby is a 1/4 acre garden on a gentle slope with views across Leicestershire. Closely planted with shrubs, perennials, lavender, roses and clematis. Two ponds, vegetable garden and many containers.

John's Wood is a 1½ -acre nature reserve planted in 2006 with 80cm native trees. The site incl a pond, wildflower meadow strip where butterflies are a feature in July. Mown paths through 18 feet high trees. Elevated viewing platform in place, further extension planned. Willoughby embroidery on display in village hall (7 July only). Church open (21 July only).

PIECEMEAL
See Nottinghamshire

38 PINE HOUSE
Gaddesby LE7 4XE. Mr & Mrs T Milward, 01664 840213, suemilward@gmail.com. *8m NE of Leicester. From A607, turn off for Gaddesby*. Home-made teas. **Adm £4, chd free. Visitors welcome by appt Apr to Oct, 10+. Coaches permitted.**
2-acre garden with fine mature trees, woodland walk, and water garden. Herb and potager garden and wisteria archway to Victorian vinery. Pleached lime trees, mixed borders with rare and unusual plants. Wide variety of tender plants in gravel garden and terracotta pot garden. Interesting topiary hedges and box trees. Grass Tennis Court and Dragon Hedge.

GROUP OPENING

39 QUORN ORCHARD GARDENS
Barrow Road, Quorn LE12 8DH. *2m S of Loughborough. From A6 take exit signed Woodhouse, Quorn & Great Central Railway. At 1st set T-lights go straight on towards Quorn village centre. At small r'about turn L into Barrow Road. Some SatNavs do not recognise Barrow Road as no through road*. Home-made teas 45 Barrow Road. **Combined adm £2.50, chd free. Sun 2 June (1-6).**

35 BARROW ROAD
Sally Ash

37 BARROW ROAD
Jacqui Fowler & Pat Manning

45 BARROW ROAD
Mr & Mrs Cox

NEW **50 BARROW ROAD, QUORN**
Ms Heather Rees

Quorn is a friendly village in the beautiful Charnwood district of Leicestershire, close to the National Forest. These neighbours and friends with a common interest in creating a beautiful green space in their own individual style, would like to invite you to share their passion for an afternoon. Three gardens are typical of 1930s urban properties with generous proportions and are created upon an old orchard. One garden belongs to Edwardian terraced Apple Tree Cottages built 1908, small but beautifully formed. Leicestershire Master Composters demonstration. Some small steps and narrow paths, but generally wheelchair friendly.

---

40 RIDGEWOLD FARM
Burton Lane, Wymeswold LE12 6UN. Robert & Ann Waterfall, 01509 881689, robert.waterfall@yahoo.co.uk. *5m SE of Loughborough. Off Burton Lane between A6006 & B676*.
Adm £3, chd free. Sat 15, Sun 16 June (2-6). Visitors also welcome by appt June to July. Coaches permitted.
2½ -acre rural garden in the Leicestershire Wolds. Conducted tours of the garden start at the sweeping drive through specimen trees. Beech, Laurel and Saxon hedges divide different areas. Lawn, rill, water feature, summer house, shrubs, rose fence, clematis arch, wisteria, ivy tunnel, rose garden, herbaceous, orchard, veg patch. Birch avenue gives view of the village. Woodland walk. Natural fish pond. Escorted tours.

Ethos of this garden is reused materials . . .

41 ROLLESTON HALL
Rolleston LE7 9EN. Mr & Mrs R Wilkinson, www.comegardenwithme.com. *8m N of Market Harborough. From Market Harborough, follow signs to Melton Mowbray B6047. Turn R at New Inn over cattle grid, down chestnut lined drive. From Uppingham, follow A47 towards Leicester, turn L onto B6047, L at New Inn*. Home-made teas. **Adm £4, chd free. Thur 11 July (10.30-4).**
A relaxed 6 acre mixture of the old and the new. Full to bursting traditional walled garden brimming with flowers, fruit and vegetables. Beautiful mixed borders, ravishing roses and lakeside walk with stunning views. A secret garden loved and lived in - whatever the weather.

42 NEW 70 STATION ROAD
Countesthorpe. LE8 5TB. Mr & Mrs Laura and Tom Hayward, 0116 2780 419, haywardlaura@hotmail.co.uk.
Approx 5m S of Leicester. Located between A5199 & A426. 10 mins from J21 of the M1. Garden located on Station Road, opposite library. Home-made teas. **Adm £2.50, chd free. Sat 20, Sun 21 July (10-4). Visitors also welcome by appt Apr to Sept.**
Newly created S facing garden. Approx 98x32 ft garden comprising several areas differing in style and content. Secret garden style veg patch. Outbuildings inc a brick and oak framed greenhouse using reclaimed materials. Plants incl a range of fruit trees, bulbs and herbaceous borders. Quirky ornamental features. Ethos of this garden is reused materials. Wildlife friendly.

43 STOKE ALBANY HOUSE
Desborough Road, Stoke Albany LE16 8PT. Mr & Mrs A M Vinton, 01858 535227, del.jones7@googlemail.com. *4m E of Market Harborough. Via A427 to Corby, turn to Stoke Albany, R at the White Horse (B669) garden ½ m on L*. **Adm £3.50, chd free (share to Marie Curie Cancer Care). Weds 5, 12, 19, 26 June; 3, 10 July (2-4.30). Groups also welcome by appt (preferably Weds) in June and July, 10+.**
4-acre country-house garden; fine trees and shrubs with wide herbaceous borders and sweeping striped lawn. Good display of bulbs in spring, roses June and July. Walled grey garden; nepeta walk arched with roses, parterre with box and roses. Mediterranean garden. Heated greenhouse, potager with topiary, water feature garden and sculptures. Featured in The Countryside magazine.

"Lemon drizzle cake, Victoria sponge ... yummy!"

SULBY GARDENS
See Northamptonshire

SUTTON BONINGTON ARBORETUM
See Nottinghamshire

44 NEW 59 THISTLETON ROAD
Market Overton, Oakham LE15 7PP. Mr Andrew Stewart JP. *7m NE of Oakham. Last house in E of village going towards Thistleton.* **Adm £4, chd free. Sun 16 June (10-4).**
Over the last 9 years, 1.8 acres of bare meadow have been converted into a restful haven for wildlife, including a large pond, shrubbery, modest arboretum with 12 specimen trees, orchard, small kitchen garden, spinney and large, colourful perennial beds. Small area of shingle to access main path.

45 THORPE LUBENHAM HALL
Lubenham LE16 9TR. Sir Bruce & Lady MacPhail. *2m W of Market Harborough. From Market Harborough take 3rd L off main rd, down Rushes Lane, past church on L, under old railway bridge and straight on up private drive.* Cream teas. **Adm £3.50, chd free. Wed 15 May (10-4).**
15 acres of formal and informal garden surrounded by parkland and arable. Many mature trees. Traditional herbaceous borders and various water features. Walled pool garden with raised beds. Ancient moat area along driveway. Gravel paths, some steep slopes and steps.

46 NEW TRESILLIAN HOUSE
67 Dalby Road, Melton Mowbray LE13 0BQ. Mrs Alison Blythe, 01664 481 997, studentsint@aol.com, www.studentsint.com. *2/3 m S Melton Mowbray. Follow signs B6047 (Dalby Road) S. Disabled parking on site otherwise park on slip rd opposite or Hamilton Drive. Please do not park on Dalby Rd.* Home-made teas. **Adm £2.50, chd free. Sun 5 May, Sat 15, Sun 16 June, Suns 4 Aug, 13 Oct (11-5). Combined with 1 Leicester Road, Sat 15, Sun 16 June (11-5). Combined adm £3.50. Visitors also welcome by appt Mar to Oct, max 20.**
3/4 -acre garden re-established by new owner between 2009 and 2012. Beautiful blue cedar trees, excellent specimen tulip tree. Parts of garden original, others reinstated with variety of plants and bushes. Original bog garden and pond. Vegetable plot. Parts left uncultivated with wild cowslips. Quiet oasis. Slate paths without steps but steep in places.

47 UNIVERSITY OF LEICESTER BOTANIC GARDEN
'The Knoll' entrance, Glebe Road, Oadby LE2 2LD. University of Leicester, 0116-271-2933, botanicgarden@le.ac.uk, www.le.ac.uk/botanicgarden. *2m SE of Leicester off A6. On outskirts of city opp race course.* Light refreshments. **Adm by donation. Sun 11 Aug (10-5). Coaches permitted.**
16-acre garden, whose formal planting centres around a restored Edwardian garden. Plantings originate from around the world and include an arboretum, a herb garden, woodland and herbaceous borders, rock gardens, a water garden, special collections of skimmia, aubretia and hardy fuchsia, and a series of glasshouses displaying temperate and tropical plants, alpines and succulents. Open daily; phone or see website for details.
NCH

GROUP OPENING

48 WALTON GARDENS
Walton LE17 5RP. *4m NE of Lutterworth. M1 J20 and, via Lutterworth follow signs for Kimcote & Walton, or from Leicester take A5199. After Shearsby turn R signed Bruntingthorpe. Follow signs.* Cream teas at The Dog & Gun (all proceeds to NGS). **Combined adm £4, chd free. Sun 30 June, Wed 3 July (11-5).**

THE MEADOWS
Mr & Mrs Falkner

NEW MULBERRY HOUSE
Mr & Mrs Karl & Hazel Busch

ORCHARDS
Mr & Mrs G Cousins
Visitors also welcome by appt May to July.
01455 556958
jennyandgraham@talktalk.net
www.grahamsgreens.com

SANDYLAND
Martin & Linda Goddard

TOAD HALL
Sue Beardmore

Small village set in beautiful south Leicestershire countryside. The five gardens at Walton are in such contrasting sizes and styles that, together, they make the perfect garden visit. There is a plantsman's garden filled with gorgeous rare plants; a Modernist garden where all the leaves are green (no variegated, gold or purple foliage) featuring the extensive use of grasses and a lovely view across the surrounding landscape; a very pretty country garden with an excellent vegetable plot, a traditional garden featuring serpentine hedging and last but not least, a really delightful enclosed cottage garden.

Our lovely garden has evolved into a peaceful haven designed to attract birds and bees . . .

49 1 WELLHOUSE CLOSE
Wigston LE18 2RQ. Barry & Mary Hayward, 07545 817664, maryehayward@googlemail.com. *4m S of Leicester. Located in Wigston Magna. By Road: From Leics at junction of Bull Head St/Welford Rd (A5199) turn R onto B582 Moat St. Then 1st L Horsewell Lane, until you pass shops on R & take next L into Laverstock Rd. 1 Wellhouse Close is 1st L on corner. By bus: either the 47 or 48 Wigston Magna, alight at Little Hill Shops.* Home-made teas. **Adm £2.50, chd free. Sats, Suns 15, 16, 29, 30 June (11-5). Visitors also welcome by appt June to Aug.**
Our lovely garden has evolved into a peaceful haven designed to attract birds and bees. You will discover very interesting planting in traditional wide borders which are brimming with a multitude of colourful herbaceous plants. We also have many varieties of hosta incl miniatures. Fleckney Communicata. Lower deck accessible. Assistance required for upper deck.

13 WESTFIELD ROAD
See Derbyshire

50 WESTVIEW
1 St Thomas's Road, Great Glen LE8 9EH. Gill & John Hadland, 01162 592170, gill@hadland.wanadoo.co.uk. *7m S of Leicester. Take either r'about from A6 into Great Glen. In village centre (War Memorial) follow NGS signs towards Burton Overy.* Home-made teas. **Adm £2, chd free. Sun 3 Mar (12-4); Suns 19 May; 14 July, 8 Sept (11-5). Combined with Gladstone Street, 14 July, adm £3, chd free. Visitors also welcome by appt Feb to Sept, max 30.**
Small walled cottage-style garden with yr-round interest. Interesting and unusual plants, many grown from seed. Formal box parterre herb garden, courtyard, herbaceous borders, small wildlife pond, greenhouse, beehives, vegetable and fruit area. Auricula display. Handmade garden sculptures and artefacts on display. Collection of Galanthus (snowdrops).

51 ◆ WHATTON GARDENS
Nr Kegworth. LE12 5BG. Lord & Lady Crawshaw, 01509 842225, www.whattonhouseandgardens.co.uk. *4m NE of Loughborough. On A6 between Hathern & Kegworth; 2½ m SE of J24 on M1.* **Adm £3.50, chd free. For NGS: Sun 16 June (11-6). For other opening times and information, please phone or see garden website.**
A wonderful extensive 15 acre C19 country house garden. Arboretum with many fine trees, large herbaceous borders, traditional rose garden, ornamental ponds, flowering shrubs and many spring bulbs. Nooks and crannies to explore. A hidden treasure and a truly relaxing experience for all the family. Garden open daily March to Oct (except Sat). Home-made teas available on NGS day. Gravel paths.

Leicestershire & Rutland County Volunteers

County Organiser Leicestershire
Colin Olle, Croft Acre, The Belt, South Kilworth, Lutterworth LE17 6DX, 01858 575791, colin.olle@tiscali.co.uk

County Treasurer Leicestershire
Martin Shave, Oak Tree House, North Road, South Kilworth, Lutterworth, LE17 6DU, 01455 556633, martinshave@kilworthaccountancy.co.uk

Publicity Leicestershire
Pete Measures, Mill House, 118 Welford Road, Leicester LE18 3SN, 01162 885409

Booklet co-ordinator
Mary Hayward, 1 Wellhouse Close, Wigston LE18 2RQ, 07545 917664, maryehayward@googlemail.com

Assistant County Organisers Leicestershire
Mary Hayward, 1 Wellhouse Close, Wigston LE18 2RQ, 01162 884018, maryehayward@googlemail.com
Verena Olle, Croft Acre, The Belt, South Kilworth, Lutterworth LE17 6DX, 01858 575791
David & Beryl Wyrko, Parkside, 6 Park Hill, Gaddesby, Leicester LE7 4WH, 01664 840385, david.wyrko1@btinternet.com

County Organiser/Publicity Rutland
Rose Dejardin, 5 Top Street, Wing, Nr Oakham LE15 8SE, 01572 737557, rosedejardin@btopenworld.com, twitter @RutlandNGS

County Treasurer Rutland
David Wood, Townsend House, Morcott Road, Wing, nr Oakham LE15 8SA, 01572 737465, rdavidwood@easynet.co.uk

LINCOLNSHIRE

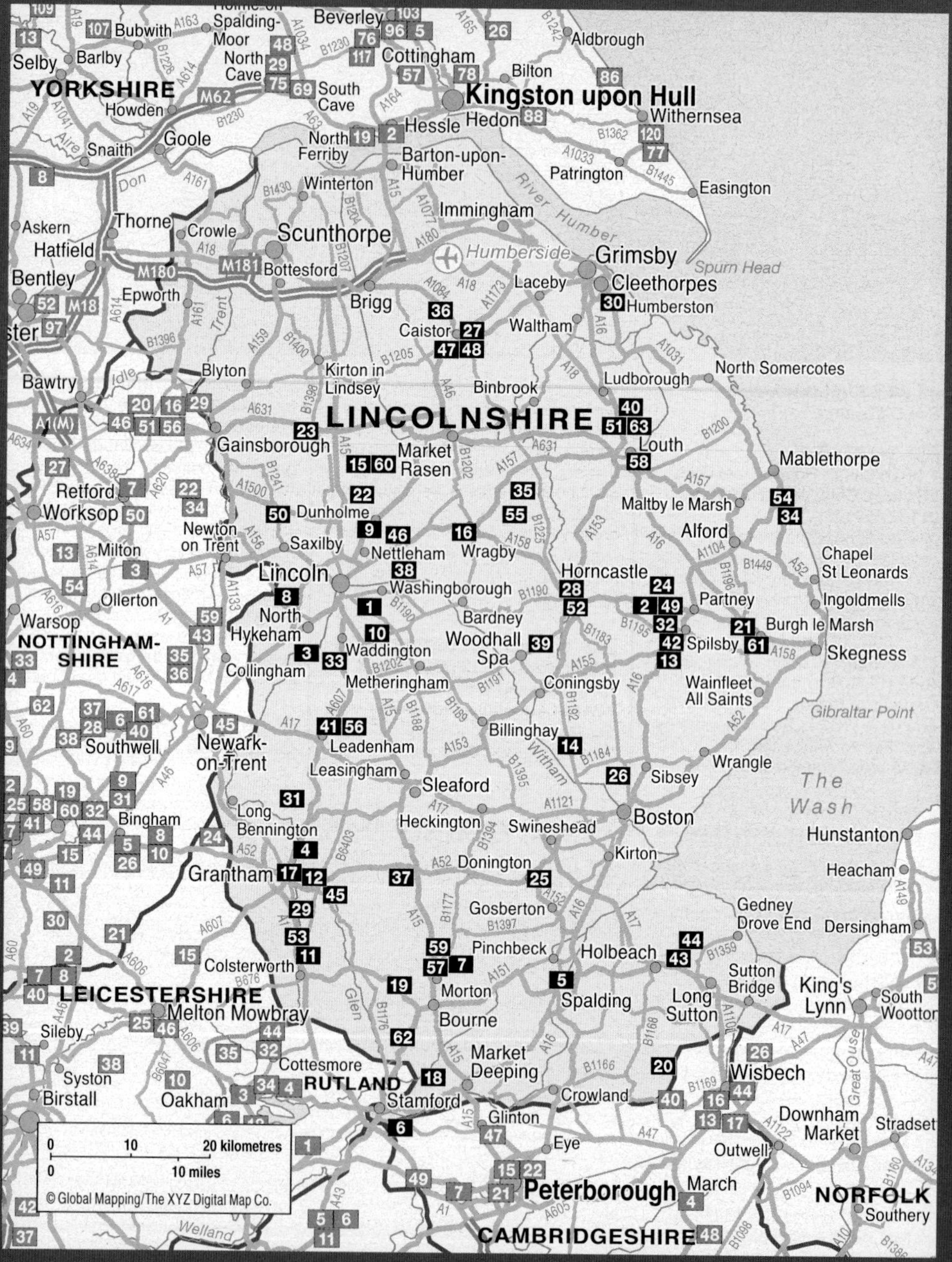

Opening Dates

February

Saturday 16
29 Little Ponton Hall

Sunday 17
29 Little Ponton Hall

Saturday 23
7 21 Chapel Street

Sunday 24
7 21 Chapel Street

March

Saturday 2
57 Walters Cottage

Sunday 3
8 Doddington Hall Gardens
57 Walters Cottage

Wednesday 20
8 Doddington Hall Gardens

Friday 29
11 Easton Walled Gardens

April

Saturday 6
6 Burghley House Private South Gardens

Sunday 7
6 Burghley House Private South Gardens
30 1 Lomond Grove

Sunday 14
19 Grimsthorpe Castle

Sunday 21
16 Goltho House
17 Grantham House
42 The Old Rectory
63 Woodlands

Saturday 27
34 Marigold Cottage

Sunday 28
34 Marigold Cottage
45 The Orchards

May

Friday 3
61 Willow Cottage

Friday 10
61 Willow Cottage

Sunday 12
1 Ashfield House
9 Dunholme Lodge
43 The Old Vicarage
44 Old White House

Friday 17
61 Willow Cottage

Saturday 18
61 Willow Cottage

Sunday 19
26 Holly House
42 The Old Rectory
51 Shepherds Hey
61 Willow Cottage
63 Woodlands

Friday 24
61 Willow Cottage

Saturday 25
4 Belton House

Sunday 26
32 Manor House

Friday 31
61 Willow Cottage

June

Sunday 2
14 Frog Hall Cottage
55 The Walled Garden

Friday 7
61 Willow Cottage

Saturday 8
47 Pottertons Nursery

Sunday 9
3 Aubourn Hall
12 Ermine Place
20 Guanock House
47 Pottertons Nursery

Thursday 13
19 Grimsthorpe Castle

Friday 14
61 Willow Cottage

National Gardens Weekend

Saturday 15
10 East Mere House
18 Greatford Mill
33 March House
38 Mulberry Croft

Sunday 16
10 East Mere House
22 Hackthorn Hall
28 Horncastle Gardens
30 1 Lomond Grove
33 March House
38 Mulberry Croft
40 Nut Tree Farm
43 The Old Vicarage
62 Witham Hall School
63 Woodlands

Friday 21
61 Willow Cottage

Saturday 22
13 Fen View

Sunday 23
25 The Hawthorns
37 The Moat
39 Nova Lodge

Friday 28
61 Willow Cottage

Saturday 29
36 Mill Farm
54 Sutton on Sea Gardens

Sunday 30
31 The Long House
36 Mill Farm
53 Stoke Rochford Hall

Many gardens offer delicious home-made teas . . . look for the tea-cup symbol . . .

July

Friday 5
61 Willow Cottage

Saturday 6
35 2 Mill Cottage

Sunday 7
2 Ashwell House
9 Dunholme Lodge
25 The Hawthorns
49 Raybecca

Friday 12
61 Willow Cottage

Saturday 13
5 The Brambles
23 Hall Farm
52 Sir Joseph Banks Tribute Garden

Sunday 14
5 The Brambles
23 Hall Farm
27 Hope House
48 Ramada
50 73 Saxilby Road
63 Woodlands

Wednesday 17
58 68 Watts Lane

Friday 19
61 Willow Cottage

Saturday 20
4 Belton House
61 Willow Cottage

Sunday 21
61 Willow Cottage

Wednesday 24
8 Doddington Hall Gardens

Friday 26
61 Willow Cottage

Sunday 28
21 Gunby Hall & Gardens
52 Sir Joseph Banks Tribute Garden

August

Friday 2
61 Willow Cottage

Sunday 4
58 68 Watts Lane

Friday 9
61 Willow Cottage

Sunday 11
24 Harrington Hall
40 Nut Tree Farm
41 The Old House
51 Shepherds Hey
56 Walnut Tree Cottage
58 68 Watts Lane
63 Woodlands

Friday 16
61 Willow Cottage

Sunday 18
58 68 Watts Lane

Friday 23
61 Willow Cottage

Sunday 25
27 Hope House
48 Ramada
58 68 Watts Lane

Monday 26
32 Manor House

Early spring is a great time to visit by appointment . . .

September

Sunday 1
23 Hall Farm

Sunday 8
52 Sir Joseph Banks Tribute Garden
63 Woodlands

Sunday 15
7 21 Chapel Street
15 The Garden House
60 West Barn

Saturday 21
4 Belton House

Sunday 29
16 Goltho House

October

Sunday 6
50 73 Saxilby Road

Sunday 20
1 Ashfield House

February 2014

Saturday 22
7 21 Chapel Street

Sunday 23
7 21 Chapel Street

Gardens open to the public

4 Belton House
6 Burghley House Private South Gardens
8 Doddington Hall Gardens
11 Easton Walled Gardens
15 The Garden House
16 Goltho House
17 Grantham House
19 Grimsthorpe Castle
21 Gunby Hall & Gardens
23 Hall Farm

By appointment only

46 Overbeck
59 10 Wendover Close

Also open by Appointment ☎

1 Ashfield House
5 The Brambles
7 21 Chapel Street
25 The Hawthorns
28 15 Elmhirst Road, Horncastle Gardens
28 Horncastle Gardens
30 1 Lomond Grove
31 The Long House
32 Manor House
33 March House
34 Marigold Cottage
36 Mill Farm
37 The Moat
39 Nova Lodge
40 Nut Tree Farm
42 The Old Rectory
43 The Old Vicarage
50 73 Saxilby Road
57 Walters Cottage
61 Willow Cottage
63 Woodlands

The Gardens

1 ASHFIELD HOUSE

Lincoln Road, Branston, Lincoln LN4 1NS. John & Judy Tinsley, 07977 505682, jmt@ashtreedevelopments.co.uk. *3m S of Lincoln. Off B1188 Lincoln Rd signed Tinsley Farms Ashfield.* Light refreshments. **Adm £3, chd free. Sun 12 May, Sun 20 Oct (11-4). Visitors also welcome by appt Feb to Nov.**

8 acre garden constructed around a planting of trees and shrubs. The main feature in the spring is the collection of some 90 flowering cherries of 40 different varieties. Sweeping lawns with massed plantings of spring flowering bulbs around a large pond. In the autumn the colours can be amazing. New magnolia collection. Early spring is a great time to visit by appointment to see the masses of bulbs. Fairly level garden. Grass paths.

♿ 🐕 ☕ ☎

2 NEW ASHWELL HOUSE

Manor Road, Hagworthingham, Spilsby PE23 4LL. Fanny Smith. *5m E of Horncastle. Horncastle to Hagworthingham turn off A158 into Bond Hayes Rd then into Manor Rd.* Light refreshments at Raybecca. **Combined adm £3, chd free (tickets from Raybecca only). Sun 7 July (2-5). Combined with Raybecca.**

Small sheltered country cottage garden. Brick steps lead to island beds with interesting plants. Some mature trees provide shade.

☕

3 AUBOURN HALL

Harmston Road, Aubourn, nr Lincoln LN5 9DZ. Mr & Mrs Christopher Nevile, www.aubournhall.co.uk. *7m SW of Lincoln. Signed off A607 at Harmston & off A46 at Thorpe.* Home-made teas. **Adm £4.50, chd free. Sun 9 June (2-5).**

Approx 8 acres. Lawns, mature trees, shrubs, roses, mixed borders, new rose garden, large prairie and topiary garden, spring bulbs and ponds. C11 church adjoining. Featured in Lincolnshire Life Magazine and Lincolnshire Today. For non-NGS open days see website.

♿ ✿ ☕

THE BEECHES

See Nottinghamshire

4 ◆ BELTON HOUSE

Grantham NG32 2LS. National Trust, 01476 566116, www.nationaltrust.org.uk. *3m NE of Grantham. On A607 Grantham to Lincoln rd. Easily reached & signed from A1 (Grantham N junction).* **Adm £10.50, chd £7. For NGS: Sats 25 May, 20 July, 21 Sept (10.30-5.30). For other opening times and**

information, please phone or see garden website.
The 35-acre gardens at Belton House are a yr-round delight. Italian Gardens with Orangery and iconic fountain, Dutch Gardens with lavender and timeless topiary lead on to woodland paths, boathouse and tranquil lakeshore. Gravel paths, cobbled driveway, some steps. Please ask at Visitor Reception for access advice or phone in advance.

5 THE BRAMBLES

27 Sherwood Drive, Spalding PE11 1QW. Kate & Len Lucas, 01775 722719, katelucas@sky.com, www.spanglefish.com/brambles garden. *3/4 m N of Spalding town centre. Take B1356 (Spalding to Pinchbeck). Sherwood Drive is on R after approx 3/4 m.* Home-made teas. **Adm £3, chd free. Sat 13, Sun 14 July (12-5). Visitors also welcome by appt July.**
The Brambles is set in a 1/3 acre of mature English garden. 3 sculptured lawns surrounded by wide, colourful borders packed with perennials and backed with classic climbers like clematis and roses. You can rest and relax on several seats throughout the garden.

6 ◆ BURGHLEY HOUSE PRIVATE SOUTH GARDENS

Stamford PE9 3JY. Burghley House Preservation Trust, 01780 752451, www.burghley.co.uk. *1m E of Stamford. From Stamford follow signs to Burghley via B1443.* **Adm £3.50, chd £2. For NGS: Sat 6, Sun 7 Apr (11-4). For other opening times and information, please phone or see garden website.**
On 6th and 7th April the Private South Gardens at Burghley House will open for the NGS with spectacular spring bulbs in parklike setting with magnificent trees and the opportunity to enjoy Capability Brown's famous lake and summerhouse. Entry to the Private South Gardens via Orangery. The Garden of Surprises, Sculpture Garden and house are open as normal. Regular admission prices apply. Gravel paths.

5 BURTON LANE
See Nottinghamshire

Manor House

7 21 CHAPEL STREET

Hacconby, Bourne PE10 0UL. Cliff & Joan Curtis, 01778 570314, cliffordcurtis@btinternet.com. *3m N of Bourne. A15, turn E at Xrds into Hacconby, L at village green.* Home-made teas. **Adm £2.50, chd free. Sat 23, Sun 24 Feb, Sun 15 Sept, Sat 22 (11-5); Sun 23 Feb 2014. Visitors also welcome by appt.**
A cottage garden behind a 300yr old cottage. Snowdrops, primroses, hellebores and many different spring flowering bulbs, colour with bulbs and herbaceous plants through the yr, autumn with asters, dahlias, salvias and many of the autumn flowering yellow daises.

CROSS LODGE
See Nottinghamshire

8 ◆ DODDINGTON HALL GARDENS

Doddington, Lincoln LN6 4RU. Claire & James Birch, 01522 812510, www.doddingtonhall.com. *5m W of Lincoln. Signed clearly from A46 Lincoln bypass & A57, 3m.* **Adm £5, chd £2.75. For NGS: Sun 3, Wed 20 Mar (11-4); Wed 24 July (11-5). For other opening times and information, please phone or see garden website.**
5 acres of romantic walled and wild gardens. Naturalised spring bulbs and scented shrubs from Feb to May. Spectacular iris display late May/early June in box-edged parterres of West Garden. Sumptuous herbaceous borders throughout summer; ancient chestnut trees; turf maze; Temple of the Winds. Fully productive, walled kitchen garden. Wheelchair access possible via gravel paths. Ramps also in use. Access map available from Gatehouse Shop. Details available on arrival.

9 DUNHOLME LODGE

Dunholme, Lincoln LN2 3QA. Hugh & Lesley Wykes. *4m NE of Lincoln. Turn off A46 towards Welton at Hand Car Wash garage. After 1/2 m turn L up long concrete rd. Garden at the top.* Home-made teas. **Adm £2.50, chd free. Sun 12 May, Sun 7 July (11-5).**
3 acre garden. Spring bulb area, shrub border, large natural pond, wild flower area, orchard. vegetable garden, private RAF Dunholme Lodge Museum and War Memorial. Local artists and book stall on both open days. Plant sales (July only). Most areas accessible but areas of loose stone and gravel.

10 EAST MERE HOUSE
Bracebridge Heath, Lincoln LN4 2JB. Mr & Mrs James Dean. *Take turning off A15 to Bardney & Mere on B1178. After 1m rd bends L, you need to turn R. After 100yds drive to East Mere House is on R.* Home-made teas. **Adm £3, chd free. Sat 15, Sun 16 June (11.30-5).**
2 acre formal country garden, recently redesigned, surrounding a stone farmhouse. Box-edged borders planted with grasses, perennials and seasonal bedding. Lawns, ornamental trees, crab apple avenue and small rose garden. Parterre planted with rosemary, lavender, santolina and alliums. Large kitchen garden with raised vegetable beds and young fruit trees on the farm-yard walls.

Native woodland areas, prairie and wild flower meadow planted with massed bulbs . . .

11 ◆ EASTON WALLED GARDENS
Easton NG33 5AP. Sir Fred & Lady Cholmeley, www.eastonwalledgardens.co.uk. *7m S of Grantham. 1m off A1. 7m S of Grantham. Follow village signposts via B6403.* **Adm £6.50, chd £2. For NGS: Fri 29 Mar (11-4). For other opening times and information, please phone or see garden website.**
12 acres of 400yr old forgotten gardens undergoing extensive renovation. Set in parkland with dramatic views. C16 garden with Victorian embellishments. Italianate terraces; yew tunnel; snowdrops and cut flower garden. David Austin roses, meadows and sweet pea collections. Cottage and vegetable gardens. Please wear sensible shoes suitable for country walking. Childrens' Trail. Featured in RHS Magazine, The Garden. Tearoom, shop and upper gardens all accessible. No access to lower gardens for wheelchair users.

ELLICAR GARDENS
See Nottinghamshire

12 NEW ERMINE PLACE
23 Hall Lane, Harrowby, Grantham NG31 9HA. Janet & Denis Manton. *Harrowby Lane out of Grantham or Harrowby off B6403.* Light refreshments. **Adm £3, chd free. Sun 9 June (11-5).**
2 acre partially walled garden developed from farmland by the current occupants over a 40yr period. Formal area with raised herbaceous borders; kitchen, herb, soft fruit and orchard gardens. Paddock with perimeter tree planting. Large well stocked eco-friendly pond. Hard landscaping, wishing well and rest area's. Partial wheelchair access. WC facilities.

13 FEN VIEW
Fen Lane, East Keal PE23 4AY. Mr & Mrs Geoffrey Wheatley. *2m SW of Spilsby. Car parking: Church Lane, in field opp church. 200yds to garden. Disabled parking at garden.* Home-made teas. **Adm £2.50, chd free. Sat 22 June (2-5).**
Sloping secluded ½ -acre garden planted to reflect the owners interest in gardening for wildlife. Designed around a number of different themed areas, ponds, vistas, sculptures and plenty of seating.

14 FROG HALL COTTAGE
Langrick Road, New York LN4 4XH. Kathy Wright. *B1192 2m S of New York Xrds. 3m N of Langrick Bridge.* Home-made teas. **Adm £2.50, chd free. Sun 2 June (2-5).**
¾ -acre plantswoman's garden. Patio with many unusual plants, stream, courtyard-style patio, large gravelled area with raised beds and an arbour, again planted for interest. Lawn with large island beds, unfenced pond. Classic-style garden planted with roses, shrubs and perennials, small paved terrace. Small nursery attached selling many unusual plants.

15 ◆ THE GARDEN HOUSE
Saxby, Market Rasen, Lincoln LN8 2DQ. Chris Neave & Jonathan Cartwright, 01673 878820, www.thegardenhousesaxby.co.uk. *8m N of Lincoln; 2¼ m E of A15. Easiest route to garden when travelling from both N & S is to approach from the A15. Take turning for Saxby & proceed 2¼ m. Garden is on L as you enter village. Car park on R.* **Adm £4, chd free. For NGS: Sun 15 Sept (11-4). For other opening times and information, please phone or see garden website.**
8-acre landscaped garden packed with interest. Yew hedging and walls enclose magical garden rooms full of roses and herbaceous plants. Long terrace, Dutch pergola and obelisk gardens link to a lavender walk. Large natural damp garden. Dry garden leading onto hillside planted with rarer trees overlooking a large reflective pond. Native woodland areas, prairie and wild flower meadow planted with massed bulbs. Wonderful views. Adjacent to C18 classical church. Featured in Lincolnshire Life. Gravel paths, steep slopes.

GOADBY MARWOOD HALL
See Leicestershire & Rutland

16 ◆ GOLTHO HOUSE
Lincoln Road, Goltho, Nr Wragby, Market Rasen LN8 5NF. Mr & Mrs S Hollingworth, 01673 857768, www.golthogardens.com. *10m E of Lincoln. On A158, 1m before Wragby. Garden on L (not in Goltho Village).* **Adm £5, chd free. For NGS: Suns 21 Apr, 29 Sept (10-4). For other opening times and information, please phone or see garden website.**
4½ -acre garden started in 1998 but looking established with long grass walk flanked by abundantly planted herbaceous borders forming a focal point. Paths and walkway span out to other features incl nut walk, prairie border, wild flower meadow, rose garden and large pond area. Snowdrops, hellebores and shrubs for winter interest.

17 ◆ GRANTHAM HOUSE
Castlegate, Grantham NG31 6SS. National Trust, 01476 564705, www.nationaltrust.org.uk. *Centre of Grantham. Follow A607 round one-way system & turn R up Castlegate at T-lights on corner before Jet station. Car park 30yrds on L & garden next L opp church.* **Adm £3, chd free. For NGS: Sun 21 Apr (2-5). For other opening times and information, please phone or see garden website.**
A delightful secret garden in a medieval setting. Created by

plantswoman Lady Molly Wyldbore-Smith and in the process of restoration. 5 acres of unusual trees and shrubs with colour themed herbaceous borders. Features incl gravel garden, iris walk and box parterre. Woodland area carpeted with bulbs and in the orchard, a wild flower meadow. Barnsdale plant stall. Gravel paths.

18 GREATFORD MILL

Greatford PE9 4QA. Mr & Mrs D Lygo. *4m E of Stamford. At T-junction in village nr Hare & Hounds PH, take route to Carlby & Braceborough. Garden is 2nd on L.* Home-made teas. **Adm £4, chd free. Sat 15 June (2-4.30).**

Lovely ½ -acre village garden overlooking St Thomas' church. Situated on the R Glen, original water wheel and open, unfenced mill pond. Informal planting of shrubs, Japanese Maples, herbaceous borders around lawn and formal parterre garden of fruit/vegetables. Large decking with seating area and prairie planting. Duck race. Featured in Garden News and Garden Answers. Some gravel paths.

19 ◆ GRIMSTHORPE CASTLE

Bourne PE10 0LY. Grimsthorpe & Drummond Castle Trust, 01778 591205, www.grimsthorpe.co.uk. *3m NW of Bourne. 8m E of A1 on A151 from Colsterworth junction.* **Adm £5.50, chd £2. For NGS: Sun 14 Apr, Thur 13 June (11-5). For other opening times and information, please phone or see garden website.**

15 acres of formal and woodland gardens incl bulbs and wildflowers. Formal gardens encompass fine topiary, roses, herbaceous borders and unusual ornamental kitchen garden. Gravel paths.

20 GUANOCK HOUSE

Guanock Gate, Sutton St Edmund PE12 0LW. Mr & Mrs Michael Coleman, 07926 552241. *16m SE of Spalding. From village church turn R, cross rd, then L Guanockgate. Garden at end of rd on R.* Home-made teas. **Adm £3, chd free. Sun 9 June (1.30-5).**

Garden designed by Arne Maynard. 5 acres. Herbaceous border, knot garden, rose garden and lime walk. Orchard, walled kitchen garden, Italian garden. Guanock House is a C16 manor house built in the flat fens of S Lincs. Plant stall. Featured in English Garden. Partial wheelchair access. Garden on different levels.

21 ◆ GUNBY HALL & GARDENS

Spilsby PE23 5SS. National Trust, 01754 890102, www.nationaltrust.org.uk. *2½ m NW of Burgh-le-Marsh. 7m W of Skegness. On A158. Signed off Gunby r'about.* **Adm £4, chd £2 (incl entry to Hall). For NGS: Sun 28 July (11-5). For other opening times and information, please phone or see garden website.**

8 acres of formal and walled gardens; old roses, herbaceous borders; herb garden; kitchen garden with fruit trees and vegetables. Greenhouses, carp pond and sweeping lawns. Tennyson's 'Haunt of Ancient Peace'. House built by Sir William Massingberd in 1700. Wheelchair access on lawn but no access in Hall.

22 HACKTHORN HALL

Hackthorn, Lincoln LN2 3PQ. Mr & Mrs William Cracroft-Eley, www.hackthorn.com. *6m N of Lincoln. Follow signs to Hackthorn. Approx 1m off A15.* Home-made teas at Hackthorn Village Hall. **Adm £3.50, chd free. Sun 16 June (1-5).**

Formal, woodland garden and productive and ornamental walled gardens surrounding Hackthorn Hall and church extending to approx 15 acres. Parts of the formal gardens designed by Bunny Guinness. The walled garden boasts a magnificent 'Black Hamburg' vine, believed to be second in size to the vine at Hampton Court. Limited wheelchair access, gravel paths, grass drives.

23 ◆ HALL FARM

Harpswell, Gainsborough DN21 5UU. Pam & Mark Tatam, 01427 668412, www.hall-farm.co.uk. *7m E of Gainsborough. On A631, 1½ m W of Caenby Corner.* **Adm £3.50, chd free. For NGS: Sat 13, Sun 14 July, Sun 1 Sept (10-5). For other opening times and information, please phone or see garden website.**

The garden is now about 3 acres, encompassing mature area, formal and informal areas, plus a new parterre filled with salad crops, herbs and annuals. There is also a sunken garden, courtyard with rill, a walled Mediterranean garden, double herbaceous borders for late summer, lawns, pond, giant chess set, and a flower and grass meadow. A short walk to a medieval moat. Free seed collecting on 1st September. Featured in GGG. Most of garden is suitable for wheelchairs.

> The walled garden boasts a magnificent 'Black Hamburg' vine . . .

24 HARRINGTON HALL

Harrington, Spilsby PE23 4NH. Mr & Mrs David Price, www.harringtonhallgardens.co.uk. *6m NW of Spilsby. Turn off A158 (Lincoln-Skegness) at Hagworthingham, 2m to Harrington.* **Adm £3, chd free. Sun 11 Aug (2-5).**

Approx 6-acre Tudor and C18 walled gardens, incl 3 walled gardens; herbaceous borders, croquet lawn leading to viewing terrace, Tennyson's High Hall Garden in 'Maud'. Organic kitchen garden, shrub borders, roses, wildlife pond and step garden. Gravel paths.

25 THE HAWTHORNS

Bicker Road, Donington PE11 4XP. Colin & Janet Johnson, 01775 822808, colinj04@hotmail.com, www.thehawthornsrarebreeds.co.uk. *½ m NW of Donington. Bicker Rd is directly off A52 opp Church Rd. Roadside parking available in Church Rd or in village centre car park.* Home-made teas. **Adm £3.50, chd free. Sun 23 June, Sun 7 July (11-4). Visitors also welcome by appt June to Aug.**

Traditional garden with extensive herbaceous borders, pond, large old English rose garden, vegetable and fruit areas with feature greenhouse. Cider orchard and area housing rare breed animals incl pigs, sheep and chickens.

26 HOLLY HOUSE

Fishtoft Drove, Frithville, Boston PE22 7ES. Sally & David Grant. *3m N of Boston. 1m S of Frithville. Unclassified rd. On W side of West Fen Drain. Marked on good maps.* Home-made teas. **Adm £3, chd free. Sun 19 May (12-5).**

Approx 1 acre informal mixed borders, scree beds, steps leading down to pond with cascade and stream. Small woodland area. Quiet garden with water feature. Extra 2½ acres devoted to wildlife, especially bumble bees and butterflies. Partial wheelchiar access with some steep and slopes.

HOLMES VILLA

See Nottinghamshire

27 HOPE HOUSE

15 Horsemarket, Caistor LN7 6UP. Sue Neave, www.hopehousegardens.co.uk. *Caistor is off A46 between Lincoln & Grimsby. Garden off Market Place down Plough Hill, then Horsemarket.* **combined adm £3, chd free. Sun 14 July, Sun 25 Aug (1-5). Combined with Ramada.**

A country garden in an attractive historic town in the heart of the Lincolnshire Wolds. Small walled garden attached to an interesting Georgian house with roses, perennials, shrubs, trees, fruit and a small raised vegetable area. Wildlife pond and formal water trough in the dining area. Yr-round colour and interest in a tranquil space created by its garden designer owner. New Caistor Arts and Heritage Centre (as seen on BBC TV). Featured in Garden News and Lincolnshire Life.

GROUP OPENING

28 HORNCASTLE GARDENS

Horncastle LN9 5AS. *Take A158 from Lincoln. Just inside 40mph turn L into Accommodation Rd. Gardens signed from here. Roadside parking only. Please park sensibly.* Home-made teas at Elmhirst Road. Ice-cream at 1 Maple Close. **Combined adm £4, chd free. Sun 16 June (11-2.30).**

40 ACCOMMODATION ROAD
Eddie & Marie Aldridge

15 ELMHIRST ROAD
Sylvia Ravenhall
Visitors also welcome by appt June to July. Daytime or evening visits welcome. 01507 526014 sylvan@btinternet.com

1 MAPLE CLOSE
Miss Chrissy Bark

The market town of Horncastle some 20 miles to the east of Lincoln on the A158 is often called 'The Gateway to the Wolds'. It is well known for its Antique and bric-a-brac shops. These three very different gardens are within easy walking distance of each other, maps provided. 40 Accommodation Road is packed with herbaceous perennials and climbers in a garden which wraps around three sides of a bungalow. The rear garden has suffered from flooding in the past, hence the raised beds. 1 Maple Close has an exposed gravelled front garden with masses of lavender. The sunny and very dry rear garden is densely planted in the cottage garden style with its mix of flowers, herbs, vegetables and fruit. 15 Elmhirst Road is a long and narrow town garden, two thirds walled, winding gravel paths and shallow steps take you around 'secret' corners. It is planted with mixed perennials, shrubs, climbers and small trees. Many hostas are grown in pots and in the ground. There are plenty of seats. Featured in Lincolnshire Today and Garden News (15 Elmhirst Road).

10 Wendover Close

29 LITTLE PONTON HALL

Grantham NG33 5BS. Mrs Alastair McCorquodale, www.littlepontonhallgardens.org.uk. *2m S of Grantham. ½ m E of A1 at S end of Grantham bypass.* Light refreshments. **Adm £5, chd free. Sat 16, Sun 17 Feb (11-4).**

3 to 4-acre garden. Massed snowdrops and aconites in Feb. Stream, spring blossom and hellebores, bulbs and river walk. Spacious lawns with cedar tree over 200yrs old. Formal walled kitchen garden and listed dovecote, with recently developed herb garden. Victorian greenhouses with many plants from exotic locations. Disabled parking. Access on hard surfaces, unsuitable on grass. Disabled WC.

30 1 LOMOND GROVE

Humberston, Grimsby DN36 4BD. Josie & Mike Ireland, 01472 319579, m.ireland1@ntlworld.com. *1m S of Cleethorpes. From A16 Peaks Parkway turn onto A1098 Hewitts Av. Turn R at r'about onto A1031 Grimsby Rd. 3rd R turn into Derwent Dr. 2nd R into Lomond*

Grove. Parking on Grimsby Rd. & nearby streets. Short walk to garden. **Adm £2.50, chd free. Sun 7 Apr, Sun 16 June (11-4). Visitors also welcome by appt.**
Small S-facing garden for alpines, bulbs, dwarf conifers and other interesting genera which grow alongside alpines. Acers grown from seed provide shade. Trillium, corydalis, primula, pulsatilla, crocus, fritillaria, anemone and sanguinaria are just some of the species grown. Raised tufa bed in alpine house and new tufa wall in the garden.

An oasis, verdant with semi tropical colours . . .

31 THE LONG HOUSE

Gelston NG32 2AE. Dr Lisanne Radice, 01400 250821, lisanne@radice.plus.com. *5m N of Grantham. 16m S of Lincoln. Between Hough-on-the-Hill & Marston.* Home-made teas. **Adm £3, chd free. Sun 30 June (2.30-5.30). Visitors also welcome by appt.**
2-acre garden with extensive views over the Vale of Belvoir. Roses in abundance, knot garden, informal arrangement of borders and a newly designed pond to encourage wildlife. Work in progress incl an extended grass bed together with a new shade garden to incorporate the existing phormium and bamboo border.

32 MANOR HOUSE

Hagworthingham, Spilsby PE23 4LN. Gill Maxim & David O'Connor, 01507 588530, vcagillmaxim@aol.com. *5m E of Horncastle. S of A158 in Hagworthingham, turn into Bond Hayes Lane downhill, becomes Manor Rd. Please follow signs down gravel track to parking area.* Home-made teas. **Adm £3, chd free (share to Holy Trinity, Hagworthingham). Sun 26 May, Mon 26 Aug (2-5). Visitors also welcome by appt May to Sept.**
2-acre garden on S-facing slope, partly terraced and well protected by established trees and shrubs. Redeveloped over 10yrs with natural and formal ponds. Shrub roses, laburnum walk, hosta border, gravel bed and other areas mainly planted with hardy perennials, trees and shrubs.

33 MARCH HOUSE

3 Harmston Park Avenue, Harmston, Lincoln LN5 9GF. Asif & Barbara Kamal, 01522 722554. *7m S of Lincoln. In the village of Harmston, off Church Lane.* Light refreshments. **Adm £2.50, chd free. Sat 15, Sun 16 June (1-5). Visitors also welcome by appt June to Sept, daytime and evening.**
The unexpected garden. Beautifully designed, lush with many unusual plants. Bird friendly with a large pond teeming with wildlife. An oasis, verdant with semi tropical colours. Very atmospheric and described by a visitor as a 'piece of paradise'.

34 MARIGOLD COTTAGE

Hotchin Road, Sutton-on-Sea LN12 2NP. Stephanie Lee & John Raby, 01507 442151, marigoldlee@btinternet.com, www.marigoldcottage.webs.com. *Turn off A52 between Sutton-on-Sea r'about & Sandilands at St Clements church (with leaning tower). Drive down Church Lane & at Y-junction take Hotchin Rd. Marigold Cottage is on L. Parking on rd is without restriction.* Home-made teas. **Adm £3, chd free. Sat 27 Apr (2-5); Sun 28 Apr (11-4). Visitors also welcome by appt May to Aug. Home-made teas available for groups.**
This plantswoman's seaside garden has doubled in size with the acquisition of adjacent land with vegetable plot, greenhouse, summerhouse, gravel garden and raised beds providing more planting and design opportunities. Look out for oriental influences from years spent in the Far East. Most of the garden is accessible along flat, paved paths.

35 2 MILL COTTAGE

Barkwith Road, South Willingham, Market Rasen LN8 6NN. Mrs Jo Rouston. *5m E of Wragby. On A157, turn R at PH in East Barkwith then immed L to South Willingham. Cottage 1m on L.* Home-made teas. **Adm £2.50, chd free. Sat 6 July (12-5).**
A garden of several defined spaces, packed with interesting features, unusual plants and well placed seating areas, created by garden designer Jo Rouston. Original engine shed, a working well, raised beds using local rock with small pond. Clipped box, alpines, roses, summerhouses and water feature. Box and lavender hedge to greenhouse and herb garden. Late season bed. Woven metal & turf tree seat. Featured in The Journal.

36 MILL FARM

Grasby, Caistor DN38 6AQ. Mike & Helen Boothman, 01652 628424, boothmanhelen@gmail.com. *3m NW of Caistor on A1084. Between Brigg & Caistor on A1084. From Cross Keys PH towards Caistor for approx 200yds.* Home-made teas. **Adm £3, chd free. Sat 29, Sun 30 June (11-4). Visitors also welcome by appt May to Sept.**
3½ -acre hill-top garden with panoramic views. Development began circa 2005. New beds and features still evolving, whilst the older beds are now maturing. New rill, rose and peony beds now completed. Remains of windmill adapted into a fernery. Plantsman's garden with a wealth of shrubs and perennials, wildlife ponds, vegetable beds and woodland area with specimen trees. Featured in Garden News.

37 THE MOAT

Newton NG34 0ED. Mr & Mrs Mike Barnes, 01529 497462. *Off A52 halfway between Grantham & Sleaford. In Newton village, opp church. Please park sensibly in village.* Home-made teas. **Adm £3, chd free. Sun 23 June (11-5). Visitors also welcome by appt June to Aug.**
Delightful 2½ acre country garden established 11yrs. Created to blend with its country surroundings and featuring island beds planted with a variety of unusual perennials, large natural pond and ha-ha, again imaginatively planted.
Topiary,courtyard and orchard. Small vegetable garden. Some gravel, sloping lawns.

38 MULBERRY CROFT
Nelson Road, Fiskerton LN3 4ER. John & Marilyn Howard. *3½ m E of Lincoln. Signed from A158 Lincoln to Skegness road. Nelson Rd is between Carpenters Arms & village church.* Home-made teas. **Adm £2.50, chd free. Sat 15, Sun 16 June (11-4).**
Plantsman's garden, cottage style, unusual and interesting plants chosen to attract birds, insects, bees, minimum chemical use. Front garden with gravelled borders of perennials, shrubs, various small trees. S-facing rear garden with mixed beds, mainly perennials incl good range of irises and peonies. Gravelled paths, wheelchair access to front garden. Rear garden viewing accessible, steps and sloping grass bank to negotiate to far end.

NORWELL GARDENS
See Nottinghamshire

39 NEW NOVA LODGE
150 Horncastle Road, Roughton Moor, Woodhall Spa LN10 6UX. Leo Boshier, 01526 354940, moxons555@btinternet.com. *On B1191. Approx 2m E of centre of Woodhall Spa on Horncastle Rd. Roadside parking.* Home-made teas. **Adm £3, chd free. Sun 23 June (11-5). Visitors also welcome by appt June to Aug.**
⅔ - acre traditional garden set within mature trees started 2009. Herbaceous beds and borders, rose and hosta beds, shrubs, ferns and grasses, large lawns 2 ponds, summerhouse, small vegetable and herb areas, 2 greenhouses. Seating to enjoy all areas.

40 NUT TREE FARM
Peppin Lane, Fotherby, Louth LN11 0UP. Mr & Mrs Hunter, 01507 602208, nuttreefarm@hotmail.com. *2m N of Louth. At end of Peppin Lane. Continue on farm track for ½ m. Transport available for those with mobility problems from Woodlands.* **Combined adm £4, chd free. Sun 16 June, Sun 11 Aug (11-5). Combined with Woodlands 16 June; combined with Shepherds Hey and Woodlands 11 Aug. Visitors also welcome by appt May to Sept.**
A garden of over an acre recently established with stunning views of the Lincolnshire Wolds. There is a sweeping herbaceous border framing the lawn, double walls planted with pelargoniums surrounding the house and a rill running from the raised terrace to the large pond. There is also an attractive brick potager. Pedigree flock of prize winning Hampshire Down sheep in fields surrounding part of garden. Honey for sale. Some gravel paths.

Lots of areas for kids to explore . . .

41 NEW THE OLD HOUSE
The Green, Welbourn, Lincoln LN5 0NJ. Mrs Stephanie Close. *Turn off A607 into S end of village, on village green opp red phone box.* Home-made teas Village Hall and wine at The Old House (4.30-6). **Combined adm £3, chd free. Sun 11 Aug (2-6). Combined with Walnut Tree Cottage.**
The formal front garden of this listed Georgian house was redesigned by Guy Petheram. Gravel, paving and pebble mosaics provide hard landscaping around beds with box hedging, clipped Portuguese laurel, lavender and roses. Herbaceous border, white hydrangea bed, and small enclosed paved garden. Welbourn Blacksmiths shop and forge dating from 1864 and still in full working order open with Friends of Forge on hand to answer questions. Some gravel.

42 THE OLD RECTORY
East Keal, Spilsby PE23 4AT. Mrs Ruth Ward, 01790 752477, rfjward@btinternet.com. *2m SW of Spilsby. Off A16. Turn into Church Lane by PO.* Home-made teas. **Adm £3, chd free. Sun 21 Apr, Sun 19 May (12-5). Visitors also welcome by appt. Refreshments by arrangement.**
Beautifully situated, with fine views, rambling cottage garden on different levels falling naturally into separate areas, with changing effects and atmosphere. Steps, paths and vistas to lead you on, with seats well placed for appreciating special views or relaxing and enjoying the peace. Dry border, vegetable garden, orchard, woodland walk, wild flower meadow.

43 THE OLD VICARAGE
Low Road, Holbeach Hurn PE12 8JN. Mrs Liz Dixon-Spain, 01406 424148, lizdixonspain@gmail.com. *2m NE of Holbeach. Turn off A17 N to Holbeach Hurn, past post box in middle of village, 1st R into Low Rd. Old Vicarage on R approx 400yds.* **Adm £3, chd free (June). Sun 12 May; Sun 16 June (1-5). Combined with Old White House adm £5, chd free (May). Visitors also welcome by appt Feb to Oct.**
2 acres of gardens with mature trees, old grass tennis court and croquet lawns surrounded by borders of shrubs, roses, herbaceous plants; shrub roses and herb garden in old paddock surrounded by informal areas with pond and bog garden, wild flowers, grasses and bulbs, fruit and vegetable gardens. Lots of areas for kids to explore. Featured in Lincolnshire Life magazine.

44 OLD WHITE HOUSE
Holbeach Hurn PE12 8JP. Mr & Mrs A Worth. *2m N of Holbeach. Turn off A17 N to Holbeach Hurn, follow signs to village, go straight through, turn R after Rose & Crown at Baileys Lane.* Home-made teas. **Combined adm £5, chd free. Sun 12 May (1-5). Combined with The Old Vicarage.**
1½ acres of mature garden, featuring herbaceous borders, roses, patterned garden, herb garden and walled kitchen garden.

45 THE ORCHARDS
Old Somerby, nr Grantham NG33 4AG. Mrs P Dean, 01476 545456, susie@dean0.plus.com. *3m E of Grantham. In School Lane, Old Somerby.* Home-made teas. **Adm £3, chd free. Sun 28 Apr (12-5).**
Yew trees dominate this 1-acre village garden created from scratch in last 12yrs on site of old farm steddings. Mixed borders, tiny pond, bog garden, fruit and vegetable area.Gravel garden. Small woodland area. Large lawn for sporting grandchildren. Some gravel.

46 OVERBECK

46 Main Street, Scothern LN2 2UW. John & Joyce Good, 01673 862200, jandjgood@btinternet.com. *4m E of Lincoln. Signed from A46 & A158. From A46 continue along Main St, pass The Bottle & Glass, village hall & nursing home. After approx 200yds Overbeck is 1st property standing back from the beck R. From the A156 turn R at The Bottle & Glass & follow directions as above.* Light refreshments. **Adm £3, chd free. Visitors welcome by appt May to Aug, daytime and evening visits. Coaches welcome.**

Approx 1/2 -acre garden in quiet village. Long herbaceous borders and colour-themed island beds with some unusual perennials. Hosta border, gravel bed with grasses, fernery, trees, numerous shrubs and climbers and large prolific vegetable and fruit area. Featured in Lincolnshire Today.

47 POTTERTONS NURSERY

Nettleton, Caistor LN7 6HX. Rob & Jackie Potterton, www.pottertons.co.uk. *1m W of Nettleton. From A46 at Nettleton turn onto B1205 (Moortown). Nursery 1 1/4 m by edge of wood.* Home-made teas. **Adm £3, chd free. Sat 8, Sun 9 June (10-4).**

Large established garden featuring extensive selection of alpines, dwarf bulbs, conifers and woodland plants. Superb landscaped rockery with stream coarse and waterfalls, pool, raised beds, troughs and island beds. Level paths mostly on mixed grass surfaces.

48 RAMADA

17 Horsemarket, Caistor, Market Rasen LN7 6UP. Peter & Gwyneth Thompson. *Caistor is off A46 between Lincoln & Grimsby. Garden off Market Place down Plough Hill on the Horsemarket.* **Combined adm £3, chd free. Sun 14 July, Sun 25 Aug (1-5). Combined with Hope House.**

Hillside garden with terraced herbaceous borders filled with perennials for yr-round interest. Small pond fed by natural spring and boggy area. Fruit trees and vegetable area. New Caistor Arts and Heritage Centre (as seen on BBC TV).

49 NEW RAYBECCA

Manor Road, Hagworthingham, Spilsby PE23 4LL. Geoff Barker & Lynne Nicholls. *5m E of Horncastle. Horncastle to Hagworthingham turn off A158 into Bond Hayes Rd then into Manor Rd.* Light refreshments. **Combined adm £3, chd free. Sun 7 July (2-5). Combined with Ashwell House.**

Front garden mainly conifers and heathers with Box hedging. Side path leads to partly shaded back garden with mature trees and fish pond. Mixed borders contain some unusual shrubs. Open view over countryside.

ROSELEA

See Nottinghamshire

50 73 SAXILBY ROAD

Sturton by Stow LN1 2AA. Charles & Tricia Elliott, 01427 788517. *9m NW of Lincoln. On B1241. Halfway between Lincoln & Gainsborough.* Home-made teas. **Adm £2.50, chd free. Sun 14 July, Sun 6 Oct (11-4). Visitors also welcome by appt May to Sept.**

Small but extensively planted garden mainly devoted to a wide selection of bold and colourful summer flowering plants followed in autumn by asters, late season grasses and autumn colouring shrubs. Large display of tender fuchsias in July. Open aspect front and rear. Small hardy plant nursery. Narrow paths in some areas.

51 SHEPHERDS HEY

Peppin Lane, Fotherby, Louth LN11 0UW. Roger & Barbara Chester. *2m N of Louth. Leave A16 to Fotherby. Peppin Lane is no-through rd running E from village centre. Please park on RH verge opp allotments.* Home-made teas at Woodlands. **Combined adm £4, chd free. Sun 19 May, Sun 11 Aug (11-5). Combined with Woodlands (May & Aug) and Nut Tree Farm (August).**

Small garden packed with unusual and interesting perennials. Open frontage gives visitors a warm welcome. It has a small pond, terraced border and steep bank side to a small stream. Rear garden takes advantage of the panoramic views over open countryside, with colour themed borders. Featured in Lincolnshire Life. Limited access to rear garden. Front garden can be viewed from road.

52 SIR JOSEPH BANKS TRIBUTE GARDEN

Bridge Street, Horncastle LN9 5HZ. Sir Joseph Banks Society. *From Horncastle Market Square 100yrds along Bridge St. Garden on L, entrance through shop.* Light refreshments. **Adm £2.50, chd free. Sat 13, Sun 28 July, Sun 8 Sept (1.30-4.30).**

Sir Joseph Banks (1743 - 1820) Tribute Garden is a courtyard providing an attractive oasis in a busy market town. It features 70 different species of plants, many collected on his voyage with Capt. Cook on HMS Endeavour. Interpretation material available. Featured in Lincolnshire Life and local press. Level gravel path.

SQUIRREL LODGE

See Nottinghamshire

Rescued from dereliction and lovingly restored by present owners . . .

53 STOKE ROCHFORD HALL

Stoke Rochford, Grantham NG33 5EJ, www.stokerochfordhall.co.uk. *6m S of Grantham W off A1. Garden on R before village.* **Adm £4, chd free. Sun 30 June (10-6).**

Stoke Rochford Hall is a superb Grade II listed Victorian manor house, surrounded by 28 acres of formal landscaped gardens and parkland. The gardens are in the Victorian style, with long herbaceous borders, rose garden, informal paths and many interesting trees and shrubs, including the Gingko Biloba or Maidenhair Tree. Traditional Sunday lunch and afternoon tea available. Hall, bars and restaurants easily accessible. Gardens accessible via gravel paths and occasional gentle slope.

THE SUMMER HOUSE

See Nottinghamshire

GROUP OPENING

54 SUTTON ON SEA GARDENS

Sutton on Sea LN12 2HE. *16m N of Skegness on A52. 7m E of Alford on A1111. 3m S of Mablethorpe on A52. The Cottage & Orchard House are on High St. Charis is in area behind. For Marigold Cottage see separate entry.* Home-made teas at Orchard House. **Combined adm £3, chd free. Sat 29 June (11-4).**

NEW CHARIS
Mrs Carol Thomas & Richard Foy

THE COTTAGE
R C Lightsey & C N Edwards

MARIGOLD COTTAGE
Stephanie Lee & John Raby
(See separate entry)

ORCHARD HOUSE
Chris & Steve Calcott

Quiet, old-fashioned seaside village, clean sandy beaches - a classic hardy plant environment! Four very different gardens will be open. On the High Street, Orchard House, a modern garden with innovative features designed to give a calming influence. Next door, The Cottage is packed with quirky features and recycling ideas. Towards Sandilands, Marigold Cottage, a plantswoman's seaside garden with oriental influences. Raised borders, secret paths and a productive kitchen garden add to the interest. Charis, in 'The Park' is a charming cottage style garden with many new features. As a result of re-designing a large area, it now incl a covered sitting space, gravel paths, new beds, a work area, and a grand 'Chicken House'. Marigold Cottage is the wheelchair friendly garden with limited access at the other three.

Panoramic view from the roof terrace . . . croquet demonstrations . . .

TRUST COTTAGE

See Nottinghamshire

55 THE WALLED GARDEN

Benniworth Road, Panton, Market Rasen LN8 5LQ. David & Jenny Eckford. *5m NE of Wragby. Turn off A157 at E Barkwith. From E turn off B1225 to Benniworth. Garden on Benniworth to Panton Rd.* Home-made teas. **Adm £3, chd free. Sun 2 June (11-5).**

Atmospheric 2-acre C18 walled garden in woodland setting. Rescued from dereliction and lovingly restored by present owners. Informal planting within a formal framework. Long herbaceous borders with gravel paths. Many unusual plants and trees. Panoramic view from the roof terrace. Croquet demonstrations Craft Stalls. Limited wheelchair access due to varying levels of gravel, step leading to garden.

56 NEW WALNUT TREE COTTAGE

6 Hall Lane, Welbourn, Lincoln LN5 0NN. Malcolm & Nina McBeath. *On A607 from Lincoln take R turn into Hall Lane by W. Nursing Home. From Leaderham take L turn. Garden is 3rd gate on L.* Light refreshments at local village hall. **Combined adm £3, chd free. Sun 11 Aug (2-6). Combined with The Old House.**

A ½ acre garden full of interesting perennials planted in long, curved borders with winding paths around central lawn, surrounded by shrubs and shady areas. Many old varieties of roses feature throughout. Welbourn Blacksmith's shop and forge dating from 1864, will be open with Friends of Forge on hand to answer questions. Gravel drive to front, some steps, narrow paths at rear.

57 WALTERS COTTAGE

6 Hall Road, Haconby, nr Bourne PE10 0UY. Ivan & Sadie Hall, 01778 571859. *3m N of Bourne A15. Turn E at Xrds to Haconby. Turn R at Hare & Hounds PH.* Home-made teas. **Adm £3, chd free. Sat 2, Sun 3 Mar (12-4). Visitors also welcome by appt Mar to Oct.**

Country cottage garden of over ¼ acre developed over the past 10 years. Various themed areas. Walled garden with hornbeam allée, topiary and rill. Woodland area with wildlife pond and plants. Sunken garden. Long herbaceous borders, lawns and collection of hostas. Garden is well-stocked with many interesting and rare plants with added features. Snowdrops, hellebores and spring bulbs.

58 68 WATTS LANE

Louth LN11 9DG. Jenny & Rodger Grasham. *½ m S of Louth town centre. Watts Lane off Newmarket (on B1200). Turn by pedestrian lights & Londis shop.* Home-made teas. **Adm £2.50, chd free. Wed 17 July (11-4); Every Sun 4 Aug to 25 Aug (11-4).**

Blank canvas of ⅕ acre in early 90s. Developed to lush, colourful, exotic to traditional plant-packed haven. A whole new world on entering from street. Generous borders, raised exotic island, long hot exotic border, ponds, stumpery, developing prairie style border. Conservatory, grapevine. Intimate seating areas along garden's journey. Featured in 'Landscape', a new national magazine. Grass pathways.

59 10 WENDOVER CLOSE

Rippingale, Bourne PE10 0TQ. Chris & Tim Bladon, 01778 440499, timbla7@btinternet.com. *5½ m N of Bourne. Rippingale is signed on the A15. On entering village at the Rippengale / Kirby Underwood Xrd, Wendover Close is 1st turning on L. Garden at end of the close.* Home-made teas. **Adm £3, chd free. Visitors welcome by appt Apr to Aug.**

Tranquil, secluded village garden of approx ½ acre containing usual and unusual herbaceous plants, shrubs and trees of general and specialist interest. Approx 30yds from main entrance to garden is gravel.

60 WEST BARN

Saxby, Lincoln LN8 2DQ. Mrs E Neave. *8m N of Lincoln; 2¼ m E of A15. 8m N of Lincoln, 2 1/4m E of A15.* Home-made teas. **Combined adm £4, chd free. Sun 15 Sept (11-4). Combined with The Garden House.**

Formal walled courtyard garden with loggia, box hedging, shrub roses, climbers and herbaceous planting. Water feature and pots with seasonal planting. Gravel paths, some steps.

61 WILLOW COTTAGE
Gravel Pit Lane, Burgh-le-Marsh PE24 5DW. Bob & Karen Ward, 01754 811450, robertward055@aol.com, www.willowcottage.webs.com. *6m W of Skegness. S of Gunby roundabout on A158, take 1st R signed Bratoft and Burgh-le-Marsh. Ist R again onto Bratoft Lane. L at T-junction, parking on R 25yds.* Home-made teas. **Adm £3, chd free. Every Fri 3 May to 30 Aug (2-5); Sat 18, Sun 19 May, Sat 20, Sun 21 July (2-5). Visitors also welcome by appt Apr to Aug Garden tours at 3pm.**
A 'Tom Sawyer' adventure! Woodland walks ponds, bridges, nooks and crannies, chance upon an enchanted hidden garden, wrapped around a delightful chocolate box English cottage. A wildlife haven, many tranquil spots to alight and relax, a photographers heaven. Victorian greenhouse, vegetable patch, chickens and all! Be sure to take tea on terrace, homemade cake from Auntie Polly's kitchen. Woodland walk homemade produce and plants for sale. Featured in Lincolnshire Today Magazine. Partial access. For assistance please ring ahead of visit.

62 WITHAM HALL SCHOOL
Witham-on-the-Hill, Bourne PE10 0JJ. Mr & Mrs C Banks, www.withamhall.com. *7m NNE of Stamford. 4m SW of Bourne. From Stamford take A6121 to Bourne. After approx 7m turn L at Xrds, signed Witham-on-the-Hill. Entrance to Witham Hall is after 1m on L.* Home-made teas. **Adm £3.50, chd free. Sun 16 June (2-5).**
One of the first gardens who opened in 1927. Now home of Witham Hall School. Formal garden with ornamental pond and paved rosewalk. Several mature cedar trees, walled garden, pupils' allotment area, herbaceous borders. 20 acres of quality sports grounds. Musical accompaniment by pupils of Witham Hall. Wheelchair access to garden only, gravel driveway.

63 WOODLANDS
Peppin Lane, Fotherby, Louth LN11 0UW. Ann & Bob Armstrong, 01507 603586, annbobarmstrong@btinternet.com, www.woodlandsplants.co.uk. *2m N of Louth. Leave bypass (A16) signed Fotherby. Woodlands is situated near far end of Peppin Lane (no through rd), running E from village centre. Please park on R verge opp allotments & walk (approx 350yds) to garden. No parking at garden & visitors are requested not to drive beyond designated area.* Home-made teas. **Single garden adm £2.50, 2 gardens £ 3.50, 3 gardens £4, chd free. Suns 21 Apr; 19 May; 16 June; 14 July; 11 Aug; 8 Sept (11-5). Combined with Nut Tree Farm (June & Aug) & Shepherds Hey (May & Aug). Visitors also welcome by appt Apr to Sept.**
A lovely mature woodland garden with many unusual plants set against a backdrop of an ever changing tapestry of greenery. A peaceful garden where wildlife is given a chance to thrive. The front garden has been developed into a crevice area for alpine plants. The nursery, featured in RHS Plantfinder, gives visitors the opportunity to purchase plants seen in the garden. Award winning professional artist's studio/gallery open to visitors. Garden News and Lincolnshire Today.

Mill Farm

Lincolnshire County Volunteers

County Organiser
Susie Dean, The Orchards, Old Somerby, Grantham NG33 4AG, 01476 565456, susie@dean0.plus.com

County Treasurer
Peter Sandberg, Croft House, Ulceby DN39 6SW, 01469 588330, peter.sandberg@btinternet.com

Publicity
Erica McGarrigle, Corner House Farm, Little Humby, Grantham NG33 4HW, 01476 585909, colinmcgarrigle@tiscali.co.uk

Leaflet Coordinator
Sylvia Ravenhall, 15 Elmhirst Road, Horncastle LN9 5AT, 01507 526014, sylvan@btinternet.com
Vic Atkinson, Belvedere, 36 Elmhirst Road, Horncastle LN9 5AT, 01507 522205, vic.atkinson@btconect.com

Assistant County Organisers
Lynne Barnes, The Moat, Newton, Sleaford NG34 0ED, 01529 497462, lynnebarnes14@googlemail.com
Helen Boothman, The Farmhouse, Mill Farm, Grasby, Barnetby DN38 6AQ, 01652 628424, boothmanhelen@gmail.com
Sally Grant, Holly House, Fishtoft Drove, Boston PE22 7ES, 01205 750486. sallygrant50@btinternet.com
Stephanie Lee, Marigold Cottage, 77 Church Lane, Sutton-on-Sea LN12 2JA, 01507 442151, marigoldlee@btinternet.com
Lizzie Milligan-Manby, Wykeham Hall Farm, East Wykeham, Ludford, Market Rasen LN8 6AU, 01507 313286, lizzie@milliganmanby.plus.com
Margaret Sandberg, Croft House, Ulceby DN39 6SW, 01469 588330, margaret.sandberg@btinternet.com
Annetta Turner, Willow Holt, Folkingham, Sleaford NG34 0SA, 01529 497215, annetta.turner@googlemail.com

LONDON

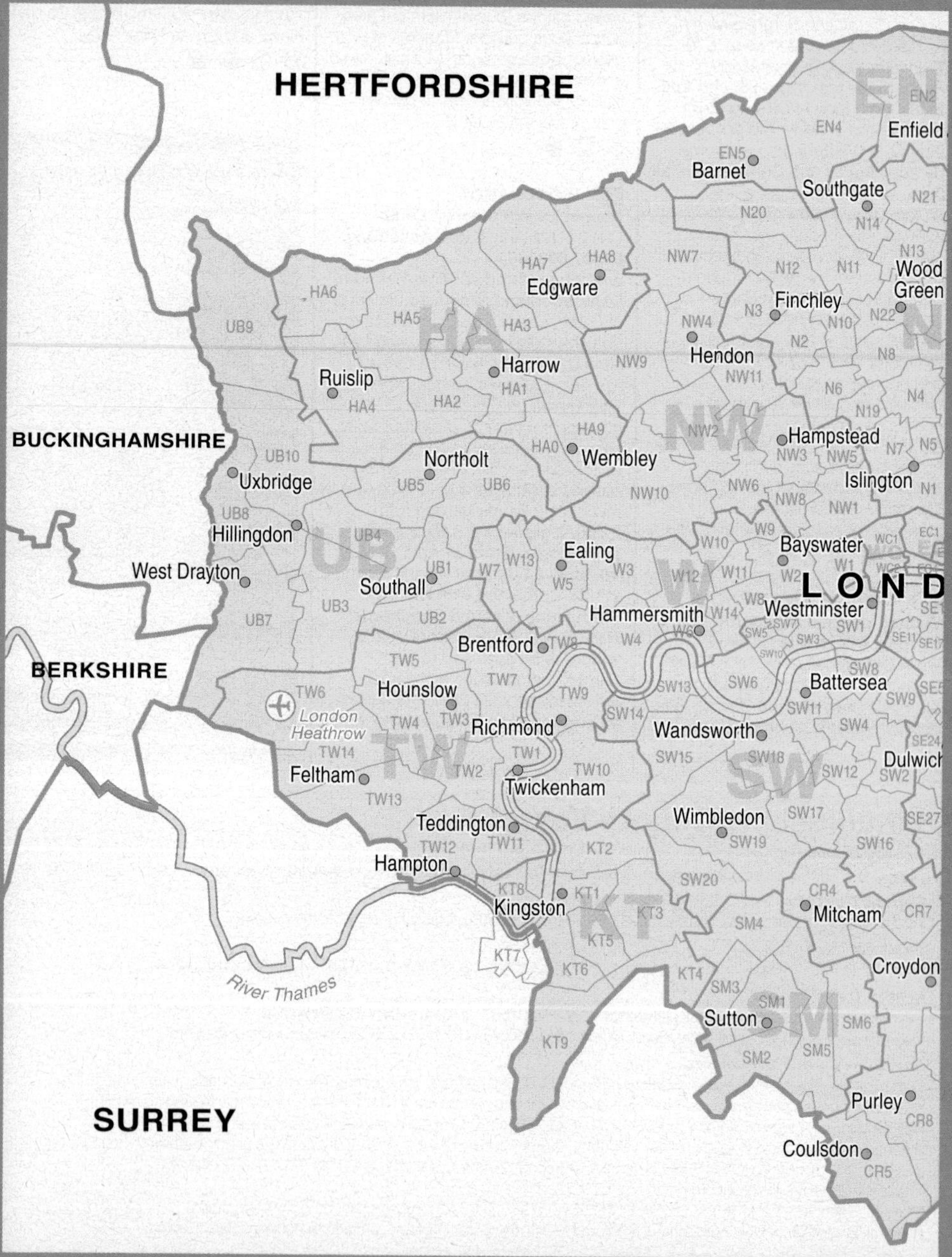
HERTFORDSHIRE
BUCKINGHAMSHIRE
BERKSHIRE
SURREY
LOND
EN
EN2
EN4
Enfield
EN5
Barnet
Southgate
N20
N21
N14
NW7
HA7
HA8
Edgware
N13
N12
N11
Wood
Green
HA6
Finchley
N22
HA5
HA
HA3
N3
N10
UB9
NW4
Hendon
N2
N8
Harrow
NW9
NW11
Ruislip
HA1
HA2
N6
N4
HA4
NW
N19
HA9
NW2
Hampstead
N7
N5
UB10
HA0
Wembley
NW3
NW5
Northolt
Islington
Uxbridge
UB5
UB6
NW10
NW6
N1
UB8
NW8
NW1
Hillingdon
UB4
UB
W9
EC1
W10
Bayswater
Ealing
W13
W1
West Drayton
UB1
W7
W5
W3
W12
W11
W2
Southall
W
UB3
W8
Westminster
UB7
UB2
Hammersmith
W14
SW7
SE1
SW1
Brentford
TW8
W4
W6
SW5
SW3
TW5
SW10
SW8
TW7
SW6
Battersea
TW6
Hounslow
TW9
SW13
SW11
SW9
London
Heathrow
TW4
TW3
Richmond
SW14
Wandsworth
SW4
SE24
TW14
TW
TW1
SW15
SW18
SW
SW12
Dulwich
Feltham
TW2
TW10
SW2
TW13
Twickenham
SW17
Wimbledon
SE27
Teddington
SW19
TW12
TW11
KT2
SW16
Hampton
SW20
CR4
KT8
KT1
Mitcham
CR7
Kingston
KT3
SM4
KT
KT5
KT7
KT6
KT4
Croydon
River Thames
SM3
SM1
SM
Sutton
SM6
KT9
SM2
SM5
Purley
CR8
Coulsdon
CR5

ESSEX
KENT
O N
EN1
EN3
N9
Edmonton
Chingford
E4
N18
Woodford
Green
IG8
IG7
RM4
RM3
RM5
RM1
IG6
Tottenham
N17
E17
E18
IG5
RM6
RM2
Romford
Walthamstow
N15
IG4
IG
IG2
RM7
RM11
E11
Ilford
IG3
RM
Upminster
RM14
N16
E10
E5
IG1
RM8
RM12
E
E7
E12
RM10
E8
E9
Stratford
E15
Barking
IG11
E2
E3
E13
E6
RM9
Rainham
RM13
E1
London
City
E14
E16
SE28
Thamesmead
DA18
SE16
DA17
SE10
SE7
SE2
SE18
SE8
Greenwich
DA8
SE15
SE14
Peckham
SE3
Lewisham
DA7
DA16
Bexleyheath
DA1
SE4
SE13
Eltham
DA6
SE
DA
SE22
SE12
SE9
DA15
DA5
Bexley
SE23
SE21
SE6
River Thames
Sidcup
DA14
SE26
Chislehurst
SE19
SE20
BR1
BR7
BR3
Bromley
SE25
BR5
BR2
BR
CR0
BR4
Orpington
Addington
BR6
CR
BR2
CR2
TN14
TN16
TN
Biggin Hill
0
5
10 kilometres
0
5 miles
© Global Mapping / The XYZ Digital Map Company

London gardens listed by postcode

Inner London postcodes

E & EC London

Spitalfields Gardens Group E1
16 Beverley Road E4
5 Brodie Road E4
Lower Clapton Gardens E5
111 Capel Road E7
42 Latimer Road E7
84 Lavender Grove E8
London Fields Gardens E8
17a Navarino Road E8
12 Bushberry Road E9
128 Cadogan Terrace E9
17 Greenstone Mews E11
Abbey Gardens E15
87 St Johns Road E17
Amwell Gardens Group EC1
The Charterhouse EC1

N & NW London

37 Alwyne Road N1
Arlington Square Gardens N1
31 Canonbury Park North N1
4 Canonbury Place N1
De Beauvoir Gardens N1
Five Canonbury Gardens N1
Islington Gardens N1
King Henry's Walk Garden N1
5 Northampton Park N1
66 Abbots Gardens N2
79 Church Lane N2
26 Ringwood Avenue N2
58 Summerlee Avenue N2
64 Summerlee Avenue N2
22 Trinity Road N2
18 Park Crescent N3
Olden Garden Community Project N5
7 The Grove N6
2 Millfield Place N6
3 The Park N6
Southwood Lodge N6
9 Furlong Road N7
16 Furlong Road N7
1a Hungerford Road N7
62 Hungerford Road N7
11 Park Avenue North N8
33 Wood Vale N10
5 Cecil Road N10
60 Church Crescent N10
19 Hillfield Park N10
66 Muswell Avenue N10
Princes Avenue Gardens N10
5 St Regis Close N10
27 Wood Vale N10
94 Brownlow Road N11
Golf Course Allotments N11
The Rose Garden at Golf Course Allotments N11
5 Russell Road N13
49 Albion Road N16
51 Albion Road N16
15 Norcott Road N16
36 Ashley Road N19
23 Myddelton Gardens N21
Alexandra Park Road Gardens N22
23 Imperial Road N22
Railway Cottages N22
70 Gloucester Crescent NW1
The Holme NW1
4 Park Village East NW1
Royal College of Physicians Medicinal Garden NW1
121 Anson Road NW2
27 Menelik Road NW2
Tanfield Avenue Gardens NW2
58A Teignmouth Road NW2
208 Walm Lane, The Garden Flat NW2
180 Adelaide Road NW3
Fenton House NW3
88 Frognal NW3
Frognal Gardens NW3
Little House A NW3
116 Hamilton Terrace NW8
4 Asmuns Hill NW11
48 Erskine Hill NW11
5 Heathgate NW11
5 Hillcrest Avenue NW11
94 Oakwood Road NW11
86 Willifield Way NW11

Inspiring examples of how much can be achieved in a very small space . . .

S, SE & SW London

Garden Barge Square at Downings Roads Moorings SE1
The Garden Museum SE1
40 Kidbrooke Gardens SE3
28 Morden Road SE3
35 Camberwell Grove SE5
Camberwell Grove Gardens SE5
24 Grove Park SE5
Roots and Shoots SE11
41 Southbrook Road SE12
Choumert Square SE15
Holly Grove Gardens Group SE15
29 Kinsale Road SE15
Lyndhurst Square Group SE15
Walworth Garden Farm SE17
Penge Gardens SE20
Ash Cottage SE21
122 Court Lane SE21
Dulwich Village Two Gardens SE21
9 Dulwich Village SE21
4 Cornflower Terrace SE22
174 Peckham Rye SE22
4 Piermont Green SE22
22 Scutari Road SE22
86 Underhill Road SE22
Tewkesbury Lodge : Over the Hill SE23
Tewkesbury Lodge: Top of the Hill SE23
5 Burbage Road SE24
2 Shardcroft Avenue SE24
South London Botanical Institute SE24
Stoney Hill House SE26
27 Thorpewood Avenue SE26
Cadogan Place South Garden SW1
Eccleston Square SW1
93 Palace Road SW2
Chelsea Physic Garden SW3
51 The Chase SW4
17 Crescent Lane SW4
Trinity Hospice SW4
35 Turret Grove SW4
All Saints Fulham Vicarage SW6
16 Daisy Lane SW6
The Hurlingham Club SW6
Bina Gardens East SW7
Natural History Museum Wildlife Garden SW7
225a Brixton Road SW9
28 Old Devonshire Road SW12
Castello House SW15
66 Woodbourne Avenue SW16
20 Eatonville Road SW17
61 Arthur Road SW19
97 Arthur Road SW19
9a Calonne Road SW19
55 Grasmere Avenue SW19
101 Pitt Crescent SW19
123 South Park Road SW19
11 Ernle Road SW20
Paddock Allotments & Leisure Gardens SW20

W London

4 Cumberland Park W3
Mill Hill Road Gardens W3
Zen Garden W3
Chiswick Mall Gardens W4
All Seasons W5
Edwardes Square W8
7 Upper Phillimore Gardens W8
57 St Quintin Avenue W10
29 Addison Avenue W11
12 Lansdowne Road W11
8 Lansdowne Walk W11
49 Loftus Road W12
6 Flanchford Road W12

Outer London postcodes

Harcourt House, Bromley BR1
36 Downs Hill, Beckenham BR3

22 Kelsey Way, Beckenham BR3
109 Addington Road, West Wickham BR4
212 Langley Way, West Wickham BR4
Elm Tree Cottage, South Croydon CR2
12 Western Road, Plaistow E13
33a Brookhill Road, Barnet EN4
207 East Barnet Road, East Barnet EN4
Elm Court Gardens, East Barnet EN4
West Lodge Park, Hadley Wood EN4
Barnet Gardens, Barnet EN5
190 Barnet Road, Barnet EN5
7 Byng Road, High Barnet EN5
54 Ferndown, Northwood Hills HA6
Treetops, Northwood HA6
20 Goldhaze Close, Woodford Green IG8
4 Stradbroke Grove, Buckhurst Hill IG9
7 Woodbines Avenue, Kingston-upon-Thames KT1
The Watergardens, Kingston-upon-Thames KT2
The Wych Elm Public House, Kingston-upon-Thames KT2
The Circle Garden, New Malden KT3
65 Farm Way, Worcester Park KT4
52A Berrylands Road, Surbiton KT5
Berrylands Gardens Group, Surbiton KT5
Little Lodge, Thames Ditton KT7
Speer Road Gardens, Thames Ditton KT7
Hampton Court Palace, East Molesey KT8
61 Wolsey Road, East Molesey KT8
239a Hook Road, Chessington KT9
12 Cedar Avenue, Upminster RM14
7 St George's Road, Twickenham TW1
Osterley Park and House, Isleworth TW7
Kew Green Gardens, Kew TW9
Trumpeters House & Sarah's Garden, Kew TW9
Kew Gardens Station Group, Kew TW9
Old Palace Lane Allotments, Richmond TW9
1 St Helena Terrace, Richmond TW9
St Michael's Convent, Richmond TW10
Stokes House, Richmond TW10
Ham House and Garden, Richmond TW10
The Old Vicarage, Richmond TW10
Ormeley Lodge, Richmond TW10
Petersham House, Richmond TW10
Hampton Hill Gardens, Hampton Hill TW12
30 St James's Road, Hampton Hill TW12

5 Burbage Road

Opening Dates

March

Wednesday 13
Hampton Court Palace (Evening - **Pre-booking essential**)

Sunday 24
7 The Grove, N6

Friday 29
Chelsea Physic Garden, SW3

April

Saturday 6
Natural History Museum Wildlife Garden, SW7
Trinity Hospice, SW4

Sunday 7
Trinity Hospice, SW4

Sunday 14
The Old Vicarage

Saturday 20
17a Navarino Road, E8

Sunday 21
84 Lavender Grove, E8

Wednesday 24
51 The Chase, SW4 (Evening)

Saturday 27
11 Ernle Road, SW20

Sunday 28
94 Brownlow Road, N11
51 The Chase, SW4
11 Ernle Road, SW20
3 The Park, N6
5 Russell Road, N13
5 St Regis Close, N10
7 Upper Phillimore Gardens, W8

May

Sunday 5
Cadogan Place South Garden, SW1
2 Millfield Place, N6
Southwood Lodge, N6

Thursday 9
Hampton Court Palace (Evening - **Pre-booking essential**)

Saturday 11
4 Canonbury Place, N1

Sunday 12
All Saints Fulham Vicarage, SW6
Eccleston Square, SW1
Elm Tree Cottage
8 Lansdowne Walk, W11
23 Myddelton Gardens, N21
15 Norcott Road, N16
The Watergardens

Wednesday 15
8 Lansdowne Walk, W11

Thursday 16
All Saints Fulham Vicarage, SW6 (Evening)

Saturday 18
9a Calonne Road, SW19

The Hurlingham Club, SW6
Spitalfields Gardens Group, E1
Tewkesbury Lodge: Over the Hill, SE23 (Evening)
Walworth Garden Farm, SE17

Sunday 19

4 Cornflower Terrace, SE22
Edwardes Square, W8
Garden Barge Square at Downings Roads Moorings, SE1
Islington Gardens, N1
Kew Gardens Station Group
Kew Green Gardens
84 Lavender Grove, E8
94 Oakwood Road, NW11
Penge Gardens, SE20
Princes Avenue Gardens, N10
Stoney Hill House, SE26
Tewkesbury Lodge: Over the Hill, SE23
Walworth Garden Farm, SE17
West Lodge Park

Tuesday 21

225a Brixton Road, SW9 (Evening)

Wednesday 22

225a Brixton Road, SW9 (Evening)
Holly Grove Gardens Group, SE15 (Evening)
12 Lansdowne Road, W11

Saturday 25

49 Albion Road, N16
51 Albion Road, N16

Japanese inspired garden with many acers, bamboo, sunken rock pool and Balinese summerhouse . . .

Sunday 26

36 Ashley Road, N19
Holly Grove Gardens Group, SE15
29 Kinsale Road, SE15
58 Summerlee Avenue, N2
86 Underhill Road, SE22

Monday 27

36 Ashley Road, N19

Tuesday 28

225a Brixton Road, SW9 (Evening)

Wednesday 29

225a Brixton Road, SW9 (Evening)

June

Sunday 2

37 Alwyne Road, N1
190 Barnet Road
31 Canonbury Park North, N1
Chiswick Mall Gardens, W4
Elm Tree Cottage
Little Lodge
Osterley Park and House
26 Ringwood Avenue, N2
Southwood Lodge, N6

Tuesday 4

225a Brixton Road, SW9 (Evening)

Wednesday 5

225a Brixton Road, SW9 (Evening)
Little Lodge

Thursday 6

The Charterhouse, EC1 (Evening)

Friday 7

212 Langley Way

Saturday 8

Hampton Hill Gardens
212 Langley Way
Osterley Park and House
7 St George's Road (Evening)

Sunday 9

66 Abbots Gardens, N2
61 Arthur Road, SW19
97 Arthur Road, SW19
5 Burbage Road, SE24
35 Camberwell Grove, SE5
Choumert Square, SE15
207 East Barnet Road
88 Frognal, NW3
9 Furlong Road, N7
16 Furlong Road, N7
Hampton Hill Gardens
1a Hungerford Road, N7
62 Hungerford Road, N7
22 Kelsey Way
212 Langley Way
Lower Clapton Gardens, E5
Olden Garden Community Project, N5
Osterley Park and House
174 Peckham Rye, SE22
St Michael's Convent
Stokes House
12 Western Road, E13
61 Wolsey Road

Friday 14

Ash Cottage, SE21 (Evening)

National Gardens Weekend

Saturday 15

180 Adelaide Road, NW3
111 Capel Road, E7
Castello House, SW15
The Circle Garden
The Garden Museum, SE1
55 Grasmere Avenue, SW19
8 Lansdowne Walk, W11
17a Navarino Road, E8
5 Northampton Park, N1 (Evening)
1 St Helena Terrace (Evening)
41 Southbrook Road, SE12
4 Stradbroke Grove
Tewkesbury Lodge: Top of the Hill, SE23 (Evening)
27 Thorpewood Avenue, SE26 (Evening)

Sunday 16

29 Addison Avenue, W11
180 Adelaide Road, NW3
Amwell Gardens Group, EC1
Arlington Square Gardens, N1
Berrylands Gardens Group
16 Beverley Road, E4
5 Brodie Road, E4
111 Capel Road, E7
Castello House, SW15
60 Church Crescent, N10
79 Church Lane, N2
The Circle Garden (Evening)
17 Crescent Lane, SW4
De Beauvoir Gardens, N1
Dulwich Village Two Gardens, SE21
9 Dulwich Village, SE21
Elm Tree Cottage
48 Erskine Hill, NW11
Frognal Gardens, NW3
55 Grasmere Avenue, SW19
116 Hamilton Terrace, NW8
239a Hook Road
40 Kidbrooke Gardens, SE3
84 Lavender Grove, E8
Little House A, NW3
London Fields Gardens, E8
Mill Hill Road Gardens, W3
15 Norcott Road, N16
Ormeley Lodge
93 Palace Road, SW2
3 The Park, N6
11 Park Avenue North, N8
18 Park Crescent, N3
101 Pitt Crescent, SW19
57 St Quintin Avenue, W10
22 Scutari Road, SE22
123 South Park Road, SW19
41 Southbrook Road, SE12
4 Stradbroke Grove
Tewkesbury Lodge: Top of the Hill, SE23
27 Thorpewood Avenue, SE26
22 Trinity Road, N2
Trumpeters House & Sarah's Garden

Monday 17

Royal College of Physicians Medicinal Garden, NW1

Tuesday 18

17 Crescent Lane, SW4 (Evening)
49 Loftus Road, W12 (Evening)

Wednesday 19

Five Canonbury Gardens, N1 (Evening)
239a Hook Road (Evening)
2 Millfield Place, N6 (Evening)

Friday 21

Roots and Shoots, SE11

Saturday 22

208 Walm Lane, The Garden Flat, NW2

Sunday 23

109 Addington Road

5 Cecil Road, N10
122 Court Lane, SE21
Lyndhurst Square Group, SE15
The Rose Garden at Golf Course Allotments, N11
5 St Regis Close, N10
South London Botanical Institute, SE24
208 Walm Lane, The Garden Flat, NW2

Friday 28
28 Morden Road, SE3 (Evening)

Saturday 29
The Holme, NW1

Sunday 30
121 Anson Road, NW2
12 Bushberry Road, E9
Camberwell Grove Gardens, SE5
36 Downs Hill
65 Farm Way
70 Gloucester Crescent, NW1
The Holme, NW1
58A Teignmouth Road, NW2
27 Thorpewood Avenue, SE26

July

Tuesday 2
Fenton House, NW3 (Evening)

Wednesday 3
King Henry's Walk Garden, N1 (Evening)

Saturday 6
All Seasons, W5
Zen Garden, W3

Sunday 7
All Seasons, W5
52A Berrylands Road
Elm Tree Cottage
Petersham House
Zen Garden, W3

Wednesday 10
Ham House and Garden

Thursday 11
116 Hamilton Terrace, NW8 (Evening)
Hampton Court Palace (Evening - **Pre-booking essential**)
Royal College of Physicians Medicinal Garden, NW1

Friday 12
27 Wood Vale, N10 (Evening)

Saturday 13
Paddock Allotments & Leisure Gardens, SW20
27 Wood Vale, N10
33 Wood Vale, N10

Sunday 14
16 Beverley Road, E4
Bina Gardens East, SW7
5 Brodie Road, E4
33a Brookhill Road
4 Cumberland Park, W3
20 Eatonville Road, SW17
Elm Court Gardens, East Barnet EN4
20 Goldhaze Close
5 Hillcrest Avenue, NW11
27 Menelik Road, NW2
Mill Hill Road Gardens, W3 (Evening)
66 Muswell Avenue, N10
17a Navarino Road, E8
28 Old Devonshire Road, SW12
2 Shardcroft Avenue, SE24
27 Wood Vale, N10
33 Wood Vale, N10

Wednesday 17
5 Hillcrest Avenue, NW11 (Evening)
28 Old Devonshire Road, SW12 (Evening)

Saturday 20
16 Daisy Lane, SW6
42 Latimer Road, E7

Sunday 21
29 Addison Avenue, W11
4 Asmuns Hill, NW11
190 Barnet Road
128 Cadogan Terrace, E9
79 Church Lane, N2
16 Daisy Lane, SW6
Elm Tree Cottage
5 Heathgate, NW11
19 Hillfield Park, N10
42 Latimer Road, E7
Railway Cottages, N22
57 St Quintin Avenue, W10
5 St Regis Close, N10
Treetops
35 Turret Grove, SW4
86 Willifield Way, NW11
66 Woodbourne Avenue, SW16

Sunday 28
Alexandra Park Road Gardens, N22
6 Flanchford Road, W12
Harcourt House
18 Park Crescent, N3
4 Piermont Green, SE22
22 Scutari Road, SE22
Tanfield Avenue Gardens, NW2
The Wych Elm Public House

August

Friday 2
212 Langley Way

Saturday 3
The Holme, NW1
212 Langley Way
Trinity Hospice, SW4

Sunday 4
109 Addington Road
Barnet Gardens
70 Gloucester Crescent, NW1
17 Greenstone Mews, E11
The Holme, NW1
212 Langley Way
Trinity Hospice, SW4

Tuesday 6
Barnet Gardens (Evening)

Sunday 11
Elm Tree Cottage
40 Kidbrooke Gardens, SE3
Old Palace Lane Allotments
86 Underhill Road, SE22

Sunday 18
54 Ferndown
20 Goldhaze Close
7 Woodbines Avenue

Sunday 25
87 St Johns Road, E17

Thursday 29
Hampton Court Palace (Evening - **Pre-booking essential**)

A unique group of riverside houses and gardens in an unspoilt quiet backwater . . .

September

Sunday 1
94 Brownlow Road, N11
Golf Course Allotments, N11
24 Grove Park, SE5
87 St Johns Road, E17

Saturday 7
Abbey Gardens, E15
111 Capel Road, E7

Sunday 8
7 Byng Road
111 Capel Road, E7
23 Imperial Road, N22
5 Russell Road, N13
Speer Road Gardens
58 Summerlee Avenue, N2
64 Summerlee Avenue, N2

Thursday 12
30 St James's Road (Evening)

Sunday 22
51 The Chase, SW4

October

Sunday 13
The Watergardens

Sunday 20
West Lodge Park

Gardens open to the public

Chelsea Physic Garden, SW3
Fenton House, NW3
The Garden Museum, SE1
Ham House and Garden
Hampton Court Palace
Natural History Museum Wildlife Garden, SW7
Osterley Park and House
Roots and Shoots, SE11

12 Western Road, E13

By appointment only

12 Cedar Avenue
4 Park Village East, NW1

Also open by Appointment ☎

180 Adelaide Road NW3
49 Albion Road, N16
61 Arthur Road, SW19
Barnet Gardens
190 Barnet Road
5 Burbage Road, SE24
Cadogan Place South Garden, SW1
35 Camberwell Grove, SE5
111 Capel Road, E7
51 The Chase, SW4
16 Eyot Gardens, Chiswick Mall Gardens, W4
16 Daisy Lane, SW6
21 Northchurch Terrace, De Beauvoir Gardens, N1
36 Downs Hill
207 East Barnet Road
Lanshaw, Elm Court Gardens, East Barnet EN4
Elm Tree Cottage
48 Erskine Hill, NW11
54 Ferndown
70 Gloucester Crescent, NW1
7 The Grove, N6
116 Hamilton Terrace, NW8
5 Hillcrest Avenue, NW11
239a Hook Road
1a Hungerford Road, N7
1 Battlebridge Court, Islington Gardens, N1
212 Langley Way
8 Lansdowne Walk, W11
Little Lodge
53 Mapledene Road, London Fields Gardens, E8
41 Mill Hill Road, W3, Mill Hill Road Gardens, W3
65 Mill Hill Road, W3, Mill Hill Road Gardens, W3
2 Millfield Place, N6
66 Muswell Avenue, N10
17a Navarino Road, E8
94 Oakwood Road, NW11
28 Old Devonshire Road, SW12
The Old Vicarage
93 Palace Road, SW2
3 The Park, N6
26 Kenilworth Road, Penge Gardens, SE20
101 Pitt Crescent, SW19
7 St George's Road
57 St Quintin Avenue, W10
5 St Regis Close, N10
41 Southbrook Road, SE12
Southwood Lodge, N6
53 Speer Road, Speer Road Gardens
Stokes House
93 Tanfield Avenue, Tanfield Avenue Gardens, NW2
58A Teignmouth Road, NW2
The Coach House, Tewkesbury Lodge: Over the Hill, SE23
27 Horniman Drive, Tewkesbury Lodge: Top of the Hill, SE23
Walworth Garden Farm, SE17
West Lodge Park
12 Western Road, E13
86 Willifield Way, NW11
33 Wood Vale, N10
Zen Garden, W3

The Gardens

ABBEY GARDENS, E15

Bakers Row, Newnham, East London E15 3NF. The Friends of Abbey Gardens. *Tube: Stratford, West Ham. DLR Abbey Rd stn at end of garden. Short walk along greenway from Olympic Stadium.* Home-made teas. **Adm £2, chd free.** **Sat 7 Sept (10-5).**

This is a unique shared community 'harvest garden' instigated by the local Friends of Abbey Gardens, then designed and developed with artists Nina Pope and Karen Guthrie (see www.somewhere.org.uk). Now up and running for 4yrs, Abbey Gardens host 3 free weekly garden club sessions where volunteers tend all the shared raised beds rather than individual plots. Garden tours, teas, produce and plant sales. Gardens also house the gatehouse ruin of a Cistercian Abbey, one of the few scheduled ancient monuments in this part of London. For more information see www.abbeygardens.org & www.whatwilltheharvestbe.com.

♿ 🐕 ✿ ☕

66 ABBOTS GARDENS, N2

East Finchley, London N2 0JH. Stephen & Ruth Kersley. *Tube: East Finchley, 6 mins walk from rear exit along the Causeway (pedestrian) to East End Rd, 2nd L into Abbots Gdns. Buses: 143 stop at Abbots Gdns on East End Rd. 102, 263 & 234 stop on East Finchley High Rd.* Home-made teas. **Adm £3, chd free.** **Sun 9 June (2-5.30).**

Combining 'grass and glass': Stephen studied garden design at Capel Manor and Ruth is a glass artist. Designed for tranquillity and yr-round interest, this garden creates a calming yet dramatic environment through plant form, colour, texture and asymmetrical geometry. Glass amphorae, feathers and mosaics catch the eye among grasses, ornamental shrubs, perennials, vegetable plot and water features.

109 ADDINGTON ROAD
Coney Hall, West Wickham BR4 9BG. Mrs Sheila Chivers. *A2022 Bromley to Croydon rd, between Glebe Way & Corkscrew Hill/Layhams Rd r'abouts. Please park on main rd.* Home-made teas. **Adm £3, chd free. Suns 23 June; 4 Aug (1-5).**
Relaxed, informal garden, divided into rooms. Winding paths lead you past hot sunny borders, cool shady areas with contrasting foliage plants, bog garden and ponds, to the apple tree with meadow flowers and cottage garden border. Hanging baskets and various containers add extra interest. Interesting, colourful garden with ponds and planting for wildlife. Very wide selection of plants.

29 ADDISON AVENUE, W11
London W11 4QS. David & Shirley Nicholson. *No entry for cars from Holland Park Ave, approach via Norland Square & Queensdale Rd. Tube: Holland Park & Shepherds Bush. Buses: 31, 94, 148, 295, 228, 316.* **Adm £2.50, chd free. Suns 16 June; 21 July (2-6). Also open nearby 57 St Quintin Ave.**
The small lawn is dominated by an ancient pear tree and surrounded by shrubs and hardy geraniums. The colour scheme is of soft blues and pinks; no yellow allowed! In June roses and clematis (a speciality here) cover the walls, while in late July phlox, salvias, and monarda make a bright splash in the centre beds. Plenty of ideas for those who think their gardens are finished by the end of June.

180 ADELAIDE ROAD, NW3
Swiss Cottage, London NW3 3PA. Simone Rothman, 07817 060206, rothmansimone@gmail.com. *Tube: Swiss Cottage, 100yds. Buses: 13, 46, 82, 113 on Finchley Rd; 31 & C11 on Adelaide Rd. 50yds from Marriott Hotel, Winchester Rd.* Home-made teas. **Adm £2.50, chd free. Sat 15 June (4-6); Sun 16 June (3-5). Visitors also welcome by appt.**
A very enchanting S-facing walled garden 25ft x 30ft, with numerous densely planted large containers on gravel, profuse and colourful. Roses, clematis and topiary. Stylish front garden with lawn, shrubs, topiary and many herbaceous plants.

49 ALBION ROAD, N16
Ground Floor Flat (bottom bell), London N16 9PP. Jane Taylor, 07980 241475, jat102@blueyonder.co.uk. *Tube: Highbury & Islington or Angel. Overground: Canonbury. Buses: 21, 73, 141, 236, 341, 476. 2 mins walk from Newington Green.* Light refreshments. **Adm £4, chd free. Sat 25 May (4-7). Combined adm with 51 Albion Road. Visitors also welcome by appt Apr to Sept.**
Now we are Six! This W-facing, approx 70ft long, N London back garden was transformed from a fox-dwelling bindweed jungle in 2007 by Society of Garden Designers designer Carol Whitehead. Slightly anarchic, loads of interesting forms, shapes and patterns and a focus on recovery and renewal this year. Accessed by metal staircase: high-heeled gardeners beware!

Two courtyard gardens with contrasting styles complement this elegant terraced setting . . .

NEW 51 ALBION ROAD, N16
London N16 9PP. Mr Roger Tolson. *Tube: Highbury & Islington or Angel. Overground: Canonbury. Buses: 21, 73, 141, 236, 341, 476. 2 mins walk from Newington Green.* Light refreshments at 49 Albion Rd. **Adm £4, chd free. Sat 25 May (4-7). Combined adm with 49 Albion Road.**
A varied and productive town garden recently emerged from family usage. Fruit trees and plants, vegetables and herbs intertwine with established planting and newly developed informal flower beds. The front garden features a flourishing British native species hedgerow. A work in progress. Steps at entrance and down to garden level.

GROUP OPENING

ALEXANDRA PARK ROAD GARDENS, N22
London N22 7BG. *Tube: Bounds Green or Wood Green, then bus 15 mins. Mainline: Alexandra Palace 3 mins. Buses: 184, W3 alight at junction of Alexandra Park Rd & Palace Gates Rd.* Home-made teas at no 272. **Combined adm £4, chd free. Sun 28 July (2-6).**

NEW 270 ALEXANDRA PARK ROAD
Dan McGiff

272 ALEXANDRA PARK ROAD
Clive Boutle & Kate Tattersall

279 ALEXANDRA PARK ROAD
Gail & Wilf Downing

289 ALEXANDRA PARK ROAD
Julie Littlejohn

300 ALEXANDRA PARK ROAD
Paul Cox & Bee Peak

On the site of the original Alexandra Park estate are five front gardens and a back garden to enjoy: the surprisingly long rear garden of a 1920s house backing onto deer enclosure and five exuberant contrasting front gardens. The back garden retains many pre-war features incl an Anderson Shelter rock garden, crazy paving and venerable trees as well as a tree house, greenhouse and wildlife-friendly eclectic planting. The front gardens all provide colour and interest for the community and are inspiring examples of how much can be achieved in a very small space. There is a profusion of colour in pots, while tall plants hide a secret hidden from the street. One steeply-sloping front garden has a semi-tropical theme, with a rill running through a riverbed rockery, disappearing under the path and dropping into a pool surrounded by beautiful stones, another is a modern re-creation of a cottage country garden, another concentrates on scent and screening planting to hide its roadside location.

NEW ALL SAINTS FULHAM VICARAGE, SW6
70 Fulham High Street, Fulham, London SW6 3LG. The Reverend Canon Joe Hawes. *Tube and also buses to Putney Bridge. Located just off Fulham High St*. Cream teas. **Adm £5, chd free. Sun 12 May (2-5.30). Evening Opening, wine, Thur 16 May (6-8.30).**
Traditional Vicarage Garden, 394ft x 197ft approx on edge of Fulham Palace grounds which give a background of mature trees enclosing five mixed shrub and herbaceous borders with tulips, alliums, large lawn and terrace with pots. 1930's Vicarage covered with mature wisteria and climbing roses. Teas served under the mature magnolia, evening drinks and canapes on the terrace. **Access to Fulham Palace and Grounds. Particular interest: Historic Bishop's Palace, replanted Walled Garden & restored Glasshouses**. Garden wheelchair accessible, disabled parking available if notified in advance. Please phone 020 7736 3264.

ALL SEASONS, W5
97 Grange Road, Ealing, London W5 3PH. Dr Benjamin & Mrs Maria Royappa. *Tube: Ealing Broadway/ South Ealing / Ealing Common: 10-15 mins walk*. Home-made teas. **Adm £3, chd free. Sat 6 July (12.30-6); Sun 7 July (12-6).**
Garden designed and planted by owners, with changes and new interesting planting. Features incl ponds, pergolas, Japanese gardens, tropical house for orchids and exotics, aviaries, recycled features, composting and rain water harvesting, orchard, kiwi, grape vines, architectural and unusual plants, collections incl ferns, bamboos, conifers and cacti. Some wheelchair access.

37 ALWYNE ROAD, N1
London N1 2HW. Mr & Mrs J Lambert. *Buses: 38, 56, 73, 341 on Essex Rd; 4, 19, 30, 43 on Upper St, alight at Town Hall; 271 on Canonbury Rd, A1. Tube: Highbury & Islington*. Home-made teas. **Adm £3.50, chd free (share to The Friends of the Rose Bowl). Sun 2 June (2-6).**
Featured in the new NGS book, The Gardens of England. The New River curves around the garden, the trees and sky are big, you could be in the country. Old fashioned roses along the river; topiary keeps things in order, pots reclaim space for colour. Teas are better than ever in the new conservatory. Look for moor hens, ducks, a heron along the New River. Shelter if it rains. Wheelchairs possible only with own assistant for 3 entrance steps.

Teas served under the mature magnolia, evening drinks and canapes on the terrace . . .

GROUP OPENING

AMWELL GARDENS GROUP, EC1
South Islington, London EC1R 1YE. *Tube: Angel, 5 mins walk. Buses: 19, 38 to Rosebery Ave; 30, 73 to Pentonville Rd*. Home-made teas at 11 Chadwell St. **Combined adm £6, chd free. Sun 16 June (2-5.30).**

11 CHADWELL STREET
Mary Aylmer & Andrew Post

LLOYD SQUARE
Lloyd Square Garden Committee.
off Amwell Street

27 MYDDELTON SQUARE
Sally & Rob Hull

NEW RIVER HEAD
The Nautilus Building, Myddelton Passage. The Residents

NEW 49 WHARTON STREET
David Sulkin & Geoffrey Milton

The Amwell Gardens Group is in a secluded corner of Georgian Clerkenwell. Contrasting gardens include Lloyd Square, a mature space with drifting borders in the centre of the Lloyd Baker Estate, and the nearby gardens surrounding the historic New River Head, where a stylish fountain and pergola have replaced the outer pond, which distributed fresh water to London. In Myddelton Square two courtyard gardens with contrasting styles complement this elegant terraced setting. New for 2013, a small garden in Wharton Street features a bandstand and musician.

121 ANSON ROAD, NW2
London NW2 4AH. Helen Marcus. *Willesden. Tube: Willesden Green or Kilburn. Thameslink: Cricklewood, 10 mins walk. Buses: 226, Dawson Road stop (at Anson Road); 16, 32, 189, 245, 260, 266, 316 to Cricklewood Broadway / Chichele Road*. **Adm £2.50 or combined adm £5.50 with 58A Teignmouth Rd, chd free. Sun 30 June (2-5.30).**
Lush country-style garden brimming with colour and year-round interest, surrounded by mature trees and shrubs creating a secluded haven. Lawned area with deep flower borders densely planted for sun and shade; wide variety of cottage garden and unusual plants, shrubs, perennials, clematis, roses. Trellises, urns and statues used to create unexpected vistas and focal points. Charming produce garden combining formal features with wild flower area, vegetables and fruit.

GROUP OPENING

NEW ARLINGTON SQUARE GARDENS, N1
London N1 7DP, www.arlingtonassociation.org.uk. *Off New North Rd via Arlington Ave or Linton St. Bus: 271*. **Combined adm £5, chd free. Sun 16 June (2-5.30).**

NEW 26 ARLINGTON AVENUE
Mr Thomas Blaikie

NEW 21 ARLINGTON SQUARE
Ms Alison Rice

NEW 25 ARLINGTON SQUARE
Mr Michael Foley

NEW 5 REES STREET
Gordon McArthur & Paul Thompson.
off New North Rd

Four gardens behind Victorian terrace houses. It is fascinating to see how each garden has used the limited space available and created an inspiring and relaxing space. Arlington Square has been transformed by the Arlington Square Association, a local residents group. Islington in Bloom - Gold Award.

♿

61 ARTHUR ROAD, SW19
Wimbledon, London SW19 7DN. Daniela McBride, 020 8947 4673, danielamcb@hotmail.com. *Tube: Wimbledon Park, then 8 mins walk. Mainline: Wimbledon, 18 mins walk.* Light refreshments. **Adm £3.50, chd free. Sun 9 June (2-6). Also open 97 Arthur Road. Visitors also welcome by appt May and June.**
In spring, the main features of this steeply sloping garden are the woodland walks, filled with bulbs, flowering shrubs and ferns. In early summer the focus moves to the many roses grown around the garden, then later the autumn colour is provided by trees and shrubs. Wheelchair access limited to top lawn and terrace, steep slopes elsewhere.

♿ ☕ ☎

97 ARTHUR ROAD, SW19
Wimbledon, London SW19 7DP. Tony & Bella Covill. *Wimbledon Park tube, then 200yds up hill on R.* Light refreshments. **Adm £3, chd free. Sun 9 June (2-6). Also open 61 Arthur Road.**
1/3 -acre garden of an Edwardian house. Garden established for more than 20yrs and constantly evolving with a large variety of plants and shrubs. It has grown up around several lawns with pond and fountains. Abundance of wildlife and a bird haven. A beautiful place with much colour, foliage and texture.

♿ 🐕 ☕

ASH COTTAGE, SE21
1B Court Lane, Dulwich Village, London SE21 7DH. Brigid Gardner. *Rail: N Dulwich (6 mins walk). Bus: P4 & 37. Tube: Brixton, then P4. Parking nearby.* **Evening Opening £3, chd free, wine, Fri 14 June (6-8.30).**
Even a garden 100ft x 40ft can provide intriguing vistas and surprises. This has three areas: a paved garden with traditional scented flowers; an orchard with mistletoe-loaded apples, mulberry, medlar, peach, fig and quince trees - with a treehouse, hammock and swing; a long vegetable garden includes over 60 herbs. They are divided by hedges and climber-covered trellis, intersected with archways.

☕

NEW **36 ASHLEY ROAD, N19**
London N19 3AF. Alan Swann & Ahmed Farooqui. *Tube: Archway & Finsbury Park. Buses and nearest bus stop: From Archway 210 to Hornsey Rise. From Finsbury Park: W7 to Heathville Rd; 210 to Hornsey Rise East, free parking in Ashley Rd and nearby streets.* Home-made teas. **Adm £3.50, chd free. Sun 26, Mon 27 May (12-7).**
A lush town garden rich in textures, colour and forms. At its best in late spring as Japanese maple cultivars display great variety of shape and colour, whilst ferns unfurl fresh, vibrant fronds over a tumbling stream and alpines and clematis burst into flower on the rockeries and pergola. Garden also includes a formal lily pond. Can only be accessed down a flight of 6 steps.

✿ ☕

Ferns unfurl fresh, vibrant fronds over a tumbling stream and alpines and clematis burst into flower . . .

4 ASMUNS HILL, NW11
Hampstead Garden Suburb, London NW11 6ET. Peter & Yvonne Oliver. *Close to Finchley Rd & N Circular. Tube: Golders Green, then buses 82,102 or 460 to Temple Fortune, then 2 mins walk along Hampstead Way, Asmuns Hill 2nd on L.* Home-made teas at 86 Willifield Way. **Adm £3, chd free. Sun 21 July (2-6). Also open 5 Heathgate & 86 Willifield Way.**
Exquisite Arts and Crafts cottage garden in the Artisan's Quarter of Hampstead Garden Suburb. Clematis and other climbers, both front and back. Mid-Summer colour from crocosmias, heleniums, salvias. Succulents, acers and other plants in pots and containers. Pond, patio, herbaceous bed, shade area. Sculptures and objets trouvés.

♿ ✿

GROUP OPENING

BARNET GARDENS
Barnet EN5 1EJ. Ron & Miriam Raymond, 07880 500617, ron.raymond91@yahoo.co.uk. *Tube: Midway between High Barnet and Totteridge & Whetstone stns, 20 mins walk. Buses: 34, 234, 263, 326, alight at junction of Great North Rd and Lynsdown Rd. Cherry Hill opp side of rd. 45 Great North Rd on the corner of Cherry Hill.* Home-made teas. **Combined adm £3, chd free. Sun 4 Aug (1-5). Evening Opening £2.50, chd free, light refreshments, Tue 6 Aug (5.30-8.30). Visitors also welcome by appt Aug.**

10 CHERRY HILL
Graham & Jean Shaddick

45 GREAT NORTH ROAD
Ron & Miriam Raymond

45 Great North Road is designed to give a riot of colour during August. 90ft x 90ft cottage style front garden is packed with interesting perennials. Tiered stands line side entrance with over 64 pots displaying a variety of flowering and foliage plants. Rear garden includes over 100 tubs and hanging baskets. Small pond surrounded by tiered beds. Named begonias a speciality. 10 Cherry Hill has a small tiered front garden full of colour and gives pleasure to all passers-by. Rear 70ft x 70ft garden is a semi formal design comprising a delightful mixture of annuals, perennials and shrubs. With several added features of interest this immaculate garden is a joy to sit in and appreciate the ambience and tranquility it offers. Partial wheelchair access to 45 Great North Road only.

♿ ✿ ☕ ☎

190 BARNET ROAD
Arkley, Barnet EN5 3LF. Hilde & Lionel Wainstein, 020 8441 4041, hildewainstein@hotmail.co.uk. *1m S of A1, 2m N of High Barnet tube. A411 Barnet Road. Tube: High Barnet then 107 bus stops opp house.* Home-made teas. **Adm £3, chd free. Suns 2 June, 21 July (2-6). Visitors also welcome by appt Apr to Aug.**
Garden designer's walled garden, approx 90ft x 36ft. Four years old, the modern asymmetric design is thickly planted in flowing, naturalistic drifts around trees, shrubs and the central pond. A changing array of interesting

containers and found objects. Hand-made beaten copper trellis divides the garden. The garden continues to evolve with a new gravel garden. National Collection of akebias. Plants, incl: akebia, propagated from the garden, for sale.

GROUP OPENING

BERRYLANDS GARDENS GROUP

Berrylands, Surbiton KT5 9AF. *2½ m S of Kingston upon Thames. From A3 take A240 joining Ewell Rd. Take Hollyfield Rd on R, cross King Charles Rd into Alexandra Drive. Map to other gardens from here.* Home-made teas at 1 The Crest. **Combined adm £5, chd free.** **Sun 16 June (2-5).**

68 ALEXANDRA DRIVE
Andy Hutchings

1 THE CREST
Robert & Julia Humphries

64 PINE GARDENS
Barbara Hutchings

A selection of three gardens all within 10 mins walk of each other, all owned by different members of the same family. The gardens are all very varied, from country cottage to jungle, chicken runs to quirky, even an enormous giant's head hidden away. Have an enjoyable afternoon being nosey, buying plants and sampling my sister's fantastic cakes. We look forward to seeing you. All three gardens appeared in the Daily Mail weekend supplement.

52A BERRYLANDS ROAD

Surbiton KT5 8PD. Dr Tim & Mrs Julia Leunig. *2m east of Kingston-upon-Thames. A3 to Tolworth; A240 (towards Kingston) for approx 1m, then R into Berrylands Rd (after Fire Stn). 52A on R after Xrds.* Home-made teas. **Adm £3, chd free.** **Sun 7 July (2.30-5.30).**
Shapes define this professionally designed garden. The 'bold verticality' of eucalyptus glaucescens, huge leaves of tetrapanex, slender cyresses, clipped hebes, cloud formed bamboo, and an S shaped lawn all in a T shaped garden. Add in a stream, a wooded area and great cakes ...

Predominantly in shade there is enough light and warmth to grow unusual and exotic plants . . .

16 BEVERLEY ROAD, E4

Highams Park, London E4 9PL. Aileen Scoular. *Mainline: Highams Park, then 3 mins walk via Hale End Rd. Buses: 212 or 275 from Walthamstow bus stn, or 275 from Woodford tube stn.* Home-made teas. **Adm £2.50, chd free.** **Suns 16 June, 14 July (12-6).**
A contemporary garden, created by garden designer owner, with densely planted herbaceous perennial borders, boundary climbers, gravelled areas and lead sculpture by 'Blazing Blacksmith', Jim Whitson. Lots of plants with foliage interest and a selection of vegetables grown in raised timber beds. The garden also has lots of insect-friendly plants and a pond with frogs, toads and newts. Featured in RHS magazine The Garden.

NEW BINA GARDENS EAST, SW7

Dove Mews, London SW7 4NH. Alice Ulm. *Pedestrian access through Dove Mews off Old Brompton Rd, or Rosary Gardens, Kensington. Tube: Gloucester Rd - 5 mins away.* **Adm £3, chd free.** **Sun 14 July (12-5).**
A private 'secret' garden of a third of an acre, hidden behind buildings. The original formal layout of 1880 is softened by generous and mature planting. Predominantly in shade there is enough light and warmth to grow unusual and exotic plants. As a winner of many London garden competitions, both plants and sculptures reflect a personal touch. Plant list available. Garden team attending opening. Paths are gravel and difficult for wheels to negotiate.

225A BRIXTON ROAD, SW9

London SW9 6LW. Deborah Nagan & Michael Johnson, www.uncommonland.co.uk. *Tube: Oval or Brixton. Buses: 3, 59, 133, 159 (Stop: Groveway) Brixton Rd is the A23; 225a is on E side, next to Mostyn Rd. Parking locally after 6.30pm.* **Evening Openings £3.50, chd free, wine, Tues, Weds 21, 22, 28, 29 May; 4, 5 June (6.30-10.30).**
Architects' listed and extended home with productive vegetable garden in modern raised beds in the front garden. To the rear - fruit and mostly perennial flowers in a rusty palette. Lower level calm garden with fish pond. Modern urban oasis with unusual materials. Featured in The London Garden Book.

5 BRODIE ROAD, E4

Chingford, London E4 7HF. Mr & Mrs N Booth. *By rail to Chingford from Walthamstow. Buses: 97, 179, 212, 313, 444. From Chingford Green at end of Station Rd (Bull on the Green PH faces you), turn L, then 2nd R (Scholars Rd), then 1st L.* Light refreshments. **Adm £2.50, chd free.** **Suns 16 June, 14 July (2-5). Also open 16 June Fairwinds & 37 Turpins Lane, see Essex.**
An east facing garden created nine years ago from a tree shaded lawn into a vibrant colourful spectacle. Packed with flowers and shrubs by an avid plantswoman with floral and textural interest along every inch of the herbaceous borders. Arches and trellis add further colour by supporting jasmine, roses and clematis. Many varieties of unusual dahlias and English roses.

33A BROOKHILL ROAD

Barnet EN4 8SE. Barbara Perry. *Brookhill Road is between East Barnet Road and Cat Hill. M25 J24 then A111 to Cockfosters. Tube: Northern line to High Barnet or Piccadilly line to Cockfosters. Buses: 384, 307.* **Adm £2.50, chd free.** **Sun 14 July (2-5).**
Small, secluded courtyard garden with an interesting collection of shrubs and lots of clematis. A tranquil space with fences covered in wisteria, roses and clematis, trees and plants in pots. A good example of what can be achieved in a small space over a short time.

94 BROWNLOW ROAD, N11
Bounds Green, London N11 2BS. Spencer Viner, www.northeleven.co.uk. *Close to N Circular. Tube: Bounds Green then 5 mins walk, direction N Circular. Corner of Elvendon Rd & Brownlow Rd*. Light refreshments. **Adm £2.50, chd free. Suns 28 Apr, 1 Sept (2-6).**
'A small courtyard for meditation'. The conception of this garden by a designer has the ability to transport the visitor to a different, foreign place of imagination and tranquillity, far away from the suburbs. Features incl reclaimed materials, trees, water, pergola, pleached limes, seating and a strong theme of pared-back simplicity. Design and horticultural advice. Featured in Ham and High and Amateur gardener journal.

5 BURBAGE ROAD, SE24
Herne Hill, London SE24 9HJ. Crawford & Rosemary Lindsay, 020 7274 5610, rl@rosemarylindsay.com, www.rosemarylindsay.com. *Nr junction with Half Moon Lane. Herne Hill and N Dulwich mainline stns, 5 mins walk. Buses: 3, 37, 40, 68, 196, 468*. **Adm £3.50, chd free. Sun 9 June (2-5). Also Open 35 Camberwell Grove, Choumert Square & 174 Peckham Rye. Visitors also welcome by appt Apr to June.**
The garden of a member of The Society of Botanical Artists. 150ft x 40ft with large and varied range of plants. Herb garden, herbaceous borders for sun and shade, climbing plants, pots, terraces, lawns. Gravel areas to reduce watering. See our website for what the papers say. Very popular plant sale. Featured in Alan Titchmarsh's 'Love your Garden'.

12 BUSHBERRY ROAD, E9
Hackney, London E9 5SX. Molly St Hilaire. *Overground stn: Homerton, then 5 mins walk. Buses: 26, 30, 388, alight last stop in Cassland Rd*. **Adm £2, chd free. Sun 30 June (2-6).**
Petite courtyard garden with water feature. Rambling roses, jasmine, vine and clematis cover the overarching pergola. 'Small but beautifully formed' ... 'a pure joy to see'.

The Holme

7 BYNG ROAD
High Barnet EN5 4NW. Mr & Mrs Julian Bishop. *Tube: High Barnet. Stn: Hadley Wood or New Barnet. Buses: 107, 263, 384 alight Ravenscroft Park or The Spires*. Home-made teas. **Adm £3, chd free. Sun 8 Sept (2-5).**
Six different borders all in one London garden. One filled with tropical plants, another 'hot' border, two with cooler coloured perennials. Lots of rare and unusual varieties with a modern design twist. Owner a Chelsea Flower Show TV producer for the past 10 yrs. Emphasis on salvias, rudbeckias, persicarias. New vegetable/cutting garden, series of raised beds and colourful pots.

CADOGAN PLACE SOUTH GARDEN, SW1
Sloane Street, London SW1X 9PE. The Cadogan Estate, 07890 452922, nicholas.barwick@cadogan.co.uk. *Entrance to garden opp 97 Sloane St*. **Adm £3.50, chd free. Sun 5 May (10-4.30). Visitors also welcome by appt Apr to Dec.**
Many surprises and unusual trees and shrubs are hidden behind the railings of this large London square. The first square to be developed by architect Henry Holland for Lord Cadogan at the end of C18, it was then called the London Botanic Garden. Mulberry trees planted for silk production at end of C17. Cherry trees, magnolias and bulbs are outstanding in spring, when the fern garden is unfurling. Award winning Hans Sloane Garden exhibited at the Chelsea Flower Show. Ponds. Spring walk on East side of garden. Feel free to bring a picnic to enjoy in the garden.

128 CADOGAN TERRACE, E9
Hackney, London E9 5HP. William Dowden. *Overground stn: Hackney Wick. Cadogan Terrace runs parallel to A102M, along edge of Victoria Park, enter by St Mark's Gate*. Home-made teas. **Adm £3, chd free. Sun 21 July (2-6).**
A tranquil yet exotic garden. Your journey begins at the Regent's Canal. You enter the upper level with its gazebo surrounded by roses, hibiscus and lavatera. You move through the middle level with its shrub borders, and finally enter the courtyard with its sunken pool. Journey's end. Adjacent nursery.

See more garden images at www.ngs.org.uk

NEW 9A CALONNE ROAD, SW19

London SW19 5HH. Mr & Mrs Neville & Marissa Quie. *Tube & Mainline: Wimbledon 15-20 mins walk. Bus: 93 on Parkside.* **Adm £3, chd free. Sat 18 May (1-6).**

Japanese inspired garden with many acers, bamboo, sunken rock pool and Balinese summerhouse. Colourful display of rhododendrons and bulbs. Bird boxes to encourage wildlife.

35 CAMBERWELL GROVE, SE5

London SE5 8JA. Lynette Hemmant & Juri Gabriel, 020 7703 6186, juri@jurigabriel.com. *From Camberwell Gn go down Camberwell Church St. Turn R into Camberwell Grove.* Light refreshments. **Adm £3.50, chd free (share to St Giles Church). Sun 9 June (12-6). Also open 5 Burbage Rd, Choumert Square & 174 Peckham Rye. Visitors also welcome by appt May to July.**

Plant-packed 120ft x 20ft garden with charming backdrop of St Giles Church. Evolved over 28yrs into a romantic country-style garden brimming with colour and overflowing with pots. In June, spectacular roses stretch the full length of the garden, both on the artist's studio and festooning an old iron staircase. Artist's studio open. Lynette has painted the garden obsessively for the past 20yrs; see NGS website. Television coverage in Japan.

GROUP OPENING

CAMBERWELL GROVE GARDENS, SE5

Camberwell, London SE5 8JE. *5 mins from Denmark Hill mainline and overgound stn. Buses: 12, 36, 68, 148, 171, 176, 185, 436. Entrance through garden rooms at rear.* Home-made teas at 81 Camberwell Grove. **Combined adm £5, chd free (share to CJD Support Network). Sun 30 June (2-6). Also open 27 Thorpewood Ave.**

81 CAMBERWELL GROVE
Alex & Jane Maitland Hudson

83 CAMBERWELL GROVE
John Hall & Robert Hirschhorn

Neighbouring walled gardens behind C18 houses in this beautiful tree-lined street. At No. 81 the owners are 5 yrs into restructuring and replanting the garden around existing features: a large Japanese maple, a tall trachycarpus palm and York stone paving. Borders filled with herbaceous perennials, roses, clematis and shade-loving ground cover; pond and bog garden. Interesting new planting scheme for borders for 2013. Pots of all sizes filled with a wide variety of planting, incl a collection of hostas. Charming clap-board garden house. No. 83 is a 90ft x 18ft beautifully designed plant-lovers' garden developed over the past 13 yrs. The emphasis is on yr-round interest, with abundant unusual planting within a formal structure of box hedging to provide varied and interesting areas of peace and privacy. Contemporary garden room, gravel and York stone paths and seating areas, calming pool and lovely views of parish church.

Flowers are planted in generous swathes creating drama and architectural impact with a bold palette of colour . . .

NEW 31 CANONBURY PARK NORTH, N1

London N1 2JU. Mr & Mrs Brian Morris. *Canonbury Park North is between Upper St and St Paul's Rd. Tube: Highbury & Islington. Buses: 19, 73, 277.* Light refreshments. **Adm £3.50, chd free. Sun 2 June (2-6).**

Tranquil, well established, west facing wooded town garden laid down predominately with mature shrubs and plants that attract wildlife with a striking clutch of silver birches, a pond and two fountains.

NEW 4 CANONBURY PLACE, N1

London N1 2NQ. Mr & Mrs Jeffrey Tobias. *Tube & Overground: Highbury & Islington. Buses: 271 to Canonbury Square. Located in the old part of Canonbury Place, off Alwyne Villas in a cul de sac.* Home-made teas. **Adm £3.50, chd free. Sat 11 May (2-5).**

A paved, 100ft garden behind a 1780 house. Spectacular mature trees enclosed in a walled garden. Mostly pots and also interesting shrubs and climbers.

CAPEL MANOR GARDENS

See Hertfordshire

111 CAPEL ROAD, E7

London E7 0JS. Jan Tallis & John Lock, 07951 762874, jantallis@btinternet.com. *2m from Stratford City. 10 mins from Forest Gate, Manor Park & Wanstead Park Overground stns. Many buses. Easy parking.* Light refreshments. **Adm £3, chd free (share to School-Home-Support). Sats, Suns 15 June (12-5), 16 June (12-4); 7 Sept (12-5), 8 Sept (12-4). Visitors also welcome by appt (a few weeks notice needed).**

90ft x 30ft urban villa garden. 7 areas: vibrant; subtle; hot; white; quiet; fernery; woodland. Large ponds - 2 wildlife ponds and 1 formal. Amazing disappearing shed (mirrors, sedum roof). Interesting small trees. Natural sculptures. No lawn! Two patios, scattered fruits. Carnivorous plant collection, lots of pots. Attached to unique modern house with balcony view. Owner's own paintings on display.

NEW CASTELLO HOUSE, SW15

40 Chartfield Avenue, Putney, London SW15 6HG. Chris Cowan & Sally Graham. *Mainline & Tube: Putney Rail Stn 10 mins walk & East Putney tube 15 mins. Buses: 14, 37, 93, 85, 39 stop at end of Chartfield Ave on Putney Hill. Free parking at weekends.* Light refreshments. **Adm £3, chd free. Sat 15, Sun 16 June (12-6).**

This is a large garden for London, which is restrained and simple with a background of borrowed trees from the Putney skyline. A structured planting arrangement around the terrace gives way to a looser planting scheme around a circular lawn and sweeping path. Flowers are planted in generous swathes creating drama and architectural impact with a bold palette and blocks of colour. Gravel paths to the garden.

5 CECIL ROAD, N10
Muswell Hill, London N10 2BU. Ben Loftus. *Off Alexandra Park Rd. Buses: 102, 299 from E Finchley or Bounds Green, alight St Andrew's Church.* **Adm £2.50, chd free.** **Sun 23 June (2-5.30). Teas & plant sale at 5 St Regis Close, also open.**
Garden designer's sloping garden featured in several magazines. Spectacular, well planted large pots (irrigated), interesting small raised pond, unusual small trees, shrubs and perennials with much emphasis on foliage and shape. Stylish garden office with green roof of bulbs, thymes etc.

12 CEDAR AVENUE
Upminster RM14 2LW. Joan & Chris Allen, 01708 224041, Chris.allenrobin@talktalk.net. *Tube: Upminster Bridge. Rail: Upminster. From A124 Upminster Rd, S into Bridge Ave, turn R into S View Drive & L into Cedar Ave.* Light refreshments. **Adm £3.50, chd free. Visitors welcome by appt June to Aug, adm incl light refreshments.**
An enchanting garden, approx 140ft x 40ft, full of colour, specimen trees, shrubs, water features, planted small rooms with secluded seating areas, fun summerhouse and fish pond. Lots of interest.

THE CHARTERHOUSE, EC1
Charterhouse Square, London EC1M 6AN. The Governors of Sutton's Hospital, www.thecharterhouse.org. *Buses: 4, 55. Tube: Barbican. Turn L out of stn, L into Carthusian St & into square. Entrance through car park.* **Evening Opening £5, chd free, wine, Thur 6 June (6-9).**
Enclosed courtyard gardens within the grounds of historic Charterhouse, which dates back to 1347. 'English Country Garden' style featuring roses, herbaceous borders, ancient mulberry trees and small pond. Various garden herbs found here are still used in the kitchen today. Buildings not open. A private garden for the Brothers of Charterhouse, not usually open to the public.

CHARTS EDGE
See Kent

51 THE CHASE, SW4
London SW4 0NP. Mr Charles Rutherfoord & Mr Rupert Tyler, 020 7627 0182, www.charlesrutherfoord.net. *Off Clapham Common Northside. Tube: Clapham Common. Buses: 137, 452.* Light refreshments. **Adm £3.50, chd free. Evening Opening, light refreshments, Wed 24 Apr (6-8); Sun 28 Apr (2-6); Sun 22 Sept (12-4). Visitors also welcome by appt.**
Member of the Society of Garden Designers, Charles has created the garden over 20yrs using 15 different species of trees. Spectacular in spring, when 1500 tulips bloom among irises and tree peonies, and in Sept with dahlias. Narrow paths lead to a mound surrounded by acanthus and topped by a large steel sculpture. Rupert's geodetic dome shelters seedlings, succulents and subtropicals. Featured on Gardeners' World.

A unique group of riverside houses and gardens situated in an unspoilt quiet backwater . . .

◆ CHELSEA PHYSIC GARDEN, SW3
66 Royal Hospital Road, London SW3 4HS. Chelsea Physic Garden self-funding charity, 020 7352 5646, www.chelseaphysicgarden.co.uk. *Tube: Sloane Square (10 mins). Bus: 170. Parking Battersea Park (charged). Entrance in Swan Walk (except wheelchairs).* **Adm £9, chd £6 (under 5s free). For NGS: Fri 29 Mar (12-6). For other opening times and information, please phone or see garden website.**
Oldest Botanic Garden in London. 3¾ acres with medicinal and herb garden, perfumery border, family order beds, historical walk, glasshouses. Cool fernery and Robert Fortune's tank pond. Guided and audio tours. Wheelchair access is via 66 Royal Hospital Rd.

CHEVENING
See Kent

GROUP OPENING

CHISWICK MALL GARDENS, W4
Chiswick, London W6 9TN. *Tube: Stamford Brook or Turnham Green. Buses: 27, 190, 267 & 391 to Young's Corner from Hammersmith, through St Peter's Sq under A4 to river. By car to Hogarth r'about, A4 (W) turn off at Eyot Gdns S, then R into Chiswick Mall.* Home-made teas at 16 Eyot Gardens & Latimer House. **Adm £2.50 each garden, chd free. Sun 2 June (2-6).**

16 EYOT GARDENS
Ms Dianne Farris.
At R-angle to Chiswick Mall where Hammersmith Terrace starts
Visitors also welcome by appt. 020 8741 1370 dianefarris@gmail.com

NEW **FIELD HOUSE**
Rupert King

LATIMER HOUSE
Looby & Paul Crean.
Next to St Nicholas Church. Entry to garden via Powells Walk next to cemetery

MORTON HOUSE
Harris Family

SWAN HOUSE
Mr & Mrs George Nissen

A unique group of riverside houses and gardens situated in an unspoilt quiet backwater. The garden at 16 Eyot Gardens has been redesigned and replanted for its 22nd yr of opening for the NGS, and with the help and inspiration of Anthony Noel has taken on a new lease of life. New this year, Latimer House's secret long walled garden features mature topiary mixed with Mr McGregor-style abundant planting, while an ancient wisteria dominates the wall. Enjoy teas in the newly-built Victorian greenhouse. At Swan House see an informal walled garden, herbaceous border, fruit trees, small vegetable garden and a tiny greenhouse. Also a small wild flower area, 2 ponds, a rill and a new knot garden.

30 Westwood Park

CHOUMERT SQUARE, SE15
London SE15 4RE. The Residents. *Via wrought iron gates off Choumert Grove. Peckham Rye mainline stn is visible from the gates, & buses galore (12, 36, 37, 63, 78, 171, 312, 345) less than 10 mins walk. Car park 2 mins*. Home-made teas & refreshments available inside the Square. **Adm £3, chd free (share to St Christopher's Hospice). Sun 9 June (1-6). Also open 5 Burbage Rd, 35 Camberwell Grove & 174 Peckham Rye.**
About 46 mini gardens with maxi-planting in Shangri-la situation that the media has described as a 'Floral Canyon', which leads to small communal 'secret garden'. This year the popular open gardens will combine with our own take on a village fete! Live music, arts, crafts and entertaining stalls. High commended in London Squares Competition. Single narrow pathway.

60 CHURCH CRESCENT, N10
Muswell Hill, London N10 3NE. Liz Gill. *Tube: Highgate, then 12 mins walk. Buses: 43, 134 along Muswell Hill Rd then 1 min walk*. Home-made teas. **Adm £3, chd free. Sun 16 June (2-6).**
Panoramic views over parkland walk and beyond set off writer's 5 yr-old garden constructed over 4 levels. Raised deck with herb-filled tubs, patio with colourful containers and mini alpine garden. Horseshoe lawn surrounded by lushly planted borders, rose covered arch leads to romantic secluded gravel area with wildlife pond.

79 CHURCH LANE, N2
London N2 0TH. Caro & David Broome. *Tube: E Finchley, then East End Rd for ¾ m, R into Church Ln. Buses: 143 to Five Bells PH, 3 min walk; 263 to E Finchley Library, 5 min walk*. Home-made teas. **Adm £3, chd free. Sun 16 June, Sun 21 July (2-6). Also open 22 Trinity Road 16 June.**
Garden writer's cottage garden with a 'twist'. Enter through 'catatorium', a plant-filled open air conservatory separating frolicking felines from bird haven beyond. Shrubs, tumbling roses and interesting perennials create a colour coordinated palette, with curved rill and hidden water features. Rustic archway leads to ferny glen with greenhouse and David's perfectly appointed Man Shed sanctuary! New for 2013 - extended borders crammed with even more unusual perennials. Gravel and stone landscaping alongside ever shrinking lawn! Columnist for Garden News 'From Where I'm Gardening'. Featured in Amateur Gardener and on ITV Love Your Garden.

THE CIRCLE GARDEN
33 Cambridge Avenue, New Malden KT3 4LD. Vincent & Heidi Johnson-Paul-McDonnell, www.thecirclegarden.com. *1¼ m N of A3 Malden junction. Bus: 213. 10 mins walk from New Malden railway station; A3 signposted for Kingston; 213 bus stop located a short distance from end of road; our house is pink!* Home-made teas. **Adm £3, chd free. Sat 15 June (2-6). Evening Opening £4, chd free, Sun 16 June (5-8).**
A welcoming front garden with cottage-style planting leading to an 'unexpected' rear garden with intriguing vistas where you will find herbaceous and annuals in mixed borders. Relax in the Japanese area, stroll through the potager and chat to our suburban hens. An ever-evolving garden with plans for further developments.

4 CORNFLOWER TERRACE, SE22
East Dulwich, London SE22 0HH. Clare Dryhurst. *5 mins walk from 63 bus stop at bottom of Forest Hill Rd. Turn into Dunstans Rd, then 2nd on L. Mainline: Peckham Rye or Honor Oak Park*. Home-made teas. **Adm £3.50, chd free. Sun 19 May (1.30-5.30). Also open Tewkesbury Lodge: Over the Hill & Stoney Hill House.**
A garden Tardis - this pretty, secluded and tiny courtyard cottage garden, in a quiet street in the heart of artistic East Dulwich, is only 50ft x 9ft. Around a sunken patio and solar fountain are clustered climbers, roses, ferns, annuals and herbs in raised beds and pots backed by a charming painted garden shed. Picture perfect.

122 COURT LANE, SE21
Dulwich, London SE21 7EA. Jean & Charles Cary-Elwes. *Buses P4, 12 (to Dulwich Library), 37, 176. Mainline: N Dulwich then 20 mins walk. Ample free parking*. Home-made teas. **Adm £3.50, chd free. Sun 23 June (2-5.30). Also open Lyndhurst Sq & South London Botanical Institute.**

Recycle – bring a bag for your plant purchases

Generously proportioned, mature garden with unusual and marginally tender shrubs which thrive in the hands of a keen propagator. Agapanthus, a signature plant followed by oleander, and a splendid clerodendron. Backing onto Dulwich Park it has a countryside feel - a true family garden with sandpit and hammock mingling with hardworking greenhouses and a super wormery, which will be demonstrated. Wheelchair access limited to terrace with good view of garden.

17 CRESCENT LANE, SW4

London SW4 9PT. Sue Phipps & Paddy Sumner. *Nr junction of Abbeville Rd and Crescent Lane, NOT in one-way part of Crescent Lane. Tube: Clapham Common, 10 mins. Buses: 137, 417, Park Hill bus stop at end of Abbeville Rd.* Home-made teas. **Adm £3.50, chd free. Sun 16 June (3-6). Evening Opening £4, chd £1, wine, Tue 18 June (6-8.30).**

Mature, tranquil garden. Lawns surrounded by roses, shrubs and trees, with a pond, backed by a yew hedge. The colour scheme is essentially pink, blue and white and the design and size are unusual for this part of London.

4 CUMBERLAND PARK, W3

Acton, London W3 6SY. Sarah Hamilton-Fairley & Richard Crofton. *E of Ealing. Tube & mainline: Acton Central & Acton Main Line stns 5 mins walk. First house N of Woodhurst Rd, on W side of Cumberland Park.* **Adm £3.50, chd free. Sun 14 July (2-5).**

A luscious, sensuous town house back garden. The deck looks over a terrace with shrubs, pots and sinks, which is bounded by a pergola laden with roses and clematis, providing views through to a lawn, more shrubs and a summerhouse. Featured in Amateur Gardening.

16 DAISY LANE, SW6

Parsons Green, London SW6 3DD. Karin Hossack, 020 7371 0292, karin@hossack.net. *Tube: Parsons Gn. Buses: 28, 295 to Sands End on Wandsworth Bridge Rd, 22 to Parsons Gn on New Kings Rd.* Home-made teas. **Adm £2.50, chd free. Sat 20 July (11-4); Sun 21 July (12-4). Visitors also welcome by appt July to Sept.**

This modern urban garden is planted in the style of a prairie garden. A sweeping wall of Molinia Karl Foerster beckons the onlooker to peep through to a large central mound covered in a bold palette of colours and textures with more than 80 varieties of grasses, perennials and shrubs.

A leafy enclave of Victorian villas next to Islington . . .

GROUP OPENING

DE BEAUVOIR GARDENS, N1

London N1 4HU. *Dalston Junction or Haggerston Station, London Overground (East London line); Highbury & Islington tube then 30 or 277 bus; Angel tube then 38, 56 or 73 bus. Street parking available.* Home-made teas at 158 Culford Road. **Combined adm £5, chd free. Sun 16 June (11-3).**

158 CULFORD ROAD
Gillian Blachford

114 DE BEAUVOIR ROAD
Nancy & Richard Turnbull

NEW 26 NORTHCHURCH ROAD
Mr Salvatore Avanzato

21 NORTHCHURCH TERRACE
Ms Nancy Korman.
Opp St Peter's Church, entry via side gate in De Beauvoir Rd
Visitors also welcome by appt May to July, refreshments by arrangement.
020 7249 4919
nancylkorman@hotmail.co.uk

Four gardens, one new this year, to explore in De Beauvoir, a leafy enclave of Victorian villas next to Islington. The area boasts some of Hackney's keenest gardeners, many having resuscitated their gardens from neglect and sensitively restored them to glory. New this year is 26 Northchurch Rd, which has a beautiful apple tree, well stocked borders and seating areas in sun and shade. 158 Culford Rd's long narrow garden has a romantic feel. A path winds through full borders with shrubs, small trees, perennials and many unusual plants.The family garden at 114 De Beauvoir Rd was designed to be wildlife-friendly and low maintenance. Decorative borders contain echinacea, penstemons, salvia and grasses. The walled garden at 21 Northchurch Terrace has a more formal feel, with deep herbaceous borders, pond, fruit trees, pergola, patio pots and herb beds. Honey tasting and seed sowing for children.

36 DOWNS HILL

Beckenham BR3 5HB. Marc & Janet Berlin, 020 8650 9377, janetberlin@hotmail.com. *1m W of Bromley. 2 mins from Ravensbourne mainline stn nr top of Foxgrove Rd.* Home-made teas. **Adm £3, chd free. Sun 30 June (2-5). Visitors also welcome by appt.**

Long, ⅔ -acre E-facing, award winning garden sloping steeply. Ponds, water courses and several varied patio areas. Many tender unusual plants and hundreds of pots. Wooded paths, dense planting of trees, shrubs and flowers, raised beds and gravel areas. Two alpine houses and greenhouse. Jazz Band.

GROUP OPENING

DULWICH VILLAGE TWO GARDENS, SE21

London SE21 7BJ. *Rail: N Dulwich or W Dulwich then 10-15 mins walk. Tube: Brixton then P4 bus passes the gardens, alight Dulwich Picture Gallery stop. Street parking.* Home-made teas at 103 Dulwich Village. **Combined adm £5, chd free (share to Macmillan, local branch). Sun 16 June (2-5). Also open 9 Dulwich Village, 22 Scutari Rd, 41 Southbrook Rd, Tewkesbury Lodge: Top of the Hill & 27 Thorpewood Ave.**

103 DULWICH VILLAGE
Mr & Mrs N Annesley

105 DULWICH VILLAGE
Mr & Mrs A Rutherford

2 Georgian houses with large gardens, 3 mins walk from Dulwich

Picture Gallery and Dulwich Park. 103 Dulwich Village is a 'country garden in London' with a long herbaceous border, lawn, pond, roses and fruit and vegetable gardens. 105 Dulwich Village is a very pretty garden with many unusual plants, lots of old-fashioned roses, fish pond and water garden. Amazing collection of plants for sale.

9 DULWICH VILLAGE, SE21
Fairfield, 9 Dulwich Village, London SE21 7BU. Helen Marsden. *Rail: N Dulwich or W Dulwich then 10-15 mins walk. Tube: Brixton then P4 bus passes the garden. Street parking*. Home-made teas. **Adm £3.50, chd free.** Sun 16 June (2-5). **Also open Dulwich Village Two Gdns, 41 Southbrook Rd, 22 Scutari Rd, Tewkesbury Lodge: Top of the Hill & 27 Thorpewood Ave.**
This stunning garden in Dulwich is a surprise on many levels; the traditional frontage belies the dramatic contemporary garden behind - almost an acre designed by the master of minimalism, Christopher Bradley-Hole. Designed on a grid, there are huge blocks of yew, gravel and box balls and raised beds for fruit and vegetables.

D

207 EAST BARNET ROAD
New Barnet, Herts EN4 8QS. Margaret Chadwick, 020 8440 0377, magg1ee@hotmail.com. *East Barnet Village. M25 J24 then A111 to Cockfosters. Tube: Northern line to High Barnet or Piccadilly line to Cockfosters. Buses: 184, 307 & 326.* Home-made teas. **Adm £3.50, chd free.** Sun 9 June (2-5). **Visitors also welcome by appt Apr to July.**
Delightful example of a minute courtyard garden 25ft x 30ft. High fences are covered with clematis, honeysuckle and passion flowers; roses and vines scramble over an arch above a seat. Small pond sustains frogs and tadpoles and water plants. An old barrel is home to the Goldfish. Many interesting and unusual plants, mainly in pots. Clever use of mirrors lends added dimensions to this pretty garden. Good use of space, packed full of plants and designed not to reveal itself all at once.

20 EATONVILLE ROAD, SW17
Tooting Bec, London SW17 7SL. Gethyn Davies & Pamela Johnson, www.pamelajohnson.co.uk. *Stns: Tooting Bec 5 min walk, Wandsworth Common 10 min walk. Buses: 219 & 319 on Trinity Rd*. Home-made teas. **Adm £3.50, chd free.** Sun 14 July (2-6). **Also open 28 Old Devonshire Rd.**
Garden designer's tiny back garden packed with far too many plants held together with cleverly concealed corsetry. Unusual plant varieties and combinations give masses of colour, shape, texture and scent and still it's a lovely garden to just sit in and watch the bees. The experiment of growing vegetables in a small space continues. Excellent plant sale and famous homemade cakes.

D

Garden designer's tiny back garden packed with plants held together with corsetry . . .

ECCLESTON SQUARE, SW1
London SW1V 1NP. Roger Phillips & the Residents, www.rogerstreesandshrubs.com. *Off Belgrave Rd nr Victoria Stn, parking allowed on Suns*. Home-made teas. **Adm £4, chd free.** Sun 12 May (2-5).
Planned by Cubitt in 1828, the 3-acre square is subdivided into mini-gardens with camellias, iris, ferns and containers. Dramatic collection of tender climbing roses and 20 different forms of tree peonies. National Collection of ceanothus incl more than 70 species and cultivars. Notable important additions of tender plants being grown and tested. Wisteria arbour, mosaic/brick patio, children's play area and secret gardens.

NCH

EDWARDES SQUARE, W8
South Edwardes Square, Kensington, London W8 6HL. Edwardes Square Garden Committee. *Tube: Kensington High St & Earls Court. Buses: 9, 10, 27, 28, 31, 49 & 74 to Odeon Cinema. Entrance in South Edwardes Square.* **Adm £4, chd free.** Sun 19 May (12.30-5).
One of London's prettiest secluded garden squares. $3^1/_2$ acres laid out differently from other squares, with serpentine paths by Agostino Agliothe, Italian artist and decorator who lived at no.15 from 1814-1820, and a beautiful Grecian temple which is traditionally the home of the head gardener. Romantic rose tunnel winds through the middle of the garden. Good displays of bulbs and blossom. Very easy wheelchair access.

GROUP OPENING

ELM COURT GARDENS
Oakhurst Avenue, East Barnet, EN4 8HA. *2 mins from Oakleigh Park Stn on First Capital Connect line to Welwyn Garden City. 10 mins walk from bus routes 184, 307, 326. M25 J24, then A111 to Cockfosters & A110 down Cat Hill to East Barnet Village*. Home-made teas. **Combined adm £4.50, chd free.** Sun 14 July (2-6).

LANSHAW
3 Elm Court, Mike & Alyne Lidgley
Visitors also welcome by appt July to Aug.
020 8361 2642
bearcat@talktalk.net

4 ELM COURT
Simon Moor & Jayne Evans

Many contrasts in these two quite different gardens, both larger than average. Front gardens - one a formal parterre, one natural, with gravel, grasses, conifers and reclaimed materials. Back gardens: one with hot annuals, perennials, shrubs, hanging baskets, water feature, two topiary beds, pink, blue, 'spiky' and heuchera beds, a 'ball' bed, greenhouse, garden and potting sheds, 2 rockeries, alpine troughs, and much more. The other is long and shady, with curving lawns, a gravel area with containers full of colour, a white bed, a rockery and the whole emphasis is on attracting pollinators - blue, pink, purple and yellow shrubs and perennials. Jayne is a successful artist and has her studio in the garden. A developing garden, still evolving and hungrily devouring cuttings, contributions and advice from all sources and gradually triumphing over poor soil, overhanging trees and lack of water. Plant crèche: plants purchased delivered locally after the event, free of charge. Raffle.

ELM TREE COTTAGE
85 Croham Road, South Croydon CR2 7HJ. Wendy Witherick & Michael Wilkinson, 020 8681 8622, elmtreecottage@sky.com. *2m S of Croydon. Off B275 from Croydon, off A2022 from Selsdon, bus 64.* **Adm £3, chd free. Suns 12 May; 2, 16 June; 7, 21 July; 11 Aug (1-4). Also open 12 May 57 West Hall Road (see Surrey). Visitors also welcome by appt May to Sept.**
Picture this! Come through the gate of our c1855 flint cottage and welcome to the Mediterranean! Meander up the sloping brick path to the sound of running water, see lemon trees, olives, palms and other drought-tolerant plants. Look inside the glasshouse and you will find agaves, cacti and succulents. Rest before you carry on your journey, past lavender, rosemary and much much more! Featured in Garden News. Steep garden, unsuitable for those unsteady on their feet. Regret no dogs or children.

6 ELMS GARDENS
See Essex

NEW **11 ERNLE ROAD, SW20**
Wimbledon, London SW20 0HH. Theresa-Mary Morton. *¼ m from Wimbledon Village, 200yds from Crooked Billet PH. Exit A3 at A238 to Wimbledon, turning L at Copse Hill. Mainline: Wimbledon or Raynes Park. Tube: Wimbledon; Bus: 200 to Christchurch then 100yds walk.* Home-made teas. **Adm £3.50, chd free. Sat 27, Sun 28 Apr (2.30-6).**
Established suburban garden of ¼ acre on sandy acid soil, spatially organised into separate sections: oak pergola framing the main vista, hidden parterre, woodland, pool, iris border, flower garden and summerhouse. Beaten gravel paths, one step up to main garden.

48 ERSKINE HILL, NW11
Hampstead Garden Suburb, London NW11 6HG. Marjorie & David Harris, 020 8455 6507. *1m N of Golders Green. Close to A406 (N Circular) & A1. Tube: Golders Green. Circular 'Hail & Ride' H2 bus from Golders Green passes door. 10 mins walk from Finchley Rd (buses 82, 102, 460 to Temple Fortune), or from Falloden Way (bus 102 to Market Place, then H2, S side only).* Self-service light refreshments. **Adm £3.50, chd free. Sun 16 June (2-6). Visitors also welcome by appt May to Sept.**
Bird-friendly garden, wrapped around artisan's cottage, stuffed with perennials, shrubs, roses and clematis. Trees incl Cotinus 'Grace', old apple tree and flowering cherry. Terrace overflowing with well-planted containers. Intriguing brick-paved area with four raised beds. Greenhouse. Second prize in 'Suburb in Bloom', London Gardens Society 'highly recommended back garden'. Nest boxes, miniature long grass areas, organic and pesticide-free. Featured in Hampstead and Highgate Express. Some single steps and narrow paths.

FAIRWINDS
See Essex

Picture this! Come through the gate of our c1855 flint cottage and welcome to the Mediterranean . . .

42 FALCONER ROAD
See Hertfordshire

65 FARM WAY
Worcester Park KT4 8SB. Mr & Mrs A Rutherford. *Off A243 from Kingston, nearest train stn Worcester Park. Bus 213 from Kingston alight at Woodbines Lane.* Cream teas. **Adm £3, chd free. Sun 30 June (12-4).**
Plant lover's 5yr-old garden with wide mixed borders bursting with colour and plants of different textures and interest, incl shrubs, roses and perennials. Assorted pots of vegetables, raised beds. Paved and decked, plenty of seating areas.

◆ FENTON HOUSE, NW3
Hampstead Grove, Hampstead, London NW3 6SP. National Trust, www.nationaltrust.org.uk. *300yds from Hampstead tube. Entrances: Top of Holly Hill & Hampstead Grove.* **For NGS: Tue 2 July (6.30-8). Pre-booking essential for Special Evening Tour £10 with wine & light refreshments. Please visit www.ngs.org.uk for information & bookings, or phone 01483 211535. For other opening times and information, please see garden website.**
Join the Gardener-in-Charge for a special evening tour. Andrew Darragh who brings over 10 yrs' experience from Kew to Fenton House will explore this timeless 1½ -acre walled garden. Laid out over 3 levels, and featuring formal walks and areas, a small sunken rose garden, a 300yr-old orchard and a kitchen garden, Andrew will present the garden and his plans for its future development.

54 FERNDOWN
Northwood Hills HA6 1PH. David Bryson & Ros Preston, 020 8866 3792, davidbryson@sky.com. *Tube: Northwood Hills 5 mins walk. R out of stn, R down Briarwood Dr then 1st R.* Cream teas. **Adm £3, chd free. Sun 18 Aug (11-5). Visitors also welcome by appt Aug to Oct.**
Subtropical escapism in suburbia. Intensely planted with a shoehorn, the garden includes many rare species of palms, bromeliads, ferns, cacti, succulents and other unusual plants. Of note are large examples of trachycarpus princeps and alcantarea. A raised deck and ponds help create a unique effect. Featured in The Independent.

GROUP OPENING

FIVE CANONBURY GARDENS, N1
St Mary's Grove, London N1 2NT. *Tube: Highbury & Islington 6 mins. Buses: 4, 19, 30, 277 to St Paul's Rd. Then, access via Compton Rd and Prior Bolton St to 36 St Mary's Grove for admission and direction map.* **Evening Opening £5, chd free, light refreshments, Wed 19 June (6.30-9).**

NEW **23 CANONBURY PLACE**

NEW **41 GRANGE GROVE**

20 ST MARY'S GROVE

NEW **26 ST MARY'S GROVE**

36 ST MARY'S GROVE

Five Canonbury Gardens are in the heart of the leafy Canonbury conservation area and close to Canonbury Square and the historic Canonbury Tower. Group includes three new gardens. 23 Canonbury Place - wildlife-friendly garden with fruit trees and flowers. 41 Grange Grove - an evergreen oasis with varied shrubs and colourful pots. Low maintenance! 20 St Mary's Grove - small, romantic garden with climber-covered walls, akebia, roses and hydrangeas. 36 St Mary's Grove - large, densely-planted 'green' garden - greenhouse, green roof, ponds, composting. Evolving front flower garden. 26 St Mary's Grove - imaginatively-planted patio garden, clever use of interesting pots. Wheelchair access to 36 St Mary's Grove only.

NEW 6 FLANCHFORD ROAD, W12

London W12 9ND. Mr & Mrs Yadav. *Tube: District line to Stamford Brook stn. Exit L from stn, down Goldhawk Rd, past petrol station to T-junction. Turn L & take 1st R into Flanchford Rd.* Light refreshments. **Adm £3, chd free.** Sun 28 July (2-6).

A family garden designed in such a way as to provide an oasis of peace and calm to adults while providing a spacious secluded play area for children at the back. The planting plan is varied and interesting and provides colour all yr round. Interest is added to the garden with a stone wall and arch with a fountain and stone bird bath. Garden is level so should be accessible to wheelchair users, although side return is narrow in places.

56 FOREST DRIVE
See Essex

NEW 88 FROGNAL, NW3

Frognal, London NW3 6XB. Mr & Mrs M. Linell. *Tube: Hampstead then 7 mins walk. Buses: 46, 268, 13, 113, 82. Garden entrance at 12B Church Row, nr corner with Frognal.* Home-made teas. **Adm £3.50, chd free.** Sun 9 June (2-6).

1/2 -acre garden hidden from view by historic high walls, designed on 2 levels with a terrace and large C19 conservatory near the house leading to lawns all surrounded by herbaceous borders and ornamental trees, shrubs and climbers, many rare, planted and underplanted for year round effect. Home propagated plants for sale. Grass and bark chip sloping paths.

Subtropical escapism in suburbia. Intensely planted with a shoehorn . . .

GROUP OPENING

FROGNAL GARDENS, NW3

Hampstead, London NW3 6UY. *Tube: Hampstead. Buses: 46, 268 to Hampstead High St. Frognal Gdns 2nd R off Church Row from Heath St.* Home-made teas. **Combined adm £5, chd free.** Sun 16 June (2-5).

5 FROGNAL GARDENS
Ruth & Brian Levy

5A FROGNAL GARDENS
Ian & Barbara Jackson

2 neighbouring gardens divided by path lined with trellises of cascading roses and clematis, underplanted with carpets of flowers. At No.5, the long narrow structured garden is romantically planted with soft colours and a profusion of unusual climbers and cottage perennials. The small, beautifully landscaped garden at 5A is a garden to enjoy and relax in with lawn, colourful flower beds and containers. 4 inch step from patio doors.

9 FURLONG ROAD, N7

Islington, London N7 8LS. Nigel Watts & Tanuja Pandit. *Tube & Overground: Highbury & Islington, 3 mins walk along Holloway Rd, 2nd L. Furlong Rd joins Holloway Rd and Liverpool Rd. Buses: 43, 271, 393.* Light refreshments. **Adm £2, chd free.** Sun 9 June (2-6). **Also open 16 Furlong Rd, 1a & 62 Hungerford Rd and Olden Garden Community Project.**

Small garden which makes clever use of an awkwardly-shaped plot. Curved lines are used to complement a modern extension. Raised beds contain a mix of tender and hardy plants to give an exotic feel and include loquat, banana, palm, cycad and tree fern. Contrasting traditional front garden. Featured in 'Small Family Gardens' and 'Modern Family Gardens' by Caroline Tilston.

16 FURLONG ROAD, N7

Islington, London N7 8LS. Charles & Ingrid Maggs. *Tube & Overground: Highbury & Islington, 3mins walk along Holloway Rd, 2nd L. Furlong Rd joins Holloway Rd and Liverpool Rd. Buses: 43, 271, 393.* Home-made teas. **Adm £3, chd free.** Sun 9 June (2-6). **Also open 9 Furlong Rd, 1a & 62 Hungerford Rd and Olden Garden Community Project.**

Exceptional aspect as garden backs onto churchyard with church tower giving a feeling of being in the country rather than just off the Holloway Rd. Informal flower borders and trellises of roses, surrounding lawn, a pond, pergola and rock garden.

GARDEN BARGE SQUARE AT DOWNINGS ROADS MOORINGS, SE1

31 Mill Street, London SE1 2AX. Mr Nick Lacey. *Close to Tower Bridge & Design Museum. Mill St off Jamaica Rd, between London Bridge & Bermondsey stns, Tower Hill also nearby. Buses: 47, 188, 381, RV1.* Home-made teas on the ArtsArk. **Adm £3.50, chd free (share to RNLI).** Sun 19 May (2-5).

Series of 7 floating barge gardens connected by walkways and bridges. Gardens have an eclectic range of plants for year round seasonal interest. Marine environment: suitable shoes and care needed. Not suitable for small children.

◆ THE GARDEN MUSEUM, SE1

Lambeth Palace Road, London SE1 7LB. Garden Museum, 020 7401 8865, www.gardenmuseum.org.uk. *E side of Lambeth Bridge. Tube: Lambeth North, Vauxhall, Waterloo. Buses: 507 Red Arrow from Victoria or*

Waterloo mainline & tube stns, also 3, 77, 344. **Adm £7.50, chd free (share to Garden Museum). For NGS: Sat 15 June (10.30-4). For other opening times and information, please phone or see garden website.**
Reproduction C17 knot garden with period plants, topiary and box hedging. Wild garden in front of graveyard area; drought planting at front entrance; themed installation planting on front border. Historic tools, information displays, changing exhibitions, shop and café housed in former church of St-Mary-at-Lambeth.

70 GLOUCESTER CRESCENT, NW1

London NW1 7EG. Lucy Gent, 020 7485 6906, gent.lucy@gmail.com. *Tube: Camden Town 2 mins, Mornington Crescent 10 mins. Metered parking in Oval Rd.* Home-made teas. **Adm £3.50, chd free. Suns 30 June; 4 Aug (2-5.30). Also open The Holme. Visitors also welcome by appt Apr to Oct.**
An oasis in Camden's urban density, where challenges of space and shade are met by resourceful planting, with an especial interest in August colour. Notice also next door on L the newly designed garden at 1 Regents Park Terrace, and next door on R the pretty cottage garden at 69 Gloucester Crescent where visitors are welcome.

20 GOLDHAZE CLOSE

Woodford Green IG8 7LE. Jenny Richmond. *By car, along A406 to Charlie Brown's r'about, L onto Chigwell Rd to T-lights. L to Broadmead Rd, 1st R Underwood Rd, L into Goldhaze Close. Tube: Woodford. Buses: 14 from South Woodford tube stn, 275 from Walthamstow Central stn.* Home-made teas. **Adm £2.50, chd free. Suns 14 July; 18 Aug (12-5).**
100ft L-shaped landscaped garden is bursting with over 100 plants grown in different types of conditions. A huge 28yr-old eucalyptus resembles a mature oak with beautiful bark. Paths lined with plants such as a strawberry tree, roses, campsis, penstemons, crocosmia and vegetables (in pots grown from seed in a greenhouse) lead to a secret decked garden for relaxation.

Ash Cottage

ALLOTMENTS

GOLF COURSE ALLOTMENTS, N11

Winton Avenue, London N11 2AS. GCAA/Haringey, www.gcaa.pwp.blueyonder.co.uk. *Tube: Bounds Green approx 1km. Buses: 102, 184, 299 to Sunshine Garden Centre, Durnsford Rd. Then Bidwell Gdns (on foot through park) to Winton Ave. Gate opp junction with Blake Rd.* Light refreshments. **Adm £3.50, chd free (share to GCAA). Sun 1 Sept (1-4.30).**
Large, long-established allotment with over 200 plots, some organic. Maintained by culturally diverse community growing wide variety of fruit, vegetables and flowers. Picturesque corners and quirky sheds - a visit feels like being in the countryside. Autumn Show on 1 Sept features prizewinning exhibits. Tours of best plots. Fresh allotment produce, chutneys, jams, cakes and light lunches all available for sale. No cars on site. Wheelchair access limited to main paths. Gravel and some uneven surfaces. WC, incl disabled.

55 GRASMERE AVENUE, SW19

Merton Park, London SW19 3DY. Glen Burnell & Roger Blanks. *1m S of Wimbledon. Tube: Morden, then 5 mins walk. Turn R out of stn, Grasmere Ave 2nd on R. By car, close to Morden Town Centre, just off one way system, Baptist Church on corner of Grasmere Ave.* Home-made teas. **Adm £3, chd £1. Sat 15, Sun 16 June (11-3).**
An oasis of calm in suburbia. Rich lush foliage, sculptured with tropical planting, sets off a subtle palette of cooling purple and white in a little haven of tranquillity in this 70ft rear garden of a 1930s London semi. Soft background music and the sound of flowing water add to the tranquil, relaxing ambiance.

17 GREENSTONE MEWS, E11

Wanstead, London E11 2RS. Mr & Mrs S Farnham, 07761 476651, farnhamz@yahoo.co.uk. *Wanstead. Tube: Snaresbrook or Wanstead, 5 mins walk. Bus: 101, 308 to Wanstead High St.* **Adm £12 (incl pre-booked lunch), regret no children. Pre-booked visitors welcome on Sun 4 Aug (12.30-4).**
Slate paved garden (20ft x 17ft). Height provided by a mature strawberry tree. A buried bath used

as a fishpond is surrounded by climbers clothing fences underplanted with herbs, vegetables, shrubs and perennials grown from cuttings; cultivated with tools stored in a shed on wheels. Ideas aplenty for small space gardening. Book sale.

7 THE GROVE, N6

Highgate Village, London N6 6JU. Mr Thomas Lyttelton, 07713 638161. *The Grove is between Highgate West Hill & Hampstead Lane. Tube: Archway or Highgate. Buses: 143, 210, 271 to Highgate Village from Archway, 214 from Camden Town*. Home-made teas. **Adm £3.50, chd free (share to The Harington Scheme). Sun 24 Mar (2-5.30). Visitors also welcome by appt in Feb & March.**

½ acre designed for max all-yr interest with its variety of conifers and other trees, ground cover, water garden, vistas, 19 paths, surprises. Exceptional camellias and magnolia in March. Article in The Ham and High. Wheelchair access to main lawn only; many very narrow paths.

24 GROVE PARK, SE5

Camberwell, London SE5 8LH. Clive Pankhurst, www.alternative-planting.blogspot.com. *Chadwick Rd end of Grove Park. Stns: Peckham Rye or Denmark Hill, both 10 mins walk. Good street parking*. Home-made teas. **Adm £3, chd free. Sun 1 Sept (2-5.30).**

A garden to surprise and delight with ponds, sunken terrace and bold, big leafed planting of exotics that reach for the sky in late summer, achieving a crescendo of colour with dark dahlias, Ricinus, bananas and tetrapanax. Huge 'secret' garden with more jungle plants, bee hives, developing potager and cutting garden. Greenhouse with carnivorous plants for the brave. Featured on BBC Gardeners' World.

◆ HAM HOUSE AND GARDEN

Ham, Richmond TW10 7RS. National Trust, www.nationaltrust.org.uk. *Mid-way between Richmond & Kingston. W of A307 on Surrey bank of R Thames. Follow NT signs*. **Adm £4.50, chd £2.25. For NGS: Wed 10 July (11-5). For other opening times and information, please see garden website.**

The beautiful C17 gardens incl Cherry Garden, featuring lavender parterres flanked by hornbeam arbours; S terrace with clipped yew cones, hibiscus and pomegranate trees; eight grass plats; maze-like wilderness; C17 orangery with working kitchen garden and licensed café and terrace. Gravel paths and some cobbles.

116 HAMILTON TERRACE, NW8

London NW8 9UT. Mr & Mrs I B Kathuria, 020 7625 6909, gkathuria@hotmail.co.uk. *Tube: Maida Vale, 5 mins walk, St John's Wood, 10 mins walk. Buses: Maida Vale 16, 98, Abbey Rd 139, 189, Finchley Rd 13, 113. Parking free after 6.30 & on Sundays*. Home-made teas. **Adm £3.50, chd free (share to St. Mark's Church). Sun 16 June (2-6). Evening Opening £5, chd free, wine, Thur 11 July (5-9). Visitors also welcome by appt May to Sept, refreshments by arrangement for groups only.**

Lush front garden full of dramatic foliage with a water feature and tree ferns. Large back garden of different levels with Yorkshire stone paving, many large terracotta pots and containers, water feature and lawn. Wide variety of perennials and flowering shrubs, many unusual, and subtropical plants, succulents, acers, ferns, hebes, climbers, roses, fuchsias and prizewinning hostas. Packed with colour and rich foliage of varied texture.

◆ HAMPTON COURT PALACE

East Molesey KT8 9AU. Historic Royal Palaces, 0844 482 7777, www.hrp.org.uk. Adm £10, wine. For NGS: Pre-booking essential Wed 13 Mar; Thur 9 May; Thur 11 July; Thur 29 Aug (6.30-8) Special evening tours with specialist talks. Please visit www.ngs.org.uk for information & bookings, or phone 01483 211535. For other opening times and information, please phone or see garden website.

Take this rare opportunity to join 4 very special NGS private tours - in the peace of the evening, after these wonderful and historic gardens have closed to the public. Experience **Spring is Here** on 13th March. On 9th May come and visit **The Heart of All** behind the scenes in the palace's glasshouse nursery. 11th July **Kings and Queens** hear about 500 years of royal garden history. Visit on 29th August for a nostalgic tour around the gardens with Anthony Boulding who is celebrating 40 years at the palace. With specialist talks, and the chance to go behind the scenes, come and learn about the 500 year history of these royal gardens and find out what goes into creating and maintaining them.

NCH

> A garden to surprise and delight with ponds, sunken terrace and bold, big leafed planting of exotics that reach for the sky . . .

GROUP OPENING

HAMPTON HILL GARDENS

Hampton Hill TW12 1DW. *4m from Twickenham/Kingston-upon-Thames. Between A312 (Uxbridge Rd) and A313 (Park Rd). Bus: 285 from Kingston stops at end of rd. Stn: Fulwell 15 mins walk*. Home-made teas. **Combined adm £5, chd free. Sat 8, Sun 9 June (2-5).**

18 CRANMER ROAD
Bernard Wigginton

30 ST JAMES'S ROAD
Jean Burman
(See separate entry)

NEW **99 UXBRIDGE ROAD**
Anne & Bob Wagner

3 gardens of diverse interest in an attractive West London suburb. With the backdrop of St James's Church spire, 18 Cranmer Rd is a colourful garden with herbaceous and exotic borders and a WW2 air raid shelter transformed as rockery and water garden with azaleas, helianthemums and foliage plants. The SE-facing garden at 30 St James's Rd is subdivided into 5 rooms. Decking with seating leads to ponds surrounded by grasses and shrubs and an African-themed thatched exterior 'sitting room'. 99 Uxbridge Rd, a wildlife-friendly, urban cottage garden. Secluded and peaceful, many pots and containers, lawn,

shrubs, flowers, fruit trees, and an organic kitchen garden. Lots of places to sit and relax. Partial wheelchair access.

HARCOURT HOUSE

Grasmere Road, Bromley BR1 4BB. Freda Davis, www.fredasgarden.co.uk. *1½ m W of Bromley. WD buses 208, 227, 320 to junction of Highland Rd.* Home-made teas. **Adm £3, chd free. Sun 28 July (2-5).**

Colourful Victorian garden with an Italian influence, wrapped around a large Victorian house. Winding pathways, newly structured rock garden, Hercules secret garden, water features, many statues, unusual objects incl French antique lamp-posts, dozens of pots, many hanging baskets and large conservatory in Victorian style. Gold Medal and Cup winner for London Gardens Society Back Garden Competition.

Relaxed family garden with a distinct cottage feel . . .

5 HEATHGATE, NW11

Hampstead Garden Suburb, London NW11 7AR. Patricia Larsen. *12 mins walk from Golders Green. Tube: Golders Green, then H2 bus stops on request at Heathgate.* Light refreshments. **Adm £3.50, chd free. Sun 21 July (2-6). Also open 4 Asmuns Hill & 86 Willifield Way.**

Set in a stunning borrowed tree-scape on the edge of Hampstead Heath, this 45ft x 25ft Arts and Crafts garden has lavishly planted traditional herbaceous borders with interesting contemporary features.

5 HILLCREST AVENUE, NW11

London NW11 0EP. Mrs R M Rees, 020 8455 0419, ruthmrees@hotmail.co.uk. *1m N of Golders Green. Tube: Golders Green. Buses: 82, 102, 460 to Temple Fortune. Walk down Bridge Lane, to Hillcrest Ave.* Home-made teas. **Adm £3.50, chd free. Sun 14 July (2-6). Evening Opening, wine, Wed 17 July (5-9). Visitors also welcome by appt May to Oct.**

Small labour-saving, low maintenance, traditional back garden with rockery, fish pond, conservatory, tree fern and secluded patio. Urban jungle front garden with drought-resistant Mediterranean plants and pseudopanax crassifolia ferox. No wheelchair access but stairlift from kitchen down to back garden.

19 HILLFIELD PARK, N10

London N10 3QT. Mr Zaki & Ruth Elia. *Off Muswell Hill Broadway, corner HSBC Bank. Buses: W7, 43, 102, 144, 134, 234. Tube: Highgate, E Finchley, Finsbury Park.* Light refreshments. **Adm £3, chd free. Sun 21 July (2-6). Also open, with home-made teas 5 St Regis Close.**

An orientalist garden in Edwardian Muswell Hill. Created by owner/designer, inspired by the original, British Raj inspired, features within the house. Three tiled terraces with ceramic containers unfold around a traditional fountain. A bespoke Eastern-style shed crowns the top terrace, while dramatic planting by Declan Buckley cocoons visitors in lush seclusion. Featured in Amateur Gardening and on ITV Love your Garden.

GROUP OPENING

NEW HOLLY GROVE GARDENS GROUP, SE15

Peckham, London SE15 5DF. *Stn: Peckham Rye 3 mins walk. Turn L into Holly Grove and L past Green towards Bellenden Rd. Buses to Rye Lane Peckham 12, 37, 63, 78, 197, 343, 363.* Home-made teas. **Combined adm £5, chd free. Evening Opening £6, chd free, wine, Wed 22 May (6.30-9); Sun 26 May (1-5). Also open 26 May, 86 Underhill Rd & 29 Kinsale Rd.**

18 HOLLY GROVE
David Woodbine

NEW 27 HOLLY GROVE
Sally & Kevin O'Brien

NEW 29 HOLLY GROVE
Jessica Nicholas

3 distinctively different small gardens in a quiet leafy Peckham cul de sac, benefitting from the shared backdrop of a high wall along their back acting as an elegant buffer and offering wind shelter to create a warm micro-climate. No 18 has a modern feel with waving grasses in the front and steel gabon-lined raised beds; No 27 neatly lines up on the diagonal with a rectangular wildlife pond, raised beds and standard roses, while at No 29 climbing hydrangeas and camellias lead visitors to an enchanting, informal, relaxed family garden with a distinct cottage feel to it with arching roses and scrambling clematis.

THE HOLME, NW1

Inner Circle, Regents Park, London NW1 4NT. Lessee of The Crown Commission. *5 mins from Baker St in Regents Park. Opp Rose Garden. Tube: Regents Park or Baker St, over York Bridge then L at Inner Circle. Buses 13, 18, 27, 30, 74, 82, 113, 139, 159, 274 to Baker St.* Teas at nearby Rose Garden Café and at 70 Gloucester Crescent (30 June & 4 Aug only). **Adm £4, chd free. Sat 29, Sun 30 June; Sat 3, Sun 4 Aug (2.30-5.30).**

4-acre garden filled with interesting and unusual plants. Sweeping lakeside lawns intersected by islands of herbaceous beds. Extensive rock garden with waterfall, stream and pool. Formal flower garden with unusual annual and half hardy plants, sunken lawn, fountain pool and arbour. Gravel paths and some steps which gardeners will help to negotiate.

239A HOOK ROAD

Chessington KT9 1EQ. Mr & Mrs D St Romaine, 020 8397 3761, derek@gardenphotolibrary.com, www.gardenphotolibrary.com. *4m S of Kingston. A3 from London, turn L at Hook underpass onto A243 Hook Rd. Garden approx 300yds on L. Parking opp in park. Buses: K4, 71, 465 from Kingston & Surbiton to North Star PH.* Home-made teas. **Adm £3, chd free (share to St Catherine of Siena Church, Chessington). Sun 16 June (2-6). Evening Opening £4.50, chd free, wine, Wed 19 June (8.30-10.30). Visitors also welcome by appt June to July.**

Garden photographer's garden. Contemporary flower garden with entertaining area, gravel garden, colour-themed herbaceous borders, fernery, pond and rose tunnel. Traditional potager with 20 varieties of fruit and 50+ varieties of vegetables and herbs. Special late night opening to show how over 500 candles and lighting, used in imaginative ways with containers and architectural foliage, can effectively transform areas of a garden at night. Images by Derek St Romaine. Featured on BBC Gardeners World, Garden Design and also in The Light Fantastic in Independent Weekend Magazine.

1A HUNGERFORD ROAD, N7
London N7 9LA. David Matzdorf, davidmatzdorf@blueyonder.co.uk, www.growingontheedge.net. *Between Camden Town & Holloway. Tube: Caledonian Rd, 6 mins walk. Buses: 29 & 253 to Hillmarton Rd stop in Camden Rd; 17, 91, 259 & 393 to last stop in Hillmarton Rd; 10 to York Way at Market Rd & 274 to junction of Market Rd & Caledonian Rd. Free parking at weekends.* **Adm £2, chd free (share to Terrence Higgins Trust). Sun 9 June (12-6). Also open 9 & 16 Furlong Rd, 62 Hungerford Rd and Olden Garden Community Project. Visitors also welcome by appt Mar to Oct.**
Unique eco-house with walled, lush front garden planted in modern-exotic style. Front garden densely planted with palms, acacia, ginger lilies, brugmansias, bananas, euphorbias, yuccas and bamboo. Floriferous 'green roof' resembling scree slope planted with agaves, aloes, yuccas, dasylirions, alpines, sedums, mesembryanthemums, bulbs, grasses, Mediterranean shrubs and aromatic herbs. Access via ladder to roof (can also be seen from below). Garden and roof each 50ft x 18ft. Featured in Small Green Roofs (Timber Press).

62 HUNGERFORD ROAD, N7
London N7 9LP. John Gilbert & Lynne Berry. *Directions as 1a Hungerford Rd.* **Adm £2.50, chd free. Sun 9 June (2-6). Also open 9 & 16 Furlong Rd, 1a Hungerford Rd and Olden Garden Community Project.**
Densely planted mature town garden at rear of Victorian terrace house which has been designed to maximise space for planting and create several different sitting areas, views and moods. NW facing with considerable shade, it is arranged in a series of paved rooms with a good range of perennials, shrubs and trees. Professional garden designer's own garden.

Eccleston Square

From tiny back plots to country estates ...

THE HURLINGHAM CLUB, SW6
Ranelagh Gardens, London SW6 3PR. The Members of the Hurlingham Club, www.hurlinghamclub.org.uk. *Main gate at E end of Ranelagh Gardens. Tube: Putney Bridge (110yds).* **Adm £5, chd free. Sat 18 May (11-4).**
Rare opportunity to visit this 42-acre jewel with many mature trees, 2-acre lake with water fowl, expansive lawns and a river walk. Capability Brown and Humphry Repton were involved with landscaping. The gardens are renowned for their roses, herbaceous and lakeside borders, shrubberies and stunning bedding displays. The riverbank is a haven for wildlife with native trees, shrubs and wild flowers. Garden Tour at 2pm.

23 IMPERIAL ROAD, N22
London N22 8DE. Kate Gadsby. *Off Bounds Green Rd between Bounds Green Tube & Wood Green Tube. 5 mins from Alexandra Palace mainline.* **Adm £2.50, chd free. Sun 8 Sept (2-6). Also open 5 Russell Rd.**
Tiny back garden overflowing with interesting and unusual plants where an inventive and inspiring approach to planting, both in raised borders and containers, has created a surprising number of perspectives. In late summer a tangle of climbers, vegetables, herbs, annuals and perennials, creates a sensational visual treat. Semi-covered deck allows enjoyment in sun and rain.

GROUP OPENING

ISLINGTON GARDENS, N1
London N1 1BE. *Tube: Kings Cross, Caledonian Road or Angel. Buses: 17, 91, 259 to Caledonian Rd.* Home-made teas at 36 Thornhill Square. **Combined adm £6 or £2 each, chd free. Sun 19 May (2-6).**

BARNSBURY WOOD
Islington Council.
Off Crescent St, N of Thornhill Square

1 BATTLEBRIDGE COURT
Wharfdale Road. Mike Jackson
Visitors also welcome by appt Mar to Oct.
07761 626310
michaeljackson215@me.com

44 HEMINGFORD ROAD
Peter Willis & Haremi Kudo

36 THORNHILL SQUARE
Anna & Christopher McKane

Walk through Islington's Georgian streets to these contrasting gardens. At Barnsbury Wood flower borders lead to Islington's hidden secret: a place of peace and relaxation, the Borough's only site of mature woodland and one of London's smallest nature reserves.
44 Hemingford Road is a surprisingly lush, country-style garden with interesting trees, shrubs, perennials, lawns and pond in a very small space. 36 Thornhill Square's 120ft long garden has old roses, hardy geraniums and clematis in curved beds giving a country garden atmosphere; also a small bonsai collection and many unusual perennials for sale. The use of sun and shade are maximised at the 35ft x 17ft plantsman's garden at 1 Battlebridge Court with its peat block terracing. Look out for the naturalised terrapins living between the nearby houseboats, a peaceful oasis only 2 mins from Kings Cross.

JULIE'S GARDEN
See Essex

Look out for the naturalised terrapins living between the nearby houseboats . . .

22 KELSEY WAY
Beckenham BR3 3LL. Janet & Steve Wright. *From Beckenham town centre, take Kelsey Park Rd, R into Manor Way. Kelsey Way is turning off this. Bus: 367 Sunday service to Village Way stop.* Home-made teas. **Adm £3.50, chd free. Sun 9 June (2-5.30).**
Multiple award winning garden. Colourful herbaceous borders with many tropical plants including bananas, colocasias, alocasias, cannas and several different varieties of brugmansias. Displays of potted plants and a conservatory with a magnificent bougainvillea. Extensive and varied vegetable garden with a large fruit cage.

GROUP OPENING

KEW GARDENS STATION GROUP
Kew TW9 4DA. Home-made teas at 355 Sandycombe Road. **Combined adm £7, chd free. Sun 19 May (2-5).**

5 ENNERDALE ROAD
Jane Tandy & Lawrence Lawson

355 SANDYCOMBE ROAD
Henry Gentle & Sally Woodward Gentle.
Garden entrance between house nos. 351 & 353 Sandycombe Road

31 WEST PARK ROAD
Anna Anderson.
By Kew Gardens Stn, on E side of railway line

Enjoy 3 varied gardens near Kew Gardens Station, all within walking distance of each other. The S-facing walled garden at 5 Ennerdale Road (approx 30m x 19m) has raised beds, mixed borders, modern sculpture, a scree bed and a large terrace with pots. 355 Sandycombe Road is an unexpectedly large urban garden on 2 levels. Terracing with wooden sleepers, bricks and decking provide distinct areas of interest incl lavenders, olives, grasses, euphorbias and other plants for sandy soils and shady areas - a garden for adults and children alike. The modern botanical garden at 31 West Park Road has an oriental twist. Emphasis is on foliage and an eclectic mix of plants, with a reflecting pool and rotating willow screens which provide varying views or privacy. Also a dry bed, shady beds, mature trees and a private paved dining area with dappled light and shade.

GROUP OPENING

KEW GREEN GARDENS
Kew, London TW9 3AH. *NW side of Kew Green. Tube: Kew Gardens. Mainline stn: Kew Bridge. Buses: 65, 391. Entrance via riverside.* Home-made teas at 67 Kew Green. **Combined adm £5, chd free. Sun 19 May (2-6).**

65 KEW GREEN
Giles & Angela Dixon

69 KEW GREEN
John & Virginia Godfrey

71 KEW GREEN
Mr & Mrs Jan Pethick

73 KEW GREEN
Sir Donald & Lady Elizabeth Insall

4 long gardens behind a row of C18 houses on the Green, close to the Royal Botanic Gardens. These gardens feature the profusely planted and traditional borders of a mature English country garden, and contrast formal gardens, terraces, lawns, laid out around tall old trees, with wilder areas and woodland and wild flower planting. One has an unusual architect-designed summerhouse, while another offers the surprise of a modern planting of espaliered miniature fruit trees.

NEW **40 KIDBROOKE GARDENS, SE3**
Blackheath, London SE3 0PD. Mrs Lynne Doughty. *Blackheath BR 10 mins walk, buses 89,108 202 to Blackheath village, street parking available.* Home-made teas. **Adm £4, chd free. Suns 16 June; 11 Aug (2-6).**
Unusually large, well-stocked, S-facing, formal garden. Beautiful herbaceous borders, summer and winter vegetable gardens, pretty pond and miniature fruit orchard. This is an old garden that was completely replanted during 2011 and has come into its own.

KING HENRY'S WALK GARDEN, N1
11c King Henry's Walk, London N1 4NX. Friends of King Henry's Walk Garden, www.khwgarden.org.uk. *Buses incl: 21, 30, 38, 56, 141, 277. Behind adventure playground on KHW, off Balls Pond Rd.* Light refreshments. **£5, chd free (share to Friends of KHW Garden). Evening Opening Wed 3 July (6.30-9).**
Vibrant ornamental planting welcomes the visitor to this hidden oasis and leads you into a verdant community garden with secluded woodland area, beehives, wildlife pond, wall-trained fruit trees, and plots used by local residents to grow their own fruit and vegetables. Live music. Art exhibition. RHS It's Your Neighbourhood National Certificate of Distinction (only six projects selected for this award,

presented at Britain in Bloom UK Finals). Second place (Community Garden) London in Bloom. Gold Award (Community Garden) Islington in Bloom. Disabled WC available.

29 KINSALE ROAD, SE15

London SE15 4HJ. A & D Dunford-Swirles. *Nr junction of E.Dulwich Rd & Peckham Rye (A2214, A2215.) Some free parking in adj streets. Rail: Peckham Rye, then 15 mins. walk. Buses: 12, 37, 63, 197, 363, 484. Tube: Brixton, then 37 bus to Peckham Rye*. Light refreshments. **Adm £2, chd free.** **Sun 26 May (2-4.30). Also open Holly Grove Gardens Group & 86 Underhill Rd.**
A tiny garden, densely planted with trees, shrubs, flowers and vegetables. Includes a micro pond and a variety of climbers scrambling up fences and walls.

212 LANGLEY WAY

West Wickham BR4 0DU. Fleur, Cliff & William Wood, 020 8249 7840, fleur.wood@ntlworld.com. *1½ m SW of Bromley. At junction of A232 (Croydon to Orpington Rd) with B265 T-lights, turn N into Baston Rd. At mini r'about junction with B251 turn L into Pickhurst Ln. Follow rd to Pickhurst PH, then 1st L into Langley Way*. Light refreshments. **Adm £3, chd free (share to National Hospital Development Foundation). Fri 7, Sat 8, Sun 9 June; Fri 2, Sat 3, Sun 4 Aug (11.30-5). Visitors also welcome by appt June to Sept.**
Not your average suburban back garden! Enter through old oak door under brick arch into cool white courtyard garden. In contrast, fiery Mediterranean terrace with marble fountain, fish, and pergola with vines. Natural cottage garden, tree house in rainforest garden, vegetable area with raised beds, greenhouses, fruit trees and chickens. Everything grown organically with emphasis on wildlife. Narrow paths, rear of garden not wheelchair accessible.

12 LANSDOWNE ROAD, W11

London W11 3LW. The Lady Amabel Lindsay. *Turn N off Holland Park Ave nr Holland Park stn or W off Ladbroke Grove halfway along. Buses: 12, 88, GL 711, 715. Bus stop & tube: Holland Park, 4 mins.* **Adm £3, chd free. Wed 22 May (2-6).**
Medium-sized garden with a 200yr-old mulberry tree as a centrepiece. It includes densely planted borders in mostly soft colours. A large terrace with massed pots and a greenhouse of climbing geraniums. Partial wheelchair access.

8 LANSDOWNE WALK, W11

London W11 3LN. Nerissa Guest, 020 7727 2660, nmguest@waitrose.com, www.8lansdownewalk.co.uk. *Tube: Holland Park, then 2 mins walk N. Buses: 94, 148*. Home-made teas. **Adm £3.50, chd free. Sun 12 May (2-6); Wed 15 May (3.30-7.30); Sat 15 June (3-6). Visitors also welcome by appt.**
Prizewinning garden, Brighter Kensington & Chelsea Scheme and Kensington Gardeners' Club. All-yr interest: specialist collection of species camellias winter and spring; choice salvias and pelargoniums summer and autumn; many clematis. Emphasis in borders and containers on foliage, texture and scent with an unusual mix of exotic and herbaceous.

42 LATIMER ROAD, E7

Forest Gate, London E7 0LQ. Janet Daniels. *8 mins walk from Forest Gate or Wanstead Park stn. From Forest Gate cross to Sebert Rd, then 3rd rd on L.* **Adm £3, chd free. Sat 20 July (11-4); Sun 21 July (11-4.30).**
Plantaholic's garden 90ft x 15ft, behind terraced house, every planting opportunity maximised. An abundance of baskets, climbers, shrubs and fruit trees. Raised koi carp pond. Step down to large secret garden containing exuberant borders, wildlife pond with gunnera, small green oasis lawn with arbour. Unusual and exotic plants, herb ladders and other quirky features. Featured in Saga Magazine.

84 LAVENDER GROVE, E8

Hackney, London E8 3LS. Anne Pauleau. *Short walk from Haggerston Stn. Train from Liverpool St to London Fields Stn. Tube from Bethnal Green then buses 106, 254 or 388 to Hackney*. **Adm £2, chd free. Suns 21 Apr; 19 May; 16 June (2-5). Also open with London Fields Gardens 16 June.**
Courtyard garden with backdrop of bamboos and palms, foil to clipped shrubs leading to wilder area mingling roses, lilies, alliums, grasses and a rather large phormium. Tulips and daffodils jostle for attention in the spring. This is a highly scented garden in midsummer. Children's quiz offered with prize on completion.

Fiery Mediterranean terrace with marble fountain, fish, and pergola with vines . . .

LITTLE HOUSE A, NW3

16A Maresfield Gardens, Hampstead, London NW3 5SU. Linda & Stephen Williams. *5 mins walk Swiss Cottage or Finchley Rd tube. Off Fitzjohn's Ave and 2 doors away from Freud Museum (signed)*. Home-made teas. **Adm £3.50, chd free. Sun 16 June (2-6).**
1920s Arts and Crafts house (not open) built by Danish artist Arild Rosenkrantz. Award-winning front and rear garden set out formally with water features, stream and sculpture. Unusual shrubs and perennials, many rare, incl *Paeonia rockii* and *Dicksonia fibrosa*. Wide collections of hellebores, roses, hostas, toad lilies, acers, clematis and astrantia.

LITTLE LODGE

Watts Road, Thames Ditton KT7 0BX. Mr & Mrs P Hickman, 020 8339 0931, julia.hickman@virgin.net. *2m SW of Kingston. Mainline stn Thames Ditton 5 mins. A3 from London; after Hook underpass turn L to Esher; at Scilly Isles turn R towards Kingston; after 2nd railway bridge turn L to Thames Ditton village; house opp library after Giggs Hill Green*. Home-made teas. **Adm £3, chd free (share to Cancer Research UK). Sun 2 June (11.30-5.30); Wed 5 June (2-5.30). Visitors also welcome by appt May to June.**
Partly walled ½ -acre informal cottage garden filled with usual and unusual shrubs, perennials, native plants and topiary. Lots of stone sinks, troughs and terracotta pots, plus a Victorian-

"Lemon drizzle cake, Victoria sponge ... yummy! "

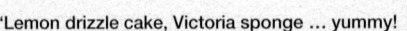

style glasshouse. Productive hidden parterre vegetable garden edged with espalier apple trees. Garden designed and maintained by owners. Plants for sale, all propagated and grown by owners.

49 LOFTUS ROAD, W12

London W12 7EH. Emma Plunket, www.plunketgardens.com. *Hammersmith. Train and tube: walk or bus from Shepherds Bush. Free street parking.* **Evening Opening £4, chd free, wine, Tue 18 June (6-9).**

Professional garden designer, Emma Plunket, opens her acclaimed walled garden. Richly planted, it is the ultimate 'hard working city garden' with all year structure and colour; fruit, vegetables and herbs. Set against a backdrop of trees, it is unexpectedly open and peaceful. Garden plan, plant list and advice.

D

GROUP OPENING

LONDON FIELDS GARDENS, E8

Hackney, London E8 3LS. *Short walk from Haggerston stn, London Overground (E London Line); train from Liverpool St to London Fields stn; or tube to Bethnal Green, then buses 106, 254 or 388 towards Hackney.* Home-made teas at 61 Lansdowne Drive. **Combined adm £6, chd free. Sun 16 June (2-5).**

61 LANSDOWNE DRIVE
Chris Thow & Graham Hart

84 LAVENDER GROVE
Anne Pauleau
(See separate entry)

36 MALVERN ROAD
Kath Harris

53 MAPLEDENE ROAD
Tigger Cullinan
Visitors also welcome by appt July to Aug.
020 7249 3754
tiggerine8@blueyonder.co.uk

84 MIDDLETON ROAD
Penny Fowler.
Down the passage on the right hand side of the house and enter through the door at the end

A diverse group of 5 gardens in London Fields, an area which takes its name from fields on the London side of the old village of Hackney. They are unexpected havens from the city's hustle and bustle, with an exciting range and variety of colours, scents and design. This year we have a large, long wildlife and sculpture garden, a fascinating plantsman's garden, lush tropical plantings, a scented cottage garden and a serene designer garden filled with the sound of running water. Expect everything from courtyards to areas of banana, from showers of roses to clusters of clematis, ponds with water lilies and giant gunnera.

GROUP OPENING

LOWER CLAPTON GARDENS, E5

Hackney, London E5 0RL. *Tube: Bethnal Green, then buses 106, 254; or Manor House, then buses 253, 254, alight Lower Clapton Rd. Pleasant 10 mins walk from Hackney Central (overground) or Hackney Downs stns.* Home-made teas at 16 and 99 Powerscroft Rd. **Combined adm £5, chd free. Sun 9 June (2-6).**

8 ALMACK ROAD
Philip Lightowlers

16 POWERSCROFT ROAD
Elizabeth Welch

91 POWERSCROFT ROAD
Mr Malcolm Fergusson

99 POWERSCROFT ROAD
Rose Greenwood

Lower Clapton is an area of mid-Victorian terraces sloping down to the R Lea. Dotted with mature trees and all with lawns, this group of gardens reflect their owner's tastes and interests. On Powerscroft Rd, no.16 has sun and space for meditation, while nos. 91 and 99 enjoy different levels, and abound with pergolas and gazebos, including one with a thatched roof. No. 8 Almack Rd is a long thin garden with two different rooms, one incl a classic blue agave named Audrey.

GROUP OPENING

LYNDHURST SQUARE GROUP, SE15

London SE15 5AR. *Rail & London Overground orbital network - Clapham Junction to Highbury & Islington; Peckham Rye (check timetables), then 5 mins walk NW. Buses: 36 from Oval tube, 171 from Waterloo, 63 from Kings Cross & 12 from Oxford Circus. Free parking in Lyndhurst Sq.* Home-made teas at 4 Lyndhurst Square. **Combined adm £7, chd free (share to Terrence Higgins Trust). Sun 23 June (1-6). Also open South London Botanical Institute & 122 Court Lane.**

1 LYNDHURST SQUARE
Josephine Pickett-Baker

3 LYNDHURST SQUARE
Stephen Haines

4 LYNDHURST SQUARE
Amelia Thorpe & Adam Russell

5 LYNDHURST SQUARE
Martin Lawlor & Paul Ward

6 LYNDHURST SQUARE
Iain Henderson & Amanda Grygelis

7 LYNDHURST SQUARE
Pernille Ahlström & Barry Joseph

Six very attractive gardens open in this small, elegant square of 1840s listed villas. Each approx 90ft x 50ft has its own shape and style as the Square curves in a U shape. No.1 is a semi-formal walled garden with a mosaic bordered lawn, gravel paths and lush flower beds. No.3 is a pretty, classic English garden with shrubs, fruit trees and sculpted topiary. A delightful greenhouse enhances the impression of peace. No.4 is for a family, with a generous lawn, vegetables and herbs, and mature fruit trees adding lushness. At No.5, the design combines Italianate and Gothic themes with roses, lavender, olives, euphorbia and ferns within yew and box parterres. Plants for sale here. No.6 is an up-to-date family garden given drama with architectural plants. A wisteria pergola frames the vegetables bordered by espaliered apples. Check the treehouse! Simplicity, Swedish style, is key at No.7, with roses and raised beds, framed by yew hedges.

> Unexpected havens from the hustle and bustle . . . range of colours, scents and design . . .

27 MENELIK ROAD, NW2
London NW2 3RJ. C Klemera. *Buses: 16, 32, 189, 316, 332 to Mill Lane on Shoot Up Hill then turn into Minster Rd, Menelik at far end. Or tube to West Hampstead then C11 bus (direction Brent Cross) to Menelik Rd.* **Adm £3.50, chd free. Sun 14 July (2-5.30).**
'Four corners of the world' laid out 20 years ago, constantly evolving and full of surprises to make you smile. Includes 'a taste of the Orient' (tea house, no tea), the allotment, piazza and colourful informal planting between strong architectural shapes. Tricky access with steps and narrow paths.

GROUP OPENING

MILL HILL ROAD GARDENS, W3
Acton, London W3 8JE. *Tube: Acton Town, turn R, Mill Hill Rd 3rd on R off Gunnersbury Ln.* Home-made teas. **Combined adm £6, chd free. Sun 16 June (2-6). Evening Opening £5, chd free, wine, Sun 14 July (6-8).**

41 MILL HILL ROAD
Marcia Hurst
Visitors also welcome by appt May to Sept.
020 8992 2632
marcia.hurst@sudbury-house.co.uk

65 MILL HILL ROAD D
Anna Dargavel
Visitors also welcome by appt Apr to Sept.
020 8992 1723
annadargavel@mac.com

Two gardens in one road encourage wildlife with ponds, a mound and a huge range of plants to attract insects. The owner at 41 Mill Hill Road describes herself as a compulsive plantaholic. The 120ft x 40ft garden features a newly created paved area with semi-circular vegetable plot. Lawn with herbaceous border and lavender hedge and a raised terrace with topiary. 65 Mill Hill Road is a typically long narrow London garden, paved, with borders and planted with fruit trees and shrubs. It is wildlife-friendly with ponds and flowers to which bees and other insect are attracted. Frogs and dragonflies abound.

2 MILLFIELD PLACE, N6
London N6 6JP, daisydogone@aol.com. *Off Highgate West Hill, E side of Hampstead Heath. Buses: C2, C11 or 214 to Parliament Hill Fields.* Home-made teas. **Adm £3.50, chd free. Sun 5 May (2-6). Evening Opening £4.50, chd free, wine, Wed 19 June (5.30-9). Visitors also welcome by appt May to Sept.**
1½ -acre spring and summer garden with camellias, rhododendrons, many flowering shrubs and unusual plants. Spring bulbs, herbaceous borders, spacious lawns, small pond and extensive views over Hampstead Heath. Easy access and/or assistance available, please ask at gate if needed.

'Four corners of the world' laid out 20 years ago, constantly evolving and full of surprises . . .

28 MORDEN ROAD, SE3
Blackheath, London SE3 0AA. Mr & Mrs R Taylor. *Stn: Blackheath BR (10 mins walk). Buses: 89, 108, 202 to Blackheath village. Street parking available.* Wine. **Adm £4, chd free (share to Look Good ... Feel Better). Evening Opening Fri 28 June (6-8.30).**
Formal front garden leads to spacious open back garden, surrounded by mature trees with interesting planting near terrace and 2 small ponds. Upper garden has lavender, grasses and a wide variety of heucheras. Lower garden emphasis is on planting for shade, incl ferns and hostas. Modern sculptures, some for sale, all round the garden. Partial wheelchair access to terrace, with good view of garden.

66 MUSWELL AVENUE, N10
London N10 2EL. Kay Thomson & Nick Wood-Glover, 07872 952959, kaythomson@valox.demon.co.uk. *1st L into Muswell Ave from Alexandra Park Rd. Tube: Bounds Green or E Finchley then bus 102 or 299, alight Colney Hatch stop.* Home-made teas. **Adm £3, chd free. Sun 14 July (2-6). Visitors also welcome by appt.**
Celtic coastal roots echo through Edwardian suburban garden. Tiny courtyard opens into Mediterranean planted terrace with oleander, jasmine and grapevine. Lawn area leads through pergola to pond with abundant wildlife, native planting, pebble beach, boat, small patio and dry stone wall's unexpected delights. Mallard ducks visit. Four contrasting atmospheres - four contrasting environments. Fish feeding - 4pm. Featured in Ham & High as 'A garden of delights'.

23 MYDDELTON GARDENS, N21
London N21 2PA. Andrew & Simon. *Stn: Winchmore Hill, then 10 mins walk. Off Green Dragon Lane, Winchmore Hill. Bus: 125 from Southgate Tube, or 329 from Enfield St. Parking available.* Home-made teas. **Adm £3.50, chd free. Sun 12 May (2-6).**
Front garden created 2004. ⅓- acre secluded back garden with mature hedges. Meandering paths lead from courtyard (with henhouse) to various areas including greenhouse, lawn with long border, bog area, 2 ponds, orchard, oriental garden, fernery and excellent compost area. All-yr interest. Garden plants and big house plants for sale.

◆ NATURAL HISTORY MUSEUM WILDLIFE GARDEN, SW7
Cromwell Road, London SW7 5BD. Natural History Museum, 020 7942 5011, www.nhm.ac.uk/wildlife-garden. *Natural History Museum. Tube: South Kensington, 5 mins walk.* **Adm by donation. For NGS: Sat 6 Apr (12-5). For other opening times and information, please phone or see garden website.**
Set in the Museum grounds, the Wildlife Garden has provided a lush and tranquil habitat in the heart of London since 1995. It reveals a varied range of British lowland habitats, incl deciduous woodland, heathland, meadow and ponds. With over 2000 plant and animal species, it beautifully demonstrates the potential for wildlife conservation in the inner city. Spring wildlife displays, workshops, activities and talks. Observation beetree. Wild flower plant sale. Nature Live talks 12.30 and 14.30. Brighter Kensington

and Chelsea Scheme Wildlife Garden Award and President's Trophy for the Best Overall Winner Green Flag Award.

17A NAVARINO ROAD, E8

London E8 1AD. Ben Nel & Darren Henderson, 07734 773990, benjamin123nel@googlemail.com. *Buses 30, 38, 242 or 277 alight Graham Rd. Short walk from Hackney Central or London Fields stns on the Overground line.* **Adm £3, chd free. Sat 20 Apr; Sat 15 June; Sun 14 July (2-5). Visitors also welcome by appt Apr to Aug.**

Established Italian and Japanese water garden reborn under new ownership. Features a square pond with Corinthian fountain, topiary yew border, lilies and Mediterranean trees. Leading to Japanese garden with pond, bridge and stream cutting the Soleirolia soleirolii landscape, with acer, cypress, ferns and bamboo, overlooked by a beautiful tea house.

15 NORCOTT ROAD, N16

Stoke Newington, London N16 7BJ. Amanda & John Welch. *Buses: 67, 73, 76, 106, 149, 243, 393, 476. Clapton & Rectory Rd mainline stns. One way system: by car approach from Brooke Rd which crosses Norcott Rd, garden in S half of Norcott Rd.* Home-made teas. **Adm £2.50, chd free. Sun 12 May; Sun 16 June (2-6).**

Developed over 30 years, open 21 years for the NGS. This year we are opening twice, firstly in May, the best time to come for our renowned plant sale, then in June for the full summer glory of our walled garden, with its pond, fruit trees and cottage-style herbaceous borders.

5 NORTHAMPTON PARK, N1

Islington, London N1 2PP. Andrew Bernhardt & Anne Brogan. *3 mins walk from Canonbury stn, 10 mins from Highbury and Islington Tube (Victoria Line).* **Evening Opening £3, chd free, wine, Sat 15 June (6-9).**

S-facing walled garden, 160 yrs old, saved from neglect and developed over the last 20 yrs. The use of arches with box and yew hedging creates contrasting areas of interest which are evolving from cool North European blues, whites and greys to 'hot' splashes of Mediterranean influence.

41 Southbrook Road

94 OAKWOOD ROAD, NW11

Hampstead Garden Suburb, London NW11 6RN. Michael Franklin, 020 8458 5846, mikefrank@onetel.com. *1m N of Golders Green. Tube: Golders Green then H2 bus stops on request at junction of Northway & Oakwood Rd. Parking free in local roads.* Home-made teas. **Adm £3.50, chd free. Sun 19 May (2-6). Visitors also welcome by appt May to July.**

A romantic cottage garden in a beautiful woodland setting. Herbaceous beds with many unusual plants. A mature garden, still developing new areas of planting.

28 OLD DEVONSHIRE ROAD, SW12

London SW12 9RB. Georgina Ivor, 020 8673 7179, georgina@balhambandb.co.uk, www.balhambandb.co.uk/page3.htm. *Off Balham High Road/A24. Balham Northern Line tube & mainline rail: 5 mins walk. Buses 155, 249, 355 stop on Balham High Rd.* Light refreshments. **Adm £3, chd free (share to Trinity Hospice). Sun 14 July (2-5.30). Evening Opening £4, chd free, wine, Wed 17 July (6-8.30). Also open 20 Eatonville Rd 14 July. Visitors also welcome by appt June to Sept.**

Walk past the Mediterranean-style front garden to a tranquil oasis at the back. A cool eucalyptus reaches for the house-tops whilst a well-established pear tree looks down on a walled garden full to bursting with planting both familiar and surprising. On the balustraded wooden balcony there are herbs in troughs and a vibrant orange trumpet vine. Article on London gardens opened for NGS in Lufthansa Inflight Magazine.

ALLOTMENTS

OLD PALACE LANE ALLOTMENTS

Old Palace Lane, Richmond TW9 1PG. Old Palace Lane Allotment Group. *Next to White Swan PH, through gate in wall. Mainline and tube: Richmond. Parking on meters in lane or round Richmond Green, or in Old Deer Park car park, entrance on A316 Twickenham Rd.* Home-made teas. **Adm £3, chd free. Sun 11 Aug (2-5).**

Secret garden in the heart of Richmond. 33 allotments on the site of Old Richmond Palace, squeezed between an ancient wall and a railway viaduct midway between Richmond Green and the river. Some resemble cottage gardens where sunflowers and sweet peas mingle haphazardly with sweetcorn and zucchini, while others sport raised beds, regimented rows of runner beans and gleaming greenhouses.

THE OLD VICARAGE

Sudbrook Lane, Richmond TW10 7AT. Matthew Collins, 07966 547779, matt.collins@talk21.com, www.orangetip.co.uk. *From Richmond, off Petersham Rd (A307), just after the Fox & Duck PH L turn into Sudbrook Lane. Limited parking onsite and free parking on Sudbrook Lane.* Home-made teas. **Adm £4, chd free.** Sun 14 Apr (11-3). **Visitors also welcome by appt.**
3-acre garden, designed by Mary Keen, focuses on encouraging wildlife, featuring wildflower meadows, a small woodland, herbaceous borders for all seasons and large, colourful cutting beds. A mass of tulips in spring, bright annuals and dahlias in summer. Chickens and outdoor tortoise colony. Narrow paths towards woodland areas.

OLDEN GARDEN COMMUNITY PROJECT, N5

Opp 22 Whistler Street, Islington, London N5 1NH. London Borough of Islington. *Tube & Overground: Highbury & Islington. L along Holloway Rd (A1) and R along Drayton Park, passing Drayton Park stn (closed w/ends) on L. Just before Arsenal Emirates Stadium, take R-hand fork of Whistler St. Garden entrance opp No.22. Buses along Holloway Rd incl: 43, 153, 271 & 393.* Home-made teas. **Adm £3.50, chd free.** Sun 9 June (2-6). **Also open 9 & 16 Furlong Rd and 1 & 62 Hungerford Rd.**
Olden Garden Community Project is a 2-acre oasis of beauty and retreat from the busy streets surrounding it. A top terrace of beautiful herbaceous borders, lawn and patio and a stunning Rambling Rector rose. On the lower slopes there is an orchard, a meadow, vegetable beds and a greenhouse. In springtime, there is blossom and golden daffodils. Islington in Bloom - Overall Winner Community Garden with Gold Award. Wheelchair access to all areas of top terrace. Disabled WC.

ORMELEY LODGE

Ham Gate Avenue, Richmond TW10 5HB. Lady Annabel Goldsmith. *From Richmond Park, exit at Ham Gate into Ham Gate Ave. 1st house on R. From Richmond, A307; after 1½ m, past New Inn on R, at T-lights turn L into Ham Gate Ave.* **Adm £4, chd free.** Sun 16 June (3-6).
Large walled garden in delightful rural setting on Ham Common. Wide herbaceous borders and box hedges. Walk through to orchard with wild flowers. Vegetable garden, knot garden, aviary. Trellised tennis court with roses and climbers.

◆ OSTERLEY PARK AND HOUSE

Jersey Road, Isleworth TW7 4RB. National Trust, 020 8232 5055, www.nationaltrust.org.uk. *4m N of Richmond. Tube: Osterley, turn L on leaving stn, 1m walk. Access via Thornbury Rd on N side of A4 between Gillette Corner & Osterley tube stn. Follow brown tourist signs. Car Park £3.50.* **Adm £4.20, chd £2.10.** For NGS: Sun 2, Sat 8, Sun 9 June (11-6). **For other opening times and information, please phone or see garden website.**
C18 garden created by the Child family, owners of Osterley Park House, in late 1700s. Currently being restored to its former glory following much research incl the discovery of documents in America showing lists of plants purchased for the garden in 1788. Highlights incl a Robert Adam designed Garden House, the Great Meadow and Mrs Child's Flower Garden.

ALLOTMENTS

PADDOCK ALLOTMENTS & LEISURE GARDENS, SW20

51 Heath Drive, Raynes Park SW20 9BE. Paddock Horticultural Society. *Stn: Raynes Park, then 10 min walk or bus 163 via Grand Drive. Buses: 57, 131, 200 to Raynes Park stn; 152 to Bushey Rd, 7 min walk via Grand Drive; 413, 5 min walk from Cannon Hill Lane via Parkway. Street parking close by.* Home-made teas. **Adm £3, chd free.** Sat 13 July (12-5).
Long established and self managed site, set in 5½ acres, situated on Cannon Hill Common. Some plots resemble cottage gardens, others are purely organic but most grow a wide varieties of fruit, vegetables and flowers. Plants, produce and jams for sale. 3rd year running winner of Best London Allotment. Paved and grass paths, mainly level.

> Children especially welcome - a treasure hunt with prizes . . . !

93 PALACE ROAD, SW2

London SW2 3LB. Charlotte & Matthew Vaight, 020 8674 2400, charlieandmatt@tiscali.co.uk. *Stn: Tulse Hill. Buses: 2, 68, 322, 432, 468.* Home-made teas. **Adm £3, chd free.** Sun 16 June (12-5). **Visitors also welcome by appt.**
Take a moment to enjoy the eye-catching front garden before heading on to the terrace, giving a full view of this contemporary cottage garden. Follow the boardwalk around the curving lawn through sculpture and perennial planting or take the 'woodland path' past the wildlife pond to the vegetable garden. Uplit in the evening.

3 THE PARK, N6

off Southwood Lane, London N6 4EU. Mr & Mrs G Schrager, 020 8348 3314, bunty@schredds.com. *3 mins from Highgate tube, up Southwood Lane. The Park is 1st on R. Buses: 43, 134, 143, 263.* Home-made teas. **Adm £3, chd free.** Sun 28 Apr, Sun 16 June (2.30-5.30). **Visitors & groups of 10 max also welcome by appt Apr to June.**
Large garden with pond and frogspawn. Informal planting with patch of snake's head fritillaries and tree peonies in April. Plants and home made jam for sale. Children especially welcome - a treasure hunt with prizes!

NEW 11 PARK AVENUE NORTH, N8

Crouch End, London N8 7RU. Mr Steven Buckley & Ms Liz Roberts. *Nearest tube Finsbury Park, nearest bus stop W3.* Home-made teas. **Adm £3, chd free. Sun 16 June (11-5).**
An exotic 250ft T-shaped garden, threaded through an old orchard and rose garden. Dramatic - mainly spiky - foliage dominates, with the focus on palms, agaves, dasylirions, aeoniums, tree ferns, nolinas, cycads, bamboos, yuccas, cacti and many species of succulents. Flowering aloes are a highlight. Rocks and terracotta pots lend a Mediterranean accent.

18 PARK CRESCENT, N3

Finchley, London N3 2NJ. Rosie Daniels. *Tube: Finchley Central. Buses: 82 to Essex Park, also 125, 460, 626, 683.* Home-made teas. **Adm £3, chd free. Suns 16 June; 28 July (2-6).**
Constantly evolving, charming small garden designed and densely planted by owner. Roses, clematis, heuchera and lots more. Mini pond, tub water feature and bird haven. Stepped terrace with lots of pots. Glass installation and sculpture by owner. Garden extension is work in progress. Hidden seating with view through garden. Secluded, peaceful, restorative.

4 PARK VILLAGE EAST, NW1

Regents Park, London NW1 7PX. Eveline Carn, 020 7388 1113, eveline@carnfamily.co.uk. *Tube: Camden Town 7 mins, Mornington Crescent 10 mins. Bus: C2 and 274, 3 mins. Garden diagonally opp The York & Albany, just off junction of Parkway/Prince Albert Rd/Gloucester Gate.* Home-made teas. **Adm £5, chd free. Visitors welcome by appt June to Aug.**
A modern Dutch aesthetic is discernible in the formal use of box and yew which provide structure and symmetry for more naturalistic planting over three terraces from behind a Regency house down to what was the Regents Canal. An unexpectedly large but skilfully landscaped town garden, punctuated with strong architectural plants, sculpture, ponds and mature trees. Working bee hives and many steps.

174 PECKHAM RYE, SE22

London SE22 9QA. Mr & Mrs Ian Bland. *Stn: Peckham Rye. Buses: 12, 37, 63, 197, 363. Overlooks Peckham Rye Common from Dulwich side.* Home-made teas. **Adm £3, chd free (share to St Christopher's Hospice). Sun 9 June (2.30-5.30). Also open 5 Burbage Rd, 35 Camberwell Grove & Choumert Square.**
Visitors call our garden an oasis of calm in Peckham. Every year the garden changes and matures. It is densely planted with a wide variety of contrasting foliage. Unusual plants are combined with old favourites. It remains easy-care and child-friendly. Garden originally designed by Jude Sharpe. Our ever-popular plant sale and famed cakes will be available again. Easy access via side alley into a flat garden.

> Constantly evolving, charming small garden . . . roses, clematis, heuchera and lots more . . .

GROUP OPENING

PENGE GARDENS, SE20

London SE20 7QG. *Nr junction A213 & A234. Short walk from Kent House (5mins) mainline stn. Buses: 176, 227, 356 & 358. Tram: Beckenham Rd.* Home-made teas. **Combined adm £5, chd free. Sun 19 May (2-5).**

43 CLEVEDON ROAD
Elizabeth Parker

26 KENILWORTH ROAD D
Mhairi & Simon Clutson
Visitors also welcome by appt Apr to Sept. Refreshments available for groups of 10+.
020 8402 3978
mhairi@grozone.co.uk
www.grozone.co.uk

Two contrasting gardens: one is a small, minimalist, modern garden with clever juxtaposition of sandstone landscaping and plants, and the other is a cottage garden. 43 Clevedon Rd is 50ft x 22ft, with unusual trees and shrubs incl snake-bark maple, sorbus cashmiriana and itea ilicifolia. Abundant rambler roses, incl Félicité Perpétue, colourful mixed borders and pots on terrace. 26 Kenilworth Rd is a garden designers' completely re-designed inspirational contemporary garden providing maximum impact in a small space. An inventive layout extends the living space with seating and large trough planters. The planting is bold and textural featuring a diverse selection of drought-tolerant Mediterranean plants providing all year round interest with seasonal colour.

PENSHURST PLACE

See Kent

PETERSHAM HOUSE

Petersham Road, Petersham TW10 7AA. Francesco & Gael Boglione, www.petershamnurseries.com. *Stn: Richmond, then 65 bus to Dysart PH. Entry to garden off Petersham Rd, through nursery. Parking very limited on Church Lane.* Light refreshments at Petersham Nurseries Café & Teahouse. **Adm £3.50, chd free. Sun 7 July (11-4).**
Broad lawn with large topiary, generously planted double borders. Productive vegetable garden with chickens. Adjoins Nursery with extensive plant sales, shop & cafe.

4 PIERMONT GREEN, SE22

East Dulwich, London SE22 0LP. Janine Wookey. *Triangle of green facing Peckham Rye at the Honor Oak end. Stns: Peckham Rye & Honor Oak. Buses: 63 (passes the door) & 12. No parking on Green but free parking on side sts nearby.* Home-made teas. **Adm £3.50, chd free. Sun 28 July (1.30-5.30). Also open 22 Scutari Rd.**
A small formal front garden faces the triangular Green with box parterres and an olive, framed by swagged 'Zepherine Drouhin' rose. In the 120ft back garden, terrace with herbs in pots leads to gravel garden with gaura and dierama. Then the vista opens up onto a circular lawn edged with deep borders. A vegetable garden and a shady yellow exotic garden complete the picture.

© Marianne Majerus

62 Hungerford Road

101 PITT CRESCENT, SW19

London SW19 8HR. Karen Grosch, 020 8893 3660, info@whettonandgrosch.co.uk, www.karensgarden.org.uk. *Tube: Wimbledon Park 10 mins walk. Bus: 156 along Durnsford Rd. Limited parking in Pitt Crescent.* Home-made teas. **Adm £3, chd free. Sun 16 June (2-6). Also open 123 South Park Rd. Group of 10+ also welcome by appt.**

Secluded terraced garden packed with well structured subtle plant combinations, great design ideas for long sloping garden overlooked by busy railway. Top walled terrace with greenhouse, garden studio, mature trees, scented climbers and atmospheric seating areas. Creative use of reclaimed and donated materials.Original sculpture. New features for 2013. Wheelchair access to lower terrace only.

GROUP OPENING

PRINCES AVENUE GARDENS, N10

Muswell Hill, London N10 3LS. *Buses: 43 & 134 from Highgate tube; also W7, 102, 144, 234, 299. Princes Ave opp M&S in Muswell Hill Broadway, or John Baird PH in Fortis Green.* Home-made teas at No. 17. **Combined adm £3.50, chd free. Sun 19 May (2-6).**

15 PRINCES AVENUE
Eliot & Emma Glover

28 PRINCES AVENUE
Ian & Viv Roberts

In a beautiful Edwardian avenue in the heart of Muswell Hill Conservation Area, two very different gardens reflect the diverse life-styles of their owners. The large S-facing family garden at No.15 has been designed for entertaining and yr-round interest. White and blue themed beds with alliums and a wide variety of perennials and shrubs frame an *exceptional* lawn. A Wendy house and hidden wooden castle provide delight for children of all ages. Charming annexe garden at No.17 where tea can be enjoyed. No.28 is a well-established traditional garden reflecting the charm typical of the era. Mature trees, shrubs, mixed borders and newly planted woodland garden creating an oasis of calm just off the bustling Broadway.

GROUP OPENING

RAILWAY COTTAGES, N22

Alexandra Palace, London N22 7SL. *Tube: Wood Green, 10 mins walk. Stn: Alexandra Palace, 3 mins. Buses: W3, 184, 3 mins. Free parking in Bridge Rd, Buckingham Rd, Palace Gates Rd, Station Rd, Dorset Rd.* Home-made teas at 2 Dorset Rd. **Combined adm £3.50, chd free. Sun 21 July (2-5.30). Also open 19 Hillfield Park & 5 St Regis Close.**

2 DORSET ROAD
Jane Stevens

14 DORSET ROAD
Cathy Brogan

22 DORSET ROAD
Mike & Noreen Ainger

A row of historical railway cottages, tucked away from the bustle of Wood Green near Alexandra Palace, takes the visitor back in time. Two front gardens, 14 and 22, one nurtured by the grandson of the original railway worker occupant, show a variety of planting, including aromatic shrubs, herbs, jasmine, flax, fig, fuchsia and vines. The tranquil country-style garden at 2 Dorset Rd flanks 3 sides of the house. Hawthorn topiary (by the original owner) and clipped box hedges contrast with climbing roses, clematis, honeysuckle, abutilon and cottage plants. Trees incl mulberry, quince, fig, apple and a mature willow creating an opportunity for an interesting shady corner, while the demise of a big old tree has opened up new perspectives and planting challenges.

REVELEY LODGE

See Hertfordshire

NEW 26 RINGWOOD AVENUE, N2

London N2 9NS. Ms J Rickards, www.jilaynerickards.com. *Nearest Tube East Finchley, 10-15 mins walk Bus 102, 234, 5-10 min walk.* Home-made teas. **Adm £3.50, chd free. Sun 2 June (2-5).**

SGD Member's own, newly planted, contemporary garden on 3 levels. Clever use of materials gives a fabulous indoor/outdoor transition. Water features sited near the patio create a relaxed atmosphere. Perennials weave through structural planting giving interest at each season - mature oak providing a perfect habitat for beautiful woodland planting. Steps may be unsuitable for disabled/very young.

◆ **ROOTS AND SHOOTS, SE11**
Walnut Tree Walk, Kennington, London SE11 6DN. Trustees of Roots and Shoots, www.rootsandshoots.org.uk. *Tube: Lambeth North. Buses: 3, 59, 159, 360. Just S of Waterloo Stn, off Kennington Rd, 5 mins from Imperial War Museum. No car parking on site.* **Adm £2, chd free. For NGS: Fri 21 June (2-7). For other opening times and information, please see garden website.**
½ -acre wildlife garden run by innovative charity providing training and garden advice. Summer meadow, observation beehives, 2 large ponds, hot borders, Mediterranean mound, old roses and echiums. Learning centre with photovoltaic roof, solar heating, rainwater catchment, three planted roofs, one brown roof. Wildlife garden study centre exhibition with photo, video and other wildlife interpretation materials.

ALLOTMENTS

NEW **THE ROSE GARDEN AT GOLF COURSE ALLOTMENTS, N11**
Winton Avenue, London N11 2AR. GCAA/Mr George Dunnion, www.gcaa.pwp.blueyonder.co.uk. *Golf Course Allotments, Winton Avenue N11 2AR. Tube Bounds Green approx 1km. Buses 102, 184, 299 to Sunshine Garden Centre Durnsford Rd. Bidwell Gardens (on foot through park) to Winton Ave. Gate opp Junction with Blake Rd.* Home-made teas served in Main Allotment Shed. **Adm £3.50, chd free. Sun 23 June (1-5.30).**
Large allotment plot displaying over 120 different roses comprising much of the history of the rose; there are Gallicas, Damasks, Albas, Portlands etc. as well as around 40 Austin roses and many others. The roses are interplanted with a wide range of perennials as well as vegetables. Colourful chards and red cabbages grasses, clematis and rare exotic plants. Owners will share their extensive knowledge with visitors. Nomination for 'Gardening Against The Odds ' award. Featured in Sunday Telegraph.

ROYAL COLLEGE OF PHYSICIANS MEDICINAL GARDEN, NW1
11 St Andrews Place, London NW1 4LE. Royal College of Physicians of London, www.rcplondon.ac.uk/museum-and-garden/garden. *Outer Circle, opp SE corner of Regents Park. Exit Regents Park tube station, turn R, go 100yds, L to Outer Circle, 150yds on R.* **Adm £4, chd free. Mon 17 June; Thur 11 July (10-4.30).**
1300 different plants used in conventional and herbal medicines around the world during the past 3000 yrs; plants named after physicians and plants with medical implications. The plants are labelled, and arranged by continent except for the plants from the College's Pharmacopoeia of 1618. Guided tours all day, explaining the uses of the plants, their histories and stories about them. Books about the plants in the medicinal garden will be for sale. Featured in numerous publications. Wheelchair ramps at steps.

Simple, unfussy with a contemporary feel, calm, quiet and peaceful . . .

5 RUSSELL ROAD, N13
Bowes Park, London N13 4RS. Angela Kreeger. *Close to N Circular Rd and Green Lanes. Tube: Bounds Green, 10 mins walk. Mainline: Bowes Park, 3 mins walk. Numerous bus routes. Off Whittington Rd.* Home-made teas. **Adm £3, chd free. Suns 28 Apr; 8 Sept (2-6). Also open 23 Imperial Rd 8 Sept.**
A 'poem for the eyes', Full, generous planting. Billowing, overflowing, balanced by flat, open lawn, and airy, dreamy planting in small woodland, a pebble garden marks the border. Not manicured. Simple, unfussy with a contemporary feel, calm, quiet and peaceful. Many spring plants and bulbs, many pots. Autumn is rusty, looser and soft. A different pleasure. Golden in sunlight. New small bespoke greenhouse reminiscent of Dungeness and Hastings.

7 ST GEORGE'S ROAD
St Margarets, Twickenham TW1 1QS. Richard & Jenny Raworth, 020 8892 3713, jraworth@gmail.com, www.raworthgarden.com. *1½ m SW of Richmond. Off A316 between Twickenham Bridge & St Margarets r'about.* **Evening Opening £5.50, chd free, wine, Sat 8 June (6-8). Visitors also welcome by appt May to July.**
Exuberant displays of Old English roses and vigorous climbers with unusual herbaceous perennials. Massed scented crambe cordifolia. Pond with bridge converted into child-safe lush bog garden. Large N-facing luxuriant conservatory with rare plants and climbers. Pelargoniums a speciality. Sunken garden and knot garden. Pergola covered with climbing roses and clematis. Featured in The Garden and Readers Digest 'The Most Amazing Gardens in Britain and Ireland'.

1 ST HELENA TERRACE
TW9 1NR. Christina Gascoigne, christina@christinagascoigne.com. *Tube & mainline stn: Richmond, then 10 mins walk via Richmond Green. St Helena Terrace in Friars Ln, 50yds from river, just beyond car park.* **Evening Opening £5, chd free, wine, Sat 15 June (6-8).**
Small secret studio garden on 3 levels of brick terraces, around 35ft curving fish pond with a 5ft waterfall tumbling over natural rocks. Unusual plants in pots with huge gunnera in a pot. Partial wheelchair access, small dogs allowed.

30 ST JAMES'S ROAD
Hampton Hill TW12 1DQ. Jean Burman. *Between A312 (Uxbridge Rd) and A313 (Park Rd). Bus: 285 from Kingston stops at end of rd (15 mins walk). Stn: Fulwell (20 mins walk).* **Evening Opening £3.50, chd free, wine, Thur 12 Sept (7-10).**
Lovely SE-facing garden (35ft x 90ft) with tasteful features throughout, subdivided into 5 rooms of interest. Decking with seating leads to ponds,

surrounded by grasses and shrubs and an African-themed thatched exterior 'sitting room'. Fairy lights and candles make this perfect for a magical evening's visit.

87 ST JOHNS ROAD, E17
London E17 4JH. Andrew Bliss. *From Walthamstow tube 15 mins walk through the charming old village of Walthamstow or 275 or 212 bus from bus stn opp tube stn. Alight stop just after Texaco/Somerfield on L, St Johns Rd on corner.* Home-made teas. **Adm £3, chd free. Sun 25 Aug; Sun 1 Sept (1-5).**
A typical terrace garden measuring 15ft x 25ft (plus the side bit!) with concrete screed on slabs, has been transformed into an oasis of raised borders, decking, slate and bamboo walling, water features, canopies & pebble mosaics. A calming purple, blue & white planting ensures utter relaxation. The garden owner is an artist who creates beautiful and eye-catching mirror mosaics on roof slates and other objets trouvés, for use in garden or home.

ST MICHAEL'S CONVENT
56 Ham Common, Ham, Richmond TW10 7JH. Community of the Sisters of the Church. *2m S of Richmond. From Richmond or Kingston, A307, turn onto the common at the Xrds nr New Inn, 100yds on the R adjacent to Martingales Close. Mainline trains to Richmond & Kingston also tube to Richmond, then bus 65 from either to Ham Common.* **Adm £3, chd free. Sun 9 June (2-5).**
4-acre organic garden comprises walled vegetable garden, orchards, vine house, ancient mulberry tree, extensive borders, meditation and Bible gardens.

57 ST QUINTIN AVENUE, W10
London W10 6NZ. Mr H Groffman, 020 8969 8292. *1m from Ladbroke Grove or White City tube. Buses: 7, 70 from Ladbroke Grove stn; 220 from White City, all to North Pole Rd. No parking restrictions on Sundays.* Home-made teas. **Adm £3, chd free. Sun 16 June; Sun 21 July (2-6). Also open 29 Addison Ave. Visitors also welcome by appt June to July.**
30ft x 40ft walled garden; wide selection of plant material incl evergreen and deciduous shrubs for foliage effects. Patio area mainly furnished with bedding material, colour themed. Focal points throughout. Refurbished with new plantings and special features. Floral display for 2013 to commemorate HM The Queen's Diamond Anniversary of the Coronation. Featured in local press to commemorate visit by HRH The Earl of Wessex to view Diamond Jubilee floral display.

A calming purple, blue and white planting ensures utter relaxation . . .

5 ST REGIS CLOSE, N10
Alexandra Park Road, London N10 2DE. Ms S Bennett & Mr E Hyde, 020 8883 8540, suebearlh@yahoo.co.uk. *2nd L in Alexandra Park Rd from Colney Hatch Lane. Tube: Bounds Green or E Finchley then bus 102 or 299. Alight at St Andrew's Church on Windermere Rd. Bus: 43 or 134 to Alexandra Park Rd.* Home-made teas. **Adm £3.50, chd free. Suns 28 Apr; 23 June; 21 July (2-6.30). Also open 5 Cecil Rd 23 June, 19 Hillfield Park & Railway Cottages 21 July. Visitors also welcome by appt, refreshments by arrangement.**
A cornucopia of sensual delights! Artists' garden renowned for unique architectural features and delicious cakes. Baroque temple, pagodas, oriental raku-tiled mirrored wall conceals plant nursery. Compost heap with medieval pretensions alongside American Gothic shed. Maureen Lipman's favourite garden, combining colour, humour and trompe l'oeil with wildlife-friendly ponds, waterfalls, weeping willow and lawns. Imaginative container planting and abundant borders, creating an inspirational and re-energising experience. Open studio with ceramics and prints. Featured on BBC Gardener's World. Wheelchair access to all parts of garden unless waterlogged.

22 SCUTARI ROAD, SE22
East Dulwich, London SE22 0NN. Sue Hillwood-Harris & David Hardy. *S side of Peckham Rye Park. B238 Peckham Rye/Forest Hill Rd, turn into Colyton Rd (opp Herne Tavern). 3rd rd on R. Bus: 63. Stn: East Dulwich.* Home-made teas. **Adm £3, chd free. Sun 16 June; Sun 28 July (2-6). Also open 9 Dulwich Village, Dulwich Village Two Gardens 16 June & 4 Piermont Green 28 July.**
Our inspirational labour of love, created from scratch 9yrs ago, continues to evolve. It has a cottagey area, water, trees, ferns and many attractive shrubs. Palatially-housed chickens produce eggs (subject to feathery whim) which are used in cakes of memorable standard. Steps and narrow paths may make access difficult for less mobile visitors. Featured in numerous publications and on BBC Open Gardens programme.

NEW 2 SHARDCROFT AVENUE, SE24
Herne Hill, London SE24 0DT. Catriona Andrews. *Short walk from Herne Hill rail station and bus stops. Buses: 3, 68, 196, 201, 468 to Herne Hill. Parking in local streets.* Home-made teas. **Adm £3, chd free. Sun 14 July (2-6).**
A recently designed modernist garden with loose, naturalistic planting. Geometric terracing accommodates a natural slope, framing vistas from the house. Drought tolerant beds with cascading perennials and grasses, scented courtyard, formal wildlife pond, woodland glade with fire pit and green roofed shed provide wildlife habitats and a feast for the senses. Planted ecologically to benefit wildlife. Nesting boxes and log piles.

SOUTH LONDON BOTANICAL INSTITUTE, SE24
323 Norwood Road, London SE24 9AQ. www.slbi.org.uk. *Mainline stn: Tulse Hill. Buses: 68, 196, 322 & 468 stop at junction of Norwood & Romola Rds.* Home-made teas. **Adm £2.50, chd free (share to South London Botanical Institute). Sun 23 June (2-5). Also open 122 Court Lane & Lyndhurst Square Group.**
London's smallest botanical garden, densely planted with 500 labelled species grown in a formal layout of

themed borders. Wild flowers flourish alongside medicinal herbs. Carnivorous, scented, native and woodland plants are featured, growing among rare trees and shrubs. The pond is home to frogs, newts, dragonflies. The fascinating SLBI building is also open. Unusual plants for sale.

123 SOUTH PARK ROAD, SW19

Wimbledon, London SW19 8RX. Susan Adcock. *Mainline & tube: Wimbledon, 10 mins; S Wimbledon tube 5 mins. Buses: 57, 93, 131, 219 along High St. Entrance in Bridges Rd (next to church hall) off South Park Rd.* Home-made teas. **Adm £3. Sun 16 June (2-6). Also open 101 Pitt Crescent.**

This small L shaped garden has a high deck amongst trees overlooking a woodland area, patio with pots, several small water containers, a fish pond, and a secluded courtyard with raised beds for flowers and herbs, as well as a discreet hot tub. Lots of ideas for giving a small space atmosphere and interest.

41 SOUTHBROOK ROAD, SE12

Lee, London SE12 8LJ. Barbara & Marek Polanski, 020 8333 2176, polanski101@yahoo.co.uk. *Off Sth Circular at Burnt Ash Rd. Mainline stns: Lee & Hither Green, both 10 mins walk.* Home-made teas. **Adm £3.50, chd free. Sat 15, Sun 16 June (2-5.30). Also open Tewkesbury Lodge: Top of the Hill & 27 Thorpewood Avenue. Visitors also welcome by appt June 2-5.30pm.**

Developed over 10yrs, this large garden has a formal layout, with wide mixed herbaceous borders full of colour and interest, surrounded by mature trees, framing sunny lawns, a central box parterre and an Indian pergola. Ancient pear trees festooned in June with clouds of white 'Kiftsgate' and 'Rambling Rector' roses. Discover fishes and damsel flies in 2 lily ponds. Many places to sit and relax. Enjoy home-made tea and cake in a small classical garden building. Side access just wide enough for wheelchairs.

SOUTHVIEW

See Essex

SOUTHWOOD LODGE, N6

33 Kingsley Place, Highgate, London N6 5EA. Mr & Mrs C Whittington, 020 8348 2785, suewhittington@hotmail.co.uk. *Tube: Highgate then 6 min walk up Southwood Ln. 4 min walk from Highgate Village along Southwood Ln. Buses: 143, 210, 214, 271.* Home-made teas. **Adm £3.50, chd free. Sun 5 May; Sun 2 June (2-5.30). Visitors also welcome by appt Apr to July. Refreshments by arrangement.**

Secret garden hidden behind C18 house (not open), laid out last century on steeply sloping site, now densely planted with shrubs, climbers and perennials. Ponds, waterfall, frogs and newts. Lots of different topiary shapes formed from self-sown yew trees. Many unusual plants grown and propagated for sale - rare pelargoniums a speciality. Brand new greenhouse should make anything possible! Toffee hunt for children. Featured on BBC Gardeners World and in Ham and High.

GROUP OPENING

NEW SPEER ROAD GARDENS

Thames Ditton KT7 0PJ. *2m SW of Kingston. Mainline: Thames Ditton 5 mins walk. By car: A3 to Scilly Isles r'about, L towards Hampton Court, R at next r'about down Embercourt Rd to Thames Ditton stn, under railway bridge then L into Speer Rd.* Home-made teas. **Combined adm £5, chd free (share to Born Too Soon Kingston Hospital). Sun 8 Sept (11.30-5).**

NEW 53 SPEER ROAD
Mrs Jayne Thomas
Visitors also welcome by appt Sept to Dec.
07762 023761
tjayne@btconnect.com

NEW UNDERWOOD
37 Speer Road. Diana Brown & Dave Matten

2 contrasting gardens within 4 mins walking distance of each other.
53 Speer Rd is a garden designers family garden, transformed to provide areas of interest with large mixed shrub and herbaceous borders, planted to give a long season of interest including a late season display of colour. Ornamental trees and silver birches create a calm woodland setting with a wild meadow. Many plants from designers gardens at Hampton Court.
Underwood is an 1920s landscaped garden, maintained by present owners to the original design with emphasis on imaginative and carefully clipped topiary. The boundary is edged by 7 small fish pools, which also mark an ancient public right of way for villagers to drive their sheep to pastures beyond. The garden is an evocative reminder of the '20s. Croquet on the lawn at Underwood.

Ancient pear trees festooned in June with clouds of white 'Kiftsgate' and 'Rambling Rector' roses . . .

GROUP OPENING

NEW SPITALFIELDS GARDENS GROUP, E1

London E1 6QH. *Tube: Liverpool St, 6 mins walk; Aldgate East, 10 mins walk. Overground: Shoreditch High St, 4 mins. Bus: 33. No parking: CP Whites Row, Commercial Street.* **Combined adm £10, chd free. Sat 18 May (10-5).**

NEW 4 FOURNIER STREET
Ms Eleanor Jones

NEW 34 HANBURY STREET
Mr Philip Vracas

21 PRINCELET STREET
Marianne & Nicholas Morse

NEW 21 WILKES STREET
Rupert Wheeler

A group of gardens within the Spitalfields conservation area. Often described as hidden treasures behind some of London's finest Georgian houses. 2013 will be the first time gardens in the area have opened as a group. 4 Fournier Street is a large, south-facing garden beside Christ Church - semi-formal with box and yew hedges. Tree peonies, irises, clematis and climbing roses.
34 Hanbury Street - an arabesque walled garden with central double

fountain surrounded by lavender, roses and acanthus. 21 Princelet Street (C17 house) a north-facing walled garden with shade loving plants - hostas and hellebores. Climbers and roses plus interesting architectural pieces. 21 Wilkes Street - a contemporary garden on three levels within a redundant factory behind C18 Huguenot weavers' house. Moat, bridge, light-wells, rock pool and raised beds. Roses, jasmines and vines.

STOKES HOUSE
Ham Street, Richmond TW10 7HR. Peter & Rachel Lipscomb, 020 8940 2403, rlipscomb@virginmedia.com. *2m S of Richmond. From Richmond or Kingston, A307, turn onto Ham Common at Xrds nr New Inn. 65 bus from either Richmond or Kingston to Ham Common. 200yds down Ham St from Ham Pond on L opposite Evelyn Rd cul de sac.* Home-made teas. **Adm £3.50, chd free. Sun 9 June (2-5). Visitors & groups of up to 10 also welcome by appt May to Sept.**
Originally an orchard, this ½ -acre walled country garden is abundant with roses, clematis and perennials. There are mature trees incl ancient mulberries and wisteria. The yew hedging, pergola and box hedges allow for different planting schemes throughout the year. Compost area. Supervised children are welcome to play on the slide and swing. Georgian house, herbaceous borders, brick garden, wild garden, large compost area and interesting trees. Many plants for sale at June opening. Featured in Parish magazine. Double doors from street with 2 wide steps that will take a wheelchair.

STONEY HILL HOUSE, SE26
Rock Hill, London SE26 6SW. Cinzia & Adam Greaves. *Stn: Sydenham, Gipsy Hill or Sydenham Hill stns. Buses: to Crystal Palace or 363 along Sydenham Hill, house at end of cul-de-sac on L.* Home-made teas. **Adm £3.50, chd free. Sun 19 May (2-6). Also open 4 Cornflower Terrace & Tewkesbury Lodge: Over the Hill.**
Garden and woodland of approx 1-acre providing a secluded green oasis in the city. Paths meander through a woodland of mature rhododendron, oak, yew and holly trees, offset by pieces of contemporary sculpture. The planting in the top part of the garden is fluid and informal.

4 STRADBROKE GROVE
Buckhurst Hill IG9 5PD. Mr & Mrs Brighten. *Between Epping & Woodford, 5m from M25 J26. Tube: Buckhurst Hill, turn R cross rd to Stradbroke Grove.* Home-made teas. **Adm £2.50, chd free. Sat 15, Sun 16 June (2-5).**
Secluded garden, designed to enhance its strong sloping aspect. Central gravelled bed. Rose-screened vegetable and fruit garden. Large lawn with good herbaceous borders and pergola to disguise conifer hedge.

NEW **58 SUMMERLEE AVENUE, N2**
London N2 9QH. Edwina & Nigel Roberts. *Tube to East Finchley, cross main rd, Summerlee Ave is located off Southern Rd. Walking distance from Muswell Hill.* Home-made teas. **Adm £3, chd free. Sun 26 May; Sun 8 Sept (2-7). Also open 64 Summerlee Ave 8 Sept.**
Small garden with beautiful acer, densely planted borders with mixture of shrubs and herbaceous perennials and spring and summer bulbs. Fences clothed with climbing roses, wisteria, clematis and honeysuckle. Woodland planting under acer. Small wildlife pond and planting is chosen to attract birds and insects. Several seating areas arranged to allow different views of garden.

NEW **64 SUMMERLEE AVENUE, N2**
London N2 9QH. Ms Ana Sanchez Martin. *Tube to East Finchley, cross main rd, Summerlee Ave is located off Southern Rd. Walking distance from Muswell Hill.* **Adm £3, chd free. Sun 8 Sept (2-7). Also open 58 Summerlee Avenue.**
Maximalist contemporary garden; lush, bold planting, counter pointed by graphic elements. An oxidised moongate creates a dramatic invitation into the exotic garden. The afternoon sun makes the planting sing. Strong sustainable ethos, only UK materials are used; oxidised steel from Essex, sweet chestnut from Herefordshire and handmade bricks from Yorkshire.

D

The afternoon sun makes the planting sing . . .

GROUP OPENING

NEW **TANFIELD AVENUE GARDENS, NW2**
London NW2 7SB. *Tube: Neasden, then ½ m walk. Bus: 182, 245, 332 and others to Neasden Library: 300yds walk.* Home-made teas at 93 Tanfield Avenue. **Combined adm £6 or £3.50 each, chd free. Sun 28 July (2-6).**

72 TANFIELD AVENUE
Mr Orod Ohanians

93 TANFIELD AVENUE
Mr James Duncan Mattoon
Visitors also welcome by appt May to Sept.
020 8830 7410

2 rather exotic gardens within yds of each other on opposite sides of the road. 72 Tanfield Ave is a long, uphill sloping garden, densely planted with exotic trees and shrubs 4 yrs ago. Designed to be a 'mini botanical garden', packed with exotic plants from China, New Zealand, Australia, Chile, central America, Middle East, Mediterranean, S Africa and Britain. Plants carefully chosen to survive, with a bit of care, in the British climate and complemented by rocks, pond, waterfall and bog garden. Over 400 species of plants. 93 Tanfield Ave is a shorter, very steep, downhill sloping garden, exotically planted as a paradise garden just 2 yrs ago. A professional plantsman's fabulous fantasy hillside paradise! Recently created yet almost heaven already! Arid/tropical deck with panoramic views descends to vividly planted Mediterranean and subtropical oasis on a circular layout. Packed with rare and unusual plants e.g. Bougainvillea, punica, luma. Tranquil jungle shade terrace and secret summerhouse. Plants for sale at 93 Tanfield Avenue.

58A TEIGNMOUTH ROAD, NW2
Cricklewood, London NW2 4DX. Drs Elayne & Jim Coakes, 020 8208 0082, elayne@coakes.co.uk. *Tube: Willesden Green or Kilburn 10 mins walk. Buses: 16, 32, 189, 226, 260, 266, 316, 332, 460. Teignmouth Rd just off Walm Ln.* Home-made teas. **Adm £3.50 or combined adm £5.50 with 121 Anson Rd, chd free. Sun 30 June (3-7). Visitors & groups of up to 15 people also welcome by appt Mar to Oct.**

Award winning front garden and back garden with eclectic planting schemes including colour co-ordinated beds, pergola with wisteria, climbing roses and 30+ clematis, 2 ponds, water feature, hardy, and unusual plants. Rainwater harvesting with integral watering system, native plants and organic treatment means a home for many frogs and bees. Some areas accessible only by stepping stones. Deep pond.

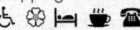

GROUP OPENING

TEWKESBURY LODGE: OVER THE HILL, SE23
Forest Hill, London SE23 3DE. *Off S Circular (A205) behind Horniman Museum & Gardens. Stn: Forest Hill, 10 mins walk. Buses: 176, 185, 312, P4. Combined admission: £6, accompanied children free. Buy tickets at any of the gardens.* Home-made teas at 6 Tewkesbury Ave (Sun 19 May). **Combined adm £6, chd free. Evening Opening, wine, Sat 18 May (5-8); Sun 19 May (2-6). Also opening 4 Cornflower Terrace & Stoney Hill House.**

THE COACH HOUSE
3 The Hermitage. Pat Rae
Visitors also welcome by appt.
020 8699 6326
pat@patrae.co.uk
patrae.co.uk

NEW **6 TEWKESBURY AVENUE**
Rowena Lowe

25 WESTWOOD PARK
Beth & Steph Falkingham-Blackwell

30 WESTWOOD PARK
Jackie McLaren

Four very different hillside gardens within a short walk of each other. Discover a sculptor's creative courtyard 'container' garden crammed with unusual plants and the artist's sculptures and ceramics (for sale); imaginative plant combinations in a garden designer's country-style garden with meandering paths through deep curving borders which contain plants and shrubs to cope with dense shade, full sun, and dry banks; a terraced front garden full of plants set in gravelled beds and a peaceful organic garden to the rear with flower, fruit and vegetable beds. Opening this year for the first time is a recently landscaped garden, terraced to take advantage of the views of London and provide an outdoor living space. As well as mature fruit trees and raised beds for vegetables, the enthusiastic gardener is exploring planting styles in this evolving very new garden. Art, sculpture and many plants for sale.

28 Horniman Drive

GROUP OPENING

NEW **TEWKESBURY LODGE: TOP OF THE HILL, SE23**
Forest Hill, London SE23 3DE. *Off South Circular (A205) behind Horniman Museum & Gardens. Station: Forest Hill, 10 mins walk. Buses: 176, 185, 312, P4. Tickets at 27 Horniman Drive.* Home-made teas At 53 Ringmore Rise. **Combined adm £6, chd free. Evening Opening, wine, Sat 15 June (5-8); Sun 16 June (2-6). Also open Dulwich Village Two Gardens, 9 Dulwich Village, 41 Southbrook Ave & 27 Thorpewood Ave.**

27 HORNIMAN DRIVE
Rose Agnew
Visitors also welcome by appt Apr to Oct.
020 8699 7710
roseandgraham@talktalk.net

28 HORNIMAN DRIVE
Frankie Locke

53 RINGMORE RISE
Valerie Ward

These 3 gardens are within a short walk of each other on a hill with spectacular views over London and the North Downs. A small SE-facing garden has borders with rich colours within formal outlines to complement a modern extension plus mini meadow and a tranquil vegetable area with seating, greenhouse and compost. A hilltop country garden is in 2 sections, evolving from the owner's love of growing vegetables, with raised beds, a fruit cage, green house, chicken run and working and wildlife areas with 'bug hotel'. The front garden of another, inspired by Beth Chatto's dry garden, has stunning borders in soft mauves, yellows and white, interspersed with drifts of red and purple poppies. Great views. Plants for sale at 28 Horniman Drive.

27 THORPEWOOD AVENUE, SE26

Sydenham, London SE26 4BU. Barbara & Gioni Nella. *1/2 m from Forest Hill Stn. Just off the S Circular (A205) turning up Sydenham Hill nr Horniman Gdns or Dartmouth Rd from Forest Hill stn. Buses: 122, 176, 312 to Thorpewood Ave.* Home-made teas. **Adm £3.50, chd free (share to Bromley Branch of NSPCC). Evening Opening £4.50, chd free, wine, Sat 15 June (6-9); Sun 16, Sun 30 June (2-5). Also open 15/16 June Tewkesbury Lodge: Top of the Hill, Dulwich Village Two Gardens, 9 Dulwich Village & 30 June Camberwell Grove Gardens.**

Mature tree-bordered 1/2 -acre garden on gently sloping site. Mixed borders with lots of interesting shrubs and perennials. Formal vegetable plot and gravel slope growing Mediterranean and alpine plants, pond and varied sitting areas. Small 'jungle' growing bamboos, bananas and tree ferns. Interesting plants for sale.

TREETOPS

Sandy Lane, Northwood HA6 3ES. Mrs Carole Kitchner. *Opp Northwood HQ. Tube: Northwood, 10 mins walk. Bus 8 stops at the bottom of lane. Parking in Lane.* Home-made teas. **Adm £3.50, chd free. Sun 21 July (2-6).**

Nestling in quiet lane in Northwood conservation area, sloping garden with long terrace and large pots. Rose-covered pergola, water feature, small lawn, wide variety unusual shrubs incl magnolia grandiflora, paulownias, trochodendron. Peaking in high summer, heleniums, agapanthus, lobelias, eryngiums, crocosmias present a vibrant vision - well worth a visit!

TRINITY HOSPICE, SW4

30 Clapham Common North Side, London SW4 0RN. Trinity Hospice, www.trinityhospice.org.uk. *Tube: Clapham Common. Buses: 35, 37, 137 stop outside.* **Adm £2.50, chd free. Sat 6, Sun 7 Apr; Sat 3, Sun 4 Aug (10-3).**

Trinity's 2-acre gardens have been a haven of peace, and a place of joy, for many thousands of patients and their families for more than 100 yrs. Recently restored as a memorial to Lanning Roper and replanted for all year interest with soft colours. Features incl a large carp lake, ancient mulberry trees and display of spring bulbs. Ramps and pathways.

Peaking in high summer, heleniums, agapanthus, lobelias, eryngiums, crocosmias present a vibrant vision - well worth a visit . . . !

22 TRINITY ROAD, N2

East Finchley. N2 8JJ. Janet Maitland. *Tube: East Finchley 12 mins walk. Bus: 263 to library, turn L into Church Lane, R into Trinity Rd. Car: turn into Trinity Rd from Long Lane, off Church Lane.* **Adm £2.50, chd free. Sun 16 June (2-5). Also open 79 Church Lane.**

Densely planted courtyard of vivid contrasts. Cottage garden plants mingle happily with elegant ferns and grasses. A majestic black bamboo towers over pots of dainty annuals. Neatly clipped box accentuates sprawling climbers. Giant trachycarpus palm falls over a feathery tamarix. Sturdy fig tree guards a small pond.

TRUMPETERS HOUSE & SARAH'S GARDEN

Richmond TW9 1PD. Baron & Baroness Van Dedem & Mrs Pamela Franklyn. *Richmond riverside. 5 mins walk from Richmond Station via Richmond Green in Trumpeter's Yard Parking only on Richmond Green and in Old Deer Park car park.* Home-made teas. **Adm £5, chd free. Sun 16 June (2-6).**

The 2-acre garden is on the original site of Richmond Palace. Long lawns stretch from the house to banks of the River Thames. There are clipped yews, a box parterre and many unusual shrubs and trees, a rose garden and oval pond with carp. The ancient Tudor walls are covered with roses and climbers. Discover Sarah's secret garden behind the high walls.

223 TUBBENDEN LANE

See Kent

37 TURPINS LANE

See Essex

35 TURRET GROVE, SW4

Clapham Old Town, London SW4 0ES. Wayne Amiel, www.turretgrove.com. *Off Rectory Grove. 10 mins walk from Clapham Common Tube and Wandsworth Rd Mainline. Buses: 87, 137.* Home-made teas. **Adm £3, chd free. Sun 21 July (10-5).**

This garden shows what can be achieved in a small space (8m x 25m). The owners, who make no secret of disregarding the rule book, describe this visual feast of intoxicating colours as 'Clapham meets Jamaica'. This is gardening at its most exuberant, where bananas, bamboos, gingers, tree ferns and fire-bright plants flourish beside the traditional. Featured in The Independent (Anna Pavord).

86 UNDERHILL ROAD, SE22

East Dulwich, London SE22 0QU. Claire & Rob Goldie. *Between Langton Rise & Melford Rd. Stn: Forest Hill. Buses: P13, 363, 63, 176, 185 and P4.* Home-made teas. **Adm £3.50, chd free. Sun 26 May; Sun 11 Aug (2-6). Also open Holly Grove Gardens Group & 29 Kinsale Rd 26 May, Elm Tree Cottage 11 Aug.**

A family space bursting with colour. Mixed bed of medicinal, fragrant and edible planting. Secluded seating set amongst gravel and bamboo with a rabbit hutch under a grass roof. Enjoy tea and cake in the garden room built on tyres. A new water feature this year with a rill running across the gravel garden.

7 UPPER PHILLIMORE GARDENS, W8
London W8 7HF. Mr & Mrs B Ritchie. *From Kensington High St turn into Phillimore Gdns or Campden Hill Rd; entrance at rear in Duchess of Bedford Walk.* Light refreshments. **Adm £2.50, chd free. Sun 28 Apr (2-6).**
Well planned mature garden on different levels creating areas of varied character and mood. Pergola with Italian fountain and fishpond, lawn with border plants leading to the sunken garden with rockery. Also groundcover, mature trees (making a secluded haven in central london), flowering shrubs and a fine display of spring bulbs.

208 WALM LANE, THE GARDEN FLAT, NW2
London NW2 3BP. Miranda & Chris Mason, www.thegardennw2.co.uk. *Tube: Kilburn. Garden at junction of Exeter Rd & Walm Lane. Buses: 16, 32, 189, 226, 245, 260, 266, 316 to Cricklewood Broadway, then consult A-Z.* Home-made teas, wine & Pimms. **Adm £3.50, chd free. Sat 22, Sun 23 June (2-7).**
Large S-facing oasis of green with big sky. Meandering lawn with island beds, fishpond with fountain, curved and deeply planted borders of perennials and flowering shrubs. Shaded mini woodland area of tall trees underplanted with rhododendrons, ferns and hostas with winding path from oriental-inspired summerhouse to secluded circular seating area. Woodwind Ensemble, Latin Guitar Duo, String Quartet providing entertainment throughout the weekend. Raffle prizes.

WALTHAM ABBEY
See Essex

WALWORTH GARDEN FARM, SE17
Braganza Street/Manor Place, Kennington, London SE17 3BN. Trustees of Walworth Garden Farm, 020 7582 2652, kevinmoore@walworthgardenfarm.org.uk, www.walworthgardenfarm.org.uk. *Tube: Kennington, 500yds down Braganza St, corner of Manor Place.* **Adm £2, chd free. Sat 18, Sun 19 May (10-4.30). Visitors welcome by appt.**
Walworth Garden Farm is an oasis in Southwark. From a derelict site this charity has created a productive garden full of organically grown fruit and vegetables surrounded by colourful flowerbeds. It is a working garden with greenhouses, a large newly constructed apiary, bee hives, ponds (a haven for wildlife) and a vital part of the local community providing training and development in horticulture. Majority of garden accessible by wheelchair uses.

For the tree-lover this is a must-see garden . . . attractive to wildlife . . .

THE WATERGARDENS
Warren Road, Kingston-upon-Thames KT2 7LF. The Residents' Association. *1m E of Kingston. From Kingston take A308 (Kingston Hill) towards London; after approx ½ m turn R into Warren Rd.* **Adm £4, chd £1. Sun 12 May; Sun 13 Oct (2-4.30).**
Japanese landscaped garden originally part of Coombe Wood Nursery, planted by the Veitch family in the 1860s. Approx 9 acres with ponds, streams and waterfalls. Many rare trees which, in spring and autumn, provide stunning colour. For the tree-lover this is a must-see garden. Gardens attractive to wildlife.

WEST LODGE PARK
Cockfosters Road, Hadley Wood EN4 0PY. Beales Hotels, 020 8216 3904, headoffice@bealeshotels.co.uk. *2m S of Potters Bar. On A111. J24 from M25 signed Cockfosters.* Afternoon Cream Teas are available in the hotel, booking in advance advisable. **Adm £4, chd free. Sun 19 May (2-5); Sun 20 Oct (1-4). Visitors also welcome by appt.**
Open for the NGS for over 25yrs, the 35-acre Beale Arboretum consists of over 800 varieties of trees and shrubs, incl National Collection of Hornbeam cultivars (Carpinus betulus) and 2 planned collections (Taxodium and Catalpa). Network of paths through good selection of conifers, oaks, maples and mountain ash - all specimens labelled. Beehives and 2 ponds. Stunning collection within the M25.
NCH

12 WESTERN ROAD, E13
Plaistow E13 9JF. Elaine Fieldhouse, 020 8470 3681, fhouse@btinternet.com. *Stn: Upton Park, 3mins walk. Buses: 58, 104, 330, 376.* Home-made teas. **Adm £3, chd free. Sun 9 June (1-6). Visitors & small groups of up to 10 also welcome by appt June.**
Urban oasis, 85ft garden designed and planted by owners. Relying more heavily on evergreen, ferns, foliage and herbaceous planting. Rear of garden leads directly onto a 110ft allotment - part allotment, part extension of the garden - featuring topiary, medlar tree, mulberry tree, 2 ponds, small fruit trees, raised beds and small iris collection.

86 WILLIFIELD WAY, NW11
Hampstead Garden Suburb, London NW11 6YJ. Diane Berger, 020 8455 0455, dianeberger@hotmail.co.uk. *1m N of Golders Green. Tube: Golders Green, then H2 bus to Willifield Way. Buses 82, 102, 460 to Temple Fortune, walk along Hampstead Way, turn L at The Orchard.* Home-made teas. **Adm £2.50, chd £1. Sun 21 July (2-6). Also open 4 Asmuns Hill & 5 Heathgate. Visitors also welcome by appt June to Sept.**
Cottage garden with a contemporary twist with colour-themed herbaceous borders designed for yr-round interest, wildlife pond, gazebo, rose and clematis-clad pergola and interesting, mature shrubs and perennials. Winner of Hampstead Garden Suburb garden competition. Teas served on communal lawns in front of this historic Arts and Crafts cottage.

61 WOLSEY ROAD
East Molesey KT8 9EW. Jan & Ken Heath. *Rail: From Hampton Court stn ½ m towards E Molesey, into Wolsey Rd*. Home-made teas. **Adm £3, chd free.** Sun 9 June (2-5).
Romantic garden of two halves. Part is shaded by two large copper beech trees with woodland planting and shade-loving plants. The second, reached through a beech arch, has cottage garden planting, pond and wooden obelisks covered in roses and sweet peas. Beautiful octagonal summerhouse overlooks pond. Plenty of seating and interesting ideas.

27 WOOD VALE, N10
London N10 3DJ. Mr & Mrs A W Dallman. *Muswell Hill 1m. A1 to Woodman PH; signed Muswell Hill. From Highgate tube, take Muswell Hill Rd, sharp R into Wood Lane leading to Wood Vale*. Home-made teas. **Adm £3.50, chd free.** Evening Opening £5, chd free, wine, Fri 12 July (6-9); Sat 13, Sun 14 July (1.30-6). **Also open 33 Wood Vale 13 & 14 July.**
One of London's most popular gardens. Winner of London Gardens Society best large garden. An unexpected adventure unfolds through herbaceous borders, winding paths with water features, to lawn with orchard, vegetable garden and greenhouses. Enjoy refreshments and celebrate our 26th year of opening. We would love to see you.

33 WOOD VALE, N10
Highgate, London N10 3DJ. Mona Abboud, 020 8883 4955, monaabboud@hotmail.com. *Tube: Highgate, 10 mins walk. Buses: W3, W7 to top of Park Rd*. **Adm £2, chd free.** Sat 13, Sun 14 July (2-6). **Also open 27 Wood Vale. Visitors also welcome by appt Apr to Oct.**
The garden is entered via a steep but safe staircase with a good view of the living sedum roof of the greenhouse. A relatively formal Italienate area with unusual Mediterranean shrubs and trees leads to a meandering path between two 30 metre mixed borders of soft coloured perennials and grasses. This garden is constantly developing and at the far end a new rockery and bog garden are being established.

NEW **7 WOODBINES AVENUE**
Kingston Upon Thames KT1 2AZ. Mr Tony Sharples & Mr Paul Cubert. *Kingston-upon-Thames. Accessed by rd from Portsmouth Rd or by foot from Penrhyn Rd, located opp Kingston University. By train: Surbiton Stn, then bus 71, 281, K2 or K3 from outside Waitrose. From Kingston Stn, go to Eden St bus station then bus 281 or 71, exit at Kingston University*. Home-made teas. **Adm £3.50, chd free.** Sun 18 Aug (1-5.30).
We have used a 70ft plot to create a 'tall' garden with trees, evergreen structure and perennials. We have been inspired by the deep borders at Wisely and Hampton Court to create 'depth' to provide variety, texture and interest around the garden. Whilst a N-facing spot we have maximised the benefit from the south facing back wall to creat a garden of contrasts from shade to sun. Wide herbaceous borders, a box hedge topiary garden and a hot summer terrace providing a contrast.

Roses and herbaceous plants with a subtropical twist using bananas and palms . . . a tranquil oasis in an urban setting . . .

66 WOODBOURNE AVENUE, SW16
London SW16 1UT. Brian Palmer & Keith Simmonds. *Off Streatham High Rd (A23) by Barclay's Bank. Enter from Garrads Rd by Tooting Bec Common (by car only)*. Home-made teas. **Adm £3, chd £0.50.** Sun 21 July (1-6).
A popular garden (19th year of opening) that is constantly evolving. Cottage-style front garden 40ft x 60ft containing roses and herbaceous plants with a subtropical twist using bananas and palms. Rear garden approx 40ft x 80ft with contrasting cool green and white colour palette, rare shrubs, trees and hidden sitting areas, creating a tranquil oasis in an urban setting. Take-away service for our renowned home-made cakes. Crazy-paved paths, narrow wheelchair access in places, small height difference from terrace to lawn.

THE WORLD GARDEN AT LULLINGSTONE CASTLE
See Kent

THE WYCH ELM PUBLIC HOUSE
93 Elm Road, Kingston-upon-Thames KT2 6HT. Janet Turnes, www.thewychelm.co.uk. *Stn: Kingston, 10 mins walk. 8 mins walk Kingston Gate, Richmond Park*. Home-made teas. **Adm £3, chd free.** Sun 28 July (12-6).
Prize-winning floriferous garden famed for its brilliant colourful display from eaves to pavement. Back garden features pampered exotic plants creating a Mediterranean atmosphere. Many unusual species lovingly tended by plantaholic licensee. Cool, shady corner and hot colours on the terrace. Pergola, festooned with exotic climbers, protects banana and other tender plants. Jean Griffin from Radio Kent and Radio Surrey/Sussex and Jim Buttress VMH AHRHS will be attending to answer your garden questions.

ZEN GARDEN, W3
55 Carbery Avenue, Acton, London W3 9AB. Three Wheels Buddhist Centre, 020 8248 2542, threewheels@threewheels.co.uk, www.threewheels.co.uk. *Tube: Acton Town 5 mins walk, 200yds off A406*. Home-made teas. **Adm £3, chd free.** Sat 6, Sun 7 July (2-5.30). **Visitors also welcome by appt.**
Pure Japanese Zen garden (so no flowers) with 12 large and small rocks of various colours and textures set in islands of moss and surrounded by a sea of grey granite gravel raked in a stylised wave pattern. Garden surrounded by trees and bushes outside a cob wall. Oak-framed wattle and daub shelter with Norfolk reed thatched roof. Japanese tea ceremony demonstration and talks by designer/creator of the garden. Buddha Room open to visitors.

London County Volunteers

County Organiser

Penny Snell, Moleshill House, The Fairmile, Cobham, Surrey KT11 1BG, 01932 864532, pennysnellflowers@btinternet.com

County Treasurer

Richard Raworth, 7 St George's Road, St Margarets, Twickenham TW1 1QS, 07831 476088, raworth.r@blueyonder.co.uk

Booklet Distributor

Joey Clover, 13 Fullerton Road, London SW18 1BU, 020 8870 8740, joeyclover@dsl.pipex.com

Assistant County Organisers

NW London Susan Bennett & Earl Hyde, 5 St Regis Close, Alexandra Park Road, Muswell Hill, London N10 2DE, 020 8883 8540, suebearlh@yahoo.co.uk
Caroline Broome, 79 Church Lane, London N2 0TH, 020 8444 2329, carosgarden@virginmedia.com

SW London Joey Clover as above

Islington Nell Darby Brown, 26 Canonbury Place, London N1 2NY, 020 7226 6880, pendarbybrown@blueyonder.co.uk
Gill Evansky, 25 Canonbury Place, London N1 2NY, 020 7359 2484

E London Teresa & Stuart Farnham, 17 Greenstone Mews, London E11 2RS, 020 8530 6729, farnhamz@yahoo.co.uk

Outer W London Julia Hickman, Little Lodge, Watts Road, Thames Ditton KT7 0BX, 020 8339 0931, julia.hickman@virgin.net

Hampstead Ruth Levy, 5 Frognal Gardens, London NW3 6UY, 020 7435 4124, ruthlevy@tiscali.co.uk

Hackney Philip Lightowlers, 8 Almack Road, London E5 0RL, 07910 850276, plighto@gmail.com

Outer NW London James Duncan Mattoon, 93 Tanfield Avenue, Neasden, London NW2 7SB, 020 8830 7410, jamesmattoon@msn.com

SW & Outer London Sue Phipps, 17 Crescent Lane, London SW4 9PT, 020 7622 7230, sue@crescentlane.co.uk

W London, Barnes & Chiswick Jenny Raworth, 7 St George's Road, St Margarets, Twickenham TW1 1QS, 020 8892 3713, jraworth@googlemail.com

Highgate, St John's Wood & Holland Park Sue Whittington, Southwood Lodge, 33 Kingsley Place, London N6 5EA, 020 8348 2785, suewhittington@hotmail.co.uk

SE London Janine Wookey, 4 Piermont Green, London SE22 0LP, 020 8693 1015, j.wookey@btinternet.com

NORFOLK

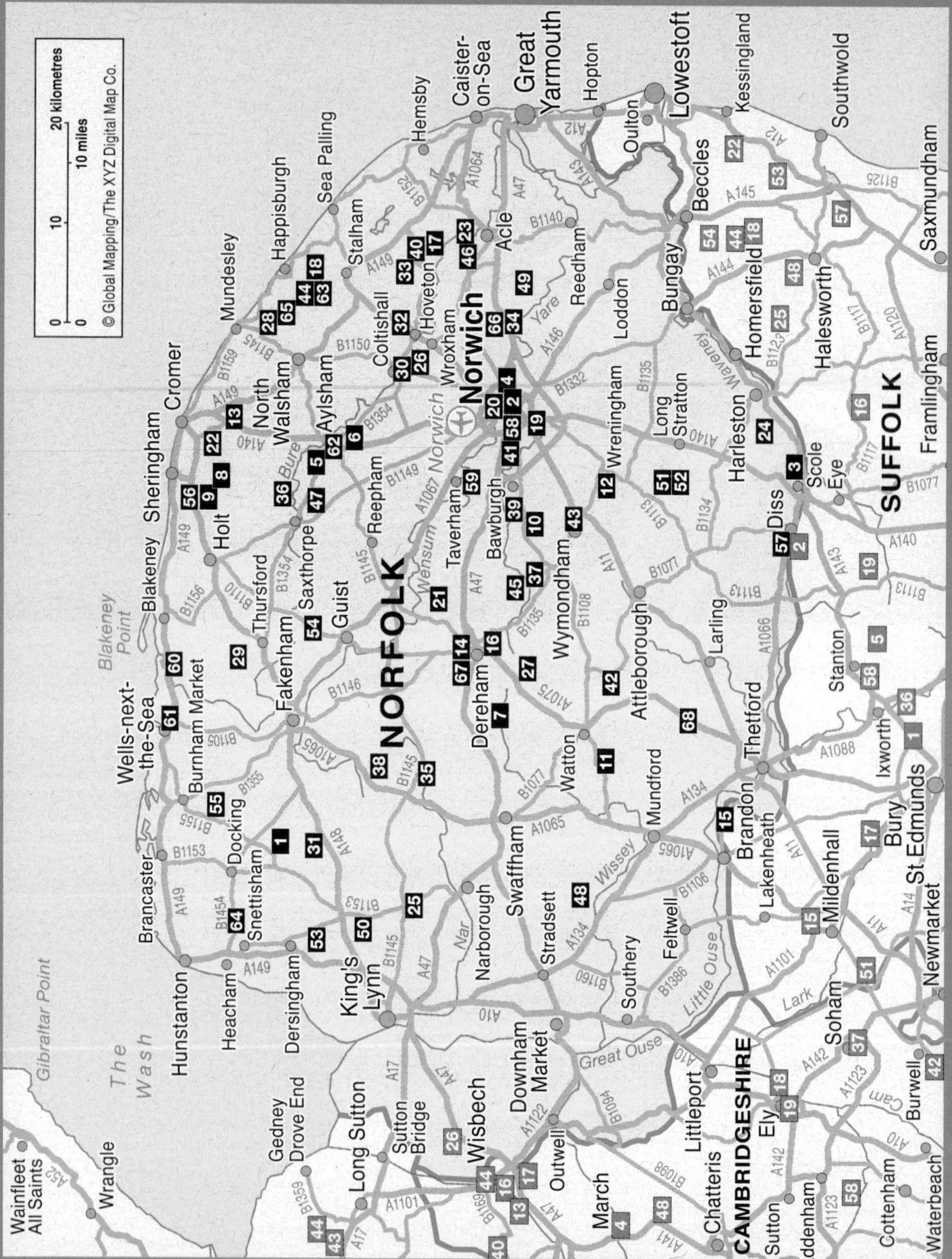
0 10 20 kilometres
0 10 miles
© Global Mapping/The XYZ Digital Map Co.
NORFOLK
SUFFOLK
CAMBRIDGESHIRE
Norwich
Great Yarmouth
Lowestoft
Caister-on-Sea
Hopton
Kessingland
Southwold
Saxmundham
Hemsby
Sea Palling
Happisburgh
Mundesley
Cromer
Sheringham
Blakeney
Blakeney Point
Wells-next-the-Sea
Burnham Market
Brancaster
Docking
Snettisham
Hunstanton
Heacham
Dersingham
King's Lynn
Gibraltar Point
The Wash
Wainfleet All Saints
Wrangle
Gedney Drove End
Long Sutton
Sutton Bridge
Wisbech
Outwell
March
Chatteris
Downham Market
Littleport
Ely
Sutton
Soham
Cottenham
Waterbeach
Burwell
Newmarket
Mildenhall
Lakenheath
Brandon
Bury St Edmunds
Ixworth
Stanton
Thetford
Larling
Diss
Scole
Eye
Framlingham
Harleston
Homersfield
Halesworth
Bungay
Beccles
Outon
Loddon
Reedham
Acle
Wroxham
Hoveton
Coltishall
Stalham
North Walsham
Aylsham
Reepham
Holt
Thursford
Saxthorpe
Fakenham
Guist
Taverham
Bawburgh
Wymondham
Wreningham
Long Stratton
Attleborough
Dereham
Swaffham
Narborough
Watton
Mundford
Stradsett
Southery
Feltwell
Great Ouse
Little Ouse
Wissey
Nar
Wensum
Bure
Yare
Waveney
Lark
Cam

Opening Dates

February

Sunday 10
35 Lexham Hall

Sunday 24
1 Bagthorpe Hall
30 Horstead House

Thursday 28
9 Chestnut Farm

March

Sunday 3
9 Chestnut Farm

Sunday 17
36 Mannington Hall

Sunday 24
25 Gayton Hall
29 Hindringham Hall

Friday 29
15 Desert World Gardens

Saturday 30
15 Desert World Gardens

Sunday 31
12 The Conifers
15 Desert World Gardens
68 Wretham Lodge

April

Monday 1
15 Desert World Gardens
68 Wretham Lodge

Saturday 13
18 East Ruston Old Vicarage

Sunday 21
7 Bradenham Hall
49 Plovers Hill
66 16 Witton Lane

May

Sunday 5
49 Plovers Hill

Monday 6
28 Hill Cottage
49 Plovers Hill
65 Witton Hall

Sunday 12
11 Clermont House
32 Hoveton Hall Gardens

Sunday 19
3 Billingford Hall
9 Chestnut Farm
33 How Hill Farm
35 Lexham Hall
44 The Old Rectory, Ridlington
63 West View

Monday 20
35 Lexham Hall

Thursday 23
56 Sheringham Park

Sunday 26
45 The Old Rectory, Brandon Parva

Monday 27
6 Bolwick Hall
60 Warborough House

June

Saturday 1
55 Shammer House

Sunday 2
47 Oulton Hall
55 Shammer House
67 Wood Hill, Gressenhall

Thursday 6
56 Sheringham Park

Saturday 8
43 167 Norwich Road

Sunday 9
13 Daisy Cottage
28 Hill Cottage
43 167 Norwich Road

Tuesday 11
8 Chaucer Barn

Friday 14
36 Mannington Hall (Evening)

National Gardens Weekend

Saturday 15
55 Shammer House
64 Wethered Manor

Sunday 16
12 The Conifers
17 The Dutch House
22 Felbrigg Hall
27 High House Gardens
48 Oxburgh Hall
55 Shammer House
64 Wethered Manor

Wednesday 19
27 High House Gardens

Saturday 22
19 Eaton Rise Gardens

Sunday 23
11 Clermont House
24 Furze House
38 Manor House Farm, Wellingham
51 Sand Pit Farm North
52 Sandpit Farm South

Saturday 29
24 Furze House

Sunday 30
4 Bishop's House
21 Elsing Hall Gardens
24 Furze House
39 4 Mill Road
40 The Mowle
42 Northacre Village Gardens
57 Sundown

July

Tuesday 2
39 4 Mill Road

Saturday 6
2 The Bear Shop

Sunday 7
2 The Bear Shop
26 Heggatt Hall

Friday 12
37 Manor Farm, Coston (Afternoon & Evening)

Saturday 13
5 Blickling Hall Estate

Sunday 14
20 68 Elm Grove Lane
23 The Firs
41 North Lodge
46 Orchard Cottage

Sunday 21
41 North Lodge
62 West Lodge

Sunday 28
7 Bradenham Hall
14 Dale Farm
58 Two Norwich Community Gardens
60 Warborough House

Tranquil garden with several sitting areas, free-roaming bantams and dovecote . . .

August

Saturday 3
10 Church Farm
24 Furze House

Sunday 4
16 Dunbheagan
24 Furze House
39 4 Mill Road
50 Rectory Cottage

Monday 5
24 Furze House

Tuesday 6
39 4 Mill Road

Sunday 11
49 Plovers Hill
54 Severals Grange

Sunday 18
13 Daisy Cottage
48 Oxburgh Hall

Tuesday 20
32 Hoveton Hall Gardens

You are always welcome at an NGS garden!

September

Saturday 7
61 Wells-Next-The-Sea Gardens

Sunday 8
7 Bradenham Hall
61 Wells-Next-The-Sea Gardens

Wednesday 11
35 Lexham Hall

Sunday 15
22 Felbrigg Hall
27 High House Gardens
59 The Urban Jungle Gardens

Wednesday 18
27 High House Gardens

October

Saturday 12
5 Blickling Hall Estate
18 East Ruston Old Vicarage

January 2014

Tuesday 28
40 The Mowle

Gardens open to the public

5 Blickling Hall Estate
7 Bradenham Hall
18 East Ruston Old Vicarage
22 Felbrigg Hall
29 Hindringham Hall
31 Houghton Hall Walled Garden
32 Hoveton Hall Gardens
36 Mannington Hall
36 Mannington Hall
48 Oxburgh Hall
53 Sandringham Gardens
54 Severals Grange
56 Sheringham Park
59 The Urban Jungle Gardens

By appointment only

34 Lake House

Also open by Appointment

3 Billingford Hall
9 Chestnut Farm
12 The Conifers
14 Dale Farm
16 Dunbheagan
17 The Dutch House
21 Elsing Hall Gardens
24 Furze House
25 Gayton Hall
29 Hindringham Hall
39 4 Mill Road
40 The Mowle
49 Plovers Hill
57 Sundown
62 West Lodge

The Gardens

1 BAGTHORPE HALL

Bagthorpe PE31 6QY. Mr & Mrs D Morton, 01485 578528, dgmorton@hotmail.com. *3½ m N of East Rudham, off A148. At King's Lynn take A148 to Fakenham. At East Rudham (approx 12m) turn L opp The Crown, 3½ m into hamlet of Bagthorpe. Farm buildings on L, wood on R, white gates set back from road, at top of drive.* Home-made teas and home-made organic soups, made from veg from the farm. **Adm £3.50, chd free. Sun 24 Feb (11-4).**
Snowdrops carpeting woodland walk.

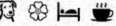

A beautiful cottage garden full of hot and pastel shades with a koi pond . . .

BATTELEYS COTTAGE
See Suffolk

2 THE BEAR SHOP

Elm Hill, Norwich NR3 1HN. Robert Stone. *Norwich City Centre. From St Andrews, L to Princes St, then L to Elm Hill. Garden at side of shop through large wooden gate and along alleyway.* **Adm £3, chd free. Sat 6, Sun 7 July (11-5).**
Considered to be based on a design by Gertrude Jekyll, a small terraced garden behind a C15 house in the historic Cathedral Quarter of Norwich. Enjoy the tranquillity of the riverside.

3 BILLINGFORD HALL

Billingford, Diss IP21 4HN. Sir Rupert & Lady Mann, 01379 740314, rosie.mann@electramail.co.uk. *4m E of Diss, 1½ m E of Scole. Take A143 towards Great Yarmouth, by-passing Scole, after 1½ m see Billingford Horseshoes PH on R. Past PH, turn L by lodge cottage and sign to church and Billingford Hall is up hill past church.* Tea. **Adm £3.50, chd free. Sun 19 May (11-5.30). Visitors also welcome by appt May to July.**
A visually pretty traditional English garden with herbaceous and shrub borders, stunning views over Waveney Valley. Also, a formal walled garden with shrub, climbing roses and clematis, box-edged borders and fruit trees. An unusual feature is the thatched roof dovecote in the adjacent park.

4 BISHOP'S HOUSE

Bishopgate, Norwich NR3 1SB. The Bishop of Norwich. *City centre. Entrance opposite Law Courts on Bishopgate on N side of Cathedral (not through The Close). Through Archway on R. Public car parking nearby. No parking at garden.* Home-made teas. **Adm £3, chd free. Sun 30 June (1-5).**
4-acre walled garden dating back to C12. Extensive lawns with specimen trees. Borders with many rare and unusual shrubs. Spectacular herbaceous borders flanked by yew hedges. Rose beds, meadow labyrinth, kitchen garden, woodland walk and long border with hostas and bamboo walk. Popular plant sales. Gravel paths, slopes.

5 ◆ BLICKLING HALL ESTATE

Aylsham, Norwich NR11 6NF. National Trust, 01263 738030, www.nationaltrust.org.uk/blickling. *14m N of Norwich just off the A140. 14m N of Norwich via A140. 1½ m NW of Aylsham on N side of B1354.* **Adm £8.90, chd £4.45. For NGS: Sats 13 July; 12 Oct (10.30-5.30). For other opening times and information, please phone or see garden website.**
Four centuries of good husbandry have made this 55 acre garden one of the greatest in England. Lord Lothian brought in Norah Lindsay, the society gardener, to create the garden you see today which changes through the seasons and complements the Jacobean house. 18C Orangery, Doric style temple, secret garden, beautiful double borders and parterre, lake, azaleas, rhododendrons, topiary and yew hedges. Kitchen garden open. Wheelchairs and powered mobility vehicles available to borrow. WC, gravel paths.

6 BOLWICK HALL

Marsham NR10 5PU. Mr & Mrs G C Fisher. *8m N of Norwich off A140. On A140 towards Aylsham, at Marsham take 1st R after Plough PH, then next R onto private rd to front of Hall.* Home-made teas. **Adm £4, chd free. Mon 27 May (1-5).**

Landscaped gardens and park surrounding a late Georgian hall and stable block (not open). The original design is attributed to Humphry Repton. The current owners have rejuvenated the herbaceous and shrub borders and clad the walls of the house in old roses. Enjoy a woodland walk around the lake as well as as stroll through the working vegetable and fruit garden.

7 ◆ BRADENHAM HALL

Bradenham, Thetford IP25 7QP. Chris & Panda Allhusen, 01362 687279, www.bradenhamhall.co.uk. *6m E of Swaffham. 5m W of East Dereham off A47. Turn S signed Wendling & Longham. 1m turn S signed Bradenham, 2m.* **Adm £5, chd free. For NGS: Sun 21 Apr, Sun 28 July, Sun 8 Sept (2-5.30). For other opening times and information, please phone or see garden website.**

A garden for all seasons. Flower gardens, formally designed and richly planted, formal rose gardens, paved garden, unusual climbers, herbaceous and shrub borders, traditional kitchen gardens with 2 glasshouses. Arboretum of over 800 different trees, all labelled. Massed daffodils in spring. A delight and an education. Groups by appt. Featured in Country Life & House and Gardens.

8 CHAUCER BARN

Holt Road, Gresham NR11 8RL. James Mermagen, www.chaucerbarn.com. *3m S of Sheringham. Turn off A149 nr junction of A149 & A1082 signed Gresham/E Beckham. Turn L at T junction. 1st building in Gresham. 1st gravel drive on L of sharp L bend.* Light refreshments. **Adm £3.50, chd free. Tue 11 June (2-6).**

5-acre garden created by owner over 20 years in ruins of farmyard. Uphill drive flanked by topiary leads to award winning barn conversion. Knot/herb garden leads to lawn flanked by walled herbaceous borders and pergola leading through contemporary topiary garden to stunning views over rolling hills to woodland. Woodland path leads downhill to wild flower meadow and young arboretum.

68 Elm Grove Lane

9 CHESTNUT FARM

Church Road, West Beckham NR25 6NX. Mr & Mrs John McNeil Wilson, 01263 822241, john@mcneil-wilson.freeserve.co.uk. *2½ m S of Sheringham. Mid-way between Holt & Cromer. 1m S off the A148 at the Sheringham Park entrance. Sign post indicates 'By Rd to W Beckham'. Chestnut Farm located behind the village sign. Lots of free parking, WC.* Light refreshments, home-made cakes and light lunches served all day. **Adm £4.50, chd free. Thur 28 Feb; Sun 3 Mar (11-4); Sun 19 May (11-5). Visitors also welcome by appt Feb to Sept. Refreshments by arrangement.**

A 3 acre garden for all seasons, created over many years by enthusiastic plant lovers. Lawns, formal areas, herbaceous borders, vegetables and fruit. Woodland garden, specimen trees and shrubs. In the spring there are over 60 varieties of snowdrops, with crocus, hellebores and daphnes planted in natural surroundings. There is always something to see. Plant sales and visiting nurseries at all openings. Refreshments on Sunday events. Featured in The Garden, Gartner leicht gemacht (Germany) Gardens Illustrated, the Norfolk magazine etc. Wheelchair access weather permitting.

10 NEW CHURCH FARM

The Street, Wramplingham, Wymondham NR18 0RU. Mr Peter Howard, peted.howard@hotmail.co.uk. *7m W of Norwich, 3m N of Wymondham. Leave Norwich on B1108 Watton Rd. Wramplingham is signed to the L just before Barford or 2nd L after chevroned double bends. Through the village to a sharp LH bend at war memorial. Garden is 1st house on L. Ample car parking is just beyond. From Wymondham follow signposts for Wramplingham off Tuttles Lane East. After 3m Church Farm is situated on R down the hill from the church.* Light refreshments. **Adm £3.50, chd free. Sat 3 Aug (11-5).**

An half acre garden of two eras. One a vista of calm formality packed with colourful herbaceous borders, some edged with lavender punctuated with a perfumed rose pergola. The other a beautiful cottage garden full of hot and pastel shades with a koi pond. The gardens have an overall relaxing feel. Large gravel areas access gardens and one has 3 steps to negotiate.

Visit a garden in your own time – look out for the ☎

11 CLERMONT HOUSE

Little Cressingham IP25 6LY. Mr & Mrs John Davies, www.clermonthousegarden.com. *3m SW of Watton on the Brandon Rd. Signed only off the B1108 at Little Cressingham. Turn S onto School Rd. The garden is ½ m on L.* Home-made teas. **Adm £4.50, chd free. Suns 12 May; 23 June (2-5.30).**

Established since 1984, 13 acres. Woodland garden and walks with spring flowering bulbs, bluebells and shrubs; Arboretum, walled garden and mixed borders, lake, lawns and turf labyrinth. You can sense the close harmony with nature as you wander through the garden. Mown paths open up vistas as they weave through the maturing trees, wild flowers and water features. Stunning views across open countryside. Some gravel paths and steep slope to pond.

12 THE CONIFERS

Wymondham Road, Wreningham NR16 1AT. Sue Sayers & Barry Layton, 01508 489654, sue.sayers@yahoo.co.uk. *7m S of Norwich. 4m E Wymondham, 300yds W of Wreningham centre. From A11 follow signs towards Mulbarton, 2nd R turn to Pennys Green, R at T-junction, R into Wymondham Road. From Norwich A140 - B1113, turn R at Bird in Hand PH, 2nd R into Wymondham Road. 300 yds on R.* Home-made teas. **Adm £3.50, chd free. Sun 31 Mar (1-4); Sun 16 June (1-5). Visitors also welcome by appt Apr to July.**

1½ -acre garden with 3 ponds and bog garden, herbaceous and shrub borders, rose pergolas and statuary. Informal area featuring many trees inc walnut, medlar,larch, birch and oak. In spring blossom and massed planting of daffodils and narcissi. New pond area and planting for 2013.

13 DAISY COTTAGE

Chapel Road, Roughton, Norwich NR11 8AF. Miss Geraldine Maelzer & Miss Anne Callow. *3½ m S of Cromer. A140 from Norwich, in Roughton Village take B1436, signed Felbrigg Hall NT. Daisy Cottage is 150yds on L.* Light refreshments. **Adm £4, chd free. Suns 9 June; 18 Aug (11-5).**

2 acre garden with areas dedicated for wildlife, incl stream, pond, bog garden and more formally a Japanese style garden with a thatched tea house. Among its features are herbaceous borders, vegetable garden and apiary, chickens and ducks. Produce and plants for sale. Bees and bugs in the garden demo. Featured on BBC Norfolk Radio garden party. Limited wheelchair access to pathed areas only.

You can sense the close harmony with nature as you wander through the garden . . .

14 DALE FARM

Sandy Lane, Dereham NR19 2EA. Graham & Sally Watts, 01362 690065, grahamwatts@dsl.pipex.com. *16m W of Norwich. 12m E of Swaffam. From A47 take B1146 signed to Fakenham, turn R at T-junction, ¼ m turn L into Sandy Lane (before pelican crossing).* Home-made teas. **Adm £4, chd free. Sun 28 July (11-5). Visitors also welcome by appt June to Aug.**

2 acre plant lover's garden with spring fed lake. Over 700 plant varieties featured in exuberantly planted borders and waterside gardens. Kitchen garden, orchard, naturalistic planting areas, gravel garden and sculptures. Gravel drive and some grass paths. Wide range of plants for sale incl rare hydrangeas.

15 DESERT WORLD GARDENS

Thetford Road (B1107), Santon Downham IP27 0TU. Mr & Mrs Barry Gayton, 01842 765861. *4m N of Thetford. On B1107 Brandon 2m.* Light refreshments. **Adm £3.50, chd free. Fri 29, Sat 30, Sun 31 Mar; Mon 1 Apr (10-5).**

1¼ acres plantsman's garden, specialising in tropical and arid plants. Hardy succulents - sempervivums, hanging gardens of Babylon (plectranthus). Main garden - bamboos, herbaceous primula theatre, spring/summer bulbs, particularly lilies. Over 70 varieties of magnificent magnolias. View from roof garden. Radio Cambridge gardener. Glasshouses cacti/succulents 12500, viewing by appt only on a different day. In the heart of man made Thetford forest. Plant identifications and demonstrations if asked. Plant hunts each day, win prizes. Featured in New Landscape Magazine and on Countrywide Gardeners Question Time Roadshow.

16 DUNBHEAGAN

Dereham Road, Westfield NR19 1QF. Jean & John Walton, 01362 696163, jandjwalton@btinternet.com. *2m S of Dereham. From Dereham take A1075 towards Shipdham. Turn L at Premier Food Store (Westfield Rd). At staggered Xrds continue straight ahead down narrow lane. Garden 4th on L. Disabled parking in drive. Please respect our neighbours & park carefully.* Home-made teas. **Adm £4, chd free. Sun 4 Aug (12.30-5.30). Visitors also welcome by appt May to Sept.**

Prepare to be amazed at the amount of colour from rare, unusual and more recognisable flowers, trees and shrubs in this 1.4 acre plantsman's garden. Planted for year round interest with masses of colour into late summer. We try to provide the 'wow' factor. Come along to relax and enjoy'. Reepham Ensemble playing 2-4pm. Featured in local press, Garden News. Gravel driveway.

17 THE DUTCH HOUSE

Ludham NR29 5NS. Mrs Peter Seymour, 01692 678225. *5m W of Wroxham. B1062 Wroxham to Ludham 7m. Turn R by Ludham village church into Staithe Rd. Garden ¼ m from village.* Home-made teas. **Adm £4, chd free. Sun 16 June (2-5). Visitors also welcome by appt June to July.**

Romantic 2½ acre garden originally designed and planted by painter Edward Seago. Informal borders lead to wild areas of old fashioned roses and shrubs. Steep bridge and uneven paths through Marsh and Wood lead one to Womack water (limited access). Wheelchair access limited to main part of garden.

18 ◆ EAST RUSTON OLD VICARAGE
East Ruston, Norwich NR12 9HN. Alan Gray & Graham Robeson, 01692 650432, www.eastrustonoldvicaragegardens.co.uk. *3m N of Stalham. Turn off A149 onto B1159 signed Bacton, Happisburgh. After 2m turn R 200yds N of East Ruston Church (ignore sign to East Ruston).* **Adm £7.50, chd £1. For NGS: Sats 13 Apr; 12 Oct (2-5.30). For other opening times and information, please phone or see garden website.**
20-acre exotic coastal garden incl traditional borders, exotic garden, desert wash, sunk garden, topiary, water features, walled and Mediterranean gardens. Many rare and unusual plants, stunning plant combinations, wild flower meadows, old-fashioned cornfield, vegetable and cutting gardens.

GROUP OPENING

19 NEW EATON RISE GARDENS
Norwich NR4 6QD. *1½ m S of Norwich City centre. From the outer Norwich Ring Rd take A 140 Ipswich Road, then 3rd L, Broadhurst Rd, then L at Welsford Road. Gardens on L after about 100 metres. For 20 Constabe Rd, Broadhurst Rd, then 1st L into Constable Rd. Tickets & directions available at all gardens.* Home-made teas at the United Reformed Church, Ipswich Road. **Combined adm £4, chd free. Sat 22 June (11-5).**

NEW 20 CONSTABLE ROAD
Jan Paulger

NEW 69 WELSFORD ROAD
Elizabeth George

NEW 81 WELSFORD ROAD
Mr & Mrs J Bryce

NEW 86 WELSFORD ROAD
Anne Curran

A group of small town gardens with a variety of designs and content.
20 Constable Road is a small mature town garden designed by the owner with unusual trees, shrubs and architectural plants to be deliberately green throughout the year. Bird's paradise. 69 Welsford Road a pretty small garden with a large collection of shrubs, perennials and fuchsias. Small pond, patio and bird feeders. 81 Welsford Small town garden with a variety of shrubs, perennials and small trees. Garden incl various features with a small wildlife pond. Seating and patio area available for use at different times of the day.
86 Welsford Road is a cottage style garden with lawn, shrubs and quite a lot of flowers. Wheelchair access to most areas.

ELM GARDENS
See Cambridgeshire

Owners endeavour to redefine a suburban garden and to provide inspiration when viewed from his studio window . . .

20 NEW 68 ELM GROVE LANE
Norwich NR3 3LF. Selwyn Taylor. *1¾ m Nof Norwich city centre. Proceed from Norwich city centre to Magdalen Street, then onto Magdalen Rd, bear L to St Clements Hill, turn L into Elm Grove Lane. Number 68 is at the bottom of the hill on the RH-side.* Home-made teas. **Adm £3, chd free. Sun 14 July (11-4).**
This extended living/working space is the owner's endeavour to redefine a suburban garden and to provide inspiration when viewed from his studio window. Aesthetic values, initially took precedent over gardening know-how, but over 30 years a more balanced approach has resulted in an eclectic array of informal planting, rich in colour and form and full of surprises.

21 NEW ELSING HALL GARDENS
Elsing Hall, Elsing, Dereham NR20 3DX. Patrick Lines & Han Yang Yap, 01362 637 866, patrick.lines@gmail.com, www.elsinghall.com. *6km NW of Dereham. N Tuddenham exit from A47, on N side of A47 turn R at Lodge PH & R after about 1½ m (just after Hall Farm), 1st drive on L. Elsing exit from A1067, turn R at T junction after the bridge, turn R at Xrds, proceed for about 1½ m, 1st drive on R just after sign to Peaseland Green on L.* **Adm £4, chd free. Sun 30 June (11-4). Visitors also welcome by appt May to July.**
15th century fortified manor house (not open) with working moat. 10 acre gardens and 10 acre park surrounding the house. Significant collection of old roses, walled garden, formal garden, marginal planting, Gingko avenue, viewing mound, moongate, pinetum and terraced garden. Finalist Daily Telegraph/Country Life - England's Favourite House competition.

ELY GARDENS 1
See Cambridgeshire

22 ◆ FELBRIGG HALL
Felbrigg NR11 8PR. National Trust, 01263 837444, www.nationaltrust.org.uk. *2½ m SW of Cromer. S of A148; main entrance from B1436.* **Adm £4.75, chd £2. For NGS: Suns 16 June; 15 Sept (11-5). For other opening times and information, please phone or see garden website.**
Large pleasure gardens; mainly lawns and shrubs; orangery with camellias; large walled garden restored and restocked as fruit, vegetable, herb and flower garden; dovecote; dahlias; wooded parks. Botanical interest. 1 electric and 2 manual wheelchairs available.

23 NEW THE FIRS
27 Prince Of Wales Road, Upton, Norwich NR13 6BW. Jayne Armes. *3m W of Acle. From A47 go to Acle r'about and take exit by petrol station into Acle. With petrol station on L proceed approx 200yds and turn R keeping co-op directly on your L. Follow to T-junction and turn L passing vet and school on L. After 500yds Amber Lodge on R. Take 1st R to Upton Village. Follow this road through village until road bears sharp Linto Prince of Wales Rd. The Firs approx 400 metres on L with car parking in paddock oppe.* Home-made teas at Orchard Cottage. **Adm £4, chd free. Sun 14 July (11-5). Combined with Orchard Cottage.**
⅓ acre garden created from a paddock over the last 12 years consisting of mature ornamental trees

and shrubs also incorporating smaller areas of interest with cottage style borders with a small raised pond. Countryside views, with Upton boat dyke a short distance away. Initial gravel incline into garden.

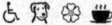

THE FORMER RECTORY
See Suffolk

24 FURZE HOUSE
Harleston Road, Rushall, Diss IP21 4RT. Philip & Christine Greenacre, 01379 852375 or 07967966698, philip@furzehouse.com, www.furzehouse.com. *2m W of Harleston. A140 r'about to Dickleburgh Village, turn R at church, then 3m on L. If coming on A143 Harleston r'about to Diss, turn R 500 yds to Upper Harman's Lane, turn L at T-junction, 1st house ½ m on R.* Light refreshments, teas, cakes & ploughman's. **Adm £3.50, chd free. Sun 23, Sat 29, Sun 30 June; Sat 3, Sun 4, Mon 5 Aug (10-6). Visitors also welcome by appt.**
2-acre plantsman's garden comprising herbaceous and shrub borders with cottage style planting in profusion. Lawned paths flow around many new island beds, incorporating established specimen trees, intensively planted with unusual shrubs and many special perennials. Established, informal wildlife pond, large rockery/ scree area with water feature. 2 Haygrove polytunnels protecting tender and special specimens.

GABLE HOUSE
See Suffolk

25 GAYTON HALL
Gayton PE32 1PL. The Earl & Countess of Romney, 015536 36259, ciciromney@tiscali.co.uk. *6m E of King's Lynn. On B1145; R on B1153. R down Back St 1st entrance on L.* Home-made teas. **Adm £4, chd free. Sun 24 Mar (12-5). Visitors also welcome by appt Mar to Oct.**
20-acre water garden, with over 2 miles of paths. Lawns, woodland, lakes, streams and bridges. Many unusual trees and shrubs. Spring bulbs and autumn colour. Traditional and waterside borders. Primulas, astilbes, hostas, lysichitums, gunneras and magnificent rambling roses through trees and yews in June. Gravel and grass paths.

Heggatt Hall

© Nicola Stocken Tomkins

GISLINGHAM GARDENS
See Suffolk

IVY CHIMNEYS
See Suffolk

26 HEGGATT HALL
Horstead NR12 7AY. Mr & Mrs Richard Gurney. *6m N of Norwich. Take B1150 North Walsham rd out of Norwich go for N 6m. R at small Xrds signed Heggatt Hall. Turn L at T-junction house 400yds on L.* Light refreshments. **Adm £4, chd free. Sun 7 July (12-5).**
Elizabethan house (not open) set in large gardens surrounded by parkland with ancient chestnut trees. Herbaceous border, sunken garden. Walled knot/rose garden leading into kitchen garden with wisteria walk and further flower beds. Some Gravel paths and steps.

HENSTEAD EXOTIC GARDEN
See Suffolk

27 HIGH HOUSE GARDENS
Blackmoor Row, Shipdham, Thetford IP25 7PU. Mr & Mrs F Nickerson. *6m SW of Dereham. Take the airfield or Cranworth Rd off A1075 in Shipdham. Blackmoor Row is signed.* Home-made teas. **Adm £4, chd free. Suns, Weds 16, 19 June; 15, 18 Sept (2-5.30).**
Plantsman's garden with colour-themed herbaceous borders with extensive range of perennials. Box-edged rose and shrub borders. Woodland garden, pond and bog area. Newly planted orchard and vegetable garden. Wildlife area. Glasshouses. Featured in Amateur gardening magazine, Eastern Daily Press Norfolk. Gravel paths.

Spread the word about the NGS: tell your family and friends

28 HILL COTTAGE
School Road, Edingthorpe NR28 9SY. Shirley Gilbert. *3m NE of North Walsham. Off B1150 halfway between North Walsham & Bacton, leave main rd at Edingthorpe Green & continue straight towards Paston for 3/4 m. Cottage on L at top of hill. Parking in adjacent field.* Tea. **Adm £4, chd free. Mon 6 May; Sun 9 June (11-5).**
Cottage garden, approx 1/4 acre, surrounding former farm workers' cottages. Organically cultivated, never watered and densely planted with both traditional and unusual varieties of drought resistant climbers, shrubs, perennials and annuals. Fruit, vegetable and herb gardens, greenhouse and pond. A real butterfly and wildlife paradise. Small nursery. Member of Norfolk Cottage Garden Society. Photos may be taken with owner's permission. Garden Workshops. Featured in Amateur Gardener.

29 ◆ HINDRINGHAM HALL
Blacksmiths Lane, Hindringham NR21 0QA. Mr & Mrs Charles Tucker, 01328 878226, www.hindringhamhall.org. *7m from Holt/Fakenham/Wells. Off A148 @ Thursford Crawfish PH signed Hindringham. After village hall L into Holme Lane (after the church). Follow signs to parking. Sat Nav takes you down a private rd - do not use it.* Home-made teas at the hall. **Adm £5, chd free. For NGS: Sun 24 Mar (10.30-4). For opening times and information, please phone or see garden website.**
Tudor Manor House surrounded with complete 13thC. moat. Victorian nut walk, formal beds and wild Garden. Surrounding the moat are thousands of narcissi (32 varieties), a working walled vegetable garden and stream garden ablaze with hellibore and primula. Carving of female legs with head buried in ground. Open every Weds Apr to Oct 10-4.30. Coaches by appt Apr to Sept. Featured in The English Garden.

30 HORSTEAD HOUSE
Mill Road, Horstead, Norwich NR12 7AU. Mr & Mrs Matthew Fleming. *6m NE of Norwich. B1150 Norwich to North Walsham rd. Turn down Mill Road at mini r'about by Recruiting Sargeant PH. House at far end of Mill Rd by Mill Pond. Disabled parking only - park nearby on road or in village.* Home-made teas. **Adm £3.50, chd free. Sun 24 Feb (11-4).**
Millions of beautiful snowdrops carpet the woodland setting, which has also been recently planted with scented winter flowering shrubs. A stunning feature are the dogwoods growing on a small island in R Bure, which flows through the garden. Small walled garden. River Bure. Wheel chair access to main snowdrop area.

Millions of beautiful snowdrops carpet the woodland setting shrubs . . .

31 ◆ HOUGHTON HALL WALLED GARDEN
New Houghton, King's Lynn PE31 6UE. The Cholmondeley Gardens Trust, 01485 528569, www.houghtonhall.com. *11m W of Fakenham. 13m E of King's Lynn. Signed from A148.* **For opening times and information, please phone or see garden website.**
Superbly laid-out award-winning 5-acre walled garden divided by clipped yew hedges into 'garden rooms', incl large mixed kitchen garden. Magnificently colourful 120m double herbaceous border. Rose parterre with over 120 varieties. Fountains, incl 'Waterflame' by Jeppe Hein, glasshouse, statues, rustic temple and croquet lawn. Plants on sale. Owing to special exhibition in House during 2013 please refer to website (houghtonhall.com) for specific admission details. Gravel and grass paths. Electric buggies available for use in the walled garden.

32 ◆ HOVETON HALL GARDENS
nr Wroxham NR12 8RJ. Mr & Mrs Andrew Buxton, 01603 782558, www.hovetonhallgardens.co.uk. *8m N of Norwich. 1m N of Wroxham Bridge. Off A1151 Stalham Rd - follow brown tourist signs.* **Adm £7, chd £3.50. For NGS: Sun 12 May, Tue 20 Aug (10.30-5). For other opening times and information, please phone or see garden website.**
15-acre gardens and grounds taking you through the seasons. Featuring daffodils, azaleas, rhododendrons and hydrangeas in woodland. Mature walled herbaceous and kitchen gardens. Tearooms open serving light lunches and afternoon tea. Gift shop and plant sales available. Guided walks and nature trails for children. A varied events programme runs throughout the open season. Please visit our website for more details. Under 4's free, OAP's £6.50. Wheelchair users and carers £5.

33 HOW HILL FARM
Ludham NR29 5PG. Mr P D S Boardman. *2m W of Ludham. On A1062; then follow signs to How Hill. Farm garden S of How Hill.* Home-made teas in Thatched Barn. **Adm £4, chd free. Sun 19 May (1-5).**
Broadland garden. 2 very different gardens around the house. 3rd garden started 1968 on green field site with 3 acre broad dug 1978 with views of Turf Fen Mill, R Ant and Reedham Marshes. Approx 12 acres incl Broad, 4 ponds, site of old Broad with 100yr old Tussock sedges 5ft tall, approx 1 acre of indigenous ferns under oak and alder. Paths through rare conifers, rhododendrons, azaleas, ornamental trees, shrubs and herbaceous plants. Collection of holly species and varieties. Various very old stone carvings used for seats, excellent vistas.

KENILWORTH SMALLHOLDING
See Cambridgeshire

THE LABURNUMS
See Suffolk

34 LAKE HOUSE
Postwick Lane, Brundall NR13 5LU. Mrs Janet Muter, 01603 712933. *5m E of Norwich. On A47; take Brundall turn at r'about. Turn R into Postwick Lane at T-junction.* Tea. **Adm £4, chd free. Visitors welcome by appt 14 Jan to 14 Dec, refreshments by arrangement.**
In the centre of Brundall Gardens, a series of ponds descends through a wooded valley to the shore of a lake. Steep paths wind through a variety of shrubs and flowers in season, which attract many kinds of rare birds, dragonflies and mammals. This is an historic water garden.

35 LEXHAM HALL
nr Litcham PE32 2QJ. Mr & Mrs Neil Foster. *2m W of Litcham. 6m N of Swaffham off B1145.* Home-made teas. **Adm £5, chd free. Sun 10 Feb (11-4); Sun 19, Mon 20 May; Wed 11 Sept (11-5).**
Fine C17/C18 Hall (not open). Parkland with lake and river walks. Formal garden with terraces, yew hedges, roses and mixed borders. Traditional kitchen garden with crinkle crankle wall. Extensive collection of scented, winter flowering shrubs and woods, carpeted with snowdrops. 3-acre woodland garden with azaleas, rhododendrons, camellias, spring bulbs, and fine trees. A major new planting scheme in the walled garden. Dogs on leads welcome Feb only.

Traditional kitchen garden with crinkle crankle wall . . .

36 ◆ MANNINGTON HALL
nr Saxthorpe/Corpusty NR11 7BB. The Lord & Lady Walpole, 01263 584175, www.manningtongardens.co.uk. *18m NW of Norwich. 2m N of Saxthorpe via B1149 towards Holt. At Saxthorpe/Corpusty follow sign posts to Mannington.* **Adm £6, chd free, concessions £5. For NGS: Sun 17 Mar (12-5). Evening Opening, wine, light refreshments, Fri 14 June (6-9). For other opening times and information, please phone or see garden website.**
20 acres feature shrubs, lake, trees and roses. Heritage rose and period gardens. Borders. Sensory garden. Extensive countryside walks and trails. Moated manor house and Saxon church with C19 follies. Wild flowers and birds. Gravel paths, one steep slope.

37 MANOR FARM, COSTON
Coston Lane, Coston, nr Barnham Broom NR9 4DT. Mr & Mrs J O Hambro. *10m W of Norwich. Off B1108 Watton Rd. Take B1135 to Dereham at Kimberley. After approx 300yds sharp L bend, go straight over down Coston Lane.* Cream teas and light refreshments. Picnics welcome. **Adm £5, chd free. Afternoon & evening opening Fri 12 July (3-8).**
Approx 3 acre country garden, several small garden rooms with both formal and informal planting. Walled kitchen garden, white, grass and late summer gardens, roses, herbaceous and shrub borders. Wild flower areas with ponds. Many interesting plants. Plant sale,. Some gravel paths and steps.

38 MANOR HOUSE FARM, WELLINGHAM
nr Fakenham, Kings Lynn PE32 2TH. Robin & Elisabeth Ellis, www.manor-house-farm.co.uk. *7m from Fakenham. 8m from Swaffham, ½ m off A1065 N of Weasenham. Garden is beside the church.* Home-made teas. **Adm £4.50, chd free. Sun 23 June (11-5).**
Charming 4-acre garden surrounds an attractive farmhouse. Many interesting features. Formal quadrants with obelisks. 'Hot Spot' with grasses and gravel. Small arboretum with specimen trees, pleached lime walk, vegetable parterre and rose tunnel. Unusual 'Taj' garden with old-fashioned roses, tree peonies, lilies and pond. Small herd of Formosan Sika deer. Featured in local Press and Country Life Magazine. Some gravel and a few steps negotiable with assistance.

39 4 MILL ROAD
Marlingford NR9 5HL. Mrs Jean Austen, 01603 880396, jeanausten101@btinternet.com. *6m W of Norwich. A47 to B1108 Watton Rd junction, 3rd on R. Bear R past mill & garden on R after village hall, (parking) before The Bell. From Easton, signed opp Des Amis.* Home-made teas. **Adm £3, chd free. Suns, Tues 30 June; 2 July; 4, 6 Aug (12-7). Visitors also welcome by appt June to Aug.**
Take home ideas from this small garden packed with unusual features. Designed as a collection of garden rooms divided by hedges, paths, arches and pleached limes. Colour-themed borders, Japanese garden, pond, vegetables and fruit. Wind sculpture. Views to the water meadows beyond. A children's trail, plenty of seats to sit, relax and enjoy the view. Children's trail. Featured in Amateur Gardening and Garden News. Two small steps, ramps available.

40 THE MOWLE
Staithe Road, Ludham NR29 5NP. Mrs N N Green, 01692 678213, ann@mowlegreen.fsnet.co.uk. *5m E of Wroxham. A1062 Wroxham to Ludham 7m. Turn R by Ludham village church into Staithe Rd. Garden ¼ m from village.* Home-made teas. **Adm £4.50, chd free. Sun 30 June (1.30-5.30); Tue 28 Jan 2014. Visitors also welcome by appt.**
Approx 2½ acres running down to marshes. The garden incl several varieties of catalpa. Japanese garden and enlarged wildlife pond with bog garden. A special border for gunnera as in Aug 2008 we were given full National Collection status. Boardwalk into wild area. Gunneras featured in the RHS 'The Garden'. 85% of the garden is acessable to wheelchairs.
NCH

NETHERHALL MANOR
See Cambridgeshire

41 NORTH LODGE
51 Bowthorpe Road, Norwich NR2 3TN. Bruce Bentley & Peter Wilson. *1½ m W of Norwich City Centre. In Bowthorpe Rd off Dereham Rd, turn after 150 metres L through cemetery gates (opp end of Bond St) to North Lodge. Parking restricted, can park outside gates. Bus services 5, 16, 19, 20, 21, 22, 23 and 24 stop at Dereham Rd - Bowthorpe Rd junction.* Home-made teas. **Adm £3, chd free. Suns 14, 21 July (11-5).**
Town garden 0.1 acre to Victorian Gothic Cemetery Lodge (not open), created from barren, challenging triangular plot over past 10yrs. Strong structure and attention to internal vista incl Gothic conservatory, formal pond, pergola, and classical-style summerhouse. Predominantly herbaceous planting. Adjacent associated historic parkland cemetery also worth a visit. New front garden planned for 2013. Featured on BBC Radio Norfolk Garden Club. Sloping gravel entrance drive, some width restriction. Access to main garden via three shallow steps or steep brickweave slope.

GROUP OPENING

42 NEW NORTHACRE VILLAGE GARDENS

Caston, Attleborough NR17 1DG. *From Watton head S towards Thetford via the A1075. At the Thompson Xrds (also posted Wayland prison) turn L. Follow the road into Caston, turn L just after village sign.* Teas at Cherry Tree Cottage. **Combined adm £4, chd free. Sun 30 June (11-4).**

NEW CHERRY TREE COTTAGE
Teresa & Geoff Mayes

NEW WILLOW FARM
Clive & Sandra Middleton

Cherry Tree Cottage, Plantsmans cottage garden which has evolved over a period of 10 years, to the front are grass walkways leading through the beautifully maintained shrub and herbaceous borders with the occasional topiary giving structure and interest. A simple evolving knot garden with sundial can be found at its centre. To the rear is a small gravelled garden planted with perennials, shrubs androck plants. Willow Farm, an overgrown field in 2002 evolving into a diverse family garden. Mixed shrub, perennial and herbaceous borders, vegetable gardens, small orchard with unusual fruit trees and a cold glasshouse with a variety of tomatoes and peppers. A natural pond with planted perimeter banks and wild area supporting varied wildlife.

43 NEW 167 NORWICH ROAD

Wymondham NR18 0SJ. Rachel & Richard Dylong. *3/4 m N of Wymondham centre. A47 to Wymondham. Take centre exit,straight to Waitrose and turn L at r'about. Garden on R after 1/4 m on the RH side of the old Norwich/Hethersett rd.* Home-made teas and homemade ice creams for sale. **Adm £3, chd free. Sat 8, Sun 9 June (10-4).**

In our 1/4 -acre town garden, created from a blank canvas 10 years ago, meandering pathways round a circular lawn to a secluded tropical haven, on to a sunken pergola, greenhouse with a cactus collection and a fruit and vegetable plot. We love to recycle and experiment. Featured in Amateur Gardening.

45 THE OLD RECTORY, BRANDON PARVA

Stone Lane, Brandon Parva NR9 4DL. Mr & Mrs S Guest. *9m W of Norwich. Leave Norwich on B1108 towards Watton, turn R at sign for Barnham Broom. L at T-junction, stay on rd approx 3m until L next turn to Yaxham. L at Xrds.* Home-made teas. **Adm £4, chd free. Sun 26 May (11-5).**

4-acre, mature garden with large collection (70) specimen trees, huge variety of shrubs and herbaceous plants combined to make beautiful mixed borders. The garden comprises formal lawns and borders, woodland garden including rhododendrons, pond garden, walled garden and pergolas covered in wisteria, roses and clematis which create long shady walkways. Croquet lawn open for visitors to play. Featured in EDP and Norfolk Magazine.

44 THE OLD RECTORY, RIDLINGTON

Ridlington, nr North Walsham NR28 9NZ. Peter & Fiona Black, www.oldrectorynorthforfolk.co.uk. *4m E of North Walsham 4m N of Stalham. Take B1149 Stalham to Bacton Rd, turn left at By Way to Foxhill sign continue to Xrds turn R past farm continue for 1/2 m house on R.* Home-made teas. **Combined adm £5, chd free with West View. Sun 19 May (12-5).**

A tranquil 2 acre garden around a former rectory. Established trees and some topiary. Mixed borders of shrubs, perennials, roses and bulbs, raised vegetable beds. A peaceful spot for a cup of tea! Stalham Brass Band 2-4pm. Childrens treasure hunt. BBQ 12-2. Gravel drive and some paths might be difficult if wet.

46 NEW ORCHARD COTTAGE

34 Prince Of Wales Road, Upton, Norwich NR13 6EW. Mike & Linda Brown. *3m W of Acle. Follow directions to The Firs where the car park for both properties will be. Turn R out of the car parking area and Orchard Cottage is the 3rd property on R (approx 400 metres).* Home-made teas. **Adm £4, chd free. Sun 14 July (11-5). Combined with The Firs.**

A 3/4 acre cottage garden with extensive traditional borders of shrubs and herbaceous plants. Planting to attract bees and butterflies. Small orchard and vegetable garden. Wildlife and wetland area against a backdrop of mature trees. Nearby is a public footpath to an observation platform to Upton Broad. Suitable footwear needed. Plants for sale at The Firs. Some shingle paths and a small bridge but garden is flat with additional grass paths.

Croquet lawn open for visitors to play . . .

47 OULTON HALL

Oulton, Aylsham NR11 6NU. Bolton Agnew. *4m W of Aylsham. From Aylsham take B1354. After 4m Turn L for Oulton Chapel, Hall 1/2 m on R. From B1149 (Norwich/Holt rd) take B1354, next R, Hall 1/2 m on R.* **Adm £5, chd free. Sun 2 June (1-5).**

C18 manor house (not open) and clocktower set in 6-acre garden with lake and woodland walks. Chelsea designer's own garden - herbaceous, Italian, bog, water, wild, verdant, sunken and parterre gardens all flowing from one tempting vista to another. Developed over 15yrs with emphasis on structure, height and texture, with a lot of recent replanting in the contemporary manner.

48 ◆ OXBURGH HALL

Oxborough PE33 9PS. National Trust, 01366 328926, www.nationaltrust.org.uk. *7m SW of Swaffham. At Oxborough on Stoke Ferry rd.* **Adm £4.50, chd £2.25. For NGS: Suns 16 June; 18 Aug (11-5). For other opening times and information, please phone or see garden website.**

Hall and moat surrounded by lawns, fine trees, colourful borders; charming parterre garden of French design. Orchard and vegetable garden. Woodland walks. A garden steward is on duty on open days to lead 4 free tours throughout the day. A map is available on arrival showing suitable paths for wheelchair access.

49 PLOVERS HILL

Buckenham Road, Strumpshaw NR13 4NL. Jan Saunt, 01603 714587, jan@saunt.vispa.com. *9m E of Norwich. Off A47 at Brundall continuing through to Strumpshaw village. Turn R 300yds past PO, then R at T-junction. Plovers Hill is 1st on R up the hill.* Home-made teas. **Adm £3.50, chd free. Sun 21 Apr; Sun 5, Mon 6 May; Sun 11 Aug (11-5). Combined with 16 Witton Lane adm £4.50, 21 April. Visitors also welcome by appt Apr to Sept.**

1-acre garden of contrasts, small C18 house (not open) with RIBA award winning orangery. Formal lawn hedged with yew and lesser species, huge mulberry, gingko, liquidambar and Japanese bitter orange, herbaceous borders with a range of varied plants and spring bulbs. Kitchen garden with orchard and soft fruits. Garden sculptures. Water feature. Cast aluminium silver birches. To the main part of the garden, some gentle steps to teas.

Created from a largely concrete and rubble farmyard using reclaimed materials . . .

50 NEW RECTORY COTTAGE

St. Andrews Lane, Congham, King's Lynn PE32 1DU. Jonathan & Sarah Beart. *3m E of King's Lynn. From King's Lynn, take the A148 signed to Fakenham & Cromer. After 2m from Knight's Hill r'about, turn R at the signpost to Roydon. ½ m further, turn L into St Andrew's Lane to Congham. Once in the village, turn into Church Hill where parking is adjacent to the Church.* Light refreshments and homemade teas. **Adm £4, chd free. Sun 4 Aug (11-5.30).**

An established plant-lover's cottage garden in ¾ acre, next to the Church (which will be open). Borders filled with a wide variety of herbaceous plants; shaded beds; gravel garden; mature trees; wildlife pond and shrubbery. A tranquil garden with several sitting areas, free-roaming bantams and dovecote. Plants for sale.

REDISHAM HALL

See Suffolk

RYDAL MOUNT

See Suffolk

51 NEW SAND PIT FARM NORTH

Overwood Lane, Forncett St. Peter, Norwich NR16 1LW. Christina Wakeford, christa.wake@gmail.com. *12m S of Norwich. Leave A140 at Long Stratton, Swan Lane, signed South Norfolk Council. Follow rd for approx 3m. In Forncett the rd bends R uphill at Mill Rd. At top of hill turn L onto Overwood Lane and take the 2nd farm track on the R. Car parking will be in an adjacent field.* Home-made teas. **Adm £4, chd free. Sun 23 June (11-5). Combined with Sandpit Farm South.**

A tranquil and structured cottage garden with bountiful planting,designed to complement the small C17 farmhouse. Created from a largely concrete and rubble farmyard using reclaimed materials. Hidden surprises and many creative touches. Sun/shade borders, small vegetable plot, a few hens, insect sanctuary, wildflower meadow with maze.

52 NEW SANDPIT FARM SOUTH

Overwood Lane, Forncett St. Peter, Norwich NR16 1LW. Cynthia Finlayson. *12m S of Norwich. Leave A140 at Long Stratton, Swan Lane, signed South Norfolk Council. Follow rd for approx 3m. In Forncett the rd bends R uphill at Mill Rd. At top of hill turn L onto Overwood Lane and take the 2nd farm track on the R. Car parking will be in an adjacent field.* Home-made teas. **Adm £4, chd free. Sun 23 June (11-5). Combined with Sandpit Farm North.**

One acre country garden developed over the last 5 years for colour and year round interest. Open, flowing design with island beds and features incl abundantly planted mixed borders, orchard meadow, annual mini-meadows, wisteria and old rose pergolas. Access is down an unmade farm track. Sloping garden with gravel paths and rough grass.

53 ◆ SANDRINGHAM GARDENS

Sandringham PE35 6EN. 01485 545408, www.sandringhamestate.co.uk. *6m NW of King's Lynn. By gracious permission, the House, Museum & Gardens at Sandringham will be open.* **For opening times and information, please phone or see garden website.**

60 acres of formal gardens, woodland and lakes, with rare plants and trees. Donations are given from the Estate to various charities. Gravel paths (not deep), long distances - please tel or visit website for our Accessibility Guide.

54 ◆ SEVERALS GRANGE

Holt Road, Wood Norton NR20 5BL. Jane Lister, 01362 684206, www.hoecroft.co.uk. *8m S of Holt, 6m E of Fakenham. 2m N of Guist on LH-side of B1110. Guist is situated 5m SE of Fakenham on A1067 Norwich rd.* **Adm £3, chd free. For NGS: Sun 11 Aug (2-5). For other opening times and information, please phone or see garden website.**

The gardens surrounding Severals Grange and the adjoining nursery Hoecroft Plants are a perfect example of how colour, shape and form can be created by the use of foliage plants, from large shrubs to small alpines. Movement and lightness is achieved by interspersing these plants with a wide range of ornamental grasses, which are at their best in late summer. New herbaceous borders opened in 2012 providing addtional mid to late summer interest. Extensive range of ornamental grasses and shrubs in various garden settings.

55 NEW SHAMMER HOUSE

Shammer, North Creake, Fakenham NR21 9LN. Charles Polito & Judi Tussaud. *At Shammer Xrds (between Stanhoe & North Creake) take road south marked 'to farm only'. After ⅓ m turn L into farm entrance.* Home-made teas. **Adm £4, chd free. Sats, Suns 1, 2, 15, 16 June (10-4).**

Walled garden in outstanding rural location with well stocked borders. Gravel drive and paths.

Warborough House

56 ◆ SHERINGHAM PARK
Wood Farm Visitors Centre, Upper Sheringham NR26 8TL. National Trust, 01263 820550, www.nationaltrust.org.uk/sheringham. *2m SW of Sheringham. Access for cars off A148 Cromer to Holt Rd, 5m W of Cromer, 6m E of Holt, signs in Sheringham town.* **For NGS: Thur 23 May; Thur 6 June (10-5). For other opening times and information, please phone or see garden website.**
80 acres of species rhododendron, azalea and magnolia. Also numerous specimen trees incl handkerchief tree. Viewing towers, waymarked walks, sea and parkland views. No adm charge to Sheringham Park, car park charge payable, £4.80 for non NT members. Special walkway and WCs for disabled. 1½ m route is assessable for wheelchairs, mobility scooters available to hire.

57 SUNDOWN
Hall Lane, Roydon, Diss IP22 5XL. Liz Bloom, 01379 642074, liza.bloom@yahoo.co.uk. *2m W of Diss. From Diss take A1066 Thetford Rd, after Roydon White Hart PH, turn R into Hall Lane. From Thetford on A1066, approx 1m after Blooms of Bressingham, turn L into Hall lane.* Home-made teas. **Adm £3.50, chd free. Sun 30 June (11-5). Visitors also welcome by appt Apr to Sept.**
1-acre plantsman's garden established over 40yrs ago. Densely planted with wide variety of unusual perennials, shrubs and trees for colour and foliage yr-round. Woodland walk with rhododendrons and other woodland favourites. Recently developed areas incl ornamental kitchen garden and terrace area with water features and a new informal pond and decking.

GROUP OPENING

58 NEW TWO NORWICH COMMUNITY GARDENS
Off Dereham Road, Norwich NR2 3AZ. Norwich City Council. *¾ to 1 m W of city centre From A11 straight to Inner ring rd, turn L and continue to Dereham Rd Turn L then 1st L into Valentine St for Grapes Hill garden, or continue through T-lights at Heigham Rd then 1st L into Belvoir St. Belvedere Centre and its car park are on L where rd ends. Belvedere garden is accessed through The Belvedere Centre or via the foot and cycle path and through a small gate L in wall beyond the children's play area.* Home-made teas Belvedere Centre Garden. **Combined adm £3, chd free. Sun 28 July (10-5).**

NEW THE BELVEDERE CENTRE GARDEN
Belvedere Community Centre.
There is limited parking in a small car park outside the community centre
http://thebelvedere.co.uk

NEW GRAPES HILL COMMUNITY GARDEN
Grapes Hill Community Garden Group.
On foot from W side of the bottom of Grapes Hill beside St. Benedict's View Business Units or off Dereham Rd from Valentine St. By vehicle from Valentine St (turn L at garages and follow road to its end). Parking by the garden is very limited. Further parking at Cathedral Retail Park (off Westwick Street) & St Andrew's car park.
www.grapeshillcommunitygarden.org

Two small community gardens with space for local residents to grow a range of garden plants from vegetables, fruit and flowers to shrubs and trees. Belvedere Centre Garden the garden, first created about twenty-five years ago, was extensively redesigned and replanted in 2012 by a team of volunteers. It includes a sunny bank with herbaceous border, a shade border and slate paths with grasses and ferns. Grapes Hill Community Garden this garden was created from a piece of tarmac in autumn 2010 and was planted up by volunteers. It contains raised vegetable beds, a wildflower meadow and mini-orchard, a lawn, herbs, ornamental flowers and shrubs. The emphasis is on edible plants, including many with edible flowers. Art and crafts fair at Belvedere centre, donation to NGS.

A peaceful spot for a moment of relaxation and a cup of tea . . .

59 ◆ THE URBAN JUNGLE GARDENS

Ringland Lane, Old Costessey NR8 5BG. Urban Jungle, 01603 744997, www.urbanjungle.uk.com. *5m W of Norwich. From Norwich: on A1074 Dereham Rd. After 3m turn R at Longwater Rd, at T-junction turn L into West End for 1m, turn R into Ringland Lane. Garden 200yds on R. From A1067 Fakenham Rd: turn L into Sandy Lane, then on to Taverham Lane and down to T-junction, turn L into Ringland Lane. Garden 200yds on R.* **Adm £3, chd free. For NGS: Sun 15 Sept (11-5). For other opening times and information, please phone or see garden website.**

Rare collectors' species with the best of exotic jungle garden with traditional plants displayed in garden compositions that demonstrate a wide range of styles and climate zones. Two vertical gardens, exotic and herbaceous borders, woodland garden. New for 2012 a prairie-style garden with ornamental grasses, and late flowering perennials.

60 WARBOROUGH HOUSE

Wells Road, Stiffkey NR23 1QH. Mr & Mrs J Morgan. *13m N of Fakenham, 4m E of Wells Next The Sea. On A149 in centre of Stiffkey Village, opp Post Office and Stores. Coasthopper bus stop outside garden. Garden Entrance is off the main road and parking is signposted. Please DO NOT park on the main road in the village as it is very narrow and will cause severe congestion.* Home-made teas. **Adm £4, chd free. Mon 27 May; Sun 28 July (1-5).**

7 acre garden on a steep chalk slope, surrounding C19 house (not open) with views across the Stiffkey valley and to the coast. Woodland walks, formal terraces, shrub borders, lawns and walled garden create a garden of contrasts. Garden is on a slope which is steep in parts. Paths are gravel, bark chip or grass and may be uneven.

GROUP OPENING

61 WELLS-NEXT-THE-SEA GARDENS

Wells-Next-The-Sea NR23 1DP. *10m N of Fakenham. B1105 from Fakenham and off A149 Kings Lynn to Cromer rd.* Home-made teas at Caprice. **Combined adm £5, chd free. Sat 7, Sun 8 Sept (11-5).**

CAPRICE
Clubb Lane. David & Joolz Saunders.
Coasthopper/Norfolk Green Bus to 'The Buttlands' follow NGS signs 1min from stop. Town Centre garden few metres walk from 'The Buttlands' - (a tree-lined Georgian green square)

7 MARKET LANE
Hazel Ashley.
Off Burnt St. Follow NGS signs Close to two other gardens

NORFOLK HOUSE
Burnt Street. Katrina & Alan Jackson.
Next to Poacher Cottage

NEW OSTRICH HOUSE
Burnt Street. Mr Stuart Rangeley-Wilson & Ms Janey Burland.
Opp Norfolk House & Poacher Cottage

POACHER COTTAGE
Burnt Street. Roger & Barbara Oliver.
Next door to Norfolk House. Coasthopper + X29 buses pass the house

Wells-next-the-Sea is a small friendly costal town on the glorious North Norfolk coast. Popular with families, walkers and bird watchers. The harbour has shops, cafes, fish and chips and a mile walk along The Run leads to the Lifeboat Station and Wells Beach. Wells is served by Norfolk Green Coast Hopper bus (Cromer-Kings Lynn) or NG 29 from Fakenham. Car park at Stearmans Yard behind the Ark Royal, the Buttlands or Market Lane where one of the gardens is situated. Advisable to tour gardens on foot. The route around the 5 gardens takes in the Parish Church of St Nicholas, the High St with its beautiful once shop windows and the tree lined Georgian green square, The Buttlands. The 5 town gardens, though small, demonstrate a variety of design and planting approaches incorporating herbaceous borders, 'cottage', shrubs and fruit. Wheelchair access at most gardens.

62 WEST LODGE

Aylsham NR11 6HB. Mr & Mrs Jonathan Hirst, jonathan.hirst@brickcourt.co.uk. *1/4 m NW of Aylsham. Off B1354 Blickling Rd out of Aylsham, turn R down Rawlinsons Lane, garden on L.* Home-made teas. **Adm £5, chd free. Sun 21 July (12-5). Visitors also welcome by appt Please email.**

9-acre garden with lawns, splendid mature trees, rose garden, well-stocked herbaceous borders, ornamental pond, magnificent C19 walled kitchen garden (maintained as such). Georgian house (not open) and outbuildings incl a well-stocked tool shed (open) and greenhouses. Most of the garden is easliy accessible to wheelchair users. Some recently repaired gravel areas a bit more difficult.

63 WEST VIEW

Youngmans Lane, East Ruston, nr Stalham NR12 9JN. Chris & Bev Hewitt. *3 m N of Stalham. Take B1149 Stalham to Bacton Rd turn L after East Ruston Church, continue 3/4 m turn L by Butchers Arms PH (Oak Lane), turn R into Youngmans Lane, 1st house on L.* **Combined adm £5, chd free with The Old Rectory, Ridlington. Sun 19 May (12-5).**

1 acre plantsmans garden incl borders with trees and shrubs underplanted with carpets of hellebores and bulbs, pergolas with roses and clematis, greenhouse with many interesting plants, a summer

border with mixed perennials, vegetable parterre, tropical border, orchard and pond. Gravel Paths.

64 WETHERED MANOR
Sedgeford, Hunstanton PE36 5LR. William & Louise Barber, 01485 570983. *From Heacham follow rd to Sedgeford, past war memorial them immed on L after sharp bend. From Docking 1/4 m into village, follow carrstone wall to entrance on R.* Home-made teas. **Adm £4, chd free.** **Sat 15, Sun 16 June (11-5).**
Georgian house surrounded by mature trees and ever evolving herbaceous borders, pergolas, roses, mixed borders, pleached hedging and lawn. With it's variety of 'rooms' there is always a surprise around the corner, including a walled garden.The conservatory is a peaceful spot for a moment of relaxation and a cup of tea to enjoy the plumbago and unusual abundant climbing geraniums. Home made produce and plant stall. Georgian house encirlced by mature trees and lawns. The borders are on different levels which creates interest and encourages expressive planting.

WHITE HOUSE FARM
See Suffolk.

65 WITTON HALL
nr North Walsham NR28 9UF. Sally Owles. *3 1/2 m from North Walsham. Off B1150 halfway between North Walsham & Bacton. Take R fork to Bacton Woods picnic area, driveway 200yds on L.* Light lunches & teas. **Adm £3, chd free.** **Mon 6 May (11-4).** **Also open Hill Cottage.**
A natural woodland garden. Walk past the handkerchief tree and wander through carpets of English bluebells, rhododendrons and azaleas. Walk from the garden down the field to the church. Stunning views over farmland to the sea. Wheelchair access difficult if wet.

66 16 WITTON LANE
Little Plumstead NR13 5DL. Sally Ward & Richard Hobbs. *5m E of Norwich. From B1140 Norwich to Acle rd after railway xing, turn R at 2nd Xrds, signed Little Plumstead next to Brick Kilns PH. Take 2nd L into School Lane, then 2nd R into Witton Lane. From A47 Norwich to Yarmouth rd take L signed Witton Green & Great Plumstead just past pylons. Then 1st R into Witton Lane keep going for 1 1/2 m, garden on L.* Light refreshments. **Adm £3, chd free.** **Sun 21 Apr (11-4).** **Combined with Plovers Hill adm £4.50.**
An 'Aladdin's Cave' for the alpine and woodland plant enthusiast. Tiny garden with wide range of rare and unusual plants will be of great interest with its species tulips, daffodils, scillas, dog's tooth violets, many more bulbous plants and an abundance of trilliums and wood anemones. A garden indeed for the plant specialist. National Collection of Muscari. Featured in The Garden when our National Collection of Muscari was featured. Very difficult due to narrow paths.

NCH

67 WOOD HILL, GRESSENHALL
East Dereham NR19 2NR. Mr & Mrs John Bullard. *2m W of East Dereham. A47 to East Dereham. Exit Dereham on the old A47, heading West, down the hill from the market place, past The George Hotel. 2nd R into Rushmeadow Rd. Proceed for 1m, over small brick hump back bridge. Entrance to our drive is immed on R.* Home-made teas. **Adm £4, chd free.** **Sun 2 June (2-5).**
3 acres, the Garden is set in mature parkland, includes water features, statues/stones, lily pond, varied rose gardens, yew hedging, vegetable garden, lawns with floodlighting for mature hardwood trees. One of East Anglia's oldest Tulip trees and beautiful oaks and copper Beech.

WOOTTENS
See Suffolk

68 WRETHAM LODGE
East Wretham IP24 1RL. Mr Gordon Alexander. *6m NE of Thetford. A11 E from Thetford, L up A1075, L by village sign, R at Xrds then bear L.* Teas in Church. **Adm £4, chd free.** **Sun 31 Mar; Mon 1 Apr (12-5).**
In spring masses of species tulips, hellebores, fritillaries, daffodils and narcissi; bluebell walk. In June hundreds of old roses. Walled garden, with fruit and interesting vegetable plots. Mixed borders and fine old trees. Double herbaceous borders. Wild flower meadows.

An 'Aladdin's Cave' for the alpine and woodland plant enthusiast . . .

Norfolk County Volunteers

County Organisers
Fiona Black, The Old Rectory, Ridlington, North Walsham NR28 9NZ, 01692 650247, blacks7@email.com
Anthea Foster, Lexham Hall, King's Lynn PE32 2QJ, 01328 701341, antheafoster@lexhamestate.co.uk

County Treasurer
Neil Foster, Lexham Hall, King's Lynn PE32 2QJ, 01328 701288, neilfoster@lexhamestate.co.uk

Publicity
Graham Watts, Dale Farm, Sandy Lane, Dereham NR19 2EA, 01362 690065, grahamwatts@dsl.pipex.com

Booklet Coordinator
Sue Guest, The Old Rectory, Stone Lane, Brandon Parva, Norwich NR9 4DL, 01362 858317, guest63@btinternet.com

Assistant County Organisers
Panda Allhusen, Bradenham Hall, Bradenham, Thetford IP25 7QP, 01362 687243/687279, panda@bradenhamhall.co.uk
Jenny Dyer, Orchard Barn,4 Lacey's Farm, Long Lane, Colby,NR11 7EF, 01263 761811, jandrdyer@btinternet.com
Stephanie Powell, Creake House, Wells Road, North Creake, Fakenham NR21 9LG, 01328 730113, stephaniepowell@creake.com
Jan Saunt, Plovers Hill, Buckenham Road, Strumpshaw NR13 4NL, 01603 714587, jan@saunt.vispa.com

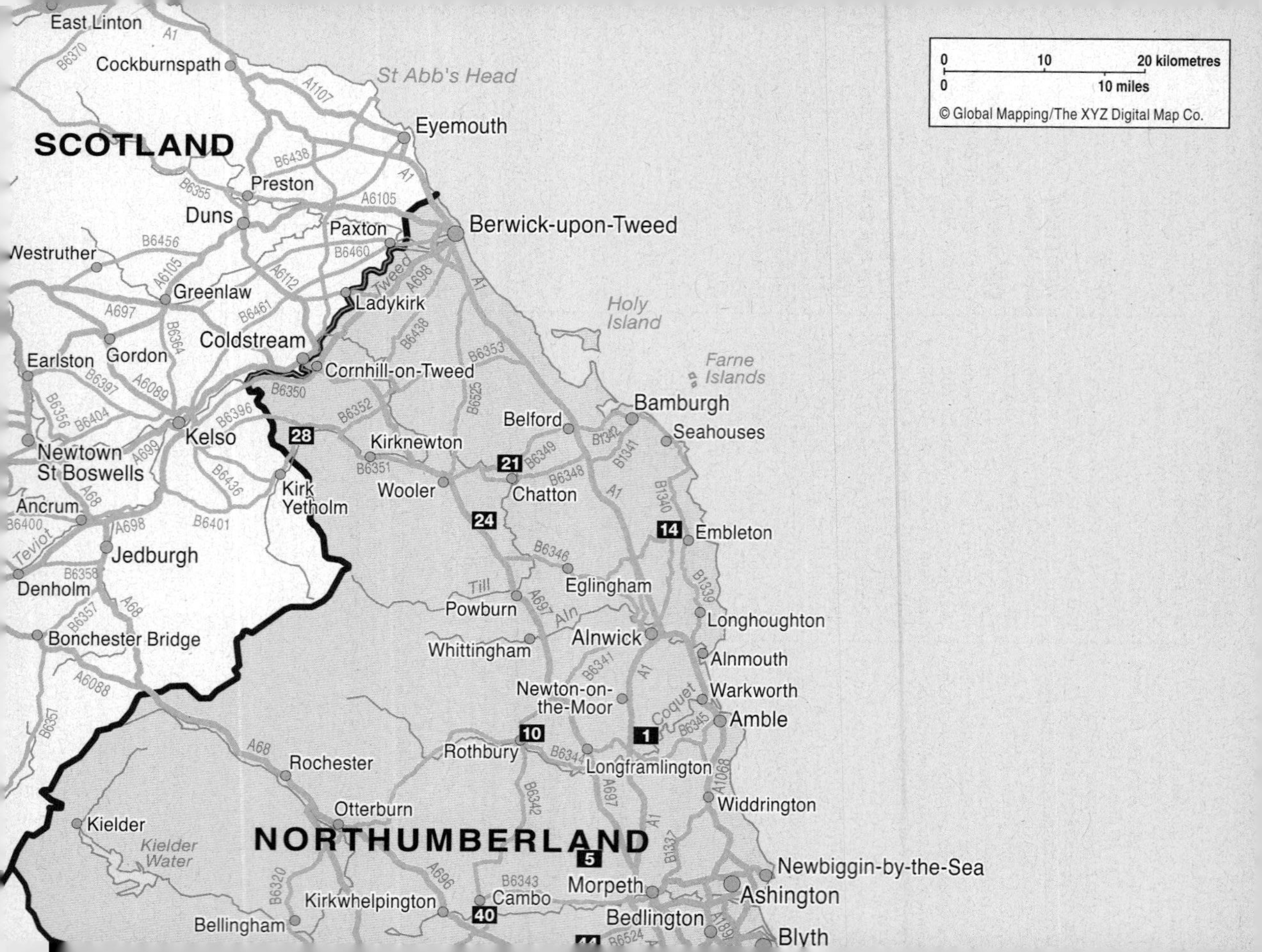

SCOTLAND
NORTHUMBERLAND
East Linton
Cockburnspath
St Abb's Head
Eyemouth
Preston
Duns
Paxton
Berwick-upon-Tweed
Westruther
Greenlaw
Ladykirk
Coldstream
Earlston
Gordon
Cornhill-on-Tweed
Holy Island
Farne Islands
Bamburgh
Seahouses
Belford
Kelso
Newtown St Boswells
Kirknewton
Wooler
Chatton
Kirk Yetholm
Ancrum
Jedburgh
Denholm
Embleton
Eglingham
Powburn
Bonchester Bridge
Longhoughton
Alnwick
Whittingham
Alnmouth
Newton-on-the-Moor
Warkworth
Amble
Rothbury
Longframlington
Rochester
Widdrington
Otterburn
Kielder
Kielder Water
Newbiggin-by-the-Sea
Morpeth
Ashington
Cambo
Kirkwhelpington
Bedlington
Bellingham
Blyth
Tweed
Till
Aln
Coquet
Teviot
0 10 20 kilometres
0 10 miles
© Global Mapping/The XYZ Digital Map Co.

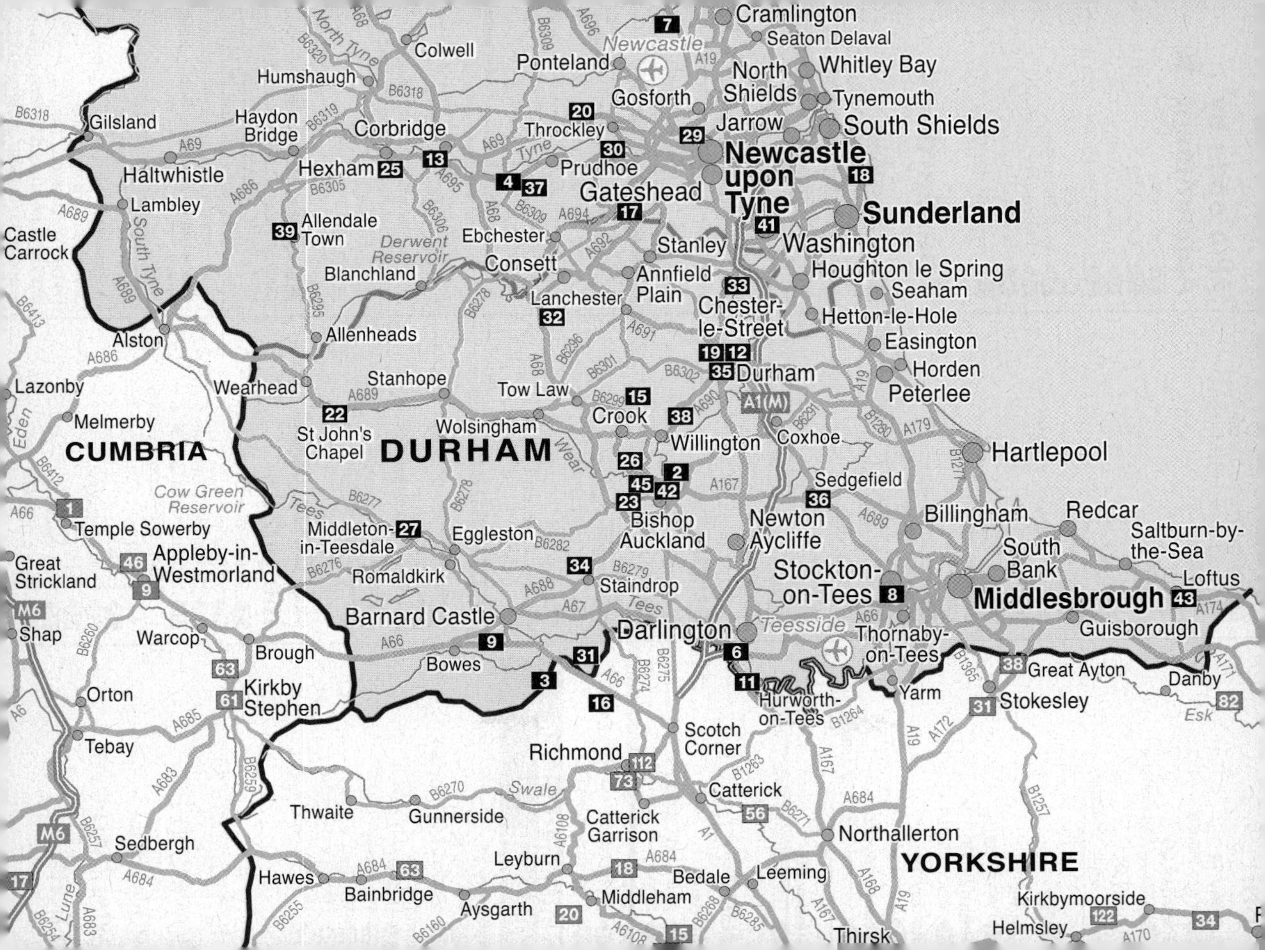

DURHAM
CUMBRIA
YORKSHIRE
Cramlington
Seaton Delaval
Whitley Bay
North Shields
Tynemouth
South Shields
Newcastle upon Tyne
Gateshead
Sunderland
Washington
Houghton le Spring
Seaham
Hetton-le-Hole
Easington
Horden
Peterlee
Hartlepool
Colwell
Ponteland
Gosforth
Jarrow
Humshaugh
Haydon Bridge
Corbridge
Throckley
Prudhoe
Hexham
Gilsland
Haltwhistle
Lambley
Castle Carrock
Allendale Town
Ebchester
Consett
Stanley
Annfield Plain
Chester-le-Street
Blanchland
Lanchester
Durham
Alston
Allenheads
Wearhead
Stanhope
Tow Law
Crook
Willington
Coxhoe
Lazonby
Melmerby
St John's Chapel
Wolsingham
Sedgefield
Bishop Auckland
Newton Aycliffe
Billingham
Redcar
Saltburn-by-the-Sea
Temple Sowerby
Middleton-in-Teesdale
Eggleston
Stockton-on-Tees
South Bank
Middlesbrough
Loftus
Great Strickland
Appleby-in-Westmorland
Romaldkirk
Staindrop
Barnard Castle
Darlington
Thornaby-on-Tees
Guisborough
Shap
Warcop
Brough
Bowes
Great Ayton
Danby
Orton
Kirkby Stephen
Hurworth-on-Tees
Yarm
Stokesley
Tebay
Scotch Corner
Richmond
Catterick
Thwaite
Gunnerside
Catterick Garrison
Northallerton
Sedbergh
Leyburn
Hawes
Bainbridge
Bedale
Leeming
Middleham
Aysgarth
Kirkbymoorside
Helmsley
Thirsk
Newcastle
Teesside
Cow Green Reservoir
Derwent Reservoir
North Tyne
South Tyne
Tyne
Wear
Tees
Swale
Eden
Lune
Esk
A1(M)
M6

Opening Dates

March

Sunday 17
29 Moorbank Botanic Garden

April

Sunday 14
42 West House

Saturday 20
5 Bide-a-Wee Cottage

Sunday 21
31 The Old Vicarage,

May

Sunday 12
40 Wallington

Saturday 18
1 Acton House

Sunday 19
24 Lilburn Tower

Wednesday 22
29 Moorbank Botanic Garden (Evening)

Sunday 26
3 Barningham Village Gardens

June

Sunday 2
2 Auckland Castle
7 Blagdon

Sunday 9
11 Croft Hall
41 Washington Old Hall

National Gardens Weekend

Saturday 15
16 The Forge
27 Middleton-in-Teesdale

Sunday 16
8 Briarcroft
16 The Forge
28 Mindrum
32 Oliver Ford Garden
39 Thornley House

Wednesday 19
12 Crook Hall & Gardens

Sunday 23
9 Browside

Saturday 29
14 Fallodon Hall

Sunday 30
4 The Beacon
13 Dilston Physic Garden & Northumberland Medicinal Plants

July

Sunday 7
16 The Forge
22 High Hill Top
44 Whalton Manor Gardens

Saturday 13
10 Cragside

Sunday 14
15 The Fold
21 Hetton House
25 Loughbrow House
35 St Margaret's Allotments
36 Sedgefield Gardens
40 Wallington

Sunday 21
6 Blackwell Gardens
29 Moorbank Botanic Garden
45 Woodside House

August

Saturday 3
5 Bide-a-Wee Cottage

Sunday 4
23 2 Hillside Cottage
38 4 Stockley Grove

Sunday 11
30 No. 2 Ferndene

September

Sunday 8
17 Gibside
29 Moorbank Botanic Garden

Sunday 22
20 Halls of Heddon

Gardens open to the public

5 Bide-a-Wee Cottage
10 Cragside
12 Crook Hall & Gardens
13 Dilston Physic Garden & Northumberland Medicinal Plants
17 Gibside
20 Halls of Heddon
34 Raby Castle
40 Wallington
41 Washington Old Hall

By appointment only

18 Glebe Farm
19 14 Grays Terrace
26 10 Low Row
33 25 Park Road South
37 Skara Brae

Also open by Appointment ☎

15 The Fold
22 High Hill Top
23 2 Hillside Cottage
25 Loughbrow House
28 Mindrum
30 No. 2 Ferndene
35 St Margaret's Allotments
39 Thornley House
45 Woodside House

Ha-ha, spring flowers in the woodland, extending over 5 acres . . .

The Gardens

1 ACTON HOUSE

Felton, Morpeth NE65 9NU. Mr Alan & Mrs Eileen Ferguson. *N of Morpeth. On old A1 N of Felton. Take turning to Acton, follow rd for 1/2 m until fork. Take R fork and follow signs*. Home-made teas. **Adm £4, chd free. Sat 18 May (1-4).**
This stunning walled garden has structure, colour and variety of planting, with displays of late Spring bulbs, abundant herbaceous perennials and different grasses. Planted in the spring of 2011, it has sections devoted to fruit and vegetables, David Austin rose borders, standard trees and climbers spreading over the brick walls. Additional mixed borders, ha-ha, spring flowers in the woodland, extending over 5 acres. Herbaceous perennial section incls species and varieties favoured by butterflies and bees (info available). May opening for spring perspective.
♿ ✿ ☕

2 AUCKLAND CASTLE

Market Place, Bishop Auckland DL14 7NR. Auckland Castle Trust. *Centre of Bishop Auckland. Follow brown signs to Castle*. Home-made teas. **Adm by donation. Sun 2 June (2-5).**
Gates open for free access to approx 5 acres of castle grounds laid extensively to lawns with 1/4 mile of gravel path walkways and herbaceous borders. The amphitheatre-shaped bowling green is one of the delights of the grounds.

Prestigious views from a raised walkway overlook Auckland Park, and the R Wear. First open to the public 1927. Several professional plant sellers, with some unusual plants. Castle will be open: entrance fee payable. Wheelchair access to grounds. For access to castle, please ring for details.

GROUP OPENING

3 BARNINGHAM VILLAGE GARDENS

Barningham DL11 7DW. Kay Duggan, www.plantsmancorner.co.uk. *6m SE of Barnard Castle. 9m W of Scotch Corner turn S off A66 at Greta Bridge, or from A66 Motel via Newsham.* Home-made teas at Barningham Village Hall. **Combined adm £4, chd free. Sun 26 May (12-5).**

6 interesting and varied gardens and one private nursery in the beautiful village of Barningham on the edge of the Yorkshire Dales. The gardens are intimate reflections of their owners' style and character; all in a delightful setting. The nursery has a collection of rarer cornus, holly, maple and conifer species.

4 THE BEACON

10 Crabtree Road, Stocksfield NE43 7NX. Derek & Patricia Hodgson. *12m W of Newcastle upon Tyne. From A69, Stocksfield turn off, into village. Pass station then cricket ground, on L.Turn R into Cadehill Rd & next R into Crabtree Rd. As Crabtree Rd is a cul de sac please park in Cadehill or main rds. If you like a good walk, park in the stn car park.* Cream teas. **Adm £3.50, chd free. Sun 30 June (2-6).**

This garden has been created over the last 14 years and illustrates how to make a garden, with lots of interest at different levels, on a steep site. Water gently runs through it, and it is planted with acers, apple and lilac trees, roses, rhododendron and herbaceous perennials. There are quiet, tranquil places to sit. Featured in Amateur Gardening Magazine and on Look North TV Programme.

5 ◆ BIDE-A-WEE COTTAGE

Stanton, Morpeth NE65 8PR. Mr M Robson, 01670 772238, www.bideawee.co.uk. *7m NNW of Morpeth. Turn L off A192 out of Morpeth at Fairmoor. Stanton is 6m along this rd.* **Adm £3, chd free. For NGS: Sat 20 Apr (1.30-4.30); Sat 3 Aug (1.30-5). For other opening times and information, please phone or see garden website.**

Unique secret garden created over the last 35 yrs out of a small sandstone quarry, it features rock and water. Unusual perennials are woven within a matrix of ferns, trees and shrubs. The garden contains the National Collection of centaurea, and many other plants seldom seen. Partial wheel chair access.

NCH

GROUP OPENING

6 NEW BLACKWELL GARDENS

45 / 46 Blackwell, Darlington DL3 8QT. Cath & Peter Proud / Christopher & Yvonne Auton. *SW of Darlington next to the R Tees. 1/2 way along Blackwell, which links Bridge Road (on A66 just past Blackwell Bridge) and Carmel Road.* Cream teas with home-made jams, cheese scones, teas and coffees. **Combined adm £4, chd free. Sun 21 July (12-5).**

Two contrasting town gardens. No. 46 is a plantsman's garden - compact but with a collection of unusual plants and trees, a pond and a summerhouse. No. 45 rises from the R Tees up to a garden with many mature trees, a wildlife meadow, pond, a herb and Mediterranean garden, shady borders, lawns and a colourful herbaceous border.

7 BLAGDON

Seaton Burn NE13 6DE. Viscount Ridley, www.blagdonestate.co.uk. *5m S of Morpeth on A1. A1 N of Newcastle 8m, turn on to B1318 towards Seaton Burn then L at r'about (Holiday Inn) and follow signs to Blagdon. Entrance to parking area signed.* Home-made teas. **Adm £4, chd free. Sun 2 June (1-4.30).**

Unique 27 acre garden encompassing formal garden with Lutyens designed 'canal', Lutyens structures and walled kitchen garden. Valley with stream and various follies, quarry garden and woodland walks. Large numbers of ornamental trees and shrubs planted over many generations. National Collections of Acer, Alnus and Sorbus. Trailer ride around the estate (small additional charge) and market stalls selling local produce. Limited wheelchair access.

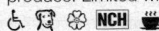

NCH

Hetton House

8 BRIARCROFT
27 Barnard Avenue, Grangefield, Stockton-on-Tees TS19 7AB. Mr Glenn Sunman. *1½ m W of Stockton centre. From A66 follow signs to Hartburn. Turn L into Greens Lane and follow yellow signs. Parking in Gainford Road please.* Home-made teas. **Adm £3.50, chd free. Sun 16 June (1-5).**
Beautiful wildlife-friendly garden designed by an award-winning design team. The centre piece is a wisteria-clad pergola on a formal lawn. A living willow arbour and tunnel lead to a small kitchen garden and tranquil reflective pool. Another feature is a small wild flower orchard bound by a dry-stone wall. Limited wheelchair access.

Pretty rose garden and mature box Italianate parterre are beautifully set . . .

9 BROWSIDE
Boldron, Barnard Castle DL12 9RQ. Mr & Mrs R D Kearton. *3m S of Barnard Castle. On A66 3m W of Greta Bridge, turn R to Boldron, then proceed ½ m. Entrance opp junction. From Barnard Castle take A67 to Bowes, after 2m turn L to Boldron.* Home-made teas. **Adm £2.50, chd free. Sun 23 June (1-5.30).**
1¼ acres with unusual water features and large collection of conifers and acers, wide range of plants and imaginative stone objects. Wonderfully tranquil seating areas. Wheelchair access to most of garden.

10 ◆ CRAGSIDE
Rothbury NE65 7PX. National Trust, 01669 620333, www.nationaltrust.org.uk. *13m SW of Alnwick. (B6341); 15m NW of Morpeth (A697).* **Adm £8.90, chd £4.50. For NGS: Sat 13 July (10-5). For other opening times and information, please phone or see garden website.**
The Formal Garden is in the 'High Victorian' style created by the 1st Lord and Lady Armstrong. Including orchard house, carpet bedding, ferneries and Italian terrace. New double herbaceous border for 2013. The largest sandstone Rock Garden in Europe with its tumbling cascades. Extensive grounds of over 1000 acres famous for Rhododendrons in June, large lakes and magnificent conifer landscape. The House, mainly the design of Norman Shaw, with its very fine arts and crafts interiors is worth a separate visit. Limited access to the Formal Garden.

11 CROFT HALL
Croft-on-Tees DL2 2TB. Mr & Mrs Trevor Chaytor Norris. *3m S of Darlington. On A167 to Northallerton, 6m from Scotch Corner. Croft Hall is 1st house on R as you enter village from Scotch Corner.* Home-made teas. **Adm £4, chd free. Sun 9 June (2-5).**
A lovely lavender walk leads to a Queen Anne-fronted house (not open) surrounded by a 5-acre garden, comprising a stunning herbaceous border, large fruit and vegetable plot, two ponds and wonderful topiary arched wall. Pretty rose garden and mature box Italianate parterre are beautifully set in this garden offering peaceful, tranquil views of open countryside. Some gravel paths.

12 ◆ CROOK HALL & GARDENS
Sidegate, Durham City DH1 5SZ. Maggie Bell, 0191 384 8028, www.crookhallgardens.co.uk. *Centre of Durham City. Crook Hall is short walk from Durham's Market Place. Follow the tourist info signs. Parking available at entrance.* **Adm £6.50, chd £5. For NGS: Wed 19 June (11-5). For other opening times and information, please phone or see garden website.**
Described in Country Life as having 'history, romance and beauty'. Intriguing medieval manor house surrounded by 4 acres of fine gardens. Visitors can enjoy magnificent cathedral views from the 2 walled gardens. Other garden 'rooms' incl the silver and white garden, and an orchard, moat, pool, maze and Sleeping Giant give added interest! Featured in national press, House Beautiful, Country Life, 25 Beautiful Gardens, Choice, etc and on television.

13 ◆ DILSTON PHYSIC GARDEN & NORTHUMBERLAND MEDICINAL PLANTS
nr Corbridge NE45 5QZ. Prof Elaine Perry, 07897 533875, www.dilstonphysicgarden.com. *1m W of Corbridge, 2m E of Hexham. On B695 between Corbridge & Hexham,just W of the junction with B6529. Car park on W side of main garden, entrance where Dilston Scout Camp is 5min walk (footpath).* **Adm £3, chd free. For NGS: Sun 30 June (1-4). For other opening times and information, please phone or see garden website.**
This garden, dedicated to the healing power of plants, has been established as an education and research venue. It is not a garden of finely tended herbaceous borders. Set in 2-acres beside the Devil's Water, over 800 plants are grown for their medicinal, magical or mind altering powers, each with a sign providing valuable information on the plant and its uses. Whilst being educational, Dilston is also designed for fun. It is child friendly, with places and sculptures that will keep children amused. This is a unique and quirky garden for those with a sense of adventure. Freshly picked and prepared herbal teas to order. For children - animal trail, chamomile lawn to lie on, kids play area with safe herbs for children to discover, kids drawing hut.

14 FALLODON HALL
Alnwick NE66 3HF. Mr & Mrs Mark Bridgeman. *5m N of Alnwick on A1. Turn R on B6347, and turn into Fallodon gates after 2m.* Home-made teas in stable yard. **Adm £3, chd free. Sat 29 June (2-5).**
12 acre garden, incl a 30 metre border, finishing beside a hot greenhouse and bog garden. The C18 walls of the kitchen garden surround cutting and vegetable borders and fruit greenhouse. The sunken garden from 1898 has recently been replanted by Natasha McEwen. Woodlands, pond and arboretum. Home-made teas in stable yard, and plant sale, predominantly of Fallodon plants. Featured in The Journal. Limited wheelchair access.

15 THE FOLD
High Wooley, Stanley Crook DL15 9AP. Mr & Mrs G Young, 01388 768412, gfamyoung@madasafish.com. *3m N of Crook. On A690 S from Durham turn R at Brancepeth Xrds (opp sign to Castle), After 3m follow yellow signs. From A1 going N on A68 take B6299 before Tow Law then after approx 2m follow yellow signs.* Home-made teas. **Adm £3.50, chd free. Sun 14 July (2-5). Visitors also welcome by appt Apr to Sept.**
Large, cottage-style garden, approx 1/2 acre at 700ft and with splendid views over countryside. Winner of Alan Siggens Memorial Award 2011: Beautiful Durham. Herbaceous borders and island beds. Ponds and numerous mature trees. Small roof garden, wide range of plants, many grown from seed and cuttings. Emphasis on colour, harmony and texture. Tour by garden owner at 3.30pm. Featured in Northern Echo.

Mixed borders leading to an old land hay meadow . . .

16 NEW THE FORGE
Ravensworth, Richmond DL11 7EU. Mr & Mrs Peter & Enid Wilson. *7m N of Richmond. Travel 5 1/2 m W on the A66 from Scotch Corner. Turn L to Ravensworth and follow NGS signs.* Cream teas. **Adm £2.50, chd free. Sat 15 June (4-7); Sun 16 June (2-5); Sun 7 July (2-7).**
The Blacksmith's Secret Garden - the garden is hidden from view behind The Forge House, Cottage and Blacksmith's Forge. It has a small wildlife pond with two natural stone features. There is a variety of trees, shrubs and mixed borders leading to an old land hay meadow. Wheelchair access across gravel path.

17 ◆ GIBSIDE
nr Rowlands Gill, Tyne and Wear NE16 6BG. National Trust, 01207 541820, www.nationaltrust.org.uk/gibside. *6m SW of Gateshead. Entrance on B6314 between Burnopfield & Rowlands Gill. Follow brown signs from A1 exit N of Metrocentre on to the A694. Regular bus service from Newcastle upon Tyne.* Light refreshments Potting Shed Cafe offers fresh seasonal lunches, home baked cakes and delicious afternoon teas. **Adm £7.50, chd £4. For NGS: Sun 8 Sept (10-6). For other opening times and information, please phone or see garden website.**
C18 landscape park designed by Stephen Switzer for one of the richest men in Georgian England, George Bowes, and his celebrated daughter Mary Eleanor. Inner pleasure grounds with tree lined avenue and productive walled garden, plus miles of woodland and riverside walks in the Derwent Valley. Ongoing restoration of the gardens and woodland, one of the National Trust's most ambitious such projects. Guided talks by the landscape gardener; see the walled garden come back to life as we restore it.

18 GLEBE FARM
Moor Lane, Whitburn, Sunderland SR6 7JP. John & Kathryn Moor, 0191 529 3120, kmoor@sky.com. *2m N of Sunderland. From junction of A19 & A184, follow A184 E through W & E Boldon. After passing Dog Track on L turn L at r'about onto A1018 towards South Shields. Take 2nd R (after 1m) onto Moor Lane. Farm & parking on R on entering village.* Light refreshments. **Adm £3, chd free. Groups welcome by appt May to Aug.**
This lovely garden is on the edge of the picturesque village of Whitburn. Its 3/4 acre has a range of colours, moods and styles - lawned and gravelled areas surrounded by herbaceous borders with David Austin roses, a wide variety of shrubs and herbaceous perennials. Ornamental trees, herb garden and small woodland. Views of the sea, and the North York Moors (on a good day). Featured on BBC Look North.

19 NEW 14 GRAYS TERRACE
Redhills, Durham DH1 4AU. Mr Paul Beard, 0191 384 1558. *Just off A167 on W side of Durham. 1/2 m S of A167 / A691 r'about, turn L into Redhills Lane. When road turns R with no entry sign, Grays Terrace is ahead. No.14 is at the very end.* **Adm by donation. Visitors welcome by appt Apr to Aug.**
A steeply sloping garden of about 2/3 acre with a superb view over Durham Cathedral, Castle and surroundings. Very informal garden; no bedding and a significant wild area. Planting is mixed with interest throughout the yr. Many unusual and rare plants. Particularly knowledgeable owner who is happy to escort groups round the garden.

20 NEW ◆ HALLS OF HEDDON
West Heddon Nursery, Heddon-On-The-Wall, Newcastle Upon Tyne NE15 0JS. Mr David Hall, 01661 852445, www.hallsofheddon.co.uk. *Approx. 5m W of Newcastle upon Tyne. Approx. 1m NW of Heddon on the Wall signposted off the B6318 (Military Road) at the bridge crossing the A69.* Refreshments. **Adm by donation. For NGS: Sun 22 Sept (10.30-4). For other opening times and information, please phone or see garden website.**
Halls is a world renowned family owned nursery, full of plants set against the backdrop of an orginal heated wall garden. But September sees a spectacular display of colour and foliage in its dahlia and chrysanthemum trial fields. Row upon row of brilliant hues of plants arranged to show type, colour and height. It lifts the spirits as winter approaches and makes a dahlia/chrysanthemum lover of every gardener. An introductory talk with a question and answer session will be provided in the morning and the afternoon by David Hall. Wheelchair access is possible but pathways can be tricky if it has been very wet!

21 HETTON HOUSE
Wooler NE71 6ET. Mr & Mrs J Lovett, www.janelovett.com. *2 1/2 m N of Chatton. 4m E of Wooler. On B6349. Signed between Chatton & Wooler on B6348.* Home-made teas. **Adm £4, chd free. Sun 14 July (2-6).**
3 acres of s-facing mature gardens. Large mixed herbaceous, rose and shrub borders. Informal, pretty paved garden. New Spring garden. Greenhouse, productive kitchen garden, lawns with ornamental trees and shrubs. Fine views across the beautiful Glendale Valley.

22 HIGH HILL TOP
St John's Chapel DL13 1RJ. Mr & Mrs I Hedley, 01388 537952. *7m W of Stanhope. On A689. Turn L into Harthope Rd after Co-op shop in St John's Chapel. Up hill for ½ m past the Animal Hotel. Garden next house on L.* Home-made teas. **Adm £3, chd free. Sun 7 July (10-4). Visitors also welcome by appt June to Sept.**
See what can be achieved in an exposed garden at 1200ft. Mixed planting includes a wonderful collection of sorbus, hostas, ferns, eucalyptus and candelabra primulas. The magnificent backdrop of the North Pennines offers stunning views from a garden full of thoughtfully placed pathways, interesting bridges and still and flowing water with associated planting. Featured in Amateur Gardening and North East Life.

23 2 HILLSIDE COTTAGE
Low Etherley, Bishop Auckland DL14 0EZ. Mrs M Smith, 01388 832727, mary@maryruth.plus.com. *3m W of Bishop Auckland. From Bishop Auckland take B6282 to Etherley. Turn R opp no. 63 Low Etherley into Heritage Railway Trail (signed), follow the road down and round to the white cottage. From A68 take B6282 for ½ m, then turn L as above. Parking available at Greencroft Farm on B6282 east of the cottage.* Home-made teas. **Adm £3, chd free. Sun 4 Aug (1.30-5). Visitors also welcome by appt Mar to Oct.**
The large island beds featuring conifers, heathers and perennials, are bordered by grass paths with views over Weardale. Interesting shrubs and trees grow throughout the garden. A greenhouse has tender plants and vegetables. There is a fruit cage, fruit trees, vegetable beds and herbs. Two ponds and naturally managed areas attract wildlife. Tucked away at the bottom of the garden are beehives. Featured on local radio. It is possible to negotiate most of the garden using shallow steps.

24 LILBURN TOWER
Alnwick NE66 4PQ. Mr & Mrs D Davidson. *3m S of Wooler. On A697.* Home-made teas. **Adm £4, chd free. Sun 19 May (2-6).**
10 acres of magnificent walled and formal gardens set above river; rose parterre, topiary, scented garden, Victorian conservatory, wildflower meadow. Extensive fruit and vegetable garden, large glasshouse with vines. 30 acres of woodland with walks. Giant lilies, meconopsis around pond garden. Rhododendrons and azaleas. Also ruins of Pele Tower, and C12 church. Home made teas. Limited wheelchair access.

Hellebores, snowdrops, daffodils, bluebells and tulips, with later summer flowering perennials . . .

25 LOUGHBROW HOUSE
Hexham NE46 1RS. Mrs K A Clark, 01434 603351, patriciaclark351@btinternet.com. *1m S of Hexham. Take B6306 from Hexham, signed Blanchland, after ¼ m take RH-fork. After a further ¼ m you come to another fork, lodge gates are at intersection. Garden ½ m up the drive.* Home-made teas. **Adm £3, chd free. Sun 14 July (2-5). Visitors also welcome by appt Mar to Oct.**
Country house garden with sweeping, colour themed herbaceous borders set around large lawns. Unique Lutyens inspired rill with grass topped bridges. Old fashioned roses. Part walled kitchen garden and paved courtyard. Bog garden with pond. Wildflower meadow with specimen trees. Woodland quarry garden with rhododendrons, azaleas, hostas and rare trees. Home made jams and chutneys. Featured in Hexham Courant and The Northumbrian.

26 10 LOW ROW
North Bitchburn, Crook DL15 8AJ. Mrs Ann Pickering, 01388 766345, keightleyann@yahoo.co.uk. *3m NW of Bishop Auckland. From Bishop Auckland take A689 (N) to Howden-le-Wear. R up Bank before petrol stn, 1st R in village at 30mph sign.* **Adm £2. Visitors welcome by appt.**
Quirky, original and truly organic garden: 90% grown from seeds and cuttings. Created without commercially bought plants or expense. Environmentally friendly. A haven for wildlife: frogs have colonised a bath! Sloping garden with a myriad of paths and extensive views over the Wear valley. Beautiful yr-round from snowdrops to autumn leaves. Open all yr except Tuesdays. Book by phone or e-mail. Good food at Red Lion in village. Featured on TV and in Amateur Gardening, Northern Echo.

GROUP OPENING

27 NEW MIDDLETON-IN-TEESDALE
Market Place, Middleton-In-Teesdale, Barnard Castle DL12 0QG. *Gardens are all located in the village. Tickets and map with directions to each garden available from several, clearly marked, village locations.* Home-made teas in village hall. **Combined adm £4, chd free. Sat 15 June (1-5).**
4+ gardens will be open in this delightfully picturesque village, showing a variety of sizes, designs and planting.

28 MINDRUM
Mindrum, nr Cornhill on Tweed & Yetholm TD12 4QN. Mrs V Fairfax, 01890 850246, ginny@mindrumgarden.co.uk, www.mindrumgarden.co.uk. *6m SW of Coldstream, 9m NW of Wooler. Off B6352, 4m N of Yetholm. 5m from Cornhill on Tweed.* Home-made teas. **Adm £3.50, chd free. Sun 16 June (2-6). Visitors also welcome by appt May to Sept, adm £5 incl guided walk. Coach tours welcome. Lunch can be pre-booked.**
3 acres of romantic planting with old fashioned roses, lilies, herbs, sweet peas, scented shrubs, and intimate garden areas hedged by yew. Glasshouses with vines, jasmine. Large hillside rock garden with water leading to a pond, delightful stream, woodland and wonderful views across Bowmont valley with further river walks. Plants galore. Large plant sale, mostly home grown. Limited wheelchair access due to landscape. Blue badge parking close to house.

High Hill Top

29 MOORBANK BOTANIC GARDEN

University of Newcastle, Claremont Road, Newcastle upon Tyne NE2 4NL. University of Newcastle, www.ncl.ac.uk/biology/about/facilities/Moorbank/. *3/4 m from Newcastle Haymarket. W end of Claremont Rd, just E of Cat & Dog Shelter. Shared entrance with Town Moor Superintendents Farm (blue gate). 12 mins walk up Claremont Rd from Exhibition Park entrance r'about. No parking in garden. On st parking.* Home-made teas. **Adm £3, chd free. Sun 17 Mar (1-4); Evening Opening Wed 22 May, wine (4-8); Suns 21 July; 8 Sept (2-5).**

Hidden behind a high wall is a 3 acre university botanic garden with collections of rare conifers, rhododendrons, sorbus, pond, perennials, herb garden, wildflower meadow, including plant collections originally from Kilbryde Gardens, Corbridge. Extensive plantings under glass with tropical plants, succulents, insectivorous plants. Economically valuable plants; pomegranate, pineapple, date palm.

30 NEW NO. 2 FERNDENE

2 Holburn Lane Court, Ryton NE40 3PN. Maureen Kesteven, 0191 4135937, maureen@patrickkesteven.plus.com. *In Ryton Old Village, 8m W of Gateshead. On Holburn Lane, off B6317. Park in car park next to the Co-op on High Street, cross road and walk through Ferndene Park, or park near Village Green in Old Ryton Village.* Home-made teas. **Adm £4, chd free. Sun 11 Aug (1-4.30). Visitors also welcome by appt Apr to May.**

A garden of approx. 3/4 acre developed over the last 3 years, it is surrounded by mature trees. Informal areas of herbaceous perennials, a more formal box bordered area, vegetable patch, wildlife pond, bog and fern gardens, with lots of early interest - hellebores, snowdrops, daffodils, bluebells and tulips, with later summer flowering perennials. 1 1/2 acre mixed broadleaf wood being restored.

31 THE OLD VICARAGE,

Hutton Magna, nr Richmond, N Yorkshire DL11 7HJ. Mr & Mrs D M Raw. *8m SE of Barnard Castle. 6m W of Scotch Corner on A66. Turn R, signed Hutton Magna. Continue to, and through, village. Garden 200yds past village on L, on corner of T-junction.* Home-made teas. **Adm £3, chd free. Sun 21 Apr (2-5.30).**

S-facing garden, elevation 450ft. Plantings, since 1978, now maturing within original design contemporary to 1887 house (not open). Cut and topiary hedging, old orchard, rose and herbaceous borders featuring hellebores in profusion, with tulips and primulas. Large and interesting plant sale.

32 OLIVER FORD GARDEN

Longedge Lane, Rowley, Consett DH8 9HG. Bob & Bev Tridgett, www.gardensanctuaries.co.uk. *5m NW of Lanchester. From Castleside approx 1m S on A68 turn L to Lanchester 1/2 m on L. From Lanchester B6296 signed Satley approx 2m turn R at Woodlea Manor, garden 2.9m on R.* Light refreshments. **Adm £3, chd free. Sun 16 June (1-5).**

Spectacular 1 1/2 -acre woodland garden that includes rare acers, stewartia, betula and prunus. Stream, wildlife pond and bog garden. Japanese maple and dwarf rhododendron garden. 80 sq metre rock garden containing a significant collection of dwarf conifers. Large insect nectar garden. Orchard and 1 1/2 -acre upland meadow. Annual wild flower area.

33 25 PARK ROAD SOUTH

Chester le Street DH3 3LS. Mrs A Middleton, 0191 388 3225. *4m N of Durham. A167 N towards Chester le Street. L at r'about (Durham Rd) to town centre. 1st R for parking and rear access to garden only. S from A1 - 3rd r'about then R as above.* Home-made teas. **Adm £2.50, chd free. Visitors welcome by appt May to July.**

Plantswoman's garden with all-yr round interest, colour, texture and foliage. Unusual perennials, grasses, shrubs and container planting. Cool courtyard garden using foliage only. Small front gravel garden. Lots of unusual plants for sale! Featured in North East Life magazine.

34 ◆ RABY CASTLE
Staindrop, Darlington DL2 3AH. Lord Barnard, 01833 660202, www.rabycastle.com. *12m NW of Darlington, 1m N of Staindrop. On A688 8m NE of Barnard Castle.* **For opening times and information, please phone or see garden website.**
C18 walled gardens set within the grounds of Raby Castle. Designers such as Thomas White and James Paine have worked to establish the gardens, which now extend to 5 acres, displaying herbaceous borders, old yew hedges, formal rose gardens and informal heather and conifer gardens. Assistance will be needed for wheelchairs.

ALLOTMENTS

35 ST MARGARET'S ALLOTMENTS
Margery Lane, Durham DH1 4QG, 0191 386 1049, carolereeves21@btinternet.com. *From A1 take A690 to city centre/Crook. Straight ahead at T-lights after passing 4 r'abouts. Pedestrians walk up Sutton St from big r'about at viaduct. Allotments L in Margery Lane.* Home-made teas. **Combined adm £2.50, chd free. Sun 14 July (2-5). Visitors also welcome by appt June to Sept.**
5 acres of 82 allotments against the spectacular backdrop of Durham Cathedral. This site has been cultivated since the Middle Ages, and was saved from development 20yrs ago, allowing a number of enthusiastic gardeners to develop plots which display a great variety of fruit, vegetables and flowers. Display about successful campaign to save the allotments from development. Live music on the community plot. Guided Tours. Art in the Allotments. Featured in Northern Echo Garden News.

GROUP OPENING

36 SEDGEFIELD GARDENS
Sedgefield TS21 2AE. *Village green. Sedgefield is E of the A1(M), ajacent to the r'about junctions of the A177 and A689.* Home-made teas at Ceddesfeld Hall, adjacent to village green. **Combined adm £3.50, chd free. Sun 14 July (1-5).**
Selection of 8-10 gardens in a beautiful town, featuring water gardens, cottage planting and oriental display. Northumbria in Bloom Gold award winners. Sedgefield boasts the magnificent C13 St Edmund's church set on traditional village green. Marquee on village green selling various garden crafts. Limited wheelchair access.

Added interest of statuary and water features, including small stream at bottom of the garden . . .

37 NEW SKARA BRAE
20 Tynedale Gardens, Stocksfield NE43 7EZ. Ann Mates, 01661 843175. *14m W of Newcastle upon Tyne. 9m E of Hexham. A1/A69 then B6309 into Stocksfield Village. From W, past station and cricket ground. At Quaker meeting house turn into New Ridley Rd. 2nd R is Tynedale Gardens.* Tea. **Adm £2.50, chd free. Visitors welcome by appt June to Aug, Sat, Mon or Tue. Minibuses acceptable.**
A developing summer cottage-style garden, with established shrubs and herbaceous planting, that is continuously being improved, on SW-facing site 150ft x 40ft. Added interest of statuary and water features, including small stream at bottom of the garden.

38 4 STOCKLEY GROVE
Brancepeth DH7 8DU. Mr & Mrs Bainbridge. *5m W of Durham City. Take the A690 from Durham to Brancepeth. No parking allowed in Stockley Grove. Please park in the Castle car park which is signposted and walk to the garden following the signs. Transport to the garden is available for those who need it.* Home-made teas. **Adm £4, chd free. Sun 4 Aug (2-5).**
A stunning ½ -acre garden with inspirational planting to provide yr-round colour and interest. Landscaped with hidden grassy paths with many unusual trees, shrubs and plants incl wildlife pond, rockery area and water features.

39 THORNLEY HOUSE
Thornley Gate, Allendale, Northum NE47 9NH. Ms Eileen Finn, 01434 683255, enquiries@thornleyhouse.co.uk, www.thornleyhouse.co.uk. *1m W of Allendale. From Allendale town, down hill from Allendale Inn to 5 rd junction, 1m away.Thornley House is big house in field opposite, with private drive leading to it from jnct.* Home-made teas. **Adm £4, chd free (share to Brooke Charity for Working Animals). Sun 16 June (2-5). Visitors also welcome by appt.**
1-acre country garden with perennials, wildflowers, shrubs, conifers, stream and pond. Vegetables and fruit, rose avenue and peaceful woodland reached across field. A feline theme is evident throughout this child-friendly garden. Seek and find quiz is available for family fun. Maine Coon cats and ornamental animals enhance this garden. Featured in The Northumbrian magazine.

40 ◆ WALLINGTON
Cambo NE61 4AR. National Trust, 01670 774389, www.nationaltrust.org.uk/wallington. *12m W of Morpeth 20m NW Newcastle. From N B6343; from S via A696 from Newcastle, 6m W of Belsay, B6342 to Cambo.* **Adm £7, chd £3.50. For NGS: Suns 12 May; 14 July (10-5). For other opening times and information, please phone or see garden website.**
Walled, terraced garden with fine herbaceous and mixed borders; Edwardian conservatory; 100 acres woodland and lakes. House dates

from 1688 but altered, interior greatly changed c1740; exceptional rococo plasterwork by Francini brothers. Head Gardener's Question Time 12-4 both days. 12th May Create your own Container Planting with Wallington bedding to take away. (Charge made for NGS) 14th July Music in the Garden with local artist. Wheelchair access limited to top terrace in Walled Garden but elsewhere possible with care and support.

Pergolas and walls, festooned with rambling roses and clematis . . .

41 ◆ WASHINGTON OLD HALL
The Avenue, Washington Village NE38 7LE. National Trust, 0191 416 6879, www.nationaltrust.org.uk. *7m SE of Newcastle upon Tyne. Exit A1 J64 onto A195 then follow brown signs to Washington Old Hall. From A19 & other routes take A1231 & follow brown signs to Washington Old Hall in Washington Village, next to church on the hill.* Home-made teas Friends tearoom in the garden (run by volunteers). **Adm £2, chd free. For NGS: Sun 9 June (12-4). For other opening times and information, please phone or see garden website.**
The picturesque stone manor house and its gardens provide a tranquil oasis in an historic setting. It contains a formal Jacobean garden with box hedging borders around evergreens and perennials, vegetable garden, wild flower nut orchard with bee hives. Places to sit out and enjoy a picnic or afternoon tea. Refreshments supplied by Friends of Washington Old Hall. The wild flower nut orchard and the knot garden. Bargain plant sale. The garden has a lift which allows wheelchair users full access to the whole area.

42 NEW WEST HOUSE
5 Etherley Lane, Bishop Auckland DL14 7QR. Dr & Mrs R McManners. *Park in Bondgate car park, Bishop Auckland. 250 metre walk to house; route clearly signed.* Home-made teas. **Adm £3, chd free. Sun 14 Apr (2-5).**
A domestic, semi-rustic town garden surrounding 3 sides of this mid C19 town house. Probably originally laid out in 1856, there is now a more recent terraced garden on the site of the original orchard. To the rear of the house is a small, walled 'Dutch Yard Garden', complete with fountain which may well have been enjoyed by Sir Edward Elgar during his many visits to West House. Wheelchair access to viewing point.

44 WHALTON MANOR GARDENS
Whalton NE61 3UT.
Mr & Mrs T R P S Norton, www.whaltonmanor.co.uk. *5m W of Morpeth. On the B6524, the house is at the east end of the village and will be signed.* **Adm £4, chd free. Sun 7 July (2-5.30).**
The historic Whalton Manor, altered by Sir Edwin Lutyens in 1908, is surrounded by 3 acres of magnificent walled gardens, designed by Lutyens with the help of Gertrude Jekyll. The gardens have been developed by the Norton family since the 1920s and incl extensive herbaceous borders, 30yd peony border, rose garden, listed summerhouses, pergolas and walls, festooned with rambling roses and clematis. Partial wheelchair access. Some stone steps.

45 WOODSIDE HOUSE
Witton Park, Bishop Auckland DL14 0DU. Charles & Jean Crompton, 01388 609973, j.crompton@talktalk.net. *2m N of Bishop Auckland. From Bishop Auckland take A68 to Witton Park. In village please park in Main St. Then follow signs down track next to St Paul's Church. Parking for disabled at the garden. DO NOT follow sat nav.* Home-made teas. **Adm £4, chd free. Sun 21 July (1-5). Visitors also welcome by appt May to Sept.**
Stunning 3-acre, mature, undulating garden full of interesting trees, shrubs and plants. Superbly landscaped with island beds, flowing herbaceous borders, an old walled garden, rhododendron beds, 3 ponds and vegetable garden. Delightful garden full of interesting and unusual features, much to fire the imagination. Limited wheelchair access.

North East County Volunteers

County Organisers
County Durham Jean Morley, The Willows, Lumley Lane, Kirkby Fleetham, Northallerton DL7 0SH, 01609 748066, morley@the-willows.wanadoo.co.uk
Northumberland and Tyne and Wear Maureen Kesteven, No. 2 Ferndene, Holburn Lane Court, Ryton NE40 3PN, 0191 4135937, maureen@patrickkesteven.plus.com

County Treasurers
County Durham Gill Naisby, 44 Whitebridge Drive, Darlington DL1 3TY, 01325 381324, gillnaisby@tiscali.co.uk
Northumberland and Tyne and Wear David Oakley, david@susie-white.co.uk

Publicity
County Durham Kay Duggan, Braeside, Barningham, Richmond, North Yorkshire DL11 7DW, 01833 621455, kay@kayduggan.fsnet.co.uk
Northumberland and Tyne and Wear Susie White, 07941 077595, susie@susie-white.co.uk

Assistant County Organisers
County Durham Shanah Smailes, The Stables, Chapman's Court, Catterick Village, North Yorkshire DL10 7UE, 01748 812887, shanah@talktalk.net
Northumberland and Tyne and Wear Patricia Fleming, Wooperton Hall, Alnwick NE66 4XS 01668 217009
Northumberland and Tyne and Wear Natasha McEwen, Fowberry Mains Farmhouse, Wooler NE71 6EN, 01668 282092

NORTHAMPTONSHIRE

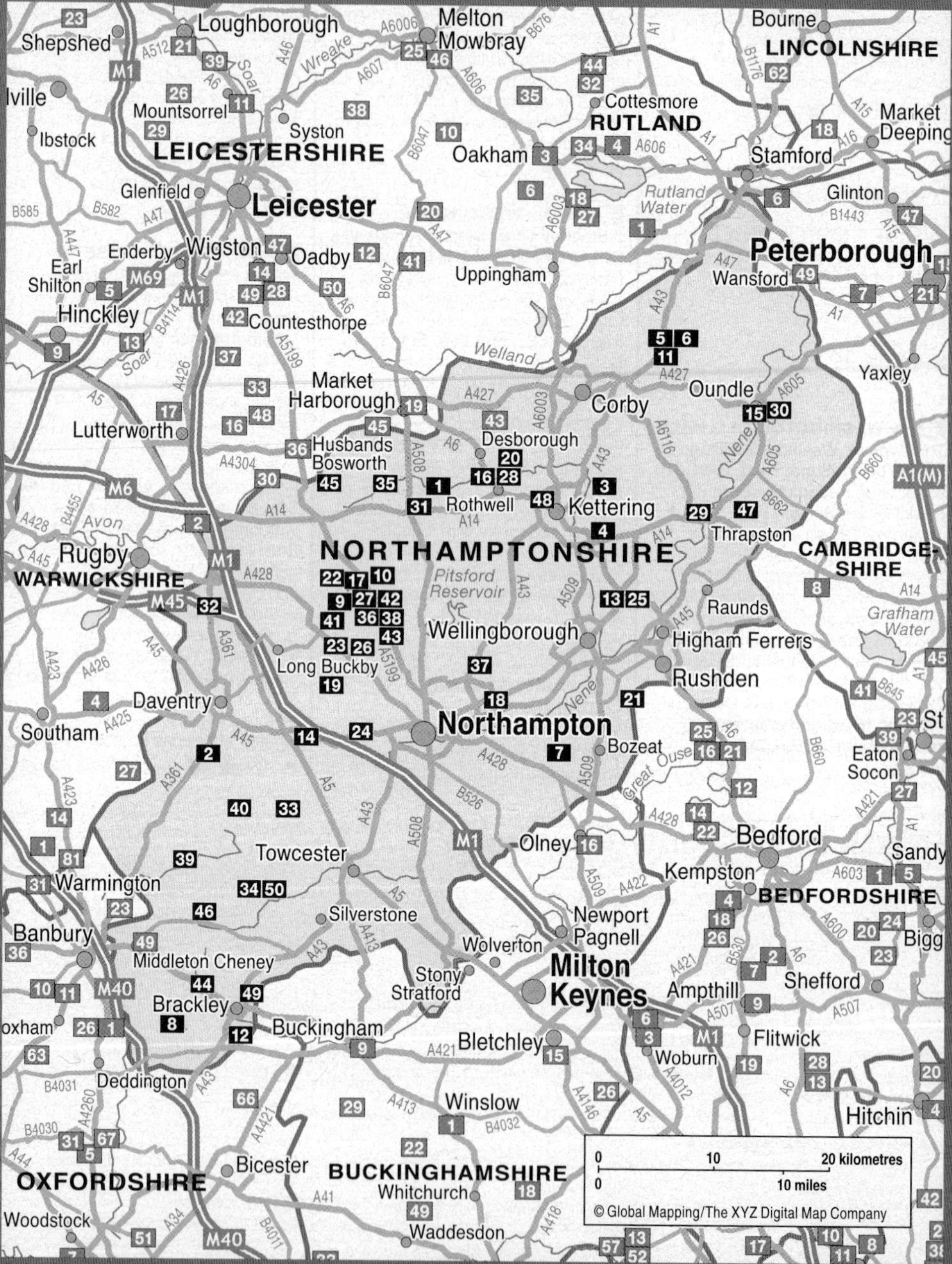

Opening Dates

February

Saturday 23
3 Boughton House

Sunday 24
3 Boughton House
30 Jericho
42 Rosemount

March

Sunday 3
21 Greywalls

Sunday 24
38 Mulberry Cottage

Saturday 30
35 The Maltings

Sunday 31
35 The Maltings

April

Monday 1
35 The Maltings

Saturday 6
4 Briarwood

Sunday 7
4 Briarwood

Sunday 14
14 Flore Gardens
33 Litchborough Gardens

Sunday 21
10 Cottesbrooke Hall Gardens
34 Lois Weedon House

Thursday 25
45 Sulby Gardens

Saturday 27
22 Guilsborough Gardens
23 Haddonstone Show Gardens

Sunday 28
22 Guilsborough Gardens
23 Haddonstone Show Gardens

May

Saturday 4
12 Evenley Wood Garden

Sunday 5
12 Evenley Wood Garden
19 Great Brington Gardens

Tuesday 7
9 Coton Manor Garden

Sunday 12
20 Greenway
43 Spratton Gardens

Tuesday 14
31 Kelmarsh Hall

Sunday 19
8 Charlton Gardens
11 Deene Park
30 Jericho
47 Titchmarsh House

Thursday 23
20 Greenway (Evening)

Sunday 26
35 The Maltings
49 Turweston Gardens

Monday 27
35 The Maltings

June

Sunday 2
13 Finedon Gardens
40 Preston Capes Gardens

Thursday 6
25 67-69 High Street (Evening)

Saturday 8
47 Titchmarsh House

Sunday 9
2 Badby and Newnham Gardens
18 Great Billing Village
24 Harpole Gardens
32 Kilsby Gardens
48 Top Lodge

Thursday 13
25 67-69 High Street (Evening)

National Gardens Weekend

Sunday 16
6 Bulwick Hall
15 Foxtail Lilly
20 Greenway
39 The Old Rectory

Thursday 20
25 67-69 High Street (Evening)
45 Sulby Gardens

Saturday 22
14 Flore Gardens

Sunday 23
14 Flore Gardens
28 Hostellarie
29 Islip Gardens
46 Sulgrave Gardens

Thursday 27
13 67-69 High Street (Evening)

Sunday 30
1 Arthingworth Open Gardens
13 Finedon Gardens
50 Weedon Lois & Weston Gardens

July

Sunday 7
7 Castle Ashby Gardens

Sunday 14
41 Ravensthorpe Gardens
44 Steane Park

Saturday 20
35 The Maltings

Sunday 21
5 Bulwick Gardens
35 The Maltings

Sunday 28
16 Froggery Cottage
37 Moulton Open Gardens

August

Sunday 11
27 Hollowell Gardens

Sunday 18
36 Manor Lodge

Thursday 22
45 Sulby Gardens

Saturday 31
23 Haddonstone Show Gardens

September

Sunday 1
23 Haddonstone Show Gardens

Sunday 8
26 Holdenby House Gardens

Our gardens have been chosen because they are all different in spirit . . .

October

Thursday 3
45 Sulby Gardens

Saturday 26
3 Boughton House

Sunday 27
3 Boughton House

February 2014

Sunday 23
30 Jericho

Gardens open to the public

3 Boughton House
7 Castle Ashby Gardens
9 Coton Manor Garden
10 Cottesbrooke Hall Gardens
11 Deene Park
12 Evenley Wood Garden
23 Haddonstone Show Gardens
26 Holdenby House Gardens
31 Kelmarsh Hall
44 Steane Park

You are always welcome at an NGS garden!

By appointment only

17 Gower House

Also open by Appointment ☎

1 Bosworth House, Arthingworth Open Gardens
1 11 Oxendon Road, Arthingworth Open Gardens
4 Briarwood
5 Bulwick Gardens
6 Bulwick Hall
14 The Old Bakery, Flore Gardens
15 Foxtail Lilly
16 Froggery Cottage
21 Greywalls
22 Dripwell House, Guilsborough Gardens
24 The Close, Harpole Gardens
24 19 Manor Close, Harpole Gardens
25 67-69 High Street
27 Ivy Cottage, Hollowell Gardens
30 Jericho
32 Pytchley House, Kilsby Gardens
35 The Maltings
41 Mill House, Ravensthorpe Gardens
41 Ravensthorpe Nursery, Ravensthorpe Gardens
42 Rosemount
47 Titchmarsh House
48 Top Lodge

The Gardens

GROUP OPENING

1 ARTHINGWORTH OPEN GARDENS

Arthingworth, nr Market Harborough LE16 8LA. *6m S of Market Harborough. From Market Harborough via A508 after 4m take L to Arthingworth. From Northampton, A508 turn R just after Kelmarsh.* Home-made teas at Bosworth House and village hall. **Combined adm £5, chd free. Sun 30 June (2-6).**

BOSWORTH HOUSE
Mr & Mrs C E Irving-Swift
Visitors also welcome by appt Apr to Aug. Guided tour (approx 1hr) by owner. 01858 525202

1 CHURCH FARM WAY
Mr & Mrs J Ingleby

3 CHURCH FARM WAY
Mr & Mrs P Reeve

10 OXENDON ROAD
Mr & Mrs J Audley

NEW **1 OXENDON ROAD**
Mr & Mrs Charles Blake

11 OXENDON ROAD
Nr & Mrs B Cunningham
Visitors also welcome by appt Apr to Aug. 01858-525365 bc@ukzero.co.uk

SCHOOL HOUSE
Mr & Mrs R Tinkler

1 SUNNYBANK
Miss Jane Perry

Arthingworth welcomes you with 7 gardens to visit. From 'The good life' to 'to the manor born' or nearly, come and enjoy the diversity. We aim to give the visitors an afternoon of 'discovery'. Our gardens have been chosen because they are all different in spirit, tended by young and weathered gardeners, some with stunning views, some traditional (herbaceous borders, vegetables), some walled, some artisan, even a secret and a futurist one. And when you come, you can enjoy home baked cakes and a cup of tea either in the village hall or at Bosworth house. The village is looking forward to welcoming you. Wheelchair access not available at all gardens.

GROUP OPENING

2 BADBY AND NEWNHAM GARDENS

Daventry NN11 3AR. *3m S of Daventry. E side of A361. Maps provided for visitors.* Home-made teas at Badby and Newnham Churches. **Combined adm £4, chd free. Sun 9 June (2-6).**

THE BANKS
Newnham. Sue Styles & Geoff Chester
www.suestyles.co.uk

HILLTOP
Newnham. David & Mercy Messenger

THE LILACS
Badby. Matthew and Ruth Moser

SHAKESPEARES COTTAGE
Badby. Sarah & Jocelyn Hartland-Swann

SOUTHVIEW COTTAGE
Badby. Alan and Karen Brown

TRIFIDIA
Badby. Colin & Shirley Cripps

Six gardens in two beautiful villages with attractive old houses of golden-coloured Hornton stone set around their Village greens. In Badby there are four gardens of differing styles. A wisteria-clad thatched cottage with modern sculptures, a terraced garden with vegetables and orchard and a newly developed garden with views over the Village. The fourth garden with pond, conservatory, glasshouses and vegetables has unusual plants and aims for yr-round interest. In Newnham, there is a 3-acre organic garden around a picturesque C17 thatched cottage with lawns, densely planted borders, vegetable and cutting garden and paddocks with feature trees and the garden of a garden designer with pools, herbaceous borders, vegetables and herbs developed as rooms among mature trees.

The village is looking forward to welcoming you . . .

BARTON ABBEY
See Oxfordshire

3 ◆ BOUGHTON HOUSE

Geddington, Kettering NN14 1BJ. Duke of Buccleuch & Queensberry, KBE, 01536 515731, www.boughtonhouse.org.uk. *3m NE of Kettering. From A14, 2m along A43 Kettering to Stamford, turn R in to Geddington, House entrance 1½ m on R.* **Adm £5, chd £2. For NGS: Sats, Suns 23, 24 Feb; 26, 27 Oct (11-3). For other opening times and information, please phone or see garden website.**

The Northamptonshire home of the Duke and Duchess of Buccleuch. The garden opening incl opportunities to see the historic walled kitchen garden and herbaceous border incl the newly created sensory and wildlife gardens. The wilderness woodland will open for visitors to view the spring flowers or the autumn colours. As a special treat the garden originally created by Sir David Scott (cousin of the Duke of Buccleuch) will also be open.

Nortoft Grange, Guilsborough Gardens

4 BRIARWOOD
4 Poplars Farm Road, Barton Seagrave, Kettering NN15 5AF. Elaine Christian & William Portch, 01536 522169, www.elainechristian-gardendesign.co.uk. *1½ m SE of Kettering town centre. J10 off A14 - turn onto Barton Rd (A6) towards Wicksteed Park. R into Warkton Lane, after 200m R into Poplars Farm Road*. Delicious home-made lunches, cakes and teas. **Adm £3, chd free. Sat 6, Sun 7 Apr (10.30-4). Visitors also welcome by appt Apr & July only.**
A garden in two parts with quirky original sculptures and many faces: An S-facing lawn and colourful borders with spring bulbs, blossom trees, summer colour, hedging, palms, climbers, lily pond, and sunny terrace; secondly, a secret garden with summerhouse, small orchard, raised bed potager and water feature. Crafts for sale and children's quiz.

BUCKINGHAM GARDENS
See Buckinghamshire

GROUP OPENING

5 BULWICK GARDENS
Bulwick NN17 3DZ. *10m SW of Stamford. ½ m off A43*. Cream teas at Bulwick Hall. **Combined adm £4, chd free. Sun 21 July (2.30-5.30).**

BULWICK HALL
Mr & Mrs G T G Conant
(See separate entry)

19 CHURCH LANE
David Haines

THE SHAMBLES
Roger Glithero

Unspoilt Northamptonshire stone conservation village. Interesting C14 church and PH. Bulwick Hall is a formal terraced 8 acre walled garden leading to river and island, 50 metre double herbaceous borders, topiary, walled kitchen garden. C17 wrought iron gates, C19 orangery and C17 arcade. Peacocks and rare breed hens. 19 Church Lane is a small cottage garden with courtyard and water feature. The Shambles has an original village well, lawns, hedges and stone walls. Featured in Stamford Mercury, Northants Evening Telegraph and on Rutland Radio. Disabled parking at Bulwick Hall. Wheelchair access to Bulwick Hall only.

6 BULWICK HALL
NN17 3DZ. Mr & Mrs G T G Conant, 01780 450245, timdavconant@bulwick.com. **Adm £4, chd free. Sun 16 June (2.30-5.30). Visitors also welcome by appt anytime.**
Formal terraced 8-acre walled garden leading to river and island. Double herbaceous borders, holly walk ending at attractive C17 wrought iron gates. C19 orangery and C17 arcade, large kitchen garden, fine mature trees, topiary, peacocks. (House not open). Plant stall.

7 ◆ CASTLE ASHBY GARDENS
Northampton NN7 1LQ. Earl Compton, 01604 695200, www.castleashbygardens.co.uk. *6m E of Northampton. 1½ m N of A428; turn off between Denton & Yardley Hastings. Follow brown tourist signs*. **Adm £5, chd £4.50 (under 10 free). For NGS: Sun 7 July (10-5.30). For other opening times and information, please phone or see garden website.**
25-acres within a 10,000 acre estate of both formal and informal gardens, incl Italian gardens with orangery and arboretum with lakes, all dating back to the 1860s. Rare breed farmyard, tea-rooms and gift shop. Gravel paths.

GROUP OPENING

8 CHARLTON GARDENS
Banbury OX17 3DR. *7m SE of Banbury, 5m W of Brackley. From B4100 turn off N at Aynho, or from A422 turn off S at Farthinghoe. Parking at village hall*. Home-made at teas Walnut House. **Combined adm £5, chd free. Sun 19 May (2-5.30).**

8 CARTWRIGHT ROAD
Miss Valerie Trinder

CHARLTON LODGE
Mr & Mrs Andrew Woods

THE CROFT
Mr & Mrs R D Whitrow

ELLESMERE
Rod & Wendy Cone

HOME FARM HOUSE
Mrs N Grove-White

WALNUT HOUSE
Sir Paul & Lady Hayter

Pretty stone village with a selection of gardens large and small, incl a paved courtyard with tubs, containers and climbers; a cottage garden with colourful planting, interesting corners and lovely views; a walled garden with roses and clematis; a large garden behind C17 farmhouse with colour-themed borders, separate small gardens and a hot gravel garden created in 2011; a large terraced garden with a 140ft-long herbaceous border and raised-bed vegetable patch, overlooking a lake; and a mainly dry gravel garden with good perennials, grasses and bamboos.

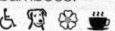

CHURCH GREEN GARDENS
See Buckinghamshire

9 ◆ COTON MANOR GARDEN
Nr Guilsborough, Northampton NN6 8RQ. Mr & Mrs Ian Pasley-Tyler, 01604 740219, www.cotonmanor.co.uk. *10m N of Northampton, 11m SE of Rugby. From A428 & A5199 follow tourist signs.* **Adm £6, chd £2. For NGS: Tue 7 May (12-5.30). For other opening times and information, please phone or see garden website.**
10-acre garden set in peaceful countryside with old yew and holly hedges, extensive herbaceous borders containing many unusual plants, rose, water, herb and woodland gardens, famous bluebell wood, wild flower meadow. Adjacent specialist nursery with over 1000 plant varieties propagated from the garden. Some narrow paths inaccessible to wheelchair users. Please note, site is on a slope so not all areas are accessible.

10 ◆ COTTESBROOKE HALL GARDENS
Cottesbrooke NN6 8PF. Mr & Mrs A R Macdonald-Buchanan, 01604 505808, www.cottesbrooke.co.uk. *10m N of Northampton. Signed from J1 on A14. Off A5199 at Creaton, A508 at Brixworth.* **Adm £5.50, chd £3. For NGS: Sun 21 Apr (2-5.30). For other opening times and information, please phone or see garden website.**
Award winning gardens by Geoffrey Jellicoe, Dame Sylvia Crowe, James Alexander Sinclair and more recently Arne Maynard. Formal gardens and terraces surround Queen Anne house with extensive vistas onto the lake and C18 parkland containing many mature trees. Wild and woodland gardens, which are exceptional in Spring, a short distance from the formal areas. Most of garden accessible. Paths are grass, stone and gravel. Access map identifies best route.

COWPER & NEWTON MUSEUM GARDENS
See Buckinghamshire

11 ◆ DEENE PARK
Nr Corby, Deene NN17 3EW. Mr Edmund & The Hon Mrs Brudenell, 01780 450278, www.deenepark.com. *6m N of Corby. Off A43 between Stamford & Corby.* **Adm £6, chd £3. For NGS: Sun 19 May (2-5). For other opening times and information, please phone or see garden website.**
Interesting garden set in beautiful parkland. Large parterre with topiary designed by David Hicks echoing the C16 decoration on the porch stonework, long mixed borders, old-fashioned roses, Tudor courtyard and white garden. Lake and waterside walks with rare mature trees in natural garden. Wheelchair access available to main features of garden.

12 ◆ EVENLEY WOOD GARDEN
Evenley, Brackley NN13 5SH. Timothy Whiteley, 07776 307849, www.evenleywoodgarden.co.uk. *¾ m S of Brackley. Turn off at Evenley r'about on A43 & continue through village towards Mixbury before taking 1st turn L.* **Adm £5, chd £1. For NGS: Sat 4, Sun 5 May (11-5). For other opening times and information, please phone or see garden website.**
This 60-acre woodland is a plantsman's garden with a huge variety of plants all of which are labelled. Mainly trees, shrubs, bulbs and lilies. Many magnolias, azaleas, rhododendrons and camellias. All paths are grass.

Garden set in peaceful countryside with famous bluebell wood . . .

GROUP OPENING

13 FINEDON GARDENS
Finedon NN9 5JN. *2m NE of Wellingborough. 6m SE Kettering. All gardens individually signed from A6/A510 junction.* Home-made teas at 67-69 High Street. **Combined adm £3, chd free. Sun 2, Sun 30 June (2-6).**

29 EASTFIELD CRESCENT
Terry & Linda Goodman

67-69 HIGH STREET
Mary & Stuart Hendry
(see separate entry)

11 THRAPSTON ROAD
John & Gillian Ellson

All three gardens are very different - everything from vegetables to flowers on show. **67-69 High Street** is an ever evolving garden of ⅓ acre of C17 cottage (not open) Mixed borders, many obelisks and containers. Planting for varied interest Spring to Autumn.
29 Eastfield Crescent This is a garden in 4 sections. Lawn with mixed borders and pond with bridge leading to paved area with containers, water feature and arbour seat. Fruit and vegetable garden with 2 greenhouses. Shady end section with borders and summerhouse. Front garden with varied hanging baskets and containers.
11 Thrapston Road ⅓ acre cottage garden with lawns and mixed borders, gravel and paved seating areas with planters and water features. Pergola, rose arches, summer house and tree house. Mixed vegetable plot, soft fruit and apple trees. Large selection of home-raised plants for sale at some locations- all proceeds to the NGS. Generally good access for wheelchairs but with some gravel paths and grassed areas.

GROUP OPENING

14 FLORE GARDENS
Flore NN7 4LQ. *7m W of Northampton. 2m W of J16 M1. 5m E of Daventry on A45. Garden map provided at official free car park, signed from A45. Coaches welcome, please phone 01327 341225 for parking advice.* Light refreshments at Chapel School Room (Apr), Chapel Schoolroom and Church (June). **Combined adm £5, chd free (June only, share to All Saints Church Flower Festival). Sun 14 Apr (2-6); Sat 22, Sun 23 June (11-6).**

BLISS LANE NURSERY
Geof & Chris Littlewood

24 BLISS LANE
John & Sally Miller

THE CROFT
John & Dorothy Boast

THE GARDEN HOUSE
Edward & Penny Aubrey-Fletcher.
Open June dates only

38 HIGH STREET
Pat, Joan & Anne Harrison.
Open June dates only

3 MEADOW FARM CLOSE
Eric & Jackie Ingram.
Open April date only

4 MEADOW FARM CLOSE
Bob & Lynne Richards.
Open April date only

THE OLD BAKERY
John Amos & Karl Jones
Visitors also welcome by appt Apr to Aug. 01327 349080 yeolbakery@aol.com www.johnnieamos.co.uk

RUSSELL HOUSE
Peter Pickering & Stephen George

Flore gardens have been open for many years as part of the Flore Flower Festival and the partnership with the NGS started in 1992. Flore is an attractive village with views over the upper Nene valley, a C12 Church and Victorian Chapel which are also open in June with floral displays. We have a varied mix of gardens, developed by friendly and enthusiastic owners, that provide interest throughout the year. There is an interesting selection of garden structures, incl greenhouses, and gazebos and summerhouses with seating providing opportunities to rest while admiring the gardens. In spring we have early flowering perennials, interesting shrubs, and bulbs in pots and border drifts. There is planting for all situations incl shade and full sun. The June gardens incl formal and informal designs with lots of roses, clematis and many varieties of trees, shrubs, perennials, fruit, vegetables and herbs. Gardens open in association with Flore Flower Festival. Wheelchair access possible in most gardens, some assistance may be required.

Some unusual plants and quirky oddities . . .

15 FOXTAIL LILLY
41 South Road, Oundle PE8 4BP. Tracey Mathieson, 01832 274593, tracey@foxtail-lilly.co.uk, www.foxtail-lilly.co.uk. *1m town centre. From A605 at Barnwell Xrds take Barnwell Rd, 1st R to South Rd.* Home-made teas. **Adm £3.50, chd free. Sun 16 June (10.30-5). Visitors also welcome by appt May to July.**
A cottage garden where perennials and grasses are grouped creatively together amongst gravel paths, complementing one another to create a natural look. Some unusual plants and quirky oddities create a different and colourful informal garden. Lots of flowers for cutting, shop in barn. New meadow pasture turned into new cutting garden.

16 FROGGERY COTTAGE
85 Breakleys Road, Desborough NN14 2PT. Mr John Lee, 01536 760002, johnlee@froggerycottage85.fsnet.co.uk. *6m N of Kettering. 5m S of Market Harborough. Signed off A6 & A14.* Home-made teas. **Adm £3, chd free. Sun 28 July (11.30-5.30). Visitors also welcome by appt May to Aug.**
3/4 -acre plantsman's garden full of rare and unusual plants. NCCPG Collection of 435 varieties of penstemons incl dwarfs and species. Artefacts on display incl old ploughs and garden implements. Workshops throughout the day.

NCH

17 GOWER HOUSE
Guilsborough, Northampton NN6 8PY. Ann Moss, 01604 740755, cattimoss@aol.com. *Off High St by Ward Arms, through PH car park.* Light refreshments. **Adm £5, chd free. Visitors welcome by appt Apr to July. Visits in association with Dripwell House only.**
Although Gower House garden is small it is closely planted with specimen trees, shrubs, perennials, orchids, thyme lawn, wild flowers and alpines, some rare or unusual, with foliage colour being important. Several seating areas designed for elderly relatives incorporating recycled materials. Soft fruit and vegetable garden, shared with Dripwell, is an important part of our gardening. Very steep site unsuitable for those with mobility problems.

GROUP OPENING

18 GREAT BILLING VILLAGE
Northampton NN3 9HA. *3m E of Northampton. off A4500.* Home-made teas at 20 Elwes Way. **Combined adm £4, chd free. Sun 9 June (1.30-5.30).**

20 ELWES WAY
Cindy & John Evitt

FIELD VIEW
Anner Fehnert

PLANTATION HOUSE
Freddie Rayner

20 STANDING STONES
Mrs Janet James

The village is listed in the Domesday Book and parts still retain the old atmosphere with the C12 church of St Andrew and the old rectory. At one time the Elwes family owned almost the whole village. They lived in Billing Hall, sadly demolished in 1956. Today the only tangible links are The Elwes Arms, Elwes Way and Lady Winefride's Walk. One garden is in the conservation area, which is predominately stone-built. A short walk away, across open parkland by the church; the other gardens are in a recent development, in the grounds of the old Hall. Behind conventional facades lie unexpected delights. In one you could imagine being on a beach, another is formal, with clipped hedges and a cricket pavilion. One has a series of garden rooms around old farm buildings. A warm welcome awaits.

GROUP OPENING

19 GREAT BRINGTON GARDENS

NN7 4JJ. *7m NW of Northampton. Off A428 Rugby Rd. 1st L turn past main gates of Althorp. Free parking. Programmes & maps available.* Teas at parish church, morning coffee and lunches in the Reading Room. **Combined adm £4.50, chd free. Sun 5 May (11-5).**

7 BEDFORD COTTAGES
Mrs Felicity Bellamy

FOLLY HOUSE
Sarah & Joe Sacarello

NEW **66 MAIN STREET**
Mr & Mrs A Clayton

THE OLD RECTORY
Mr & Mrs R Thomas

ROSE COTTAGE
David Green & Elaine MacKenzie

THE STABLES
Mrs A George

Great Brington is renowned for its warm welcome with dozens of parish volunteers helping on the day: manning the free car park and plant stall, serving lunches and teas, stewarding and providing information about the village and its gardens. A particularly picturesque, predominately stone and thatch village, Great Brington is well worth a visit in its own right. The C12 church, rated as one of Simon Jenkins' 1000 Best, has connections with the Spencers of Althorp and George Washington. Our Open Gardens provide immense variety from a small cottage garden with a summerhouse to a 3-acre formal garden complete with an extensive vegetable patch and orchard. Many of the gardens continue to evolve each year; several have unique water features; most are planned and maintained by their owners. Featured in local press and on radio/television. Wheelchair access at some gardens only.

Trifidia

Spread the word about the NGS: tell your family and friends

20 GREENWAY

Pipewell Road, Desborough NN14 2SN. Robert Bass, 01536 760934. *6m NW of Kettering, 5m SE of Market Harborough. On B576. 150 metres E of Pipewell Rd railway bridge & Travis Perkins builders' yard.* Home-made teas. **Adm £3, chd free. Sun 12 May (2-6). Evening Opening £3, chd free, wine, Thur 23 May (6-9); Sun 16 June (2-6).**
Constantly evolving arboretum style garden set in 1/3 acre with over 100 acers (Japanese maple) in containers and open planting. Front and rear areas with a Japanese influence, Torii gate, teahouse and lanterns. Garden structures, water features, statuary, sculptures and containers to provide yr-round interest, incl gothic folly with fernery. Covered seating areas for contemplation.

21 GREYWALLS

Farndish NN29 7HJ. Mrs P M Anderson, 01933 353495, patricia@greywalls.tradaweb.net. *2½ m SE of Wellingborough. A609 from Wellingborough, B570 to Irchester, turn to Farndish by cenotaph. House adjacent to church.* Light refreshments. **Adm £3, chd free. Sun 3 Mar (12-4). Visitors also welcome by appt Mar to June. Coaches welcome.**
2-acre mature garden surrounding old vicarage (not open). Over 100 varieties of snowdrops, drifts of hardy cyclamen and hellebores. Alpine house and raised alpine beds. Water features and natural ponds with views over open countryside. Rare breed hens.

Wine and nibbles . . .

GROUP OPENING

22 GUILSBOROUGH GARDENS
Guilsborough NN6 8PT. *10m NW of Northampton. 10m E of Rugby. Between A5199 & A428. J1 off A14. Car parking in field on Hollowell Rd out of Guilsborough. Maps provided.* Home-made teas in village hall. **Combined adm £5, chd free. Sat 27, Sun 28 Apr (2-6).**

DRIPWELL HOUSE
Mr J W Langfield & Dr C Moss
Visitors also welcome by appt Apr to July. Visits in association with Gower House only.
01604 740140
cattimoss@aol.com

FOUR ACRES
Mark & Gay Webster

THE GATE HOUSE
Mike & Sarah Edwards

GUILSBOROUGH HOUSE
Mr & Mrs John McCall

NORTOFT GRANGE
Lady Lowther

OAK DENE
Mr & Mrs R A Darker

THE OLD HOUSE
Richard & Libby Seaton Evans

THE OLD VICARAGE
John & Christine Benbow

Eight varied village gardens in attractive rural setting. Two small cottage-style gardens, one belonging to a keen flower arranger, the other a secret walled garden crammed with fruit, flowers and vegetables. The remaining gardens are larger, ranging from a magical woodland garden on a very steep site to formal gardens with sweeping lawns, mature trees and beautiful views. There is plenty of room to sit and relax. Walled kitchen gardens and a potager are an important part of our gardening. Plants for sale will incl both the rare and unusual from our plantsmen's gardens, a true highlight here. Dripwell House, open for the NGS since 1986, was originally an individual garden as was Nortoft Grange. There is thus a lot to see and visitors find that they need the whole afternoon. Information point, maps on The Green. Church open. Disabled access at Four Acres, Guilsborough House, Oak Dene, The Old House & The Old Vicarage only. Featured in local press. Not all gardens suitable for wheelchair users. Dogs not permitted at all gardens.

23 ◆ HADDONSTONE SHOW GARDENS
The Forge House, Church Lane, East Haddon, Northampton NN6 8DB. Haddonstone Ltd, 01604 770711, www.haddonstone.com. *7m NW of Northampton. Brown tourism signs from A428. Located in centre of village opp school.* **Adm £2.50, chd free. For NGS: Sat 27, Sun 28 Apr, Sat 31 Aug, Sun 1 Sept (11-5). For other opening times and information, please phone or see garden website.**
See Haddonstone's classic garden ornaments in the beautiful setting of the walled Manor gardens inc planters, fountains, statuary, bird baths, sundials, balustrading and follies. Garden is on different levels with roses, clematis, climbers, herbaceous borders, ornamental flowers, topiary, specimen shrubs and trees. New: star jasmin walk, wildflower meadow, contemporary garden and statue walk. Wheelchair access to all areas of main garden.

HAMMOND ARBORETUM
See Leicestershire & Rutland

GROUP OPENING

24 HARPOLE GARDENS
Harpole NN7 4BX. *4m W Northampton. On A45 towards Weedon. Turn R at The Turnpike Hotel into Harpole. Village maps given to all visitors.* Home-made teas at The Close. **Combined adm £4, chd free. Sun 9 June (1-6).**

BRYTTEN-COLLIER HOUSE
James & Lucy Strickland

THE CLOSE
Michael Orton-Jones
Visitors also welcome by appt.
01604 830332
michael@orton-jones.com

19 MANOR CLOSE
Caroline & Andy Kemshed
Visitors also welcome by appt June.
01604 830512
carolinekemshed@live.co.uk

MILLERS
Mrs M Still

THE OLD DAIRY
David & Di Ballard

Attractive Northamptonshire village well known for its annual scarecrow festival (2nd weekend Sept). Enjoy a lovely farmhouse garden with an acre of lawn, mixed borders, mature trees, views overlooking the farm and strawberry field. Visit a partly walled S-facing garden with wonderful herbaceous borders, many climbing roses and clematis and a beautiful tree house. See a sheltered cottage garden with clematis, roses and luxuriant planting. View a smaller garden (40 x 10yd) belonging to a more recently constructed house. This is a flower arranger's garden of interesting design with water features and mixed borders. Take tea in an old fashioned country garden with large lawn, herbaceous borders and mature trees. An interesting and varied afternoon is guaranteed with a warm welcome to all. Wheelchair access at Brytten-Collier House, The Close and The Old Dairy only.

25 67-69 HIGH STREET
Finedon NN9 5JN. Mary & Stuart Hendry, 01933 680414, sh_archt@hotmail.com. *6m SE Kettering, J A6 & A510. 6m SE Kettering, Garden signed from A6/A510 junction.* **Evening Openings £3.50, chd free, wine, Thurs 6, 13, 20, 27 June (5-8.30). Visitors also welcome by appt Feb to Oct. Evening visits with wine and 'nibbles'.**
Constantly evolving, 1/3 -acre rear garden of C17 cottage (not open). Mixed borders, many obelisks and containers, kitchen garden and herb bed, rope border. Spring garden with snowdrops, bluebells and hellebores; Summer and Autumn borders all giving varied interest from Feb through to Oct. Plant surgery by local expert. Bring along your plants or questions. Home raised plants for sale. Featured on BBC Radio Northampton. Most areas accessible via hard paved paths, with some gravel paths and grass.

HILLESDEN HOUSE
See Buckinghamshire

26 ◆ HOLDENBY HOUSE GARDENS

Northampton NN6 8DJ. Mr & Mrs James Lowther, 01604 770074, www.holdenby.com. *6m NW of Northampton. From A5199 or A428 between East Haddon & Spratton. Follow brown tourist signs. Signed from A5199 & A428.* **Adm £5, chd £3.50. For NGS: Sun 8 Sept (1-5). For other opening times and information, please phone or see garden website.**

The 20 acre, Grade I listed garden set in stately lawns and hedges, has several special features. Away from the formal gardens lie the terraces of the Elizabethan rose garden - one of the best preserved examples of their kind. There is also a delightful walled kitchen garden with the original Victorian greenhouse. Cream teas served in the tea-room. Featured in local press, re location for BBC's Great Expectations. Gravel paths.

We have been complimented on our welcoming atmosphere . . .

GROUP OPENING

27 HOLLOWELL GARDENS

Hollowell NN6 8RR. *8m N of Northampton. ½ m off A5199, turn off at Creaton.* Light refreshments at Village Hall. **Combined adm £3.50, chd free. Sun 11 Aug (11-5).**

HILLVIEW
Jan & Crawford Craig

IVY COTTAGE
Rev John & Mrs Wendy Evans
Visitors also welcome by appt June to Aug. Tea or wine available depending on time of visit. revjohnwenevans@yahoo.co.uk

ROSEMOUNT
Mr & Mrs J Leatherland
(See separate entry)

Small village with church built approx 150yrs ago using sandstone from Duston Quarry and the Village Hall was the local school until its closure about 40yrs ago. The gardens open are **Rosemount** with its collections of clematis, mimulus and salvias. **Ivy Cottage** is a semi-wildlife garden with orchard, vegetable garden and model railway. **Hillview** is a traditional country garden incl a lily pond dating from the 1930s. No wheelchair access at Hillview, limited access at remaining gardens. Steep hills.

28 HOSTELLARIE

78 Breakleys Road, Desborough NN14 2PT. Stella & Stan Freeman. *6m N of Kettering. 5m S of Market Harborough. Signed from centre of Desborough.* Home-made teas. **Adm £3, chd free. Sun 23 June (1.30-5.30).**

Over 180ft long town garden divided into rooms of different character, courtyard garden, colour themed flower beds, ponds and water features, cottage gardens, fruit and vegetable areas all linked by lawns and grass paths. We have been complimented on our welcoming atmosphere, good value teas, and our hosta collection.

GROUP OPENING

29 ISLIP GARDENS

Islip, nr Kettering NN14 3JY. *1m from A14 J12. Leave A14 at J12, join A6116. Follow signs for Islip Village & NGS signs.* Tea in Village Hall. **Combined adm £4, chd free. Sun 23 June (12-5).**

NEW CHAPTER HOUSE
Penny Pedroli & David Sobey

HEADMASTERS HOUSE
Julie & Bob Lymn

8 LOWICK ROAD
Dawn & Richard Scrutton

3 lovely gardens, from broad, bordered drive leading to ever-changing rear garden with colourful mix of shrubs to a split level garden with apple and pear trees. Plantsman's small garden to the rear of a late Georgian cottage with a collection of clematis, hellebore, hardy geraniums and Japanese acers, a variety of sculptural plants in raised beds, incl pots and borders. Charming collection of C17/18 stone cottages under thatched, pantiles and slate roofs. C15 church. Islip is listed in the Domesday Book and has prehistoric, Roman & Anglo Saxon sites.

30 JERICHO

42 Market Place, Oundle PE8 4AJ. Stephen & Pepita Aris, 01832 275416, stephenaris@btinternet.com. *East Jericho. From Oundle Market Place, find Hambleton Bakery, go through red door & down yard to garden.* **Adm £3, chd free. Sun 24 Feb (12-4); Sun 19 May (12-5); Sun 23 Feb 2014. Visitors also welcome by appt Mar to July.**

Inspired by Vita Sackville-West 50 years ago, the 100m, S-facing, walled garden is divided into a series of 'secret' spaces. House (not open) is clothed in wisteria, clematis and roses. A plant-led garden with massive hornbeam hedge, clipped box and lavender. Over 50 labelled species roses, plus a 'hot' border. Featured in Peterborough Evening Telegraph.

31 NEW ◆ KELMARSH HALL

Main Road, Kelmarsh, Northampton NN6 9LY. The Kelmarsh Trust, 01604 686543, www.kelmarsh.com. *Directions from A14; Exit at J2 & head N towards Market Harborough. The village of Kelmarsh is 500m from A14. The entrance gates on L at Kelmarsh Xrds, 500m N of A14. Directions from A508; The Hall is 5m S of Market Harborough (on R) and 11m N of Northampton (on L). The entrance gates on Kelmarsh village Xrds (on R coming N, or L coming S).* **Adm £5, chd £3.50**

Kelmarsh Hall is an C18 country house, set in gardens inspired by society decorator Nancy Lancaster and surrounded by woodland and an estate of rolling Northamptonshire countryside. Hidden gems in the gardens incl a double border, sunken garden, a 30m long border, rose garden and at the heart of it all, a historic walled kitchen garden. Featured in Country Living and The English Garden.

GROUP OPENING

32 KILSBY GARDENS

Kilsby Village CV23 8XP. *5m SE of Rugby. 6m N of Daventry on A361. From Rugby on A428 turn R onto B4038. From J18 on M1 take A428 towards Rugby. At junction with A5 going S turn L. Entrance to Kilsby on R just after 30mph sign.* **Combined adm £4, chd free. Sun 9 June (1-5).**

6A ESSEN LANE
Phil & Lilian Francis

12 MAIN ROAD
Mrs S Cornes

MICKELHOME
Mr & Mrs R Mason

PYTCHLEY HOUSE
Mr & Mrs T F Clay
Visitors also welcome by appt Apr to Aug. 4 weeks notice required.
01788 822373
the.clays@tiscali.co.uk

RAINBOW'S END
Mr & Mrs J Madigan

12 RUGBY ROAD
Mr & Mrs T Hindle

5 THE LAWNS
Charles Smedley

Kilsby is a stone and brick village with historic interest, home of St Faith's Church dating from the C12. The village was the site of one of the first skirmishes of the Civil War in 1642 and also gave its name to Stephenson's nearby lengthy rail tunnel built in the 1830s. This year 7 attractive gardens will be open, all within easy walking distance within the village. Some of the gardens open alternate years so there is always something new to see - and there are always plants for sale too. Visitors have commented on the friendly welcome so do please come and see us.

Wonderful display of tulips in the spring . . .

GROUP OPENING

33 LITCHBOROUGH GARDENS

Litchborough NN12 8JQ. *10m SW of Northampton, nr Towcester. Please use car park nr village green. Maps provided.* Home-made teas in Village Hall. **Combined adm £4, chd free (share to St Martins Church, Litchborough). Sun 14 Apr (2-6).**

BRUYERE COURT
Mr M Billington

2 KILN LANE
Anna Steiner

4 KILN LANE
Roger & Angela Linnell

LITCHBOROUGH HALL
Mr & Mrs Robert Heygate

NEW THE OLD SCHOOL HOUSE
Mr & Mrs Phillips

ORCHARD HOUSE
Mr & Mrs B Smith

41 TOWCESTER ROAD
Ian & Vanessa Lowery

Litchborough Gardens offer a wonderful, diverse selection of gardens varying in size from several acres to the more conventional small back garden. On show is a landscape architects country garden designed for low maintenance, a small family garden featuring a play area with willow tunnel and vegetable patch. Visit a modern cottage garden offering a wonderful display of tulips in the spring and spectacular views over the countryside and a large garden with clipped yews, extensive woodland and winding walks through specimen trees and around the lake. Lastly, but most definitely not least, admire the ornamental lakes with rock stream and fountain and the rhododendrons, azaleas and herbaceous borders in this 3 acre landscape garden. A garden for every taste.

34 LOIS WEEDON HOUSE

Weedon Lois NN12 8PJ. Sir John & Lady Greenaway. *From S or W go to Weston village (N of Helmdon) then E to Weedon Lois. Pass church & village green on L. After sharp R bend Weedon Lois House is 2nd entrance on R. From N or E, in Wappenham go N for approx 1½m & on sharp L bend entrance lodge to house is on the L.* Cream teas. **Adm £4, chd free. Sun 21 Apr (2-5.30).**

Large garden with terraces and fine views, lawns, pergola, water garden, mature yew hedges, pond. During 2012 over 11,000 spring bulbs have been planted. Access to most areas but some slopes and steps.

35 THE MALTINGS

10 The Green, Clipston LE16 9RS. Mrs Hamish Connell & Mr William Connell, 01858 525336, j.connell118@btinternet.com. *4m S of Market Harborough, 9m W of Kettering, 10m N Northampton. From A14 take J2, A508 N. After 2m turn L for Clipston. 2 houses away from Old Red Lion PH.* Cream teas. **Adm £3, chd free. Sat 30 Mar (2-6); Sun 31 Mar, Mon 1 Apr, Sun 26, Mon 27 May (11-6); Sat 20 July (2-6); Sun 21 July (11-6). Visitors also welcome by appt. Light Refreshments and wine available.**

¾ acre sloping plantsman's garden designed for yr round interest by the present owner. Many unusual plants, shrubs, old and new trees. Over 60 different clematis, wild garden walk, spring bulb area, over 30 different species roses, 2 ponds connected by a stream, bog garden. Fruit, vegetables and greenhouse. Home made cake stall. Swing and slide for children. Partial wheelchair access. Gravelled drive, some narrow paths, some steps.

THE MANOR HOUSE, STEVINGTON
See Bedfordshire

36 NEW MANOR LODGE

Creaton Road, Teeton, Northampton NN6 8LH. Mr & Mrs Louise and David Lakin. *8m NNW of Northampton. Signed from A5199 at Spratton to parking on Spratton-Ravensthorpe rd. Short walk through Teeton village to garden.* **Adm £3, chd free. Sun 18 Aug (1.30-5.30).**

⅓ acre garden transformed over the last 10 years by the present owners. Relaxed and varied planting with lots of year-round colour. Planting and seating areas designed to maximise the views over the beautiful countryside. Small bog garden, kitchen garden with several raised beds and soft fruit. Views over open countryside can be enjoyed while you take afternoon tea.

Jericho

© Nicola Stocken Tomkins

MIDDLETON CHENEY GARDENS
See Oxfordshire

THE MOAT HOUSE
See Bedfordshire

GROUP OPENING

37 MOULTON OPEN GARDENS
Moulton NN3 7UX. *N of Northampton town. Turn L off A43 at small r'about to Overstone Rd. Follow rd to The Co-op in village centre, bear L, then take next R after approx 300 metres into Cross St which leads into West St. Take 1st L into Pound Lane, Village Hall car park is just up on R.* Light refreshments at Village Hall. **Combined adm £5, chd free. Sun 28 July (11-5).**

NEW **38 ARNSBY CRESCENT**
Mr Fritz De Zutter

BAYTREE COTTAGE
Ian Longstaff

NEW **33 BOUGHTON ROAD**
Mr & Mrs Christoph & Celia Boueke

NEW **32 CROSS STREET**
Dr John Gill

DAIRY FARMHOUSE
Angela & John Campling

NEW **DENE COTTAGE**
Jenny & David Aarons

NEW **MANOR FARM**
Peter and ChrisThompson

NEW **4 THE PADDOCKS**
Mr Russell Moore

ROSEARIE-DE-LA-NYMPH
Peter Hughes, Mary Morris, Irene Kay & Jeremy Stanton

Moulton is a typical Northamptonshire village which has a distinctive character. There are many historic and visually interesting houses built from local stone. This year nine gardens are open, including five opening for the first time. We vary the mix of gardens opening from year to year, so there is always something new to see and a variety of gardening styles to enjoy.

38 MULBERRY COTTAGE
6 Yew Tree Lane, Spratton, Northampton NN6 8HL. Michael & Morley Heaton. *6½ m NNW of Northampton. From Northampton on A5199 turn R at Brixworth Rd. Pass church & turn R opp butchers, approx 150yrds along Yew Tree Lane. Park at far end of lane or in Church Rd.* Home-made teas. **Adm £2.50, chd free. Sun 24 Mar (2-5).**
Half acre garden, which has much spring interest incl hellebores and a small woodland area. Own propagated plants for sale.

OAK TREE HOUSE
See Leicestershire & Rutland

39 THE OLD RECTORY
Eydon, Daventry NN11 3QE. Sir John & Lady Parsons. *10m NE of Banbury, 8m S of Daventry. At the edge of Eydon on the Culworth rd.* Home-made teas. **Adm £3, chd free. Sun 16 June (2-6).**
2-acre garden with glorious view and fine vistas. Mixed borders, shrubberies, specimen trees, walled kitchen garden and small arboretum. Wheelchair access to most of garden.

ORCHARD HOUSE
See Leicestershire & Rutland

OUSE MANOR
See Bedfordshire

PARK END THATCH
See Bedfordshire

GROUP OPENING

40 PRESTON CAPES GARDENS
Daventry NN11 3TF. *6m SW of Daventry. 13m NE of Banbury. 3m N of Canons Ashby. Parking for Little Preston at Old West Farm - follow signs. For Preston Capes parking off High St - follow signs.* Delicious lunches and teas at Little Preston. **Combined adm £4.50, chd free. Sun 2 June (12-5).**

CITY COTTAGE
Mrs Gavin Cowen

NORTH FARM
Mr & Mrs Tim Coleridge

THE OLD RECTORY
Luke & Victoria Bridgeman

OLD WEST FARM
Mr & Mrs Gerard Hoare

VILLAGE FARM
Trevor & Julia Clarke

A varied selection of gardens in a beautiful unspoilt south

Northamptonshire ironstone village mostly with wonderful views. Gardens range from classical country style to large extensive with woodland walk and ponds. Local sandstone houses and cottages. Norman Church. (Wonderful views). Limited wheelchair access in some parts of the gardens.

GROUP OPENING

41 RAVENSTHORPE GARDENS

Ravensthorpe NN6 8ES. *7m NW of Northampton. Signed from A5199 and the A428. Mill House immed on R as you turn off A428 down Long Lane. 1m from village.* Home-made teas at Village Hall. **Combined adm £4, chd free. Sun 14 July (1-5).**

MILL HOUSE
Ken and Gill Pawson
Visitors also welcome by appt June to Aug.
01604 770103
gill@gpplanning.co.uk

THE OLD FORGE HOUSE
Bryan & Anna Guest

QUIET WAYS
Russ & Sally Barringer

RAVENSTHORPE NURSERY
Mr & Mrs Richard Wiseman
Visitors also welcome by appt. Tea/coffee/biscuits by prior arrangement.
01604 770548
ravensthorpenursery@hotmail.com

TREETOPS
Ros and Gordon Smith

Attractive village in Northamptonshire uplands near to Ravensthorpe reservoir and Top Ardles Wood Woodland Trust which have bird watching and picnic opportunities. 5 very different established and developing gardens set in beautiful countryside displaying a wide range of plants, many of which are available from the Nursery, offering inspirational planting, quiet contemplation, beautiful views, gardens encouraging wildlife, fruit and vegetable gardens owned by Heritage Seed Library Guardian, rose garden and woodland walk.

ROLLESTON HALL
See Leicestershire & Rutland

42 ROSEMOUNT

18 Church Hill, Hollowell NN6 8RR. Mr & Mrs J Leatherland, 01604 740354. *10m NW of Northampton, 5m S J1 A14. Between A5199 and A428. Parking at village hall.* Light refreshments at Village Hall. **Adm £3.50, chd free. Sun 24 Feb (11-3). Visitors also welcome by appt Feb to Aug.**

The Leatherlands have been developing this ½-acre garden for over 50yrs. Both are keen and knowledgeable plantspeople, who love collecting and propagating their favourite plants, many of which are for sale. In August the garden is full of colour and interest with usual shrubs, herbaceous and clematis. Feb opening features their collection of nearly 200 different snowdrops, many hellebores and unusual spring bulbs, some for sale. Featured in local press and on Radio Northampton. Limited wheelchair access.

Tea and cake, how yummy . . . !

GROUP OPENING

43 SPRATTON GARDENS

Spratton NN6 8HL. *6½ m NNW of Northampton. From Northampton on A5199 turn L at Holdenby Rd for Spratton Grange Farm, after ½ m turn L up long drive. For other gardens turn R at Brixworth Rd. Car parking in village well signed with close access to first garden. Maps given to all visitors.* Light refreshments at St. Andrew's Church. **Combined adm £5, chd free. Sun 12 May (11-5).**

DALE HOUSE
Fiona & Chris Cox

THE GRANARY
Stephanie Bamford and Mark Wilkinson

11 HIGH STREET
Philip & Frances Roseblade

MULBERRY COTTAGE
Michael & Morley Heaton
(See separate entry)

SPRATTON GRANGE FARM
Dennis & Christine Yardy

THE STABLES
Pam & Tony Woods

WALTHAM COTTAGE
Norma & Allan Simons

The old part of the picturesque village has many late C17 stone built houses and turn of the C19/20 brick-built ones. These line the route between the seven inner village gardens, which are of a very varied nature. One is more formal with courtyard, walled garden and orchard, another a natural stream and pond, one has a 300yr old Holm (evergreen) oak. 3 gardens are cottage-style, with one well-stocked with tulips. Many interesting shrubs with good use of foliage colour. 3 gardens show how much can be made of a small area. Several gardens have fine views over rolling agricultural countryside. The garden outside of the village centre was created from a farm and at 2 acres is the largest. Natural pond, bog garden and beautiful courtyard where once cows stood. One of the gardens will be hosting a massive plant sale. Attractive village with C12 Grade I Norman church which is a very fine example and its many interior features can be admired whilst enjoying some light refreshments. Disabled access at most gardens.

44 ◆ STEANE PARK

Brackley NN13 6DP. Lady Connell, 01280 705899, www.steanepark.co.uk. *2m from Brackley towards Banbury. On A422, 6m E of Banbury.* **Adm £4.50, chd free. For NGS: Sun 14 July (11-4). For other opening times and information, please phone or see garden website.**

Beautiful trees in 80 acres of parkland, old waterway and fishponds, 1620 church in grounds. The gardens are constantly being updated in sympathy with old stone house and church. Limited wheelchair access.

STOKE ALBANY HOUSE
See Leicestershire & Rutland

45 NEW SULBY GARDENS
Sulby, Northampton NN6 6EZ. Mrs Alison Lowe. *16m NW of Northampton, 2m NE of Welford off A5199. Travelling N through Welford on A5199 past Wharf House hotel take 1st R, signed Sulby & Sibbertoft. After sharp R bend, followed by sharp L bend, Police Helicopter HQ is on L. Immed turn R at Home Farm sign (pheasants). At staggered junction with red letter box, turn R, Sulby Gardens is 1st driveway on L. Park outside gate on grass.* **Adm £4, chd free. Thurs 25 Apr; 20 June; 22 Aug (2-5.30); Thur 3 Oct (2-5).**
Unusual property covering 12 acres comprising working Victorian Kitchen Garden, Orchard, and C19 Ice House, plus Nature Reserve incl woodland, ponds, stream and wildflower meadows.

GROUP OPENING

46 SULGRAVE GARDENS
Banbury OX17 2RP. *8m NE of Banbury. Just off B4525 Banbury to Northampton rd, 7m from J11 off M40.* Home-made teas at Asby House. Manor Road. **Combined adm £4, chd free. Sun 23 June (2-6).**

CHURCH COTTAGE
Hywel & Ingram Lloyd

FERNS
George & Julia Metcalfe

THE HERB SOCIETY GARDEN AT SULGRAVE MANOR
The Herb Society

MILL HOLLOW BARN
David Thompson

RECTORY FARM
Mr & Mrs C Smyth-Osbourne

NEW ◆ SULGRAVE MANOR
The Sulgrave Manor Trust

SUNNYMEAD
Bob & Jean Bates

THREEWAYS
Alison & Digby Lewis

THE WATERMILL
Mr & Mrs A J Todd

Small historic village with lovely stone houses. C14 church and C16 manor house, home of George Washington's ancestors. Award winning community owned and run village shop. Nine gardens opening, including one returning this year, a real plantsman's garden. All gardens have been sympathetically and excitingly planted for a wide range of sites incl a small old cottage garden with container grown vegetable, a mature 1/4 -acre garden, contemporary garden designed by Alexander-Sinclair set around C17 water mill and pond, an extensive 7-acre garden with an arboretum and ponds. Sulgrave Manor gardens and the National Garden of Herb Society based at the Manor has grown a range of herbs that the Founding Fathers would have taken to America. Wheelchair access not possible at all gardens.

THORPE LUBENHAM HALL
See Leicestershire & Rutland

Look out for gardens open by appointment and visit at a time to suit you . . . !

47 TITCHMARSH HOUSE
Chapel Street, Titchmarsh NN14 3DA. Sir Ewan & Lady Harper, 01832 732439, jennifer.harper3@virginmedia.com. *2m N of Thrapston. 6m S of Oundle. Exit A14 at A605 J, Titchmarsh signed as turning to E.* Tea at Community Shop (19 May) & BBQ lunches at Village Fete (8 June). **Adm £3, chd free. Sun 19 May (2-6); Sat 8 June (12-5). Visitors also welcome by appt Apr to June.**
4 1/2 -acres extended and laid out since 1972. Cherries, magnolias, herbaceous, irises, shrub roses, range of unusual shrubs, walled borders and ornamental vegetable garden. Most of the garden can be visited without using steps.

TOFTE MANOR LABYRINTH & GARDEN
See Bedfordshire

48 TOP LODGE
Violet Lane, Glendon, nr Kettering NN14 1QL. Glenn & Anne Burley, 01536 511784, glennburley@btconnect.com. *3m NW of Kettering. Take A6003 to Corby, off r'about W of Kettering turn L onto Glendon Rd, signed at T-lights, approx 2m L into Violet Lane.* Light refreshments. **Adm £3, chd free. Sun 9 June (2-5.30). Visitors also welcome by appt May to Aug.**
1 1/2 -acre garden which is full of pleasant surprises around every corner. Large collection of plants, some rare and unusual shrubs plus a good selection of climbing roses and clematis. Woodland area, pond with stream and waterfalls, gravel, secluded garden and a children's garden. Access mostly on grass.

GROUP OPENING

49 TURWESTON GARDENS
Brackley NN13 5JY. *2m E of Brackley. A43 from M40 J10. On Brackley bypass turn R on A422 towards Buckingham, 1/2 m turn L signed Turweston.* Cream teas at Versions Farm. **Combined adm £4, chd free. Sun 26 May (2-5.30).**

OATLEYS HALL
Caroline & Ralph Grayson

TURWESTON HOUSE
Mr & Mrs C Allen

TURWESTON MILL
Mr & Mrs Harry Leventis

VERSIONS FARM
Mrs E T Smyth-Osbourne

Charming unspoilt stone built village in a conservation area. 4 quite large beautiful gardens. The Mill with bridges over the millstream and a spectacular waterfall, wildlife pond and newly designed kitchen garden. A 3-acre plantsman's garden with old stonewalls, terraces, pond and small water garden. 5-acre garden with woodland and pond. Formal terrace designed by James Alexander-Sinclair in 2008. 5-acre garden with lake, woodland walk with magnificent trees. Walled garden with flowers and vegetables.

GROUP OPENING

50 WEEDON LOIS & WESTON GARDENS

Weedon Lois, Towcester NN12 8PJ. Sir John & Lady Greenaway. *7m W of Towcester. 7m N of Brackley. Old Barn & Hillside are on High St, Weedon Lois. Home Close, Kettle End is just off High St & Ridgeway Cottage is on Weston High St.* Cream teas at Weston Community Centre. **Combined adm £4.50, chd free.** Sun 30 June (2-5.30).

NEW **HILLSIDE**
Mrs Karen Wilcox

HOME CLOSE
Clyde Burbidge

OLD BARN
Mr & Mrs John Gregory

RIDGEWAY COTTAGE
Jonathan & Elizabeth Carpenter

Two adjacent villages in South Northants with a handsome medieval Church in Weedon Lois. The extension churchyard contains the graves of the poets Dame Edith Sitwell and her brother Sir Sacheveral Sitwell who lived in Weston Hall. There are three gardens in Weedon Lois comprising a plantsman's garden, an award winning garden and new this year a garden with lovely stone terracing. In Weston there is a charming cottage garden and teas being provided in the Community Centre.

Dripwell House, Guilsborough Gardens

Northamptonshire County Volunteers

County Organisers

David Abbott, Wroxton Lodge, 1 Church Hill, Finedon, Wellingborough NN9 5NR, 01933 680363, d_j_abbott@btinternet.com
Gay Webster, Four Acres, The Green, Guilsborough NN6 8PT, 01604 740203, gay.webster6@gmail.com

County Treasurer & Publicity

Michael Heaton, Mulberry Cottage, Yew Tree Lane, Spratton NN6 8HL, 01604 846032, ngs@mimomul.co.uk

Assistant County Organisers

Philippa Heumann, The Old Vicarage, Broad Lane, Evenley, Brackley NN13 5SF, 01280 702409, philippaheumann@andreas-heumann.com
Geoff Sage, West Cottage, West End, West Haddon NN6 7AY, 01788 510334, geoffsage@aol.com

NOTTINGHAMSHIRE

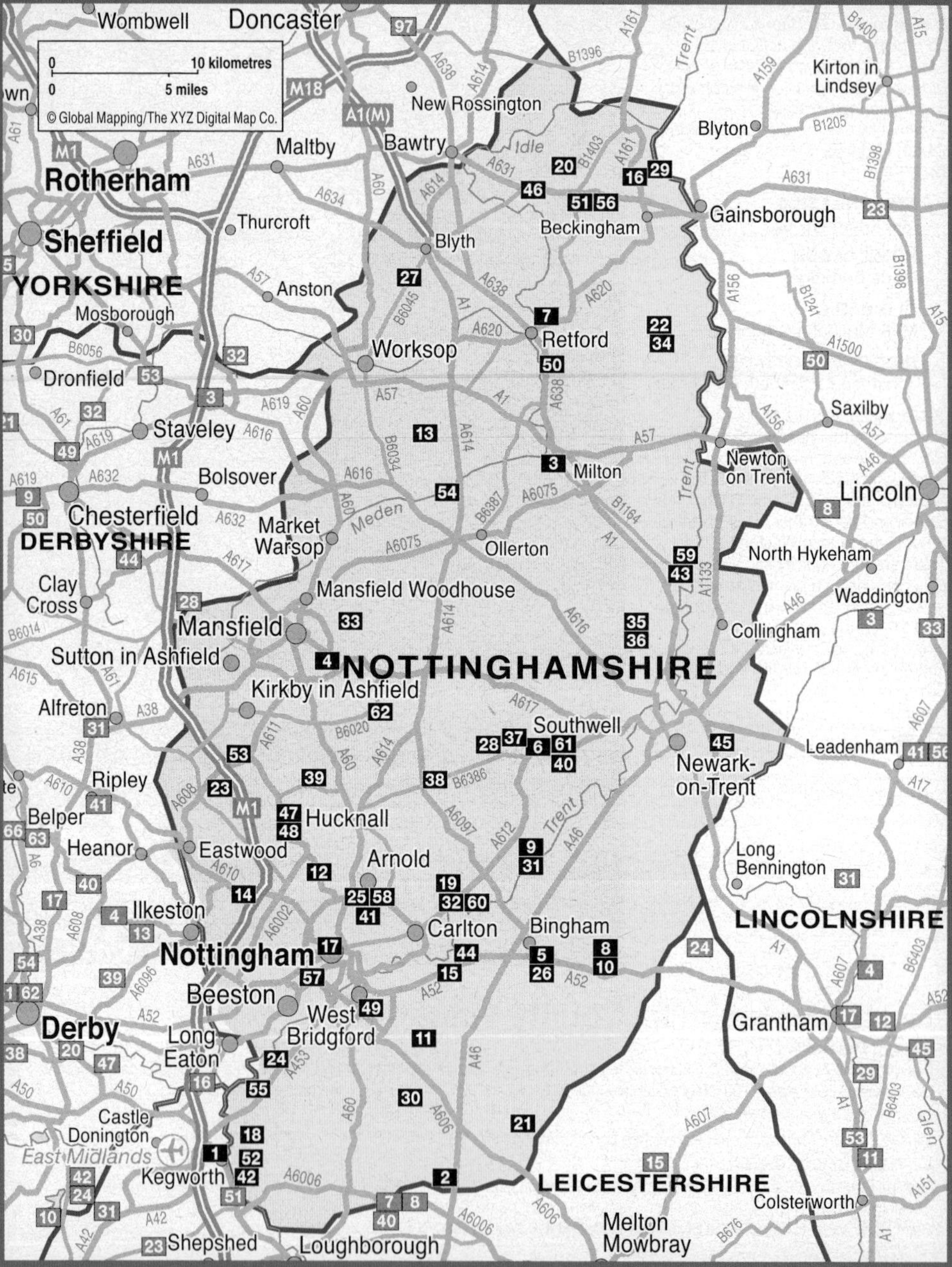

Opening Dates

February

Sunday 17
3 The Beeches

Wednesday 20
3 The Beeches

March

Sunday 24
3 The Beeches

Sunday 31
45 Roselea

April

Sunday 7
23 Felley Priory

Sunday 14
9 Capability Barn

Sunday 21
3 The Beeches
21 Elm House

Sunday 28
53 Sycamores House

Formal pond and seating areas to relax and enjoy something refreshing . . .

May

Sunday 12
16 Cross Lodge
26 Granby House
60 Woodpeckers

Sunday 19
31 Hoveringham Gardens
36 Norwell Nurseries

Sunday 26
19 Dumbleside
32 61 Lambley Lane
39 Papplewick Hall

Monday 27
28 Holbeck Lodge
29 Holmes Villa
37 The Old Vicarage

Wednesday 29
1 25 Ashby Road

June

Saturday 1
6 Bishop's Manor

Sunday 2
6 Bishop's Manor
31 Hoveringham Gardens

Friday 7
30 Home Farm House, 17 Main Street (Evening)

Sunday 9
2 Baxter Farm
17 Darby House
30 Home Farm House, 17 Main Street

Wednesday 12
9 Capability Barn

National Gardens Weekend

Saturday 15
28 Holbeck Lodge
37 The Old Vicarage
43 The Poplars
59 Woodbine Farmhouse

Sunday 16
5 Bingham Gardens
20 Ellicar Gardens
33 29 Lime Grove
43 The Poplars
45 Roselea
51 The Summer House
53 Sycamores House
56 Trust Cottage
58 6 Weston Close
59 Woodbine Farmhouse

Wednesday 19
44 Riseholme, 125 Shelford Road (Evening)

Saturday 22
61 The Workhouse

Sunday 23
7 Bolham Manor
11 Charnwood
38 Oxton Village Gardens
47 78 Sandy Lane
48 96 Sandy Lane

Sunday 30
11 Charnwood
12 The Chimes
35 Norwell Gardens
46 Rye Hall Farm

July

Wednesday 3
35 Norwell Gardens (Evening)

Saturday 6
54 Thoresby Hall Hotel & Spa
62 Young Gardeners at 3 Primary Schools

Sunday 7
18 Davryl
21 Elm House
37 The Old Vicarage
41 48 Penarth Gardens
50 Squirrel Lodge

Wednesday 10
54 Thoresby Hall Hotel & Spa

Saturday 13
13 Clumber Park Walled Kitchen Garden
54 Thoresby Hall Hotel & Spa

Sunday 14
25 The Glade
58 6 Weston Close

Wednesday 17
54 Thoresby Hall Hotel & Spa

Saturday 20
12 The Chimes (Evening)
54 Thoresby Hall Hotel & Spa

Sunday 21
4 335 Berry Hill Lane
15 Cornerstones
55 Thrumpton Hall

Wednesday 24
1 25 Ashby Road
41 48 Penarth Gardens (Evening)
54 Thoresby Hall Hotel & Spa

Saturday 27
54 Thoresby Hall Hotel & Spa

Sunday 28
22 The Elms
42 Piecemeal
44 Riseholme, 125 Shelford Road

August

Sunday 4
42 Piecemeal
47 78 Sandy Lane

Sunday 11
12 The Chimes
15 Cornerstones
24 The Forge

Sunday 18
57 University of Nottingham Gardens

Sunday 25
37 The Old Vicarage

September

Sunday 1
8 5 Burton Lane
10 Cedarwood

Thursday 5
6 Bishop's Manor

Saturday 7
52 Sutton Bonington Arboretum

Sunday 8
34 Lodge Mount

Sunday 15
20 Ellicar Gardens
50 Squirrel Lodge

October

Sunday 13
36 Norwell Nurseries

Gardens open to the public

- 13 Clumber Park Walled Kitchen Garden
- 23 Felley Priory
- 27 Hodsock Priory Gardens
- 36 Norwell Nurseries
- 61 The Workhouse

By appointment only

- 14 7 Collygate
- 40 Park Farm
- 49 The Small Exotic Garden

Also open by Appointment ☎

- 2 Baxter Farm
- 3 The Beeches
- 7 Bolham Manor
- 8 5 Burton Lane
- 9 Capability Barn
- 10 Cedarwood
- 15 Cornerstones
- 17 Darby House
- 19 Dumbleside
- 20 Ellicar Gardens
- 22 The Elms
- 26 Granby House
- 28 Holbeck Lodge
- 29 Holmes Villa
- 31 Church House, Hoveringham Gardens
- 31 Hoveringham Gardens
- 31 West Farm House, Hoveringham Gardens
- 34 Lodge Mount
- 37 The Old Vicarage
- 38 Crows Nest Cottage, Oxton Village Gardens
- 38 Home Farm Cottage, Oxton Village Gardens
- 41 48 Penarth Gardens
- 42 Piecemeal
- 44 Riseholme, 125 Shelford Road
- 45 Roselea
- 47 78 Sandy Lane
- 53 Sycamores House
- 55 Thrumpton Hall
- 58 6 Weston Close
- 60 Woodpeckers

The Gardens

1 25 ASHBY ROAD

Kegworth, Derby DE74 2DH. Richard & Leigh Woods. *10m S of Nottingham. 6m N of Loughborough. From A6 turn into High St (opp Boots, next to Flying Horse PH). Follow for 500 metres into Ashby Rd.* Home-made teas. **Adm £2.50, chd free. Wed 29 May; Wed 24 July (2-7).**

Plant lovers' garden, packed with traditional, rare and unusual plants. Mixed borders throughout this relatively small garden (8 metres x 40 metres) giving flower, foliage, colour and interest all yr. Also several specimen trees incl oak, liquidambar and liriodendron. No lawn to speak of, just a bit of grass! Formal pond and seating areas to relax and enjoy something refreshing.

Stroll across the croquet lawn, down mown paths into the old orchard . . .

2 BAXTER FARM

Willoughby on the Wolds LE12 6SY. Peter & Pru Tatham, 01509 880975, docpetertatham@gmail.com. *10m S of Nottingham, 12m N of Leicester. About ¼ m off A46 at E end of Main St.* Ploughmans lunch and home-made teas. **Adm £3, chd free. Sun 9 June (12-5). Visitors also welcome by appt 15 May to 31 July.**

Old farmhouse and barns. 1-acre garden planted over last 25yrs. Conservatory, old cattle drinking pond now planted, herbaceous borders, informal plantings of old roses, hardy geraniums, primulas, salvias and many climbers. Pergola, Chinese garden, beech and yew hedged walks. Kitchen garden.

3 THE BEECHES

The Avenue, Milton, Tuxford, Newark NG22 0PW. Margaret & Jim Swindin, 01777 870828, james91.swindin@mypostoffice.co.uk. *1m S A1 Markham Moor. Exit A1 at Markham Moor, take Walesby sign into village (1m). From Main Street, L up The Avenue.* Home-made teas. **Adm £3, chd free. Sun 17, Wed 20 Feb (11-4); Suns 24 Mar, 21 Apr (2-5). Visitors also welcome by appt Feb to Apr.**

1-acre garden full of colour and interest to plant enthusiasts looking for unusual and rare plants. Spring gives some 250 named snowdrops together with hellebores and early daffodils. The lawn is awash with crocus, fritillarias, anemones, narcissi and cyclamen. Large vegetable garden on raised beds. Lovely views over open countryside. Newcastle Mausoleum (adjacent) open. Featured on BBC TV Belmont, Newark Advertiser, Nottingham Post and Daily Telgraph. Some gravel paths, steps and slopes.

4 335 BERRY HILL LANE

Mansfield NG18 4JB. Sheila Whalley. *2m S of Mansfield. Berry Hill Lane joins A60 Nottingham Rd and goes through to A614 Southwell Rd opp Oak Tree PH.* Home-made teas. **Adm £3, chd free. Sun 21 July (1-5).**

A 'Tardis Garden' with herbaceous borders, water features, statuary, mature trees. Various features. Terraced steps lead down to large patio and summerhouse. Marquees will be erected if wet.

GROUP OPENING

5 NEW BINGHAM GARDENS

NG13 8BG. *8m E of Nottingham. From A46 or A52 follow signs for Bingham then NGS signs to gardens off Long Acre on main rd through centre of Bingham. All gardens accessed off Long acre.* Teas at 8A Fisher Lane and 22 Long Acre East. **Combined adm £4, chd free. Sun 16 June (2-5).**

8A FISHER LANE
Michael & Sylvia Bennett

GRANBY HOUSE
Maureen & John Gladwin
(See separate entry)

NEW 22 LONG ACRE EAST
Sue Hull

The gardens consist of a large plantsmans' garden, small terraced town garden and formal contemporary designed garden. Something for everyone.

6 BISHOP'S MANOR

Bishop's Drive, Southwell NG25 0JR. The Rt Rev & Mrs P Butler. *Centre of Southwell, end of Bishops Dr on S side of Minster. Close to War Memorial Park.* Home-made teas. **Adm £3.50, chd free. Sat 1, Sun 2 June (1-5); Thur 5 Sept (1-4).**

Mature Edwardian gardens surrounding the medieval walls of the Archbishops of York's Palace. Delightful enclosed garden within the ruined walls incl a herb knot garden and quadruple Medieval privy, overlooked by Southwell Minister and the Great Hall. Woodland areas. Southwell Minster- Embroidery Exhibition (June). Gravel paths.

7 NEW BOLHAM MANOR

Bolham Way, Bolham, Retford DN22 9JG. Pam & Butch Barnsdale, 01777 703528, pamandbutch@bolham-manor.com, www.bolham-manor.com. *1m from Retford. A620 Gainsborough Rd from Retford, turn L onto Tiln Lane signed 'A620 avoiding low bridge'. Past Carr Hill School, at sharp R bend take rd directly ahead signed 'Tiln Lane' & immed L onto Bolham Way, then 150 yds L down drive.* Home-made teas. **Adm £3.50, chd free. Sun 23 June (1-5). Visitors also welcome by appt May to July.**

Enjoy this much loved 3-acre garden with its stream of meadow flowers, mature trees, herbaceous borders, and meandering terraced planting down to the ponds and cave. Stroll across the croquet lawn, down mown paths into the old orchard where Paul's Himalyan Musk and other ramblers are there to greet you. Wheelchair access limited to parts of garden.

88 BROOK STREET

See Leicestershire & Rutland

109 BROOK STREET

See Leicestershire & Rutland

8 5 BURTON LANE

Whatton in the Vale NG13 9EQ. Mr & Ms Faulconbridge, 01949 850942, jpfalconbridge@hotmail.co.uk. *3m E of Bingham. Follow signs to Whatton from A52 between Bingham & Elton. Garden nr Church in old part of village. Will be signed.* Home-made teas at Cedarwood. **Combined adm £4, chd free. Sun 1 Sept (1-5). Combined with Cedarwood. Visitors also welcome by appt May to Sept.**

Medium-sized, organic, wildlife-friendly garden. Attractive fruit and vegetable areas at front and side. Back has romantic atmosphere. Scented plants and seating. Large beds have stepping stone paths with great variety of plants, incl rarities, climbers, wild flowers and herbs. Also features hot gravel garden, pond, shade planting and trained fruit. Historic church.

Crows Nest Cottage, Oxton Village Gardens

© Nicola Stocken Tomkins

9 CAPABILITY BARN

Gonalston Lane, Hoveringham NG14 7JH. Malcolm & Wendy Fisher, 0115 966 4322. *8m NE of Nottingham. A612 from Nottingham through Lowdham. Take 1st R into Gonalston Lane. 1m on L.* **Adm £3, chd free. Sun 14 Apr; Wed 12 June (1-5). Visitors also welcome by appt Apr to June.**

This large country garden continues to evolve with new features and plantings. Enjoy colourful displays of spring bulbs in April and rich varied herbaceous displays from early summer onwards. All this within a framework of mature trees and wonderful countryside views. Daffodils, hostas and ornamental grasses all star in their seasons.

10 CEDARWOOD

Burton Lane, Whatton in the Vale NG13 9EQ. Louise Bateman, 01949 850227, louise.bateman@hotmail.co.uk. *3m E of Bingham. Cedarwood is a cedar-clad bungalow in the old part of Whatton, around the corner from the church and set back off the rd.* Home-made teas. **Combined adm £4, chd free. Sun 1 Sept (1-5). Combined with 5 Burton Lane. Visitors also welcome by appt May to July. Please ring to discuss requirements.**

Cedarwood is a 1/3 -acre plantswoman's garden developed over 7yrs where flowers dominate; incl a rose garden, formal pond, bog garden, raised alpine bed and beautiful mixed plantings. Majority of plants are grown from seed by the owner and this enables frequent experiments with planting combinations, on a tight budget.

11 CHARNWOOD
120 Cotgrave Lane, Tollerton NG12 4FY. Kate & Peter Foale, www.katescuttings.net. *5m SE Nottingham. From Wheatcroft r'about, A606 Melton, turn L at 2nd set T-lights signed Cotgrave. After 1m turn L. From A46 take A606. After 5m turn R at T-lights.* Home-made teas. **Adm £3.50, chd free (share to Friends of South Wolds Community School). Sun 23, Sun 30 June (1-5).**
1-acre garden with many mature trees and shrubs developed over 25 yrs by obsessive plantswoman and patient husband. New summer opening with early perennials, roses and clematis. Large well-established water lily pond with jetty. Seaside gravel garden, unusual sculptures, 'secret' bamboo garden. Come and get lost in the tranquility of this plant-lover's garden. Featured on BBC East Midlands Today. Some grassy slopes and bark paths.

12 THE CHIMES
37 Glenorchy Crescent, Heronridge NG5 9LG. Stan & Ellen Maddock. *4m N of Nottingham. A611 towards Hucknall, onto Bulwell Common, turn R at Tesco, Top Valley, up to island, turn L, 100yds. 1st L, then 2nd L onto Glenorchy Crescent, down to bottom.* Cream teas. **Adm £3, chd free. Sun 30 June (12-5). Evening Opening £5, chd free, wine, Sat 20 July (6-9); Sun 11 Aug (12-5).**
We would like to invite you to visit our small but well stocked garden. Full of roses, peonies, lilies and much more. We have a small pond and plenty of pots and baskets. Winner of silver gilt award Nottingham in Bloom - best front garden.

13 ◆ CLUMBER PARK WALLED KITCHEN GARDEN
Clumber Park, Worksop S80 3AZ. National Trust, 01909 476592, www.nationaltrust.org.uk. *4m S of Worksop. From main car park or main entrance follow directions to the Walled Kitchen Garden.* **Adm £3, vehicle entry to park £5.80, chd free. For NGS: Sat 13 July (10-5). For other opening times and information, please phone or see garden website.**
Beautiful 4-acre walled kitchen garden, growing unusual and old varieties of vegetables, fruits, herbs and ornamentals, incl magnificent recently extended 400ft long double herbaceous borders. 450ft long glasshouse with grape vines, peaches, nectarines and figs. Museum of gardening tools. New soft fruit garden and rose garden. Featured on BBC2 - Great British Food Revival. Gravel paths and slopes.

Enjoy tea and delicious home-made cake in a beautiful setting . . .

14 7 COLLYGATE
Swingate, Kimberley NG16 2PJ. Doreen Fahey & John Arkinstall, 01159 192690. *6m W of Nottingham. From M1 J26 take A610 towards Nottingham. L at next island on B600 into Kimberley. At Sainsbury's mini island take L. L at top. Park on this rd, in 500yds Collygate on R.* **Adm £3, chd free. Visitors welcome by appt May to Aug.**
Delightful garden created by serious plant enthusiasts and tucked away at the end of a short narrow lane in Swingate. It greets you with an impact of unexpected colour and delights you with the variety and sensitivity of the planting. A peaceful backwater in an urban setting.

15 CORNERSTONES
15 Lamcote Gardens, Radcliffe-on-Trent, Nottingham NG12 2BS. Judith & Jeff Coombes, 0115 8458055, judith.coombes@gmail.com, www.cornerstonesgarden.co.uk. *4m E of Nottingham. From A52 take Radcliffe exit at RSPCA junction, then 2nd L just before hairpin bend.* Home-made teas. **Adm £3, chd free. Sun 21 July; Sun 11 Aug (1.30-5.30). Visitors also welcome by appt July and Aug.**
Plant lovers garden, approaching ½ acre. Flowing colour-themed and specie borders, with rare, exotic and unusual plants, provide a wealth of colour and interest, whilst the unique fruit and vegetable garden generates an abundance of produce. Bananas, palms, fernery, fish pond, bog garden, lovely new summerhouse area and greenhouse. Enjoy tea and delicious home-made cake in a beautiful setting. Some bark paths and unfenced ponds.

7 THE CRESCENT
See Leicestershire & Rutland

16 NEW CROSS LODGE
Beckingham Road, Walkeringham DN10 4HZ. John & Betty Roberts. *A620 from Retford or A631 from Bawtry/Gainsborough and A161 to Walkeringham. Garden is on A161. Parking at Village Hall on A161 approx 150 metres N of garden (postcode DN10 4JF).* Home-made teas at Walkeringham Village Hall. **Adm £2.50, chd free. Sun 12 May (1-5).**
Ever changing 1¼-acre garden with successive displays of spring and summer flowers. Rhododendron walk in which there are over 50 varieties is at its best in May. Shrubs and perennial borders, rockeries, roses, conifers, old orchard and small woodland with large pond. Access to all main features excluding pond-side paths.

17 DARBY HOUSE
10 The Grove, Southey Street, Nottingham NG7 4BS. Jed Brignal, 07960 065042, jedbrignal@yahoo.co.uk, www.jedbrignal.co.uk. *¾m NE of city centre take A610, turn R into Bentinck Rd, turn R at lights into Southey St.* Light refreshments. **Adm £3, chd free. Sun 9 June (2-5). Visitors also welcome by appt Jan to Oct.**
Unusual city garden designed and developed by artist owner. A tranquil oasis in unlikely location. Victorian walled garden with ponds, gazebos and fairy-tale shady area surrounded by mature trees. Wide variety of rare and unusual perennials incl hardy geraniums. Also home to charming construction formed from stained glass. House (1849) and garden provide temporary home and sanctuary for actors, writers, dancers and other creative visitors. Rare plant nursery and bespoke craft stalls. Wheelchair access limited to terrace.

18 DAVRYL
9 The Green, Kingston-on-Soar, Nottingham NG11 0DA. David & Beryl Elliott. *10m SW of Nottingham. From J24 of M1, A6 to Loughborough, then 1st L signed Kingston. From Nottingham, SE on A453, turn L, through Ratcliffe on Soar, then 1st L under railway. Opp village green, 4th cottage from church, path by telephone box.* Cream teas. **Adm £2.50, chd free. Sun 7 July (2-6).**
Located in small, peaceful village. Garden borders filled with colourful perennials, annuals and bulbs as well as mature trees and shrubs. Lawn runs down to brook and small pond. Plenty of secluded seating for teas.

DODDINGTON HALL GARDENS
See Lincolnshire

19 DUMBLESIDE
17 Bridle Road, Burton Joyce NG14 5FT. Mr P Bates, 01159 313725. *5m NE of Nottingham. In Burton Joyce turn off A612, Nottingham to Southwell rd into Lambley Lane. Bridle Rd is an impassable looking rd to R. Car parking easiest beyond garden.* Home-made teas at nearby United Reformed Church. **Combined adm £4, chd free. Sun 26 May (2-6). Combined with 61 Lambley Lane. Visitors also welcome by appt Apr to Dec.**
2-acre garden of varied habitat. Raised gravel beds for small sun lovers. Natural springs planted with primulas, fritillaries; the stream runs beside woodland paths, bordered by shade loving tree ferns, arisaemas and trilliums. 50yd mixed border. Stepping stones to meadow/orchard, with bulbs and extensive wild flowers in grass. Steep slopes towards stream.

20 ELLICAR GARDENS
Ellicar House, Carr Road, Gringley-on-the-Hill DN10 4SN. Will & Sarah Murch, 01777 817218 / 07850 034195, enquiries@inspirational-gardens.co.uk, www.inspirational-gardens.co.uk. *Gringley on the Hill. Turn L onto Leys Ln (after school) and follow road approx 1½ m. Ellicar Gardens is on L opp cream house.* Home-made teas. **Adm £3, chd free. Sun 16 June; Sun 15 Sept (1-5). Combined with The Summer House and Trust Cottage, adm £4.00, chd free, Sun 16 June. Visitors and groups also welcome by appt Mar to Oct. Refreshments by arrangement.**
Young, vibrant and naturalistic, this 5-acre family garden is a wildlife hotspot. Enjoy our sweeping gravel garden, new rose garden, wildflower meadows, orchard, woodland walk, winter garden, bog garden and beautiful natural swimming pool. Children love exploring the school garden, willow maze and tree house. Garden visitors are greeted by our pet pigs, ponies, geese, goats and guinea fowl. Some uneven ground and gravel wide paths.

Children love exploring the school garden, willow maze and tree house . . .

21 ELM HOUSE
Main Street, Hickling, Melton Mowbray LE14 3AJ. David & Deborah Chambers. *12m E of Nottingham. 7m W of Melton Mowbray. From Nottingham take A606 E. After crossing A46 turn L at Bridgegate Lane signed Hickling. In village turn R at T-junction. Elm House is last on R.* Home-made teas. **Adm £3, chd free. Sun 21 Apr; Sun 7 July (1-5).**
Large interesting garden with many different areas. Lovely in spring with more than 25 varieties of magnolia and many spring bulbs. Other features incl a railway garden, seaside garden, small walled garden, woodland area and pond with fish. Newly-formed stumpery. Level garden with some gravel paths.

22 THE ELMS
Main Street, North Leverton DN22 0AR. Tim & Tracy Ward, 01427 881164, tracy@wardt2.fsnet.co.uk. *5m E of Retford, 6m SW of Gainsborough. From Retford take rd to Leverton for 5m, into North Leverton with Habblesthorpe.* **Adm £2.50, chd free. Sun 28 July (2-5). Visitors also welcome by appt June to Sept.**
This garden is very different, creating an extension to the living space. Inspiration comes from tropical countries, giving a Mediterranean feel. Palms, bamboos and bananas, along with other exotics, create drama and yet make a statement true to many gardens, that of peace and calm. North Leverton Windmill will be open for visitors. The garden is fully viewable however access onto decked and tiled areas is restricted.

23 ◆ FELLEY PRIORY
Underwood NG16 5FJ. Miss Michelle Upchurch for the Brudenell Family, 01773 810230, www.felleypriory.co.uk. *8m SW of Mansfield. Off A608 ½ m W M1 J27.* **Adm £4, chd free. For NGS: Sun 7 Apr (10-4). For other opening times and information, please phone or see garden website.**
Garden for all seasons with yew hedges and topiary, snowdrops, hellebores, herbaceous borders and rose garden. There are pergolas, a white garden, small arboretum and borders filled with unusual trees, shrubs, plants and bulbs. The grass-edged pond is planted with primulas, bamboo, iris, roses and eucomis. Bluebell woodland walk. Extremely rare orchard of daffodils.

FIRVALE ALLOTMENT GARDEN
See Yorkshire

24 THE FORGE
Barton in Fabis, Nottingham NG11 0AE. Angela Plowright & Paul Kaczmarczuk. *6m SW of Nottingham. Off A453 between Clifton and M1 J24. From Nottingham, 1st R signed Barton-in-Fabis, approx 1½ m from Crusader PH r'about. The Forge is 1st house on R at bottom of hill by red phone box. From M1, approx 3½ m along A453, take 2nd L signed Barton. Car parking & toilets in village.* Tea and cakes available in barn. **Adm £3, chd free. Sun 11 Aug (2-6).**
A pretty and interesting cottage garden divided into several intimate 'rooms', overflowing with perennials, herbs and shrubs. Many plants chosen to attract butterflies and bees. Original buildings incl old farmyard with wildflowers, pond and agricultural bygones. Barton in Fabis - Small Village category winner, E Midlands in Bloom Competition and Judges' Award for community work to create wildlife friendly habitats in churchyard.

Church House, Hoveringham Gardens

25 NEW THE GLADE
2A Woodthorpe Avenue, Nottingham NG5 4FD. Tony Hoffman. *A60 Mansfield Rd from Nottingham. After Sherwood shops turn R at T-lights by Woodthorpe Park into Woodthorpe Drive. 2nd L into Woodthorpe Avenue.* Home-made teas. **Adm £3, chd free. Sun 14 July (1-5). Also opening 6 Weston Close.**
Exquisite medium-sized garden developed over 8 yrs on the site of a former Great Western Railway track with very free draining soil which allows Mediterranean plants to thrive. Feature plants incl tree ferns, 30 ft high bamboos, fan palms, acers and other shrubs rarely seen. The railway arch, enclosed in trellis work, provides shade for a variety of ferns and hostas.

26 GRANBY HOUSE
8 Long Acre, Bingham NG13 8BG. Maureen & John Gladwin, 01949 836340, gladwin897@btinternet.com. *8m E of Nottingham. From A46 or A52 follow signs for Bingham. Follow NGS signs to garden.* **Adm £3, chd free. Sun 12 May (2-5). Visitors also welcome by appt May to Sept.**
Town centre garden of just under 1/3 acre, previously a thriving nursery. Lots of nooks and crannies, borders with wide variety of shrubs and plants. Formal pond, woodland plant area and bog garden. Wisteria in bloom May. Featured in Garden News - Garden of the Week.

134 HERRICK ROAD
See Leicestershire & Rutland

27 ◆ HODSOCK PRIORY GARDENS
Blyth, Worksop S81 0TY. Sir Andrew & Lady Buchanan, 01909 591204, www.snowdrops.co.uk. *4m N of Worksop off B6045. Blyth-Worksop rd approx 2m from A1M. Well signed locally.* **For opening times and information, please phone or see garden website.**
Enjoy exploring our estate and nearby attractions. Visitors to the snowdrops can enjoy a leisurely walk through the gardens and woods. See our website for special offers, opening times and full details of our snowdrop events, talk and tours. Some paths difficult for wheelchairs when wet.

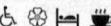

28 HOLBECK LODGE
Manor Fields, Halam, Newark NG22 8DU. Paul & Jane Oakley, 01636 813896, pauloakley07@btinternet.com. *1½ m W of Southwell. From B6386 in Halam village 350yds past church, R into Manor Fields. Parking on Radley Rd.* **Combined adm £4, chd free. Mon 27 May; Sat 15 June (1-5). Combined with The Old Vicarage. Visitors also welcome by appt June and July.**
Starting with a blank canvas in 2001 when Holbeck Lodge was built, this ½ -acre garden was designed and planted to flow from semi-formal to more natural planting bordering open countryside. A vegetable garden with raised beds is contained by a rose trellis, leading through herbaceous beds, hostas, roses, betula, sorbus and several spectacular Cornus Kousa. Bordering beck. Some sloping areas may not be suitable for wheelchairs.

29 HOLMES VILLA
Holmes Lane, Walkeringham, nr Gainsborough DN10 4JP. Peter & Sheila Clark, 01427 890233, clarkshaulage@aol.com. *4m NW of Gainsborough. A620 from Retford or A631 from Bawtry/Gainsborough & A161 to Walkeringham then towards Misterton. Follow yellow signs for last mile. Allocated parking for disabled visitors.* Home-made teas. **Adm £2, chd free. Mon 27 May (1-5). Visitors also welcome by appt.**
1¾ -acre plantsman's interesting and inspirational garden; surprises around every corner with places to sit and ponder, gazebos, arbours, ponds, hosta garden, unusual perennials and shrubs for flower arranging. Lots of ideas to copy. Old tools, wildlife pond and scarecrows A flower arranger's artistic garden. Specialist plant sale. Driftwood stall bric-a-brac. Featured in Lincolnshire Today, Epworth Bells and Yorkshire Post.

30 HOME FARM HOUSE, 17 MAIN STREET
Keyworth, Nottingham NG12 5AA. Graham & Pippa Tinsley. *7m S of Nottingham. Follow signs to Keyworth from A60 or A606 and head for the church. Garden about 50yds on L. Some parking on Main St. Car parking at village hall and public car park on Bunny Lane.* Home-made teas (Sun 9 June only).

Adm £3, chd free. **Evening Opening £3, chd free, wine, Fri 7 June (6-9); Sun 9 June (1-5).**
Large atmospheric garden hidden behind old farmhouse in the village centre. Beech walk, orchard, ponds, turf mound, pergolas, new summer house, winter garden and old garden with herbaceous borders. High yew hedges hide a secret rose garden. Many trees incl cedars, oaks and chestnuts. A place to be explored. Access via gravel yard.

THE HOMESTEAD
See Leicestershire & Rutland

GROUP OPENING

31 NEW HOVERINGHAM GARDENS
Gonalston Lane, Hoveringham NG14 7JH. *Centre of Hoveringham village. 6m NE of Nottingham. Signed from A612 Nottingham to Southwell rd, on Southwell side of Lowdham.* Home-made teas. **Combined adm £4, chd free. Sun 19 May; Sun 2 June (1-5).**

CHURCH HOUSE
Alex & Sue Allan
Visitors also welcome by appt Apr to June with West Farm House.
07976 966795
suziewoo109@hotmail.com

WEST FARM HOUSE
Dr R S & Mrs C D Torr
Visitors also welcome by appt Apr to June with Church House.
01159 664771
richard-torr1@tiscali.co.uk

2 contrasting gardens in the centre of Hoveringham village near St Michael's Church. West Farm House is a large cottage-style garden and Church House is a small, but perfectly formed, walled garden. Both gardens host a wide range of features and plants, with specialist collections in each. Cacti and succulent collection at West Farm House. Auricula theatre and Japanese area at Church House. West Farm House has featured in Nottingham Evening Post and Weekly News. Gravel at both gardens and narrow, uneven access at Church House, very difficult for wheelchairs.

32 61 LAMBLEY LANE
Burton Joyce NG14 5BG. Mr Richard Powell. *6m N of Nottingham. In Burton Joyce turn off A612 (Nottingham to Southwell rd) into Lambley Lane.* Home-made teas at nearby United Reform Church. **Combined adm £4, chd free. Sun 26 May (2-6). Combined with Dumbleside.**
Approx ¾ acre of spring flowering shrubs, plants and bulbs. Mixed borders, greenhouse and terrace. Cacti, vegetable garden, fruit trees, colourful display of azaleas and camellias. Steep drive to entrance.

The garden was specifically designed for opening as part of the NGS . . .

33 29 LIME GROVE
Forest Town, Mansfield NG19 0HR. Laurence & Margaret Brown. *2m E of Mansfield. On B6030 through Forest Town on Clipstone Road West. Lime Grove R turn immed before Shell filling station. (Caution-narrow entry.) Parking in field adjacent number 20 on R.* Cream teas. **Adm £3, chd free. Sun 16 June (1-5).**
Beautifully laid out plant lovers' garden of 1.3 acres. Large neat front garden with topiary and many varieties of colourful perennials all year round. Rear garden is a gardener's joy with lawn, irregular colourful herbaceous borders, beds and koi pond. All varieties of planting with specimen trees leading through to nursery and vegetable beds.

34 NEW LODGE MOUNT
Town Street, South Leverton, Retford DN22 0BT. Mr & Mrs A Whitton-Jones, 01427 884949, a.wj@live.co.uk. *4m E of Retford. Opp Bradley's Garage on Town Street.* Home-made teas. **Adm £3, chd free. Sun 8 Sept (10-5). Visitors also welcome by appt.**
Following organic principles, an orchard and large vegetable and fruit plots are complemented by an area of unusual perennial edibles, and helpful plants, with a view to self-sufficiency. Originally a field, much of the ½ -acre garden, although planned on paper for years, was landscaped within a few months during 2012 in order to fulfil an ambition following Helen's terminal cancer diagnosis. Helen's aunt also had cancer and the garden was specifically designed for opening as part of the NGS to fulfil the desire to raise money for cancer charities.

LONG CLOSE
See Leicestershire & Rutland

MOUNTAIN ASH
See Leicestershire & Rutland

GROUP OPENING

35 NORWELL GARDENS
Nr Newark. NG23 6JX. *6m N of Newark. Off A1 at Cromwell turning, take Norwell Rd at bus shelter.* Tea in Village Hall (June) and Norwell Nurseries (July). **Combined adm £4, chd free. Sun 30 June (2-5). Evening Opening £4, chd free, Wed 3 July (6.30-9).**

NEW THE BAKEHOUSE
Mr Peter Jones

NEW FAUNA FOLLIES
Mrs Sheila Wright

4 MOORLANDS CLOSE
Jackie Musgrove

NORWELL ALLOTMENT PARISH GARDENS
Norwell Parish Council

◆ NORWELL NURSERIES
Andrew & Helen Ward
(See separate entry)

THE OLD FORGE
Adam & Hilary Ward

THE OLD MILL HOUSE, NORWELL
Mr & Mrs M Burgess

SOUTHVIEW COTTAGE
Margaret & Les Corbett

Range of different, very appealing gardens all making superb use of the beautiful backdrop of a quintessentially English village and countryside. They incl an outstanding plantsman's garden with over 2,500 different plants radiating from a 'Monet' pond. 32 allotments of different sizes are tended by gardeners from all generations growing fruit, vegetables and a wealth of cut flowers. Also walled gardens, water features, sun and shade gardens, a mature verdant garden with unusual trees and shrubs providing a luxuriant stage for pools of perennial colour, gardens where innovative features abound with lush and colourful plantings incl roses and grasses. A tiny, quirky garden shows what can be done when space is restricted but ideas are not and the development of a family garden will allow visitors to follow its progress over the next few yrs. A modern house with angular lines is echoed by a bold, evolving contemporary garden which manages to blend effortlessly into the rolling countryside. The beautiful medieval church and its peaceful churchyard with grass labyrinth will be open. The church will be celebrating the diamond jubilee of the installation of the church clock.

Bounteous borders of unusual herbaceous plants, clematis, roses, shrubs and trees . . .

36 ◆ NORWELL NURSERIES
Woodhouse Road, Norwell NG23 6JX. Andrew & Helen Ward, 01636 636337, www.norwellnurseries.co.uk. *6m N of Newark. Off A1 at Cromwell turning, take rd to Norwell at bus stop.* **Adm £2.50, chd free. For NGS: Sun 19 May; Sun 13 Oct (2-5). For other opening times and information, please phone or see garden website.**
Jewel box of over 2,500 different, beautiful and unusual plants sumptuously set out in a ¾ -acre plantsman's garden incl shady garden with orchids, woodland gems, cottage garden borders, alpine and scree areas. Pond with opulently planted margins. Extensive herbaceous borders and effervescent colour-themed beds. New borders every year. Autumn opening features UK's largest collection of hardy chrysanthamums. Featured in Great Gardens to Visit and Gardens-Guide.com. Grass paths, no wheelchair access to woodland paths.

37 THE OLD VICARAGE
Halam Hill, nr Southwell NG22 8AX. Mrs Beverley Perks, 01636 812181, perks.family@talk21.com. *1m W of Southwell. On approach to Halam village down hill on L or from A614 through Farnsfield & Edingley villages over Xrds in Halam, last house on R. Park diagonally into beech hedge on verge (with interactive speed sign) for ease of parking & reversing, back onto rd when leaving or park in village up Radley Rd.* Home-made teas. **Mon 27 May; Sat 15 June; Sun 7 July; Sun 25 Aug (1-5). Combined with Holbeck Lodge, adm £4.00, chd free, 27 May and 15 June. Adm £3.50, chd free, 7 July and 25 Aug. Visitors also welcome by appt May to Sept.**
This beautifully planted, organic, relaxing garden on south facing hillside, offers history, wonder and design. Bounteous borders of unusual herbaceous plants, clematis, roses, shrubs and trees. There are hidden nooks and crannies, varied wildlife ponds, swimming pool planting, orchard, productive kitchen garden, new wildflower meadow with glorious views - soak up the peace and quiet, slightly disturbed by our friendly chickens. Beautiful C12 Church open only short walk through village or across field through attractive churchyard - rare C14 stained glass window. Featured in Gardening News - Garden of the Week. Slopes but cheerful help available.

GROUP OPENING

38 OXTON VILLAGE GARDENS
Southwell NG25 0SS. Oxton Village Gardens. *5m W of Southwell. From B6386 turn into Oxton Village (Blind Lane), Home Farm Cottage is on L opp The Green Dragon PH & Roman Way is on corner opp. Wesley Grange is at end of Chapel Lane behind PH. Turn R at T-junction into Forest Rd. Crow's Nest Cottage is 200yds on R. Turn L into Main St and take New Rd to the water splash. Turn R and find The White Bungalow and Pilgrim Cottage on L along Water Lane.* Home-made teas at Crows Nest Cottage. **Combined adm £5, chd free. Sun 23 June (12-6).**

CROWS NEST COTTAGE
Joan Arnold & Tom Heinersdorff
Visitors also welcome by appt Mar to Sept (combined with Home Farm Cottage if date convenient).
01159 653789
trebleclef.arnold@btinternet.com

HOME FARM COTTAGE
Pauline Hansler
Visitors also welcome by appt Apr to Sept (combined with Crow's Nest Cottage if date convenient).
01159 655860
jhansler410@btinternet.com

NEW PILGRIM COTTAGE
Mike & Sue Hulme

ROMAN WAY
Corby & Lewie Lewington

NEW WESLEY GRANGE
Judith & Phil Meats

NEW THE WHITE BUNGALOW
Sue & Robin Aldridge

Enjoy 6 very different gardens in this lovely, rural village. In Blind Lane, Roman Way, a bijoux garden, has a sunny rockery, manicured lawn, water feature and shady corners. Home Farm Cottage is a delightful, traditional cottage garden, crammed full of unusual plants - an ever-changing, surprising garden with narrow paths and hidden corners. Along Chapel Lane, Wesley Grange's gravelled courtyard garden is set around a converted barn with a sunny Mediterranean feel. Up Forest Road, Crow's Nest Cottage is a larger, bird-friendly garden with ponds, running water, scented beds and lovely clematis. On Water Lane, The White Bungalow with its colourful stream edge has a neat vegetable plot and grass play area for grandchildren as well as colourful borders of shrubs and herbaceous perennials. Further down is Pilgrim Cottage a mature wildlife-friendly garden with lots of 'rooms' packed with plants. A few quirky touches make the garden interesting but still with a cottage garden feel. Access with help in some of the gardens.

39 PAPPLEWICK HALL
Blidworth Waye, Papplewick NG15 8FE. Mr & Mrs J R Godwin-Austen, www.papplewickhall.co.uk. *7m N of Nottingham. N end of Papplewick village on B683, off A60. Parking at Hall.* **Adm £3.50, chd free (share to St James's Church, Papplewick). Sun 26 May (2-5).**
This historic, mature, 8-acre garden, mostly shaded woodland, abounds with rhododendrons, hostas, ferns, and spring bulbs. Section of paths are gravel.

40 PARK FARM
Crink Lane, Southwell NG25 0TJ. Dr & Mrs Ian Johnston, 01636 812195, v.johnston100@gmail.com. *1m SE of Southwell. A612 from Southwell towards Newark, take rd to Fiskerton and 200yds up hill turn R into Crink Lane. Park Farm is on 2nd bend.* **Adm £3, chd free. Visitors welcome by appt.**
3-acre garden with extensive borders comprising a large range of plants, shrubs and trees, many unusual. Woodland garden, oak arches with roses, long flower borders, large wild flower meadow, pond and ha-ha complement the garden with spectacular views across fields to The Minster. Wild flower meadow, roses, long herbaceous borders, rock garden, large wildlife pond, woodland garden, rare trees, shrubs, and herbaceous plants. Featured in the Newark Advertiser.

41 48 PENARTH GARDENS
Sherwood Vale, Nottingham NG5 4EG. Josie & Geoff Goodlud, 01159 609067. *Approx 2½ m N of Nottingham. Take B684 (Woodborough Rd) from Nottingham, turn L after Autopark Garage into Woodthorpe Rd, turn L again into Penarth Rise, L again into Penarth Gardens.* Home-made teas. **Adm £3, chd free. Sun 7 July (12-5). Evening Opening adm £4, chd free, wine, Wed 24 July (6-9). Visitors also welcome by appt July and Aug.**
One of Nottingham city's hidden gems is to be found in the unlikely setting of the old Nottingham Brickwork Quarry. The landscape has been transformed with pathways, steps and a summer house. Clever planting with trees, fences, bamboos, palms and specimen shrubs, lead to flowing herbaceous borders which provide colour and interest with many unusual plants. Featured in Nottinghamshire Today and Nottingham Evening Post.

42 PIECEMEAL
123 Main Street, Sutton Bonington, Loughborough LE12 5PE. Mary Thomas, 01509 672056, admet123@btinternet.com. *2m SE of Kegworth (M1 J24). 6m NE of Loughborough. Almost opp St Michael's Church and near to Sutton Bonington Hall.* **Adm £2.50, chd free. Sun 28 July; Sun 4 Aug (1-6). Visitors (individuals and small groups) also welcome by appt June to Aug. For larger groups, please contact to discuss.**
Plant enthusiast's tiny, walled garden with an amazing collection of shrubs, perennials and annuals thriving in around 400 terracotta pots of various sizes. Huge range of plants, many unusual and not fully hardy. Busy herbaceous borders. Distinctive foliage and colour combinations provide interest from spring to autumn. Conservatory. Fern-filled well. A jungle by mid summer.

PINE HOUSE
See Leicestershire & Rutland

43 NEW THE POPLARS
60 High Street, Sutton-On-Trent, Newark NG23 6QA. Sue & Graham Goodwin-King. *7m N of Newark. Leave A1 at Sutton/Carlton/Normanton-on-Trent junction. In Carlton turn L onto B1164. Turn R into Hemplands Lane then R into High Street. 1st house on R. Limited parking, but more at Woodbine Farm.* **Combined adm £3.50, chd free. Sat 15 June (1-5); Sun 16 June (11-5). Combined with Woodbine Farmhouse.**
½ acre of lawns and garden 'rooms' made over many years on the site of a Victorian market garden and flower nursery. Unique iron balcony overlooking pond, terrace, oriental style gravel garden and rock scree. 'Jungle' with castaway's shack and treehouse, black and white garden, hot border, fernery, woodland area, walled potager and many sitting stops. Unusual and rare plantings. Some topiary.

QUORN ORCHARD GARDENS
See Leicestershire & Rutland

RIDGEWOLD FARM
See Leicestershire & Rutland

'Jungle' with castaway's shack and treehouse . . .

44 RISEHOLME, 125 SHELFORD ROAD
Radcliffe on Trent NG12 1AZ. John & Elaine Walker, 0115 9119867, john.walker@nottingham.ac.uk. *4m E of Nottingham. From A52 follow signs to Radcliffe. In village centre take turning for Shelford (by Co-op). Approx ¾ m on L.* Home-made teas. **Evening Opening adm £4 (incl wine), chd free, Wed 19 June (6-9); adm £3, chd free, Sun 28 July (2-6). Visitors also welcome by appt May to Sept.**
Just under ½ acre designed for colour, texture and movement. Many unusual varieties, hardy perennials, grasses. Formal front garden with packed borders incl hot/cool colour-themed beds and prairie-style borders. Back garden has flowing curves with informal planting, gazebo, pond and jungle area with exotic planting. Colour and interest all year.

45 ROSELEA
40 Newark Road, Coddington, Newark NG24 2QF. Bruce & Marian Richmond, 01636 676737, richmonds.roselea@tiscali.co.uk. *1½ m E of Newark. Leave A1 signed Coddington, from N take 1st turn L before main T-junction, Roselea is 1st white house straight ahead. From S turn L at T-junction signed Coddington. Cross over A1, turn L (signed Grantham) then turn immed R. Roselea is 1st white house straight ahead.* Home-made teas. **Adm £2.50, chd free. Sun 31 Mar; Sun 16 June (11-5). Visitors also welcome by appt Mar to Sept.**
Picturesque plantsman's garden.

Mixed borders, shrubs, roses, clematis and geraniums. Hellebores, daffodils, cyclamen and alpines. Many unusual plants. Hostas and ferns in pots. Small alpine area. Pergolas covered with climbers. Compost area. Places to sit and ponder. Come and enjoy home-made cakes and teas. Spring opening - hellebores, cyclamen, daffodils and alpines. Wheelchair access to front garden only.

Visit this newly established garden and be inspired by the contemporary feel . . .

46 NEW RYE HALL FARM

Eel Pool Road, Everton, Doncaster DN10 5DR. Mr & Mrs Tim Shuldham. *Between villages of Everton & Mattersey. Take rd towards Mattersey off A631, turn L onto Eel Pool Rd, Rye Hall Farm is 1st property on L. From Ranskill B6045, go through Mattersey, turn R onto Eel Pool Rd.* Home-made teas. **Adm £2.50, chd free. Sun 30 June (12.30-4).**

Visit this newly established garden and be inspired by the contemporary feel. There is an impressive mixture of trees, shrubs, herbaceous plants and attractive grasses. Enjoy mown paths through the long grass and the productive fruit and vegetable garden. At the centre of this 1/2 acre family garden is a beautiful pond with gravel surround planted with reeds, dierama, iris and grasses. Partial wheelchair access.

47 78 SANDY LANE

Hucknall NG15 7GP. Alan & Linda Foster, 01159 534609. *7m N of Nottingham, 5 mins walk from Hucknall market. On Hucknall by-pass A611 from Nottingham 1st R then 4th L. On A611 from Mansfield or Linby, 1st L then 4th R.* Teas at 96 Sandy Lane (June) and 78 Sandy Lane (Aug). **Adm £2.50, chd free. Sun 23 June; Sun 4 Aug (1-5). Combined with 96 Sandy Lane, adm £3.00, chd free, Sun 23 June. Visitors also welcome by appt June to Sept.**

1/4 -acre plant lovers' garden, colourful in all seasons and bursting with perennials, annuals, grasses and shrubs. Superb collection of hostas and other shade loving plants. Lots of paths and seats. Two frog friendly ponds and chickens taking centre stage. Borders still overflowing and awash with colour till late autumn. Grass paths, 2 small slopes.

48 96 SANDY LANE

Hucknall NG15 7GP. Helen Rose. *7m N of Nottingham, 5 mins walk from Hucknall market. On Hucknall by-pass A611 from Nottingham 1st R then 4th L. On A611 from Mansfield or Linby, 1st L then 4th R.* Teas. **Combined adm £3, chd free. Sun 23 June (1-5). Combined with 78 Sandy Lane.**

Medium sized, low maintenance, child-friendly garden with steps down to lawned and planted area with summerhouse. Wheelchair access only to patio area.

73 SAXILBY ROAD

See Lincolnshire

49 THE SMALL EXOTIC GARDEN

26 Selby Road, West Bridgford, Nottingham NG2 7BL. Tim & Jenny Martin, 01159 813657, jennyandtim@tiscali.co.uk. *2m SE of Nottingham, off A52 ring rd. Selby Rd is sandwiched between (& runs parallel to) Melton Rd (A606) & Musters Rd. It can be accessed from either rd via Devonshire Rd or Boundary Rd.* **Adm £2.50, chd free. Visitors welcome by appt 27 July to 11 Aug. Weekends and eves only. Adm £4, incl wine (evening visits only), chd free.**

Small green oasis planted for foliage effect. Ornamental vegetable patch, patio with bamboo bed and exotic potted plants. 3 steps down to lower garden with bark paths encircling desert style beds and 'mini jungle' beyond with wildlife pond and secluded 'jungle' hut. New 'al fresco' dining area and patio water feature. Featured in Garden News.

50 SQUIRREL LODGE

2 Goosemoor Lane, Retford DN22 7JA. Peter & Joan Whitehead. *1m S of Retford on A638. Last R turn before railway bridge.* Home-made teas. **Adm £2.50, chd free. Sun 7 July; Sun 15 Sept (2-5).**

A warm welcome awaits you at a garden which has been skilfully crafted into a corner plot. Well kept lawns, mature trees, small ponds. Walled vegetable garden, quirky features and a wide variety of plants ensure colour until the first frosts appear. Apple pie and cream (subject to availability), cream teas (15 Sept). Ordsall Scarecrow Festival. Many wonderful exhibits (14 & 15 Sept).

51 THE SUMMER HOUSE

High Street, Gringley on the Hill, Doncaster DN10 4RF. Helena Bishop. *From High St turn up gravel drive opposite Bluebell PH.* Home-made teas at Ellicar Gardens. **Combined adm £4, chd free. Sun 16 June (1-5). Combined with Ellicar Gardens and Trust Cottage.**

A charming English garden, lovingly planted with outstanding views framed by overflowing borders. The romantic rose garden, wildflower meadow and white border are maturing and the water garden with stream makes a stunning focal point. Sloped gravel drive.

52 SUTTON BONINGTON ARBORETUM

University Campus, College Road, Sutton Bonington LE12 5RD. University of Nottingham, www.nottingham.ac.uk. *2m SE of Kegworth. From J24 M1, take A6 towards Loughborough. Take 1st L off A6, then on bend, turn R and, at Xrds, R again - all turns signed Sutton Bonington. Proceed along College Rd and on L turn into University campus. Follow signs for parking.* **Adm £3, chd free. Sat 7 Sept (2-5).**

Sutton Bonington Arboretum is a little-known resource that began life during the 'Plant a Tree in '73' campaign. The arboretum has an interesting collection of over 300 evergreen and deciduous trees. Notable specimens incl big cone pine, Corsican pine, cedar, eucalyptus, American chestnut, maple & Persian ironwood. Picnic area, cafe, guided tour.

From tiny back plots to country estates ...

Norwell Allotment Parish Gardens, Norwell Gardens

53 NEW SYCAMORES HOUSE
Salmon Lane, Annesley Woodhouse, Nottingham NG17 9HB. Lynne & Barrie Jackson, 01623 750466, landbjackson@gmail.com. *From M1 J27 follow Mansfield signs to Badger Box T-lights. Turn L up Forest Rd. Gate is 2 metres after brow of hill 'No Footway for 600yds' sign on L. From Mansfield follow Derby Rd to Badger Box. Turn R up Forest Rd, then as above. Please park considerately on rd.* Home-made teas. **Adm £3, chd free. Sun 28 Apr, Sun 16 June (1-5). Visitors also welcome by appt May to July.**
A young garden of about 1½ acres on a gentle southerly slope. A grassy field in 2005, it now comprises traditional herbaceous borders along with wilder areas and a large, productive, organic vegetable garden and orchard. There is still much to develop and the garden will continue to evolve over the coming years as plants, trees and hedges mature and new spaces are planted. A couple of short steep slopes. Gravel paths near house, grass further down. Ramp available for entrance steps.

54 THORESBY HALL HOTEL & SPA
Thoresby Park, nr Ollerton NG22 9WH. Warner Leisure Hotels, 01623 821000, www.warnerleisurehotels.co.uk. *N of Nottingham. Exit A1signed A614 Nottingham - Leicester. After 4m at the r'about take exit signed Thoresby Hall Hotel. Entrance 1m on L.* **Adm £3.50. Every Wed & Sat 6 July to 27 July (9-4).**
Thoresby Hall gardens are famous for their beauty. Set in 30-acres of Sir Humphry Repton designed gardens, featuring a Grade I listed Victorian rose garden with rare species. Formal terraced gardens. Gravel paths.

55 THRUMPTON HALL
Thrumpton NG11 0AX. Miranda Seymour, 01159 830333, www.thrumptonhall.com. *7m S of Nottingham. M1 J24 take A453 towards Nottingham. Turn L to Thrumpton village & continue to Thrumpton Hall.* **Adm £3, chd free. Sun 21 July (2-5). Visitors also welcome by appt Jan to Nov.**
2-acres incl lawns, rare trees, lakeside walks, flower borders, rose-garden and box-bordered sunken herb garden, all enclosed by C18 ha-ha and encircling a Jacobean house. Garden is surrounded by C18 landscaped park and is bordered by a river. Rare opportunity to visit Thrumpton Hall (separate ticket). Jacobean mansion, unique carved staircase, Great Saloon, State Bedroom, Priest's Hole.

TRESILLIAN HOUSE
See Leicestershire & Rutland

Follow the path through the woodland walk . . .

56 NEW TRUST COTTAGE
Cross Hill, Gringley-On-The-Hill, Doncaster DN10 4RE. Mr Paul Reed. *From Market Cross end of High St go down hill. Trust Cottage is 2nd house on R, covered in Virginia creeper.* Home-made teas at Ellicar Gardens. **Combined adm £4, chd free. Sun 16 June (1-5). Combined with Ellicar Gardens and The Summer House.**
Small, secluded, walled cottage garden located in the centre of the village. Narrow paths link a number of seating areas and are bordered by roses, clematis, herbaceous borders and wisteria. Wide variety of plants.

57 UNIVERSITY OF NOTTINGHAM GARDENS
University Park, Nottingham NG7 2RD, www.nottingham.ac.uk. *Nr centre of Nottingham. Suggest visitors use University Park's N entrance on A52 adjacent to Queens Medical Centre r'about. Tickets on sale in Millennium Garden, well signed on campus.* Light refreshments. **Adm £3, chd free. Sun 18 Aug (1.30-5).**
University Park has many beautiful gardens incl the award-winning Millennium Garden with its dazzling flower garden, timed fountains and turf maze, the huge Lenton Firs rock garden, the dry garden and Jekyll garden. During summer the walled garden will be alive with exotic plantings. In total, 300 acres of landscape and gardens. Picnic area, cafe, walking tour. Some gravel paths and steep slopes. Accessible minibus provided to reach all main areas.

58 6 WESTON CLOSE
Woodthorpe NG5 4FS. Diane & Steve Harrington, 01159 857506, di.harrington@o2.co.uk. *3m N of Nottingham. A60 Mansfield Road from city centre. After Sherwood shops turn R at T-lights by Woodthorpe Park into Woodthorpe Drive. 2nd L into Grange Road. R into The Crescent, R into Weston Close. Park in The Crescent.* Home-made teas. **Adm £3, chd free. Sun 16 June; Sun 14 July (1-5). Also opening The Glade. Visitors also welcome by appt June to Aug. Adm price incl refreshments.**
Set on a substantial slope with 3 separate areas, dense planting creates a full, varied yet relaxed display incl many scented roses, clematis and a collection of dozens of mature hostas in the impressive colourful rear garden. Large plant sale packed with good value home propagated plants. Occasional craft stalls. Featured as garden of the week in Garden News.

WHATTON GARDENS
See Leicestershire & Rutland

59 NEW WOODBINE FARMHOUSE
Ingram Lane, Sutton-on-Trent, Newark NG23 6RT. Peter & Jennie Searle, www.jenniesearle.co.uk. *7m N of Newark. Leave A1 at Sutton/Carlton/Normanton junction. Turn L onto B1164 in Carlton. Garage on L, take next R along Main St. Follow rd till school on L & church on R, bear R along Ingram Lane. Woodbine Farmhouse on L.* Home-made teas. **Combined adm £3.50, chd free. Sat 15 June (1-5); Sun 16 June (11-5). Combined with The Poplars.**
Colourful artist's garden surrounding C18 farmhouse. Jennie's studio gallery open. Herbaceous borders, quirky sculptures. Follow the path through the woodland walk. Rediscovered well now full of ferns. Walled courtyard garden with water feature. Wild garden with pond. Fruit and vegetable garden.

Children sow and harvest fruit and vegetable crops for school dinners . . .

60 WOODPECKERS
35 Lambley Lane, Burton Joyce, Nottingham NG14 5BG. Lynn & Mark Carr, 01159 313237, info@woodpeckersdining.co.uk. *6m N of Nottingham. In Burton Joyce, turn off A612 (Nottingham to Southwell rd) into Lambley Lane, garden on L.* Light refreshments. **Adm £3.50, chd free. Sun 12 May (12-5). Visitors also welcome by appt Mar to Nov.**
4 acres of mature woodland and formal gardens with spectacular views over the Trent Valley. Over 500 rhododendrons and azaleas. Balustraded terrace for teas or pimms. Glade with 200 yr-old cedars overlooking ponds, waterfalls and croquet lawn. Bog garden and sunken area below ha-ha, created in 2009 and planted to tempt the eye onwards towards ancient well. Gravel and grass paths, steep slopes.

61 ◆ THE WORKHOUSE
Upton Road, Southwell NG25 0PT. Rachel Harrison, 01636 817260, www.nationaltrust.org.uk. *1m E of Southwell on A612. Signed from centre of Southwell.* **Adm £7, chd £3.50. For NGS: Sat 22 June (12-4). For other opening times and information, please phone or see garden website.**
Originally started in 1825 to provide food and labour for the pauper inmates, the north side was cultivated to provide potatoes, and the south was used to grow vegetables and a pasture for two cows. Volunteers have been recreating the kitchen garden using traditional techniques and heirloom varieties of produce. Compact stone paths between beds allow for close inspection of growing areas.

GROUP OPENING

62 NEW YOUNG GARDENERS AT 3 PRIMARY SCHOOLS
Abbey Gates, Haywood Avenue, Blidworth, Mansfield NG21 0RE. ***Abbey Gates***: From A60 S of Mansfield take Longdale Lane opp Newstead Abbey L onto Vernon Ave, L at T-junction. Park in village hall. **Blidworth Oaks**: From A60 take B6020 or Dale Lane from A614. Belle Vue Lane is opp shops, next to Gym. School is on R between nos 16 & 18. **Lake View**: from M1 J28 take A38 Mansfield & A617 (Newark). At 2nd r'about take 3rd exit to Rainworth. Over T-lights, 1st R on Warsop Lane, follow Sure Start sign. R onto Thoresby Rd into Rainworth Water Rd. Use school car park. Home-made teas. **Combined adm £4, chd free. Sat 6 July (11-4).**

NEW ABBEY GATES PRIMARY SCHOOL
Head Teacher: Kate Cumberpatch
www.abbeygatesprimaryschool.co.uk

NEW BLIDWORTH OAKS PRIMARY SCHOOL
Head Teacher: Celia Lassetter
www.blidworthoaks.co.uk

NEW LAKEVIEW PRIMARY SCHOOL
Head Teacher: Miss S Warrington
www.lakeviewprimary.org

The wooded grounds of Abbey Gates encourage eco and environmental study. The pond/wildlife area has a viewing platform for close study and a developing wildflower area. Children sow and harvest fruit and vegetables crops for school dinners. The 'Matisse' garden, designed by the children has seating areas, decorative box and bamboo screens and colour themed flowering plants. Blidworth Oaks has different gardening environments. Children are enthusiastically involved in an allotment where SPUD the scarecrow protects our fruit and vegetables. In our Eco Garden, where wild flowers, bird tables and a newly acquired pond attract wildlife and in the inner courtyard, where an enchanted statue comes to life! Lake View is fortunate to have substantial grounds of natural beauty set within views of rolling fields adjacent to the 'Lake'. Visit class allotments, the developing meadow bank and herbaceous border area, planted to attract wild life and the story garden, incorporating a planned sensory area. All gardens are accessible for wheelchair users, via some slopes and gravel paths.

Nottinghamshire County Volunteers

County Organiser
Georgina Denison, Ossington House, Newark NG23 6LD, 07710 344118, campden27@aol.com

County Treasurer
Rowan & Janet McFerran, Juxta Mill, Main Street, Norwell NG23 6JN 01636 636921 rowancf@btinternet.com

Publicity
Barry Cope, 196 Tamworth Road, Sawley, Long Eaton, NG10 3GS, 01159 728309, the_copes@hotmail.com

Booklet Coordinator
Robert & Pauline Little, 10 Chestnut Way, Repton DE65 6FQ 01283 702267 plittle@hotmail.com

Assistant County Organisers
Joan Arnold, Crows Nest Cottage, Forest Road, Oxton NG25 0SZ, 01159 653789, trebleclef.arnold@btinternet.com
Ian Cooke, 14 Park Close, Mapperley NG3 5FB, 01159 524755, iankcooke@ntlworld.com
Judy Geldart, Hopbine Farm, Main Street, Ossington, Newark NG23 6LJ, 01636 823832, petergeldart@btinternet.com
Pauline Hansler, Home Farm Cottage, Blind Lane, Oxton NG25 0SS, 01159 655860, pauline2603@me.com
Beverley Perks, The Old Vicarage, Halam Hill, Halam NG22 8AX, 01636 812181, perks.family@talk21.com
Mary Thomas, Piecemeal, 123 Main Street, Sutton Bonington, Loughborough LE12 5PE, 01509 672056, admet123@btinternet.com

OXFORDSHIRE

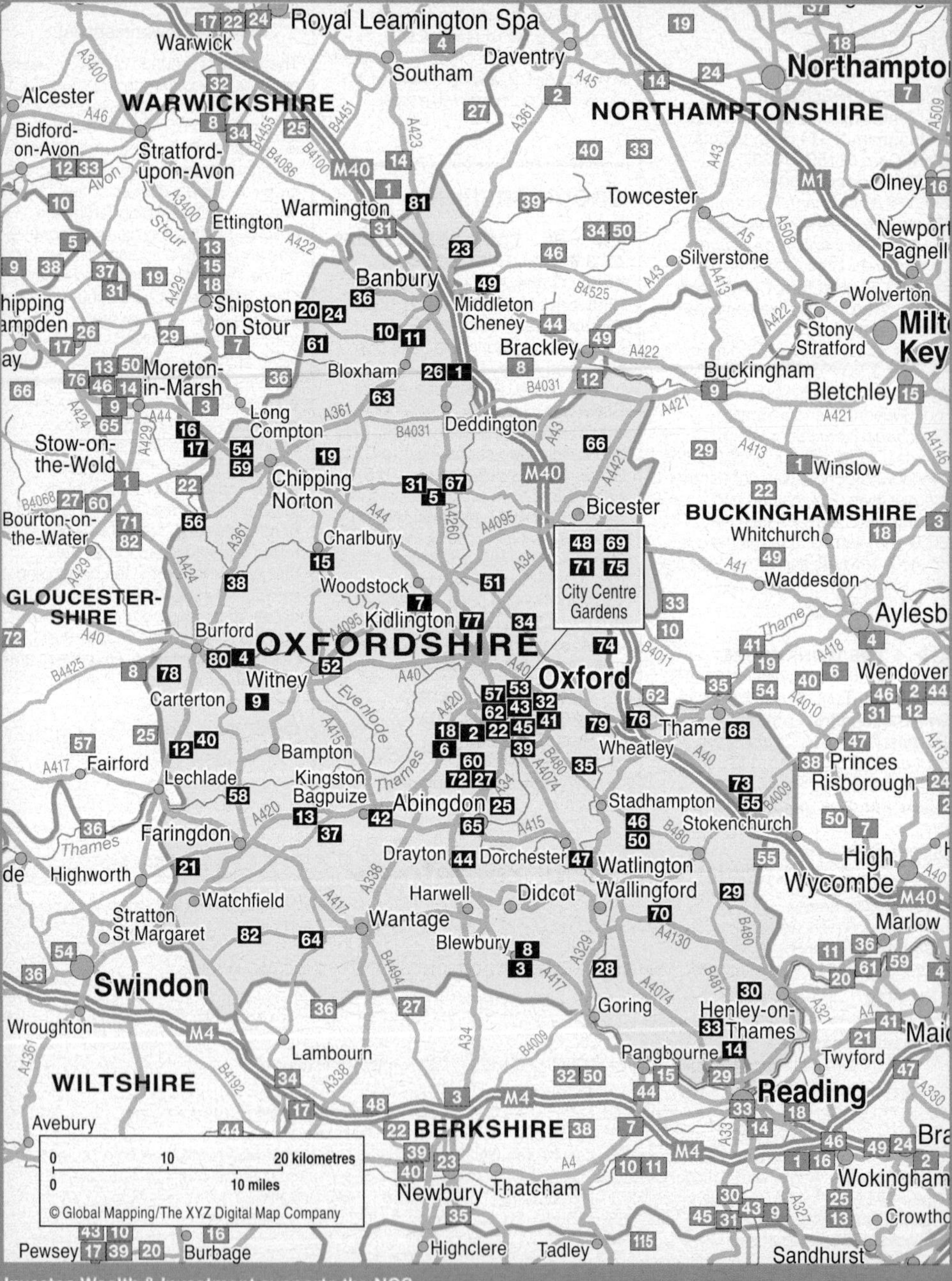

Opening Dates

February

Tuesday 12
54 Old Rectory

March

Sunday 10
51 Monks Head

Sunday 17
42 Kingston Bagpuize House
75 Wadham College

Sunday 24
3 Ashbrook House
69 Trinity College
76 Waterperry Gardens

April

Monday 1
40 Kencot Gardens

Sunday 7
13 Buckland Lakes
24 Epwell Mill
45 Magdalen College

Sunday 14
20 Church Farm Field
44 Lime Close

Saturday 20
57 50 Plantation Road

Sunday 21
34 Hollyhocks
51 Monks Head
57 50 Plantation Road

Wednesday 24
81 Wildwood

Saturday 27
57 50 Plantation Road

Sunday 28
11 Broughton Grange
57 50 Plantation Road

May

Wednesday 1
82 Woolstone Mill House

Sunday 5
12 Broughton Poggs & Filkins Gardens

Monday 6
64 Sparsholt Manor

Wednesday 8
82 Woolstone Mill House

Wednesday 15
82 Woolstone Mill House

Saturday 18
6 36 Bertie Road
18 14 Chawley Lane
27 Foxcombe Hall

Sunday 19
31 The Grove
34 Hollyhocks
37 Home Farm House
43 Lady Margaret Hall
51 Monks Head

Monday 20
37 Home Farm House

Wednesday 22
82 Woolstone Mill House

Sunday 26
5 Barton Abbey
15 Charlbury Gardens

Wednesday 29
33 Hearns House
81 Wildwood
82 Woolstone Mill House

Friday 31
33 Hearns House

Sit back, relax and enjoy the view . . .

June

Sunday 2
20 Church Farm Field
23 Eaves Cottage
24 Epwell Mill
25 Failford
70 Troy & Gould's Grove Farmhouse
77 Wayside
80 Whitehill Farm

Wednesday 5
82 Woolstone Mill House

Saturday 8
63 South Newington House

Sunday 9
63 South Newington House
67 Steeple Aston Gardens

Tuesday 11
30 Greys Court

Wednesday 12
82 Woolstone Mill House

National Gardens Weekend

Saturday 15
7 Blenheim Palace
11 Broughton Grange
37 Home Farm House
52 32 New Yatt Road
57 50 Plantation Road
63 South Newington House
81 Wildwood

Sunday 16
8 Blewbury Gardens
9 Brize Norton Gardens
11 Broughton Grange
32 Headington Gardens
37 Home Farm House
39 Iffley Gardens
52 32 New Yatt Road
55 The Old Vicarage
56 The Old Vicarage, Bledington
57 50 Plantation Road
59 Salford Gardens
61 Sibford Gower Gardens
63 South Newington House
81 Wildwood

Tuesday 18
29 Greenfield Farm (Evening)

Wednesday 19
82 Woolstone Mill House

Thursday 20
73 Upper Chalford Farm

Sunday 23
4 Asthall Manor
22 Corpus Christi College
49 Middleton Cheney Gardens
62 Somerville College Gardens
68 Thame Gardens
73 Upper Chalford Farm
78 Westwell Manor
79 Wheatley Gardens

Wednesday 26
55 The Old Vicarage
82 Woolstone Mill House

Friday 28
46 The Manor
50 Mill Barn

Sunday 30
1 Adderbury Gardens
38 Hunters Lodge
46 The Manor
50 Mill Barn
53 North Oxford Gardens

July

Wednesday 3
82 Woolstone Mill House

Wednesday 10
82 Woolstone Mill House

Sunday 14
16 Chastleton Glebe
17 Chastleton House and Garden
28 Green and Gorgeous, The Cutting Garden
72 Uplands
73 Upper Chalford Farm
75 Wadham College

Wednesday 17
82 Woolstone Mill House

Sunday 21
14 Chalkhouse Green Farm
48 Merton College Oxford Fellows' Garden

You are always welcome at an NGS garden!

Wednesday 24
- 33 Hearns House
- 82 Woolstone Mill House

Friday 26
- 33 Hearns House

Sunday 28
- 10 Broughton Castle
- 11 Broughton Grange
- 52 32 New Yatt Road
- 69 Trinity College

Wednesday 31
- 81 Wildwood
- 82 Woolstone Mill House

August

Wednesday 7
- 82 Woolstone Mill House

Sunday 11
- 2 Appleton Dene

Wednesday 14
- 82 Woolstone Mill House

Sunday 18
- 47 Manor House
- 58 Radcot House
- 72 Uplands

Wednesday 21
- 82 Woolstone Mill House

Wednesday 28
- 81 Wildwood
- 82 Woolstone Mill House

September

Sunday 1
- 3 Ashbrook House
- 20 Church Farm Field
- 24 Epwell Mill

Wednesday 4
- 82 Woolstone Mill House

Sunday 8
- 42 Kingston Bagpuize House

Wednesday 11
- 82 Woolstone Mill House

Wednesday 18
- 71 University of Oxford Botanic Garden
- 82 Woolstone Mill House

Sunday 22
- 76 Waterperry Gardens

Wednesday 25
- 82 Woolstone Mill House

October

Sunday 6
- 58 Radcot House

Gardens open to the public

- 7 Blenheim Palace
- 10 Broughton Castle
- 17 Chastleton House and Garden
- 30 Greys Court
- 42 Kingston Bagpuize House
- 48 Merton College Oxford Fellows' Garden
- 71 University of Oxford Botanic Garden
- 76 Waterperry Gardens

By appointment only

- 19 Chivel Farm
- 21 Clock House
- 26 Fairfield
- 35 Home Close
- 36 Home Farm
- 41 10 Kennett Road
- 60 The Sheiling
- 65 64 Spring Road
- 66 Springhill House

Also open by Appointment ☎

- 2 Appleton Dene
- 3 Ashbrook House
- 8 Blewbury Manor, Blewbury Gardens
- 14 Chalkhouse Green Farm
- 20 Church Farm Field
- 24 Epwell Mill
- 25 Failford
- 28 Green and Gorgeous, The Cutting Garden
- 29 Greenfield Farm
- 32 40 Osler Road, Headington Gardens
- 33 Hearns House
- 34 Hollyhocks
- 44 Lime Close
- 47 Manor House
- 51 Monks Head
- 55 The Old Vicarage
- 56 The Old Vicarage, Bledington
- 63 South Newington House
- 67 Primrose Gardens, Steeple Aston Gardens
- 72 Uplands
- 73 Upper Chalford Farm
- 74 Upper Green
- 77 Wayside
- 79 Breach House Garden, Wheatley Gardens
- 79 The Manor House, Wheatley Gardens
- 79 The Studio, Wheatley Gardens
- 79 Wheatley Gardens
- 80 Whitehill Farm

The Gardens

GROUP OPENING

1 ADDERBURY GARDENS

Adderbury OX17 3LS. *3m S of Banbury. J10 M40, onto A43 signed Northampton, then B4100 to Adderbury; or A4260 S from Banbury. Maps supplied & displayed at each garden & at various other venues*. Home-made teas Church House. (Library) High Street. **Combined adm £5, chd free (share to Katharine House Hospice).** **Sun 30 June (2-6).**

NEW **CANALIA**
Mr Jeffrey Moore

CROSSHILL HOUSE
Mr & Mrs Gurth Hoyer Millar
www.oxoniangardener.co.uk

THE OLD VICARAGE
Christine & Peter Job

PLACKETTS
Dr D White

SORBROOK MANOR
Mr & Mrs Robin Thistlethwayte

Attractive Ironstone village, with 5 gardens ranging from quite small to very large. **Crosshill House** 4-acre classic Victorian walled garden and grounds with ha-ha. **The Old Vicarage** Walled front garden, large rear garden stretching from ha ha to small lake and flood meadows. Unusual plants and trees. Japanese maple plantation. **Placketts** 1/5 acre walled garden with sheltered gravel courtyard, main garden exposed, with views. Plethora of colourful plants throughout the yr with late summer colour. **Canalia** notable for remarkable collection of Mints. Wheelchair access at Crosshill House, restricted access at Placketts. Dogs allowed at Crosshill House & The Old Vicarage.

♿ 🐕 ✿ ☕

In spring the banks are a mass of daffodils . . .

Adderbury Gardens

2 APPLETON DENE
Yarnells Hill, Botley, Oxford OX2 9BG. Mr & Mrs A Dawson, 07701 000977, annrobe@aol.com. *3m W of Oxford. Take W rd out of Oxford, through Botley Rd, pass under A34, turn L in to Westminster Way. Yarnells Hill is 2nd R. Park at top of hill/Lime Rd. House 200 metres at end of rd.* Home-made teas. **Adm £3, chd free. Sun 11 Aug (11-5). Visitors also welcome by appt May to Aug. Please phone in advance.**
Beautiful secluded new garden set in a hidden valley bordered by woods and a field. The 1/4 -acre garden on a steeply sloping site surrounds a mature tulip tree. There is a skillfully incorporated level lawn area overlooked by deep borders incl a wide variety of plants for long seasonal interest. There will also be some outdoor floral displays.

3 ASHBROOK HOUSE
Blewbury OX11 9QA. Mr & Mrs S A Barrett, 01235 850810, janembarrett@me.com. *4m SE of Didcot. Turn off A417 in Blewbury into Westbrook St. 1st house on R. Follow yellow signs for parking in Boham's Road.* Home-made teas. **Adm £4, chd free. Sun 24 Mar, Sun 1 Sept (2-6). Visitors also welcome by appt Mar to Sept. Light refreshments by arrangement.**
The garden where Kenneth Grahame read Wind in the Willows to local children and where he took inspiration for his description of the oak doors to Badger's House. Come and see - you may catch a glimpse of Toad and friends in this 3 1/2 -acre chalk and water garden in a beautiful spring-line village. In spring the banks are a mass of daffodils and in late summer the borders are full of unusual plants. Plant sale (April only).

4 ASTHALL MANOR
Asthall, nr Burford OX18 4HW. Rosanna Pearson, www.asthallmanor.com. *3m E of Burford. At r'about between Witney & Burford on A40, take turning to Minster Lovell. Turn immed L (signed to Asthall). At bottom of hill, follow avenue of trees & look for car park signs. From N, go to Shipton-under-Wychwood, turn L at Shaven Crown & follow rd straight through to Swinbrook. Go through Swinbrook, turn L at Xrds after cricket pitch. Follow signs.* Home-made teas in village. **Adm £6, chd free. Sun 23 June (2-6).**
6-acres of garden surround this C17 manor house (not open) once home to the Mitford family and overlooking the Windrush Valley. The gardens, designed by I & J Bannerman in 1998, offer 'a beguiling mix of traditional and contemporary'. Exuberant scented borders, sloping box parterres, wild flowers, a gypsy waggon, a turf sculpture and a hidden lake are all part of the mix. Featured in The English Garden. Limited wheelchair access. No disabled WC.

AVON DASSETT GARDENS
See Warwickshire

5 BARTON ABBEY
Steeple Barton OX25 4QS. Mr & Mrs P Fleming. *8m E of Chipping Norton. On B4030, 1/2 m from junction of A4260 & B4030.* Home-made teas. **Adm £4, chd free. Sun 26 May (2-5).**
15-acre garden with views from house (not open) across sweeping lawns and picturesque lake. Walled garden with colourful herbaceous borders, separated by established yew hedges and espalier fruit, contrasts with more informal woodland garden paths with vistas of specimen trees and meadows. Working glasshouses and fine display of fruit and vegetables.

6 36 BERTIE ROAD

Cumnor, Oxford OX2 9PS. Esther & Neil Whiting. *3½ m W of Oxford. Take W rd out of Oxford, through Botley & continue up hill. At car showrooms turn R. Park in Bertie/Norreys Rd.* Home-made teas at 14 Chawley Lane. **Combined adm £4, chd free. Sat 18 May (2-5.30). Combined with 14 Chawley Lane.**
Professionally designed developing garden planted in 2008 in pleasant suburban setting. Structured layout, relaxed planting, incl hemerocallis and ornamental grasses. Small area of gravel path.

7 ◆ BLENHEIM PALACE

Woodstock OX20 1PX. His Grace the Duke of Marlborough, www.blenheimpalace.com. *8m N of Oxford. Bus: S3 Oxford-Chipping Norton, alight Woodstock.* **Adm £4, chd £2. For NGS: Sat 15 June (9-5.30). For other opening times and information please see website.**
Blenheim Gardens, originally laid out by Henry Wise, include the formal Water Terraces and Italian Garden by Achille Duchêne, Rose Garden, Arboretum, and Cascade. The Secret Garden, opened in 2004, offers a stunning garden paradise in all seasons. Blenheim Lake, created by Capability Brown and spanned by Vanburgh's Grand Bridge, is the focal point of over 2,000 acres of landscaped parkland. The Pleasure Gardens complex incl the herb and lavender garden and Butterfly House. Other activities incl the Marlborough Maze, putting greens, adventure play area, giant chess and draughts. Some gravel paths, terrain can be uneven in places. Dogs allowed in park only.

GROUP OPENING

8 BLEWBURY GARDENS

Blewbury OX11 9QB. *4m SE of Didcot. On A417. Follow yellow signs for car parks.* Home-made teas at The Manor (all proceeds to the NGS). **Combined adm £5, chd free. Sun 16 June (2-6).**

BLEWBURY MANOR
Mr & Mrs M R Blythe
Visitors also welcome by appt Apr to July.
07901 551216
richard.roslyn1@btinternet.com

BROOKS END
Jean & David Richards

GREEN BUSHES
Phil Rogers

HALL BARN
Malcolm & Deirdre Cochrane

NOTTINGHAM FEE HOUSE
Mrs Carolyn Anderson

STOCKS
Norma & Richard Bird

As celebrated by Rachel de Thame in Gardener's World. Six gardens in charming downland village. **Blewbury Manor** Manor House with moat set in a garden of about 10 acres. Features incl a parterre; flower garden, herbaceous and mixed borders; pergola; vegetable and herb garden; stream planting and woodland area; lake and sunken gravel gardens. Large traditional courtyard with late season flowering borders **Brooks End** 1960's bungalow, newly designed garden with colour themed beds, damp border, hidden garden, small orchard, new shady border area added, greenhouse and vegetable garden. **Green Bushes** Created by plant lover Rhon (dec'd 2007) around C16 cottage. Colour themed borders, ponds and poolside planting, alpine troughs, ferns, pleached limes and roses. **Hall Barn** Extends over 4 acres with traditional herbaceous borders, kitchen garden and a croquet lawn. C16 dovecote, thatched cob wall and clear chalk streams. **Nottingham Fee House** ⅓ -acre garden surrounding early C17 house. Hard landscaping designed by Robin Williams (2005). But original planting now mostly replaced to provide seasonal interest with unusual perennials and clipped Boxes and gravel paths. **Stocks** Early cruck-constructed thatched cottage, surrounded by densely planted lime tolerant herbaceous perennials offering tiers of colour yr-round. Plant Stall in the car park.

Come and see . . . you may catch a glimpse of Toad and friends . . .

GROUP OPENING

9 BRIZE NORTON GARDENS

Brize Norton OX18 3LY. *3m SW of Witney. Brize Norton village, S of A40, between Witney & Burford. Parking at various locations in village.* Home-made teas. **Combined adm £4, chd free. Sun 16 June (1-6).**

BARNSTABLE HOUSE
Mr & Mrs P Butcher

17 CHICHESTER PLACE
Mr & Mrs D Howard

CHURCH FARM HOUSE
Philip & Mary Holmes

CLUMBER
Mr & Mrs S Hawkins

THE COTTAGE
G & J A Griffin

16 DAUBIGNY MEAD
Bob & Margaret Watts

2 ELM GROVE
Brian De'Ath & Joy Lee

GAYLYN
Mrs B Wallace

GRANGE FARM
Mark & Lucy Artus

MIJESHE
Mr & Mrs M Harper

3 MINSTER ROAD
James & Sarah Jane Gillies

PAINSWICK HOUSE
Mr & Mrs T Gush

RAMSHEAD COTTAGE
Mrs A Elsmore

ROSEDALE
Mr & Mrs S Finlayson

95 STATION ROAD
Mr & Mrs P A Timms

STONE COTTAGE
Mr & Mrs K Humphris

Pretty village on the edge of the Cotswold's offering 16 gardens open for your enjoyment. You can see a wide variety of planting incl a bog garden, ornamental trees, herbaceous borders, ornamental grasses and traditional fruit and vegetable gardens. Features incl a Mediterranean style patio, courtyard garden, water features, C14 dovecote plus many gardens where you can just sit and relax. Some gardens have limited wheelchair access, some have gravel paths.

10 ◆ BROUGHTON CASTLE
Nr Banbury OX15 5EB. Lord Saye & Sele, 01295 276070, www.broughtoncastle.com. *2½ m SW of Banbury. On Shipston-on-Stour rd (B4035).* **Adm £4, chd free. For NGS: Sun 28 July (2-5). For other opening times and information, please phone or see garden website.**
1 acre; shrubs, herbaceous borders, walled garden, roses, climbers seen against background of C14-C16 castle surrounded by moat in open parkland. House also open with extra charge.

11 BROUGHTON GRANGE
Wykham Lane, Broughton OX15 5DS, www.broughtongrange.com. *¼ m out of village. From Banbury take B4035 to village of Broughton. At the Saye & Sele Arms PH turn L up Wykham Lane (one way). Follow rd out of village along lane for ¼ m. Entrance on R.* **Adm £6, chd free. Sun 28 Apr, Sat 15, Suns 16 June, 28 July (10-5).**
An impressive 25 acres of gardens and light woodland in an attractive Oxfordshire setting. The centrepiece is a large terraced walled garden created by Tom Stuart-Smith in 2001. Vision has been used to blend the gardens into the countryside. Good early displays of bulbs followed by outstanding herbaceous planting in summer. Formal and informal areas combine to make this a special site incl newly laid arboretum with many ongoing projects.

GROUP OPENING

12 BROUGHTON POGGS & FILKINS GARDENS
GL7 3JH, 01367 860875. *3m N of Lechlade. 5m S of Burford. Just off A361 between Burford & Lechlade.* Home-made teas at Filkins village hall. **Combined adm £5, chd free. Sun 5 May (2-6).**

BROUGHTON HALL
Karen & Ian Jobling

BROUGHTON POGGS MILL
Charlie & Avril Payne

FIELD COTTAGE
Peter & Sheila Gray

FILKINS HALL
Filkins Hall Residents

LITTLE PEACOCKS
Colvin & Moggridge

PEACOCK FARMHOUSE
Pauline & Peter Care

PIGEON COTTAGE
Lynn Savege

PIP COTTAGE
G B Woodin

ST PETER'S HOUSE
John Cambridge

NEW THE STONE HOUSE
Mr & Mrs Roland and Jackie Cullum

NEW THE TALLOT
Mr & Mrs Don Stowell

NEW TAYLOR COTTAGE
Mr & Mrs Ian & Ronnie Bailey

WILLOW COTTAGE
Sue Logan

13 gardens in these beautiful and vibrant Cotswold stone twin villages. Scale and character vary from the grand landscape setting of Filkins Hall and the equally extensive but more intimate Broughton Hall, to the small but action-packed Pigeon Cottage and The Tallot, a new opening. Broughton Poggs Mill has a rushing mill stream with an exciting bridge, Little Peacocks is a serene composition of spaces (Brenda Colvin's own garden) and Pip Cottage combines topiary, box hedges and a fine rural view. In these and the other equally exciting gardens horticultural interest abounds. Maps available. Plant stall by professional local nursery, Swinford Museum of Cotswolds tools and artefacts and Cotswold Woollen Weavers. Many gardens have gravel driveways but most suitable for wheelchair access. Some gardens do not welcome dogs.

13 BUCKLAND LAKES
nr Faringdon SN7 8QW. The Wellesley family. *3m NE of Faringdon. Signed to Buckland off A420, lane between 2 churches. Minibus shuttle available between car park & tea rooms.* Home-made teas at Memorial Hall. **Adm £4, chd free (share to RWMT (community bus)). Sun 7 Apr (2-5).**
Six acres of parkland surround the lakeside walk, designed by Richard Woods; fine trees; daffodils; shrubs. Norman church adjoins garden. C18 icehouse; thatched boathouse; exedra. Children must be supervised due to large expanse of open water which is unfenced.

BURROW FARM
See Buckinghamshire

Vision has been used to blend the gardens into the countryside . . .

14 CHALKHOUSE GREEN FARM
nr Kidmore End RG4 9AL. Mr & Mrs J Hall, 01189 723631, chgs@btinternet.com, www.chgs.info. *2m N of Reading, 5m SW of Henley-on-Thames. Situated between A4074 & B481. From Kidmore End take Chalkhouse Green Rd. Follow yellow signs.* Home-made teas. **Adm £3.50, chd free. Sun 21 July (2-6). Visitors also welcome by appt.**
1-acre garden and open traditional farmstead. Herbaceous borders, herb garden, shrubs, old-fashioned roses, trees incl medlar, quince and mulberries, walled ornamental kitchen garden. New cherry orchard. Rare breed farm animals incl an ancient breed of British White cattle, Suffolk Punch and Percheron horses, donkeys, Berkshire pigs, piglets, chickens, ducks and turkeys. Plant and jam stall, donkey rides, swimming in covered pool, trailer rides, farm trail, horse logging demonstration, bee display. Limited wheelchair access.

Waterperry Gardens

GROUP OPENING

15 CHARLBURY GARDENS

Charlbury OX7 3PP. *6m SE of Chipping Norton. Large Cotswold village on B4022 Witney-Enstone Rd.* Home-made teas at Charlbury Memorial Hall. **Combined adm £4, chd free.** Sun 26 May (2-4).

GOTHIC HOUSE
Mr & Mrs Andrew Lawson

THE PRIORY GARDEN
Dr D El Kabir & Colleagues

2 varied gardens in the centre of this large Cotswold village, in the context of traditional stone houses. Gothic House. 1/3 -acre walled garden designed with sculpture and colour in mind. New area of planted squares replaces lawn. False perspective, pleached lime walk, trellis, terracotta containers. The Priory Garden has 1 acre of formal terraced topiary gardens with Italianate features. Foliage colour schemes, shrubs, parterres with fragrant plants, old roses, water features, sculpture and inscriptions aim to produce a poetic, wistful atmosphere. Arboretum of over 3 acres. Borders R Evenlode. Incl wildlife garden and pond.

16 CHASTLETON GLEBE

Moreton-in-Marsh GL56 0SZ. Prue Leith. *Chastleton. 3m SE of Moreton-in-Marsh off A44 / 4m NW of Chipping Norton.* **Combined adm £5, chd free.** Sun 14 July (2-6). **Combined with Chastleton House.**
5 acres, old trees, terraces (one all red); small lake, island; Chinese-style bridge, pagoda; views; rose tunnel. Vegetable and flower parterres. Gravel paths & grass areas dependent on weather.

17 ◆ CHASTLETON HOUSE AND GARDEN

Chaselton, Moreton-in-Marsh GL56 0SU. National Trust, 01608 674981, www.nationaltrust.org.uk. *at Chastleton House NT. Follow brown signs for Chastleton House from A44 between Morton in Marsh & Chipping Norton.* **Combined adm £5, chd free.** For NGS: Sun 14 July (2-6). **Combined with Chastleton Glebe. For other opening times and information, please phone or see garden website.**
Chastleton is a historic garden that represents the decline of one family from 1607-1991. Made up of various rooms, it still shows how certain areas were accessed depending on your status in the Jacobean household. The garden has a variety of topiaries, shrubs, fruit, vegetables, trees and herbaceous planting with an ancient feel. It has 2 croquet lawns and is home of croquet. Garden tours, meet garden volunteers and gardener. Plant/produce stall, honey from the garden for sale, meet the bee keeper, garden fruit advice. Gravel, some slopes and steps.

18 14 CHAWLEY LANE

Cumnor, Oxford OX2 9PX. Alice & Paul Munsey. *3m W of Oxford. From W Oxford, at top of Cumnor Hill, turn R opp Jaguar garage into Chawley Lane. Garden 50 metres on R. Parking in Norreys and Bertie Road.* Home-made teas. **Combined adm £4, chd free.** Sat 18 May (2-5.30). **Combined with 36 Bertie Road.**
Plantsman's 1/2 -acre garden with wide and interesting range of plants, many unusual. Owner has a particular interest in alpines and woodland plants. Lovely views over valley and Wytham Woods. Area of developing 'meadow'. Well laid out vegetable garden. One slight slope. Small step to WC.

19 CHIVEL FARM

Heythrop OX7 5TR. Mr & Mrs J D Sword, 01608 683227, rosalind.sword@btinternet.com. *4m E of Chipping Norton. Off A361 or A44.* Light refreshments. **Adm £4, chd free.** Visitors welcome by appt **Mar to Oct. Admission fee dependent on group size.**
Beautifully designed country garden, with extensive views, designed for continuous interest. Colour-schemed borders with many unusual trees, shrubs and herbaceous plants. Small formal white garden. Conservatory.

20 CHURCH FARM FIELD
Church Lane, Epwell, Banbury OX15 6LD. Mr V D & Mrs D V D Castle, 01295 788473. *7½ m W of Banbury on N side of Epwell. Field to be found on North Side of Epwell Village.* **Adm £2, chd free. Suns 14 Apr, 2 June, 1 Sept (2-6). Visitors also welcome by appt Apr to Sept.**
Woods; arboretum with wild flowers (planting started 1992); over 90 different trees and shrubs in 4½ acres. Paths cut through trees for access to various parts.

21 CLOCK HOUSE
Coleshill SN6 7PT. Denny Wickham & Peter Fox, 01793 762476, denny.andrews@virgin.net. *3½ m SW of Faringdon. On B4019.* Tea at Coleshill Village Shop and Cafe. **Adm £2, chd free. Visitors welcome by appt. Refreshments available.**
Rambling garden on hilltop overlooking NT parkland and Vale of the White Horse. On the site of Coleshill House, burnt down in 1952, the floor plan has been laid out as a garden with lavender and box 'walls' and gravel 'rooms' full of self-sown butterfly-attracting flowers. Exuberant, not too tidy, garden with unusual plants; walled garden; vegetables.

22 CORPUS CHRISTI COLLEGE
Merton Street, Oxford OX1 4JF. Mr C Holmes, Domestic Bursar. *Entrance from Merton St.* **Adm £2, chd free. Sun 23 June (2-6).**
David Leake, the College gardener since 1979, eschewing chemicals and sprays, has created a marvellous 'wild' garden by blending a huge range of wild and cultivated flowers into a vivid, yet harmonious, landscape. In amongst beautiful buildings and with wonderful views of Christ Church meadows from the mound beside the ancient city wall, the Corpus garden is a real treasure.

CUDDINGTON GARDENS
See Buckinghamshire

DANESFIELD HOUSE
See Buckinghamshire

DAYLESFORD HOUSE
See Gloucestershire

23 EAVES COTTAGE
Cropredy Lane, Williamscot OX17 1AD. Ken & Sandra Atack. *3m NE of Banbury. From J11 M40 take A361 to Daventry. After 3m L into Williamscot. Eaves Cottage on L at end of village.* Home-made teas. **Adm £4, chd free (share to Pancreatic Cancer UK). Sun 2 June (2-5).**
Cottage garden set in 1-acre of C17 house with SE facing sloped aspect. Planted for yr-round interest with many different shrubs, trees and herbaceous borders. Pond, stream and bog area with natural planting. Newly cultivated large vegetable and fruit area.

Flowers selected for scent, novelty, nostalgia and naturalistic style . . .

24 EPWELL MILL
nr Banbury OX15 6HG. Mrs William Graham & Mrs David Long, caroline.long@talk21.com. *7m W of Banbury. Between Shutford & Epwell, ½ m outside Epwell.* Home-made teas. **Adm £2.50, chd free. Suns 7 Apr, 2 June, 1 Sept (2-5.30). Visitors also welcome by appt Apr to Sept. Please apply by email.**
Medium-sized peaceful garden, interestingly landscaped in open country, based around former watermill, with terraced pools. Spring bulbs in April, azaleas in June and early autumn colour in September. White double border; productive vegetable garden; a haven for wild birds. Open under the NGS since 1963.

25 FAILFORD
118 Oxford Road, Abingdon OX14 2AG. Mr & Mrs P Aylward, 01235 523925, liz@dreamfisher.co.uk. *A34 S, take N Abingdon turn, turn L at top of slip rd toward Abingdon, continue straight on at r'about into Oxford Rd. Failford is on R. A34 N, take Abingdon turn, follow signs into Abingdon centre & out towards Oxford. Keep on Oxford Rd pass Boundary House, over T-lights take 2nd L into service rd. NGS signs will be in use.* Light refreshments. **Adm £3, chd free. Sun 2 June (11-4). Visitors also welcome by appt Apr to Nov.**
This town garden won Abingdon in Bloom best large back garden competition. Both formal and informal areas, an extension of the home. Walkways through shaded area, arches, kitchen garden, grasses, roses, topiaries, acers, hostas, heucheras. A wide variety of planting and features, within an area 570sq.ft. Featured in Garden News.

26 FAIRFIELD
Cross Hill Road, Adderbury, Banbury OX17 3EQ. Mr Mike & Mrs Val Adams, 01295 810109. *Cross Hill Road, Adderbury. From A4260 follow rd via Adderbury. House 900yds on L.* Light refreshments. **Adm £5, chd free. Visitors welcome by appt June to Sept.**
This exquisite, tiny, paved garden is a tapestry of beautiful plants and a patchwork of colour, interwoven with a selection of unusual and interesting clematis and climbers. Notable for late summer colour.

FOLLY FARM
See Berkshire

27 NEW FOXCOMBE HALL
Boars Hill, Oxford OX1 5HR. The Open University in the South. *3m S of Oxford. From Oxford Ring rd S follow signs for Wootton & Boars Hill. At Berkley Rd turn R. At 1st bend to L look for car park on L.* Light refreshments. **Adm £3, chd free. Sat 18 May (11-3).**
Come and explore 15 acres of beautiful garden at Foxcombe Hall, home to the Open University in the South since 1976 and formerly owned by Lord Randall Berkeley. The grounds are mostly natural woodland and incl an artificial lake, Italian garden with terrace and rockery, spring flowers, rhododendrons and magnolias. The grounds are not usually open to the public. Indoor display of cactii and succulents. Presentation at 1 pm 'Aloe, aloe and useful succulents'. Limited wheelchair access. Some paths very slippery when wet.
NCH

28 GREEN AND GORGEOUS, THE CUTTING GARDEN
Little Stoke, Wallingford OX10 6AX. Rachel Siegfried, 07977 445041, www.greenandgorgeousflowers.co.uk. *3m S of Wallingford. Off B4009 between N & S Stoke; follow single track rd down to farm.* Home-made teas. **Adm £3.50, chd free. Sun 14 July (12-5). Visitors also welcome by appt June to Aug.**
6-acre working flower farm next to R Thames. Organically grown cut flowers (many unusual varieties) in large plots and polytunnels, planted with combination of annuals, bulbs, perennials, roses and shrubs, plus some herbs, vegetables and fruit to feed the workers! Flowers selected for scent, novelty, nostalgia and naturalistic style. Floristry demonstrations. Featured on BBC Gardeners World and in The English Garden Magazine. Short grass paths, large concrete areas.

29 GREENFIELD FARM
Christmas Common, nr Watlington OX49 5HG. Andrew & Jane Ingram, 01491 612434, abingram@hotmail.co.uk. *4m from J5 of M40, 7m from Henley. J5 M40; A40 towards Oxford for $\frac{1}{2}$ m; turn L signed Christmas Common. $\frac{3}{4}$ m past Fox & Hounds PH. Turn L at Tree Barn sign.* **Evening Opening £4, chd free, Tue 18 June (6-8). Visitors also welcome by appt June to Sept.**
10-acre wild flower meadow, surrounded by woodland, established 16 yrs ago under the Countryside Stewardship Scheme. Traditional Chiltern chalkland meadow in beautiful peaceful setting with 100 species of perennial wild flowers, grasses and 5 species of orchids. $\frac{1}{2}$ m walk from parking area to meadow. Opportunity to return via typical Chiltern beechwood. A guided tour at 6.00pm. The tour will last approx 2 hours and is $1\frac{1}{2}$ miles long.

30 ◆ GREYS COURT
Rotherfield Greys, Henley-on-Thames RG9 4PG. National Trust, 01491 628529, www.nationaltrust.org.uk. *2m W of Henley-on-Thames. Signed from Nettlebed taking B481. Direct route from Henley-on-Thames town centre (unsigned for NT): follow signs to Badgemore Golf Club towards Rotherfield Greys, about 3m out of Henley.* **Adm £4, chd free. For NGS: Tue 11 June (11-5). For other opening times and information, please phone or see garden website.**
The tranquil gardens cover 9 acres and surround a Tudor house with many alterations, as well as a Donkey Wheel and Tower. They incl lawns, a maze and small arboretum. The highlights are the series of enchanting walled gardens, a colourful patchwork of interest set amid medieval walls. Meet the gardeners and volunteers who look after the gardens. Limited wheelchair access. Loose gravel paths in garden, slopes and some cobbles.

31 THE GROVE
North Street, Middle Barton, Chipping Norton OX7 7BZ. Ivor & Barbara Hill. *7m E Chipping Norton. On B4030, 2m from junction A4260 & B4030, opp Carpenters Arms PH. Parking in street.* Home-made teas. **Adm £3, chd free. Sun 19 May (1.30-5).**
Mature informal plantsman's garden. $\frac{1}{3}$ acre planted for all year interest around C19 Cotswold Stone cottage (not open). Numerous borders with wide variety of unusual shrubs, trees and hardy plants; several species weigela syringa viburnum and philadelphus. Pond area, well-stocked greenhouse. Plant list available. Home-made preserves for sale. Wheelchair access to most of garden.

GROUP OPENING

32 HEADINGTON GARDENS
Old Headington OX3 9BT. *2m E from centre of Oxford. After T-lights, centre of Headington, towards Oxford, 2nd turn on R into Osler Rd. Gardens at end of rd in Old Headington.* Tea at Ruskin College. **Combined adm £4, chd free (share to Ruskin College). Sun 16 June (2.30-5.30).**

THE COACH HOUSE
Mr & Mrs David Rowe

40 OSLER ROAD
Nicholas & Pam Coote
Visitors also welcome by appt Apr to Sept. Refreshments available.
07804 932748
pamjcoote@gmail.com

37 ST ANDREWS ROAD
Judith & David Marquand

35 ST ANDREWS ROAD
Mrs Alison Soskice

WHITE LODGE
Denis & Catharine Macksmith and Roger & Frances Little

Headington was an Anglo-Saxon settlement at the centre of the royal domain of Mercian kings high above the Cherwell and Thames. The village is remarkable for its mature trees, high stone walls, narrow lanes and Norman church (1142). The 5 gardens provide a rare glimpse behind the walls. **The Coach House** combines a formal setting with hedges, lawn and flowers and a sunny courtyard on 2 levels. **40 Osler Road** is a well-established garden with an Italian theme brimming with exotic planting. **White Lodge** provides a large park-like setting for a Regency property and **35 & 37 St Andrews Road** are 2 delightful smaller cottage gardens, one incl vegetables and planted for all-yr interest.

Home-made preserves for sale . . .

33 HEARNS HOUSE
Gallowstree Common RG4 9DE. John & Joan Pumfrey, 01189 722848, joanpumfrey@lineone.net. *5m N of Reading, 5m W of Henley. From A4074 turn E at Cane End.* Home-made teas. **Adm £4, chd free. Wed 29, Fri 31 May, Wed 24, Fri 26 July (11-5). Visitors also welcome by appt May to Aug. Introductory talk by owner.**
2-acre garden provides yr-round interest with pergolas, crinkle-crankle walls, sculpture, ponds. Inspirational variety of indigenous and exotic planting. Some self-sown plants are allowed to flourish where they enhance the original design. The nursery is full of wonderful plants propagated from the garden. National Collections of brunnera and omphalodes.

NCH

34 HOLLYHOCKS
North Street, Islip, nr Kidlington OX5 2SQ. Avril Hughes, 01865 377104, ahollyhocks@btinternet.com. *3m NE of Kidlington. From A34 - exit Bletchingdon/Islip. B4027 direction Islip, turn L into North St.* Home-made teas. **Combined adm £5, chd free.** **Sun 21 Apr (2-5); Sun 19 May (2-5.30). Combined with Monkshead. Visitors also welcome by appt Mar to Sept.**
Plantswoman's small garden brimming with yr-round interest. Divided into areas with bulbs, herbaceous borders, roses, clematis, shade and woodland planting with a particular interest in ferns. There are several alpine troughs as well as lots of pots around the house. 5 steps into garden, disabled access through house.

35 HOME CLOSE
Southend, Garsington OX44 9DH. Ms M Waud & Dr P Giangrande, 01865 361394. *3m SE of Oxford. Southend. N of B480. Opp Garsington Manor.* **Adm £4, chd free. Visitors welcome by appt Apr to Sept. Refreshments by arrangement.**
2 acre garden with listed house (not open) and listed granary. Unusual trees and shrubs planted for all-year round effect. Terraces, walls and hedges divide the garden and the planting reflects a Mediterranean interest. One acre mixed tree plantation separated from garden by traditional style deer fence.

36 HOME FARM
Balscote OX15 6JP. Mr Godfrey Royle, 01295 738194. *5m W of Banbury. ½ m off A422.* Light refreshments. **Adm £3, chd free. Visitors welcome by appt.**
Formerly a plant lover's peaceful garden, but now redesigned as a gravel garden by Zizi 3D garden design, with flowering shrubs and mature trees and a unique Balscote-sur-Mer theme. Two lawns give a feeling of spaciousness, and a small terrace has views of surrounding countryside.

37 HOME FARM HOUSE
Pusey, Faringdon SN7 8QB. Mr & Mrs Hugh Buchanan. *Take B4508 marked to Pusey from Oxford ñ Swindon A420. After 1m turn L into no through rd beside 3 Georgian cottages. Garden ½ m further on R.* Cream teas. **Adm £4, chd free. Sun 19, Mon 20 May, Sat 15, Sun 16 June (2-6).**
A newly formed garden in a particularly peaceful, rural setting, which has been created over the last 10yrs. Features are a walled garden, courtyard garden, seasonal shrubs, peonies, irises and rose garden. Partial wheelchair access. Steep slope to rose garden and some gravel paths.

HOSTAS AT 25 SIMONS LANE
See Berkshire

38 NEW HUNTERS LODGE
High Street, Shipton-Under-Wychwood OX7 6DG. Mrs Madeline Taylor. *Opp Mawles Lane & nr Shaven Crown Hotel.* Home-made teas. **Adm £3, chd free. Sun 30 June (2-4).**
Just over ¾ acre. Recently re-established with many perennials. Vegetable garden, orchard and rose garden.

A newly formed garden in a particularly peaceful, rural setting . . .

GROUP OPENING

39 IFFLEY GARDENS
Iffley, Oxford OX4 4EJ. *2m S of Oxford. Within Oxford's ring rd, off A4158 from Magdalen Bridge to Littlemore r'about. Map provided at each garden.* Teas at village hall. **Combined adm £5, chd free. Sun 16 June (2-6).**

15 ABBERBURY ROAD
Allen & Boglarka Hill

65 CHURCH WAY
Jacqueline Woodfill

86 CHURCH WAY
Helen Beinart & Alex Coren

122 CHURCH WAY
Sir John & Lady Elliott

6 FITZHERBERT CLOSE
Tom & Eunice Martin

THE MALT HOUSE
Mrs Helen Potts

THE THATCHED COTTAGE
Martin & Helen Foreman

Secluded old village with renowned Norman church, featured on cover of Pevsner's Oxon Guide. Visit 7 gardens ranging in variety and style from an English cottage garden with Californian plants to a small professionally designed Japanese style garden, with maples and miniature pines. Varied planting throughout the gardens incl herbaceous borders and shade loving plants, roses, fine specimen trees and plants in terracing. Features incl water features, formal gardens, small lake and riverbank. Plant sale at The Malt House.

KEMPSFORD MANOR
See Gloucestershire

GROUP OPENING

40 KENCOT GARDENS
Kencot, nr Lechlade GL7 3QT. *5m NE of Lechlade. E of A361 between Burford & Lechlade. Village maps available.* Home-made teas in Village Hall. **Combined adm £4, chd free. Mon 1 Apr (2-6).**

THE ALLOTMENTS
Amelia Carter Trust

DE ROUGEMONT
David & Susan Portergill

HILLVIEW HOUSE
John & Andrea Moss

IVY NOOK
Gill & Wally Cox

KENCOT HOUSE
Tim & Kate Gardner

THE MALT HOUSE
Gareth & Lynne John

MANOR FARM
Jane & Jonathan Fyson

PINNOCKS
Joy & John Coxeter

WELL HOUSE
Gill & Ian Morrison

Allotments with the emphasis on organic vegetables, flowers and soft fruit. De Rougemont ½ acre of bulbs, flowers, soft fruit cage, apples and pears, grape vines in greenhouse and 1920s well. Hillview House 2 acre garden with lime tree drive, established trees, shrubs, borders and abundant spring flowers incl daffodils and aconites, a lovely family garden. Ivy Nook inherited from plantsmen parents is a yr-long mass of flowers, shrubs and borders, rockery and small pond with waterfall under magnolia and old apple. Kencot House 2 acres with gingko tree, shrubs and 50 varieties of clematis: wonderful backdrop to abundant spring bulbs. The new owners are keen to retain the haven of tranquillity for wildlife and garden ambience. The Malt House was transformed from gravel parterres to a more open, relaxed format of lawn, roses and herbaceous borders. Water features in corners with fruit trees and productive grape vine framing the late mediaeval stone buildings. Manor Farm Grade II C17 house (not open). 2 acre garden with bulbs, wood anemones, fritillaria in mature orchard with varieties of old English apples, quince, medlar and mulberry. Ancient Black Hamburg vine, geese, chickens and 2 alpacas in paddock. Pinnocks 2 gardens divided by the house. Mixed shrub and herbaceous borders, spring bulbs and flowers, no space left unplanted incl roadside with daffodils. Wow factor old magnolia. Well House, ⅓ acre garden with mature trees and hedges, miniature woodland glade, wildlife pond with waterfall and small bog area. Island beds and mixed borders all year.

♿ 🐕 ✿ ☕

Magdalen meadow, where purple and white snake's-head fritillaries can be found . . .

41 10 KENNETT ROAD
Headington, Oxford OX3 7BJ. Linda & David Clover, 01865 765881, lindaclover@yahoo.co.uk. *2m E of Oxford in Central Headington. S side of London Rd in Central Headington.* **Adm £3, chd free. Visitors welcome by appt.**
Small (20'X90') densely-planted suburban oasis created for year-round interest. It includes a sheltered patio, mixed shrub and herbaceous planting, secluded fernery, small unfenced wildlife pond and an unparalled view of 'Untitled 1986' Headington's world-famous roof top sculpture.

☎

42 ◆ KINGSTON BAGPUIZE HOUSE
Kingston Bagpuize, nr Abingdon OX13 5AX. Mrs Francis Grant, 01865 820259, www.kingstonbagpuizehouse.com. *5m W of Abingdon. In Kingston Bagpuize just off A415, ¼ m S of A415/A420 and accessed from Rectory Lane.* **Adm £5, chd free. For NGS: Sun 17 Mar, Sun 8 Sept (2-5). For other opening times and information, please phone or see garden website.**
Notable collection of unusual trees, incl magnolias, shrubs, perennials, snowdrops and other bulbs, providing yr-round interest and colour. Large mixed borders, interesting summer flowering trees and shrubs. Restoration of copses and new planting in garden and parkland continues. House open - extra charge of £2.50. Featured in Sunday Times. Gravel and grass paths. Disabled WC.

♿ ✿ ☕

43 LADY MARGARET HALL
Norham Gardens, Oxford OX2 6QA. Principal & Fellows of Lady Margaret Hall. *1m N of Carfax. From Banbury Rd, R at T-lights into Norham Gdns.* Cream teas. **Adm £3, chd free. Sun 19 May (2-5.30).**
Beautiful college garden, full of interesting plants, wonderful buildings and riverside walk. One of the best college gardens, great trees, plenty of seats, the perfect retreat, grasses a speciality, 10 acres to wander at your leisure.

✿ ☕

LAPLANDS FARM
See Buckinghamshire

44 LIME CLOSE
35 Henleys Lane, Drayton, Abingdon OX14 4HU. M C de Laubarede, mail@mclgardendesign.com. *2m S of Abingdon. Henleys Lane is off main rd through Drayton.* Cream teas. **Adm £4, chd free (share to CLIC Sargent Care for Children). Sun 14 Apr (2-5.30). Visitors also welcome by appt Feb to June.**
3-acre mature plantsman's garden with rare trees, shrubs, perennials and bulbs. Mixed borders, raised beds, pergola, unusual topiary and shade borders. Herb garden designed by Rosemary Verey. Listed C16 house (not open). Cottage garden designed by MCL Garden Design, focusing on colour combinations and an iris garden with over 100 varieties of tall bearded irises. Many winter bulbs, hellebores and shrubs. Plants for sale from Phoenix Plants Nursery.

♿ 🐕 ✿ ☕ ☎

LORDS WOOD
See Buckinghamshire

LOWER LOVETTS FARM
See Berkshire

LYDIARD PARK WALLED GARDEN
See Wiltshire

45 MAGDALEN COLLEGE
Oxford OX1 4AU. Magdalen College, www.magd.ox.ac.uk. *Entrance in High St.* **Adm £5, chd £4. Sun 7 Apr (1-6).**
60 acres incl deer park, college lawns, numerous trees 150-200yrs old; notable herbaceous and shrub plantings. Magdalen meadow, where purple and white snake's-head fritillaries can be found, is surrounded by Addison's Walk, a tree-lined circuit by the R Cherwell developed since the late C18. Ancient herd of 60 deer. Some uneven ground. Not all areas are accessible for wheelchairs.

♿ ☕

46 NEW THE MANOR
Mill Lane, Chalgrove, Oxford OX44 7SL. Paul & Rachel Jacques. *12m E of Oxford. Chalgrove is 12m E of Oxford and 4m from Watlington off B480. The Manor is W of Chalgrove, 300yds S of Lamb PH. Parking is in field behind The Manor.* Cream teas. **Combined adm £5, chd free. Fri 28, Sun 30 June (2-5). Combined with Mill Barn.**

The Manor garden has a lake and wildlife areas. Mixed shrub and herbaceous beds surround the C15, Grade 1 listed Manor house. The kitchen garden incl hotbeds and companion planting. Parking on mown grass; gravel paths, some shallow steps.

47 MANOR HOUSE

Manor Farm Road, Dorchester-on-Thames OX10 7HZ. Mr & Mrs S H Broadbent, 01865 340101, mab2@o2.co.uk. *8m SSE of Oxford. Off A4074, signs from village centre. Parking at Bridge Meadow 400 metres. Disabled parking at house.* **Adm £3, chd free. Sun 18 Aug (2-5.30). Visitors also welcome by appt.**

2-acre garden in beautiful setting around Georgian house (not open) and mediaeval abbey. Spacious lawn leading to riverside copse of towering black poplars from which there are fine views of Dorchester Abbey. Terrace with rose and vine covered pergola around lily pond. Colourful herbaceous borders, small orchard and vegetable garden. Gravel paths.

48 ◆ MERTON COLLEGE OXFORD FELLOWS' GARDEN

Merton Street, Oxford OX1 4JD. Merton College. *Merton Street runs parallel to High Street.* **Adm £4.50, chd free. For NGS: Sun 21 July (2-5).**

Ancient mulberry, said to have associations with James I. Specimen trees, long mixed border, recently-established herbaceous bed. View of Christ Church meadow.

GROUP OPENING

49 MIDDLETON CHENEY GARDENS

OX17 2ST. *3m E of Banbury. From M40 J11 follow A422, signed Middleton Cheney. Map available at all gardens.* Home-made teas at Peartree House. **Combined adm £5, chd free. Sun 23 June (1-6).**

NEW 19 GLOVERS LANE
Mr Michael Donohoe & Jane Rixon

NEW 21 GLOVERS LANE
Mr & Mrs Richard Walmsley

The Old Vicarage

© Nicola Stocken Tomkins

NEW 20 HORTON ROAD
Steve and Vicky Paxton

38 MIDWAY
Margaret & David Finch

PEARTREE HOUSE
Roger & Barbara Charlesworth

19 Glovers Lane has a strong modern design with flowing curves that create an elegant, serene feeling echoed in a cool, restrained water feature. Planted for foliage and texture as well as colour. 21 Glovers Lane has a bold modern design incorporating formal elements of oak pergola, water feature, box-edged beds, pleached trees and smooth paving contrasting with colourful beds and borders. 20 Horton Road is exuberant with lush, dense planting with a greenhouse, exotic pot plants, dovecote and bog garden. A summerhouse entices you across a Japanese-style bridge over a large carp pond. At 38 Midway mature small front and back gardens planted in great profusion create a powerful sensation of a private, intimate haven including a pond and waterfall. Peartree House is a mature garden with an air of mystery and romance full of hidden corners and surprises. An extensive water feature enhances the other worldly atmosphere emphasising the ever-changing sight and sound of water.

50 NEW MILL BARN

25 Mill Lane, Chalgrove OX44 7SL. Pat Hougham. *12m E of Oxford. Chalgrove is 12m E of Oxford & 4m from Watlington off B480. Mill Barn is in Mill Lane on the W of Chalgrove, 300 yds S of Lamb PH. Parking in field behind The Manor.* Cream teas at The Manor. **Combined adm £5, chd free. Fri 28, Sun 30 June (2-5). Combined with The Manor, Chalgrove.**

Mill Barn has an informal cottage garden with a variety of flowers, shrubs and fruit trees including medlar, mulberry and quince in sunny and shaded beds. Wheelchair-friendly brick paths with rose arches and a pergola leading to a vegetable plot surrounded by a cordon of fruit trees all set in a mill stream landscape. Brick paths and lawn.

51 MONKS HEAD
Weston Road, Bletchingdon OX5 3DH. Sue Bedwell, 01869 350155. *Approx 4m N of Kidlington. From A34 take B4027 to Bletchingdon, turn R at Xrds into Weston Rd.* Home-made teas. **Adm £5, chd free. Suns 10 Mar; 21 Apr (2-5); 19 May (2-5.30). Combined with Hollyhocks 21 Apr & 19 May, adm £5. Visitors also welcome by appt Mar to May.**
Plantaholics' garden for all-yr interest. Bulb frame and alpine area, greenhouse.

52 32 NEW YATT ROAD
Witney OX28 1NZ. Montserrat & Nigel Holmes. *½ m NE of Witney town centre. Turn off A4095 towards Wood Green. Follow New Yatt Rd in NE direction. Garden is close to District Council offices (Elmfield).* **Adm £3, chd free. Sat 15, Sun 16 June, Sun 28 July (2-6).**
An exuberant, plantswoman's suburban oasis, brimming with traditional and unusual plants in a small, but long, rear garden to an Edwardian house. Features a 70 metre mixed herbaceous border with over 60 old fashioned roses. Also contains island beds, small shrubbery, vegetable patch plus a patio crammed with exotic and tender container plants. Short but flat shingle driveway to access garden.

GROUP OPENING

53 NORTH OXFORD GARDENS
Oxford OX2 6UL. *¾ m N of Oxford City Centre. N of city centre, within Oxford ring rd, ¼ m S of Summertown on E side of Banbury Rd A4165.* Home-made teas at Bishop's House. **Combined adm £3.50, chd free. Sun 30 June (2-5).**

13 BELBROUGHTON ROAD
Dr Jennie Turner

BISHOP'S HOUSE
Mrs Wendy Pritchard

Two interesting but very different gardens dating from the 1920s within the North Oxford conservation area. **13 Belbroughton Road** is a mature garden with a sunken area which is part of the original 1920s garden. It is well stocked with a range of unusual and interesting plants and incl an ornamental vegetable garden. **Bishop's House** is a large mature garden currently being restored. It is divided into different rooms and features well stocked herbaceous borders, an Italian garden, a bamboo forest with walkway, a woodland area and an orchard with vegetable garden. This will probably be the last time that these gardens will be open to the public under the NGS. The paths are mostly of grass or gravel with some slopes.

Romantic vicarage garden lovingly rejuvenated and enjoyed by the present family . . .

54 OLD RECTORY
Salford, Chipping Norton OX7 5YL. Mr & Mrs N M Chambers. *Salford. 2m W of Chipping Norton. Off A44 Oxford-Worcester Rd.* Tea. **Adm £3, chd free. Tue 12 Feb (10-1).**
This 1½ acre garden will be opening in February for the first time for the snowdrops and aconites. There are also winter flowering shrubs. Partial wheelchair access.

THE OLD RECTORY FARNBOROUGH
See Berkshire

55 THE OLD VICARAGE
Aston Rowant, nr Watlington OX49 5ST. Julian & Rona Knight, 01844 351315, jknight652@aol.com. *Between Chinnor & Watlington, off B4009. From M40 J6, take B4009 towards Chinnor & Princes Risborough. After 1m L signed Aston Rowant village only.* Home-made teas at local church. **Adm £4, chd free. Sun 16, Wed 26 June (2-6). Visitors also welcome by appt June to Oct.**
Romantic, 1¾ -acre vicarage garden lovingly rejuvenated and enjoyed by the present family. Centered around a croquet lawn surrounded by beds brimming with shrubs and herbaceous plants, hot bed and roses. Lushly planted pond leading through a pergola overflowing with roses and clematis to a tranquil green garden. Small vegetable and cutting garden.

56 THE OLD VICARAGE, BLEDINGTON
Main Road, Bledington, Chipping Norton OX7 6UX. Sue & Tony Windsor, 01608 658525, tony.windsor@tiscali.co.uk. *6m SW of Chipping Norton. 4m SE of Stow-on-the-Wold. On the main st, B4450, through Bledington. NOT next to church.* Home-made teas. **Adm £3.50, chd free. Sun 16 June (2-6). Visitors also welcome by appt Apr to July. Refreshments by prior arrangement.**
1½ -acre garden around a late Georgian (1843) vicarage (not open). Borders and beds filled with hardy perennials, shrubs and trees. Informal rose garden with 350 David Austin roses. Small pond and vegetable patch. Paddock with trees, shrubs and herbaceous border. Planted for yr-round interest. Gravel driveway, gentle sloped garden.

57 NEW 50 PLANTATION ROAD
Oxford OX2 6JE. Philippa Scoones. *Central Oxford. N on Woodstock Rd take 2nd L. Coming into Oxford on Woodstock Rd turn R after Leckford Rd. No disabled parking nr house.* **Adm £3.50, chd free. Sat 20, Sun 21, Sat 27, Sun 28 Apr, Sat 15, Sun 16 June (2-6).**
Surprisingly spacious small city garden. North facing front garden, side alley filled with shade-loving climbers, lawn with mature and unusual plants including Mount Etna Broom, conservatory, terraced area and secluded water garden with rill, woodland plants and alpines.

PYT HOUSE
See Berkshire

58 RADCOT HOUSE
Radcot OX18 2SX. Robin & Jeanne Stainer, www.radcothouse.com. *1¼ m S of Clanfield. On A4095 between Witney & Faringdon, 300yds N of Radcot bridge.* Cream teas. **Adm £5, chd free. Sun 18 Aug, Sun 6 Oct (2-6).**

Approx $2\frac{1}{2}$ acres of dramatic yet harmonious planting in light and shade, formal pond, fruit and vegetable cages. Convenient seating at key points enables relaxed observation and reflection. Extensive use of grasses and unusual perennials and interesting sculptural surprises. Financial Times: 'An exhuberant new garden...' The Oxford Mail: 'The best gardens must offer drama, surprise and contrast and you can find all three here... Radcot House is a gem...'.

Masses of roses, wisteria and clematis clamber over walls and pergolas . . .

GROUP OPENING

59 SALFORD GARDENS

Salford OX7 5YN. *2m W of Chipping Norton. Off A44 Oxford-Worcester Rd.* Tea in Salford village hall. **Combined adm £4, chd free.** **Sun 16 June (2-6).**

NEW GREYSANDS HOUSE
DJ & LJ Stevens

JUNIPERS
Mr M Edmunds

WILLOW TREE COTTAGE
Mr & Mrs J Shapley

Willow Tree Cottage Small walled twin gardens with shrub and herbaceous borders, many clematis; one garden created from old farmyard with large alpine garden. Small grass beds. Plantsman's garden with many interesting plants. **Greysands House** New garden. Completely re-landscaped. Only 6 yrs old. Walls, pond, raised beds, fantastic views, interesting corners. **Junipers** A small garden, essentially designed for family use. The beds are planted in a cottage garden style with a variety of perennials and roses.

SHEEPDROVE ORGANIC FARM
See Berkshire

60 THE SHEILING

Bedwells Heath, Boars Hill, Oxford OX1 5JE. Sue & Tony Shepherd, 01865 739033. *3m S of Oxford. From S ring rd A4142 at J with A34 follow signs to Wootton & Boars Hill. 1m turn R into Berkley Rd signed Old Boars Hill & Scout Camp. At bend turn into Bedwells Heath. Garden $\frac{1}{4}$ m on L. Parking Berkley Rd, Jarn Way & Ridgeway.* **Adm £4, chd free.** **Visitors welcome by appt Apr to Sept.**

Delightful N-facing hillside garden set amongst mature Scots pines, oaks and silver birch. Spring garden of $\frac{2}{3}$ acre planted with unusual rhododendrons, azaleas, magnolias, camellias, pieris, hellebores and spring bulbs. Stream cascading to naturalised pond surrounded by acers. Wheelchair access to top garden only.

GROUP OPENING

61 SIBFORD GOWER GARDENS

Sibford Gower OX15 5RX. *7m W of Banbury. Nr the Warwickshire border, S of B4035, in centre of village nr Wykham Arms PH.* Home-made teas The Manor House. **Combined adm £4, chd free.** **Sun 16 June (2-6).**

BUTTSLADE HOUSE
Mrs Diana Thompson

CARTER'S YARD
Sue & Malcolm Bannister

GOWERS CLOSE
Judith Hitching & John Marshall

GREEN ACRES
Paul & Margaret Hobson

THE MANOR HOUSE
Michael Donovan & Alison Jenkins

Charming small village off the beaten track, with thatched stone cottages. Four gardens open, all different, all very interesting. The cottage gardens complement the ancient houses they surround. Masses of roses, wisteria and clematis clamber over walls and pergolas. Box parterres, clipped yew hedges, herb gardens, bosky borders in pinks and purples plus productive kitchen gardens. Some new and innovative planting with unusual plants. plus a woodland walk with mown paths, rare trees and wild flowers.

62 SOMERVILLE COLLEGE GARDENS

Woodstock Road, Oxford OX2 6HD. Somerville College. *$\frac{1}{2}$ m E of Carfax Tower. Enter from Woodstock Rd, S of Radcliffe Infirmary.* **Adm £2.50, chd free (share to Friends of Oxford Botanic Garden).** **Sun 23 June (2-6).**

Approx 2 acres, robust college garden planted for yr-round interest. Formal bedding, colour-themed and extensive vibrant old-fashioned mixed herbaceous borders.

63 SOUTH NEWINGTON HOUSE

Barford Road, South Newington OX15 4JW. Mr & Mrs David Swan, 01295 721866, claire_ainley@hotmail.com. *6m SW of Banbury. South Newington is between Banbury & Chipping Norton. Take Barford Rd off A361, 1st L after 100yds in between oak bollards. For Sat Nav use OX15 4JL.* Home-made teas. **Adm £4.50, chd free.** **Sat 8 June (1.30-5.30); Sun 9 June (1-5); Sat 15 June (1.30-4.30); Sun 16 June (1-5).** **Visitors also welcome by appt.**

Meandering tree lined drive leads to 2 acre garden full of unusual plants, shrubs and trees. Richly planted herbaceous borders designed for yr-round colour. Organic garden with established beds and rotation planting scheme. Orchard full of fruit trees with pond encouraging wildlife. A family garden beautifully designed to blend seamlessly into the local environment. Resident bee keeper with observation hive. Garden treasure hunt with prizes for children and adults. Some gravel paths but generally full access for wheelchair users.

64 SPARSHOLT MANOR

nr Wantage OX12 9PT. Sir Adrian & Lady Judith Swire. *$3\frac{1}{2}$ m W of Wantage. Off B4507 Ashbury Rd.* Home-made teas in adjacent village hall. **Adm £3, chd free.** **Mon 6 May (2-6).**

Lakes and wildfowl; ancient boxwood, wilderness and summer borders. Wheelchair access in most of the garden.

65 NEW **64 SPRING ROAD**
Abingdon OX14 1AN. Mrs Janet Boulton, j.boulton89@btinternet.com, www.janetboulton.co.uk. *S Abingdon from A34 take L turn after police station into Spring Rd. Minute's drive to number 64 on L.* **Adm £6.** **Visitors welcome by appt June to Oct, (limited numbers only).**
An artists garden (4.5 x 30.5 m) behind a Victorian terrace house, narrow with steps. Predominantly green it contains numerous sculptures with inscriptions relating to art, history and the human spirit'.
☎

66 **SPRINGHILL HOUSE**
Main Street, Hethe OX27 8ES. Mrs Penny Jacoby, 01869 277971, peezweezel@gmail.com. *4m N of Bicester. L off A4421 N from Bicester. Follow signs to Hethe.* Home-made teas. **Adm £4, chd free. Visitors welcome by appt May to Aug.**
A secret 1¾ -acre garden cascading down a slope to a delightfully planted extensive pond. The walled garden area is heavily planted with many varieties of plants. There are over 200 roses, a Mediterranean garden incl many tender and exotic plants (no wheelchair access), a vegetable garden and small arboretum. True plantswoman's garden. No wheelchair access to Mediterranean garden.
♿ 🐕 ✿ ☕ ☎

STEANE PARK
See Northamptonshire

GROUP OPENING

67 **STEEPLE ASTON GARDENS**
Steeple Aston OX25 4SP. *14m N of Oxford, 9m S of Banbury. ½ m E of A4260.* **Combined adm £5, chd free. Sun 9 June (11.30-6).**

ACACIA COTTAGE
Jane & David Stewart

CANTERBURY HOUSE
Peter & Harriet Higgins

KRALINGEN
Mr & Mrs Roderick Nicholson

THE LONGBYRE
Mr Vaughan Billings

PAYNE'S HILL HOUSE
Tim & Caroline Edwards

THE POUND HOUSE
Mr & Mrs R Clarke

PRIMROSE GARDENS
Richard & Daphne Preston
Visitors also welcome by appt Apr to Aug.
01869 340512
richard.preston5@btopenwolrd.com

TOUCHWOOD
Gary Norris

Steeple Aston, often considered the most easterly of the Cotswold villages, is a beautiful stone built village with gardens that provide a huge range of interest. A stream meanders down the hill as the landscape changes from sand to clay. The 8 open gardens include: small floriferous cottage gardens, large landscaped gardens, natural woodland areas, ponds and bog gardens, themed borders. No wheelchair access at Primrose Gardens or Touchwood.
♿ 🐕 ✿ ☕

GROUP OPENING

68 **THAME GARDENS**
Thame OX9 3LA. *From M40 J7/8 follow signs to Thame Mid-way between Oxford & Aylesbury on A418.* Home-made teas. **Combined adm £5, chd free. Sun 23 June (2-5.30).**

19 CHINNOR ROAD
Dr Wendie Norris

NEW **10 HAMILTON ROAD**
Lesley Winward & Wendy Reid

7 NEWBARN CLOSE
Mary & Brian Dover

12 PARK TERRACE
Maggie & Colin Sear

THE STABLES
Pam & Roger Smith

Five gardens set in the historic market town of Thame, including a secluded garden planted with herbaceous beds and a small vegetable plot; a well-stocked garden designed to contrast with a modern bungalow, with borders brimming with perennials and climbers; a walled garden with raised

Green Bushes

beds containing fruit trees and in-filled with climbers, perennials and annual bedding, also handmade pots and sculptures. Rejoining the group this year is a small, quiet retreat planted with foliage for late summer colour and easy care perennials. New to the group is a colourful cottage-style garden filled with pots, pools and perennials where children can take part in a quiz with edible prizes.

THE TITHE BARN
See Berkshire

Wildlife pond inhabited by great crested and smooth newts in spring . . .

69 TRINITY COLLEGE
Oxford OX1 3BH. Dr C R Prior, Garden Master, www.trinity.ox.ac.uk. *Central Oxford. Entrance in Broad St.* Home-made teas. **Adm £2.50, chd free. Sun 24 Mar, Sun 28 July (2-5).**
Historic main College Gardens with specimen trees incl aged forked catalpa, spring bulbs, fine long herbaceous border and handsome garden quad originally designed by Wren. President's Garden surrounded by high old stone walls, mixed borders of herbaceous, shrubs and statuary. Fellows' Garden: small walled terrace, herbaceous borders; water feature formed by Jacobean stone heraldic beasts. Award-winning lavender garden and walk-through rose arbour.

70 TROY & GOULD'S GROVE FARMHOUSE
Ewelme, Wallingford OX10 6PY. David & Tania Ruck-Keene & Mrs Anstey Wild. *3m NE of Wallingford. From roundabout on A4074/A4130 take exit signed Ewelme, RAF Benson (Clacks Lane). Approx 1½ m turn R at T-junction towards Henley.* Home-made teas. **Adm £3.50, chd free. Sun 2 June (2-5).**
An early C19 Grade II farmhouse, formally home of Jerome K Jerome, in a setting of fields and paddocks is surrounded by 1½ acres of garden, which is a mixture of mature formal and natural design and planting. Extensive lawns end in a Ha-Ha and across the fields are stunning views of Oxfordshire. A gazebo and summerhouse, where Jerome and HG Wells are known to have worked, are delightful. The adjoining cottage garden at Gould's Grove Farmhouse has interesting shrubs and Jacob sheep. Grey garden and new vegetable garden under construction.

71 ◆ UNIVERSITY OF OXFORD BOTANIC GARDEN
Rose Lane, Oxford OX1 4AZ. University of Oxford, 01865 286690, www.botanic-garden.ox.ac.uk. *1m E of Oxford city centre. Bottom of High St in central Oxford, on banks of the R Cherwell by Magdalen Bridge & opp Magdalen College Tower.* **Adm £4.50, chd free. For NGS: Wed 18 Sept (9-5). For other opening times and information, please phone or see garden website.**
The Botanic Garden contains more species of plants per acre than anywhere else on earth. These plants are grown in 7 glasshouses, water and rock gardens, large herbaceous border, walled garden and every available space. In total there are over 6,000 different plants to see. National Collection of Euphorbia. Gravel paths.
NCH

72 NEW UPLANDS
Old Boars Hill, Oxford OX1 5JF. Mr & Mrs C Sanders, 01865 739486, sandersc4@hotmail.com. *3m S Oxford. From S ring rd towards A34 follow signs to Wootton & Boars Hill. At junction up Hinksey Hill turn R. After 1m turn R into Berkley Rd & follow rd around L bed & then R bend to Jarn Mound. Parking in lane.* Home-made teas. **Adm £3.50, chd free. Suns 14 July (2-4), 18 Aug (2-6). Visitors also welcome by appt.**
A hidden ⅓ -acre garden with borrowed views and colour throughout the year. You will find dry shade borders, wildlife pond inhabited by great crested and smooth newts in spring and damselflies and dragonflies later plus an extensive range of herbaceous plants, bulbs, roses and clematis.

73 UPPER CHALFORD FARM
between Sydenham & Postcombe OX39 4NH. Mr & Mrs Paul Rooksby, 01844 351320. *4½ m SE of Thame. M40 J6, then A40. At Postcombe turn R signed Chalford (turn L if on A40 from Oxford direction). After 1m on LH-side at 1st telegraph pole. (House is ½ -way Sydenham to Postcombe).* Cream teas. **Adm £3.50, chd free. Thur 20 June (4-7); Sun 23 June, Sun 14 July (2-5.30). Visitors also welcome by appt.**
Jacobean farmhouse garden, old roses, shrubs and perennials. Unusual trees and an ancient black pine. Hidden gardens with different plantings and peaceful places to sit. Spring-fed pond and stream with damp planted banks leading to reclaimed woodland with treehouse. Reopening after 2 years allowing for new landscaping and bog garden to establish. Short gravel drive from car park. Nearer drop-off possible.

74 UPPER GREEN
OX33 1BU. Susan & Peter Burge 01865 351310 *From Headington/ Green Rd r'about on Oxford ring rd, take Bayswater rd signed Barton & Crematorium. After 1m, turn R & immed L at staggered Xrds, following signs to Horton cum Studley. On entering village, follow main road up hill & turn L at T junction. Upper Green is on R after 250 yds.* **Adm £3.50, chd free. Visitors welcome by appt.**
½-acre garden. Views to the Chilterns. Incl gravel garden, mixed borders, small potager, bog area and small pond (great crested newts in residence). Old apple trees. The garden is a carpet of colour with a wide range of perennials, bulbs and shrubs.

75 WADHAM COLLEGE
Parks Road, Oxford OX1 3PN. The Warden & Fellows. *Central Oxford. Parks Road.* **Adm £2, chd free. Sun 17 Mar, Sun 14 July (2-5).**
5 acres, best known for trees, spring bulbs and mixed borders. In Fellows' main garden, fine ginkgo and *Magnolia acuminata*; bamboo plantation; in Back Quadrangle very large *Tilia tomentosa* 'Petiolaris'; in Mallam Court white scented garden est 1994; in Warden's garden an ancient tulip tree; in Fellows' private

garden, Civil War embankment with period fruit tree cultivars, recently established shrubbery with unusual trees and ground cover amongst older plantings.

♿

THE WALLED GARDEN
See Buckinghamshire

WARMINGTON VILLAGE GARDENS
See Warwickshire

A garden designed to admire and enjoy . . . !

76 ◆ WATERPERRY GARDENS
Waterperry, nr Wheatley OX33 1JZ. School of Economic Science, 01844 337264, www.waterperrygardens.co.uk. *9m E of Oxford. M40 J8 from London (turn off Oxford-Wheatley, 1st L to Wheatley, follow brown rose symbol). J8A from Birmingham (turn R Oxford-Wheatley over A40, 1st R Wheatley, follow brown rose symbol. We are 2½ m N of Wheatley.* **Adm £6.50, chd free. For NGS: Sun 24 Mar (10-5.30); Sun 22 Sept (10-3.30). For other opening times and information, please phone or see garden website.**
Waterperry Gardens are an inspiration. 8 acres of landscaped gardens incl rose and formal knot garden, water lily canal, riverside walk and one of the country's finest purely herbaceous borders. There's also a plant centre, garden shop, teashop, art gallery, museum and Saxon church. National Collection of Kabschia and Silver Saxifrages. Fritillaries looking fantastic for April opening. Michaelmas weekend coincides with Sept NGS open day. Riverside Walk may be inaccessible to wheelchair users if very wet.

♿ ❀ NCH ☕

77 WAYSIDE
82 Banbury Road, Kidlington OX5 2BX. Margaret & Alistair Urquhart, 01865 460180, alistairurquhart@ntlworld.com. *5m N of Oxford. On R of A4260 travelling N through Kidlington.* **Adm £3, chd free. Sun 2 June (2-6). Visitors also welcome by appt May to June.**
¼ -acre garden with wide variety of plants and mature trees; mixed borders with hardy geraniums, clematis and bulbs. Woodland garden with extensive collection of hardy ferns. Conservatory, and (new for 2013) large fern house with a collection of unusual species of tree ferns and tender exotics. Limited access for wheelchairs.

❀ ☕ ☎

78 WESTWELL MANOR
Westwell, nr Burford OX18 4JT. Mr Thomas Gibson. *2m SW of Burford. From A40 Burford-Cheltenham, turn L ½ m after Burford r'about on narrow rd signed Westwell. After 1½ m at T-junction, turn R & Westwell Manor (with the Sphinxes atop the gates), is 2nd house on L opp the pond.* Home-made teas in village. **Adm £5, chd free (share to St Marys Church, Westwell). Sun 23 June (2.30-6).**
6 acres surrounding old Cotswold manor house (not open), knot garden, potager, shrub roses, herbaceous borders, topiary, earth works, moonlight garden, rills and water garden, auricula ladder.

❀ ☕

GROUP OPENING

79 WHEATLEY GARDENS
High Street, Wheatley OX33 1XX. *5m E of Oxford. Leave A40 at Wheatley, turn into High St. Gardens at W end of High St. Access from the High St, the original Oxford to London Rd, before it climbs onto the Shotover plain.* Cream teas at Manor House Garden. **Combined adm £4.50, chd free. Sun 23 June (2-6). Visitors also welcome by appt.**

BREACH HOUSE GARDEN
Liz Parry
Visitors also welcome by appt. 01865 876278

THE MANOR HOUSE
Mrs Edward Hess
Visitors also welcome by appt. 01865 875022 ehess@hotmail.co.uk

THE STUDIO
S & A Buckingham
Visitors also welcome by appt June and July. ann.buckingham@alexlive.com

Three adjoining gardens in the historic coaching village of Wheatley. Breach House Garden has an established main area with extensive shrubs and perennials, also a more contemporary reflective space with a wild pond. The Manor House is a 1½ -acre garden surrounding an Elizabethan manor house (not open). Formal box walk, herb garden, cottage garden with rose arches and a shrubbery with old roses. A romantic oasis in this busy village. The Studio is a cottage-style walled garden developed from what was once a farm yard. Herbaceous borders, climbing roses and clematis, shrubs, vegetable plot and fruit trees. All in all a lovely little collection of gardens set in the busy village of Wheatley. Various musical events. Wheelchair accessible with assistance, although there are gravel paths, 2 shallow steps and grass.

♿ 🐕 ☕ ☎

WHICHFORD & ASCOTT GARDENS
See Warwickshire

80 WHITEHILL FARM
Widford nr Burford OX18 4DT. Mr & Mrs Paul Youngson, 01993 823218, a.youngson@virgin.net, www.whitehillfarmnursery.co.uk. *1m E of Burford. From A40 take turn signed Widford. Follow signs to Whitehill Farm Nursery.* Home-made teas. **Adm £3.50, chd free. Sun 2 June (2-6). Visitors also welcome by appt May to Aug.**
2 acres of hillside gardens and woodland with spectacular views overlooking Burford and Windrush valley. Informal plantsman's garden being continuously developed in various areas. Herbaceous and shrub borders, ponds and bog area, old-fashioned roses, ground cover, ornamental grasses, bamboos and hardy geraniums.

🐕 ❀ ☕ ☎

81 WILDWOOD
Farnborough OX17 1EL. Mr & Mrs M Hart. *5m N of Banbury, 8m S of Southam. On A423 at Oxon/Warwicks border. Next to Farnborough Garden Centre.* Home-made teas. **Adm £3, chd free.**

Wed 24 Apr, Wed 29 May, Sat 15, Sun 16 June, Wed 31 July, Wed 28 Aug (2-5).
Delightful ½ -acre garden in the country set amongst mature trees and shrubs providing a haven for wildlife. Garden is stocked with many unusual plants and shrubs and also contains interesting rustic garden features, many of which are made by the owner. Cut flower garden. Rare plants for sale.

WITTINGTON ESTATE
See Buckinghamshire

82 WOOLSTONE MILL HOUSE
Woolstone, nr Faringdon SN7 7QL. Mr & Mrs Anthony Spink, 01367 820219, pennyspink@gmail.com.
7m W of Wantage. 7m S of Faringdon. Woolstone is a small village off B4507 below Uffington White Horse Hill. Home-made teas. **Adm £4, chd free. Every Weds 1 May to 25 Sept (2-5).**
2-acre garden in pretty hidden village. Stream runs through garden. Large mixed herbaceous and shrub circular border bounded by yew hedges. Small gravel, cutting, kitchen and bog gardens. Topiary. Medlars and old-fashioned roses. Tree house with spectacular views to Uffington White Horse and White Horse Hill. C18 mill house and barn, not open. Partial wheelchair access.

WORMINGHALL GARDENS
See Buckinghamshire

South Newington House

Oxfordshire County Volunteers

County Organisers
Marina Hamilton-Baillie, Rectory House, Church Green, Stanford in the Vale, SN7 8HU, 01367 710486, marina_hamilton_baillie@hotmail.com
David White, Placketts, High Street, Adderbury, Banbury OX17 3LS, 01295 812679, david.white@doctors.org.uk

Treasurer
David White, Placketts, High Street, Adderbury, Banbury OX17 3LS, 01295 812679, david.white@doctors.org.uk

Publicity & North West Oxon
Priscilla Frost, 27 Ditchley Road, Charlbury, Chipping Norton OX7 3QS, 01608 810578, info@oxconf.co.uk

Booklet Coordinator
Catherine Pinney, Pond House, Pyrton, Watlington OX49 5AP, 01491 612638

Assistant County Organisers
Lyn Baldwin, 9 Toy Lane, Chipping Norton OX7 5FH, 01608 642754, elynnbalswin@gmail.com
Graham & Rosemarie Lenton, The Old School, 25A Standlake Road, Ducklington, Witney OX29 7UR, 01993 899033, grahamlenton@btopenworld.com
John & Joan Pumfrey, Hearns House, Gallows Tree Common, Reading RG4 9DE, 01189 722848, joanpumfrey@lineone.net
Charles & Lyn Sanders, Uplands, Old Boars Hill, Oxford OX1 5JF, 01865 739486, sandersc4@hotmail.com

SHROPSHIRE

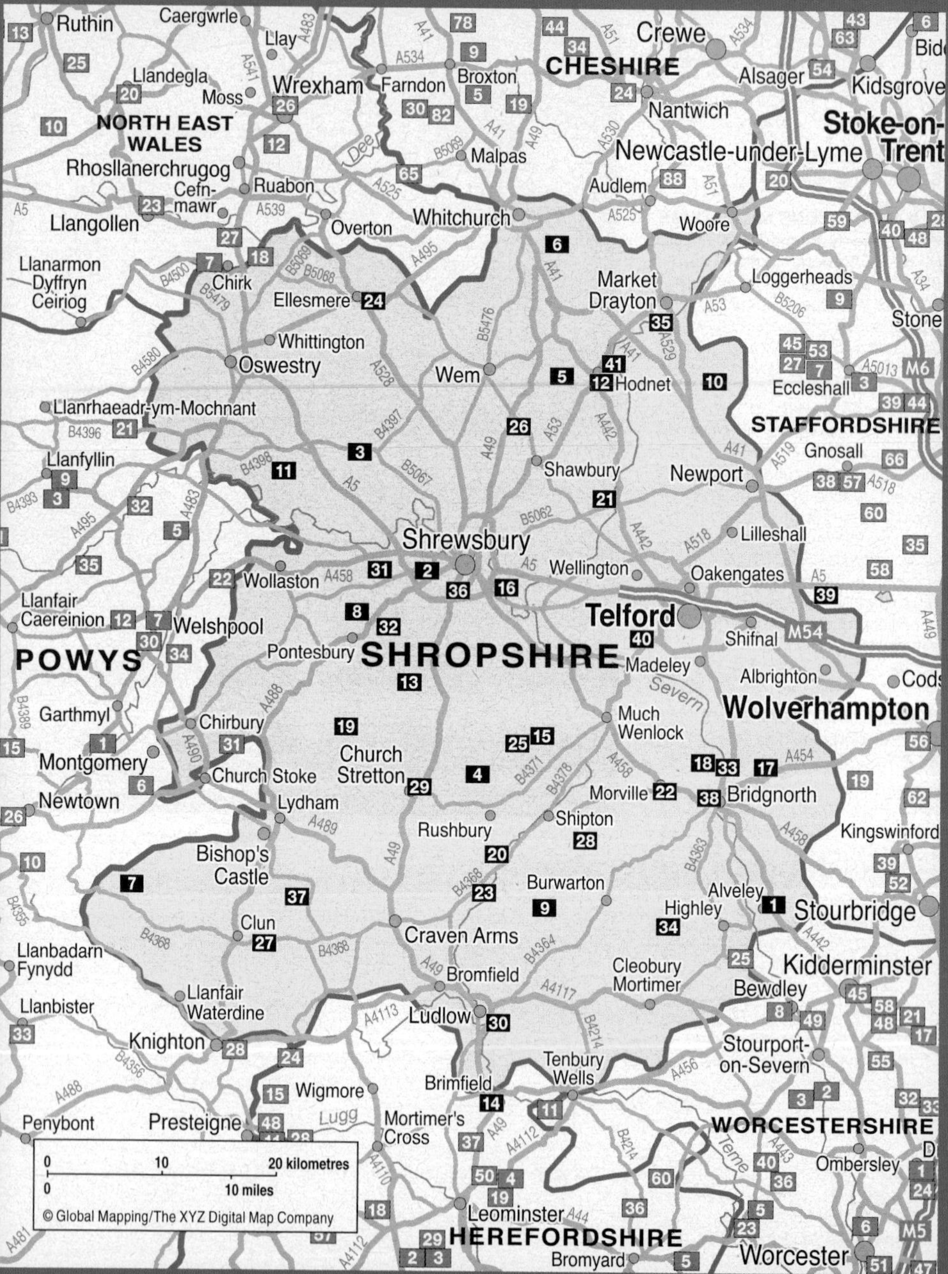

SHROPSHIRE
CHESHIRE
NORTH EAST WALES
STAFFORDSHIRE
POWYS
WORCESTERSHIRE
HEREFORDSHIRE
Ruthin
Caergwrle
Llay
Wrexham
Farndon
Broxton
Crewe
Alsager
Kidsgrove
Nantwich
Stoke-on-Trent
Newcastle-under-Lyme
Llandegla
Moss
Rhosllanerchrugog
Cefn-mawr
Ruabon
Llangollen
Overton
Malpas
Whitchurch
Audlem
Woore
Llanarmon Dyffryn Ceiriog
Chirk
Ellesmere
Market Drayton
Loggerheads
Stone
Whittington
Oswestry
Wem
Hodnet
Eccleshall
Llanrhaeadr-ym-Mochnant
Llanfyllin
Shawbury
Newport
Gnosall
Lilleshall
Shrewsbury
Wellington
Oakengates
Wollaston
Llanfair Caereinion
Welshpool
Telford
Shifnal
Pontesbury
Madeley
Albrighton
Cods
Garthmyl
Chirbury
Much Wenlock
Wolverhampton
Montgomery
Church Stretton
Church Stoke
Newtown
Lydham
Morville
Bridgnorth
Rushbury
Shipton
Kingswinford
Bishop's Castle
Burwarton
Alveley
Highley
Stourbridge
Clun
Craven Arms
Llanbadarn Fynydd
Bromfield
Cleobury Mortimer
Kidderminster
Bewdley
Llanfair Waterdine
Llanbister
Ludlow
Knighton
Stourport-on-Severn
Tenbury Wells
Brimfield
Wigmore
Penybont
Presteigne
Mortimer's Cross
Ombersley
Leominster
Bromyard
Worcester
Dee
Severn
Teme
Lugg
0 10 20 kilometres
0 10 miles
© Global Mapping/The XYZ Digital Map Company

Opening Dates

February

Sunday 24
20 Millichope Park

April

Monday 1
25 Preen Manor

Tuesday 2
27 Radnor Cottage

Friday 5
38 8 Westgate Villas (Evening)

Sunday 7
38 8 Westgate Villas

Sunday 14
21 Moortown

Tuesday 23
3 Brownhill House

Saturday 27
18 Lyndale House

May

Friday 3
41 Wollerton Old Hall

Sunday 5
13 Holly Grove
16 Longner Hall

Monday 6
20 Millichope Park

Sunday 12
5 The Citadel
24 Oteley

Sunday 19
1 Ancoireán

Tuesday 21
3 Brownhill House

Friday 24
41 Wollerton Old Hall

Sunday 26
29 3 Scotsmansfield
37 Walcot Hall

Monday 27
10 Goldstone Hall Gardens
37 Walcot Hall

Tuesday 28
27 Radnor Cottage

June

Sunday 2
33 Stanley Hall
40 Windy Ridge

Wednesday 5
8 Edge Villa

Thursday 6
25 Preen Manor

Sunday 9
7 Crossways
19 Marehay Farm
22 Morville Hall Gardens

National Gardens Weekend

Saturday 15
26 Preston Hall
28 Ruthall Manor

Sunday 16
12 Hodnet Hall Gardens
28 Ruthall Manor
31 Shoothill House

Monday 17
28 Ruthall Manor

Tuesday 18
3 Brownhill House

Saturday 22
30 Secret Garden

Sunday 30
14 Holmcroft

July

Wednesday 3
39 Weston Park

Tuesday 9
23 Mynd Hardy Plants

Thursday 11
25 Preen Manor

Sunday 14
2 Bowbrook Allotment Community
23 Mynd Hardy Plants
40 Windy Ridge

Sunday 21
1 Ancoireán
15 Jessamine Cottage

Sunday 28
6 The Croft
10 Goldstone Hall Gardens
36 Valducci Flower & Vegetable Gardens

August

Sunday 4
18 Lyndale House
34 Stiggley Cottage

Wednesday 7
10 Goldstone Hall Gardens

Sunday 11
4 Cardington Gardens
10 Goldstone Hall Gardens
11 Hall Farm Nursery

Sunday 18
40 Windy Ridge

Sunday 25
15 Jessamine Cottage

September

Sunday 1
8 Edge Villa

Sunday 15
40 Windy Ridge

October

Sunday 6
25 Preen Manor

Gardens open to the public

15 Jessamine Cottage
39 Weston Park
41 Wollerton Old Hall

By appointment only

9 Field House
17 Lower Hall
32 Sibberscote Manor
35 7 Tennyson Close

Also open by Appointment ☎

1 Ancoireán
3 Brownhill House
7 Crossways
8 Edge Villa
10 Goldstone Hall Gardens
13 Holly Grove
14 Holmcroft
19 Marehay Farm
24 Oteley
25 Preen Manor
26 Preston Hall
27 Radnor Cottage
28 Ruthall Manor
31 Shoothill House
40 Windy Ridge

A wonderful place for children to run, play and discover, shared with contented animals, flowers, fruit and vegetables and a 'green man' hiding in the woodland garden . . .

The Gardens

ABERNANT
See Powys

1 ANCOIREÁN
24 Romsley View, Alveley WV15 6PJ. Judy & Peter Creed, 01746 780504, pdjc@me.com. *6m S Bridgnorth off A442 Bridgnorth to Kidderminster rd. N from Kidderminster, turn L just after Royal Oak PH, S from Bridgnorth turn R after Squirrel PH. Take 3rd turning R into Romsley View after 50yds bear R & follow NGS signs to bottom of rd, last house in the corner on R.* Home-made teas. **Adm £3, chd free. Sun 19 May; Sun 21 July (1-5). Visitors also welcome by appt May to July, min group 20.**
Natural garden layout on several levels, developed over 30yrs, with a large variety of herbaceous plants and shrubs. Water features, wooded area with bog garden containing numerous varieties of ferns and hostas. Features incl chickens in wooded area, stumpery and ornamental grass border. New colourful alpine scree for 2013. Selection of plants and bird and insect boxes for sale. Close to Severn Valley Railway and Country Park and Dudmaston Hall NT. Featured in Shropshire Star, Express & Star, Shropshire Life Magazine.

BIRCH TREES
See Staffordshire, Birmingham & West Midlands

ALLOTMENTS

2 BOWBROOK ALLOTMENT COMMUNITY
Mytton Oak Road, Shrewsbury SY3 5BT, www.bowbrookallotments.co.uk. *½ m from Royal Shrewsbury Hospital. From A5 Shrewsbury bypass take B4386 following signs for hospital. Allotments situated ½ m along B4386. (Mytton Oak Rd) on R.* **Combined adm £3.50, chd free. Sun 14 July (1-5).**
This award winning 4-acre site which opened in Spring 2009 and which has featured in a variety of gardening magazines has 68 productive plots displaying wide-ranging cultivation methods. Organic techniques incl companion planting and attracting natural predators are encouraged. Green spaces throughout the site are designed to attract wildlife and encourage community involvement. Nest boxes, bat boxes and insect shelters abound. The site features an interest trail, 2 orchards, picnic area, wild flowers, wildlife areas and 'Gardens of the Seasons'. Local environmental groups and schools welcomed. The community has a website (see above) and regular newsletters for members. Children enjoy the trail, willow den and tunnel, turf maze and sensory garden. The site boasts a compost toilet and information hut. Surplus produce is delivered weekly to the local hospice. Displays by Shropshire Hardy Plant Society, RSPB. Children's quiz sheets. Featured in Grow It and Edible Garden magazines. RHS Heart of England in Bloom Awards, Level 5 Outstanding award and RHS Award of Distinction.

'It was a lovely experience wandering through the pretty village and being treated to marvellous gardens . . .'

BROOK FARM
See Worcestershire

3 BROWNHILL HOUSE
Ruyton XI Towns SY4 1LR. Roger & Yoland Brown, 01939 261121, brownhill@eleventowns.co.uk, www.eleventowns.co.uk. *10m NW of Shrewsbury on B4397.* Home-made teas. **Adm £3.50, chd free. Tues 23 Apr; 21 May; 18 June (1.30-5.30). Visitors also welcome by appt Apr to July, individuals or groups.**
'Has to be seen to be believed'. A unique hillside garden (over 700 steps) bordering R Perry. Wide variety of styles and plants from formal terraces to woodland paths, plus large kitchen garden. Kit cars on show. Featured in GGG.

GROUP OPENING

4 CARDINGTON GARDENS
nr Church Stretton SY6 7JZ, www.cardington.org.uk. *5m NE of Church Stretton. From Shrewsbury, take A49 S, turn L at Leebotwood just past The Pound Inn for Cardington. From Ludlow/Church Stretton, turn R off A49 at T-lights on to B4371 turn L at Wall for Cardington. From Much Wenlock, take B4371 turn R at Longville for Cardington.* Home-made teas, at Gulley Green and Village Hall, smoked salmon & champagne at New Inn House. **Combined adm £5, chd free. Tickets from Village Hall and outlying gardens. Sun 11 Aug (1-6).**
Cardington is a Conservation Village and one of the prettiest in the county, nestling with its outlying hamlets under Caer Caradoc in the beautiful upland hill country of S Shropshire in an area of Outstanding Beauty. We have an enthusiastic band of gardeners ready to welcome you to one of the most attractive group of openings in the Marches. A typical quote from a previous opening: 'The whole day was a lovely experience wandering through the pretty village and being treated to marvellous gardens with splendid tea and cakes'. The TEN gardens which will delight and inspire you include: Immaculate cottage gardens and topiary. Vicarage garden with magnificent views and sweeping lawns. Vegetable and fruit gardens. Formal gardens and water gardens. Romantic roomed garden with annual wild flower meadow. 10 acre conservation garden, natural ponds and wonderful planting. Butterfly meadow. Featured in Shropshire Magazine, national and local press and on Radio Shropshire. Limited wheelchair access.

CARTREF
See Powys

CHIRK CASTLE
See North East Wales

CHOLMONDELEY CASTLE GARDEN
See Cheshire & Wirral

Holly Grove

5 THE CITADEL
Weston-under-Redcastle SY4 5JY. Mr Beverley & Mrs Sylvia Griffiths, www.thecitadelweston.co.uk. *12m N of Shrewsbury on A49. At Xrds turn for Hawkstone Park, through village of Weston-under-Redcastle, 1/4 m on R beyond village.* Home-made teas. **Adm £3.50, chd free. Sun 12 May (2-5.30).**
Imposing castellated house (not open) stands in 4 acres. Mature garden, with fine trees, rhododendrons, azaleas, acers and camellias. Herbaceous borders; walled potager and Victorian thatched summerhouse provide added interest. Paths meander around and over sandstone outcrop at centre.

6 NEW THE CROFT
Ash Magna, Whitchurch SY13 4DR. Peter & Shiela Martinson. *2m S of Whitchurch. From Whitchurch bypass take A525 Newcastle (A530 Nantwich). 'Ash' signed at r'about. Park at Village Hall, 2m. Follow signs to garden, 200 metres walk.* Home-made teas. **Adm £3, chd free. Sun 28 July (1-5).**
How much food can be produced on just over an acre whilst still indulging a love of colour and the natural world? A wonderful place for children to run, play and discover, shared with contented animals, flowers, fruit and vegetables and a 'green man' hiding in the woodland garden. Music by local Folk Band. Sheep, pigs and chickens. Pond dipping.

7 NEW CROSSWAYS
Craven Arms, Newcastle-on-Clun SY7 8QT. Robin & Polly Smith, 01686 670890. *4m W of Newcastle-on-Clun. 1m off B4368. From Clun, proceed to Newcastle-on-Clun on B4368. Continue on B4368 for 4m. Turn R before Stonebridge signed Crossways. Cottage at top of junction.* Home-made teas. **Adm £3, chd free. Sun 9 June (2-5). Visitors also welcome by appt May and June.**
1 acre cottage garden surrounding a C17 cottage nearly 1400ft in South Shropshire Hills and overlooking Rhos Fiddle Wildlife reserve.
Densely planted with a wide variety of plants. Of particular interest are the hardy herbaceous perennials, some less well known and unusual. Himilayan plants, such as Meconopsis and Primula Florindea thrive here. There is a pond, rockery, 2 large vegetable areas, woodland and 4 acre species-rich wild flower meadow. Winner of Shropshire Show Garden Competition.

CWM-WEEG
See Powys

DINGLE NURSERIES & GARDEN
See Powys

8 EDGE VILLA
Edge, nr Yockleton SY5 9PY. Mr & Mrs W F Neil, 01743 821651, bill@billfneil.fsnet.co.uk. *6m SW of Shrewsbury. From A5 take either A488 signed to Bishops Castle or B4386 to Montgomery for approx 6m then follow NGS signs.* Home-made teas. **Adm £3, chd free. Wed 5 June (9.30-1); Sun 1 Sept (2-5). Visitors also welcome by appt May to Aug, min group 20.**
Two acres nestling in South Shropshire hills. Self-sufficient vegetable plot. Chickens in orchard, foxes permitting. Large herbaceous borders. Dewpond surrounded by purple elder, irises, candelabra primulas and dieramas. Large selection of fragrant roses. Comprehensive plant stall. Teas in sheltered courtyard. Wed 5 June is a morning opening with plant sale. Some gravel paths.

THE ELMS
See Staffordshire, Birmingham & West Midlands

9 FIELD HOUSE
Clee St Margaret SY7 9DT. Dr & Mrs John Bell, 01584 823242, bellbrownclee@thelittlefield.co.uk. *8m NE of Ludlow. Turning to Stoke St Milborough & Clee St Margaret, 5m from Ludlow, 10m from Bridgnorth along B4364. Through Stoke St Milborough to Clee St Margaret. Ignore R turn to Clee Village. Field House on L.* **Adm £3.50, chd free. Visitors welcome by appt June and July.**
1-acre garden created since 1982 for yr-round interest. Mixed borders; rose walk; pool garden; herbaceous borders. Lovely views, in a tranquil rural setting with donkeys and sheep.

10 GOLDSTONE HALL GARDENS
Goldstone, Market Drayton TF9 2NA. Miss Victoria Cushing, 01630 661202, enquiries@goldstonehall.com. *5m N of Newport on A41. Follow brown signs from Hinstock. From Shrewsbury A53, R for A41 Hinstock & follow brown signs.* Cream teas. **Adm £3.50, chd free. Mon 27 May; Sun 28 July; Wed 7, Sun 11 Aug (2-5). Visitors also welcome by appt Apr to Oct, min group 10.**
Mature setting of Goldstone Hall; large well ordered kitchen garden with raised beds and herbal walkway cover over a third of an acre. Double tiered herbaceous border backed onto a south facing wall. Award winning oak framed pavilion perfect for afternoon tea. All in five acres of ground and gardens.

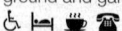

11 HALL FARM NURSERY
Vicarage Lane, Kinnerley, Oswestry SY10 8DH. Christine & Nick Ffoulkes Jones, www.hallfarmnursery.co.uk. *10m NW of Shrewsbury. 2m off A5 mid-way between Shrewsbury & Oswestry. Off A5 at Wolfshead Island onto B4396, then 1st L towards Kinnerley. In Kinnerley turn opp Church into Vicarage Lane.* Home-made teas. **Adm £3, chd free. Sun 11 Aug (10-4).**
Nursery display beds with a wide range of herbaceous plants and raised beds with alpines and scree plants. Creative container plantings. Lots of unusual perennials in shade beds. RHS Partner Nursery with a range of lectures and events. Some grass and gravel paths.

HEATH HOUSE
See Staffordshire, Birmingham & West Midlands

HILLSIDE
See North East Wales

A willow tunnel takes you to the long borders and then through the moon gate . . .

12 HODNET HALL GARDENS
Hodnet, nr Market Drayton TF9 3NN. Mr & The Hon Mrs Heber-Percy, www.hodnethallgardens.org. *5½ m SW of Market Drayton. 12m NE Shrewsbury. At junction of A53 & A442.* Light refreshments. **Adm £5, chd £2.50. Sun 16 June (12-5).**
60-acre landscaped garden with series of lakes and pools; magnificent forest trees, great variety of flowers, shrubs providing colour throughout season. Unique collection of big-game trophies in C17 tearooms. Kitchen garden. For details please see website.

13 HOLLY GROVE
Church Pulverbatch SY5 8DD. Peter & Angela Unsworth, 01743 718221, angela.unsworth@btinternet.com. *6m S of Shrewsbury. Midway between Stapleton & Church Pulverbatch. From A49 follow signs to Stapleton & Pulverbatch.* Home-made teas. **Adm £4, chd free. Sun 5 May (2-6). Visitors also welcome by appt Apr to July, min group 10.**
3-acre garden set in S Shropshire countryside. Yew and beech hedges enclosing 'rooms', box parterres, pleached limes, vegetable garden, rose and herbaceous borders containing many rare plants. Arboretum, lake and wild flower meadows. Opportunity to see rare White Park cattle and Soay sheep. Featured on 'Alan's Garden Secrets' The 17th Century Garden.

14 HOLMCROFT
Wyson Lane, Brimfield, nr Ludlow SY8 4NW. Mr & Mrs Michael Dowding, 01584 711743, carole953@live.co.uk, www.anenglishcottageonline.com. *4m S of Ludlow. 6m N of Leominster. From Ludlow or Leominster leave A49 at the Salway Arms PH, turn into lane signed Wyson Only. From Tenbury Wells cross the A49 opp the Salway Arms into Wyson Lane.* Home-made teas & cream teas. **Adm £4, chd free. Sun 30 June (2-5.30). Visitors also welcome by appt June to Aug, min group 20.**
C17 thatched cottage set in terraced gardens of ¾ acre. Sunken, gravel and woodland garden with walk to fern bank and stumpery. Orchard and kitchen garden with views of Mortimer Forest and Clee Hill. A willow tunnel takes you to the long borders and then through the moon gate. Only the woodland walk is inaccessible for wheelchairs.

HUNTERS END
See Worcestershire

15 ◆ JESSAMINE COTTAGE
Kenley, Shrewsbury SY5 6NS. Lee & Pamela Wheeler, www.stmem.com/jessamine-cottage. *6m W of Much Wenlock. Signed from B4371 Much Wenlock to Church Stretton Rd and from A458 Shrewsbury to Much Wenlock Rd at Harley.* **Adm £4, chd £1. For NGS: Suns 21 July; 25 Aug (2-6). For other opening times and information, please phone or see garden website.**
'A slice of heaven' and 'inspirational': typical comments from visitors to this 3-acre garden which incl mature wildlife pond, mixed island beds, lime avenue, large kitchen garden; parterre; stream and woodland. All-season colour is provided by a rose garden and ornamental trees, large range of attractive perennials and shrubs. Groups by appointment. Featured in Shropshire Star, Shropshire Magazine, Shropshire Life and Gardening Which?.

16 LONGNER HALL
Atcham, Shrewsbury SY4 4TG. Mr & Mrs R L Burton. *4m SE of Shrewsbury. From M54 follow A5 to Shrewsbury, then B4380 to Atcham. From Atcham take Uffington rd, entrance ¼ m on L.* Home-made teas. **Adm £4, chd free. Sun 5 May (2-5).**
A long drive approach through parkland designed by Humphry Repton. Walks lined with golden yew through extensive lawns, with views over Severn Valley. Borders containing roses, herbaceous and shrubs, also ancient yew wood. Enclosed walled garden containing mixed planting, garden buildings, tower and game larder. Short woodland walk around old moat pond. 1-acre walled garden currently being restored now open to visitors. Woodland walk not suitable for wheelchairs.

The unusual and the oddities of plant life, in mixed borders of 'controlled' confusion . . .

17 LOWER HALL
Worfield WV15 5LH. Mr & Mrs C F Dumbell, 01746 716607, chrisdumbell@googlemail.com. *3½ m E of Bridgnorth. ½ m N of A454 in village centre.* **Adm £4, chd free. Visitors welcome by appt May to July, min group 20.**
4 acres on R Worfe. Garden developed by present owners. Courtyard with fountain, walled garden with old-fashioned roses, clematis and mixed borders. Water garden with pool, primula island and rock garden. Woodland garden with rare trees incl magnolias, paper bark and Japanese maples.

18 LYNDALE HOUSE
Astley Abbots, Bridgnorth WV16 4SW. Bob & Mary Saunders. *2m out of Bridnorth off B4373. From High Town Bridgnorth take B4373 Broseley Rd for 1½ m, then take lane signed Astley Abbotts & Colemore Green.* Home-made teas. **Adm £3, chd free. Sat 27 Apr; Sun 4 Aug (2-5).**
1½ acre garden with large pristine lawns that surround a pool and waterfall. Many borders are crammed with unusual perennials and shrubs. A wealth of spring bulbs and hellebores start the season. The terrace garden is planted with roses, iris and alliums. Topiary garden planted in 2011. New for 2013 a stumpery and fernery. Entrance available without steps - please ask.

MAESFRON HALL AND GARDENS
See Powys

19 MAREHAY FARM
Gatten, Ratlinghope SY5 0SJ. Stuart & Carol Buxton, 01588 650289. *6½ m W of Church Stretton. 6m S of Pontesbury, 9m NNE of Bishops Castle. 1½ m from 'The Bridges' Xrds & the intersection of the Longden, Pulverbatch & Bishops Castle rd and the minor rd from Church Stretton to the Stiperstones.* Home-made teas. **Adm £3, chd free. Sun 9 June (11-6). Visitors also welcome by appt May to July. Refreshments with prior notice of numbers.**
In 1982 a building society surveyor reported 'there is no garden and at this height (1100ft), elevation and aspect there never will be!' Since 1990, on heavy boulder clay a 1½ acre woodland/water garden evolved, with primulas, hostas, iris, damp/shade tolerant perennials. Rhododendrons, azaleas, various conifers, trees, roses and shrubs complementing the location. A secret garden within the Shropshire Hill AONB. A 'primularium' is being developed. A mini arboretum as the wood is interplanted. Wheelchairs with assistance, some gravel.

MILL COTTAGE
See Powys

20 MILLICHOPE PARK
Munslow, Craven Arms, Munslow SY7 9HA. Mr & Mrs Frank Bury, 01584 841841, frank@bflap.co.uk. *8m NE of Craven Arms. From Ludlow (11m) turn L off B4368, just ½ m outside village of Munslow.* Home-made teas. **Adm £5, chd free. Sun 24 Feb; Mon 6 May (2-6).**
Historic landscape gardens covering 14 acres with lakes, cascades dating from C18, woodland walks and wildflowers. Extensive shows of snowdrops in late winter and bluebells in spring. Rare opportunity to see the Bouts Viola. UK's largest collection of hardy, perennial, scented violas. Many varieties for sale. Limited wheelchair access, incl WC.

21 MOORTOWN
nr Wellington TF6 6JE. Mr David Bromley. *8m N of Telford. 5m N of Wellington. Take B5062 signed Moortown 1m between High Ercall & Crudgington.* Home-made teas. **Adm £5, chd £1. Sun 14 Apr (2-5).**
Approx 1-acre plantsman's garden. Here may be found the old-fashioned, the unusual and even the oddities of plant life, in mixed borders of 'controlled' confusion. In April double primroses, anemones and antique daffodils are specialties. February 2014 opening to view collection of snowdrops, see NGS website for date and times.

GROUP OPENING

22 MORVILLE HALL GARDENS
Bridgnorth WV16 5NB. *3m W of Bridgnorth. On A458 at junction with B4368.* Home-made teas in Morville Church. **Combined adm £5, chd free (share to Morville Church). Sun 9 June (2-5).**

THE COTTAGE
Mrs J Bolton

THE DOWER HOUSE
Dr Katherine Swift

1 THE GATE HOUSE
Mr & Mrs Rowe

2 THE GATE HOUSE
Mrs G Medland

MORVILLE HALL
Dr & Mrs J C Douglas & The National Trust

An interesting group of gardens that surround a beautiful Grade I listed mansion (not open). The Cottage has a walled cottage garden which is currently being re-developed. The Dower House is a horticultural history lesson about Morville Hall which incl a turf maze, cloister garden, Elizabethan knot garden, C18 canal garden, Edwardian kitchen garden and more. It is the setting of Katherine Swift's bestselling book 'The Morville Hours', and the sequel 'The Morville Year'. 1 & 2 The Gate House are cottage-style gardens with colourful borders, formal areas, lawns and wooded glades. The 4-acre Morville Hall (NT) garden has a parterre, medieval stew pond, shrub borders and large lawns, all offering glorious views across the Mor Valley. Mostly all level but areas of gravel in some gardens.

23 MYND HARDY PLANTS

Delbury Hall Estate, Mill Lane, Diddlebury, Craven Arms SY7 9DH. Mr Mark Zenick, www.myndhardyplants.co.uk. *8m W of Craven Arms. 1m off B4368, Craven Arms to Bridgnorth, through village of Diddlebury, turn R at Mynd Hardy Plants sign.* Home-made teas. **Adm £3, chd free. Tue 9, Sun 14 July (1-5).**

Commercial nursery within old walled garden, offering and selling more than 800 varieties of herbaceous perennials. Speciality is hemerocallis with more than 150 day lily varieties, American hybrids, field grown. More than 80% of day lily varieties cannot be seen elsewhere in the UK. Gravel and grass paths.

24 OTELEY

Ellesmere SY12 0PB. Mr & Mrs R K Mainwaring, 01691 622514. *1m SE of Ellesmere. Entrance out of Ellesmere past Mere, opp Convent nr to A528/495 junction.* Home-made teas. **Adm £3, chd free. Sun 12 May (1-5). Visitors also welcome by appt May to July, min group 10. Refreshments by arrangement. Coaches welcome by appt.**

10 acres running down to Mere, incl walled kitchen garden; architectural features; many interesting trees, rhododendrons and azaleas, incl wild woodland walk, views across Mere to Ellesmere Church. Wheelchair access if dry.

PEAR TREE COTTAGE
See Worcestershire

PEAR TREE COTTAGE
See North East Wales

PONT FAEN HOUSE
See Powys

POWIS CASTLE GARDEN
See Powys

© Julia Stanley

Every garden visit makes a difference

25 PREEN MANOR

Church Preen SY6 7LQ. Mrs Ann Trevor-Jones, 01694 771207. *6m W of Much Wenlock. Signed from B4371.* **Adm £5, chd free. Mon 1 Apr (2-5); Thurs 6 June; 11 July (2-6); Sun 6 Oct (2-5). Visitors also welcome by appt June to July.**

6-acre garden on site of Cluniac monastery and Norman Shaw mansion. Kitchen, chess, water and wild gardens. Fine trees in park; woodland walks. Developed for over 30yrs with changes always in progress. Harvest produce stall & Thanksgiving in church adjacent to garden (Oct).

26 PRESTON HALL

Preston Brockhurst SY4 5QA. C C & L Corbet, 01939 220312, corbetleil@btinternet.com. *8m N of Shrewsbury on A49.* Teas in the house kitchen. **Adm £4, chd free. Sat 15 June (2.30-5.30). Visitors also welcome by appt Apr to Oct. Corbet Bed Embroideries talk.**

A large informal garden with interesting trees (planted about 1995). Large oval herbaceous border. Formal garden in front of 1700 stone house (not open) and large sunken courtyard at the back. Walled garden with a newly restored 1911 Cricket Pavilion (open), meadow walk with small pond and ducks. You may play tennis and there will be garden games for children. Grass paths, courtyard has steps.

PRIEST WESTON GARDENS
See Powys

QUARRY HOUSE
See Powys

TY'N Y BRYN
See Powys

QUEEN ANNE COTTAGE
See North East Wales

27 RADNOR COTTAGE

Clun SY7 0JA. Pam & David Pittwood, 01588 640451. *7m W of Craven Arms. 1m E of Clun on B4368.* Home-made teas. **Adm £3, chd free (share to Home-Start S Shropshire). Tues 2 Apr; 28 May (2-6). Visitors also welcome by appt Mar to June.**

2 acres on S-facing slope, overlooking Clun Valley. Wide variety of garden habitats all densely planted. Incl sunny terracing with paving and

dry-stone walling; alpine troughs; cottage garden borders; damp shade for white flowers and gold foliage; pond, stream and bog garden; orchard; rough grass with naturalised bulbs and wild flowers.

RHOSDDU HOUSE
See Powys

ROWAN
See Powys

ROWLEY HOUSE FARM
See Staffordshire, Birmingham & West Midlands

Very old fruit trees and stunning views of the Cleehills . . .

28 RUTHALL MANOR
Ditton Priors, Bridgnorth WV16 6TN. Mr & Mrs G T Clarke, 01746 712608, clarke@ruthall.orangehome.co.uk. *7m SW of Bridgnorth. Ruthall Rd signed nr garage in Ditton Priors.* Home-made teas. **Adm £3.50, chd free. Sat 15, Sun 16, Mon 17 June (12-6). Visitors also welcome by appt May to Aug.**
1-acre garden with ha-ha and old horse pond planted with candelabra primulas, iris and bog plants. Rare specimen trees. Designed for easy maintenance with lots of ground cover and unusual plants. Gravel art garden and other areas for low maintenance incl stumpery. New features being added year by year. Featured in Shropshire Magazine, Life & Star.

29 3 SCOTSMANSFIELD
Burway Road, Church Stretton SY6 6DP. Mr & Mrs Knowles. *Limited parking in Burway Rd, please use town car park.* Home-made teas. **Adm £3, chd free. Sun 26 May (2-5).**
Architect designed Arts and Crafts garden set at the foot of the Longmynd in an AONB. Facing SW overlooking Church Stretton. Rock garden, formal rose garden with perennial beds, York-paved terraces and steps. Lower lawn enclosed by yew hedges; vegetable garden. New parterre. Sloping site. Arts and Crafts house (not open).

30 SECRET GARDEN
21 Steventon Terrace, Steventon New Road, Ludlow SY8 1JZ. Mr & Mrs Wood. *Park & ride available, bus 702, stops outside garden.* Home-made teas. **Adm £3, chd free. Sat 22 June (12-6).**
½ -acre of very secret S-facing garden, divided into different sections, roses, herbaceous borders, lawn and summer house. Developed over 30yrs by present owners. Terraced vegetable garden and greenhouses. ¼ -acre project incl poly tunnel, vegetable plot, chickens, completed in 2011. New for 2013 Mediterranean style terrace garden and small stumpery. Second award in Ludlow in Bloom.

31 SHOOTHILL HOUSE
Ford, Shrewsbury SY5 9NR. Colin & Jane Lloyd, 01743 850795, jane@lloydmasters.com. *5m W of Shrewsbury. From A458 turn L towards Shoothill (signed).* Home-made teas. **Adm £3.50, chd free. Sun 16 June (2-6). Visitors also welcome by appt June to Sept, min group 10.**
6-acre garden, incl small wood with swamp garden, wild flower meadows, tree house and several lawned areas surrounded by mixed borders. Large well maintained Victorian greenhouse in renovated walled kitchen garden. New areas of garden created in 2012. Mature wildlife pond surrounded by species trees and shrubs with extensive views over Welsh hills.

32 SIBBERSCOTE MANOR
Lea Cross, Shrewsbury SY5 8JF. Lady Kingsland, 01743 860985. *5m S of Shrewsbury. Take A488 S off Shrewsbury bypass, 4m take L turn in Lea Cross to Arscott.* Home-made teas. **Adm £6, chd free. Visitors welcome by appt May to Aug, min group 20.**
Garden created to complement C16 timbered farmhouse (not open). Lovely views over 4-acre lake and S Shropshire hills. Artistically planted with roses, herbaceous and shrub borders, interesting topiary and showing a collection of sculpture. Teas in renovated farm buildings. Mown walk round lake with nesting swans and much wildlife. Wheelchair access on gravel and grass.

33 STANLEY HALL
Bridgnorth WV16 4SP. Mr & Mrs M J Thompson. *½ m N of Bridgnorth. Leave Bridgnorth by N gate; B4373; turn R at Stanley Lane. Pass Golf Course Club House on L & turn L at Lodge.* Home-made teas. **Combined adm £4, chd free. Sun 2 June (2-6).**
Drive ½ m with rhododendrons, azaleas, fine trees and chain of pools. Restored ice-house. Woodland walks with steps, slopes and pools. Also open **The Granary** (Mr & Mrs Jack Major) Charming small trellis garden. Profusion of flowers in hanging baskets and herbaceous borders. **Dower House**, (Mr & Mrs Colin Wells) Come and see start of new project. Featured in Bridgnorth Journal.

34 STIGGLEY COTTAGE
1 Pound Lane, Stottesdon, Kidderminster DY14 8UJ. Ray & Denise Ingram. *Between Bridgnorth & Cleobury Mortimer signed from from B4364. The B4194 from Bewdley joins B4363 4m from village. Look for yellow signs.* Home-made teas. **Adm £4, chd free. Sun 4 Aug (1-6).**
New this year, prizewinning exhibition vegetables, shown at national level. Baskets, containers and borders brimming with colour, very old fruit trees and stunning views of the Cleehills. Sorry no dogs, own Belgian shepherds in residence. Featured in Shropshire Life, Shropshire Star, Express and Star.

SUGNALL HALL, WALLED KITCHEN GARDEN
See Staffordshire, Birmingham & West Midlands

TAN-Y-LLYN
See Powys

35 7 TENNYSON CLOSE
Market Drayton TF9 1NQ. Mr & Mrs Les & Pat Lacey, 01630 698131. *1m W of Market Drayton town centre. On A53 from Shrewsbury take 2nd exit, signed Market Drayton West, at Island Close Muller factory. Continue ¾ m. Turn sharp R at Kings Head Inn into Buntingsdale Rd. Just beyond church, turn L into Wordsworth Drive,*

then 2nd L Tennyson Close. Light refreshments. **Adm £3, chd free. Visitors welcome by appt May to Sept 10 days notice required for any arranged visits.**
Created to exploit its 30 degree south facing slope to best advantage, wandering pathways introduce individual gardens sections; azalea, conifer and shrub beds, woodland, formal parterre, grand rock gardens, thatched gazebo and courtyard. Designed for easy maintenance. Gardener's World magazine wrote, 'Whichever angle you view it from, Les's garden is magnificent'.

36 VALDUCCI FLOWER & VEGETABLE GARDENS

Vicarage Road Site, Meole Brace, Shrewsbury SY3 9EZ. Luigi Valducci. *2m W of Shrewsbury. Meole Brace Garden & Allotment Club. On A5 exit at Dobbies r-about, direction Shrewsbury. Follow sign for Nuffield Hospital, opp hospital Stanley Lane, follow Stanley Lane until you reach Vicarage Rd. Car park on R, garden on L.* Home-made teas. **Adm £4, chd free. Sun 28 July (12-5).**
An Italian style of gardening focusing on unusual vegetables and flowers. The Valducci Horticultural site has been featured in many national and regional magazines and ITV Midland Today. Visited by 16 international judges (Europe, USA, Canada). The National Collection of *Brugmansias* has won 7 golds in shows. Speciality vegetables chicory - endives etc. A garden and allotment with many quotations scattered around the ground, amusing and intellectual plus an innovative aspect ... of vision and sound.
NCH

37 WALCOT HALL

Lydbury North SY7 8AZ. Mr & Mrs C R W Parish, www.walcothall.com. *4m SE of Bishop's Castle. B4385 Craven Arms to Bishop's Castle, turn L by Powis Arms, in Lydbury North*. Home-made teas. **Adm £3.50, chd free. Sun 26, Mon 27 May (1.30-5.30).**
Arboretum planted by Lord Clive of India's son, Edward. Cascades of rhododendrons, azaleas amongst specimen trees and pools. Fine views of Sir William Chambers' Clock Towers, with lake and hills beyond. Walled kitchen garden; dovecote; meat safe; ice house and mile-long lakes. Outstanding ballroom where excellent teas are served. Russian wooden church, grotto and fountain now complete and working; tin chapel. Beautiful borders and rare shrubs. Lakeside replanted, and water garden at western end re-established. The garden adjacent to the ballroom is accessible via a sloping bank, as is the walled garden and arboretum.

Japanese style teahouse and zen garden and path in Chinese style . . .

38 8 WESTGATE VILLAS

Salop Street, Bridgnorth WV16 4QX. Bill & Marilyn Hammerton. *From A458 Bridgnorth bypass, take rd into Bridgnorth at Ludlow Rd r'about signed town centre. At T-junction (pay & display parking at council offices here) turn R, garden 100 yds on L just past entrance to Victoria Rd*. **Adm £3.50, chd free. Evening Opening £5, chd free, canapes & wine, Fri 5 Apr (7-9.30); Sun 7 Apr (2-5.30).**
Town garden having formal Victorian front garden with box hedging and water feature to complement house. Back garden has a shade border, lawn, small knot garden and orchard, together with a strong oriental influence incl Japanese style teahouse and zen garden and path in Chinese style. Music and garden lighting at evening opening.

39 ◆ WESTON PARK

Weston-under-Lizard, Shifnal TF11 8LE. The Weston Park Foundation, www.weston-park.com. *6m E of Telford. Situated on A5 at Weston-under-Lizard. J12 M6 & J3 M54*. **Adm £5, chd £3. For NGS: Wed 3 July (10.30-6). For other opening times and information, please phone or see garden website.**
Capability Brown landscaped gardens and parkland. Formal gardens restored to original C19 design, rose garden and long border together with colourful adjacent Broderie garden. Orchard in the walled garden. New for 2013 - Lady Anne Memorial Garden created in memory of Lady Anne Cowdray who grew up at Weston. Disabled route map available on request.

THE WICKETS

See Staffordshire, Birmingham & West Midlands

40 WINDY RIDGE

Church Lane, Little Wenlock, Telford TF6 5BB. George & Fiona Chancellor, 01952 507675, fionachancellor@btinternet.com, www.gardenschool.co.uk. *2m S of Wellington. Follow signs for Little Wenlock from N (J7, M54) or E (off A5223 at Horsehay). Parking signed. Do not rely on Sat Nav*. Home-made teas. **Adm £4, chd free. Suns 2 June; 14 July; 18 Aug; 15 Sept (12-5). Visitors also welcome by appt May to Sept, min group 10. Suitable for coaches.**
'Stunning' and 'inspirational' are how visitors frequently describe this multi-award-winning ⅔ -acre village garden. The strong design and exuberant colour-themed planting (over 1000 species, mostly labelled) offer a picture around every corner. The grass and perennial gravel garden has created a lot of interest and versions are now appearing in gardens all over the country! Featured in the Shropshire magazine and on Radio Shropshire. Some gravel paths but help available.

41 ◆ WOLLERTON OLD HALL

Wollerton, Market Drayton TF9 3NA. Lesley & John Jenkins, www.wollertonoldhallgarden.com. *4m SW of Market Drayton. On A53 between Hodnet & A53-A41 junction. Follow brown signs*. **Adm £6, chd free. For NGS: Fris 3, 24 May (12-5). For other opening times and information, please phone or see garden website.**
4-acre garden created around C16 house (not open). Formal structure creates variety of gardens each with own colour theme and character. Planting is mainly of perennials, the large range of which results in significant collections of salvias, clematis, crocosmias and roses. Featured regularly in national press. Nominated in the Countryfile Magazine Awards for 'Most Beautiful Garden'.

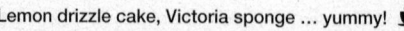

"Lemon drizzle cake, Victoria sponge ... yummy!"

Millichope Park

Shropshire County Volunteers

County Organiser
Chris Neil, Edge Villa, Edge, Yockleton, Shrewsbury SY5 9PY, 01743 821651, bill@billfneil.fsnet.co.uk ,

County Treasurer
Melinda Laws, 50 Sheinton Street, Much Wenlock TF13 6HU, 01952 727237, melinda@mlaws.freeserve.co.uk

Publicity
Allison Walter, Holly Cottage, Great Argoed, Mellington, nr Church Stoke SY15 6TH, allison.walter2@btinternet.com

Leaflet Coordinator
Fiona Chancellor, Windy Ridge, Little Wenlock, Telford TF6 5BB, 01952 507675, fionachancellor@btinternet.com

Assistant County Organisers
Bill Neil, Edge Villa, Edge, Yockleton, Shrewsbury SY5 9PY, 01743 821651
Penny Tryhorn, The Granary, Folley Road, Ackleton WV6 7JL, 01746 783931

SOMERSET, BRISTOL AREA & SOUTH GLOUCESTERSHIRE incl Bath

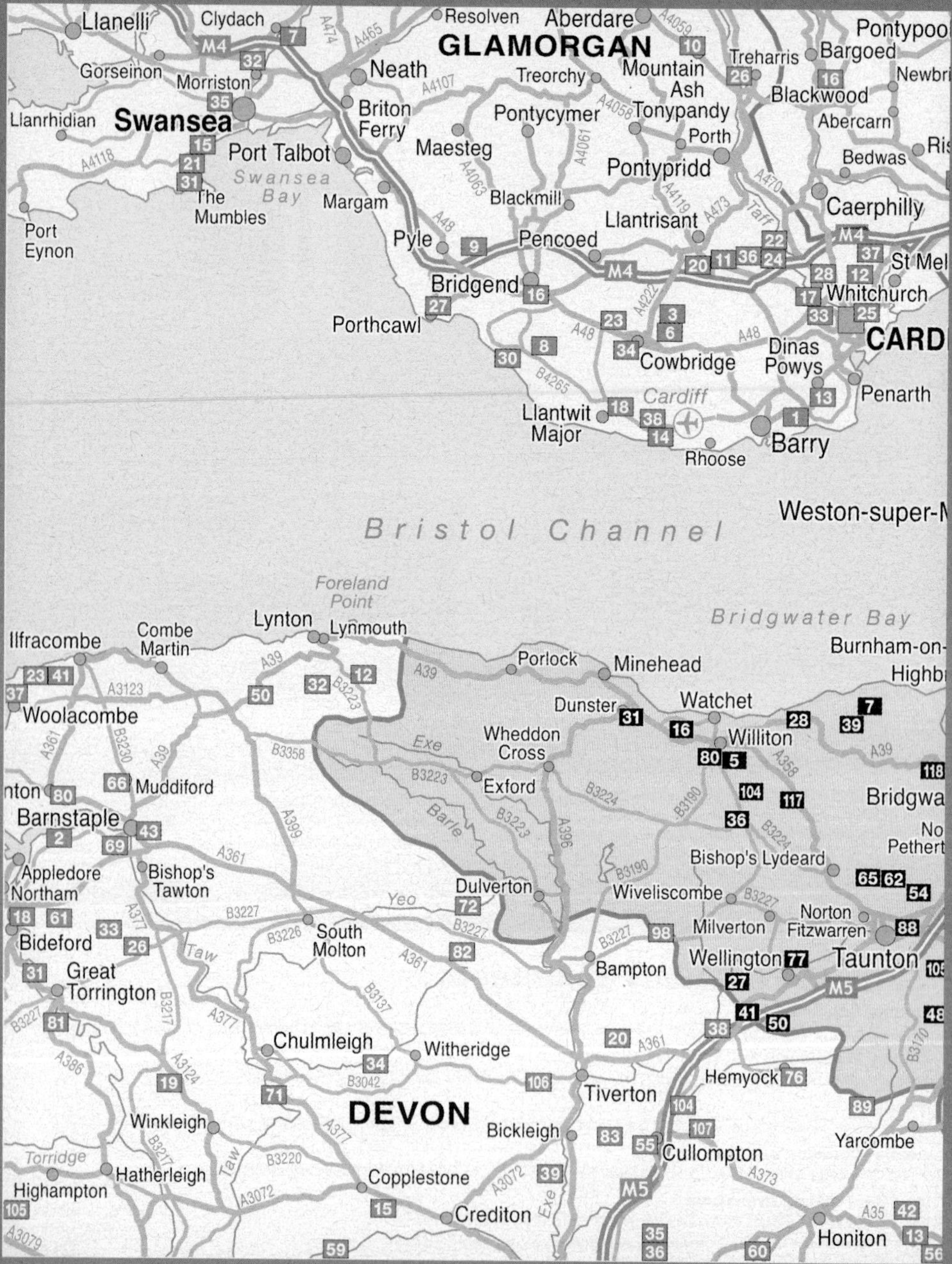

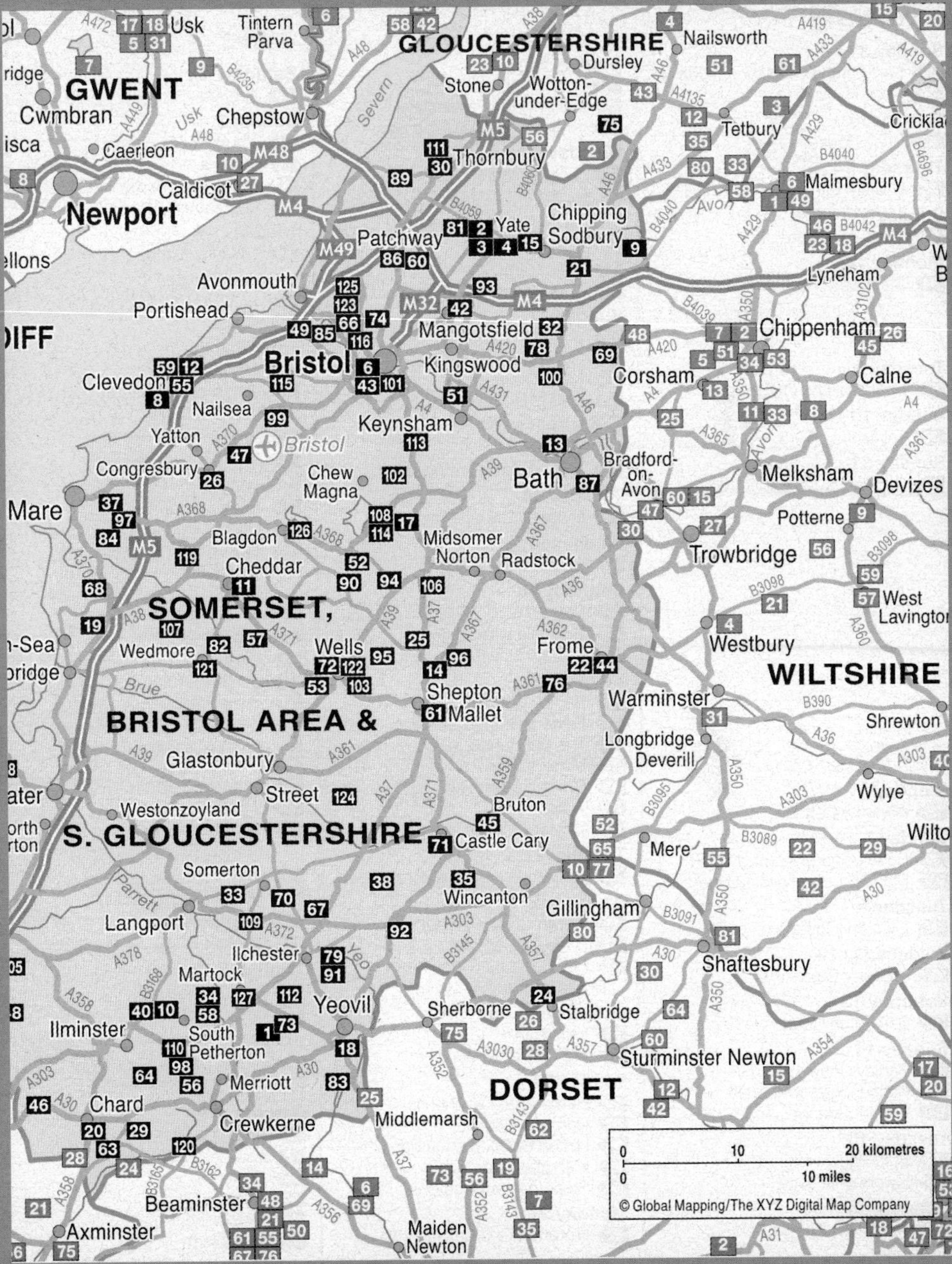
GWENT
GLOUCESTERSHIRE
SOMERSET,
BRISTOL AREA &
S. GLOUCESTERSHIRE
WILTSHIRE
DORSET
Usk
Tintern Parva
Nailsworth
Dursley
Stone
Wotton-under-Edge
Tetbury
Cwmbran
Chepstow
Caerleon
Caldicot
Newport
Thornbury
Malmesbury
Chipping Sodbury
Yate
Patchway
Avonmouth
Portishead
Lyneham
Mangotsfield
Chippenham
Bristol
Kingswood
Corsham
Calne
Clevedon
Nailsea
Yatton
Keynsham
Congresbury
Chew Magna
Bath
Bradford-on-Avon
Melksham
Devizes
Mare
Blagdon
Midsomer Norton
Radstock
Potterne
Trowbridge
Cheddar
West Lavington
Wedmore
Wells
Frome
Westbury
Shepton Mallet
Warminster
Shrewton
Longbridge Deverill
Glastonbury
Street
Wylye
Westonzoyland
Bruton
Castle Cary
Mere
Somerton
Wincanton
Gillingham
Langport
Ilchester
Shaftesbury
Martock
Yeovil
Sherborne
Stalbridge
Ilminster
South Petherton
Sturminster Newton
Merriott
Chard
Crewkerne
Middlemarsh
Beaminster
Axminster
Maiden Newton
0 10 20 kilometres
0 10 miles
© Global Mapping/The XYZ Digital Map Company

Opening Dates

January

Sunday 27
51 Hanham Court

February

Sunday 3
34 East Lambrook Manor Gardens
89 Rock House

Sunday 10
89 Rock House

Thursday 14
75 Newark Park

Sunday 17
94 Sherborne Garden

Monday 18
94 Sherborne Garden

March

Tuesday 5
54 Hestercombe Gardens

Sunday 10
39 Fairfield

Sunday 31
29 Cricket House and Gardens

Lots of new gardens . . . !

April

Monday 1
36 Elworthy Cottage

Sunday 7
90 Rose Cottage & Coley Court
102 Stanton Court Nursing Home

Tuesday 9
36 Elworthy Cottage

Wednesday 10
103 Stoberry Garden

Saturday 13
10 Barrington Court

Sunday 14
11 Bartley Cottage
50 Hangeridge Farmhouse
120 Wayford Manor

Tuesday 16
13 Bath Priory Hotel
36 Elworthy Cottage

Saturday 20
124 Westbrook House

Sunday 21
70 Midney Gardens
119 Watcombe
126 The Yeo Valley Organic Garden at Holt Farm

Saturday 27
64 Little Garth

May

Sunday 5
18 1 Braggchurch
50 Hangeridge Farmhouse
87 Prior Park Landscape Garden

Monday 6
18 1 Braggchurch

Friday 10
65 Little Yarford Farmhouse

Saturday 11
64 Little Garth
65 Little Yarford Farmhouse

Sunday 12
8 6 Ashton Close
28 Court House
61 Kilver Court
65 Little Yarford Farmhouse
66 Lucombe House

Monday 13
65 Little Yarford Farmhouse

Tuesday 14
36 Elworthy Cottage

Wednesday 15
47 Goblin Combe House

Saturday 18
34 East Lambrook Manor Gardens
55 Highdale Villa
71 The Mill House

Sunday 19
11 Bartley Cottage
16 Binham Grange Gardens
71 The Mill House
72 Milton Lodge
80 Orchard Wyndham
119 Watcombe
120 Wayford Manor

Tuesday 21
16 Binham Grange Gardens

Wednesday 22
47 Goblin Combe House
67 Lytes Cary Manor
92 Self Realization Meditation Healing Centre Garden

Saturday 25
64 Little Garth
69 Marshfield Gardens

Sunday 26
50 Hangeridge Farmhouse
52 Harptree Court
56 Hinton St George Gardens
69 Marshfield Gardens
107 Stone Allerton Gardens

Monday 27
56 Hinton St George Gardens
107 Stone Allerton Gardens

Tuesday 28
36 Elworthy Cottage
122 Wellfield Barn

Thursday 30
59 Jasmine Cottage
117 Vellacott

June

Saturday 1
38 Esotera

Sunday 2
25 Church Farm House
38 Esotera
118 The Walled Gardens of Cannington

Tuesday 4
36 Elworthy Cottage

Wednesday 5
47 GOBLIN COMBE House
119 Watcombe

Thursday 6
7 Ash Cottage
59 Jasmine Cottage
117 Vellacott

Friday 7
70 Midney Gardens

Saturday 8
51 Hanham Court
64 Little Garth
78 The Old Rectory, Doynton
111 Thornbury Park Estate/The Sheiling School
125 18 Woodgrove Road

Sunday 9
8 6 Ashton Close
11 Bartley Cottage
17 Bishop Sutton Gardens
26 Congresbury Gardens
51 Hanham Court
72 Milton Lodge
74 16 Montroy Close
84 3 Palmer's Way
111 Thornbury Park Estate/The Sheiling School

Tuesday 11
54 Hestercombe Gardens

Wednesday 12
113 Tranby House

Thursday 13
7 Ash Cottage
59 Jasmine Cottage

National Gardens Weekend

Saturday 15
2 Acton Court
7 Ash Cottage
38 Esotera
40 Farndon Thatch
43 1 Frobisher Road
64 Little Garth

You are always welcome at an NGS garden!

68 The Manor
79 The Old Rectory, Limington
82 Overbrook Cottage
83 Owl Cottage
86 Pretoria Road Allotments
97 52 South Lawn
98 South Meade
101 95 St Johns Lane
110 1 The Pheasant
121 Wedmore Gardens
124 Westbrook House
125 18 Woodgrove Road

Sunday 16
2 Acton Court
5 Aller Farmhouse
25 Church Farm House
35 Eastfield
38 Esotera
40 Farndon Thatch
43 1 Frobisher Road
68 The Manor
73 Montacute House
77 Nynehead Court
79 The Old Rectory, Limington
82 Overbrook Cottage
83 Owl Cottage
95 Sole Retreat
97 52 South Lawn
98 South Meade
101 95 St Johns Lane
104 Stogumber Gardens
108 Stowey Gardens
110 1 The Pheasant
112 Tintinhull
121 Wedmore Gardens
123 West Bristol Gardens

Monday 17
25 Church Farm House
35 Eastfield

Wednesday 19
47 GOBLIN COMBE House

Thursday 20
9 Badminton House
59 Jasmine Cottage
100 Special Plants
117 Vellacott

Saturday 22
6 22 Ambra Vale
42 29 Four Acre Avenue

Sunday 23
6 22 Ambra Vale
42 29 Four Acre Avenue

Wednesday 26
22 9 Catherston Close
47 GOBLIN COMBE House

Thursday 27
59 Jasmine Cottage

Saturday 29
46 Glebe Cottage and Old Rectory Cottage
64 Little Garth
97 52 South Lawn

Sunday 30
14 The Beeches
41 Fernhill
44 Frome Gardens
46 Glebe Cottage and Old Rectory Cottage
48 Goddards Orchard
62 Kingston St Mary Secret Gardens
84 3 Palmer's Way
85 Penny Brohn Cancer Care
97 52 South Lawn

July

Wednesday 3
22 9 Catherston Close
48 Goddards Orchard

Thursday 4
59 Jasmine Cottage
117 Vellacott

Saturday 6
76 Nunney Gardens

Sunday 7
28 Court House
29 Cricket House and Gardens
116 University of Bristol Botanic Garden

Delicious home-made teas . . .

Wednesday 10
22 9 Catherston Close
67 Lytes Cary Manor

Thursday 11
59 Jasmine Cottage
113 Tranby House

Friday 12
70 Midney Gardens

Saturday 13
40 Farndon Thatch
64 Little Garth
91 Rugg Farm

Sunday 14
25 Church Farm House
30 Daggs Allotments
31 Dunster Castle Gardens
34 East Lambrook Manor Gardens
40 Farndon Thatch
50 Hangeridge Farmhouse
72 Milton Lodge
77 Nynehead Court
81 Organic Blooms
91 Rugg Farm
109 Sutton Hosey Manor
127 Yews Farm

Monday 15
127 Yews Farm

Tuesday 16
13 Bath Priory Hotel

Wednesday 17
25 Church Farm House

Thursday 18
59 Jasmine Cottage
100 Special Plants
117 Vellacott

Saturday 20
10 Barrington Court
97 52 South Lawn
114 Truffles
115 Tyntesfield

Sunday 21
19 Brent Knoll Gardens
55 Highdale Villa
57 Honeyhurst Farm
95 Sole Retreat
97 52 South Lawn
114 Truffles

Monday 22
98 South Meade

Tuesday 23
98 South Meade

Wednesday 24
98 South Meade

Thursday 25
59 Jasmine Cottage
98 South Meade

Friday 26
98 South Meade

Saturday 27
64 Little Garth
98 South Meade

Sunday 28
21 Camers
27 Cothay Manor & Gardens
99 Southfield Farm

August

Thursday 1
12 Barum
59 Jasmine Cottage

Sunday 4
41 Fernhill

Thursday 8
12 Barum
59 Jasmine Cottage

Saturday 10
64 Little Garth

Sunday 11
20 20 Bubwith Road
45 Gants Mill & Garden
50 Hangeridge Farmhouse

Monday 12
20 20 Bubwith Road

Thursday 15
12 Barum
59 Jasmine Cottage
100 Special Plants

Friday 16
32 Dyrham Park

Saturday 17
32 Dyrham Park

Sunday 18
25 Church Farm House
60 Jen's Gardyn
88 Priorswood Allotments
94 Sherborne Garden
113 Tranby House

Saturday 24
64 Little Garth

Sunday 25
20 20 Bubwith Road
36 Elworthy Cottage
41 Fernhill
60 Jen's Gardyn
103 Stoberry Garden

Monday 26
20 20 Bubwith Road

. . . year-round interest with wildlife in mind . . .

September

Sunday 1
66 Lucombe House
118 The Walled Gardens of Cannington

Tuesday 3
36 Elworthy Cottage

Wednesday 4
106 Ston Easton Park

Saturday 7
64 Little Garth
83 Owl Cottage

Sunday 8
50 Hangeridge Farmhouse
61 Kilver Court
83 Owl Cottage
102 Stanton Court Nursing Home

Tuesday 10
67 Lytes Cary Manor

Sunday 15
15 Beechwell House

Tuesday 17
117 Vellacott

Thursday 19
100 Special Plants
117 Vellacott

Friday 20
70 Midney Gardens

Saturday 21
64 Little Garth

Sunday 22
11 Bartley Cottage
111 Thornbury Park Estate/The Sheiling School

October

Thursday 17
100 Special Plants

Sunday 20
29 Cricket House and Gardens

November

Friday 15
103 Stoberry Garden (Evening)

February 2014

Sunday 2
89 Rock House

Sunday 9
34 East Lambrook Manor Gardens
89 Rock House

Gardens open to the public

2 Acton Court
10 Barrington Court
16 Binham Grange Gardens
27 Cothay Manor & Gardens
28 Court House
31 Dunster Castle Gardens
32 Dyrham Park
34 East Lambrook Manor Gardens
36 Elworthy Cottage
51 Hanham Court
54 Hestercombe Gardens
61 Kilver Court
67 Lytes Cary Manor
70 Midney Gardens
72 Milton Lodge
73 Montacute House
75 Newark Park
87 Prior Park Landscape Garden
94 Sherborne Garden
100 Special Plants
106 Ston Easton Park
112 Tintinhull
115 Tyntesfield
116 University of Bristol Botanic Garden
118 The Walled Gardens of Cannington
126 The Yeo Valley Organic Garden at Holt Farm

By appointment only

1 Abbey Farm
3 Algars Manor
4 Algars Mill
24 Cherry Bolberry Farm
33 East End Farm
37 14 Eskdale Close
49 16 Gordano Gardens
53 Henley Mill
58 Ina's Orchard
63 Lift The Latch
93 Serridge House
96 Somerfoss
105 Stoke St Mary Gardens

Also open by Appointment ☎

5 Aller Farmhouse
8 6 Ashton Close
11 Bartley Cottage
14 The Beeches
18 1 Braggchurch
19 Copse Hall, Brent Knoll Gardens
21 Camers
25 Church Farm House
40 Farndon Thatch
41 Fernhill
42 29 Four Acre Avenue
46 Glebe Cottage, Glebe Cottage and Old Rectory Cottage
50 Hangeridge Farmhouse
56 Hooper's Holding, Hinton St George Gardens
57 Honeyhurst Farm
59 Jasmine Cottage
62 Kingston St Mary Secret Gardens
64 Little Garth
65 Little Yarford Farmhouse
66 Lucombe House
74 16 Montroy Close
77 Nynehead Court
79 The Old Rectory, Limington
82 Overbrook Cottage
84 3 Palmer's Way
89 Rock House
90 Rose Cottage, Rose Cottage & Coley Court
91 Rugg Farm
95 Sole Retreat
97 52 South Lawn
104 Knoll Cottage, Stogumber Gardens
107 Badgers Acre, Stone Allerton Gardens
109 Sutton Hosey Manor
119 Watcombe
122 Wellfield Barn
123 4 Haytor Park, West Bristol Gardens
123 159 Westbury Lane, West Bristol Gardens
124 Westbrook House
127 Yews Farm

Visit a garden in your own time – look out for the ☎

The Gardens

1 ABBEY FARM

Montacute TA15 6UA. Mr & Mrs A McFarlane, 07831 334086, ct.fm@btopenworld.com. *4m from Yeovil. Follow A3088, take slip rd to Montacute, turn L at T-junction into village. Turn R between Church & King's Arms (no through rd).* Home-made teas by arrangement. **Adm £4, chd free. Visitors welcome by appt June to July.**

2½ acres of mainly walled gardens on sloping site, provide the setting for Cluniac Medieval Priory gatehouse. Interesting plants incl roses, shrubs, grasses, clematis. Herbaceous borders, white garden, gravel garden. Small arboretum. Pond for wildlife - frogs, newts, dragonflies. Fine mulberry, walnut and monkey puzzle trees. Seats for resting. Gravel area & one steep slope.

2 ◆ ACTON COURT

Latteridge Road, Iron Acton, Bristol BS37 9TL, www.actoncourt.com. *10m NE of Bristol. On B4059 near junction with B4058. Brown sign for Acton Court.* **Adm £4, chd free. For NGS: Sat 15, Sun 16 June (11-5). For other opening times and information, please see garden website.**

3 acres: walled wildflower meadow plus abundance of old English and wild roses on grounds of Tudor Manor House (not open on NGS days). Organic kitchen garden cultivated on medieval lines which produces vegetables, culinary and medicinal herbs. The site is Soil Association Certified. Owl habitat & breeding barn. Grass paths, kitchen garden not accessible - gravel path/step.

3 ALGARS MANOR

Station Road, Iron Acton BS37 9TB. Mrs B Naish, 01454 228372, bhnaish@gmail.com. *9m N of Bristol. 3m W of Yate/Chipping Sodbury. Turn S off Iron Acton bypass B4059, past village green, 200yds, then over level Xing (Station Rd).* **Combined adm £4, chd free. Combined with Algars Mill. Groups of 10+ welcome by appt.**

2 acres of woodland garden beside R Frome, mill stream, native plants mixed with collections of 60 magnolias and 70 camellias, eucalyptus and other unusual trees and shrubs. Mar/Apr camellias, magnolias; Apr/May/June rhododendrons, azaleas; Oct autumn colours. Limited wheelchair access, gravel paths, some steep slopes.

The Manor

4 ALGARS MILL

Station Road, Iron Acton BS37 9TD. Mr & Mrs John Wright, 01454 228373, marilyn@algarsmill.plus.com. *9m N of Bristol. 3m W of Yate/Chipping Sodbury. (For directions see Algars Manor).* **Combined adm £4, chd free. Combined with Algars Manor. Groups welcome by appt (see Algars Manor).**

2-acre woodland garden bisected by R Frome; spring bulbs, shrubs; very early spring feature (Feb-Mar) of wild Newent daffodils. 300-400yr-old mill house (not open) through which millrace still runs.

5 ALLER FARMHOUSE

nr Williton TA4 4LY. Mr & Mrs Richard Chandler, 01984 633702. *7m E of Minehead, 1m S of Williton. From A358 (½ m S of Williton) opp garage, through Sampford Brett, then Capton; curve R, down hill to Aller Farm. Exit from car park (NOT back past house) on continuation of drive, ¾ m to Williton onto A39.* Cream teas Orchard Mill. **Adm £4, chd free. Sun 16 June (2-5.30). Visitors also welcome by appt Apr to Sept.**

2-3 acres. Hot, dry, sunny, S-facing, surrounded by pink stone walls and sub-divided into 5 separate compartments by same. 'Cliff Garden' is old 3-sided quarry. Old magnolias, figs, Judas, etc; newer acacias; many unusual and/or tender plants incl eremurus, cantua, beschorneria, dendromecon, echiums in variety and buddleia colvilei. Partial wheelchair access.

6 22 AMBRA VALE

Clifton Wood, Bristol BS8 4RW. Joyce Poole. *Off A4 Hotwells Rd nr Holy Trinity Church. Garden entrance in Ambrose Rd next to Ambrose Villas.* Light refreshments. **Adm £3.50, chd free. Sat 22, Sun 23 June (1-6).**

Part-walled small town garden with romantic feel. Informal planting incl grasses, ferns, exotics, fig and vine. Lots of interesting features incl statues, mosaics and secluded seating areas. 2 wildlife ponds with water features, fish and frogs. Plenty of hidden corners for bird watching and restive contemplation with a glass of wine.

7 ASH COTTAGE

Shurton, Bridgwater TA5 1QF. Barbara & Peter Oates. *8m W of Bridgwater. From A39 nr Holford, follow signs to Stogursey then to Shurton. From A39 at Cannington follow signs to Hinkley Point then Shurton.* Cream teas. **Adm £3.50, chd free.** **Thur 6, Thur 13, Sat 15 June (2-5).**

Tranquil cottage garden in rural area, approx 2/3 acre, wrapping around 3 sides of early C16 cottage (not open). Colour-themed borders and flowerbeds incl island bed, with raised 40ft border reached by steps from either end. Some areas have been replanted since last opening 2 years ago. Natural stream with planted banks runs through garden. Children must be supervised at all times. Some gravel paths and shallow steps.

Some areas replanted since last opening 2 years ago . . .

8 6 ASHTON CLOSE

Clevedon BS21 7UT. Helen & Roy Goodchild, 01275 874547, rg007f5966@blueyonder.co.uk. *12m W of Bristol. M5 J20. Follow ring rd L onto Southern Way. Past sports centre on R, next turning on R (Westerleigh Rd), Ashton Close on R at end.* Home-made teas. **Adm £3, chd free.** **Sun 12 May, Sun 9 June (11-4). Visitors also welcome by appt.**

Japanese inspired creation representing your progress through life. Emphasis on varied use of rocks and planting which convey reminders of places visited. Acers, flowering shrubs and trees are designed to form a continuing series of pictures with yr-round interest. Old clay pit provides wildlife-friendly pond.

9 BADMINTON HOUSE

Badminton GL9 1DB. Duke & Duchess of Beaufort, www.badmintonestate.co.uk. *4m N of M4 J18. From M4 J18, 1st exit onto A46/Bath Rd. Follow yellow arrows.* Lunch/teatime refreshments. **Adm £10, chd free.** **Thur 20 June (10-4).**

Designed by Russell Page and Francois Goffinet, Badminton House gardens combine formality, structure and openness. The Duke and Duchess of Beaufort are passionate about plants and have made their mark on the garden's many different aspects, incl formal south garden and a walled garden. Local nurseries will be selling plants.

10 ◆ BARRINGTON COURT

Barrington, Ilminster TA19 0NQ. National Trust, 01460 241938, barringtoncourt@nationaltrust.org.uk, www.nationaltrust.org.uk. *5m NE of Ilminster. In Barrington village on B3168. Follow brown National Trust signs.* **Adm £10.50, chd £5.20.** **For NGS: Sat 13 Apr, Sat 20 July (10-5). For other opening times and information, please phone or see garden website.**

Well known garden constructed in 1920 by Col Arthur Lyle from derelict farmland (the C19 cattle stalls still exist). Gertrude Jekyll suggested planting schemes for the layout. Paved paths with walled rose and iris, white and lily gardens, large kitchen garden. Some paths a little uneven.

11 BARTLEY COTTAGE

Birch Hill, Cheddar BS27 3JP. Mr & Mrs S Cleverdon, 01934 740387/07737 132214. *Cheddar town centre. Follow signs for Cheddar Gorge. Follow yellow signs. Parking on rd.* Home-made teas. **Adm £2.50, chd free.** **Suns 14 Apr; 19 May; 9 June; 22 Sept (2-5). Visitors also welcome by appt.**

Small garden filled with over 100 very rare and unusual conifers which will surprise our visitors with differing colours, shapes and textures. Large koi pond. Tranquil oriental-style garden with large outdoor bonsai. New for 2013, spring bulbs and Japanese tea house. Greenhouse with collection of succulents (sempervivums). Spectacular views of Cheddar Gorge. Featured in Mendip Times (Sept Garden of the Month) and Somerset Country Gardener.

12 BARUM

50 Edward Road, Clevedon BS21 7DT. Marian & Roger Peacock, www.barum.pwp.blueyonder.co.uk. *12m W of Bristol. M5 J20, follow signs to pier, continue N, past Walton Park Hotel, turn R at St Mary's Church. Up Channel Rd, over Xrds, turn L into Edward Rd at top.* **Adm £3, chd free.** **Thur 1, Thur 8, Thur 15 Aug (1.30-4.30).**

Informal 1/3 -acre plantsman's garden, reclaimed by the owners from years of neglect. Now crammed with shrubs and perennials from around the world, incl tender and exotic species using the clement coastal climate and well-drained soil. The vegetable patch uses a no-tread bedding system.

13 BATH PRIORY HOTEL

Weston Road, Bath BA1 2XT. Jane Moore, Head Gardener, www.thebathpriory.co.uk. *Close to centre of Bath. From Bath centre take Upper Bristol Rd, turn R at end of Victoria Park & L into Weston Rd.* Home-made teas. **Adm £3, chd free.** **Tue 16 Apr; Tue 16 July (2-5).**

Discover 3 acres of mature walled gardens. Quintessentially English, the garden has billowing borders, croquet lawn, wild flower meadow and ancient specimen trees. Spring is bright with tulips and flowering cherries; autumn alive with colour. Perennials and tender plants provide summer highlights while the kitchen garden supplies herbs, fruit and vegetables to the restaurant. Gravel paths and some steps.

NCH

14 THE BEECHES

High Street, Oakhill BA3 5AS. Wendy Hounsfield, 01749 841776, wjh1@me.com. *2½ m N of Shepton Mallet. From Oakhill Church, turn into High St, ¼ m on L (parking on High St).* Home-made teas. **Adm £3.50, chd free.** **Sun 30 June (2-6). Visitors also welcome by appt 1st June to 1st Sept, adm £4.50.**

3/4 -acre. Magical, peaceful garden brimming with colour. Walled garden, rose walk, formal vegetable garden. Terraced garden with many places to sit and linger. A flower arranger's delight. Featured in Somerset Country Gardener, local press and radio.

Treat yourself to a plant from the plant stall

15 BEECHWELL HOUSE
51 Goose Green, Yate BS37 5BL. Tim Wilmot, www.beechwell.com. *10m NE of Bristol. From centre of Yate (Shopping & Leisure Centre) or Station Rd B4060, turn N onto Church Rd. After 1/2 m turn L onto Greenways Rd then immediately R onto continuation of Church Rd. Goose Green starts after 200yds. After 100yds take R-fork, garden 100yds on L. Limited parking*. Home-made teas. **Adm £3, chd free.** **Sun 15 Sept (1-5).**
Enclosed, level, subtropical garden created over last 23 yrs and filled with exotic planting, incl palms (over 6 varieties), tree ferns, yuccas, agaves and succulent bed, rare shrubs, bamboos, bananas, aroids and other architectural planting. Wildlife pond and koi pond. C16 40ft deep well. Rare plant raffle every hour. Some narrow pathways.

BERKELEY CASTLE
See Gloucestershire

16 ◆ BINHAM GRANGE GARDENS
Old Cleeve, Minehead TA24 6HX. Stewart & Marie Thomas, 01984 640056, mariethomas@btconnect.com. *4m E of Dunster. Take A39 for Minehead, R at Xrds after Washford to Blue Anchor, past Old Cleeve, garden on L*. **Adm £3.50, chd free.** **For NGS: Sun 19, Tue 21 May (2-5). For other opening times and information, please phone or see garden website.**
Established garden set in 300 acres of farmed Somerset countryside with extensive views. Parterre garden to the front of house, Italian-style garden, pergola, island beds, cutting and vegetable garden. Splendid Irises in the spring. Plants for the senses working with the seasons. Interesting and unusual plants. View the dairy herd coming for milking from the Garden Terrace. Views of West Somerset steam train passing the farm. Featured in Exmoor, Somerset Life and Period House magazines.

GROUP OPENING

17 BISHOP SUTTON GARDENS
BS39 5UP. *10m W of Bath. Village on A368 Bath to Weston-super-Mare, nr Chew Valley Lake. Turn off main rd at Red Lion PH, into Sutton Hill Rd. Park in rd. 2 gardens on A368. Follow signs*. Home-made teas at Truffles. **Combined adm £5, chd free.** **Sun 9 June (2-6).**

CEDAR VALE
Sutton Hill Road. Mr & Mrs D Thompson

NEW 2 CHURCH COTTAGES
Church Lane. Ms Fay Hollomon

TRUFFLES
Sally Monkhouse
(See separate entry)

42 WOODCROFT
Wick Road. Ann & Mervyn Williams

A welcome awaits you in the 4 gardens. Whether you aspire to very small scale gardening to larger gardens, examples can be found in the village. Something for everyone from different planting schemes to back-saving ideas. Wild areas, secret areas, creative hard landscaping softened by time. Come and sit and enjoy the wonderful views and countryside. Delicious home-made teas. Parking in road.

Free range chickens and call ducks with young . . .

18 1 BRAGGCHURCH
93 Hendford Hill, Yeovil BA20 2RE. Veronica Sartin, 01935 473841/471508. *Walking distance of Yeovil centre. Approaching Yeovil on A30 from The Quicksilver Mail PH r'about, go halfway down Hendford Hill, 1st driveway on R. Roadside parking at Southwoods (next R down hill) and Public Car Park at bottom of Hendford Hill*. Home-made teas. **Adm £3.50, chd free.** **Sun 5, Mon 6 May (2-6). Visitors also welcome by appt May, refreshments by arrangement.**
Old garden of undulating lawns and mature trees evolving, since May 2002, to semi-wild, nature-friendly, woodland garden with a few surprises within the new planting - refurbished tree house, dancing figures, Anderson shelter, pond, more willow weaving, retreat with poetry, medlar tree enclosure, rhododendron hideaway and courtyard curios.

GROUP OPENING

19 BRENT KNOLL GARDENS
TA9 4DF. *2m N of Highbridge. Off A38 & M5 J22*. Cream teas Copse Hall. **Combined adm £6, chd free.** **Sun 21 July (2-6).**

COPSE HALL
Hill Lane. Mrs S Boss & Mr A J Hill.
From A38 follow signs to Woodlands Hotel then L into car park
Visitors also welcome by appt, max 30.
01278 760301
susan.boss@gmail.com

PEN ORCHARD
Brent Street. Major and Mrs John Harper.
From A38, just past Post Office on R

NEW UNDERKNOLL
Brent Street. Mr & Mrs Peter Osborn.
From A38 after Red Cow PH on R

The distinctive hill of Brent Knoll, an iron age hill fort, is well worth climbing 449ft for the 360° view of hills incl Glastonbury Tor and levels. Lovely C13 church renowned for its bench ends. Copse Hall: S-facing Edwardian house (not open) on lower slopes of Knoll. Front garden newly designed with curving slopes and paths. Ha-ha, wild area and kitchen garden remain. Views to Quantock and Polden Hills. Kitchen garden enclosed by Crinkle Crankle wall, has heritage vegetables, wall fruit, kiwifruit and feijoas amongst the usual fruit and vegetables. New front garden is now pretty well established and colourful. Pen Orchard is a lovely garden with several developments since last open. Underknoll - the garden is laid out to lawns and flower beds with thought for wildlife. The house was once the village bakery. At the top of the orchard is a compound containing free range chickens and call ducks with young. There may be llamas and black sheep on the hill above and a section A pony, Blue. Wheelchair access in all gardens, some restricted.

Bath Priory Hotel

20 20 BUBWITH ROAD

Chard. TA20 2BN. Paul & Barbara Blackburn. *A30 or A358 to Chard. At T-lights surrounded by 2 churches, school and garage, take Axminster rd (A358), L at mini r'about into Milfield Rd, next R. Garden on L before 2nd R turn. From Axminster, pass police stn on L before mini r'about, R into Milfield Rd.* Home-made teas. **Adm £2.50, chd free. Sun 11, Mon 12, Sun 25, Mon 26 Aug (1-5).**
Surprising oasis for a small young garden. Full of perennials, shrubs, herbaceous plants, trees, lawn area, deck, arches and containered acers. To the rear, gently winding paths lead you to a surprise round every corner. At front, unusual parking incorporated into cottage-style planting. Featured in Real Homes magazine.

BURROW FARM GARDENS

See Devon.

21 CAMERS

Old Sodbury BS37 6RG. Mr & Mrs A G Denman, 01454 322430, dorothydenman@camers.org, www.camers.org. *2m E of Chipping Sodbury. Entrance in Chapel Lane off A432 at Dog Inn.* Home-made teas. **Adm £4, chd free. Sun 28 July (2-5). Groups of 20+ welcome by appt Feb to Oct. Small parties may enter directly from A432.**
Elizabethan farmhouse (not open) set in 4 acres of constantly developing garden and woodland with spectacular views over Severn Vale. Garden full of surprises, formal and informal areas planted with very wide range of species to provide yr-round interest. Parterre, topiary, Japanese garden, bog and prairie areas, waterfalls, white and hot gardens, woodland walks. Some steep slopes.

22 9 CATHERSTON CLOSE

Frome. BA11 4HR. Dave & Prue Moon. *15m S of Bath. Town centre W towards Shepton Mallet (A361). R at Sainsburys r'about, follow lane for ½ m. L into Critchill Rd. Over Xrds then 1st L Catherston Close.* **Adm £2.50, chd free. Weds 26 June; 3, 10 July (12-5). Also open with The Bastion 30 June (see Frome Gardens).**
⅓ -acre town garden. Colour-themed shrub and herbaceous borders, pond, patios, pergolas and wild meadow areas, with extensive views of countryside. Productive vegetable and fruit garden with greenhouse. Exhibition of garden photography by owner displayed in summerhouse. Featured on BBC Radio Somerset and in local press and Somerset Country Gardener. 7 times gold winner in Frome-in-Bloom. Several shallow steps, gravel paths.

24 CHERRY BOLBERRY FARM

Furge Lane, Henstridge BA8 0RN. Mrs Jenny Raymond, 01963 362177, cherrybolberryfarm@tiscali.co.uk. *6m E of Sherborne. In centre of Henstridge, turn R at small Xrds signed Furge Lane. Continue straight up the lane, over 2 cattle grids, garden at top of lane on R.* Tea. **Adm £4, chd free. Visitors welcome by appt June/July.**
37 yr-old award-winning, owner-designed and maintained 1-acre garden planted for yr-round interest with wildlife in mind. Colour-themed island beds, shrub and herbaceous borders, unusual perennials and shrubs, old roses and specimen trees. Vegetable and flower cutting garden, greenhouses, nature ponds. Wonderful extensive views. Garden surrounded by our dairy farm which has been in the family for nearly 100 years. You will see Jersey cows, sheep, horses and hens!

CHEVITHORNE BARTON

See Devon

CHIFFCHAFFS
See Dorset

25 CHURCH FARM HOUSE
Turners Court Lane, Binegar, Radstock BA3 4UA. Susan & Tony Griffin, 01749 841628, smgriffin@beanacrebarn.co.uk, www.beanacrebarn.co.uk. *4m NE of Wells. On A37 Binegar (Gurney Slade), at George Inn, follow sign to Binegar. 1m past PH & Church to Xrds, Binegar Green, turn R, 300mtrs, turn R. From Wells B3139, 4m turn R signed Binegar. 1m to Xrds, turn L, 300mtrs turn R. Park in field on L.* **Adm £3.50, chd free. Sun 2, Sun 16, Mon 17 June; Sun 14, Wed 17 July; Sun 18 Aug (11-5). Visitors also welcome by appt June to Aug.**
Goddess Flora demands further tribute! More grass must be sacrificed for further planting. The Wiry Old Owl oversees 2 walled gardens. Contemporary cottage style planting, unusual perennials in deep borders give interest all seasons. Progressive colourist design in S garden, insect attractive planting in old farmyard gravel & prairie patch guarded by Green Man's living willow throne. Featured in Mendip Times (Garden of the Month) and local press and radio. Gravel forecourt, 2 shallow steps.

GROUP OPENING

26 CONGRESBURY GARDENS
Congresbury, Bristol BS49 5DN. *Approx halfway between Bristol and Weston-super-Mare. 13m S of Bristol on A370. At traffic lights in Congresbury turn R onto High St B3133 and look for signs.* Morning coffee and cake at Moorway, teas at Middlecombe Nursery and Yeo Meads. **Combined adm £5, chd free. Sun 9 June (10.30-4.30).**

NEW LABURNUM COTTAGE
20 Pauls Causeway. Mrs Mary Gilbert.
From High St R at Memorial into Broad St. L into Pauls Causeway. Laburnum next door to Old Inn PH

NEW MARTY'S GARDEN
Mr John Dunster.
Woodhill is lane off the Congresbury-Yatton road B3133. Marty's Garden is at Woodhill Nursery ¾ m along lane on R, 3rd hole in the hedge

MIDDLECOMBE NURSERY
Nigel J North.
On the edge of Congresbury, on the Bristol side, turn to Wrington along the Wrington Rd off A370 Weston to Bristol rd. Garden 250yds on L
www.middlecombenursery.co.uk

MOORWAY
30 The Causeway. Brian & Julie Gosling.
Along High St, after t-lights, R hand bend and sharp R turn off

NEW 29 STONEWELL LANE
Mike & Janet Sweeting.
Stonewell Lane is after PO and shops in High St, continue to bottom, 29 is the bungalow with 2 odd chimney pots

YEO MEADS
Debbie Fortune & Mark Hayward.
150yds along High St from Ship & Castle PH on L. Park in Ship and Castle public car park

Village group of 6 strikingly contrasting gardens. A large family size vegetable plot with herbaceous borders and mature trees overlooking cricket field. Large garden with many trees amongst which is a 350 year old Cedar of Lebanon which fell in 2007 but survives as a feature, together with Victorian pond and thatched octagonal summerhouse. A 3 acre nursery site in country setting with a series of different gardens, owned by Nigel North, a regular contributor to BBC Radio Bristol. A tranquil rear garden with emphasis on scented plants and unusual trees. A 1 acre garden with borders of herbaceous plants and alstroemeria plus a rare clematis bred at Cannington College. A garden to encourage wildlife with borders, mature trees, a pond and herbaceous perennials.

27 ◆ COTHAY MANOR & GARDENS
Greenham, nr Wellington TA21 0JR. Mr & Mrs Alastair Robb, 01823 672283, cothaymanor@btinternet.com, www.cothaymanor.co.uk. *5m SW of Wellington. At M5 J26 or 27 take A38. Approx 4m follow signs marked Greenham and Cothay Manor, take turning. After 1m follow brown signs marked Cothay Manor and finger posts marked Cothay. In narrow lane, L at Y junction, signed Cothay. Cothay Manor is 1m on L. Car park end of drive on R.* **Adm £7.50, chd £3.50. For NGS: Sun 28 July (2-6). For other opening times and information, please phone or see garden website.**
Few gardens are as evocatively romantic as Cothay. Laid out in 1920s and replanted in 1990s within the original framework, Cothay encompasses a rare blend of old and new. Plantsman's paradise set in 12 acres of magical gardens. Antiques; garden shop; tea room. Sorry, no picnicing in gardens. Sunday house tours 11:45 and 2:15. £6.75, advance booking recommended. Events throughout year - see our website for dates. Partial wheelchair access, gravel paths.

Goddess Flora demands further tribute! More grass must be sacrificed for further planting . . .

28 ◆ COURT HOUSE
East Quantoxhead TA5 1EJ. East Quantoxhead Estate (Hugh Luttrell Esq), 01278 741 271, hugh_luttrell@yahoo.co.uk. *12m W of Bridgwater. Off A39; house at end of village past duck pond. Enter by Frog Lane (Bridgwater/Kilve side from A39). Car park 50p in aid of church.* **Adm £4, chd free. For NGS: Sun 12 May, Sun 7 July (2-5). For other opening times and information, please phone.**
Lovely 5 acre garden; trees, shrubs, many rare and tender; herbaceous and 3 acre woodland garden with spring interest and late summer borders. Traditional kitchen garden (all chemical free). Views to sea and Quantocks. Groups welcome by appointment, proceeds not to NGS. Gravel and stone paths, some mown grass paths.

29 CRICKET HOUSE AND GARDENS

Nr Chard TA20 4DD. Warner Leisure Hotels, 01460 30111. *3m E of Chard. On A303, Cricket St Thomas Wildlife Park signed from M3, M4, M5.* Light refreshments. **Adm £4. Suns 31 Mar; 7 July, 20 Oct (11-4).**

The grounds were designed by a student of Capability Brown. Mixture of mature trees in beautiful setting along valley with chain of lakes. Brand new 'Otter Garden' alongside rose, grotto and water gardens, with formal and mixed borders. Beautiful spring and autumn display. Worth visiting at any time of year. Sorry, no children. Featured in Somerset Country Gardener. Some gravel paths and steep slopes.

ALLOTMENTS

30 DAGGS ALLOTMENTS

High Street, Thornbury BS35 2AW, www.thornburyallotments.com. *Park in free car park off Chapel St.* Home-made teas/soft drinks. **Combined adm £3, chd free. Sun 14 July (2-5).**

Thornbury is a historic market town and has been a regular winner of awards in the RHS Britain in Bloom competition. 105 plots, all in cultivation, many organic, including vegetables, soft fruit, herbs and flowers for cutting. Narrow, steep, grass paths between plots. Many plot holders will be available to answer any questions you may have about the plots, cultivation techniques and varieties grown. Short talk on the history of Daggs since 1546.

DICOT
See Devon

31 ◆ DUNSTER CASTLE GARDENS

Dunster TA24 6SL. National Trust, 01643 821314, www.nationaltrust.org.uk. *3m SE of Minehead. NT car park approached direct from A39 Minehead to Bridgwater rd, nr to A396 turning. Car park charge to non-NT members.* **Adm £4.80, chd free. For NGS: Sun 14 July (10-4.30). For other opening times and information, please phone or see garden website.**

Hillside woodland garden surrounding fortified mansion, previously home to the Luttrell family for 600yrs. Terraced areas, interlinked by old carriage drives and paths, feature tender plants. Fine views over polo lawns and landscape with C18 features. Winter interest border. Dream garden with dahlia displays in main season. Play elements within the River gardens.

DURCOMBE WATER
See Devon

Olive trees, palms, agapanthus. A hint of France in Somerset . . .

32 ◆ DYRHAM PARK

Bath SN14 8ER. National Trust, 01179 371330, www.nationaltrust.org.uk/dyrham-park. *8m N of Bath, 12m E of Bristol. On Bath to Stroud road (A46), 2m S of Tomarton interchange with M4, exit 18. Sat nav use SN14 8HY.* **Adm £5, chd £2.60. For NGS: Fri 16, Sat 17 Aug (10-5). For other opening times and information, please phone or see garden website.**

C17 mansion with formal gardens on W side, lawns, herbaceous borders, fine yew hedges, ponds and cascade. Nichols orchard with perry pear trees. Continuing project to refresh new areas. On E side of house is a C17 orangery traditionally used for citrus plants. Steep slopes in park, cobbles in courtyard. Disabled WC.

33 EAST END FARM

Pitney, Langport TA10 9AL. Mrs A M Wray, 01458 250598. *2m E of Langport. Please telephone for directions.* **Adm £3, chd free. Visitors welcome by appt June.**

Approx $1/3$ acre. Timeless small garden of many old-fashioned roses in beautiful herbaceous borders set amongst ancient listed farm buildings. Mostly wheelchair access.

34 ◆ EAST LAMBROOK MANOR GARDENS

East Lambrook TA13 5HH. Mike & Gail Werkmeister, 01460 240328, enquiries@eastlambrook.com, www.eastlambrook.com. *2m N of South Petherton. Follow brown tourist signs from A303 South Petherton r'about or B3165 Xrd with lights N of Martock.* **Adm £5.50, concessions £5, chd free. For NGS: Sun 3 Feb, Sat 18 May, Sun 14 July, Sun 9 Feb 2014 (10-5). For other opening times and information, please phone or see garden website.**

The quintessential English cottage garden created by 20th century gardening legend Margery Fish. A plantsman's paradise with old-fashioned and contemporary plants grown in a relaxed and informal manner to create an extraordinary garden of great beauty and charm. With noted collections of snowdrops, hellebores and geraniums and the excellent specialist Margery Fish Plant Nursery. Snowdrops Feb. Art exhibitions: Kaye Parmenter May, Moish Sokal July. Also open Feb/May/June/July daily; Mar/Apr/Aug to Oct Tue to Sat and BH Mons; (10-5). Featured on BBC Gardeners' World, local radio and TV and in The English Garden, Somerset Life and others. Partial wheelchair access only due to narrow paths and steps.

35 EASTFIELD

Pound Lane, Yarlington, Wincanton BA9 8DQ. Lucy McAuslan-Crine. *3m W of Wincanton. A303 Wincanton exit, follow A371 to Castle Cary, Shepton Mallet, L on bend to Yarlington (2m). 2nd or 3rd R to Yarlington. At Xrds follow lane past front of Stags Head to end, entrance and parking at rear of Eastfield.* Tea. **Adm £3.50, chd free. Sun 16, Mon 17 June (2-5).**

Approx $1/2$ acre made up of small gardens each with a different planting style. Mixture of tender and hardy herbaceous plants and shrubs incl olive trees, palms, agapanthus. A hint of France in Somerset. Ponds, roof garden, organic kitchen garden, young orchard, greenhouse, conservatory with beds filled with citrus plants. Featured in Garden Answers.

36 ◆ ELWORTHY COTTAGE
Elworthy, Taunton TA4 3PX. Mike & Jenny Spiller, 01984 656427, mike@elworthy-cottage.co.uk, www.elworthy-cottage.co.uk. *12m NW of Taunton. On B3188 between Wiveliscombe & Watchet.* **Adm £3, chd free. For NGS: Mon 1, Tues 9, 16 Apr; Tues 14, 28 May; 4 June; Sun 25 Aug, Tue 3 Sept (11-5). For other information, please phone or see garden website.**
1-acre plantsman's garden in tranquil setting. Island beds, scented plants, clematis, unusual perennials and ornamental trees and shrubs to provide yr-round interest. In spring, pulmonarias, hellebores and more than 100 varieties of snowdrops. Planted to encourage birds, bees and butterflies, lots of birdsong. Wild flower areas, decorative vegetable garden, living willow screen. Stone ex privy and pigsty feature. Adjoining nursery. Also open Thurs Apr - Aug incl (10-5) or by appt. Featured in Somerset Country Gardener.

37 14 ESKDALE CLOSE
Weston-Super-Mare BS22 8QG. Janet & Adrian Smith, 01934 414543, nanandpops14@hotmail.co.uk. *1½ m E of WSM town centre. J21 M5, 1½ m (B3440) towards WSM town centre. L at chevrons into Corondale Rd, 1st R into Garsdale Rd. Park halfway along and take footpath beside no. 37. From town centre take B3440 towards Bristol. After 1½ m keep straight on at mini r'about then 1st R into Corondale Rd.* Tea. **Adm £2.50, chd free. Visitors welcome by appt 27 Apr to 31 Aug, max group 30.**
Unexpected size for town garden, containing over 250 different plants. Interesting and naturally planted in cottage style. Four areas: pond with seating, packed borders with climbing roses, Mediterranean garden and conifer rockery. A wisteria archway leads to a productive area of fruit trees, vegetable plot and herb garden. No wheelchair access to vegetable patch.

38 ESOTERA
Foddington, nr Babcary TA11 7EL. Andrew & Shirley Harvey. *6m E of Somerton, 6m SW of Castle Cary. Signs to garden off A37 Ilchester to Shepton Mallet and B3153 Somerton to Castle Cary. (Old) A303 from Sparkford.* Home-made teas. **Adm £4, chd free. Sat 1, Sun 2, Sat 15, Sun 16 June (11-5).**
2-acre established informal country garden housing 3 wildlife ponds. Large prairie border. Contemporary new potting shed with shrubs and herbaceous planting. Mature trees, boxed topiary, courtyard and meadow walk leading to shepherd hut. New Olympic hen house. Children must be supervised at all times.

39 FAIRFIELD
Stogursey, Bridgwater TA5 1PU. Lady Acland Hood Gass. *7m E of Williton. 11m W of Bridgwater. From A39 Bridgwater to Minehead rd turn N; garden 1½ m W of Stogursey on Stringston rd. No coaches. For directions please phone 01278 732251.* **Adm £3.50, chd free. Sun 10 Mar (2-5).**
Woodland garden with bulbs, shrubs and fine trees; paved maze. Views of Quantocks and sea.

40 FARNDON THATCH
Puckington, Ilminster TA19 9JA. Bob & Jane St John Wright, 01460 259845, info@bandbinsomerset.com, wwwbandbinsomerset.com. *3m N of Ilminster. From Ilminster take B3168 to Langport. Through Puckington village, last house on L. No parking at house, directions on arrival.* Home-made teas. **Adm £3, chd free. Sats, Suns 15, 16 June; 13, 14 July (1-6). Visitors also welcome by appt 3 June to 26 July.**
With panoramic views to die for, this 1-acre plantaholic's garden comes complete with C16 thatched cottage. Banks and borders brimming with shrubs and perennials. Planted for yr-round interest. Terrace and courtyard with pots; sculptures, vegetable garden, fine trees and lawns and areas of natural tranquility. An undulating garden following the contours of the land. Featured in Somerset Country Gardener. Some wheelchair access.

41 FERNHILL
nr Wellington TA21 0LU. Peter & Audrey Bowler, 01823 672423, muldoni@hotmail.co.uk, http://sampfordarundel.org.uk/fernhill/. *3m W of Wellington. On A38, White Ball Hill. Past Beam Bridge Hotel stay on A38 at top of hill, follow signs on L into garden & car park. Disabled parking at front of house.* **Adm £3, chd free. Sun 30 June, Sun 4, Sun 25 Aug (2-5). Groups of 10-30 also welcome by appt 15 June to 15 Sept.**
In approx 2 acres, a delightful garden to stir your senses, with a myriad of unusual plants and features. Intriguing almost hidden paths, leading through English roses, and banks of hydrangeas. Scenic views stretching up to the Blackdowns and its famous monument. Truly a Hide and Seek garden . . . for all ages. Featured in Somerset Country Gardener. Wheelchair access to terrace and other parts of garden from drive.

FORDE ABBEY GARDENS
See Dorset

Newly constructed contemporary cascade . . .

FOSSLEIGH
See Devon

42 29 FOUR ACRE AVENUE
Downend, Bristol BS16 6PD. Anne & Lyndon Heal, 0117 9562149, a.heal168@btinternet.com. *From A4174 ring rd take A432 towards Downend (Willy Wicket r'about), after ⅔ m R into Four Acre Rd, immed L into Four Acre Ave, 1st bungalow on R.* Home-made teas. **Adm £3, chd free. Sat 22, Sun 23 June (2-5). Visitors also welcome by appt June to July.**
Large colourful suburban garden transformed with good architecture and numerous climbers. Densely-planted borders with perennials, shrubs, trees, unusual and tropical plants. Large ornamental fish pond. Moon window. Small productive vegetable patch. Newly-constructed walk through pergola adorned with roses and clematis covering raised beds and seating area. Newly constructed contemporary cascade.

FRANKHAM FARM
See Dorset

43 1 FROBISHER ROAD
Ashton Gate, Bristol BS3 2AU. Karen Thomas. *2m SW of city centre. Bristol City FC on R, next R Duckmoor Rd, 5th turning L before bollards.* Home-made teas. **Combined adm £4, chd free. Sat 15, Sun 16 June (2-6). Combined with 95 St John's Lane, Bedminster.**
Relax and lose yourself among trees, closely planted perennials and annuals, 2 little ponds. A garden full of surprises, with seating areas. Original stain glass panel in front door, 63ft frontage in an interesting, compact, city garden.

GROUP OPENING

44 FROME GARDENS
BA11 4HR. *15m S of Bath. Town centre W towards Shepton Mallet (A361). At Sainsbury's r'about turn R, follow lane for ½ m, L into Critchill Rd, over Xrds then 1st L for Catherston Close. The Bastion Garden in town centre on Cork St.* Home-made teas at The Bastion Garden. **Combined adm £3, chd free. Sun 30 June (12-5).**

THE BASTION GARDEN
Mrs Karen Harvey.
Access to garden via Zion Path, next to Catherine House Care Home opp Cork St car park

9 CATHERSTON CLOSE
Dave & Prue Moon
(See separate entry)

2 varied gardens. The Bastion Garden: C18 extensively restored. Features reveted banks, raised platforms, yew hedges and pond. Emphasis on shape and form not extensive floral planting. Colourful 50-metre curved border of David Austin roses with low box hedging. 9 Catherston Close: 1/3-acre town garden. Colour-themed shrub and herbaceous borders, pond, patios, pergolas and wild meadow areas. Productive vegetable and fruit garden, greenhouse. Exhibition of garden photography by owner displayed in summerhouse. Featured in local press and radio. Some gravel and slopes.

45 GANTS MILL & GARDEN
Gants Mill Lane, Bruton BA10 0DB. Elaine & Greg Beedle, www.gantsmill.co.uk. *½ m SW of Bruton. From Bruton centre take Yeovil rd, A359, under railway bridge, 100yds uphill, fork R down Gants Mill Lane. Parking for wheelchair users.* Home-made teas. **Adm £6, chd £4. Sun 11 Aug (2-5).**
¾ -acre garden. Clematis, rose arches and pergolas; streams, ponds, waterfalls. Riverside walk to top weir; delphiniums, day lilies, 100+ dahlia varieties; also vegetable, soft fruit and cutting flower garden. The garden is overlooked by the historic watermill, open on NGS day. Firm wide paths round the garden. Narrow entrance to mill not accessible to wheelchairs. WC.

GROUP OPENING

46 GLEBE COTTAGE AND OLD RECTORY COTTAGE
Whitestaunton TA20 3DL. *3m W of Chard. Signs to Whitestaunton from A303 and A30.* Home-made teas. **Combined adm £3, chd free. Sat 29, Sun 30 June (2-6).**

GLEBE COTTAGE
Mr & Mrs R White
Visitors also welcome by appt 1 July to 28 July. 01460 68074

OLD RECTORY COTTAGE
Mr S Pook

Nestling in the Blackdown hills in an AONB is the idyllic Hamlet of Whitestaunton. The church of St Andrew dates from BC. Glebe Cottage, with a partly walled garden, houses an abundance of roses, honeysuckle, lupins, delphiniums and many highly scented plants. Next door at Old Rectory Cottage is an evolving wild flower garden (with a new pond) to encourage wildlife. Homemade cream teas.

47 GOBLIN COMBE HOUSE
Plunder Street, Cleeve, Bristol BS49 4PQ. Mrs H R Burn. *10m S of Bristol. On A370, turn L onto Cleeve Hill Rd just before Lord Nelson Inn. After 300yds turn L onto Plunder St, first drive on R. Car parking near bottom of drive just beyond Plunder St turning.* Home-made teas. **Adm £3.50, chd free (share to Greenpeace Environmental Trust). Weds 15, 22 May; 5, 19, 26 June (11-5).**
2-acre terraced garden with interesting collection of trees, shrubs and borders, surrounded by orchards, fields and woodlands. Magnificent views. Wide range of plants.

Evolving wild flower garden to encourage wildlife . . .

48 GODDARDS ORCHARD
Staple Fitzpaine, Taunton TA3 5SP. Dianne & Brian Hood. *4m S of Taunton. Centre of village. Car park adjoining Greyhound Inn. 2½ m from A358. 99 bus stop in village.* Home-made teas. **Adm £3.50, chd free. Sun 30 June, Wed 3 July (2-5.30).**
The ½ -acre sloping cottage-style flower garden is terraced, with steps and some narrow pathways where a profusion of perennials intermingle with wild flowers in a series of island flowerbeds and rooms, rose archways and ponds. The ½ -acre wildlife woodland beside stream has a bridge to the meadow and large (traditional) vegetable plot, the whole area of about 4 acres. Steps and narrow pathway. Irregular surfaces in woodland and meadow.

49 16 GORDANO GARDENS
Easton in Gordano BS20 0PD. Mr & Mrs Milsom, 01275 373463. *5m W of Bristol. M5 J19 Gordano Services, exit Bristol. 1st L for Easton-in-Gordano, past King's Arms PH. Park in church hall car park by football field (BS20 0PR). Walk through field directly behind scout hut.* **Adm £3, chd free. Visitors welcome by appt July.**
Cottage-style garden 80ft long with many pretty and unusual features incl decked area, natural pond with waterfall, grasses and herbaceous plants.

50 HANGERIDGE FARMHOUSE
Wrangway, Wellington TA21 9QG. Mrs J M Chave, 01823 662339, hangeridge@hotmail.co.uk. *2m S of Wellington. 1m off A38 bypass signed Wrangway. 1st L towards Wellington Monument, over mway bridge 1st R.* Home-made teas. **Adm £3, chd free. Suns 14 Apr; 5, 26 May; 14 July; 11 Aug; 8 Sept (2-5). Groups welcome by appt.**
Informal, relaxing, mature family garden set under Blackdown Hills. Seats to enjoy views across Somerset landscape. Atmospheric mix of herbaceous borders and this lovely and still-evolving garden contains wonderful flowering shrubs, heathers, mature trees, rambling climbers and seasonal bulbs. Content and design belie its 1-acre size. Garden not to be missed.

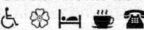

51 ◆ HANHAM COURT
Ferry Rd, Hanham Abbots, South Gloucestershire BS15 3NT, 07800 536628, info@hanhamcourtgardens.co.uk, www.hanhamcourtgardens.co.uk. *5m E of Bristol centre. Old Bristol Rd A431 from Bath, through Willsbridge (past Queen's Head), L at mini r'about, down Court Farm Rd for 1m. Drive entrance on L at bend.* **Adm £5, chd free. For NGS: Sun 27 Jan, Sat 8, Sun 9 June (1.30-5.30). For other opening times and information, please phone or see garden website.**
Hanham Court Gardens develops this rich mix of bold formality, water, woodland, orchard, meadow and kitchen garden with emphasis on scent, structure and romance, set amid a remarkable cluster of manorial buildings between Bath and Bristol. Also open to the public early May - late August, please see website for further details. Partial wheelchair access via slopes.

52 HARPTREE COURT
East Harptree BS40 6AA. Mrs Richard Hill & Mr & Mrs C Hill, 01761 221729, www.harptreecourt.co.uk. *8m N of Wells. A39 Bristol Rd to Chewton Mendip, then B3114 to E Harptree, gates on L. From Bath, A368 Weston-super-Mare Rd to W Harptree, follow signs for E Harptree.* Cream teas. **Adm £3.50, chd free. Sun 26 May (2-5).**
Spacious garden designed when the house was built in 1797. 2 ponds linked by romantic waterfall and stream, flanked by large trees. Lily pond and formal garden. Pleached limes. Walled garden comprising herbaceous borders, fruit trees, soft fruit and large productive area for growing cut flowers and vegetables, incl many unusual and heritage varieties such as crimson-flowered broad beans and purple podded peas. Featured in Somerset Life, local press and radio as well as BBC2's Great British Bake Off.

Knoll Cottage

HEDDON HALL
See Devon

53 HENLEY MILL
Henley Lane, Wookey BA5 1AW. Peter & Sally Gregson, 01749 676966, millcottageplants@gmail.com, www.millcottageplants.co.uk. *2m W of Wells. Off A371 towards Cheddar. Turn L into Henley Lane, driveway 50yds on L through white pillars to end of drive.* Home-made teas. **Adm £3.50, chd free. Visitors welcome by appt Apr to 29 Sept, teas/home-made cake by arrangement.**
2½ acres beside R Axe. Scented garden with roses, hydrangea borders, shady 'folly garden' and late summer borders with grasses and perennials. New zig-zag boardwalk at river level. Ornamental kitchen garden. Rare Japanese hydrangeas. The garden is on one level, but the paths can get a bit muddy after heavy rain.

54 ◆ HESTERCOMBE GARDENS
Cheddon Fitzpaine TA2 8LG. Mr P White, Hestercombe Gardens Trust, 01823 413923, info@hestercombe.com, www.hestercombe.com. *4m N of Taunton. Follow tourist signs.* **Adm £9.70, chd £3.60. For NGS: Tue 5 Mar, Tue 11 June (10-5). For other opening times and information, please phone or see garden website.**
Georgian landscape garden designed by Coplestone Warre Bampfylde, Victorian terrace/shrubbery and stunning Edwardian Lutyens/Jekyll formal gardens together make up

50 acres of woodland walks, temples, terraces, pergolas, lakes and cascades. Restored Watermill and Barn, Lesser Horseshoe bats and art gallery. Featured in Somerset County Gazette, The Garden, Telegraph Gardening, Garden History Society, Somerset Life. Gravel paths, steep slopes, steps - All Abilities Route marked out.

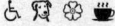

55 NEW HIGHDALE VILLA
14 Sunnyside Road, Clevedon BS21 7TE. Steve & Miriam Thornton. *1m from J20 M5 motorway, short walk from middle of town. From M5 head towards town centre/Curzon cinema. At cinema lights turn L and immed R up Hillside Rd. 2nd R into Sunnyside Rd. Highdale approx 80 metres on R. Ample street parking.* **Adm £2.50, chd free. Sat 18 May; Sun 21 July (1-5).**
Delightful small garden 80' x 30', front garden will interest those who enjoy unusual perennials. Deep borders, shrubs, 25+ trees. Year round colour. Pond with secluded seating area. The garden has been open for various charities and featured in BBC 'Easy Gardening' magazine. Chickens. Shallow steps to garden. WC.

GROUP OPENING

56 HINTON ST GEORGE GARDENS
TA17 8SA. *3m N of Crewkerne. N of A30 Crewkerne-Chard; S of A303 Ilminster Town Rd, at r'about signed Lopen & Merriott, then R to Hinton St George.* Cream teas at Hoopers Holding. **Combined adm £6, chd free. Sun 26, Mon 27 May (2-5.30).**

40 CHURCH STREET
Caroline Van den Berg-Adams.
Corner of High St opp village cross

END HOUSE
West Street. Helen Newman

HOOPER'S HOLDING
45 High Street. Ken & Lyn Spencer-Mills
Visitors also welcome by appt 1 May to 12 Aug, £2.50. 01460 76389 kenlyn@devonrex.demon.co.uk

THE OLD RECTORY
Church Street. Robert & Caroline Duval.
Adjacent to churchyard

THE OLIVE GARDEN
Lopen Road. Pat Read

5 cottage gardens varying in size and style in beautiful hamstone village. C15 church. Country seat of the Earls of Poullett for 600yrs until 1973. Hooper's Holding: ½ -acre garden in colour compartments. Rare plants, many exotics, garden mosaics and sculptures. End House has sweeping lawns, gravel gardens and interesting trees and shrubs (approx ½ acre). The Olive Garden is a loving restoration of a site which had been neglected for decades. The intriguing and totally organic garden at 40 High Street reveals and unfolds its secrets as you pass from one compartment to the next. The Old Rectory is a traditional vicarage garden with mature trees and shrubs. Featured in Somerset Country Gardener. Wheelchair access to 3 gardens.

HODGES BARN
See Gloucestershire

Featured in BBC 'Easy Gardening' magazine . . .

57 HONEYHURST FARM
Honeyhurst Lane, Rodney Stoke, Cheddar BS27 3UJ. Don & Kathy Longhurst, 01749 870322, donlonghurst@btinternet.com. *4m E of Cheddar. From A371 between Wells and Cheddar, turn into Rodney Stoke signed Wedmore. Pass church on L and continue for almost 1m.* Home-made teas. **Adm £3, chd free. Sun 21 July (2-5). Groups of 10-30 also welcome by appt 1 Apr to 7 Sept, £4.**
⅔ -acre part walled rural garden with babbling brook and 4-acre cider orchard, with views. Specimen hollies, copper beech, paulownia, yew and poplar. Pergolas, arbour and numerous seats. Mixed informal shrub and perennial beds with many unusual plants. Pots planted with shrubs, hardy and half-hardy perennials. Level, grass and some shingle. Featured in Wells Life.

IFORD MANOR
See Wiltshire

58 NEW INA'S ORCHARD
Silver Street, South Petherton TA13 5BY. Joy & David Hook, 01460 249 200. *Park in village car park. L out of village car park into Prigg Lane for 100m to Silver St. R then immed L into drive marked Manor Lodge. follow gravel drive to end.* **Adm £3. Small groups, max 10, welcome by appt 15 Apr to 7 June, refreshments available at café in village centre.**
Small (approx 1/3-acre) garden created to surround a C15 hamstone cottage. Mature mulberry and an ancient medlar are all that remain of the original orchard. Garden incl well-stocked mixed borders, courtyard garden, gravel garden, vegetable garden and small stream and pond. Partial wheelchair access.

59 JASMINE COTTAGE
26 Channel Road, Clevedon BS21 7BY. Margaret & Michael Redgrave, 01275 871850, margaret@bologrew.net, http://jasminecottage.bologrew.net. *12m W of Bristol. M5 J20. From Clevedon seafront travel N (0.8m), via Wellington Terrace, follow winding rd to St Mary's Church, R into Channel Rd, approx 100yds on L. Bus: Bristol - Clevedon route 361, alight Cambridge Rd, 5 mins from garden.* **Adm £3, chd free. Thur 30 May; 6, 13, 20, 27 June; 4, 11, 18, 25 July; 1, 8, 15 Aug (11-4). Visitors also welcome by appt 30 May to 20 June.**
Cottage garden with a difference. ⅓ acre with intriguing re-designed layout. New beds and borders are abundant with unusual plant varieties incl rhodochiton, dicentra macrocapnos and salvias, which are home grown and usually for sale. Early June delights with scented wisterias, old-fashioned sweet peas and roses. Salvias and tender perennials augment the feast of colour July onwards. RHS Partner Garden. Featured in Somerset Life.

60 JEN'S GARDYN
4 Wroxham Drive, Little Stoke BS34 6EJ. Jennifer & Gary Ellington, http://www.jensgardyn.moonfruit.com. *5m N of Bristol city centre. From Cribbs Causeway r'about go*

S on A38. Over next r'about, L into Stoke Lane, 4th L into Braydon Ave, 1st L into Wroxham Dr. Light refreshments. **Adm £3, chd free. Sun 18, Sun 25 Aug (1-5).**
Inconceivably just 15' x 31'... Astonishingly vibrant, intimate, exotic jungle! Collections of palms, bamboos, grasses, cycads, hostas, fuchsias, clematis and fernery. Organically grown, aromatic, culinary, medicinal and magical herbs! Wildlife stream, goldfish pools, fragrant living arbor. Beautiful sculptures, shell grotto and tropical eye-candy galore! Inspirational and dynamic...a plantaholics paradise! Free herb tasting and talks. Featured on BBC Gardeners World, local press and radio.

KIA-ORA FARM & GARDENS
See Devon

61 ◆ KILVER COURT
Kilver St, Shepton Mallet BA4 5NF. Roger Saul, 01749 340410, charlotte@kilvercourt.com, www.kilvercourt.com. *Directly off A37, opposite Magners Cider factory*. Light refreshments. **Adm £4, concessions £3.50, chd free on NGS open days only. For normal admission see Kilver Court website. On NGS days RHS and Friends of Kilver Court cards are not accepted. For NGS: Sun 12 May, Sun 8 Sept (10-4). For other opening times and information, please phone or see garden website.**
Created in 1800s and restored in 1960s by the Showering family, who commissioned George Whiteleg to recreate his gold medal winning Chelsea garden. Millpond, boating lake, herbaceous borders and parterre with the most stunning feature being the Grade II listed viaduct built for the Somerset and Dorset railway. Local press and radio. Some slopes, rockery is not accessible but can be viewed.

GROUP OPENING

62 NEW KINGSTON ST MARY SECRET GARDENS
Kingston St. Mary, Taunton TA2 8HR, 01823 451673, gaye.fox@btinternet.com. *3.5m N of Taunton. Take Kingston Road North out of Taunton,signed in centre of village*. Cream teas and family-friendly activities in adjacent Village Hall. **Combined adm £4, chd free. Sun 30 June (2-6). Groups also welcome to both gardens by appt May to Aug.**

NEW MYRTLE COTTAGE
Church Lane. Gaye Fox

NEW WINPENNY COTTAGE
Winpenny Lane. Mrs Carla Griffith

Magical gardening in a small space: plants, design, art, conservation and much more. Myrtle Cottage: Gaye Fox an artist/designer with high walled garden. Rose-filled patio leads by 'secret' gate into the garden with its wild flower meadow, gazebo, herbaceous beds, stream and jungle, seating to savour its varying moods. Artist's work on show in studio. Myrtle Cottage featured in Somerset Life. Winpenny Cottage: organic gardening on a pocket handkerchief with abundance of exotic plants from around the world, a pond, mini jungle and collection of succulents. Wheelchair access to everywhere except the jungle walk at Myrtle Cottage, limited at Winpenny Cottage.

63 LIFT THE LATCH
Blacklands Lane, Forton, Chard TA20 2NF. Pauline & David Wright, 01460 64752, davidwright@ltlpublishing.freeserve.co.uk. *1½ m S of Chard. Blacklands Lane is off B3162 at E end of Forton from Chard*. **Adm £3, chd free. Visitors welcome by appt Jan to 20 Dec.**
Stunning country garden, densely planted with wide range of deciduous and evergreen trees, shrubs and perennials to produce spectacular colour throughout the year. The planting is arranged in descending terraces around large wildlife pond bordered by small stream, and also includes a raised ornamental Koi pond. Limited wheelchair access to upper terrace of garden only.

64 LITTLE GARTH
Dowlish Wake, Ilminster TA19 0NX. Roger & Marion Pollard, 01460 52594. *2m S of Ilminster. Turn R off Ilminster to Crewkerne rd at Kingstone Cross, then L, follow Dowlish Wake sign. Turn L at Glebe Cottage (white cottage) before reaching church. Turn R following signs. Speke Hall car park in front of nearby church may be used*. **Adm £3, chd free. Sats 27 Apr; 11, 25 May; 8, 15, 29 June; 13, 27 July; 10, 24 Aug; 7, 21 Sept (10.30-5.30). Visitors also welcome by appt 27 Apr to 21 Sept.**
½ -acre plantsman's garden for all seasons with many interesting and unusual perennials. Although essentially cottage style, emphasis is placed on the artistic arrangement of plants, using foliage, grasses and colour themes. Refreshments, plants for sale and public toilets at nearby Cider Mill, proceeds to Cider Mill.

Magical gardening in a small space: plants, design, art, conservation and much more . . .

65 LITTLE YARFORD FARMHOUSE
Kingston St Mary, Taunton TA2 8AN. Brian Bradley, 01823 451350, yarford@ic24.net. *3½ m N of Taunton. From Taunton on Kingston St Mary rd. At 30mph sign turn L at Parsonage Lane. Continue 1¼ m W, to Yarford sign. Continue 400yds. Turn R up concrete rd*. Light refreshments and cream teas. **Adm £4, chd free. Fri 10 May (11-5); Sat 11, Sun 12 May (2-6); Mon 13 May (11-5). Visitors also welcome by appt 14 May to 13 Sept. Guided tours of trees.**
This unusual garden embraces a C17 house (not open) overgrown with a tapestry of climbing plants. The 3 ponds exhibit a wide range of aquatic gems. Of special interest is the tree collection of rare and unusual cultivars, both broad leaf and conifer, all differing in form and colour including weeping and fastigiate. The 3 acres are a delight to both artist and plantsman. Mostly wheelchair access.

Somerset Lodge Garden

66 LUCOMBE HOUSE
12 Druid Stoke Ave, Stoke Bishop, Bristol BS9 1DD. Malcolm Ravenscroft, 01179 682494, famrave@gmail.com. *4m NW of Bristol centre. On L at top of Druid Hill. Garden on R 200m from junction.* Cream teas. **Adm £3, chd free. Sun 12 May, Sun 1 Sept (2-5). Visitors also welcome by appt.**
Woodland area with over 30 mature trees planted in last 3 yrs underplanted with bluebells and white foxgloves. Separate semi-formal area, formal patio and small herb garden. Untouched wild area under 200yr-old Lucombe oak. Landscape gardeners will be on site and happy to answer questions. Rough paths in woodland area, 2 steps to patio.

67 ◆ LYTES CARY MANOR
Nr Kingsdon TA11 7HU. National Trust, 01458 224471, www.nationaltrust.org.uk/lytes-cary-manor. *3m SE of Somerton. Signed from Podimore r'about at junction of A303, A37, take A372.* **Adm £9, chd £4.50. For NGS: Wed 22 May (10.30-5); Wed 10 July, Tue 10 Sept (11-5). For other opening times and information, please phone or see garden website.**
Arts and Crafts style garden with many contrasts, topiary and mixed borders. Home of medieval herbalist Henry Lyte. Estate walks: Garden and Behind the Scenes tour at 2pm. Simple food kiosk and seating.

68 NEW THE MANOR
Lympsham, Weston-super-Mare BS24 0DT. James & Lisa Counsell. *5m S of Weston-super-Mare and 5m N of Burnham on Sea. From M5 J22, take A370 towards Weston-super-Mare and drive through East Brent, until you reach L turn towards Lympsham village. From Weston, take A370 towards Taunton, through Bleadon, R after 1m. Drive down Lymspham road ½ m to cricket pitch and school on R. Entrance to garden through 2 stone gateposts on L, school on R at junction of Church Rd, Lympsham Rd and Rectory Way.* Home-made teas. **Adm £4, chd free. Sat 15, Sun 16 June (2-5.30).**
Early C19 gothic pinnacled, castellated Rectory Manor House with 2 octagonal towers set in 10 acres of formal and semi-formal garden surrounded by paddocks and farmland. The garden's main features are its carefully preserved, fully working Victorian kitchen garden and greenhouse, an arboretum of trees from all parts of the world, large stocked fish pond and a beautiful old rose garden.

GROUP OPENING

69 MARSHFIELD GARDENS
Marshfield SN14 8LR. *7m NE of Bath. From Bath A46 to Cold Ashton r'about, turn R onto A420. Marshfield 2m. From M4 J18, turn R onto A46 and L at Cold Ashton r'about. From Chippenham A420 8m W. Follow yellow arrows into village. Parking, see signs on the day.* **Combined adm £5, chd free. Sat 25, Sun 26 May (1-5).**

NEW BRAMLEY COTTAGE
Sheepfair Lane. Mr & Mrs Glyn Watkins

42 HIGH STREET
Mary & Simon Turner.
Access from back lane

43 HIGH STREET
Linda & Denis Beazer

44 HIGH STREET
Mr Paul Sawyer

111 HIGH STREET
Joy & Mervyn Pierce.
Bristol end of village

NEW 113 HIGH STREET
Kirstie Long.
Access via drive at side of house

NEW 116 HIGH STREET
Mr Doug Bond

NEW 3 OLD SCHOOL COURT
Mrs R Crew

4 OLD SCHOOL COURT
Mrs Jenny Wilkinson

WEIR COTTAGE
Weir Lane. Ian & Margaret Jones

NEW YEELES HOUSE
24 Back Lane. Kay and Peter Little.
Entry halfway down Back Lane

11 gardens in large, interesting village. Late spring gardens with newly-planted vegetable plots; 5 new gardens. 111 High St open for lunches and teas 12 noon (proceeds to Marshfield Almshouses). Gardens open 1pm. 25 May - guided walk by Cotswold Wardens around access trail of Marshfield (01225 891229 for info). Plants for sale in some gardens. Regrettably no disabled access except for teas.

MATARA GARDENS OF WELLBEING
See Gloucestershire

70 ◆ MIDNEY GARDENS
Mill Lane, Midney, Somerton TA11 7HR. David Chase and Alison Hoghton, 01458 274250, davidandalison@midneygardens.co.uk, www.midneygardens.co.uk. *1m SE of Somerton. 100yds off B3151. From Podimore r'about on A303 take A372. After 1m R on B3151 towards Street. After 2m L on bend into Mill Lane.* Home-made teas. **Adm £3.50, chd free. For NGS: Sun 21 Apr, Fri 7 June, Fri 12 July, Fri 20 Sept (11-5). For other opening times and information, please phone or see garden website.**
New 1-acre plantsman's garden, where unusual planting combinations, interesting use of colour, subtle themes and a natural flowing style create a garden full of variety and inspiring ideas. Incl seaside garden, Clarice Cliff inspired garden, white garden, vegetables and borders. Nursery offers herbaceous perennials, alpines, herbs and grasses. Featured in Somerset Country Gardener.

71 THE MILL HOUSE
Torbay Road, Castle Cary BA7 7DR. Peter Davies. *Do not go into Castle Cary Town Centre, but follow signs to Torbay Rd Industrial Estate (W). Entrances to Trading Estate on L. Park on Trading estate rds. Garden 200yds on R up Torbay Rd.* Cream teas. **Adm £3.50, chd free. Sat 18, Sun 19 May (2-5.30).**
Approx 1-acre terraced sloping garden, with stream and waterfalls. Emphasis on natural look. Many interesting plants mingled with native flora. Bog garden with selection of candelabra and farina primulas, rodgersias and hostas; vegetable plot, orchard and paddock. Limited wheelchair access, steep slopes.

72 ◆ MILTON LODGE
Old Bristol Road, Wells BA5 3AQ. Simon Tudway Quilter, 01749 672168, www.miltonlodgegardens.co.uk. *½ m N of Wells. From A39 Bristol-Wells, turn N up Old Bristol Rd; car park first gate on L.* **Adm £5, chd free. For NGS: Sun 19 May, Sun 9 June, Sun 14 July (2-5). For other opening times and information, please phone or see garden website.**
Mature Grade II, terraced garden conceived c1900. Sloping ground transformed into architectural terraces with profusion of plants, capitalising on views of Wells Cathedral and Vale of Avalon. 1960, garden lovingly restored to former glory, orchard replaced with raised collection of ornamental trees. Cross Old Bristol Rd to 7-acre woodland garden, the Combe, natural peaceful contrast to formal garden at Milton Lodge. First opened for NGS 1962. Open Tues, Weds, Suns, BHs, Easter - 31 Oct (2-5).

Picturesque village . . . 2 contrasting gardens . . .

73 ◆ MONTACUTE HOUSE
Montacute TA15 6XP. National Trust, 01935 823289, grahame.meaden@nationaltrust.org.uk, www.nationaltrust.org.uk. *4m W of Yeovil. NT signs off A3088 & A303.* **Adm £11, chd £5.50 incl house. For NGS: Sun 16 June (10-5). For other opening times and information, please phone or see garden website.**
Magnificent Elizabethan house with contemporary garden layout. Fine stonework provides setting for informally planted mixed borders and old roses; range of garden features illustrates its long history. 80% wheelchair access.

74 16 MONTROY CLOSE
Henleaze, Bristol BS9 4RS. Sue & Rod Jones, 0117 9624599. *3½ m N of Bristol city centre. On B4056 continue past all shops, R into Rockside Dr (opp Eastfield Inn). Up hill, across Xrds into The Crescent. Montroy Close is 3rd turning on L.* Home-made teas. **Adm £3, chd free. Sun 9 June (2-5.30). Visitors also welcome by appt June.**
Large SW-facing town garden on corner plot. 20 ft stream, informal pond with pebble beach, pergola and seats. Lawn with curving flower beds incl ferns, shrubs, perennials, climbers, small rock garden with water feature, unusual partitioned greenhouse with alpine bench. 8 ft wide arch with climbers. Hanging baskets and many pots of fuchsias. Width of gateway: 79cm.

75 ◆ NEWARK PARK
Ozleworth GL12 7PZ. National Trust, 01453 842644, www.nationaltrust.org.uk/newarkpark. *2m E of Wotton-under-Edge. Follow signs to Ozleworth off A4135 Tetbury to Dursley road. Disabled drop off/parking at house.* Tea/coffee and cake. **Adm £7.10, chd £3.70. For NGS: Thur 14 Feb (11-4). For other opening times and information, please phone or see garden website.**
Wild woodland garden with a good display of snowdrops and aconites. Wonderful views to the South. Limited wheelchair access, steep slopes.

GROUP OPENING

76 NUNNEY GARDENS
Horn Street, Nunney, Nr Frome BA11 4NP. *3m SW of Frome. A361 from Glastonbury, turn left at Nunney Catch signed Nunney. At Market Place turn left over bridge, up Castle Hill to Quarry Car Park on right. Walk back down Castle Hill, Horn St on right before bridge.* Teas at the artist's workshop - Somerset Lodge. **Combined adm £5, chd free. Sat 6 July (11-4).**

THE MILLER'S HOUSE
17 Horn Street. Caroline Toll

SOMERSET LODGE GARDEN
Lord and Lady Watson
www.karenwatson.co.uk

Picturesque village clustered around C15 church, duck pond fed by Nunney Brook, ruined medieval castle with moat and market square.
2 contrasting gardens, Miller's House: garden of person who considers herself to be an untidy planter! Over small steps, top garden is accessible, part of remaining garden and millpond can be seen from here. Many seats to enjoy views of mostly perennial garden, rockeries, terraced borders, veg. patch leading to bridge over Nunney Brook, shrubbery and wild walk, encouraging nature alongside brook and leat which feeds

the romantic millpond. Small modern sculptures incorporated in garden. Somerset Lodge: unusual garden created over 15 years from rough pasture by artist owner and first time gardener. Signature colour blue. Garden is a patchwork with different aspects, unusual topiaries, tall yew pyramids, drifts of lavender and rampant roses lead to glorious meadow with large drifts of various Rugosa roses and orchard of unusual hawthorns. Artist's ceramic sculptures incorporated into garden. Adjoining farmyard still a work in progress. Featured in Somerset Country Gardener, local press and radio. Very limited wheelchair access in both gardens.

77 NYNEHEAD COURT

Nynehead, Wellington TA21 0BN. Nynehead Care Ltd, 01823 662481/07834 773441. *2m S of Wellington. M5 J26 B3187 towards Wellington. R on r'about marked Nynehead & Poole, follow lane for 1 m, take Milverton turning at fork.* Cream teas in Orangery. **Adm £3, chd free. Sun 16 June, Sun 14 July (2-5). Visitors also welcome by appt. Large groups must book 1 month in advance.**

Nynehead Court Gardens are on English Heritage's list of gardens of historic interest. Once the ancestral home of the Sanford family. Gardens laid out during the Victorian period, points of interest - pinetum, ice house, parterre and extended walks within parkland of old estate. Garden tours by head gardener, Justin Cole, start 2pm prompt (tour lasts 1 hr approx). Featured in Mendip Times. Gravel paths, slight slopes, cobbled yard (ice house).

78 NEW THE OLD RECTORY, DOYNTON

18 Toghill Lane, Doynton, Bristol BS30 5SY. Edwina & Clive Humby. *At heart of village of Doynton, between Bath and Bristol. Follow Toghill Lane up from The Holy Trinity Church about 500 metres, around cricket field to car park field. Signs to garden.* Home-made teas. **Adm £3.50, chd free. Sat 8 June (11-3).**

Doynton's Grade II-listed Georgian Rectory's walled garden and extended 15-acre estate. Renovated over 12 years, it sits within an area of natural beauty. Garden has diversity of modern and traditional elements, fused to create atmospheric series of garden rooms. It is both a landscaped and large kitchen garden, featuring a canal, vegetable plots, fruit cages and tree house. Partial wheelchair access, some narrow gates and uneven surfaces.

79 THE OLD RECTORY, LIMINGTON

Church St, Limington, nr Yeovil BA22 8EQ. John Langdon & Paul Vintner, 01935 840127, jdlpv@aol.com. *2m E of Ilchester. From A303 exit on A37 to Yeovil/Ilchester. At 1st r'about L to Ilchester/Limington. 2nd R to Limington. Continue 1½ m.* Cream teas. **Adm £3.50, chd free. Sat 15, Sun 16 June (2-6). Visitors also welcome by appt, prebook by email or telephone.**

Romantic walled gardens of 1½ acres. Formal parterres, herbaceous borders. Many unusual shrubs and trees incl 200 yr-old lucombe oak, liriodendron, paulownia, davidia, laburnocytisus, leycesteria and poncirus. Extensive planting of bulbs incl galanthus, anemone blanda, winter aconites, tulips and alliums. New this year we will be including a garden design clinic to be run by a member of The Society of Garden Designers and past Chelsea judge. Please bring along photographs or drawings of any problem areas in your garden for suggestions and advice. Featured in Somerset Country Gardener. Gravel drive, one gentle slope only.

THE OLD RECTORY, NETHERBURY

See Dorset

THE OLD VICARAGE

See Devon

80 ORCHARD WYNDHAM

nr Williton TA4 4HH. The Trustees. *7m SE of Minehead, 16m from Taunton. Out of Williton take A39 towards Minehead then signed L and up long drive to house. Exit past Bakelite Museum.* Teas in adjacent Bakelite Museum. **Adm £3, chd free. Sun 19 May (2.30-5.30).**

Garden of historic house (not open on NGS days) in parkland setting: woods, interesting old trees, borders, rose walk, 2 small lakes, wild garden.

81 ORGANIC BLOOMS

Latteridge Road (Latteridge Hill), Latteridge, Bristol BS37 9TS. Jo & Chris Wright, www.organicblooms.co.uk. *5m W of Yate. 6m from J16 of M5, on B4059 that runs between A38 and Iron Acton. Look for green corrugated steel fence that borders site and main road. Approx 200 metres from Latteridge duck pond and green, heading towards A38.* Light refreshments. **Adm £3, chd free. Sun 14 July (12-4).**

Working cut flower nursery run as social enterprise. We specialise in growing traditional cut flower crops from sweet williams and anemone to zinnias, dahlias and sweetpeas. Flowers are grown using organic principles. Hand-tied bouquet demonstration. Tour and talk on organic gardening. Our paths are woodchip, so access may be more difficult in very wet conditions.

New garden design clinic . . .

82 OVERBROOK COTTAGE

Lower Cocklake, nr Wedmore BS28 4HF. Margaret Castle, 01934 712420, m.castle105@btinternet.com. *1m E of Wedmore. Take B3151 from Wedmore towards Cheddar for 1m. Turn R following sign to Draycott & Nyland. Cottage after 3 bungalows on R.* Light refreshments, cream teas, home-made gluten and dairy free cakes available. **Adm £2.50, chd free. Sat 15, Sun 16 June (11-6). Visitors also welcome by appt June to July 3 vehicles, if more please consult. 15 people max.**

Cottage garden developed over 14 yrs when lawns were dug up, soil and stone imported to create raised beds; gravel paths laid and a steep learning curve began! Now established with many plants, shrubs, fruit and vegetables growing side-by-side. Vertical posts carry clematis, honeysuckle and roses. Gravel paths.

83 OWL COTTAGE
Coker Marsh, East Coker, Yeovil BA22 9JZ. Sue Richards. *4m S of Yeovil. Take A37 out of Yeovil (to Dorchester), straight on at Red House r'about, next R for E Coker, next R, 1st house on R.* Home-made teas. **Adm £3, chd free. Sats, Suns 15, 16 June; 7, 8 Sept (2-5.30).**
450 yr old thatched cottage with well in 1/2 -acre garden planted for yr-round interest. Herbaceous borders, trees, shrubs and vegetables. Chickens in 1/2 -acre paddock. Situated on outskirts of lovely village of East Coker (TS Elliott buried here, William Dampier born in village). Garden is divided into smaller areas. Small pond, and several home bred dalias. Vegatables. Some gravel.

84 3 PALMER'S WAY
Hutton, Weston-super-Mare BS24 9QT. Mary & Peter Beckett, 01934 815110, macbeckett@tiscali.co.uk. *3m S of Weston-super-Mare. From A370 (N or S) follow signs to Hutton. L at PO, 1st L into St Mary's Rd, 2nd R to car park. Very limited disabled parking at garden.* Home-made teas. **Adm £3, chd free. Sun 9, Sun 30 June (2-5.30). Visitors also welcome by appt June/July, Wednesdays only.**
Average suburban plot, no long vistas or space for your daily constitutional (too many plants!) but enjoy strolling this densely packed plantsman's garden or sit and admire the 'informal tapestry' of fruit trees among unusual perennials, herbs, grasses, hardy geraniums, wildlife ponds and box knot garden. Home-made preserves using locally-grown produce for sale. Some steps. Wheelchair access more limited if wet.

PEMBERLEY LODGE
See Gloucestershire

PEN MILL FARM
See Dorset

85 NEW PENNY BROHN CANCER CARE
Chapel Pill Lane, Pill, North Somerset BS20 0HH. Penny Brohn Cancer Care, www.pennybrohncancercare.org. *4m W of Bristol. Off A369. Clifton Suspension Bridge to M5 (J19 Gordano Services). Follow signs to Penny Brohn Cancer Care and to Pill and Ham Green.* Home-made teas. **Adm £3.50, chd free. Sun 30 June (11-5).**
Penny Brohn Cancer Care's 3.5-acre tranquil garden surrounds a Georgian mansion with many mature trees, wild flower meadow, newly-developed flower garden, cedar summerhouse, fine views from historic gazebo overlooking R Avon, courtyard gardens with water features. The garden is maintained by volunteers and plays an active role in the Charity's Living Well with Cancer approach. Music. Some gravel and grass paths.

We have built our own garden room from recycled materials . . .

ALLOTMENTS

86 PRETORIA ROAD ALLOTMENTS
Patchway, Bristol BS34 5PX. www.growpretoria.org. *6m N of Bristol city centre. From Cribbs Causeway A4018 follow signs for Patchway onto Highwood Rd. At r'about, 2nd exit, L onto Durban Rd. R onto Cavendish Rd then immed L onto Pretoria Rd. Entrance to allotments between houses 84 and 86. Some parking on site, otherwise please park considerately in neighbouring rds.* Home-made teas. **Adm £3.50, chd free. Sat 15 June (11-3).**
Large allotment site on flat ground. Grass paths between plots. Vegetables, soft fruits (incl grapes and hops), trees, herbs and flowers. Shop selling garden sundries, jams, pickles and handmade cards. Many plot-holders will be available to answer questions. Plants and produce for sale. Disabled access WC. Partial disability access, grass pathways between plots.

87 ◆ PRIOR PARK LANDSCAPE GARDEN
Ralph Allen Drive, Bath BA2 5AH. National Trust, 01225 833422, www.nationaltrust.org.uk. *1m S of Bath. Visitors are advised to use public transport as there is no parking at Prior Park or nearby, except for disabled visitors. Telephone for 'How to Get There' leaflet.* Light refreshments, situated by the lakes. **Adm £6.30, chd £3.30. For NGS: Sun 5 May (10-5.30). For other opening times and information, please phone or see garden website.**
Beautiful and intimate C18 landscape garden created by Bath entrepreneur Ralph Allen (1693-1764) with advice from the poet Alexander Pope and Capability Brown. Sweeping valley with magnificent views of city. Palladian bridge and lakes. Wilderness restoration, completed in 2007, involved reinstating the serpentine lake, cascade and cabinet to their former glory. Drifts of wild garlic carpeting the woodlands. Limited wheelchair access (the wilderness and view point are accessible, steep slopes, gravel paths and steps in rest of garden).

ALLOTMENTS

88 NEW PRIORSWOOD ALLOTMENTS
Obridge, Taunton TA2 7PZ. Taunton Deane. *Obridge Road. Signed off A3259 Priorswood Rd to W of viaduct and Obridge PH. Large green gate before railway tunnel. Parking on nearby roads.* Cream teas. **Combined adm £4, chd free. Sun 18 Aug (2-5.30).**
Gardening for all! Over 100 individual plots in 5.5 acres, all very different, growing seasonal fruit and vegetables, herbs and flowers. We have built our own garden room from recycled materials as our Community centre. We also have an orchard where Taunton Transition Group will demonstrate Seasonal Cooking. Teas at Garden Room, plant stall and preserves on sale. Children's Discovery Trail. Limited wheelchair access.

PRIORY HOUSE
See Wiltshire

REGENCY HOUSE
See Devon

89 ROCK HOUSE
Elberton BS35 4AQ. Mr & Mrs John Gunnery, 01454 413225. *10m N of Bristol. 3½ m SW Thornbury. From Old Severn Bridge on M48 take B4461 to Alveston. In Elberton, take 1st turning L to Littleton-on-Severn & turn immed R.* **Adm £3, chd free (share to St Johns Church, Elberton). Suns 3, 10 Feb 2013; Suns 2, 9 Feb 2014 (11-4). Visitors also welcome by appt 27 Jan to 29 Sept, incl groups.**
1-acre walled garden undergoing improvement. Pond and old yew tree, mixed borders, cottage garden plants and developing woodland with many snowdrops.

Colourful courtyard with old farm implements . . .

GROUP OPENING

90 ROSE COTTAGE & COLEY COURT
East Harptree/Coley BS40 6BY. *5m N of Wells, 15m S of Bristol BS40 6BY/6AN. Please see individual gardens for directions.* Home-made teas at Rose Cottage. **Combined adm £4.50, chd free. Sun 7 Apr (2-5).**

COLEY COURT
Coley. Mrs M J Hill.
From A39 at Chewton Mendip take B3114 for 2m, before E Harptree turn R signed Coley and Hinton Blewitt. From E Harptree, R at bottom of High St onto B3114 towards Chewton Mendip for 1m, L at sign to Coley

ROSE COTTAGE
East Harptree. Bev & Jenny Cruse.
From B3114 turn into High St in East Harptree. L at Clock Tower and immed R into Middle St, up hill for 1m. From B3134 take East Harptree turning opp Castle of Comfort, continue 1½ m. Car parking in field opp cottage
Visitors also welcome by appt 8 Apr to 31 July Rose Cottage only, adm £3.50, home-made teas.
01761 221627
bandjcruse@gmail.com

2 contrasting gardens. Coley Court: early Jacobean house (not open). 1-acre garden, stone walls, spring bulbs; 1-acre old mixed orchard. Rose Cottage: 1-acre hillside cottage garden with panoramic views over Chew Valley. Garden is carpeted with primroses, spring bulbs and hellebores and in summer with roses and hardy geraniums. It is bordered by stream and established mixed hedges. Plenty of seating areas to enjoy the views and teas. Wildlife area and pond in corner of car park field. Rose Cottage award winner Bath in Bloom. Featured in local press and radio.

91 RUGG FARM
Church Street, Limington, nr Yeovil BA22 8EQ. Morene Griggs, Peter Thomas & Christine Sullivan, 01935 840503, griggsandthomas@btinternet.com. *2m E of Ilchester. From A303 exit on A37 to Yeovil/ Ilchester. At 1st r'about L to Ilchester/Limington, 2nd R to Limington. Continue 1½ m.* Cream teas. **Adm £4, chd free. Sat 13, Sun 14 July (2-5.30). Visitors also welcome by appt July to Sept.**
2-acre garden created since 2007 around former farmhouse and farm buildings. Diverse areas of interest. Ornamental, kitchen and cottage gardens, lawn and borders, courtyard container planting, orchard, wildlife meadows and pond, developing shrubberies, woodland plantings and walk (unsuitable for wheelchairs). Featured metalwork designs. Exuberant annuals and perennials throughout. Compost Champion in residence. Featured in Somerset Country Gardener. Some gravel paths.

92 SELF REALIZATION MEDITATION HEALING CENTRE GARDEN
Laurel Lane, Queen Camel BA22 7NU. SRMHC Charitable Trust, 01935 850266, info@selfrealizationcentres.org, www.selfrealizationcentres.org. *6m NE of Yeovil. A359 S from Sparkford r'about (on A303) to Queen Camel. Garden 100yds off High St, R after school and before Hair Studio. Restricted mobility parking at SRMHC centre. Follow signs for other car parking.* Cream teas. **Adm £3.50, chd free. Wed 22 May (2-5).**
Peaceful 3-acre garden with varied vistas, trees and lawns, surrounding spiritual retreat and training Centre. Stunning herbaceous borders and fragrant old roses around C17 farmhouse (not open). Wildflower tumps, pond, newly planted maze, herb beds and meditation room garden. Oriental garden and koi pond by arrangement only. Gravel drive and some uneven flagstone paths. Steps avoidable with detour.

93 SERRIDGE HOUSE
Henfield Road, Coalpit Heath BS36 2UY. Mrs J Manning, 01454 773188. *9m N of Bristol. On A432 at Coalpit Heath T-lights (opp church), turn into Henfield Rd. R at PH, ½ m small Xrds, house with iron gates on corner. At junction of Henfield Rd and Ruffet Rd, parking on Henfield Rd.* Cream teas/refreshments by arrangement. **Adm £4 afternoon/£5 evening, chd free. Groups of 10+ welcome by appt July to Aug.**
2½ -acre garden with mature trees, heather and conifer beds, island beds mostly of perennials, woodland area with pond. Colourful courtyard with old farm implements. Lake views and lakeside walks. Unique tree carvings.

SHAPCOTT BARTON ESTATE
See Devon

94 ◆ SHERBORNE GARDEN
Litton, Norton-Radstock BA3 4PP. Mr & Mrs John Southwell, 01761 241220. *15m S of Bristol. 15m W of Bath, 7m N of Wells. On B3114 Chewton Mendip to Harptree rd, ½ m past The Kings Arms. Car park in field.* **Adm £4, chd free. For NGS: Sun 17, Mon 18 Feb; Sun 18 Aug (11-4). For other opening times and information, please phone.**
4½ -acre gently sloping garden with small pinetum, holly wood and many unusual trees and shrubs. Cottage garden leading to privy. 3 ponds linked by wadi and rills with stone and wooden bridges. Hosta walk leading to pear and nut wood. Rondel and gravel gardens with grasses and phormiums. Collections of day lilies, rambling and rose species. Good

labelling. Plenty of seats. Featured on Radio Bristol for presentation of *Prunus Incisa Variegata* after 30 yrs garden opening for NGS.

SHUTELAKE
See Devon

SNAPE COTTAGE PLANTSMAN'S GARDEN
See Dorset

95 SOLE RETREAT

Haydon Drove, Haydon, West Horrington, Wells BA5 3EH. Jane Clisby, 01749 672648/ 07790 602906, janeclisby@aol.com, www.soleretreat.co.uk. *3m NE of Wells. From Wells take B3139 to the Horringtons. Keep on main road. after 3m L for Sole Retreat Reflexology, garden 50yds on L.* Refreshments. **Adm £3, chd free.** Suns 16 June; 21 July (11-5). **Visitors also welcome by appt 1 - 31 July, adm £3.50, chd free.**

It is a challenge to garden at almost 1000ft on the Mendip Hills AONB, close to the cathedral city of Wells. Peaceful garden full of old garden favourites set in 1/3 acre. Cottage garden style within dry stone walls and raw face bedrock. 9 differing areas incl sun terrace, water feature and pool, therapy and hidden contemplation gardens, fernery and vegetable plot. Best Overall Garden in the Parish Garden in Bloom 2011. Local press and radio features. Some gravel.

96 SOMERFOSS

Bath Road, Oakhill, Radstock BA3 5AG. Ewan & Rosemary Curphey, 01749 840542, ECurphey@aol.com. *3m N of Shepton Mallet. From Oakhill School ¼ m N on A367. Parking in lay-by on R.* Refreshments by arrangement. Individuals and groups welcome day or eve by appt **15 May to 14 Aug, adm £4, chd free.**

Descend drive, an unusual and surprising garden awaits you at Somerfoss. The S-facing valley provides several different plant areas and beds full of unusual shrubs and perennials. Particular features, natural rock area with Mediterranean feel and damp area with stand of wild orchids flowering in June. Large raised deck, great place to view garden and enjoy a cup of tea or coffee with

Badgers Acre

homemade cake. Featured in local press and radio. Steep slopes, steps and uneven ground.

97 NEW 52 SOUTH LAWN

Locking, Weston-Super-Mare BS24 8AD. Bill & Shirley Marlow, 01934 822077, sparra52@hotmail.co.uk. *2 m E of Weston-super-Mare. M5 J21 onto A370, L at 2nd r'about onto A371. Over 1st r'about, R into Locking Village just before garage onto Elm Tree Rd then 2nd R into South Lawn. Last bungalow on R.* Home-made teas. **Adm £3, chd free.** Sat 15, Sun 16, Sat 29, Sun 30 June; Sat 20, Sun 21 July (11-5). **Visitors also welcome by appt June to Aug.**

Garden reflects owners' creative interests and innovative ideas, not only in the evergreen and fragrant planting; the variety of textures, topiary, colours and themes stimulate the imagination. Stroll around winding pathways into attractive rooms with seating areas in which to relax and enjoy the unusual features. Gaudi-style mosaic features. Original sculptures and folly, stained glass features amongst evergreen and fragrant planting with a variety of seating areas to relax and enjoy an interesting garden. Scrumptious cakes.

98 SOUTH MEADE

Meade Lane, Seavington St Mary TA19 0QL. Charo & Robin Ritchie. *3m E of Ilminster. Via B3168 to Seavington St Michael, near PH turn down Water St to Seavington Millennium Hall, shop and café for Car Parking signs and Map directions to garden. Children 6+ only.* Home-made teas/light bites at village cafe. **Adm £3, chd free.** Sat 15, Sun 16 June (11-4); Mon 22 to Sat 27 July (2-6). **Also open 1 The Pheasant 15th/16th June, combined adm £4.00, chd free.**

Beautiful country views all around. Mix of herbaceous, shrubs, roses and over 100 clematis are dotted around the garden. Absorb nature sitting in the Mediterranean patio and special Japanese pond areas. The searching for garden perfection is what fills my heart with joy. Exhibition of watercolour floral art.

99 SOUTHFIELD FARM

Farleigh Road, Backwell, Bristol BS48 3PE. Pamela & Alan Lewis. *6m S of Bristol. On A370, 500yds after George Inn towards WSM. Farm directly off main rd on R with parking.* Home-made teas. **Adm £4, chd free.** Sun 28 July (2-5).

2-acre owner-designed garden of rooms with lovely views. Mixed shrub and herbaceous borders, perennials, roses, climbers, pergolas and arbours with seating. Formal and wildlife ponds. Orchard, vegetable garden, terracing and courtyards. Paths to 1-acre maturing copse and to large pond with bird hides and seating. Tearoom in old stable courtyard. Wheelchair access to most areas. Some gravel. Small courtyard and terrace only accessible by steps.

100 ◆ SPECIAL PLANTS

Greenways Lane, Nr Cold Ashton SN14 8LA. Derry Watkins, 01225 891686, www.specialplants.net. *6m N of Bath. From Bath on A46, turn L into Greenways Lane just before r'about with A420.* **Adm £4, chd free. Coaches welcome by appointment only. For NGS: Thurs 20 June; 18 July; 15 Aug; 19 Sept; 17 Oct (11-5). For other opening times and information, please phone or see garden website.**
Architect-designed ¾ -acre hillside garden with stunning views. Started autumn 1996. Exotic plants. Gravel gardens for borderline hardy plants. Black and white (purple and silver) garden. Vegetable garden and orchard. Hot border. Lemon and lime bank. Annual, biennial and tender plants for late summer colour. Spring-fed ponds. Bog garden. Woodland walk. Allium alley. Free list of plants in garden. Featured in Somerset Country Gardener, Gardens Illustrated, The Garden and BBC Gardeners' World magazines.

SPRINGDALE

See Devon

101 NEW 95 ST JOHNS LANE

Bedminster, Bristol BS3 5AB. Anna Henderson. *SW of Bristol Centre. Few mins SW of Temple Meads Station. Main road up to junction, R into St Johns Lane, down to r'about, 2nd exit following main rd, 5th house on L.* **Combined adm £4, chd free. Sat 15, Sun 16 June (2-6). Combined with1 Frobisher Rd, Ashton Gate.**
Delightful small rear garden behind 1930s semi on busy road. Planted out just 3 years ago on totally neglected site. Very heavily planted with climbers, bamboos, gunnera, indian bean tree, hostas, tetrapanax, and many perennials. 3 seating areas. Side entrance to garden - limited wheelchair access down centre path through garden.

102 STANTON COURT NURSING HOME

Stanton Drew BS39 4ER. Pam Townsend. *5m S of Bristol. From Bristol on A37, R onto B3130 signed Chew Magna. 1.4m, L at old thatched toll house into Stanton Drew, 1st property on L.* Light lunches/cream teas. **Adm £2.50, chd free. Sun 7 Apr; Sun 8 Sept (1-4).**
2 acres of tranquil gardens around gracious Georgian House (grade II listed). Mature trees, extensive herbaceous borders with many interesting plants and spring bulbs. Large vegetable garden, fruit trees and soft fruit bushes; raised beds planted by local primary school. Gardener Judith Chubb Whittle keeps this lovely garden interesting in all seasons. Wheelchair access to most parts.

Mystical Evening on 15 November . . .

103 STOBERRY GARDEN

Stoberry Park, Wells BA5 3LD. Frances & Tim Young, 01749 672906, stay@stoberry-park.co.uk, www.stoberry-park.co.uk. *½ m N of Wells. From Bristol - Wells on A39, L into College Rd and immed L through Stoberry Park.* Light refreshments. **Adm £5, chd free. Wed 10 Apr, Sun 25 Aug (2-5.30). Evening Opening £5, chd free, wine, Fri 15 Nov (5-8).**
With breathtaking views over Wells and the Vale of Avalon, this 6-acre family garden planted sympathetically within its landscape provides a stunning combination of vistas accented with wildlife ponds, water features, sculpture, 1½ -acre walled garden, sunken garden, gazebo, potager, lime walk. Colour and interest in every season; spring bulbs, irises, roses, acer glade, salvias. A Mystical Evening on 15 November from (5-8). Featured in local press and radio.

GROUP OPENING

104 STOGUMBER GARDENS

TA4 3SZ. *11m NW of Taunton. On A358. Signed to Stogumber, W of Crowcombe. Maps given to all visitors.* Home-made teas in Village Hall. **Combined adm £5, chd free. Sun 16 June (2-6).**

BRAGLANDS BARN
Kingswood. Simon & Sue Youell
www.braglandsbarn.com

BROOK HOUSE
Brook Street. Jan & Jonathon Secker-Walker

CRIDLANDS STEEP
Mrs A M Leitch

HIGHER KINGSWOOD
Fran Vesey

KNOLL COTTAGE
Elaine & John Leech
Visitors also welcome by appt 1 Apr to 31 Oct, £3.
01984 656689
john@knoll-cottage.co.uk
www.knoll-cottage.co.uk

POUND HOUSE
Barry & Jenny Hibbert

6 delightful and very varied gardens in picturesque village at edge of Quantocks. 2 surprisingly large gardens in village centre, a semi-wild garden, and 3 very large gardens on outskirts of village, with many rare and unusual plants. Conditions range from waterlogged clay to well-drained sand. Features include a walled garden, ponds, bog gardens, rockery, vegetable and fruit gardens, a collection of over 80 different roses, even a cider-apple orchard. Fine views of surrounding countryside. Dogs on leads allowed in 5 gardens. Wheelchair access to main features of all gardens.

GROUP OPENING

105 STOKE ST MARY GARDENS

Taunton TA3 5BY, 01823 442556, stepcroc@btinternet.com, www.rebeccapow.com. *2½ m SE of Taunton. From M5 J25 take A358 S towards Ilminster. Turn 1st R after 1½ m. 1st R in Henlade then 1st L signed Stoke St Mary. Car parking in village hall car park, no parking at either garden.* Home-made teas either garden. **Combined adm £5,**

chd free. Fyrse Cottage and Tuckers Farmhouse open together by appointment. Visitors welcome by appt 1 Apr to 30 Sept.

FYRSE COTTAGE
Miss S Crockett

TUCKERS FARMHOUSE
Rebecca Pow & Charles Clark.
Two doors down from PH
www.rebeccapow.com

Village nestles below beautiful backdrop of Stoke Hill. C13 church (with stained glass windows by the renowned Patrick Reyntiens), popular Half Moon Inn, playground at nearby Village Hall. Fyrse Cottage: designed by owner landscape architect, Stephanie Crockett, secluded cottage garden with oriental flavour. ½ acre of lush planting with pond, pergola, lots of sculptures and Chinese pots. Birch avenue leading to ½ -acre wildlife area. Gravel and flower gardens. Oil paintings and cards for sale. Tuckers Farmhouse: gardening journalist Rebecca Pow's family garden in lovely rural location. Formal/cottage-style extending to natural with wildlife. Jekyll-style border and 'busy persons' gravel/grass border. Topiary, exotic planting in courtyard, pear tree avenue. Fruit garden, raised bed vegetable garden, a very small smallholding. Emphasis on wildlife gardening with mown paths through wild grasses and trees. Personal tours by Stephanie and Rebecca! Featured in Kitchen Garden, Amateur Gardening, Somerset Life and on BBC Somerset 'What's Growing On'. Wheelchair access to Tuckers Farmhouse.

106 ◆ STON EASTON PARK

Ston Easton BA3 4DF, 01761 241631, info@stoneaston.co.uk, www.stoneaston.co.uk. *On A37 between Bath & Wells. Entrance to Park from main rd A37 in centre of village, opp bus shelter.* **Adm £3.50, chd £1. For NGS: Wed 4 Sept (10.30-4). For other opening times and information, please phone or see garden website.**

A hidden treasure in the heart of the Mendips. Walk through the glorious parkland of the historic 30 acres of Repton landscape, alongside the quietly cascading River Norr, to the productive walled Victorian kitchen garden. Visit the octagonal rose garden, stunning herbaceous border, numerous colourful flowerbeds, fruit cage and orchard. The parkland at Ston Easton Park is now the only remaining Humphry Repton landscape in Somerset. His 'Red Book', a facsimile demonstrating his plans in 'before' and 'after' stages, illustrated in wonderful watercolours, can be found in the hotel reception. Local press and radio features. Gravel paths, steep slopes, shallow steps.

There is something of interest for everyone . . .

GROUP OPENING

107 STONE ALLERTON GARDENS

Stone Allerton, Axbridge BS26 2NW. *2m from A38, signed from Lower Weare.* Home-made teas. **Combined adm £5, chd free. Sun 26, Mon 27 May (2-5.30).**

BADGERS ACRE
New Road. Lucy Hetherington & Jim Mathers.
Please phone for directions
Visitors also welcome by appt 1 Apr to 30 June, please request refreshments when booking.
01934 713159
lucyhetherington@btinternet.com

NEW FERN COTTAGE
Mrs Alison Smith

GREENFIELD HOUSE
Mr & Mrs Bull

Three distinctly different beautiful gardens on the edge of the Somerset levels. Badgers Acre: 1-acre garden. Colour themed mixed borders. Secret walk, pond and colourful rockery. Semi-circular tulip and allium bed surrounded by box. Vegetable potager with pergola draped in rambling roses and clematis. Greenfield House: 4 main gardens: grass, shrub, colour and cottage. Many unusual plants in vast range of perennials, shrubs and bulbs. Garden created from garden centre bargains. Ponds and chickens. Fern Cottage: Charming small cottage garden full of interesting plants and ideas.

GROUP OPENING

108 NEW STOWEY GARDENS

Bristol BS39 5UP. *10m W of Bath. Stowey Village A368 between Bishop Sutton and Chelwood. Follow signs for parking in field.* Home-made teas. **Combined adm £6, chd free. Sun 16 June (2-6).**

NEW DORMERS
Stowey Bottom. Mr & Mrs G Nicol

NEW 1 STOWEY CROSS COTTAGE
Stowey Bottom. Deborah & Kim Heather

NEW STOWEY MEAD
Stowey. Mr Victor Pritchard

NEW VICARAGE COTTAGE
Stowey. Mr & Mrs P Haggett

The 4 gardens are all new to the NGS and provide a varied and interesting afternoon's viewing. From some large, informal and interesting planting to designer-planned and loved smaller gardens there is something of interest for everyone. All within 10 mins walk of parking area, natural progression from one to another. Delicious home-made teas for sale (partly in aid of the ancient Church as well as the NGS charities).

109 SUTTON HOSEY MANOR

Long Sutton TA10 9NA. Roger Bramble, 0207 390 6700, rbramble@bdbltd.co.uk. *2m E of Langport, on A372. Gates N of A372 at E end of Long Sutton.* Home-made teas. **Adm £4, chd £2. Sun 14 July (2.30-6). Visitors also welcome by appt Aug to Sept.**

3 acres, of which 2 walled. Lily canal through pleached limes leading to amelanchier walk past duck pond; rose and juniper walk from Italian terrace; Judas tree avenue; Ptelea walk. Ornamental potager. Drive-side shrubbery. Music by players of Sinfonia of Westminster.

110 NEW 1 THE PHEASANT
Water Street, Seavington, Ilminster TA19 0QH. Lis Tope. *Fronting Water Street 300 yards down on right hand side from village. From Ilminster travel east along old A303 for 3 miles.On approaching Seavington St. Michael pass garage on left and turn sharp right into Water Street. Garden is approximately 300 yards down on the right. From South Petherton enter village and turn left into Water Street immediately after The Volunteer pub.* **Sat 15, Sun 16 June (11-4). Open with Southmeade, combined admission £4, chd free.**
A small recently landscaped cottage garden with a range of herbaceous perennials. No wheelchair access.

111 THORNBURY PARK ESTATE/THE SHEILING SCHOOL
The Sheiling School, Park Road, Thornbury BS35 1HP. Camphill Communities Thornbury. *12m N of Bristol, off A38. From Thornbury High St, down Castle St towards Thornbury Castle. This leads into Park Rd, bearing R, past castle and St Mary's Church on L. Pass high stone wall on L for entrance to estate and gardens. Parking further on, next L at Castle School.* Home-made teas. **Adm £4, chd free. Sat 8, Sun 9 June; Sun 22 Sept (11-4.30).**
Estate comprises 15 acres of mature parkland with many magnificent trees, together with 35 acres of biodynamic/ organic farmland, hay meadow, orchard, walled garden with secluded artist's garden behind it. Ponds, stream and small woodland trails. A rarely seen part of Thornbury's conservation area. Sensory garden with bog garden, pond, stream, flow form, and sculptures, flower meadow, grass labyrinth, biodynamic fruit and vegetables, cut flower garden, farm animals. Crafts and art from our school community. New for 2013 - prairie style meadow with emphasis on late summer and autumn flowers. Featured in Daily Telegraph Gardening 'Portrait of the garden as a place of art and therapy'. Wheelchair access to some areas difficult but most of parkland estate accessible.

112 ◆ TINTINHULL
nr Yeovil BA22 8PZ. National Trust, 01935 823289, www.nationaltrust.org.uk. *5m NW of Yeovil. Tintinhull village. Signs on A303, W of Ilchester.* **Adm £7, chd £3.50. For NGS: Sun 16 June (10-7). For other opening times and information, please phone or see garden website.**
C17 and C18 house (part open). Famous 2-acre garden in compartments, developed 1900 to present day, influenced by Hidcote; many good and uncommon plants. Featured in Somerset Country Gardener. Care, uneven paths.

113 TRANBY HOUSE
Norton Lane, Whitchurch, Bristol BS14 0BT. Jan Barkworth. *5m S of Bristol. 1/2 m S of Whitchurch. Leave Bristol on A37 Wells Rd, through Whitchurch village, 1st turning on R signed Norton Malreward.* Home-made teas. **Adm £3.50, chd free. Wed 12 June, Thur 11 July (1-4); Sun 18 Aug (2-5).**
1 1/4 -acre well-established informal garden, designed and planted to encourage wildlife. Wide variety of trees, shrubs and cottage garden plants; ponds and wild flower meadow. Garden still evolving to provide colour and interest from spring to autumn. Plants for sale in aid of The Wildlife Trust.

114 TRUFFLES
Church Lane, Bishop Sutton, Bristol BS39 5UP. Sally Monkhouse. *10m N of Wells. On A368 Bath to Weston-Super-Mare rd take rd opp Bishop Sutton PO/stores towards Hinton Blewett. 1st R into Church Lane.* Home-made teas. **Adm £3.50, chd free. Sat 20, Sun 21 July (2-6).**
2 acres, intriguing and surprising, relaxing garden set in countryside. Formal and semi-formal planting linked with meandering paths. Secret Sylvan valley and small stream, amphitheatre, wildlife pond, wild flower bed and meadows. 1/4 -acre kitchen garden with long, large waist-high raised beds, herb and rose garden, new flower borders. Lots of seating. Featured in Somerset Country Gardener. Gravel and grass paths, some slopes and steps. Parking at top of drive.

115 ◆ TYNTESFIELD
Wraxall BS48 1NX. National Trust, 0844 800 4986, www.nationaltrust.org.uk/ tyntesfield. *7m SW of Bristol. Nr Nailsea, entrance off B3128. Follow brown signs.* **Adm £9, chd £4.50. For NGS: Sat 20 July (10-6). For other opening times and information, please phone or see garden website.**
Remarkably intact Victorian garden with formal bedding display, rose garden, and a productive walled kitchen garden which offers produce for sale to the public, and supplies the Cow Barn Kitchen on site. The grounds also include an arboretum, wildflower meadows and an orangery. Talks and demonstrations throughout the day. Steep slopes, steps and gravel paths throughout garden. Courtesy bus from Visitor Centre to Kitchen Garden.

© Rowan Isaac

"Lemon drizzle cake, Victoria sponge ... yummy!"

116 ◆ UNIVERSITY OF BRISTOL BOTANIC GARDEN
Stoke Park Road, Stoke Bishop, Bristol BS9 1JG. University of Bristol, 0117 3314906, botanic-gardens@bristol.ac.uk, www.bristol.ac.uk/Depts/BotanicGardens. *1/4 m W of Durdham Downs. By car from city centre, proceed across Downs towards Stoke Bishop, crossing T-lights at edge of Downs. Stoke Park Rd, 1st turning R off Stoke Hill and garden is 100 yds along on R. Parking in walled garden car park or on Open Day alternative arrangements signed opp garden entrance in Churchill Hall Car Park.* Light refreshments. **Adm £4.50, chd free.** **For NGS: Sun 7 July (10-5). For other opening times and information, please phone or see garden website.**
Exciting contemporary Botanic Garden with organic flowing network of paths which lead visitors through collections of Mediterranean flora, rare natives, useful plants (incl European and Chinese herbs) and those that illustrate plant evolution. Large floral displays illustrating pollination/flowering plant evolution. Glasshouses, home to Giant Amazon Waterlily, tropical fruit and medicinal plants, orchids and cacti. Unique sacred lotus collection. Special tours of garden throughout day; plants for sale; refreshments. Wheelchair available to borrow from Welcome Lodge. Wheelchair friendly route through garden available upon request, also accessible WC.
♿ ❀ ☕

Growing collection of clematis . . . !

117 VELLACOTT
Lawford, Crowcombe TA4 4AL. Kevin & Pat Chittenden. *9m NW of Taunton. Off A358, signed Lawford. For directions phone 01984 618249.* Home-made teas. **Adm £3, chd free.** **Thurs 30 May; 6, 20 June; 4, 18 July; Tue 17, Thur 19 Sept (12-5).**
1-acre informal garden on S. facing slope with lovely views of the Quantock and Brendon Hills. Profusely stocked with wide selection of herbaceous plants, shrubs and trees. Other features include ponds, ruin and potager. Plenty of places to sit and enjoy the surroundings. Featured in Somerset Country Gardener. Not suitable for wheelchairs.
❀ ☕

VENN CROSS RAILWAY GARDENS
See Devon

118 ◆ THE WALLED GARDENS OF CANNINGTON
Bowling Green (Church St), Cannington TA5 2HA. Bridgwater College, 01278 655042, walledgardens@bridgwater.ac.uk, canningtonwalledgardens.co.uk. *3m NW of Bridgwater. On A39 Bridgwater-Minehead rd - at 1st r'about in Cannington 2nd exit, through village. War memorial, 1st L into Bowling Green (Church St) then 1st L.* **Adm £3.50, chd free. For NGS: Sun 2 June, Sun 1 Sept (10-5). For other opening times and information, please phone or see garden website.**
Lying within the grounds of medieval priory, the gardens have undergone extensive redevelopment over last few yrs. Features, both classic and contemporary, incl hot herbaceous border, stunning blue garden, sub-tropical walk, Victorian-style fernery and large botanical glasshouse. Gravel paths.
♿ ❀ ☕

119 WATCOMBE
92 Church Road, Winscombe BS25 1BP. Peter & Ann Owen, 01934 842666, peter.o@which.net. *From Axbridge, A371 to A38. R up hill, next L into Winscombe Hill. After 1m reach The Square. Pink house on L after further 150yds down hill. From Bristol, take A38 S; straight on through Sidcot T-lights, pass Texaco garage on R, next R into Winscombe Hill, then as above.* Home-made teas incl gluten-free cake/cream teas. **Adm £3, chd free. Sun 21 Apr, Sun 19 May, Wed 5 June (2-5). Visitors also welcome by appt Apr to July.**
3/4 -acre mature Edwardian garden with colour-themed, informally planted mixed borders. Topiary, box hedging, lime walk, pleached hornbeams, orchard, vegetable plot, 2 small formal ponds, many unusual trees and shrubs. Strong framework separating several different areas of the garden; pergola with varied wisteria; lime walk; unusual topiary; growing collection of clematis! See video clips on http://www.threesixtyvr.co.uk/tours/Watcombe_2/Watcombe.html. Most areas accessible by wheelchair with minimal assistance.
♿ 🐕 ❀ ☕ ☎

WATERDALE HOUSE
See Wiltshire

120 WAYFORD MANOR
Wayford, Crewkerne TA18 8QG. *3m SW of Crewkerne. Turning N off B3165 at Clapton; or S off A30 Chard to Crewkerne Rd.* Light refreshments. **Adm £5, chd free. Sun 14 Apr, Sun 19 May (2-5).**
The mainly Elizabethan manor (not open) mentioned in C17 for its 'fair and pleasant' garden was redesigned by Harold Peto in 1902. Formal terraces with yew hedges and topiary have fine views over W Dorset. Steps down between spring-fed ponds past mature and new plantings of magnolia, rhododendron, maples, cornus and, in season, spring bulbs, cyclamen, giant echium. Primula candelabra, arum lily, gunnera around lower ponds. Featured in Somerset Country Gardener.
🐕 ☕

GROUP OPENING

121 NEW WEDMORE GARDENS
9m W of Wells. 4m from A38 signed from Lower Weare. On B3139 between Wells and Burnham-on-Sea. Sat Nav postcode BS28 4AB. Maps given to all visitors. Parking in village car park Cheddar Road or street parking. Home-made teas St Mary's Church, Church Street. **Combined adm £5, chd free.**
Sat 15, Sun 16 June (2-6).

NEW ALLINGTON HOUSE
The Borough. Barbara and Martin Horton

NEW COTSWOLD
Guildhall Lane. John and Jill Morse

NEW DAMSON COTTAGE
Plud Street. Anne and Michael Blandford

NEW MANOR LODGE
Manor Lane. Jean and Philip Hamlin

NEW POUND COTTAGE
Combe Batch. Margaret and David Kitson

5 distinctive secret gardens in lovely Saxon village in heart of Somerset countryside, views of Mendips. Wedmore won 2 Gold Awards in RHS Britain in Bloom competition. Allington House: SW facing corner plot in heart of village. Makeover 2010 with gravelled areas bordered by shrub and flowerbeds established formal plantings retained. Cotswold: small retirement garden, series of rooms. Hot coloured planters contrast with coolness of ferns on edge of Wedmore Brook. Damson Cottage: short walk from centre, small walled cottage garden with borders of clematis, roses, honeysuckle. Vegetable patch, fruit cage, greenhouse. Manor Lodge: walled garden evolved over 50 years, grown from cuttings and village plant sales, scrambling to create tranquil retreat. Fruit trees & bushes, modest vegetable patch. Pound Cottage: new S-facing terraced garden for old cottage. Excavated 2011, planted 2012 to create colour and yr. round interest. Top terrace gravel for free seeding. Many tubs and pots for seasonal changes. Plant stall at church.

122 WELLFIELD BARN
Walcombe Lane, Wells BA5 3AG. David & Virginia Nasmyth, 01749 675129, david.nasmyth@talktalk.net. *½ m N of Wells. From A39 Bristol to Wells rd turn R at 30mph sign into Walcombe Lane. Entrance at 1st cottage on R, parking signed*. Home-made teas. **Adm £3.50, chd free. Tue 28 May (11-5). Visitors also welcome by appt 29 May to 30 June, max 29 seat coach on site.**
1½ -acre gardens, made by owners over the past 17yrs from concrete farmyard. Ha-ha, wonderful views, pond, lawn, mixed borders, formal sunken garden, grass walks and interesting young and semi-mature trees. Structured design integrates house and garden with landscape. New areas under development. Special interest plants are the hardy geranium family. Featured as garden of the month in May edition of Mendip Times; local press and radio features. Moderate slopes in places.

Five distinctive secret group gardens . . .

GROUP OPENING

123 WEST BRISTOL GARDENS
BS9 2LR/2PY. *3m NW of Bristol city centre. Please see individual gardens for directions*. Home-made teas. **Combined adm £5, chd free. Sun 16 June (2-6).**

4 HAYTOR PARK
BS9 2LR. Mr & Mrs C J Prior. *Edge of Coombe Dingle. From A4162 Inner Ring Rd between A4 Portway & A4108 Falcondale Rd, take turning into Coombe Bridge Ave, Haytor Park is 1st turning L. No parking in Haytor Park*
Groups also welcome by appt Apr to Aug. 07779 203626 p.l.prior@gmail.com

159 WESTBURY LANE
Coombe Dingle BS9 2PY. Maureen Dickens. *L A4162/Sylvan Way, B4054/Shirehampton Rd, R to Westbury Lane. 1st house on R*
Visitors also welcome by appt May to Sept. 01179 043008 159jmd@googlemail.com

Pair of interesting and contrasting gardens. 4 Haytor Park: Do come and discover dreaming dragons, shady glades, plant-stuffed borders and hidden seats. Pass under flower-swathed arches to tiny ponds and sunny spaces encircled with pots and paraphernalia. Where does it all end, at the green-roofed hideaway or beyond the secret garden? 159 Westbury Lane: Gently sloping garden. Large patio at rear, walled beds, pond and many other features. Some common and unusual plants with successional planting to give colour throughout yr. Closely planted in owner's style. From patio, garden is seen through rambler and other climber-covered wooden archways. Garden now coming into shape and changing rapidly as plants fill out. Lots of half-hidden artefacts and mirror feature.

124 WESTBROOK HOUSE
West Bradley BA6 8LS. Keith Anderson and David Mendel, 01458 850604, mail@westbrook-bed-breakfast.co.uk. *4m E of Glastonbury. From A361 at W Pennard follow signs to W Bradley (2m)*. **Adm £3.50, chd free (share to West Bradley Church). Sat 20 Apr, Sat 15 June (11-5). Visitors also welcome by appt.**
4 acres comprising 3 distinct gardens with formal layout around house which leads to meadow and orchard with spring bulbs, species roses and lilacs. Planting and layout began 2004. Featured in The English Garden.

WESTON HOUSE
See Dorset

WILLAND OLD VILLAGE GARDENS
See Devon

WOLVERHOLLOW
See Dorset

WOOD BARTON
See Devon

125 18 WOODGROVE ROAD
Henbury, BRISTOL BS10 7RE. Peter & Ruth Whitby. *4m N of Bristol. M5 J17, follow B4018, R at 3rd r'about signed Blaise Castle. R opp Blaise Castle car park - rd next to Avon riding centre*. Home-made teas. **Adm £3, chd free. Sat 8, Sat 15 June (2-5).**
Medium-sized garden divided into 3 sections. Traditional flower garden with Bonsai display and small wildlife pond. Cottage garden with greenhouse and plant sale area. Small orchard with dwarf fruit trees and small vegetable garden. Peter's art studio open for sale of watercolour and oil paintings, 10% to NGS. Gravel path from patio.

13 WOOLLEY GREEN
See Wiltshire

126 ◆ THE YEO VALLEY ORGANIC GARDEN AT HOLT FARM

Bath Road, Blagdon BS40 7SQ. Mr & Mrs Tim Mead, 01761 461650, gardens@holtfarmsgroup.co.uk, www.theyeovalleyorganicgarden.co.uk. *12m S of Bristol. Off A368 Weston-super-Mare to Bath rd, between Blagdon & Ubley. Entrance to Yeo Valley Organic Garden is approx ½ m outside Blagdon towards Bath, on LH-side, then follow garden signs passed the dairy.* **Adm £5, chd free. For NGS: Sun 21 Apr (10-5). For other opening times and information, please phone or see garden website.**

The only organic ornamental garden as certified by the Soil Association, 6.5 acres of contemporary planting, quirky sculptures, bulbs in their thousands, purple palace, glorious meadows and posh veggie patch. Great views, green ideas, light lunches and teas available. Garden lectures, events, workshops and exhibitions held throughout the year. Featured in Country Living and Telegraph.

127 YEWS FARM

East Street, Martock TA12 6NF. Louise & Fergus Dowding, 01935 822202, louise@louisedowding.co.uk, www.louisedowding.co.uk. *In the small town of Martock. Turn off main road through village at Market House, onto East St, past PO, garden 150 yds on R between Nag's Head and White Hart.* Home-made teas. **Adm £4.50, chd free. Sun 14, Mon 15 July (2-6). Groups of 20-50 also welcome by appt 1 May to 22 Aug.**

1 acre of theatrical planting in large walled garden. Outsized plants in jungle garden. Sculptural planting for height, shape, leaf and texture. Self-seeded gravel garden, box and bay ball border, espalier apples, cloud pruning. Working organic kitchen garden. Hens, pigs and orchard. We grow the Martock broad bean, the only known survivor of a mediaeval variety of broad bean. Visitors may throw Beauty of Bath apples to the pigs. Child friendly garden, with hammocks, swing etc. Featured in Edible Garden and Cottage Homes & Interiors magazines and on BBC2 The Great British Food Revival. Mostly wheelchair access.

Bristol Area County Volunteers

County Organiser
Su Mills, 3 Over Court Mews, Over Lane, Almondsbury BS32 4DG, 01454 615438, susanlmills@gmail.com

County Treasurer
Ken Payne, 2 Old Tarnwell, Stanton Drew, Bristol BS39 4EA, 01275 333146, kg.payne@yahoo.co.uk

Booklet Co-ordinator/County Booklet Advertising
Jean Damey, 2 Hawburn Close, Brislington, Bristol BS4 2PB, 0117 9775587, jeandamey@gmail.com

Assistant County Organisers
Angela Conibere, Christmas Cottage, Church Rd, Oldbury-on-Severn BS35 1QA, 01454 413828, aeconibere@hotmail.com
Graham Guest, The Caves, Downside Road, Backwell BS48 3DH, 01275 472393, gandsguest@btinternet.com
Christine Healey, The Walled Garden, The Street, Olveston, BS35 4DR, 01454 612795, christine.healey@uwclub.net
Margaret Jones, Weir Cottage, Weir Lane, Marshfield, Chippenham SN14 8NB, 01225 891229, ian@weircott.plus.com
Jeanette Parker, The School Yard, 2 High St, Wickwar GL12 8NE, 01454 299699, jeanette_parker@hotmail.co.uk
Jane Perkins, Woodland Cottage, Oldbury-on-Severn BS35 1PL, 01454 414570, janekperkins@gmail.com

Somerset County Volunteers

County Organiser
Lucy Hetherington, Badgers Acre, Stone Allerton, Axbridge BS26 2NW, 01934 713159, lucyhetherington@btinternet.com

County Treasurer
David Bull, Greenfield House, Stone Allerton, Nr Axbridge BS26 2NH, 01934 712609, d.bull08@btinternet.com

Publicity
Roger Peacock, Barum, 50 Edward Road, Clevedon BS21 7DT, 01275 341584, barum@blueyonder.co.uk

Presentations
Dave & Pru Moon, 9 Catherston Close, Frome BA11 4HR, 01373 473381, davidmoon202@btinternet.com

Group Tour Coordinator
Dilly Bradley, Little Yarford Farmhouse, Kingston St Mary, Taunton TA2 8AN, 01823 451350, yarford@ic24.net

Booklet Distribution
Chris & Dianne McKinley, Grove Rise, Downhall Drive, Wembdon, Bridgwater TA6 7RT, 01278 421675, chrismckinley80@hotmail.com

Photographer
Simon Parry, 90 Moorland Road, Weston-Super-Mare, Avon BS23 4HT, 01934 420201, simon@imagesbysimonparry.co.uk

Beneficiaries
Sarah Wilcox, Epworth, Kingston St. Mary, Taunton TA2 8HZ, 01823 451402, wilcoxsarah@hotmail.co.uk

Assistant County Organisers
Brian & Dilly Bradley, Little Yarford Farmhouse, Kingston St Mary, Taunton TA2 8AN, 01823 451350, yarford@ic24.net
Patricia Davies-Gilbert, Coombe Quarry, West Monkton, Taunton TA2 8RE, 01823 412187, pdaviesgilbert@btinternet.com
Alison Highnam, Candleford, Fernhill, East Stour, Nr Gillingham SP8 5ND, 01747 838133, allies1@btinternet.com
Laura Howard, The Old Manse, Fivehead, Taunton TA3 6QH, 01460 282911, laurafivehead@btinternet.com
Rosemary Lee, 6 Buttle Close, Shepton Beauchamp TA19 0LU, 01460 249594, rosemary2410@plus.net
Judith Stanford, Bowden Hill Cottage, Chilcompton, Radstock BA3 4EN, 01761 233045, judithstanford.ngs@hotmail.co.uk

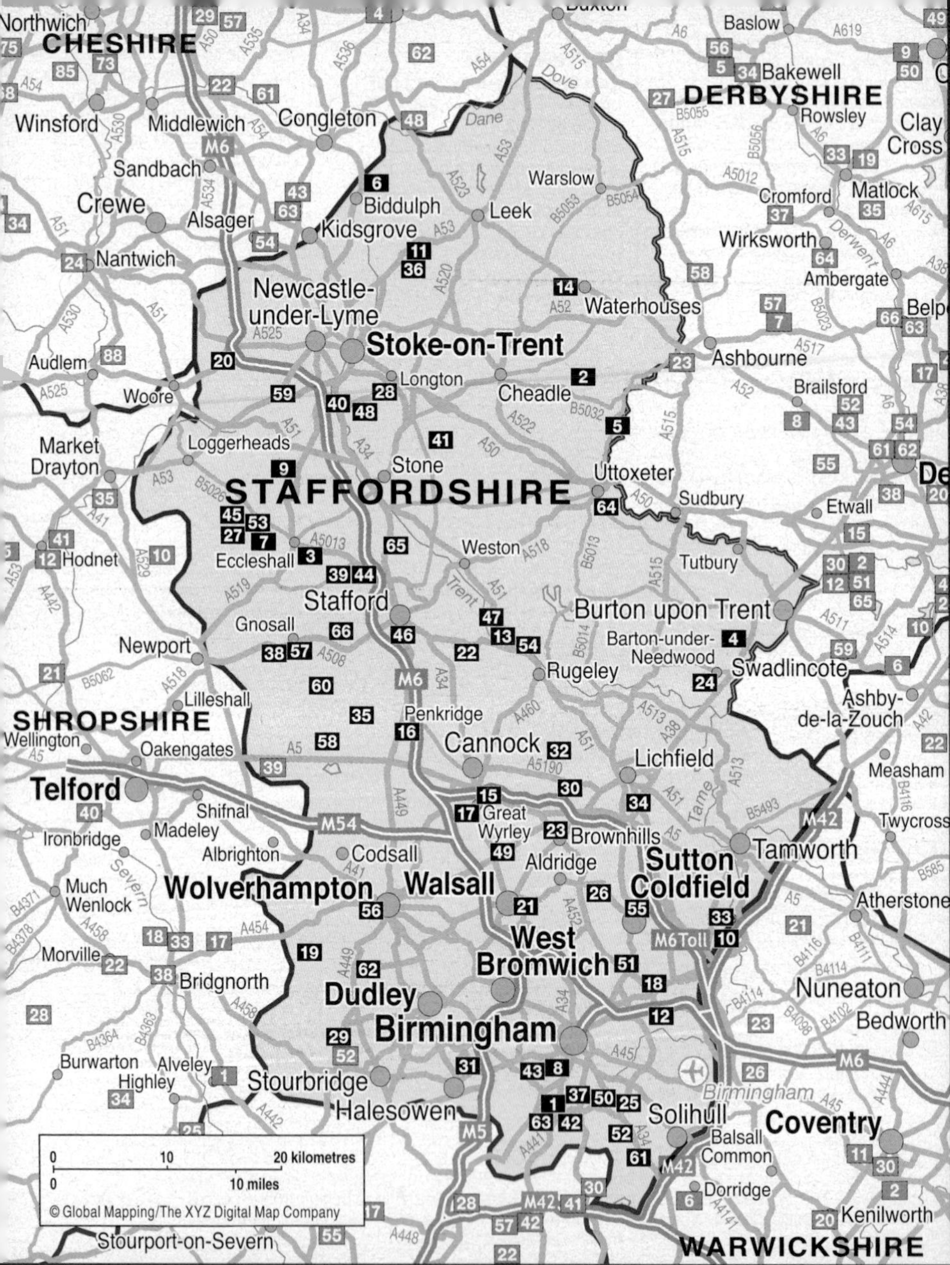

nvestec Wealth & Investment supports the NGS

Opening Dates

February

Sunday 24
21 Four Seasons

March

Sunday 10
18 198 Eachelhurst Road

Sunday 24
46 23 St Johns Road

April

Sunday 7
34 Millennium Garden

Wednesday 10
8 Birmingham Botanical Gardens

Sunday 28
43 Pereira Road Gardens

May

Sunday 5
25 Hall Green Gardens
66 Yew Tree Cottage

Monday 6
27 Heath House

Wednesday 8
8 Birmingham Botanical Gardens

Saturday 11
21 Four Seasons

Sunday 12
17 Dorset House
21 Four Seasons
61 Wits End

Two gardens as different as Monet's soft pastel colours are to Vincent's bright sunflowers . . .

Friday 17
46 23 St Johns Road (Evening)

Saturday 18
21 Four Seasons

Sunday 19
1 Acorns Children's Hospice
5 The Beeches
12 Castle Bromwich Hall Gardens
47 The Secret Garden
54 Tanglewood Cottage

Saturday 25
40 The Old Dairy House

Sunday 26
26 Hamilton House
27 Heath House
40 The Old Dairy House
49 Small But Beautiful
66 Yew Tree Cottage

Monday 27
10 Bridge House

June

Sunday 2
22 The Garth
44 The Pintles

Friday 7
13 Coley Cottage
47 The Secret Garden

Sunday 9
3 Ashcroft and Claremont
34 Millennium Garden
55 91 Tower Road
56 19 Waterdale

Wednesday 12
4 Bankcroft Farm

Friday 14
2 Alton Towers Gardens
61 Wits End

National Gardens Weekend

Saturday 15
6 Biddulph Grange Garden
31 13 Lansdowne Road
41 The Old Vicarage

Sunday 16
31 13 Lansdowne Road
41 The Old Vicarage
59 Wilkins Pleck
61 Wits End
63 Woodbrooke Quaker Study Centre

Wednesday 19
4 Bankcroft Farm

Sunday 23
13 Coley Cottage
33 Middleton Hall
37 Moseley Gardens South
38 The Mount, Coton, Gnosall
45 Rowley House Farm
47 The Secret Garden
48 Silverwood

Saturday 29
28 High Trees
65 Yarlet House

Sunday 30
5 The Beeches
11 Brooklyn
22 The Garth
24 Grafton Cottage
30 Kosynook
43 Pereira Road Gardens
44 The Pintles
51 190 Station Road
57 West View

July

Sunday 7
7 Birch Trees
14 Colour Mill
27 Heath House
39 The Mount, Great Bridgeford
58 The Wickets
61 Wits End

Thursday 11
58 The Wickets

Saturday 13
56 19 Waterdale (Evening)
64 Woodleighton Grove Gardens

Sunday 14
16 4 Dene Close
31 13 Lansdowne Road
32 Lilac Cottage
35 Mitton Manor
36 Moorfield
64 Woodleighton Grove Gardens

Sunday 21
17 Dorset House
23 The Good Life
24 Grafton Cottage
25 Hall Green Gardens
50 56 St Agnes Road
66 Yew Tree Cottage

Saturday 27
54 Tanglewood Cottage

Sunday 28
5 The Beeches
18 198 Eachelhurst Road
39 The Mount, Great Bridgeford
49 Small But Beautiful
59 Wilkins Pleck

August

Friday 2
61 Wits End

Sunday 4
9 The Bowers
24 Grafton Cottage
61 Wits End

Saturday 10
21 Four Seasons

Sunday 11
20 10 Fern Dene
24 Grafton Cottage

Wednesday 14
13 Coley Cottage
47 The Secret Garden

Thursday 22
14 Colour Mill

Saturday 24
26 Hamilton House (Evening)

Sunday 25
7 Birch Trees
23 The Good Life
58 The Wickets

Monday 26
7 Birch Trees
10 Bridge House

September

Sunday 1

5 The Beeches

Friday 13

54 Tanglewood Cottage (Evening)

Sunday 22

31 13 Lansdowne Road

53 Sugnall Hall, Walled Kitchen Garden

Sunday 29

53 Sugnall Hall, Walled Kitchen Garden

October

Sunday 13

29 John's Garden

Saturday 26

21 Four Seasons

Sunday 27

21 Four Seasons

Gardens open to the public

2 Alton Towers Gardens

6 Biddulph Grange Garden

8 Birmingham Botanical Gardens

12 Castle Bromwich Hall Gardens

33 Middleton Hall

53 Sugnall Hall, Walled Kitchen Garden

By appointment only

15 12 Darges Lane

19 The Elms

42 Paul's Oasis of Calm

52 172 Stonor Road

60 Willow Cottage

62 The Wombourne Wodehouse

Also open by Appointment

5 The Beeches

7 Birch Trees

9 The Bowers

10 Bridge House

14 Colour Mill

16 4 Dene Close

17 Dorset House

22 The Garth

24 Grafton Cottage

25 16 Burnaston Road, Hall Green Gardens

25 37 Burnaston Road, Hall Green Gardens

25 36 Ferndale Road, Hall Green Gardens

25 120 Russell Road, Hall Green Gardens

31 13 Lansdowne Road

35 Mitton Manor

36 Moorfield

38 The Mount, Coton, Gnosall

39 The Mount, Great Bridgeford

43 50 Pereira Road, Pereira Road Gardens

45 Rowley House Farm

46 23 St Johns Road

47 The Secret Garden

51 190 Station Road

54 Tanglewood Cottage

56 19 Waterdale

58 The Wickets

61 Wits End

64 Karibu, Woodleighton Grove Gardens

64 Woodleighton Grove Gardens

66 Yew Tree Cottage

The Gardens

1 NEW ACORNS CHILDREN'S HOSPICE

103 Oak Tree Lane, Selly Oak, Birmingham B29 6HZ. Mr Chris Reed, www.acorns.org.uk. *From Selly Oak: past old hospital and school on L. Garden on brow and bend of hill. Just after Selly Oak School turn L opp turning for Langleys Rd. From Cotteridge: Linden Rd A4040 past Cadburys on R. Garden on R at top of hill opp turning for Langleys Rd.* Home-made teas. **Adm £4, chd free. Sun 19 May (12-4.30).**

4 beautifully designed gardens. Delightful children's garden in the centre, large rear garden intended to provide wonderful multisensory experience, memorial garden using water and stone to signify perpetual remembrance and striking quiet garden utilising natural greys and silvers to create a sense of peace and tranquillity. Wheelchair entrance via gate at front and side of building.

2 ◆ ALTON TOWERS GARDENS

Alton, Stoke on Trent ST10 4DB. Alton Towers Resort, 01538 703344, www.altontowers.com. *6m N of Uttoxeter. From A50, follow 'brown signs' for Alton Towers. At the theme park follow signs for Alton Towers Hotel. Enter garden through the Alton Towers Hotel.* **Adm £4, chd free. For NGS: Fri 14 June (3.30-6). For other opening times and information, please phone or see garden website.**

Alton Tower's magnificent early C19 gardens, designed by the flamboyant 15th Earl of Shrewsbury, feature pools, pagoda fountain, statues, mature trees, shrubs, rhododendrons and azaleas set in a steep sided valley with steep walks and viewing terraces. Access via the 1m long 'woodland walk' from the Alton Towers Hotel. Refreshments in hotel. One of the first gardens in Staffordshire to 'Open' for the NGS in 1932. Unfortunately the historic nature of the gardens makes them unsuitable for wheelchair users or those with limited mobility.

Garden using water and stone to signify perpetual remembrance . . .

GROUP OPENING

3 NEW ASHCROFT AND CLAREMONT

Eccleshall ST21 6JP. *7m W of Stafford. J14 M6. At Eccleshall end of A5013 the garden is 100 metres before junction with A518. On street parking nearby.* Home-made teas at Ashcroft. **Combined adm £4, chd free. Sun 9 June (2-5).**

ASHCROFT
Peter & Gillian Bertram

NEW CLAREMONT
Maria Edwards

Two gardens as different as Monet's soft pastel colours are to Vincent's bright sunflowers. Ashcroft is a 1-acre wildlife-friendly garden, pond and covered courtyard. Rooms flow seamlessly around the Edwardian house. Herb bed, treillage, greenhouse with raised beds. Find the topiary peacock that struts in the gravel bed. In the woodland area Gollum lurks in the steps of the ruin. Claremont is a small town garden its design based on feng shui principles. Manicured lawns, herbaceous borders, shrubs, perennials and annuals. Constantly evolving with colour and new features, maintaining interest throughout the year. Come and be inspired!

ASKEW COTTAGE
See Derbyshire

4 BANKCROFT FARM
Tatenhill, Burton-on-Trent DE13 9SA. Mrs Penelope Adkins. *2m SW of Burton-on-Trent. Take Tatenhill Rd off A38 Burton-Branston flyover. 1m, 1st house on L approaching village. Parking on farm.* **Adm £3, chd free. Weds 12, 19 June (2-5).**
Lose yourself for an afternoon in our 1½-acre organic country garden. Arbour, gazebo and many other seating areas to view ponds and herbaceous borders, backed with shrubs and trees with emphasis on structure, foliage and colour. Productive fruit and vegetable gardens, wildlife areas and adjoining 12-acre native woodland walk. Picnics welcome. Gravel paths.

5 THE BEECHES
Mill Street, Rocester ST14 5JX. Ken & Joy Sutton, 01889 590631, joy@joy50.orangehome.co.uk. *5m N of Uttoxeter. On B5030, turn R into village by JCB factory. By Red Lion PH & mini r'about take rd for Marston Montgomery. Garden 250yds on R, car park at JCB Academy.* Home-made teas. **Adm £3, chd free. Suns 19 May; 30 June; 28 July; 1 Sept (1.30-5). Visitors also welcome by appt May to Aug.**
Stroll along the driveway containing island beds planted with mixed shrubs and perennials, and enter a stunning plant lover's garden of approx ⅔ acre, enjoying views of surrounding countryside. Box garden, mixed shrubs incl rhododendrons and azaleas, vibrant colour-themed herbaceous borders, roses, clematis and climbing plants, fruit trees, pools and late flowering perennials also raised vegetable and soft fruit garden, yr-round garden. Gold award and overall winner East Staffs Brighter Borough gardens. Wheelchair access to most of the garden.

6 ◆ BIDDULPH GRANGE GARDEN
Grange Road, Biddulph ST8 7SD. National Trust, 01782 517999, www.nationaltrust.org.uk. *3½ m SE of Congleton. 7m N of Stoke-on-Trent off A527, Congleton to Biddulph rd.* **Adm £7, chd £3.50. For NGS: Sat 15 June (11-5.30). For other opening times and information,**

4 Dene Close

please phone or see garden website.
Amazing Victorian garden created by Darwin contemporary and correspondent James Bateman as an extension of his beliefs, scientific interests and collection of plants. Visit the Italian terrace, Chinese inspired garden, dahlia walk and the oldest surviving golden larch in Britain brought from China by the great plant hunter Robert Fortune. Featured in the Independent as one of the 10 Best Gardens to visit.

7 BIRCH TREES
Copmere End, Eccleshall ST21 6HH ST21 6HH. Susan & John Weston, 01785 850448, johnweston123@btinternet.com. *1½ m W of Eccleshall. On B5026, turn at junction signed Copmere End. After ½ m straight across Xrds by Star Inn.* Home-made teas. **Adm £3, chd free. Sun 7 July; Sun 25, Mon 26 Aug (1.30-5.30). Also open Heath House & The Mount, Great Bridgeford 7 July. Visitors also welcome by appt June to Sept. Adm £4.50, tea and biscuits incl.**
Surprising ½ acre SW-facing sun trap which takes advantage of the 'borrowed landscape' of the surrounding countryside. Take time to explore the pathways between the island beds which contain many unusual herbaceous plants, grasses and shrubs; also vegetable patch, stump bed, alpine house and water features. Featured in local press.

8 ◆ BIRMINGHAM BOTANICAL GARDENS
Westbourne Road, Edgbaston B15 3TR. Birmingham Botanical & Horticultural Society, 01214 541860, www.birminghambotanicalgardens.org.uk. *1½ m SW of the centre of Birmingham. From J6 M6 take A38(M) to city centre. Follow underpasses signed Birmingham West to A456. At Fiveways island turn L onto B4217 (Calthorpe Rd) signed Botanical Gardens.* **Adm £7, chd £4.75. For NGS: Weds 10 Apr; 8 May (9-7). For other opening times and information, please phone or see garden website.**
Extensive botanical garden set in a green urban environment with a comprehensive collection of plants from throughout the world growing in the glasshouses and outside. Four stunning glasshouses take you from tropical rainforest to arid desert. Fifteen acres of beautiful landscaped gardens. Roses, alpines, perennials, rare trees and shrubs. Playground, Children's Discovery Garden, Gallery.

BOLESWORTH CASTLE
See Cheshire & Wirral

9 THE BOWERS
Church Lane, Standon, nr Eccleshall ST21 6RW. Maurice & Sheila Thacker, 01782 791244, metbowers@gmail.com. *5m N of Eccleshall. Take A519 & at Cotes Heath turn L signed Standon. After 1m turn R at Xrds by church, into Church Lane ½ m on L.* Home-made teas. **Adm £3, chd free. Sun 4 Aug (1-5). Visitors also welcome by appt June to Aug. Min 10, adm £4 incl light refreshments.**
Come and share our tranquil ⅓ acre cottage style garden. Meander around the grass paths which enclose colour -themed borders containing over 200 clematis and many hardy geraniums and hostas. You will see height, blossom and flowers in abundance. Our garden is always evolving with new features each year. Small water feature, obelisks, arches and trellising. Many unusual and rare clematis. Some gravel paths may prove difficult.

A plant lovers' country cottage garden in the heart of the old village of Endon . . .

10 BRIDGE HOUSE
Dog Lane, Bodymoor Heath B76 9JF. Mr & Mrs J Cerone, 01827 873205, janecerone@btinternet.com. *5m S of Tamworth. From A446 at the Belfry, head 1m N on A4091, R at sign into Bodymoor Heath Lane. ¾ m into village, immediately after hump back bridge turn R into Dog Lane. Parking usually in field on R.* Home-made teas. **Adm £3.50, chd free. Mons 27 May; 26 Aug (2-5). Visitors also welcome by appt Apr to Sept.**
1-acre garden surrounding converted public house. Divided into smaller areas with a mix of shrub borders, azalea and fuchsia, herbaceous and bedding, orchard, kitchen garden and wild flower meadow. Pergola walk, wisteria, formal fish pool, pond and lawns. Kingsbury Water Park and RSPB Middleton Lakes Reserve located within a mile.

11 NEW BROOKLYN
Gratton Lane, Endon, Stoke-on-Trent ST9 9AA. Janet & Steve Howell. *4m W of Leek. 6m from Stoke-on-Trent on A53. Turn at Black Horse PH into centre of village. R into Gratton Lane. 1st house on R. Parking signed in village.* Home-made teas. **Adm £3, chd free. Sun 30 June (12-5).**
A plant lovers' country cottage garden in the heart of the old village of Endon. Small, pretty front garden, borders overflowing with geraniums, astrantia, Alliums and roses. Shady area features hostas and ferns. Steep steps to rear garden with large, well-stocked borders, pond, summerhouse and rural views.

12 ◆ CASTLE BROMWICH HALL GARDENS
Chester Road, Castle Bromwich, Birmingham B36 9BT. Castle Bromwich Hall & Gardens Trust, 0121 749 4100, www.cbhgt.org.uk. *4m E of Birmingham. 1m J5 M6 (exit N only).* **Adm £4.50, chd £1. For NGS: Sun 19 May (12-4). For other opening times and information, please phone or see garden website.**
A delightful 10-acre English formal walled garden. Comprising orchards, formal period planting schemes and a unique kitchen garden of the C17 and early C18. An all-season garden.

10 CHESTNUT WAY
See Derbyshire

13 COLEY COTTAGE
Coley Lane, Little Haywood ST18 0UU. Yvonne Branson, 01889 882715, yvonnebranson0uu@btinternet.com. *5m SE of Stafford. A51 from Rugeley or Weston signed Little Haywood. ½ m from Seven Springs. A513 Coley Lane from Red Lion PH past Back Lane, 100yds on L opp red post box.* Home-made teas. **Adm £2.50, chd free. Fri 7, Sun 23 June; Wed 14 Aug (11-4.30). Also open The Secret Garden.**
A plant lover's cottage garden, full of subtle colours and perfume, every inch packed with plants. Clematis and old roses covering arches, many hostas and agapanthus, a wildlife pool, all designed to attract birds and butterflies. This garden is now 6yrs old, trees, roses and herbaceous planting has become well established. Featured on Radio Stoke.

14 COLOUR MILL
Winkhill, Leek ST13 7PR. Bob & Jackie Pakes, 01538 308680, robert.pakes@virgin.net, http://colourmill.webplus.net. *7m E of Leek. From Leek follow A523 to Ashbourne. On entering Winkhill look for red telephone box on L. Colour Mill is 200yds past telephone box on R. with a wooden hanging sign indicating turn immed before 50mph sign.* Home-made teas. **Adm £3, chd free. Sun 7 July; Thur 22 Aug (1.30-5.30). Visitors also welcome by appt July to Sept.**
¾ -acre S-facing garden, created in the shadow of a former iron foundry, set beside the delightful R Hamps frequented by kingfisher and dipper. Informal planting in a variety of rooms surrounded by beautiful 7ft beech hedges. Large organic vegetable patch complete with greenhouse. Maturing trees provide shade for the interesting seating areas.

15 12 DARGES LANE
Great Wyrley WS6 6LE. Mrs A Hackett, 01922 415064, annofdarges@orange.net. *2m SE of Cannock. From A5 take A34 towards Walsall. Darges Lane is 1st turning on R (over brow of hill). House on R on corner of Cherrington Drive.* **Adm £3, chd free. Visitors welcome by appt Apr to Aug.**
¼ -acre well-stocked enthusiastic plantsman's garden on two levels. Foliage plants are a special feature, together with shrubaceous borders containing rare and unusual plants, divided into areas that link with each other. The use of an extensive collection of clematis gives height in small spaces. Objects of art are eased into every corner, and the owner's own artwork is available to view. Constant updating gives fresh interest to both owner and visitors.

16 4 DENE CLOSE

Penkridge ST19 5HL. David & Anne Smith, 01785 712580. *6m S of Stafford. On A449 from Stafford. At far end of Penkridge turn L into Boscomoor Lane, 2nd L into Filance Lane, 3rd R Dene Close. Please park with consideration in Filance Lane. Disabled only in Dene Close.* Home-made teas. **Adm £3, chd free. Sun 14 July (11-5). Visitors also welcome by appt June to Aug, coaches permitted.**

A medium-sized garden of many surprises. Vibrant colour-themed herbaceous areas incl a long 'rainbow border'. Many different grasses and bamboos creating texture and interest in the garden. Attractive display of many unusual hostas shown for great effect 'theatre style'. Shady area for ferns etc. Water feature. Summerhouse and quiet seating areas within the garden. Featured in Express and Star and local press.

We have a summer opening this year so even if you have been before please come again . . . !

17 DORSET HOUSE

68 Station Street, Cheslyn Hay WS6 7EE. Mary & David Blundell, 01922 419437, david.blundell@talktalk.net. *2m SE of Cannock. J11 M6. A462 towards Willenhall, L at island, follow rd to next island. R into one-way system (Low St), at T-junction L into Station St. A5 Bridgetown L over M6 toll rd to island, L into Coppice Rd. At T-junction R into Station St.* Home-made teas. **Adm £3, chd free. Suns 12 May; 21 July (11-5). Visitors also welcome by appt May to Aug, min 10.**

Step back in time with a visit to this inspirational ½ -acre garden which incorporates country cottage planting at its very best. Unusual rhododendrons, acers, shrubs and perennials planted in mixed borders. Clematis-covered arches and hidden corners with water features including stream and wildlife pool all come together to create a haven of peace and tranquillity. Featured in Express and Star.

DOVE COTTAGE

See Derbyshire

18 NEW 198 EACHELHURST ROAD

Sutton Coldfield B76 1EW. Mrs Jacqui Whitmore. *5mins N of Birmingham. From N at J6 take slip road L to A38(m) towards Lichfield/ Birmingham NE. At r'about take 3rd exit onto A38/Tyburn Rd. Straight at T-lights at Lidl & continue on Tyburn Rd. Next r'about 2nd exit Eachelhurst Rd.* Home-made teas. **Adm £3, chd free. Suns 10 Mar; 28 July (1-5).**

A long garden approx 210ft x 30ft divided by arches and pathways. Plenty to explore incl wildlife pond, cottage garden and hanging baskets leading to formal garden with box-lined pathways, well, stocked borders, willow gazebo and chicken house then through to raised decking area, overlooking Pype Hayes golf course, with summer house and bar and Mediterranean plants.

19 THE ELMS

Post Office Road, Seisdon, Wolverhampton WV5 7HA. Mr Alec Smith & Ms Susan Wilkinson, 01902 893482, kissjewellery@gmail.com. *6m W of Wolverhampton. From Wolverhampton: A454 Bridgnorth rd. At Shipley (Fox PH) take Fox Rd Seisdon 1m T-junction. L by Seven Stars PH over bridge, L into Post Office Rd. Garden 500yds on R.* Tea. **Adm £3.50, chd free. Visitors welcome by appt Mar to Aug. Guided tour by owner, min 10, max 30.**

4-acre garden surrounding large country house. Walled tropical style garden around swimming pool. Large mixed herbaceous borders with all-yr interest. Over 125 roses around garden pergolas and hidden areas. Kitchen garden with box hedging. Many unusual plants most named. New and ancient trees. Victorian bandstand from Ilfracombe pier. Fully restored by present owner. Some slopes.

20 10 FERN DENE

Madeley, Crewe CW3 9ER. Martin & Stella Clifford-Jones. *10m W of Newcastle under Lyme. Madeley is on A525 between Keele/Woore. Enter Moss Lane next to Madeley Pool. 2nd R, Charles Cotton Drive. At end turn R then L into the Bridle Path, 1st R to Fern Dene.* Home-made teas. **Adm £3, chd free. Sun 11 Aug (2-5).**

The garden is dominated by a huge range of beautiful trees and shrubs, designed for yr-round interest. The ponds and woodland area attract wildlife whilst owners' passion for plants provides a rich and diverse habitat. We have a summer opening this year so even if you have been before please come again!

21 FOUR SEASONS

26 Buchanan Road, Walsall WS4 2EN. Marie & Tony Newton, www.fourseasonsgarden.co.uk. *Adjacent to Walsall Arboretum. From M6 J7 take A34 Walsall. At double island take 3rd exit A4148 onto Ring Rd. Over 2 islands, at large junction turn R A461 (signed Lichfield). At 1st island take 3rd exit Buchanan Ave, fork R into Buchanan Rd. From M6 J10 take A454 towards Walsall. Continue onto Blue Lane W/A4148. Continue to follow A4148. At large junction filter L onto A461. At 1st island take 3rd exit onto Buchanan Ave, fork R into Buchanan Rd. Extensive parking in rd or ave.* Tea. **Adm £3.50, chd free. Sun 24 Feb; Sat 11, Sun 12, Sat 18 May; Sat 10 Aug; Sat 26, Sun 27 Oct (10-5).**

Stunning tapestry of colour in all seasons. Suburban, S-facing ⅓ acre, gently sloping to arboretum. 180 acers, 350 azaleas, bulbs, hellebores, camellias, perennials, begonias, bright conifers, topiary and shrubs. Interesting barks and berries. Many 'rooms'. Themes include contrast of red, blue and yellow. Jungle, oriental pagoda, bridges, water features and stone ornaments. Some steps. WC. Featured on BBC Radio 4 Gardeners' Question Time and BBC News photo gallery website and in Daily Mail, Telegraph, Daily Mirror, Sun, Daily Express, National Geographic Traveller (China).

© Clive Nicholls

22 THE GARTH
2 Broc Hill Way, Milford, Stafford ST17 0UB. Mr & Mrs David Wright, 01785 661182, anitawright1@yahoo.co.uk, www.anitawright.co.uk. *4½ m SE of Stafford. A513 Stafford to Rugeley rd; at Barley Mow turn R (S) to Brocton; L after ½ m.* Cream teas. **Adm £3, chd free. Suns 2, 30 June (2-6). Visitors also welcome by appt.**
½ -acre garden of many levels on Cannock Chase AONB. Acid soil loving plants. Series of small gardens, water features, raised beds. Rare trees, island beds of unusual shrubs and perennials, many varieties of hosta and ferns. Ancient sandstone caves. Featured on BBC Radio Stoke and in Express & Star.

23 THE GOOD LIFE
35 Ogley Road, Brownhills, Walsall WS8 6BB. Mr & Mrs Emery. *¼ m from Brownhills centre. From N on Brownhills High St (A452), turn L onto Ogley Rd (B5011).* Home-made teas. **Adm £2.50, chd free. Suns 21 July; 25 Aug (12-5).**
Hidden behind a normal looking suburban house is our little glimpse of heaven. Wander along our long and interesting garden split over three levels with a large variety of shrubs, climbers, perennials and bedding plants. Up on the top level is our work area with vegetable patches and free range chickens.

24 GRAFTON COTTAGE
Barton-under-Needwood DE13 8AL. Margaret & Peter Hargreaves, 01283 713639, marpeter@talktalk.net. *6m N of Lichfield. Leave A38 for Catholme S of Barton, follow sign to Barton Green, L at Royal Oak, ¼ m.* Cream teas. **Adm £3, chd free (share to Alzheimers Research Trust). Suns 30 June; 21 July; 4, 11 Aug (11.30-5). Visitors also welcome by appt June to Aug, min adm £60 per group.**
This is where the bees and owners work overtime producing a traditional cottage garden, admired over the years. A visitor commented it's like indulging in a memorable meal which lingers on the palate'. What hits you immediately is the use of colour in divided areas, variety of unusual herbaceous plants and perfume from old fashioned roses, sweet peas, violas, dianthus, phlox and lilies. Particular interests are viticella clematis, delphiniums, cottage garden annuals and use of foliage plants. Featured ion ITV Love Your Garden and in Country Living, Gardens Illustrated.

GROUP OPENING

25 HALL GREEN GARDENS
Burnaston Road, Birmingham B28 8DH, 0121 608 2397. *Off A34, 3m city centre, 6m from M42 J4. Take A34 to Hall Green, turn into Colebank Rd, turn 1st R into Southam Rd, 1st L into Burnaston Rd.* Home-made teas at 16 Burnaston Rd. **Combined adm £3.50, chd free. Suns 5 May; 21 July (2-5.30).**

16 BURNASTON ROAD
Howard Hemmings & Sandra Hateley
Visitors also welcome by appt May to Sept.
0121 624 1488
howard.hemmings@blueyonder.co.uk

37 BURNASTON ROAD
Mrs Carolyn Wynne-Jones
Visitors also welcome by appt May to July.
0121 608 2397

36 FERNDALE ROAD
Mrs A A Appelbe & Mrs E A Nicholson
Visitors also welcome by appt.
0121 777 4921

120 RUSSELL ROAD
Mr David Worthington
Visitors also welcome by appt May to Sept, weekends and school hols only, groups max 20.
0121 624 7906
hildave@hotmail.com

NEW 19 STAPLEHURST ROAD
Mrs Sheena Terrace

A group of 5 suburban gardens, each unique in style. They incl a S-facing lawned and border garden with interesting features incl a log display, selection of conifers, water feature and various artefacts around the garden. 'Find IT' quiz for children. A tranquil garden with curving borders containing many different perennials, shade areas, soft fruit and vegetables and a surprise around the corner. Florist's large suburban garden with many unusual plants giving yr round interest. The garden is divided into distinct areas, large ornamental garden with pool and waterfalls, tree and soft fruit garden. Plantsman's newly refurbishedgarden featuring formal raised pool and hosta collection. Many unusual perennials and, opening for the first time, a shady garden with mature trees, pond, cottage style borders and vegetable area. Limited wheelchair access to 19 Staplehurst Rd and none to 16 Burnaston Rd. Steps to garden at 19 Staplehurst Rd and 16 Burnaston Rd not accessible.

An NGS day to remember, so join us for afternoon tea, home-made cakes to die for and a few hours of 'cup cake' heaven . . .

26 HAMILTON HOUSE
Roman Grange, Roman Road, Little Aston Park, Sutton Coldfield B74 3GA. Philip & Diana Berry. *3m N of Sutton Coldfield. Follow A454 (Walsal Rd) & enter Roman Rd, Little Aston Pk. Roman Grange is 1st L after church but enter rd via pedestrian gate.* Home-made teas. **Adm £3.50, chd free. Sun 26 May (2-5). Evening Opening wine, Sat 24 Aug (7.30-10).**
½ -acre N-facing English woodland garden in tranquil setting, making the most of challenging shade, providing haven for birds and other wildlife. Large pond with stone bridge, pergolas, water features, box garden with a variety of roses and herbs. Interesting collection of rhododendrons, hostas, ferns and old English roses. An NGS day to remember, so join us for afternoon tea, home-made cakes to die for and a few hours of 'cup cake' heaven. Sip a glass of chilled Pimm's punch at leisure whilst listening to music and admire - (or not) the art of our garden. There are many new features this year so please come and see what we have tried to achieve. Featured in local press and The Journal.

27 HEATH HOUSE
Offley Brook, nr Eccleshall ST21 6HA. Dr D W Eyre-Walker, 01785 280318. *3m W of Eccleshall. From Eccleshall take B5026 towards Woore. At Sugnall turn L, after 1½ m turn R immed by stone garden wall. After 1m straight across Xrds.* Light refreshments. **Adm £3.50, chd free (share to Adbaston Church). Mon 6, Suns 26 May; 7 July (2-5.30). Also open Birch Trees and The Mount, Great Bridgeford 7 July.**
1½ -acre country garden of C18 miller's house in lovely valley setting, overlooking mill pool. Plantsman's garden containing many rare and unusual plants in borders, bog garden, woodland, alpine house, raised bed and shrubberies and incl slowly expanding collection of hardy terrestrial orchids.

28 HIGH TREES
18 Drubbery Lane, nr Longton Park ST3 4BA. Peter & Pat Teggin. *5m S of Stoke-on-Trent. Off A5035, midway between Trentham Gardens & Longton. Opp Longton Park.* Cream teas. **Adm £3, chd free. Sat 29 June (2-5).**
Garden designer and plantswoman's pretty, perfumed hidden garden. Colourful herbaceous plants juxtapose to create a rich woven tapestry of spires, flats and fluffs interwoven with structure planting and focal points. An ideas garden continuing to inspire, evoking orderly diversity. All within two minutes walk of a Victorian park and views to the fields of Barlaston.

29 JOHN'S GARDEN
Ashwood Lower Lane, Ashwood, nr Kingswinford DY6 0AE. John Massey, www.ashwoodnurseries.com. *5m S of Wolverhampton. 1m past Wall Heath on A449 turn R to Ashwood along Doctors Lane. At T-junction, turn L, park at Ashwood Nurseries. Otherwise look for brown signs on A449 into Ashwood Lower Lane. Park as above.* **Adm £5, chd free. Sun 13 Oct (10-4).**
A plantsman's garden bordered by the Staffordshire and Worcestershire canal, incorporating many innovative design features in a natural setting. The garden contains a huge plant collection, where flowers and foliage blend in perfect harmony. Autumn brings fruits, berries and foliage colour to the garden as well as many late summer flowers. Tearooms at Ashwood Nurseries. Disabled access difficult if very wet.

30 KOSYNOOK
25 Cannock Road, Burntwood WS7 0BL. Mr & Mrs Brian & Judith Littler. *5m W of Lichfield. Midway between Cannock & Lichfield on A5091, 200yds from Swan Island. Parking at shopping centre.* Home-made teas. **Adm £3, chd free. Sun 30 June (1-5).**
⅓ acre of lovingly maintained S-facing flat garden, stocked with a large variety of shrubs and plants that give an all-yr- round impressive viewing. Several water features a dovecote pond & ornaments are to be seen along with a variety of hanging baskets and tubs containing a beautiful array of colour. Mature trees. Ample seating is available. Best rear garden Burntwood In Bloom.

31 13 LANSDOWNE ROAD
Hurst Green, Halesowen B62 9QT. Mr Peter Bridgens, 0121 421 7796, peterwbridgens@hotmail.co.uk. *7m W of Birmingham. Leave M5 at J2, 1st exit of r'about on A4123 Wolverhampton Rd. After ½ m turn R onto B4169 Causeway Green Rd, 2nd L into Grafton Rd, continue onto Lansdowne Rd.* Home-made teas. **Adm £3, chd free. Sat 15, Sun 16 June; Sun 14 July; Sun 22 Sept (2.30-5.30). Visitors also welcome by appt June to Oct, groups max 30.**
A plantsman's suburban garden designed to ensure maximum use of space. The garden features rare and unusual plants, incl Pardancanda, Buddleia agathosma, Stewartia, Halesia, Schizandra. Water features and bog area. The mixed borders are planted giving a long season of interest. Attention paid to plant association and colour themes. The garden presents a softly planted look with a tropical twist.

LATIMERS REST
See Warwickshire

32 LILAC COTTAGE
Chapel Lane, Gentleshaw, nr Rugeley WS15 4ND. Mrs Sylvia Nunn, www.lilaccottagegarden.co.uk. *5m NW of Lichfield. Approx midway between Lichfield & Rugeley on A51 at Longdon, turn W into Borough Lane signed Cannock Wood & Gentleshaw. Continue 1m to T-junction. L for 1½ m to Gentleshaw. From Burntwood, A5190 head N on*

Rugeley Rd at Burntwood Swan island; turn L at Xrds approx ½ m past Nags Head PH, over Xrds to Gentleshaw. Parking only at village hall. Roadside disabled & elderly parking only at Lilac Cottage. SatNavs tend to take visitors down narrow single-track lanes so do follow directions above. Home-made teas. **Adm £3, chd free. Sun 14 July (11.30-5).**
Stunning 1-acre plant-enthusiast's country garden; inspirational colour-themed borders, unusual perennials, shrubs, roses and clematis. Lush bog garden and wildlife pond, spectacular vibrant 'hot' border, cool shady walk, new stumpery. Enjoy the ambience of three tranquil seating areas and fragrant roses throughout the garden. Unusual perennials for sale. See our website for more information & photos. Close to ancient Iron Age Fort 'Castle Ring' on Cannock Chase and Gentleshaw Common (SSSI). West Midland Hedgehog Rescue attraction. Featured in BBC Gardeners' World magazine, Express & Star and local press. Some gravel paths and limited disabled access to certain areas.

Fine Edwardian and Victorian villas hiding wonderful secret gardens . . .

LITTLE MORETON HALL
See Cheshire & Wirral

MARLBROOK GARDENS
See Worcestershire

MAXSTOKE CASTLE
See Warwickshire

74 MEADOW ROAD
See Worcestershire

33 ◆ MIDDLETON HALL
Tamworth B78 2AE. Middleton Hall Trust, 01827 283095, www.middleton-hall.org.uk. *4m S of Tamworth, 2m N J9 M42. On A4091 between The Belfry & Drayton Manor.* **Adm £3, chd £1. For NGS: Sun 23 June (1-5). For other opening times and information, please phone or see garden website.**
Two walled gardens set in 40 acres of grounds surrounding Grade 2 Middleton Hall, the C17 home of naturalists Sir Francis Willoughby and John Ray. Large colour-themed herbaceous borders radiating from a central pond, restored gazebo, pergola planted with roses and wisteria. Courtyard garden with raised beds. Musical entertainment in the Hall.

34 MILLENNIUM GARDEN
London Road, Lichfield WS14 9RB. Carol Cooper. *1m S of Lichfield. Off A38 along A5206 towards Lichfield ¼ m past A38 island towards Shoulder of Mutton PH. Park in field on L.* Home-made teas. **Adm £3.50, chd free. Suns 7 Apr; 9 June (1-5).**
2-acre garden with many flower beds, host of golden daffodils. Millennium bridge over landscaped water garden, leading to attractive walks along rough mown paths through maturing woodland, and seasonal wild flowers, Uneven surfaces and gravel paths.

35 MITTON MANOR
Mitton ST19 5QW. Mrs E A Wilson, 07970 457457, eag@eguk.co.uk. *2m W of Penkridge. At Texaco island on A449 in Penkridge turn W into Bungham Lane. Turn R at end then immed L. Keep R at the fork after single file bridge. House is 1½ m from bridge on R. Car park in field before house.* Cream teas. **Adm £4.50, chd free. Sun 14 July (11.30-4.30). Visitors also welcome by appt July to Sept.**
This 7-acre country garden was started in 2001 and has been developed from an overgrown wilderness. The garden surrounds a Victorian manor (not open) and contains rooms of different styles, formal box/topiary, prairie planting and natural woodland bordered by a stream. Stunning vistas, water features and sculpture. Live music. Many levels and gravel paths.

36 MOORFIELD
Post Lane, Endon, Stoke-on-Trent ST9 9DU. Ian & June Sellers, 01782 504096. *4m W of Leek. 6m from Stoke-on-Trent A53. Turn into Station Rd over railway line, canal bridge with lights, 1st on L opp Endon Cricket Club.* Home-made teas. **Adm £3, chd free. Sun 14 July (1.30-5). Visitors also welcome by appt June to Aug.**
Flower arranger's delight situated in ⅓ acre. This colourful garden has a variety of different styles ranging from herbaceous borders to areas with a Mediterranean feel. The garden incl many structural features such as unusual wooden tree stumps to a spacious summerhouse. Wide variety of unusual plants. Featured in Leek Post Times and on Radio Stoke.

GROUP OPENING

37 MOSELEY GARDENS SOUTH
Birmingham B13 9TF. *3m city centre. Halfway between Kings Heath and Moseley village. From A435 turn at the main Moseley T-lights on to St Mary's Row/Wake Green Rd. 1st R, Oxford Rd, then 1st R, School Rd. Prospect Rd is 3rd on L, Ashfield Rd is 4th on R.* Home-made teas at 51 Valentine Road. **Combined adm £4, chd free. Sun 23 June (2-6).**

NEW **39 ASHFIELD AVENUE**
Judy Cottrell

7 ASHFIELD ROAD
Hilary Bartlett

14 PROSPECT ROAD
Jan Birtle & Mark Wilson

19 PROSPECT ROAD
Tony White

65 SCHOOL ROAD
Wendy Weston

51 VALENTINE ROAD
Clare Goulder

WILD ROSE COTTAGE
Rosemary Chatfield

Come and explore our 7 beautiful and varied urban plots, from small city gardens to a ½ acre of spreading lawns with mature trees. Moseley itself is an attractive area, with many fine Edwardian and Victorian villas hiding wonderful secret gardens. Some of our front gardens are worth seeing too! The street containers and hanging baskets of award-winning Moseley in Bloom enhance the area at this time of year. We have wildlife and koi ponds, plus a variety of other water features, fruit and vegetable cultivation, outdoor artworks, chickens and ducks and as many different design ideas as gardeners. These incl wildlife, child-friendly, and easy maintenance gardens. Amongst our special features on Open Day are a quiz or treasure trail for children and live classical music, drifting from the windows of a house into the garden. Meet our gardeners, browse plant and preserve stall, and enjoy tea and home-made cakes in a quintessentially English setting. Formal and wildlife-friendly water features, well-stocked, mature borders, scree garden, bog garden, chickens, outdoor artworks, a great variety of seating areas. Featured in local interest magazine (called B13) & Moseley Society newsletter. Partial wheelchair access.

38 THE MOUNT, COTON, GNOSALL

Gnosall ST20 0EQ. Andrew & Celia Payne, 01785 822253, ac.payne@waitrose.com. *8m W of Stafford. 4m E of Newport. From Stafford take A518 W towards Newport/Telford. Go through Gnosall, over canal. Garden on edge of Gnosall Village, on LH-side of A518. Parking approx 200yds signed up lane.* Home-made teas. **Adm £3, chd free. Sun 23 June (2-5.30). Visitors also welcome by appt June to July.**
Established 3/4 -acre colourful country garden divided into garden rooms. Wildlife friendly with wild flower meadow, small pond and bog area. Over 100 different varieties of hosta, huge Kiftsgate rose, interesting and colourful containers, attractive trees, unusual perennials and raised vegetable beds, there is something for everyone.

39 THE MOUNT, GREAT BRIDGEFORD

33 Newport Road, Great Bridgeford, Stafford ST18 9PR. Adrian Hubble, 01785 282423, crocus88@btinternet.com. *2m NW of Stafford. From J14 M6 take A5013 to Great Bridgeford. Turn L on to B5405. Park at village hall on L, or with consideration in Jasmine Rd on R. Short walk.* Light refreshments. **Adm £3, chd free. Suns 7, 28 July (1.30-5.30). Also open Birch Trees and Heath House 7 July. Visitors also welcome by appt July. Minimum charge £60, refreshments by arrangement.**
The garden consists of 6 quite distinct areas each with beds and borders with their own colour schemes planted with rare and choice plants spread over 1/3 acre. Raised beds, vegetable and alpine gardens and water feature. New for 2013 a blue and white bed and a Roman style feature. A garden of harmonies and contrasts guaranteed to provoke planting ideas.

It's my piece of heaven. . . .

40 THE OLD DAIRY HOUSE

Trentham Park, Stoke-on-Trent ST4 8AE. Philip & Michelle Moore. *S edge of Stoke-on-Trent. Behind Trentham Gardens on rd to Trentham Church and Trentham Park Golf Club. From A34 turn into Whitmore Rd B5038. 1st L and follow NGS signs. Visitors are requested to park in the church car park.* Home-made teas. **Adm £3, chd free. Sat 25, Sun 26 May (1-5).**
Grade 2 listed house (not open) designed by Sir Charles Barry forms backdrop to this 2-acre garden in parkland setting. Shaded area for rhododendrons, azaleas plus expanding hosta and fern collection. Mature trees, 'cottage garden' and long borders. Narrow brick paths in vegetable plot. Large courtyard area for teas.

41 THE OLD VICARAGE

Fulford, nr Stone ST11 9QS. Mike & Cherry Dodson. *4m N of Stone. From Stone A520 (Leek). 1m R turn to Spot Acre and Fulford, turn L down Post Office Terrace, past village green/PH, take 2nd L. Good parking.* Home-made teas. **Adm £3.50, chd free. Sat 15, Sun 16 June (2-5).**
On edge of attractive village, 1 1/2 acres of formal garden on a sloping site around Victorian house. Relaxed herbaceous borders, roses, pretty small pond with seating area, summerhouse and appropriate planting for light and shade among the mature trees. Organic vegetables in raised beds, greenhouse, chickens and fruit cage to keep the kitchen well supplied. A lovely scenic walk around 2-acre reclaimed lake with a 'wilder' feel and native specie planted to encourage wildlife. Waterfall, new arboretum, acer and fern glade, jetty and fishing hut to sit and enjoy (managed!) nature. Wheelchair access to most areas.

ORCHARD VILLA
See Cheshire & Wirral

PACKINGTON HALL
See Warwickshire

42 PAUL'S OASIS OF CALM

18 Kings Close, Kings Heath, Birmingham B14 6TP. Mr Paul Doogan, 0121 444 6943. *4m from city centre. 5m from the M42 J4. Take A345 to Kings Heath High St then B4122 Vicarage Rd. Turn L onto Kings Rd then R to Kings Close.* **Adm £2.50, chd free. Visitors welcome by appt May to Aug.**
Garden cultivated from nothing into a little oasis. Measuring 18ftx70ft. It's small but packed with interesting and unusual plants, water features and 7 seating areas. It's my piece of heaven.

GROUP OPENING

43 PEREIRA ROAD GARDENS

Harborne, Birmingham B17 9JN. *1/2 m N of Harborne High Street. Between Gillhurst Rd & Margaret Grove, 1/4 m from Hagley Rd or 1/2 m from Harborne High St.* Home-made teas at 12 Pereira Road, neighbouring garden open only for refreshments. **Combined adm £3.50, chd free. Suns 28 Apr; 30 June (2-5).**

14 PEREIRA ROAD
Mike Foster

48 PEREIRA ROAD
Rosemary Klem.
Not open 28 April

50 PEREIRA ROAD
Peg Peil
Visitors also welcome by appt Feb to Nov, groups max 20. 07905 892831 (after 6.30pm)

55 PEREIRA ROAD
Emma Davies & Martin Commander.
Not open 28 April

Group of 4 different urban gardens. No.14 is a well established suburban garden with mixed herbaceous and shrub borders. Wildlife-friendly with 2 ponds and wild flower area. Ongoing alterations provide new area of interest each year. No. 48 is a S-facing sloping, tiered garden with mature shrubs and koi pond. No. 50 is a plantaholic's paradise with over 1000 varieties, many rare, incl fruits, vegetables, herbs, grasses and large bed of plants with African connections. Over 100 varieties on sale - see how they grow. No. 55 is a sloping garden, incl gravelled beds with mixed planting, grasses and a small pond. All gardens have steps.

Amazing selection of home-made cream teas to eat in the garden or take away. More than just an Open Garden, we like to think of it as a garden party . . . !

44 NEW THE PINTLES

18 Newport Road, Great Bridgeford ST18 9PR. Peter & Leslie Longstaff. *J14 M6 take A5013 towards Eccleshall. In Great Bridgeford turn L onto B5405. Car park on L after ½ m in front of Village Hall.* Home-made teas. **Adm £3, chd free. Suns 2, 30 June (1-5).**
Traditional semi-detached house in a semi-rural location. Medium-sized garden designed to be wildlife friendly, including vegetable plot, pool, weather station, 2 greenhouses and collection of 200 cacti and succulents. Plenty of seating and a surprise at the end. Shows what can be done with a traditional plot.

RODE HALL

See Cheshire & Wirral

45 ROWLEY HOUSE FARM

Croxton, Stafford ST21 6PJ. Tony & Beryl Roe, 01630 620248. *4m W of Eccleshall. Between Eccleshall & Loggerheads on B5026. At Wetwood Xrds turn for Fairoak. Take 1st L turn & continue for ¾ m.* **Adm £3.50, chd free. Sun 23 June (2-5). Visitors also welcome by appt June to July.**
Quiet country garden, part reclaimed from farm rick-yard. Shrub roses in orchard, soft fruits, vegetables and water feature incl. Extensive views towards the Wrekin and Welsh hills from adjacent land at 570ft, with plantings of 95 varieties of 7 species of ilex, various corylus and specimen trees. Children - How many owls are there? (ornamental). Gravel paths.

46 23 ST JOHNS ROAD

Rowley Park, Stafford ST17 9AS. Colin & Fiona Horwath, 01785 258923, fiona_horwath@yahoo.co.uk. *½ m S of Stafford Town Centre. Just a few mins from J13 M6. Off A449 just after Rising Brook. Through entrance into private park, please park considerately.* **Adm £3, chd free. Sun 24 Mar (2-5). Evening Opening £4, chd free, wine, Fri 17 May (6.30-9). Visitors also welcome by appt Apr to Aug.**
Pass through the black and white gate of this Victorian house into a part-walled gardener's haven, encouraging birds and other wildlife with an organic approach. Bulbs and shady woodlanders in Spring, many herbaceous plants and climbers. Sit and enjoy home-made cakes, by pond or Victorian-style greenhouse. Gardener is keen Hardy Planter and sows far too many seeds so always something good for sale!

47 THE SECRET GARDEN

3 Banktop Cottages, Little Haywood ST18 0UL. Derek Higgott & David Aston, 01889 883473, poshanddeks@yahoo.co.uk. *5m SE of Stafford. A51, from Rugeley or Weston signed Little Haywood ½ m from Seven Springs. A513 Coley Lane from public houses at Back Lane, R into Coley Grove. Entrance to garden in Coley Grove.* Cream teas. **Adm £3, chd free. Sun 19 May; Fri 7, Sun 23 June; Wed 14 Aug (11-4). Also open Coley Cottage (not 19 May) & Tanglewood Cottage 19 May. Visitors also welcome by appt June to Aug.**
Wander past the other cottage gardens and through the evergreen arch and there before you a fantasy for the eyes and soul. Stunning garden approx ½ acre, created over the last 25yrs. Strong colour theme of trees and shrubs, underplanted with perennials, 1000 bulbs and laced with clematis; other features incl water, laburnum and rose tunnel and unique buildings. Is this the jewel in the crown? Raised gazebo with wonderful views over untouched meadows and Cannock Chase, also new features to be discovered. HPS plant sale in village hall 20 May. Featured on BBC Radio Gardeners' Question Time, Radio Stoke & on Gardeners' World. Some slopes.

48 SILVERWOOD

16 Beechfield Road, Trentham ST4 8HG. Aki & Sarah Akhtar. *3m S of Stoke on Trent. From A34 Trentham Gardens r'about take A5035 Longton Rd. After Nat West Bank turn R into Oaktree Rd. From Longton (A50) follow A5035 into Trentham. After PH take L turn into Oaktree Rd, which becomes Beechfield Rd. Parking limited.* Home-made teas. **Adm £3, chd free (share to Breast Cancer Campaign). Sun 23 June (2-5).**
Designed for tranquillity and all year interest, this is a small, secluded town garden for plant collectors. Plants for shade, cornus kousa, roses and bamboos. Limited wheelchair access.

49 SMALL BUT BEAUTIFUL

6 Fishley Close, Bloxwich WS3 3QA. John & Julie Quinn. *1m NE of Bloxwich. Turn at side of Bloxwich Golf Club on A34, L at island, L at Costcutter into Fishley Lane, park at Saddlers PH (garden 5 mins walk).* Home-made teas. **Adm £3, chd free. Suns 26 May; 28 July (10-4).**
This 10m x 10m garden is just what it says - small but very beautiful. All-year-round colour is achieved with clever planting of unusual shrubs and mature acers mixed with flowering perennials. A stunning water feature complements a Japanese area and every corner of the garden is used to its best potential. Great ideas used to make a big impact with low maintenance. Featured in local press.

50 56 ST AGNES ROAD

Moseley, Birmingham B13 9PN. Michael & Alison Cullen. *3m from city centre. From centre of Moseley take St Mary's Row which becomes Wake Green Rd. After ½ m turn R into St Agnes Rd.* Home-made teas. **Adm £3, chd free. Sun 21 July (1-5.30).**

Immaculately maintained, medium-sized, urban garden with curving borders surrounding a formal lawn punctuated with delicate acers and contemporary sculpture. Seating by a Victorian-style fish pond with a fountain and waterfall offers a peaceful setting to enjoy the tranquillity of this elegant garden.

51 190 STATION ROAD

Boldmere, Sutton Coldfield B73 5LH. Jenny & Bill Baker, 0121 244 2916, furfuls2000@yahoo.co.uk. *Leave M6 at J6 following signs for Birmingham NE A38. Then take A5127 signed to Sutton Coldfield. Turn L into Station Rd after 3m.* Home-made teas in adjoining garden. **Adm £3, chd free. Sun 30 June (11-5). Visitors also welcome by appt June to Sept. Groups 10 max welcomed at weekends.**
Medium-sized suburban garden designed for visual impact with colour and interest provided predominantly by foliage. Many different acers and hostas grown in containers. Mints, herbs, shrubs, trees and bedding also grown in pots. Greenhouse, small rockery and tortoise enclosure. Featured in Garden News as 'Garden of the Week'. and local press.

52 172 STONOR ROAD

Hall Green, Birmingham B28 0QJ. Mrs O Walters, 0121 745 2894, gwenowalt@yahoo.co.uk. *Off A34 Birmingham to Stratford Rd at Robin Hood island nr Birmingham/Solihull border. Approaching island along A34 from Shirley take 1st exit (Baldwins Ln). Stonor Rd is 2nd L. Follow rd round keeping to R at fork in rd. If coming from Hall Green, Baldwins Lane is 4th exit.* Home-made teas. **Adm £3, chd free. Visitors welcome by appt Apr to July, groups max 10.**
Dedicated plantswoman's back garden 19 metres x 10 metres with wide variety of plants from alpine gravel bed at top to choice woodlanders at the bottom. Trilliums, fritillaries, podophyllum ferns etc. Acers, clematis and other climbers. Small conservatory with half-hardy shrubs and perennials. Mediumsized front garden with interesting, shrubs, perennials and bulbs. Wheelchair access to front garden only.

Lilac Cottage

53 ◆ SUGNALL HALL, WALLED KITCHEN GARDEN

Sugnall, Stafford ST21 6NF. Dr & Mrs David Jacques, 01785 850820, www.sugnall.co.uk. *2½ m NW of Eccleshall. Just off B5026 Eccleshall to Loggerheads Rd. Turn at the Sugnall Xrds & use the Sugnall Business Centre car park.* **Adm £3, chd free. For NGS: Sun 22, Sun 29 Sept (10.30-4.30). For other opening times and information, please phone or see garden website.**
Historic walled kitchen garden of 1737, renovated for the C21. Work in progress, e.g. glass houses still to be repaired, but most of the 2 acres is under cultivation with 200 apple and pear dwarf pyramids, 50 fan-trained wall fruit and a wide variety of produce within the quarters. Apple tasting. Disabled wc.

54 TANGLEWOOD COTTAGE

Crossheads, Colwich ST18 0UG. Dennis & Helen Wood, 01889 882857, shuvitdog@hotmail.com. *5m SE of Stafford. A51 from Rugeley or Weston, signed Colwich, into village - Main Rd. Past church on L and school on R, under bridge & up hill, immed on R turn into Railway Lane (Crossheads) continue approx ¼ m (it does lead somewhere). Parking signed.* Home-made teas in conservatory. **Adm £3, chd free. Sun 19 May (10.30-3); Sat 27 July (11-3). Evening Opening £4, chd free, wine & BBQ in new courtyard, Fri 13 Sept (7-10). Also open The Secret Garden 19 May. Visitors also welcome by appt May to Sept all catering requirements can be catered for. Min 10.**
A large country cottage garden with small rooms of interest. Mixed borders, koi carp pool, tranquil seated areas, vegetables and fruit, chickens and aviary. An array of wonderful perennials. A garden of peace and tranquillity, recently described as a spiritual garden. Year on year people spend many hours relaxing with us. New courtyard planned for 2013. Art and jewellery display and sale. Winner of Stafford in Boom and of Haywoods large garden. Featured in Express and Star. Lots of gravel paths, people with walking sticks seem to manage quite well.

7 TENNYSON CLOSE

See Shropshire

55 91 TOWER ROAD

Four Oaks, Sutton Coldfield B75 5EQ. Heather & Gary Hawkins. *3m N Sutton Coldfield. From A5127 at Mere Green island, turn onto Mere Green Rd, L at St James Church, L again onto Tower Road.* Home-made teas. **Adm £3, chd free. Sun 9 June (1.30-5.30).**

163ft S-facing garden with sweeping borders and island beds planted with an eclectic mix of shrubs and perennials. Fishpond, cast iron water feature and hiding griffin enhance your journey around the garden. The ideal setting for sunbathing, children's hide and seek and lively garden parties. Amazing selection of home-made cream teas to eat in the garden or take away. More than just an Open Garden, we like to think of it as a garden party! Featured in Garden News.

56 19 WATERDALE

Compton, Wolverhampton WV3 9DY. Anne & Brian Bailey, 01902 424867, m.bailey1234@btinternet.com. *1½ m W of Wolverhampton city centre. From Wolverhampton Ring Rd take A454 towards Bridgnorth. Turn L into Waterdale off A454 Compton Rd West. Car park available at Compton Grange on R of Compton Rd W, opp Linden Lea - 5 mins walk or park on main road. Limited parking for less able in Waterdale.* Home-made teas. **Adm £3, chd free. Sun 9 June (1.30-5.30). Evening Opening £5, chd free, Sat 13 July (6.30-9.30). Visitors also welcome by appt June to Sept, min 10, max 30.**

Secluded town garden which gradually unfolds from the sunny terrace and upper garden, through shady fernery to gothic folly and on to Japanese garden, complete with teahouse, hidden by towering bamboo. The return journey leads to summerhouse and shell grotto. Densely planted, in spite of dry conditions, incl many unusual perennials and shrubs. At the evening opening in July visitors are invited to come for pudding and coffee and enjoy a stroll round the garden. Featured in the Wolverhampton Magazine and Express & Star.

57 WEST VIEW

Cross Street, Gnosall ST20 0BX. Bev & John Smith. *8m W of Stafford. From Stafford take A518 W towards Newport/Telford. Park on Methodist Chapel car park (on R of A518) cross rd, R past Heath Garage, L into The Rank & R into Cross St, garden 2nd house on L.* Home-made teas. **Adm £3, chd free. Sun 30 June (1-5).**

Take a journey through our gem of a garden and be prepared to be surprised. Travel via the pot filled decking and down through the archway, or descend the steps under the scented pergola by the stream and through the arbour. Either way, you enter a hidden oasis of calm and colour where flowers and foliage blend in perfect harmony. Enjoy!

WESTACRES
See Worcestershire

WESTON PARK
See Shropshire

58 THE WICKETS

47 Long Street, Wheaton Aston ST19 9NF. Tony & Kate Bennett, 01785 840233, ajtonyb@tiscali.co.uk. *8m W of Cannock, 10m N of Wolverhampton. M6 J12 turn W towards Telford on A5. Across A449 Gailey r'about A5 for 1½ m turn R signed Stretton. 150yds turn L signed Wheaton Aston, 2½ m turn L ½ m over canal bridge garden on R. Or Bradford Arms Wheaton Aston 2m.* **Adm £3, chd free. Sun 7, Thur 11 July; Sun 25 Aug (1.30-5). Visitors also welcome by appt July to Sept.**

On the edge of the village near the Shropshire Union Canal and large gardens; features range from a fernery, grasses beds to a dry stream, many baskets and even a cricket match! Seating areas offer varied viewing points of the hidden back garden while you enjoy our tea and cakes. 2 steps in garden.

59 WILKINS PLECK

off Three Mile Lane, Whitmore, nr Newcastle-under-Lyme ST5 5HN. Sheila & Chris Bissell, www.wilkinspleckgarden.com. *5m SW from Newcastle-under-Lyme. Take A53 SW from Newcastle-under-Lyme. At Whitmore turn R at Mainwaring Arms PH. Signed R at Cudmore Fisheries. Please NO Dogs in car park in field at landowner's request.* Home-made teas. **Adm £5, chd free. Suns 16 June; 28 July (1-5).**

5½ acres of paradise in North Staffordshire in the true Arts & Crafts Tradition. A series of enclosed gardens, parterres and yew hedges. Pleached lime avenue. Herbaceous borders which move from cool colours to hot. Pyramidal roofed summerhouse. Beyond lies a lake spanned by two Monet-style bridges, and young arboretum. See website for more information. Featured in Period Living Magazine.

60 WILLOW COTTAGE

High Street, Church Eaton ST20 0AG. Sue & Jeremy Bach, 01785 823085, jeremy.bach@btinternet.com. *7½ m SW of Stafford. From Stafford take A518 SW. At Haughton turn L signed Church Eaton. At T-junction (church on R) turn R into Church Eaton High St. Car park at end of High St at Royal Oak PH.* Home-made teas. **Adm £3, chd free. Visitors welcome by appt June to Aug. Min adm £60, max 30 visitors.**

Behind the country cottage frontage is an oasis of flower and colour. The gentle sound of water welcomes you to walk amongst the herbaceous beds, water features, ponds and vegetable plot. Sit in some of the quiet corners of this garden and enjoy the passing wildlife.

61 WITS END

59 Tanworth Lane, Shirley B90 4DQ. Sue Mansell, 0121 744 4337, wits-end@hotmail.co.uk. *2m SW of Solihull. Take B4102 from Solihull for 2m. R at island onto A34. After next island (Sainsbury's) Tanworth Lane 1st L off A34.* Home-made teas. **Adm £2.50, chd free. Sun 12 May (2-5); Fri 14 June (11-3); Sun 16 June; Sun 7 July (2-5); Fri 2 Aug (11-3); Sun 4 Aug (2-5). Visitors also welcome by appt Apr to Sept, group min 10.**

Interesting all-yr-round plantaholic's cottage-style garden. Perennials and shrubs, many unusual in various shaped beds (some colour co-ordinated) plus spectacular late summer border. New ponds with waterfalls, rill and bog, hot alpine and cool shady rockeries, woodland area with extensive shade loving plants. Various containers displaying an array of sempervivum and jovibarba.

62 THE WOMBOURNE WODEHOUSE

Wolverhampton WV5 9BW. Mr & Mrs J Phillips, 01902 892202. *4m S of Wolverhampton. Just off A449 on A463 to Sedgley.* **Adm £5, chd free. Visitors welcome by appt Apr to July. Small or large groups welcome, preferably weekdays.**

18-acre garden laid out in 1750.

Rhododendrons, azaleas, woodland walk and 180 different varieties of tall bearded irises in walled kitchen garden (mid May to early June), 66yd herbaceous border, also 2 small borders and water garden (June and July). Partial wheelchair access.

63 WOODBROOKE QUAKER STUDY CENTRE
1046 Bristol Road, Selly Oak B29 6LJ. Woodbrooke Quaker Study Centre, 0121 472 5171, enquiries@woodbrooke.org.uk, www.woodbrooke.org.uk. *4m SW of Birmingham. On A38 Bristol Rd, S of Selly Oak, opp Witherford Way.* Cream teas. **Adm £4, chd free. Sun 16 June (2.30-5.30).**
10 acres of organically-managed garden and grounds. Grade II listed house (not open), former home of George Cadbury. Herbaceous and shrub borders, walled garden with herb garden, potager and cutting beds, Chinese garden, orchard, arboretum, Victorian boat house, lake and extensive woodland walks. Very fine variety of trees. Our Garden Manager and other staff will be on hand to help visitors to identify the key garden features and make the most of their visit. Garden tours and short talks will be available. Freshly baked cakes and hot drinks will be available to purchase. Some paths may be unsuitable for wheelchair access depending on the weather.

WOODEND COTTAGE
See Derbyshire

GROUP OPENING

64 WOODLEIGHTON GROVE GARDENS
Woodleighton Grove, Uttoxeter ST14 8BX, 01889 563930, cityofgold@lineone.net. *SE of Uttoxeter. From Uttoxeter take B5017 (Marchington). Go over Town Bridge, turn L, then R into Highwood Road, pass turning to Racecourse. After ¼ m turn R.* Home-made teas Karibu, 9 Woodleighton Grove. **Combined adm £3.50, chd free. Sat 13 July (11-5); Sun 14 July (1-5). Visitors & groups also welcome by appt June to July. Coaches welcome.**

APOLLONIA
Helen & David Loughton

KARIBU
Graham & Judy White

These two adjacent gardens demonstrate varied and fascinating approaches to design, layout and planting, and are said to have inspired and given many people ideas for their own gardens. Apollonia is a plantaholics garden on several levels, with strong structure, incl summerhouse, greenhouse, fruit arch, natural stream and some steep steps. Unusual and interesting planting includes bamboos, bananas, hostas and agaves. Karibu is a distinctive and intriguing garden with a number of absorbing features. Informally planted on two levels, with a natural stream, summerhouse, greenhouse, folly and gazebo. Archways, bridges, steps and a boardwalk lead to a selection of tranquil resting places. The garden discreetly houses many fascinating artefacts, plus a collection of antique horticultural and agricultural hand tools. The greenhouse contains nearly 400 cacti and succulents, jam and marmalade made with 'Staffordshire Honey', on sale. Quiz and garden search are available for anyone interested. Wheelchair access limited to top gardens and greenhouses.

65 YARLET HOUSE
Yarlet, Stafford ST18 9SU. Mr & Mrs Nikolas Tarling. *2m S of Stone. Take A34 from Stone towards Stafford, turn L into Yarlet School and L again into car park.* Light refreshments. **Adm £4, chd free (share to Staffordshire Wildlife Trust). Sat 29 June (9.30-12.30).**
4 acre garden with extensive lawns, walks, lengthy herbaceous borders and traditional Victorian box hedge. Water gardens with fountain and rare lilies. Sweeping views across Trent Valley to Sandon. Victorian School Chapel. 9 hole putting course. Boules pitch. Yarlet School Art Display. Gravel paths.

66 YEW TREE COTTAGE
Podmores Corner, Long Lane, nr White Cross, Haughton, Stafford ST18 9JR. Clive & Ruth Plant, 01785 282516, pottyplantz@aol.com. *4m W of Stafford. Take A518 W Haughton, turn R Station Rd (signed Ranton) 1m, then turn R at Xrds ¼ m on R.* Home-made teas. **Adm £3, chd free. Suns 5, 26 May; 21 July (2-5). Visitors also welcome by appt May to July.**
Hardy Planter's garden brimming with unusual plants. All-yr-round interest incl meconopsis, trillium, arisaema and dierama. ½ -acre incl pond, gravel garden, herbaceous borders, vegetable garden and plant sales area. Covered courtyard with oak-timbered vinery to take tea in if the weather is unkind, and seats in the garden for lingering on sunny days. Some grass paths so hard going in wet.

YEW TREE HOUSE GARDEN & SPECIAL PERENNIALS NURSERY
See Cheshire & Wirral

Staffordshire County Volunteers

County Organisers
Susan & John Weston, Birch Trees, Copmere End, Eccleshall, Stafford ST21 6HH, 01785 850448, johnweston123@btinternet.com

County Treasurer and Booklet Co-ordinator
John Weston, Birch Trees, Copmere End, Eccleshall, Stafford ST21 6HH, 01785 850448, johnweston123@btinternet.com

Assistant County Organisers
Jane Cerone Bridge House, Dog Lane, Bodymoor Heath, Sutton Coldfield B76 9JF, 01827 873205, janecerone@btinternet.com
Pat Teggin, High Trees, 18 Drubbery Lane, Stoke-on-Trent ST3 4BA, 01782 318453, pat.teggin@btinternet.com
Sheila Thacker The Bowers, Bowers, Standon, Stafford ST21 6RW, 01782 791244, metbowers@gmail.com

SUFFOLK

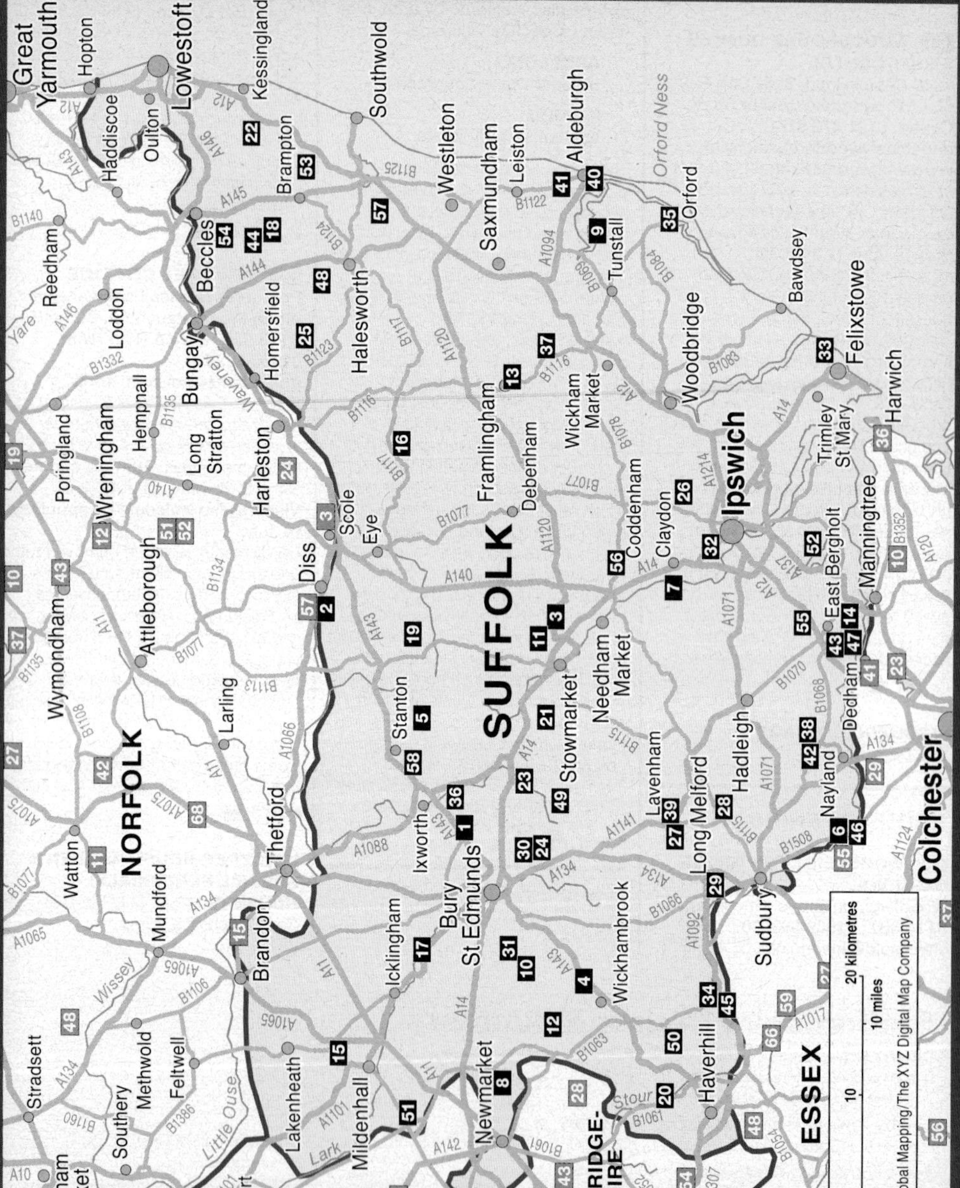
SUFFOLK
NORFOLK
ESSEX
CAMBRIDGE-SHIRE
Great Yarmouth
Hopton
Lowestoft
Kessingland
Haddiscoe
Oulton
Southwold
Westleton
Saxmundham
Leiston
Aldeburgh
Orford Ness
Orford
Tunstall
Brampton
Beccles
Reedham
Loddon
Halesworth
Homersfield
Bungay
Hempnall
Wreningham
Poringland
Long Stratton
Harleston
Framlingham
Debenham
Wickham Market
Woodbridge
Bawdsey
Felixstowe
Trimley St Mary
Harwich
Ipswich
Coddenham
Claydon
Scole
Eye
Diss
Attleborough
Wymondham
Stanton
Needham Market
Stowmarket
Larling
Thetford
Ixworth
Bury St Edmunds
Lavenham
Long Melford
Hadleigh
East Bergholt
Manningtree
Dedham
Nayland
Colchester
Sudbury
Watton
Mundford
Brandon
Icklingham
Wickhambrook
Haverhill
Methwold
Feltwell
Stradsett
Southery
Lakenheath
Mildenhall
Newmarket
Downham Market
Littleport
Soham
Burwell
Linton
Yare
Waveney
Wissey
Little Ouse
Great Ouse
Lark
Stour
0 10 20 kilometres
0 10 miles
© Global Mapping/The XYZ Digital Map Company

Opening Dates

February

Sunday 17
7 Blakenham Woodland Garden
18 Gable House

March

Saturday 23
58 Wyken Hall
Sunday 24
58 Wyken Hall
Sunday 31
56 Woodwards

April

Every Tue, Wed, Thur, Fri, Sat & Sun in April
57 Woottens
Monday 1
25 The Laburnums
Sunday 7
5 The Beeches
7 Blakenham Woodland Garden
20 Great Thurlow Hall
48 Rydal Mount
Tuesday 9
56 Woodwards
Sunday 21
14 East Bergholt Place - The Place for Plants

Full to capacity with many rare and unusual shrubs, trees and perennials . . .

May

Every Tue, Wed, Thur, Fri, Sat & Sun in May
57 Woottens
Saturday 11
26 Larks' Hill
Sunday 12
7 Blakenham Woodland Garden
14 East Bergholt Place - The Place for Plants
51 Street Farm
Sunday 19
9 Church Farm
33 Old Felixstowe Gardens
42 The Priory
55 Windmill Cottage
Sunday 26
21 Green Farmhouse
27 Lavenham Hall
56 Woodwards
Monday 27
11 Columbine Hall

June

Every Tue, Wed, Thur, Fri, Sat & Sun in June
57 Woottens
Sunday 2
1 Barton Mere
8 Brinkley Gardens
18 Gable House
Sunday 9
15 The Former Rectory
31 Moat House
53 Uggeshall Hall

National Gardens Weekend

Saturday 15
3 Bays Farm
26 Larks' Hill
32 428 Norwich Road
52 Tattingstone Place
Sunday 16
3 Bays Farm
24 Home Farm House
29 Long Melford Group
30 The Lucy Redman Garden
32 428 Norwich Road
34 Orchard House
47 Rosemary
49 Smallwood Green Gardens
Tuesday 18
56 Woodwards
Sunday 23
13 28 Double Street
20 Great Thurlow Hall
23 Hessett House
28 Little Waldingfield Gardens
35 Orford Gardens
50 Southleigh
Sunday 30
22 Henstead Exotic Garden
36 Pakenham Gardens
41 Priors Oak
43 Ravenscroft

July

Every Tue, Wed, Thur, Fri, Sat & Sun in July
57 Woottens
Sunday 7
16 Frythe Barn
38 Polstead Mill
Saturday 13
26 Larks' Hill
54 White House Farm
Sunday 14
2 Batteleys Cottage
37 Parham Hall
44 Redisham Hall
Sunday 21
45 Riverside House
56 Woodwards
Sunday 28
46 Rosedale
Tuesday 30
56 Woodwards

August

Every Tue, Wed, Thur, Fri, Sat & Sun in August
57 Woottens
Sunday 4
10 Cobbs Hall
Tuesday 6
56 Woodwards
Saturday 10
19 Gislingham Gardens
26 Larks' Hill
Sunday 11
19 Gislingham Gardens
Sunday 18
4 Beech Hall
39 Prentice Street
Sunday 25
56 Woodwards

September

Every Tue, Wed, Thur, Fri, Sat & Sun in September
57 Woottens
Sunday 8
16 Frythe Barn
Saturday 14
58 Wyken Hall
Sunday 15
40 Priors Hill, Aldeburgh
58 Wyken Hall
Sunday 22
17 Fullers Mill

October

Tuesday 1
57 Woottens

February 2014

Sunday 16
18 Gable House

Gardens open to the public

7 Blakenham Woodland Garden
14 East Bergholt Place - The Place for Plants

You are always welcome at an NGS garden!

- 17 Fullers Mill
- 57 Woottens
- 58 Wyken Hall

By appointment only

- 12 Dip-on-the-Hill

Also open by Appointment ☎

- 2 Batteleys Cottage
- 3 Bays Farm
- 4 Beech Hall
- 9 Church Farm
- 10 Cobbs Hall
- 16 Frythe Barn
- 21 Green Farmhouse
- 26 Larks' Hill
- 28 The Priory, Little Waldingfield Gardens
- 31 Moat House
- 32 428 Norwich Road
- 33 41 Westmorland Road, Old Felixstowe Gardens
- 36 Fen House, Pakenham Gardens
- 38 Polstead Mill
- 40 Heron House, Priors Hill, Aldeburgh
- 41 Priors Oak
- 43 Ravenscroft
- 46 Rosedale
- 48 Rydal Mount
- 49 Smallwood Farmhouse, Smallwood Green Gardens
- 54 White House Farm
- 55 Windmill Cottage
- 56 Woodwards

The Gardens

1 BARTON MERE

Thurston Road, Great Barton IP31 2PR. Mr & Mrs C O Stenderup. *2m E of Bury St Edmunds. From Bury St Edmunds on A143 through Gt Barton turn R at Bunbury Arms PH. Entrance ½ m on L. From Thurston take Gt Barton Rd from railway bridge. Entrance 1½ m on R.* Home-made teas. **Adm £4, chd free. Sun 2 June (2-5).**

C16 house (not open) with later Georgian façade, set in 50 acres of parkland. Extensive lawns with views over the Mere. Rose garden & herbaceous borders mostly surrounded by C16 walls,two courtyards and large conservatory. Productive vegetable garden,old orchard and beautiful grass tennis court. Gravel paths.

2 NEW BATTELEYS COTTAGE

The Ling, Wortham, Diss IP22 1ST. Mr & Mrs Andy & Linda Simpson, 07949 204820, lindaruth11@googlemail.com. *3m W of Diss. Turn signed from A143 Diss/Bury Rd at Wortham village. Follow rd to T- junction by church, turn R. At top of hill turn L, signed Roydon, (Rectory Rd). Follow rd down hill and round sharp L corner. Garden on L around corner.* Home-made teas. **Adm £3.50, chd free. Sun 14 July (1-6). Visitors also welcome by appt Apr to Sept. Refreshments may be available for groups by arrrangement.**

Recently renovated still developing 1 acre garden with voluptuous plantings of wide range of perennials and grasses. Mature and more recently planted trees and shrubs. Ponds and stream, potager garden, fruit and vegetable garden, orchard and meadow area. Varied local habitat and mixed planting in the garden makes this a haven for birds. Wheelchair access available to most parts of the garden, gravel, grass and bark paths.

> Varied local habitat and mixed planting . . . makes this a haven for birds . . .

3 BAYS FARM

Forward Green, Earl Stonham, Stowmarket IP14 5HU. Richard & Stephanie Challinor, 01449 711286, stephanie@baysfarmsuffolk.co.uk, www.baysfarmsuffolk.co.uk. *3½ m E of Stowmarket. J50 A14, take A1120 direction Stowupland. Proceed through Stowupland on A1120 for 1m, at sharp L bend turn R signed Broad Green. 1st house on R.* Home-made teas. **Adm £4, chd free. Sat 15, Sun 16 June (2-5). Visitors also welcome by appt.**

New opening date - after 2 years of opening in July come in June to enjoy a different aspect to this 2-acre plantsman's garden extensively renovated and beautifully designed. Formal gardens comprising shady borders, scented and sun-loving beds with woodland and butterfly planting. Large kitchen gardens, greenhouse, lovely herb garden, orchard and wild-flower area. BBC Breakfast TV showing how Bays Farm were dealing with the hosepipe ban and the continuing focus on water conservation. Gravel paths.

4 BEECH HALL

Depden IP29 4BU. Mrs J Bolton, 01284 850220. *Midway between Bury St Edmunds & Haverhill on A143, take 1st R turn after Chedburgh.* Home-made teas. **Adm £3, chd free. Sun 18 Aug (1-5). Visitors also welcome by appt.**

9 acres of beautiful gardens with herbaceous borders and mixed variety of mature trees. New woodland walk with pond and various shrubs. Two summerhouses are situated in the garden together with large pond with Monet-style bridge. Partial wheelchair access.

5 THE BEECHES

Grove Road, Walsham-le-Willows IP31 3AD. Dr A J Russell. *11m E of Bury St Edmunds. From A143 to Diss take turning for Walsham-le-Willows. At Xrds in village turn R, church on L. After 100yds turn L. The Beeches is on L just over the bridge.* Tea. **Adm £3.50, chd free (share to St Marys Church, Walsham-le-Willows). Sun 7 Apr (2-5).**

150yr-old, 3-acre garden, which incl specimen trees, pond, stream, potager, memorial garden, lawns and a variety of beds. Stream area landscaped. Mediterranean bed and camellia bed. Gravel paths.

BETH CHATTO GARDENS

See Essex

6 BEVILLS

Sudbury Road, Bures CO8 5JW. Mr & Mrs G T C Probert. *4m S of Sudbury. Just N of Bures on the Sudbury rd B1508.* Home-made teas. **Adm £3, chd £3. Mon 6 May (2-5).**

A beautiful house (not open) overlooking the Stour Valley with parkland trees, hills and woodland. The gardens are formal and Italianate in style with hedges and lawns flanked by Irish yews and mature specimen trees. Terraces, borders, ponds, vistas and woodland walks. Spring bulbs and bluebell wood. Gravel paths.

BILLINGFORD HALL
See Norfolk

7 ◆ BLAKENHAM WOODLAND GARDEN
Little Blakenham, Ipswich IP8 4LZ. Lord & Lady Blakenham, www.blakenhamwoodlandgarden.org.uk. *4m NW of Ipswich. Follow signs at Little Blakenham, 1m off B1113.* **Adm £3.50, chd free. For NGS: Suns 17 Feb; 7 Apr; 12 May (10-5). For other opening times and information, please see garden website.**
Beautiful 6-acre woodland garden with variety of rare trees and shrubs. Chinese rocks and a landscape sculpture. Especially lovely in spring with daffodils, camellias, magnolias and bluebells followed by roses in early summer. Special snowdrop opening February 17th. Partial wheelchair access.
♿

GROUP OPENING

8 NEW BRINKLEY GARDENS
Newmarket CB8 8ST. *Brinkley is S of Newmarket on B1061. From Newmarket turn L into village High St. The Old Rectory in Hall Lane & The Grove at the Carlton end of the street will be signed to the L.* Home-made teas. **Combined adm £4, chd free. Sun 2 June (1.30-5.30).**

NEW THE GROVE
Dr & Mrs Alexander Gimson.
At Carlton end of the High Street, opposite open field

NEW THE OLD RECTORY
Mrs Julie Coley.
Hall Lane is a turning off Brinkley High St

Two lovely gardens, one of one acre and one of two acres in the attractive village of Brinkley. The Grove 1-acre garden surrounding C19 house (not open), with mature yew trees and beech hedges. Walled garden area has established shrubs and wisteria, with new beds and planting created over the last 8 years. This incl a winter/spring bed with narcissi and hellebores, a dry bed with irises, terrace beds with tulips and a mixed herbaceous border along the curved wall. The Old Rectory two acre garden started in 1973. Interesting trees planted to supplement beech, yew and chestnut already there. Mixed Herbaceous borders. Traditional potager with box hedges planted in 1993. Small woodland area still being developed
♿ ☕

Columbine Hall

BYNDES COTTAGE
See Essex

CHIPPINS
See Essex

9 NEW CHURCH FARM
Tunstall Road, Iken, Woodbridge IP12 2ER. Mrs Caroline Erskine, 01728 687485, cerskine30@btinternet.com. *From A12 take A1094 towards Aldeburgh. At Snape Church turn R to Snape. Past Snape Maltings turn L signed Orford. At next Xrds turn L signed Iken. Entrance to garden on R after 1m.* Tea. **Adm £3, chd free. Sun 19 May (2-5.30). Visitors also welcome by appt Apr to Sept.**
Two acre area surrounded by mature alders and pines. Many young specimen trees and shrubs planted over the last five years. Mixed planting of perennials, grasses and smaller shrubs.
♿ 🐕 ☕ ☎

10 COBBS HALL
Great Saxham IP29 5JN. Dick & Sue Soper, 01284 850678, soperdoc@gmail.com. *4½ m W of Bury St Edmunds. A14 exit to Westley. R at Westley Xrds. L fork at Little Saxham signed Hargrave & Chevington. Approx 1½ m to sign on R turn. Mustard-coloured house 300yds on L.* Home-made teas. **Adm £3.50, chd free (share to St Andrews Church, Gt Saxham). Sun 4 Aug (2-6). Visitors also welcome by appt June to Aug.**
2 acres of lawns and borders, ornamental trees, large fish/lily pond. Parterre, folly, walled kitchen garden, fernery/stumpery, grass tennis court and pretty courtyard.
♿ ✿ ☕ ☎

11 COLUMBINE HALL
Gipping Road, Stowupland, Stowmarket IP14 4AT. Hew Stevenson & Leslie Geddes-Brown, www.columbinehall.co.uk. *1½ m NE of Stowmarket. Turn N off A1120 opp Total garage across village green, then R at T-junction into Gipping Rd. Garden on L just beyond derestriction sign.* Home-made teas. **Adm £4, chd free. Mon 27 May (2-6).**
George Carter's formal garden and herb garden surround moated medieval manor (not open). Outside the moat, vistas, stream, ponds and bog garden, Mediterranean garden, colour-themed vegetable garden, cutting garden, orchards and parkland. Gardens developed since 1994 with constant work-in-progress, incl transformed farm buildings and eyecatchers.
♿ 🐕 ✿ ☕

Visit a garden in your own time – look out for the ☎

12 NEW DIP-ON-THE-HILL
Ousden, Newmarket CB8 8TW. Dr & Mrs. Geoffrey Ingham, 01638 500329, gki1000@cam.ac.uk. *5m E of Newmarket; 7m W of Bury St Edmunds. From Newmarket: Ousden signed at junction of B1063 & B1085, garden 1m from junction. From Bury St Edmunds follow signs for Little Saxham & Hargrave. Parking at village hall*. Tea. **Adm £4, chd free. Visitors welcome by appt July to Sept.**
Approx one acre in a dip on a S-facing hill based on a wide range of architectural/sculptural evergreen trees, shrubs and groundcover: pines; grove of Phillyrea latifolia; 'cloud pruned' hedges; palms; large bamboo; ferns; range of kniphofia and croscosmia.

13 NEW 28 DOUBLE STREET
Framlingham, Woodbridge IP13 9BN. Mr & Mrs David Clark. *Just 250yds from Market Hill (main square) of Framlingham. Leave square from top left (NE) corner into Church Street. Double St is 100yds on the R opp the main church entrance. Car parking in main square & near to Framlingham Castle.* **Adm £2.50, chd free. Sun 23 June (12-5).**
A recently developed town garden featuring roses together with a wide range of perennials and shrubs. Conservatory, greenhouse, gazebo, summerhouse and terrace full of containers all add interest to the garden. Good views of Framlingham's roofscape. Fine shingle access drive with two ramps.

14 ◆ EAST BERGHOLT PLACE - THE PLACE FOR PLANTS
East Bergholt CO7 6UP. Mr & Mrs Rupert Eley, 01206 299224, www.placeforplants.co.uk. *2m E of A12, 7m S of Ipswich. On B1070 towards Manningtree, 2m E of A12. Situated on the edge of East Bergholt*. **Adm £6, chd free. For NGS: Suns 21 Apr; 12 May (2-5). For other opening times and information, please phone or see garden website.**
20-acre garden originally laid out at the turn of the last century by the present owner's great grandfather. Full of many fine trees and shrubs, many seldom seen in East Anglia. A fine collection of camellias, magnolias and rhododendrons, topiary, and the National Collection of deciduous Euonymus. In dry conditions there is wheelchair access to the main and central top part of the garden. It is essential to ring prior to check conditions.
NCH

15 THE FORMER RECTORY
The Street, Eriswell, Brandon IP27 9BH. Bernard & Marian Ransome. *3m NE of Mildenhall. From Fiveways r'about at Barton Mills on A11 take A1065 towards Brandon, after approx 2m turn L onto B1112. On approaching Eriswell Village garden on L of War Memorial next to Church*. Home-made teas. **Adm £3.50, chd free. Sun 9 June (1-5).**
1 acre consisting of shrub and perennial borders surrounded by lawned area containing specimen trees offering many different aspects. Unusual features incl cathedral style pergola with clock tower and water fountain and short woodland walk. Well stocked vegetable garden divided by grass paths.

Take a stroll via a willow tunnel, spinney with bee hives and bog garden . . .

FOUNTAIN FARM
See Essex

16 FRYTHE BARN
Wilby Road, Stradbroke, Eye IP21 5JP. Don & Carol Darling, 01379 388098, caroldon01@gmail.com. *11m SE of Diss, 10m N of Framlingham. From Framlingham B1118 to Stradbroke through Wilby, after ³/₄ m sharp LH bend (Neaves Lane on R) then 2nd driveway on R. Frythe Barn to R of drive. From Diss B1118 to Stradbroke. Centre of village R at church, immed L, Wilby Rd (B1118) ³/₄ m out of village, sharp LH bend, driveway on L 50yds after bend.* Home-made teas. Gluten and dairy free options available. **Adm £4, chd free. Suns 7 July; 8 Sept (1-5). Visitors also welcome by appt Mar to Oct.**
A maze of concrete and brick buildings transformed in 6 yrs into a delightfully relaxing 2 acre garden.Take a stroll via a willow tunnel, spinney with bee hives and bog garden through the orchard to a leafy arbour, surrounded by flowing grasses. View from here the large pond and stream to the left, sensitively planted borders to the right and Italian style patio in front of the renovated barn. Wild life area, large grass beds, pond, mixed borders, roses. No wheelchair access to spinney/wild flower meadow.

17 ◆ FULLERS MILL
West Stow IP28 6HD. Fullers Mill Trust, www.fullersmillgarden.org.uk. *6m NW of Bury St Edmunds. Turn off A1101 Bury to Mildenhall Road, signed West Stow Country Park, go past Country Park continue for ¹/₄ m, garden entrance on R.* **Adm £4, chd free. Sun 22 Sept (2-5). For other opening times and information, see garden website.**
An enchanting 7 acre garden on the banks of R Lark. A beautiful site of light, dappled woodland with a plantsman's paradise of rare and unusual shrubs, perennials and marginals planted with great natural charm. Euphorbias and lilies are a particular feature. A garden with interest in every season. In late Sept colchicums in flower incl outstanding white variety. Also yellow crocus-like Sternbergia should be in bloom. Partial wheelchair access around garden.

18 GABLE HOUSE
Halesworth Road, Redisham, Beccles NR34 8NE. John & Brenda Foster. *5m S of Beccles. From Bungay A144 to Halesworth for 5m, turn L at St Lawrence School, 2m to Gable House. From A12 Blythburgh take A145 to Beccles, at Brampton Xrds L to Station Rd. 3m on at junction is Gable House*. Soup Lunches for February Snowdrop Days. Home-made teas. **Adm £3.50, chd free (share to St Peter's Church, Redisham). Sun 17 Feb (11-4); Sun 2 June (11-5); Sun 16 Feb 2014.**
1-acre plantsman's garden of all-year interest. Vast collection of snowdrops,

cyclamen, hellebores etc for the February opening. The June open day brings colour and variety from shrub roses, perennials and interesting trees and shrubs. Greenhouses contain rare bulbs and tender plants. Vast collection of snowdrops for the February Open Day Many unusual trees and shrubs. Featured in The Garden and Gardens Illustrated.

GROUP OPENING

19 GISLINGHAM GARDENS

Eye IP23 8JT. *4m W of Eye. Gislingham $2^1/_2$ m W of A140. 9m N of Stowmarket, 8m S of Diss. Disabled parking at Ivy Chimneys. No parking on Dunton Drive.* Home-made teas at Aughton House. **Combined adm £3, chd free. Sat 10, Sun 11 Aug (11-4).**

AUGHTON HOUSE
Mill Street. Anthony & Dee Ambler

IVY CHIMNEYS
Mill Street. Iris & Alan Stanley

2 varied gardens in a picturesque village with a number of Suffolk timbered houses. Ivy Chimneys is planted for yr round interest with ornamental trees, some topiary, exotic borders and fishpond set in an area of Japanese style. Wisteria draped pergola supports a productive vine. Also a separate ornamental vegetable garden. New Aughton House lies alongside Ivy Chimneys and has $^1/_2$ acre garden professionally designed in 2005. Still maturing it has vivid late summer colour, a cottage garden, formal garden and many interesting features.

20 GREAT THURLOW HALL

Haverhill CB9 7LF. Mr & Mrs George Vestey. *12m S of Bury St Edmunds, 4m N of Haverhill. Great Thurlow village on B1061 from Newmarket; $3^1/_2$ m N of junction with A143 Haverhill/Bury St Edmunds rd.* Home-made teas. **Adm £4, chd free. Suns 7 Apr; 23 June (2-5).**
River walk newly restored and trout lake with extensive display of daffodils and blossom. Spacious lawns, shrubberies and roses. Walled kitchen garden.

21 GREEN FARMHOUSE

The Green, Shelland, Stowmarket IP14 3JE. Miss Rosemary Roe, 01449 736591. *4m NW of Stowmarket, 10m SE of Bury St Edmunds. A14 westbound take A1308 signed Haughley/Wetherden, over A14. Follow sign to Wetherden, turn L Harleston then follow NGS signs. A14 east bound take Wetherden/HaughleyPark turning (just past A1088), turn R signed Buxhall, follow NGS signs.* Light refreshments. **Adm £3.50, chd free. Sun 26 May (11-5). Visitors also welcome by appt June, adm incl refreshments.**
2 acre garden surrounding thatched cottage (not open), overlooking a private green. Established shrub/herbaceous borders with lawns and vistas, natural pond, courtyard garden and small feature gardens. A wide variety of plants. Also a developing wild flower meadow and trees with wonderful views of the Suffolk countryside.

HANNAMS HALL
See Essex

HEDINGHAM CASTLE
See Essex

The spring garden is awash with colour - snowdrops, aconites, hellebores, daffodils and much more . . .

22 HENSTEAD EXOTIC GARDEN

Church Road, Henstead, Beccles, Suffolk NR34 7LD. Andrew Brogan, www.hensteadexoticgarden.co.uk. *Equal distance between Beccles, Southwold & Lowestoft approx 5m. 1m from A12 turning after Wrentham (signed Henstead) very close to B1127.* Home-made teas. **Adm £3.50, chd £1. Sun 30 June (11-4).**
2-acre exotic garden featuring 100 large palms, 20+ bananas and 200 bamboo plants. 2 streams, 20ft tiered walkway leading to Thai style wooden covered pavilion. Mediterranean and jungle plants around 3 large ponds with fish. Suffolk's most exotic garden. Newly extended this year. Newly installed composting toilet straight out of Lord of the Rings/Harry Potter! It is 15ft tall with framed glass windows! Featured on Gardeners World, Look East, filmed by National Geographic TV. Featured in The Daily Telegraph and many publications.

23 HESSETT HOUSE

Drinkstone Road, Beyton, Bury St Edmunds IP30 9AH. Mr & Mrs Richard Holt. *5m E of Bury St Edmunds. 1m up Drinkstone Rd, from Beyton on R.* Home-made teas. **Adm £3, chd free. Sun 23 June (2-6).**
Large country garden with S-facing lawns, looking over the ha ha to parkland planted with native mature trees and a young copse. The rose garden is set in 16 formal beds of mature old fashioned roses backed by a pergola of roses and clematis. Shrub beds border the lawns. Swimming pool and tennis court gardens with hedges of yew and viburnum and beech hedge of impressive size. A gate leads through to young arboretum and beds of hydrangea. Gravel paths, grassed areas.

24 HOME FARM HOUSE

Rushbrooke IP30 0EP. Anita Wigan. *3m SE of Bury St Edmunds. A14 J44, proceed towards town centre, after 50yds 1st exit from r'bout then immed R. Proceed $^3/_4$ m to T-junction, turn L, follow rd for 2m Rushbrooke Church on L, turn R into drive opp church.* Home-made teas. **Adm £4, chd free. Sun 16 June (2-5). Also open The Lucy Redman Garden.**
3 acre walled garden with mixed shrubs and herbaceous borders, roses and formal lawns. 1-acre kitchen garden plus glasshouses with peaches, apricots, nectarines, grapes and figs etc. 5-acre parkland with moat garden, specimen trees and orchard. Small cottage garden alongside moat.

KIRTLING TOWER
See Cambridgeshire

Southleigh

25 NEW THE LABURNUMS
St. James South Elmham, Halesworth IP19 0HN. Mrs Jane Bastow. *6m W of Halesworth, 7m E of Harleston & 6m S of Bungay Parking at nearby village hall. For disabled parking please phone to arrange.* Home-made teas. **Adm £3.50, chd free. Mon 1 Apr (11-5).**
This one acre garden is 20 years old and is packed with annuals, perennials, flowering shrubs and trees and areas dedicated to wildflowers.The spring garden is awash with colour- snowdrops, aconites, hellebores, daffodils and much more. There are three ponds, a sunken garden and two glasshouses. This garden opened for Help For Heroes in May 2012. The owner is a Chelsea Gold medal winner and still exhibits each year at Chelsea, planting a trade stand for a local Sculptor. Gravel drive. Limited access to from garden. Steps to sunken garden. Concrete path in back garden.

26 LARKS' HILL
Clopton Road, Tuddenham St Martin IP6 9BY. Mr John Lambert, 01473 785248, jrlambert@talktalk.net. *3m NE of Ipswich. From Ipswich take B1077, go through village, take the Clopton Rd and Larks' Hill is on brow of the hill on L.* Home-made teas. **Adm £4, chd free. Sats 11 May; 15 June; 13 July; 10 Aug (2-6). Visitors also welcome by appt May to Aug.**
The gardens of 8 acres comprise woodland, field and more formal areas, and fall away from the house to the valley floor. A hill within a garden and in Suffolk at that! Hilly garden with a modern castle keep with an interesting and beautiful site overlooking the gentle Fynn valley and the village beyond.

27 NEW LAVENHAM HALL
Hall Road, Lavenham, Sudbury CO10 9QX. Mr & Mrs Anthony Faulkner. *Next to Lavenham's iconic church & close to High St. From Lavenham High St turn up Hall Rd (opp Greyhound pub). After 200 metres is a white 5 bar gate on the L which is the front drive for the Hall and entrance for those on foot. Follow signs for Parking.* **Adm £4, chd free. Sun 26 May (11-6.30).**
5 acre garden built around the ruins of the original ecclesiastical buildings on the site and the village's one acre fishpond. The garden includes deep borders of herbaceous planting with sweeping vistas and provides the perfect setting for the sculptures which Kate makes in her studios at the Hall and exhibits nationally and internationally. 40 garden sculptures on display. There is a gallery in the grounds which displays a similar number of indoor sculptures. Note large number of gravel paths and slopes within the garden.

Two very different gardens situated in this ancient and picturesque village . . .

GROUP OPENING

28 NEW LITTLE WALDINGFIELD GARDENS

Sudbury CO10 0SW. *4m E of Sudbury. The Priory is in the centre of the village, 100yds down Church Rd from The Street. The Maltings is situated on The Street towards the end of the village towards Monks Eleigh.* Tea In the Parish Rooms opposite The Priory. **Combined adm £5, chd free. Sun 23 June (10-5).**

NEW THE MALTINGS
Mrs Sally Furlonger.
Garden is at edge of the village. Pass the PH on L, and approx 400yds beyond, a cream painted house, with the gate on the far side. Enter grounds through white 5 bar gate. Plenty of parking. Garden accessed through wooden door leading into the courtyard,

NEW THE PRIORY
Mrs Laura Paul.
Please park on the playing fields, signed in the centre of the village. Opp the Swan PH is Church Rd, walk down this road and garden is 100yds down opp the church of St Lawrence
Visitors also welcome by appt June.
01787 247335
laura.priory@btinternet.com

The Maltings is very informal. A sunny courtyard leading to a walled garden. The principal feature is a long west facing herbaceous border. The east facing border is planted with a mixture of shrubs and perennials. Beyond the walled garden is a meadow and woodland, bisected by a small stream reached via a 200yd mown ride. A small pond, recently re-landscaped is behind the driveway. Caution, deep water. The Priory has a 2 acre garden, some of which is still a work in progress. The main lawn in front of the house is surrounded by herbaceous borders. There is a separate rose garden too. From the main lawn there is access to a raised vegetable and cutting garden. To the other side of house there is a swimming pool area which has raised herbaceous borders with a summer house. Wheelchair access restricted to certain areas.

LODE GARDENS
See Cambridgeshire

GROUP OPENING

29 LONG MELFORD GROUP

Hall Street, Sudbury COI0 9JQ. *2m N of Sudbury, 12m S of Bury St Edmunds. On village high street, opp The Bull Hotel.* **Combined adm £4, chd free. Sun 16 June (2-5.30).**

CONDUIT HOUSE
The Green. Nicholas & Fiona Pearson

SUN HOUSE
Hall Street. Lord Dixon-Smith

Two very different gardens situated in this ancient and picturesque village. The magnificent Holy Trinity Church looks down over the village green towards Conduit House whose large country house style garden offers zones of planting and hidden areas incl a scented garden, vegetable garden and massive herbaceous border. Sun House displays a plethora of contrasts in an established setting. Long Melford is famous for its long High Street along which there are plenty of interesting shops, galleries, PH and restaurants. The village also boasts two stately homes Kentwell Hall and Melford Hall.

30 THE LUCY REDMAN GARDEN

6 The Village, Rushbrooke, Bury St Edmunds IP30 0ER. Lucy Redman & Dominic Watts, www.lucyredman.co.uk. *3m E of Bury St Edmunds. From A14 Bury St Edmunds E Sudbury exit, proceed towards town centre. After 50yds, 1st L exit from r'about and immed R. ¾ m to T-junction, turn L, follow rd for 2m. Before church turn R between white houses, past brick well, thatched house on L.* Tea/coffee/cake (NGS day). **Adm £3, chd free. Sun 16 June (2-5). Also open Home Farm House.**

Thatched cottage with ¾ -acre quirky plantsman's family garden with impressive colour-coordinated borders - unusual shrubs, roses, grasses and perennials. Stone parterre, sculptures, unusual bulb and rhizome garden, decorative vegetable garden. 20m Celtic sculpture topped with 250 Sedum and Sempervivium. Woven metal turf tree seat/ fencing and lawn edging by Dominic's business. Garden visited by Beth Chatto. Featured in Dream Gardens of England book and GGG. Gravel paths.

447 MAIN ROAD
See Essex

31 MOAT HOUSE

Little Saxham, Bury St. Edmunds IP29 5LE. Mr & Mrs Richard Mason, 01284 810941, rnm333@live.com. *2m W of Bury St Edmunds. Leave A14 J42 - through Westley Village, at Xrds R towards Barrow/Saxham 1.3m L (follow signs).* Home-made teas. **Adm £3.50, chd free. Sun 9 June (1-5). Visitors also welcome by appt May to Aug, adm incl tea.**

Set in a 2 acre historic and partially moated site. This tranquil mature garden has been developed by the present owners over 20yrs. Bordered by mature trees the garden is in various sections incl a sunken garden, rose and clematis arbours, herbaceous bordered by box hedging, small arboretum. Featured in Country Homes and Interiors.

32 428 NORWICH ROAD

Ipswich IP1 5DU. Robert & Gloria Lawrence, 01473 743673, globoblaw@talktalk.net. *1½ m W of Ipswich town centre. On A1156 Norwich Rd garden is 200yds W of railway bridge.* Cream teas. STRAWBERRY CREAM TEAS WILL BE AVAILABLE. **Adm £2.50, chd free. Sat 15, Sun 16 June (2-5). Visitors also welcome by appt June to July.**

⅓ acre garden with sunken terrace and small pond leading up to lawn with rose beds, herbaceous border and dry stone garden. Lawn leads to bog garden, island mixed bed and on to orchard (17 fruit trees), asparagus bed, small vegetable plot with composting area and greenhouse.

GROUP OPENING

33 NEW OLD FELIXSTOWE GARDENS

41,Westmorland Road, Felixstowe IP11 9TJ. Mrs Diane Elmes. *corner of Wrens Park and Westmorland Road. Come into Felixstowe on A154 to r'about take 1st exit-Grove Road on to next r'about, turn R into Beatrice Ave, L at next r'about - High Road East, follow road approx 1¼ m to Cliftlands car park, turn L into Westmorland Rd.* Tea, cakes and scones at 41 Westmorland Road. **Combined adm £3.50, chd free. Sun 19 May (11-5).**

NEW 33 FERRY ROAD
Peter & Monica Smith

NEW FERRYFIELDS
Mr & Mrs Paul Smith.
Follow signs to Felixstowe Golf Club, Ferry Rd is opp Golf Club. Ferryfields is about ¼ m on L

NEW 41 WESTMORLAND ROAD
Mrs Diane Elmes.
No. 41 on corner of Wrens Park
Visitors also welcome by appt May to Sept.
01394 284647
dianeelmes@talktalk.net

Three very different gardens either close to the sea or the River Deben. 33 Ferry Road is a large irregular shaped garden with established trees, shrubs, herbaceous borders and vegetables. It is well established but is constantly evolving. Ferryfields has mature gardens of ⅓ -acre with lawns, borders and informal island beds with shrubs and perennials, greenhouses, pond and gazebo. With views over the Deben Estuary . The owners of 41 Westmorland Road moved into their house four years ago, since when they have recovered the garden by taking down 21 leylandii trees and various other dead trees. It is now full of perennials and has interesting and eclectic features.

♿ 🐕 ☕ ☎

OLIVERS
See Essex

34 ORCHARD HOUSE

22 Nethergate Street, Clare CO10 8NP. Gillian & Geoffrey Bray. *100yds from centre of Clare. On L of Nethergate St (A1092) from direction of Stoke-by-Clare. Limited on-street parking. Please use Country Park car park off Well Lane.* Home-made teas. **Adm £3, chd free. Sun 16 June (1.30-5).**

A surprisingly large garden for a town house. We redesigned, re-landscaped and replanted it in 2007/08 and maintain it entirely by ourselves. The long formal garden is divided into areas of different interest, which incl a tranquil pond garden, herb garden, colour-themed borders and productive kitchen garden. Wild area with newly planted trees and meadow flowers. Gravel drive on slight slope, before hard paths reached.

♿ ✿ ☕

Quite a young garden with very much work in progress . . .

GROUP OPENING

35 NEW ORFORD GARDENS

High Street, Woodbridge IP12 2NW. *Enter village on B1084. Continue past the Kings Head, then bear L by the Church onto the High Street. Anders is 200 yards on the RHside. For Brundish Lodge when entering Orford, the church is on L. Follow the road round to the L and up High St. Do not follow the main road down to the quay. Brundish Lodge where the road widens out. Please enter by wrought iron gate.* **Combined adm £3, chd free. Sun 23 June (2-6).**

NEW ANDERS
Mrs Sue Johnston.

NEW BRUNDISH LODGE
Mrs Elizabeth Spinney.

Two very different gardens with varied planting situated in the picturesque village of Orford. Anders is a garden of about an acre. It is informal and has evolved over the years. It has views of the R Ore and the North Sea. It suffers from strong winds and light soil. The mixed shrubberies have an emphasis on fragrance and colour. There are herbaceous beds and an orchard with many different fruit trees. Brundish Lodge is a garden of about one third of an acre. It was completely redesigned, reconstructed and replanted in 2005. It is therefore, quite a young garden with very much work in progress. It has beds which are a mixture of shrubs, herbaceous plants and grasses grouped around a central lawn.

♿

GROUP OPENING

36 PAKENHAM GARDENS

Fen Road, Bury St. Edmunds IP31 2LP, www.fenhouse.net. *5m NE of Bury St Edmunds. Off A143, 11m NW of Stowmarket A14 & A1088. 11m S of Thetford A1088 & A143. On entering Great Barton approx 1m, take R turn at Bunbury Arms signed Thurston/Pakenham. Turn L towards Pakenham through village, L past Agri Centre signed Watermill. Fen House ¼ m on R. Pelambech 1m on L.* Cream teas at Fen House. **Combined adm £3.50, chd free. Sun 30 June (11-5).**

FEN HOUSE 🛏
Lynn & Glynn Patterson-Evans
Visitors also welcome by appt May to Sept.
01359 234968
glynn.evans@hotmail.co.uk

PELAMBECH
Mr & Mrs A Jacobi

Two quite different gardens in picturesque village with a working watermill and windmill. Fen House is a beautiful half acre garden created on two levels accessed via steps or slope. Large pond with waterfall, numerous beds, incl collection of hostas, mature trees, shrubs, pergola and folly, small courtyard garden complete with red telephone box. Pelambech, a delight to wander around this pretty cottage garden of approx two thirds of an acre built on two levels. Interesting and colourful at most times of the year. This established garden has various water features and many attractive trees. Fen house only wheelchair access only.

♿ ✿ 🛏 ☕ ☎

37 PARHAM HALL
Hall Hill, Parham, Woodbridge IP13 9AB. Mr & Mrs A Paul. *3m SE of Framlingham. Off B1116 between Framlingham & Wickham Market.* Home-made teas. **Adm £4, chd free. Sun 14 July (2-5.30).**
8 acre formal and informal garden surrounded by lawn. Fine fully productive serpentine walled kitchen garden with fan trained and cordon fruit. Vine glasshouse. Small formal courtyard with herbs and scented plants, adjacent to sunken greenhouse and potting shed. The 390th Bomb group Memorial Air Museum and the Museum of the British Resistance Organisation Auxiliary Units is open in Parham on Sundays 11-5.

PARSONAGE HOUSE
See Essex

PEPPERS FARM
See Essex

38 NEW POLSTEAD MILL
Mill Lane, Polstead, Colchester CO6 5AB. Mrs Lucinda Bartlett, 01206 265969, lucyofleisure@hotmail.com. *Satnav finds the garden. Mill Lane lies between Polstead and Stoke by Nayland, the entrance to the Mill Lane is opp a small red post box. Polstead Mill is 1st house on R, with the car parking in a field on the R.* Home-made teas. **Adm £4, chd free. Sun 7 July (2.30-5.30). Visitors also welcome by appt May to Sept.**
The garden has formal and informal areas, a wild flower meadow and a large kitchen garden. The R Box runs through the garden and there is a mill pond, which gives opportunity for damp gardening, while much of the rest of the garden is arid and is planted to minimise the need for watering.

GROUP OPENING

39 NEW PRENTICE STREET
Lavenham, Sudbury CO10 9RD. *Behind Woolstaplers Cottage. From the Market Square walk down Prentice Street almost to the bottom.* Home-made teas. **Combined adm £3.50, chd free. Sun 18 Aug (11-5).**

NEW ORANGE HOUSE
Mr James Soane.
Prentice Street runs down the hill from the Market Square. ½ way down on RH-side

NEW WOOLSTAPLERS COTTAGE
Mr & Mrs Geoff & Sue Heald.
Walk down Prentice Street and you will find Woolstaplers Cottage is a Pretty Pink Cottage on your L

2 very different gardens, one recently designed behind a newly built modern property, the other behind a typical Lavenham medieval building. Orange House is a newly created garden which is divided into several rooms with formal lawn borders, a small orchard and fruit garden. Steps lead down a path to a lower area of oval lawn flanked on one side by an established shrubbery and on the other by a contemporary herbaceous border. The potager is set on an axis with a charming summerhouse complete with a planted roof. Woolstaplers Cottage has a beautiful small garden which will surprise and delight you with its tropical plants. It is packed full of rare and exotic specimens along with over 30 Roses, Clematis, Hostas, Ivy, Heuchera and Dahlias. Look for the rare Spotty Dotty and the Exotic Tetra Panax, Dicksonia Tara and Clerodendrons.

The potager is set on an axis with a charming summerhouse complete with a planted roof . . .

GROUP OPENING

40 NEW PRIORS HILL, ALDEBURGH
IP15 5ET. *At the r'about which is the junction of A1094 (Saxmundham Rd) and B1122 (Leiston Road), take A1094 E (Victoria Rd) into Aldeburgh. About 100 metres from the r'about, take Park Rd off to the R. After about 400 metres, Priors Hill Rd will branch off to the R (tennis courts on R).* Home made teas and soft drinks at Stanny. **Combined adm £5, chd free. Sun 15 Sept (2-5).**

HERON HOUSE
Mr Jonathan Hale.
Heron House is the last house on Priors Hill Rd on your R, at the junction where it rejoins Park Road
Visitors also welcome by appt Apr to Oct.
01728 452200
jonathanrhhale@aol.com

NEW LONGCROFT
Dr. and Mrs. Charles Twort

NEW STANNY
Kimberley & Angus Robertson

NEW WESTCROFT
Mr & Mrs John Thompson

Four gardens situated in Priors Hill Road with enviable views over the River Alde and the sea. All gardens are on a slope which gives the opportunity for terracing and associated planting. Heron House consists of two acres with views over coastline, river and marshes. Unusual trees, herbaceous beds, shrubs and ponds with waterfall in large rock garden, stream and bog garden. Interesting attempts to grow half hardy plants in the coastal micro-climate. Longcroft has a terrace going down to a lawn with a herbaceous border and then on to an orchard and vegetable garden. Many roses, clematis and a heather bed. Stanny is terraced over three levels. Many established camellias, hydrangea, grasses and mature trees, which incl Holm Oaks, Scots Pine, Japanese Maples and Strawberry Trees. Waterfall, large natural pond and wild flower meadow along with some exotic planting. Westcroft is a town garden with views of the river and sea. Please note the garden has a pond and children must be supervised. Wheelchair access with difficulty in some instances.

41 PRIORS OAK
Leiston Road, Aldeburgh IP15 5QE. Mrs Trudie Willis, 01728 452580, trudie.willis@dinkum.free-online.co.uk. *1m N of Aldeburgh on B1122. Garden on L opp RSPB Reserve.* Home-made teas. **Adm £3, chd free. Sun 30 June (2-6). Visitors also welcome by appt Mar to Sept.**

10-acre wildlife and butterfly garden. Ornamental salad and vegetable gardens with companion planting. Herbaceous borders, ferns and Mediterranean plants. Pond and wild flower acid grassland with a small wood. Skirting the wood are a 100 Buddlias in around 30 varieties forming a perfumed tunnel. Very tranquil and fragrant garden with grass paths and yearly interest. Rich in animal and bird life. Specialist butterfly garden, as seen in SAGA magazine, renovated railway carriages, tortoise breeding, wildlife walks.

♿ ✿ ☕ ☎

42 THE PRIORY

Stoke-by-Nayland, Colchester CO6 4RL. Mr & Mrs H F A Engleheart. *5m SW of Hadleigh. Entrance on B1068 to Sudbury (NW of Stoke-by-Nayland).* Home-made teas. **Adm £4, chd free. Sun 19 May (2-5).**

Interesting 9-acre garden with fine views over Constable countryside; lawns sloping down to small lakes and water garden; fine trees, rhododendrons and azaleas; walled garden; mixed borders and ornamental greenhouse. Wide variety of plants. Gravel paths, some slopes.

♿ 🐕 ✿ ☕

43 NEW RAVENSCROFT

Askins Road, East Bergholt, Colchester CO7 6SN. Mr D Milner, 01206 299343, jodavidrayner@btinternet.com. *9m NE of Colchester. Turn off the A12 onto B1070 signed East Bergholt. Take 1st R (Hadleigh Rd) then take 2nd L (Elm Rd) Please park in Elm Rd. Askins Rd is approx. 100yds on RH-side. Ravenscroft is 2nd property on L (30yds) on a narrow, unmade, cul-de-sac lane.* Home-made teas. **Adm £3, chd free. Sun 30 June (11-5). Visitors also welcome by appt Mar to Sept.**

Garden Designer and Plantaholic's small walled garden. It is full to capacity with many rare and unusual shrubs, trees and perennials. Interesting features incl a folly, large pond, an almost secret box-edged parterre, and studios with paintings for sale.

✿ ☕ ☎

44 REDISHAM HALL

nr Beccles NR34 8LZ. The Palgrave Brown Family. *5m S of Beccles. From A145, turn W on to Ringsfield-Bungay rd. Beccles, Halesworth or Bungay, all within 5m.* Light refreshments. **Adm £4, chd free. Sun 14 July (2-6).**

C18 Georgian house (not open). 5-acre garden set in 400 acres parkland and woods. Incl 2-acre walled kitchen garden (in full production) with peach house, vinery and glasshouses. Lawns, herbaceous borders, shrubberies, ponds and mature trees.

♿ ☕

45 RIVERSIDE HOUSE

Stoke Road, Clare, Sudbury CO10 8NS. Mr & Mrs A C W Bone, www.clare.bulbs.co.uk/garden. *On Haverhill side of Clare on A1092, 500yds from town centre.* **Adm £3.50, chd free. Sun 21 July (12-5).**

Peaceful walled country garden leading down to the R Stour. Fine lawns, trees, shrubs and mixed herbaceous beds. Annuals are a speciality. Some gravel paths.

♿ 🐕

ROOKWOODS

See Essex

46 ROSEDALE

40 Colchester Road, Bures CO8 5AE. Mr & Mrs Colin Lorking, 01787 227619, rosedale40@btinternet.com. *6m SE of Sudbury. 9m NW of Colchester on B1508. As you enter the village of Bures, garden on L. From Sudbury follow signs through village towards*

Great Thurlow Hall

©Harpur GL

Colchester, garden on R as you leave village. Home-made teas. **Adm £3, chd free. Sun 28 July (12-5.30). Visitors also welcome by appt. Preferably evenings & weekends.**
Approx 1/3 -acre plantsman's garden developed over the last 20 years,containing many unusual plants, herbaceous borders, pond and a stunning collection of approx 60 Agapanthus in full flower.

47 ROSEMARY
Rectory Hill, East Bergholt CO7 6TH. Mrs N E M Finch, 01206 298241. *9m NE of Colchester. Turn off A12 onto B1070 to East Bergholt, 1st R Hadleigh Rd; bear L at end of rd. At junction with Village St turn R, pass Red Lion PH, post office & church. Garden 100yds down from church on L.* Home-made teas. **Adm £3.50, chd free. Sun 16 June (2-5.30).**
This romantic garden, which appeals particularly to artists, has been developed over 35yrs. Planted to reveal paths and vistas. Many flowering trees and shrubs, much admired 'tapestry' bed with mixed hellebores, bulbs and appropriate ground cover. 2 bog beds, and unusual trees. Planted for all seasons. Over 100 old-fashioned roses.

48 RYDAL MOUNT
Grays Lane, Wissett, Halesworth IP19 0JP. Mr & Mrs A Witherby, 01986 873339, witherbys@btinternet.com. *2m W of Halesworth. From A12 exit onto A144 signed Halesworth/Bungay. Turn R into Halesworth, straight over 3 r'abouts then 1st L into Wissett Rd. Follow rd to Wissett, past church in Wissett, Grays Lane is next turning on R. Garden 1st house on L.* Home-made teas. **Adm £5, chd free. Sun 7 Apr (11-5). Visitors also welcome by appt Apr to Aug, adm incl teas.**
Fine vistas of daffodils shown off by flowering cherries, and ornamental trees. Primroses and cowslips in abundance. Roses predominate in June with many beds. Climbers and ramblers are supported by superb pergolas. 2 ponds, fine shrubbery, young orchard with orchids, chickens, geese and bees. Kitchen garden, polytunnel, and soft fruit. New Victorian greenhouse. Bird boxes for sale. Demonstration of bee-keeping.

SHRUBS FARM
See Essex

GROUP OPENING

49 SMALLWOOD GREEN GARDENS
Bradfield St George, nr Bury St Edmunds IP30 0AJ. *1/2 m from Bradfield Woods. On main rd between Hessett & Felsham. From A14 take Beyton turn off, S through Hessett. 2m from Hessett on Felsham rd. From A134 turn at Little Whelnetham, through Bradfield St George, past Bradfield Woods, turn L towards Hessett.* Home-made teas at Smallwood House (Martins Nursery). **Combined adm £4, chd free. Sun 16 June (11-5).**

SMALLWOOD FARMHOUSE
Smallwood Green. Widget & Tim Finn.
Pink farmhouse in dip on L
Visitors also welcome by appt May to Aug.
01449 736358
widget.finn@gmail.com

SMALLWOOD HOUSE
Bradfield St George. Richard & Susan Martin.
Follow the brown signs to Bradfield Woods in Bradfield St George
www.martinsnurseries.co.uk

Two adjacent gardens with different styles of herbaceous gardening in the hamlet of Smallwood Green. Smallwood House has a relatively new garden full of herbaceous perennials with two distinctive styles of gardening on view. Smallwood Farmhouse, a C16 farmhouse is a backdrop to a romantic mature 3-acre garden with old roses, clematis, honeysuckle rambling through trees, paths winding through ancient meadow to Ruby dome, with a variety of habitats.

50 SOUTHLEIGH
Valley Wash, Hundon CO10 8EJ. Paula Halson & Mike Laycock, www.southleighhouse.co.uk. *3 1/2 m NW of Clare. 5m NE of Haverhill, 10m S of Bury St Edmunds. A143 out of Haverhill, turn R at Grey's Lane to Barnardiston/Hundon. Follow rd to Hundon sign then 1/2 m on L, or take B1063 from Clare to Chilton St/Hundon.* Home-made teas. **Adm £3.50, chd free. Sun 23 June (10-4).**
Lovely 1/2 -acre cottage garden surrounding thatched cottage (not open) dating from 1640, situated on outskirts of village. Garden restored in recent yrs to incl both cottage-style planting and more formal borders. Music. Ramp up to main lawn.

SPENCERS
See Essex

Fine vistas of daffodils shown off by flowering cherries, and ornamental trees . . . primroses and cowslips in abundance . . .

51 STREET FARM
North Street, Freckenham IP28 8HY. David & Clodagh Dugdale. *3m W of Mildenhall. From A11 exit at Kennett to Chippenham. Through Chippenham and take 1st R then 1st R to Freckenham. North St on L by village cross, Street Farm 2nd on L.* Home-made teas. **Adm £4, chd free. Sun 12 May (11-5).**
Approx 1 acre of landscaped garden, with several mature trees. The garden incl a water cascade, pond with island and a number of bridges. Formal box garden, rose pergola, herbaceous borders and hornbeam walk. Gravel paths with steps and slopes. Featured in Homes and Gardens.

52 NEW TATTINGSTONE PLACE
Tattingstone Park, Tattingstone, Ipswich IP9 2NF. Mrs Sarah Chevenix-Trench. *From Ipswich take A137 towards Manningtree. At the Tattingstone/Bentley Xrds turn L (Wheatsheaf PH). Continue through the village where there are five sharp bends then a fruit & vegetable stall on R. Garden is approx 150yds on L(second entrance).* Home-made teas. **Adm £4, chd free. Sat 15 June (11-5).**

Kitchen garden, lime avenue, informal and formal pond, formal box parterre of herbaceous and roses within, large new pyramids, informal rambling rose garden, large terraced herbaceous garden, large oak pergola with rose clematis and vines, stone and gravel gardens, orchard and wild flower meadows, rose arches, millennium standing stone and large collection of lavender, agapanthus and iris. Glorious vistas over Alton Water. Limited wheelchair access to all parts of the garden although some areas have bark or stone paths which may make access more difficult.

TUDOR ROOST
See Essex

53 UGGESHALL HALL
Uggeshall, Beccles NR34 8BG. Stevie & Bob Nicholson. *6m W of Southwold, 6.8m S of Beccles. A12 from S, turn L at Wangford bypass to Uggeshall & Stoven, take 1st R then R again, garden 250 metres on L. A12 from Lowestoft, R after Frostenden to Clay Common, garden 1m on R. A145 from Beccles, L at Brampton xrds, 2nd L and garden $\frac{1}{2}$ m on L.* Tea. **Adm £3.50, chd free. Sun 9 June (2-6).**
2 acre, relaxed style, country garden of contrasting areas, curved paths and circular lawn lead to a gravel garden at the front of the house, to the side a large pond with walkways and platform, walled garden with beds and trees, an orchard, avenue of lime trees, vegetable garden and formal area with box hedging and pergola covered in old fashioned roses.

WASHLANDS
See Essex

54 WHITE HOUSE FARM
Ringsfield, Beccles NR34 8JU. James & Jan Barlow, 07780 901233 (gardener), coppertops707@aol.com. *2m SW of Beccles. From Beccles take B1062 towards Bungay, after $1\frac{1}{2}$ m turn L, signed Ringsfield. Continue for approx 1m. Parking opposite Ringsfield Church. Garden 300yds on L over small white railed bridge.* Light refreshments. **Adm £3.50, chd free. Sat 13 July (10.30-4.30). Visitors also welcome by appt Tuesday - Friday, daytime or evening, not weekends.**
Tranquil park-type garden approx 30 acres, bordered by farmland and with fine views. Comprising formal areas, copses, natural pond, ornamental pond, woodland walk, vegetable garden and orchard. Picnickers welcome. NB The ponds and beck are unfenced. Wheelchair access limited to the areas around the house.

55 WINDMILL COTTAGE
Mill Hill, Capel-St-Mary, Ipswich IP9 2JE. Mrs E M Cox, 01473 311121, gaandemcox@btinternet.com. *3m SW of Ipswich. Turn off A12 at Capel-St-Mary. At far end of village on R after $1\frac{1}{4}$ m.* Tea. **Adm £3, chd free. Sun 19 May (2-5). Visitors also welcome by appt May to June.**
$\frac{1}{2}$ -acre plantsman's cottage-style garden. Island beds, pergolas with clematis and other climbers. Many trees and shrubs, wildlife ponds and vegetable plot.

56 WOODWARDS
Blacksmiths Lane, Coddenham, Ipswich IP6 9TX. Marion & Richard Kenward, 01449 760639, richardwoodwards@btinternet.com. *7m N of Ipswich. From A14 turn onto A140, after $\frac{1}{4}$ m take B1078 towards Wickham Market, Coddenham is on route. Ample parking for coaches.* Home-made teas. **Adm £2.50, chd free. Suns, Tues 31 Mar; 9 Apr; 26 May; 18 June; 21, 30 July; 6, 25 Aug (10-5.30). Visitors also welcome by appt mid March to late Aug.**
Award winning S-facing gently sloping garden of $1\frac{1}{2}$ acres, overlooking the rolling Suffolk countryside. Designed and maintained by owners for yr-round colour and interest, lots of island beds, well stocked with 1000s of bulbs, shrubs and perennials, vegetable plot, numerous hanging baskets for spring and summer. Well manicured lawns, with large mature trees. More than 25000 bulbs have been planted over the last 3yrs, for our spring display. An unusual exhibition of photographic images bonded on to natural surfaces. It is an artistic combination that marries this beautiful setting with innovative sculptural forms, Sun July 21. Featured in W.I. Life Magazine and East Anglian Daily Times.

57 ◆ WOOTTENS
Blackheath Road, Wenhaston IP19 9HD. Mrs E Loftus, 01502 478258, www.woottensplants.co.uk. *18m S of Lowestoft. On A12 & B1123, follow signs to Wenhaston.* **Adm by donation. For NGS: Every Tue to Sun 2 Apr to 1 Oct (9.30-4). Woottens Bearded Iris Field - end of May to mid June. For other opening times and information, please phone or see garden website.**
Small romantic garden- redesigned in 2003. Overflowing with hardy perennials. Geraniums, Agapanthus, Irises, Anemones, Hostas, to admire and inspire. Woottens Bearded Iris Field - over two acres of scent and colour.

Large collection of lavender, agapanthus and iris . . . glorious vistas over Alton Water . . .

58 ◆ WYKEN HALL
Stanton IP31 2DW. Sir Kenneth & Lady Carlisle, 01359 250287, www.wykenvineyards.co.uk. *9m NE of Bury St Edmunds. Along A143. Follow signs to Wyken Vineyards on A143 between Ixworth & Stanton.* **Adm £3.50, chd free. For NGS: Sats, Suns 23, 24 Mar; 14, 15 Sept (10-6). For other opening times and information, please phone or see garden website.**
4-acre garden much developed recently; knot and herb garden; old-fashioned rose garden, wild garden, nuttery, pond, gazebo and maze; herbaceous borders and old orchard. Woodland walk, vineyard. Resturant and shop.

© Harpur GL

Suffolk County Volunteers

County Organiser

Jenny Reeve, 6a Church Walk, Mildenhall IP28 7ED, 01638 715289, j.reeve05@tiscali.co.uk

County Treasurer

David Reeve, 6a Church Walk, Mildenhall, Bury St. Edmunds IP28 7ED, 01638 715289, j.reeve05@tiscali.co.uk

Publicity & Booklet Coordinator

Catherine Horwood Barwise, Richmond House, 20 Nethergate Street, Clare, Sudbury CO10 8NP, 01787 279315, catherine@richmondhouse-clare.com

Assistant County Organisers:

Gilly Beddard, The Old School, School Road, Sudbourne IP12 2BE, 01394 450468
Francis Boscawen, Moat Farm, Dennington, Woodbridge IP13 8BZ, 01728 638768
Yvonne Leonard, Crossbills, Field Road, Mildenhall IP28 7AL, 01638 712742, yj.leonard@btinternet.com
Barbara Segall, Primrose Cottage, Edgworth Road, Sudbury CO10 2TG, 01787 312046 barbara@bsegall.com
Dick Soper, Cobbs Hall, Cobbs Hall Lane, Great Saxham, Bury St Edmunds, IP29 5JN, 01284 850678, soperdoc@gmail.com

Recycle – bring a bag for your plant purchases

SURREY

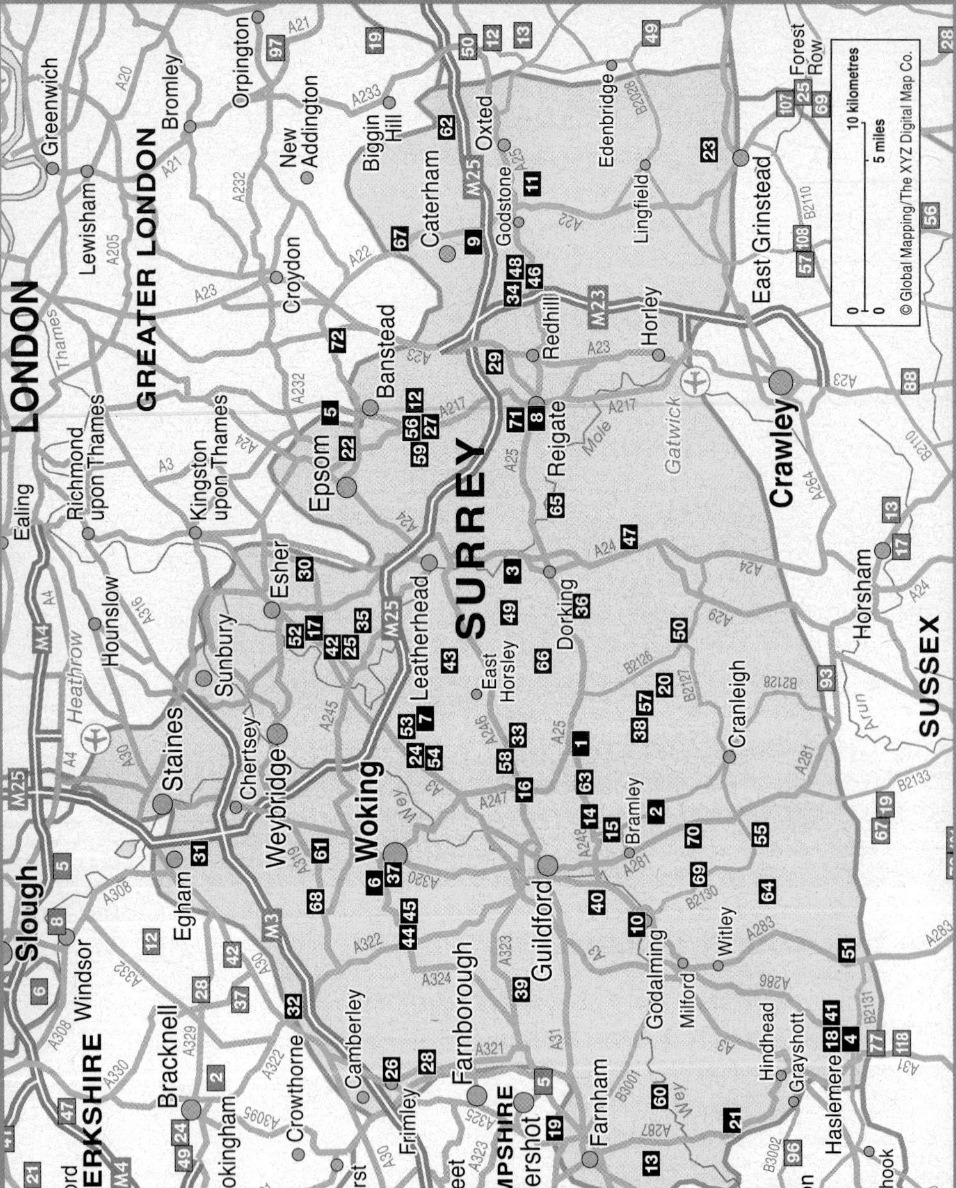
LONDON
GREATER LONDON
SURREY
BERKSHIRE
HAMPSHIRE
SUSSEX
Greenwich
Lewisham
Bromley
Orpington
New Addington
Biggin Hill
Croydon
Ealing
Richmond upon Thames
Kingston upon Thames
Hounslow
Heathrow
Slough
Windsor
Twyford
Wokingham
Bracknell
Crowthorne
Sandhurst
Camberley
Frimley
Fleet
Farnborough
Aldershot
Farnham
Egham
Staines
Sunbury
Chertsey
Weybridge
Esher
Woking
Epsom
Banstead
Caterham
Oxted
Godstone
Redhill
Reigate
Leatherhead
East Horsley
Dorking
Guildford
Bramley
Godalming
Milford
Witley
Cranleigh
Hindhead
Grayshott
Haslemere
Liphook
Bordon
Edenbridge
Lingfield
East Grinstead
Forest Row
Horley
Gatwick
Crawley
Horsham
Thames
Mole
Wey
Arun
0 10 kilometres
0 5 miles
© Global Mapping/The XYZ Digital Map Co.

Opening Dates

February

Sunday 17
29 Gatton Park

March

Saturday 16
70 Wintershall Manor

Sunday 17
1 Albury Park

Sunday 24
16 Clandon Park

Sunday 31
8 Caxton House
9 The Chalet

April

Tuesday 2
64 Vann

Wednesday 3
64 Vann

Thursday 4
64 Vann

Friday 5
64 Vann

Saturday 6
64 Vann

Sunday 7
9 The Chalet
20 Coverwood Lakes
64 Vann

Sunday 14
20 Coverwood Lakes
69 Winkworth Arboretum

Sunday 21
20 Coverwood Lakes
56 41 Shelvers Way

Saturday 27
24 Dunsborough Park

Sunday 28
20 Coverwood Lakes
41 The Manor House

May

Saturday 4
70 Wintershall Manor

Sunday 5
13 Chestnut Cottage
21 Crosswater Farm

Monday 6
20 Coverwood Lakes
21 Crosswater Farm
64 Vann
66 Walton Poor House

Tuesday 7
64 Vann

Wednesday 8
64 Vann

Thursday 9
64 Vann

Friday 10
64 Vann

Saturday 11
17 Claremont Landscape Garden
32 Hall Grove School
64 Vann
68 Westways Farm

Sunday 12
20 Coverwood Lakes
33 Hatchlands Park
38 Knowle Grange
40 Loseley Park
64 Vann
68 Westways Farm

Monday 13
11 Chauffeur's Flat

Tuesday 14
11 Chauffeur's Flat
31 Great Fosters

Wednesday 15
11 Chauffeur's Flat
31 Great Fosters

Thursday 16
11 Chauffeur's Flat

Friday 17
11 Chauffeur's Flat

Saturday 18
11 Chauffeur's Flat
19 56 Copse Avenue
62 Titsey Place Gardens

Sunday 19
11 Chauffeur's Flat
14 Chilworth Manor
19 56 Copse Avenue

Friday 24
51 Ramster

Saturday 25
34 The Hawthorns

Sunday 26
13 Chestnut Cottage
23 Dormans Park Safari
47 The Old Croft
67 57 Westhall Road

Monday 27
47 The Old Croft
67 57 Westhall Road

June

Saturday 1
24 Dunsborough Park

Sunday 2
53 Rose Cottage

Saturday 8
54 7 Rose Lane

Sunday 9
64 Vann

Monday 10
64 Vann

Tuesday 11
64 Vann

Wednesday 12
64 Vann

Thursday 13
64 Vann

Friday 14
64 Vann

National Gardens Weekend

Saturday 15
4 Bardsey
11 Chauffeur's Flat
18 Cleeves
26 16 Farm Road
35 Heathside
55 The Round House
61 Timber Hill
62 Titsey Place Gardens
64 Vann
65 Vicarage Cottage
66 Walton Poor House
67 57 Westhall Road (Evening)

Sunday 16
4 Bardsey
7 Bridge End Cottage
10 Charterhouse
11 Chauffeur's Flat
12 Chelsfield
18 Cleeves
22 Culverkeys
25 Fairmile Lea
26 16 Farm Road
28 Frimley Green Gardens
30 21 Glenavon Close
35 Heathside
39 Longer End Cottage
42 Moleshill House
55 The Round House
58 Stuart Cottage
61 Timber Hill
65 Vicarage Cottage
66 Walton Poor House
67 57 Westhall Road (Evening)

Something of interest to see whichever way you turn . . .

Monday 17
11 Chauffeur's Flat

Tuesday 18
11 Chauffeur's Flat

Wednesday 19
11 Chauffeur's Flat

Thursday 20
11 Chauffeur's Flat

Friday 21
3 Ashleigh Grange (Evening)
11 Chauffeur's Flat

Saturday 22
11 Chauffeur's Flat
60 Tilford Cottage

Sunday 23
3 Ashleigh Grange
6 Birch Cottage
11 Chauffeur's Flat
15 Chinthurst Lodge
27 The Firs
37 Horsell Allotments
45 141 Oakway
52 Rose Briar
60 Tilford Cottage

Wednesday 26
3 Ashleigh Grange
15 Chinthurst Lodge

Friday 28
60 Tilford Cottage (Evening)

Saturday 29
60 Tilford Cottage

Sunday 30
48 The Old Rectory
60 Tilford Cottage

July

Saturday 6
71 Woodbury Cottage

Sunday 7
71 Woodbury Cottage

Saturday 13
62 Titsey Place Gardens

Sunday 14
22 Culverkeys
25 Fairmile Lea
42 Moleshill House
49 Polesden Lacey
55 The Round House
58 Stuart Cottage

Saturday 20
2 Appletrees

Sunday 21
2 Appletrees
44 19 Oak Tree Road
56 41 Shelvers Way
72 48 Woodmansterne Lane

Saturday 27
2 Appletrees (Evening)

August

Saturday 3
4 Bardsey
59 35 Tadorne Road

Sunday 4
4 Bardsey
26 16 Farm Road
46 Odstock
59 35 Tadorne Road

Saturday 10
5 Bethany
47 The Old Croft

Sunday 11
5 Bethany
47 The Old Croft
58 Stuart Cottage

Saturday 17
50 Pratsham Grange
62 Titsey Place Gardens

Sunday 18
50 Pratsham Grange

Sunday 25
43 Norwood Farm

Saturday 31
71 Woodbury Cottage

September

Sunday 1
71 Woodbury Cottage

Wednesday 4
71 Woodbury Cottage

Saturday 14
24 Dunsborough Park

Sunday 15
36 Hill Farm
38 Knowle Grange

October

Sunday 6
1 Albury Park
69 Winkworth Arboretum

Saturday 12
66 Walton Poor House

Sunday 13
17 Claremont Landscape Garden
66 Walton Poor House

Sunday 20
20 Coverwood Lakes
33 Hatchlands Park

February 2014

Sunday 16
29 Gatton Park

Gardens open to the public

16 Clandon Park
17 Claremont Landscape Garden
21 Crosswater Farm
29 Gatton Park
33 Hatchlands Park
40 Loseley Park
49 Polesden Lacey
51 Ramster
62 Titsey Place Gardens
64 Vann
69 Winkworth Arboretum

By appointment only

57 Spurfold
63 Vale End

Also open by Appointment ☎

2 Appletrees
3 Ashleigh Grange
4 Bardsey
8 Caxton House
15 Chinthurst Lodge
18 Cleeves
22 Culverkeys
26 16 Farm Road
30 21 Glenavon Close
35 Heathside
38 Knowle Grange
46 Odstock
50 Pratsham Grange
55 The Round House
56 41 Shelvers Way
58 Stuart Cottage
60 Tilford Cottage
61 Timber Hill
66 Walton Poor House
68 Westways Farm
71 Woodbury Cottage

Beautiful gardens tended by passionate owners . . .

The Round House © Leigh Clapp

The Gardens

1 ALBURY PARK

Albury GU5 9BH. Trustees of Albury Estate. *5m SE of Guildford. From A25 take A248 towards Albury for 1/4 m, then up New Rd, entrance to Albury Park immed on L.* Home-made teas. **Adm £3.50, chd free. Suns 17 Mar; 6 Oct (2-5).**

14-acre pleasure grounds laid out in 1670s by John Evelyn for Henry Howard, later 6th Duke of Norfolk. 1/4 m terraces, fine collection of trees, lake and river. Gravel path and slight slope.

23 ANGLESEY ROAD

See Hampshire

2 APPLETREES

Stonards Brow, Shamley Green, Guildford GU5 0UY. Mr & Mrs A Hodgson, 01483 898779, thodgson@uwclub.net. *5m SE of Guildford. A281 Guildford to Horsham rd, turn L at Shalford on B2128 via Wonersh to Shamley Green. Turn R before Red Lion PH, then R into Sweetwater Lane. At top of lane turn R into Stonards Brow or follow signs to car park when entering village. From Ewhurst/Cranleigh turn L at village stores, proceed down Hullbrook Lane following signs to Longacre School car park.* Cream teas & light refreshments. **Adm £4, chd free. Sat 20 July (12-4) with lunchtime BBQ; Sun 21 July (2-6). Evening Opening £6.50, chd free, wine, Sat 27 July (6-9). Visitors also welcome by appt in July.**

1/4 -acre garden with many interesting features. Several small water features incl koi pond. Summerhouse, greenhouses, raised railway sleeper beds, pergolas. Shrub and perennial borders. Patio and gravel area with several colourful containers. Raised vegetable beds; jungle beds with bananas and an elevated walkway; small Japanese garden. Obelisks and clematis, all on a sandy loam soil. An ideas garden. Music in the Garden on Sat 27 July from The Pete Spence Trio Jazz Group. Limited wheelchair access. Parking for disabled reserved outside house.

3 ASHLEIGH GRANGE

off Chapel Lane, Westhumble RH5 6AY. Clive & Angela Gilchrist, 01306 884613, ar.gilchrist@btinternet.com. *2m N of Dorking. From A24 at Boxhill/ Burford Bridge follow signs to Westhumble. Through village & L up drive by ruined chapel (1m from A24).* Home-made teas. **Adm £3.50, chd free (share to Barnardo's). Evening Opening £5.50, chd free, wine, Fri 21 June (6-8); Sun 23, Wed 26 June (2-5.30). Visitors also welcome by appt May to July.**

Plant lover's chalk garden on 3 1/2 -acre sloping site in charming rural setting with delightful views. Many areas of interest incl rockery and water feature, raised ericaceous bed, prairie-style bank, foliage plants, woodland walk, fernery and folly. Large mixed herbaceous and shrub borders planted for dry alkaline soil and widespread interest.

4 BARDSEY

11 Derby Road, Haslemere GU27 1BS. Maggie & David Boyd, 01428 652283, maggie.boyd@live.co.uk, www.bardseygarden.co.uk. *1/4 m N of Haslemere station. Turn off B2131 (which links A287 to A286 through town) 400yds W of station into Weydown Rd, 3rd R into Derby Rd, garden 400yds on R.* Home-made teas. **Adm £4, chd free. Sats, Suns 15, 16 June; 3, 4 Aug (11-5). Visitors also welcome by appt June to Aug.**

Relax in this 2-acre garden in the heart of Haslemere. Wander through fragrant herb and rose parterres bordered by lavender and box. Enjoy the herbaceous borders, raised vegetable beds and fruit garden. In the lower garden watch ducks and dragonflies in the natural ponds and the reflection of a tree carving. Classic MGs on view. First third of garden level, other two thirds sloping.

BEECHENWOOD FARM
See Hampshire

BERRYLANDS GARDENS GROUP
See London

52A BERRYLANDS ROAD
See London

5 BETHANY

87 Sandy Lane, South Cheam SM2 7EP. Brian & Pam West & Mrs D West. *2m W of Sutton. Approx 1m S of Cheam village, or from A217 turn into Northey Ave. At small r'about L into Sandy Lane, then approx 100yds on L.* Home-made teas. **Adm £3.50, chd free. Sat 10, Sun 11 Aug (1-5.30).**

1/3 -acre plantsman's garden with a subtropical feel where palm trees, tree ferns, banana trees, agave and bamboo surround the wide lawn. Vibrant coloured dahlias and a large collection of cannas make this an exciting August garden. Behind pretty summerhouse is vegetable garden and greenhouses.

Enter a 1-acre tapestry of magical secret gardens with magnificent views . . .

6 BIRCH COTTAGE

5 High Street, Horsell, Woking GU21 4XA. Celia & Mel Keenan. *Entrance on High St opp Bullbeggars Lane.* Home-made teas. **Adm £3.50, chd free. Sun 23 June (11-4). Also open Horsell Allotments.**

Created since 1999, smallish garden designed to reflect the 400yr old Grade II listed cottage. Knot-style box garden in front; at the rear, courtyard with planted pots and hanging baskets, rill water feature, gravel garden, active dovecote, archway with climbing roses through to the kitchen garden, with greenhouse. Shrubs and perennials throughout.

7 NEW BRIDGE END COTTAGE

Ockham Lane, Ockham GU23 6NR. Clare & Peter Bevan. *Nr RHS Gardens at Wisley. Travel S on A3, take the B2039 to Horsley/Ockham. Enter Wisley r'about, take 1st exit L and after 1/2 m turn L at Ockham Memorial Cross into Ockham Lane. House on the R after Cricket Club.* Home-made teas. **Adm £3.50, chd free. Sun 16 June (11-5).**

A 2-acre country garden with several different areas of interest including perennial borders, mature trees, pond and streams, herb parterre, fruit trees, soft fruit cage, vegetable patch and a large wild flower meadow in the making. Limited wheelchair access.

BURY COURT
See Hampshire

8 CAXTON HOUSE

67 West Street, Reigate RH2 9DA. Bob Bushby, 01737 243158. *On A25 towards Dorking, approx 1/4 m W of Reigate on L. Parking on rd.* Cream teas. **Adm £3.50, chd free. Sun 31 Mar (2-5). Groups of 10+ also welcome by appt Mar to Sept.**

Lovely large spring garden with wildlife wood, 2 well-stocked ponds, large collection of hellebores and spring flowers. Pots planted with colourful displays. Interesting plants in conservatory. Small Gothic folly built by owner. Herbaceous borders with grasses, perennials, spring bulbs and parterre. New bed with wild daffodils and wild flower meadow. Antique dog cart completes the picture.

9 THE CHALET

Tupwood Lane, Caterham CR3 6ET. Miss Lesley Manning & Mr David Gold. *1/2 m N of M25 J6. Exit J6 of M25 onto A22 going N. After 1/2 m take sharp 1st L into Tupwood Lane. Car park immediately on the R in field. Wheelchair and disabled access parking at top of the hill via Tupwood Lane.* Home-made teas. **Adm £4, chd free (share to St Catherine's Hospice). Suns 31 Mar; 7 Apr (11-4.30).**

55 acres. Carpets of tens of thousands of daffodils; lakes, ornamental ponds, koi pond and waterfall. Ancient woodlands, grasslands and formal garden. Large planted terraces. Beautiful Victorian mansion (not open). Woodland and garden trail. On view, a limited edition 'Blue Train' Bentley, Silver Phantom Rolls Royce and various vintage and classic cars. Partial wheelchair access, some steep slopes. 3 large unfenced ponds.

10 CHARTERHOUSE

Hurtmore Road, Godalming GU7 2DF. The Headmaster The Reverend John Witheridge & Mrs Sarah Witheridge. *1/2 m N of Godalming town centre at top of Charterhouse Hill. Follow signs for Charterhouse from A3 & Godalming town centre.* Home-made teas. **Adm £5, chd free. Sun 16 June (2.30-5).**

Extensive grounds with mature trees and mixed borders around beautiful old buildings. Two historical borders planted with species available prior to 1872, based on the writings of William Robinson; several enclosed individual gardens. Headmaster's garden, originally designed by Gertrude Jekyll, with long herbaceous border, pergola, mixed borders, Lutyens summerhouse and double dry stone wall.

CHARTWELL
See Kent

11 CHAUFFEUR'S FLAT

Tandridge Lane, Tandridge RH8 9NJ. Mr & Mrs Richins. *2m E of Godstone. Turn off A25 for Tandridge. Take drive on L past church. Follow arrows to circular courtyard.* Home-made teas. **Adm £3, chd free (share to Sutton & Croydon MS Therapy Centre). Mon 13 May to Sun 19 May incl (10-5); Sat 15 June to Sun 23 June incl (10-5).**

Enter a 1-acre tapestry of magical secret gardens with magnificent views. Touching the senses, all sure-footed visitors may explore the many surprises on this constantly evolving exuberant escape from reality. Imaginative use of recycled materials creates an inspired variety of ideas, while wild and specimen plants reveal an ecological haven.

12 NEW CHELSFIELD

Hill Lane, Kingswood, Tadworth KT20 6DZ. Pat & Mike Gibson. *1/2 m S of junction between A217 and A240 at Burgh Heath. Turning on L signed to Kingswood Station, Hill Lane is 2nd turning on L (steep turn). Chelsfield is 3rd on the R.*

Adm £4, chd free. **Sun 16 June (2-5.30).**
Enthusiast's ½ -acre garden planted for yr round interest, developed and maintained by owners. Gentle S-facing slope with mixed borders (shrubs, perennials, roses, clematis); specimen trees; agave and cacti; orchard; soft fruit; kitchen garden with raised beds and compost area; greenhouse and propagation area.

13 CHESTNUT COTTAGE

15 Jubilee Lane, Boundstone, Farnham GU10 4SZ. Mr & Mrs David Wingent. *2½ m SW of Farnham. From A31 r'about take A325 to Petersfield, ½ m bear L. At mini r'about into School Hill, ½ m over staggered Xrds, into Sandrock Hill Road, 4th turn R after PH.* Home-made teas. **Adm £3, chd free.** **Sun 5, Sun 26 May (2-5.30).**
½ -acre garden created by owners on different levels. Rhododendrons, azaleas, acers and conifers. Long pergola with wisteria and roses, attractive gazebo copied from the original at NT Hunting Lodge in Odiham. Peaceful setting. Plant expert John Negus will be in attendance.

14 CHILWORTH MANOR

Halfpenny Lane, Chilworth, Guildford GU4 8NN. Mia & Graham Wrigley. *3½ m SE of Guildford. From centre of Chilworth village turn into Blacksmith Lane. 1st drive on R on Halfpenny Lane.* Home-made teas. **Adm £5, chd free.** **Sun 19 May (11-5).**
Extensive grounds of lawns and mature trees around C17/C18 manor on C11 monastic site. Substantial C18 terraced walled garden laid out by Sarah, Duchess of Marlborough, with herbaceous borders, topiary and fruit trees. Original stewponds integrated with new Japanese-themed garden and woodland garden and walk. Paddock home to alpacas. Ongoing restoration project aims to create a contemporary and practical garden sensitive to its historic context. Garden walks at 11.30, 12.30, 1.30 & 2.30.

15 CHINTHURST LODGE

Wonersh Common Road, Wonersh, Guildford GU5 0PR. Mr & Mrs M R Goodridge, 01483 535108, michaelgoodridge@ymail.com. *4m S of Guildford. From A281 at Shalford turn E onto B2128 towards Wonersh. Just after Waverley sign, before village, garden on R.* Home-made teas. **Adm £4, chd free.** **Sun 23, Wed 26 June (12-5.30).** **Visitors also welcome by appt May to July, wine is also available.**
1-acre yr-round enthusiast's atmospheric garden, divided into rooms. Herbaceous borders, white garden, specimen trees and shrubs, gravel garden with water feature, small kitchen garden, fruit cage, 2 wells, ornamental ponds, herb parterre and millennium parterre garden. Some gravel paths, which can be avoided.

C18 terraced walled garden . . . with herbaceous borders, topiary and fruit trees . . .

THE CIRCLE GARDEN

See London

16 ◆ CLANDON PARK

West Clandon, Guildford GU4 7RQ. National Trust, 01483 222482, www.nationaltrust.org.uk. *3m E of Guildford on A247. From A3 follow signs to Ripley to join A247 via B2215.* **Adm £4.20, chd free.** **For NGS: Sun 24 Mar (11-4.30).** **For other opening times and information, please phone or see garden website.**
Garden around the house laid out informally, apart from parterre beneath S front. To the S a mid-C18 grotto. Principal front faces parkland, laid out in the style of Capability Brown around 1770. Created in 1901, Dutch garden modelled on the pond garden at Hampton Court Palace. Large bulb and daffodil field looks stunning in spring.

17 ◆ CLAREMONT LANDSCAPE GARDEN

Portsmouth Road, Esher KT10 9JG. National Trust, 01372 467806, www.nationaltrust.org.uk. *1m SW of Esher. On E side of A307 (no access from A3 bypass).* **Adm £7.20, chd £3.60.** **For NGS: Sat 11 May, Sun 13 Oct (10-5.30).** **For other opening times and information, please phone or see garden website.**
One of the earliest surviving English landscape gardens, begun by Vanbrugh and Bridgeman before 1720 and extended and naturalised by Kent and Capability Brown. Lake, island with pavilion; grotto and turf amphitheatre; viewpoints and avenues. Free guided walk at 2pm both NGS days with member of the gardening team. Access maps available with recommended route.

18 CLEEVES

Weydown Road, Haslemere GU27 1DT. Peter & Sue Morgan, 01428 642757, petermorgan@cleeves2.demon.co.uk. *Just over ½ m from Haslemere station. R out of station, under railway bridge, R into Weydown Rd, approx ½ m up on R.* Home-made teas. **Adm £4, chd free.** **Sat 15, Sun 16 June (11-5).** **Groups of 20+ also welcome by appt May to Sept.**
This 2-acre garden has been landscaped and developed over thirty years with designs and advice from John Brookes. It has 8-10 different 'rooms' which are full of surprises. Strategically positioned benches allow visitors to enjoy the perspectives and the tranquillity. Visitors have described the garden as 'magical'.

19 NEW 56 COPSE AVENUE

Farnham GU9 9EA. Lyn & Jimmy James. *Approx 1½ m N of Farnham. From A31 at Shepherd and Flock r'about take A325 towards Farnborough. At 2nd r'about take last exit signed Weybourne. After approx 1m turn L at Xrds with T-lights into Upper Weybourne Lane. Take 2nd R into Oakland Ave. Continue to T-Junction, turn L. Parking in local residential roads.* Home-made teas. **Adm £3.50, chd free.** **Sat 18, Sun 19 May (12-5).**
A fascinating and unusual 1-acre garden in a residential area. The garden was originally landscaped in the late 1960s following the plans of a Chelsea Flower Show garden, but was subsequently allowed to become very overgrown. The present owners have restored many of the original features and are adding innovative areas of planting and interest.

©Nicola Stocken Tomkins

COTTAGE FARM
See Kent

20 COVERWOOD LAKES
Peaslake Road, Ewhurst GU6 7NT. The Metson Family, 01306 731101, www.coverwoodlakes.co.uk. *7m SW of Dorking. From A25 follow signs for Peaslake; garden ½ m beyond Peaslake on Ewhurst rd.* Light refreshments. **Adm £5, chd £2. Suns 7, 14, 21, 28 Apr; Mon 6, Sun 12 May (2-6); Sun 20 Oct (11-4.30).**
14-acre landscaped garden in stunning position high in the Surrey Hills with 4 lakes and bog garden. Extensive rhododendrons, azaleas and fine trees. 3½ -acre lakeside arboretum. Marked trail through the 180-acre working farm with Hereford cows and calves, sheep and horses, extensive views of the surrounding hills.

21 ◆ CROSSWATER FARM
Crosswater Lane, Churt, Farnham GU10 2JN. Mrs E G Millais & Family, 01252 792698, www.rhododendrons.co.uk. *6m S of Farnham, 6m NW of Haslemere. From A287 turn E into Jumps Rd ½ m N of Churt village centre. After ¼ m turn acute L into Crosswater Lane & follow signs for Millais Nurseries.* **Adm £3.50, chd free. For NGS: Sun 5, Mon 6 May (10-5). For other opening times and information, please phone or see garden website.**
Idyllic 6-acre woodland garden. Plantsman's collection of rhododendrons and azaleas, incl rare species collected in the Himalayas, hybrids raised by the owners. Everything from alpine dwarfs to architectural large-leaved trees. Ponds, stream and companion plantings incl sorbus, magnolias and Japanese acers. Trial gardens of new varieties. Woodland garden and specialist plant centre. RHS Chelsea Gold Medal. Grass paths may be soft after rain.

22 CULVERKEYS
20A Longdown Lane North, Ewell, Epsom KT17 3JQ. Anne Salt, 020 8393 6861. *1m E of Epsom, 1m S of Ewell Village. Leave Ewell bypass (A24) by Reigate Rd (A240) to pass Nescot on L. Turn R in ¼ m.* **Adm £3, chd free. Suns 16 June, 14 July (2-5). Visitors also welcome by appt May to Sept.**
A romantic somewhat secret garden on the edge of Epsom Downs. Meandering paths pass borders planted to capacity with interesting and unusual plants. Arches smothered in climbers reveal secluded corners and running water soothes the spirit. Designed for yr-round interest, shrubs and trees play host to many clematis.

GROUP OPENING

23 DORMANS PARK SAFARI
Dormans Park, East Grinstead RH19 2NB. *Between Lingfield and East Grinstead. Two entrances to Dormans Park: from East Grinstead, on A264 turn L after hospital down rd to Dormansland, entrance on L after 1m. Or from A22 to Lingfield, follow rd at 2nd r'about to Felcourt, bear L into Blackberry Lane then turn L follow signs. Entrance nr Dormans stn. Please buy a ticket and collect a map (showing directions and parking) at one of the 2 entrances to the Park.* Light refreshments at Lake House and Castanas. **Combined adm £6, chd free. Sun 26 May (10-4.30).**

BENTLEY
Andrew & Annabel Simpson

BRAEKENAS
Ann Lindfield

CASTANAS
Mrs A Brown

LAKE HOUSE
The Rousell family

LOENWOOD
Maria Osmore

Second year of this Safari. 5 gardens have been chosen to take part and all gardens offer something quite different, combining to make a unique experience. Dormans Park dates back to 1887 and originally comprised 218 acres of farmland and coppiced woodland. Following the arrival of the railway, plots were sold off for development by the Bellaggio Estate. Today the Park offers an interesting variety of houses old and new. Some have architectural interest and history, but all have beautiful gardens tended by passionate owners. There will be gardens where picnics are allowed (and WCs) so possibility to make a day out, buying tea, coffee and cakes in 2 gardens. Wheelchair access to most gardens.

24 DUNSBOROUGH PARK
Ripley GU23 6AL. Baron & Baroness Sweerts de Landas Wyborgh, www.dunsboroughpark.com. *6m NE of Guildford. Entrance across Ripley Green via The Milkway opp Wylie & Mar*. Home-made teas. **Adm £5, chd free. Sats 27 Apr; 1 June; 14 Sept (2-6).**
Extensive walled gardens of 6 acres redesigned by Penelope Hobhouse and Rupert Golby, structured with box hedging creating different garden rooms. Exciting herbaceous borders with beautiful standard wisterias. 70ft ginkgo hedge and ancient mulberry tree. Atmospheric water garden with life-size gunnera/rhododendrons. Festival of Tulips with 10,000 bulbs and large cut flower garden. Spectacular dahlias in September.

ELM TREE COTTAGE
See London

ETON COLLEGE GARDENS
See Berkshire

25 NEW FAIRMILE LEA
Portsmouth Road, Cobham KT11 1BG. Steven Kay. *2m NE of Cobham. On A307 Esher to Cobham Rd, next to car park by A3 bridge, by Moleshill House at entrance to Waterford Close. Fairmile Lea 200 metres up lane from car park*. Home-made teas. **Adm £5.50, chd free. Suns 16 June (11-2); 14 July (2-5). Combined adm with Moleshill House.**
Large Victorian sunken garden with pond. An old acacia tree stands in the midst of the lawn. Interesting planting on a large mound camouflages an old underground air raid shelter. Caged vegetable garden. Formality adjacent to wilderness.

26 16 FARM ROAD
Frimley, Camberley GU16 8TE. Norma & Bob Stephens, 01276 62162, bobandnorma@virginmedia.com. *1½ m from M3 J4. From J4 (M3) follow signs for Frimley Pk Hospital. At Hospital r'about take Chobham Rd (opp Hospital entrance). At mini r'about 1st L into Bicknell Rd, 1st R into Farm Rd. 16 is just before shops on L. Please be considerate when parking*. Light refreshments. **Adm £2.50, chd free. Sat 15 June (11-5); Sun 16 June (2-5); Sun 4 Aug (11-5). Groups of 10-20 also welcome by appt June to Sept.**
Small (60ft x 35ft) beautiful and well maintained, superbly structured on three levels with steps. Whilst the garden is small, it is a garden that should not be rushed. In addition to planting there are numerous quirky ornaments and features that add to this garden's charm incl a small pond with fish, frogs and newts.

27 NEW THE FIRS
The Hoppety, Tadworth KT20 5RQ. Timothy & Sue Edwards. *3m from J8 M25. Take A217 N towards Sutton. At 3rd r'about take 2nd exit, B2220 towards Walton on the Hill. The Hoppety is 5th turning on L. No parking in The Hoppety, use adjoining roads*. Home-made teas. **Adm £3, chd free. Sun 23 June (2-5.30).**
A ⅓ -acre cottage garden intensively planted with bulbs, herbaceous plants, annuals and climbers. An exciting secret knot garden is well hidden at the end of the path flanked by more borders and two greenhouses full of tender plants. Something of interest to see whichever way you turn. Wheelchair access to first half of garden only.

GROUP OPENING

28 NEW FRIMLEY GREEN GARDENS
Frimley Green GU16 6HE. *3m S of Camberley. From M3 J4 follow A325 to Frimley Town Centre, head towards Mytchett and Frimley Green (B3411) for 1m. Turn R at The Green R into The Hatches. On street parking, please be considerate of our neighbours*. Home-made teas at Wildwood. **Combined adm £5, chd free. Sun 16 June (11-5).**

NEW ELMCROFT
Mrs Geraldine Huggon

NEW OAKLEIGH
22 The Hatches. Mrs Angela O'Connell

NEW TABOR
7 Bedford Crescent. Susan Filbin

NEW WILDWOOD
34 The Hatches. Annie Keighley

Four very different gardens in the delightful village of Frimley Green. Start your adventure at Oakleigh or if parking available, at Elmcroft. Tickets and a map are available at all the gardens. Enjoy designer chic - and how to get the best from a small space - at Tabor. Experience a romantic cottage garden at Wildwood and unusual varieties rub shoulders with cottage classics at Elmcroft where no space is wasted. And look for surprises at charming and colourful Oakleigh. A warm welcome awaits. Some great plants for sale at Elmcroft. Gravel drives at Elmcroft and Wildwood. Two steps at Oakleigh.

Festival of Tulips with 10,000 bulbs and large cut flower garden . . .

FROGMORE HOUSE GARDEN
See Berkshire

FROYLE GARDENS
See Hampshire

29 ◆ GATTON PARK
Rocky Lane, Merstham RH2 0TW. Royal Alexandra & Albert School, 01737 649068, www.gattonpark.com. *3m NE of Reigate. 5 mins from M25 J8 (A217) or from top of Reigate Hill, over M25 then follow sign to Merstham. Entrance is off Rocky Lane accessible from Gatton Bottom or A23 Merstham*. **Adm £4.50, chd free. For NGS: Suns 17 Feb 2013 (11-4); 16 Feb 2014. For other opening times and information, please phone or see garden website.**
Gatton Park is the core 250 acres of the estate originally laid out by Capability Brown. Gatton also boasts a Japanese garden, rock and water garden and Victorian parterre nestled within the sweeping parkland. Stunning displays of snowdrops and aconites in February and March. Free activities for children. Limited wheelchair access.

30 NEW 21 GLENAVON CLOSE

Claygate, Esher KT10 0HP. Selina & Simon Botham, 01372 210570, selina@designsforallseasons.co.uk, www.designsforallseasons.co.uk. *At A3 junction take A244 towards Esher, turn R at T-lights into Milbourne Lane, continue straight through village. Bear R/straight on at both mini r'abouts. After Holy Trinity Church and recreation ground turn L into Causeway, diagonally straight over is Glenavon Close. No parking in Glenavon Close, please park in the surrounding residential roads.* Home-made teas. **Adm £3, chd free. Sun 16 June (11-6). Groups of 20+ also welcome by appt June to Oct, you are welcome to bring a picnic.**

A relaxing 66ft x 92ft secluded garden created by garden designer Selina Botham and her husband Simon. Swathes of grasses and perennials surround a spacious lawn. Curving paths invite exploration and lead you through a sensory trail which encourages rest and connection with nature. A magnificent willow is the setting for a pond, deck and garden office. Organic sculpture by Claire Knights.

Curving paths invite exploration and lead you through a sensory trail . . .

31 GREAT FOSTERS

Stroude Road, Egham TW20 9UR. The Sutcliffe Family, 01784 433822, reception@greatfosters.co.uk, www.greatfosters.co.uk. *1m S of Egham. On A30 at T-lights opp Virginia Water, turn down Christchurch Rd B389. Continue over r'about and after railway bridge turn L at T-lights into Stroude Rd. Great Fosters approx 3/4 m on R.* Full range of refreshments available, afternoon tea £21 per person (not NGS). **Suggested donation £4.50, chd free. Tue 14, Wed 15 May (11-6).**

Within the 50-acre estate, this wonderful and inspiring garden has been beautifully restored over the last 20yrs. Framed on 3 sides by a Saxon moat, a knot garden of intricate design has fragrant beds of flowers and herbs and is bordered by clipped hedges and topiary. Beyond, find a grass amphitheatre, large lake, wisteria-draped Japanese bridge, sunken rose garden, 'secret' gardens & lily pond. Partial wheelchair access.

32 HALL GROVE SCHOOL

London Road (A30), Bagshot GU19 5HZ. Mr & Mrs A R Graham. *6m SW of Egham. M3 J3, follow A322 1m until sign for Sunningdale A30, 1m E of Bagshot, opp Long Acres garden centre, entrance at footbridge. Ample car park.* Home-made teas. **Adm £5, chd free. Sat 11 May (2-5).**

Formerly small Georgian country estate, now co-educational preparatory school. Grade II listed house (not open). Mature parkland with specimen trees. Historical features incl ice house, old walled garden, heated peach wall. New lake, woodland walks, rhododendrons and azaleas. Live music at 3pm.

HAMPTON HILL GARDENS
See London

HANGING HOSTA GARDEN
See Hampshire

33 ◆ HATCHLANDS PARK

East Clandon, Guildford GU4 7RT. National Trust, 01483 222482, www.nationaltrust.org.uk. *4m E of Guildford. Off A246. A3 from London, follow signs to Ripley to join A247 & via W Clandon to A246. From Guildford take A25 then A246 towards Leatherhead at W Clandon.* **Adm £4.20, chd free. For NGS: Suns 12 May, 20 Oct (11-6). For other opening times and information, please phone or see garden website.**

Garden and park designed by Repton in 1800. Follow one of the park walks to the stunning bluebell wood in spring (40 mins round walk over rough and sometimes muddy ground - Tramper vehicle available to borrow). South of the house, a small parterre designed by Gertrude Jekyll in 1913 to flower in early June. In autumn enjoy the changing colours on the long walk.

34 THE HAWTHORNS

Pendell Road, Bletchingley RH1 4QJ. The Hawthorns School. *1m N of Bletchingley. Turn off A25 by Red Lion in Bletchingley along Little Common Lane. School over Xrds at bottom of hill.* Home-made teas. **Adm £5, chd free. Sat 25 May (1-5).**

A new heritage trail leads visitors through the remnants of what was once one of the most famous late Victorian gardens in Surrey. Pendell Court is now home to The Hawthorns School, the pupils of which are actively engaged in conserving what remains of Sir George Macleay's arboretum. Trail incl muddy and uneven ground.

35 HEATHSIDE

10 Links Green Way, Cobham KT11 2QH. Miss Margaret Arnott & Mr Terry Bartholomew, 01372 842459, m.a.arnott@btinternet.com. *1 1/2 m E of Cobham. Off A245 Cobham to Leatherhead rd. From Cobham take 4th turning L after Esso Garage into Fairmile Lane. Straight on at mini-r'about into Water Lane for 1/2 m. Links Green Way 3rd on L.* Home-made teas. **Adm £3.50, chd free. Sat 15, Sun 16 June (1-5). Visitors also welcome by appt, afternoon tea or wine & canapés for evening visits.**

1/3 -acre terraced garden planted for yr-round interest, beautiful in any season. Spring bulbs and alpines, herbaceous borders, roses and clematis in summer, leaf colour and berries in autumn and winter, all set off by harmonious landscaping with pergola, parterre, ponds, obelisks and urns. Many inspirational ideas.

36 NEW HILL FARM

Logmore Lane, Westcott, Dorking RH4 3JY. Helen Thomas. *1m W of Dorking. Turn off A25 onto Logmore Lane past church. Bear R just after church for parking on the heath. Well signed. Please note garden is at Hill Farm, not Hill Farm House or Hill Farm Barn which are neighbouring properties.* Home-made teas. **Adm £3.50, chd free. Sun 15 Sept (11-5.30).**

1 3/4 -acre recently redesigned garden set in the magnificent Surrey Hills landscape. The garden has a wealth of different natural habitats to encourage wildlife, and planting areas

which come alive through the different seasons. A wildlife pond, woodland walk, a tapestry of heathers and glorious late summer grasses and perennials. A garden to be enjoyed by all. Everyone welcome. Pond dipping, nature trail and drawing competition. Working excavation and restoration of lime kiln, display of drawings, planting plans, and photos of redesign. Sloping garden, most areas are accessible to wheelchair users. Most paths are grass so care needed if very wet.

239A HOOK ROAD
See London

37 HORSELL ALLOTMENTS
Bullbeggars Lane, Horsell, Woking GU21 4SQ. Horsell Allotments Association, http://horsellalots.wordpress.com. *1½ m W of Woking. From Woking follow signs to Horsell, along High St, Bullbeggars Lane at Chobham end of Village. Disabled parking only at Allotments*. **Adm £3.50, chd free.** Sun 23 June (11-4). **Also open Birch Cottage.**
With over 100 individual plots growing a variety of flowers, fruit and vegetables, showcasing a mixture of modern, well-known, heritage and unusual vegetables, many not seen in supermarkets. Two working beehives with informative talks. Vegetable and herb plants for sale. Chairman's weekly column in Woking edition of Surrey Advertiser. Grass paths, may be uneven in places.

38 KNOWLE GRANGE
Hound House Road, Shere, Guildford GU5 9JH. Mr P R & Mrs M E Wood, 01483 202108, prmewood@hotmail.com. *8m S of Guildford. From Shere (off A25), through village for ¾ m. After railway bridge, continue 1½ m past Hound House on R (stone dogs on gatepost). After 100yds turn R at Knowle Grange sign, go to end of lane*. Home-made teas. **Adm £6, chd free.** Suns 12 May, 15 Sept (11-5). **Visitors also welcome by appt May to Sept, mini buses only.**
80-acre idyllic hilltop position. Extraordinary and exciting 7-acre gardens, created from scratch since 1990 by Marie-Elisabeth Wood, blend the free romantic style with the strong architectural frame of the classical tradition. Walk the rural one-mile Bluebell Valley Unicursal Path of Life and discover its secret allegory. Featured in Most Beautiful Gardens in Britain book and on Austrian/German TV. Deep unfenced pools, high unfenced drops.

LITTLE GABLES
See Kent

LITTLE LODGE
See London

Walk the rural one-mile Bluebell Valley Unicursal Path of Life . . .

39 LONGER END COTTAGE
Normandy Common Lane, Normandy GU3 2AP. Ann & John McIlwham. *4m W of Guildford on A323. At War Memorial Xrds in Normandy turn R into Hunts Hill Rd then 1st R into Normandy Common Lane*. Home-made teas. **Adm £3.50, chd free.** Sun 16 June (1-5).
1½ -acre garden divided into rooms with wide variety of plants, shrubs and trees incl roses, delphiniums, tree ferns, gunnera, grasses etc. Knot garden, laburnum walk, wild flower meadow, folly and small stumpery add to the attraction of the garden. Featured in Period Homes & Gardens. Uneven drive.

40 ◆ LOSELEY PARK
Guildford GU3 1HS. Mr & Mrs M G More-Molyneux, 01483 304440/405112, www.loseley-park.com. *4m SW of Guildford. Leave A3 at Compton S of Guildford, on B3000 for 2m. Signed. Guildford stn 2m, Godalming stn 3m. If using SatNav, type in Stakescorner Rd, not postcode*. **Adm £5, chd £2.25.** For NGS: Sun 12 May (11-5). **For other opening times and information, please phone or see garden website.**
Delightful 2½ -acre walled garden. Award-winning rose garden (over 1,000 bushes, mainly old-fashioned varieties), extensive herb garden, fruit/flower garden, white garden with fountains, and spectacular organic vegetable garden. Magnificent vine walk, herbaceous borders, moat walk, ancient wisteria and mulberry trees. Wild flower meadow.

LOWDER MILL
See Sussex

41 THE MANOR HOUSE
Three Gates Lane, Haslemere GU27 2ES. Mr & Mrs Gerard Ralfe. *1m NE of Haslemere. From Haslemere centre take A286 towards Milford. Turn R after Museum into Three Gates Lane. At T-Junction turn R into Holdfast Lane. Can park on R.* Home-made teas. **Adm £5, chd free (share to Etshelengele Crèche).** Sun 28 Apr (12-5).
Described by Country Life as 'The hanging gardens of Haslemere', The Manor House gardens are in a valley of the Surrey Hills. One of Surrey inaugural NGS gardens, they are still under restoration. Fine views, six acres, water gardens.

42 MOLESHILL HOUSE
The Fairmile, Cobham KT11 1BG. Penny Snell, www.pennysnellflowers.co.uk. *2m NE of Cobham. On A307 Esher to Cobham Rd next to free car park by A3 bridge, at entrance to Waterford Close*. Refreshments at Fairmile Lea. **Adm £5.50, chd free.** Suns 16 June (11-2); 14 July (2-5). **Combined adm with Fairmile Lea.**
Romantic garden. Short woodland path leads from dovecote to beehives. Informal planting contrasts with formal topiary box and garlanded cisterns. Colourful courtyard and pots, conservatory, fountains, bog garden. Pleached avenue, new circular gravel garden replacing most of the lawn. Some vegetables. Music in the garden on 14th July. Garden 5 mins from Claremont Landscape Garden, Painshill Park & Wisley, also adjacent excellent dog-walking woods. Featured in Financial Times.

43 NORWOOD FARM
Effingham Common Road, Effingham, Leatherhead KT24 5JF. Judith & Mervyn Gardner. *Approx 5m from J10, M25. 800yds SE of Effingham Junction stn, towards Effingham*. Home-made teas. **Adm £5, chd free. Sun 25 Aug (11-5).**
C15 listed Hall house and 100ft long listed barn surrounded by over 10 acres of immaculate gardens. There are extensive, well-stocked herbaceous borders and shrubberies, a formal area with fish pond and a white garden. Two duck ponds linked by a stream, woodland walk and a large area planted with specimen trees. Most areas accessible for wheelchair users.

Beautiful 5-acre garden with many diverse areas of natural beauty . . .

44 19 OAK TREE ROAD
Knaphill GU21 2RW. Barry & Pam Gray. *5m NW of Guildford. From A3 take A322 Bagshot Rd, continue through Worplesdon, straight over at Brookwood Xrds. 1st turning on L into Oak Tree Rd (opp Sainsbury's).* Home-made teas. **Adm £3, chd free. Sun 21 July (11-5).**
Colourful front garden of informal bedding, baskets and containers featuring tender perennials and annuals grown by owners. Back garden (approx 80ft x 35ft) has lawn, patio, small pond, trees, shrubs and perennials for foliage, texture, scent and yr-round interest. 3 greenhouses, fruit trees and vegetables. No wasted space in this delightful garden.

45 NEW 141 OAKWAY
Woking GU21 8TR. Mrs Molly Arch. *2½ m W of Woking, Hermitage Woods Estate, St Johns. From Woking take A324 signed Aldershot, continue straight over r'about, at 2nd r'about turn L signed M3/Woking Crematorium. At r'about take 2nd exit into Hermitage Rd, at mini r'about turn L into Amis Rd. Take 1st R into Batten Ave, garden ½ way round horseshoe beyond grassed r'about.* Home-made teas. **Adm £3, chd free. Sun 23 June (11-4). Also open Birch Cottage & Horsell Allotments.**
Approx 140ft x 24ft, this slightly narrowing garden is an oasis for wildlife. Walking under the oak trees you will discover decaying log piles, a bug hotel and eventually a large pond. Herbaceous, nectar-rich flowers fill the borders. Fruit and vegetables grow in unusual containers. Ramp for wheelchair access, grass to main features.

46 ODSTOCK
Castle Square, Bletchingley RH1 4LB. Averil & John Trott, 01883 743100. *3m W of Godstone. Just off A25 in Bletchingley. At top of village nr Red Lion PH. Parking in village, no parking in Castle Square. Disabled parking by gate*. Home-made teas. **Adm £3, chd free. Sun 4 Aug (11-5). Groups of 10+ welcome by appt.**
⅔ -acre plantsman's garden maintained by owners and developed for all-yr interest. Special interest in grasses and climbers, approx 80 at last count. Japanese features; dahlias. No-dig, low-maintenance vegetable garden. Children's quiz. Short gravel drive. Some paths too narrow for wheelchairs.

OLD BUCKHURST
See Kent

47 THE OLD CROFT
South Holmwood, Dorking RH5 4NT. David & Virginia Lardner-Burke, www.lardner-burke.org.uk. *3m S of Dorking. From Dorking take A24 S for 3m. Turn L at sign to Leigh-Brockham into Mill Road. ½ m on L, 2 free car parks in NT Holmwood Common. Follow signs for 500yds along woodland walk. Can be very muddy.* ***Disabled and elderly: for direct access tel 01306 888224.*** Home-made teas. **Adm £5, chd free. Sun 26, Mon 27 May; Sat 10, Sun 11 Aug (2-6).**
Beautiful 5-acre garden with many diverse areas of natural beauty, giving a sense of peace and tranquillity. Stunning vistas incl lake, bridge, pond fed by natural stream running over rocky weirs, bog gardens, roses, perennial borders, elevated viewing hide, tropical bamboo maze, curved pergola of rambling roses, unique topiary buttress hedge, many specimen trees and shrubs. Visitors return again and again.

48 THE OLD RECTORY
Sandy Lane, Brewer Street, Bletchingley RH1 4QW. Mr & Mrs A Procter. *3m W of Godstone. Just off A25 in Bletchingley. At top of village nr Red Lion PH, turn R into Little Common Lane then R at Cross Rd into Sandy Lane. Parking near house, disabled parking in courtyard*. Home-made teas. **Adm £4, chd free. Sun 30 June (11-4).**
Georgian Manor House (not open). Quintessential Italianate topiary garden, statuary, box parterres, courtyard with columns, water features, antique terracotta pots. Much of the 4-acre garden is the subject of ongoing reclamation. This incl the ancient moat and woodland with fine specimen trees and walled kitchen garden. Sunken and exotic garden under construction. Featured in Country Living. House and garden film location for BBC Emma and The Secret Interview. Gravel paths.

49 ◆ POLESDEN LACEY
Great Bookham, Dorking RH5 6BD. National Trust, 01372 452048, www.nationaltrust.org.uk. *Nr Dorking, off A246 Leatherhead to Guildford rd. 1½ m S of Great Bookham, well signed.* **Adm £7.40, chd £3.70. For NGS: Sun 14 July (10-5). For other opening times and information, please phone or see garden website.**
Designed as the perfect setting for Mrs Greville, a famous Edwardian hostess, to entertain royalty and the best of society, Polesden Lacey has beautiful formal gardens with something to offer for every season, as well as glorious views over the rolling Surrey Hills. Wheelchairs and battery cars available from Visitor Reception, it is advisable to pre-book.

50 PRATSHAM GRANGE
Tanhurst Lane, Holmbury St Mary RH5 6LZ. Alan & Felicity Comber, 01306 621116, alancomber@aol.com. *12m SE of Guildford, 10m SW of Dorking. From A25 take B2126. 2m after Holmbury church turn L into Tanhurst Lane. House 2nd on L after ¼ m. From A29 take B2126. Before Forest Green turn R on B2126 signed Holmbury. After ¼ m turn R into Tanhurst Lane.* **Adm £4, chd free. Sat 17, Sun 18 Aug (12-5). Groups also welcome by appt June to Aug.**
4-acre garden around late Victorian

"Lemon drizzle cake, Victoria sponge ... yummy!"

house in a stunning setting overlooked by Holmbury Hill and Leith Hill. The garden has been created over the last 7yrs and is surrounded by mature oaks, laurels, rhododendrons and paddocks. Features incl herbaceous borders, kitchen garden, ponds, knot garden and rose, hydrangea and fuchsia beds. To feature in Surrey Life Magazine. Some slopes and gravel paths. Deep ponds.

51 ◆ RAMSTER

Chiddingfold GU8 4SN. Mr & Mrs Paul Gunn, 01428 654167, www.ramsterevents.com. *1½ m S of Chiddingfold. On A283 1½ m S of Chiddingfold; large iron gates on R.* **Adm £6, chd free.** **For NGS: Fri 24 May (10-5). For other opening times and information, please phone or see garden website.**

A stunning, mature woodland garden set in over 20 acres, famous for its rhododendron and azalea collection and its carpets of bluebells in Spring. Enjoy a peaceful wander down the woodland walk, explore the bog garden with its stepping stones, or relax in the tranquil enclosed Tennis Court Garden. Tea house, WC are accessible and some paths suitable for wheelchairs.

NCH

52 NEW ROSE BRIAR

Winterdown Road, West End, Esher KT10 8LP. Jane Saville, www.designsforallseasons.co.uk. *West End village nr Garson's Farm Garden Centre. From A3 Cobham exit follow A307 towards Esher. Just before Claremont Landscape garden turn L into West End Lane. At pond on green turn L into Winterdown Rd. Park in Garson's Farm Garden Centre, walk back two houses from the entrance to number 42 Rose Briar.* Cream teas. **Adm £3, chd free. Sun 23 June (11-6).**

Approx ⅓ -acre, a beautifully secluded garden designed by Selina Botham to complement the quintessentially English village setting. A traditional garden with grass parterre and overflowing herbaceo us beds and borders. Formal yew and box hedging contrast with abundant informal planting. Features of interest include a mature mulberry tree, summerhouse, and quirky tree house. Close to Garson's Farm garden centre & fruit picking. Also village green and duck pond and extensive woodland walks. Claremont is ½ m away.

D

The Old Rectory

© Leigh Clapp

53 NEW ROSE COTTAGE

Elm Corner, Ockham, Woking GU23 6PX. Helen Cowell. *Nr Wisley Gardens, on southbound side of A3 opp entrance to Wisley. From J10 on M25 travel S on A3 keeping in the LH lane, take sharp L turn off A3 signed Elm Corner just before footbridge. Follow NGS signs along single track road and park in field.* Home-made teas. **Adm £3.50, chd free. Sun 2 June (11-5).**

1-acre cottage garden starts with a vegetable garden enclosed in fan-trained fruit trees. Deep borders surround the C18 cottage and a rose arch takes you through to a tulip tree and laburnum walk with box balls and alliums. Next a large pond with resident terrapin and Koi carp. Finally the 12ft x 12ft knot garden with bird and frog topiary gives a formal ending to the garden journey. Rose Cottage is minutes from Wisley Gardens, close to Polesden Lacey (NT), Claremont Landscape Gardens (NT) and Painshill Park. Parking for disabled visitors reserved outside house.

54 NEW 7 ROSE LANE

Ripley, Woking GU23 6NE. Mindi McLean. *Just off Ripley High St on Rose Lane, 3rd house on L next to shoe repair shop.* Home-made teas. **Adm £3, chd free. Sat 8 June (10-4).**

7 Rose Lane is a small but perfectly formed village-centre garden behind an historic listed cottage. It has 3 'rooms' a traditional perennial flower garden laid to lawn; a vegetable and fruit garden with Agriframe orchard and a working garden with greenhouse, compost bins, shed and chicken run. It is a perfect example of how to make the most of a cottage garden. Monthly Ripley Farmers Market held on 8 June from 9-1.

55 THE ROUND HOUSE
Dunsfold Road, Loxhill GU8 4BL. Mrs Sue Lawson, 01483 200375, roundhouseloxhill@gmail.com. *4m S of Bramley. Off A281, at Smithbrook Kilns turn R to Dunsfold. Follow to T-junction. Go R (B2130). After 1.2m Park Hatch on R, enter park, follow drive to garden.* Home-made teas. **Adm £3.50, chd free. Sat 15, Sun 16 June; Sun 14 July (2-6). Groups of 10+ also welcome by appt June to July, occasional visits accepted in Sept.**
2½ -acre walled Victorian garden with far-reaching views from the top of the garden. Continuing renewal programme since 2002. Colourful mixed beds with perennials, roses and interesting statuary. Water cascades. Apple and plum orchard. Serpentine paths between shrubs and wild flowers. 75 metre lavender walk. Ornamental fish pond and wild flower orchard. Gravel paths and steep slopes.

SANDY SLOPES
See Hampshire

SHALFORD HOUSE
See Sussex

56 41 SHELVERS WAY
Tadworth KT20 5QJ. Keith & Elizabeth Lewis, 01737 210707, kandelewis@ntlworld.com. *6m S of Sutton off A217. 1st turning on R after Burgh Heath T-lights heading S on A217. 400yds down Shelvers Way on L.* Home-made teas. **Adm £3, chd free. Suns 21 Apr, 21 July (2-5.30). Visitors and groups of 10+ also welcome by appt May to Aug.**
Visitors say 'one of the most colourful back gardens in Surrey'. In spring, a myriad of small bulbs with specialist daffodils and many pots of colourful tulips. Choice perennials follow, with rhododendrons and azaleas. Cobbles and shingle support grasses and self-sown plants with a bubble fountain. Annuals, phlox and herbaceous plants ensure colour well into Sept. A garden for all seasons. Featured in Surrey Life and Alan Titchmarsh calendar.

SOUTHGATE
See Berkshire

SPEER ROAD GARDENS
See London

57 SPURFOLD
Radnor Road, Peaslake GU5 9SZ. Mr & Mrs A Barnes, 01306 730196, spurfold@btinternet.com. *8m SE of Guildford. A25 to Shere. Turn R through Shere village & up hill. Over railway bridge, 1st L to Peaslake. In Peaslake turn L after village stores Radnor Rd. Approx ½ m up single track lane fork left up steep drive and then left at top, see signs to car park.* Home-made teas. **Adm £5, chd £2. Groups of 20+ welcome by appt May to Aug, evening visits, refreshments by arrangement.**
4 acres, large herbaceous and shrub borders, formal pond with Cambodian Buddha head, sunken gravel garden with topiary box and water feature, terraces, beautiful lawns, mature rhododendrons and azaleas, woodland paths, and gazebos. Garden contains unique collection of Indian elephants and other objets d'art. Topiary garden created 2010 and new formal lawn area created in 2012.

Colourful, curvaceous garden with lots of variety and hidden corners . . .

STONEWALL PARK
See Kent

58 STUART COTTAGE
Ripley Road, East Clandon GU4 7SF. John & Gayle Leader, 01483 222689, www.stuartcottage.com. *4m E of Guildford. Off A246 or from A3 through Ripley until r'about, turn L and continue through West Clandon until T-lights, then L onto A246. East Clandon 1st L.* Home-made teas. **Adm £3.50, chd free. Suns 16 June, 14 July, 11 Aug (1-5). Groups of 20+ also welcome by appt May to Sept.**
This much visited ½ -acre garden seems to please many, being planted to offer floral continuity through the seasons. In June, the romance of the rose walk combines with the sound of water, in July, flowerbeds are floriferous with soft coordinated colours and scented plants, in August, vibrant colours will lift the spirits and in September, tender perennials reach their zenith. Access to all the garden for wheelchairs.

SUNNINGDALE PARK
See Berkshire

59 35 TADORNE ROAD
Tadworth KT20 5TF. Dr & Mrs J R Lay. *6m S of Sutton. On A217 to large r'about, 3m N of M25 J8. Take B2220 signed Tadworth. Tadorne Rd 2nd on R.* Home-made teas. **Adm £3, chd free. Sat 3, Sun 4 Aug (1.30-5.30).**
Colourful, curvaceous garden with lots of variety and hidden corners. We have bright herbaceous borders, shrubby island beds, flower-covered pergolas, secluded seating areas, potager-style vegetable plot, pebble patch, wild woodland corner and varied patio display - all in ⅓ acre! Delicious home-made teas served in plant-filled conservatory. Gravel drive at entrance.

60 TILFORD COTTAGE
Tilford Road, Tilford GU10 2BX. Mr & Mrs R Burn, 01252 795423, rodburn@tiscali.co.uk, www.tilfordcottagegarden.co.uk. *3m SE of Farnham. From Farnham station along Tilford Rd. Tilford Cottage opp Tilford House. Parking by village green.* **Adm £6, chd free. Sat 22, Sun 23 June (10.30-4.30). Evening Opening, wine, Fri 28 June (6-9); Sat 29, Sun 30 June (10.30-4.30). Visitors and groups of 10+ also welcome by appt Mar to Oct, refreshments by arrangement.**
Artist's garden designed to surprise, delight and amuse. Formal planting, herb and knot garden. Numerous examples of topiary combine beautifully with the wild flower river walk. Japanese and water gardens, hosta beds, rose, apple and willow arches, treehouse and fairy grotto all continue the playful quality especially enjoyed by children. Dogs on lead

please! Beekeeper demonstrations. Holistic centre open for taster sessions. Art studio open for viewing. Some gravel paths and steep slopes.

61 TIMBER HILL

Chertsey Road, Chobham GU24 8JF. Mr & Mrs Nick Sealy, 01932 873875, nicksealy@chobham.net, www.laviniasealy.co.uk. *4m N of Woking. 2½ m E of Chobham and ⅓ m E of Fairoaks aerodrome on A319 (N side). 1¼ m W of Ottershaw, J11 M25.* Home-made teas. **Adm £4, chd free. Sat 15, Sun 16 June (1-5). Visitors and groups of 20+ also welcome by appt.**

Beautifully situated 15-acre garden, woodland garden and park with views to N Downs. Fine specimens of oaks, liquidambar and liriodendron. Early witch hazel walk (by appt), new plantings of oaks, beech, cherry and acers. Many camellias and magnolias shelter behind banks of rhododendron ponticum. Drifts of narcissi, daffodils and spring bulbs; shrub and ground-cover borders. Bluebells and azaleas in early May. Good help for disabled and wheelchair users.

62 ◆ TITSEY PLACE GARDENS

Titsey Hill, Oxted RH8 0SD. The Trustees of the Titsey Foundation, 01273 715356, www.titsey.org. *3m N of Oxted. A25 between Oxted & Westerham. Follow brown signs to Titsey Estate from A25 at Limpsfield or see website directions.* **Adm £4.50, chd free. For NGS: Sats 18 May; 15 June; 13 July; 17 Aug (12.30-5). For other opening times and information, please phone or see garden website.**

One of the largest surviving historic estates in Surrey. Magnificent ancestral home and gardens of the Gresham family since 1534. Walled kitchen garden restored early 1990s. Golden Jubilee rose garden. Etruscan summer house adjoining picturesque lakes and fountains. 15 acres of formal and informal gardens in idyllic setting within the M25. Tearooms with delicious home-made teas 12:30-5 on open days. Dogs allowed in picnic area, car park and woodland walks. Good wheelchair access and disabled carpark alongside tearooms.

Formal clipped yew walk with rope swags festooned with wisteria, roses and vines . . .

UPPER PRYORS

See Kent

63 VALE END

Chilworth Road, Albury GU5 9BE. Mr & Mrs John Foulsham, 01483 202594, daphne@dfoulsham.freeserve.co.uk. *4m SE of Guildford. From Albury take A248 W for ¼ m.* Home-made teas. **Adm £3.50, chd free. Visitors welcome by appt Apr to Sept.**

1-acre walled garden arranged on many levels in idyllic setting overlooking mill pond. Spring garden and wild flower meadow give way to borders richly planted with roses, shrubs, perennials and annuals. Formal clipped yew walk with rope swags festooned with wisteria, roses and vines. Attractive hidden courtyard, gravel garden and steps by pantiled cascade lead up to fruit, vegetable and sunken herb garden. Delightful stream, lake and woodland walk from garden on public footpaths. Featured in Gardens Illustrated.

64 ◆ VANN

Hambledon GU8 4EF. Mrs M Caroe, 01428 683413, www.vanngarden.co.uk. *6m S of Godalming. A283 to Wormley. Turn L at Hambledon. On NGS days only, follow yellow Vann signs for 2m. Please park in field, not in road.* **Home-made teas Mon 6 May only (2-6). Adm £5, chd free. For NGS: Tue 2 to Sun 7 Apr incl (10-6); Mon 6 May (2-6); Tue 7 to Sun 12 May incl (10-6); Sun 9 to Sat 15 June incl (10-6). For other opening times and information, please phone or see garden website.**

5-acre English Heritage registered garden surrounding Tudor and William and Mary house (not open) with Arts and Crafts additions by W D Caröe incl a Bargate stone pergola. At the front, brick-paved original 'cottage' garden; to the rear, ¼ -acre pond, yew walk with rill and Gertrude Jekyll water garden. Snowdrops and hellebores, spring bulbs, Fritillaria meleagris in March. Island beds, crinkle crankle wall, orchard with wild flowers, vegetable garden. Centenary garden and woodland. Featured in Gardens Illustrated and Surrey Life. Deep water. Water garden paths not suitable for wheelchairs, but many others are. Please ring prior to visit to request disabled parking.

65 VICARAGE COTTAGE

Brockham Green, Betchworth RH3 7JS. Mrs K Harman. *2m E of Dorking. Take signed rd from A25 between Dorking and Reigate, then ½ m to Brockham Green. No parking on Green, considerate parking on rd please.* Home-made teas. **Adm £3.50, chd free. Sat 15, Sun 16 June (11-5).**

½ -acre cottage garden situated on the Green, next to church and in one of Surrey's most beautiful villages. Designed to complement the 400yr-old cottage. Gently curving borders surround a central ancient yew tree, with a mix of flowers, shrubs and roses. Pond, small wild flower meadow and kitchen garden. Wheelchair access to most areas. This year again featuring Wind in the Willows. The little houses where the characters lived on the riverbank will be set around the pond area, only visible from the woodland path. All will be created using natural materials. Lovely river walk to Betchworth Village. Village Flower Show Sat 15 June 2-4.

66 WALTON POOR HOUSE

Ranmore RH5 6SX. Prue Calvert, 01483 282273, wnscalvert@btinternet.com. *6m NW of Dorking. From Dorking take rd to Ranmore, continue for approx 4m, after Xrds 1m on L. From A246 at East Horsley go S into Greendene, 1st L Crocknorth Rd, 1m on R.* Home-made teas. **Adm £3.50, chd free. Mon 6 May; Sat 15, Sun 16 June; Sat 12, Sun 13 Oct (12-5). Visitors and groups of 20+ also welcome by appt Apr to Oct.**

Tranquil, almost secretive, 4-acre mostly wooded garden in N Downs AONB, planted to show contrast between colourful shrubs and mature trees. Paths wind through garden to pond, hideaway dell and herb garden, planted to show the use of aromatic plants and shrubs. Specialist nursery with wide variety of herbs, shrubs and aromatic plants. Herb talks, recipe leaflets and refreshments available for groups by appt. Grass paths.

67 57 WESTHALL ROAD

Warlingham CR6 9BG. Robert & Wendy Baston. *Approx 3m from M25, J6. Travelling N on A22 at r'about in centre of Whyteleafe turn R onto B270 towards Warlingham. Sharp R after going under railway bridge. Parking on roads above no. 57.* Home-made teas. **Adm £3, chd free (share to Warlingham Methodist Church). Sun 26, Mon 27 May (2-5). Evening Openings £3, chd free, wine, Sat 15, Sun 16 June (6-9.30). Also open 12 May Elm Tree Cottage, see London.**

Reward for the sure-footed - many steep steps to 3 levels! Swathes of tulips and alliums. Mature kiwi and grape vines. Mixed borders. Raised vegetable beds. Box, bay, cork oak and yew topiaries. 'Amphitheatre' of potted plants on lower steps. Stunning views of Caterham and Whyteleafe from top garden. Featured in Surrey Life.

68 WESTWAYS FARM

Gracious Pond Road, Chobham GU24 8HH. Paul & Nicky Biddle, 01276 856163, nicolabiddle@rocketmail.com. *4m N of Woking. From Chobham Church proceed over r'about towards Sunningdale, 1st Xrds R into Red Lion Rd to junction with Mincing Lane.* Home-made teas. **Adm £3.50, chd free. Sat 11 May (11-5); Sun 12 May (11-4). Visitors also welcome by appt Apr to June.**

Open 6-acre garden surrounded by woodlands planted in 1930s with mature and some rare rhododendrons, azaleas, camellias and magnolias, underplanted with bluebells, erythroniums, lilies and dogwood; extensive lawns and sunken pond garden. Working stables and sandschool. Lovely Queen Anne House (not open) covered with listed *Magnolia grandiflora*. Victorian design glasshouse.

WHEATLEY HOUSE

See Hampshire

WHISPERS

See Hampshire

69 ◆ WINKWORTH ARBORETUM

Hascombe Road, Godalming GU8 4AD. National Trust, 01483 208477, www.nationaltrust.org.uk. *2m SE of Godalming on B2130. By rd: nr Hascombe, 2m SE of Godalming on E side of B2130. By bus: 42/44 Guildford to Cranleigh (stops at Arboretum).* **Adm £7, chd £3.50. For NGS: Sun 14 Apr, Sun 6 Oct (10-6). For other opening times and information, please phone or see garden website.**

This dramatic hillside Arboretum perfectly demonstrates what Dr Fox, the Arboretum's creator, described as 'using trees and shrubs to paint a picture'. Impressive displays of daffodils, bluebells and azaleas await in spring. Picnic by the lake in summer. Don't miss the stunning autumnal display created by maples, cherries and tupelos. Guided walk with member of the garden team. Steep slopes.

70 WINTERSHALL MANOR

Bramley GU5 0LR. Mr & Mrs Peter Hutley. *3m S of Bramley Village. On A281 turn R, then next R. Wintershall Drive next on L. Bus: AV33 Guildford to Horsham, alight Palmers Cross, 1m.* **Adm £3.50, chd free (share to St Anna's Children's Home, Ghana). Sats 16 Mar, 4 May (2-5).**

2-acre garden and 200 acres of park and woodland. Bluebell walks in spring, wild daffodils, rhododendrons, specimen trees. Lakes and flight ponds; superb views. Chapel of St Mary, stations of Cross, Rosary Walk and St Francis Chapel.

Relax on the pond's deck amongst darting dragonflies and enjoy tea by the chicken run . . .

61 WOLSEY ROAD

See London

71 WOODBURY COTTAGE

Colley Lane, Reigate RH2 9JJ. Shirley & Bob Stoneley, 01737 244235. *1m W of Reigate. M25 J8, A217 (direction Reigate). Immed before level Xing turn R into Somers Rd, cont as Manor Rd. At very end turn R into Coppice Lane & follow signs to car park. Garden is 300yds walk from car park. Approach from A25 not recommended.* Home-made teas. **Adm £3.50, chd free. Sat 6 July; Sun 7 July; Sat 31 Aug; Sun 1 Sept; Wed 4 Sept (Sats & Wed 2-5, Suns 11-5). Groups of 10+ also welcome by appt July to Sept.**

Cottage garden of just under 1/4 acre, made and maintained by owners. Garden is stepped on a slope, enhanced by its setting under Colley Hill and N Downs Way. We grow a rich diversity of plants, incl perennials, annuals and tender ones, with many plants in pots. The garden is colour-themed, and still looking great in Sept.

72 48 WOODMANSTERNE LANE

Wallington SM6 0SW. Joanne & Graham Winn. *4 1/2 m NE of Banstead. From A217 take A2022 towards Purley (Winkworth Rd). Stay on A2022 for 2.4m. Take L turn as rd bends sharp R. Park on rd (not on verges/curbs - traffic wardens!).* Home-made teas. **Adm £4, chd free. Sun 21 July (12.30-4.30).**

Approx 1/3 acre. Part of former smallholding, converted by garden designer Joanne Winn and husband Graham. Built around the original orchard's remaining fruit trees, the bold, curvy design is softened by a sumptuous palette of perennials and grasses. Pop into the secluded kitchen garden, relax on the pond's deck amongst darting dragonflies and enjoy tea by the chicken run. Featured in Surrey Life. Partial wheelchair access, some gravel and narrow paths, raised deck and boardwalk.

THE WYCH ELM PUBLIC HOUSE

See London

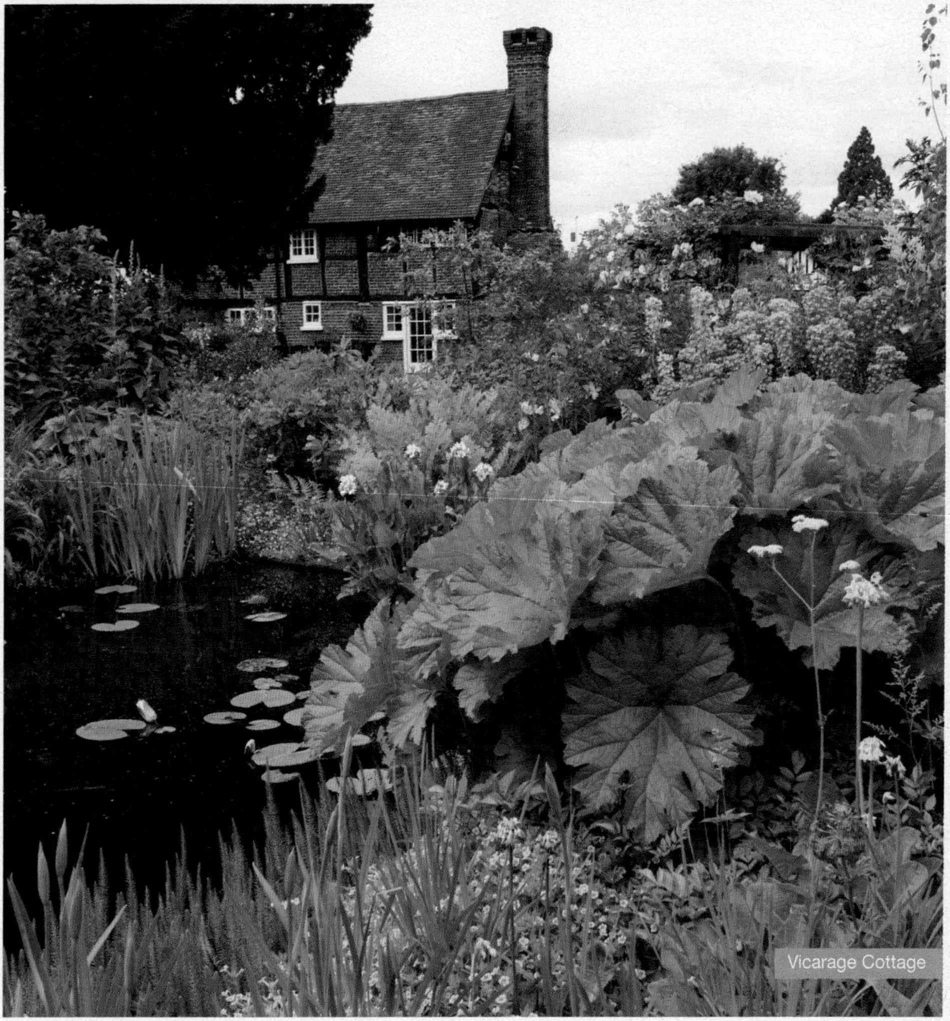

© Leigh Clapp

Surrey County Volunteers

County Organiser

Maggie Boyd, Bardsey, 11 Derby Road, Haslemere GU27 1BS, 01428 652283, maggie.boyd@live.co.uk

County Treasurer

David Boyd, Bardsey, 11 Derby Road, Haslemere GU27 1BS, 01428 652283, dhboyd@live.co.uk

Publicity

Mary Farmery, Fairlawn, Camilla Drive, Westhumble RH5 6BU 01306 640225, maryfarmery@hotmail.com

Group Tour Organiser

Margaret Arnott, Heathside, 10 Links Green Way, Cobham KT11 2QH, 01372 842459, m.a.arnott@btinternet.com

Assistant County Organisers

Margaret Arnott, Heathside, 10 Links Green Way, Cobham KT11 2QH, 01372 842459
Anne Barnes, Spurfold, Radnor Road, Peaslake, Guildford GU5 9SZ, 01306 730196
Annie Keighley, Wildwood, 34 The Hatches, Frimley Green GU16 6HE, 01252 838660, annie.keighley12@btinternet.com
Keith Lewis, 41 Shelvers Way, Tadworth KT20 5QJ, 01737 210707
Shirley Stoneley, Woodbury Cottage, Colley Lane, Reigate RH2 9JJ, 01737 244235
Jean Thompson, Norney Wood, Elstead Road, Shackleford, Godalming GU8 6AY, 01483 425633, norney.wood@btinternet.com

Plant specialists: look for the Plant Heritage symbol NCH

SUSSEX

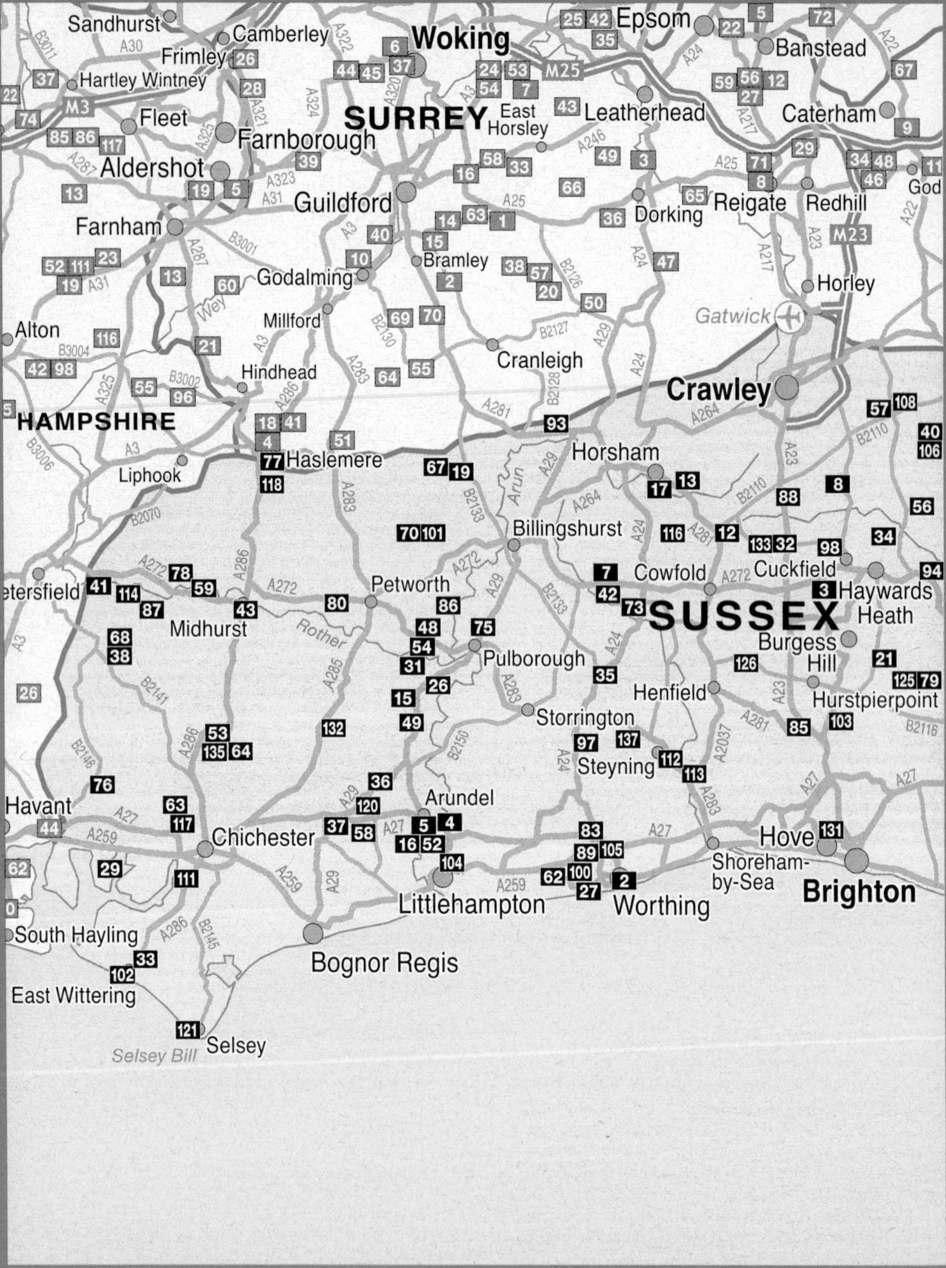
Sandhurst
Camberley
Woking
Epsom
Banstead
Frimley
Hartley Wintney
SURREY
East Horsley
Leatherhead
Caterham
Fleet
Farnborough
Aldershot
Guildford
Dorking
Reigate
Redhill
God
Farnham
Bramley
Godalming
Horley
Gatwick
Alton
Millford
Cranleigh
Hindhead
Crawley
HAMPSHIRE
Horsham
Liphook
Haslemere
Billingshurst
Cowfold
Cuckfield
etersfield
Petworth
Haywards Heath
Midhurst
SUSSEX
Pulborough
Burgess Hill
Henfield
Hurstpierpoint
Storrington
Steyning
Havant
Arundel
Chichester
Hove
Shoreham-by-Sea
Brighton
Littlehampton
Worthing
South Hayling
Bognor Regis
East Wittering
Selsey Bill
Selsey
Wey
Arun
Rother

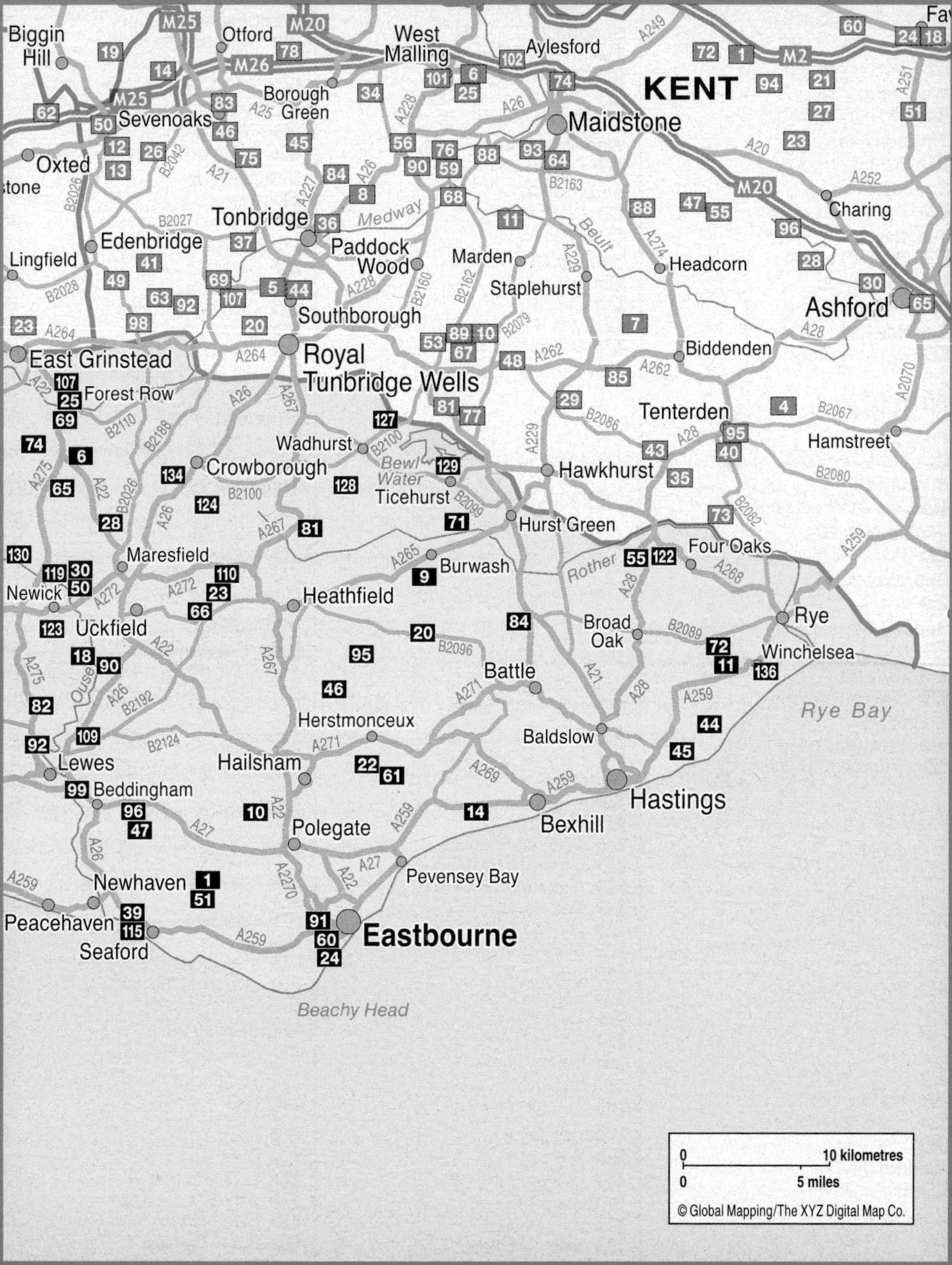
KENT
Biggin Hill
Otford
West Malling
Aylesford
Maidstone
Borough Green
Sevenoaks
Oxted
Tonbridge
Edenbridge
Lingfield
Paddock Wood
Marden
Staplehurst
Headcorn
Charing
Ashford
Southborough
Royal Tunbridge Wells
East Grinstead
Forest Row
Biddenden
Tenterden
Hamstreet
Wadhurst
Crowborough
Bewl Water
Ticehurst
Hawkhurst
Hurst Green
Four Oaks
Maresfield
Burwash
Newick
Heathfield
Uckfield
Rother
Rye
Broad Oak
Winchelsea
Battle
Rye Bay
Herstmonceux
Baldslow
Lewes
Hailsham
Hastings
Beddingham
Bexhill
Polegate
Pevensey Bay
Newhaven
Peacehaven
Seaford
Eastbourne
Beachy Head
Medway
Beult
Ouse
M25
M20
M26
M2
0
10 kilometres
0
5 miles
© Global Mapping/The XYZ Digital Map Co.

Opening Dates

February

Thursday 7
82 McBean's Orchids

Friday 8
82 McBean's Orchids

Tuesday 12
103 Pembury House

Wednesday 13
103 Pembury House

Thursday 14
103 Pembury House

Sunday 17
80 The Manor of Dean

Tuesday 19
103 Pembury House

Wednesday 20
103 Pembury House

Thursday 21
103 Pembury House

March

Friday 8
103 Pembury House

Sunday 17
80 The Manor of Dean

Wednesday 20
128 Tidebrook Manor

Saturday 23
35 Dachs

Sunday 24
35 Dachs

Saturday 30
76 Lordington House

Sunday 31
19 Bradstow Lodge
71 King John's Lodge

April

Monday 1
76 Lordington House

Wednesday 3
15 Bignor Park
105 6 Plantation Rise

Saturday 6
22 Butlers Farmhouse
105 6 Plantation Rise
111 Rymans

Sunday 7
22 Butlers Farmhouse
54 The Grange
85 Newtimber Place
111 Rymans

Wednesday 10
15 Bignor Park

Saturday 13
80 The Manor of Dean

Sunday 14
54 The Grange
80 The Manor of Dean
100 Palatine School Gardens

Wednesday 17
15 Bignor Park

Saturday 20
114 Sandhill Farm House

Sunday 21
97 The Old Vicarage
110 Rose Cottage
114 Sandhill Farm House
134 Warren House

Wednesday 24
15 Bignor Park

Saturday 27
38 Down Place
46 Fineoaks

Sunday 28
38 Down Place
46 Fineoaks
78 Malt House
92 Offham House

Enjoy a home-made tea on the lawn . . .

May

Wednesday 1
48 Fittleworth House

Saturday 4
124 Stone Cross House

Sunday 5
16 4 Birch Close
30 Clinton Lodge
41 Durford Mill House
59 Hammerwood House
62 Highdown Gardens
78 Malt House
93 The Old Farmhouse
124 Stone Cross House

Monday 6
16 4 Birch Close
78 Malt House
93 The Old Farmhouse
134 Warren House

Tuesday 7
119 Sheffield Park and Garden

Wednesday 8
9 Bateman's
48 Fittleworth House

Saturday 11
65 Holly House
69 Kidbrooke Park

Sunday 12
3 Ansty Gardens
6 Ashdown Park Hotel
12 Beedinglee
59 Hammerwood House
65 Holly House
84 Mountfield Court
118 Shalford House

Wednesday 15
8 Balcombe Gardens
48 Fittleworth House
135 West Dean Gardens

Friday 17
25 Caxton Manor
107 2 Quarry Cottages

Saturday 18
25 Caxton Manor
107 2 Quarry Cottages

Sunday 19
7 Bakers House
12 Beedinglee
53 Gardeners' Cottage
57 Grove Farm House
74 Legsheath Farm
80 The Manor of Dean
134 Warren House

Wednesday 22
48 Fittleworth House
123 Sparrow Hatch

Thursday 23
123 Sparrow Hatch

Saturday 25
40 Duckyls Holt
106 The Priest House
109 Ringmer Park

Sunday 26
5 Arundel Gardens group
10 Bates Green
11 Beauchamps
17 Blue Jays
33 Cookscroft
40 Duckyls Holt
71 King John's Lodge
110 Rose Cottage
125 Stonehealed Farm
132 Upwaltham Barns

Monday 27
5 Arundel Gardens group
17 Blue Jays
33 Cookscroft
40 Duckyls Holt
71 King John's Lodge
132 Upwaltham Barns
134 Warren House

Wednesday 29
48 Fittleworth House

June

Saturday 1
28 Chestnut Farm
34 Copyhold Hollow
37 Denmans Garden
77 Lowder Mill
121 Solent Cottage

You are always welcome at an NGS garden!

Sunday 2
28 Chestnut Farm
34 Copyhold Hollow
77 Lowder Mill
92 Offham House
121 Solent Cottage

Monday 3
30 Clinton Lodge

Wednesday 5
48 Fittleworth House

Thursday 6
62 Highdown Gardens

Saturday 8
35 Dachs
43 54 Elmleigh
65 Holly House
86 North Springs
87 Nyewood House
136 Winchelsea's Secret Gardens

Sunday 9
2 Ambrose Place Back Gardens
35 Dachs
36 Dale Park House
43 54 Elmleigh
58 Halfpenny Cottage
61 Gardens & Grounds of Herstmonceux Castle
65 Holly House
81 Mayfield Gardens
87 Nyewood House

Wednesday 12
48 Fittleworth House

Thursday 13
120 Slindon Gardens
130 Town Place

Friday 14
101 Parsonage Farm
105 6 Plantation Rise (Evening)

National Gardens Weekend

Saturday 15
8 Balcombe Gardens
24 51 Carlisle Road
38 Down Place
46 Fineoaks
51 Follers Manor
65 Holly House
70 Kiln Copse Farm
76 Lordington House
88 Nymans
95 Old School House
97 The Old Vicarage
108 Ridge House
114 Sandhill Farm House
115 Seaford & Bishopstone Gardens
117 Sennicotts
131 11 Tredcroft Road

Sunday 16
7 Bakers House
14 Bexhill Gardens
15 Bignor Park
17 Blue Jays
19 Bradstow Lodge
24 51 Carlisle Road
38 Down Place
46 Fineoaks
47 Firle Place Herb Garden
51 Follers Manor
60 Hardwycke
65 Holly House
67 Jacaranda
70 Kiln Copse Farm
71 King John's Lodge
72 Knellstone House
88 Nymans
93 The Old Farmhouse
94 Old Scaynes Hill House
95 Old School House
96 Old Vicarage
97 The Old Vicarage
114 Sandhill Farm House
115 Seaford & Bishopstone Gardens
120 Slindon Gardens
125 Stonehealed Farm
131 11 Tredcroft Road

Tuesday 18
1 Alfriston Clergy House

Wednesday 19
48 Fittleworth House

Thursday 20
128 Tidebrook Manor

Friday 21
44 Fairlight End

Saturday 22
27 Channel View
41 Durford Mill House
43 54 Elmleigh
44 Fairlight End
50 Fletching Garden Trio
64 Historic Gardens
108 Ridge House
111 Rymans

Sunday 23
3 Ansty Gardens
27 Channel View
41 Durford Mill House
43 54 Elmleigh
50 Fletching Garden Trio
64 Historic Gardens
73 Knepp Castle
108 Ridge House
110 Rose Cottage
111 Rymans
130 Town Place

Monday 24
64 Historic Gardens

Tuesday 25
64 Historic Gardens

Wednesday 26
48 Fittleworth House
64 Historic Gardens
123 Sparrow Hatch

Thursday 27
64 Historic Gardens
75 Little Hill (Evening)
123 Sparrow Hatch

Friday 28
64 Historic Gardens

Saturday 29
13 4 Ben's Acre
18 Bradness Gallery
40 Duckyls Holt
106 The Priest House

Sunday 30
18 Bradness Gallery
40 Duckyls Holt
75 Little Hill
116 Sedgwick Park House
130 Town Place
133 Warninglid Gardens

Bug hunt and fact sheet for children . . .

July

Tuesday 2
39 Driftwood

Wednesday 3
48 Fittleworth House

Thursday 4
116 Sedgwick Park House (Evening)

Friday 5
80 The Manor of Dean (Evening)

Sunday 7
89 Oak Grove College
100 Palatine School Gardens
102 33 Peerley Road
118 Shalford House
130 Town Place
137 Wiston House

Wednesday 10
48 Fittleworth House

Thursday 11
122 South Grange

Friday 12
113 St Mary's House Gardens

Saturday 13
97 The Old Vicarage
98 Orchard House
113 St Mary's House Gardens

Sunday 14
10 Bates Green
23 Cabbages & Kings
94 Old Scaynes Hill House
98 Orchard House

Wednesday 17
48 Fittleworth House
112 Saffrons

Friday 19
- 61 Gardens & Grounds of Herstmonceux Castle
- 88 Nymans (Evening)

Sunday 21
- 66 The Hundred House
- 83 Mill House
- 112 Saffrons
- 115 Seaford & Bishopstone Gardens

Monday 22
- 66 The Hundred House

Sunday 28
- 21 Burgess Hill Gardens
- 63 4 Hillside Cottages

Monday 29
- 21 Burgess Hill Gardens

A warm welcome for all . . .

August

Saturday 3
- 45 Fairlight Hall

Sunday 4
- 83 Mill House

Monday 5
- 30 Clinton Lodge

Tuesday 6
- 45 Fairlight Hall

Saturday 10
- 127 Three Chimneys

Sunday 11
- 39 Driftwood
- 80 The Manor of Dean
- 127 Three Chimneys

Wednesday 14
- 32 Colwood House
- 105 6 Plantation Rise

Friday 16
- 42 Durrance Manor (Evening)

Saturday 17
- 22 Butlers Farmhouse
- 52 70 Ford Road
- 105 6 Plantation Rise

Sunday 18
- 22 Butlers Farmhouse
- 32 Colwood House
- 42 Durrance Manor
- 52 70 Ford Road
- 79 Malthouse Farm
- 90 The Oast House

Tuesday 20
- 79 Malthouse Farm

Saturday 24
- 13 4 Ben's Acre

Sunday 25
- 60 Hardwycke
- 93 The Old Farmhouse

Monday 26
- 93 The Old Farmhouse
- 126 Sussex Prairies

September

Sunday 1
- 27 Channel View
- 67 Jacaranda
- 118 Shalford House

Wednesday 4
- 9 Bateman's

Saturday 7
- 122 South Grange

Sunday 8
- 101 Parsonage Farm
- 109 Ringmer Park
- 122 South Grange

Saturday 14
- 111 Rymans
- 114 Sandhill Farm House
- 136 Winchelsea's Secret Gardens

Sunday 15
- 10 Bates Green
- 15 Bignor Park
- 111 Rymans
- 114 Sandhill Farm House

Friday 20
- 128 Tidebrook Manor

Sunday 22
- 71 King John's Lodge
- 80 The Manor of Dean

October

Tuesday 8
- 119 Sheffield Park and Garden

Sunday 13
- 6 Ashdown Park Hotel

Friday 18
- 97 The Old Vicarage

February 2014

Tuesday 11
- 103 Pembury House

Wednesday 12
- 103 Pembury House

Thursday 13
- 103 Pembury House

Tuesday 18
- 103 Pembury House

Wednesday 19
- 103 Pembury House

Thursday 20
- 103 Pembury House

March 2014

Friday 7
- 103 Pembury House

Gardens open to the public

- 1 Alfriston Clergy House
- 4 Arundel Castle & Gardens - The Collector Earl's Garden
- 9 Bateman's
- 10 Bates Green
- 30 Clinton Lodge
- 37 Denmans Garden
- 55 Great Dixter House, Gardens & Nurseries
- 61 Gardens & Grounds of Herstmonceux Castle
- 62 Highdown Gardens
- 64 Historic Gardens
- 71 King John's Lodge
- 82 McBean's Orchids
- 88 Nymans
- 106 The Priest House
- 113 St Mary's House Gardens
- 119 Sheffield Park and Garden
- 126 Sussex Prairies
- 135 West Dean Gardens

By appointment only

- 20 Brightling Down Farm
- 26 Champs Hill
- 29 Chidmere Gardens
- 31 Coates Manor
- 49 Five Oaks Cottage
- 56 Great Lywood Farmhouse
- 68 Kent House
- 91 Ocklynge Manor
- 99 Oxsetton
- 104 Pindars
- 129 Tinkers Bridge Cottage

Also open by Appointment ☎

- 7 Bakers House
- 8 46 Westup Farm Cottages, Balcombe Gardens
- 8 Winterfield, Balcombe Gardens
- 12 Beedinglee
- 13 4 Ben's Acre
- 14 26 Winston Drive, Bexhill Gardens
- 16 4 Birch Close
- 19 Bradstow Lodge
- 21 47 Leylands Road, Burgess Hill Gardens
- 21 30 Sycamore Drive, Burgess Hill Gardens
- 22 Butlers Farmhouse
- 24 51 Carlisle Road
- 25 Caxton Manor
- 27 Channel View

Visit a garden in your own time – look out for the ☎

The Gardens

1 ◆ ALFRISTON CLERGY HOUSE

Alfriston BN26 5TL. National Trust, 01323 871961, www.nationaltrust.org.uk. *4m NE of Seaford. Just E of B2108, in Alfriston village, adjoining The Tye & St Andrew's Church. Bus: RDH 125 from Lewes, Autopoint 126 from Eastbourne & Seaford.* **Adm £4.65, chd £2.35. For NGS: Tue 18 June (10.30-4.30). For other opening times and information, please phone or see garden website.**

Enjoy the scent of roses, admire the vegetable garden and orchard in a tranquil setting with views across the River Cuckmere. Visit this C14 thatched Wealden hall house, the first building to be acquired by the National Trust in 1896. Our gardener will be available to talk to you about this peaceful cottage garden. Limited wheelchair access.

♿

Gardeners' Cottage

GROUP OPENING

2 AMBROSE PLACE BACK GARDENS

Richmond Road, Worthing BN11 1PZ. *Worthing Town Centre. Entry points: Ambrose Villa, corner Portland Rd and Richmond Rd; No 1, next to St Paul's Church; No 10, opp Worthing Library.* Afternoon teas/cakes (2 - 4.45pm) at 'Way-In Café', Worthing Tabernacle Church by £2.50 prepaid ticket only from Entry points. **Combined adm £5, chd free. Sun 9 June.**

1 AMBROSE PLACE
Mrs M M Rosenberg.
Entry point for visitors

3 AMBROSE PLACE
Tim & Fiona Reynoldson

4 AMBROSE PLACE
Mark & Caroline Robson

5 AMBROSE PLACE
Pat & Sue Owen

6 AMBROSE PLACE
Catherine Reeve

7 AMBROSE PLACE
Mark & Susan Frost

8 AMBROSE PLACE
Claire & Steve Hughes

9 AMBROSE PLACE
Anna & Derek Irvine

10 AMBROSE PLACE
Alan & Marie Pringle

11 AMBROSE PLACE
Mrs M Stewart

12 AMBROSE PLACE
Peter & Nina May

13 AMBROSE PLACE
Malcolm & Hilary Leeves

NEW **14 AMBROSE PLACE**
Mr & Mrs A Marks

AMBROSE VILLA
122 Portland Place. Mark & Christine Potter.
Entry point for visitors

The highly acclaimed back gardens of Ambrose Place are indeed a 'horticultural phenomenon' in their rich panoply of styles, plantings and layouts. Behind a classic Regency Terrace, itself the architectural jewel of Worthing, the gardens draw inspiration from such exotic diversity as Morocco, Provence and the Alhambra to the more traditional sources of the English Cottage and Victorian gardens. All within the typically limited space of a terrace (NB seriously restricted disabled access), a variety of imaginative water features add to the charm and attraction for all gardeners and prove that small can be beautiful. Do come and enjoy our special spaces! As this is the 30th anniversary year of opening, the Mayor of Worthing will officially open the gardens on Sunday 9 June 2013. Featured on BBC Radio 'Dig-it ' programme, in Worthing Herald, West Sussex Gazette and other local media.

GROUP OPENING

3 ANSTY GARDENS

Ansty nr. Haywards Heath RH17 5AS. *3m W of Haywards Heath on A272. 1m E of A23.* Home-made teas The Barn House (May) & Apple Tree Cottage (June). **Combined adm £5, chd free. Sun 12 May, Sun 23 June (1.30-6).**

APPLETREE COTTAGE
Mr & Mrs G J Longfield

THE BARN HOUSE
Mr & Mrs Michael Dykes

3 LAVENDER COTTAGES
Derry Baillieux

NEW **LITTLE ORCHARD**
Harry & Charlotte Lloyd Owen

SPRINGFIELD
David & Julie Pyrah

WHYDOWN COTTAGE
Mrs M Gibson & Lance Gibson.
Open May only

Ansty's gardens offer interesting contrast. Parking is in a field opp the lane leading to Whydown Cottage (open in May only) or if too wet try the Council car park at the Ansty end of Deaks Lane. Whydown Cottage covers an acre with the occasional water feature and an atmospheric woodland including an Embothrium. Onward along the bridleway to 3 Lavender Cottages with an attractive garden to the front and pretty brick courtyard to the rear with cottage flowers. Close by picturesque Appletree Cottage (C16) set in 2 acres with herbaceous beds, vegetable garden and fruit cage with wonderful views. Springfield's 1 acre offers mature trees and large pond, also camellias, azaleas, and rhododendrons plus herbaceous border. The Barn House of an acre has a walled garden, large pond, veg garden and to the front a formal design of clipped box and pergolas. Little Orchard is a 3 acre garden with informal plantings of trees and shrubs, family friendly woodland and fine views. Limited wheelchair access at 3 Lavender Cottages, no wheelchair access at Springfield.

4 ◆ ARUNDEL CASTLE & GARDENS - THE COLLECTOR EARL'S GARDEN

BN18 9AB. Arundel Castle Trustees Ltd, 01903 882173, www.arundelcastle.org. *Arundel Castle, Arundel. In the centre of Arundel, N of A27.* **For opening times and information, please phone or see garden website.**
Home of the Duke & Duchess of Norfolk. 40 acres of grounds and gardens. The Collector Earl's Garden with hot subtropical borders and wild flowers. English herbaceous borders. 2 restored Victorian glasshouses with exotic fruit and vegetables. Walled flower and organic kitchen gardens. C14 Fitzalan Chapel white garden.

GROUP OPENING

5 ARUNDEL GARDENS GROUP

BN18 9HL. *1/4 m W of Arundel town centre. Take Ford Rd exit off main A27 r'about by river. All 3 locations well signed.* Home made teas at Torton Top. **Combined adm £4, chd free. Payments only at Torton Top or Birch Close. Sun 26, Mon 27 May (2-5).**

4 BIRCH CLOSE
Elizabeth & Mike Gammon
(See separate entry)

NEW **20 DALLAWAY ROAD**
Mr Geoff Allen

TORTON TOP
36 Torton Hill Road. Barry & Lucy Hopkins

The ancient town of Arundel sits impressively on a hilltop overlooking the River Arun with its Norman Castle and imposing Cathedral. Town centre full of interesting shops, pubs and restaurants and these three gardens are situated in Torton Hill, a residential area close by. Torton Top, has mature gardens of 1/2 acre with ancient oak trees and large lawn areas interspersed with well stocked beds and borders full of specimen shrubs, acers, clematis, roses and annuals. Delightful natural pond feature with waterfall. New 20 Dalloway Road is a delightful split level woodland garden, designed 14 years ago, in a peaceful setting with many specimen shrubs and trees. Lovely Summer House in the woodland corner with garden seating. 4 Birch Close - 0.4 acre of woodland garden with wide range of mature trees and shrubs with many hardy perennials. Extensive selection of spring flowers and over 100 clematis all in a tranquil setting with meandering pathways and ample seating.

Delightful split level woodland garden in a peaceful setting with many specimen shrubs and trees . . .

6 ASHDOWN PARK HOTEL

Wych Cross RH18 5JR. Mr Kevin Sweet, 01342 824988, reservations@ashdownpark.co.uk, www.elitehotels.co.uk. *6m S of E Grinstead. Take A22, 3m S of Forest Row turn L at Wych Cross by garage, 1m on R. From M25 take M23 S, exit J10 on A264 to E Grinstead. Approach from S on A22, turn R at Wych Cross.* Teas (not for NGS). **Adm £5, chd free. Suns: 12 May, 13 Oct (2-5).**
186 acres of parkland, grounds and gardens surrounding Ashdown Park Hotel. Our 'Secret Garden' is well worth a visit with many new plantings. Large number of deer roam the estate and can often be seen during the day. Enjoy and explore the woodland paths, quiet areas and views. Featured in Sussex Life & local press. Some gravel paths and uneven ground with steps.

7 ▶ BAKERS HOUSE
Bakers Lane, Shipley RH13 8GJ. Mr & Mrs Mark Burrell, 01403 741215, margot@dragons.me.uk. *5m S of Horsham. Take A24 to Worthing, then A272 W, 2nd turn to Dragon's Green. L at George & Dragon PH, Bakers Lane then 300yds on L.* Home-made teas. **Adm £5, chd free. Suns: 19 May, 16 June (2-6). Visitors also welcome by appt May to June.**
Large parkland garden with great oaks, lake, laburnum tunnel, rose walks of old-fashioned roses, scented knot garden, olive and lemon walk, bog gardens and big kitchen garden with potager. Featured in numerous publications. Gravel paths, partial wheelchair access.

GROUP OPENING

8 ▶ BALCOMBE GARDENS
RH17 6JJ. *3m N of Cuckfield on B2036. From J10A on M23, follow B2036 S for 2½ m.* Tea at Krawden. **Combined adm £5, chd free. Wed 15 May, Sat 15 June (12-5).**

KRAWDEN
Victoria Road. Ann & Eddie Bryant

46 WESTUP FARM COTTAGES
Chris & Sarah Cornwell.
¼ m N of stn, turn L off B2036 immed before Balcombe Primary School (signed) ¾ m
Visitors also welcome by appt Apr to Oct, groups of 4+. 01444 811891

WINTERFIELD
Sue & Sarah Howe.
Just N of stn, R into Newlands ¼ m signed
Visitors also welcome by appt Apr to Sept, groups of 4+. 01444 811380

Balcombe is an ancient village with 55 listed buildings incl the C15 parish church of St Mary's. The village hall contains interesting murals on the theme of War and Peace, while nearby is the famous Ouse Valley Viaduct and beautiful woods, lakes, millpond and reservoir. The three gardens opening for the NGS will especially appeal to plant-lovers and are full of variety and interest. Hidden in the countryside of the High Weald, Westup Farm cottage garden contains unique and traditional features linked by intimate paths through lush and subtle planting, while Winterfield contains as many trees and shrubs as can be crammed into ½ acre! There are also wild flowers, gravelled areas, alpine troughs, a secret garden, pond and borders. Krawden offers roses, herbaceous borders, fruit and vegetables, a Mediterranean area with gravel and water feature. Featured in Sussex Living magazine. Wheelchair access at Winterfield and Krawden only.

9 ▶ ◆ BATEMAN'S
Burwash TN19 7DS. National Trust, 01435 882302, www.nationaltrust.org.uk. *6m E of Heathfield. ½ m S of A265 on rd leading S at W end of Burwash, or N from Woods Corner (B2096). Pick up and drop off point available.* **Adm £9.50, chd £4.75. For NGS: Wed 8 May, Wed 4 Sept (10-4.30). For other opening times and information, please phone or see garden website.**
Bateman's is an idyllic spot, loved by Rudyard Kipling until the end of his life. Nestled in a shallow valley, the house and garden were a joy and an inspiration to him, from the formal lawns and clipped yew hedges to the romantic meadow with the meandering river flowing through it. Water levels permitting, the mill will be grinding. Most of the garden is accessible. There are some slopes and the paths are uneven.

10 ▶ ◆ BATES GREEN
Tye Hill Road, Arlington, Hailsham BN26 6SH. Carolyn & John McCutchan, 01323 485152, www.batesgreen.co.uk. *3½ m SW of Hailsham and of A22. Midway between the A22 & A27 2m S of Michelham Priory. Bates Green is in Tye Hill Rd (N of Arlington Village) 350yds S of Old Oak Inn.* **Adm £4, chd free. For NGS: Suns 26 May; 14 July; 15 Sept (11-5). For other opening times and information, please phone or see garden website.**
Plantsman's 2-acre tranquil garden, of interest through the seasons. Springtime including narcissi, primroses, violets, early tulips and coloured stems of cornus. Summer progresses with alliums, hardy geraniums, kniphofias, hemerocallis, grasses, crocosmias and organic vegetables. Autumn peaks with asters, cyclamen, colchicum, dahlias, heleniums, miscanthus, and verbenas. Most areas are wheelchair accessible.

Rose walks of old-fashioned roses, scented knot garden, olive and lemon walk . . .

11 ▶ BEAUCHAMPS
Float Lane, Udimore, Rye TN31 6BY. Matty & Richard Holmes. *3m W of Rye. 3m E of Broad Oak Xrds. Turn S off B2089 down Float Lane ½ m.* Home-made teas. **Adm £4, chd free. Sun 26 May (2-6).**
Now open again, nestling in the beautiful Brede Valley, this lovely informal garden, maintained by its owners, displays a wide range of unusual herbaceous plants, shrubs and trees incl a fine specimen of *Cornus controversa* 'Variegata'. Small orchard, kitchen garden and copse. Good display of irises, many for sale, with other home-propagated herbaceous plants. Full access by wheelchair difficult after any recent rainfall.

12 ▶ NEW ▶ BEEDINGLEE
Brighton Road, Lower Beeding, Horsham RH13 6NQ. Mrs Jo Longley, 01403 891251, jolongley@tiscali.co.uk. *4m SE of Horsham on A281. Beedinglee is on A281 between Cowfold and Mannings Heath, approx ½ m from South Lodge Hotel. Look out for a red post box on a stalk; the entrance to Beedinglee is almost opposite on the other side of the road.* Home-made teas. **Adm £4, chd free. Suns 12, 19 May (11.30-5). Groups of 10-20 also welcome by appt June to Oct.**
Originally part of the Leonardslee Estate, the planting of the 6-acre

Victorian/Edwardian garden disappeared during the hurricane of 1987, when over 100 mature trees blew down. The present garden has evolved since then with many interesting and unusual trees and shrubs. Still an informal garden there are hidden paths and a secret garden.

13 4 BEN'S ACRE

Horsham RH13 6LW. Pauline Clark, 01403 266912, brian.clark8850@yahoo.co.uk, www.youtube.com, search Pauline & Brian's Sussex Garden. *From A281 via Cowfold after Hilliers Garden Centre on L take 2nd R by restaurant into St Leonards Rd which runs into Comptons Lane. 5th R into Heron Way after mini r'about, 2nd L Grebe Crescent, 1st L Ben's Acre.* Home-made teas. **Adm £3, chd free.** Sats 29 June; 24 Aug (1-5). **Visitors also welcome by appt June to Sept 15-40 people.**

On the edge of St Leonards Forest. Described as a little piece of heaven and a horticultural cornucopia with delights at every corner. Only 100ft x 45ft using steps and terraces to take you up gently to borders planted to capacity with interesting pot pourri of colour, texture and form. Secretive seating areas and top terrace to enjoy the garden while having your pot of tea and cake. Featured on front cover of gardening book and in Amateur Gardening.

GROUP OPENING

14 BEXHILL GARDENS

Bexhill TN39 4QB. *½ m W of centre of Bexhill. Proceed to Little Common r'about on A259, then see directions for each garden.* Home-made teas at 57 Barnhorn Road. **Combined adm £5, chd free.** Sun 16 June (11-5).

1 ASHCOMBE DRIVE
Richard & Liz Chown.
Exit r'about S into Cooden Sea Rd, 3rd L into Kewhurst Ave, 1st L into Ashcombe Dr, 400yds on R

57 BARNHORN ROAD
Trevor Oldham & John Vickers.
At r'about continue on A259 (Barnhorn Rd) towards Eastbourne, approx 450yds. Garden on L

89 COODEN DRIVE
Carole & Ian Woodland.
From Little Common r'about exit into Cooden Sea Rd. At Cooden Beach follow rd round to L into Cooden Drive, garden approx 1m on R

6 DARESBURY CLOSE
Ms M Carpenter.
Turning near Orchard Cottage. Look for signs

37 GRANGE COURT DRIVE
Mr & Mrs Clarke.
Follow instructions as below from A259 onto A269. 1st L into Woodsgate Park. 1st R Buxton Drive. 1st L

ORCHARD COTTAGE
22 Gatelands Drive
Pat McCarthy.
From Little Common keep on A259 for approx 1.2 m towards Hastings. Turn L at T-lights (Viking chip bar) onto A269 London. Take 1st L into Woodsgate Park then 4th R into Gatelands Drive

NEW **24 RIDERS BOLT**
Margaret & Michael Steer.
½ m E of Little Common r'about on A259 turn L by bus shelter Broad Oak Lane 1st R Courthope Drive 1st R Riders Bolt

NEW **THE TULIP TREE**
20 Chestnut Walk
Pearse & Andrea Carty.
On the r'about take exit skirting RH-side of The Wheatsheaf PH into Chestnut Walk. Halfway down on R

NEW **26 WINSTON DRIVE**
Ron & Clare Brazier.
Exit r'about E towards Hastings. After 1m, turn R into Sutherland Ave immed R into Collington Lane East, R Eden Drive, 1st L Winston Drive 100yds on L
Visitors also welcome by appt June to Aug.
01424 844177
ronbrazier@talktalk.net

An attractive Edwardian residential seaside town famous for its De la Warr Pavilion arts centre. Also noted for the enthusiastic gardeners who open to the public. Orchard Cottage has a truly interesting plantswoman's newly designed garden with clever use of trellis supporting a variety of climbers. Wonderful variety of plants for sale. Daresbury Close is a secluded, partly-walled 80ft garden with mixed planting of acers, shrubs and perennials. With paintings on show, Grange Court Drive is a small, informal, colourful family garden, planted with shrubs, flowers, fruit trees and vegetables. Riders Bolt new this year, is a mix of trees, shrubs and herbaceous borders full of mixed perennials with dark and variegated foliage. Cooden Drive is a plant lover's garden with large numbers of herbaceous plants, shrubs and trees. At Ashcombe Drive discover a delightful hide-away garden. Returning visitors will notice some changes this year. Another new garden this year at Winston Drive with 275 plant species and 5 water features. Then enjoy a delicious home-made tea at Barnhorn Road, a

Saffrons

© Leigh Clapp

pleasant, spacious garden with lots of lawn and beds. Orchard Cottage awarded Certificate of Excellence & Best ECO Award at Bexhill in Bloom. Some of the gardens have wheelchair access. The Tulip Tree has a wide variety of flowers, roses, clematis, and exotics, mainly from seed. Shade plants. Unusual trees. Wildlife and ornamental ponds. Wormery

15 BIGNOR PARK

Pulborough RH20 1HG. The Mersey Family, www.bignorpark.co.uk. *5m S of Petworth and Pulborough. Well signed from B2138. Nearest village Sutton.* Home-made teas. **Adm £4, chd free. Every Wed 3 Apr to 24 Apr (2-5); Sun 16 June, Sun 15 Sept (2-5.30).**

11 acres of garden to explore, with magnificent views of S Downs. Interesting trees, shrubs, wild flower areas with swathes of daffodils in spring. The walled flower garden has been replanted. Plenty of seats for contemplation, and shelter if it rains. Temple, Greek loggia, Zen pond and unusual sculptures. A peaceful garden with no traffic noise. Floral Fringe Fair 19 & 20 May (see website). Wheelchair access possible in shrubbery, not easy in walled garden.

All in a tranquil setting with secluded corners, meandering paths and plenty of seating . . .

16 4 BIRCH CLOSE

Arundel BN18 9HN. Elizabeth & Mike Gammon, 01903 882722. *1m S of Arundel. From A27/A284 r'about at W end of Arundel take Ford Rd. After ½ m turn R into Maxwell Rd and follow signs.* Home-made teas. **Adm £3, chd free. Sun 5, Mon 6 May (2-5). Also opening 26, 27 May with Arundel Gardens Group. Visitors also welcome by appt Apr to May.**

0.4 acre of woodland garden on edge of Arundel. Wide range of mature trees and shrubs with many hardy perennials. Emphasis on extensive selection of spring flowers and clematis (over 100 incl 11 montana). All in a tranquil setting with secluded corners, meandering paths and plenty of seating.

17 BLUE JAYS

Chesworth Close, Horsham RH13 5AL. Stella & Mike Schofield. *5 mins walk SE of St Mary's Church. From A281 (East St) L down Denne Rd, L to Chesworth Lane, R to Chesworth Close. Garden at end of close with 4 disabled parking spaces. Other parking in Denne Rd car park; some spaces in Denne Rd, Normandy and Queensway, free on Suns.* Home-made teas. **Adm £3, chd free (share to The Badger Trust). Sun 26, Mon 27 May, Sun 16 June (12-5).**

Wooded 1-acre garden with rhododendrons, camellias and azaleas. Candelabra primulas and ferns edge the R Arun. Primroses and spring bulbs border woodland path and stream. Cordylines, gunneras, flower beds, a pond and a fountain are set in open lawns. An arch leads to the vegetable plot and orchard bounded by the river. Large WW2 pill box in the orchard; visits inside with short talk are available.

18 BRADNESS GALLERY

Spithurst Road, Spithurst, Barcombe BN8 5EB. Michael Cruickshank & Emma Burnett, www.emmaburnett.co.uk. *5m N of Lewes. Bradness Gallery lies midway between the villages of Barcombe & Newick in Spithurst, Parking in field. Less mobile visitors can drive into entrance to drop off, then park by Gallery.* Home-made teas. **Adm £4, chd free. Sat 29, Sun 30 June (11-6).**

Delightful and tranquil mature, organic, wildlife garden with trees, scented shrubs, old roses, herbaceous borders and wild garden planting. A wooded stream flows along the bottom and two large ponds are home to wild ducks, dragonflies and frogs. Also raised beds for vegetables and cut flowers. Camomile patch. Delicious home-made teas and cakes. Lovely new tearoom for rainy days. Surrounded by fields and cows. Gallery will be open showing original paintings, prints and cards by owners www.englishlandscapepaintings.co.uk. Featured in Sussex Life, Sussex Living, Gardening News and Amateur Gardening. Lower half of garden slopes to stream and ponds. Ground is uneven.

19 BRADSTOW LODGE

The Drive, Ifold, Billingshurst RH14 0TE. Ian & Elizabeth Gregory, 01403 753248, elysian@ukgateway.net. *1m S of Loxwood. From A272/A281 take B2133 (Loxwood). ½ m S of Loxwood take the Plaistow Rd, after 800yds turn R into The Drive (by village shop). Follow signs. Parking in The Drive only, please park considerately.* **Adm £3.50, chd free. Sun 31 Mar (2-5); Sun 16 June (1-6). 16 June combined adm £5 with Jacaranda. Visitors also welcome by appt Apr to Sept For groups only.**

A series of 'garden rooms' with a variety of planting for year round interest create the effect of a much larger garden than half an acre. Bulbs, trees and shrubs, water features, formal topiary, raised beds and containers, greenhouses and vegetable garden give structure, texture and interest. Wheelchair access is possible but not to all areas of the garden due to narrow gravel paths. Unsuitable for powered wheelchairs.

20 BRIGHTLING DOWN FARM

Brightling Down, nr Woods Corner TN21 9LL. Mr & Mrs P Stephens, 01689 852144/01435 831118, valstephens29@btinternet.com. *1m from Woods Corner. At Swan PH at Woods Corner, take road opp signed Brightling. Take 1st L, signed Burwash. Almost immed, turn into 1st driveway on L.* Light refreshments. **Adm £7, chd free. Groups welcome by appt June to Sept, max 20, no coaches.**

The garden has several different areas incl a Zen garden, water garden, walled vegetable garden with 2 large greenhouses, herb garden and herbaceous borders. The garden makes clever use of grasses and is set amongst woodland, with stunning countryside views.

D

GROUP OPENING

21 NEW BURGESS HILL GARDENS
RH15 0GH. *8m N of Brighton. Burgess Hill can be reached by public transport. Collect map at either 30 Sycamore Drive or 14 Barnside Ave, both gardens off Folders Lane (B2113).* Home-made teas at Marle Place. **Combined adm £5, chd free. Sun 28, Mon 29 July (1-5).**

NEW 14 BARNSIDE AVENUE
Mr & Mrs Knight

NEW 47 LEYLANDS ROAD
Diane & Stephen Rabson.
Leylands Rd lies between the London Rd (B2036) and Wivelsfield Stn
Visitors also welcome by appt July to Aug, max 10.
01444 247937

NEW MARLE PLACE COMMUNITY GARDEN
Leylands Road. Steve Bridger.
Leylands Rd runs between London Rd and Wivelsfield Stn

NEW THE OLD VICARAGE
27 Crescent Road. Tina & Martin Harboard

NEW 9 SYCAMORE DRIVE
Peter Machin & Martin Savage

NEW 30 SYCAMORE DRIVE
John Smith & Kieran O'Regan.
Off Folders Lane (B2113) at the Ditchling Common end
Visitors also welcome by appt June to Aug Talk plants, design and enjoy.
01444 871888
jsarastroo@aol.com

NEW 59 SYCAMORE DRIVE
Steve & Debby Gill.
Follow map from first garden

This diverse group of seven is a mixture of established and small new gardens. Three of the group are a great example of what can be achieved over a four year period from a blank canvas in a new development while close by is 14 Barnside, a wisteria clad house with a family lawn and borders. Next is Marle Place which is an adult community centre. Here local people including some with learning difficulties are actively involved in creating an amazing garden. Just down the road is a garden packed with an array of plants and a wildlife pond. Finally, the Victorian Old Vicarage, is the oldest garden of the group with bay topiary, fig and jasmine along with statuary and greenhouses. Some of gardens have partial wheelchair access.

Constantly revised planting to maintain the magical and secluded atmosphere . . . art, cards & jewellery stalls . . .

22 BUTLERS FARMHOUSE
Butlers Lane, Herstmonceux BN27 1QH. Irene Eltringham-Willson, 01323 833770, irene.willson@btinternet.com. *3m E of Hailsham. Take A271 from Hailsham, go through village of Herstmonceux, turn R signed Church Rd then approx 1m turn R. Do not use SatNav!* Home-made teas (Apr) & cream teas (Aug). **Adm £3.50 (Apr) & £5 (Aug), chd free. Sat 6, Sun 7 Apr, Sat 17, Sun 18 Aug (2-5). Visitors also welcome by appt Apr to Oct, refreshments by arrangement.**
Lovely rural setting for 1-acre garden surrounding C16 farmhouse (not open) with views of S Downs. Pretty in spring with primroses and hellebores. Mainly herbaceous with rainbow border, small pond with dribbling frogs and Cornish-inspired beach corners. Restored to former glory, as shown in old photographs, but with a few quirky twists such as a poison garden and a secret jungle garden. Newest project is the restoration of a large wildlife pond in the field. Relax and listen to live jazz in the garden in August. Featured on Channel 4 'Four in a Bed' and in Swiss Life Style magazine. Most of garden accessible by wheelchair.

23 CABBAGES & KINGS
Wilderness Barns, Wilderness Lane, Hadlow Down TN22 4HU. System Professional Ltd, www.sysprogardens.teamcreative.co.uk. *5m E of Uckfield. ½ m S of A272, centre of Hadlow Down, ½ m down Wilderness Lane from A272, then see turning on L. Follow signs.* Wine, cream teas, coffee & home-made cakes. **Adm £4.50, chd free. Sun 14 July (10-4).**
System Professional took proud ownership of Ryl Nowell's contemporary garden in September 2006 and started a major restoration exercise that is ongoing to this day to restore the garden back to its former glory. Head Gardener Tim Penney, formally RBG Kew, has been overseeing the project. The garden comprises of semi-walled herbaceous and ornamental planting with stunning views overlooking open countryside. The garden also features undulating lawns leading down to a small and tranquil lake. Limited wheelchair access.

24 51 CARLISLE ROAD
Eastbourne BN21 4JR. Mr & Mrs N Fraser-Gausden, 01323 722545, n.fg@sky.com. *200yds inland from seafront (Wish Tower), close to Congress Theatre.* Home-made teas. **Adm £3, chd free. Sat 15, Sun 16 June (2-5). Visitors also welcome by appt May to June.**
Walled, S-facing garden (82ft sq) with mixed beds intersected by stone paths and incl small pool. Profuse and diverse planting. Wide selection of shrubs, old roses, herbaceous plants and perennials mingle with specimen trees and climbers. Constantly revised planting to maintain the magical and secluded atmosphere. Art, cards & jewellery stalls.

25 CAXTON MANOR
Wall Hill, Forest Row RH18 5EG. Adele & Jules Speelman, 01342 823102. *1m N of Forest Row, 2m S of E Grinstead. From A22 take turning to Ashurstwood, entrance on L after ⅓ m, or 1m on R from N.* Home-made teas. **Adm £4.50, chd free. Fri 17, Sat 18 May (2-5). Also open 2 Quarry Cottages (separate admission). Visitors also welcome by appt Apr to Sept. Adm £20 per person incl tour, talk & teas.**
Delightful 5 acre Japanese-inspired

gardens planted with mature rhododendrons, azaleas and acers, surrounding large pond with boat house, massive rockery and waterfall, beneath the home of the late Sir Archibald McIndoe (house not open). Japanese tea house and Japanese-style courtyard.

26 CHAMPS HILL

Waltham Park Road, Coldwaltham, Pulborough RH20 1LY. Mr & Mrs David Bowerman, 01798 831205, m.bowerman@btconnect.com. *3m S of Pulborough. On A29, turn R to Fittleworth into Waltham Park Rd; garden 400 metres on R.* **Adm £4, chd free. Groups of 10+ welcome by appt.**
27 acres of acid-loving plants around sand pits and woodland. Sculptures, superb views and year-round interest.

27 CHANNEL VIEW

52 Brook Barn Way, Goring-by-Sea, Worthing BN12 4DW. Jennie & Trevor Rollings, 01903 242431, tjrollings@gmail.com. *Goring-by-Sea. 1m W of Worthing, near seafront. Turn S off A259 into Parklands Ave, L at T-junction into Alinora Crescent. Brook Barn Way is immed on L.* Home-made teas. **Adm £3.50, chd free. Sat 22, Sun 23 June, Sun 1 Sept (1-5). Visitors also welcome by appt May to Sept.**
Mature owner-designed garden by the sea, imaginatively blending traditional Tudor cottage garden with subtropical, Mediterranean and antipodean planting. Unusually designed structures, paths, arches and pond combine dense planting with shady viewpoints and sunny patios. Inter-connecting garden 'rooms' ensure multiple perspectives and hidden vistas. Great variety of home-grown plants for sale.

28 NEW CHESTNUT FARM

Fords Green, Nutley, Uckfield TN22 3LL. Diana Hurrell & Peter Smith, 01825 712444. *Southern end of Nutley Village, opp Village Green. Head S through Nutley on A22 until reaching Nutley Arms PH on L. Garden is down very bumpy and steep track. Limited passing places. Less adventurous visitors may prefer to park in the Village and walk.* Home-made teas. **Adm £4, chd free. Sat 1, Sun 2 June (2-5.30). Visitors also welcome by appt Apr to Sept.**
A naturalistic garden in the heart of the Ashdown Forest developed over 20yrs by the current owners. Approx one-acre garden on a variety of levels and including lawns, large mixed borders, seasonal planting, spring-fed pond and waterfall, vegetable garden, small integral orchard, extensive bird and insect life. Look out for the topiary teddy bear!

Look out for the topiary teddy bear . . . !

29 CHIDMERE GARDENS

Chidham Lane, Chidham, Chichester PO18 8TD. Jackie & David Russell, 01243 572287, info@chidmere.com, www.chidmerefarm.com. *6m W of Chichester at SE end of Chidham Lane by pond in village.* Light refreshments. **Adm £5, chd free. Groups of 10-20 welcome by appt.**
Wisteria-clad C15 house surrounded by yew and hornbeam hedges situated next to Chidmere pond. Garden incl white garden, formal rose garden, well-stocked herbaceous borders and springtime woods. 8 acres of orchards with wide selection of heritage and modern varieties of apples, pears and plums incl 200yr old varieties of Blenheim Orange and Bramley Seedling. Chidmere Pond (almost 5 acres) is a natural wildlife preserve. Chidmere Farm apple juice available. Featured in Country Life and Chichester Observer. Limited wheelchair access.

30 ◆ CLINTON LODGE

Fletching, Uckfield TN22 3ST. Lady Collum, 01825 722952, www.clintonlodgegardens.co.uk. *4m NW of Uckfield. From A272 turn N at Piltdown for Fletching, 1½ m. Car park available (weather permitting) so please do not park in street.* ***Please follow signs to parking in field behind house.*** **Adm £5, chd free. For NGS: Sun 5 May, Mon 3 June, Mon 5 Aug (2-5.30). For other opening times and information, please phone or see garden website.**
6-acre formal and romantic garden, overlooking parkland, with old roses, William Pye water feature, double white and blue herbaceous borders, yew hedges, pleached lime walks, copy of C17 scented herb garden, medieval-style potager, vine and rose allée, wild flower garden. Canal garden, small knot garden, shady glade and orchard. Caroline and Georgian house, not open.

31 COATES MANOR

Fittleworth RH20 1ES. Mrs G H Thorp, 01798 865356. *3½ m SW of Pulborough. Turn off B2138 signed Coates.* **Adm £3.50, chd free. £5 with light refreshments by arrangement. Visitors welcome by appt.**
1-acre, mainly shrubs and foliage of special interest, surrounding Elizabethan house (not open). Flowing design punctuated by clipped shrubs and specimen trees. Paved walled garden with interesting perennials, clematis, scented climbers and smaller treasures. Cyclamen, nerines, amaryllis, berries and coloured foliage give late season interest. Featured in The English Garden.

32 COLWOOD HOUSE

Cuckfield Lane, Warninglid RH17 5SP. Mr & Mrs Patrick Brenan, 01444 461831, rbrenan@me.com. *6m W of Haywards Heath, 6m SE of Horsham. Entrance on B2115 (Cuckfield Lane). From E, N & S, turn off A23, turn W towards Warninglid for ¾ m. From W come through Warninglid village.* **Adm £5, chd free (share to Seaforth Hall). Wed 14, Sun 18 Aug (2-5). Groups of 10+ also welcome by appt Mar to Aug.**
12 acres of garden, with mature and specimen trees from the late 1800s, lawns and woodland edge. Formal parterre, rose and herb gardens. 100ft terrace and herbaceous border overlooking flower-rimmed croquet lawn. Cut turf labyrinth and forsythia tunnel. Water features, Statues and gazebos. Pets' cemetery. Giant chessboard. Lake with island. Gravel paths, some slopes.

33 COOKSCROFT
Bookers Lane, Earnley, nr Chichester PO20 7JG. Mr & Mrs J Williams, 01243 513671, williams.cookscroft@virgin.net, www.cookscroft.co.uk. *6m S of Chichester. At end of Birdham Straight A286 from Chichester, take L fork to E Wittering B2198. 1m on, before sharp bend, turn L into Bookers Lane. 2nd house on L.* Home-made teas. **Adm £4, chd free. Sun 26, Mon 27 May (1-5). Visitors also welcome by appt.**
This is a garden for all seasons which delights the visitor. Started in 1988, it features Cottage, Woodland and Japanese gardens, water features and borders of perennials, with a particular emphasis on S Hemisphere plants. Unusual plants for the plantsman to enjoy, many grown from seed. Grass paths, unfenced ponds.

34 COPYHOLD HOLLOW
Copyhold Lane, Borde Hill, Haywards Heath RH16 1XU. Frances Druce, 01444 413265, ngs@copyholdhollow.co.uk, www.copyholdhollow.co.uk. *2m N of Haywards Heath. Follow signs for Borde Hill Gardens. With BHG on L, over brow of hill and take 1st R signed Ardingly. Garden ½ m.* Home-made teas. **Adm £3.50, chd free. Sat 1, Sun 2 June (1-4). Visitors also welcome by appt Apr to Oct, adm £4, teas by arrangement (Extra £3).**
Cottage garden in a hollow, with woodland garden above. Spring-fed pond with dam and waterfall edged with damp-loving perennials. The oak stumpery gives way to a rock garden on the way to the crow's nest and the whole garden is planted for yr-round interest. Crow's nest viewing platform slung between two oak trees affording far-reaching views of garden and countryside. Very steep slopes.

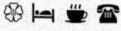

35 DACHS
Spear Hill, Ashington RH20 3BA. Bruce Wallace. *Approx 6m N of Worthing. From A24 at Ashington onto B2133 Billingshurst Rd, R into Spear Hill. We are the first house in Spear Hill and the garden also runs along the Billingshurst Road.* Home-made teas. **Adm £4, chd free. Sats, Suns: 23, 24 Mar; 8, 9 June (2-5.30).**
A waterlogged field turned into a beautiful garden of about 2 acres. Incl white garden, bog area, stream and unusual design of bridges. Several other themed beds with perennials of different textures and colours. Wide range of daffodils, narcissi, some snowdrops, fritillaria and iris in the spring.

Natural wild flower meadow renowned for its collection of native orchids . . .

36 DALE PARK HOUSE
Madehurst BN18 0NP. Robert & Jane Green, 01243 814260, robertgreen@farming.co.uk. *4m W of Arundel. Take A27 E from Chichester or W from Arundel, then A29 (London) for 2m, turn L to Madehurst & follow red arrows.* Home-made teas. **Adm £4, chd free. Sun 9 June (2-5). Visitors also welcome by appt May to July. Wine.**
Set in parkland on S Downs with magnificent views to the sea. Large walled garden with 200ft herbaceous border, mixed borders and rose garden. Gravel sunken garden. Rose and clematis arches, interesting collection of hostas, foliage plants and shrubs, orchard and kitchen garden.

37 ◆ DENMANS GARDEN
Denmans Lane, Fontwell BN18 0SU. Michael Neve & John Brookes, 01243 542808, www.denmans-garden.co.uk. *5m from Chichester & Arundel. Off A27, ½ m W of Fontwell r'about.* **Adm £4.95, chd £3.95. For NGS: Sat 1 June (9.30-5). For other opening times and information, please phone or see garden website.**
Denmans is a unique 4 acre garden designed for yr-round interest through use of form, colour and texture. Owned by Michael Neve and John Brookes MBE, renowned garden designer and writer. It is a garden full of ideas to be interpreted within smaller home spaces. Award-winning café and plant centre.

DORMANS PARK SAFARI
See Surrey

38 DOWN PLACE
South Harting, Petersfield GU31 5PN. Mr & Mrs D M Thistleton-Smith, 01730 825374, selina@downplace.co.uk. *1m SE of South Harting. B2141 to Chichester, turn L down unmarked lane below top of hill.* Home-made teas. **Adm £3.50, chd free (share to Friends of Harting Church). Sats, Suns: 27, 28 Apr; 15, 16 June (2-6). Groups of 15+ also welcome by appt, adm includes refreshment.**
7-acre hillside, chalk garden on the N side of S Downs with fine views of surrounding countryside. Extensive herbaceous, shrub and rose borders on different levels merging into natural wild flower meadow renowned for its collection of native orchids. Fully stocked vegetable garden and greenhouses. Spring flowers and blossom. Substantial top terrace and borders accessible to wheelchairs.

39 DRIFTWOOD
4 Marine Drive, Bishopstone, Seaford BN25 2RS. Geoff Stonebanks & Mark Glassman, 01323 899296, geoffstonebanks@gmail.com, www.driftwoodbysea.co.uk. *Clearly signed from A259 between Seaford & Newhaven. Turn L into Marine Drive from Bishopstone Rd, 2nd on R. Please park carefully in street.* Light refreshments. **Adm £3.50, chd free. Tue 2 July, Sun 11 Aug (11-5). Also opening 16, 17 June & 21 July with Seaford & Bishopstone Gardens. Visitors and groups of up to 20 also welcome by appt June to Aug.**
A multi award winning bright beach-inspired plot that fully embraces its location with imaginative planting, cleverly combining wooden and rusted metal features with the landscape. Densely packed, no exposed soil, home to over 400 different varieties of plants and shrubs in coastal gravel and cottage beds, with space to sit and admire the sea views. An immaculate, lawnless, gem, 112ft x 48ft. Garden decorations and Daily Mail National Garden Competition Blue Plaque Holder and Winner for Garden News Gardener of the Year Best Small Garden. Extensive coverage in national/local press and in numerous publications. Steep drive but help readily available.

40 DUCKYLS HOLT

Selsfield Road, West Hoathly RH19 4QN. Mrs Diana Hill & Miss Sophie Hill. *4m SW of East Grinstead, 6m E of Crawley. At Turners Hill take B2028. After 1m S fork L to West Hoathly. Garden on R immed beyond 30mph sign, very limited disabled parking at garden; parking difficult as busy road, some parking in village centre.* Home-made teas. **Adm £3.50, chd free. Sat 25, Sun 26, Mon 27 May, Sat 29, Sun 30 June (11-6). Also open 25 May & 29 June The Priest House, combined adm £4.**

Delightful cottage garden of approx 2 acres on many different levels. Small herb garden, colourful formal and informal plantings, herbaceous borders, rose border and formal rose garden, lots of pots and baskets - a riot of colour. Mature azaleas and rhododendrons in season. Very limited parking.

41 DURFORD MILL HOUSE

West Harting, Petersfield GU31 5AZ. Mrs John Jones. *3m E of Petersfield. Just off A272 between Petersfield and Rogate, signed Durford Mill and The Hartings. Cross medieval bridge, follow parking signs. From S, past village shop (South Harting) on L, take 1st L signed West Harting (Durford Mill House approx 2m).* Home-made teas. **Adm £3.50, chd free. Sun 5 May, Sat 22, Sun 23 June (2-5.30).**

Come and relax in our peaceful mill garden with it's meandering stream and quiet places to sit. Wander along the paths and over the bridges among the flowers, shrubs and beautiful trees. Finishing up with delicious home-made cakes and tea.

42 DURRANCE MANOR

Smithers Hill Lane, Shipley RH13 8PE. Gordon & Joan Lindsay, 01403 741577, jlindsay@dsl.pipex.com. *7m SW of Horsham. Take A24 to A272 (S from Horsham, N from Worthing), then turn W towards Billingshurst. Go 1.7m to 2nd turning on L Smithers Hill Lane signed to Countryman PH. Durrance Manor 2nd on L.* **Adm £4.50, chd free. Evening Opening, wine & light refreshments Fri 16 Aug (6-8.30); Sun 18 Aug (2-6). Visitors also welcome by appt May to Sept.**

2-acre site surrounding medieval hall house (not open) with Horsham stone roof. Uninterrupted views to S Downs and Chanctonbury Ring over ha-ha. Many different gardens including colourful long borders, Japanese-style gardens, shade gardens, large pond, wild flowering meadow and orchard, greenhouse and vegetable garden.

© Nicola Stocken Tomkins

43 54 ELMLEIGH

Midhurst GU29 9HA. Wendy Liddle, 07796 562275, wendyliddle@btconnect.com. *¼ m W of Midhurst, off A272. Wheelchair users please use designated parking spaces at top of drive, phone on arrival for assistance.* Home-made teas. **Adm £3. Sat 8, Sun 9, Sat 22, Sun 23 June (10-5). Visitors and groups also welcome by appt June to Sept.**

Come and walk around this beautiful, award-winning garden on the edge of Midhurst. Planted with majestic Scots pines, shrubs, perennials and annuals - small, but packed with interest, a tapestry of unusual plants giving all-season colour. Many raised beds and numerous statues. A child-friendly garden. New attraction is a wild life pond. Award winner of Midhurst Garden in Bloom and Chichester Residential Garden award.

EMSWORTH GARDENS

See Hampshire

44 FAIRLIGHT END

Pett Road, Pett, Hastings TN35 4HB. Chris & Robin Hutt, 07774 863750, chrishutt@btopenworld.com. *From Hastings take A259 to Rye. At White Hart Beefeater turn R into Friars Hill. Descend into Pett village. Park in village hall car park, opp house.* Home-made teas, Pimms & wine. **Adm £4, chd free (share to Pett Village Hall). Fri 21, Sat 22 June (11-5). Groups of 10-30 also welcome by appt May to Sept.**

3-acre sloping garden with lovely views, paved terrace, lawn and ancient cherry tree, kitchen garden with 30 raised beds, wild flower meadow with mown paths, large orchard, two natural ponds joined by a stream and terraced herbaceous borders. Extensive new landscaping and planting this year. Steep paths, unfenced ponds.

45 FAIRLIGHT HALL
Martineau Lane, Hastings TN35 5DR. Mr & Mrs D Kovitz, www.fairlighthall.co.uk. *2m E of Hastings. A259 from Hastings towards Dover/Rye, 2m turn R into Martineau Lane.* Cream teas and light refreshments in walled garden. **Adm £5, chd free. Sat 3, Tue 6 Aug (10-4).**
A stunning garden in E Sussex, planted and restored over the last 4yrs. The formal gardens extend over 7 acres and surround the Victorian Gothic mansion. Features semi-tropical woodland avenues, a huge contemporary walled garden with amphitheatre and two 110m perennial borders above and below ha-ha with far-reaching views across Rye Bay. Featured in Hastings Observer. Most of the garden can be viewed by wheelchair-but tell us so we can put you in a disabled parking place.

Culinary and native wild herbs, planted organically in zones of colour . . .

46 FINEOAKS
Hammer Lane, Cowbeech, Heathfield TN21 9HF. Brian & Brenda Taylor. *5m S of Heathfield, 5m N of Hailsham. From Cowbeech 1m, on LH-side side.* Home-made teas. **Adm £4, chd free. Sat 27, Sun 28 Apr, Sat 15, Sun 16 June (1-6). Also open 15, 16 June Old School House (separate admission).**
An immaculate 3½ -acre garden in lovely countryside. Along the northern boundary runs a trout stream, flowing in spring, trickling in summer. The lawns are punctuated with island beds planted idiosyncratically with a mixture of shrubs, herbaceous and bedding plants. Further afield an orchard, large vegetable and fruit garden, greenhouse and woodland (bluebell walk in April). Nearer the house a pond, fountain and pretty rockery. Home-made organic jams and marmalades for sale.

47 NEW FIRLE PLACE HERB GARDEN
Firle Place, Firle, Lewes BN8 6LP. Lady Gage, firleplaceherbgarden.co.uk. *Located within main grounds of Firle Place, making up a part of its walled gardens. Clearly signed just before you enter main village of Firle, approx 300yds from turn off of A27, 4m from Lewes. Parking provided in park, short walk to garden.* Teas (Also available The Old Vicarage). **Adm £3, chd free. Sun 16 June (2-5). Also open The Old Vicarage at Firle (separate admission).**
Lady Gage's fascinating walled wilderness, 130ft x 200ft, originally part of the kitchen gardens for Firle Place, being transformed into newly planted tranquil herb garden. A unique work in progress, started in the winter of 2011, already home to a wide range of unusual medicinal, culinary and native wild herbs, planted organically in zones of colour. Herbal Teas, a selection of fresh infusions made from the plants in the garden.

48 FITTLEWORTH HOUSE
Bedham Lane, Fittleworth, Pulborough RH20 1JH. Edward & Isabel Braham, 01798 865074. *3m SE of Petworth. Just off A283, midway between Petworth and Pulborough, 200yds along lane signed Bedham.* **Adm £4, chd free. Every Wed 1 May to 17 July (2-5). Visitors also welcome by appt.**
3-acre garden with working walled kitchen garden growing a wide range of fruit, vegetables and flowers. Large glasshouse and old potting shed. Rhododendrons, roses, fountain, mixed borders. Magnificent cedar overlooks wisteria-covered Georgian house (not open) and croquet lawn. Wild garden, long grass areas, wildlife pond, spring bulbs. Gardeners on hand to answer questions.

49 FIVE OAKS COTTAGE
West Burton, nr Pulborough RH20 1HD. Jean & Steve Jackman, 07939 272443, jeanjackman@hotmail.com. *5m S of Pulborough. Please ring or email for directions.* **Adm £3.50, chd free. Visitors welcome by appt July. Individuals or small groups of friends.**
An artist's garden. Quirky and naturalistic, designed to attract wildlife. We would love you to visit, parking is limited please ring or email first. Good teas nearby. Plants, metal plant supports and cards for sale. Wildlife garden.

GROUP OPENING

50 FLETCHING GARDEN TRIO
Fletching, nr Uckfield TN22 3SP. *4m NW of Uckfield. From A272 turn N at Piltdown or North Chailey for Fletching.* Home-made teas North Hall. **Combined adm £5, chd free. Sat 22, Sun 23 June (2-5.30).**

THE GRANARY
Mill Lane. Pauline & Mike Tiplady

NORTH HALL
North Hall Lane. Celia & Les Everard
Visitors also welcome by appt 24-30 June.
01825 791103
indigodogs@yahoo.co.uk

1 WHITES COTTAGES
Gillian & Colin Smith

Fletching village is centred around the Parish Church of St Andrew and St Mary the Virgin which in 1264 Simon de Montfort visited on the eve of the battle of Lewes. The village borders Sheffield Park Garden (NT), famed for its autumn colour. Three lovely gardens, maintained by owners, are planted to please the senses and are packed with interest. The Granary is a charming 1-acre garden bordering the River Ouse with a vibrant cutting and kitchen garden and a newly landscaped courtyard and a riverside orchard with decked seating area. North Hall surrounds a C16 house (not open) where roses and clematis scramble through mature shrubs. There is a vast array of plants and a moated terrace adds interest to a romantic garden. 1 Whites Cottages is a delightful little cottage garden with a surprise around every corner incl a small gypsy caravan and free running ducks. See NGS website for full details.

51 NEW FOLLERS MANOR
Seaford Road, Alfriston, Polegate BN26 5TT. Geoff & Anne Shaw, www.facebook.com/FollersManor Garden. *½ m S of Alfriston. From Alfriston travel uphill towards Seaford. Park on L in paddock before garden.*

Entrance to garden next door to Alfriston Youth Hostel immed before road narrows. Light refreshments. **Adm £4, chd free. Sat 15, Sun 16 June (2-5.30).**
Contemporary garden designed by Ian Kitson attached to C17 listed historic farmhouse. Entrance courtyard, sunken garden, herbaceous displays, wildlife pond, wild flower meadows, woodland area and beautiful views of the South Downs. Winner of Sussex Heritage Trust Award. Featured on Gardeners' World, C4's Landscape Man and in numerous publications. Limited wheelchair access to some areas.

Wild flower meadows, woodland area and beautiful views of the South Downs . . .

52 70 FORD ROAD

Arundel BN18 9EX. Tony & Lizzie Gilks, 01903 884981, timespan70@tiscali.co.uk. *1/2 m W of Arundel. From the Arundel/Ford r'about on the A27 take the exit to Bognor Regis/Littlehampton. Our Garden is approximately 1000 yds on the right hand side. From Littlehampton/Bognor direction we can be found one mile from Ford Railway station, as you enter Arundel we are situated on the left hand side two houses past Maxwell Road*. **Adm £3, chd free. Sat 17, Sun 18 Aug (2-5). Visitors also welcome by appt 4 May -15 Sept, max 20.**
A must see immaculate town garden with ingenious ideas of how to incorporate well stocked flower beds with year round colour and texture, herbs, fruit and vegetable beds producing a wonderfully lush sanctuary in which to relax.

53 GARDENERS' COTTAGE

West Dean, nr Chichester PO18 0RX. Jim Buckland & Sarah Wain. *6m N of Chichester. Follow signs to West Dean Gardens and park in Gardens car park. Follow signs to cottage*. Home-made teas. **Adm £3, chd free. Sun 19 May (11-5).**
Small serene and secluded theatrical retreat with strong emphasis on texture, foliage and good structure created by trees, topiary, labyrinthine paths, interesting spaces. Separate courtyard garden with pond.

54 THE GRANGE

Fittleworth RH20 1EW. Mr & Mrs W Caldwell. *3m W of Pulborough. A283 midway Petworth-Pulborough; in Fittleworth turn S onto B2138 then turn W at Swan PH. Coming from the South turn left off A29 onto B2138 at Bury Gate then left again at Swan PH*. Home-made teas. **Adm £4, chd free. Suns: 7, 14 Apr (2-5.30).**
3-acre garden gently sloping to R Rother. Formal areas enclosed by yew hedges comprising colour-themed beds and herbaceous borders around pretty C18 house (not open). Small potager and orchard. Large collection of hellebores and more bulbs planted for 2013. Snakeshead fritillaries a feature in April. Plants for sale. Featured in Ten Landscapes by Michael Balston. Gravel paths.

55 ◆ GREAT DIXTER HOUSE, GARDENS & NURSERIES

Northiam TN31 6PH. Great Dixter Charitable Trust, 01797 252878, www.greatdixter.co.uk. *8m N of Rye. 1/2 m NW of Northiam off A28*. **For opening times and information, please phone or see garden website.**
Designed by Edwin Lutyens and Nathaniel Lloyd whose son, Christopher, officiated over these gardens for 55yrs, creating one of the most experimental and constantly changing gardens of our time. Wide variety of interest from clipped topiary, wild meadow flowers, natural ponds, formal pool and the famous long border and exotic garden. A long and varied season is aimed for. A wide range of educational study days and workshops held.

56 GREAT LYWOOD FARMHOUSE

Lindfield Road, Ardingly RH17 6SW. Richard & Susan Laing, 01444 892500, splaing@btinternet.com. *2 1/2 m N of Haywards Heath. Take B2028 for Ardingly. 2m from centre of Lindfield, turn L down single track*. Home-made teas/wine or light refreshments by arrangement. **Adm £7.50 incl refreshments, chd free. Visitors welcome by appt June to July.**
Approx 1 1/2 -acre terraced garden surrounding C17 Sussex farmhouse (not open). Lovely views to S Downs. Featuring lawns and grass walks, mixed borders, rose garden, kitchen garden and orchard, walled garden with dovecote. Terracing and lovely views to the South Downs.

57 GROVE FARM HOUSE

Paddockhurst Road, Turners Hill RH10 4SF. Mr & Mrs Piers Gibson. *1/4 m W of Turners Hill on B2110. The garden is on the edge of the village of Turners Hill; entrance is on the Paddockhurst Rd (B2110), 1/4 m W of village Xrds*. Home-made teas. **Adm £5, chd free. Sun 19 May (2-5).**
4-acre classic terraced garden with views of S Downs. The garden includes a yew maze, ha-ha, lime walk, herb and vegetable gardens, and a pond in a woodland setting. Circular yew maze, herb and vegetable gardens, shrub and herbaceous borders, woodland pond. Garden extends over a series of terraces, has several flights of steps.

58 HALFPENNY COTTAGE

Copse Lane, Walberton BN18 0QH. Sue & Dave Settle, 01243 542399, settle92@btinternet.com. *5m from Chichester & Arundel. Off A27 at Fontwell r'about, past petrol stn to end of village. At last mini r'about turn R onto West Walberton Lane, Copse Lane next on L*. Home-made teas. **Adm £3.50, chd free. Sun 9 June (1-5.30). Visitors also welcome by appt in May and June.**
Delightful 1/2 -acre garden designed and planted by the present owners in a romantic cottage style with different colour-themed borders using a palette of soft colours, winding brick paths, rose pergola. Mediterranean garden, green oak gazebo and enclosed kitchen garden. Lots of interesting perennial planting combinations.

59 HAMMERWOOD HOUSE

Iping, Midhurst GU29 0PF. Mr & Mrs M Lakin, 07785 776222, amandalakin@me.com. *3m W of Midhurst. Just off A272. 3m out of Midhurst towards Petersfield. Turn R, go over bridge, past church. Approx 400 yds, turn R at green triangle.*

Driveway immed on R. Home-made teas. **Adm £5, chd free. Sun 5, Sun 12 May (2-5). Visitors also welcome by appt Apr to May.**
Large S-facing garden with lots of mature shrubs, including camellias, rhododendrons and azaleas. An arboretum with a variety of flowering and fruit trees. The old yew and beech hedges give a certain amount of formality to this traditional English garden. Tea on the terrace is a must with the most beautiful view of the S Downs. For the more energetic, there is a woodland walk. Wheelchair access limited, garden set on slope.

60 NEW HARDWYCKE

Southfields Road, Eastbourne BN21 1BZ. Lois Machin, 01323 729391, loisandpeter@yahoo.co.uk. *Centre of Eastbourne, Upperton. A259 towards Eastbourne, Southfields Rd on R just before junction with A2270 (Upperton Rd). Limited parking available, public car park (pay) in Southfields Rd. 5mins walk from station. Bus stops 1 & 1a.* **Adm £3.50, chd free. Sun 16 June, Sun 25 Aug (11-5). Visitors also welcome by appt May to Aug, max 12. Refreshments by arrangement.**
Delightful S-facing town garden mainly of chalky soil, with many usual and unusual plants. Separate vegetable garden with restored 1920's summer house. Wide selection of shrubs including 50 types of clematis. L shaped garden that has 2 spaces 70ft x 50ft and 18ft x 50ft. 2 slight steps to rear garden area, accessible with care.

61 ◆ GARDENS & GROUNDS OF HERSTMONCEUX CASTLE

Herstmonceux, Hailsham BN27 1RN. Bader International Study Centre, Queen's University (Canada), 01323 833816, www.herstmonceux-castle.com. *Located between Herstmonceux & Pevensey on the Wartling Rd. From Herstmonceux take A271 to Bexhill, 2nd R signed Castle. Do not use SatNav.* **Adm £6, chd £3, concessions £4.95. For NGS: Sun 9 June, Fri 19 July (10-6). For other opening times and information, please phone or see garden website.**
Herstmonceux is renowned for its magnificent moated castle set in beautiful parkland and superb Elizabethan walled gardens, leading to delightful discoveries such as our rhododendron, rose and herb gardens and onto our woodland trails. Take a slow stroll past the lily covered lakes to the 1930s folly and admire the sheer magnificence of the castle. The Gardens & Grounds first opened for the NGS in 1927. Limited wheelchair access to formal gardens.

62 ◆ HIGHDOWN GARDENS

33 Highdown Rise, Littlehampton Road, Goring-by-Sea, Worthing BN12 6FB. Worthing Borough Council, 01903 501054, www.highdowngardens.co.uk. *3m W of Worthing. Off A259. Stn: Goring-by-Sea, 1m.* **Adm by donation. For NGS: Sun 5 May, Thur 6 June (10-6). For other opening times and information, please phone or see garden website.**
Famous garden created by Sir Frederick Stern situated in chalk pit and downland area containing a wide collection of plants. Many plants were raised from seed brought from China by great collectors like Wilson, Farrer and Kingdon-Ward. Open all year round. Mainly grass paths, hillside garden. Wheelchair access limited.
NCH

Pembury House

© Leigh Clapp

63 4 HILLSIDE COTTAGES

Downs Road, West Stoke PO18 9BL. Heather & Chris Lock, 01243 574802, chlock@btinternet.com. *3m NW of Chichester. From A286 at Lavant, head W for 1½ m, nr Kingley Vale.* Home-made teas. **Adm £3, chd free. Sun 28 July (2-5). Groups of 10-30 also welcome by appt June to Aug.**
Garden 120ft x 27ft in a rural setting. Densely planted with mixed borders and shrubs. Large collection of roses, mainly New English shrub roses; walls, fences and arches covered with mid and late season clematis; baskets overflowing with fuchsias. A profusion of colour and scent in a well maintained small garden.

64 ◆ HISTORIC GARDENS

Town Lane, Singleton, Chichester PO18 0EU. Weald & Downland Open Air Museum, 01243 811348, www.wealddown.co.uk. *6m S of Midhurst, 6m N of Chichester. Middle of Singleton village, the gardens are part of the Museum site.* **Adm £11, chd £6, concessions £10.50, family £31. For NGS: Sat 22 June to Fri 28 June incl (11-5). For other**

Plant specialists: look for the Plant Heritage symbol NCH

opening times and information, please phone or see garden website.
The award-winning Museum has 50 historic building exhibits. Explore our six period gardens to discover the folklore, heritage and history of the plants that met the needs of ordinary country folk through the centuries. Heritage varieties are grown and used at the Museum for historic home life demonstrations and courses. Celebrating Historic Gardens Week, incl Herbarium exhibition, demonstrations, guided talks and tours. Heritage seeds and herbs on sale. some rough paths.

65 NEW HOLLY HOUSE
Beaconsfield Road, Chelwood Gate, Haywards Heath RH17 7LF. Mrs Deirdre Birchell, www.hollyhousebnb.co.uk. *7m E of Haywards Heath. From Nutley village on the A22 turn off at Dine Asia signed Chelwood Gate 2m. Chelwood Gate village hall will be on R, Holly House is opp village hall.* Home-made teas. **Adm £3, chd free. Sats, Suns: 11, 12 May; 8, 9, 15, 16 June (2-5.30).**
An acre of English garden providing views and cameos of plants and trees round every corner with many different areas giving constant interest, a fish pond and a wildlife pond beside a grassy area with many shrubs and flower beds. Among the trees and winding paths there is a cottage garden which is a profusion of colour and peace. Exhibition of paintings and cards by owner. The whole of the garden is accessible by wheelchair in good weather, but it is not easy.

66 THE HUNDRED HOUSE
Pound Lane, Framfield TN22 5RU. Dr & Mrs Michael Gurney. *4m E of Uckfield. From Uckfield take B2102 through Framfield. 1m from centre of village turn L into Pound Lane, then 3/4 m on R.* Home-made teas. **Adm £4, chd free. Sun 21, Mon 22 July (2-5).**
Delightful garden with panoramic views set in the grounds of the historic The Hundred House. Fine stone ha-ha. 1 1/2 -acre garden with mixed herbaceous borders, productive vegetable garden, greenhouse, ancient yew tree, pond area with some subtropical plants, secret woodland copse and orchard. Beech hedge, field and butterfly walk, Wildflower meadow under development. Bear hunt for young children.

67 JACARANDA
Chalk Road, Ifold, Loxwood RH14 0UE. Brian & Barbara McNulty, 01403 751532, bam101@btinternet.com. *1m S of Loxwood. From A272/A281 take B2133 (Loxwood). 1/2 m S of Loxwood take Plaistow rd. 3rd R into Chalk Rd. Follow signs for parking & garden.* Home-made teas. **Adm £3, chd free. Sun 16 June (1-6); Sun 1 Sept (2-5). Also open 16 June Bradstow Lodge. Groups of 10-30 also welcome by appt Apr to Sept.**
Tranquil wildlife-friendly 1/4 -acre garden created over past 13yrs. Large sweeping borders are home to many interesting trees and shrubs plus a wide variety of perennials, roses and clematis. Various seating areas allow different perspectives of the garden. Over 60 hostas in pots. Kitchen garden with raised bed plus greenhouse, potting area and compost bins. Wheelchair users can park in the driveway.

Cottage garden which is a profusion of colour and peace . . .

68 KENT HOUSE
East Harting, nr Petersfield GU31 5LS. Mr & Mrs David Gault, 01730 825206. *4m SE of Petersfield. On B2146 at South Harting take Elsted to Midhurst rd E for 1/2 m. Just W of Turkey Island, turn N up no through road for 400yds.* Light refreshments. **Adm £4, chd free. Visitors welcome by appt May to Aug.**
1 1/2 -acre garden with fine trees, ha-ha, shade-loving plants for Apr and May, walled garden, exceptional views of the Downs from pretty Georgian house (not open). Mixed borders of unusual shrubs and herbaceous plants.

69 KIDBROOKE PARK
Priory Road, Forest Row RH18 5JA. Michael Hall School, 01342 822275 reception. *1/2 m from village centre. Approaching from N on A22: at mini r'about outside Parish Church in village, turn R down Priory Rd, then approx 1/2 m on L.* Variety of refreshments at Mansion Market. **Adm £5, chd free (share to Michael Hall Steiner Waldorf School). Sat 11 May (11-4).**
Kidbrook Mansion (1734) is now home to Michael Hall Steiner Waldorf School. Grounds landscaped by Humphry Repton still retain many of his original vistas, including lakes, cascades, ornamental bridges and C19 greenhouses. Rather a 'romantic lost gardens' feel. Original kitchen garden in full use as a prolific biodynamic plot. Weedy, but wonderful. Much to explore in 60 acres-boggy in places. Organic produce for sale. Lively 'Mansion Market' offering variety of artisan products and crafts.

70 KILN COPSE FARM
Kirdford RH14 0JJ. Bill & Pat Shere. *4m NE of Petworth. Take A283 from Petworth then fork R signed Kirdford & Balls Cross. Through Balls Cross, over narrow bridge then 400yds on L.* Home-made teas. **Adm £3.50, chd free. Sat 15, Sun 16 June (1-5.30).**
2-acre all yr round garden on clay that has gradually evolved to blend with the natural woodland surroundings. Many informal mixed shrub and herbaceous borders, low-maintenance conifer border, spacious lawns, vegetable garden and ponds with ducks. Enjoy a home-made tea on the lawn in this lovely setting. Partial wheelchair access.

71 ◆ KING JOHN'S LODGE
Sheepstreet Lane, Etchingham TN19 7AZ. Jill Cunningham, 01580 819232, harry@kingjohnsnursery.co.uk, www.kingjohnsnursery.co.uk. *2m W of Hurst Green. A265 Burwash to Etchingham. Turn L before Etchingham Church into Church Lane which leads into Sheepstreet Lane after 1/2 m. L after 1m.* **Adm £4, chd free. For NGS: Sun 31 Mar (12-4); Sun 26, Mon 27 May, Sun 16 June, Sun 22 Sept (2-5). For other opening times and information, please phone or see garden website.**

4-acre romantic garden for all seasons surrounding an historic listed house (not open). Formal garden with water features, rose walk and wild garden and pond. Rustic bridge to shaded ivy garden, large herbaceous borders, old shrub roses and secret garden. Further 4 acres of meadows, fine trees and grazing sheep. Nursery and Shop. Featured in Country Life. Garden is mainly flat. Stepped areas can usually be accessed from other areas. No disabled WC.

72 KNELLSTONE HOUSE

Udimore, Rye TN31 6AR. Linda & Stuart Harland, 01797 222410, info@knellstonehouse.co.uk, www.knellstonehouse.co.uk. *3m W of Rye. B2089 on R past Float Lane going towards Rye.* Home-made teas. **Adm £5, chd free. Sun 16 June (2-5.30). Visitors also welcome by appt May to July.**

This 3½-acre garden surrounds a beautiful C15 house (not open). Separate areas accommodate the sloping landscape, exploiting the stunning views across the Brede Valley to the sea. There is a small wood, wildlife pond and formal pool courtyard as well as a parterre for cut flowers and produce, hydrangea bank, plus many other features, pathways and viewing points. Stunning views towards the sea and over the Brede Valley, within an Area of Outstanding Natural Beauty. Limited wheelchair access, gravel paths and some slopes.

73 NEW KNEPP CASTLE

Knepp Castle, West Grinstead, Horsham RH13 8LJ. Sir Charles & Lady Burrell. *8m S of Horsham. Turning to Shipley off the A272. ½ m to entrance on L. Follow driveway through the parkland.* Home-made teas. **Adm £5, chd free. Sun 23 June (11-5).**

Recently designed and re-planted garden surrounding Knepp Castle (Castle not open to the public). Main garden dominated by three old Cedar of Lebanon, clipped box and a Ha Ha over looking the lake, sympathetic planting to reflect the landscape. Also approx 2 acres of walled garden containing vegetables, fruit, flowers, herbs and pool garden.

74 LEGSHEATH FARM

nr Forest Row RH19 4JN. Mr & Mrs M Neal, 01342 810230, legsheath@btinternet.com. *4m S of E Grinstead. 2m W of Forest Row, 1m S of Weirwood Reservoir.* Home-made teas. **Adm £5, chd free (share to Holy Trinity Church, Forest Row). Sun 19 May (2-5.30). Visitors welcome by appt.**

Panoramic views over Weirwood reservoir. Exciting 10-acre garden with woodland walks, water gardens and formal borders. Of particular interest, clumps of wild orchids, fine davidia, acers, eucryphia and rhododendrons. Mass planting of different species of meconopsis on the way to ponds.

LEYDENS
See Kent

75 LITTLE HILL

Hill Farm Lane, Codmore Hill, Pulborough RH20 1BW. Barbara & Derek James. *1m N of Pulborough. Hill Farm Lane off A29 by The Rose PH, garden 10th on L. Overflow parking in field before garden entrance, follow signs.* Home-made teas. **Adm £4, chd free. Evening Opening, wine, Thur 27 June (5-7); Sun 30 June (2-4).**

4 acres of formal gardens with sunken rose garden and pond, tiered rock garden with waterfall and pond, rose and grape arbour in middle of box-hedged beds, hidden rhododendron dell. Some annuals, perennials, shrubs, trees and small orchard, vegetable plot and fruit cage. Wild flowers. Some gravel and stone paths, but many areas accessible for wheelchairs.

76 LORDINGTON HOUSE

Lordington, Chichester PO18 9DX. Mr & Mrs John Hamilton, 01243 375862, hamiltonjanda@btinternet.com. *7m W of Chichester. On W side of B2146, ½ m S of Walderton, 6m S of South Harting. Ask for directions at gate.* Home-made teas. **Adm £4, chd free. Sat 30 Mar, Mon 1 Apr, Sat 15 June (1.30-4.30). Visitors also welcome by appt Apr to Sept. No Coaches.**

Early C17 house (not open) and walled gardens. Clipped yew and box, lawns, borders and fine views. Vegetables, fruit and poultry in old kitchen garden. Carpet of daffodils in spring. Nearly 100 roses planted since 2008. Various trees both mature and young. Lime avenue planted in 1973 to replace elms. Overlooks farmland, Ems Valley and wooded slopes of S Downs, all in AONB and SD National Park. Gravel paths, uneven paving, slopes. Wheelchair access possible to all areas of the garden.

Streams, waterfalls, innovative and quirky container planting . . .

77 LOWDER MILL

Bell Vale Lane, Fernhurst, Haslemere GU27 3DJ. Anne & John Denning, 01428 644822, john@denningconsultancy.co.uk, www.lowdermill.com. *1½ m S of Haslemere. 6m N of Midhurst. Follow A286 out of Midhurst towards Haslemere, through Fernhurst and take 2nd R after Kingsley Green into Bell Vale Lane. Lowder Mill approx ½ m on R.* Home-made teas. **Adm £3.50, chd £1.50. Sat 1 June (11-5.30); Sun 2 June (10.30-5.30). Groups welcome by appt only, close to opening dates.**

C17 mill house and former mill set in 3-acre garden. The garden has been restored, since 2002, with the help of Bunny Guinness. Interesting assortment of container planting forming a stunning courtyard between house and mill. Streams, waterfalls, innovative and quirky container planting around the potting shed and restored greenhouse. Raised vegetable garden. Rare breed chicken and ducks, as well as resident kingfishers. Renowned for superb home-made teas, served overlooking the mill lake. Extensive plant stall, mainly home propagated Choir singing on Sunday 2nd June at 11am. Featured in numerous publications.

78 MALT HOUSE
Chithurst Lane, Rogate GU31 5EZ. Mr & Mrs G Ferguson, 01730 821433, g.ferguson34@btinternet.com. *3m W of Midhurst. From A272, 3½ m W of Midhurst turn N signed Chithurst then 1½ m, very narrow lane; or at Liphook turn off A3 onto old A3 (B2070) for 2m before turning L to Milland, then follow signs to Chithurst for 1½ m.* Home-made teas. **Adm £4, chd free. Sun 28 Apr, Sun 5, Mon 6 May (2-6). Visitors also welcome by appt. Refreshments by arrangement.**
6 acres; flowering shrubs incl exceptional rhododendrons and azaleas, leading to 50 acres of arboretum and lovely woodland walks plus many rare plants and trees.

79 MALTHOUSE FARM
Streat Lane, Streat, Hassocks BN6 8SA. Richard & Helen Keys, 01273 890356, helen.k.keys@btinternet.com. *2m SE of Burgess Hill. From Ditchling B2116, 1m E of Westmeston, turn L signed Streat. 2m on L immed after railway bridge.* Home-made teas. **Adm £4, chd free. Sun 18, Tue 20 Aug (2-5.30). Visitors also welcome by appt Apr to Sept, adm £7 includes tea/coffee and cake.**
Rural garden with wonderful views to the S Downs. Garden divided into rooms. Box parterre, herbaceous and shrub borders, kitchen garden. Young orchard leading to partitioned area with grass walks through field. Unique water feature. Snail mound. Pond with wildlife. Chickens. Featured in Sussex Living.

80 THE MANOR OF DEAN
Tillington, Petworth GU28 9AP. Mr & Mrs James Mitford, 07887 992349, emma@mitford.uk.com. *3m W of Petworth. On A272 from Petworth to Midhurst. Pass through Tillington village. A272 then has short section of dual carriageway. Turn R at end of this section and proceed N, entrance to garden approx ½ m.* Home-made teas. **Adm £3.50, chd free. Sun 17 Feb, Sun 17 Mar, Sat 13, Sun 14 Apr, Sun 19 May (2-5). Evening Opening, wine, Fri 5 July (5-8); Sun 11 Aug, Sun 22 Sept (2-5). Groups of 10+ also welcome by appt Mar to Sept.**
Approx 3 acres. Traditional English garden, herbaceous borders, a variety of early-flowering bulbs and snowdrops, spring bulbs, grass walks and steps. Walled kitchen garden partly in use for household. Lawns, rose garden and informal areas with views of South Downs. Garden under a long-term programme of improvements.

A variety of early-flowering bulbs and snowdrops, spring bulbs, grass walks . . .

GROUP OPENING

81 MAYFIELD GARDENS
TN20 6TE. *10m S of Tunbridge Wells. Turn off the A267 into Mayfield. Car parks available by Memorial Hall and by turning S off High St by Budgens. Detailed map will be available from all gardens.* Home-made teas at Yeomans & Warren House. **Combined adm £5, chd free. Sun 9 June (11-5).**

HOOPERS FARM
Andrew & Sarah Ratcliffe

NEW MAYFIELD PRIMARY SCHOOL
Ms Teresa Cass

MEADOW COTTAGE
Adrian & Mo Hope

TEW COTT
Jon & Sue Barnes

WARREN HOUSE
Chris Lyle & Pat Robson

YEOMANS
Paul & Jenny Ziegler

Mayfield is a beautiful Wealden village with several old pubs and interesting historical connections. There are six very different gardens to visit. All are in the village centre, except for Warren House with its sculpture trail. The gardens vary in size and style including a formal parterre, colour-themed and cottage-style planting, wild flower meadows, woodland and vegetables. Many have far-reaching, panoramic views over beautiful countryside. Mayfield Primary School garden is included this year for the first time. It is planted and maintained by the pupils. Come and support the gardeners of the future!

82 NEW ◆ MCBEAN'S ORCHIDS
Resting Oak Hill, Cooksbridge, Lewes BN8 4PR. Mr Jim Durrant, 01273 400228, www.mcbeansorchids.co.uk. *A275 1m N of Cooksbridge Stn, 4m N of Lewes. As above.* **Adm £4, chd free. For NGS: Thur 7, Fri 8 Feb (10-3.30). For other opening times and information, please phone or see garden website. Coaches welcome.**
A selection of orchids bred by McBeans since 1879 on this site. Includes tropical plants award winning cymbidium and oncidium orchids plus other plants of interest from around the world. Working nursery tour plus exotic growing house display with shop full of plants to buy. Wheelchair access to shop and display house. Flight of 4 steps for nursery tour.

83 MILL HOUSE
Mill Lane, High Salvington, Worthing BN13 3DE. Paul & Fran Thornton. *3m N of Worthing. From A24 turn R up Bost Hill & sharp L at top of hill. From A27 turn into Salvington Hill. Follow round to R at top of hill & turn R immed after windmill.* Home-made teas. **Adm £3.50, chd free. Suns 21 July, 4 Aug (2-5).**
A pretty chalk garden situated on the South Downs. Enter through a tranquil contemporary courtyard into a 140ft x 40ft rear garden. There are raised beds, woodland, shade, bog, productive vegetable and alpine gardens. Pergolas surround a feature sunken garden with a raised pond surrounded by intensely planted beds including tropical plants. High Salvington windmill (1750) postmill will be open both days (small entry charge), within 200yds of garden. Regret not suitable for the less mobile - many steps.

Look out for the NGS yellow arrows...

84 MOUNTFIELD COURT
nr Robertsbridge TN32 5JP. Mr & Mrs Simon Fraser. *3m N of Battle. On A21 London-Hastings; 1/2 m from Johns Cross.* Home-made teas. **Adm £3.50, chd free. Sun 12 May (2-5).**
3-acre wild woodland garden; walkways through exceptional rhododendrons, azaleas, camellias and other flowering shrubs; fine trees and outstanding views. Small paved herb garden. Recently restored walled garden.

85 NEWTIMBER PLACE
Newtimber BN6 9BU. Mr & Mrs Andrew Clay, 01273 833104, andy@newtimberholidaycottages.co.uk, www.newtimberplace.co.uk. *7m N of Brighton. From A23, take A281 towards Henfield. Turn R at small Xrds signed Newtimber in approx 1/2 m. Go down Church Lane, garden is at end of lane on L.* Home-made teas. **Adm £4, chd free. Sun 7 Apr (2-5.30).**
Beautiful C17 moated house (not open). Gardens and woods full of bulbs and wild flowers in spring. Herbaceous border and lawns. Moat flanked by water plants. Mature trees. Wild garden, ducks, chickens and fish. Wheelchair access across lawn to some of garden, tea room and toilets.

86 NORTH SPRINGS
Bedham, nr Fittleworth RH20 1JP. Mr & Mrs R Haythornthwaite. *Between Fittleworth and Wisborough Green. From Wisborough Green take A272 towards Petworth. Turn L into Fittleworth Rd signed Coldharbour. Proceed 1 1/2 m. From Fittleworth take Bedham Lane off A283 and proceed for approx 3m NE. Limited parking.* Home-made teas. **Adm £4, chd free. Sat 8 June (2-6).**
Hillside garden with beautiful views surrounded by mixed woodland. Focus on structure with a wide range of mature trees and shrubs. Stream, pond and bog area. Abundance of roses, clematis, hostas, rhododendrons and azaleas.

87 NYEWOOD HOUSE
Nyewood, nr Rogate GU31 5JL. Mr & Mrs C J Wright, 01730 821563, s.warren.wright@gmail.com. *4m E of Petersfield. From A272 at Rogate take South Harting rd for 1 1/2 m. Turn L at pylon towards South Downs Hotel. Nyewood House 2nd on R over cattle grid.* Cream teas. **Adm £3.50, chd free. Sat 8, Sun 9 June (2-6). Visitors also welcome by appt Apr to June.**
Victorian country house garden with stunning views of S Downs. 3 acres comprising formal gardens with rose walk and arbours, pleached hornbeam, colour-themed herbaceous borders, shrub borders, lily pond and fully stocked kitchen garden with greenhouse. Wooded area featuring spring flowers followed by wild orchids and wild flowers. Featured on best gardens to visit in Sussex, in Sussex Life and Midhurst & Petworth Observer.

88 ◆ NYMANS
Handcross RH17 6EB. National Trust, 01444 405250, www.nationaltrust.org.uk. *4m S of Crawley. On B2114 at Handcross signed off M23/A23 London-Brighton rd. Bus: 73 from Hove or Crawley & 271 from Haywards Heath.* **Adm £10.50, chd £5.50. For NGS: Sat 15, Sun 16 June (10-5); Fri 19 July (5-8) Jazz in the Garden: Doors open 5pm for picnics. Adm £10, chd £5, bookings through box office 0844 249 1895. For other opening times and information, please phone or see garden website.**
In the late C19 the unusually creative Messel family bought the Nymans estate in the High Weald of Sussex with the intention of making a dream country house. Inspired by both the setting and the soil, they created one of the country's great gardens with experimental designs and plants from around the world. Free activities to pick up and do every day. For garden lovers there is a well stocked plant and garden centre including the Nymans Collection of plants propagated at Nymans Nursery. Featured in Mid-Sussex Times.

89 OAK GROVE COLLEGE
The Boulevard, Worthing BN13 1JX. *1m W of Worthing. Turn S off A2032 at r'about onto The Boulevard, signed Goring. School entrance 1st on L (shared entrance with Durrington High School).* Teas at Palatine School. **Adm £4, chd free. Sun 7 July (2-5). Combined adm with Palatine School.**
An inspiring example of how special needs children have transformed their school grounds into a green oasis. Extensive and unusual planting, features include water-wise, memorial and herb gardens, large sensory courtyard, sculptures, mosaics, and large food growing area. Living willow, reclaimed woodland, outdoor textiles and outdoor performance area.

Abundance of roses, clematis, hostas, rhododendrons and azaleas . . .

90 THE OAST HOUSE
Elms Farm, Isfield TN22 5XG. Richard & Ann Montier, annmontier@me.com. *5m NE of Lewes. 1 1/2 m off A26 Lewes (5m) to Uckfield (4m). From A272 turn R at Piltdown, take R fork after The Peacock. Isfield 2m. Car parking at adjacent village hall, disabled parking only at The Oast House.* **Adm £5, chd free (share to Cancer Research UK). Sun 18 Aug (2-5). Groups of 10+ also welcome by appt July to Sept.**
One of 25 beautiful gardens named in Sussex Life. A delightful two-acre garden using a variety of planting to attract wildlife especially bees and butterflies. A lake has been created out of what was a farm pond and the spoil used to form a double helix mound giving views of the South Downs. Visitors say 'inspirational planting', 'a hidden treasure'.

91 OCKLYNGE MANOR
Mill Road, Eastbourne BN21 2PG. Wendy & David Dugdill, 01323 734121, ocklyngemanor@hotmail.com, www.ocklyngemanor.co.uk. *Close to Eastbourne District General Hospital. Take A22 (Willingdon Rd) towards old Town, turn L into Mill Rd just before parade of shops.* **Adm £3.50, chd free. Visitors welcome by appt May to Sept.**
Hidden oasis behind an ancient, flint wall. Informal and tranquil, 1/2 -acre

chalk garden with sunny and shaded places to sit. Use of architectural and unusual trees. Rhododendrons, azaleas and acers in containers. Garden evolved over 20yrs, maintained by owners. Georgian house (not open), former home of Mabel Lucie Attwell.

92 OFFHAM HOUSE

Offham BN7 3QE. Mr S Goodman & Mr & Mrs P Carminger. *2m N of Lewes on A275. From Lewes follow directions to Haywards Heath A275, at Offham pass Blacksmith Arms on L, Offham House is at brow of hill on L. Cooksbridge Station 1/2 m, Lewes Station 2.2m.* Home-made teas. **Adm £4.50, chd free. Suns 28 Apr; 2 June (1-5).**

Romantic garden with fountains, flowering trees, double herbaceous border, long peony bed. 1676 Queen Anne house (not open) with well-knapped flint facade. Herb garden. Walled kitchen garden with glasshouses, coldframes, chickens and friendly pigs. Teas on lawn/conservatory. Featured in Viva Lewes and Period Homes and Interiors. Some steep slopes and gravel paths.

93 THE OLD FARMHOUSE

Hermongers Lane, Rudgwick RH12 3AL. Caspian Robertson, 01403 824034, surreygardens@googlemail.com, www.musicmindspirit.org. *Between Horsham & Cranleigh. 1/4 m N of Rudgwick on B2128 at Cox Green turn R (E) into Hermongers Lane. 1/2 m, parking signed. Disabled parking available.* Home-made teas. **Adm £5, chd free (share to Mind Music Spirit Trust). Sun 5, Mon 6 May; Sun 16 June; Sun 25, Mon 26 Aug (1-6). Visitors also welcome by appt May to Sept.**

1-acre traditional garden set about C16 Grade II listed Farmhouse (not open) and barns open as tearoom and concert hall. Features incl knot garden, rose garden, espalier avenue of fruit trees. Water features and walks. Fine views. Live music events in magnificent C17 converted barn. This year featuring Caspian's 'RHS Gold Medal' and 'Best In Show': 'A La Mode' Dining Garden. Wheelchair access to main garden and concert hall.

North Hall

© Leigh Clapp

94 OLD SCAYNES HILL HOUSE

Clearwater Lane, Scaynes Hill RH17 7NF. Sue & Andy Spooner, 01444 831602, a_spooner@btopenworld.com. *2m E of Haywards Heath. On A272, 50yds down Sussex border path beside BP Garage shop, & opp Inn on the Green.* ***No parking at garden*** (drop off only), please park considerately in village. Home-made teas. **Adm £4, chd free. Suns 16 June; 14 July (2-5). Visitors also welcome by appt June to July, max 30. Refreshments by arrangement.**

In memory of Sarah Robinson. Entrance archway with steps leading to peaceful 1-acre naturalistic garden on S-facing slope of clay. Mature trees and shrubs, several colourful herbaceous borders and island beds. Many roses, hemerocallis and ornamental grasses, small wild flower meadow with orchids, fruit and vegetable area and natural-looking pond.

95 NEW OLD SCHOOL HOUSE

Rushlake Green, Heathfield TN21 9QD. Lady Shawcross. *2 m SE of Heathfield, 4m NE of Hailsham. Proceed to Rushlake Green. Garden at side of green nr Village Hall, parking available around village green.* Home-made teas at Fineoaks. **Adm £3, chd free. Sat 15, Sun 16 June (1-6). Also open Fineoaks (separate admission).**

Small pretty garden with lawns, borders, vegetable garden/potager. Nepalese Garden and garden house called 'Villa Nepal' and Himalayan mountain art work on fencing. Goldfish pond with koi. Attractive country views. Some steps.

96 NEW OLD VICARAGE

The Street, Firle, Lewes BN8 6NR. Mr & Mrs Charlie Bridge. *Off A27 5m E of Lewes. Signed from main road.* Home-made teas by Firle Primary School. **Adm £4, chd free. Sun 16 June (2-5). Also open Firle Place Herb Garden.**

Garden originally designed by Lanning Roper in the 1960's. Previously opened under NGS in 1970's 80's and 90's. 4 acre garden set around a Regency vicarage (not open). Features a walled garden with vegetable parterre and flower borders, wild flower meadow, pond, pleached limes. Over 100 roses. Wonderful Downland views.

97 THE OLD VICARAGE

The Street, Washington RH20 4AS. Meryl & Peter Walters, 07766 761926, meryl.walters@btopenworld.com. *2½ m E of Storrington, 4m W of Steyning. From Washington r'about on A24 take A283 to Steyning. 500yds R to Washington. Pass Frankland Arms, R to St Mary's Church*. Home-made teas 13 July in Village Hall with Village Day. **Adm £4.50. Sun 21 Apr, Sat 15, Sun 16 June (10.30-4.30); Sat 13 July (2-5); Fri 18 Oct (10.30-4). Visitors also welcome by appt Apr to Oct, max 30.**

3½ -acre garden, set around 1832 Regency-style house (not open). Front is formally laid out with topiary, a large lawn and mixed border. To the rear some mature trees dating back to C19, herbaceous border, new large pond and stunning uninterrupted 20 mile view to the N Downs. Stream and woodland area. 15 June Live music and Painting Day (donation to NGS). 16 June Father's Day trail. Featured in Sussex Life.

Packed full of ideas and interesting plants using every inch of space . . .

98 NEW ORCHARD HOUSE

Staplefield Road, Cuckfield, Haywards Heath RH17 5HY. Dr. and Mrs. Andrew Winskill. *Approx 1m W of Cuckfield. Weald Chase is a private drive 200yds to W of Haywards Heath Rugby Club on B2115 Cuckfield to Handcross Rd. Weald Chase turning is immed before 50mph de-restriction sign. After entering Weald Chase follow gravelled drive round to the R through two stone pillars, carry on to the end. The garden is entered through the gap in the Leylandii hedge*. Home-made teas. **Adm £4, chd free. Sat 13, Sun 14 July (2-5).**

Large family garden with greenhouses, herbaceous borders, vegetable plot, grasses bed, a small North American Prairie meadow, shrubberies, heather bed, rhododendron walk, an orchard, a walled courtyard and wild area which includes a childrens play area. There is also an extensive compost area. The courtyard contains container planting and a part raised, part sunk pond. Full wheelchair access.

99 OXSETTON

Southerham, Lewes BN8 6JN. Peter & Jean Burges, 01273 472851. *Nr junction of A26 & A27. From A27, turn N towards Lewes, take 1st R to Southerham, through industrial estate. Continue for approx ½ m, garden on L*. **Adm £3.50, chd free. Visitors welcome by appt Apr to Sept. Small garden so smaller groups preferred.**

Small walled garden built on existing farmyard. Ancient flint horse trough, old well. Raised beds containing a variety of interesting herbaceous plants, roses, clematis etc. Many containers filled with shrubs, trees, steep steps to part of the garden. Seating areas. Partial wheelchair access.

100 PALATINE SCHOOL GARDENS

Palatine Road, Worthing BN12 6JP. Mrs N Hawkins, 01903 242835, nhawkins@wsgfl.org.uk, www.palatineschool.org/. *Turn S off A2032 at r'about onto The Boulevard, signed Goring. Take R turn at next r'about into Palatine Rd. School approx 100yds on R*. Home-made teas. **Adm £3.50, chd free. Suns 14 Apr; 7 July (2-5). Combined adm £4 on 7 July with Oak Grove College. Visitors also welcome by appt Apr to July not during school hours.**

This is a many-roomed mature garden with varied planting. Constructed by teachers, volunteers and children with special needs, it never ceases to surprise visitors. Wildlife corner, large and small ponds, themed gardens and children's outdoor art features, along with rockeries, living willow, labyrinth, mosaics and interesting tree collection. South & South East in Bloom Special Schools Silver Gilt Winner.

101 PARSONAGE FARM

Kirdford RH14 0NH. David & Victoria Thomas. *5m NE of Petworth. From centre of Kirdford (before church) turn R, through village, past Forresters PH on R. Entrance on L, just past R turn to Plaistow*. Home-made teas. **Adm £5, chd free (share to Churchers College). Fri 14 June, Sun 8 Sept (2-6).**

Major garden under development now growing to maturity with fruit theme and many unusual plants. Formally laid out gardens on a grand scale, C18 walled garden with borders in apricot, orange, scarlet and crimson, topiary walk, pleached lime allée, tulip tree avenue, rose borders, vegetable garden with trained fruit, lake, turf amphitheatre, recently planted autumn shrubbery and jungle walk.

102 33 PEERLEY ROAD

East Wittering PO20 8PD. Paul & Trudi Harrison. *7m S of Chichester. From A286 take B2198 to Bracklesham. Turn R into Stocks Lane then L at Royal British Legion into Legion Way & follow rd round to Peerley Rd half way along*. **Adm £2.50, chd free. Sun 7 July (12-4).**

Small garden 65ft x 32ft, 110yds from sea. Packed full of ideas and interesting plants using every inch of space to create rooms and places for adults and children to play. A must for any suburban gardener. Specialising in unusual plants that grow well in seaside conditions with advice on coastal gardening.

103 PEMBURY HOUSE

Ditchling Road (New Road), Clayton, nr Hassocks BN6 9PH. Nick & Jane Baker, 01273 842805, jane.baker47@btinternet.com, www.pemburyhouse.co.uk. *6m N of Brighton, off A23. On B2112, 110 m from A273. Disabled parking at the house, otherwise parking at village green clearly signed. Garden can be reached by public transport*. Homemade teas and light refreshments. **Adm £4, chd free. Tue 12, Wed 13, Thur 14, Tue 19, Wed 20, Thur 21 Feb; Fri 8 Mar Special Hellebore Day (all dates 11-4). 2014 dates: Tues, Weds, Thurs 11, 12, 13, 18, 19, 20 Feb. Thur 7 Mar 2014 Special Hellebore Day. Groups of 15+ also welcome by appt Feb to Mar.**

Depending on the vagaries of the season, winter-flowering shrubs, hellebores and drifts of snowdrops are at their best in February. Special Hellebore Day on 8th March. Winding paths give a choice of walks through the 2+ acres of garden which is in the

South Downs National Park and enjoys views to the Downs. Small 25yr old woodland. Wellies, macs and winter woollies advised. Hellebores and snowdrops for sale. Featured on Japanese TV and Garten Träume magazine. Limited disabled access in wet weather.

104 PINDARS

Lyminster, nr Arundel BN17 7QF. Mr & Mrs Clive Newman, 01903 882628, pindars@tiscali.co.uk. *2m S of Arundel. Lyminster on A284 between A27 & A259. 1m S of A27 Pindars on L.* Home-made teas. **Visitors welcome by appt May to July groups of 10-30. Adm £6 to incl home-made refreshments.**

Owner-maintained garden created over 40yrs. Many mature trees form an enclosed peaceful space with lots of seating to enjoy vistas. Interesting and ever-changing herbaceous plants, bulbs and shrubs are planted for long-lasting colour and interest. A relaxed atmosphere, warm welcome and delicious home-made teas await visitors. Parking for larger groups is available by prior arrangement in neighbouring field. Some gravel paths not wheelchair accessible.

105 6 PLANTATION RISE

Worthing BN13 2AH. Nigel & Trixie Hall, 01903 262206, trixiehall@btinternet.com. *2m from seafront on outskirts of Worthing. A24 meets A27 at Offington r'about. Proceed into Offington Lane. Take 1st R into The Plantation, 1st R again to Plantation Rise. Please park in The Plantation, short walk to Plantation Rise.* Home-made teas. **Adm £3.50, chd free. Wed 3, Sat 6 Apr (2-5); Evening opening £4, chd free, light refreshments, Fri 14 June (6-9); Wed 14, Sat 17 Aug (2-5). Visitors also welcome by appt Mar to Aug.**

Our garden is 70ft x 80ft but has been landscaped to give the appearance of being much larger - a surprise awaits you! With pond, summerhouse, patio areas and pergolas. Silver birches, evergreen shrubs, azaleas, rhododendrons and acers. Heathers in Spring to ensure year round colour. WC available on request. Some steps.

106 ◆ THE PRIEST HOUSE

North Lane, West Hoathly RH19 4PP. Sussex Archaeological Society, 01342 810479, www.sussexpast.co.uk. *4m SW of East Grinstead. Turn E to West Hoathly 1m S of Turners Hill at the Selsfield Common junction on B2028. 2m S turn R into North Lane. Garden ¼ m further on.* **Adm £2, chd free. For NGS: Sat 25 May, Sat 29 June (10.30-5.30). Also open both dates Duckyls Holt, combined adm £4. For other opening times and information, please phone or see garden website.**

C15 timber-framed farmhouse with cottage garden on fertile acid clay. Large collection of culinary and medicinal herbs in a small formal garden and mixed with perennials and shrubs in exuberant borders. Long-established yew topiary, box hedges and espalier apple trees provide structural elements. Traditional fernery and small secluded shrubbery. Adm to Priest House Museum £1 for NGS visitors.

A warm welcome and delicious home-made teas await visitors . . .

107 2 QUARRY COTTAGES

Wall Hill Road, Ashurst Wood, East Grinstead RH19 3TQ. Mrs Hazel Anne Archibald. *1m S of E Grinstead. From N turn L off A22 from E Grinstead, garden adjoining John Pears Memorial Ground. From S turn R off A22 from Forest Row, garden on R at top of hill.* Home-made teas. **Adm £3, chd free. Fri 17, Sat 18 May (2-5). Also open Caxton Manor (separate admission).**

Peaceful little garden that has evolved over 40yrs in the present ownership. A natural sandstone outcrop hangs over an ornamental pond; mixed borders of perennials and shrubs with specimen trees. Many seating areas tucked into corners. Highly productive vegetable plot. Terrace round house revamped 2013. Florist and gift shop in barn. Featured in Sussex Life. Steep slopes.

108 RIDGE HOUSE

East Street, Turners Hill RH10 4PU. Mr & Mrs Nicholas Daniels, 01342 715344, nickanwyn@supanet.com. *4m SW of East Grinstead. 3m E of Crawley. On B2110, 5m SE of J10 M23. Via A264 & B2028. 30yds E of Crown PH on Turners Hill Xrds. Parking at recreation ground E of Ridge House.* Home-made teas. **Adm £3.50, chd free. Sats: 15, 22, Sun 23 June (2-5.30). Visitors also welcome by appt May to Aug.**

A magical view of the High Weald greets the visitor, with all-yr interest being offered by Nigel's Garden in its quiet corner together with the mixed borders, dell with its pond and the productive vegetable garden. Large beautifully manicured bi-coloured Leylandii hedge plus other shrubs. Paths lead to unexpected vistas, and the large compost heaps and Victorian greenhouse with its reservoir should not be missed. Solar panels and 5,000 gallon underground reservoir with water collected from roof. Mainly flat, some steep slopes.

109 RINGMER PARK

Ringmer, Lewes BN8 5RW. Deborah & Michael Bedford. *On A26 Lewes to Uckfield rd. 1½ m NE of Lewes, 5m S of Uckfield.* Home-made teas. **Adm £5, chd free. Sat 25 May, Sun 8 Sept (2-5).**

Densely-planted 8-acre formal garden with soft edges. Emphasis is on continuous flowering from spring to Oct, with bold and dramatic blocks of colour. Features incl a striking hot garden, white garden, rose gardens, pergola covered with roses and clematis, double herbaceous borders, a new grasses garden and much more. Outstanding views of S Downs. Local press.

110 ROSE COTTAGE

Hall Lane, Hadlow Down TN22 4HJ. Ken & Heather Mines, 01825 830314, kenmines@hotmail.com. *6m NE of Uckfield. After entering village on A272, turn into Hut Lane next to the New Inn. Follow signs.* Home-made teas. **Adm £4, chd free. Suns: 21 Apr; 26 May; 23 June (2-5.30). Groups of 10+ also welcome by appt Apr to July.**

Plantsman's ⅔ -acre garden with views across an Area of Outstanding Natural Beauty. Old roses, exuberant planting and luxuriance within a strong design create a garden that visitors refer to as harmonious, tranquil and evoking memories of childhood. Self-seeding is encouraged, so constantly changing. David Newman sculptures are integral to the design, further enhanced by Victorian church stonework. Bug hunt and fact sheet for children. Some gravel paths.

♿ ❀ ☕ ☎

111 RYMANS

Apuldram, Chichester PO20 7EG. Mrs Michael Gayford, 01243 783147, suzanna.gayford@talktalk.net. *1m S of Chichester. Take Witterings rd, at 1½ m SW turn R signed Dell Quay. Turn 1st R, garden ½ m on L.* Home-made teas. **Adm £4, chd free.** **Sats, Suns: 6, 7 Apr; 22, 23 June; 14, 15 Sept (2-5). Visitors also welcome by appt Apr to Sept.**

Walled and other gardens surrounding lovely C15 stone house (not open); bulbs, flowering shrubs, roses, ponds, potager. Many unusual and rare trees and shrubs. In late spring the wisterias are spectacular. The heady scent of hybrid musk roses fills the walled garden in June. In late summer the garden is ablaze with dahlias, sedums, late roses, sages and Japanese anemones. Featured in Sussex Life.

🐕 ❀ ☕ ☎

112 SAFFRONS

Holland Road, Steyning BN44 3GJ. Tim Melton & Bernardean Carey. *6m NE of Worthing. Exit r'about on A283 at S end of Steyning bypass into Clays Hill Rd. 1st R into Goring Rd; 4th L into Holland Rd. Parking in Goring Rd and Holland Rd.* Home-made teas. **Adm £3.50, chd free.** **Wed 17, Sun 21 July (2-5.30).**

¾ -acre garden behind an Edwardian house. Broad lawns studded with ornamental trees; borders containing Japanese maples, cherries and magnificent bamboos interspersed with grasses and rhododendrons. Herbaceous beds with contrasting textures and glorious colours including buddleia, agapanthus, eryngiums and fragrant lilies. Fruit and vegetable garden. Featured in Sussex Life and in 25 Gardens to Visit in Sussex.

🐕 ❀ ☕

113 ◆ ST MARY'S HOUSE GARDENS

Bramber BN44 3WE. Peter Thorogood & Roger Linton, 01903 816205, www.stmarysbramber.co.uk. *1m E of Steyning. 10m NW of Brighton in Bramber Village off A283.* **Adm £4, chd free. For NGS: Fri 12, Sat 13 July (2-5.30). For other opening times and information, please phone or see garden website.**

Five acres incl charming formal topiary, ivy-clad 'Monks' Walk', large *Ginkgo biloba*, and magnificent Magnolia grandiflora around charming timber-framed medieval house. Victorian 'Secret' gardens incl splendid 140ft fruit wall, Rural Museum, terracotta garden, delightful Jubilee Rose Garden, heated pineapple pits and English Poetry Garden. In the heart of the S Downs National Park. All parts of the gardens are accessible by wheelchair.

♿ ❀ ☕

© Leigh Clapp

"Lemon drizzle cake, Victoria sponge ... yummy! ☕"

114 SANDHILL FARM HOUSE

Nyewood Road, Rogate GU31 5HU. Rosemary Alexander, 01730 818373, r.a.alexander@talk21.com, www.rosemaryalexander.co.uk. *4m SE of Petersfield. From A272 Xrds in Rogate, take rd S signed Nyewood/Harting. Follow rd for approx 1m over small bridge. Sandhill Farm House on R, over cattle grid.* Home-made teas and wine (Evening visits). **Adm £3.50, chd free. Sats, Suns 20, 21 Apr; 15, 16 June; 14, 15 Sept (2-5). Groups of 10+ also welcome by appt Mar to Oct.**

Front and rear gardens are broken up into garden rooms, incl small kitchen garden. Front garden incl small woodland area planted with early spring flowering shrubs and bulbs, white garden and hot dry terraced area. Rear garden has mirror borders, small decorative vegetable garden and 'red' border. Grit and grasses garden. Organic and environmentally friendly. Home of author and Principal of The English Gardening School. Featured in The Garden and Saga magazine. Gravel paths, a few steps.

♿ ❀ D ☕ ☎

GROUP OPENING

115 SEAFORD & BISHOPSTONE GARDENS

A259 midway between Brighton & Eastbourne, both 12m. All gardens signed from A259 (3.5m trail). For Driftwood, follow signs to Bishopstone village between Seaford and Newhaven, take L into Marine Drive, 2nd on R. For 8 Sandgate Close, follow signs to Alfriston at E side of Seaford, turn R into Hillside Ave, L into Hastings Ave, R into Deal Close and R into Sandgate Close. Maps for other gardens at either venue. Home-made teas at Driftwood (all dates) also 15 June at Barrack Cottage & 16 June, 21 July at 1

Sandgate Close. **Combined adm £5, chd free.** Sat 15, Sun 16 June, Sun 21 July (11-5).

BARRACK COTTAGE
Bishopstone, BN25 3LL. David & Karen Allam.
Follow signs to Bishopstone village, past the church, cottage down-hill on R

NEW **1 BUCKTHORN CLOSE**
Seaford, BN25 4NY. Roger & Jane Bullock.
From A259 going towards Eastbourne, turn R into Sutton Ave, 1st L at mini r'about into Kingston Ave. Follow road round to L (becomes Kingston Way), Buckthorn Close is 2nd cul-de-sac L.
Visitors also welcome by appt June to Aug.
01323 301967
bullock.abbs@talktalk.net

DRIFTWOOD
Geoff Stonebanks & Mark Glassman
(See separate entry)

NEW **ELIZABETH COTTAGE**
Seaford, BN25 3EH. Sue Wright

8 SANDGATE CLOSE
Seaford, BN25 3LL. Aideen & Denis Jones
Visitors also welcome by appt June to July, groups of up to 20 people.
01323 899452
deniswjones@gmail.com
www.sandgateclosegarden.co.uk

5 totally unique gardens. Daily Mail finalist and Winner Garden News Gardener of Year Best Small Garden, Driftwood home to over 400 varieties of plants and shrubs, cleverly combining wooden and metal features with the landscape with space to sit and admire the view. Sandgate Close, a green and tranquil haven with a delightful mix of trees, shrubs and perennial borders, with gazebo, summer house, water features, sweet pea arches, and courtyard garden. Both with no lawn. Barrack Cottage, partly walled, 5 acre chalk garden, with rose garden and several garden rooms in Bishopstone Village. Two new gardens, 1 Buckthorn Close and Elizabeth Cottage, the former an integrated combination of flowers, fruits and vegetables. The garden majors on 3D landscaping to create mood and enclosure and yet preserve views and openness, the latter a small but delightful garden stocked with cottage plants mature ginkgo and silver birch. Home-made jam at Sandgate Close. Featured in Amateur Gardening magazine. Driftwood featured extensively in national/local press. Wheelchair access to 8 Sandgate Close and 1 Buckthorn close only, Steep drive at Driftwood but help readily available.

Beautiful hilly setting with streams, ponds, waterfall . . .

116 SEDGWICK PARK HOUSE
Horsham RH13 6QQ. John & Clare Davison, 01403 734930, clare@sedgwickpark.com, www.sedgwickpark.co.uk. *1m S of Horsham off A281. Take A281 towards Cowfold/Brighton. Hillier Garden Centre on R, then 1st R into Sedgwick Lane. After Sedgwick sign post, enter N gates of Sedgwick Park. Enter also by W gates via Broadwater Lane, from Copsale or Southwater A24.* Home-made teas. **Adm £5, chd free.** Sun 30 June (1-5). Evening Opening Thur 4 July (6-9), wine. **Groups of 10+ also welcome by appt Apr to Sept, ground floor of house also available for tours.**
Extensive parkland, meadows and woodland. Formal gardens landscaped by Harold Peto featuring 20 interlinking pools, cascades and impressive water garden known as 'The White Sea'. Large Horsham stone terraces and lawns look out onto clipped yew hedging and specimen trees. Original secluded rosewalk and mature herbaceous borders, set in the grounds of this Grade II listed Ernest George Mansion. Some of the finest views of S Downs, Chanctonbury Ring and Lancing College. New turf labyrinth and organic vegetable garden with chickens. Uneven paving, slippery when wet; unfenced ponds and swimming pool.

117 SENNICOTTS
West Broyle, Chichester PO18 9AJ. Mr & Mrs James Rank, www.sennicotts.com. *2m NW of Chichester. From Chichester take B2178 signed Funtington for 2m. Entrance on R. Long drive, ample parking nr house. From Fishbourne turn N marked Roman Palace then straight on until T-junction. Entrance opp Salt Hill Rd.* Home-made teas. **Adm £4, chd £0.50.** Sat 15 June (2-6).
Historic gardens set around a Regency villa (not open). Extensive rhododendron and azalea borders. Working walled kitchen and cutting garden. Avenues and walks. Fountain. Views across mature Sussex parkland to S Downs. Lots of space for children. A warm welcome for all. Level garden, access on grass, some gravel paths.

118 SHALFORD HOUSE
Square Drive, Kingsley Green GU27 3LW. Sir Vernon & Lady Ellis. *2m S of Haslemere. Just S of border with Surrey on A286. Square Drive is at brow of hill, to the E. Turn L after 0.2m and follow rd to R at bottom of hill.* Home-made teas. **Adm £5, chd free.** Sun 12 May, Sun 7 July, Sun 1 Sept (2-6).
Highly regarded 10-acre garden designed and created from scratch over last 18 yrs. Beautiful hilly setting with streams, ponds, waterfall, sunken garden, good late borders, azaleas, walled kitchen garden, wild flower meadow with orchids, prairie-style plantation and stumpery merging into further 7-acre woodland. Additional 30-acre arboretum with beech, rhododendrons, bluebells, ponds, Japanese-themed area and specimen trees. Children's woodland trail.

119 ◆ SHEFFIELD PARK AND GARDEN
Sheffield Park TN22 3QX. National Trust, 01825 790231, www.nationaltrust.org.uk. *10m S of E Grinstead. 5m NW of Uckfield; E of A275.* **Adm £8, chd free.** For NGS: Tues 7 May, 8 Oct (10.30-5.30, last admission 4.30). **For other opening times and information, please phone or see garden website.**
Magnificent 120 acres (40 hectares) landscaped garden laid out in C18 by Capability Brown and Humphry Repton. Further development in early

yrs of this century by its owner Arthur G Soames. Centrepiece is original lakes, with many rare trees and shrubs. Beautiful at all times of the year, but noted for its spring and autumn colours. National Collection of Ghent azaleas. Natural play trail for families on South Park. Large number of Champion Trees-87 in total. Garden largely accessible for wheelchairs - please call for any access information.

NCH

GROUP OPENING

120 SLINDON GARDENS

Slindon, nr Arundel BN18 0RE. *4m W of Arundel. From Slindon Xrds on A29 turn N into village. Follow rd up village for approx ½ m. The Well House on L just past Church Hill, park in farm opp.* Home-made teas The Well House. **Combined adm £4, chd free.** Thur 13, Sun 16 June (2-5).

COURT COTTAGE
BN18 0RE. Mark & Clare Bacchus

NEW **MANCHESTER HOUSE**
BN18 0RD. Ms Niki Adamson

THE WELL HOUSE
BN18 0RS. Sue & Patrick Foley

The pretty National Trust village of Slindon has many fine listed buildings and lovely walks on the Downs. Enjoy three contrasting gardens, within a short stroll of each other. Court Cottage features 'hot' and 'cool' island borders, linked by an arch of roses and clematis, and a splendid, mature beech hedge. There is a small orchard and raised vegetable beds. New this year, Manchester House has a small formal garden, featured in the Bognor Regis Observer, laid out with box hedging enclosing beds stocked with many scented roses and perennials. Enjoy a delicious home-made tea in the delightful romantic setting of the old, walled garden at The Well House (featured in the Chichester Observer). There is much to delight incl traditional herbaceous beds stocked with mixed perennials, shrubs and roses, a small vegetable and cutting garden and side garden designed around a pool. Interesting plants propagated from our gardens for sale. Dogs allowed at Court Cottage only. Restricted wheelchair access to Manchester House.

121 SOLENT COTTAGE

35 Clayton Road, Selsey, Chichester PO20 9DF. Liz Shackleton & David Bradley, 01243 602150, lizshackleton@btinternet.com. *8m S of Chichester on the coast at Selsey. Take B2145 from Chichester to Selsey, continue through the village towards the sea. Clayton Rd is last rd on R, garden is named Solent Cottage ¼ m on L.* **Adm £3.50, chd free.** Sat 1, Sun 2 June (2-5). **Visitors also welcome by appt June to Sept, please contact well in advance.**
Fully exposed coastal garden. Cultivated and indigenous plants, artworks, shingle and driftwood. Galleried greenhouse connecting front garden. Raised vegetable beds. Shrubs and herbaceous garden, climbers, pergola and decking. Garden pond water feature and 'sea mirror'. Ornamental grasses and perennials with grass bank and seat. Hedges, grasses and wildlife area. Display of textile art. Featured on BBC Gardeners World and in Coast Magazine and Chichester Observer.

Jacob sheep graze the surrounding pastures . . .

122 SOUTH GRANGE

Quickbourne Lane, Northiam, Rye TN31 6QY. Linda & Michael Belton, 01797 252984, belton.northiam@virgin.net. *Between A268 & A28, 1km E of Northiam. From Northiam centre follow Beales Lane into Quickbourne Lane, or Quickbourne Lane leaves A286 approx ⅔ km S of A28/A286 junction.* Light refreshments. **Adm £3.50, chd free.** Thur 11 July (2-5); Sat 7, Sun 8 Sept (11-5). **Visitors also welcome by appt Apr to Oct.**
Hardy Plant Society member's garden combining grasses, herbaceous perennials, shrubs, trees, raised beds, wildlife pond for yr-round interest. Vegetable plot. Orchard incl meadow flowers, fruit cage with willow windbreak. Woodland is left wild. House roof runoff diverted to pond and bulk storage. Many home propagated plants for sale. We are becoming older folk who garden without assistance and like to think that visitors can see what they too might achieve.

123 SPARROW HATCH

Cornwell's Bank, nr Newick BN8 4RD. Tony & Jane Welfare. *5m E of Haywards Heath. From A272 turn R into Oxbottom Lane (signed Barcombe), ½ m fork L into Narrow Rd, continue to T-junction & park in Chailey Lane (no parking at house).* Cold drinks available. **Adm £3, chd free.** Weds, Thurs 22, 23 May; 26, 27 June (2-5).
Delightful ⅓ -acre plantsman's cottage garden, wholly designed, made and maintained by owners. Many features incl 2 ponds, formal and wildlife, herbaceous borders, shady dell, vegetables, herbs, alpines. Planned for owners' enjoyment and love of growing plants, both usual and unusual. Plants for sale, propagated and grown by garden owner.

124 STONE CROSS HOUSE

Alice Bright Lane, Crowborough TN6 3SH. Mr & Mrs D A Tate. *½ m S of Crowborough. At Crowborough T-lights (A26) turn S into High St, & shortly R into Croft Rd. Straight over 2 mini r'abouts into Alice Bright Lane. Garden on L at next Xrds about 1½ m from T-lights.* Home-made teas. **Adm £4, chd free.** Sat 4, Sun 5 May (2-5.30).
Beautiful 9-acre country property with gardens containing a delightful array of azaleas, acers, rhododendrons and camellias, interplanted with an abundance of spring bulbs. The very pretty cottage garden has interesting examples of topiary and unusual plants. Jacob sheep graze the surrounding pastures. Mainly flat, no steps. Gravel drive.

125 STONEHEALED FARM

Streat Lane, Streat BN6 8SA. Lance & Fiona Smith, 01273 891145, afionasmith@hotmail.com. *2m SE of Burgess Hill. From Ditchling B2116, 1m E of Westmeston, turn L (N) signed Streat, 2m on R immed after railway bridge.* Home-made teas. **Adm £4, chd free (share to St Peter & St James Hospice).** Sun 26 May, Sun 16 June (2-5).

Visitors also welcome by appt May to Sept Minimum of 10.
C17 house (not open) in beautiful rural setting. Sheltered garden 'rooms' link with areas open to views of the South Downs. Paths wind through relaxed informal planting of trees, shrubs, climbers and unusual perennials, around ponds, through a vegetable garden and extending out into surrounding fields. Wonderful overview from a raised platform in an ancient oak tree. Delicious home-made teas served under cover. Some gravel paths and steps.

126 ◆ SUSSEX PRAIRIES

Morlands Farm, Wheatsheaf Road, Henfield BN5 9AT. Paul & Pauline McBride, 01273 495902, www.sussexprairies.co.uk. *2m E of Henfield on B2116 Wheatsheaf Rd (also known as Albourne Rd).* **Adm £6, chd free. For NGS: Mon 26 Aug (11-5). For other opening times and information, please phone or see garden website.**
Exciting Prairie garden of approx 6 acres planted in the naturalistic style using 30,000 plants and 600 different varieties. A colourful garden featuring a huge variety of unusual ornamental grasses. Expect layers of colour, texture and architectural splendour. Surrounded by mature oak trees with views of Chanctonbury Ring and Devil's Dyke on the S Downs. Permanent Sculpture collection & exhibited sculpture throughout the season. Rare breed sheep and pigs. Featured in Landscape magazine and The Telegraph. Woodchip paths may be difficult for wheelchairs.

127 THREE CHIMNEYS

Cousley Wood, Wadhurst TN5 6QU. Mr & Mrs James Burnett-Hitchcock. *2m N of Wadhurst. From Wadhurst take B2100 to Lamberhurst. Pass school on R, approx 1½ m to SDR Motors & Old Vine PH on R. Opp pub turn L, continue to Xrds, turn R to Hook Green. 200yds R again, garden on corner.* Home-made teas. **Adm £4.50, chd free. Sat 10 Aug (2-5); Sun 11 Aug (1-4).**
3½ -acre garden surrounding C15 house (not open). Incl an arboretum, orchard, pool garden, formal lawn and herbaceous borders. A constantly evolving garden where some wild flowers mix with more formal planting and wildlife is encouraged. Featured in local press. Wheelchair access via grass and gravel paths.

128 TIDEBROOK MANOR

Tidebrook, Wadhurst TN5 6PD. *Between Wadhurst & Mayfield. From Wadhurst take B2100 towards Mark Cross, L at Best Beech PH, down-hill, 200m past church on R,then a drive on the left.* **Adm £5, chd free. Wed 20 Mar, Thur 20 June, Fri 20 Sept (10-4).**
4-acre garden developed over the last decade with outstanding views of the Sussex countryside. In the 'Arts and Crafts' tradition the garden features large mixed borders, intimate courtyards, meadows, hydrangea walk, kitchen garden with raised beds, a willow platt and a wild woodland of particular interest in the spring. A lively and stimulating garden throughout the yr. Tours with Head Gardener Edward Flint at 11am and 2pm £2 extra. Wheelchair access possible, not in woodland area.

129 TINKERS BRIDGE COTTAGE

Tinkers Lane, Ticehurst TN5 7LU. Mrs M A Landsberg, 01580 200272. *11m SE of Tunbridge Wells. From B2099 ½ m W Ticehurst, turn N to Three Leg Cross for 1m, R after Bull Inn. House at bottom of hill.* Light refreshments. **Adm £5, chd free. Visitors welcome by appt Apr to July Coffee and biscuits available.**
12 acres landscaped; stream garden nr house (not open) leading to herbaceous borders, wildlife meadow with ponds and woodland walks. Disabled access over grass.

130 TOWN PLACE

Ketches Lane, Freshfield, nr Sheffield Park RH17 7NR. Dr & Mrs Anthony McGrath, 01825 790221, mcgrathsussex@hotmail.com, www.townplacegarden.org.uk. *5m E of Haywards Heath. From A275 turn W at Sheffield Green into Ketches Lane for Lindfield. 1¾ m on L.* Cream teas. **Adm £5, chd free. Thur 13, Sun 23, Sun 30 June, Sun 7 July (2-6). Groups of 20+ also welcome by appt June to July.**
3 acres with over 600 roses, 150ft herbaceous border, walled herb garden, ornamental grasses, ancient hollow oak, orchard and potager. 'Green' Priory Church and Cloisters. C17 Sussex farmhouse (not open). Featured in Countryside and Gardens Illustrated.

Roam at leisure, relax and enjoy at every season . . .

131 11 TREDCROFT ROAD

Hove BN3 6UH. Barbara Kennington, bk@bkennington.com. *East of Hove Park. Tredcroft Rd runs between Woodruff Ave and Shirley Drive.* Home-made teas. **Adm £3, chd free. Sat 15, Sun 16 June (12-5). Visitors also welcome by appt June to Aug.**
110ft x 50ft town garden on 4 levels facing NW, on clay soil. Designed and landscaped 4 yrs ago, this wildlife-friendly garden is now well established and boasts many unusual and creative features incl sculptures, a pebble mosaic, an exotic pool garden, shaded walk, many perennials and grasses and a working vegetable garden. Featured in The English Garden.

132 UPWALTHAM BARNS

Upwaltham GU28 0LX. Roger & Sue Kearsey, 01798 343145. *6m S of Petworth. 6m N of Chichester on A285.* Light refreshments. **Adm £4, chd free (share to St Mary's Church). Sun 26, Mon 27 May (11-5.30). Visitors also welcome by appt May to Sept.**
Unique farm setting has been transformed into a garden of many rooms. Entrance is a tapestry of perennial planting to set off C17 flint barns. At the rear, walled terraced garden redeveloped and planted with an abundance of unusual plants. Extensive vegetable garden. Landscaping in walled garden in progress. Roam at leisure, relax and enjoy at every season, lovely views of S Downs and C12 Shepherds Church (open to visitors). Some gravel paths.

GROUP OPENING

133 WARNINGLID GARDENS

Warninglid, Haywards Heath RH17 5TR. *Midway between Haywards Heath & Horsham, both 6m. From S at B2115 Xrds (Cuckfield/Warninglid Lane). From E, N & S turn off A23 W towards Warninglid for 3/4 m. From W come through Warninglid village. Free parking adjacent to rec ground next to Pavilion, street parking limited for disabled access, drop off for elderly visitors.* Cream teas & light refreshments in Pavilion. **Combined adm £5, chd free.** **Sun 30 June (2-6).**

APRIL COTTAGE
Spronketts Lane. Alan Griffin.
1 1/2 m down the hill from the village towards Wineham

NEW **BEECHES**
Cuckfield Lane. Mr & Mrs C Steel

BLACKMANS COTTAGE
Diana Housego-Woolgar

NEW **GLENWOOD COTTAGE**
Mr & Mrs Peter & Susanna Lye

1 HERRINGS COTTAGES
Mr A L Brown

2 HERRINGS COTTAGES
Jan & Alan Lambert

OLD BARN COTTAGE
Alison & David Livesley

OLD PLACE
Carey Phelan

OLD POST
Mariola & Bob Clark

Warninglid is a pretty medieval village set in a conservation area & it's architecture provides a perfect back drop to the gardens on view. Several of the gardens are sited in The Street and on Spronketts Lane, part of the old smuggling route from the south coast, heading from the village towards Wineham. The gardens are in the main cottage style, but in different ways reflect the distinctive approach of each owner. The cultivated woodland garden in Cuckfield Lane gives another interesting gardening perspective. Terraces, shrubs and water features are used to enhance the natural landscapes and offer variety and contrast to the visitor. Featured in Sussex Living.

134 WARREN HOUSE

Warren Road, Crowborough TN6 1TX. Mr & Mrs M J Hands, 01892 663502, michaelhands443@btinternet.com. *1 1/2 m SW of Crowborough Cross. From Crowborough Cross towards Uckfield A26, 4th turning on R. 1m down Warren Rd. From South 2nd L after Blue Anchor.* Home-made teas. **Adm £4, chd free.** **Suns, Mons 21 Apr; 6, 19, Sun 27 May (2-5).** **Groups of 20+ also welcome by appt Apr to June.**

Beautiful house (not open) steeped in history with 9-acre garden and views over Ashdown Forest. Series of gardens old and new, displaying wealth of azaleas, rhododendrons, impressive variety of trees and shrubs. Sweeping lawns framed by delightful walls and terraces, woodlands, ponds, wildlife area. Largely maintained by owner. Come and see how to simplify your gardening!

135 ◆ WEST DEAN GARDENS

West Dean PO18 0QZ. Edward James Foundation, 01243 818221, www.westdean.org.uk. *5m N of Chichester. On A286, midway between Chichester & Midhurst.* **Adm £8.10, chd £0.90.** **For NGS: Wed 15 May (10.30-5).** **For other opening times and information, please phone or see garden website.**

35-acre historic garden in tranquil downland setting. 300ft long Harold Peto pergola, mixed and herbaceous borders, rustic summerhouses, water and spring garden, specimen trees. 2 1/2 -acre walled garden contains fruit collection, 13 Victorian glasshouses, apple store, large working kitchen garden, extensive plant collection. Circuit walk (2 1/4 m) climbs through parkland to 45-acre St Roche's Arboretum. Featured in national/ international press and in Gardens Illustrated. Most areas of the walled garden and grounds are accessible.

GROUP OPENING

136 WINCHELSEA'S SECRET GARDENS

Winchelsea TN36 4EJ. *2m W of Rye, 8m E of Hastings. Purchase ticket for all gardens at first garden visited; a map will be provided, also showing the location of teas.* **Combined adm £5, chd free.** **Sats: 8 June; 14 Sept (1-5.30).**

THE ARMOURY
Mr & Mrs A Jasper

CLEVELAND HOUSE
Mr & Mrs J Jempson.
Open June only

CLEVELAND PLACE
Sally & Graham Rhodda.
open June only

KING'S LEAP
Philip Kent.
open Sept only

MAGAZINE HOUSE
Susan & Stuart Stradling

2 MONEYSELLERS
George & Lorna Challand.
open June only

PERITEAU HOUSE
Dr & Mrs Lawrence Youlten

RYE VIEW
Howard Norton & David Page

Rye View

© Nicola Stocken Tomkins

Take your Group to an NGS garden

NEW **STRAND HOUSE**
Mrs Mary Sullivan & Mr Hugh Davie.
open Sept only

NEW **2 STRAND PLAT**
Mr & Mrs Anthony and Gillian Tugman.
open June only

TRUNCHEONS
Monica Edge-Partington.
open June only

THE WELL HOUSE
Alice Kenyon

Winchelsea is a beautiful medieval town founded in 1288 by Edward I. For nearly 200 years, as a Cinque Port, it was a major trading centre. Now all that remains of that time are the medieval merchants' cellars and the old streets, built on a grid system, behind whose old walls are the Secret Gardens. Two gardens return to the list for the June opening and we add two exciting new ones. 7 gardens also open in September; a new departure for us. Guided tours of medieval cellars both dates at 10.30am, £5, booking essential, 01797 229525 (mornings) or cellars@winchelsea.com. Beautiful church of St Thomas open to visitors. Town information at www.winchelsea.net and www.winchelsea.com. Wheelchair access to most gardens; see map for details.

♿ ✿ ☕

137 **WISTON HOUSE**
Steyning Road, Wiston BN44 3DD. Mr & Mrs R H Goring & Wilton Park. *A24 Washington r'about, take A283 to Steyning.* Home-made teas. **Adm £5, chd free. Sun 7 July (1.30-5).**

Nestled at the foot of the S Downs within a landscaped park, Wiston House has a Victorian garden under restoration. Features incl a conservatory, terraced lawns with herbaceous borders, a cascade, woodland garden, Italian parterre, herb garden, walled vegetable garden and Victorian greenhouses. Gravel paths.

♿ ✿ ☕

Sussex County Volunteers

East & Mid Sussex

County Organiser

Irene Eltringham-Willson, Butlers Farmhouse, Butlers Lane, Herstmonceux BN27 1QH, 01323 833770, irene.willson@btinternet.com

Treasurer

Peter Willson, Butlers Farmhouse, Butlers Lane, Herstmonceux BN27 1QH, 01323 833770, peter.willson2@btopenworld.com

Publicity Officer and ACO

Geoff Stonebanks, Driftwood, 4 Marine Drive, Bishopstone BN25 2RS, 01323 899296, ngseastsussex@gmail.com

Assistant County Organisers

Jane Baker, Pembury House, Ditchling Road (New Road), Clayton, Hassocks, 01273 842805, jane.baker47@btinternet.com
Lynne Brown, 26 Cornwall Gardens, Brighton BN1 6RJ, 01273 556439, brown.lynne@ntlworld.com
Diane Gould, Heronbrook, Perrymans Lane, High Hurstwood, nr Uckfield, 01825 732253, heron.brook@btinternet.com
Jasmine Hart, Roundstone House, Town Littleworth, Cooksbridge BN8 4TH, 01273 400427, jasminehart111@yahoo.co.uk
Richard & Matty Holmes, Beauchamps, Float Lane, Udimore TN31 6BY, 01797 223055, mrholmes@rye.hivetelecom.net
Philippa Hopkins, Birchover Cottage, 10 Maypole Road, Ashurstwood RH19 3QN, 01342 822090, piphop@waitrose.com
Jean Kendrick, Brinkers, Brinkers Lane, Wadhurst TN5 6LS, jm.kendrick@virgin.net
Susan Laing, Great Lywood Farmhouse, Lindfield Road, Ardingly RH17 6SW, 01444 892500, lainghome@btinternet.com
Jan Newman, Dormers, 25 Mill Lane, East Hoathly, Lewes BN8 6QB, 01825 840916
Sara Turner, 9 Terminus Avenue, Bexhill TN39 3LS, 01424 210716, sara.kidd@virgin.net
Liz Warner, 10 Roundhay Avenue, Peacehaven BN10 9TQ, 01273 586050, elizabeth55warner@btinternet.com

West Sussex

County Organiser

Jane Allen, Dyers House, Pickhurst Road, Chiddingfold GU8 4TG, 01428 683130, jane.allen01@talktalk.net

Treasurer

Peter Edwards, Quince Cottage, The Street, Bury, Pulborough RH20 1PA, 01798 831900, peteredwards425@btinternet.com

Assistant County Organisers

Paula Baker, 077877 23462, jp.baker@tinyworld.co.uk
Sanda Belcher, The Courtyard, Linchmere GU27 3NG, 01428 723259, sandabelcher@tiscali.co.uk
Jane Burton, Church Farmhouse, Ford Water Road, Lavant, Chichester PO18 0AL, 01243 527822
Diana Cave, Old Barkfield, Plaistow RH14 0PU, 01403 871254
Lesley Chamberlain, Dew Cottage, Beaumont Road, Broadwater, Worthing BN14 8HG, 01903 820813, chamberlain_lesley@hotmail.com
Elizabeth Gammon, 4 Birch Close, Arundel BN18 9HN, 01903 882722, e.gammon@toucansurf.com
Jane Lywood, Battlehurst Farm, Kirdford, Billingshurst RH14 0LJ, 01403 820225, jmlywood@aol.com
Claudia Pearce, Worthing, 07985 648216, claudiapearce17@gmail.com
Fiona Phillips, Old Erringham Cottage, Steyning Road, Shoreham-by-Sea BN43 5FD, 01273 462285, fiona.h.phillips@btinternet.com
Susan Pinder, 30 Townfield, Kirdford RH14 0LZ, 01403 820430, nasus.rednip@virgin.net
Sue Shipway, Browns House, The Street, Sutton, nr Pulborough RH20 1PS, 01798 869206, shipway@arunvalley.net

(for Birmingham & West Midlands see Staffordshire)

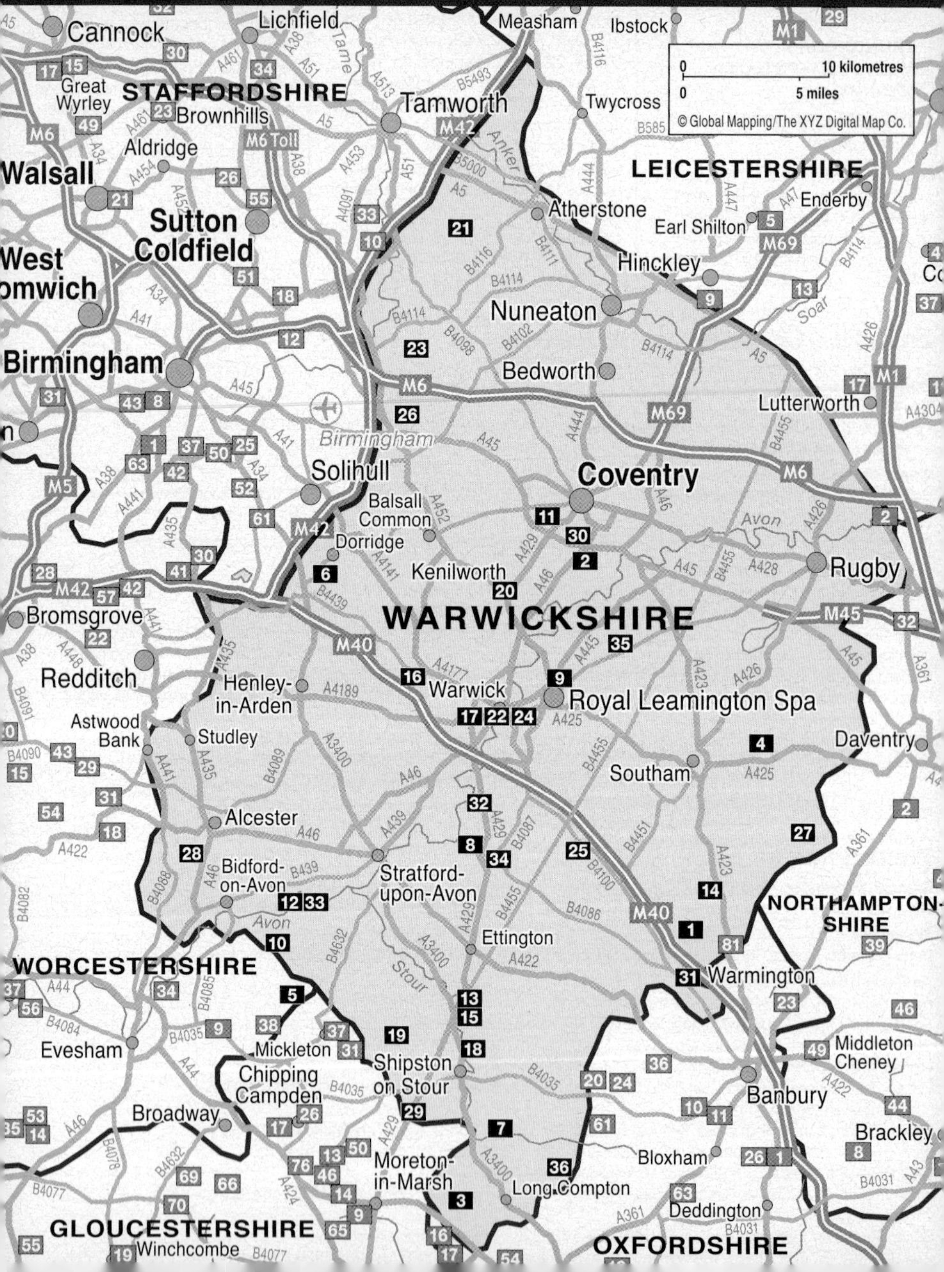

Opening Dates

April

Open every day in April
4 Bridge Nursery

Sunday 7
19 Ilmington Gardens

Sunday 21
6 Broadacre

Sunday 28
29 Stretton-on-Fosse Gardens

May

Open every day in May
4 Bridge Nursery

Monday 6
11 Earlsdon Gardens

Sunday 26
3 Barton House
5 Broad Marston & Pebworth Gardens

Monday 27
5 Broad Marston & Pebworth Gardens

Wednesday 29
7 Burmington Grange

June

Open every day in June
4 Bridge Nursery

Sunday 2
20 Kenilworth Gardens

Saturday 8
35 Weston-under-Wetherley Gardens

Sunday 9
10 Dorsington Gardens
35 Weston-under-Wetherley Gardens
36 Whichford & Ascott Gardens

National Gardens Weekend

Saturday 15
14 The Granary

Sunday 16
7 Burmington Grange
14 The Granary
18 Honington Village Gardens
21 Latimers Rest
23 Maxstoke Castle
27 Priors Marston Manor

Sunday 23
25 The Old Rectory
30 Styvechale Gardens
31 Warmington Village Gardens

Thursday 27
28 Ragley Hall Gardens

Saturday 29
33 Welford-on-Avon & District

Sunday 30
15 Halford Gardens
16 Hatton Gardens
32 Wasperton Gardens
33 Welford-on-Avon & District

July

Open every day in July
4 Bridge Nursery

Sunday 7
26 Packington Hall

Sunday 14
1 Avon Dassett Gardens
34 Wellesbourne Allotments

Sunday 21
29 Stretton-on-Fosse Gardens

Tuesday 30
13 Folly Lodge

Visit a group opening and really make a day of it . . .

August

Open every day in August
4 Bridge Nursery

Sunday 4
2 Avondale Nursery
14 The Granary
21 Latimers Rest

Saturday 24
14 The Granary

Sunday 25
2 Avondale Nursery
14 The Granary

Monday 26
2 Avondale Nursery
14 The Granary

Tuesday 27
13 Folly Lodge

September

Open every day in September
4 Bridge Nursery

Sunday 1
20 Kenilworth Gardens

Saturday 21
17 Hill Close Gardens

October

Open until 13 th October
4 Bridge Nursery

Gardens open to the public

2 Avondale Nursery
4 Bridge Nursery
8 Charlecote Park
17 Hill Close Gardens
22 The Master's Garden
24 The Mill Garden
28 Ragley Hall Gardens

By appointment only

9 19 Church Lane
12 Elm Close

Also open by Appointment ☎

1 The Limes, Avon Dassett Gardens
3 Barton House
6 Broadacre
13 Folly Lodge
14 The Granary
21 Latimers Rest
27 Priors Marston Manor
29 Court House, Stretton-on-Fosse Gardens

The Gardens

GROUP OPENING

1 AVON DASSETT GARDENS

Southam CV47 2AE. *7m N of Banbury. From M40 J12 turn L & L again B4100. 2nd L into village. Park in village & at top of hill.* Home-made teas at Old Mill Cottage. **Combined adm £5, chd free (share to The Churches Conservation Trust). Sun 14 July (2-6).**

AVON HOUSE
Mrs L Dunkley

THE COACH HOUSE
Diana & Peter Biddlestone

HILL TOP FARM
Mrs N & Mr D Hicks

THE LIMES 🛏
John & Diane Anderson
Visitors also welcome by appt.
01295 690245
dianeanderson2006@yahoo.co.uk

OLD MILL COTTAGE
Mike & Jill Lewis

THE OLD NEW HOUSE
Mr & Mrs W Allan

THE OLD RECTORY
Lily Hope-Frost

NEW **ORCHARD END**
Mrs Jill Burgess

POPPY COTTAGE
Bob & Audrey Butler

Pretty Hornton Stone village sheltering in the lee of the Burton Dassett hills, well wooded and with parkland setting, The Old Rectory mentioned in Domesday Book. Wide variety of gardens incl kitchen gardens, gravel and tropical gardens. Range of plants incl alpines, herbaceous, perennials, roses, climbers and shrubs. Art Exhibition. Two churches open. Wheelchair access to most properties.

AVON HOUSE
See Leicestershire & Rutland

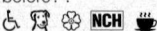

2 ◆ AVONDALE NURSERY
at Russell's Nursery, Mill Hill, Baginton CV8 3AG. Mr Brian Ellis, 02476 673662, www.avondalenursery.co.uk. *3m S Coventry. At junction of A45/A46 take slip rd to Baginton, 1st L to Mill Hill. Opp Old Mill Inn.* **Adm £3, chd free. For NGS: Sun 4, Sun 25, Mon 26 Aug (11-4). For other opening times and information, please phone or see garden website.**
Vast array of flowers and ornamental grasses, incl national collections of *Sanguisorba*, *Aster Novae-angliae* and *Anemone nemorosa*. A vast cornucopia of plants, this garden is a well-labelled reference book illustrating the unusual, exciting and even some long-lost treasures. Adjacent nursery is a plantaholic's delight. Visitors often remark 'Why have I not visited this garden before?'.

NCH

BARRACCA
See Leicestershire & Rutland

3 BARTON HOUSE
Barton-on-the-Heath GL56 0PJ. Mr & Mrs I H B Cathie, 01608 674303, hamish.cathie@thebartonfarms.com. *2m W of Long Compton. 2m W off A3400 Stratford-upon-Avon to Oxford rd; $1\frac{1}{4}$ m N off A44 Chipping Norton to Moreton-in-Marsh rd.* **Adm £5, chd £2.50. Sun 26 May (2-6). Visitors also welcome by appt spring to autumn.**
$6\frac{1}{2}$ acres with mature trees, azaleas, species and hybrid rhododendrons, magnolias, moutan tree peonies. National collections of *Arbutus* and *Catalpa*. Japanese garden, rose garden, secret garden and many rare and exotic plants. Victorian kitchen garden. Exotic garden with palms, cypresses and olive trees established 2002. Vineyard planted 2000 - free wine tasting. Manor house by Inigo Jones (not open). Featured in Gloucestershire Echo, Cotswold Life etc. Some gravel paths and some steps. Can be slippery but generally wheelchair friendly. Dogs strictly only on leads.

NCH

The children grow vegetables and then cook them, sometimes inviting parishioners to join them for lunch . . .

BRIDGE HOUSE
See Staffordshire, Birmingham & West Midlands

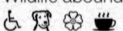

4 ◆ BRIDGE NURSERY
Tomlow Road, Napton, nr Southam CV47 8HX. Christine Dakin & Philip Martino, 01926 812737, www.bridge-nursery.co.uk. *3m E of Southam. Brown tourist sign at Napton Xrds on A425 Southam to Daventry rd.* **Adm £2.50, chd free. For NGS: Mon 1 Apr to Sun 13 Oct incl (10-4). For other opening times and information, please phone or see garden website.**
Be inspired by the range of rare and unusual plants thriving in heavy clay soil. Our $1\frac{1}{2}$ -acre garden is a fine example of mind over matter! Large pond and bamboo grove. Hedgerow walk, butterfly border, cutting garden. Wildlife abounds.

GROUP OPENING

5 BROAD MARSTON & PEBWORTH GARDENS
Stratford-upon-Avon CV37 8XZ. *9m SW of Stratford-upon-Avon. On B439 at Bidford turn L towards Honeybourne, after 3m turn L at Xrds signed Pebworth.* Home-made teas at Pebworth Village Hall. **Combined adm £5, chd free. Sun 26, Mon 27 May (2-6).**

BANK FARM HOUSE
Craig & Erica Chapman

BANK HOUSE
Clive & Caroline Warren

FELLY LODGE
Maz & Barrie Clatworthy

ICKNIELD BARN
Sheila Davies

IVYBANK NCH
Mr & Mrs R Davis

THE KNOLL
Mr & Mrs K Wood

NOLAN COTTAGE
Gill & Ron Thomas

Broad Marston, a small hamlet with a priory and manor (not open), modern houses and thatched cottages, lies at the lowest point of the parish and the gardens are all on the level. The gardens in Pebworth, $\frac{1}{2}$ m away, run down the hill topped by St. Peter's simple C13 church. At the bottom of the hill lies the Primary School with a thriving garden. The children grow vegetables and then cook them, sometimes inviting parishioners to join them for lunch. Among the houses here you will find the Village Hall and two small but interesting gardens very different in character, this is another area with old thatched cottages, and properties of various ages. On the outskirts of the village is Fibrex Nursery, holders of the National Pelargonium and ivy collections, Ivybank, their private garden is open. In the 2010 winter (18 degrees of frost) and a following very dry summer, much was lost in the gardens giving owners the chance to change and review. 2012's early drought and then above-average rainfall was also difficult. But we still have 7 very interesting gardens to visit.

Bring a bag for plants – help us give more to charity

6 BROADACRE
Grange Road, Dorridge, Solihull B93 8QA. Mr John Woolman, 07818 082885, john@jgwoolman.plus.com. *Approx 3m SE of Solihull. From J4 on M42 follow A3400 toward Hockley Heath for just under 1m. At r'about turn L on Box Trees Rd. After 600 metres turn R on Earlswood Rd. After 100 metres follow Earlswood Rd (R) at junction. After 400 metres turn R on Grange Rd. Broadacre is 100 metres on the R.* Home-made teas. **Adm £3, chd free. Sun 21 Apr (2-6). Visitors also welcome by appt.**
Broadacre is a semi-wild garden attractively landscaped with pools, lawns and trees and with two adjoining wild flower meadows. The garden is at its best when the fruit trees are blossoming in the spring. Bring stout footwear to follow the nature-trail around the meadows. Lovely venue for a spring picnic. Pets welcome. Dorridge Cricket club is in the grounds.

BURBAGE GARDENS
See Leicestershire & Rutland

7 BURMINGTON GRANGE
Cherington, Shipston on Stour CV36 5HZ. Mr & Mrs Patrick Ramsay. *2m E of Shipston-on-Stour. Take Oxford Rd (A3400) from Shipston-on-Stour, after 2m turn L to Burmington, go through village & continue for 1m, turn L to Willington & Barcheston, on sharp L bend turn R over cattle grid.* **Adm £5, chd free. Wed 29 May; Sun 16 June (2-6).**
Planted 10 yrs ago, $1\frac{1}{2}$ -acre garden with far-reaching views over the North Cotswold hills. Small vegetable garden, sunken rose garden with herbaceous and shrub borders. Small orchard and tree walk with unusual trees incl *Chitalpa tashkentensis* and *Koelreuteria paniculata*.

CASTLE BROMWICH HALL GARDENS
See Staffordshire, Birmingham & West Midlands

8 ◆ CHARLECOTE PARK
Wellesbourne, Warwick CV35 9ER. National Trust, 01789 470277, www.nationaltrust.org.uk/charlecote. *5m E of Stratford-upon-Avon, 6m S of Warwick, 1m W of Wellesbourne. From J15 of M40 take A429 towards Cirencester & follow signs for Charlecote Park. From Stratford-upon-Avon follow B4086 towards Wellesbourne & follow signs for Charlecote Park.* **For opening times and information, please phone or see garden website.**
Charlecote Park has been home to the Lucy family for more than 800yrs. The gardens incl a formal parterre, woodland walk, the herbaceous border and the wider parkland which is a Capability Brown landscape offering picturesque views across the River Avon. A herd of fallow deer has been in the park since Tudor times. Charlecote Park was one of the first gardens to open in support of NGS back in 1927. Please note there are gravel paths around the grounds.

A country atmosphere, satisfying to the horticultural connoisseur . . .

9 19 CHURCH LANE
Lillington, Leamington Spa CV32 7RG. David & Judy Hirst, 01926 422591. *$1\frac{1}{2}$ m NE Leamington Spa. Take A445 towards Rugby. Church Lane on R just beyond r'about junction with B4453. Garden on corner of Hill Close. Enter via front door (brick archway) in Hill Close.* **Adm £3, chd free. Visitors welcome by appt Mar to July, Suns and Mons only. Max group size 16.**
Camellias, spring bulbs and many hellebores greet the early visitor to this plantsperson's cottage-style garden. Many unusual plants in all seasons, with pleasingly combined herbaceous areas, clematis, raised beds and alpine containers. A country atmosphere, satisfying to the horticultural connoisseur.

DAIRY COTTAGE
See Leicestershire & Rutland

GROUP OPENING

10 DORSINGTON GARDENS
Dorsington CV37 8AR. *6m SW of Stratford-upon-Avon. On B439 from Stratford turn L to Welford-on-Avon, then R to Dorsington. Free shuttle bus service & map incl.* Home-made teas in marquee at The Old Manor Garden. **Combined adm £6, chd free. Sun 9 June (12-5).**

THE BARN
Mr & Mrs P Reeve

COLLETTS FARM
Mr & Mrs D Bliss

CRABTREE FARM COTTAGE
Mr & Mrs David Boulton

DORSINGTON ARBORETUM
Mr F Dennis

DORSINGTON HOUSE
Mr & Mrs I Kolodotschko

2 DORSINGTON MANOR
Mr & Mrs C James

3 DORSINGTON MANOR
Mr & Mrs E Rusling

9 DORSINGTON MANOR
Pat and Derek Hudson

1 GLEBE COTTAGES
Mr & Mrs A Brough

MANOR FARM HOUSE
Mr A Smart & Miss L Burfoot

THE MOAT HOUSE
Mr & Mrs R Vaudry

THE OLD MANOR
Mr F Dennis

THE OLD RECTORY
Mr & Mrs Nigel Phillips

SAPPHIRE HOUSE
Mrs D Sawyer

THE WELSHMAN'S BARN
Mr F Dennis

Dorsington is a Domesday hamlet with a secret ... it is revealed one magic day in June - a spectacle of glorious gardens, tea and cake, plants, vintage Rolls Royces, statues and farm animals. These gardens offer an array of different styles such as young cottage gardens, productive kitchen gardens, stone terracing and climbing roses, orchards and gurgling brooks, ultra modern, futuristic and minimal. You can wander among the life-size statues at Welshman's Barn together with Oz maze and Japanese garden. Featured in Historic Gardens in Warwickshire and Daily Telegraph magazine.

GROUP OPENING

11 EARLSDON GARDENS

Earlsdon CV5 6FS. *Turn towards Coventry at A45/A429 T-lights. Take 3rd L into Beechwood Ave, continue ½ m to St Barbara's Church at Xrds with Rochester Rd. Maps & Tickets at St Barbara's Church Hall*. Light refreshments at St Barbara's Church Hall. **Combined adm £3, chd free. Mon 6 May (11-4).**

43 ARMORIAL ROAD
Gary & Jane Flanagan

3 BATES ROAD
Victor & Judith Keene

40 HARTINGTON CRESCENT
Viv & George Buss

114 HARTINGTON CRESCENT
Liz Campbell & Denis Crowley

65 KNOLL DRIVE
Sue & Rob Horne

36 PROVIDENCE STREET
Rachel Culley & Steve Shiner

54 SALISBURY AVENUE
Peter & Pam Moffit

2 SHAFTESBURY ROAD
Ann Thomson & Bruce Walker

23 SPENCER AVENUE
Susan & Keith Darwood

8 THE SPINNEY
Professor Michael & Eleni Tovey

35 WARWICK AVENUE
Anne-Marie Greene & Peter Gillam

Varied selection of town gardens from small to more formal with interest for all tastes incl a mature garden with deep borders bursting with spring colour, a large garden with extensive lawns and an array of rhododendrons, azaleas and large mature trees; a densely planted town garden with sheltered patio area and wilder woodland and a surprisingly large garden offering interest to all ages! There is also a pretty garden set on several levels with hidden aspects, a large peaceful garden with water features and vegetable plot and a large mature garden in a peaceful surrounding. Plantaholic's garden with a large variety of plants, clematis and small trees, some unusual and a woodland setting providing the backdrop to a garden of many contrasts incl a terrace of subtropical plants.

12 ELM CLOSE

Welford on Avon CV37 8PT. Eric & Glenis Dyer, 01789 750793, glenisdyer@gmail.com. *5m SW of Stratford, off B4390. Elm Close is between Welford Garage & The Bell Inn*. Home-made teas. **Adm £3, chd free. Visitors welcome by appt Feb to Sept. Min group 15, max 50.**
Drifts of snowdrops, aconites, erythroniums and hellebores in spring are followed by species peonies, sumptuous tree peonies, herbaceous peonies and delphiniums. Colourful Japanese maples, daphnes and cornus are underplanted with hostas, heucheras, and brunneras. Then agapanthus, phlox, asters, salvias and hydrangeas extend the seasons, with hundreds of clematis providing yr-round colour. Sloping gravel front drive.

13 FOLLY LODGE

Idicote Road, Halford CV36 5DG, Mike & Susan Solomon, 01789 740183,ss@follylodge.eclipse.co.uk. *3m NE Shipston-on-Stour. On A429 (Fosse Way). In Halford take turning to Idlicote*. Home-made teas. **Adm £3.50, chd free. Tue 30 July, Tue 27 Aug (2-5). Combined with Halford Gardens Sun 30 June (2-5.30). Visitors also welcome by appt May to Sept.**
A relaxing, informal garden with hidden corners and special spaces. Overflowing beds and borders are a patchwork of colour and shape. Added to the myriad of plants are many sculptures, incl Susan's ceramics.

14 NEW THE GRANARY

Wharf Road, Fenny Compton, Southam CV47 2FE. Lucy & Mike Davies, 01295 770033, bookings@the-granary.co.uk. *7m S of Southam. On A423 Southam to Banbury rd. 200 yds S of turning to Fenny Compton turn R into service rd signed Fenny Compton Wharf. Follow NGS signs*. Home made teas and light refreshments. **Adm £4, chd free. Sat 15, Sun 16 June; Sat 24, Sun 25, Mon 26 Aug (10.30-5.30). Visitors also welcome by appt June to Aug.**
Attractive 1 acre canal-side garden with views of the Oxford canal and Dassett Hills. Recent additions include herbaceous beds, water feature and herb garden. Beyond is a ⅓ acre kitchen plot comprising a vegetable area (grown on organic principles), a poly-tunnel for propagation and salad crops, fruit-cage and orchard. There is also a copse of native British trees in the 3 acre paddock. There are steps down to the herb garden and up to the vegetable area.

THE GRANGE
See Leicestershire & Rutland

GREEN WICKET FARM
See Leicestershire & Rutland

Drifts of snowdrops, aconites, erythroniums and hellebores in spring . . .

GROUP OPENING

15 NEW HALFORD GARDENS

Idlicote Road, Halford, Shipston-on-Stour CV36 5DG. *3m NE Shipston-on-Stour. On A429 (Fosse Way). In Halford take turning to Idlicote. Garden 200 yds on R.* **Combined adm £4, chd free. Sun 30 June (2-5.30).**

NEW **1 AYLWORTH COTTAGES**
Sue Lyons

FOLLY LODGE
Mike & Susan Solomon, (See separate entry)

NEW **19 THE CLOSE**
Amanda & Henry Probert

Small, medium and large - 3 gardens created and cared for by women gardeners. Sue's garden is very small, but every inch is full of plants and interesting objects. Amanda's garden is specifically managed to make it attractive to wildlife. Susan's garden is a place for contemplation, with plenty of plants and artwork. Featured in Cotswold Life. Mostly level, but gravel paths.

The Old Manor, Dorsington Gardens

120 RUSSELL ROAD
See Staffordshire, Birmingham & West Midlands

GROUP OPENING

16 HATTON GARDENS

Station Road, Hatton, Warwick CV35 7LG. *2m NW of Warwick. J15 M40, take A46 signed Coventry. After 1m exit L onto A4177 Birmingham Rd. After approx 1m bear L onto B4439 Hockley Rd. Station Rd 1m on L signed Hatton Station.* **Combined adm £4, chd free. Sun 30 June (12-4).**

CATCHAMA CROFT
Heather & David Howell

CHUMLEYWOOD
Ann & Peter Thomas

Within 2 miles of the historic town of Warwick, close to Hatton Country World and Hatton Flight, are two unique, contrasting, hidden gardens backing on to the Grand Union Canal. Chumleywood has unusual specimen trees, including a magnificent Tulip tree. This 1-acre garden incl ponds, original well and mixed borders, rose garden parterre and kitchen garden. A mature and well-stocked orchard and woodland area leads down to the canal. Catchama Croft is a plantsman's acre garden of all yr-round interest with ponds, scree areas and unusual trees and shrubs interspersed with seasonal planters. A large vegetable and fruit garden completes the picture. Also to be found, aviary and wild area for free-range chickens.

17 ◆ HILL CLOSE GARDENS

Bread & Meat Close, Warwick CV34 6HF. Hill Close Gardens Trust, 01926 493339, www.hillclosegardens.com. *Town centre. Entry from Friars St by Bread & Meat Close. Car park by entrance next to racecourse. 2hrs free parking. Disabled parking outside the gates.* **Adm £3.50, chd £1 under 5yrs free. For NGS: Sat 21 Sept (11-5). For other opening times and information, please phone or see garden website.**

Restored Grade II* Victorian leisure gardens comprising 16 individual hedged gardens, 8 brick summerhouses. Herbaceous borders, heritage apple and pear trees, C19 daffodils, many varieties of asters and chrysanthemums. Heritage vegetables. Plant Heritage border, auricula theatre, Victorian style glasshouse. Children's garden. Gardener's walk 2nd Fri in month. Visitors can admire our large collection of asters and wide range of other late flowering plants in our herbaceous borders. There are over 40 varieties of chrysanthemum, as well as helianthus, nerines and schizostylis. Wheelchair available which can be booked in advance by phone. Access route indicated on plan of the gardens.

GROUP OPENING

18 HONINGTON VILLAGE GARDENS

Shipston-on-Stour CV36 5AA. *1½ m N of Shipston-on-Stour. Take A3400 towards Stratford-upon-Avon then turn R signed Honington.* Home-made teas. **Combined adm £5, chd free. Sun 16 June (2-6).**

HOME FARM
Mr Guy Winter

HONINGTON GLEBE
Mr & Mrs J C Orchard

HONINGTON HALL
B H E Wiggin

MALT HOUSE RISE
Mr & Mrs M Underhill

THE OLD COTTAGE
Liz Davenport

THE OLD HOUSE
Mr & Mrs I F Beaumont

ORCHARD HOUSE
Mr & Mrs Monnington

SHOEMAKERS COTTAGE
Christopher & Anne Jordan

STABLE COTTAGE
Mr Shaun de Wolf

C17 village, recorded in Domesday, entered by old toll gate. Ornamental stone bridge over the R Stour and interesting church with C13 tower and late C17 nave after Wren. 9 super gardens. 2-acre plantsman's garden consisting of rooms planted informally with yr-round interest in contrasting foliage, texture, lilypool and parterre. Extensive lawns and fine mature trees with river and garden monuments. Small garden that is well stocked with interesting established shrubs and container plants and a structured cottage garden formally laid out with box hedging and small fountain. Small, developing garden created by the owners with informal mixed beds and borders.

Stunning rambling gardens with wonderful planting and views . . .

GROUP OPENING

19 ILMINGTON GARDENS
Ilmington CV36 4LA. *8m S of Stratford-upon-Avon. 8m N of Moreton in Marsh. 4m NW of Shipston-on-Stour off A3400. 3m NE of Chipping Campden.* Home-made teas and refreshments at Village Hall. **Combined adm £5, chd free (share to Warwickshire and Northamptonshire Air Ambulance). Sun 7 Apr (2-6).**

THE BEVINGTONS
Mr & Mrs N Tustain

NEW **CHERRY ORCHARD**
Mr Angus Chambers

COMPTON SCORPION
Mr & Mrs T Karlsen.

FOXCOTE HILL
Mr & Mrs Michael Dingley

FROG ORCHARD
Mr & Mrs Jeremy Snowden

GRUMP COTTAGE
Mr & Mrs Martin Underwood

ILMINGTON MANOR
Mr Martin Taylor

PARK FARM HOUSE
Mike & Lesley Lane

Ilmington is an ancient hillside Cotswold village 2m from the Fosse Way with two good pubs and splendid teas at the Village Hall. Buy your ticket at the beautiful Elizabethan Manor House (next to the Red Lion PH in the centre of the village) and wander round the three acres of clipped yews, spring flowers and drifts of daffodils. Walk 200yds up to Foxcote Hill, a beautiful Georgian house behind which are acres of stunning rambling gardens with wonderful planting and views. Proceed to Grump Cottage, a small stone cottage near the Catholic chapel on the Upper Green, behind which is a fascinating terraced walled garden planted in 2010. Move on to nearby Frog Lane, and enjoy the lovingly tended cottage gardens of Park Farmhouse, Cherry Orchard and Frog Orchard. Cross the village to The Bevingtons, a large cottage garden at the end of Valanders Lane, between the Manor ponds and the Norman Church and revel in ancient peace. Drive 2m to Compton Scorpion Farm, a C18 farmhouse with a stunning garden and views on a remote hillside. Morris Men will play around the village.

GROUP OPENING

20 KENILWORTH GARDENS
Kenilworth, Warwickshire CV8 1BT. *Gardens are located in the small town of Kenilworth. Tickets & maps are available at all gardens. Refreshments available at Fieldgate at junction of A452 (Fieldgate Lane) & A429 (New St) in Kenilworth & Old Town centre. Free parking is available in Abbey Fields car park with additional parking on High St, Fieldgate Lane, Chase Lane & Malthouse Lane.* Home-made teas at Fieldgate. **Combined adm £4, chd free. Sun 2 June, Sun 1 Sept (1-5).**

NEW **14C FIELDGATE LANE**
Mrs Sandra Aulton

ABBEY HILL
Pam Vaughan

FIELDGATE
Liz & Bob Watson

25 MALTHOUSE LANE
David & Linda Pettifor

NEW **TYROES**
Mrs Jo Stevens

Kenilworth was historically a very important town in Warwickshire, which now has one of England's best castle ruins and plenty of pubs and good restaurants. The position of the Abbey is marked by the lovely Abbey Fields, around which four of the gardens open in June are situated. In 2012 three gardens opened. This year we welcome two new gardens to the group. All the gardens have won awards in the Kenilworth in Bloom garden competition, with 3 attaining Best in Class.

KILSBY GARDENS
See Northamptonshire

21 LATIMERS REST
Hipsley Lane, Baxterley CV9 2HS. Gerald & Christine Leedham, 01827 875526, christine_leedham@yahoo.co.uk. *3m S of Atherstone on B4116. From A5 Atherstone, at island, take Merevale Lane to Baxterley. From M42 J9 take A4097 for Kingsbury. At island follow signs to Hurley & Baxterley, garden nr church.* Home-made teas. **Adm £5, chd free. Sun 16 June, Sun 4 Aug (12.30-5). Visitors also welcome by appt June to Sept.**
2½ acres of wonderful contrasts. Formal lawns and ponds with colourful flower beds and giant hanging baskets give way to hostas and ferns with medieval moat backdrop. Feature rose gardens with over 40 standard roses. Small arboretum with specimen trees, vegetable gardens, greenhouses and chickens.

22 ◆ THE MASTER'S GARDEN
Lord Leycester Hospital, Warwick CV34 4BH. The Governors, 01926 491422, www.lordleycester.com. *W end of Warwick High St, behind ancient Hospital buildings.* **For opening times and information, please phone or see garden website.**
Restored historic walled garden hidden behind the medieval buildings of this home for retired ex-servicemen, also open to the public. Mixed shrub and herbaceous planting with climbing roses and clematis, Norman arch, ancient Egyptian Nilometer, thatched summerhouse, gazebo, knot garden and C18 pineapple pit. Seasonal produce and plants for sale.

23 MAXSTOKE CASTLE
Coleshill B46 2RD. Mr & Mrs M C Fetherston-Dilke. *2½ m E of Coleshill. E of Birmingham, on B4114. Take R turn down Castle Lane, Castle drive 1¼ m on R.* Home-made teas. **Adm £7, chd £4.50. Sun 16 June (11-5).**
Approx 5 acres of garden and grounds with herbaceous, shrubs and trees in the immed surroundings of this C14 moated castle. No wheelchair access to house.

MEADOW FARM
See Worcestershire

MIDDLETON HALL
See Staffordshire, Birmingham & West Midlands

24 ◆ THE MILL GARDEN
55 Mill Street, Warwick CV34 4HB. Julia (née Measures) Russell & David Russell, 01926 492877. *Off A425 beside old castle gate, at the bottom of Mill St. Use St Nicholas car park.* **Adm £1.50, chd free. 1 Apr - 30 Oct incl (9-6).**
This garden lies in a magical setting on the banks of the R Avon beneath the walls of Warwick Castle. Winding paths lead round every corner to dramatic views of the castle and ruined medieval bridge. This informal cottage garden is a profusion of plants, shrubs and trees. Beautiful all-yr. Limited wheelchair access. Unsuitable for electric wheelchairs.

25 THE OLD RECTORY
Lighthorne, Warwick CV35 0AR. The Hon Lady Butler. *10m S of Warwick just off B4100. From village green head for Church. At lych gate turn R up lane. Entrance on R. Parking straight on.* Home-made teas. **Adm £4, chd free. Sun 23 June (2-6).**
An old established garden sheltered by brick walls surrounding the C17 rectory. Sloping lawns with two fine copper beeches lead down to the house. Roses adorn the house and garden walls. Main part of garden accessible for wheelchair users but steep slope in part.

THE OLD STABLES
See Leicestershire & Rutland

26 PACKINGTON HALL
Meriden, Nr Coventry CV7 7HF. Lord & Lady Aylesford. *Midway between Coventry & Birmingham on A45. Entrance 400yds from Stonebridge island towards Coventry. Use postcode CV7 7HE for SatNav.* Home-made teas. **Adm £5, chd free. Sun 7 July (2.30-5.30).**
Packington is the setting for an elegant Capability Brown landscape. Designed from 1750 in 100 acres of parkland which sweeps down to a lake incl 1762 Japanese bridge. Mirrored terrace beds glow with perennials. Nearby is the Millennium Rose Garden planted with old fashioned roses complete with flowers, hips and haws. Delicious W.I teas.

COLDOR
See Leicestershire & Rutland

FARMWAY
See Leicestershire & Rutland

JOHN'S WOOD
See Leicestershire & Rutland

PEREIRA ROAD GARDENS
See Staffordshire, Birmingham & West Midlands.

4 PODEN COTTAGES
See Worcestershire

Wonderful walled kitchen garden provides seasonal produce and cut flowers for the house . . .

27 PRIORS MARSTON MANOR
The Green, Priors Marston CV47 7RH. Dr & Mrs Mark Cecil, 01788 891439, whewitt15@yahoo.co.uk. *8m SW of Daventry. Off A361 between Daventry & Banbury at Charwelton.* Home-made teas. **Adm £4, chd free. Sun 16 June (2-6). Visitors also welcome by appt (Mon, Tue, Thurs, Fri) June to Aug. For groups, advanced booking is advised.**
Arrive through the newly planted rotunda garden and explore the manor gardens. Greatly enhanced by present owners to relate back to a Georgian manor garden and pleasure grounds. Wonderful walled kitchen garden provides seasonal produce and cut flowers for the house. Herbaceous flower beds and a sunken terrace with water feature by William Pye. Lawns lead down to the lake around which you can walk amongst the trees and wildlife with stunning views up to the house and garden aviary. Limited wheelchair access.

PUMP COTTAGE
See Worcestershire

28 ◆ RAGLEY HALL GARDENS
Alcester B49 5NJ. Marquess & Marchioness of Hertford, 01789 762090, www.ragleyhall.com. *8m W of Stratford-upon-Avon. 2m SW of Alcester, off A435/A46.* **Adm £5, chd free. For NGS: Thur 27 June (11-3). For other opening times and information, please phone or see garden website.**
24 acres of gardens, predominantly mature broadleaved trees, within which a variety of cultivated and non-cultivated areas have been blended to achieve a garden rich in both horticulture and bio-diversity. The winter garden, spring meadows and bulbs make way for summer meadows, herbaceous borders and annual bedding. New rose garden has been planted and looks stunning from late June through to Sept. Wheelchair access map available.

172 STONOR ROAD
See Staffordshire, Birmingham & West Midlands

GROUP OPENING

29 NEW STRETTON-ON-FOSSE GARDENS
Stretton on Fosse, Moreton-in-Marsh GL56 9SD. *Stretton on Fosse off the A429 between Moreton in Marsh & Shipston-on-Stour. Court House is in centre of vllage next to St Peter's Church. Parking either in rd outside Church or at village hall at bottom of village opp The Plough Inn.* Home-made teas. **Combined adm £5, chd free. Suns 28 Apr; 21 July (2-6).**

COURT HOUSE
Christopher White
Visitors also welcome by appt Feb to Dec.01608 663811 mum@star.co.uk

NEW OLD BEAMS
Mrs Hilary Fossey

Court House is a continually evolving, 4-acre garden with yr-round interest and colour. Walled kitchen garden, fernery and winter garden: spring bulbs, herbaceous borders, rose garden, and wild flowers in the paddocks and orchards. Article in Cotswold Life in 2011. Old Beams is a walled cottage garden on a slope with traditional cottage garden plants, small lawn, rockery, fruit cage and vegetable garden.

"Lemon drizzle cake, Victoria sponge ... yummy!"

GROUP OPENING

30 STYVECHALE GARDENS
Knoll Drive, Coventry CV3 5DE. *Tickets & map listing gardens available from St Thomas More RC Church Hall CV3 5DE. From A45 take B4113 (Leamington Rd) towards Coventry. Take 2nd R (Baginton Rd), then 2nd L (Watercall Av.) Continue past 2 R turns, church is on your R. For further information contact suepountney@btinternet.com.* Home-made teas. **Combined adm £3.50, chd free. Sun 23 June (11-5).**

43 ARMORIAL ROAD
Gary & Jane Flanagan

164 BAGINTON ROAD
Fran & Jeff Gaught

166 BAGINTON ROAD
Wilf & Ann Hawes

16 DELAWARE ROAD
Val & Roy Howells

2 THE HIRON
Sue & Graham Pountney

A collection of lovely, mature, suburban gardens, each one different in style and size. Come and enjoy the imaginatively planted herbaceous borders, spectacular roses, water features, fruit and vegetable patches, cottage garden planting and shady areas - something for everyone and plenty of ideas for you to take home. Relax in the seating areas and enjoy the warm, friendly welcome you will receive from us all. There will be refreshments available and plants for sale in some of the gardens. Other gardens will be open on the day.

A knot garden and a pleached hornbeam pathway are to be found in the lovely garden . . .

WALTON GARDENS
See Leicestershire & Rutland

GROUP OPENING

31 WARMINGTON VILLAGE GARDENS
Banbury OX17 1BU. *5m NW of Banbury. Take the B4100 N from Banbury after 5m turn R across short dual carriageway into Warmington. From the N take J12 off M40 onto B4100.* Home-made teas at Village Hall. **Combined adm £5, chd free. Sun 23 June (2-6).**

AGDON HOUSE
Mr & Mrs P Grenet

GROVE FARM HOUSE
Richard & Kate Lister

KIRK LEE
Mr & Mrs L Albrighton

THE MANOR HOUSE
Mr & Mrs G Lewis

OLD RECTORY FARMHOUSE
Dr & Mrs J Deakin

SPRINGFIELD HOUSE
Jenny & Roger Handscombe
01295 690286
jenny.handscombe@virgin.net

WESTERING
Mr & Mrs R Neale

1 THE WHEELWRIGHTS
Ms E Bunn

Warmington, at the edge of the Cotswolds is an exceptionally attractive village with its C17 Hornton stone houses set around the village green. In front of the Pond is **The Manor House** with its Elizabethan Knot garden, and topiary. **Kirk Lee** on 3 levels with its cascade has panoramic views across the valley. **Wheelwrights** features a small pond surrounded by many varieties of heuchera and allium. **Springfield House** with its gravel garden is terraced and informal. **Old Rectory Farmhouse** is a developing garden with a small wooded area. A knot garden and a pleached hornbeam pathway are to be found in the lovely garden at **Grove Farm. Agdon House** and **Westering** have colourful herbaceous borders with many unusual plants. Do visit St Michael's Church at the top of the village containing the Millennium Tapestry.

GROUP OPENING

32 NEW WASPERTON GARDENS
Wasperton CV35 8EB. *4m S of Warwick. On A429, turn R between Barford & Wellesbourne; gardens near end of village.* Home-made teas at Cedar House. **Combined adm £6, chd free. Sun 30 June (2-5).**

CEDAR HOUSE
Mr & Mrs D L Burbidge

NEW DOVECOTE
Sylvia Fenwick

Two gardens at end of village. Large mature vicarage garden, colourful herbaceous borders, island bed and walled garden; grass garden, woodland walk. Small informal garden designed and planted over last nine years: packed with variety of trees, shrubs and flowers arranged in colour groupings. Some gravel and rough paths.

GROUP OPENING

33 WELFORD-ON-AVON & DISTRICT
Welford-on-Avon CV37 8PT. *5m SW of Stratford-upon-Avon. Off B4390.* Tea in the village hall. **Combined adm £5, chd free. Sat 29, Sun 30 June (2-6).**

ARDENCOTE
Mike & Sally Luntley

NEW 2 CHAPEL STREET
Mr Rod Scarrott

NEW DUNELM
Mr & Mrs Paul & Colleen King

9 QUINEYS LEYS
Ann Raff

NEW RIVERCOT
Mrs Elaine Selby

NEW SOUTHLAWNS
Mr & Mrs Amanda & Guy Kitteringham

WATERMILL COTTAGE
Martin & Sheila Greenwood

In addition to its superb position on the river, with serene swans, dabbling ducks and resident herons, Welford-on-Avon has a beautiful church, an excellent family butcher's shop, a very convenient general store and selection of PHs serving great food. Just down the road is a highly popular farm-shop where seasonal fruit and vegetables are much in demand. With its great variety of house styles, incl an abundance of beautiful cottages with thatched roofs and chocolate-box charisma, Welford also has an army of keen gardeners (5yr old garden club has over 100 members!) The gardens open for the NGS range from a plot with fantastic topiary, herb knot and live willow weaving, to a walled garden, gardens with fun sculptures, flowerpot men, prairie planting and water features, all with a glorious array of containers and hanging baskets. Fruit and vegetable areas are also integral to these gardens for all seasons.

ALLOTMENTS

34 WELLESBOURNE ALLOTMENTS

Kineton Road, Wellesbourne, Warwick CV35 9NE. *5m E of Stratford-upon-Avon. On Kineton Rd (B4086) E side of Wellesbourne.* Home-made teas. **Adm £3, chd free. Sun 14 July (2-5).**

The 3-hectare Wellesbourne allotment site with 96 members is one of the oldest in the country. Its impressive range of vegetables from ridiculously large to miniscule, delicious fruits and beautiful flowers offers much of interest to novice, experienced gardeners and young enthusiasts. There will be a demonstration of our excellent under soil irrigation system. Plants and produce for sale. Scarecrow display - vote for the best scarecrow! Afternoon teas, Stratford Grammar School for Girls Jazz Band, Stratford Beekeepers. Tarmac driveway allows wheelchair access to length of allotments. Level site.

GROUP OPENING

35 NEW WESTON-UNDER-WETHERLEY GARDENS

Leamington Spa CV33 9BW. *3m NE of Leamington Spa on B4453.* Home-made teas at Weston Village Hall. **Combined adm £3, chd free. Sat 8, Sun 9 June (12.30-5.30).**

NEW 4 ALDERMAN WAY
Mr Paddy Taylor

NEW 7 ALDERMAN WAY
Jane Jones

NEW 8 ALDERMAN WAY
Tracy & Bill Byrne

NEW 10 ALDERMAN WAY
Alastair Rodda

NEW 23 ALDERMAN WAY
Lynne Williams

NEW GLEBE COTTAGE
Stephen Evans

NEW GLEBE HOUSE
Ian & Pippa Jamie

NEW THE OLD FORGE
Sarah & Peter Haine

NEW 13 RUGBY ROAD
Jean Smith

NEW 5 RUGBY ROAD
Mrs Brenda Boardman

NEW 12 SIMPKINS CLOSE
Sue & Chris Garden

Eleven gardens opening for the first time incl established gardens with rolling lawns, orchards, sheep and chickens; cottage gardens new and old; field views, artisan studio, pergolas and patios. Water features, lily ponds, vegetable gardens, raised beds and packed herbaceous borders; in fact, almost every style and size of garden. The village has a C12 parish church, St Michaels; a recently-built village hall where NGS visitors can enjoy refreshments; and a village pub, The Bull Inn.

GROUP OPENING

36 WHICHFORD & ASCOTT GARDENS

Whichford and Ascott, Shipston-on-Stour CV36 5PP. *6m SE of Shipston-on-Stour. Turn E off A3400 at Long Compton for Whichford. Car park opposite church.* Home-made teas at St Michael's church. **Combined adm £5, chd free. Sun 9 June (1.30-5.30).**

ASCOTT LODGE
Charlotte Copley

BROOK HOLLOW
John & Shirley Round

NEW MURTON COTTAGE
Hilary & David Blakemore

THE OLD HOUSE
Terry & Barbara Maher

NEW PLUM TREE COTTAGE
Janet Knight

WHICHFORD HILL HOUSE
Mr & Mrs John Melvin

THE WHICHFORD POTTERY
Jim & Dominique Keeling
www.whichfordpottery.com

This group of gardens reflects a range of several garden types and sizes. The two villages are in an area of outstanding natural beauty. They nestle within a dramatic landscape of hills, pasture and woodland, which is used to picturesque effect by the garden owners. Fine lawns, mature shrub planting and much interest to plantsmen provide a peaceful visit to a series of beautiful gardens. Many incorporate the inventive use of natural springs, forming ponds, pools and other water features. Classic cottage gardens contrast with the romantic acres of the C14 Old House, while other gardens adopt variations on the traditional English garden of herbaceous borders, climbing roses, yew hedges and walled enclosures. Other amenities are the C12 church, where teas are served in the churchyard; also the internationally renowned pottery and a PH serving meals. Some gardens are not appropriate for wheelchair users.

With fantastic topiary, herb knot and live willow weaving . . .

WITHYBED GREEN
See Worcestershire

WITS END
See Staffordshire, Birmingham & West Midlands

WOODBROOKE QUAKER STUDY CENTRE
See Staffordshire, Birmingham & West Midlands

Ragley Hall Gardens

© Heather Edwards

Warwickshire Volunteers

County Organiser

Julia Sewell, Dinsdale House, Baldwins Lane, Upper Tysoe, Warwick CV35 0TX, 01295 680234, sewelljulia@btinternet.com

County Treasurer

Susan Solomon, Folly Lodge, Idlicote Road, Halford, Shipston-on-Stour, Warwicks, CV36 5DG, 01789 740183, SS@follylodge.eclipse.co.uk

Publicity

Peter Pashley, Millstone, Mayfield Avenue, Stratford upon Avon CV37 6XB, 01789 294932, peter@peterpash.mail1.co.uk
Di Reeds, 18 Paddock Lane, Stratford-upon-Avon CV37 9JE, 01789 414212, digardengate@hotmail.com

Booklet Coordinator

Janet Neale, Westering, The Green, Warmington, Banbury OX17 1BU, 01295 690515, janetneale5@gmail.com

Assistant County Organiser

David Ainsworth, 1 Evenlode Close, Stratford-upon-Avon CV37 7EL, 01789 292487, dainsworth@btinternet.com
Keith Browne, 1a Williams Road, Radford Semele, Leamington Spa CV31 1UR, 01926 420284, keith_browne@hotmail.com
Elspeth Napier, 17 Simpson Road, Shipston-on-Stour CV36 4JT, 01608 666278, elspeth@cherryvilla.demon.co.uk
Sal Renwick, 75 Blue Lake Road, Dorridge, Solihull B93 8BH, 01684 770215, sal.renwick@blueyonder.co.uk

Join us on Facebook and spread the word

WILTSHIRE

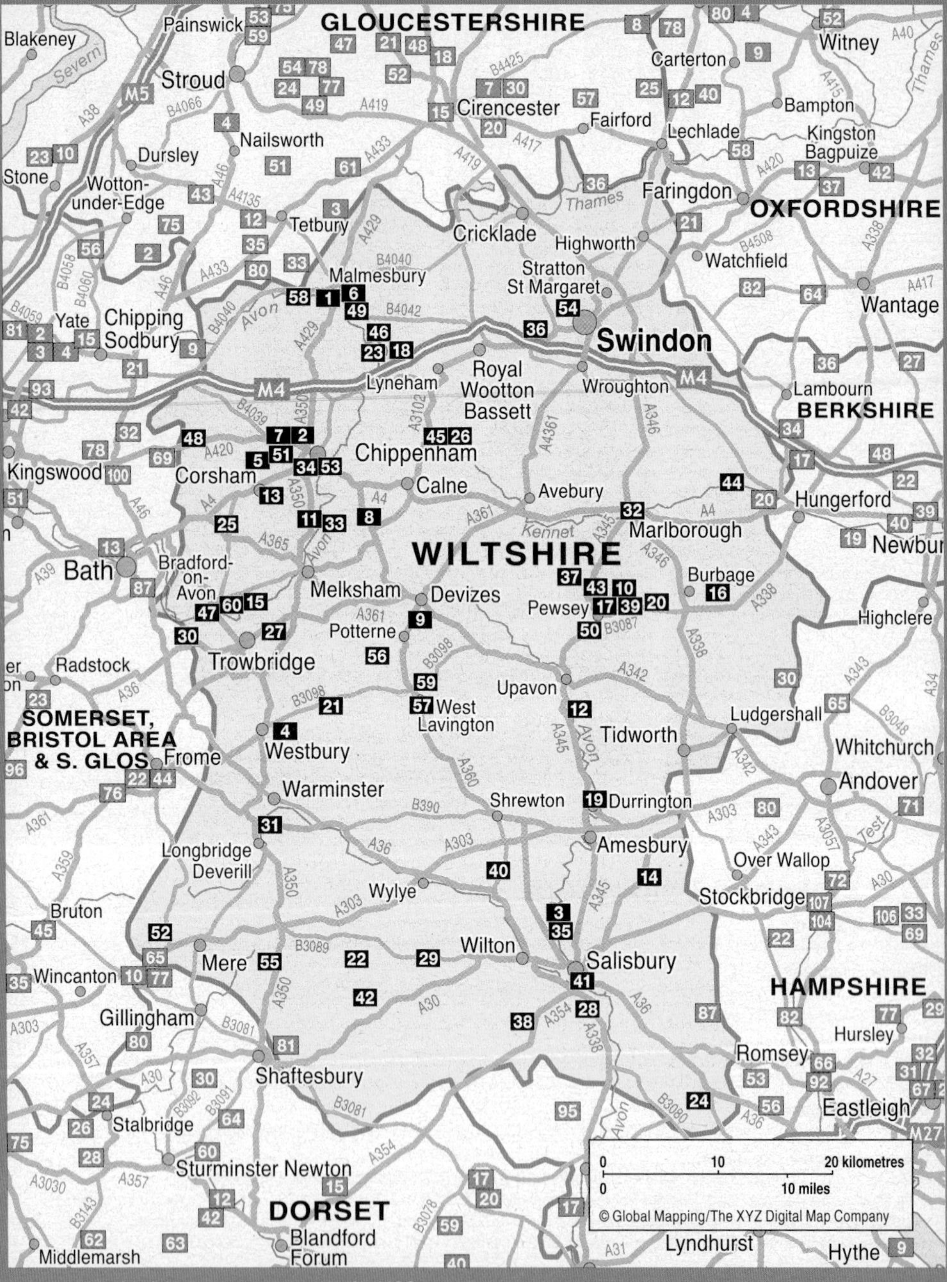
GLOUCESTERSHIRE
OXFORDSHIRE
BERKSHIRE
WILTSHIRE
SOMERSET, BRISTOL AREA & S. GLOS
HAMPSHIRE
DORSET
Swindon
Chippenham
Bath
Salisbury
Trowbridge
Devizes
Marlborough
Malmesbury
Corsham
Calne
Melksham
Westbury
Warminster
Pewsey
Amesbury
Tidworth
Wilton
Mere
Shaftesbury
Cricklade
Highworth
Royal Wootton Bassett
0 10 20 kilometres
0 10 miles
© Global Mapping/The XYZ Digital Map Company

Opening Dates

February

Saturday 9
33 Lacock Abbey Gardens

Sunday 10
33 Lacock Abbey Gardens

Saturday 16
33 Lacock Abbey Gardens

Sunday 17
3 Avon Cottage
33 Lacock Abbey Gardens

March

Sunday 17
1 Abbey House Gardens
3 Avon Cottage
14 Cottage in the Trees

Sunday 24
22 Fonthill House

Sunday 31
40 The Mill House

April

Sunday 7
13 Corsham Court

Sunday 14
9 Broadleas House Gardens
14 Cottage in the Trees
56 Wellaway

Sunday 21
3 Avon Cottage
10 Broomsgrove Lodge
35 Little Durnford Manor
47 Priory House

Friday 26
59 Windmill Cottage

Saturday 27
31 Job's Mill

Sunday 28
2 Allington Grange
30 Iford Manor
43 Oare House

May

Saturday 4
52 Stourhead Garden

Sunday 5
55 Waterdale House

Sunday 12
5 Biddestone Manor
9 Broadleas House Gardens
14 Cottage in the Trees
21 Edington Gardens
28 Horatio's Garden
48 Ridleys Cheer

Friday 17
41 Mompesson House

Sunday 19
2 Allington Grange
13 Corsham Court

Wednesday 22
51 Sheldon Manor

Friday 24
59 Windmill Cottage

Sunday 26
11 Cantax House
29 Hyde's House
49 River Barn
54 Twigs Community Garden

Monday 27
60 13 Woolley Green

June

Sunday 2
16 Crofton Lock House
42 North Cottage & Woodview Cottage
60 13 Woolley Green

Wednesday 5
50 Sharcott Manor

Friday 7
59 Windmill Cottage

Saturday 8
16 Crofton Lock House

Sunday 9
24 Hamptworth Estate
25 Hazelbury Manor Gardens
35 Little Durnford Manor
42 North Cottage & Woodview Cottage
45 The Old Vicarage

Tuesday 11
15 The Courts

Wednesday 12
45 The Old Vicarage

Friday 14
38 Manor House

People welcome to draw and paint in the garden by appointment . . .

National Gardens Weekend

Saturday 15
10 Broomsgrove Lodge
14 Cottage in the Trees
26 Hilmarton Group Gardens
31 Job's Mill
37 Manor Farm
38 Manor House
44 The Old Mill
57 West Lavington Manor

Sunday 16
9 Broadleas House Gardens
12 Chisenbury Priory
14 Cottage in the Trees
18 Dauntsey Gardens
19 Durrington Village Gardens
26 Hilmarton Group Gardens
32 10 Kingsbury Street
37 Manor Farm
44 The Old Mill
49 River Barn

Wednesday 19
19 Durrington Village Gardens

Friday 21
59 Windmill Cottage

Saturday 22
23 Great Somerford Gardens

Sunday 23
7 Bolehyde Manor
23 Great Somerford Gardens
27 Hilperton House

Tuesday 25
15 The Courts

Saturday 29
17 Dane Brook
39 Milkhouse Water Farm

Sunday 30
6 Blicks Hill House
17 Dane Brook
39 Milkhouse Water Farm
40 The Mill House
43 Oare House
46 The Pound House
58 Whatley Manor

July

Wednesday 3
50 Sharcott Manor

Friday 5
59 Windmill Cottage

Sunday 14
20 Easton Royal Gardens

Friday 19
59 Windmill Cottage

Saturday 20
4 Beggars Knoll Chinese Garden

Sunday 21
4 Beggars Knoll Chinese Garden
54 Twigs Community Garden

You are always welcome at an NGS garden!

Saturday 27
17 Dane Brook
39 Milkhouse Water Farm

Sunday 28
17 Dane Brook
36 Lydiard Park Walled Garden
39 Milkhouse Water Farm
53 Sweet Briar Cottage

August

Sunday 4
16 Crofton Lock House
34 130 Ladyfield Road
47 Priory House

Wednesday 7
50 Sharcott Manor

Saturday 10
17 Dane Brook

Sunday 11
9 Broadleas House Gardens
17 Dane Brook
44 The Old Mill

September

Wednesday 4
50 Sharcott Manor

Wednesday 11
38 Manor House

Sunday 15
28 Horatio's Garden
50 Sharcott Manor
56 Wellaway

February 2014

Saturday 8
33 Lacock Abbey Gardens

Sunday 9
33 Lacock Abbey Gardens

Saturday 15
33 Lacock Abbey Gardens

Sunday 16
33 Lacock Abbey Gardens

Sunday 23
3 Avon Cottage

Gardens open to the public

1 Abbey House Gardens
8 Bowood Rhododendron Walks
13 Corsham Court
15 The Courts
30 Iford Manor
33 Lacock Abbey Gardens
36 Lydiard Park Walled Garden
40 The Mill House
41 Mompesson House
51 Sheldon Manor
52 Stourhead Garden
54 Twigs Community Garden
55 Waterdale House

Also open by Appointment ☎

3 Avon Cottage
4 Beggars Knoll Chinese Garden
5 Biddestone Manor
7 Bolehyde Manor
12 Chisenbury Priory
14 Cottage in the Trees
18 The Coach House, Dauntsey Gardens
32 10 Kingsbury Street
38 Manor House
42 North Cottage & Woodview Cottage
45 The Old Vicarage
46 The Pound House
47 Priory House
49 River Barn
50 Sharcott Manor
53 Sweet Briar Cottage
57 West Lavington Manor
59 Windmill Cottage

The Gardens

1 ◆ ABBEY HOUSE GARDENS

Malmesbury Town Centre SN16 9AS. Ian & Barbara Pollard, 01666 827650, www.abbeyhousegardens.co.uk. *5m N of J17 M4. Beside C12 Abbey. Parking in town centre (short stay) or follow brown signs to long stay (via steps to gardens).* **Adm £8, chd £3. For NGS: Sun 17 Mar (11-5.30). For other opening times and information, please phone or see garden website.**
Beside Malmesbury's Abbey Church and straddling the R Avon, this spectacular 5-acre garden, home to The Naked Gardeners, has brought praise from around the world. Spring bulbs begin the display, as 70,000 tulips bloom from March to May.

ALDERLEY GRANGE
See Gloucestershire

Visit a group opening and really make a day of it . . . !

2 ALLINGTON GRANGE

Allington, Chippenham SN14 6LW. Mrs Rhyddian Roper, www.allingtongrange.com. *2m W of Chippenham. Take A420 W. 1st R signed Allington Village, entrance 1m on L.* Home-made teas. **Adm £3, chd free. Suns 28 Apr; 19 May (2-5).**
Informal country garden of approx 1½ acre, around C17 farmhouse (not open) with a diverse range of plants. Mixed and herbaceous borders, colour themed; white garden with water fountain. Pergola lined with clematis and roses. Walled potager. Small orchard with chickens. Wildlife pond with natural planting. Many spring bulbs. Mainly level with ramp into potager. Dogs on leads.

ASHLEY GRANGE
See Gloucestershire

3 AVON COTTAGE

Lower Woodford, Salisbury SP4 6NQ. Mr & Mrs Trevor Shepherd, 01722 782295, dotty.sas@gmail.com. *4m N of Salisbury. Off Woodford Valley Rd, between A360 & A345.* Home-made teas. **Adm £4.50, chd free. Suns 17 Feb; 17 Mar (1-4); 21 Apr (2-5); 23 Feb 2014. Visitors also welcome by appt Feb to Apr, Weds and Fris only.**
Garden planted for year round interest incl bulbs, large drifts of snowdrops and narcissi, flowering shrubs and perennials in woodland, along stream and in borders with tulips in pots. Mature evergreen hedges break up the level site which is under continual development. Lovely views and abundant wildlife. Featured in Country Living and Wiltshire magazine. Gravel drive and tree roots on woodland paths.

☎

BATH PRIORY HOTEL
See Somerset, Bristol & South Gloucestershire

4 BEGGARS KNOLL CHINESE GARDEN

Newtown, Westbury BA13 3ED. Colin Little & Penny Stirling, 01373 823383, silkendalliance@talktalk.net. *1m SE of Westbury. Turn off B3098 at White Horse Pottery, up hill towards the White Horse for ½ m. Disabled parking at end of drive. Main parking 300yds up hill.* Home-made teas.

Adm £3.50, chd free. Sat 20, Sun 21 July (2-6). **Visitors also welcome by appt May to July.**
This inspirational 1-acre garden is filled with colourful plantings set against a backdrop of Chinese pavilions, gateways, statues and dragons. Pathways and mosaic pavements wind around ponds and rocks. Rare Chinese shrubs, mature trees, and flower-filled borders form a haven of serenity. A large potager houses chickens, and pigs live in the woods. Spectacular views too! Art exhibition. Featured in Garden News and Wiltshire Magazine.

BEVERSTON CASTLE
See Gloucestershire

5 BIDDESTONE MANOR

Chippenham Lane, Biddestone SN14 7DJ. Rosie Harris, Head Gardener, 01249 713211. *5m W of Chippenham. On A4 between Chippenham & Corsham turn N. From A420, 5m W of Chippenham, turn S. Use car park.* Home-made teas. **Adm £5, chd free.** Sun 12 May (2-5). **Visitors also welcome by appt Mar to June.**
Stroll through our 8 peaceful acres of wide lawns, lake and ponds, arboretum and roses. Kitchen and cutting gardens and orchard. Then join us for tea in the formal front garden. Beautiful C17 Manor House (not open) with ancient dovecote. Maybe spot the bee orchids and kingfisher. Garden photography for sale.

6 BLICKS HILL HOUSE

Blicks Hill, Malmesbury SN16 9HZ. Alan & Valerie Trotman. *1/2 m E of Malmesbury. On A429 Malmesbury bypass, turn off 1/2 way between r'abouts.* Home-made teas. **Adm £3.50, chd free.** Sun 30 June (11-5.30).
Stunning, and having the wow factor is how visitors describe this garden situated on a 1-acre stepped and sloping site. Mature trees give a backdrop to the colourful beds and borders which have all been created since 2004. Unique pergola leading to a woodland glade, water feature and stream constructed in green slate, hanging baskets, tubs and bedding plants add extra impact. Very much a plantsman's garden. Gradual slope.

Cantax House

7 BOLEHYDE MANOR

Allington SN14 6LW. The Earl & Countess Cairns, 01249 443056, amandamcairns@gmail.com. *1 1/2 m W of Chippenham. On Bristol Rd (A420). Turn N at Allington Xrds. 1/2 m on R. Parking in field.* Home-made teas. **Adm £4, chd free.** Sun 23 June (2.30-6). **Visitors also welcome by appt June to July (weekdays preferred).**
Series of gardens around C16 manor house (not open), enclosed by walls and topiary. Formal framework densely planted with many interesting shrubs and climbers, especially roses. Mixed borders. Blue walk of alliums and agapanthus. Inner courtyard with troughs full of tender plants. Collection of tender pelargoniums Vegetable/fruit garden and greenhouse. Some steps.

8 ◆ BOWOOD RHODODENDRON WALKS

Calne SN11 9PG. The Marquis of Lansdowne, 01249 812102, www.bowood.org. *3 1/2 m SE of Chippenham. Located off J17 M4 nr Bath & Chippenham. Entrance off A342 between Sandy Lane & Derry Hill villages. Follow brown signs.* **Adm £6.50, chd free. For opening times and information, please phone or see garden website.**
This 60-acre woodland garden of azaleas and rhododendrons is one of the most exciting of its type in the country. From the individual flowers to the breathtaking sweep of colour formed by hundreds of shrubs, surrounded by carpets of bluebells, this is a garden not to be missed. Planting began in 1850 and some of the earliest known hybrids feature among the collection. The Rhododendron Walks are located 2m from Bowood House and Gardens.

9 BROADLEAS HOUSE GARDENS

Devizes SN10 5JQ. Mr & Mrs Cardiff. *1m S of Devizes. From Hartmoor Rd turn into Broadleas Park, follow rd for 350 metres then turn R into estate. PLEASE NOTE, NO ACCESS from A360 Potterne Rd.* **Adm £5, chd free.** Suns 14 Apr; 12 May; 16 June; 11 Aug (2-5.30).
6-acre garden, a sheltered dell planted with many unusual trees and shrubs. Azaleas, rhododendrons and magnolias. Herbaceous borders, perennial garden full of interesting plants and a new orchard and bee garden. Some of the paths in the dell are quite steep.

10 BROOMSGROVE LODGE
New Mill, Pewsey SN9 5LE. Diana Robertson, www.britainsfinest.co.uk. *2m E of Pewsey. From A345 take B3087 Burbage Rd, after 1½ m L to New Mill, through village & past canal. Park in field*. Home-made teas. **Adm £4, chd free. Sun 21 Apr; Sat 15 June (11.30-5).**
Alongside stunning views of Martinsell Hill discover the imaginatively planted herbaceous borders, in spring full of tulips and forget-me-nots. Large vegetable garden, greenhouse and tunnel. Sunken terrace full of vibrantly planted pots where tea is served and a 4-acre field to wander around, admire the views and enjoy a picnic.

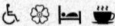

THE BUILDINGS
See Hampshire

11 CANTAX HOUSE
Lacock SN15 2JZ. Andrew & Deborah van der Beek, www.deborahvanderbeek.com. *3m S of Chippenham. Off A350 between Chippenham & Melksham. Please use signed public car park (except disabled). Entrance to garden in Cantax Hill*. Home-made teas. **Adm £4.50, chd free (share to Amnesty International). Sun 26 May (2-6).**
Queen Anne former vicarage (not open). Medium-sized garden of colour, pattern and scent straddling the Bide Brook. Designed and maintained by sculptor owner for 25yrs; both common and unusual plants including wildflower sports; hornbeam spire, yew castle and other topiary; old orchard wild garden; sculpture by owner and friends. Images by Lynn Keddie. Featured in many publications incl RHS The Garden.

12 CHISENBURY PRIORY
East Chisenbury SN9 6AQ. Mr & Mrs John Manser, john.manser@shaftesbury.co.uk. *3m SW of Pewsey. Turn E from A345 at Enford then N to E Chisenbury, main gates 1m on R*. Cream teas. **Adm £4, chd free. Sun 16 June (2-6.30). Visitors also welcome by appt.**
Medieval Priory with Queen Anne face and early C17 rear (not open) in middle of 5-acre garden on chalk. Mature garden with fine trees within clump and flint walls, herbaceous borders, shrubs, roses. Moisture-loving plants along mill leat, carp pond, orchard and wild garden, many unusual plants. Front borders redesigned in 2009 by Tom Stuart-Smith.

Designed with a painter's eye to provide riotous colour and sculptural form . . .

CONHOLT PARK
See Hampshire

13 ◆ CORSHAM COURT
Corsham SN13 0BZ. Mr James Methuen-Campbell, 01249 701610, www.corsham-court.co.uk. *4m W of Chippenham. Signed off A4 at Corsham*. **Adm £3, chd £1.50. For NGS: Sun 7 Apr; 19 May (2-5.30). For other opening times and information, please phone or see garden website.**
Park and gardens laid out by Capability Brown and Repton. Large lawns with fine specimens of ornamental trees surround the Elizabethan mansion. C18 bath house hidden in the grounds. Spring bulbs, beautiful lily pond with Indian bean trees, young arboretum and stunning collection of magnolias. Wheelchair (not motorised) access to house gravel paths in garden.

14 COTTAGE IN THE TREES
Tidworth Rd, Boscombe Village, nr Salisbury SP4 0AD. Karen & Richard Robertson, 01980 610921, robertson909@btinternet.com. *7m N of Salisbury. Turn L of A338 just before Social Club. Continue past church, turn R after bridge to Queen Manor, cottage 150yds on R*. Home-made teas. **Adm £2.50, chd free. Suns 17 Mar (11-4); 14 Apr; 12 May (1-4); Sat 15, Sun 16 June (2-5). Visitors also welcome by appt Mar to Aug.**
Enchanting ½ -acre cottage garden, immaculately planted with a water feature, raised vegetable patch, small wildlife pond and gravel garden. Spring bulbs, hellebores and pulmonarias give a welcome start to the season, with pots and baskets, roses and clematis. Mixed borders of herbaceous plants and shrubs giving all-yr interest. Featured in Salisbury Life.

COTTAGE ROW
See Dorset

15 ◆ THE COURTS
Holt, Trowbridge BA14 6RR. National Trust, 01225 782875, www.nationaltrust.org.uk. *2m E of Bradford-on-Avon. S of B3107 to Melksham. In Holt follow NT signs, park at village hall & at overflow car park when signed*. **Adm £7, chd £3.50. For NGS: Tues 11, 25 June (11-5). For other opening times and information, please phone or see garden website.**
Beautifully kept but eclectic garden. Yew hedges divide garden compartments with colour themed borders and organically shaped topiary. Water garden with 2 pools, temple, conservatory and small kitchen garden split by an apple allée, all surrounded by 3½ acres of arboretum with specimen trees. Wheelchair access map available.

16 CROFTON LOCK HOUSE
Crofton, Great Bedwyn, Marlborough SN8 3DW. Michael & Jenny Trussell. *1m W of Great Bedwyn. 4m W of Hungerford. Lock 62 on K&A canal towpath between Great Bedwyn & Crofton. Signs from A4 Marlborough - Hungerford at Great Bedwyn turning, & A338 Burbage - Hungerford at East Grafton. Limited parking. Garden 8-10 mins walk along towpath*. Home-made teas. **Adm £2.50, chd free. Sun 2, Sat 8 June; Sun 4 Aug (2-6).**
¾ -acre garden in idyllic setting around 200 yr old lock keeper's cottage. Garden comprises herbaceous beds designed with a painter's eye to provide riotous colour and sculptural form from spring to autumn, leading at rear into small orchard, collection of apple and soft fruit trees, raised-bed vegetables. Artists studio open. People welcome to draw and paint in the garden by appointment. Off grid house relying on sun and wind for electricity, own water supply. Selection of unusual plants for sale. Crofton steam pumping station and Wilton Windmill close by.

17 DANE BROOK
Milkhouse Water, Pewsey SN9 5JX. Mr & Mrs P Sharpe, www.danebrook.co.uk. *1m NE of Pewsey. From Pewsey take B3087 Burbage Rd. After approx 3/4 m turn L to Milkhouse Water. Dane Brook is 1st on R after railway bridge.* Home-made teas. Gluten free available. **Adm £3, chd free (share to Swift Medics). Sats & Suns 29, 30 June; 27, 28 July; 10, 11 Aug (12.30-5). Combined with Milkhouse Water Farm (June & July), combined adm £5, chd free.**
Approx one acre of gardens, incl herbaceous beds, shrubs, trees, semi formal garden, roses, oxbow pond with planted banks and thatched summer house. Tree lined river walk runs the length of the garden, leading to a shrubbery. Also lawns and paved areas with planted containers. Far reaching views from paddocks. Craft shop with handmade gifts and accessories, home-made sweets, jams, chutney, rare breed sheep and lambs, vintage tractor, horses. Featured in Wiltshire Life. Wheelchair accesible in dry weather with exception of pond and stream.

GROUP OPENING

18 DAUNTSEY GARDENS
Chippenham SN15 4HW. *5m SE of Malmesbury. Approach via Dauntsey Rd from Gt Somerford, 1 1/4 m from Volunteer Inn.* Home-made teas at Idover House. **Combined adm £5, chd free. Sun 16 June (1.30-5).**

THE COACH HOUSE
Col & Mrs J Seddon-Brown
Visitors also welcome by appt May to Aug. 01249 720972 g.seddonbrown@btinternet.com

DAUNTSEY PARK
Mr & Mrs Giovanni Amati

THE GARDEN COTTAGE
Miss Ann Sturgis

IDOVER HOUSE
Mr & Mrs Christopher Jerram

THE OLD POND HOUSE
Mr & Mrs Stephen Love

This group of 5 gardens, centred around the historic Dauntsey Park Estate, ranges from the Classical C18 country house setting of Dauntsey Park, with spacious lawns, old trees and views over the R Avon, to mature country house gardens and traditional walled gardens. Enjoy the formal rose garden in pink and white, old fashioned borders and duck ponds at Idover House, and the quiet seclusion of The Coach House with its thyme terrace and gazebos, climbing roses and clematis. Here, mop-headed pruned crataegus prunifolia line the drive. The Garden Cottage has a traditional walled kitchen garden with organic vegetables, apple orchard, woodland walk and yew topiary. Meanwhile the 2 acres at The Old Pond House are both clipped and unclipped! Large pond with lilies and fat carp, and look out for the giraffe and turtle.

GROUP OPENING

19 NEW DURRINGTON VILLAGE GARDENS
Durrington, Salisbury SP4 8AQ. *10m N of Salisbury. Turn off A303 N onto A345, after approx 2m turn R at sign to village centre.* **Combined adm £5, chd free. Sun 16, Wed 19 June (1-5). Also Opening Cottage in the Trees (16 June).**

NEW TRANTOR HOUSE
Mrs Jane Turner

NEW WEST END MANOR
Mrs Pippa Cranston

2 gardens in an historic village which has neolithic origins, 2m NE of Stonehenge and close to the R Avon. West End Manor is a 1 1/4 acre walled garden rising gently westward from a C18 farmhouse. Lavender surrounds white roses. Mixed borders, loosely colour themed, surround lawns. Water burbles gently into a small raised pond in the south garden. Orchard, coppice, vegetable and soft fruit garden. Currently the old vegetable garden is being redesigned for easy maintenance. Trantor House is an oak framed house on country lane surrounded by approx 2/3 acre of both formal and informal garden. Attractive mixed and herbaceous colour themed borders, rose garden, wildlife pond and stream. Summer house, raised vegetable beds and new wildflower meadow. Chickens, sloping garden with steps. Plant stall incl large variety of perennial geraniums. Some grassy slopes.

DYRHAM PARK
See Somerset, Bristol & South Gloucestershire

Large pond with lilies and fat carp, and look out for the giraffe and turtle . . .

GROUP OPENING

20 NEW EASTON ROYAL GARDENS
Pewsey SN9 5LY. *4m E of Pewsey, 1m W of Burbage. From Pewsey take B3087 for Burbage for 4m to Easton Royal. From Burbage r'about on A338 take B3087 for 1m to village Xrds. Park in playing field at Xrds. All gardens within easy walking distance, maps provided.* Home-made teas at Copes Cottage. **Combined adm £5, chd free. Sun 14 July (2-6).**

NEW CHAPEL COTTAGE
Tricia & Allan Duncan

NEW COPES COTTAGE
Sarah Townsend-Rose & Colin Sibun

NEW EASTON GRANGE
Mr & Mrs Jane & Robert Hector

3 contrasting gardens to enjoy in this historic conservation village. Easton Grange has been cleverly designed by its owners in the last 5 yrs and shows what can be achieved in a modern house small garden. A plantswoman's garden, packed with many interesting flowers, shrubs and trees. Chapel Cottage has colourful wide borders, vegetables, mature trees and distant views. Copes Cottage has a delightful cottage garden with a stunning gravel garden, mixed borders, vegetables, meadow and distant views. The soil in the gardens is greensand, two of the gardens are exposed to the winds. Copes Cottage has limited wheelchair access.

GROUP OPENING

21 EDINGTON GARDENS

Edington, nr Westbury BA13 4QF. *4m NE of Westbury. On B3098 between Westbury & West Lavington. Park off B3098 in church car park, or car park nr B3098 & Monastery Rd junction, or iTinhead Rd for Becketts House. Overflow parking on verge in Monastery Rd beyond church. Village minibus available to take visitors from church car park to Becketts Hse. Gardens map provided.* Home-made teas in Parish Hall (nr The Old Vicarage). **Combined adm £4, chd free.** **Sun 12 May (2-6).**

BECKETTS HOUSE
Mr & Mrs David Bromhead

THE OLD VICARAGE NCH
Mr J N d'Arcy

2 varied gardens on greensand, both with lovely views, are open in this historic village. Both are large gardens with fine views, full of colour, interest and ideas. Among the highlights are an arboretum with a growing range of unusual trees and an avenue of fastigiate hornbeams, herbaceous borders, gravel garden, wide range of interesting bulbs, magnolias, roses, fruit and vegetables - and even some long-established Japanese knotweed. The Old Vicarage is home to a National Collection of evening primroses, with over 20 species. Grade I C14 church open.

NCH

22 FONTHILL HOUSE

nr Tisbury SP3 5SA. The Lord Margadale of Islay, www.fonthill.co.uk/gardens. *13m W of Salisbury. Via B3089 in Fonthill Bishop. 3m N of Tisbury.* Home-made teas. **Adm £6, chd free.** **Sun 24 Mar (2-6).**
Large woodland garden. Daffodils, rhododendrons, azaleas, shrubs, bulbs; magnificent views; formal garden. Limited wheelchair access.

FRITHAM LODGE
See Hampshire

GANTS MILL & GARDEN
See Somerset, Bristol & South Gloucestershire

GILBERTS NURSERY
See Hampshire

GROUP OPENING

23 GREAT SOMERFORD GARDENS

Chippenham SN15 5JB. *4m SE of Malmesbury. 4m N of M4 between J16 & J17; 2m S of B4042 Malmesbury to Royal Wootton Bassett Rd; 3m E of A429 Cirencester to Chippenham Rd. Cross river bridge in Great Somerford, parking opposite The Mount & additional parking on Dauntsey Rd opp allotments.* Home-made teas at The Mount. **Combined adm £5, chd free (share to Great Ormond Street Hospital Children's Charity Reg. No 235825).** **Sat 22, Sun 23 June (1.30-5).**

CLEMATIS
Arthur & Iris Scott

GREAT SOMERFORD'S FREE GARDENS & ALLOTMENTS
In trust to Great Somerford Parish Council

THE MOUNT
Mr & Mrs McGrath

THE OLD POLICE HOUSE
Diane Hunt

SOMERFORD HOUSE
Mr & Mrs Hyde

Great Somerford is a medium-sized village, with a lovely walk by R Avon. Maintained by very active gardeners, two well-established 3-acre gardens and two charming smaller ones with Gt Somerford's Free Gardens and Allotments. Endowed in 1809 by the village rector, these are thought to be the oldest continuously cultivated allotments in the country. The gardens offer a wide range of interest. Clematis, although small, has perennials, a collection of approx 20 clematis, herbaceous borders, shrubs and a pond. At The Mount 2 acres of lawns, herbaceous beds, shrubs, nuttery, large trees, fruit and vegetables and a recently created natural swimming pond. An adjacent historic house is open for viewing. Somerford House, developed over 30yrs, features roses, shrubs, old wisteria, perennials, rockery and pool, vegetables and soft fruit. The Old Police House is a 15yr old re-established 1/4 acre garden with herbaceous borders, perennials, shrubs, cottage garden plants, pergola and pond. Gardening with a smile. Limited wheelchair access.

24 NEW HAMPTWORTH ESTATE

Landford, Hamptworth, Salisbury SP5 2DR. Mr & Mrs Donald Anderson, www.hamptworthestate.co.uk. *10m S of Salisbury. Leave M3 at J2 and head N on A36 towards Salisbury. Through villages of Wellow & Plaitford (approx 4 m). Past Golden Acres garden centre on L, take next turn L signed to Hamptworth. After 1/2 m turn R into Hamptworth Rd. Continue past Hamptworth Golf Club & Hamptworth Lodge on L after 1m.* **Adm £4, chd free.** **Sun 9 June (10-4).**
Originally dating from early C17 but research indicates there could have been a garden on this site in the early C12. With the construction of a late Georgian house in early C19, a garden layout very similar to that of today was almost certainly put in place at the same time. Features incl an archery lawn, sunken pond, summer houses and beautiful terracing.

Housekeeper's cream teas and home made cakes . . . !

25 HAZELBURY MANOR GARDENS

Wadswick, Box SN13 8HX. Mr L Lacroix. *5m SW of Chippenham, 5m NE of Bath. From A4 at Box, A365 to Melksham, at Five Ways junction L onto B3109 toward Corsham, 1st L at top of hill, drive immed on R.* Home-made teas. **Adm £5, chd free.** **Sun 9 June (2-5.30).**
8 Acres of Grade II landscaped organic gardens around C15 fortified manor (not open). Edwardian garden with yew hedges and topiary, beech stilt hedges, laburnum tunnel and pleached lime avenue. A large variety of plants, shrubs fill 5000 sq metres of planting, many herbal and native species. Productive vegetable gardens, orchards and a circle of megaliths. Wildflower drive from butterfly rich common.

HIDEAWAY
See Hampshire

HILLTOP
See Dorset

GROUP OPENING

26 HILMARTON GROUP GARDENS

Church Road, Hilmarton, Calne SN11 8SE. *On A3102 between Calne and Lyneham. Turn of A3102, opp The Duke PH, into village, follow signs to car park. Directions to gardens will be provided.* Home-made teas at Hilmarton Community Room. **Combined adm £5, chd free. Sat 15, Sun 16 June (1-5).**

HAMLYN HOUSE
Mr & Mrs John & Brenda Reeves

10 POYNDER PLACE
Mrs Marion Jeary

WEAVERS
Sheron & Mel Wilkins

3 gardens with their own individual charm. An interesting tiered garden, previous winner of the SW 'HTV Garden of the Year' competition. An informal family garden with established tree, shrubs and herbaceous borders, a fun garden to visit. A cottage garden set out with different 'rooms' and lawns linked by a leafy pergola. WC incl disabled. Gravel drive at 10 Poynder Place and Weavers. No wheelchair access to Hamlyn House.

27 HILPERTON HOUSE

The Knap, Hilperton, Trowbridge BA14 7RJ. Mr & Mrs Chris Brown. *1½ m NE of Trowbridge. Follow A361 towards Trowbridge and turn R at r'about signed Hilperton. House is next door to St Michael's Church in the Knapp off Church St.* Cream teas and home-made cakes. **Adm £4, chd free. Sun 23 June (2-6).**

2½ acres well stocked borders, small stream leading to large pond with fish, water lilies, waterfall and fountain. Fine mature trees incl unusual specimens. Walled fruit and vegetable garden, small woodland area. Rose walk with roses and clematis, 160yr old vine in conservatory of Grade II listed house, circa 1705 (not open). Activity sheets for children. Some gravel and lawns. Conservatory not wheelchair accessible.

HOOKSHOUSE POTTERY
See Gloucestershire

28 NEW HORATIO'S GARDEN

Duke of Cornwall Spinal Treatment Centre, Salisbury Hospital NHS Foundation Trust, Odstock Road, Salisbury SP2 8BJ. Tina Crossley (Head Gardener). *Follow the hospital signs out of Salisbury & use entrance B (southern entrance) off main rd. Continue across 4 pedestrian crossings & use Car Park 10 at end of rd. Walking from car park turn R & continue down the hill. Horatio's Garden entrance is opp entrance to car park.* Home-made teas. **Adm £3, chd free (share to Horatio's Garden Friends). Sun 12 May, Sun 15 Sept (2-5).**

Horatio's Garden is a small garden which opened in September 2012 and was designed by Cleve West for patients with spinal cord injury at the Duke of Cornwall Spinal Treatment Centre, Salisbury. It was built from donations given in memory of Horatio Chapple who was a volunteer at the centre in his school holidays. Low limestone walls, which present the form of the spine divide the densely planted beds and double as seating. Everything in the garden has been designed to benefit patients during their long stays in hospital. The Garden is run by a Head Gardener and a team of volunteers, called Horatio's Garden Friends.

29 HYDE'S HOUSE
Dinton SP3 5HH. Mr George Cruddas. *9m W of Salisbury. Off B3089 nr Dinton Church on St Mary's Rd.* Home-made teas at Thatched Old School Room. **Adm £4.50, chd free. Sun 26 May (2-5).**
3 acres of wild and formal garden in beautiful situation with series of hedged garden rooms. Numerous shrubs, flowers and borders, all allowing tolerated wild flowers and preferred 'weeds'. Large walled kitchen garden, herb garden and C13th dovecote (open). Charming C16/18th Grade I listed house (not open), with lovely courtyard. Free walks around park and lake. Steps, slopes and gravel paths.

30 ◆ IFORD MANOR
Lower Westwood, Bradford-on-Avon BA15 2BA. Mrs Cartwright-Hignett, 01225 863146, www.ifordmanor.co.uk. *7m S of Bath. Off A36, brown tourist sign to Iford 1m. Or from Bradford-on-Avon or Trowbridge via Lower Westwood village (brown signs).* **Adm £5, chd £4.50. For NGS: Sun 28 Apr (2-5). For other opening times and information, please phone or see garden website.**
Very romantic award-winning, Grade I listed Italianate garden famous for its tranquil beauty. Home to the Edwardian architect and designer Harold Peto 1899-1933. The garden is characterised by steps, terraces, sculpture and magnificent rural views. (House not open.). Housekeeper's cream teas and home made cakes. Featured in The English Garden magazine. Please see website for wheelchair access details.

INHOLMES
See Berkshire

31 JOB'S MILL
Five Ash Lane, Crockerton BA12 8BB. Lady Silvy McQuiston. *1½ m S of Warminster. Down lane E of A350, S of A36 r'about.* Home-made teas. **Adm £3.50, chd free. Sats 27 Apr (2-5); 15 June (2-6).**
Surrounding an old converted water mill, a delightful medium-sized terraced garden through which R Wylye flows. Riverside and woodland walks, vegetable garden, orchard, herbaceous border and water garden.

Everything in the garden has been designed to benefit patients during their long stays in hospital . . .

32 10 KINGSBURY STREET
Marlborough SN8 1HU. Tom & Jill Otley, 01672 516506, tomotley@btinternet.com. *100yds from Marlborough Town Hall. From E end of Marlborough High St, go to L of the Town Hall & proceed up Kingsbury St. No 10 is on the L, facing down the hill. No parking on site.* Home-made teas. **Adm £3.50, chd free. Sun 16 June (2-5). Visitors also welcome by appt May to Aug.**
A town garden of approx ½ acre, entirely walled, terraces, beds, lawns, water, other decorative features; large pergola, C18 summer house and kitchen garden. N.B lots of steps - no handrails. The design packs a lot into a small space and shows what can be done to make the most of a site on a hill.

KINGSTON BAGPUIZE HOUSE
See Oxfordshire

33 ◆ LACOCK ABBEY GARDENS
Chippenham SN15 2LG. National Trust, 01249 730459, www.nationaltrust.org.uk. *3m S of Chippenham. Off A350. Follow NT signs. Use public car park just outside Abbey.* **Adm £5, chd £2.50. For NGS: Sats & Suns 9, 10, 16, 17 Feb (11-4); 8, 9, 15, 16 Feb 2014. For other opening times and information, please phone or see garden website.**
Woodland garden with carpets of aconites, snowdrops, crocuses and daffodils. Botanic garden with greenhouse, mediaeval cloisters and magnificent trees. Mostly level site, some gravel paths.

34 130 LADYFIELD ROAD
Ladyfield Road, Chippenham SN14 0AP. Philip & Pat Canter and Chippenham Town Council. *1m SW of Chippenham. Between A4 Bath and A420 Bristol rds. Signed off B4528 Hungerdown Lane which runs between the A4 & A420.* Home-made teas. **Adm £3, chd free. Sun 4 Aug (1.30-5.30).**
Very pretty small garden with more than 30 clematis, climbing roses and a small fish pond. Curved neat edges packed with colourful herbaceous plants and small trees. 2 patio areas with lush lawn, pagoda and garden arbour. Next to garden are allotments with 15 gardens owned by Chippenham Town Council. Garden of the week in Weekly Garden News and featured in Amateur Gardening. Wheelchair access to allotments on main drive way only.

35 LITTLE DURNFORD MANOR
Salisbury SP4 6AH. The Earl & Countess of Chichester. *3m N of Salisbury. Just beyond Stratford-sub-Castle.* Home-made teas. **Adm £3.50, chd £1. Sun 21 Apr; Sun 9 June (2-6).**
Extensive lawns with cedars, walled gardens, fruit trees, large vegetable garden, small knot and herb gardens. Terraces, borders, sunken garden, water garden, lake with islands, river walks, labyrinth walk. Gravel paths, some narrow. Steep slope and some steps.

LITTLECOTE HOUSE HOTEL
See Berkshire

36 ◆ LYDIARD PARK WALLED GARDEN
Lydiard Tregoze, Swindon SN5 3PA. Swindon Borough Council, 01793 770401, www.lydiardpark.org.uk. *3m W Swindon, 1m from J16 M4. Follow brown signs from W Swindon.* **Adm £2.50, chd £1. For NGS: Sun 28 July (11-5). For other opening times and information, please phone or see garden website.**
Beautiful ornamental C18 walled garden. Trimmed shrubs alternating with individually planted flowers and bulbs incl rare daffodils and tulips, sweet peas, annuals and wall-trained fruit trees. Park and children's playground. Unique features including well and sundial. Park Cafe open.

37 MANOR FARM
Huish, Marlborough SN8 4JN. Mr & Mrs J Roberts. *3m NW of Pewsey. Huish is signed from A345 by White Hart PH in Oare. Follow lane for 1m into Huish, turn R immed after row of thatched cottages on L.* Home-made teas. **Adm £3, chd free. Sat 15, Sun 16 June (2-5).**
A stunning setting of sweeping downland has influenced the design of this intriguing and extensive garden. Varied planting gives yr-round interest and there are both modern and tradional areas. The garden features a pleached lime walk, gravel garden, woodland pond, herbaceous borders together with many species of clematis and rose. Some paths too narrow for wheelchairs.

38 MANOR HOUSE
Stratford Tony, Salisbury SP5 4AT. Mr & Mrs Hugh Cookson, 01722 718496, lucindacookson@stratfordtony.co.uk, www.stratfordtony.co.uk. *4m SW of Salisbury. Take minor rd W off A354 at Coombe Bissett. Garden on S after 1m. Or from Wilton turn R off A3094 past Salisbury racecourse. Turn L at Xrds and follow signs.* Home-made teas. **Adm £4, chd free. Fri 14 June (4-7); Sat 15 June, Wed 11 Sept (2-5). Visitors also welcome by appt. Please telephone or see garden website.**
Varied 4-acre garden with all yr interest. Formal and informal areas. Small lake fed from R Ebble, waterside planting, herbaceous borders with colour from spring to late autumn. Pergola-covered vegetable garden, formal parterre garden, orchard, shrubberies, roses, specimen trees, winter colour and structure, many original contemporary features and places to sit and enjoy the downland views. Featured in Wiltshire Magazine. Some gravel.

MARSHFIELD GARDENS
See Somerset, Bristol & South Gloucestershire

Birdsong is phenomenal in spring and summer . . .

39 MILKHOUSE WATER FARM
Milkhouse Water, Pewsey SN9 5JX. Mrs S Glover. *From Pewsey take B3087 Burbage rd. After about ¾ m turn L to Milkhouse Water. Garden 2nd house on R.* Home-made teas at Dane Brook.
Combined adm £5, chd free (share to Swift Medics). Sats & Suns 29, 30 June; 27, 28 July (12.30-5). Combined with Dane Brook.
A beautiful cottage garden incl a natural pond area, bluebell wood, parterre formal box garden and paddocks with alpacas. The terraced area around the cottage displays wisteria, vines, clematis and many beautiful roses. There is a small vegetable and fruit garden, home to our hens. Each area has seating to enjoy the gardens. There will be wool, crafts from the wool and eggs for sale.

40 ◆ THE MILL HOUSE
Berwick St James, Salisbury SP3 4TS. Diana Gifford Mead, 01722 790331, www.millhouse.org.uk. *8m NW of Salisbury. S of A303, N of A36, on B3083, S end of village.* **Adm £3.50, chd free. For NGS: Sun 31 Mar; Sun 30 June (2-6). For other opening times and information, please phone or see garden website.**
Surrounded by the R Till, millstream and a 10-acre traditional wet water meadow, this garden of wildness supports over 300 species of old fashioned roses rambling from the many trees. It is filled with butterflies, moths and insects. Birdsong is phenomenal in spring and summer. Herbaceous borders crammed with plants of yesteryear, unforgettable scents. Glorious spring bulbs. SSSI. Open all yr-round.

41 ◆ MOMPESSON HOUSE
The Close, Salisbury SP1 2EL. National Trust, 01722 335659, www.nationaltrust.org.uk. *Enter Cathedral Close via High St Gate, Mompesson House on R.* **Adm £1, chd free. For NGS: Fri 17 May (11-4.30). For other opening times and information, please phone or see garden website.**
The appeal of this comparatively small but attractive garden is the lovely setting in Salisbury Cathedral Close, with a well-known Queen Anne house (not open). Planting as for an old English garden with raised rose and herbaceous beds around the lawn. Climbers on pergola and walls, shrubs and small lavender walk. Cake stall.

42 NORTH COTTAGE & WOODVIEW COTTAGE
Tisbury Row, Tisbury SP3 6RZ. Jacqueline & Robert Baker, Diane McBride, 01747 870019, robert.baker@pearceseeds.co.uk. *12m W of Salisbury. From A30 turn N through Ansty, L at T-junction, towards Tisbury. From Tisbury take Ansty rd. Entrance nr junction signed Tisbury Row.* Home-made teas & lunches. **Combined adm £3, chd free. Sun 2, Sun 9 June (11-5). Visitors also welcome by appt May to Aug.**
Two cottage gardens side by side tucked away in a beautiful corner of S Wiltshire. Many corners to explore and secret hideaways to reveal. Pottery and sculpture to find which enhance the garden and orchard. Herbaceous borders, fruit trees, ponds, vegetable garden, wildflowers, and smallholding with sheep, poultry and cattle. And, most importantly, glorious home-made lunches and teas. Pottery and handicrafts all made by garden owners. Ceramics featured in and part of the Wylye Valley Arts Trail.

43 OARE HOUSE

Rudge Lane, Oare, Nr Pewsey SN8 4JQ. Sir Henry Keswick. *2m N of Pewsey. On Marlborough Rd (A345).* Home-made teas. **Adm £4, chd free (share to The Order of St John). Sun 28 Apr; Sun 30 June (10-5).**

Fine house (not open) in large garden with large trees, hedges, spring flowers, woodlands, extensive lawns and kitchen garden. Limited wheelchair access.

44 THE OLD MILL

Ramsbury SN8 2PN. Annabel & James Dallas. *8m NE of Marlborough. From Marlborough head to Ramsbury. At The Bell PH follow sign to Hungerford. Garden behind yew hedge on R 100yds beyond The Bell.* Home-made teas. **Adm £4, chd free. Sat 15, Sun 16 June; Sun 11 Aug (2-6).**

Water running through multitude of channels no longer drives the mill but provides backdrop for whimsical garden of pollarded limes, colour themed borders and naturalistic planting. Paths meander by streams and over small bridges. Vistas give dramatic views of downs beyond. New kitchen/herb garden and cutting bed give added interest.

THE OLD RECTORY, DOYNTON

See Somerset, Bristol & South Gloucestershire

45 THE OLD VICARAGE

Hilmarton, Swindon Road, Hilmarton SN11 8SB. Lesley & George Hudson, 07802 741293, lesleyhudson@outlook.com. *4m S of Royal Wootton Bassett on A3102 between Lynham & Calne. On main rd next to the Duke PH. Park signed to Paddock behind house.* Home-made teas. **Adm £3.50, chd free. Sun 9, Wed 12 June (12-5). Visitors also welcome by appt Apr to Sept, wine available on request for evening visits.**

7-acre plot incl a Victorian walled garden, ornamental pond, wisteria-covered pergola, blue and white herbaceous border, Italianate secret garden, woodland garden, colourful herbaceous borders flanked by lawns and a herb garden. Adjacent to the formal garden are two paddocks incorporating a wildflower meadow (in June), orchard and kitchen garden. Featured in Wiltshire magazine & WI Life. Limited wheelchair access, some gravel paths.

ORDNANCE HOUSE

See Hampshire

46 THE POUND HOUSE

Little Somerford SN15 5JW. Mr & Mrs Michael Baines, 01666 823212, squeezebaines@yahoo.com. *2m E of Malmesbury on B4024. In village turn S, leave church on R. Car park on R before railway bridge.* Home-made teas. **Adm £3.50, chd free. Sun 30 June (2-5.30). Visitors also welcome by appt May to Sept.**

Large well planted garden surrounding former rectory attached to C17 house. Mature trees, hedges and spacious lawns. Well-stocked herbaceous borders, roses, shrubs, pergola, parterre, swimming pool garden, water, ducks, chickens, alpacas and horses. Raised vegetable garden and lots of places to sit!

Chisenbury Priory

PRIOR PARK LANDSCAPE GARDEN
See Somerset, Bristol & South Gloucestershire

47 PRIORY HOUSE
Market Street, Bradford-on-Avon BA15 1LH. Mr & Mrs Tim Woodall, trwwoodall@yahoo.com. *Town centre. Park in town centre. Take A363 signed Bath up Market St. House 500yds.* Home-made teas. **Adm £3, chd free. Suns 21 Apr; 4 Aug (2-5.30). Visitors also welcome by appt Apr to Aug.**
3/4 -acre town garden, mostly formal. Spring garden of narcissi, tulips and hellebores. Late summer borders of herbaceous plants, grasses and hydrangeas. Knot garden in front of part Georgian house is an interpretation of the sash windows. Steep slopes and steps at bottom of garden.

48 RIDLEYS CHEER
Mountain Bower SN14 7AJ. Mr & Mrs A J Young, www.ridleyscheer.co.uk. *9m WNW of Chippenham. At The Shoe, on A420 8m W of Chippenham, turn N then take 2nd L & 1st R.* Cream teas. **Adm £4, chd free. Sun 12 May (2-5).**
Largely informal garden; mixed borders, lawns, interesting collection of shrubs and trees incl acers, magnolias, liriodendrons, tree peonies, deutzias, daphnes, oaks, beech, birch and hollies. Some 130 rose varieties; old-fashioned and modern shrub roses, and magnificent tree ramblers. Potager, miniature box garden, arboretum, 3-acre wild flower meadow, plus new 1/2 -acre meadow. Dew pond.

49 RIVER BARN
Cowbridge Farm, Swindon Road, Malmesbury SN16 9LZ. Finn and Nicki Spicer, 01666 825670, nickiwhite18@yahoo.co.uk, www.riverbarn.org.uk. *1m SE of Malmesbury. From the Malmesbury r'about take the Wooton Bassett Rd (B4042) for 1km. Turn L towards Cowbridge Mill, signed visitors car park. Follow signs to open garden.* Home-made teas. **Adm £4, chd free. Suns 26 May; 16 June (11-5.30). Visitors also welcome by appt May to June.**
3 acre garden in a sublime river setting as part of former model farm. Planting commenced in 2007 to create an arboretum with wild flower areas and wildlife pond. Walled courtyard garden with koi pond, rose pergola, mosaics and rich planting. Formal terraced lawn overlooking Avon. Pigmy pinetum. Stone circle. Fruit and vegetable garden. Dragonflies breeding in wildlife pond. Wildflower areas teeming with butterflies, moths, honey bees, solitary bees and bumblebees. R Avon with swans, ducks, moorhens, dabchicks, kingfishers.

ROOKSNEST
See Berkshire

Wildflower areas teeming with butterflies, moths, honey bees, solitary bees and bumblebees . . .

50 SHARCOTT MANOR
Pewsey SN9 5PA. Captain & Mrs D Armytage, 01672 563485. *1m SW of Pewsey. Via A345 from Pewsey towards Salisbury. Turn R signed Sharcott at grass triangle. 400yds up lane, garden on L over cattle-grid.* Home-made teas. **Adm £4, chd free. Weds 3 July; 7 Aug; 4 Sept (11-5); Sun 15 Sept (2-6). Visitors also welcome by appointment 1 June - 15 Sept.**
6-acre plantsman's garden on greensand, planted for yr-round interest. Wide range of trees and shrubs, densely planted mixed borders with many unusual plants and climbers. Magnificent tree ramblers. Woodland walk carpeted with spring bulbs around 1/2 -acre lake. Good autumn colour. Small vegetable garden, ornamental water fowl. Gravel and narrow grass paths, grass slope.

51 ◆ SHELDON MANOR
Chippenham SN14 0RG. Kenneth & Caroline Hawkins, 01249 653120, www.sheldonmanor.co.uk. *1 1/2 m W of Chippenham. Take A420 W. 1st L by the Allington Farm Shop, signed Chippenham RFC, entrance approx 1/2 m on R.* **For NGS: Wed 22 May (2-4). For other opening times and information, please phone or see garden website.**
Wiltshire's oldest inhabited manor house with C13 porch and C15 chapel. Gardens with ancient yews, mulberry tree and profusion of old-fashioned roses blooming in May and June. New this yr - an opportunity to have a private tour of Sheldon Manor and it's historical gardens. Enjoy lunch or afternoon tea. £22.50 per head (incl a £2.50 donation to NGS). House open, £3.50 per person.

STOCKBRIDGE GARDENS
See Hampshire

52 ◆ STOURHEAD GARDEN
Stourton, Warminster BA12 6QD. National Trust, 01747 841152, www.nationaltrust.org.uk. *3m NW of Mere on B3092. Follow NT signs, The property is very well signed from all main rds incl A303.* **Adm £7.70, chd £4.20. For NGS: Sat 4 May (9-7). For other opening times and information, please phone or see garden website.**
One of the earliest and greatest landscape gardens in the world, creation of banker Henry Hoare in 1740s on his return from the Grand Tour, inspired by paintings of Claude and Poussin. Planted with rare trees, rhododendrons and azaleas over last 250yrs. Wheelchaire accessable and buggy available.

53 SWEET BRIAR COTTAGE
19 Gladstone Road, Chippenham, Wiltshire SN15 3BW. Paul & Joy Gough, 01249 656005, paulgough@btopenworld.com. *Chippenham Town Centre. In town centre, turn off A4 Ave La Fleche into Gladstone Rd. Park in Borough Parade car parks. Garden just above car park opp Angel Hotel.* Home-made teas. **Adm £3, chd free. Sun 28 July (1.30-5.30). Visitors also welcome by appt Apr to Oct.**
Nearly an acre of walled garden restored in 2006, visitors are still amazed that such a large garden can exist within a town centre location. Low box-edged herbaceous borders planted to encourage wildlife. Slate paths. Vegetables grown organically in 4ft beds. Large collection of roses, ornamental and fruit trees. Featured in Gardeners World Magazine, Wiltshire Wildlife Trust Golden Gardens and local press.

54 ◆ TWIGS COMMUNITY GARDEN

Manor Garden Centre, Cheney Manor Industrial Estate, Swindon SN2 2QJ. RF TWIGS, 01793 523294, www.richmondfellowship.org.uk/twigs. *From Great Western Way, travel under Bruce St bridges onto Rodbourne Rd. At next r'about take 1st L into Cheney Manor Industrial Estate. Proceed through estate, take 2nd exit on next r'about. Opp Pitch & Putt course. Take signs on R to Manor Garden Centre.* **Adm £3, chd free. For NGS: Sun 26 May; Sun 21 July (1-5). For other opening times and information, please phone or see garden website.**

Twigs is a delightful 2-acre community garden, created and maintained by volunteers. Features incl seven individual display gardens, ornamental pond, plant nursery, Iron Age round house, artwork, fitness trail, separate 1-acre organic allotment site, Swindon beekeepers and the haven, overflowing with wild flowers. Live folk music on patio. Willow working activity. Featured on Great British Gardens. Most areas wheelchair accessible. Disabled WC.

55 ◆ WATERDALE HOUSE

East Knoyle SP3 6BL. Mr & Mrs Julian Seymour, 01747 830262. *8m S of Warminster. N of East Knoyle, garden signed from A350. DO NOT use Sat Nav.* **Adm £4, chd free. For NGS: Sun 5 May (2-6). For other opening times and information, please phone.**

4-acre mature woodland garden with rhododendrons, azaleas, camellias, maples, magnolias, ornamental water, bog garden, herbaceous borders. Bluebell walk. New shrub border created by storm damage mixed with agapanthus and half hardy salvias. Limited wheelchair access.

56 WELLAWAY

Close Lane, Marston SN10 5SN. Mr & Mrs P Lewis. *5m SW of Devizes. From A360, Devizes to Salisbury, R in Potterne. Through Worton. L at end of village signed to Marston, Close Lane ½ m on L.* Home-made teas. **Adm £4, chd free. Sun 14 Apr; Sun 15 Sept (2-6).**

2-acre flower arranger's garden comprising herbaceous borders, orchard, vegetable garden, ornamental and wildlife ponds, lawns and naturalised areas. Planted since 1979 for yr-round interest. Shrubberies and rose garden, other areas underplanted with bulbs or ground cover. Springtime particularly colourful with daffodils, tulips and hellebores.

57 WEST LAVINGTON MANOR

1 Church Street, West Lavington SN10 4LA. Mr & Mrs Andrew Doman, andrewdoman01@gmail.com. *6m S of Devizes, on A360. House opp White St, where parking available.* Home-made teas. **Adm £6, chd free (share to West Lavington Youth Club). Sat 15 June (12-6). Visitors also welcome by appt.**

A 5-acre walled garden first established in C17 by John Danvers who brought Italianate gardens to the UK. Variety of formal and informal areas incl herbaceous border, Japanese garden, rose garden, orchard and arboretum with some outstanding specimen trees all centred around a trout stream and duck pond. Colour gardens, cutting garden are formal courtyard established 2010 are developing well. Featured in Wiltshire Magazine - A Garden of Moods.

WESTONBIRT SCHOOL GARDENS

See Gloucestershire

58 WHATLEY MANOR

Easton Grey SN16 0RB. Christian Landolt & Alix Landolt, www.whatleymanor.com. *4m W of Malmesbury. From A429 at Malmesbury take B4040 signed Sherston. Manor 2m on L.* **Adm £4.50, chd free. Sun 30 June (2-5).**

12 acres of English country gardens with 26 distinct rooms each with a strong theme based on colour, scent or style. Original 1920s plan inspired the design and combines classic style with more contemporary touches. Specially commissioned sculptures.

WINCOMBE PARK

See Dorset

59 WINDMILL COTTAGE

Kings Road, Market Lavington SN10 4QB. Rupert & Gill Wade, 01380 813527. *5m S of Devizes. Turn E off A360 1m N of West Lavington, 2m S of Potterne. At top of hill turn L into Kings Rd, L into Windmill Lane after 200yds. Limited parking.* Home-made teas. **Adm £3, chd free. Fris 26 Apr; 24 May; 7, 21 June; 5, 19 July (2-5). Visitors also welcome by appt May to July.**

1-acre cottage-style, wild-life friendly garden on greensand. Mixed beds and borders with long season of interest. Roses on pagoda, large vegetable patch for kitchen and exhibition at local shows, polytunnel and greenhouse. Whole garden virtually pesticide free for last 15yrs. Small bog garden by wildlife pond. Secret glade with prairie. Some second-hand materials awaiting reuse. Featured in Amateur Gardening.

Springtime particularly colourful with daffodils, tulips and hellebores . . .

60 13 WOOLLEY GREEN

Woolley Green, Bradford-on Avon BA15 1TX. Mr A Dark & Mrs S Dark. *1½ m NE of Bradford-on-Avon. Just off B3105 at Woolley Green.* **Adm £2.50, chd free. Mon 27 May, Sun 2 June (2-6).**

C18 converted coach house with impressive gothic entrance arch in ⅔ acre of gardens. Cottage garden with mixed herbaceous borders, shrubs, roses, set around independent terraced lawns. Mature trees, paddock and free range chickens and ducks. Also studio barn and vegetable garden with half standard fruit trees. Exhibition of architectural drawings of Bradford-upon-Avon.

Little Durnford Manor

Wiltshire County Volunteers

County Organisers

Sean & Kena Magee, Byams House, Willesley, Tetbury GL8 8QU, 01666 880009, spbmagee@googlemail.com

Publicity/Booklet Coordinator

Tricia Duncan, Chapel Cottage, Easton Royal, Pewsey SN9 5RU, 01672 810443, tricia@windward.biz

Assistant County Organisers

Sarah Coate, Colts Corner, Upper Woodford, Salisbury SP4 6PA, 01722 782365
Jo Hankey, Mill Cottage, Burcombe, Wilton SP2 0EJ, 01722 742472, rbhankey@gmail.com
Shirley Heywood, Brook House, Kingston Deverill, Warminster BA12 7HF, 01985 844486
Diana Robertson, Broomsgrove Lodge, New Mill, nr Pewsey SN9 5LE, 01672 810515, diana@broomsgrovelodge.co.uk
Anne Shand, Ashton House, Worton, Devizes SN10 5RU, 01380 726249, anneshand@btinternet.com

WORCESTERSHIRE

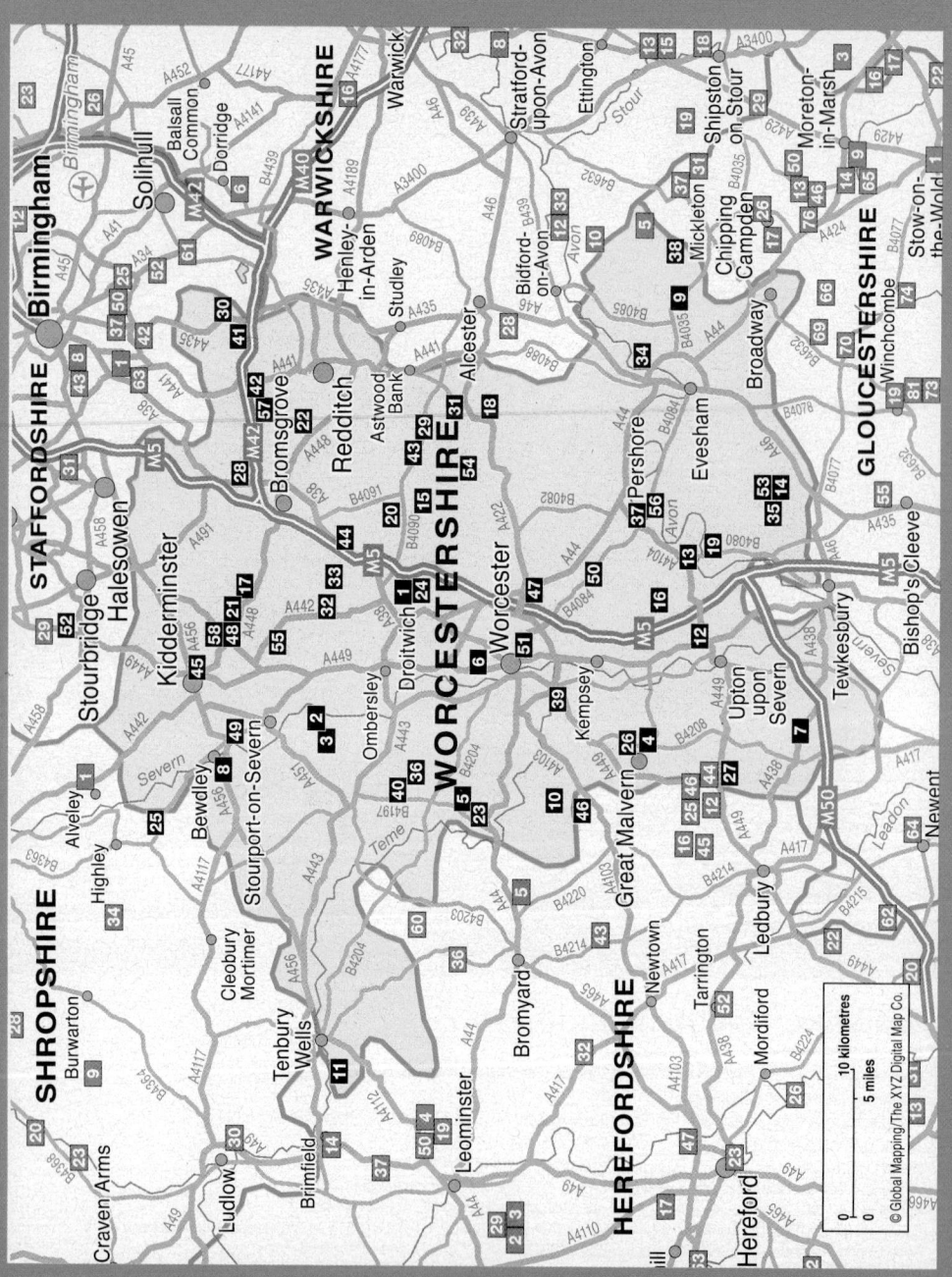

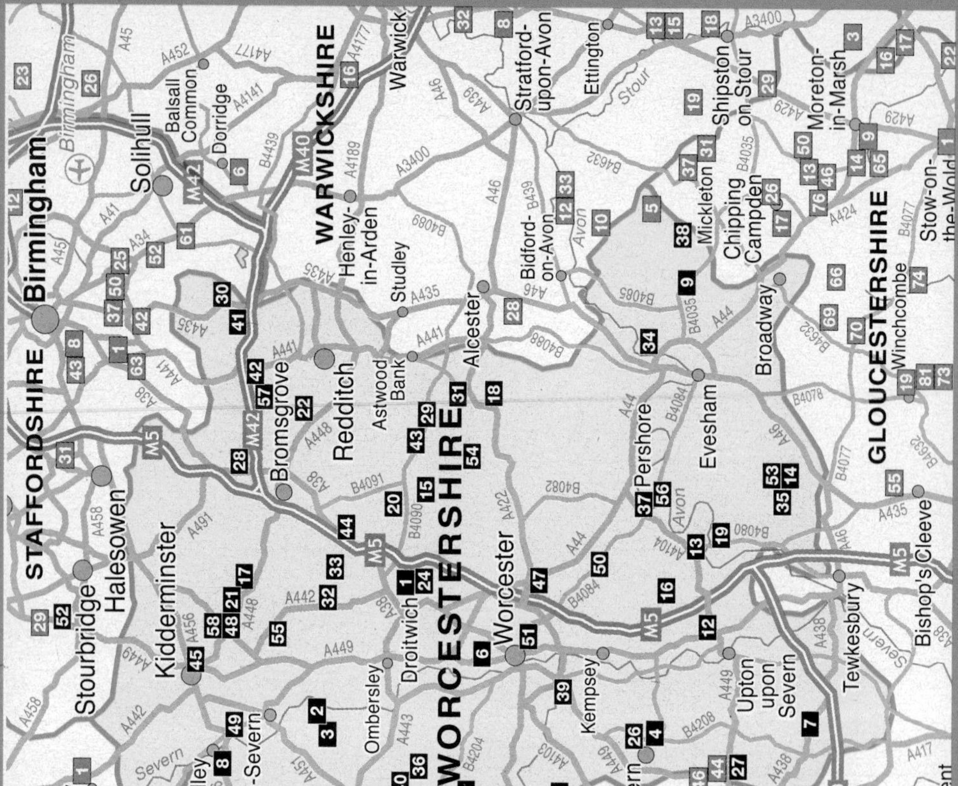

Opening Dates

February

Wednesday 20
17 Dial Park

March

Open every Thursday in March
43 Red House Farm

Sunday 3
40 1 Prickley Bungalows

Sunday 10
40 1 Prickley Bungalows

Sunday 17
27 Little Malvern Court
40 1 Prickley Bungalows

Sunday 24
40 1 Prickley Bungalows

Friday 29
47 Spetchley Park Gardens

Sunday 31
38 4 Poden Cottages
40 1 Prickley Bungalows

Many unusual trees and shrubs make this a garden to visit at all seasons . . .

April

Open every Thursday in April
43 Red House Farm

Monday 1
38 4 Poden Cottages

Saturday 6
12 Bylane
51 The Walled Garden
55 Whitlenge Gardens

Sunday 7
40 1 Prickley Bungalows
54 White Cottage
55 Whitlenge Gardens

Wednesday 10
51 The Walled Garden

Thursday 11
43 Red House Farm

Sunday 14
1 24 Alexander Avenue
15 The Cottage
40 1 Prickley Bungalows

Monday 15
15 The Cottage

Sunday 21
10 Bridges Stone Mill
40 1 Prickley Bungalows

Wednesday 24
16 Croome Park

Saturday 27
46 Shuttifield Cottage

Sunday 28
40 1 Prickley Bungalows

May

Open every Thursday in May
43 Red House Farm

Saturday 4
13 1 Church Cottage
46 Shuttifield Cottage

Sunday 5
13 1 Church Cottage
39 Pond House
40 1 Prickley Bungalows

Monday 6
13 1 Church Cottage
27 Little Malvern Court

Wednesday 8
24 Hiraeth

Saturday 11
33 New House Farm, Elmbridge
55 Whitlenge Gardens

Sunday 12
33 New House Farm, Elmbridge
40 1 Prickley Bungalows
55 Whitlenge Gardens

Saturday 18
22 Hewell Grange (by appointment only)
46 Shuttifield Cottage

Sunday 19
22 Hewell Grange (by appointment only)
40 1 Prickley Bungalows
49 Toll House Cottage

Thursday 23
6 5 Beckett Drive

Saturday 25
12 Bylane
26 22 Layton Avenue

Sunday 26
26 22 Layton Avenue
28 Marlbrook Gardens
40 1 Prickley Bungalows

June

Open every Thursday in June
43 Red House Farm

Saturday 1
5 The Barton
30 74 Meadow Road
55 Whitlenge Gardens

Sunday 2
5 The Barton
30 74 Meadow Road
55 Whitlenge Gardens

Saturday 8
36 Pear Tree Cottage
46 Shuttifield Cottage

Sunday 9
7 Birtsmorton Court
36 Pear Tree Cottage
42 Rectory Cottage

National Gardens Weekend

Saturday 15
1 24 Alexander Avenue
11 Brook Farm
12 Bylane
13 1 Church Cottage
24 Hiraeth
26 22 Layton Avenue
37 Pershore Gardens
38 4 Poden Cottages
51 The Walled Garden
54 White Cottage

Sunday 16
1 24 Alexander Avenue
11 Brook Farm
13 1 Church Cottage
24 Hiraeth
37 Pershore Gardens
38 4 Poden Cottages
54 White Cottage

Wednesday 19
51 The Walled Garden

Saturday 22
2 Astley Country Gardens
19 Eckington Gardens
32 New House Farm, Cutnall Green

Sunday 23
2 Astley Country Gardens
19 Eckington Gardens
32 New House Farm, Cutnall Green
58 The Woodlands

Sunday 30
6 5 Beckett Drive
18 6 Dingle End
56 Wick Village
57 Withybed Green

July

Open every Thursday in July
43 Red House Farm

Wednesday 3
24 Hiraeth

Saturday 6
12 Bylane
21 Harvington Hall
46 Shuttifield Cottage

Sunday 7
21 Harvington Hall
28 Marlbrook Gardens
38 4 Poden Cottages
45 The Shrubbery Nursing Home
47 Spetchley Park Gardens

Saturday 13
20 Hanbury Hall
32 New House Farm, Cutnall Green

Sunday 14
1 24 Alexander Avenue
20 Hanbury Hall
32 New House Farm, Cutnall Green
58 The Woodlands

Saturday 20
52 Westacres

Sunday 21
49 Toll House Cottage
52 Westacres

Wednesday 24
6 5 Beckett Drive (Evening)

Sunday 28
3 Astley Towne House
24 Hiraeth

August

Open every Thursday in August
43 Red House Farm

Saturday 3
34 Offenham Gardens
46 Shuttifield Cottage

Sunday 4
34 Offenham Gardens
39 Pond House
45 The Shrubbery Nursing Home

Wednesday 7
24 Hiraeth

Saturday 24
28 Marlbrook Gardens (Evening)
46 Shuttifield Cottage

Sunday 25
3 Astley Towne House
28 Marlbrook Gardens

Saturday 31
55 Whitlenge Gardens

September

Open every Thursday in September
43 Red House Farm

Sunday 1
45 The Shrubbery Nursing Home
55 Whitlenge Gardens

Saturday 7
12 Bylane
46 Shuttifield Cottage

Saturday 14
33 New House Farm, Elmbridge

Sunday 15
15 The Cottage
33 New House Farm, Elmbridge

Monday 16
15 The Cottage

Sunday 29
3 Astley Towne House
18 6 Dingle End

Gardens open to the public

16 Croome Park
20 Hanbury Hall
21 Harvington Hall
27 Little Malvern Court
43 Red House Farm
44 Riverside Gardens at Webbs
47 Spetchley Park Gardens
48 Stone House Cottage Gardens
55 Whitlenge Gardens

By appointment only

4 Barnard's Green House
8 Bowcastle Farm
9 Bretforton Manor
14 Conderton Manor
22 Hewell Grange
23 High View
25 Hunters End
29 Meadow Farm
31 Morton Hall
35 Overbury Court
41 Pump Cottage
50 The Tynings
53 Whitcombe House

A walk through this long, narrow garden . . . a recent visitor describing it as 'a magical mystery tour' . . .

Also open by Appointment ☎

1 24 Alexander Avenue
6 5 Beckett Drive
11 Brook Farm
12 Bylane
13 1 Church Cottage
15 The Cottage
17 Dial Park
19 Mantoft, Eckington Gardens
24 Hiraeth
28 Marlbrook Gardens
28 Oak Tree House, Marlbrook Gardens
28 Round Hill Garden, Marlbrook Gardens
28 Saranacris, Marlbrook Gardens
30 74 Meadow Road
32 New House Farm, Cutnall Green
33 New House Farm, Elmbridge
40 1 Prickley Bungalows
45 The Shrubbery Nursing Home
46 Shuttifield Cottage
49 Toll House Cottage
52 Westacres
54 White Cottage
58 The Woodlands

The Gardens

1 24 ALEXANDER AVENUE

Droitwich Spa WR9 8NH. Malley & David Terry, 01905 774907, terrydroit@aol.com. *1m S of Droitwich. Droitwich Spa towards Worcester A38. Or from M5 J6 to Droitwich Town centre.* **Adm £3, chd free. Sun 14 Apr; Sat 15, Sun 16 June; Sun 14 July (2-5.30). Visitors also welcome by appt Mar to Sept.**
Beautifully designed giving feeling of space and tranquillity. 100+ clematis varieties interlacing high hedges. Borders with rare plants and shrubs. Sweeping curves of lawns and paths to woodland area with shade-loving plants. Drought-tolerant plants in S-facing gravel front garden. Alpine filled troughs. April spring bulbs, June clematis. Featured in GGG, Daily Telegraph 50 Best Small Gardens to visit. Wheelchair access most of the garden.
♿ ❀ ☎

GROUP OPENING

2 ASTLEY COUNTRY GARDENS

Astley, nr Stourport-on-Severn DY13 0SG, 01299 823769, rogchrisrussell@btinternet.com. *3m SW of Stourport-on-Severn. Take A451 out of Stourport, turn L onto B4196 for Worcester. Start at Astley Village Hall where map and descriptions of gardens are available. Car parking available at each location as distances between most gardens too great to walk.* Light refreshments and homemade cakes available at Astley Towne House and Longmore Hill Farmhouse. **Combined adm £5, chd free. Sat 22, Sun 23 June (1-6).**

ASTLEY TOWNE HOUSE
Tim & Lesley Smith
(See separate entry)

LITTLE LARFORD
Seed Green Lane. Lin & Derek Walker.

LONGMORE HILL FARMHOUSE
Larford Lane. Roger & Christine Russell

THE WHITE HOUSE
Dunley. Tony & Linda Tidmarsh

THE WHITE HOUSE - ASTLEY BURF
John & Joanna Daniels

A wonderful range of 5 country gardens of great variety, in picturesque, peaceful and colourful settings. These include the garden of a Grade II listed half timbered house with sub tropical planting, stumpery with tree ferns and woodland temple, underground grotto and water features; classical style garden with a variety of features celebrating events in the owner's family; ½ - acre garden with mixed borders, 'wheel' herbery and large paddock with specimen trees overlooking the Severn Valley; a Grade II listed C16 farmhouse garden with mixed borders, small feature courtyard leading to a part-walled terrace and lily pond.

3 ASTLEY TOWNE HOUSE

Astley DY13 0RH. Tim & Lesley Smith, www.astleytownehousesubtropicalgarden.co.uk. *School Lane, Astley nr. Stourport on Severn, Worcestershire. 3m W of Stourport on Severn. On B4196 Worcester to Bewdley Road.* Home-made teas. **Adm £4, chd free. Suns 28 July; 25 Aug; 29 Sept (1-5).**
2½ -acres garden of a Grade II listed timber building (not open), incl sub-tropical planting. Stumpery garden with tree ferns and woodland temple. Mediterranean garden, tree house, revolving summerhouse and underground grotto with shell mosaics and water features. Teas/cakes and plant stall within the garden. Featured in WI magazine and Gardeners' World.

4 BARNARD'S GREEN HOUSE

Hastings Pool, Poolbrook Road, Malvern WR14 3NQ. Mrs Sue Nicholls, 01684 574446. *1m E of Malvern. At junction of B4211 & B4208.* **Adm £3, chd free. Visitors welcome by appt, refreshments provided depends on size of group.**

Confetti Field, Wick Village

With a magnificent backdrop of the Malvern Hills, this 2 acre old-fashioned English garden is a plantsman's paradise. The main feature is a magnificent cedar in addition to a large number of rare and mature trees. At its best in Spring is the woodland, covered with euphorbia robbiae, hellebore, daffodils and leucojum and the cedar border which is awash with anemone blanda, daffodils and primroses. In summer and autumn the herbaceous borders are ablaze with colour including two rockeries and white and red borders. There is also a vegetable plot surrounding a rose-covered gazebo, known as the Millennium Dome.

5 THE BARTON

Berrow Green, Martley WR6 6PL. David & Vanessa Piggott. *1m S of Martley. On B4197 between Martley & A44 at Knightwick, corner of lane to Broadheath. Parking & lunches (12.30 to 2.30) at Admiral Rodney PH opp.* Home-made teas. **Adm £3, chd free. Sat 1, Sun 2 June (1-5).**
Started in 2003 this ½ -acre colourful cottage-style garden contains unusual trees, shrubs and herbaceous planting. Large pond with herbaceous terracing, wildlife pond, colour-themed gardens, gravel and grass beds. Roses, clematis and uncommon climbers decorate pergola, arbour and trellises. Vegetable garden. Ornamental features and sculptures. Book sale. Featured in Worcestershire Life.

6 5 BECKETT DRIVE
Northwick, Worcester WR3 7BZ. Jacki & Pete Ager, 01905 451108, peteandjacki@tiscali.co.uk. *1½ m N of Worcester city centre. Cul-de-sac off A449 Ombersley Rd directly opp Grantham's garage, 1m S of Claines r'about on A449.* Home-made teas. **Adm £3, chd free. Thur 23 May (2-5); Sun 30 June (10-5). Evening Opening £4, chd free, wine, Wed 24 July (6-9). Visitors also welcome by appt June to Aug.**
A plantsman's garden with a wide variety of colourful planting in distinctly different settings. Hot borders give way to a raised alpine area and a sun-loving bed before moving into a shade garden with hostas and ferns. A walk through this long, narrow garden reveals a number of surprising features, a recent garden visitor describing it as 'a magical mystery tour'. Compost advisors in attendance.

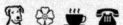

7 BIRTSMORTON COURT
nr Malvern WR13 6JS. Mr & Mrs N G K Dawes. *7m E of Ledbury. On A438.* Home-made teas. **Adm £4.50, chd free. Sun 9 June (2-5.30).**
Fortified manor house (not open) dating from C12; moat; Westminster pool laid down in Henry VII's reign at time of consecration of Westminster Abbey. Large tree under which Cardinal Wolsey reputedly slept in shadow of ragged stone. White garden, potager, topiary.

8 BOWCASTLE FARM
Tanners Hill, Bewdley DY12 2LN. Thelma & Cedric Quayle, 01299 403585, Quayle@phonecoop.coop. *1m W of Bewdley town centre. OS ref: SO769752. Take the Bewdley by-pass. On the 3rd r'about (or 1st if coming from Ludlow) take the B4190 signed 'Town Centre'. In about ½ m turn off at Hop Pole Inn, bear L in 100 yds down Tanners Hill. Follow single track rd approx 500 yds. Farm on L(signed).* Home-made teas. **Adm £5 incl refreshments, chd free. Visitors welcome by appt Apr to Sept.**
½ -acre garden, set among C18 farm buildings and old cherry, pear and apple orchards (SSSI), with fine long views. Informal planting of interesting trees, shrubs and herbaceous, around a lawn, old cider press and stone troughs, pond and seating. An ever-growing collection of clematis and beginnings of a new orchard/arboretum. Featured in Garden News and winner of Bewdley in Bloom-Large Garden. Some narrow paths of bark and gravel. Stout shoes recommended in orchard.

9 BRETFORTON MANOR
Main Street, Bretforton, Evesham WR11 7JH. Mr & Mrs M L Chambers, 01386 832148, angela-m-chambers@hotmail.co.uk. *4m E of Evesham, 6½ m N of Broadway. Centre of Bretforton village, next to church.* Light refreshments. **Adm £5, chd free. Visitors welcome by appt.**
5 acre garden recently redesigned and replanted. Containing mixed and herbaceous borders, an exotic border, scented walk and many tender and unusual plants. Hedges and topiary both old and new, several water features and many listed buildings and structures. The orchard has been extended and now contains a wide variety of fruit and specimen trees. The dovecote, aviary, apiary, cider barn and old village stocks are all listed. Waterfall and ponds. Featured in Gloucestershire Weekend Echo, 'Tranquil refuge from outside world'. Gravel paths, unfenced ponds.

An exotic border, scented walk and many tender and unusual plants . . .

10 BRIDGES STONE MILL
Alfrick Pound WR6 5HR. Sir Michael & Lady Perry. *6m NW of Malvern. From Worcester, take the A4103 Hereford rd to Bransford, at Bank House Hotel r'about take minor rd towards Leigh & Suckley. After 200yds, fork L towards Suckley. After 3m sign announces arrival at Alfrick Pound. 300yds beyond that, entrance gate to Bridges Stone Mill on L.* Home-made teas. **Adm £4, chd free. Sun 21 Apr (2-5.30).**
Formerly a cherry orchard adjoining the mainly C19 water mill, this is now a 2½ -acre garden laid out with trees, shrubs, mixed beds and borders. Small lake, stream and brook. The garden is bounded by 200yd stretch of Leigh Brook (an SSSI), and a mill stream from the mill's own weir. Extensive all-yr round planting. Ornamental vegetable parterre completes the picture.

BROAD MARSTON & PEBWORTH GARDENS
See Warwickshire

11 BROOK FARM
Berrington, nr Tenbury Wells WR15 8TJ. Sarah & William Wint, 01584 819868, sarah@brookfarmberrington.com, www.brookfarmberrington.com. *2m W of Tenbury Wells. From Tenbury take A4112 towards Leominster. After about 3m, pass St Michael's church on L, continue for a further mile. Turn R down Hayes Lane, signed Berrington, and continue 1½ m to T-junction. Brook Farm on L. If using satnav, the garden is about 500 metres N along Hayes Lane from post code destination.* Home-made teas in Conservatory for NGS days, and group visits, £2.50. **Adm £3.50, chd free. Sat 15, Sun 16 June (2-6). Visitors also welcome by appt May to Oct. Self Service Teas.**
A relaxed country garden. It's been described as a cottage garden, wildlife garden and chaotic garden. To paraphrase the lovely Eric Morecambe 'They're all the right plants, just not necessarily in the right order'. 1½ -acre garden, 7 acres woodland and wilderness. His and her guides, teas, some weeds. One of Alastair Sawday's special places to stay for Garden lovers; reviewed by the Galloping Gardener. Limited wheelchair access to the garden over gravel and grass, which is passable unless it's very wet.

12 BYLANE
Worcester Road, Earls Croome WR8 9DA. Shirley & Fred Bloxsome, 01684 592489, shirleymay70@hotmail.co.uk. *1m N of Upton on Severn turning. On main A38 directly past Earls Croome Garden Centre, signed Bridle Way. Directly behind Earls Croome Garden Centre.* Home-made teas. **Adm £3, chd free. Sats 6 Apr; 25 May; 15 June; 6 July; 7 Sept (11-4). Visitors also welcome by appt Apr to Sept.**

Please give one months notice. Adm £5 incl tea.
Herbaceous garden, paddock with pond (wildlife), small vegetable garden, chickens, wood with mature trees and bluebells. Sensible shoes needed. Picnic area, private parties welcome.

CAVES FOLLY NURSERIES
See Herefordshire

13 1 CHURCH COTTAGE
Defford WR8 9BJ. John Taylor, 01386 750863, ann98sheppard@btinternet.com. *3m SW of Pershore. A4104 Pershore to Upton rd, turn into Defford, black & white cottage at side of church. Parking in village hall car park.* Home-made teas. **Adm £2.50, chd free. Sat 4, Sun 5, Mon 6 May; Sat 15, Sun 16 June (11-5). Visitors also welcome by appt May to Sept.**
True countryman's 1/3 -acre garden. Interesting layout, with new Japanese -style feature. Specimen trees; water features; vegetable garden; aviary, poultry and cider making. Featured in Amateur Gardening.

14 CONDERTON MANOR
Conderton, nr Tewkesbury GL20 7PR. Mr & Mrs W Carr, 01386 725389, carrs@conderton.wanadoo.co.uk. *5 1/2 m NE of Tewkesbury. On Bredon - Beckford rd or from A46 take Overbury sign at Beckford turn.* Light refreshments in the house. **Adm £4. Visitors welcome by appt.**
7-acre garden, recently replanted in a contemporary style with magnificent views of Cotswolds. Flowering cherries and bulbs in spring. Formal terrace with clipped box parterre; huge rose and clematis arches, mixed borders of roses and herbaceous plants, bog bank and quarry garden. Many unusual trees and shrubs make this a garden to visit at all seasons. Visitors are particularly encouraged to come in spring and autumn. This is a garden/small arboretum of particular interest for tree lovers. Some gravel paths and steps - no disabled WC.

15 THE COTTAGE
Broughton Green, Droitwich WR9 7EF. Terry Dagley, 01905 391670. *5m E of Droitwich. 8m S of Bromsgrove. From Droitwich take B4090 4m towards Feckenham. Turn R at sign Broughton Green & Earls Common. 1m (just before T junction) Cottage up track on R, 300yds.* Tea. **Adm £3.50, chd free. Suns, Mons 14, 15 Apr; 15, 16 Sept (2-5). Visitors also welcome by appt Mar to Sept.**
Plantsmans 1/2 -acre garden, structured by formal hedges, topiary and mature fruit trees. Yr round colour and interest provided by unusual plants and shrubs. Special 9 month coloured grass area Sept to May by bulbs and tubers, plus crocus lawns in spring and autumn. Featured in Period Living.

Visitors have described the garden as magical, inspirational and one of the best kept secrets of Worcestershire . . . !

16 ◆ CROOME PARK
nr High Green WR8 9DW. National Trust, 01905 371006, www.nationaltrust.org.uk/main/w-croome. *4m W of Pershore. Signed from A38 & B4084.* **Adm £6.50, chd £3. For NGS: Wed 24 Apr (10-5.30). For other opening times and information, please phone or see garden website.**
730 acre landscape park designed by Capability Brown in mid C18. Restored pleasure grounds, with shrubberies, flowering studs, garden buildings and statuary, ornamental lake and restored parkland. Featured in local and national press, regional and national television, incl Time Team, Countryfile, BBC Breakfast. Ask at reception for alternative parking for wheelchair users.

17 DIAL PARK
Chaddesley Corbett DY10 4QB. David & Olive Mason, 01562 777451, olivemason75@btinternet.com. *4 1/2 m from Kidderminster, 4 1/2 m from Bromsgrove. On A448 midway between Kidderminster & Bromsgrove. Limited parking at garden, or park in village or at village hall (if available).* **Adm £3, chd free. Wed 20 Feb (11-4). Visitors also welcome by appt Individuals or groups. Refreshments by arrangement.**
Approx 3/4 acre garden in rural setting. Planted with a wide variety of plants providing interest throughout the year. Specialities incl a large collection of snowdrops, old daffodils and hardy ferns. Small collection of country tools and bygones. Featured in RHS Garden, Gardens Illustrated.

18 NEW 6 DINGLE END
Inkberrow, Worcester WR7 4EY. Mr & Mrs Glenn & Gabriel Allison. *12m E of Worcester. A422 from Worcester. At the 30mph sign in Inkberrow turn R down Appletree Lane then 1st L up Pepper St. Dingle End is 4th on R of Pepper St. Limited parking in Dingle End but street parking on Pepper St.* Home-made teas. **Adm £3, chd free. Suns 30 June; 29 Sept (11-5).**
Over 1 acre garden with formal area close to the house opening into a flat area featuring a large pond, stream and weir with apple orchard and woodland area. Large vegetable garden incl an interesting variety of fruits. Garden designed for wildlife.

GROUP OPENING

19 ECKINGTON GARDENS
Manor Road, Eckington, Pershore WR10 3BH, 01386 751924, lynnglaze@cmail.co.uk. *5 gardens - 2 in Manor Rd, 3 in or close to New Rd/Nafford Rd. A4104 (from B4084 through Pershore) to Upton & Defford, L turn B4080 to Tewkesbury/ Eckington. At Xrds in centre of Eckington (by war memorial): Turn R into Drakesbridge Rd/Hammock Rd & then L into Manor Rd for Brook House & Court Gate Cottage. Turn L into New Rd (signed The Combertons), leading to Nafford Rd for The Mantoft (fomerly The Croft), Hilltop & Nafford House. Four gardens within 1/2 m radius, Nafford House further out.* Tea, coffee, soft drinks & cakes at Brook House. Wine & soft drinks available at The Mantoft **Combined adm £5, chd free. Sat 22, Sun 23 June (11-5).**

BROOK HOUSE
Manor Road. George & Lynn Glaze

NEW **COURT GATE COTTAGE**
Manor Road. Mr & Mrs David & Yvonne Walton.

HILLTOP
Nafford Road. Richard & Margaret Bateman.
Park on road - easy walk from Mantoft. Disabled drivers can drive right to house/garage for parking

MANTOFT
Upper End. Mr & Mrs M J Tupper.
Changed Name - was -The Croft. Park on road - garden has electric gates, admission requires pressing a button on a VDU screen to obtain entrance
Visitors also welcome by appt please telephone for further info.
01386 750819

NAFFORD HOUSE
Nafford Road. Janet & John Wheatley.
Enter village of Eckington over river bridge at T lights on B4080 from Pershore to Tewkesbury at Xrds in centre of Eckington (by war memorial): Turn L into New Rd (signed the Combertons) & follow for 3 m, on L at top of hill
01386 750233

5 very diverse gardens; a traditional open cottage garden with koi pond; a cottage garden broken into smaller areas; a formal and structured walled garden with topiary; a garden enhanced by magnificent views through hedging windows; a natural wooded garden sloping down to the riverside. Set in/close to lovely village of Eckington with riverside parking and picnic site. Brook House 1 acre cottage garden with herbaceous beds and koi pond surrounded by rockery. Court Gate Cottage ²/₃ acre cottage garden, broken into 'rooms', with wildlife pond, summer house and vegetable garden. Mantoft - formal walled garden with fish pond, topiary and dew pond, with ducks and geese. Hedges and stone paths, gazebo overlooking garden. Hilltop - 1 acre garden with sunken garden/pond, rose garden, herbaceous borders and formal hedging having 'windows' linking to extensive countryside views. Nafford House 2 acre mature natural garden/wood with slopes to R Avon, formal gardens around house and magnificent wisteria. Featured in Amateur Gardening - Hilltop. Limited wheelchair access at Nafford House to wooded area and slopes to river.

Little Larford, Astley Country Gardens

Every garden visit makes a difference

HALL GREEN GARDENS
See Staffordshire, Birmingham & West Midlands

20 ◆ HANBURY HALL
School Road, Hanbury, Droitwich WR9 7EA. National Trust, 01527 821214, www.nationaltrust.org.uk/hanburyhall. *3m NE of Droitwich. 6m S of Bromsgrove. Signed off B4090 and B4091*. **Adm £6.70, chd £3.60. For NGS: Sat 13, Sun 14 July (10.30-5). For other opening times and information, please phone or see garden website.**
Re-creation of C18 formal garden by George London. Parterre, fruit garden and wilderness. Mushroom house, orangery and ice house, William and Mary style house dating from 1701. Opportunity to meet the gardeners and to see behind the scenes in the Walled Garden. Buggy available to bring visitors from the car park to the front of the property and wheelchairs are available from the Hall.

21 ◆ HARVINGTON HALL
Harvington, Kidderminster DY10 4LR. The Roman Catholic Archdiocese of Birmingham, 01562 777846, www.harvingtonhall.com. *3m SE of Kidderminster. ½ m E of A450 Birmingham to Worcester Rd & about ½ m N of A448 from Kidderminster to Bromsgrove*. **Adm £3, chd £1. For NGS: Sat 6, Sun 7 July (11.30-4). For other opening times and information, please phone or see garden website.**
Romantic Elizabethan moated manor house with island gardens, small Elizabethan-style herb garden, all tended by volunteers. Tours of the Hall, which contains secret hiding places and rare wall paintings, are also available. Wheelchair access to gardens, Malt House Visitor Centre, tea room and shop.

22 HEWELL GRANGE
Hewell Lane, Tardebigge, Redditch B97 6QS. HMP Hewell, 01527 785050, alison.bramham-smith@hmps.gsi.gov.uk. *2m NE of Redditch. HMP Hewell is situated on B4096. Sat Nav postcode B97 6QQ. Follow signs to Grange Resettlement Unit*. Light refreshments. **Adm £5, chd £2.50. Sat 18, Sun 19 May (10-3.30). Visitors by appointment only on specified days and times.**

All visitors must follow a booking procedure and due to Prison environment, must follow security procedures.
Hewell Grange is an C18 landscape park and lake laid out by Lancelot Brown and modified around 1812 by Humphry Repton. The grounds of this prison feature rhododendrons and azaleas, restored Repton bridge, formal garden, water tower, and rock garden. Grounds have mature woodland. Not a flower garden. Please note - Visitors to the garden will be shown the garden features in escorted small groups. The garden tour may be over 60 minutes. Therefore, visitors must be physically able to walk for this length of time. There are uneven surfaces in the grounds so sensible walking footwear is essential. Hearing Dogs for the deaf demonstration and Hawk demonstration. Lakeside walk and bluebell walk. Featured in The Village magazine.

23 HIGH VIEW

Martley WR6 6PW. Mike & Carole Dunnett, 01886 821559, mike.dunnett@virgin.net. *1m S of Martley. On B4197 between Martley & A44 at Knightwick.* Home-made teas. **Adm £4, chd free. Visitors welcome by appt June to Sept.**
Intriguing and mature 2½ acre garden developed over 40yrs. Visitors have described the garden as magical, inspirational and one of the best kept horticultural secrets of Worcestershire! With its superb views over the Teme valley, vast range of plants and many interesting features, it is a garden not to be missed. Steps and steep slopes so appropriate foot wear required.

24 HIRAETH

30 Showell Road, Droitwich WR9 8UY. Sue & John Fletcher, 07752 717243 / 01905 778390, jfletcher@inductotherm.co.uk. *1m S of Droitwich. On The Ridings estate. Turn off A38 r'about into Addyes Way, 2nd R into Showell Rd, 500yds on R. Follow the yellow signs!* Home-made teas. **Adm £3, chd free. Wed 8 May (1-5.30); Sat 15, Sun 16 June (2-6); Wed 3 July (1-5.30); Sun 28 July (2-6); Wed 7 Aug (1-5.30). Visitors also welcome by appt May to Aug.**
'A haven on the way to heaven' - description in Visitors Book. Front and rear gardens contain unusual plants, traditional cottage garden, herbaceous, hostas, ferns, arches, pool, waterfall, 200yr-old stile, oak sculptures, metal animals, birds etc including, giraffes, elephant. An oasis of colours in a garden not to be missed.

25 HUNTERS END

Button Bridge Lane, Button Bridge. Kinlet, Bewdley DY12 3DW. Norma & Colin Page, 01299 841055, norma_and_colin@hotmail.co.uk. *6m NW of Bewdley. A4194 from Bewdley at Button Bridge, turn R down Button Bridge Lane, garden ¾ m on L (look for horses heads).* Light refreshments. **Adm £3, chd free. Visitors welcome by appt June to Sept.**
This ¾ -acre garden with plants and decorative features will create a smile and a laugh from beginning to end of your tour. Soak up the atmosphere and tranquillity of the garden. Relax in one of the many seating areas and enjoy your tea and cake. Even more flower beds are being created. Some gravel. Partly sloping.

Relax in one of the many seating areas and enjoy your tea and cake . . .

13 LANSDOWNE ROAD

See Staffordshire, Birmingham & West Midlands

26 22 LAYTON AVENUE

Malvern WR14 2ND. Brian & Jenny Bradford, WR14 2ND. *From Worcester approach Malvern on A449.Turn L at r'about onto Townsend Way (signed A4208 Welland). After 3 r'abouts take 2nd R into Charles Way then 2nd L into Layton Avenue. From Upton approach Malvern on A4211. Take 3rd exit at Barnards Green r'about, Pickersleigh Rd. After 1m turn R at T- lights (signed A4208 Worcester). Take 2nd L (Charles Way) then 2nd L into Layton Avenue.* Home-made teas. **Adm £3, chd free. Sat 25, Sun 26 May (11-4); Sat 15 June (11-5).**
Totally changed over 7 years and now maturing this is a garden to linger in. The latest addition is a wisteria and clematis draped pergola entrance opening onto lawns with beds and borders packed full of interesting plants and trees. A streamside garden and ornamental fish pond complete its attraction. Exhibition in the conservatory of paintings, carvings and ceramic sculptures by Jenny. Featured in Malvern Gazette (week before opening).

27 ◆ LITTLE MALVERN COURT

Little Malvern WR14 4JN. Mrs T M Berington, 01684 892988, www.littlemalverncourt.co.uk. *3m S of Malvern. On A4104 S of junction with A449.* **Adm £5, chd 50p. For NGS: Sun 17 Mar, Mon 6 May (2-5). For other opening times and information, please phone or see garden website.**
10 acres attached to former Benedictine Priory, magnificent views over Severn valley. Garden rooms and terrace around house designed and planted in early 1980s; chain of lakes; wide variety of spring bulbs, flowering trees and shrubs. Notable collection of old-fashioned roses. Topiary hedge and fine trees. The May Bank Holiday - Flower Festival in the Priory Church. Very limited wheelchair access.

GROUP OPENING

28 MARLBROOK GARDENS

Braces Lane, Marlbrook, Bromsgrove B60 1DY. *2m N of Bromsgrove. 1m N of M42 J1, follow B4096 signed Rednal, turn L at Xrds into Braces Lane. 1m S of M5 J4, follow A38 signed Bromsgove, turn L at T-lights into Braces Lane. Parking available.* Home-made teas at St Luke's Church (Suns). **Combined adm £5, chd free. Suns 26 May; 7 July (1.30-5.30). Evening Opening £6 incl wine, chd free, Sat 24 Aug (6.30-10); Sun 25 Aug (1.30-5.30). Visitors also welcome by appt May to Sept. Coaches welcome, viewing for 1, 2 or all gardens.**

OAK TREE HOUSE
504 Birningham Road.
Di & Dave Morgan
Visitors also welcome by appt May to Sept. Coaches welcome. Refreshments available.
0121 445 3595
meandi@btinternet.com

ROUND HILL GARDEN
24 Braces Lane. Lynn & Alan Nokes
Visitors also welcome by appt May to Sept. Coaches welcome. Refreshments available.
0121 445 5520
alyn.nokes@btinternet.com

SARANACRIS
28a Braces Lane. John & Janet Morgan
Visitors also welcome by appt May to Sept. Coaches welcome. Refreshments available.
0121 445 5823
saranacris@btinternet.com

One group, three unique gardens, rated by one national paper in the top 50 small gardens worth visiting. Individually stunning gardens, together they're a wonderful experience of contrasting styles and topography from gentle slopes to a former sand quarry's steep terraces. Jungle, traditional and cottage styles, overflowing with plants for sun and shade, incl rare, exotics and vegetables areas. Streams, ponds, patios, artefacts, sculptures, glasshouses and special collections add to the individuality. Recognised for excellence and continually evolving, many repeat visitors enjoy sharing with us their new discoveries. Visit us during the year and at our Saturday evening celebration in August, journey through a myriad of lights sparkling throughout all the gardens, with a glass of wine in hand. Visitor's comments 'Having visited all three gardens, all were unique and beautiful in different ways, will visit again', S & L from Worcestershire. 'This is what gardening is all about! absolutely fabulous', D.H. from Yorkshire. Garden Quiz for children at Gardens. Featured in Worcestershire Life, Amateur Gardening.

29 MEADOW FARM

33 Droitwich Road, Feckenham B96 6RU. Robert & Diane Cole, 01527 821156, meadowfarm33@aol.com, www.meadowfarm33.co.uk. *1/2 m W of Feckenham. On B4090, Droitwich Rd, opposite Berrow Hill Lane.* Home-made teas. **Adm £5, chd free.** **Visitors welcome by appt May to Aug. Groups of 20+.**
1-acre plantsmans garden created since 1999 by enthusiastic husband and wife team, and intensively planted with herbaceous perennials. Particularly colourful between June and Sept, but planted for all season interest. 1 1/4 -acre wild flower meadow, and 3/4 -acre nursery, not normally open to the public.

Soft plantings around pools and teahouse, into fritillary meadows with wild roses and towering redwoods . . .

30 74 MEADOW ROAD

Wythall B47 6EQ. Joe Manchester, 01564 829589, joe@cogentscreenprint.co.uk. *4m E of Alvechurch. 2m N from J3 M42. On A435 at Beckets Farm r'about take rd signed Earlswood/Solihull. Approx 250 metres turn L into School Drive, then L into Meadow Rd.* Light refreshments. **Adm £2.50, chd free.** **Sat 1, Sun 2 June (1-5). Visitors also welcome by appt May to Sept.**
Vastly improved urban garden dedicated to woodland, shade-loving plants. 'Expect the unexpected' in a few tropical and foreign species. Meander through the garden under the majestic pine, eucalyptus and silver birch. Sit and enjoy the peaceful surroundings and see how many different ferns and hostas you can find.

31 NEW MORTON HALL

Morton Hall Lane, Holberrow Green, Redditch B96 6SJ. Mrs A Olivieri, 01386 791820, mortonhall61@hotmail.co.uk. *Between B4090 & A422 signed Inkberrow' then signed Holberrow Green. At circular wooden bench around tree in center of hamlet, turn up Morton Hall Lane. The gates to Morton Hall on your RH-side. Press intercom to be admitted.* Home-made teas. **Adm £5 incl tea & cake, chd free.** **Visitors welcome by appt Apr to Sept, groups max 20.**
An elegant stroll garden around a late Georgian house (not open), with potager, hot coloured borders, formalised flower garden, wisteria arbour, large rock garden leading to soft plantings around pools and teahouse, into fritillary meadows with wild roses and towering redwoods. Living roof, Mediterranean plantings, and Ha-Ha with views over vale of Evesham'.

MOSELEY GARDENS SOUTH
See Staffordshire, Birmingham & West Midlands

32 NEW HOUSE FARM, CUTNALL GREEN

Kidderminster Road, Cutnall Green, Droitwich Spa WR9 0PW. Mrs Rachel Barnes, 01299 851013, barnes.p7@sky.com. *Within grounds of New House Farm and Hatfield Interiors. A442 Droitwich to Kidderminster rd. From Droitwich you pass the village sign on left, New House Farm is on RH-side. From Kidderminster past The Chequers PH on R as you pass Rajdoot on L, New House Farm on R.* Home-made teas, tearoom within grounds. **Adm £4, chd free.** **Sats, Suns 22, 23 June; 13, 14 July (10-5). Visitors also welcome by appt June to July.**
1 acre country garden surrounding Victorian farmhouse (not open), offering many old features, with new planting schemes and views over open countryside giving this garden a wealth of interest. The creativity is abundant due to resident designer who runs an interior design/craft shop and tea room. Artistic and creative features and aspirational ideas. Some gravel pathways and steps.

33 NEW HOUSE FARM, ELMBRIDGE

Elmbridge Lane, Elmbridge WR9 0DA. Charles & Carlo Caddick, 01299 851249, Carlocaddick@hotmail.com. *2 1/2 m N of Droitwich Spa. From Droitwich take A442 to Cutnall Green. Take lane opp The Chequers PH and proceed 1m to T-junction, turning L towards Elmbridge Green & Elmbridge. Continue along lane passing church and church hall. At T-junction turn R into Elmbridge Lane, garden on L.* Home-made teas. **Adm £4, chd free.** **Sats, Suns 11, 12 May; 14, 15 Sept (2-4.30). Visitors also welcome by appt Apr to Oct.**
This charming garden surrounding an

early C19 red brick house, has a wealth of rare trees and shrubs under planted with unusual bulbs and herbaceous plants. Special features are the 'perry wheel', ornamental vegetable gardens. Water garden, dry garden, rose garden, mews, the retreat, potager and greenhouse. Topiary and tropical plants complete the effect. New plant nursery with many exotics for sun and shade. Dahlias from The National Collection. Plant clearance sale.

GROUP OPENING

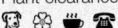

34 NEW OFFENHAM GARDENS

WR11 8RW. *Approaching Offenham on B4510 from Evesham, L into village signed Offenham and ferry ³/₄ m. Follow road round into village & to church. Park in Village Hall car park opp church. NO PARKING AVAILABLE IN VILLAGE OTHER THAN CAR PARK. Gardens 5 mins walk from car park. R out of car park down to maypole. L at maypole into Church St. Keep L in Church St, gardens next to each other on R. Combined ticket at each garden.* Home-made teas. **Combined adm £3, chd free. Sat 3, Sun 4 Aug (11-5).**

NEW LANGDALE
Sheila & Adrian James
www.adrianjames.org.uk

NEW WILLOWAY
Stephen & Linda Pitts

Offenham is a picturesque village in the heart of the Vale of Evesham, with thatched cottages and traditional maypole Two gardens of diverse interests from woodland and wildlife to herbaceous and exotic.Langdale a plantsman's garden, designed for all year round interest, with some areas still under development. Relaxed lawns and borders in a variety of styles, from woodland to hot exotic, leading down to a productive vegetable garden. Willoway this oasis of sound and colour is initially hidden by the traditional front garden. A corridor of Hostas leads the visitor to the patio, a lush carpet of lawn, and then, via the bamboo curtain, to the oriental area ponds and waterfalls. Acers and a stunning Silver Birch Tree.

THE ORCHARDS
See Herefordshire

35 OVERBURY COURT

nr Tewkesbury GL20 7NP. Mr & Mrs Bruce Bossom, 01386 725111, garden@overburyestate.co.uk. *5m NE of Tewkesbury. Village signed off A46.* **Adm £3.50, chd free. Visitors welcome by appt.**
Georgian house 1740 (not open); landscape garden of same date with stream and pools; daffodil bank and grotto. Plane trees, yew hedges; shrubs; cut flowers; coloured foliage; gold and silver, shrub rose borders. Norman church adjoins garden. Some slopes, while all the garden can be viewed, parts are not accessible to wheelchairs.

PAUL'S OASIS OF CALM
See Staffordshire, Birmingham & West Midlands

Strategically placed seating . . . the garden exudes a quirky and humorous character with the odd surprise . . .

36 NEW PEAR TREE COTTAGE

Witton Hill, Wichenford, Worcester WR6 6YX. Pamela & Alistair Thompson, www.peartreecottage.me. *13m NW of Worcester & 2m NE of Martley. From Worcester, take A449 N to Ombersley, follow A4133 to Holt Heath. Turn R on the A443 and 1st L to Ockeridge, 3rd R signed Martley & Kings Green, 1st R signed Witton Hill. Pear Tree Cottage is on the RH-side. From Martley take B4197 towards Stourport, 1st R into Horn Lane, 1st L to Prickley Green, keep R & Pear Tree Cottage is at the top of hill on L.* **Adm £3.50. Sat 8, Sun 9 June (11-6).**
A Grade II listed black and white cottage (not open) with SW-facing gardens and views across orchards to Abberley clock tower. The gardens extend to approx. ³/₄ acre and comprise of gently sloping lawns with mixed and woodland borders, shade and plenty of strategically placed seating. The garden exudes a quirky and humorous character with the odd surprise! Wonderful Views. An exhibition of mixed media artwork featuring artists from around Worcestershire and Gloucestershire. The 'Gardeners' Loo' is available to visitors. Most areas are accessible by wheelchair.

GROUP OPENING

37 PERSHORE GARDENS

Pershore WR10 1BG, www.visitpershore.co.uk. *On the B4084 between Worcester & Evesham. Tickets & maps can be obtained from Number 8 Community Arts Centre opp the Angel Hotel or from any garden on the open days. Tickets also available in advance from Pershore Town Hall & 'Blue' in Broad St.* Home-made teas at The Primary School & Number 8 Community Arts Centre, 8 High Street. **Combined adm £5, chd free. Sat 15, Sun 16 June (1-5).**
Explore 20 large and small gardens in the attractive market town of Pershore. These include gardens tucked away behind Georgian town houses, gardens which sweep down to the River Avon, tiny courtyards and walled gardens and a Primary School garden.

PHELPS COTTAGE GARDEN
See Herefordshire

THE PICTON GARDEN
See Herefordshire

38 4 PODEN COTTAGES

Honeybourne WR11 7PS. Patrick & Dorothy Bellew. *6m E of Evesham. At the Gate Inn take the Pebworth, Long Marston Rd, turn Right at end of the Village for Mickleton. 1m on Mickleton Rd.* Home-made teas. **Adm £3, chd free. Sun 31 Mar; Mon 1 Apr (12-5); Sat 15, Sun 16 June; Sun 7 July (2-5).**
¹/₃ acre cottage garden which has been planted by the owners. Paths wind through mixed herbaceous borders. Roses old and modern, shrubs, small terrace and pond. Fine views over the Cotswold Hills. All-yr colour. Gravel drive at entrance.

39 NEW POND HOUSE

Ham Lane, Powick, Worcester WR2 4RD. Robin & Jill Wallace. *A422 approx 2m from Worcester & 6m Malvern. M5 exit 7, towards Malvern. In Powick village on Worcester to Malvern rd, go around island with black & white house in middle as though starting to head back the way you came. Turn very sharp L up Kings End Road. ½ m at top of hill, a track goes straight on (signed 'Private Road') where the lane corners L. The track bears L down-hill and a field entrance will be signed 100yds on L.* Tea. **Adm £3, chd free. Sun 5 May (1.30-5); Sun 4 Aug (1.30-5.30).**

Buried in the Worcestershire countryside is this unusual 1-acre garden, progressing into 4 acres of woodland with streams and ponds surrounded by bluebells and wild garlic in spring. Steep slopes criss-crossed with a mile of paths and bridges. The aim is maximum effect with minimal maintenance using wild flowers and interesting pruning. Suggest good walking shoes.

40 1 PRICKLEY BUNGALOWS

Hockhams Lane, Martley WR6 6QP. Megan Griffiths, 01886 812523. *7m NW of Worcester. Situated 2m from Martley on the B4197 (N), between Martley and Gt Witley. Park on roadside.* **Adm £3, chd free. Every Sun 3 Mar to 26 May (11-3). Visitors also welcome by appt Mar to Oct.**

This stunning ⅓ acre cottage garden provides colour and form all year round with two ponds, woodland area and vegetable plot. Good selection of plants for sale.

41 PUMP COTTAGE

Hill Lane, Weatheroak, nr Alvechurch B48 7EQ. Barry Knee & Sue Hunstone, 01564 826250, barryknee.1947@btinternet.com, www.pumpcottage.org.uk. *3m E of Alvechurch. 1½ m from J3 M42 off N-bound c'way of A435 (signed Alvechurch). Parking in adjacent field.* Home-made teas. **Adm £3, chd free. Visitors welcome by appt Apr to Sept, individuals or groups welcome. Adm £5 incl home made teas.**

Described by visitors as 'A secret wonderland, surprises at every turn'. C19 cottage, rural setting. Enchanting, romantic 1 acre plantaholic's garden with yr-round interest. Colourful borders, roses, rockery, fernery, water features, bog garden, natural pond, water lilies and wildlife area. Victorian styled greenhouse, creative features, artefacts and ornaments, Continually evolving. Garden ironwork for sale. Featured in Worcestershire Life as one of top 50 gardens to visit. Limited wheelchair access.

RAGLEY HALL GARDENS

See Warwickshire

> Maximum effect with minimal maintenance using wild flowers and interesting pruning . . . .

42 RECTORY COTTAGE

Old Rectory Lane, Alvechurch B48 7SU. *From A441 at Alvechurch, turn into Old Rectory Lane, continue along, after sharp R bend, next house on L.* Cream teas. **Adm £3, chd free. Sun 9 June (1-6).**

Courtyard garden with pergolas and many plants including roses and hostas. Aviary with budgerigars. Wonderful long, riverside gardens - secret garden, waterside borders, patios, 'dragon's den', bridge, ponds, waterfall.

43 ◆ RED HOUSE FARM

Flying Horse Lane, Bradley Green, nr Redditch B96 6QT. Mrs M M Weaver, 01527 821269, www.redhousefarmgardenandnursery.co.uk. *7m W of Redditch, 7m E of Droitwich. On B4090 Alcester to Droitwich Spa. Ignore sign to Bradley Green. Turn opp The Red Lion PH.* **Adm £2, chd free. For NGS: Every Thur 7 Mar to 26 Sept (12-5). For other opening times and information, please phone or see garden website.**

Created as a peaceful haven from its working farm environment, this mature country garden offers yr-round interest. In densely planted borders a wide range of traditional favourites rub shoulders with the newest of introductions and make each visit a pleasurable and rewarding experience. Adjacent nursery open daily 10-5.

44 ◆ RIVERSIDE GARDENS AT WEBBS

Wychbold, nr Droitwich WR9 0DG. Webbs of Wychbold, 01527 860000, www.webbsdirect.co.uk. *2m N of Droitwich Spa. 1m N of M5 J5 on A38. Follow tourism signs from M5.* **For opening times and information, please phone or see garden website.**

2½ acres. Themed gardens incl National Collection of Shrubby Potentilla. Colour spectrum, tropical and dry garden, David Austin Rose collection, grassery and bamboozelum. New Wave gardens opened 2004, designer Noel Kingsbury, to create natural seasonal interest with grasses and perennials. The patio gardens are 6 themed gardens which showcase what to do with a small space. Open all yr, except Christmas & Boxing Day and Easter Sunday.

NCH

45 NEW THE SHRUBBERY NURSING HOME

Birmingham Road, Kidderminster DY10 2JZ. Mr Aidan Tagg (Gardener), 01562 68122, aidantagg@hotmail.com, www.shrubberynursing.co.uk. *Head towards the centre of Kidderminster on the Birmingham Rd. We are just off Tabbs Gardens - between Holy Trinity School & the Territorial Army building.* Cream teas, cold drinks. Tea, coffee & hot chocolate. **Adm £3, chd free. Suns 7 July; 4 Aug; 1 Sept (9-4). Visitors also welcome by appt.**

The Shrubbery Nursing Home is an historic Georgian property, located close to the centre of Kidderminster and surrounded by beautiful, colour-filled gardens specifically designed for the residents to experience and enjoy. Croquet on the main lawn. Full, flat wheelchair access.

From tiny back plots to country estates ...

46 SHUTTIFIELD COTTAGE
Birchwood, Storridge WR13 5HA. Mr & Mrs David Judge, 01886 884243, judge.shutti@btinternet.com. *8m W of Worcester. Turn R off A4103 opp Storridge Church to Birchwood. After 1¼ m L down steep tarmac drive. Please park on roadside but drive down if walking is difficult.* Home-made teas. **Adm £4, chd free. Sats 27 Apr; 4, 18 May; 8 June; 6 July; 3, 24 Aug; 7 Sept (1.30-5). Visitors also welcome by appt Apr to Sept.**
Superb position and views. Unexpected 3-acre plantsman's garden, extensive herbaceous borders, primula and stump bed, many unusual trees, shrubs, perennials, colour-themed for all-yr interest. Walks in 20-acre wood with ponds, natural wild areas, anemones, bluebells, rhododendrons, azaleas are a particular spring feature. Large old rose garden with many spectacular mature climbers. Good garden colour throughout the yr. Small deer park, vegetable garden. Wildlife ponds, wild flowers and walks in 20 acres of ancient woodland. Featured in The Cotswold Life Magazine.

47 ◆ SPETCHLEY PARK GARDENS
Spetchley WR5 1RS. Mr John Berkeley, 01453 810303, www.spetchleygardens.co.uk. *2m E of Worcester. On A44, follow brown signs.* **Adm £6, chd free. For NGS: Fri 29 Mar, Sun 7 July (11-6). For other opening times and information, please phone or see garden website.**
Surrounded by glorious countryside and deer park, virtually hidden from the road, this 30-acre Victorian paradise, belonging to the Berkeley family has been lovingly created by successive generations and boasts an enviable collection of plant treasures from every corner of the globe. The Spetchley Revival Project, aimed at restoring Spetchley's heritage and making it a hub for local tourism, has received a development grant from the Heritage Lottery Fund. Gravel paths.

56 ST AGNES ROAD
See Staffordshire, Birmingham & West Midlands

STANTON VILLAGE GARDENS
See Gloucestershire

Mantoft, Eckington Gardens

48 ◆ STONE HOUSE COTTAGE GARDENS
Stone DY10 4BG. James & Louisa Arbuthnott, 01562 69902, www.shcn.co.uk. *2m SE of Kidderminster. Via A448 towards Bromsgrove, next to church, turn up drive.* **Adm £3, chd free. For opening times and information, please phone or see garden website.**
A beautiful and romantic walled garden adorned with unusual brick follies. This acclaimed garden is exuberantly planted and holds one of the largest collections of rare plants in the country. It acts as a shop window for the adjoining nursery. Open Wed to Sat late March to early Sept 10-5. Limited wheelchair access.

49 TOLL HOUSE COTTAGE
Stourport Road, Bewdley DY12 1PU. Joan & Rob Roberts, 01299 402331, robertroberts292@o2.co.uk. *1m S of Bewdley. 2m N of Stourport, 3m W of Kidderminster. On A456 between Bewdley & Stourport, opp Blackstone car park & picnic site (free parking). Disabled parking on drive.* Home-made teas. **Adm £3, chd free. Suns 19 May; 21 July (10-5). Visitors also welcome by appt May to Sept, groups max 30.**
Developing ½ acre garden started in 2008 in 2 sections. Cottage garden with a collection bulbs, herbaceous and shrubs for year round colour including lawn. A small arboretum with grass walkways and summerhouse. A large pool with waterfall and beach for wildlife. Vegetable garden with raised beds in large fruit cage. A painters garden. Gallery for woodturning and paintings also open for viewing.

50 THE TYNINGS
Church Lane, Stoulton, nr Worcester WR7 4RE. John & Leslie Bryant, 01905 840189, johnlesbryant@btinternet.com. *5m S of Worcester; 3m N of Pershore. On the B4084 (formerly A44) between M5 J7 & Pershore. The Tynings lies beyond the church at the extreme end of Church Lane. Ample parking.* Light refreshments. **Adm £3, chd free. Visitors welcome by appt May to Sept.**
Acclaimed plantsman's ½ -acre garden, generously planted with a large selection of rare trees and shrubs. Features incl specialist collection of lilies, many unusual climbers and rare ferns. The colour continues into late summer with dahlia, berberis, euonymus and tree colour. Surprises around every corner. You will not be disappointed. Lovely

views of adjacent Norman Church and surrounding countryside. Plants labelled and plant lists available.

51 THE WALLED GARDEN

6 Rose Terrace, off Fort Royal Hill, Worcester WR5 1BU. Julia & William Scott. *1/2 m from cathedral. Via Fort Royal Hill, off London Rd (A44). Park on 1st section of Rose Terrace & walk the last 20yds down track.* **Adm £3, chd free. Sats, Weds 6, 10 Apr; 15, 19 June (1-5).**

In this peaceful oasis of scent and colour, a tapestry of culinary and medicinal herbs, vegetables, flowers and fruit grow organically. History, symmetry and historic tributes are the foundation of this C19 walled kitchen garden which is seasonally evolving with new projects and planting schemes. Featured on BBC's Hereford and Worcester Radio and in The Little Book of Worcestershire Gardens.

52 WESTACRES

Wolverhampton Road, Prestwood, Stourbridge DY7 5AN. Mrs Joyce Williams, 01384 877496. *3m W of Stourbridge. A449 in between Wall Heath (2m) & Kidderminster (6m). Ample parking Prestwood Nurseries (next door).* Home-made teas. **Adm £3, chd free. Sat 20, Sun 21 July (11-4). Visitors also welcome by appt.**

3/4 -acre plant collector's garden, many different varieties of acers, hostas, shrubs. Woodland walk, large koi pool, covered tea area with home-made cakes. Come and see for yourselves, you won't be disappointed. Plant sales.

53 WHITCOMBE HOUSE

Overbury, nr Tewkesbury GL20 7NZ. Faith & Anthony Hallett, 01386 725206, faith@whitcombeassocs.co.uk. *9m S of Evesham. From M5 J9, A46 towards Evesham to r'about junction with A435 & B4077, 1st exit down small lane. From Cheltenham, A435 to A46/B4077 r'about (above) (2nd exit). From Evesham, R off A46 at Beckford Inn. From Tewkesbury, B4080 through Bredon, then straight on via Kemerton to Overbury.* Teas. **Adm £3.50, chd free. Visitors welcome by appt Apr to Sept. Evening appts (with wine) also possible. We are very happy to consider last minute requests for afternoon and evening visits although refreshments may not be available.**

1 acre planted for every season in an idyllic Cotswold stone setting. Spring bulbs give way to cool blue and white, allium and flowering shrubs are followed by cascading roses, summer pastels and fiery oranges, red and yellows. The spring-fed stream flows through colourful moisture loving plants. Asters, cosmos and yet more roses provide late summer colour. Lots of seats for relaxation. For wheelchair access please contact us in advance for details.

Colour-filled gardens specifically designed for the residents to experience and enjoy . . .

54 WHITE COTTAGE

Earls Common Road, Stock Green, nr Inkberrow B96 6SZ. Mr & Mrs S M Bates, 01386 792414, smandjbates@aol.com. *2m W of Inkberrow, 2m E of Upton Snodsbury. A422 Worcester to Alcester, turn at sign for Stock Green by Red Hart PH, 1 1/2 m to T- junction, turn L.* Refreshments will only be served if the weather is fine, NGS days. **Adm £3, chd free. Sun 7 Apr; Sat 15, Sun 16 June (11-5). Visitors also welcome by appt Mar to Oct, groups max 30.**

2-acres, herbaceous and shrub beds, stream and spring wild flower area, rose garden, raised woodland bed, large specialist collection of hardy geraniums and echinacea. New raised vegetable bed. Featured in Worcestershire Life and Period Living. Gravel drive to the gate but it is manageable.

55 ◆ WHITLENGE GARDENS

Whitlenge Lane, Hartlebury DY10 4HD. Mr & Mrs K J Southall, 01299 250720, www.whitlengegardens.co.uk. *5m S of Kidderminster, on A442. Take A449 from Kidderminster towards Worcester, then L at T-lights A442 (signed Droitwich) over small island, 1/4 m, 1st R into Whitlenge Lane. Follow signs. From Worcester along A449 keep on dual carriageway through Hartlebury until goes into single track, turn R at lights (A450) R at island (A442 Droitwich) then 1/4 m turn R into Whitlenge Lane.* **Adm £3, chd free. For NGS: Sats, Suns 6, 7 Apr; 11, 12 May; 1, 2 June; 31 Aug; 1 Sept (10-5). For other opening times and information, please phone or see garden website.**

3 acre show garden of professional designer with over 800 varieties of trees, shrubs etc. Twisted pillar pergola, camomile lawn, waterfalls and pools. Mystic features of the Green Man, 'Sword in the Stone' and cave fernery. Walk the labyrinth and take refreshments in The Garden 'Design Studio' tearoom. 400 sq metre grass labyrinth, 2 1/2 metre brick moongate with 4 cascading waterfalls, deck walk through giant gunnera leaves, camomile paths through herb gardens, childrens play and pet corner. Organic and locally sourced homemade food, plant nursery. Open daily 9 - 5 not xmas week. Featured in Worcester Life.

GROUP OPENING

56 WICK VILLAGE

Pershore WR10 3NU, 01386 550007, kate.tudorhall@gmail.com. *Wick village. 1m E of Pershore on B4084. Sign post to Wick is almost opposite Pershore Horticultural College.* Several locations for home made teas. **Combined adm £5, chd free. Sun 30 June (1-6).**

THE BARN
Main Street. Alison and David Scott

CONFETTI FIELD
Yock Lane. Charles Hudson www.confettidirect.co.uk

LAMBOURNE HOUSE
Main Street. Mr & Mrs G Power

THE OLD FORGE
Main Street. Sean & Elaine Young

TUDOR HALL D
Main Street. Mr & Mrs A Smart

VENEDIGER
Wick House Close. Alan & Barbara de Ville

5 WICK HOUSE CLOSE
Jill & Martin Willams

WILLOW CORNER
Wick House Close. Marjorie Donaldson

WOODWARDS HOUSE
Cooks Hill. Garth & Lynne Raymer

WYKE MANOR
Main Street. Charles Hudson

Wick has a delightful combination of gardens for 2013 many of which have been updated in different ways since 2011 when we last opened. We have the spectacle of the confetti fields in bloom (weather permitting!) as well as the romantic Wyke Manor gardens that have evolved over several hundred years. There are gardens with ponds and resident wildlife, gardens with horticulturally challenging places, lots of well stocked herbaceous borders and productive vegetable plots. To make your visit more leisurely we are also running a mini bus service up and down the village to save your feet for those well-tended lawns. Wick is the home of The Real Flower Petal Company. Featured on Countryfile & in many magazine articles. Many of the gardens are suitable for wheel chair access.

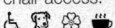

The site is compact and in a charming environment . . .

GROUP OPENING

57 WITHYBED GREEN

Alvechurch B48 7PP. *3m N of Redditch. W edge of Alvechurch, 11m SW of Birmingham. 6 mins from J2 of M42 where signed N to Birmingham. At next r'about turn L signed Alvechurch. From Redditch A441 to Bordesley r'about, then take 1st exit on B4120 to Alvechurch, From Alvechurch centre take Tanyard Lane or Bear Hill. Follow NGS signs along Snake Lane & Withybed Lane. By rail Alvechurch, with a pleasant 15 min stroll along towpath.* Home-made teas at The New Smithy, Withybed Green. **Combined adm £5, chd free.** **Sun 30 June (1-6).**

FAIRVIEW
Bryan & Angela Haycocks.
200yds past Crown Inn turn R Birches Lane, 200yds down Birches Lane, enter through 5 bar gate on L

2 FRONT COTTAGES
Ann & Clive Southern

NEW **4 FRONT COTTAGES**
Alvechurch. Leon Southern

6 FRONT COTTAGES
Mr & Mrs Horne

THE MOUSEHOLE
4 Forward Cottages. David & Lucy Hastie

6 REAR COTTAGES
John Adams & Amelda Brown

SELVAS COTTAGE
Birches Lane. Mr & Mrs J L Plewes

7 varied gardens (one new this year) opening biennially. Withybed Green is a secret hamlet to the W of Alvechurch set between semi-wooded hillsides and the Birmingham Worcester Canal. The gardens provide a range of sizes and styles to give interest for all - incl a rose garden, ancient woodland, allotments, small cottage gardens and a stream-side walk. The site is compact and in a charming environment and you can easily walk round all seven. The houses and cottages mostly date from C19, built for farm workers, nail makers, canal and railway builders. Withybed has its own canal-side pub, The Crown.

WOLFERLOW HOUSE
See Herefordshire

58 THE WOODLANDS

Dunclent, Stone, Kidderminster DY10 4AY. Pat & Phil Gaskin, 01562 740795, thewoodlands1@yahoo.co.uk. *2m SE of Kidderminster. A448 Bromsgrove Rd. Turn into Dunclent Lane, follow signs down narrow lane onto unadopted rd, short distance.* Home-made teas. **Adm £3.50, chd free.** **Suns 23 June; 14 July (11.30-5).** **Visitors also welcome by appt June to Aug.**
Intriguing approx 3/4 -acre garden in rural woodland, open fields haven. Developed last 8yrs, designed on various levels, with secret winding paths, steps to coloured themed herbaceous/shrub borders, large vegetable garden, tomato/cucumber greenhouses. Courtyard, waterfall, pergola walk, fish pond, swimming pool, hanging baskets and tubs of flowers all grown in the greenhouse. Featured in Express and Star Newspaper.

Worcestershire County Volunteers

County Organiser
Judy Berrow, Tythe Barn House, Chaddesley Corbett DY10 4QB, 01562 777014, jdberrow@btinternet.com

County Treasurer
Cliff Woodward, 11 Trehernes Drive, Pedmore, Stourbridge DY9 0YX, 01562 886349

Publicity
David Morgan, Oak Tree House, 504 Birmingham Road, Marlbrook B61 0HS, 0121 445 3595, meandi@btinternet.com

Advertising & Leaflet Coordinator
Alan Nokes, 24 Braces Lane, Marlbrook, Bromsgrove B60 1DY, 0121 445 5520, alyn.nokes@btinternet.com

Assistant County Organisers
Richard Armitage, 11 Myatts Field, Harvington, Evesham WR11 8NG, 01386 871211
Mike George, 55 Hawkwood Crescent, Worcester WR2 6BP, 01905 427567
Lynn Glaze, Brook House, Manor Road, Eckington, nr Pershore WR10 3BH, 01386 751924 lynnglaze@cmail.co.uk
Marion Scholey, 105 Hewell Road, Barnt Green B45 8NM, 0121 445 1329, marl2910@aol.com

YORKSHIRE

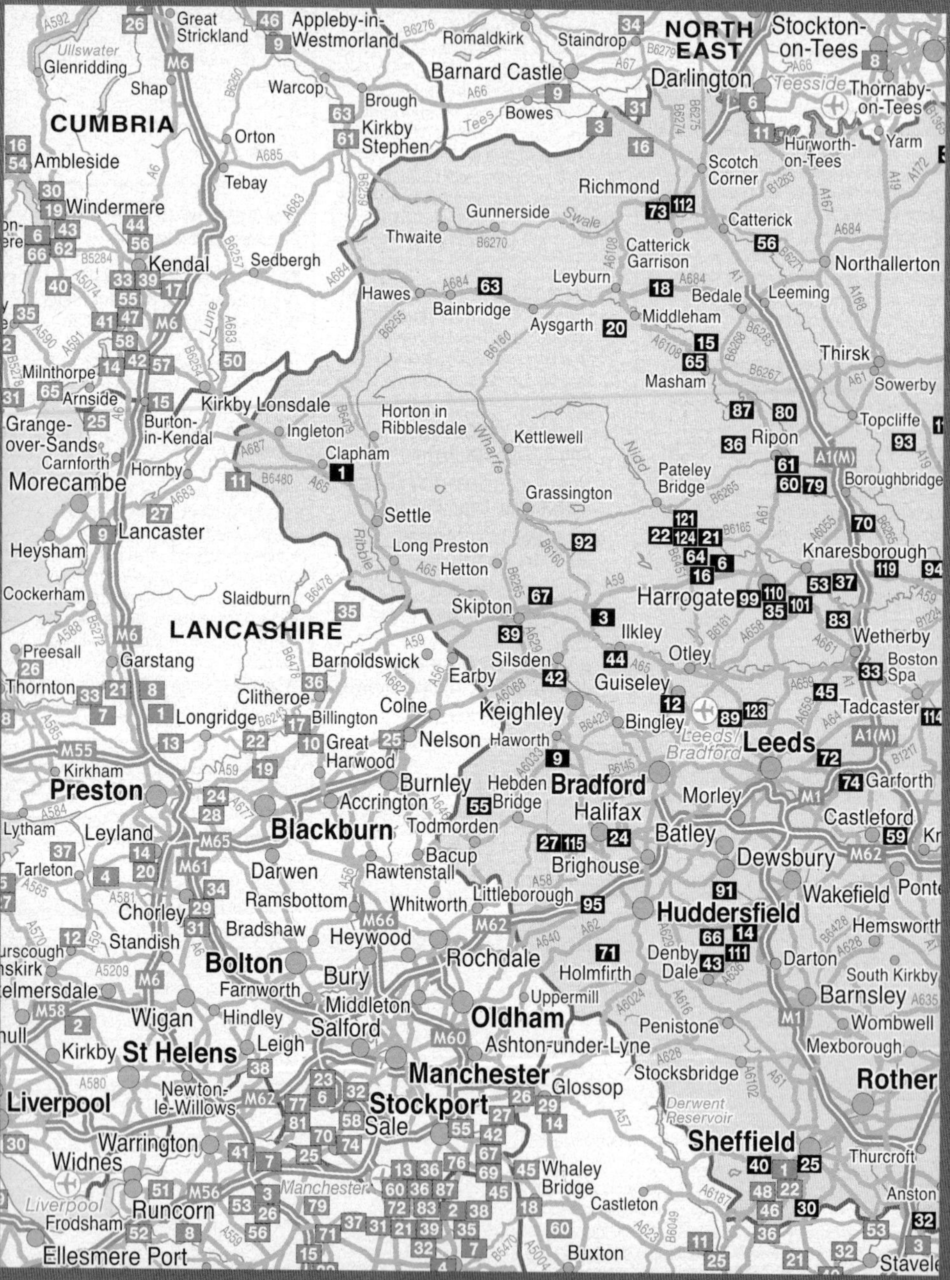

NORTH EAST
CUMBRIA
LANCASHIRE
Great Strickland
Appleby-in-Westmorland
Romaldkirk
Staindrop
Stockton-on-Tees
Ullswater
Glenridding
Shap
Warcop
Barnard Castle
Darlington
Teesside
Thornaby-on-Tees
Brough
Bowes
Orton
Kirkby Stephen
Tees
Hurworth-on-Tees
Yarm
Ambleside
Tebay
Scotch Corner
Richmond
Windermere
Gunnerside
Swale
Catterick
Thwaite
Catterick Garrison
Northallerton
Kendal
Sedbergh
Leyburn
Hawes
Bainbridge
Bedale
Leeming
Middleham
Aysgarth
Lune
Thirsk
Milnthorpe
Masham
Sowerby
Arnside
Kirkby Lonsdale
Grange-over-Sands
Burton-in-Kendal
Horton in Ribblesdale
Topcliffe
Ingleton
Kettlewell
Ripon
Carnforth
Clapham
Nidd
Wharfe
Morecambe
Hornby
Pateley Bridge
Boroughbridge
Grassington
Heysham
Lancaster
Settle
Ribble
Long Preston
Hetton
Knaresborough
Cockerham
Slaidburn
Skipton
Harrogate
Ilkley
Wetherby
Preesall
Garstang
Barnoldswick
Silsden
Otley
Boston Spa
Thornton
Earby
Guiseley
Clitheroe
Colne
Keighley
Bingley
Tadcaster
Longridge
Billington
Nelson
Haworth
Leeds/Bradford
Leeds
Great Harwood
Kirkham
Preston
Burnley
Hebden Bridge
Bradford
Garforth
Accrington
Halifax
Morley
Lytham
Leyland
Blackburn
Todmorden
Batley
Castleford
Bacup
Dewsbury
Tarleton
Darwen
Rawtenstall
Brighouse
Wakefield
Ramsbottom
Whitworth
Littleborough
Chorley
Huddersfield
Bradshaw
Heywood
Hemsworth
Standish
Bolton
Rochdale
Darton
Bury
Holmfirth
Denby Dale
South Kirkby
Farnworth
Uppermill
Barnsley
Middleton
Wigan
Hindley
Oldham
Penistone
Wombwell
Salford
Kirkby
St Helens
Leigh
Ashton-under-Lyne
Mexborough
Manchester
Stocksbridge
Glossop
Liverpool
Newton-le-Willows
Stockport
Derwent Reservoir
Sale
Warrington
Sheffield
Widnes
Thurcroft
Whaley Bridge
Runcorn
Castleton
Liverpool
Frodsham
Anston
Ellesmere Port
Buxton

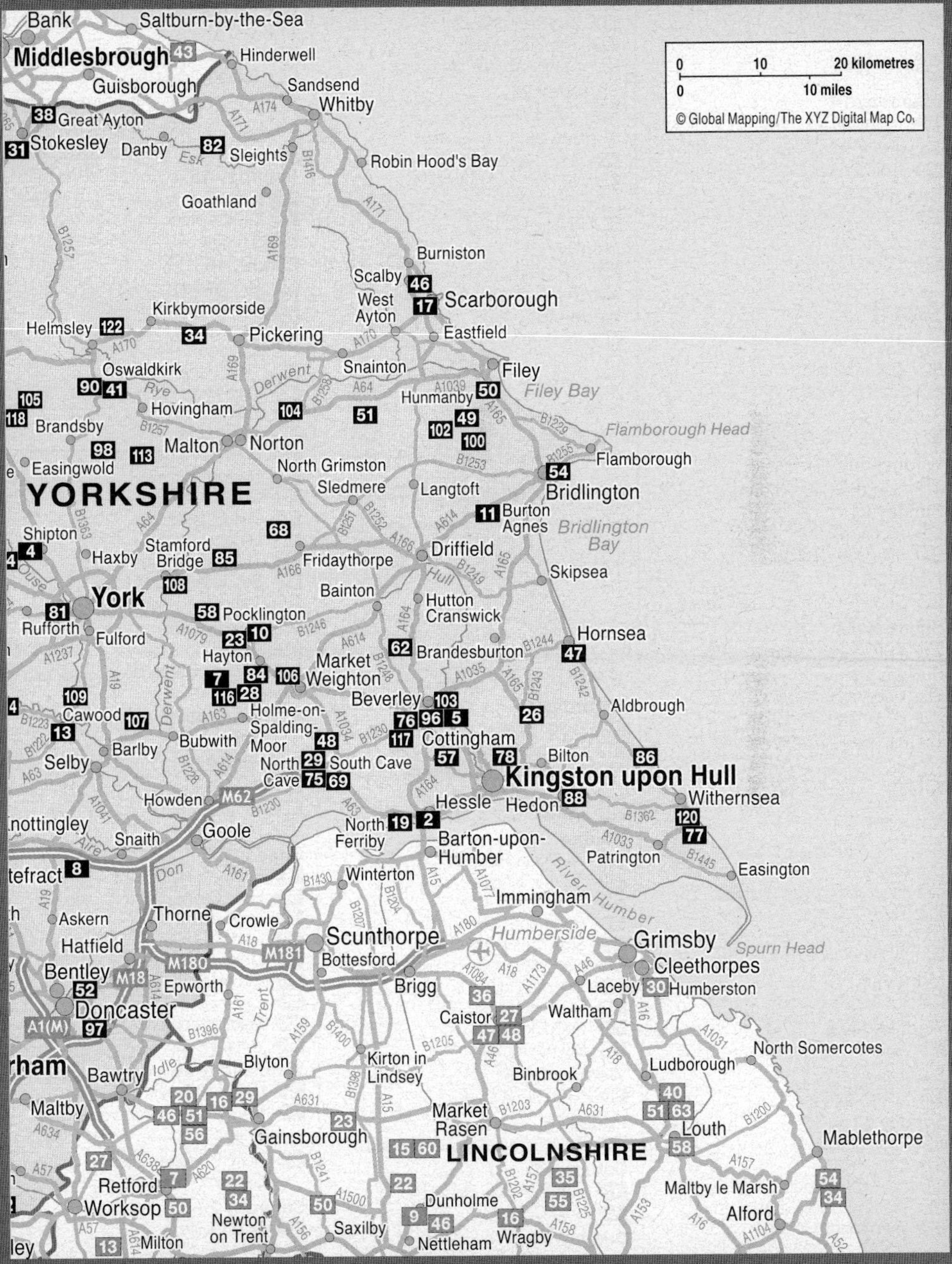
0 10 20 kilometres
0 10 miles
© Global Mapping/The XYZ Digital Map Co.
Middlesbrough
Saltburn-by-the-Sea
Hinderwell
Guisborough
Sandsend
Whitby
Great Ayton
Stokesley
Danby
Sleights
Robin Hood's Bay
Goathland
Burniston
Scalby
West Ayton
Scarborough
Kirkbymoorside
Helmsley
Pickering
Eastfield
Oswaldkirk
Snainton
Filey
Filey Bay
Hovingham
Hunmanby
Brandsby
Flamborough Head
Malton
Norton
Flamborough
Easingwold
North Grimston
Sledmere
Langtoft
Bridlington
YORKSHIRE
Burton Agnes
Bridlington Bay
Shipton
Haxby
Stamford Bridge
Fridaythorpe
Driffield
Skipsea
York
Bainton
Hutton Cranswick
Pocklington
Rufforth
Fulford
Hornsea
Hayton
Market Weighton
Brandesburton
Beverley
Aldbrough
Cawood
Holme-on-Spalding-Moor
Cottingham
Bubwith
Barlby
Bilton
Selby
North Cave
South Cave
Kingston upon Hull
Howden
Hessle
Hedon
Withernsea
Knottingley
Snaith
Goole
North Ferriby
Barton-upon-Humber
Patrington
Pontefract
Winterton
Easington
Immingham
River Humber
Askern
Thorne
Crowle
Hatfield
Scunthorpe
Humberside
Grimsby
Spurn Head
Bottesford
Cleethorpes
Bentley
Epworth
Brigg
Laceby
Humberston
Doncaster
Caistor
Waltham
North Somercotes
Rotherham
Bawtry
Blyton
Kirton in Lindsey
Binbrook
Ludborough
Maltby
Market Rasen
Gainsborough
Louth
Mablethorpe
LINCOLNSHIRE
Retford
Maltby le Marsh
Worksop
Dunholme
Alford
Newton on Trent
Saxilby
Nettleham
Wragby
Milton

Opening Dates

February

Sunday 17
23 Devonshire Mill

Wednesday 20
1 Austwick Hall

March

Thursday 14
48 Hotham Hall

Thursday 21
48 Hotham Hall

Sunday 24
37 Goldsborough Hall

Saturday 30
28 Ellerker House

April

Sunday 7
15 Clifton Castle
28 Ellerker House

Sunday 14
14 The Circles Garden

Wednesday 17
92 Parcevall Hall Gardens

Sunday 21
43 Highfields
114 Vicarage House

Friday 26
105 Shandy Hall Gardens (Evening)

Saturday 27
10 Burnby Hall Gardens

Sunday 28
74 Millrace Nursery
93 3 Pilmoor Cottages
99 RHS Garden Harlow Carr

May

Saturday 4
16 Cold Cotes

Sunday 5
32 Firvale Allotment Garden
98 Rewela Cottage
113 Terrington House
116 Weathervane House

Monday 6
119 Whixley Gardens

Wednesday 8
3 Beacon Hill House

Saturday 11
16 Cold Cotes

Sunday 12
33 Four Gables
64 Low Hall
109 Stillingfleet Lodge
115 Warley House Garden
121 Woodlands Cottage

Saturday 18
2 Beacon Garth
16 Cold Cotes
31 Fir Trees Cottage

Sunday 19
2 Beacon Garth
19 The Court
43 Highfields
51 Jackson's Wold
97 The Red House
106 Shiptonthorpe Gardens

Saturday 25
16 Cold Cotes

Sunday 26
25 34 Dover Road
40 16 Hallam Grange Croft
100 The Ridings
102 Rustic Cottage

Monday 27
8 Bridge Farm House
89 The Orchard

Wednesday 29
44 5 Hill Top

Stroll along formal borders, labyrinth paths and discover hidden woods . . .

June

Saturday 1
16 Cold Cotes
49 Hunmanby Grange
56 Langton Farm (Evening)
57 Linden House
87 Old Sleningford Hall

Sunday 2
25 34 Dover Road
28 Ellerker House
44 5 Hill Top
49 Hunmanby Grange
52 Jasmine House
57 Linden House
73 Millgate House
87 Old Sleningford Hall
101 Rudding Park
112 Swale Cottage

Wednesday 5
35 6 Fulwith Avenue

Friday 7
24 Dove Cottage Nursery Garden

Saturday 8
11 Burton Agnes Hall
16 Cold Cotes

Sunday 9
11 Burton Agnes Hall
36 Galphay Manor
45 Hillbark
53 Kelberdale
62 Lockington Gardens
90 Oswaldkirk Hall

Wednesday 12
107 Skipwith Hall

Friday 14
24 Dove Cottage Nursery Garden
105 Shandy Hall Gardens (Evening)

National Gardens Weekend

Saturday 15
9 Brookfield
16 Cold Cotes
88 Omega

Sunday 16
9 Brookfield
15 Clifton Castle
26 Dowthorpe Hall & Horse Pasture Cottage
38 The Granary
42 High Hall
47 Hornsea Gardens
58 Linden Lodge
74 Millrace Nursery
80 Norton Conyers
82 Oatmill Cottage
83 The Old Hall
88 Omega
97 The Red House
109 Stillingfleet Lodge
113 Terrington House

Wednesday 19
9 Brookfield
119 Whixley Gardens

Friday 21
24 Dove Cottage Nursery Garden

Saturday 22
16 Cold Cotes
56 Langton Farm
124 Yorke House

Sunday 23
6 Birstwith Hall
46 Holly Croft
51 Jackson's Wold
58 Linden Lodge
76 Molecroft Cottage
86 Old Rectory Cottage
95 2 Prospect Place
106 Shiptonthorpe Gardens
124 Yorke House

Wednesday 26
66 Lower Crawshaw
70 Marton Cum Grafton Gardens

Friday 28
24 Dove Cottage Nursery Garden

Saturday 29
16 Cold Cotes

Sunday 30
30 Fernleigh
59 Little Eden
66 Lower Crawshaw
77 Neakins House
94 The Priory
122 Wytherstone Gardens

July

Wednesday 3
27 Edgeholme
53 Kelberdale

Friday 5
24 Dove Cottage Nursery Garden
95 2 Prospect Place (Evening)

Saturday 6
16 Cold Cotes
20 Coverham Abbey
103 St John RC Primary School

Sunday 7
22 Dacre Banks & Summerbridge Gardens
45 Hillbark
73 Millgate House
75 Millview Cottage
100 The Ridings
102 Rustic Cottage

Thursday 11
63 Lodge Yard

Friday 12
24 Dove Cottage Nursery Garden
78 Neasden Primary School

Saturday 13
13 Cawood Gardens
16 Cold Cotes
50 Hunmanby School
68 Manor Farm
85 The Old Rectory

Sunday 14
7 Boundary Cottage
13 Cawood Gardens
71 Meltham, Pavilion Way Gardens
78 Neasden Primary School
82 Oatmill Cottage
85 The Old Rectory
89 The Orchard
91 Overthorpe J I & N School

Wednesday 17
39 The Grange

Friday 19
24 Dove Cottage Nursery Garden
72 Mere'stead (Evening)

Saturday 20
16 Cold Cotes

Sunday 21
37 Goldsborough Hall
42 High Hall
72 Mere'stead
81 The Nursery
98 Rewela Cottage
73 Stamford Bridge Gardens
120 Withernsea Gardens

Wednesday 24
17 Combe Hay
81 The Nursery (Afternoon & Evening)

Friday 26
24 Dove Cottage Nursery Garden

Saturday 27
16 Cold Cotes

Sunday 28
21 Cow Close Cottage
30 Fernleigh
60 Littlethorpe Gardens
65 Low Sutton
93 3 Pilmoor Cottages
96 Queensgate & Kitchen Lane Allotments

Wednesday 31
21 Cow Close Cottage
39 The Grange

Spectacular 'triumphal arch' is an amazing display of climbers, pots and water feature . . .

August

Friday 2
24 Dove Cottage Nursery Garden

Saturday 3
16 Cold Cotes

Sunday 4
111 Sue Proctor Plants Nursery Garden

Wednesday 7
39 The Grange

Friday 9
24 Dove Cottage Nursery Garden

Saturday 10
16 Cold Cotes

Sunday 11
41 Havoc Hall

Wednesday 14
12 Butterfield Heights
35 6 Fulwith Avenue
63 Lodge Yard

Friday 16
24 Dove Cottage Nursery Garden

Saturday 17
16 Cold Cotes

Sunday 18
59 Little Eden
74 Millrace Nursery

Friday 23
24 Dove Cottage Nursery Garden

Saturday 24
16 Cold Cotes

Sunday 25
30 Fernleigh
54 23 Lambert Road

Friday 30
24 Dove Cottage Nursery Garden

Saturday 31
16 Cold Cotes
56 Langton Farm (Evening)

September

Friday 6
24 Dove Cottage Nursery Garden

Saturday 7
16 Cold Cotes

Sunday 8
7 Boundary Cottage
109 Stillingfleet Lodge

Friday 13
24 Dove Cottage Nursery Garden

Saturday 14
16 Cold Cotes

Sunday 15
93 3 Pilmoor Cottages

Friday 20
24 Dove Cottage Nursery Garden

Saturday 21
16 Cold Cotes

Friday 27
24 Dove Cottage Nursery Garden

Saturday 28
16 Cold Cotes

October

Sunday 6
28 Ellerker House

February 2014

Wednesday 26
1 Austwick Hall

Gardens open to the public

4 Beningbrough Hall & Gardens
10 Burnby Hall Gardens
11 Burton Agnes Hall
18 Constable Burton Hall Gardens
51 Jackson's Wold
55 Land Farm
79 Newby Hall & Gardens
80 Norton Conyers
92 Parcevall Hall Gardens
99 RHS Garden Harlow Carr
104 Scampston Walled Garden
105 Shandy Hall Gardens
109 Stillingfleet Lodge
123 York Gate

By appointment only

- 5 Beverley Hidden Town Gardens
- 29 Fawley House
- 34 Friars Hill
- 61 Littlethorpe Manor
- 67 Lower Heugh Cottage Garden
- 69 39 Market Place
- 84 The Old Priory
- 110 Stonehaven
- 117 26 West End
- 118 The White House

Also open by Appointment

- 2 Beacon Garth
- 3 Beacon Hill House
- 6 Birstwith Hall
- 8 Bridge Farm House
- 9 Brookfield
- 13 Cawood Gardens
- 16 Cold Cotes
- 19 The Court
- 21 Cow Close Cottage
- 22 Dacre Banks & Summerbridge Gardens
- 22 Riverside House, Dacre Banks & Summerbridge Gardens
- 26 Dowthorpe Hall & Horse Pasture Cottage
- 30 Fernleigh
- 32 Firvale Allotment Garden
- 37 Goldsborough Hall
- 39 The Grange
- 43 Highfields
- 47 Hornsea Gardens
- 47 New House, Hornsea Gardens
- 47 Nutkins, Hornsea Gardens
- 48 Hotham Hall
- 52 Jasmine House
- 53 Kelberdale
- 56 Langton Farm
- 57 Linden House
- 58 Linden Lodge
- 59 Little Eden
- 60 Greencroft, Littlethorpe Gardens
- 64 Low Hall
- 74 Millrace Nursery
- 82 Oatmill Cottage
- 85 The Old Rectory
- 89 The Orchard
- 90 Oswaldkirk Hall
- 91 Overthorpe J I & N School
- 93 3 Pilmoor Cottages
- 95 2 Prospect Place
- 98 Rewela Cottage
- 100 The Ridings
- 102 Rustic Cottage
- 107 Skipwith Hall
- 73 Daneswell House, Stamford Bridge Gardens
- 73 Grove Lodge, Stamford Bridge Gardens
- 73 Mill Timber, Stamford Bridge Gardens
- 73 Stamford Bridge Gardens
- 111 Sue Proctor Plants Nursery Garden
- 113 Terrington House
- 116 Weathervane House
- 119 Ash Tree House, Whixley Gardens
- 119 Cobble Cottage, Whixley Gardens
- 119 Whixley Gardens
- 121 Woodlands Cottage
- 124 Yorke House

Sumptuous planting for late summer colour, unusual herbaceous plants, shrubs and trees . . .

The Gardens

12 ANSELL ROAD
See Derbyshire

1 AUSTWICK HALL

Town Head Lane, Austwick, nr Settle LA2 8BS. James Culley & Michael Pearson, www.austwickhall.co.uk. *5m W of Settle. From A65 to Austwick Village. Pass Game Cock Inn on L. After Primary School turn L up Town Head Lane. No parking adjacent to hall, please park in village.* Home-made teas. **Adm £3.50, chd free. Wed 20 Feb (12-4); Wed 26 Feb 2014.**
Set in the dramatic limestone scenery of the Dales the garden nestles into a steeply wooded hillside. Extensive drifts of common single and double snowdrops are an impressive sight with examples of over 50 other varieties. Sculptures along the trail add further interest.Woodland paths may be slippery in wet weather so sensible footwear recommended.

BARLBOROUGH GARDENS
See Derbyshire

BARNINGHAM VILLAGE GARDENS
See North East

2 BEACON GARTH

Redcliff Road, Hessle, Hull HU13 0HA. Ivor & June Innes, 01482 646140, ivorinnes@mac.com. *$4^{1}/_{2}$ m W of Hull. Humber Bridge r'about. Toward Hessle. R at T-lights. Travel toward river along Heads Lane, over Xrds into Woodfield Lane, approx $^{1}/_{2}$ m sharp bend L. House on RH-side at junction of Cliff Rd & Redcliff Rd. Parking on foreshore car park.* Home-made teas in hall of the house. **Adm £4, chd free. Sat 18, Sun 19 May (12-5). Visitors also welcome by appt Apr to Sept.**
Edwardian, Arts & Crafts House (not open) and S-facing garden set in $3^{1}/_{2}$ acres, in an elevated position overlooking the Humber. Stunning sunken rock garden with bulbs and specimen trees, hostas and ferns. Mature trees, large lawns and herbaceous borders. Gravel paths, box hedges and topiary. Child friendly. Partial wheelchair access.

3 BEACON HILL HOUSE

Langbar, nr Ilkley LS29 0EU. Mr & Mrs H Boyle, 01943 607544. *4m NW of Ilkley. $1^{1}/_{4}$ m SE of A59 at Bolton Bridge.* Home-made teas. **Adm £3.50, chd free (share to Riding for the Disabled). Wed 8 May (1.30-5). Visitors also welcome by appt May to Sept.**
Look over the garden wall onto a grouse moor. This 7-acre 'intake', steeply sloping but gardened since 1848, is a spring paradise with early rhododendrons, magnolias and bulbs. Roses, large scented rhododendrons and borders take over, some unusual trees, an established liriodendron, pterostyrax, hoherias and several species of eucryphia.

4 NEW ◆ BENINGBROUGH HALL & GARDENS

Beningbrough, York YO30 1DD. National Trust, 01904 472027, www.nationaltrust.org.uk. *8m N of York. Easily accessed from A19 or over toll bridge & country roads from A59.* **For opening times and information, please phone or see garden website.**
Each visit to Beningbrough Hall and Gardens is a friendly, relaxed and inspiring journey. Visit our famous pear arch and working walled garden which supplies the Walled Garden Restaurant. Stroll along formal borders, labyrinth paths and discover hidden woods. Guided walks are available during the main season. Or enjoy a walk in our extensive surrounding parkland. New for 2013 - Beningbrough at War tells the story of the air crews billeted during WWII.

GROUP OPENING

5 NEW BEVERLEY HIDDEN TOWN GARDENS

Beverley HU17 8JH, 01482 8639191, a_aveyard@hotmail.com. *Centre of Beverley*. **Combined adm £3.50, chd free. St Matthews only, £2.50. Groups of up to 10 by appointment, (1-5). Parking limited. Visitors welcome by appt June and July.**

NEW 30 RAILWAY STREET
Wendy Munday

NEW 32 RAILWAY STREET
M Williamson

NEW 34 RAILWAY STREET
Sharon Clay

NEW 16 ST MATTHEWS COURT
Annegret Aveyard

Four town gardens. 16 St Matthews Court: front garden overlooking spectacular West Towers of Beverley Minster. A rich collection of hellebores, tulips, grasses and other spring flowers. Hidden garden at back features many perennials, roses, climbers, annuals and grasses, Mediterranean area with different succulents and small pond with water plants. Has been described as giving a Continental feel with its modern art work. 30 Railway Street: through spectacular 'triumphal arch' is an amazing display of climbers, pots and water feature. 32 Railway Street: after extensive building work, a garden is in the making. 34 Railway Street: paved, creatively planted courtyard. All 3 Railway Street gardens have a S aspect and tender plants thrive. The town has many tearooms.

☎

6 BIRSTWITH HALL

High Birstwith, nr Harrogate HG3 2JW. Sir James & Lady Aykroyd, info@birstwithhall.co.uk. *5m NW of Harrogate. Between Hampsthwaite & Birstwith villages, close to A59 Harrogate/Skipton Rd*. Home-made teas. **Adm £3.50, chd free. Sun 23 June (2-5). Visitors and groups also welcome by appt May to July. Coaches permitted.**
Large 8-acre garden nestling in secluded Yorkshire dale with formal garden and ornamental orchard, extensive lawns, picturesque stream, large pond and Victorian greenhouse.

♿ 🐕 ✿ ☕ ☎

7 BOUNDARY COTTAGE

Seaton Ross, York YO42 4NF. Roger Brook, www.nodiggardener.co.uk. *5m SW of Pocklington. From A64 York, take Hull exit & immed B1228, approx 9m, then follow signs Seaton Ross. From M62 Howden N on B1228 approx 11m, R turn to Seaton Ross. Garden 1m before Seaton Ross. From Hull turn R 100yds before Seaton Ross*. Light refreshments. **Adm £4, chd free. Suns 14 July; 8 Sept (11-4.30).**
Lecturer and creator of Bolton Percy churchyard garden, Roger Brook's own no-dig garden. 1500 different plant varieties, many rare, provide colour all yr round. The acre garden has numerous and varied intimate features, visually connected in sweeping views. Horticulturally unorthodox, especially the fruit and vegetables, the overall effect is dramatic. The garden holds the National Collection of Dicentra. Very friendly rheas in the field next door! Artist in the garden. Access to all parts of the garden. Some pushing required on fescue lawns. WC access up a step.

♿ 🐕 ✿ NCH ☕

8 BRIDGE FARM HOUSE

Long Lane, Great Heck, nr Selby DN14 0BE. Barbara & Richard Ferrari, 01977 661277, barbaraferrari@mypostoffice.co.uk. *6m S of Selby. 3m E of M62 (J34) A19 turn E at r'about to Snaith onto A645. R at T-lights then L at T junc on to Main St past Church at T-junction straight across into field car park*. Tea in church opposite. **Adm £3, chd free. Mon 27 May (12-4). Visitors also welcome by appt May to June.**
2-acre garden, divided by ½ m of hedges, to house a varied collection of plants, many unusual. Garden developed by owners from 2002, including bog, gravel, ponds and 130ft long double mixed borders. Happy hens, extensive compost heaps and wildlife.

♿ ✿ ☕ ☎

Fernleigh

9 BROOKFIELD

Jew Lane, Oxenhope, nr Keighley BD22 9HS. Mrs R L Belsey, 01535 643070. *5m SW of Keighley. Take A629 towards Halifax. Fork R onto A6033 towards Haworth. Follow signs to Oxenhope. Turn L at Xrds in village. Continue through village to fork in rd. Turn R into Jew Lane.* Home-made teas. **Adm £3, chd free.** **Sat 15, Sun 16, Wed 19 June (1-5). Visitors also welcome by appt May to July.**

1-acre, intimate garden, incl large pond with island and mallards. Many varieties of candelabra and primulas, florindae, azaleas, rhododendrons. Unusual trees and shrubs, screes, greenhouses and conservatory. Series of island beds. Children's quiz and garden notes 'A walk round the garden'.

10 NEW ◆ BURNBY HALL GARDENS

33 The Balk, Pocklington, York YO42 2QF. Sara Waddington, 01759 307125, www.burnbyhallgardens.com. *In the centre of Pocklington, follow brown signs from both directions of A1079.* **Adm by donation. For NGS: Sat 27 Apr (10-5.30 last adm 4.30). For other opening times and information, please phone or see garden website.**

Beautiful 9 acre garden, containing 2 lakes which are home to a National Collection of Hardy Water Lilies. The gardens have many different features incl a rockery, secret garden, stumpery, formal beds, Victorian garden and natural shrubbery. 25 April to 3 May we are holding our first tulip festival.

NCH

11 ◆ BURTON AGNES HALL

Burton Agnes, Driffield YO25 4NB. Mrs S Cunliffe-Lister, 01262 490324, www.burtonagnes.com. *Between Driffield & Bridlington on A614. on A614.* **Sat 8, Sun 9 June Gardener Fair (11-5). Donation to NGS. For other opening times and information, please phone or see garden website.**

Beautiful award-winning gardens of Burton Agnes Hall are home to 3,000 different plant species, herbaceous borders, a jungle garden, potager, coloured gardens, giant games, a maze and collection of campanulas. Surrounded by lawns, topiary yews, fountains and a woodland walk. Collections of hardy geraniums, clematis, penstemons and unusual perennials.

12 NEW BUTTERFIELD HEIGHTS

4 Park Crescent, Guiseley, Leeds LS20 8EL. Vicky & Trevor Harris. *From Guiseley A65 (Otley-Leeds) A6038 r'about follow A6038 Bradford Rd towards Shipley. Park Crescent ½ m on L. Please park in Southway/ Tranmere Park opp and surrounding rds.* Home-made teas. **Adm £2.50, chd free. Wed 14 Aug (11-5).**

Hardy plantswoman's garden with view towards Otley Chevin. Restoration of this dark, damp plot since 1998 revealed 1930s landscape on 3 levels linked by steps. Sumptuous planting for late summer colour, unusual herbaceous plants, shrubs and trees. Winding gravel paths and tall perennials, secluded Japanese corner. Small pond, newly planted box parterre and steep steps to paved area.

GROUP OPENING

13 CAWOOD GARDENS

Cawood, Selby YO8 3UG. *On B1223 5m N of Selby & 7m SE of Tadcaster. Between York & A1 on B1222. Village maps given at all gardens.* Home-made teas at each garden. **Combined adm £4, chd free. Sat 13, Sun 14 July (12-5). Visitors also welcome by appt June to Aug.**

9 ANSON GROVE
Tony & Brenda Finnigan
01757 268888,
beeart@btinternet.com

21 GREAT CLOSE
David & Judy Jones
01757 268571
dave-judyjones@hotmail.co.uk

These two contrasting gardens in an attractive historic village are linked by a pretty riverside walk to the C11 church and Memorial garden and across the Castle Garth to the remains of Cawood Castle. 9 Anson Grove is a small garden with tranquil pools and secluded sitting places. Narrow winding paths and raised areas give views over oriental-style pagoda, bridge and Zen garden. 21 Great Close is a flower arranger's garden, designed and built by the owners. Interesting trees and shrubs combine with herbaceous borders incl many grasses. Two ponds are joined by a stream, winding paths take you to the vegetable garden and summerhouse, then back to the colourful terrace for views across the garden and countryside beyond. Crafts and paintings on sale at 9 Anson Grove.

These two contrasting gardens are linked by a pretty riverside walk . . .

14 THE CIRCLES GARDEN

8 Stocksmoor Road, Midgley, nr Wakefield WF4 4JQ. Joan Gaunt. *Equidistant from Huddersfield, Wakefield & Barnsley, W of M1. Turn off A637 in Midgley at the Black Bull PH (sharp bend) onto B6117 (Stocksmoor Rd). Please park on L adjacent to houses.* Home-made teas. **Adm £3, chd free. Sun 14 Apr (1.30-5).**

Plantswoman's ½ -acre garden on gently sloping site overlooking fields and woods. Designed and maintained by owner. Interesting herbaceous, bulb and shrub plantings linked by grass and gravel paths, a woodland area with mature trees, spring and summer meadows, fernery, greenhouse, fruit trees, viewing terrace with pots. South African plants, ferns, hollies and small bulbs are particular interests.

15 CLIFTON CASTLE

Ripon HG4 4AB. Lord & Lady Downshire. *2m N of Masham. On rd to Newton-le-Willows & Richmond. Gates on L next to red telephone box.* Home-made teas. **Adm £3.50, chd free. Suns 7 Apr; 16 June (2-5).**

Fine views, river walks, wooded pleasure grounds with bridges and follies. Cascades, wild flower meadow and C19 walled kitchen garden. Gravel paths and steep slopes to river.

16 COLD COTES

Cold Cotes Road, nr Kettlesing, Harrogate HG3 2LW. Penny Jones, Ed Loft, Doreen & Joanna Russell, 01423 770937, info@coldcotes.com, www.coldcotes.com. *7m W of Harrogate. Off A59. After Black Bull PH turn R to Menwith Hill/Darley.* Light refreshments. **Adm £3.50, chd free. Every Sat 4 May to 28 Sept (11-5). Visitors also welcome by appt May to Sept.**

Large peaceful garden with expansive views at ease in its rural setting. Series of discrete gardens incl formal areas, stream-side walk, pond, bog garden. Oudolf-inspired sweeping herbaceous borders peak in late summer. Chatto-inspired woodland garden underplanted with bulbs and perennials for spring to autumn interest. Tearoom and nursery specialising in shade and moisture-loving perennials.

17 COMBE HAY

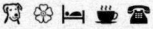

Stepney Drive, Scarborough YO12 5DJ. The George Edward Smart Homes. *1m W of Scarborough. From Whitby take A171. After Scarborough Hospital follow sign for A170 onto Stepney Drive. From Thirsk follow A170 to sixth form college, L at r'about 150 metres on R. A64 into Scarborough L onto A171 follow signs for Thirsk A170. At r'about L Stepney Drive.* **Adm £3.50, chd free. Wed 24 July (10-4).**

Situated in attractive and tranquil landscape grounds of approx 4½ acres. The award-winning garden is designed for relaxation, with summerhouses and seating areas to admire the large variety of trees and shrubs/colourful herbaceous/annual borders. Other features of interest incl orchard, vegetable garden and pond.

18 ◆ CONSTABLE BURTON HALL GARDENS

Constable Burton, nr Leyburn DL8 5LJ. Mr Charles Wyvill, 01677 450428, www.constableburton.com. *3m E of Leyburn. Constable Burton Village. On A684, 6m W of A1.* **Adm £4, chd 50p. For opening times and information, please phone or see garden website.**

Large romantic garden with terraced woodland walks. Garden trails, shrubs, roses and water garden. Display of daffodils and over 5000 tulips planted annually amongst extensive borders. Fine John Carr house (not open) set in splendour of Wensleydale countryside.

19 THE COURT

Humber Road, North Ferriby HU14 3DW. Guy & Liz Slater, 01482 633609, liz@guyslater.karoo.co.uk. *7m W of Hull. Travelling E on A63 towards Hull, follow sign for N Ferriby. Through village to Xrds with war memorial, turn R & follow rd to T-junction with Humber Rd. Turn L & immed R into cul-de-sac, last house on L.* Home-made teas. **Adm £3, chd free. Sun 19 May (1-5). Visitors also welcome by appt Feb to July.**

Romantic and restful with hidden seating areas offering different vistas. Roses and clematis scrambling up walls and trees. 2 summerhouses, small pond and waterfall with secluded arbours and historical items. A long tunnel of wisteria, clematis and laburnum leads to a little path with Betula jacquemontii, small stumpery, and grown up swing.

20 COVERHAM ABBEY

Middleham, Leyburn DL8 4RL. Mr & Mrs Nigel Corner. *A6108 to Middleham then Coverdale rd out of Middleham following signs to 'The Forbidden Corner', past pond on R. Drive at bottom of steep bank on L before Church.* Home-made teas. **Adm £3.50, chd free. Sat 6 July (2-5).**

Stunning gardens set in the heart of tranquil Coverdale. Within the grounds of C13 premonstratensian Abbey ruins, a large intricate knot garden, mixed borders, parterre and yew rondel with rose arches. Some areas being developed. Wild flower meadow.

21 NEW COW CLOSE COTTAGE

Stripe Lane, Hartwith, Harrogate HG3 3EY. William Moore & John Wilson, 01423 779813, cowclose1@btinternet.com. *8m NW of Harrogate. From A61 (Harrogate-Ripon) at Ripley take B6165 to Pateley Bridge. 1m beyond Burnt Yates turn R signed Hartwith (1m) on to Stripe Lane. Parking Available.* Home-made teas. **Adm £3, chd free. Sun 28, Wed 31 July (11-5). Visitors also welcome by appt July and Aug, refreshments available on request.**

⅔ -acre recently redeveloped country garden on sloping site with stream and far reaching views. Large borders with drifts of interesting, well-chosen, later flowering summer perennials and some grasses contrasting with woodland shade and streamside plantings. Gravel path leading to vegetable area. Terrace and seating with views of the garden and beyond. New orchard and meadow walk to view-point.

Romantic and restful with hidden seating areas . . . roses and clematis scrambling up walls and trees . . .

CROFT HALL

See North East

GROUP OPENING

22 DACRE BANKS & SUMMERBRIDGE GARDENS

Nidderdale HG3 4EW. *4m SE of Pateley Bridge, 10m NW of Harrogate, 10m N of Otley on B6451 & B6165. Parking at each garden. Maps available to show garden locations.* Home-made teas at Yorke House & Low Hall. **Combined adm £6, chd free. Sun 7 July (11-5). Visitors also welcome by appt, see seperate gardens below.**

LOW HALL
Mrs P A Holliday
(See separate entry)

RIVERSIDE HOUSE
Joy Stanton.
B6451 from Dacre, please park in yard of Nidderdale Sawmill (on L before bridge). From Ripley, turn L at Xrds near PH, go over bridge and park in sawmill on R. From Pateley Bridge, turn R at Xrds near PH, go over bridge and park in sawmill on R. Walk across bridge into Riverside Lane, garden at end terrace house
Visitors also welcome by appt. 01423 780596 joy.stanton@btinternet.com

WOODLANDS COTTAGE
Mr & Mrs Stark
(See separate entry)

YORKE HOUSE
Tony & Pat Hutchinson
(See separate entry)

Dacre Banks and Summerbridge Gardens are situated in the beautiful countryside of Nidderdale and designed to take advantage of the scenic Dales landscape. The gardens are linked by an attractive walk along the valley and may be accessed individually by car. Low Hall has a romantic walled garden set on different levels around the historic C17 family home (not open) with extensive herbaceous borders, shrubs, climbing roses and tranquil water garden. Riverside House is a mysterious waterside garden on many levels, supporting many shade-loving plants and incorporates a Victorian folly, fernery, courtyard and naturalistic riverside plantings. Woodlands Cottage is designed to harmonise with boulder-strewn woodland whilst also having varied areas of formal and informal planting, a wild flower meadow and productive fruit and vegetable garden. Yorke House has colour-themed borders, attractive waterside plantings and secluded millennium garden full of fragrant plants and rambling roses. Visitors welcome to use orchard picnic area at Yorke House.

DAM STEAD
See Derbyshire

23 NEW DEVONSHIRE MILL
Canal Lane, Pocklington, York YO42 1NN. Sue & Chris Bond, www.devonshiremill.co.uk. *1m S of Pocklington. Situated on Canal Lane, Pocklington off A1079 at The Wellington Oak PH.* Home-made teas. **Adm £3, chd free. Sun 17 Feb (11-4).**
Early spring features double snowdrops (mainly galanthus flore pleno) in old orchards, hellebores and ferns in a woodland setting. The house is a 200yr old Grade II listed watermill. An intimate garden with different areas and mill stream. Organic principles used to encourage wildlife. Productive vegetable gardens with raised beds, polytunnel, greenhouses, hen run and well-stocked herbaceous borders.

122 DOBCROFT ROAD
See Derbyshire

Hunmanby Grange

Clive Nicholls

24 DOVE COTTAGE NURSERY GARDEN
Shibden Hall Road, Hipperholme, nr Halifax HX3 9XA. Kim & Stephen Rogers, www.dovecottagenursery.co.uk. *1m W of Hipperholme. 2m E of Halifax. J26 M62 take A58 Halifax. Turn 2nd L after Hipperholme T-lights (4m from J26) at pet store down Tanhouse Hill. Cont for 1/2 m. From Halifax turn L off A58 signed Claremount, Horley Green. Straight on over bridge continue 1/2 m.* **Adm £2.50, chd free. Every Fri 7 June to 27 Sept (10-5).**
Hedges and green oak gates enclose 1/3 -acre sloping garden, generously planted by nursery owners over 15yrs. A beautiful mix of late summer perennials and ornamental grasses. Winding paths and plenty of seats incl a romantic oak tulip arbour. Plants for sale in nursery.

25 NEW 34 DOVER ROAD
Hunters Bar, Sheffield S11 8RH. Marian Simpson. *1 1/2 m SW of city centre. From A61 (ring rd) A625 Moore St/Eccleshall Rd for approx 1m. Dover Rd on R.* Home-made teas. **Adm £3, chd free. Suns 26 May; 2 June (10-5). Also open 16 Hallam Grange Croft 26 May.**
Colourful, small town garden packed with interest and drama, combining formality with exotic exuberance. Attractive alpine area replacing old driveway, many interesting containers and well-stocked borders. Conservatory, seating areas and lawns complement unusual plants and planting combinations. Featured in Yorkshire Post & Sheffield Telegraph.

26 DOWTHORPE HALL & HORSE PASTURE COTTAGE
Skirlaugh, Hull HU11 5AE. Mr & Mrs J Holtby, 01964 562235, john.holtby@farming.co.uk, www.dowthorpehall.com. *6m N of Hull, 8m E of Beverley. From Hull A165 towards Bridlington. Through Ganstead & Coniston. 1m S of Skirlaugh on R, (long drive white railings and sign at drive end).* Refreshments available by arrangement. **Adm £5, chd free. Sun 16 June (11-5). Visitors also welcome by appt May to July.**
Dowthorpe Hall: 3 1/2 acres, large herbaceous borders, lawns, shady area, pond with bridge, scree garden,

hardy garden, orchards and vegetable potager. Horse Pasture Cottage: small cottage garden, herbaceous border and woodland water feature. Gravel, lawns, no steps.

27 NEW EDGEHOLME
Stock Lane, Warley, Halifax HX2 7RW. Mrs S L Ryan. *2m W of Halifax. From Halifax take A646 (Burnley). Turn R up Windleroyd Lane approx 1m after A58, A646 junction (King Cross). Turn L at T-junction into Stock Lane. Park on rd before Warley Village.* Cream teas. **Adm £3, chd free. Wed 3 July (1-5).**
Terraced country house garden complementing 1910 Arts & Crafts house (not open). Colourful mixed herbaceous borders, paths and steps link the lower and upper areas. Natural hillside stream enters via stone trough, flowing into formal pond and rill then descending to large informal bog garden in a shrub and woodland setting.

28 ELLERKER HOUSE
Everingham, York YO42 4JA. Mrs R Los & Mr M Wright, 01430 861465. *15m SE of York. 5½ m from Pocklington. On rd towards Harswell on R.* Home-made teas. **Adm £3.50, chd free. Sat 30 Mar; Sun 7 Apr; Sun 2 June; Sun 6 Oct (12-5).**
5 acres of garden on sandy soil. Lots of spring bulbs, mature trees, formal lawn and extensive grass area. Woodland walkway around lake. Traditional oak and thatched breeze hut. Several seating areas with views of the garden. Rose archway, herbaceous borders. Wheelchair access to main part of garden but not around lake.

29 FAWLEY HOUSE
7 Nordham, North Cave HU15 2LT. Mr & Mrs T Martin, 01430 422266, louisem200@hotmail.co.uk. *15m W of Hull. M62 E, J38 turn L to North Cave. On B1230 E of village, turn L before church. After bridge and L hand bend, house 3rd on L.* Home-made teas. **Adm £6, chd free. Groups welcome by appt Feb to Sept, admission incl home-made tea. Individual visitors can ring to join a group.**
Tiered, 2½ -acre garden with lawns, mature trees, formal hedging and gravel pathways. Lavender beds, mixed shrub/herbaceous borders, hot borders. Apple espaliers, pears, soft fruit, vegetable and herb gardens. Terrace with pergola and vines. Sunken garden with white border. Woodland with naturalistic planting and spring bulbs, hellebores, ferns. Quaker well, stream and spring area.

30 FERNLEIGH
9 Meadowhead Avenue, Meadowhead, Sheffield S8 7RT. Mr & Mrs C Littlewood, 01142 747234. *4m S of Sheffield city centre. From Sheffield city centre. A61, A6102, B6054 r'about, exit B6054 towards Holmesfield. 1st R Greenhill Ave, then 2nd R Meadowhead Ave. From M1 J33, A630 to A6102 (Chesterfield) then follow directions above.* Home-made teas. **Adm £2.50, chd free. Suns 30 June; 28 July; 25 Aug (1-5). Visitors also welcome by appt Apr to Aug.**
Plantswoman's ⅓ -acre cottage style garden. Large variety of unusual plants set in differently planted sections to provide all-yr interest. Auricula theatre and paved area for drought resistant plants in pots. Seating areas to view different aspects of garden. Patio, gazebo and greenhouse. Miniature log cabin with living roof. Sempervivum, alpine displays and wildlife 'hotel'. Featured in Sheffield Star and Yorkshire Post.

31 FIR TREES COTTAGE
Stokesley TS9 5LD. Helen & Mark Bainbridge, www.firtreespelargoniums.co.uk. *1m S of Stokesley. On A172, signed Pelargonium Exhibition.* Home-made teas. **Adm £3.50, chd free. Sat 18 May (1-4.30).**
1-acre mixed shrubaceous borders, large rockeries, spring bulbs, species tulips, mature conifers, fritillaries, erythroniums and secluded ornamental pond. Hosta collection and garden sculpture. Tranquil garden surrounded by farmland with views to Cleveland Hills and Roseberry Topping. Designed and maintained by owners since 1992 with low maintenance in mind. Pelargonium Exhibition - features mature award-winning show plants. Over 76 RHS gold medals on display around glass house. Nursery featured in The English Garden. Gravel drive.

ALLOTMENTS

32 FIRVALE ALLOTMENT GARDEN
Winney Hill, Harthill, nr Worksop S26 7YN. Don & Dot Witton, 01909 771366, donshardyeuphorbias @btopenworld.com, www.euphorbias.co.uk. *12m SE of Sheffield, 6m W of Worksop. M1 J31 A57 to Worksop. Turn R to Harthill. Allotments at S end of village, 26 Casson Drive at N end on Northlands Estate.* Light refreshments at 26 Casson Drive. **Adm £2.50, chd free. Sun 5 May (1-4). Visitors also welcome by appt Apr to July.**
Large allotment containing 13 island beds displaying 500+ herbaceous perennials incl the National Collection of hardy Euphorbias with approx 100 varieties in flower. Organic vegetable garden. Refreshments, WC, plant sales at 26 Casson Drive - small garden with mixed borders, shade and seaside garden. Featured on BBC Gardeners' World.

NCH

Natural hillside stream enters via stone trough, flowing into formal pond and rill . . .

33 FOUR GABLES
Oaks Lane, Boston Spa, nr Wetherby LS23 6DS. David & Anne Watts, www.fourgables.co.uk. *1m SE of Wetherby off A659 in Boston Spa. Please park on Boston Spa High Street (A659) 400yds W of church.* Home-made teas. **Adm £3, chd free. Sun 12 May (12.30-5).**
Many surprises in this ½ -acre garden surrounding Grade II listed Arts and Crafts home (not open). Some original garden hard landscaping densely planted in the style of 'The Wild Garden' by William Robinson. Fine specimen trees, hellebores, wood anemone, dicentra, tree peony, aquilegia and fritillaria. Ponds, deep well, 30ft wood sculpture, and various garden features. Attractive courtyard with seating areas and raised beds.

34 FRIARS HILL
Sinnington YO62 6SL. Mr & Mrs C J Baldwin, 01751 432179, friars.hill@abelgratis.co.uk. *4m W of Pickering. On A170.* **Adm £3, chd free. Visitors welcome by appt Mar to Sept.**
Plantswoman's 1¾ -acre garden containing over 2500 varieties of perennials and bulbs, with yr-round colour. Early interest with hellebores, bulbs and woodland plants. Herbaceous beds. Hostas, delphiniums, old roses and stone troughs. Excellent Autumn colour.

Tranquil garden surrounded by farmland with views to Cleveland Hills and Roseberry Topping . . .

35 NEW 6 FULWITH AVENUE
Harrogate HG2 8HR. Vanda & David Hartley. *1½ m S of Harrogate. A61 (Harrogate-Leeds). From town centre straight over 2 r'abouts and continue through main T-lights. 3rd L (Fulwith Mill Lane) 1st R Fulwith Avenue. Parking in rd.* Light refreshments. **Adm £2.50, chd free. Weds 5 June; 14 Aug (11-5).**
A small town garden designed to appear larger by use of focal points, including a mirror trompe l'oeil, with paths and hidden corners encircling a central lawn. Dry stone walls, sunken pond and summerhouse give structure and provide backdrop to the extensive range of foliage and flowers giving interest all year.

36 GALPHAY MANOR
Galphay, nr Ripon HG4 3NJ. Mr & Mrs Andrew Duncan. *5m W of Ripon. From B6265 turn R at Studley Royal cricket club, signed Galphay. Follow signs in village. Car parking in village & paddock.* Home-made teas. **Adm £3.50, chd free. Sun 9 June (1-5).**
Large tranquil 3-acre family garden in the heart of picturesque Dales village with Edwardian features incl water garden and ornamental pond. Sweeping spacious lawns lead to rose and clematis arches and woodland walk. Restored herbaceous border, topiary and box parterre. Potager style kitchen garden, herbs and fruit cages.

THE GARDEN HOUSE
See Lincolnshire

37 GOLDSBOROUGH HALL
Church Street, Goldsborough HG5 8NR. Mr & Mrs M Oglesby, 01423 867321, info@goldsboroughhall.com, www.goldsboroughhall.com. *2m SE of Knaresborough. 3m W of A1M. Off A59 (York-Harrogate) carpark 300yds past PH on R.* Cream teas. **Adm £5, chd free (share to St Mary's Church). Sun 24 Mar (12-4); Sun 21 July (12-5). Visitors also welcome by appt.**
Previously opened for NGS from 1928-30 and now beautifully restored by present owners (re-opened in 2010). 11-acre garden and formal landscaped grounds in parkland setting and Grade II*, C17 house, former residence of the late HRH Princess Mary, daughter of George V and Queen Mary. Gertrude Jekyll inspired replanted 120ft double herbaceous borders and rose garden. ¼ -mile lime tree walk planted by royalty circa 1920 underplanted with 50,000 naturalised daffodils. Woodland walk and specimen trees. St Mary's Church also open. Featured in local and national press. Gravel paths and some steep slopes.

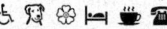

38 THE GRANARY
Langbaurgh Grange, Great Ayton, Middlesbrough TS9 6QQ. Helen Jones. *¼ m W of Great Ayton. Entrance to Langbaurgh Grange in trees on S side of B1292 ¼ m from junction with A173, (Sat Navs sometimes misleading) The Granary is furthest building from rd. Follow signs for parking.* Home-made teas. **Adm £3.50, chd free. Sun 16 June (2-5).**
A plantswoman's much-loved country garden reclaimed from ⅙ -acre brown field site over the last 20 yrs. Narrow paths lead through distinct areas separated by windbreak hedges, each having its own mood. Varied planting is influenced by local conditions as well as the owner's interest in plant-hunting and photography.

39 THE GRANGE
Carla Beck Lane, Carleton, Skipton BD23 3BU. Mr & Mrs R N Wooler, 07740 639135, margaret.wooler@hotmail.com. *1½ m SW of Skipton. Turn off A56 (Skipton-Clitheroe) into Carleton. Keep L at Swan PH, continue to end of village & turn R into Carla Beck Lane. From Skipton town centre follow A6131. Turn R to Carleton.* Home-made teas. **Adm £5, chd free (share to Sue Ryder Care Manorlands Hospice). Weds 17, 31 July; 7 Aug (12.30-4.30). Visitors also welcome by appt July and Aug. Adm incl guided tour and refreshments.**
Over 4 acres set in the grounds of Victorian house (not open) with mature trees and panoramic views towards The Gateway to the Dales. The garden has been restored by the owners over the last 2 decades with many areas of interest being added to the original footprint. Bountiful herbaceous borders with many unusual species, rose walk, parterre, mini-meadows and water features. Large greenhouse and raised vegetable beds. Oak seating placed throughout the garden invites quiet contemplation, a place to 'lift the spirit'. Featured on ITVs The Dales. Gravel paths and steps.

40 NEW 16 HALLAM GRANGE CROFT
Fulwood, Sheffield S10 4BP. Tricia & Alistair Fraser, 01142 306508, tricia.fraser@talktalk.net. *Approx 4m SW of Sheffield city centre. Follow A57 (Glossop). 1½ m after University turn L after petrol station. After 1m turn L (at top of hill) and follow signs.* Home-made teas. **Adm £2.50, chd free. Sun 26 May (12-5). Also open 34 Dover Road. Visitors and groups also welcome by appt.**
Developed over 20yrs, a plantswoman's SE-facing sloping wildlife-friendly garden. Backed by mature trees with established perennial and shrub planting including many unusual hardy geraniums. Shady areas, pond, summerhouse, greenhouse and vegetable plots. Raised bed, rockery and decking area feature alpines and sun-loving perennials.

41 HAVOC HALL
York Rd, Oswaldkirk, York YO62 5XY. David & Maggie Lis, www.havochall.co.uk. *21m N of York. On B1363, 1st house on R as you enter Oswaldkirk from S and last house on L as you leave village from N.* Home-made teas. **Adm £4, chd free. Sun 11 Aug (12-5.30).**
Started in 2009, comprising 8 areas incl knot, herbaceous, mixed shrub and flower gardens, courtyard, vegetable area and orchard, woodland walk and large lawned area with hornbeam trees and hedging. To the S is a 2-acre wild flower meadow and small lake. Some steps but these can be avoided.

42 HIGH HALL
St Stephen's Road, Steeton, nr Keighley BD20 6SB. Roger & Christine Lambert. *3m W of Keighley. Enter Steeton village from A629. Turn R at T-lights, then R after 100yds down St Stephens Rd. Entrance on L immed after church. No parking, except disabled, adj to garden. Please follow signs for parking in the village.* Home-made teas. **Adm £3.50, chd free. Suns 16 June; 21 July (12-5).**
2-acre surprising suburban Arts & Crafts garden and historic house (not open) adjacent to St Stephens Church. Formal walled garden with tanks, pond, belvedere, pergola, dovecote, summerhouse and ancient yew, herbaceous planting in formal beds connected by gravel paths. Walled kitchen garden with vegetable beds and fruit trees. Natural woodland area and small croquet lawn. Historical notes available. Exhibition by Jackie Sumerfield, local artist, and display of Alexander Keighley photographs.

43 HIGHFIELDS
Manorstead, Skelmanthorpe, Huddersfield HD8 9DW. Julie & Tony Peckham, 01484 864336, julie-tony@tiscali.co.uk. *8m SE of Huddersfield. M1 (J39) A636 towards Denby Dale. Turn R in Scissett village (B6116) to Skelmanthorpe. Just before humped zebra crossing turn L (Barrowstead), continue to top of hill.* **Adm £2, chd free. Suns 21 Apr; 19 May (2-5). Visitors also welcome by appt Apr to June.**
Small garden which shows creativity within metres rather than acres! Re-opening this year after refurbishment and upgrading of hard landscaping and planting. New summerhouse and patio area with alpine beds. Larger of two ponds has been replanted and has boardwalk. New acer woodland border. Spring/early summer garden with bulbs, woodland plants and alpines.

Original Edwardian potting shed leading to wild flower area with steps, mown path to rustic hut . . .

44 5 HILL TOP
Westwood Drive, Ilkley LS29 9RS. Lyn & Phil Short. *1/2 m S of Ilkley, Turn S at town centre T-lights up Brook St, cross The Grove taking Wells Rd up to the Moors.* Home-made teas. **Adm £3, chd free. Wed 29 May; Sun 2 June (11-4.30).**
Delightful 2/3 -acre steep garden on edge of Ilkley Moor. Sheltered woodland underplanted with naturalistic, flowing tapestry of foliage, shade-loving flowers, shrubs and ferns amongst large moss covered boulders. Natural stream, bridges, meandering gravel paths and steps lend magic to 'Dingley Dell'. Lawns, large rockery and summerhouse with stunning views. Steep steps, slopes and gravel paths.

45 HILLBARK
Church Lane, Bardsey, nr Leeds LS17 9DH. Tim Gittins & Malcolm Simm, www.hillbark.co.uk. *4m SW of Wetherby. Turn W off A58 into Church Lane, garden on L before church.* Home-made teas. **Adm £4, chd free. Suns 9 June; 7 July (11-5).**
Award-winning 1-acre country garden. 3 S-facing levels, hidden corners; surprise views. Formal topiary, relaxed perennial planting. Dramatic specimen yew. Ornamental ponds, summerhouse overlooking gravel, rock and stream gardens, large natural pond with ducks. Marginal planting incl bamboo. Woodland area. Large rambling roses. Unusual ceramics.

46 NEW HOLLY CROFT
28 Station Road, Scalby, Scarborough YO13 0QA. Mrs Christine Goodall. *From Scarborough take Whitby Road A171. At Scalby Xrds turn by tennis court into Station Rd. Garden is approx 400 metres on R.* Home-made teas. **Adm £3, chd free. Sun 23 June (11.30-5.30).**
2/3 -acre sloping garden leading from house to Scalby Beck. Lawned formal area near house has circular pond, pergola, large beech tree and clipped box. Sundial garden has mixed borders, fruit bushes, raised vegetable beds, original Edwardian potting shed leading to wild flower area with steps, mown path to rustic hut. Gate and steps lead steeply down through woodland area to bench by river. Wheelchair access to terrace overlooking garden.

GROUP OPENING

47 HORNSEA GARDENS
Hornsea HU18 1UR. *12 NE of Beverley. On B1242 S-side of Hornsea between Freeport & golf course. Directions to New House from Nutkins signed.* Tea at Nutkins. **Combined adm £4, chd free. Sun 16 June (11-4). Visitors to both gardens also welcome by appt.**

NEW HOUSE
Mrs Kate Willans.
N end of Cliff Rd, opp bus garage. Garden is halfway down L fork
Visitors also welcome by appt May to July.
01964 534502
kwkatewillans32@gmail.com

NUTKINS
72 Rolston Road. Alan & Janet Stirling
Visitors also welcome by appt.
01964 533721
ashornsea@aol.com

Two gardens set in the popular seaside town. One large garden divided into different areas with a sense of fun, and a smaller garden, a real gem with plants for the enthusiast. Hornsea has seaside attractions, as well as the Mere, Museum, Freeport and Honeysuckle Farm nearby. Nutkins covers 3/4 acre with herbaceous borders, bog garden, streamside walk and woodland garden with pergolas, gazebo and plenty of seating to linger and enjoy different views of the garden and see light play on many pieces of stained glass. New House has a small garden, very close to the sea, packed with both hardy and tender herbaceous planting in borders and island beds; a wildlife pond and succulent collection, with paved areas and seating. Wheelchair access at Nutkins.

48 HOTHAM HALL
Hotham YO43 4UA. Stephen & Carolyn Martin, 01430 422054, carolynandstephenmartin @btinternet.com. *15m W of Hull. J38 of M62 turn towards North Cave, follow signs for Hotham.* Light refreshments. **Adm £5, chd £2.50 incl refreshments. Thurs 14, 21 Mar (11-2.30). Visitors also welcome by appt Feb to Aug.**
C18 Grade II house (not open), stable block and clock tower in mature parkland setting with established gardens. Lake with bridge over to island walk (arboretum). Garden with Victorian pond and mixed borders. Many spring flowering bulbs. Children's play area, garden games.

49 HUNMANBY GRANGE
Wold Newton YO25 3HS. Tom & Gill Mellor. *12½ m SE of Scarborough. Hunmanby Grange is home of Wold Top Brewery, a farm between Wold Newton & Hunmanby on rd from Burton Fleming to Fordon.* **Adm £3.50, chd free. Sat 1, Sun 2 June (11-5).**
3-acre garden created over the last 30 yrs from exposed open field, on top of Yorkshire Wolds nr coast. Hedges and fences now provide shelter from wind, making series of gardens with yr-round interest and seasonal highlights. Wold Top Brewery open with garden. Steps can be avoided by using grass paths and lawns. Pond garden not completely accessible to wheelchairs but can be viewed from gateway.

50 NEW HUNMANBY SCHOOL
Priest Close, Hunmanby, Filey YO14 0QH. Mrs Lisa Woolridge. *From Scarborough S on A64. At r'about 1st exit (A1039) toward Filey. Take R fork up White Gate Hill, along Malton Rd to Hunmanby. 2nd exit at r'about (Castle Hill). Turn L (Stonegate) and immed L (Northgate). Turn 1st R (Owston Rd). Turn R (Priest Cl). From Bridlington N on A165 for 7m (over 2 r'abouts). Turn L onto Moor Rd and bear L onto Filey Rd. Continue onto Stonegate. Turn R (Outgates Ln). Take 2nd L (Outgates Cl). Turn L onto Priest Cl. Limited parking.* Home-made teas. **Adm £3, chd free. Sat 13 July (10.30-4).**
The extensive grounds include a sensory bed, vegetable garden, nectar bed, rivers of wild flowers, wildlife garden with pond, living willow classroom, sculpture, Japanese courtyard, and orchard. 3 times winners of Yorkshire in Bloom (Gold). Voted Best in Category at Scarborough in Bloom awards ceremony for 3 consecutive years. Some areas of rough terrain may not be suitable for wheelchairs.

51 ◆ JACKSON'S WOLD
Sherburn, Malton YO17 8QJ. Mr & Mrs Richard Cundall, 07966 531995, www.jacksonswoldgarden.com. *11m E of Malton, 10m SW of Scarborough. A64 in Sherburn. T-lights take Weaverthorpe Rd. 100 meters right fork to Helperthorpe and Luttons.1m to top of hill turn L at garden sign. Do not use Sat Nav.* **Adm £3, chd free. For NGS: Suns 19 May; 23 June (1-5). For other opening times and information, please phone or see garden website.**
2-acre garden with stunning views of the Vale of Pickering. Walled garden with mixed borders, numerous old shrub roses underplanted with unusual perennials. Woodland paths lead to further shrub and perennial borders. Lime avenue with wild flower meadow. Traditional vegetable garden with roses, flowers and box edging framed by Victorian greenhouse. Adjoining nursery.

52 JASMINE HOUSE
145 The Grove, Wheatley Hills, Doncaster DN2 5SN. Ray & Anne Breame, 01302 361470. *2m E of Doncaster. 1m E of Doncaster Royal Infirmary off A18. Turn R into Chestnut Ave (Motor Save on corner).* **Adm £2.50, chd free. Sun 2 June (1-5). Visitors also welcome by appt mid May to Aug.**
Colourful tropical to traditional, plant-packed haven. A real surprise awaits you on entering this town 'garden for all seasons'. Climbers festoon archways that lead to enclosed gardens displaying the gardener's love of rare and unusual plants, from ferns and alpines to bonsai and tender perennials.

53 KELBERDALE
Wetherby Road, Knaresborough HG5 8LN. Stan & Chris Abbott, 01423 862140, kelberdale@gmail.com. *1m S of Knaresborough. On B6164 Wetherby rd. House on L immed after ring rd (A658) r'about.* **Adm £3, chd free. Sun 9 June (10-6); Wed 3 July (10-4). Visitors also welcome by appt Mar to Sept.**
Winner of 3 national awards, this owner-made and maintained plantsman's garden overlooking the R Nidd has a bit of everything. Full of yr round interest with large traditional herbaceous border, colour themed beds, pond and bog garden, alpine house and troughs and vegetable garden. The wild garden with large pond and meadow is a haven for wildlife. Wheelchair access limited but help will be given.

Rivers of wild flowers . . . living willow classroom . . .

54 NEW 23 LAMBERT ROAD
Bridlington YO16 6RD. S Earnshaw. *North Bridlington. Take A164 or A165 to Bridlington. At Scarborough Rd double r'about follow signs for Sewerby & Flamborough. At next r'about turn R. Continue across next r'about to T-lights and turn L. Lambert Rd is 2nd turning L.* **Adm £2.50, chd free. Sun 25 Aug (11-4).**
Recently created small town garden on clay soil. Shaded areas planted with ferns, hostas, heucheras and hellebores contrast with sunny beds of herbaceous perennials and colourful containers of bedding plants. The planting area has been designed to provide year round interest culminating in a blaze of colour in late summer.

55 ◆ LAND FARM
Colden, Hebden Bridge HX7 7PJ. Mr J Williams, 01422 842260, www.landfarmgardens.co.uk. *8m W of Halifax. From Halifax at Hebden Bridge go through 2 sets T-lights. Take turning circle to Heptonstall. Follow signs to Colden. After 2¾ m turn R at Edge Lane 'no through' rd, follow signs from bus stop at Colden.* **For opening times and information, please phone or see garden website.**
6 acres incl alpine, herbaceous, formal and newly developing woodland garden, meconopsis varieties in June, cardiocrinum giganteum in July. Elevation 1000ft N-facing. C17 house (not open). Art Gallery and garden sculpture. Garden listed on Lap Map as being one of the best 80 gardens of England and Wales. Look for scupltures on Google Earth. Limited wheelchair access.

56 LANGTON FARM
Great Langton, Northallerton DL7 0TA. Richard & Annabel Fife, 01609 748446, annabel@fsmail.net. *5m W of Northallerton. B6271 in Great Langton between Northallerton and Scotch Corner.* Home-made teas. **Adm £4, chd free. Evening Openings, wine, Sats 1 June; 31 Aug (5.30-8.30); Sat 22 June (2-6). Visitors also welcome by appt.**
Riverside garden comprising formal and informal gravel areas, nuttery, romantic flower garden with mixed borders and pebble pool. Organic. Featured in The English Garden.

THE LEYLANDS
See Derbyshire

57 LINDEN HOUSE
16 Northgate, Cottingham HU16 4HH. Eric Nicklas & Mrs Pat Plaxton, 01482 847788, mrnick@mrnick.karoo.co.uk. *4m NW of Hull. From A164 turn onto B1233 signed Cottingham, garden on L 50yds before railway Xing. From A1079, turn onto B1233, straight on at bowling club, over Xing then 50yds on R.* Light refreshments. **Adm £2.50, chd free (share to Hospice in Hull). Sat 1, Sun 2 June (10.30-5). Visitors also welcome by appt.**
This interesting small garden with a thoughtfully curved lawn, numerous shrubs, pond and aviary which blend well together. Featured in Cottingham Advertiser.

58 LINDEN LODGE
Newbridge Lane, nr Wilberfoss, York YO41 5RB. Robert Scott & Jarrod Marsden, 07900 003538, rdsjsm@gmail.com. *10m E of York. A1079 Hull/York rd, E of Wilberfoss and NW of Barmby Moor. Do not go into Wilberfoss village, take turn signed Bolton, onto Bolton Lane. At Xrds turn L, garden after Bolton Hall on R.* Cream teas served in the marquee. **Adm £4, chd free. Suns 16, 23 June (1-5.30). Groups also welcome by appt Apr to Oct. Individual visitors can ring to join a group.**
6 acres with a 1-acre garden, owner-designed and constructed since 2000, with many choice, unusual plants and trees. Gravel paths edged with box and lavender lead to herbaceous/mixed borders, wildlife pond and summerhouse. Kitchen garden, glasshouse, orchard and woodland area and formal garden with pond and water feature. 5 acres of developing meadow, wild flowers and Shetland sheep. Crafts. Featured in 100 Inspirational Gardens of England, Yorkshire Post, East Riding Journal and Amateur Gardening. Gravel paths and shallow steps.

59 LITTLE EDEN
Lancaster Street, Castleford WF10 2NP. Melvyn & Linda Moran, 01977 514275, melvynmoran609@btinternet.com. *2½ m NW of M62 J32. A639 (Castleford). 1st r'about 2nd exit B6136 (Ferrybridge). At top of hill turn L at T-lights (Fryston Rd), straight over next r'about, 3rd R (Elizabeth Drive) 2nd L (Dunderdale Cres), 3rd L (Lancaster St).* Home-made teas. **Adm £3, chd free. Suns 30 June, 18 Aug (10-4). Also open 18 Aug, Millrace Nursery. Visitors also welcome by appt June to Oct.**
Plant lovers' small hidden oasis of unusual, tender, exotic and tropical plants in the midst of large housing estate. Trellis and archway festooned with climbers, colourful pots and hanging baskets. Herbaceous perennials, succulents, tree ferns, palms, bananas, pond and a decorative summerhouse. Featured on BBC Gardeners' World, various magazines & local and national press.

GROUP OPENING

60 LITTLETHORPE GARDENS
nr Ripon HG4 3LS. *1½ m SE of Ripon. Off A61 bypass follow signs to Littlethorpe. Turn R at church. From Bishop Monkton follow signs to Ripon (Knaresborough Rd), turn R to Littlethorpe. The gardens are approx ½ m apart.* Home-made teas at Greencroft. **Combined adm £4.50, chd free. Sun 28 July (12-5).**

GREENCROFT
David & Sally Walden
Visitors also welcome by appt end June to mid Aug.
01765 602487
s.walden@talk21.com

KIRKELLA
Jacky Barber

Littlethorpe is a small village characterised by houses interspersed with fields. Greencroft is a ½ -acre informal garden made by the owners. Special ornamental features incl gazebo, temple pavilions, formal pool, stone wall with mullions, and gate to rose pergola leading to a cascade water feature. Long herbaceous borders packed with colourful late flowering perennials, annuals and exotics culminate in circular garden with views through to large wildlife pond and surrounding countryside. Kirkella is a small garden recently created by plantswoman and flower arranger to give constant interest. Gravel garden to the front with Mediterranean feel. Densely planted hidden paved rear garden with decorative summerhouse; hostas, half-hardy perennials, salvias, succulents, desirable small shrubs, many in pots and containers. A willow hedge conceals a small productive vegetable plot.

61 LITTLETHORPE MANOR
Littlethorpe, Ripon HG4 3LG. Mr & Mrs J P Thackray, thackray@littlethorpemanor.com, www.littlethorpemanor.com. *Outskirts of Ripon by racecourse. Ripon bypass A61. Follow Littlethorpe Rd from Dallamires Lane r'about to stable block with clock tower. Map supplied on application.* Home-made teas. **Adm £8, chd free. Visitors welcome by appt only May to Sept, incl guided tour.**
11 acres. Walled garden based on cycle of seasons with box, herbaceous, roses, gazebo. Sunken garden with white rose parterre and herbs. Brick pergola with white wisteria, blue and yellow borders. Terraces with ornamental pots. Formal lawns with fountain pool, hornbeam towers and yew hedging. Box headed hornbeam drive with Aqualens water feature. Parkland with lake, late summer plantings and classical pavilion. Cut flower garden. Spring bulbs and winter garden. Gravel paths, some steep steps.

GROUP OPENING

62 NEW LOCKINGTON GARDENS
Driffield YO25 9SR. *7m N of Beverley. Lockington is on Thorpe Rd between A164 & B1248. Park in church car park and follow signs to gardens.* Home-made teas. **Combined adm £4, chd free. Sun 9 June (10-6).**

NEW PENNY COTTAGE
42 Thorpe Road. Sue & John Rowson

NEW THORPE LODGE
Dead Lane. Mrs Jane Warburton

Two small gardens in the village of Lockington. Penny Cottage is a small, well-maintained garden on different levels with conifers, selection of herbaceous perennials and climbers. Small raised vegetable plot. Thorpe Lodge a cottage garden on the site of an old orchard. Interesting shrubs and trees creating contrast and shade. Wildlife pond, summer house and vegetable patch.

Small hidden oasis of unusual, tender, exotic and tropical plants . . .

63 LODGE YARD
Main Street, Askrigg, nr Leyburn DL8 3HQ. Holiday Property Bond. *On main st of Askrigg, opp The White Rose Hotel, through the arch. Parking in public car park or nr church. Limited disabled parking at Lodge Yard.* **Adm £4, chd free. Thur 11 July; Wed 14 Aug (11-3).**
A garden with stunning views of the Yorkshire Dales, sheltered by stone walls softened with climbers incl many roses and clematis. Large terraced garden at rear created by sleepers topped by box hedging and abundant mixed planting. Wild flower area, with fruit trees. Slowworm Havens. Courtyard gardens. Steep slopes and gravel paths.

64 LOW HALL
Dacre Banks, Nidderdale HG3 4AA. Mrs P A Holliday, 01423 780230, pamela@pamelaholliday.co.uk. *10m NW of Harrogate. On B6451 between Dacre Banks and Darley.* Tea. **Adm £3, chd free. Sun 12 May (1.30-5). Also open with Dacre Banks & Summerbridge Gardens, 7 July. Visitors also welcome by appt.**
A romantic walled garden set on differing levels designed to complement historic C17 family home (not open). Spring bulbs, rhododendrons; azaleas round tranquil water garden. Asymmetric rose pergola underplanted with auriculas and lithodora links orchard to the garden. Extensive herbaceous borders, shrubs and climbing roses give later interest.

65 LOW SUTTON
Sutton Lane, Masham HG4 4PB. Steve & Judi Smith, www.lowsutton.co.uk. *1½ m W of Masham. From Masham towards Leyburn (A6108). L into Sutton Lane, single track tarmac rd. Low Sutton ¼ m on L.* Home-made teas. **Adm £3, chd free. Sun 28 July (1-5).**
Developing since 2007 a fresh approach to cottage gardening. Concentric circular floral colour wheel surrounded by scented roses and clematis. Abundant variety of fruit and vegetables decoratively grown in raised beds, fruit cage, greenhouse and coldframe. Perennial border, grasses, fernery and courtyard surround the house, all set within 6-acre smallholding.

66 LOWER CRAWSHAW
off Stringer House Lane, Emley, nr Huddersfield HD8 9SU. Mr & Mrs Neil Hudson. *8m E of Huddersfield. From Huddersfield turn R to Emley off A642 (Paul Lane). From M1 J39 (A636) direction Denby Dale, 1m after Bretton r'about turn R to Emley, ½ m beyond Emley village turn R (Stringer House Lane) continue for ½ m. Blind corner on approach to field carpark, please take care of oncoming cars.* Home-made teas. **Adm £4, chd free. Wed 26, Sun 30 June (12-5).**
Large country garden with extensive views, 650ft high on E slopes of the Pennines, created by the owners since 1996. The garden surrounds the 1690s farmhouse and old barns that enclose the courtyard. A stream is dammed on several levels and opens into two natural ponds with marginal planting. Enclosed rose garden underplanted with soft coloured perennials. Walled vegetable garden, soft fruit and small orchard.

67 LOWER HEUGH COTTAGE GARDEN
14 Kirk Lane, Eastby, nr Skipton BD23 6SH. Trevor & Marian Nash, 01756 793702, mnash862@gmail.com. *2½ m NE of Skipton. Follow A59/65 N ring rd around Skipton, turn at signs for Skipton, Embsay (railway) & Eastby. Alternatively follow rd past Skipton Castle from central Skipton. After ½ m, turn for Embsay. In Embsay follow signs for Eastby & Barden onto Kirk Lane.* Light refreshments. **Adm £6, chd free. Visitors welcome by appt.**

Japanese Kaiyushiki stroll through Garden. Hosting Professor Fukuhara, one of the world's leading Japanese Garden Designers for a workshop led by him in late 2011, was a privilege. His Emperor Garden design for the outer Roji extension within this one acre Kaiyushiki stroll garden has proved inspirational for the many visitors during 2012. Uniquely, this little piece of the Orient, high in the Yorkshire Dales is all Japanese in style. Its many gardens are explained during the 90 minute conducted tour enhancing the understanding of the history, religion, philosophy and concepts behind Japanese garden design. This all year round garden, created and maintained by the owners, is perhaps best seen from March to October yet can be spectacular in the winter. The tour is followed by appropriate refreshments included in the entry fee. Limited wheelchair access.

Enclosed rose garden underplanted with soft coloured perennials . . .

68 MANOR FARM
Thixendale, Malton YO17 9TG. Charles & Gilda Brader, 01377 288315, manorfarmthixendale@hotmail.com. *10m SE of Malton. Unclassified rd through Birdsall, ½ m up hill, turn L at Xrds for Thixendale - 3m, 1st farm on R. 17m E of York, turn off A166 rd at top of Garrowby Hill, follow signs for Thixendale, 4m turn into village, drive through to end, farm on L.* Home-made teas. **Adm £3.50, chd free. Sat 13 July (10-6).**
Main lawn surrounded by shrub and herbaceous borders. Ruined shed, small knot garden, little arbour, running water and rocks. Topiary and pots throughout garden. Central pergola to new bespoke summerhouse, formal pool with sphere, set in stone flagged trellised area. Through curved pergola to alpines planted among farm stones, small courtyard, into garden room overflowing with plants.

69 39 MARKET PLACE
South Cave, Brough HU15 2BS. Lin & Paul Holland, 01430 421874, paulandlin@btinternet.com. *12m W of Hull. From A63 turn N to South Cave on A1034. House on L opp PO, before Xrds.* Home-made teas. **Adm £3, £5.00 incl tea, chd free. Visitors welcome by appt May to Sept.**
Small walled garden with eclectic planting. Established trees, cottage garden plants and evergreen shrubs. Rockeries, gravel fernery with grasses and water feature. Interesting stonework and lots of nooks and crannies.

GROUP OPENING

70 MARTON CUM GRAFTON GARDENS
nr Boroughbridge, York YO51 9QJ. *2½ m S of Boroughbridge. A1m J48 off A168, nr Boroughbridge.* Home-made teas at Marton village hall. **Combined adm £3.50, chd free. Wed 26 June (1-5).**

SHIPPEN BOWER
Marton. Jim & Cynthia Foster

SPRINGFIELD
Grafton. Chris Woods & Molly Naish

WELL HOUSE
Grafton. Glen Garnett

Marton cum Grafton are adjacent villages overlooking the York Plain. The two Grafton cottage gardens are away from the village centre and nestle into the hillside with long views to the White Horse and Hambleton Hills. Well House extends to over 1½ acres and has evolved over 35 years and continues to change. Flowing colourful borders, climbers and rambling roses and ornamental shrubs of interest. Orchard with geese, ducks and chickens. Adjacent below lies Springfield with box parterre to the front and a rear paved garden overflowing with cottage garden plants, ramblers and shrub old roses. Narrow box lined paths lead to vegetable garden and orchard with copper marans and silky bantams. In Marton village an enclosed small garden with colourful tapestry of perennials, annuals, hanging baskets, pots and shrubs wraps itself around Shippen Bower.

GROUP OPENING

71 MELTHAM, PAVILION WAY GARDENS

nr Huddersfield HD9 5QN. *4m NW of Holmfirth, 5m SW of Huddersfield. From Huddersfield ring rd take A616 to Lockwood then B6108 to Meltham town centre. At Xrds turn R onto B6107. Straight ahead at 1st mini r'about, turn R at 2nd mini r'about. Turn R into Pavilion Way. Parking in field at end.* Teas at The Pig Sty. **Combined adm £3.50, chd free. Sun 14 July (2-5.30).**

THE ARTIST'S GARDEN
88 Pavilion Way. Karen Rogers

BATWOMAN'S GARDEN
82 Pavilion Way. Jean & Brian Walters

THE PIG STY
73 Pavilion Way. Mary & Jonathan Harrison

With far reaching views, Pavilion Way is a well-designed modern development completed in 2000 on the site of Meltham Silica brickworks. The three gardens illustrate imaginative use of space and are full of interest. The Pig Sty is a small end plot looking over woodland towards Castle Hill with modern 'pod' summerhouse surrounded by black bamboo and red dogwoods. Compact raised vegetable beds, greenhouse, mixed shrubs and unusual ornaments. Rare breed woolly Mangalitsa pigs. Batwoman's Garden is a small compact enclosed feature-full rear garden. Evergreen shrubs, climbers and grapevine covered pergola give privacy. Colourful pots, fruit, herbs and tiny pond all designed to attract wildlife. A retired florist has made the vibrant and colourful S-facing Artist's Garden against a backdrop of trees. Paved area with pots, pergola and summerhouse leads to steep terracing and seating overlooking the valley and hills beyond.

72 MERE'STEAD

28 Kelmscott Garth, Manston Crossgates, Leeds LS15 8LB. Mr & Mrs Renzi. *6m E of Leeds. 1m from M1 J46 follow A63 towards Leeds. Take ring road (A6120) then follow signs to Barwick-in-Elmet. At 2nd T-lights turn R (Penda's Way), then 1st L. No parking in cul-de-sac. Parking nearby at community centre.* Home-made teas. **Adm £2.50, chd free. Evening Opening, wine, Fri 19 July (5-9); Sun 21 July (12-5).**

A small enclosed English town garden with an Italian twist lovingly developed and cared for by owners. Mature trees, magnolia and cedar deodara, underplanted with interesting perennials and bulbs giving colour and foliage interest throughout the year. Arches festooned with climbers, small wildlife pond, pots with succulents, colourful summer bulbs and alpine troughs. Winner of Leeds in Bloom for past 8 years.

MILL FARM
See Lincolnshire

73 MILLGATE HOUSE

Millgate, Richmond DL10 4JN. Tim Culkin & Austin Lynch, www.millgatehouse.com. *Centre of Richmond. House located at bottom of Market Place opp Barclays Bank. Just off corner of Market Place.* **Adm £3.50, chd free. Suns 2 June; 7 July (8-8). Also open 2 June, Swale Cottage.**

SE walled town garden overlooking R Swale. Although small, the garden is full of character, enchantingly secluded with plants and shrubs. Foliage plants incl ferns and hostas. Old roses, interesting selection of clematis, small trees and shrubs. RHS associate garden. Immensely stylish, national award-winning garden. Featured in GGG and on BBC Gardeners' World.

74 MILLRACE NURSERY

84 Selby Road, Garforth, Leeds LS25 1LP. Mr & Mrs Carthy, 0113 2869233, carol@millrace-plants.co.uk, www.millrace-plants.co.uk. *5m E of Leeds. On A63 in Garforth. 1m from M1 J46, 3m from A1.* Home-made teas. **Adm £3, chd free. Suns 28 Apr; 16 June; 18 Aug (1-5). Also open 18 Aug, Little Eden. Visitors also welcome by appt Apr to Sept.**

Overlooking a secluded valley, garden incl large herbaceous borders containing over 3000 varieties of perennials, shrubs and trees, many of which are unusual and drought tolerant. Garden includes an ornamental pond, vegetable garden and walled terraces leading to wildflower meadow, small woodland, bog garden and wildlife lakes. 18 Aug seed collecting opportunity. Art Exhibition, specialist nursery.

75 MILLVIEW COTTAGE
21 Church Street, North Cave, Brough HU15 2LJ. Emma Jackson. *15m W of Hull. J38 M62E turn L to North Cave B1230 E of village on R of Church St.* **Adm £2.50, chd free. Sun 7 July (12-4).**
Inspirational cottage garden, long and narrow, split into different styled sections. Rear extension, of Scandinavian influence links the house to contemporary outdoor room with terrace, raised beds, wooden walkway, water feature and exotic planting. More traditional area leads to family garden, with vegetables and greenhouse. Please be aware hidden step near back of house.

The garden is full of character, enchantingly secluded with plants and shrubs . . . Immensely stylish . . .

76 MOLECROFT COTTAGE
Northgate, Walkington HU17 8ST. Keith & Beverley Reader. *2m SW of Beverley. On B1230 in Walkington, turn R by the Dog & Duck PH.* Home-made teas. **Adm £3.50, chd free. Sun 23 June (1-5).**
The quintessential English garden. This 1-acre plot incl Yorkshire terrace with pots and pond. Traditional maintained lawn and herbaceous border area with trees, 78ft rose walk with many clematis underplanted with hostas. Hot gravel garden, vegetable plot, wild garden and orchard.

77 NEW NEAKINS HOUSE
North Leys Road, Hollym, Withernsea HU19 2QN. David & Trish Smith. *2m S of Withernsea. Enter Hollym on A1033 Hull to Withernsea Rd. Turn E at X'rds. Garden on R after double bend. Strictly no roadside parking, please park in grounds.* Home-made teas. **Adm £3, chd free. Sun 30 June (11-5).**
Quiet country garden with shrubs and choice herbaceous plantings. Specimen evergreens complement formal box topiary and hedging. Enter log arch to shady hosta walk and emerge through rose arch. Gravelled area with seating overlooks large wildlife pond. Folly wall, clothed in clematis, features iron gate leading on to bee and butterfly border. Classic cars on display. Hosta walk too narrow for wheelchairs but can be viewed from entrance.

78 NEW NEASDEN PRIMARY SCHOOL
Neasden Close, Hull HU8 0QB. Mr Graham Johnson. *East Hull. The school is signed off Bellfield Ave and Ings Rd, in Hull.* Home-made teas. Community café with food cooked and served by the children in a themed event. This will be held in one of the Schoool Halls. **Adm £2.50, chd free. Fri 12 July (10-3); Sun 14 July (10-2.30).**
An 'Open Futures' partner School and RHS Campaign for School Gardening Level 5 School where the outdoor curriculum is integral to the children's learning. Features incl an allotment, secret garden, polytunnel containing exotic plants and a Shakespeare story telling-garden. This open event will showcase the children's learning in a 'village show format' with demonstrations and child-led activites and themed gardens designed by the children. Refreshments will be provided by the community café with food cooked and served by the children. Wheelchair access available to most of the gardens.

79 ◆ NEWBY HALL & GARDENS
Ripon HG4 5AE. Mr R C Compton, 01423 322583, www.newbyhall.com. *4m SE of Ripon. (HG4 5AJ for Sat Nav). Signed from A1 & Ripon town centre.* **For opening times and information, please phone or see garden website.**
40 acres extensive gardens laid out in 1920s. Full of rare and beautiful plants. Formal seasonal gardens, stunning double herbaceous borders to R Ure and National Collection holder - Cornus. Miniature railway and adventure gardens for children. Contemporary sculpture exhibition (open June - Sept). Wheelchair map available.
NCH

9 NEWFIELD CRESCENT
See Derbyshire

80 ◆ NORTON CONYERS
Wath, Nr Ripon HG4 5EQ. Sir James & Lady Graham, 01765 640333, www.weddingsatnortonconyers.co.uk. *4m N of Ripon. Take Melmerby & Wath sign off A61 Ripon-Thirsk. Go through both villages to boundary wall. Signed entry 300 metres on R.* Home-made teas by Marie Curie Cancer Care. **Adm £5.50, chd free. For NGS: Sun 16 June (2-5). For other opening times and information, please phone or see garden website.**
Large C18 walled garden of interest to garden historians. Interesting iron entrance gate; herbaceous borders, yew hedges and Orangery (open to the public) with an attractive little pond in front. Small sales area specialising in unusual hardy plants, fruit in season. House, visited by Charlotte Brontë and inspiration for Thornfield Hall in 'Jane Eyre' is closed for major repairs. The garden retains the essential features of its original design, combined with sympathetic replanting in the English style. Borders of gold and silver plants, of old-fashioned peonies, and irises in season. Visitors frequently comment on its tranquil atmosphere. Most areas wheelchair accessible along gravel paths.

81 THE NURSERY
15 Knapton Lane, Acomb, York YO26 5PX. Tony Chalcraft & Jane Thurlow. *2½ m W of York. Follow B1224 towards Acomb & York city centre, from A1237 York ring road. Turn L at first mini r'about into Beckfield Lane. Knapton Lane 2nd L after 150 metres.* Home-made teas. **Adm £2.50, chd free. Sun 21 July (1-5). Afternoon & Evening Opening, Wed 24 July (2-8).**
Hidden attractive and productive 1-acre organic garden behind suburban house. Wide range of top and soft fruit (incl 40+ varieties apples and pears). Many different vegetables grown both outside and under cover including a large greenhouse. Productive areas interspersed with informal ornamental plantings providing colour and habitat for wildlife. Tomato tasting on 24 July.

82 OATMILL COTTAGE
Lealholm, nr Whitby YO21 2AG. Sue Morgan, 01947 897688, jpm.oatmill@btinternet.com. *9m W of Whitby. Turn from A171 to Lealholm. Parking in centre of village or by station. Garden just below station across railway line.* Home-made teas. **Adm £3, chd free. Suns 16 June; 14 July (11-4.30). Visitors also welcome by appt June to Aug.**
Cottage-style garden with a variety of herbaceous borders with drought-tolerant plants, terrace, range of mature trees and shrubs set on the hillside overlooking the picturesque village of Lealholm. Features incl formal pond and fountain, bog garden and summerhouse. Plant sales in village nursery adjacent to the garden. Art Exhibition of garden-inspired art.

Walks through groves of semi-mature hardwoods to views of open countryside . . .

83 NEW THE OLD HALL
North Deighton, Wetherby LS22 4EN. Mr & Mrs T Hare. *3m N of Wetherby on B6164. Between North Deighton and Spofforth.* Cream teas. **Adm £3.50, chd free. Sun 16 June (1-5).**
A country garden replanted 20 yrs ago to complement historic family home (not open). Clipped formal yew hedges line paths and enclose green garden rooms for croquet, orchard and a rose garden underplanted to give a spectrum of soft colour and texture. Walks through groves of semi-mature hardwoods to views of open countryside. Terrace and gravelled driveway, vegetables in raised beds. Some steps.

84 THE OLD PRIORY
Everingham YO42 4JD. Dr J D & Mrs H J Marsden, 01430 860222/07703 529112, jerryhelen@btinternet.com. *15m SE of York, 5½ m from Pocklington. 2m S of the A1079 York-Hull rd. Everingham has 3 access rds, The Old Priory is to E of Village.* Home-made teas. **Adm £3.50, chd free. Visitors welcome by appt May to June.**
Country garden of 2 acres on dry sandy loam and wet peat land. Polytunnels, walled vegetable garden. Mixed herbaceous borders drop down to bog garden where paths bridge the stream into less formal garden which leads to lake, ponds and woodland.

85 NEW THE OLD RECTORY
Bugthorpe, York YO41 1QG. Dr & Mrs P W Verow, 01759 368444, natalieverow@aol.com. *4m E of Stamford Bridge. A166, village of Bugthorpe. House 1st on R from A166 (York direction).* Light refreshments. **Adm £3.50, chd free. Sat 13, Sun 14 July (11-4). Visitors also welcome by appt in July.**
¾ -acre country garden with views of the Yorkshire Wolds. Mixed borders, ponds, stumpery, courtyard and many mature trees. Raised vegetable beds. Artist in the garden and herbaceous perennials for sale.

86 NEW OLD RECTORY COTTAGE
Rectory Lane, Tunstall, Hull HU12 0JE. Mrs P Garbutt. *6m NW of Withensea. On coast 1½ m off B1242 between Withernsea & Aldbrough via Roos. Sharp L bend into village. After church on R take 1st turn R into Rectory Lane.* Home-made teas & WC at Tunstall Village Hall. **Adm £3, chd free. Sun 23 June (1-5).**
Pretty cottage garden in peaceful seaside location, featuring arched walk with roses, clematis and honeysuckle, gravel garden and water feature. Perennial island beds and borders, clipped box with roses and lavender. Separate wildlife area with a small vegetable plot, greenhouse/work area. Public footpath to sea/cliffs, a lovely walk.

87 OLD SLENINGFORD HALL
Mickley, nr Ripon HG4 3JD. Jane & Tom Ramsden. *5m NW of Ripon. Off A6108. After N Stainley turn L, follow signs to Mickley. Gates on R after 1½ m opp cottage.* Home-made teas. **Adm £5, chd free. Sat 1, Sun 2 June (12.30-4.30).**
A large English country garden and developing 'Forest Garden'. Early C19 house (not open) and garden with original layout; wonderful mature trees, woodland walk and Victorian fernery; romantic lake with islands, watermill, walled kitchen garden; beautiful long herbaceous border, yew and huge beech hedges. Award winning permaculture forest garden. Several plant and other garden stalls. Picnics around the mill pond welcome. Reasonable wheelchair access to most parts of garden. Disabled WC at Old Sleningford Farm next to the garden.

88 NEW OMEGA
79 Magdalen Lane, Hedon, Hull HU12 8LA. Mr & Mrs D Rosindale. *6m E of Hull. Through to E Hull onto A1033. L into St Augustine's Gate through Market Place, immed R to Magdalen Gate, ahead to Magdalen Lane.* Cream teas and wine. **Adm £2.50, chd free. Sat 15, Sun 16 June (12-6).**
Front garden formalised by box hedging has densely planted borders. Small shady side garden and patio with pots precedes two long borders, two small woodland areas, mini meadow, greenhouses and newly planted orchard. A wildlife friendly garden with diverse range of perennials, ferns, shrubs and small number of trees.

89 THE ORCHARD
4a Blackwood Rise, Cookridge, Leeds LS16 7BG. Carol & Michael Abbott, 0113 2676764, michael.john.abbott@hotmail.co.uk. *5m N of Leeds centre. Off A660 (Leeds-Otley) N of A6120 ring rd bear L onto Otley Old Rd. Before radio mast turn L (Tinshill Lane). Please park in Tinshill Lane after passing council flats.* Light refreshments. **Adm £2.50, chd free. Mon 27 May; Sun 14 July (12.30-5.30). Visitors also welcome by appt Apr to July, refreshments incl.**
¼ -acre hidden suburban oasis of peace and tranquillity. Differing levels made by owners using old stone, found on site, planted for yr-round interest. Long rockery, unusual fruit tree arbour and sheltered oriental style seated area linked by narrow grass lawns and steps. Mixed perennials, bulbs and pots amongst paved and pebbled areas. Tombola in aid of Yorkshire Air Ambulance. Medal awards from Leeds in Bloom.

90 OSWALDKIRK HALL
Oswaldkirk, York YO62 5XT. David & Sara Craig, 01439 788248, sarajcraig@gmail.com. *4m E of Helmsley. Take rd through Oswaldkirk village signed Ampleforth. Pass PH and church, house last on L with long stone wall.* Home-made teas. **Adm £3.50, chd free. Sun 9 June (1-5). Visitors also welcome by appt May to July.**
4-acre garden surrounding C17 listed country house, on a slope. Stone steps lead from terrace to front lawn, ha-ha and splendid copper beeches. Large kitchen garden, orchard, stumpery, herbaceous borders, white garden, herb garden, sculpture. Fabulous views across the valley towards Howardian Hills.

91 OVERTHORPE J I & N SCHOOL
Edge Top Road, Thornhill, Dewsbury WF12 0BH. Overthorpe J I & N School, 07880 820179, dougrobbaker@hotmail.com, www.arcadialandscapes.com. *1m S of Dewsbury. Town centre on Edgetop Rd. Follow signs to Whitley & Briestfield.* Cream teas. **Adm £2.50, chd free. Sun 14 July (1-5). Visitors also welcome by appt May to Sept.**
A rare opportunity to visit the grounds of a primary school that are managed for outdoor learning, play and wildlife. Large kitchen and vegetable garden, orchard, wildlife garden and ponds, meadows, WW2 themed garden. Woodland and natural play areas, all richly planted to create opportunities for play and learning in a natural setting. Drama and music in the grounds. Refreshments provided by children from school-grown produce. Featured in Guardian Weekend Magazine.

OWL END
See Derbyshire

92 ◆ PARCEVALL HALL GARDENS
Skyreholme, nr Skipton BD23 6DE. Walsingham College, 01756 720311, www.parcevallhallgardens.co.uk. *9m N of Skipton. Signs from B6160 Bolton Abbey-Burnsall rd or off B6265 Grassington-Pateley Bridge.* **Adm £6, chd free. For NGS: Wed 17 Apr (10-5). For other opening times and information, please phone or see garden website.**
The only garden open daily in the Yorkshire Dales National Park. 24 acres in Wharfedale sheltered by mixed woodland; terrace garden, rose garden, rock garden, fish ponds. Mixed borders, spring bulbs, tender shrubs (desfontainea, crinodendron, camellias); autumn colour. Bird watching, old apple orchard for picnics.

Developed by 2 avid garden visitors who are unable to visit a garden without buying a new plant . . .

93 NEW 3 PILMOOR COTTAGES
Pilmoor. YO61 2QQ. Wendy & Chris Jakeman, 01845 501848, cnjakeman@aol.com. *20m N of York. 6m E of Boroughbridge A1M J48. Follow signs for Easingwold, turn L for Pilmoor & Sessay ½ m before Helperby. Garden 2½ m on R near railway. From A19 take rd to Hutton Sessay keep L for Sessay & Helperby. Garden on L before railway bridge.* Home-made teas. **Adm £3.50, chd free. Sun 28 Apr; 28 July; 15 Sept (11-5). Visitors also welcome by appt Apr to Sept.**
2-acre garden surrounding C19 cottages. Developed by 2 avid garden visitors who are unable to visit a garden without buying a new plant, leading to an informal style, but always with something to look at from bulbs in spring to colchicums and cyclamen in autumn. Clock-golf putting green. Miniature railway around the garden, ponds and rockery.

94 THE PRIORY
Nun Monkton, nr York YO26 8ES. Mr & Mrs R Harpin. *9m W of York, 12 E of Harrogate. E of A1M J47 off A59 signed Nun Monkton.* Light refreshments. **Adm £5, chd free. Sun 30 June (11-5).**
Large country garden at the confluence of the rivers Nidd and Ouse surrounding a William and Mary house (not open). Formal rose garden. Old walls support climbers and give a backdrop to long mixed borders, mature species trees and clipped yew walk leads to informal parkland with beck. Kitchen garden, greenhouse and glasshouse for ornamentals. Gravel paths.

95 2 PROSPECT PLACE
Outlane, nr Huddersfield HD3 3FL. Carol & Andy Puszkiewicz, 01422 376408, carol-puszkiewicz@talktalk.net. *5m N of Huddersfield. 1m N of M62. J24 (W) take A643 to J23 (E) follow A640 to Rochdale. Turn R immed before 40mph sign (Gosport Lane). Parking in adjacent field.* Home-made teas. **Adm £2.50, chd free. Sun 23 June (12-5). Evening Opening, wine, Fri 5 July (6-8). Visitors also welcome by appt June to July, groups of 6+.**
1-acre intimate garden high in Pennines (900ft). Cottage herbaceous borders and pond lead to shaded areas and secret garden with camomile lawn, colour themed borders surrounding circular bed and productive kitchen garden with trained fruit and herbs. Evolving wild area with raised wooden pathway to summerhouse, large pond, narrow stream and meadow. New for 2013 gravel garden and revamped shady area.

ALLOTMENTS

96 QUEENSGATE & KITCHEN LANE ALLOTMENTS
Beverley HU17 8NN. Beverley Town Council. *Outskirts of Beverley Town Centre. On A164 towards Cottingham, allotment site is before Victoria Rd, after double mini r'about & opp Beverley Grammar School.* Cream teas. **Adm £2.50, chd free. Sun 28 July (12-4).**
Varied allotment site of 85 plots, plus another 35 on Kitchen Lane, growing a wide variety of fruit, vegetables and flowers. Some allotment holders will be present to discuss their plots. Path for easy viewing and plots either side. Dogs on leads.

97 THE RED HOUSE
17 Whin Hill Road, Bessacarr, Doncaster DN4 7AF. Rosie Hamlin. *2m S of Doncaster. A638 S, L at T-lights for B1396, Whin Hill Rd is 2nd R. A638 N, R signed Branton B1396 onto Whin Hill.* Light refreshments. **Adm £3, chd free. Sun 19 May (12-5); Sun 16 June (2-5).**
Mature 2/3 -acre garden. Dry shade a challenge but acid loving plants a joy. Fine acers, camellia, daphne, rhododendrons, kalmia and eucryphia. Terrace and rockery stepping stones lead past and through new wave and cloud pruned shrubs to lawn with modern orb-shaped rotating summerhouse and young trees. White border conceals pond, compost and hens.

RENISHAW HALL & GARDENS
See Derbyshire

The garden has been described as 'organised chaos' . . . !

98 REWELA COTTAGE
Skewsby YO61 4SG. John Plant & Daphne Ellis, 01347 888125, plantjohnsgarden@btinternet.com. *4m N of Sheriff Hutton, 15 miles N of York. After Sheriff Hutton, towards Terrington, turn L towards Whenby & Brandsby. Turn R just past Whenby to Skewsby. Turn L into village. 400yds on R.* Home-made teas. **Adm £3.50, chd free. Suns 5 May; 21 July (12-5). Visitors also welcome by appt May and July.**
3/4 -acre ornamental garden, designed by current owner, featuring unusual trees, shrubs, and architectural plants. Other features include a pond, pergola, natural stone sunken garden, breeze house, raised vegetable garden. May for rhododendrons, azaleas, magnolias and spring bulbs. July for summer flowering plants, year round interest. Over 80 heucheras, 40 penstemons and 40 hostas in the garden. All unusual trees and shrubs have labels giving full descriptions, picture, and any cultivation notes incl propagation. Plant sales are specimens from garden. Many varieties of heuchera, heucherella and tiarelss, penstemon and herbs for sale. Featured in Garden News, Yorkshire Post and Easingwold Advertiser. Access to all parts of the garden for wheelchair users.

99 ◆ RHS GARDEN HARLOW CARR
Crag Lane, Harrogate HG3 1QB. Royal Horticultural Society, 01423 565418, www.rhs.org.uk/harlowcarr. *1 1/2 m W of Harrogate town centre. On B6162 (Harrogate - Otley).* **Adm £7.50, chd £3.75. For NGS: Sun 28 Apr (9.30-5). For other opening times and information, please phone or see garden website.**
One of Yorkshire's most relaxing yet inspiring locations! Highlights incl spectacular herbaceous borders, streamside garden, alpines, scented and kitchen gardens. 'Gardens Through Time', woodland and wild flower meadow. Betty's Tearoom, gift shop & childrens play area incl tree house. Wheelchairs and mobility scooters available. Advanced booking recommended.

100 THE RIDINGS
South Street, Burton Fleming, Driffield YO25 3PE. Roy & Ruth Allerston, 01262 470489. *11m NE of Driffield. 11m SW of Scarborough. 7m NW of Bridlington. From Driffield B1249, before Foxholes turn R to Burton Fleming. From Scarborough A165 turn R to Burton Fleming.* Home-made teas. **Adm £3, chd free. Suns 26 May; 7 July (1-5). Combined with Rustic Cottage, adm £5. Visitors also welcome by appt.**
Tranquil cottage garden designed by owners in 2001 on reclaimed site. Brick pergola and arches covered with climbers lead to secret garden with lavender edged beds. Colour-themed mixed borders with old English roses. Paved terrace with water feature and farming bygones, small potager; summerhouse and greenhouse.

101 NEW RUDDING PARK
Follifoot, nr Harrogate HG3 1JH. Mr & Mrs Simon Mackaness, www.ruddingpark.co.uk. *3m S of Harrogate off A658. Follow brown tourist signs. Use hotel entrance.* Home-made teas. **Adm £3.50, chd free. Sun 2 June (12.30-5).**
20 acres of attractive gardens and lawns around a Grade I Regency house extended and used as an hotel. Original parkland planting to designs of Humphry Repton. Formal gardens known for their collection of rhododendrons and azaleas (largest collection in Yorkshire) have recently had a major restoration. Planting adjacent to hotel is more modern with grasses and perennials, designed by Matthew Wilson.

102 RUSTIC COTTAGE
Front Street, Wold Newton, nr Driffield YO25 3YQ. Jan Joyce, 01262 470710. *13m N of Driffield. From Driffield take B1249 to Foxholes (12m), take R turning signed Wold Newton. Turn L onto Front St, opp village pond, continue up hill, garden on L.* **Adm £3, chd free. Sun 26 May; Sun 7 July (1-5). Combined with The Ridings, adm £5, 7 July. Visitors also welcome by appt Mar to Oct.**
Plantswoman's cottage garden of much interest with many choice and unusual plants. Hellebores and bulbs are treats for colder months. Old-fashioned roses, fragrant perennials, herbs and wild flowers, all grown together provide habitat for birds, bees, butterflies and small mammals. It has been described as 'organised chaos'! The owner's 2nd NGS garden. Small dogs only.

103 ST JOHN RC PRIMARY SCHOOL
Wilberforce Crescent, Beverley HU17 0BU. *1/2 m E of Beverley. From Hull A1174 to Swine Moor Lane, L Grovehill Rd. 3rd R Coltman Ave onto Wilberforce Crescent.* Cream teas. **Adm £2.50, chd free. Sat 6 July (10-4).**
Organic vegetable garden, wildlife garden, peace garden with willow sculptures, small orchard and subtropical polytunnel, with a 'global' theme. Children's craft activities and food tasting.

104 ◆ SCAMPSTON WALLED GARDEN
Scampston Hall, Scampston, Malton YO17 8NG. The Legard Family, 01944 759111, www.scampston.co.uk/gardens.

26 West End

5m E of Malton. ½ m N of A64, near the village of Rillington and signed Scampston only. **For opening times and information, please phone or see garden website.**
An exciting modern garden designed by Piet Oudolf. The 4-acre walled garden contains a series of hedged enclosures designed to look good throughout the year. The garden contains many unusual species and is a must for any keen plantsman. Featured in The English Garden and This is Y magazine.

105 ◆ SHANDY HALL GARDENS

Coxwold YO61 4AD. The Laurence Sterne Trust, 01347 868465, www.laurencesternetrust.org.uk/shandy-hall-garden.php. *N of York. From A19, 7m from both Easingwold & Thirsk, turn E signed Coxwold.* **For NGS: Evening Openings £3, chd free, Fris 26 Apr; 14 June (6.30-8.30). For other opening times and information, please phone or see garden website.**
Home of C18 author Laurence Sterne. 2 walled gardens, 1 acre of unusual perennials interplanted with tulips and old roses in low walled beds. In old quarry, another acre of trees, shrubs, bulbs, climbers and wild flowers encouraging wildlife, incl over 220 recorded species of moths. Moth trap, identification and release. Featured in Garden News. Wheelchair access to wild garden by arrangement.

GROUP OPENING

106 NEW SHIPTONTHORPE GARDENS

York YO43 3PQ. *2m NW of Market Weigton. 2nd turn off from A1079 Market Weigton Rd in Shiptonthorpe. Cairngorm on R is start point with car parking opp.* Light refreshments at Cairngorm. **Combined adm £5, chd free. Sun 19 May; Sun 23 June (11-5).**

NEW 6 ALL SAINTS
Di Thompson

NEW CAIRNGORM
Station Road. Peter & Ann Almond

NEW EAST VIEW
Town Street. Maureen Almond

NEW FIELD VIEW
Sandsfield Avenue. Mrs L Wollaston

Four contrasting gardens offering different approaches. There is a contemporary garden, a small garden showing just how much can be achieved in a limited space, a garden with gravel and evergreen planting and a cottage garden. 6 All Saints is a maze-like modern garden with a mixture of contemporary and cottage garden features. Hidden corners, water features and pond. Cairngorm Cottage a garden with gravelled area and paths. Conifers, ferns, hostas, vegetable plot, log cabin and greenhouse. East View is a hidden gem, long narrow cottage garden, with a good selection of herbaceous perennials especially hostas and ferns. Wall water feature pond near cottage and wildlife pond at the bottom of the garden. Field View a small garden intensively planted with a mixture of evergreen and deciduous small trees, shrubs and herbaceous plants to provide a tranquil and private space with all-yr-round interest and colour

Summer highlights including exuberant plantings of flowering perennials with some rare and unusual plants . . .

107 SKIPWITH HALL
Skipwith, nr Selby YO8 5SQ. Mr & Mrs C D Forbes Adam, rosalind@skipwith.com. *9m S of York, 6m N of Selby. From York A19 Selby, L in Escrick, 4m to Skipwith. From Selby A19 York, R onto A163 to Market Weighton, then L after 2m to Skipwith.* Home-made teas. **Adm £4, chd free. Wed 12 June (1-4). Groups also welcome by appt.**
4-acre walled garden of Queen Anne house (not open). Ancient mulberry, extensive mixed borders and Cecil Pinsent designed 'Richard's Garden'. Recreated working kitchen garden with 15' beech hedge, pleached fruit walks, herb maze and pool. Woodland with specimen trees and new shell house. Decorative orchard with trained fruit on walls. Secret Italian garden (under restoration). Gravel paths.

GROUP OPENING

108 STAMFORD BRIDGE GARDENS
Stamford Bridge YO41 1PD, 01759 373838, dmt17966@yahoo.co.uk. *Approx 7m E of York on A166 to Bridlington. Please use main car park in village or station car park on Church Rd.* Cream teas at Daneswell House. **Combined adm £5, chd free. Sun 21 July (12-5). Visitors also welcome by appt July and Aug.**

DANESWELL HOUSE
Brian & Pauline Clayton.
From main car park by bridge turn L and then R. Cross rd towards shops and continue up Main Street, past old corn mill. Daneswell House is at top of rd just before St Edmunds
Visitors also welcome by appt July and Aug.
01759 371446

GROVE LODGE
Mr & Mrs G Tattersall.
From main car park at bottom of village turn R. Up Viking Road to Church Road, turn R and continue bearing L onto High Catton Road. Butts Close is 1st turning on R
Visitors also welcome by appt July and Aug, coaches welcome.
01759 373838
dmt17966@yahoo.co.uk

MILL TIMBER
2 Viking Close. Mr & Mrs K Chapman
Visitors also welcome by appt July and Aug.
01759 371523

Three interesting and contrasting gardens situated in the historic village of Stamford Bridge. Grove Lodge is a plantsman's garden with a large collection of plants grown from seed or propagated from cuttings. There are small number of vegetables grown in planters, fruit trees and greenhouse that contains a variety of salad vegetables. Mill Timber has a good collection of perennials in a large sloping border. The garden is sheltered on one side by mature trees. Patio planters with summer flowers and hanging baskets displaying a kaleidoscope of colour. Daneswell House is a ¾ -acre terraced garden that sweeps down to the R Derwent. Pond and water feature with walk over bridge. Large lawned area with mixed borders and shrubs. Attracts wildlife.

109 ◆ STILLINGFLEET LODGE
Stewart Lane, Stillingfleet, nr York YO19 6HP. Mr & Mrs J Cook, 01904 728506, www.stillingfleetlodgenurseries.co.uk. *6m S of York. From A19 York-Selby take B1222 towards Sherburn in Elmet. In village turn opp church.* **Adm £4.50, chd 50p. For NGS: Suns 12 May; 16 June; 8 Sept (1-5). For other opening times and information, please phone or see garden website.**
Plantsman's garden subdivided into smaller gardens, each based on colour theme with emphasis on use of foliage plants. Wild flower meadow and natural pond. 55yd double herbaceous borders. New modern rill garden. Rare breeds of poultry wander freely in garden. Adjacent nursery. Featured in Daily Telegraph, Dalesman & The Journal. Gravel paths and lawn. No disabled WC. Ramp to cafe if needed.

110 STONEHAVEN
1a Belgrave Crescent, Harrogate HG2 8HZ. Denise & Paul Dyson, 01423 538141, paul-dyson@sky.com. *From Harrogate town centre take A61 towards Leeds. Turn 1st L at 2nd r'about down South Drive over Xrds & railway bridge. Turn 2nd R into Belgrave Crescent.* Home-made teas. **Adm £2.50, chd free. Visitors welcome by appt May to Sept.**
A gem of a small, enclosed garden recreated from 2007 on the south side of Harrogate. Partly raised and traditionally planted with an interesting selection of herbaceous perennials suitable for both sun and shade. Generously planted pergolas support roses, clematis and other climbers, underplanted with hardy cyclamen, unusual primulas, violas, hardy geraniums and much more.

111 SUE PROCTOR PLANTS NURSERY GARDEN
69 Ings Mill Avenue, Clayton West, Huddersfield HD8 9QG. Sue & Richard Proctor, 01484 866189, sueproctor@talktalk.net, www.sueproctorplants.co.uk. *9m NE of Holmfirth, 10m SW of Wakefield. Off A636 Wakefield & Holmfirth. From M1 J39 in Clayton West Village turn L signed Clayton West, High Hoyland, then R signed Kaye's F & N School. Turn 1st R to Ings Mill Avenue.* Light refreshments. **Adm £2.50, chd free. Sun 4 Aug (11-5). Visitors also welcome by appt mid May to Aug.**
Small, mainly sloping, suburban garden packed full of interest. Summer highlights incl exuberant plantings of flowering perennials with some rare and unusual plants and many varieties of hosta and crocosmia. Gravel and rock gardens show off grasses, architectural and foliage plants, ferns and hostas, especially miniatures, the nursery specialism. The Kirklees Light Railway is close by. Steam trains and many other attractions for children.

From tiny back plots to country estates ...

112 SWALE COTTAGE

Station Road, Richmond DL10 4LU. Julie Martin & Dave Dalton. *Richmond town centre. On foot, facing bottom of Market Place, turn L onto Frenchgate, then R onto Station Rd. House 1st on R.* Home-made teas. **Adm £3, chd free. Sun 2 June (1-5). Also open Millgate House.**

$^{1}/_{2}$-acre urban oasis on steep site, with sweeping views and hidden corners. Several enclosed garden rooms on different levels. Mature herbaceous, rose and shrub garden with some areas of recent improvement. Magnificent yew and cedar. Organic vegetables and soft fruit and pond. Adjacent orchard and paddock with sheep and hens. Featured in Amateur Gardening. Some gravel paths and inaccessible areas.

113 TERRINGTON HOUSE

Terrington YO60 6PU. Mr & Mrs James Fenwick, 01653 648470, lindatex7@yahoo.com. *15m NE of York. Last house in village on R if coming from Sheriff Hutton or 1st on L coming from A64 & Castle Howard rd.* Home-made teas. **Adm £4, chd free. Suns 5 May; 16 June (11-4). Visitors also welcome by appt May to July.**

Formal garden set in 3 acres with exquisite shell house, herbaceous and mixed borders. Spring: mixed beds of brunnera, narcissi, tulips, azaleas, daffodils, bluebells, rhododendrons, roses, peonies, hostas. Summer: delphiniums. Impressive trees, herb garden parterre and vegetable garden. Featured in Coast Magazine.

114 VICARAGE HOUSE

Kirkby Wharfe, nr Tadcaster LS24 9DE. Mr & Mrs R S A Hall. *1m S of Tadcaster. (A162) turn L (B1223) after 1m turn L to Kirkby Wharfe.* Home-made teas. **Adm £3.50, chd free. Sun 21 Apr (1-5).**

Secluded 1-acre country garden surrounded by mature trees, colour-themed border, extensive herbaceous borders, raised beds. Species primulae and aquilegias. New 'jewel bed', productive vegetable plot, asparagus bed, vine shaded terrace, gravel pathways.

115 WARLEY HOUSE GARDEN

Stock Lane, Warley, nr Halifax HX2 7RU. Dr & Mrs P J Hinton, www.warleyhousegardens.com. *2m W of Halifax. From Halifax take A646 (Burnley). Turn R up Windleroyd Lane approx 1m after A58, A646 junction (King Cross). Turn L at T-junction into Stock Lane. Park on rd before Warley Village.* Light refreshments. **Adm £3.50, chd free. Sun 12 May (1-5).**

Partly walled 2$^{1}/_{2}$-acre garden of demolished C18 House, renovated by the present owners. Rocky paths and Japanese style planting leads to lawns and lovely S-facing views. Alpine ravine planted with ferns and fine trees give structure to the developing woodland area. Drifts of shrubs, herbaceous plantings, wild flowers and heathers maintain constant seasonal interest. Children are welcome to play on the large lawned area. On a nice day we will also put out the croquet equipment. Limited wheelchair access to Japanese garden.

> Alpine ravine planted with ferns and fine trees give structure to the developing woodland area . . .

116 WEATHERVANE HOUSE

Mill Lane, Seaton Ross YO42 4NE. Julie & Peter Williams, 01759 318663, peteandjuliew@googlemail.com. *5m S of Pocklington. From A64 York, take Hull exit & signed B1228 approx 9m, then follow signs to Seaton Ross. From M62 Howden N on B1228 approx 11m R turn Seaton Ross. From Hull A1079 turn L at Hayton. Garden on L soon after entering village.* Home-made teas. **Adm £3, chd free. Sun 5 May (12-5). Visitors also welcome by appt April and May. Magnolias in April, azaleas and rhododendrons best in May.**

Two-acre woodland garden with magnolias, rhododendrons, azaleas, flowering trees and shrubs. A wide range of spring bulbs incl erythroniums and trilliums together with mixed herbaceous borders, lawns and circular meadow. Fruit garden, glasshouse with wide range of hardy and tender plants and large polytunnel with specimen rhododendrons and many other plants. Artist in the garden. A range of interesting and uncommon plants for sale that reflect the plants growing in the garden. Examples of plants propagated by cuttings, grafting and raised from seed are available. Gravel drive and paths but wheelchair passage possible.

WEST BARN

See Lincolnshire

117 26 WEST END

Walkington HU17 8SX. Miss Jennifer Hall, 01482 861705, jen21@jen21.karoo.co.uk. *2m SW of Beverley. On B1230, 100yds beyond Xrds in centre of village on R.* **Adm £3.50, chd free. Visitors welcome by appt June and July, refreshments by arrangement.**

Exceptionally charming and interesting 1-acre cottage garden attractive to wildlife, particularly bees. The garden opens into an old wooded gravel pit still being developed by owner. Many rare plants collected over more than 20yrs. Featured in The Journal.

118 THE WHITE HOUSE

Husthwaite YO61 4QA. Mrs A Raper, 01347 868688, audrey.husthwaite@btinternet.com. *5m S of Thirsk. Turn R off A19 signed Husthwaite. 1$^{1}/_{2}$ m to centre of village opp parish church.* **Adm £5, chd free. Visitors welcome by appt.**

Meet the gardener, an enthusiastic plantswoman, exchange ideas and visit a 1-acre country garden. Walled garden, conservatory and gardens within the garden. Herbaceous - fresh lavender and purple palette in late spring and hot summer border. Unusual plants and shrubs. Collection of clematis, landscaping, planting and bed of English and shrub roses in the old orchard. A garden for all seasons.

GROUP OPENING

119 WHIXLEY GARDENS
nr York YO26 8AR. *8m W of York, 8m E of Harrogate, 6m N of Wetherby. 3m E of A1(M) off A59 York-Harrogate. Signed Whixley.* Home-made teas at The Old Vicarage. **Combined adm £5, chd free.** **Mon 6 May; Wed 19 June (11-5). Visitors also welcome by appt May to July.**

ASH TREE HOUSE
High Street. Mr & Mrs E P Moffitt
01423 331424
epmoff@btinternet.com
Visitors also welcome by appt May to July

COBBLE COTTAGE
Rudgate. John Hawkridge & Barry Atkinson
01423 331419
johnbarry44@talktalk.net
Visitors also welcome by appt May to July

THE OLD VICARAGE
Church Street. Mr & Mrs Roger Marshall

Attractive rural yet accessible village nestling on the edge of the York Plain with beautiful historic church and Queen Anne Hall (not open). The gardens are spread throughout the village with good footpaths. A plantsman's and flower arranger's garden at Cobble Cottage has views to the Hambleton Hills. Ash Tree House further towards the village centre is a small well designed garden on a steeply sloping site with extensive rock garden and borders full of established herbaceous plants, shrubs and roses creating a tapestry of soft colour and textures achieving a cottage garden effect. In front of the Church of the Ascension stands The Old Vicarage, overlooking the old deer park, with its delightful ¾ -acre walled flower garden. The walls, house and various structures within the garden are festooned with climbers. Mixed borders, old roses, hardy and half-hardy perennials, topiary, bulbs and hellebores give interest all yr. Gravel and old brick paths lead to hidden seating areas creating the atmosphere of a romantic English garden.

GROUP OPENING

120 WITHERNSEA GARDENS
Withernsea HU19 2PJ. *23m E of Hull, 16m S of Hornsea. Enter Withernsea from A1033 onto Hollym Rd. From Hornsea, B1242, through town onto Hollym Rd.* Home-made teas, both gardens offer refreshments. **Combined adm £5, chd free.** **Sun 21 July (12-6).**

35 HOLLYM ROAD
Linda & Maurice Beever

54 HOLLYM ROAD
Mr Matthew Pottage

Two interesting, contrasting gardens opp each other in Withernsea. 35 Hollym Rd has colourful herbaceous borders planted with annuals, perennials, grasses, evergreens, shrubs and trees. Pond feature, vegetable garden and chicken runs. 54 Hollym Rd is a diverse, colourful garden containing unfamiliar plants to even the most serious of gardeners! Matthew, a true plantsman, is Garden Manager at RHS Wisley. In his own garden, yuccas stand tall in the dry garden in contrast to enormous fleshy leaves of Chatham Island forget-me-not. Mixed borders contain unusual shrubs, conifers, trees plus a potted collection of succulents and pond.

121 WOODLANDS COTTAGE
Summerbridge, Nidderdale HG3 4BT. Mr & Mrs Stark, 01423 780765, www.woodlandscottagegarden.co.uk. *10m NW of Harrogate. On the B6165 W of Summerbridge.* Tea. **Adm £3, chd free. Sun 12 May**

Skipwith Hall

"Lemon drizzle cake, Victoria sponge ... yummy!"

(1.30-5). **Also open 7 July with Dacre Banks & Summerbridge Gardens. Visitors also welcome by appt.**
A one-acre garden created by its owners making full use of its country setting with natural rock formations and woodland with wild bluebells. Several gardens within a garden, from a wild-flower meadow and woodland rock-garden to more formal herbaceous areas and a productive vegetable garden. Gravel paths with some slopes.

122 WYTHERSTONE GARDENS

Pockley, nr Helmsley, York YO62 7TE. Lady Clarissa Collin. *2m NE of Helmsley. Signed from A170.* Home-made teas. **Adm £4, chd free. Sun 30 June (10-4).**
True plantsman's garden set in 8 acres of rolling countryside on edge of N York Moors. Divided by beech hedges, creating interlinked 'feature' gardens, incl spring (large unusual clematis collection) ericaceous, terraced, fern, paeonia, foliage and bamboo garden, small arboretum. Plants not thought hardy in N England grow happily in the free draining soil. Lots of shrubs and plants for sale. Some steep slopes. Most of the garden is accessible for wheelchairs.

123 ◆ YORK GATE

Back Church Lane, Adel, Leeds LS16 8DW. Perennial, 0113 2678240, www.yorkgate.org.uk. *5m N of Leeds. 2¼ m SE of Bramhope, signed from A660. Park in Church Lane in lay-by opp church and take public footpath through churchyard to garden.* **For opening times and information, please phone or see garden website.**
One-acre masterpiece and outstanding example of late C20 garden design. A series of smaller gardens with different themes and in contrasting styles are linked by a succession of delightful vistas. Striking architectural features play a key role throughout the garden which is also noted for its exquisite detailing. Featured in Gardens Illustrated.

124 YORKE HOUSE

Dacre Banks, Nidderdale HG3 4EW. Tony & Pat Hutchinson, 01423 780456, pat@yorkehouse.co.uk, www.yorkehouse.co.uk. *4m SE of Pateley Bridge, 10m NW of Harrogate, 10m N of Otley. On B6451 near centre of Dacre Banks. Car park.* Cream teas. **Adm £4, chd free. Sat 22, Sun 23 June (11-5). Also open 7 July with Dacre Banks & Summerbridge Gardens. Visitors also welcome by appt 2 June to 4 Aug. Coaches welcome.**
Award-winning flower arranger's 2-acre garden with colour-themed borders full of flowering and foliage plants. Water feature incl large ornamental ponds and stream with attractive waterside plantings. Other features incl nut walk, rose walk, patios, gazebo, millennium garden and wildlife areas. Large collection of hosta. The garden enjoys beautiful views across Nidderdale. Orchard picnic area. 'Art in the Garden' - exhibition of paintings by professional artists. Winner Harrogate's Glorious Gardens. Featured in Yorkshire Life.

Gravel and old brick paths lead to hidden seating areas creating the atmosphere of a romantic English garden . . .

Yorkshire County Volunteers

County Organisers
East Yorks Louise Martin, Fawley House, 7 Nordham, North Cave HU15 2LT, 01430 422266, louisem200@hotmail.co.uk
North Yorks - Districts of Hambleton, Richmond, Ryedale, Scarborough & Cleveland Josephine Marks, Carlton Hall, Carlton Husthwaite, Thirsk YO7 2BR, 01845 501626, carlton331@btinternet.com
West & South Yorks & North Yorks District of Craven, Harrogate, Selby & York Bridget Marshall, The Old Vicarage, Whixley, York YO26 8AR, 01423 330474, biddymarshall@btopenworld.com

County Treasurer
Angela Pugh, Savage Garth, Nun Monkton, York YO26 8ER, 01423 330456, amjopugh@clannet.co.uk

Publicity
Felicity Bowring, Lawkland Hall, Austwick, Lancaster LA2 8AT, 01729 823551, diss@austwick.org

County Booklet Advertising
John Plant, Rewela Cottage, Main Street, Skewsby YO61 4SG, 01347 888125, plantjohnsgarden@btinternet.com

Assistant County Organisers
East Yorks Natalie Verow, The Old Rectory, Bugthorpe, York YO41 1QG, 01759 368444, natalieverow@aol.com
East Yorks Kate Willans, New House, Belvedere Park, Hornsea HU18 1JJ, 01964 534502, kwkatewillans32@googlemail.com
North Yorks Gill Mellor, Hunmanby Grange, Wold Newton, Driffield YO25 3HS, gill.mellor@btconnect.com
North Yorks Judi Smith, Low Sutton, Sutton Lane, Marsham HG4 4PB, 01765 688565, lowsutton@hotmail.co.uk
West & South Yorks Deborah Bigley, The Old Rectory, Great Langton, Northallerton DL7 0TA, 01609 748915, debsandbobbigley@aol.com
West & South Yorks Jane Cooper, The Old Vicarage, Marsh Lane, Shepley, Huddersfield, West Yorkshire HD8 8EA 01484 604232 coopers_shepley@btinternet.com
West & South Yorks Jane Hudson, Lower Crawshaw, Emley, Huddersfield HD8 9SU, 01924 840980, janehudson42@btinternet.com

Bodnant Garden, Gwynedd

The areas shown on this map are specific to the organisation of The National Gardens Scheme. The Gardens of England, listed by area, precede the Gardens of Wales.

CARMARTHENSHIRE & PEMBROKESHIRE

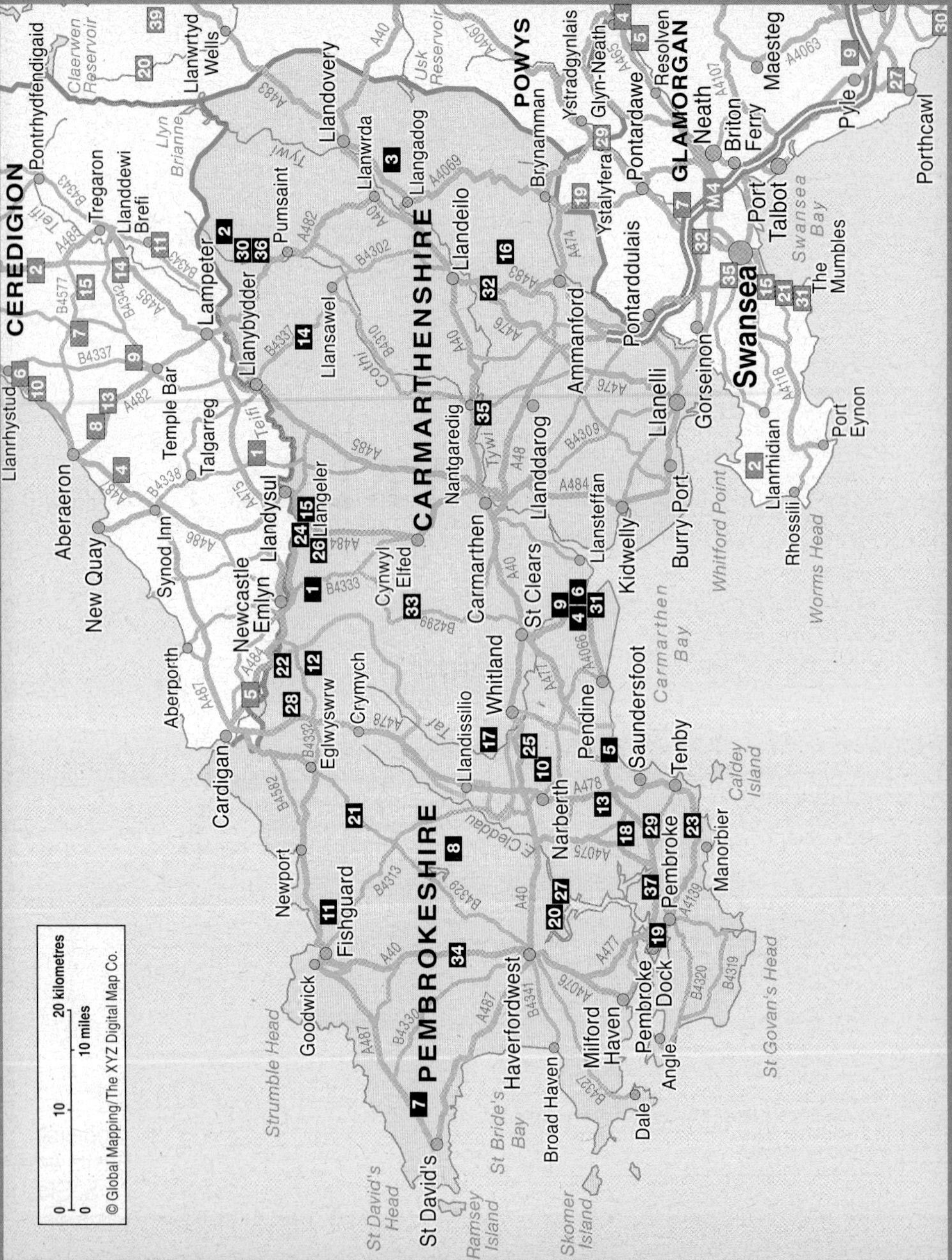

Opening Dates

February

Saturday 23
7 The Crystal Garden

Sunday 24
7 The Crystal Garden

March

Open every Sat & Sun
7 The Crystal Garden

Friday 29
7 The Crystal Garden

Sunday 31
17 Llwyngarreg

April

Open every Sat & Sun
7 The Crystal Garden

Monday 1
7 The Crystal Garden

May

Open daily from Sat 4
7 The Crystal Garden

Daily (not Wed)
21 Moorland Cottage Plants

Saturday 4
26 Pant-y-fedwen

Sunday 5
34 Treffgarne Hall

Saturday 11
5 Colby Woodland Garden

Sunday 12
5 Colby Woodland Garden
12 Ffynone
17 Llwyngarreg

Sunday 19
11 Dyffryn Fernant
36 Ty'r Maes

Sunday 26
27 Picton Castle & Gardens

June

Open daily
7 The Crystal Garden

Daily (not Wed)
21 Moorland Cottage Plants

Sunday 2
15 Glandwr

Sunday 9
1 Blaenfforest
28 Rhosygilwen Mansion
37 Upton Castle Gardens

National Gardens Weekend

Saturday 15
10 Dyffryn Farm
15 Glandwr
18 Mandrake
27 Picton Castle & Gardens
33 Tradewinds

Sunday 16
15 Glandwr
18 Mandrake
22 Nant-yr-Eryd
27 Picton Castle & Gardens
33 Tradewinds

Sunday 23
23 Norchard

Sunday 30
13 Foxways

July

Open daily
7 The Crystal Garden

Daily (not Wed)
21 Moorland Cottage Plants

Sunday 7
2 Bwlchau Duon
30 Sculptors Garden, The Old Post Office

Friday 12
19 Mead Lodge

Saturday 13
19 Mead Lodge
26 Pant-y-fedwen

Sunday 14
19 Mead Lodge
34 Treffgarne Hall

Monday 15
19 Mead Lodge

Sunday 21
29 Rosewood

Sunday 28
6 The Cors
17 Llwyngarreg
18 Mandrake

August

Open daily to 22 Aug
7 The Crystal Garden

Daily (not Wed)
21 Moorland Cottage Plants

Sunday 4
11 Dyffryn Fernant
35 Ty Castell

Sunday 11
33 Tradewinds

Sunday 18
4 The Coach House
31 Swan Cottage
36 Ty'r Maes

Saturday 31
7 The Crystal Garden

September

Open every Sat & Sun
7 The Crystal Garden

Daily (not Wed)
21 Moorland Cottage Plants

Sunday 8
11 Dyffryn Fernant

Sunday 22
17 Llwyngarreg

October

Saturday 5
7 The Crystal Garden

Sunday 6
7 The Crystal Garden

Saturday 12
7 The Crystal Garden

Sunday 13
7 The Crystal Garden

Gardens open to the public

5 Colby Woodland Garden
11 Dyffryn Fernant
27 Picton Castle & Gardens
37 Upton Castle Gardens

By appointment only

3 Cilgwyn Lodge
8 Cwm Pibau
9 Delacorse
14 Gelli Uchaf
16 Llwyn Cyll
20 Millinford
24 The Old Vicarage
25 Panteg
32 Talardd

Also open by Appointment ☎

1 Blaenfforest
6 The Cors
7 The Crystal Garden
10 Dyffryn Farm
15 Glandwr
17 Llwyngarreg
18 Mandrake
19 Mead Lodge
21 Moorland Cottage Plants
26 Pant-y-fedwen
28 Rhosygilwen Mansion
29 Rosewood
34 Treffgarne Hall
35 Ty Castell
36 Ty'r Maes

The Gardens

ALLTYRODYN MANSION
See Ceredigion

1 NEW BLAENFFOREST
Newcastle Emlyn, Carmarthenshire SA38 9JD. Sally & Russell Jones, 01559 371264, enquiries@blaenfforest.co.uk, www.cottageholidayswales.com. *2m S of Newcastle Emlyn. From Newcastle Emlyn take A484 towards Carmarthen. Turn L onto B4333. Turn R signed Capel Iwan. Take R fork onto unsigned rd. Turn R into Blaenfforest private drive signed 'Blaenfforest Cottage Holidays'. The drive is ½ m long and has a gate halfway down. From Carmarthen take A484 to Cardigan. Fork L at Cynwyl Elfed on B4333. Take 2nd turning signed Capel Iwan, on L after passing the windmills. Take R fork and cont as above.* Light refreshments. **Adm £3.50, chd free. Sun 9 June (10.30-6). Visitors also welcome by appt.**
Relaxed and tranquil gardens incl stunning views from the patio, lush planting by the wildlife ponds, interesting, tucked away corners, bees in the orchard and the Woodland Walk, deep in the valley of the R Arad. Peacocks roam freely. Children to be supervised. The Granary at Blaenfforest Featured in The Sunday Times.

Lush planting by the wildlife ponds, interesting, tucked away corners, bees in the orchard and the Woodland Walk . . .

2 NEW BWLCHAU DUON
Ffarmers, Carmarthenshire, Llanwrda SA19 8JJ. Brenda & Allan Timms, www.plantcorner.co.uk. *Ffarmers. 7m SE of Lampeter, 8m NW of Llanwrda on A482. turn to Ffarmers. Take lane opp Drovers Arms PH. Shortly after caravan site on L there is a very small Xrds, turn L up single track lane. Cont to parking area. Garden 100yds away, fairly steep walk.* Home-made teas. **Combined adm £3.50, chd free. Sun 7 July (2-6). Combined with The Old Post Office.**
1 acre, ever evolving, 'Garden Challenge', set in the foothills of the Cambrian Mountains at 1100ft. This is a 'plantaholics haven', with many unusual plants and loads of old favourites. Herbaceous beds vary from 100ft formal bed to semi wild areas, meandering paths over wooden bridge tempts a walk through newly planted natural peat bog. Rare breeds of turkeys and chickens!

3 CILGWYN LODGE
Llangadog, Carmarthenshire SA19 9LH. Keith Brown & Moira Thomas, 01550 777452, keith@cilgwynlodge.co.uk, www.cilgwynlodge.co.uk. *3m NE of Llangadog village. 4m SW of Llandovery.Turn off A40 into centre of Llangadog. Bear L in front of village shop then 1st R towards Myddfai. After 2½ m pass Cilgwyn Manor on L then 1st L. Garden ¼ m on L.* **Adm £4, chd free. Visitors welcome by appt June to Sept. Teas available upon request when booking for max 16 visitors.**
Fascinating and much-admired 1-acre garden with something for everyone. Wide variety of herbaceous plants displayed in extensive colour-themed borders, large collection of hostas, a growing collection of clematis, hardy, rare or unusual plants.Traditional vegetable and fruit garden and large waterlily pond. 'A Welsh Wonderland'. Partial wheelchair access.

4 NEW THE COACH HOUSE
Market Lane, Laugharne, Carmarthen SA33 4SB. Ms Carol Thomas. *A4066 to Laugharne, park in central car park by castle. Walk towards sea, beneath the castle. Bear L up diagonal path which joins Market Lane. Coach House on L.* **Combined adm £3.50, chd free. Sun 18 Aug (2-6). Combined with Swan Cottage.**
An intimate courtyard garden created within the castle's Coach House grounds. An eclectic and colourful mix of plants in pots and borders. Pergola, small water feature, variety of shrubs all in a sheltered setting with spectacular views across the Taf estuary. Partial wheelchair access.

5 ◆ COLBY WOODLAND GARDEN
Narberth, Amroth, Pembrokeshire SA67 8PP. National Trust, 01834 811885, www.nationaltrust.org.uk. *6m N of Tenby. 5m SE of Narberth. Signed by brown tourist signs on coast rd & A477.* **Adm £5, chd £2.50. For NGS: Sat 11, Sun 12 May (10-5). For other opening times and information, please phone or see garden website.**
8-acre woodland garden in a secluded valley with fine collection of rhododendrons and azaleas. Wildflower meadow and stream with rope swings and stepping stones for children to explore and play. Ornamental walled garden incl unusual gazebo, designed by Wyn Jones, with internal tromp l'oeil. Incl in the *Register of Historic Parks and Gardens: Pembrokeshire*. Extensive play area for children incl den building and log climbing. Free family activities incl duck racing, pond dipping, campfire lighting etc.

6 THE CORS
Newbridge Road, Laugharne, Carmarthenshire SA33 4SH. Nick Priestland, 01994 427219, nickpriestland@hotmail.com. *12m SW of Carmarthen. From Carmarthen, turn R in centre of Laugharne at The Mariners PH. At bottom of Newbridge Rd on R. Please use public car parks, 5 mins walk.* Home-made teas. **Adm £3.50, chd free. Sun 28 July (2-6). Visitors also welcome by appt. Refresments available upon request.**
Approx 2½ acres set in beautiful wooded valley bordering river. Large bog garden with ponds, *Gunnera*, bamboos and tree ferns. Exceptional, elegant plantsman's garden with unusual architectural and exotic planting incl *Tetrapanax papyrifer*, *Blechnum chilense*chusan palms and sculptures. Featured in Amateur Gardening magazine, Carmarthen Journal and other local media. Wheelchair access to garden dependant on weather conditions.

7 THE CRYSTAL GARDEN

Golwg yr Ynys, Carnhedryn, St Davids, Pembrokeshire SA62 6XT. Paul & Sue Clark, 01437 721082, susanpaulc@gmail.com, www.golwgyrynys.com. *4m E of St Davids, 11m SW of Fishguard, 2m N of Solva. Village of Carnhedryn, off A487 between Fishguard and St Davids.* **Adm £3, chd free. Sats, Suns 25 Feb - 24 March, Fri, Sat, Sun, 29, 30, 31 March, Mon 1 April Sats, Suns 6 April - 5 May (1-5); Mon 6 May to Thurs 22 Aug (incl) (1-6); Sats, Suns, 31 Aug - 13 Oct (1-5). Visitors also welcome by appt all year.**

A 3/4 acre garden for plantaholics with yr-round floral colour and foliage interest. Intriguing layout of sheltered 'rooms' full of surprises packed with unusual shrubs, perennials and garden favourites. Ever-changing outer garden we have new borders for 2013. Specialities incl hebes and hydrangeas. A warm welcome awaits. Model railway exhibition (all season), Art Wall, Glazed visitor room. Wheelchair access to outer garden.

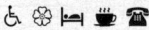

8 CWM PIBAU

New Moat, Haverfordwest, Pembrokeshire SA63 4RE. Mrs Duncan Drew, 01437 532454. *10m NE of Haverfordwest. 3m SW of Maenclochog. Off A40, take B4313 to Maenclochog, follow signs to New Moat, pass church, then 2nd concealed drive on L, 1/2 m rural drive.* **Adm by donation. Visitors welcome by appt.**

5-acre woodland garden surrounded by old deciduous woodland and streams. Created in 1978, contains many mature, unusual shrubs and trees from Chile, New Zealand and Europe, set on S-facing sloping hill. More conventional planting nearer house.

9 DELACORSE

Laugharne, Carmarthenshire SA33 4QP. Annie Hart, 01994 427728, annie.hart@ymail.com. *13m SW of Carmarthen. On A4066 from St Clears, take the 1st L after the hamlet of Cross Inn at 'no footway' rd sign. After 1/2 m at 1st bend, carry straight on along farm track for further 1/2 m. Alternatively, on foot from Laugharne, 20 mins walk along footpath up-river from Dylan Thomas Boathouse Museum.* **Adm £4, chd free. Visitors welcome by appt Apr to Oct.**

3-acre garden beside Taf Estuary in peaceful, beautiful landscape with fine views. Scented walled garden with chamomile lawn; sheltered courtyard; fernery; mixed borders with all-yr interest; living willow work; lawns; specimen trees; millpond; orchard. Carefully managed informal areas merging into woodland, reed beds and salt marsh. Extensive organic kitchen garden. Comprehensive information available on how to grow fruit, veg. and herbs. Managed 6 acre woodland providing fuel for biomass/solar heating installation. Access to all of garden except for millpond and orchard. Featured in the Kitchen Garden.

Llwyngarreg

10 DYFFRYN FARM

Lampeter Velfrey, Narberth, Pembrokeshire SA67 8UN. Dr & Mrs M J R Polson, 01834 861684, sally.polson@virgin.net. *3m E of Narberth. From junction of A40 & A478 follow signs for crematorium, continue down into Llanmill. Then uphill, at brow turn L at Bryn Sion Chapel Xrds (before Lampeter Velfrey). After 1/2 m rd turns R under railway bridge. Dyffryn Farm straight ahead.* Home-made teas. **Adm £3, chd free (share to Paul Sartori Foundation). Sat 15 June (12-5). Visitors also welcome by appt May to Oct. Refreshments availble upon request.**

Large garden, in several areas on different levels, in 'naturalised' manner (not landscaped or contrived) using secluded valley backcloth. Highlights incl 70+ bamboos; grasses, herbaceous plants, unusual shrubs; stream, pond with island and small woodland; all in relaxed style with 'hidden' havens. Children welcome.

11 ◆ DYFFRYN FERNANT
Llanychaer, Fishguard, Pembrokeshire SA65 9SP. Christina Shand & David Allum, 01348 811282, christina.shand@virgin.net, www.genuslocus.net. *3m E of Fishguard, then ½ m inland. A487 Fishguard to Cardigan. After approx 3m, at end of long straight hill, turn R signed Llanychaer with blue rd signs 'unsuitable for long vehicles'. After exactly ½ m is Dyffryn track, on L behind LH bend, with wooden sign.* **Adm £5, chd free. For NGS: Sun 19 May, Sun 4 Aug, Sun 8 Sept (11-6). For other opening times and information, please phone or see garden website.**
'I am truly inspired by this place, to see what intelligent and interesting things you can do with plants, how plants can transform a space, is really exciting. Also the way they have planned the routes and the vistas and created a narrative around this space - wonderful' - Landscape Man, Ch 4. 50 large beds of ornamental grasses and sedges. Wild marsh full of meadowsweet and angelica. Small mount giving wide views of the surrounding landscape incl Preseli uplands. Refreshments by request. Featured in The Garden and Welsh Country Magazine.

The garden is for fun and relaxation so seats abound . . .

12 FFYNONE
Newchapel, Boncath, Pembrokeshire SA37 0HQ. With the kind permission of the Honourable Robert Lloyd George, 01239 841610. *9m SE of Cardigan. 7m W of Newcastle Emlyn. From Newcastle Emlyn take A484 to Cenarth, turn L on B4332, turn L again at Xrds just before Newchapel.* Light refreshments. **Adm £3.50, chd free. Sun 12 May (1-5).**
Large woodland garden designated Grade I on Cadw Register of Historic Parks & Gardens in Wales. Lovely views, fine mature specimen trees; formal garden nr house with massive yew topiary; rhododendrons, azaleas, woodland walks and bluebells. House (also Grade I) by John Nash (1793), not open. Later additions and garden terraces by F Inigo Thomas c1904. Limited wheelchair access. Some steep paths and steps.

13 NEW FOXWAYS
Thomas Chapel, Begelly, Kilgetty, Pembrokeshire SA68 0XH. Roy & Angela Weston. *From Kilgetty take A478 to Narberth & turn L immed after the Regent Garage & signed to Thomas Chapel. Cont for apprx 1m & stay on this road through Thomas Chapel, round sharp R hand bend (ignore your SatNav wanting to turn L towards the village green). Foxways is 2nd on the R, car parking can be found by passing the house and turning into 1st opening on R (part of our neighbour's garden - if you reach Stoney Cottage you have gone too far!)* Home-made teas. **Adm £3, chd free. Sun 30 June (1-5).**
Recently developed the 3-acre garden has a wide range of plants from dry shade, cottage-garden beds to sunny bog gardens. There are waterfalls and wildlife and ornamental ponds. The garden is for fun and relaxation so seats abound, as do hidden corners to get the most from our plants and their peace and quiet. The planting is textural to complement leaf-colour, size and textures for all-season enjoyment. Limited wheelchair access.

14 GELLI UCHAF
Rhydcymerau, Llandeilo, Carmarthenshire SA19 7PY. Julian & Fiona Wormald, 01558 685119, thegardenimpressionists@gmail.com. *5m SE of Llanybydder. 1m NW of Rhydcymerau. In Rhydcymerau on the B4337 turn up Mountain Rd for Llanllwni (by BT phone box). After approx 300 yds turn R up private track cont ½ m bearing R up steep hill.* **Adm £3, chd free. Visitors welcome by appt Feb to Dec. Cream teas availble on request when booking.**
Complementing a C17 longhouse and 11 acre smallholding. Beautiful 1-acre garden. Stunning views, meadow walks and masses of flowers from Feb to Nov. Unique fruit and vegetable garden with 50+ fruit trees. Comments from visitors: 'Fabulous inspiration'; 'Magic around every corner'; 'Just my sort of paradise'. For photos see our blog http://www.thegardenimpressionists.wordpress.com. Exhibition of images and artwork created from photographs of moths and butterflies taken in the garden; and of the restoration of the house and creation of the garden. Featured in Amateur Gardening Magazine.

15 GLANDWR
Pentrecwrt, Llandysul, Carmarthenshire SA44 5DA. Mrs Jo Hicks, 01559 363729, leehicks@btinternet.com. *15m N of Carmarthen, 2m S of Llandysul, 7m E of Newcastle Emlyn. On A486. At Pentrecwrt village, take minor rd opp Black Horse PH. After bridge keep L for ¼ m. Glandwr is on R.* **Adm £3, chd free. Sun 2, Sat 15, Sun 16 June (11-5). Visitors also welcome by appt Apr to Sept.**
Delightful 1-acre cottage garden, bordered by a natural stream with country views. Some single coloured beds ahd borders, a rockery and many shrubs and climbers. Walk in the mature woodland transformed into an adventurous intriguing place, with shade loving shrubs and plants, ground covers and many surprises. Winner 'Best Garden in Llangeler Parish'.

GLANHELYG
See Ceredigion

16 LLWYN CYLL
Llandeilo, Trap SA19 6TR. Liz & John Smith, 01558 822398. *3m SE of Llandeilo. In Trap turn towards Glanaman & Llandybie (at The Cennen Arms). Llwyn Cyll is ½ m on L adjoining Llwyn Onn. Parking limited. Coach parking nearby.* **Adm £3, chd free. Visitors welcome by appt Apr to July. Home-made teas available on request.**
3½ -acre country garden of yr-round interest. Abundant, colourful terraced and walled borders, orchard, vegetable garden. Sun and shade areas with sympathetic planting. A plantsman's garden with many rarities and specimen trees. Up to 40 different magnolias in the arboretum, many in flower late Apr to early June. Scenic view of Castle Carreg Cennen. Featured on S4C.

17 LLWYNGARREG

Llanfallteg, Whitland, Carmarthenshire SA34 0XH. Paul & Liz O'Neill, 01994 240717, lizpaulfarm@yahoo.co.uk. *19m W of Carmarthen. A40 W from Carmarthen, turn R at Llandewi Velfrey, 2½ miles to Llanfallteg. Go through village, garden ½ m further on: 2nd farm on R.* Home-made teas. **Adm £3.50, chd free. Suns 31 Mar; 12 May; 28 July; Sun 22 Sept (1.30-6). Visitors also welcome by appt.**

3-acre plantaholic's haven with yr-round impact, from spring bulbs through to glorious autumn colour; tapestries of colour and texture in the many trees, interspersed with unusual shrubs and perennial underplantings. Willow tunnel welcomes visitors into a maturing shelter belt, beyond which lies the main garden with wide mixed borders. Closely planted areas in front of the house, gravel gardens behind. Woodland garden leads down to the potager. Plantsmen will linger to find many gems. Several deep ponds - children to be closely supervised. Wildlife ponds, twig piles for overwintering insects, composting, numerous living willow structures. Mentioned in Country Life magazine. Limited wheelchair access.

♿ 🐕 ❀ ☕ ☎

18 NEW MANDRAKE

Lanes End, Cresselly, Kilgetty, Pembrokeshire SA68 0SN. Brian Dawson & Barbara Pegg, 01646 651674, babsdaw@gmail.com. *Lanes End, Cresselly. On the A477 take the A4075 towards Carew - carry on for about 2m, upon entering Cresselly take R turn to Jeffreyston - carry on down lane for ½ m - Mandrake on LHS.* Home-made teas. **Adm £3, chd free. Sat 15, Sun 16 June, Sun 28 July (1-5.30). Visitors also welcome by appt May to Aug. Refreshments available on request.**

An immaculately maintained 2 acre hill top garden incorporating an extensive collection of good sized deciduous specimen trees, shrubs, herbaceous perennials, conifers, grasses and exotic plants, cleverly integrated in long wide borders and island bed against a backdrop of superb views into the distance. Fairly level access to lawns.

♿ ❀ ☕ ☎

19 MEAD LODGE

Imble Lane, Pembroke Dock SA72 6PN. John & Eileen Seal, 01646 682504, eileenseal@aol.com. *From A4139 between Pembroke and Pembroke Dock take B4322 signed Pennar and Leisure Centre. After ½ m turn L into Imble Lane. Mead Lodge at end.* Home-made teas. **Adm £3, chd free. Fri 12, Sat 13, Sun 14, Mon 15 July (11-5). Visitors also welcome by appt Apr to Sept. Refreshments available on request.**

Unexpected, secluded country garden, a relaxing oasis on S-facing slope overlooking the Pembroke River estuary. Varied ¾ acre garden reflects the owners' keen interest in ferns, grasses and herbs. Incl terraces with Chinese and Mediterranean influences, colour-themed beds, small arboretum underplanted for spring colour, fernery, vegetable garden, pond and bog garden.

🐕 ❀ ☕ ☎

Stunning mountain and moorland vistas . . .

20 MILLINFORD

The Rhos, Haverfordwest, Pembrokeshire SA62 4AL. Drs B & A Barton, 01437 762394. *3m E of Haverfordwest. From Haverfordwest on A40 to Carmarthen, turn R signed The Rhos, take turning to Millin. Turn R at Millin Chapel then immed L over river bridge.* **Adm £3, chd free. Visitors welcome by appt throughout the year. Refreshments available on request.**

Spacious, undulating and peaceful garden of 4 acres on bank of Millin Creek. Varied collection of over 125 different trees, many unusual, plus shrubs, herbaceous plants and bulbs in beautiful riverside setting. Impressive terracing and water features. Visit in spring, summer and early autumn.

☕ ☎

21 MOORLAND COTTAGE PLANTS

Rhyd-y-Groes, Brynberian, Pembrokeshire SA41 3TT. Jennifer & Kevin Matthews, 01239 891363, www.moorlandcottageplants.co.uk. *12m SW of Cardigan. 16m NE of Haverfordwest, on B4329, ¾ m downhill from cattlegrid (from Haverfordwest) and 1m uphill from signpost to Brynberian (from Cardigan).* **Adm £3, chd £0.50 (share to Paul Sartori Foundation). Every Mon, Tue, Thur, Fri, Sat & Sun 11 May to 30 Sept (10.30-5.30). Visitors also welcome by appt May to Sept.**

1½ -acre garden at 700ft on wild NE hillside. Abundantly planted, wide range of plants providing propagating material for the adjacent nursery. Secretive, enclosed areas where carpets of spring flowers give way to jungly perennials, grasses and bamboos contrast with deep, parallel herbaceous borders and new, informal shrubberies providing stunning mountain and moorland vistas, Garden entirely organic, mollusc-proof plantings. Shown on S4C Wedi3. Featured in County Life and Swansea Life.

❀ ☎

22 NANT-YR-ERYD

Abercych, Boncath, Pembrokeshire SA37 0EU. Alan & Diana Hall. *5m SE of Cardigan, 5m W of Newcastle Emlyn. Off B4332 Cenarth to Abercych, Boncath Rd. Turn N to Abercych, through village and take L fork.* Home-made teas. **Adm £2.50, chd free. Sun 16 June (11-4).**

Charming well-maintained cottage garden of 1-acre. Mature and new topiary gardens. Fernery and other displays in original outbuildings. Well worth visiting in summer. Beautiful roses including Rosa Mundi, and William Lobb, Abraham Darby, Dortmund and Himalayan Musk. Also wildflower meadow. Featured in Country Living and 'Discovering Welsh Gardens'. Limited wheelchair access.

♿ 🐕 ☕

Norchard

23 NORCHARD
The Ridgeway, Manorbier, Tenby, Pembrokeshire SA70 8LD. Ms H E Davies. *4m W of Tenby. From Tenby, take A4139 for Pembroke. 1/2 m after Lydstep, take R at Xrds. Proceed down lane for 3/4 m. Norchard on R.* Home-made teas. **Adm £4, chd free (share to Shalom House). Sun 23 June (1-5).**
Historic gardens at medieval residence. Nestled in tranquil and sheltered location with ancient oak woodland backdrop. Strong structure with formal and informal areas incl early walled gardens with Elizabethan parterre and potager (currently undergoing restoration). 1 1/2 acre orchard with old (many local) apple varieties. Mill and millpond. Extensive collections of roses, daffodils and tulips. Featured in Welsh Historic Gardens Trust's Trafodion and County Life. Gravel paths. Access to potager via steps only.

24 THE OLD VICARAGE
Llangeler, Carmarthenshire SA44 5EU. Mr & Mrs J C Harcourt, 01559 371168. *4m E of Newcastle Emlyn. 15m N of Carmarthen on A484. From N Emlyn turn down lane on L in Llangeler before church.* Cream teas. **Adm £2.50, chd free. Visitors welcome by appt. Refreshments available on request.**
A garden gem created since 1993. Less than 1 acre divided into 3 areas of roses, shrubs and a semi-formal pool with an interesting collection of unusual herbaceous plants. Ever changing scene. The last 2 winters have taken their toll so some re-invention has been needed. Optimum colour, mid-June onwards. Gravel yard - temporary ramp available.

25 NEW PANTEG
Llanddewi Velfrey, Narberth, Pembrokeshire SA67 8UU. Mr & Mrs D Pryse Lloyd, 01834 860081, d.pryselloyd@btinternet.com. *Situated off main A40 in the village of Llanddewi Velfrey. From Carmarthen - coming into the village there is a garage on your L. Just beyond garage take the 1st L turn. After about 200yrd you will come to a T-junction, turn L. Almost immed on R you will see a gateway with stone gate pillars, follow drive for about 1/2 m keeping to R. Panteg is at the end of the drive, (yellow house).* **Adm £3.50, chd free. Visitors welcome by appt Mar to Sept.**
Approached down a woodland drive, this tranquil, S-facing, large garden, surrounding a Georgian house (not open), has been developed since early 1990s. A Plantsman's garden set off by lawns on different levels. Walled garden, wisteria covered pergola. Vegetable garden, camellia and azalea bank, wild flower woodland. Many rare shrubs and plants including, Embothrium, Eucryphia and Hoheria.

Spacious lightly wooded grounds for leisurely rambling . . .

26 PANT-Y-FEDWEN
Drefelin, Drefach Felindre, Llandysul, Carmarthenshire SA44 5XB. Steven & Viki Harwood, 01559 371807, steven@harwoodsartsandcrafts.co.uk, www.harwoodsartsandcrafts.co.uk. *Drefach Felindre is signed from A484 approx 16m from Carmarthen & Cardigan, 5m from Newcastle Emlyn.* **Adm £2.50, chd free. Sat 4 May, Sat 13 July (11-4). Visitors also welcome by appt.**
Small front garden with stream, surrounded by lush architectural plantings. Hillside garden behind house, informally managed, with unusual plants and various seating areas giving views over the valley. Quirky garden of about 1/3 acre, on 5 levels, culminating in a tranquil woodland garden. For the physically adept only. Arts & Crafts for sale in Workshop.

27 ◆ PICTON CASTLE & GARDENS
The Rhos, Haverfordwest, Pembrokeshire SA62 4AS. Picton Castle Trust, 01437 751326, info@pictoncastle.co.uk, www.pictoncastle.co.uk. *3m E of Haverfordwest. On A40 to Carmarthen, signed off main rd.* **Adm £6.50, chd £4. For NGS: Sun 26 May, Sat 15, Sun 16 June (10.30-5). For other opening times and information, please phone or see garden website.**
Mature 40-acre woodland garden with unique collection of rhododendrons and azaleas, many bred over 41yrs, producing hybrids of great merit and beauty; rare and tender shrubs and trees incl *Magnolia*, myrtle, *Embothrium* and *Eucryphia*. Wild flowers abound. Walled garden with roses; fernery; herbaceous and climbing plants and large clearly-labelled collection of herbs. Exciting art exhibitions and a wide range of seasonal events. Please see website for details. Some woodland walks unsuitable for wheelchair users.

28 RHOSYGILWEN MANSION
Rhoshill, Cilgerran, Cardigan, Pembrokeshire SA43 2TW. Glen Peters & Brenda Squires, 01239 841387, enquiries@retreat.co.uk. *6m S of Cardigan. From Cardigan follow A478 signed Tenby. After 6m turn L at Rhoshill towards Cilgerran. After 1/4 m turn R signed Rhosygilwen. Mansion gates 1/2 m.* Light refreshments. **Adm £3, chd free. Sun 9 June (11-4). Visitors also welcome by appt Apr to Oct. Light refreshments available on request.**
20 acres of garden in 55 acre estate. Pretty 1/2 m drive through woodland planting. Spacious lightly wooded grounds for leisurely rambling, superb 1-acre walled garden fully productive of fruit, vegetables and flowers; authentically restored Edwardian greenhouses, many old and new trees, small formal garden. Children must be supervised please. Gravel paths around garden. Full disabled facilities.

29 ROSEWOOD
Redberth, nr Tenby, Pembrokeshire SA70 8SA. Jan & Keith Treadaway, 01646 651405. *3m SW of Kilgetty. Coming from W, turn for Sageston and almost immed R towards Redberth. 1st cottage after village boundary sign. From E, turn for Redberth and continue along old A447, 2nd cottage after village turn. Ample parking on roadside, and in field if dry.* Home-made teas. **Adm £3, chd free. Sun 21 July (1-5). Visitors also welcome by appt May to Aug.**

Intimate well-maintained $^{1}/_{4}$ -acre garden, cleverly designed in different areas. Abundant colourful mixed plantings with many exotic species and a collection of clematis in bloom all yr, but especially in Summer. A new pergola with clematis and other climbers, as well as a growing collection of grasses and ferns. In the field opposite a fruit and vegetable area with raised beds has been redeveloped. 'Pembrokeshire Life' and local press. Limited wheelchair access to parts of garden.

Planting schemes are the owner's, and seek to challenge the boundaries of what can be grown . . .

30 NEW SCULPTORS GARDEN, THE OLD POST OFFICE

Ffarmers, Llanwrda, Carmarthenshire SA19 8LQ. Mr Martin & Mrs Angela Farquharson-Duffy, www.thesculpturecollective.co.uk. *7m SE of Lampeter, 8m NW of Llanwrda,. Turning to Ffarmers village off A482, garden is in centre of village opp the Drovers Arms PH.* Home-made teas. **Combined adm £3.50, chd free.** **Sun 7 July (2-6). Combined with Bwlchau Duon.**

A compact courtyard garden with formal and informal planting on different levels, which has recently been created to form a backdrop for the garden sculptures created by the owners. One day figurative sculpture exhibition.

31 NEW SWAN COTTAGE

20 Gosport Street, Laugharne, Carmarthenshire SA33 4SZ. Geoffrey Brown. *Laugharne town centre. A4066 to Laugharne & park in central car park. Swan Cottage is a short, uphill, walk towards Pendine on the A4066.* Home-made teas. **Combined adm £3.50, chd free.** **Sun 18 Aug (2-6). Combined with The Coach House.**

A well-maintained town garden packed with great variety of plants, shrubs, trees and bamboos as well as ponds, rockeries and gravel area. Plantings show how small areas can provide colour and structure for yr long interest. Fine views overlooking the Taf estuary and the castle.

32 TALARDD

Golden Grove, Carmarthen SA32 8NN. Mr Steve Bryan, 01558 820208, steve@stevebryan.org. *1$^{1}/_{2}$ m S of Llandeilo. From Crosshands follow A476 towards Llandeilo for approx 6m. Look for white gate on R while going through a series of Z bends. 50 metres after gate there is a garage forecourt sign on R. Turn R there. At T-junction turn L & follow lane for 300 metres. From Ffairfach take A476 for approx 1m. At garage forecourt sign on the L turn L. At T-junction turn L & follow lane for 300 metres.* **Adm £4, chd free (share to Robert Dickie Charitable Trust). Visitors welcome by appt Mar to Nov. Refreshments available on request.**

The historic house is set above the stream with its banks of primulas, astilbies,*Gunnera* and diverse bog garden plants. Nearby is the productive walled kitchen garden, surrounded by beds of herbaceous plants and grasses. Elsewhere, extensive grassed areas are planted with unusual trees, shrubs and spring bulbs. There is also a riverside walk and boules court! The garden covers some 5 acres. Guided tours if requested. Wheelchair access to kitchen garden and part of woodland areas on bound gravel paths.

33 TRADEWINDS

Ffynnonwen, nr Trelech, Penybont, Carmarthenshire SA33 6PX. Stuart & Eve Kemp-Gee. *10m NW of Carmarthen. A40 W from Carmarthen approx 4m, then turn R onto B4298 to Meidrim. In Meidrim R onto B4299 to Trelech. After approx 5$^{1}/_{2}$ m turn R at Tradewinds sign, then approx $^{1}/_{2}$ m, next to 2nd farm.* **Adm £3, chd free. Sat 15, Sun 16 June (11-5); Sun 11 Aug (12-5).**

2$^{1}/_{2}$ -acre plantsman's garden with abundance of herbaceous perennials, shrubs and trees giving yr-round interest. Mixed borders, natural streams and pond. Picturesque garden in tranquil setting. 100ft grass, 100ft herbaceous and 80ft conifer borders. The arboretum incl *Quercus cerris* 'Argenteovariegata', *Aralia elata*'Variegata', *Salix fargesii* plus numerous rhododendrons and azaleas. Stream banks planted with many moisture loving plants. Vegetable plot. Many rare and unusual plants to be seen.

34 TREFFGARNE HALL

Treffgarne, Haverfordwest, Pembrokeshire SA62 5PJ. Martin and Jackie Batty, 01437 741115, bathole2000@aol.com. *7m N of Haverfordwest, signed off A40. Proceed up through village & follow rd round sharply to L, Hall $^{1}/_{4}$ m further on L.* Home-made teas. **Adm £3, chd free. Sun 5 May, Sun 14 July (1-5). Visitors also welcome by appt all yr-round.**

Stunning hilltop location with panoramic views: handsome Grade II listed Georgian house (not open) provides formal backdrop to garden of four acres with wide lawns and themed beds. A walled garden, with double rill and pergolas, is planted with a multitude of borderline hardy exotics. Also large-scale sculptures, summer broadwalk, meadow patch, gravel garden, heather bed and stumpery. Planted for yr-round interest. The planting schemes are the owner's, and seek to challenge the boundaries of what can be grown in Pembrokeshire.

35 TY CASTELL

Station Road, Nantgaredig, Carmarthen SA32 7LQ. Paul & Steve, 01267 290034, enquiries@ty-castell.co.uk, www.ty-castell.co.uk. *5m E of Carmarthen town. 10m W of Llandeilo. A40 W from Llandeilo heading to Carmarthen for 10.3m until the village of Nantgaredig L into Station Rd R after the Railway Inn. Sat Nav not accurate.* Light refreshments. **Adm £3, chd £2. Sun 4 Aug (11-5). Visitors also welcome by appt Mar to Sept. Lunch menu available.**

$^{1}/_{4}$ -acre of tranquil garden on the banks of the river Towy with walks and wildlife. Gardens segmented into chill out rooms featuring a pond and waterfall with herbaceous borders, trees, shrubs, rockery, lawned areas boasting panoramic views of the Towy valley and on the doorstep of the National Botanic and Aberglasney Gardens. Delightful riverside walks.

Treffgarne Hall

Tea Room and RSPB stand. As seen on S4C TV - Prynhawn Da and Amateur Gardening Magazine.

36 TY'R MAES

Ffarmers, Llanwrda, Carmarthenshire SA19 8JP. John & Helen Brooks, 01558 650541, johnhelen@greystones140.freeserve.co.uk. *7m SE of Lampeter. 8m NW of Llanwrda. $1^1/_2$ m N of Pumsaint on A482, opp turn to Ffarmers*. Home-made teas. **Adm £3, chd free. Sun 19 May, Sun 18 Aug (2-6). Visitors also welcome by appt. Refreshments available on request.**

Recently developed 3-acre garden with splendid views. Herbaceous and shrub beds - formal design, exuberantly informal planting, full of cottage garden favourites and many unusual plants. Burgeoning arboretum (200+ types of tree); formal and wildlife ponds, pergola, gazebos, post and rope arcade covered in climbers. Gloriously colourful; spring (rhododendrons, azaleas, primulas, 1000's bulbs); late summer (tapestry of annuals/perennials). Featured on S4C Prynhawn Da. Some gravel paths.

37 ◆ UPTON CASTLE GARDENS

Cosheston, Pembroke Dock SA72 4SE. Prue & Stephen Barlow, 01646 689996, www.uptoncastlegardens.com. *4m E of Pembroke Dock. 2m N of A477 between Carew and Pembroke Dock. Follow brown signs to Upton Castle Gardens through Cosheston.* **Adm £4, chd free. For NGS: Sun 9 June (10-4). For other opening times and information, please phone or see garden website.**

35 acres of mature gardens and arboretum with many unusual camellias, magnolias, rhododendrons and other rare trees and shrubs incl a 50yr-old *Davidia involucrata* (handkerchief tree). *Fagus sylvatica* var *'Heterophylla'*, Drimys winteri, formal rose gardens, herbaceous borders, Victorian kitchen garden, wild flower meadow, woodland walk to the estuary and C13 chapel. Incl in the register of Historic Parks & Gardens. Walk on the Wild Side. '20 Best Gardens with Cottages' - The Times. Limited wheelchair access.

Carmarthenshire & Pembrokeshire County Volunteers

County Organiser

Mrs Jane Stokes, Llyshendy, Llandeilo SA19 6YA, 01558 823233, jane.h.stokes@btinternet.com

County Treasurer

Mrs Christine Blower, Glangwilli Lodge, Llanllawddog, Carmarthen SA32 7JE, 01267 253334, cheahnwood@toucansurf.com

Publicity

Carms Mrs Jane Stokes, Llyshendy, Llandeilo SA19 6YA, 01558 823233, jane.h.stokes@btinternet.com

Assistant County Organisers

Mrs Jackie Batty, Treffgarne Hall, Treffgarne, Haverfordwest, Pembs SA62 5PJ, 01437 741115, bathole2000@aol.com

Mr Ivor Stokes, Llyshendy, Llandeilo SA19 6YA, 01558 823233, ivor.t.stokes@btopenworld.com

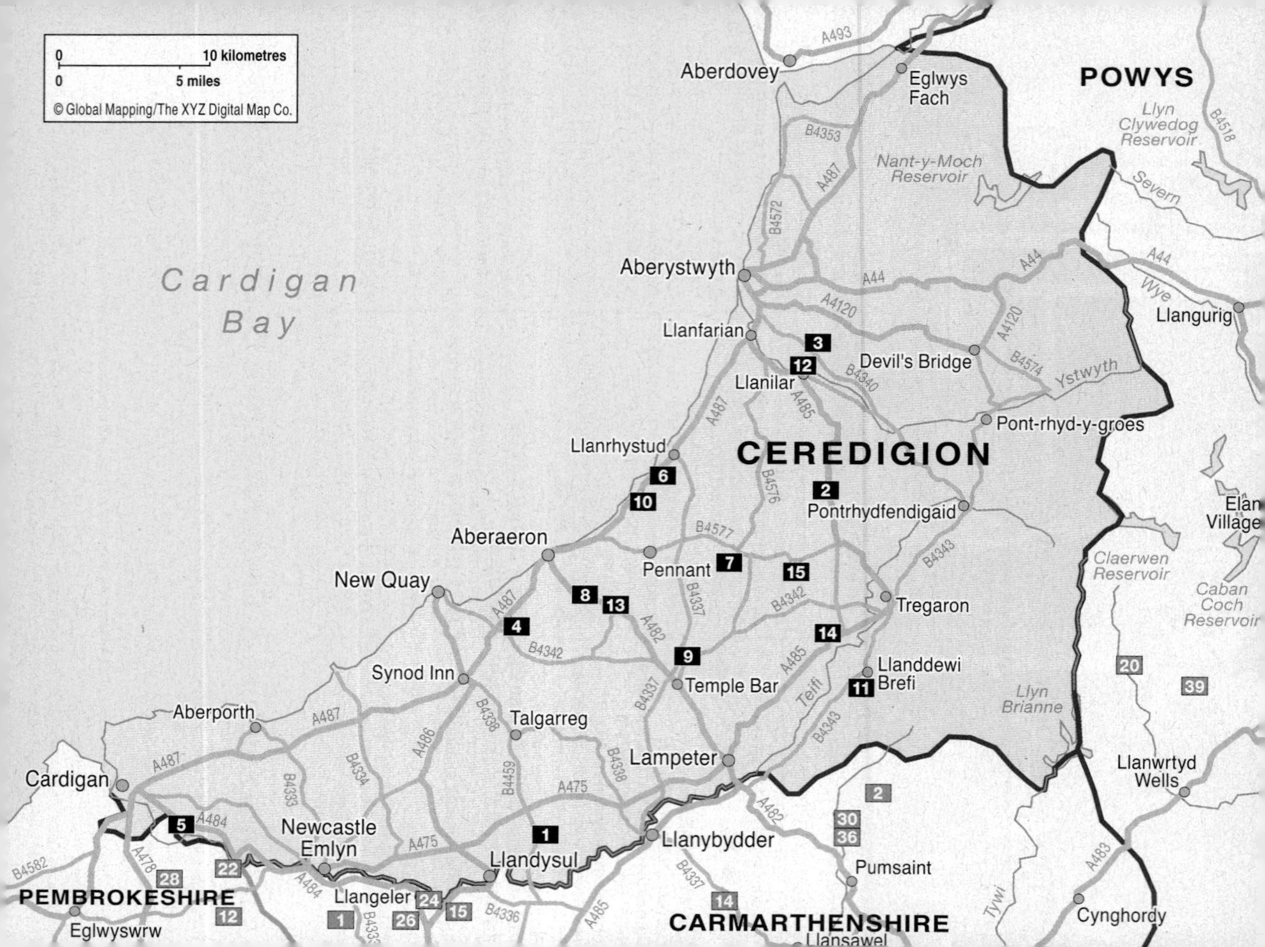

0
10 kilometres
0
5 miles
© Global Mapping/The XYZ Digital Map Co.
Cardigan Bay
POWYS
CEREDIGION
PEMBROKESHIRE
CARMARTHENSHIRE
Aberdovey
Eglwys Fach
Llyn Clywedog Reservoir
Nant-y-Moch Reservoir
Severn
Aberystwyth
Llangurig
Wye
Llanfarian
Devil's Bridge
Ystwyth
Llanilar
Pont-rhyd-y-groes
Llanrhystud
Pontrhydfendigaid
Elan Village
Aberaeron
Claerwen Reservoir
Caban Coch Reservoir
Pennant
New Quay
Tregaron
Llanddewi Brefi
Synod Inn
Temple Bar
Teifi
Llyn Brianne
Aberporth
Talgarreg
Lampeter
Llanwrtyd Wells
Cardigan
Newcastle Emlyn
Llanybydder
Pumsaint
Llandysul
Tywi
Llangeler
Cynghordy
Eglwyswrw
Llansawel
A493
B4518
B4353
A487
B4572
A44
A4120
B4574
B4340
A485
B4576
B4577
B4343
B4337
B4342
A482
A486
B4338
B4334
B4333
B4459
A475
A484
A478
B4582
B4336
A483
1
2
3
4
5
6
7
8
9
10
11
12
13
14
15
20
22
24
26
28
30
36
39

Opening Dates

May

Sunday 19
10 Llanon Group Gardens

Sunday 26
1 Alltyrodyn Mansion
3 Bwlch y Geuffordd

June

Sunday 9
12 Penbanc

National Gardens Weekend

Saturday 15
11 Pantyfod

Sunday 16
5 Glanhelyg
9 Llanllyr

Thursday 27
8 Llanerchaeron (Evening)

Sunday 30
15 Ysgoldy'r Cwrt

July

Sunday 7
7 Isfryn

Sunday 14
11 Pantyfod

Sunday 21
6 Gwynfryn

Sunday 28
13 Ty Glyn Walled Garden

August

Sunday 4
14 Yr Efail

Sunday 18
5 Glanhelyg
7 Isfryn

Sunday 25
11 Pantyfod

Gardens open to the public

8 Llanerchaeron
13 Ty Glyn Walled Garden

By appointment only

2 Bwlch y Geuffordd
4 Castell Pigyn

Also open by Appointment

1 Alltyrodyn Mansion
5 Glanhelyg
7 Isfryn
9 Llanllyr
15 Ysgoldy'r Cwrt

The Gardens

1 ALLTYRODYN MANSION

Capel Dewi SA44 4PS. Mr & Mrs Donald Usher, 01545 590206. *8m W of Lampeter, off A475. Take B4459 at Rhydowen to Capel Dewi. Entrance on R by South Lodge.* Home-made teas. **Adm £3.50, chd free (share to Capel Dewi Village Church). Sun 26 May (11-5). Visitors also welcome by appt May to Sept.**
Early C19 garden. Approx 8 acres, mostly mature woodland with many fine trees. Rare stone-built gothic cold bathhouse. Early C20 lake, Dutch garden and rhododendron plantings. Garden is best in spring when rhododendrons and azaleas are in bloom. Large and interesting plant stall available. A garden with interesting walks. Gravel paths, steep slopes and steps.

2 BWLCH Y GEUFFORDD

Bronant, Aberystwyth SY23 4JD. Mr & Mrs J Acres, 01974 251559 or 07401 987328, gayacres@aol.com. *6m NW of Tregaron. 12m SE of Aberystwyth off A485. Take turning opp Bronant school for $1\frac{1}{2}$ m then turn L up a $\frac{1}{2}$ m track.* Home-made teas. **Adm £3.50, chd 50p. Visitors welcome any time, but advisable to phone first.**
1000ft high, 3-acre, constantly evolving wildlife garden featuring a lake and several pools. There are a number of themed gardens, incl Mediterranean, cottage garden, woodland, oriental, memorial and jungle. Plenty of seating. Unique garden sculptures and buildings, incl a cave, gazebo and jungle hut. Developing as a healing garden for those dealing with cancer. Pond dipping available by appointment. 'Treasure' hunt available for children. Unique garden art and buildings.

3 BWLCH Y GEUFFORDD

New Cross, Aberystwyth SY23 4LY. Manuel & Elaine Grande. *$4\frac{1}{2}$ m SE of Aberystwyth. From Aberystwyth, turn L off A487 to A4120, (signed Devil's Bridge) then turn immed R (signed Trawsgoed). Bwlch y Geuffordd is 3m on R at bottom of small dip. Park in lay-bys opp house.* **Adm £3.50, chd free. Sun 26 May (11-5).**
Recently developed 1-acre Celtic hillside garden with lovely views of the surrounding countryside. Plenty of places to sit and look. A casual cottage garden with herbaceous borders, shrubs, trees, fish ponds, stream and waterfall. Azaleas, rhododendrons and spring bulbs. New wild flower border, courtyard area and pond. Steep slopes and steps make parts of garden unsuitable for wheelchair users or people with mobility problems.

Wildlife ponds with frogs, newts and dragonflies . . .

4 NEW CASTELL PIGYN

Llanarth SA47 0PT. Mrs Wendy Thacker, 01545 580014. *1m N of Llanarth, 3m S of Aberaeron. On A487 midway Cardigan - Aberystwyth. 1m S of Llwyncelyn, Castell Pigyn is white cottage on R. A487 is a busy trunk rd, take care when parking & pull right on to hardstanding alongside cottage.* Home-made teas. **Adm £3.50, chd free. Visitors welcome by appt Apr to Aug 11am - dusk (excluding Weds & Suns).**
Knowledgable plantswoman's garden developed from old orchard. Paths wind through herbaceous borders full of hardy geraniums, roses, shrubs and trees. Many varieties of clematis and hellebores. Bog garden, incl gunnera. Fernery, dry river bed, grasses, hostas. 4 wildlife ponds with frogs, newts and dragonflies. Old apple varieties. Seating.

5 GLANHELYG

Lon Helyg, Llechryd, Cardigan SA43 2NE. Mr & Mrs Williamson, 01239 682482, mike-annie-w@tiscali.co.uk. *3m SE of Cardigan. From Cardigan follow A484 towards Newcastle Emlyn for approx 3m. On*

reaching Llechryd take 1st L (Lon Helyg) & continue to the end. Home-made teas. **Adm £3.50, chd free. Sun 16 June, Sun 18 Aug (1.30-6). Visitors also welcome by appt May to Oct.**
Glanhelyg is 3½ -acre incl woodland, meadow and walled garden. The Victorian walled garden has been imaginatively redesigned and contains a large variety of plants, many unusual and semi-tender in a prairie-style planting. Gravel paths.

GRANDMA'S GARDEN
See Powys

6 NEW GWYNFRYN
Llanrhystud SY23 5BY. Sue Pester. *Between Llanrhystud and Llanon, on A487. 1m S of Llanrhystud, after 'Hidden Dip' rd sign. Entrance to garden where rd sign indicates L turn.* Home-made teas. **Adm £3.50, chd free. Sun 21 July (2-6).**
Large garden of 11 acres with woodland, incl over 20 varieties of cherries, paddocks, large vegetable and soft fruit areas. Lawns, herbaceous borders, pond, fuchsia hedges, poultry and other livestock. Stunning views over Cardigan Bay. Level garden, but with gravel and grass paths.

7 ISFRYN
Bethania, nr Llanon SY23 5NP. Mrs Julie Langford, 01974 272257, backyardacres@gmail.com. *15m SW Aberystwyth. B4337 from Llanrhystud or B4577 from Aberarth to Cross Inn. Turn L or continue along B4577 for 2m. At Xrds turn R. 3rd house on L. Please DO NOT use postcode for SatNav. Off road parking available in good weather.* Cream teas. **Adm £3.50, chd free. Sun 7 July, Sun 18 Aug (11-5). Visitors also welcome by appt July to Aug 12 noon-5pm. Please give at least two weeks' notice.**
5-acre garden, ever evolving shrub and herbaceous borders, kitchen garden, poultry runs, fruit areas, vegetable beds and polytunnels. 1-acre woodland with paths, field with lawns and paths, tyre plantation, a large number of young trees and shrubs, newly constructed maze, ducks, lake and wildlife areas. Children must be supervised. Eggs and plants available and maybe some produce. Featured on S4C - Prynhawn Da. Sloping garden.

8 ◆ LLANERCHAERON
Ciliau Aeron, Lampeter SA48 8DG. National Trust, 01545 570200, www.nationaltrust.org.uk. *2½ m E of Aberaeron. On A482 Lampeter to Aberaeron. Brown sign to Llanerchaeron gardens from Aberaeron and opp turning off A487.* **Adm £3.50, chd free. For NGS: Evening Opening Thur 27 June (6-9). For other opening times and information, please phone or see garden website.**
Llanerchaeron is a small C18 Welsh gentry estate set in the beautiful Dyffryn Aeron. The estate survived virtually unaltered into the C20. 2 extensive restored walled gardens produce home-grown vegetables, fruit and herbs for sale. The kitchen garden sits at the core of the estate with a John Nash villa built in 1795 and home farm, all virtually unaltered since its construction. Music, refreshments, plant and produce sales.

9 LLANLLYR
Talsarn, Lampeter SA48 8QB. Mr & Mrs Robert Gee, 01570 470900, lgllanllyr@aol.com. *6m NW of Lampeter. On B4337 to Llanrhystud.* Home-made teas. **Adm £4, chd U12 free. Sun 16 June (2-6). Visitors also welcome by appt Apr to Sept.**
Large early C19 garden on site of medieval nunnery, renovated and replanted since 1989. Large pool, bog garden, formal water garden, rose and shrub borders, gravel gardens, laburnum arbour, allegorical labyrinth and mount, all exhibiting fine plantsmanship. Yr-round appeal, interesting and unusual plants. Specialist plant fair by Ceredigion Growers Association. Featured in Country Living.

GROUP OPENING

10 NEW LLANON GROUP GARDENS
SY23 5LT. *On S edge of Llanon village 11m S of Aberystwyth on A487. The gardens are all adjacent to A487, Aberaeron to Aberystwyth rd, at S end of village of Llanon nr bridge over R Cleddan. Parking for all 3 gardens at Pugh Computers (SY23 5LP) car park just up hill on Pennant rd, opp bakery.* Home-made teas at Bron-y-Graig. **Combined adm £5, chd free. Sun 19 May (1-5.30).**

BRON-Y-GRAIG
Dr David & Mrs Gill Shepherd

NEW DOLENNOG
Mr & Mrs Meurig James

Llanllyr

Spread the word about the NGS: tell your family and friends

NEW **THE EMPORIUM**
Steve Smith & Gwenno Piette

Three small gardens with quite different characters. Dolennog is a traditional country garden with an ornamental front lawn bordered by flower beds with roses and flowering shrubs and a productive vegetable garden to the rear. Bron-y-Graig is a plantsman's garden with many unusual varieties and an intensive kitchen garden with tender fruit trees. The Emporium is a leisure garden with many seating areas, a summerhouse and a riverside path to explore. 10 room twelfth scale dolls house at Bron-y-Graig. Limited wheelchair access to all gardens.

♿ ☕

---

11 PANTYFOD
Llanddewi Brefi, Tregaron SY25 6PE. David & Susan Rowe, www.pantyfodgarden.co.uk. *About 3m S of Tregaron. From Llanddewi Brefi village square, take R fork past Community Centre, continue up hill past turning to Ffarmers, over bridge in a dip, up hill to top. Pantyfod is on R, about ¾ m from village.* Home-made teas. **Adm £3.50, chd free. Sat 15 June, Sun 14 July, Sun 25 Aug (12-5.30).**
Tranquil, intriguing, largely established 3½ -acre garden with wide variety of perennials, trees and shrubs, many unusual. Varying habitats incl terraces, woodland, mature trees, natural ponds. Hardy geraniums, Iris sibirica, grasses and rugosa roses. Wildlife friendly. Stunning, panoramic views of the Teifi Valley and mountains beyond. Gravel paths, steps and steep slopes, but level around the house.

♿ ✿ ☕

12 PENBANC
Llanilar, Aberystwyth SY23 4NY. Enfys & David Rennie. *Off A487, 6m SE of Aberystwyth. From Llanfarian take A485 signed Tregaron for 2½ m. Turn L into lane immed after Cwmaur Estate. Penbanc in ½ m, overlooking river bridge.* Home-made teas. **Adm £3.50, chd free. Sun 9 June (2-6).**
½ -acre, S-facing sloping cottage garden alongside R Ystwyth with views over valley. Established orchards, large vegetable garden and densely planted herbaceous borders created in 2005, with masses of roses, clematis, Campanula lactiflora, hardy geraniums, hostas and shrubs. Riverside wildlife walk. Limited wheelchair access. Disabled parking by house.

♿ ✿ ☕

13 ◆ TY GLYN WALLED GARDEN
Ciliau Aeron, Lampeter SA48 8DE. Ty Glyn Davis Trust, 01970 832268, www.tyglyndavistrust.co.uk. *3m SE of Aberaeron. Turn off A482 Aberaeron to Lampeter at Ciliau Aeron signed to Pennant. Entrance 700 metres on L.* **Adm £3.50, chd free. For NGS: Sun 28 July (11-5). For other opening times and information, please phone or see garden website.**
Secluded walled garden in beautiful woodland setting alongside R Aeron, developed specifically for special needs children. Terraced kitchen garden overlooks herbaceous borders, orchard and ponds with child orientated features and surprises amidst unusual shrubs and perennials. Newly planted fruit trees selected from former gardener's notebook of C19.

♿ ✿ ☕

14 NEW YR EFAIL
Llanio Road, Tregaron SY25 6PU. Mrs Shelagh Yeomans. *3m SW of Tregaron. From Lampeter; A485 towards Tregaron. Turn L at Llanio onto B4578. 2nd house on L. From: Aberystwyth. A487 then A485 towards Tregaron. Straight across at Ty'n-celyn onto B4578. Continue across at Stags Head, pass R turn to Llwynygroes. 2nd house on R.* Home-made teas. **Adm £3, chd free. Sun 4 Aug (11-4).**
Our 6 acre, mostly level plot, consists of nearly an acre of SW facing abundant herbaceous borders incl, grasses, bog and wooded garden with gravel and grass paths leading to hidden areas, many with seating and most with lovely views. Formal in design with mixed, vibrant, informal planting, a large pond and other wet areas. Sheltered fertile ½ acre vegetable and fruit garden, greenhouse and two polytunnels with new 'allotment' of hardier vegetables. Paddock with poultry run and 4-acre 'infant' native woodland with woody shrubs. Newly adopted, so new plantings are under development alongside maturing borders and vistas.

♿ 🐕 ☕

15 NEW YSGOLDY'R CWRT
Llangeitho, Tregaron SY25 6QJ. Mrs Brenda Woodley, 01974 821542. *1½ m N of Llangeitho. From Llangeitho, turn L at primary school signed Penuwch. Ysgoldy'r Cwrt is 1½ m on R. Alternatively, from Cross Inn, take B4577 past Penuwch Inn, turn R after brown sculptures in field, Ysgoldy'r Cwrt is ¾ m on L.* Home-made teas. **Adm £3.50, chd free. Sun 30 June (11-5). Visitors also welcome by appt Apr to Aug 2pm - dusk.**
Over 1-acre hillside garden, mostly newly planted, but rapidly maturing. 4 natural ponds which are a magnet for wildlife. Areas of wild flower meadow, bog, dry and woodland gardens. Rare trees, large herbaceous beds, acer collection, all bounded by a mountain stream, with 2 natural cascades, and magnificent views. Children must be supervised because of the steeply sloping ground.

✿ ☕ ☎

Ceredigion County Volunteers

County Organiser
Pat Causton, Plas Treflys, Llangwyryfon, Aberystwyth SY23 4HD, 01974 272619, dandpcauston@btinternet.com

County Treasurer
Dr David Causton, Plas Treflys, Llangwyryfon, Aberystwyth SY23 4HD, 01974 272619, dandpcauston@btinternet.com

Assistant County Organiser
Lisa Raw-Rees, The Old Mill, Water Street, Aberaeron SA46 0DG, 01545 570107, hywelrawrees@hotmail.com
Gill Shepherd, Bron-y-Graig, 4 Bont Estate, Llanon SY23 5LT, 01974 202897 lymphoedemamidwales@btinternet.com
Daphne Watson, Bwthyn Rhosyn Gwyllt, Bontgoch, Aberystwyth SY24 5DP, 01970 832025, daphnewatson77@btinternet.com

GLAMORGAN

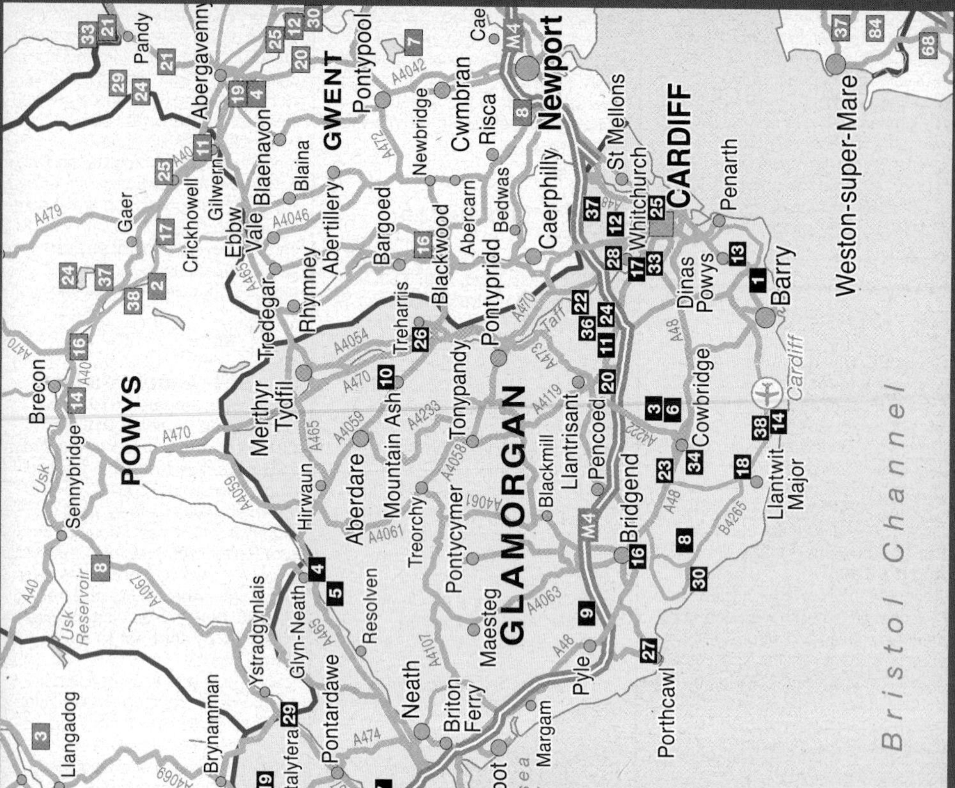
GLAMORGAN
CARMARTHENSHIRE
POWYS
GWENT
CARDIFF
Swansea
Newport
Bristol Channel
Swansea Bay
Weston-super-Mare
Barry
Penarth
Dinas Powys
Cowbridge
Llantwit Major
Bridgend
Pencoed
Llantrisant
Blackmill
Pontypridd
Caerphilly
Whitchurch
St Mellons
Bedwas
Risca
Cwmbran
Abercarn
Newbridge
Blackwood
Pontypool
Abertillery
Blaina
Blaenavon
Bargoed
Treharris
Rhymney
Tredegar
Ebbw Vale
Merthyr Tydfil
Abergavenny
Pandy
Crickhowell
Gilwern
Gaer
Brecon
Sennybridge
Usk Reservoir
Hirwaun
Aberdare
Mountain Ash
Tonypandy
Treorchy
Pontycymer
Maesteg
Glyn-Neath
Resolven
Ystradgynlais
Neath
Briton Ferry
Port Talbot
Margam
Pyle
Porthcawl
Pontardawe
Ystalyfera
Brynamman
Glanaman
Ammanford
Pontarddulais
Clydach
Morriston
Gorseinon
Llanelli
The Mumbles
Port Eynon
Llanrhidian
Rhossili
Worms Head
Whitford Point
Burry Port
Kidwelly
Llansteffan
Llanddarog
Nantgaredig
Carmarthen
Cynwyl Elfed
Llandeilo
Llangadog
Llanwrda
Cardiff
M4
0 10 20 kilometres
0 10 miles
© Global Mapping/The XYZ Digital Map Company

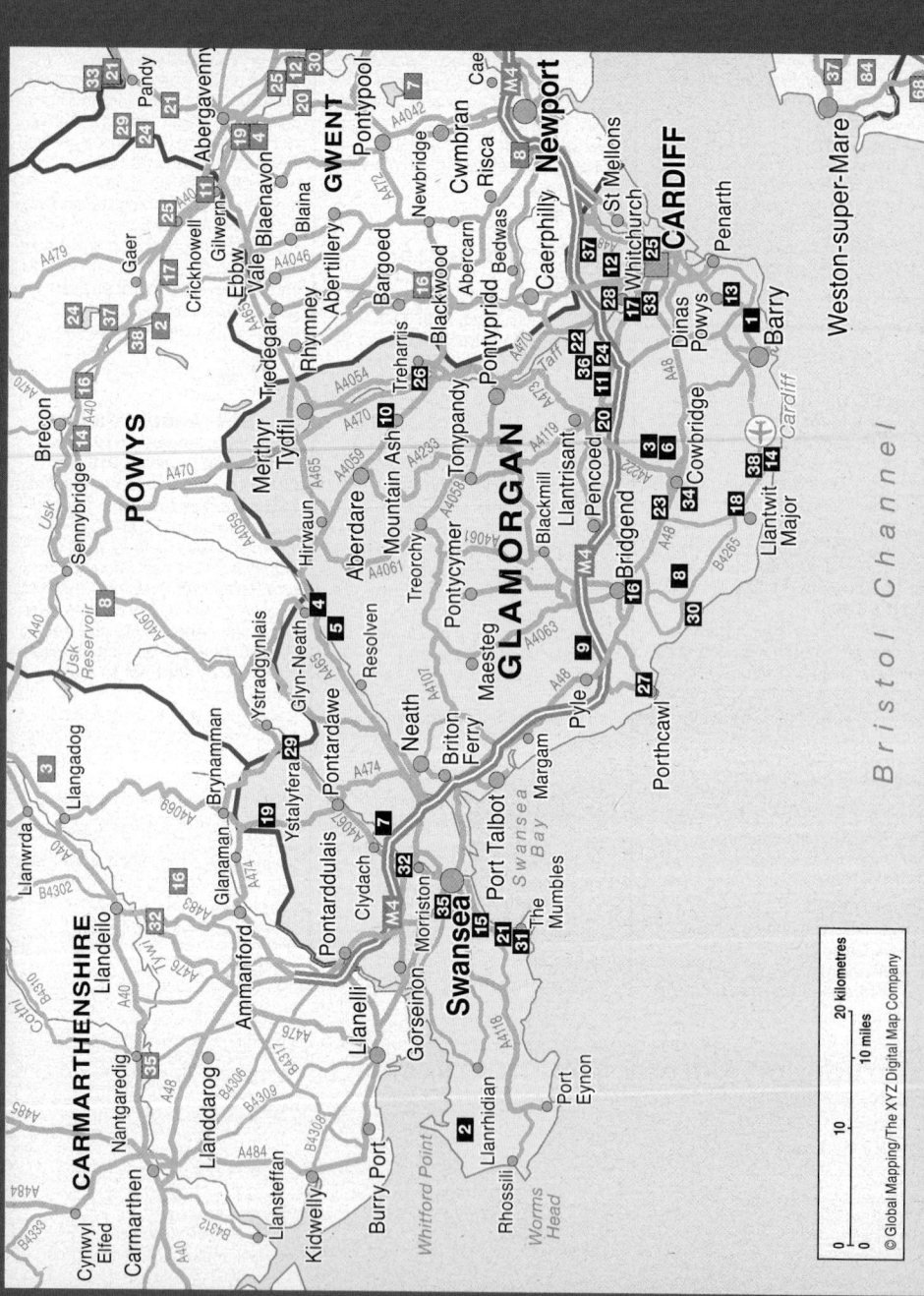

Opening Dates

April

Saturday 13
30 Slade

Sunday 14
30 Slade

Sunday 28
35 Tony Ridlers Garden

May

Sunday 5
13 Dinas Powys Village Gardens

Saturday 11
17 Llandaff Gardens

Sunday 12
12 Cyncoed & Llanishen Gardens
37 Ty'n Y Berllan

Sunday 19
21 Mumbles Gardens
31 19 Slade Gardens
35 Tony Ridlers Garden

Saturday 25
19 22 Llwyn Road
26 Pontygwaith Farm

Sunday 26
18 Llanmaes Gardens
26 Pontygwaith Farm
32 Springfield
34 St. Quintins Cottage

Monday 27
26 Pontygwaith Farm

Wednesday 29
3 Bordervale Plants

June

Saturday 8
22 The Old Post Office

Sunday 9
22 The Old Post Ofice
27 Porthcawl Gardens

National Gardens Weekend

Saturday 15
1 Barry Gardens
26 Pontygwaith Farm
29 Rhos y Bedw
30 Slade

Sunday 16
6 Bryn-y-Ddafad
12 Cyncoed & Llanishen Gardens
23 Penllyn Gardens
26 Pontygwaith Farm
28 Rhiwbina Open Gardens
29 Rhos y Bedw
30 Slade
35 Tony Ridlers Garden

Wednesday 19
3 Bordervale Plants
5 Brynheulog
20 Miskin Manor Country Hotel
36 Ty Deri

Friday 21
5 Brynheulog

Sunday 23
2 Big House Farm
9 Cefn Cribwr Garden Club
16 Heronsbridge School
24 Pentyrch Gardens in June
25 Penylan Gardens

Sunday 30
7 Brynyrenfys

July

Saturday 6
33 St Michael's College

Sunday 7
14 Gileston Manor
15 16 Hendy Close

Sunday 14
21 Mumbles Gardens
31 19 Slade Gardens
38 Wilcot

Sunday 21
11 Creigiau Village Gardens

Sunday 28
13 Dinas Powys Village Gardens
19 22 Llwyn Road

Tuesday 30
3 Bordervale Plants

A profusion of colour all year round, a real secret . . .

August

Saturday 3
1 Barry Gardens

Sunday 4
6 Bryn-y-Ddafad

Sunday 18
25 Penylan Gardens

Saturday 24
36 Ty Deri

Sunday 25
36 Ty Deri

Monday 26
3 Bordervale Plants

September

Tuesday 10
3 Bordervale Plants

Saturday 14
19 22 Llwyn Road

Sunday 22
8 Castle Upon Alun House

Gardens open to the public

3 Bordervale Plants

By appointment only

4 Bryngolwg
10 The Cottage

Also open by Appointment ☎

1 47 Aneurin Road, Barry Gardens
1 11 Arno Road, Barry Gardens
1 Belvedere Park, Barry Gardens
1 Cae Gwyn, Barry Gardens
1 1 North Walk, Barry Gardens
2 Big House Farm
5 Brynheulog
6 Bryn-y-Ddafad
7 Brynyrenfys
19 22 Llwyn Road
25 7 Cressy Road, Penylan Gardens
26 Pontygwaith Farm
30 Slade
35 Tony Ridlers Garden
37 Ty'n Y Berllan
38 Wilcot

The Gardens

GROUP OPENING

1 BARRY GARDENS
Barry CF63 2AS. *6m SW of Cardiff. From J33 on M4 take A4232 towards Cardiff following signs for the Airport. Take 2nd slip rd then at r'about take A4050 & follow signs for Barry.* Home-made teas. **Combined adm £5, chd free. Sat 15 June, Sat 3 Aug (1-5.30).**

47 ANEURIN ROAD
Dave Bryant.
Open Aug date only
Visitors also welcome by appt June to Sept.
01446 406667

11 ARNO ROAD
Debbie Palmer
Visitors also welcome by appt Feb to Sept.
01446 743642
deb.palmer@ntlworld.com

NEW BELVEDERE PARK
Drop In Centre Development Trust
Visitors also welcome by appt Jan to Dec.
01446 403549
belvederepark@dicdevelopmenttrust.com
www.dicdevelopmenttrust.com

CAE GWYN
Kay & Crandon Villis
Visitors also welcome by appt May to Aug.
01446 722450
kay.villis@hotmail.co.uk

1 NORTH WALK
Sue Hyett
Visitors also welcome by appt May to Aug.
hy_suzy@yahoo.co.uk

NEW 28 PORT ROAD EAST
Mrs Lorna Tinsley

NEW 76 PORT ROAD EAST
Ms Michele Van Duval

7 gardens of differing styles. 47 Aneurin Road is an ever changing small garden with mostly annual plants grown in over 600 containers. 11 Arno Road is a plant lovers garden filled with climbers, shrubs, perennials, alpines and ferns planted for yr-round interest. Belvedere Crescent Community Garden is a newly created garden developed by and for the local community. Cae Gwyn, 24 Port Road is a large secret garden with many attractive features incl a large pond, gravel garden, pergolas and sweeping lawns. 1 North Walk has a formal front garden with pergola festooned with roses, clematis and wisteria and a back garden with a courtyard feature, cottage garden planting and a succulent house. 28 Port Road is a mini smallholding with lots of creative, eccentric touches, lush, unmanicured, jungly feel with meandering paths. 76 Port Road is a newly developing garden with stunning views over the Vale, a wonderful old greenhouse and newly planted borders with more to come.

2 BIG HOUSE FARM

Llanmadoc, Gower, Swansea SA3 1DE. Mark & Sheryl Mead, 07831 725753, sherylandmark@tiscali.co.uk. *15m W of Swansea. M4 J47. Take A483 signed Swansea. Next r'about R A484 signed Llanelli. 2nd r'about L B4296 signed Gowerton. R at 1st T-lights onto B4295. 10m after Bury Green, R to Llanmadoc. Pass Britannia Inn, L at T-junction uphill past red tel box. 100 yds turn R. Honesty car park on R.* Home-made teas. **Adm £3, chd free. Sun 23 June (1-6). Visitors also welcome by appt.**

Award winning inspirational garden of just under an acre combines colour form and texture in this beautiful much loved Gower village, described by one visitor as 'the best I've seen this season'. Large variety of interesting plants and shrubs, with ambient cottage garden feel, Mediterranean garden, kitchen garden, beautiful views. The garden has been presented on TV and in Garden News.

Seating on different levels, so stay a while, unwind and be welcome . . .

3 ◆ BORDERVALE PLANTS

Sandy Lane, Ystradowen, Cowbridge CF71 7SX. Mrs Claire Jenkins, 01446 774036, www.bordervale.co.uk. *8m W of Cardiff. 10 mins from M4. Take A4222 from Cowbridge. Turn R at Ystradowen postbox, then 3rd L & proceed ½ m, following brown signs. Garden on R. Parking in rd past corner.* **Adm £3, chd free. For NGS: Weds 29 May, 19 June, Tue 30 July, Mon 26 Aug, Tue 10 Sept (10-5). For other opening times and information, please phone or see garden website.**

Within mature woodland valley (semi-tamed), with stream and bog garden, extensive mixed borders; mini wild flower meadow, providing diverse wildlife habitats. Children must be supervised. The Nursery specialises in unusual perennials and cottage garden plants. Nursery open: Fri - Sun (10-5), Mar - Sept. NOT FOR NGS. Wheelchairs can access the top third of garden as well as the Nursery.

4 NEW BRYNGOLWG

Pontwalby, Glynneath, Neath SA11 5LH. Isobel Carter & Andrew Smith, 01639 720237, brynbriallu@btinternet.com, www.glynneathgardeningclub.com. *10m NW of Neath. From M4 J.43 take A465. Leave at 2nd exit A4109 to Glynneath, at T-lights turn R onto B4242. Go under flyover & park on or near Pontwalby bridge. Walk along Lvorites Row to 1st turning on L, an unmade lane with 'no parking' sign. Bryngolwg is at top of lane.* **Adm £3.50, chd free. Visitors welcome by appt May to Aug. Refreshments available.**

A visit to the Geo Heritage trail could begin at the car park on B4242 and end with tea and cake at Andrew and Isobel's developing garden which aims to integrate wildlife and traditional gardening. Much of the one acre garden has been developed since 2008 while areas of greater maturity were planted by Isobel's parents and grandparents. A real treat.

5 BRYNHEULOG

45 Heol y Graig, Cwmgwrach, Neath SA11 5TW. Lorraine Rudd, 01639 722593, lorraine.rudd@bbmax.com. *8m W of Neath. From M4 J43 take A465 to Glyneath, then rd signed Cwmgwrach. Entering village pass Dunraven PH, turn L at school sign, approx 100yds fork L into Glannant Place. Up hill, bear sharp R, approx 200yds turn L up steep track. 2nd house on L.* Home-made teas. **Adm £3.50, chd free. Wed 19, Fri 21 June (2-5). Visitors also welcome by appt May to Oct.**

This keen plantswoman's hillside garden perfectly reflects the dramatic setting and surrounding natural beauty. ¾ -acre plot with many levels with cottage style planting, tropical greenhouse, 2 other greenhouses showing Begonias and Carnations, wildflower areas, large rockery and ponds. Polytunnel houses all yr-round vegetables. Lots of scent and colour with roses and lilies.

6 BRYN-Y-DDAFAD
Welsh St Donats, Cowbridge CF71 7ST. Glyn & June Jenkins, 01446 774451, junejenkins@bydd.co.uk, www.bydd.co.uk/home/garden/. *10m W of Cardiff. 3m E of Cowbridge. From A48 follow signs to Welsh St Donats. Follow brown tourist signs from Xrds, Bryn-y-Ddafad is approx 1m from this point.* Home-made teas. **Adm £4, chd free. Sun 16 June, Sun 4 Aug (11.30-5.30). Visitors also welcome by appt Apr to Sept.**
Small courtyard garden with raised bed informally planted using pastel shades of annuals, perennials and small shrubs. The terraced rear garden has colourful raised beds and borders, mature trees and shrubs. Lily pond with water feature. Recently constructed and planted pergola of roses leads to a bridge crossing the natural stream. New bog garden and small bank of rhododendrons and azaleas. Most of the garden is accessible by wheelchair.

7 BRYNYRENFYS
30 Cefn Road, Glais, Swansea SA7 9EZ. Edith & Roy Morgan, 01792 842777. *8m N of Swansea. M4 J45, take A4067 R at 2nd r'about, then 1st R and follow yellow signs.* Home-made teas. **Adm £3.50, chd free. Sun 30 June (12-5). Visitors also welcome by appt May to Sept.**
If you love plants you'll be at home here. A small surprising garden full of interest. Unusual trees, shrubs and perennials vie for attention with the panoramic view. Wildlife and weed friendly with no bedding! Seating on different levels, so stay a while, unwind and be welcome. Croeso i bawb. Rare and unusual plants for sale.

8 CASTLE UPON ALUN HOUSE
St Brides Major, Bridgend CF32 0TN. Sir Geoffrey & Lady Inkin. *7m W of Cowbridge. Take B4265 to St. Brides Major. Opposite pond & next to Farmers Arms, take rd to Castle Upon Alun, then follow NGS signs.* Home-made teas. **Adm £5, chd free. Sun 22 Sept (1.30-6).**
Grade II listed enclave incl 2-acre walled garden which was redesigned and replanted from 1998.

5 Southcourt Road

Herbaceous borders with autumn colour. Extensive lawns. Second flowering of most roses. New area of specimen trees and shrubs outside walls.

GROUP OPENING

9 CEFN CRIBWR GARDEN CLUB
Cefn Cribwr, Bridgend CF32 0AP. *5m W of Bridgend. Cefn Cribwr is located 5m W of Bridgend on B4281.* Teas at Green Hall Community Centre. **Combined adm £3, chd free. Sun 23 June (11-5).**

NEW 6 BEDFORD ROAD
Mr John Mason

2 BRYN TERRACE
Alan & Tracy Birch

CEFN CRIBWR PRIMARY SCHOOL GARDEN & ALLOTMENTS

77 CEFN ROAD
Peter & Veronica Davies & Mr Lee

25 EAST AVENUE
Mr & Mrs D Colbridge

HILL TOP
Mr & Mrs W G Hodges

6 TAI THORN
Mr Kevin Burnell

21 WEST AVENUE
Mr Martin Morgan

Cefn Cribwr gardening club is the heart of a friendly community. The 8 diverse gardens vary from the local school allotments, an exposed mature garden, a recycled garden, a garden that has its own composting system, a chidlren's garden, a rustic garden, an artists' garden and lastly a productive vegetable garden. Just about something for everyone. Craft stalls, games, raffles, teas, plant stall, local school competition and table top sale.

10 THE COTTAGE
Cwmpennar, Mountain Ash CF45 4DB. Helen & Hugh Jones, 01443 472784, hhjones1966@yahoo.co.uk. *18m N of Cardiff. A470 from N or S. Then follow B4059 to Mountain Ash. Follow signs for Cefnpennar then Cwmpennar.* Home-made teas. **Adm £3.50, chd free. Visitors welcome by appt May to Aug.**
4 acres and 30yrs of amateur muddling have produced this enchanting garden incl bluebell wood, rhododendron and camellia shrubbery, herbaceous borders, rose garden, small arboretum, many uncommon trees and shrubs. Garden slopes NE-SW.

GROUP OPENING

11 CREIGIAU VILLAGE GARDENS
Creigiau CF15 9SE. *Creigiau village, W of Cardiff. From M4, exit at J34 (A4119) signed Llantrisant; at 1st set of T-lights, turn R by Castell Mynach PH, through village of Groes Faen & turn L after Dynevor Arms PH, follow NGS signs. From Cardiff take A4119 through Llandaff, pass over M4 & after approx 1m turn R (signed Creigiau), follow NGS signs. From N, take A470 towards Cardiff, exit at Radyr/Taffs Well, take rd to Pentyrch & continue to Creigiau, follow NGS signs. Map provided at first garden visited.* Home-made teas at 28 Maes-y-Nant and Waunwyllt. Creigiau Inn central to village, serving Sunday lunch. **Combined adm £5, chd free. Sun 21 July (11-5).**

NEW **DOL Y COED**
Mr & Mrs Ann & Will Oswald

28 MAES Y NANT
Mike & Lesley Sherwood

31 MAES Y NANT
Frances Bowyer

NEW **WAUNWYLLT**
John & Richard Hughs & Shaw

Four interesting and colourful gardens; 2 new additions at Heol Pant y Gored, 1m from Maes y Nant. The County Organiser's first reaction when visiting Waunwyllt was 'it's perfect!' Waunwyllt has been developed over the last 3yrs, taking it from a state of neglect to a tranquil garden with several colour co-ordinated rooms. Dol y Coed is an established garden on different levels, packed with colourful planting. Flower beds to front and side filled with herbaceous plants. The rear garden is a great illustration of how to garden on a slope. 28 Maes y Nant is surrounded on 3 sides by cottage style planting, with an area to the side of the house surrounded by native hedging incl a wildlife patch and area of informal mixed planting. 31 Maes y Nant is a unique architect designed garden linked by water to garden room, strong architectural elements supplemented by colourful planting. Incl a colourful 'prairie style' area alongside the property.

GROUP OPENING

12 CYNCOED & LLANISHEN GARDENS
Cyncoed, Cardiff CF23 6NA. *Leave A48 at Pentwyn, 2nd exit onto Bryn Celyn Rd, L to Pentwyn drive, R to Glyn Coed Rd. At r'about L up Hollybush Rd. Follow NGS signs to Cyncoed Crescent & Danycoed Rd. Alternatively, from Cyncoed Road, Fidlas Rd or Rhydypenau Rd follow NGS signs. Not all gardens are within walking distance. Maps will be available at first garden.* Home-made teas at 22 Dan y Coed Rd, 8 Cyncoed Cresent, Rhydypenau School (June date only). **Combined adm £4, chd free. Sun 12 May, Sun 16 June (2-6).**

8 CYNCOED CRESCENT
Alistair & Teresa Pattillo

22 DAN Y COED
Alan & Miranda Workman

KINSLEY, 3 LLYSWEN ROAD
Ms Jill Davey.
Open May date only

MOUNT COTTAGE, 166 FIDLAS ROAD
Robert Davies

RHYDYPENAU PRIMARY SCHOOL
Mr Richard Melhuish.
Open June date only

This interesting group has expanded from two to five gardens last year. Three of the four suburban gardens were carved out of woodland in the 1930's when the houses were built and they are surrounded by trees. The fourth house was originally a Victorian cottage. These gardens have a multitude of shrubs, climbing roses, clematis, hostas, succulents and ferns and many unusual plants. The owners incl sculptures and features in their gardens and spend time on landscaping. 2 of the gardens have been maintained by the same family owners for nearly half a century. The lastest addition to the group was Rhydypenau school which has a vibrant array of features incl vegetable and edible flower gardening, ponds and several wildlife areas. The school is providing inspiration to educators nationally and internationally.

Cream teas . . . yummy . . . !

GROUP OPENING

13 NEW DINAS POWYS VILLAGE GARDENS
CF64 4TL. *Dinas Powys is approx 6m SW of cardiff. Exit M4 at J33, follow A4232 to Leckwith, exit where turn R onto B4267 & follow to Merry Harrier T-lights. Turn R & follow rd into Dinas Powys. From village follow yellow signs.* Homemade cakes, incl gluten free at Long Drive. **Combined adm £4, chd free (share to Dinas Powys Voluntary Concern). Sun 5 May, Sun 28 July (12-5).**

NEW **1 ASHGROVE**
Sara Bentley

NEW **LONG DRIVE**
Margaret Hayley

NEW **18 MILL ROAD**
Edward Jenkins.
Open July date only

NEW **MILLBANK HOUSE**
Janet Wightman

NEW **ROTHBURY COTTAGE**
Joan Andrews

Five gardens in this friendly village, all with something different to offer. 1 Ashgrove is a plantaholic's garden based on permaculture principles, with many unusual perennials growing together with fruit, vegetable, a pond, woodland garden. Rothbury Cottage garden has been here for over 200yrs. In the early 1900's it was open to visitors as a tea garden and remains today a green oasis, with some unusual plants. Long Drive is an acre of mature trees, a rolling aspect with views over the golf course, plus many spring bulbs and an extensive collection of Hydrangeas. Millbank House is a hidden garden set in an old quarry, dry-stone walled terraces and steps set in rock lead to an interesting aspect, with waterfalls, ponds and cottage garden plants. 18 Mill Rd is an urban garden created 6yrs ago, from what was substantially a vegetable garden. Completely replanted, although still work in progress (isn't that always the case) it is reaching a very pleasant state of maturity. Good wheelchair access at Long Drive but limited access at other gardens.

♿ ✿ ☕

14 NEW GILESTON MANOR
Gileston. CF62 4HX. Joshua Llewelyn & Lorraine Garrad-Jones. *From Cardiff airport take B4265 W towards Llantwit Major. After 3m turn L before petrol station. Continue under bridge, turn L & follow NGS signs*. Home-made teas. **Adm £5, chd free. Sun 7 July (2.30-6).**
C18 walled garden and summer house. C19 kitchen garden and woodland/ herbaceous borders in restoration. Lawns and views across the Bristol Channel. Gardens surround the Grade II* listed manor house. Woodland and secret wall garden. Walled garden has flat gravel paths, gravel drive.

♿ ✿ 🛏 ☕

15 16 HENDY CLOSE
Derwen Fawr, Swansea SA2 8BB. Peter & Wendy Robinson. *Approx 3m W of Swansea. A4067 Mumbles Rd follow sign for Singleton Hospital. Then R onto Sketty Lane at mini r'about, turn L then 2nd R onto Saunders Way. Follow yellow signs. Please park on Saunders Way if possible*. Light refreshments.
Adm £3, chd free. Sun 7 July (2-6).
New garden which is 3yrs old. Originally the garden was covered with 40ft conifers. Cottage style, some unusual and mainly perennial plants which provide colour in Spring, Summer and Autumn. Hopefully the garden is an example of how to plan for all seasons. Featured in Amateur Gardening.

☕

16 HERONSBRIDGE SCHOOL
Ewenny Road, Bridgend CF31 3HT. Heronsbridge School. *Ewenny Rd, Bridgend. In Bridgend, from A48 turn R onto B4265 Ewenny Rd. School on R*. Cream teas. **Adm £4, chd free. Sun 23 June (10-5).**
The special needs school which won silver at Chelsea 2011. You are welcome to visit our sensory kitchen and formal gardens and our heritage orchard, with swings and a willow tunnel. Fantastic homemade cakes made by our children, display of slides from our sister schools in Botswana and Tanzania; imaginative projects for the gardens. Home grown plants for sale. Four times RHS Gold winner, Anthea Guthrie will give illustrated talk - Gardening with Children. Featured in The Guardian, Telegraph, Daily Mail, Daily Express.

♿ ✿ ☕

HILLCREST
See Gwent

GROUP OPENING

17 LLANDAFF GARDENS
Llandaff, Cardiff CF5 2QH. *1m N of Cardiff. From Llandaff city and Cathedral along Cardiff Rd, A4119. Take 2nd exit onto A4054, Bridge Rd. Turn L at bus stop into Radyr Court Rd. Park next to railings*. Home-made teas Rosemary's Garden. **Combined adm £3.50, chd free. Sat 11 May (11-4).**

GAYNORS GARDEN
Gaynor Witchard
www.witchardgardens.com

ROSEMARY'S GARDEN
Rosemary Edwards

Set in beautiful location along the R Taff and a short distance from the picturesque Llandaff Cathedral. The owners are enthusiastic gardeners who have many years of experience in horticulture and are more than happy to share their knowledge. Gaynor's Garden is a sheltered sloping garden full of spring bulbs and cottage garden plants. An arbour, octagonal greenhouse and small pond complete the scene. Under a pergola covered in a mature grapevine and clematis, a deck path leads to a quiet area at the top of the garden. Rosemary's Garden - walk through a small woodland garden with specimen Hydrangea and Rhododendron, spring bulbs, stunningly white silver birch. Raised herb bed beside a decked path leading to seasonal containers and a pergola covered in Wedding Day climbing rose. Follow a newly installed stream around a well stocked raised planting area.

✿ ☕

Hopefully the garden is an example of how to plan for all seasons . . .

GROUP OPENING

18 LLANMAES GARDENS
Llanmaes, Llantwit Major CF61 2XR. *5m S of Cowbridge. From A48 at Pentre Meyrick travel S through Llysworney to large r'about on outskirts of Llantwit Major turn L. At 1st set T-lights turn L into Llanmaes. From Barry follow 4265 to outskirts of Llantwit Major. At 2nd set T-lights turn R to Llanmaes*. Home-made teas at Old Froglands.
Combined adm £4, chd free. Sun 26 May (11-5).

OLD FROGLANDS
Dorne & David Harris

NEW WEST WINDS
Jackie & Richard Simpson

Llanmaes, a mile from Llantwit Major, is a pretty village with attractive village green with stream running through and a C13 church. Old Froglands is an historic farmhouse with streams and woodland areas linked by bridges. Ducks swim and chickens roam free. The vegetable plot is now productive. Plantings are varied with interesting foliage. West Winds is a work in progress. It was a beautiful and much loved garden that sadly became overgrown and is now being reclaimed. Pathways weave through terraces with balustrades, wooded areas and lawns with views over the village and open fields. The garden has a full range of aspects from deep shade to full sun, and is shared and enjoyed with a diverse collection of wildlife.

♿ ✿ ☕

19 NEW 22 LLWYN ROAD
Cwmgors, Ammanford SA18 1RD. Terri Darnbrook, 01269 824635, terriinwales@yahoo.co.uk. *From M4 - leave at J45. Take A4067 to Pontardawe. Follow signs to A474 signed Ammanford or Gwaun cae Gurwen. Continue along the A474 to Cwmgors. Watch out for school on R, followed by large church on R, take next rd on the R. From Ammanford side, take A474 through Gwaun cae Gurwen into Cwmgors. Look for PH on L (TJ's). Llwyn Rd is about 150yrds beyond on L.* Light refreshments. **Adm £3, chd free. Sat 25 May, Sun 28 July, Sat 14 Sept (2-5.30). Visitors also welcome by appt May to Sept.**
A well established garden with mature trees but with newer elements added. The history garden is the latest edition and incl a stone circle! Two ponds, herbaceous borders, an alpine garden with cairn, woodland areas as well as fruit and vegetable plots provide lots of interest. There is even a little secret garden hidden away with a quiet seating area. Perennials for sale.

20 MISKIN MANOR COUNTRY HOTEL
Miskin CF72 8ND. Mr & Mrs Rosenberg, 01443 224204, reservations@miskin-manor.co.uk, www.miskin-manor.co.uk. *7m W of Cardiff. Exit M4 J34, and follow signs for A4119 Llantrisant. Keep in L hand lane & exit A4119 1st L before T-lights. There is a dedicated slip rd to the hotel approx 1/2 m from M4. It is advisable to stay in nearside lane of A4119 after 50 mph speed restriction signs.* Home-made teas served at Health Club. **Adm £5, chd £2.50 (incl refreshmenst). Tickets from hotel reception. Wed 19 June (10-4).**
Miskin Manor Hotel is set in 25 acres of award-winning, landscaped gardens that would entice anyone to stop and take note. Labelled a 'hidden gem' by the media, and our 'Wales in Bloom ' award highlights our verdant credentials. Ranging from planted woodland walkways to formal yew hedge bordered lawns. Garden tours on the hour from 10.00am.

GROUP OPENING

21 MUMBLES GARDENS
Swansea SA3 5EY. *5m SW of Swansea. At r'about on Mumbles Rd (A4067) take 2nd exit, Fairwood Rd then 1st L into Westcross Lane & follow yellow signs.* Home-made teas. **Combined adm £3.50, chd free. Sun 19 May, Sun 14 July (2-6).**

5 MOORSIDE ROAD
Ceri Macfarlane & Mike Gravenor.
Open July date only

19 SLADE GARDENS
Norma & Peter Stephen
(See separate entry)

5 Moorside Road is a long, narrow garden on many levels with a wide variety of densely planted herbaceous perennials, grasses and shrubs. The garden is constantly evolving through the owners' experimentation with balance, colour and form. 19 Slade Gardens has small enclosed front and rear gardens designed to lead you around its informal planting. A garden to sit in. Close to the picturesque village of Mumbles.

22 NEW THE OLD POST OFFICE
Main Road, Gwaelod-Y-Garth, Cardiff CF15 9HJ. Ms Christine Myant. *N of Cardiff nr Radyr & Pentyrch. Off A470 at Castell Coch turn off. Take directions to Radyr then Pentyrch. Turn R just AFTER village playing fields. Drive up Main Rd. The Old Post Office is 4th house on L just after Gwaelod Inn. Parking will be signed.* Refreshments at Gwaelod Inn. **Adm £3, chd free. Sat 8, Sun 9 June (12-5).**
Situated in the popular village of Gwaelod-y-Garth on the northern edge of Cardiff this informal terraced garden provides some splendid views of the green valley and hills opposite.

GROUP OPENING

23 NEW PENLLYN GARDENS
Penllyn, Cowbridge CF71 7RQ. *17m W of Cardiff. A48 W of Cardiff towards Bridgend. Bypass Cowbridge, turn R at Pentre Meyrick, & follow yellow signs.* Home-made teas Forrest Cottage. **Combined adm £3.50, chd free. Sun 16 June (2-6).**

NEW FORREST COTTAGE
Mrs Rose Morgan

The Old Post Office

PENLLYN COURT
Mr & Mrs John Homfray

Penllyn sits in one of the most beautiful parts of the Vale of Glamorgan. Penllyn Court has a large family garden with a semi-formal walled garden, orchard with fruit trees and bulbs, stumpery, mixed plantings of shrubs and herbaceous perennials, roses. Vegetable garden and small amount of woodland plantings. Forrest Cottage is a small cottage garden, mainly herbaceous borders and lawns, great colour combinations. A treat to see please come for tea. Some gravel areas at Penllyn Court.

GROUP OPENING

24 PENTYRCH GARDENS IN JUNE

Pentyrch, Cardiff CF15 9QD. *2m N of Cardiff. M4 J32 - A470 to Merthyr. After 1/2 m exit signed Taffs Well & Radyr. 1st exit at r'about onto B4262 signed Radyr, Gwaelod & Pentyrch. Next r'about R. L at T-junction. 1st house on L.* Home-made teas at Maes-y-Gof. **Combined adm £5, chd free. Sun 23 June (11-5).**

5 DAN Y RODYN
Stephen Evans

9 HEOL Y PENTRE
Chris & Ken Rogers

MAES-Y-GOF
Jeanette & Chris Troughton

2 PENMAES
Chris & Helen Edwards

SUNNY BANK
Chris & Dave Bilham

TY DERI
Hanni & Lyn Davies
(See separate entry)

A group of 6 gardens offering something to suit all interests. MAES-Y-GOF: Medium sized cottage garden with exuberantly planted herbaceous borders, roses, clematis, ferns and palms. 5 DAN Y RODIN: Quirky use of recycling and encourages all wildlife: class winner Cardiff in Bloom. 9 HEOL-Y-PENTRE: Corner plot with perennial borders and acers. Climbers and small gravel garden. Class winner Cardiff in Bloom. 2 PENMAES: Small packed garden with roses, clematis and fuchsia. Full of colour and scent, peaceful to sit in. New water feature. SUNNY BANK: 200yr old cottage with a wisteria-covered veranda, formal terrace and informal garden. Pond with bridge leading to a summerhouse. Tries to be as organic as possible. TY DERI: Award-winning garden with water feature, herbaceous borders, raised vegetable beds and fruit cage.

A treat to see - please come for tea . . . .

GROUP OPENING

25 PENYLAN GARDENS

Penylan, Cardiff CF23 5BD. *1 1/2 m NE of Cardiff city centre. M4 J29, Cardiff E A48, then Llanedeyrn/Dock exit, towards Cyncoed & L down Penylan Hill. Marlborough Rd is L at T-lights at bottom of hill. For Oakfield St & Wordsworth Ave continue along Marlborough Rd & join A4161 towards the city centre. Approx 600yds turn R into Oakfield St. Continue for another 600yds, through the T-lights & turn R into Wordsworth Ave. Look out for NGS signs.* Home-made teas. **Combined adm £4, chd free. Sun 23 June, Sun 18 Aug (2-6).**

7 CRESSY ROAD
Victoria Thornton
Visitors also welcome by appt Aug to Sept.
02920 311215
thornton.victoria@me.com

NEW 37 ILTON ROAD
Karen Dancey.
Open August date only

102 MARLBOROUGH ROAD
Mrs Judith Griffiths.
Open June date only

NEW 61 OAKFIELD STREET
Sian Trenberth.
Open June date only

128 PENYLAN ROAD
John & Judi Wilkins

5 SOUTHCOURT ROAD
Pat & Mel Griffiths.
Open June date only

NEW 13 WORDSWORTH AVENUE
Mrs Kathryn Goding.
Open June date only

Penylan is a Victorian suburb of mostly terraced houses with small gardens and many parks. This year our group has grown to 7 gardens.The gardens open show a variety of ways of adding interest and individuality to a small space incl Mediterranean-style sunny patio areas, informal mix of cottage plants, a riot of exotic foliage, stone walled SE facing cottage garden offering colour and peace away from the busy main rd and a bijou terrace garden profusely planted with an abundance of unusual and exotic plants. Victoria Thornton and Pat and Mel Griffiths are regular winners in the Cardiff in Bloom competition. Our new gardens feature a surprisingly large city garden with deep flower beds, ponds and a dove cote; a postage stamp sized garden where trees provide an architectural framework with shade loving plants packed beneath; a natural garden with ferns, lavender and bay trees. Please note: not all gardens are within walking distance. Maps showing the gardens will be available.

26 PONTYGWAITH FARM

Edwardsville, nr Treharris CF46 5PD. Mrs D Cann, 07784 871502. *2m NW of Treharris. N from Cardiff on A470. At r'about take A4054 (old Ponytpridd to Merthyr rd), travel N towards Aberfan for approx 3m through Quakers Yard and Edwardsville. 1m after Edwardsville turn very sharp L by old black bus shelter, garden at bottom of hill.* Light refreshments. **Adm £3.50, chd free. Sat 25, Sun 26, Mon 27 May, Sat 15, Sun 16 June (10-5). Visitors also welcome by appt Apr to Sept.**

4 1/2 acre garden surrounding C17 farmhouse adjacent to Trevithick's Tramway. Situated in picturesque wooded valley. Fish pond, lawns, perennial borders, new lakeside walk, rose garden. Japanese garden. Grade II listed humpback packhorse bridge in garden, spanning R Taff. A lovely day out for all the family. Welcome to visitors on the Taff Trail (April-Sept. 10am - 5pm). Steep slope to river, gravel paths.

A garden to be savoured slowly, relax and enjoy . . .

GROUP OPENING

27 NEW PORTHCAWL GARDENS
Porthcawl CF36 5EB. *Porthcawl. M4 J37, follow the A4229 towards Porthcawl. On arriving at r'about follow yellow signs.* Home-made teas. **Combined adm £5, chd free. Sun 9 June (12-6).**

NEW 2 CWRT ISAF
Joanna Howells
www.joannahowells.co.uk

NEW 3 LIAS COTTAGES
Bryn Davies

NEWTON COTTAGE
Mr & Mrs J David

NEW SHORTLANDS
Mr Mike James

TYN-Y-CAEAU FARM
Ian John

Shortlands has recently been refurbished and the garden is now being tackled and restored to its former glory. The garden is approx acres and divided into four areas. Front garden is laid to lawns and shrubs together with mature trees, a formal Walled Garden with central Water feature, two further large lawns surrounded by mature trees and Shrubs with summer house. 2 Cwrt Isaf is a developing natural varied garden (1/3 acre) with borders, rockery, lawn, vegetable garden, soft fruit cages and fruit trees, and a shady bank with ferns. 3 Lias Cottage garden is delightful with a profusion of colour all year round,a real secret. Newton Cottage has a large informal cottage garden. Mixed borders, good variety of shrubs, climbers and herbaceous plants.Box garden. Kitchen garden. Tyn y Caeau Farm is a young garden with very interesting borders and has spectacular views over the Bristol Channel.

♿ 🐕 ✿ ☕

GROUP OPENING

28 RHIWBINA OPEN GARDENS
Rhiwbina CF14 6EL. *N Cardiff. M4 J32. 1st L to mini r'about, turn R into village at T-lights, turn R to Pen Y Dre.* Home-made teas. **Combined adm £5, chd free. Sun 16 June (11-6).**

NEW 9 GERNANT
Pat Moray

33 LON ISA
Linda Ward

7 PEN Y DRE
Christine Lewis

89 PEN-Y-DRE
Lorraine & Emil Nelz

TALIESIN
Liz Heathcote

5 very different gardens, 3 set in Rhiwbina Garden Village conservation area. 89 Pen y Dre is a small, very interesting garden with palms, tree ferns, perennials and conservatory with cacti and succulents - prize winner Cardiff in Bloom. 7 Pen y Dre is a charming garden approached from a bridge over a babbling brook. Taliesin (13 Pen y Dre) is a cottage garden with an eclectic collection of flowering trees, shrubs, roses, perennials and ferns. Entered by crossing a narrow bridge over a brook and the other 2 gardens are a real treat to be seen.

♿ ✿ ☕

29 RHOS Y BEDW
4 Pen y Wern Rd, Ystalyfera, Swansea SA9 2NH. Robert & Helen Davies. *13m N of Swansea. M4 J45 take A4067. Follow signs for Dan yr Ogof caves across 5 r'abouts. After T-lights follow NGS signs. Parking above house on rd off to R.* Home-made teas. **Adm £2, chd free. Sat 15, Sun 16 June (12-6).**
This constantly evolving garden provides a haven of peace and tranquility with spectacular views. Wander through this glorious compact garden with its array of planting areas. Perennial, herb, bog, vegetable and a new knot garden are sure to provide inspiration. A garden to be savoured slowly, relax and enjoy. Gluten free cakes available.

🐕 ✿ ☕

30 SLADE
Southerndown CF32 0RP. Rosamund & Peter Davies, 01656 880048, ros@sladewoodgarden.plus.com, www.sladeholidaycottages.co.uk. *5m S of Bridgend. M4 J35. Follow A473 to Bridgend. Take B4265 to St Brides Major. Turn R in St Brides Major for Southerndown. At Southerndown turn L opp 3 Golden Cups PH onto Beach Rd. Follow rd into Dunraven Park. Turn 1st L over cattle grid on to Slade drive.* Home-made teas. **Adm £4, chd free. Sat 13, Sun 14 Apr, Sat 15, Sun 16 June (2-6). Visitors also welcome by appt Apr to July.**
Set in 8 acres, Slade garden is an unexpected gem with masses of spring flowers. The terraced lawns, mature specimen trees, living willow arbours, rose and clematis pergola, orchard and herbaceous borders, create a very natural garden that also has extensive views over the Bristol Channel. Heritage Coast wardens will give guided tours of adjacent Dunraven Gardens with slide shows every hour from 2pm. Limited wheelchair access.

♿ ✿ 🛏 ☕ ☎

31 19 SLADE GARDENS
Norton, Swansea SA3 5QP. Norma & Peter Stephen. *5m SW of Swansea. At r'about on Mumbles Rd A4067 take 2nd exit (Fairwood Rd) then 1st L onto West Cross Lane & follow yellow signs.* Home-made teas. **Adm £3.50, chd free. Sun 19 May, Sun 14 July (2-6).**
A small enclosed front and rear garden designed to lead you around its informal planting. A garden to sit in. Narrow paths make access difficult for less mobile visitors.

✿ ☕

32 SPRINGFIELD
176 Clasemont Road, Morriston SA6 6AJ. Carole & Stuart Jones. *4m N of Swansea. From M4 J46 follow A48 E for 1m. From Morriston Cross take A48 W for 1m, garden on A48 50yds from entrance to Morriston Golf Club.* **Adm £3, chd free. Sun 26 May (2-6).**
Small informal suburban garden with interesting mix of trees, shrubs, bulbs and perennials to give yr-round interest. Incl small pond and pebble pond and many containerised plants. Several seating areas give the garden a relaxed feel. A real plantaholic's garden.

✿ ☕

"Lemon drizzle cake, Victoria sponge ... yummy! ☕"

33 NEW ST MICHAEL'S COLLEGE
54 Cardiff Road, Llandaff, Cardiff CF5 2YJ. Representative Body of the Church in Wales, www.stmichaels.ac.uk. *1m N of Cardiff. Follow signs for Llandaff (A48). In village turn L down Ely Rd at Malsters PH then L into St Michael's College car park*. Light refreshments. **Adm £3, chd free. Sat 6 July (12-5).**
The attractive gardens which won 'Cardiff in Bloom' in 2011 provide a haven of peace and tranquillity in what is a busy part of Llandaff. Musical entertainment will be provided in the Pace Chapel. Come and enjoy 'a little bit of heaven'.

34 ST. QUINTINS COTTAGE
Cowbridge CF71 7JT. Dr Malcolm & Dr Lorna Callaghan. *15 W of cardiff. From Cardiff follow bypass A48 to Cowbridge. Turn at T-lights in Cowbridge for Llanbleddian. 1st R into Broadway & then follow yellow signs*. **Adm £3, chd free. Sun 26 May (2-6).**
The garden of St Quintin's Cottage was designed by renowned garden designer Ralph Hancock and features his signature 'herringbone' paving. Stone terraces and sloping lawns are linked by winding paths and steps, to ornamental ponds with cascades. A 1940's garden providing an intimacy of place rather than exotic planting. Some unlevel paving and unfenced ponds.

35 TONY RIDLERS GARDEN
7 St Peter's Terrace, Cockett, Swansea SA2 0FW. Tony & Caroline Ridler, www.tonyridlersgarden.co.uk. *3m W of Swansea. From M4 J47 take A483 towards Swansea. At Fforestfach Cross T-lights turn R on Station Rd, A4216 at next T-lights turn L onto St Peter's Terrace*. **Adm £3. Suns 28 Apr, 19 May, 16 June (2-5). Visitors also welcome by appt Apr to June.**
'One of Britain's most compelling modern formal gardens, a delightful essay in the subtle use of balance, form and structure, and all in a third of an acre. Don't expect masses of flowers but be ready to learn many a lesson in how to design a garden' - Stephen Anderton. Regret, garden not suitable for children. Steep, narrow paths.

36 TY DERI
1 Tyn-y-Coed Road, Pentyrch CF15 9NP. Hanni & Lyn Davies. *2m N of Cardiff. M4 J32- A470 Merthyr, after 1/2 m exit signed Taffs Well & Radyr. 1st exit at r'about onto B4262 signed Radyr, Gwaelod & Pentyrch. next r'about 3rd exit. R at T-junction. R on bend signed Efail Isaf. 2nd turning L, 1st drive on R*. **Adm £3, chd free. Wed 19 June, Sat 24, Sun 25 Aug (11-5).**
Beehive, winner for Cardiff in Bloom Pentyrch District, Winner - Pentyrch Horticultural Show Vegetable and Flower Shields. A plantaholic's paradise. Steep drive, wheelchair access to front garden and car park area. Hand rails for steps.

37 NEW TY'N Y BERLLAN
Graig Llwyn Road, Lisvane, Cardiff CF14 0RP. Jeffrey Morgan, 02920 752443. *1m NE Lisvane village. From Lisvane Village take Rudry Rd. After M/W bridge turn R into Graig Llwyn Rd & follow NGS signs*. Light refreshments. **Adm £3, chd free. Sun 12 May (1-6). Visitors also welcome by appt May to June.**
A 2-acre garden set around an ancient farmhouse. Beds of azaleas, rhododendrons, camellia and mixed shrubs, set in undulating lawns designed to blend with the fields and woodlands around. The lawns are planted with trees such as oak, beech, hornbeam, ginkgo and tulip which provide interest and yr-round colour. Spring bulbs, primula and stream give natural informality to sit and dream.

38 WILCOT
Higher End, St Athans, nr Barry CF62 4LW. Jan & Tony Simmonite, 01446 753609. *6m S of Cowbridge off A48. Take B270 from Cowbridge or B4265 from Barry. Follow signs to St Athans then NGS arrows*. **Adm £3, chd free. Sun 14 July (11-5). Visitors also welcome by appt June to Sept.**
A 3/4 -acre very special garden with architectural features that lead you to meander around fishponds where waterfalls add interest to the habitat of many fish. Abundance of flowers, shrubs and trees ensures yr-round colour and interest. Fruit and vegetables. Seating invites you to stop and enjoy this labour of love.

Come and enjoy 'a little bit of heaven' . . .

Glamorgan County Volunteers

County Organiser/Booklet Coordinator
Rosamund Davies, Slade, Southerndown, Glamorgan CF32 0RP, 01656 880048, ros@sladewoodgarden.plus.com

County Treasurer
Dr Trevor Humby, 1 Ashgrove, Dinas CF64 4TL, 02920 512709, humbyt@cardiff.ac.uk

Publicity
Sara Bentley, 1 Ashgrove, Dinas, Vale of Glamorgan CF64 4TL, 02920 512709, sarajanebentley@googlemail.com

Assistant County Organiser
Sol Blytt Jordens, The Bays Farm, Overton Lane, Port Eynon, Swansea SA3 1NR, 01792 391676, solinge22@yahoo.co.uk
Melanie Hurst, Wolf House, Llysworney, Cowbridge, Vale of Glamorgan CF71 7NQ, 01446 773659, melanie@hurstcreative.co.uk
Ceri Macfarlane, 5 Moorside Road, West Cross, Swansea SA3 5EY, 01792 404906, ceri@mikegravenor.plus.com

GWENT

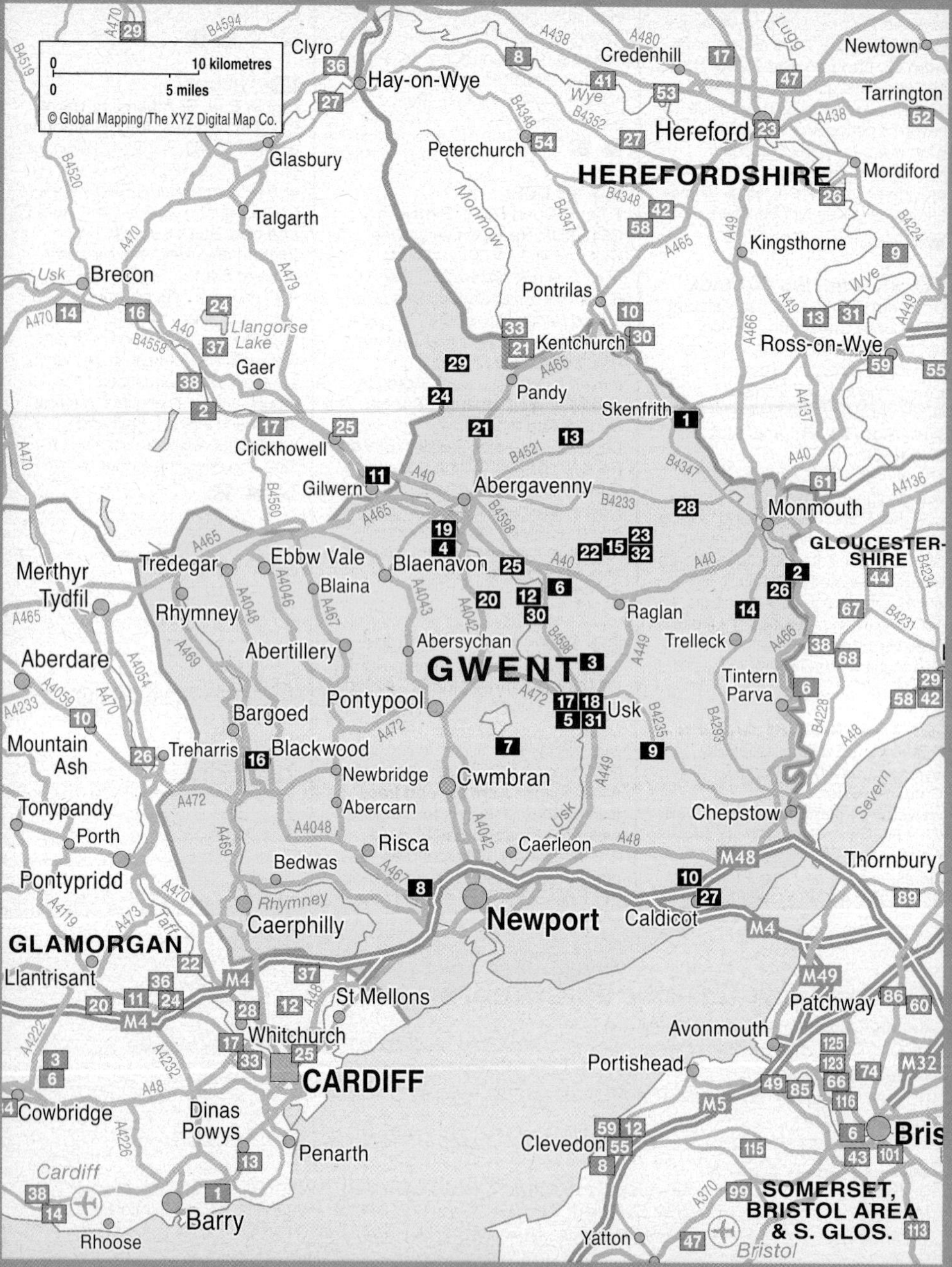

10 kilometres
5 miles
© Global Mapping/The XYZ Digital Map Co.
HEREFORDSHIRE
GWENT
GLOUCESTERSHIRE
GLAMORGAN
SOMERSET, BRISTOL AREA & S. GLOS.
Hereford
Newport
CARDIFF
Hay-on-Wye
Clyro
Glasbury
Talgarth
Brecon
Llangorse Lake
Gaer
Crickhowell
Gilwern
Abergavenny
Peterchurch
Credenhill
Newtown
Tarrington
Mordiford
Kingsthorne
Pontrilas
Kentchurch
Pandy
Skenfrith
Ross-on-Wye
Monmouth
Raglan
Trelleck
Tintern Parva
Usk
Chepstow
Caerleon
Caldicot
Thornbury
Patchway
Avonmouth
Portishead
Clevedon
Yatton
Tredegar
Ebbw Vale
Blaenavon
Blaina
Rhymney
Merthyr Tydfil
Aberdare
Abertillery
Abersychan
Pontypool
Bargoed
Blackwood
Treharris
Mountain Ash
Newbridge
Cwmbran
Abercarn
Tonypandy
Porth
Pontypridd
Risca
Bedwas
Caerphilly
Llantrisant
St Mellons
Whitchurch
Cowbridge
Dinas Powys
Penarth
Barry
Rhoose

Opening Dates

April

Sunday 14
10 Dewstow Gardens & Grottoes

Sunday 28
23 The Old Vicarage, Penrhos
32 Woodlands Farm

May

Sunday 12
14 High Glanau Manor

Saturday 18
25 Penpergwm Lodge

Sunday 19
7 Coed-y-Paen Village Gardens
25 Penpergwm Lodge

Saturday 25
16 Hillcrest

Sunday 26
16 Hillcrest
30 Trostrey Lodge

Monday 27
16 Hillcrest
30 Trostrey Lodge

Wednesday 29
11 Glangrwyney Court

June

Sunday 2
15 High House

Sunday 9
19 Llanfoist Village Gardens

National Gardens Weekend

Saturday 15
4 Castell Cwrt
24 The Pant
27 11 Severn View

Sunday 16
4 Castell Cwrt
22 Longhouse Farm
24 The Pant
26 Pentwyn Farm
27 11 Severn View

Saturday 22
12 Glebe House

Sunday 23
12 Glebe House

Saturday 29
31 Usk Open Gardens

Sunday 30
13 Glen Trothy
21 Llanthony and District Gardens
31 Usk Open Gardens

July

Saturday 13
17 5 Ladyhill Close
18 7 Ladyhill Close

Sunday 14
2 Birch Tree Well
17 5 Ladyhill Close
18 7 Ladyhill Close

Thursday 18
11 Glangrwyney Court

Saturday 27
29 Tair-Ffynnon, 'The Garden in the Clouds'.

This garden is gradually evolving amongst the ancient habitat of woodland . . .

August

Saturday 3
16 Hillcrest

Sunday 4
16 Hillcrest

Saturday 17
20 Llanover
27 11 Severn View

September

Sunday 15
10 Dewstow Gardens & Grottoes

October

Sunday 6
4 Castell Cwrt

Gardens open to the public

1 The Bell at Skenfrith
10 Dewstow Gardens & Grottoes

By appointment only

3 Brynderi
5 Castle House
6 Clytha Park
8 Croesllanfro Farm
9 Curlews
28 Sunnyside

Also open by Appointment ☎

2 Birch Tree Well
12 Glebe House
16 Hillcrest
20 Llanover
25 Penpergwm Lodge
30 Trostrey Lodge

The Gardens

BARN HOUSE
See Gloucestershire

1 ◆ THE BELL AT SKENFRITH

Skenfrith NP7 8UH. William & Janet Hutchings, 01600 750235, www.skenfrith.co.uk. *In the village of Skenfrith on B4521, opp the Norman castle. Parking in field adjacent to garden as indicated.* **Adm £3.50, chd free. For opening times and information, please phone or see garden website.**

Productive kitchen garden with formal area of raised beds edged with edible delights. Less formal area where more space consuming plants are grown. Produce grown incl herbs, salads, vegetables, flowers (edible and cutting), soft and hard fruits. All produce grown used in the restaurant at The Bell. Produce and plants for sale, depending on season. Limited access - please call beforehand so we can assist you (this would be accessed across an open field).

2 BIRCH TREE WELL

Upper Ferry Road, Penallt, Monmouth NP25 4AN. Jill Bourchier, gillian.bourchier@btinternet.com. *4m SW of Monmouth. Approx 1m from Monmouth on B4293, turn L for Penallt & Trelleck. After 2m turn L to Penallt. On entering village turn L at Xrds and R at war memorial. Then follow NGS signs & one-way system along narrow lanes.* Cream teas. **Adm £3.50, chd free.** Sun 14 July (2-6). **Visitors also welcome by appt May to Sept.**

Situated in the heart of the Lower Wye Valley this garden is gradually evolving amongst the ancient habitat of woodland, rocks and streams. As these 3 acres are shared with deer, badger and fox careful planting is constantly under review. A woodland setting with streams and boulders.

3 BRYNDERI

Wainfield Lane, Gwehelog, Usk NP15 1RG. Ann Benson, 01291 672976, mail@brynderi.co.uk, www.brynderi.co.uk. *3m N of Usk. Follow Monmouth rd signed Gwehelog, L at Hall Inn PH onto Wainfield Lane. Parking for 5 cars, disabled parking by house & in field 100metres away.* Light refreshments. **Adm £4, chd free. Visitors welcome by appt Mar to Oct.**

2 acres incl Kew fountain and pool, lawns and topiary, with colour-themed borders and vine-covered arbour. Knot garden, specimen tree collection and statues in elevated area with stunning views, fan trained fruit trees and raised beds. Wall fountain, Belgian trained fruit 'wall'. Garden owner is a garden historian and can arrange tours. Some gravel paths and slopes but main features can be viewed. Ramp available.

4 CASTELL CWRT

Llanelen, Abergavenny NP7 9LE. Lorna & John McGlynn. *1m S of From Abergavenny/Llanfoist take B4269 signed Llanelen. After passing Grove Farm turn R up single track rd. Rd climbs up steeply over canal. Approx 500yds entrance to Castell Cwrt 2nd on L. Separate disabled parking available.* Home-made teas. **Adm £3.50, chd free. Sat 15, Sun 16 June, Sun 6 Oct (2-6).**

Large informal wildlife friendly family garden on 10-acre small holding with fine views overlooking Abergavenny. Lawns with established trees, shrubs and perennial borders. Organic soft fruit and vegetable gardens. Woodland and haymeadow walks, chickens and geese, livestock in fields and family pets. Children very welcome, animals to see and space to let off steam. Hay meadow in full bloom. Some gravel paths.

5 CASTLE HOUSE

Castle Parade, Usk NP15 1SD. Mr & Mrs J H L Humphreys, 01291 672563, www.uskcastle.com. *200yds NE from Usk centre. Signed to Usk Castle, up narrow lane opp fire station, on Castle Parade in Usk. Disabled parking is available in the stableyard.* **Adm £4, chd free. Visitors welcome by appt Jan to Dec. Refreshments for groups by prior arrangement.**

Overlooked by the romantic ruins of Usk Castle, the gardens date from early C20, with yew hedges and topiary, long herbaceous border, croquet lawn and pond. The herb garden has plants that would have been used when the castle was last lived in c.1469. Castle House will also be joining the Usk Open Gardens event on Sat 29, Sun 30 June (10-5). Some areas easily accessible.

6 CLYTHA PARK

Abergavenny NP7 9BW. Sir Richard Hanbury-Tenison, 01873 840300. *Half-way between Abergavenny (4m) and Raglan (4m). On old rd signed Clytha at r'abouts at either end.* **Adm by donation. (Suggested amount £5). Visitors welcome by appt.**

Large C18 garden around 1½ -acre lake with wide lawns and good trees. Visit the 1790 walled garden or walk around the lake on a serpentine path laid out over 250 yrs ago. Ravens always around and possibly the largest Tulip tree in Wales. Garden and park layout by John Davenport. C19 arboretum with possible H. Avray Tipping influence. Gravel paths.

Glen Trothy

GROUP OPENING

7 COED-Y-PAEN VILLAGE GARDENS

Coed-Y-Paen NP4 0SS, info@coedypaen.net. *3m SW of Usk. From Usk take rd to Caerleon, 1st R to Coed-y-Paen. 1m R, 2m to village. From Newport, A4042, R at New Inn, follow signs to Llandegfedd Reservoir and Coed-y-Paen.* Home-made teas. **Combined adm £5, chd free.** Sun 19 May (11-5).

APRIL HOUSE
Mr & Mrs Dew

NEW **CARPENTERS ARMS**
Matt Hiscox

NEW **FOREST LANE**
Bart Bagnall

HONEYWELL COTTAGE
Maggie & Patrick Harkness

THE OLD SCHOOL
Carol Orchard

NEW **ORCHARD LODGE**
Carolyn Seymour & Dennis Perkins

NEW **PICTOR**
Sue & Graham Rogers

SPINDLE TREE COTTAGE
Jan & John Hargreaves

TY-PERROTT COTTAGE
Ms A Broben

WINDRUSH
Joan Stickland

Coed-y-Paen is in a beautiful, undiscovered part of Monmouthshire with wonderful views. 10 gardens from formal to quirky, humble to ambitious, newly established to mature, hilltop to forest clearing with inspiration for all. A very warm welcome awaits. Carpenters Arms PH offers Sunday lunch - booking essential.

8 CROESLLANFRO FARM

Groes Road, Rogerstone, Newport NP10 9GP. Barry & Liz Davies, 01633 894057, lizplants@gmail.com. *3m W of Newport. From M4 J27 take B4591 towards Risca. Take 3rd R, Cefn Walk (also signed 14 Locks Canal Centre). Proceed over canal bridge, continue approx 1/2 m to island in middle of lane. White farm gate opp. Limited parking.* Home-made teas. **Adm £4.50.** Visitors welcome by appt **June to Sept.**

An ever evolving 2-acre garden of contrasts. New formal courtyard on 6 levels leads to a tythe barn (open). Large sweeping borders of mass planted perennials and grasses invite the visitor to explore the paths, terracing and folly. A garden for all moods.

9 CURLEWS

Llangwm, Usk NP15 1HD. Mr & Mrs M Hatfield, 01291 652972, margarethatfield@madasafish.com. *5m E of Usk. Midway between Usk (5m) and Chepstow (8m) on the B4235. From Usk continue through Llangwm village for 1m.* Light refreshments. **Adm £4, chd free.** Visitors welcome by appt **May to Aug.**

Created by an enthusiastic plantswoman in Monmouthshire countryside, this 1 1/2 acre garden has many areas of varied planting. Numerous ways of exploring the garden offer delightful changes of perspective. Mature trees compliment clipped hedges, mixed cutting and prairie style borders and productive kitchen garden. Mature cactus collection and vintage cars. Plant stall and quiz for children.

10 ◆ DEWSTOW GARDENS & GROTTOES

Caerwent, Caldicot NP26 5AH. John Harris, 01291 431020, www.dewstowgardens.co.uk. *5m W of Chepstow. From A48 Newport to Chepstow rd, drive into the village of Caerwent. Follow the Brown tourist Daisy signs to the Gardens. Coaches permitted. Sat Nav NP26 5AH.* **Adm £5, chd free.** For NGS: Sun 14 Apr, Sun 15 Sept (10-2.30). **For other opening times and information, please phone or see garden website.**

5-acre Grade 1 listed unique garden which was buried and forgotten after World War II and rediscovered in 2000. Created around 1895 by James Pulham & Sons, the garden contains underground grottoes, tunnels and ferneries and above ground stunning water features. You will not be disappointed. Various events throughout the season. Featured on Escape to the Country plus various articles in local and national press. No access to underground areas, limited access in garden.

11 NEW GLANGRWYNEY COURT

Glangrwyney, Crickhowell, Powys NP8 1ES. Warwick & Christina Jackson. *3m W of Abergavenny. A40 (W) from Abergavenny. 200 metres after Powys County sign, turn R along the 200 metre drive to house. Small coaches only permitted.* Home-made teas. **Adm £4, chd free.** Wed 29 May, Thur 18 July (2-5).

Grade II listed 2-acre gardens in grounds of Regency house (not open) surrounded by 33 acres of parkland. Set in the Usk Valley at foot of the Black Mountains. Variety of mature rhododendrons, azaleas, magnolias, Japanese acers, catalpa and davidia. Walled garden (partly under restoration) with spacious lawns, roses and herbaceous borders.
2 cottage gardens on the estate also under construction.

Numerous ways of exploring the garden offer delightful changes of perspective . . .

12 GLEBE HOUSE

Llanvair Kilgeddin NP7 9BE. Mr & Mrs Murray Kerr, 01873 840422, joanna@amknet.com. *Midway between Abergavenny (5m) and Usk (5m). On B4598.* Home-made teas. **Adm £4, chd free.** Sat 22, Sun 23 June (2-6). **Visitors also welcome by appt.**

1 1/2 acres with herbaceous borders overflowing with colourful perennials, annuals and shrubs. S-facing terrace with climbers, ornamental vegetable garden and orchard - all surrounded by picturesque Usk Valley. Old rectory of St Mary's, Llanvair Kilgeddin with famous Victorian scraffito murals which will also be open.

13 GLEN TROTHY
Llanvetherine, Abergavenny NP7 8RB. Mr & Mrs Ben Herbert. *5m NE of Abergavenny. 6m from Abergavenny off B4521 (Old Ross Rd).* Home-made teas. **Adm £4.50, chd free. Sun 30 June (2-6).**
Victorian house (not open) in the Scottish Baronial style, set in mature parkland with a pinetum and arboretum. The walled garden has been renovated over the past 3yrs, incorporating blue and white herbaceous borders, a rose garden and ornamental vegetable garden with pear tunnel as well as an Italianate loggia.

GLIFFAES COUNTRY HOUSE HOTEL
See Powys

GROVE FARM (CELLAR GALLERY)
See Herefordshire

Visitors exploring the gardens are well-rewarded as hidden delights and surprises are revealed . . .

14 HIGH GLANAU MANOR
Lydart, Monmouth NP25 4AD. Mr & Mrs Hilary Gerrish. *4m SW of Monmouth. Situated on B4293 between Monmouth & Chepstow. Turn R into Private Road, 1/4 m after Craig-y-Dorth turn on B4293.* Home-made teas. **Adm £4.50, chd free. Sun 12 May (2-6).**
Listed Arts and Crafts garden laid out by H Avray Tipping in 1922. Original features incl impressive stone terraces with far-reaching views over the Vale of Usk to Blorenge, Skirrid, Sugar Loaf and Brecon Beacons. Pergola, herbaceous borders, Edwardian glasshouse, rhododendrons, azaleas, tulips, orchard with wild flowers and woodland walks. Owners book 'Edwardian Country Life - the story of H Avray Tipping' for sale.

15 HIGH HOUSE
Penrhos NP15 2DJ. Mr & Mrs R Cleeve. *4m N of Raglan. From r'about on A40 at Raglan take exit to Clytha. After 50 yds turn R to Llantilio Crossenny and follow garden open signs to High House - 10mins through lanes.* Home-made teas. **Adm £4, chd free. Sun 2 June (2-6).**
3-acres of spacious lawns and trees surrounding C16 house (not open) in a beautiful, hidden part of Monmouthshire. Large extended pond, orchard with chickens and ducks. S-facing terrace and extensive bed of old roses. Areas of grass with tulips, camassias, wild flowers and far reaching views.

16 HILLCREST
Waunborfa Road, Cefn Fforest, Blackwood NP12 3LB. Mr M O'Leary & Mr B Price, 01443 837029, bev.price@mclweb.net. *3m W of Newbridge. On open days follow A4048 to Blackwood town centre or A469 to Pengam T-lights, then NGS signs.* Cream teas. **Adm £4, chd free. Sat 25, Sun 26, Mon 27 May, Sat 3, Sun 4 Aug (12-6). Visitors also welcome by appt Apr to Sept.**
A cascade of secluded gardens, each having established a distinct character over the years, all within 1½ acres. With choices at every turn, visitors exploring the gardens are well-rewarded as hidden delights and surprises are revealed. Numerous, well-placed seats encourage the unhurried pace at which the gardens are best appreciated. Delicious cream teas to be enjoyed. Featured on TV. Woodland area not accessible to wheelchairs.

KENTCHURCH GARDENS
See Herefordshire

KENTCHURCH COURT
See Herefordshire

UPPER LODGE
See Herefordshire

17 5 LADYHILL CLOSE
Usk NP15 1SJ. Mrs Marion Powell. *From A449 follow Usk sign A472 into 30mph zone, 1st R after speed camera, before crossing. Park and walk up footpath behind bus shelter to garden entrance.* Home-made teas at 7 Ladyhill Close. **Combined adm £3.50, chd free. Sat 13, Sun 14 July (10-5). Combined with 7 Ladyhill Close.**
A garden bursting with topiarised shrubs, mature trees and evergreen ferns all with a lush undergrowth of annuals, perennials, grasses and ponds. The front garden is a profusion of begonias and hanging baskets all contained inside a quirky hedge.

18 7 LADYHILL CLOSE
Usk NP15 1SJ. Mr & Mrs Len & Marie Watts. *From A449 follow Usk sign A472 into 30mph zone, 1st R after speed camera, before crossing. Park and walk up footpath behind bus shelter to garden entrance.* Home-made teas. **Combined adm £3.50, chd free. Sat 13, Sun 14 July (10-5). Combined with 5 Ladyhill Close.**
This great little old fashioned garden is full of love, roses, flowers and lawns. Patio, rockery, pond and seats in the back garden; climbers and colourful annuals in the front.

LINDORS COUNTRY HOUSE
See Gloucestershire

19 LLANFOIST VILLAGE GARDENS
Llanfoist, Abergavenny NP7 9NF, Llanfoist Village Gardens. *1m SW of Abergavenny on B4246. Map provided with ticket. Most gardens within easy walking distance of the village centre. Free minibus to others.* Home-made teas. **Combined adm £5, chd free. Sun 9 June (10.30-5.30).**
Make this a great day out. Visit around 15 exciting and contrasting village gardens, both large and small, set just below the Blorenge Mountain on the edge of the Black Mountains. A number of new gardens opening along with many regulars. This is our 11th annual event. Canal boat trips and fantastic food not to be missed. Articles on gardens in local press. Wheelchair access not available at all gardens.

20 LLANOVER
nr Abergavenny NP7 9EF. Mr & Mrs M R Murray, 07753 423635, elizabeth@llanover.com, www.llanovergarden.co.uk. *4m S of Abergavenny, 15m N of Newport. On A4042 Abergavenny - Pontypool rd,*

in the village of Llanover. Home-made teas. **Adm £5, chd free. Sat 17 Aug (2-5). Visitors also welcome by appt Mar to Oct.**
15-acre listed garden and arboretum with well preserved water features and walled gardens. The Rhyd-y-meirch stream tumbles into ponds, down cascades and beneath flagstone bridges suitable for playing poo-sticks. Lawns for children to run around on or play hide and seek. In the circular walled garden the enormous herbaceous borders designed by Mary Payne are full of colour in August. Delicious home-made teas. The House (not open) is the birthplace of Augusta Waddington, Lady Llanover, nineteenth century patriot and supporter of the Welsh Language. The flock of Welsh Black Mountain Sheep which she introduced to Llanover, can still be seen grazing in the park. Gravel and grass paths, lawns.

GROUP OPENING

21 LLANTHONY AND DISTRICT GARDENS

Llanthony NP7 7LB. *5m N of Abergavenny. From Abergavenny r'about take A465 N towards Hereford. After 4.8m turn L onto Old Hereford Rd signed Pantygelli 2m. Mione is ½ m on L. Directions to the other gardens provided from here.* **Combined adm £5.50, chd free (share to Llanthony & District Garden Club). Sun 30 June (2-6).**

CRUCORNEY ALLOTMENTS
Crucorney Allotment Society

MIONE
Yvonne & John O'Neil

PERTHI CRWN
Jim Keates

TRWYN TAL
Mr & Mrs Hart

Three country gardens and a new community allotment site, set in the famously beautiful Llanthony valley of the Black Mountains, around the village of Llanvihangel Crucorney near Abergavenny. The tour incl Mione, a small, modern village garden of unusual plantsman's perennials, sheltered by a rose and clematis-clad pergola underplanted with a fine collection of ferns and a richly planted natural pool with glimpses of the Skirrid mountain beyond; Trwyn Tal, an upland farm cottage with a small modern garden on several levels, pond, a hard-working vegetable patch, and fabulous views down the Llanthony valley; Perthi-Crwn, a garden of broad terraces and stunning views, with a small, walled vegetable garden, teas and plant sales; and a new allotment scheme at Llanvihangel Crucorney, already fully subscribed and thriving (growing advice on offer during NGS openings).

Lawns for children to run around on or play hide and seek . . .

22 LONGHOUSE FARM

Penrhos, Raglan NP15 2DE. Mr & Mrs M H C Anderson. *Midway between Monmouth & Abergavenny. 4m from Raglan. Off Old Raglan/Abergavenny rd signed Clytha. At Bryngwyn/Great Oak Xrds take turn to Great Oak. In Great Oak follow NGS signs from red telephone box down narrow lane.* Home-made teas. **Adm £4, chd free. Sun 16 June (2-6).**
20 yrs, and ongoing, of developing this hidden 2 acre garden with a south facing terrace, millrace wall, pond, spacious lawns. Colourful and unusual plants varying from blossom, irises, summer bulbs, roses, vegetables to asters, grasses and a malus avenue of autumn colour. Unspoilt vistas of Monmouthshire.

THE NEUADD
See Powys

23 THE OLD VICARAGE, PENRHOS

Raglan NP15 2LE. Professor & Mrs Luke Herrmann. *3m N of Raglan. At Raglan turn off A40 for Mitchel Troy. Almost immed turn L for Tregaer. Follow signs for Tregaer, then Penrhos.* **Combined adm £6, chd free. Sun 28 Apr (2-6). Combined with Woodlands Farm, Penrhos.**
Traditional garden surrounding beautifully sited Victorian Gothic house (not open) with splendid views over Monmouthshire countryside. Rhododendrons, azaleas and magnolias, early summer roses. Also gazebo, gravel and formal kitchen gardens and ponds. All set in spacious lawns with mature trees. Plant stall.

24 THE PANT

Fforest Coal Pit, Abergavenny NP7 7LT. Dr & Mrs Jeremy Swift & Mr & Mrs Andrew Bruce. *5m N of Abergavenny. From Abergavenny take Hereford rd A465 to Llanvihangel Crucorney. Follow signs to Llanthony Abbey. After 1½ m turn L to Fforest Coal Pit. After further 1½ m, at Fiveways Xrds, turn sharp R uphill following signs.* Home-made teas. **Adm £5, chd free. Sat 15, Sun 16 June (2-6).**
2 adjoining and contrasting gardens set in secluded, spectacular Black Mountains scenery with 25 acres of landscaped woodland, orchard, knot garden, walled garden, Islamic garden and green theatre. Large dry stone turtle, ruined village, curious whale shaped lake, all with wonderful views. Welsh weather permitting, a string quartet will play in the green theatre, both days. Wheelchair users welcome but access is limited to lower gardens only.

25 PENPERGWM LODGE

nr Abergavenny NP7 9AS. Mr & Mrs Simon Boyle, 01873 840208, boyle@penpergwm.co.uk, www.penplants.com. *3m SE of Abergavenny, 5m W of Raglan. On B4598. Turn opp King of Prussia Inn. Entrance 150-yds on L.* **Adm £4, chd free. Sat 18, Sun 19 May (2-6). Visitors also welcome by appt Apr to Sept.**
3-acre garden with Jubilee tower overlooking terraced ornamental garden containing canal, cascading water and new loggia at head of canal. S-facing terraces planted with rich profusion and vibrant colours all surrounded by spacious lawns and mature trees. New brick waisted tower in 2011. Some gravel paths.

A wild garden with meadows as beautiful as anything under cultivation . . .

26 PENTWYN FARM
Penallt, Monmouth NP25 4SE. Gwent Wildlife Trust, www.gwentwildlife.org/reserves. *3m SW of Monmouth. S of Monmouth on B4293 to Mitchel Troy & Trelleck. Approx 1m from Monmouth turn L for Penallt & Trelleck, after 2m turn L to Penallt. On entering village turn L at Xrds & R at war memorial. Bear L & carry on straight ahead, along stone track. The reserve is at end of track.* Home-made teas. **Adm £3, chd free (share to Gwent Wildlife Trust).**
Sun 16 June (10-4).
A wild garden with meadows as beautiful as anything under cultivation. Gwent Wildlife Trust invites you to celebrate our 50th anniversary by viewing the wildflowers of Pentwyn Farm, famous for its orchids, teeming with butterflies and with spectacular views over the Wye Valley. Guests can also visit the Wyeswood Common, a 100 acre grassland and woodland restoration project home to the trusts flock of Hebridean sheep and lambs. Guided walks through the meadows at 11am, 1pm & 3pm.

27 11 SEVERN VIEW
Caldicot, nr Newport NP26 4AD. Sarah Dann. *3m W of Chepstow on B4245. From Newport exit M4 at Magor. Follow B4245 to Caldicot & signs to garden. From Chepstow take A48 & B4245 to Caldicot & signs to garden.* **Adm £3, chd free.**
Sat 15, Sun 16 June (10-4); Sat 17 Aug (12-10).
1/4 acre of mixed planting. Recently re-designed, retaining some more mature plants, lots of new planting of trees, shrubs and perennials. Seasonal bedding plantings in an explosion of colour. 2 unusual water features and lots of seating to encourage relaxation. Spectacular garden lighting at evening event. Limited wheelchair access.

The Pant

For anyone fit and intrepid who sees beauty in wild places - in upland wild flower meadows, dry stone walls and mountain springs . . .

28 SUNNYSIDE
The Hendre, Monmouth NP25 5HQ. Helen & Ralph Fergusson-Kelly, 01600 714928, helen_fk@hotmail.com. *4m W of Monmouth. On B4233 Monmouth to Abergavenny rd. Parking in field 50metres from garden.* Home-made teas. **Adm £3.50, chd free.** **Visitors welcome by appt only.**
Late summer colour: the last soft blooms of summer perennials and shrubs give way to the biscuit and russet tones of grasses and then bold injections of scarlet, cerise, violet and gold from bulbs, perennials and trees. All this in a sloping 1/3 acre garden on the old Rolls estate. Seating areas to enjoy views of the Monmouthshire countryside. Some gravel paths.

29 TAIR-FFYNNON, 'THE GARDEN IN THE CLOUDS'.
nr Llanvihangel Crucorney, Abergavenny NP7 7NR. Antony & Verity Woodward, www.gardenintheclouds.com. *8m N of Abergavenny. Off A465 Abergavenny-Hereford rd. At Llanvihangel Crucorney turn downhill at Skirrid PH and 1st R over hump-back bridge, then follow yellow signs. Challenging, very steep and narrow single-track lanes. Reversing may be necessary for last 1½ m. If wet, parking may be a 15-minute walk away.* Home-made teas and light refreshments. **Adm £4.50, chd free.** **Sat 27 July (2-6).**
The highest garden in the Yellow Book? Tair-Ffynnon is the inspiration behind the recent book The Garden in the Clouds. 6-acre smallholding in mountain landscape (reaching to nearly 1,600 feet) on Offa's Dyke footpath in Brecon Beacons National Park. For anyone fit and intrepid who sees beauty in wild places - in upland wild flower meadows, dry stone walls and mountain springs, forgotten farm machinery in field corners and gateways framing 70 mile views. 'The pinnacle of beauty' - The Sunday Times; 'Untamed but stunningly beautiful' - Reader's Digest. Free cup of tea.

30 TROSTREY LODGE
Bettws Newydd, Usk NP15 1JT. Roger & Frances Pemberton, 01873 840352, trostrey@googlemail.com. *4m W of Raglan. 7m E of Abergavenny. Off the old A40 (unnumbered) Abergavenny - Raglan. 1m S of Clytha Gates and 1½ m N of Bettws Newydd.* Home-made teas. **Adm £4, chd free.** **Sun 26, Mon 27 May (12-6). Visitors also welcome by appt May to June. Please call for bookings.**
See first our noble Tulip Tree (planted in 1923), walk on and our Cottage Garden waits to welcome you through ha-ha gates. Our stone walls do this garden make. (Regrettably there is no lake but views along the R Valley enlarge the vision magically). This garden's made by artistry but God provides the Tulip Tree. Good range of home grown plants for sale and new Trostrey Poppy Seed Bank.

31 USK OPEN GARDENS
Monmouthshire, Usk Town NP15 1HN, www.uskopengardens.com. *From M4 J24 take A449, proceed 8m to Usk exit. Good free parking in town. Map of gardens provided with ticket.* Refreshments at various locations. **Combined adm £7.50, chd free (Weekend ticket £10).** **Sat 29, Sun 30 June (10-5).**
Proud winner of Wales in Bloom for many years, with colourful hanging baskets and boxes - a sight not to be missed! The town is a wonderful backdrop to the 25+ gardens from small cottages packed with colourful and unusual plants to large gardens with brimming herbaceous borders. Wonderful romantic garden around the ramparts of Usk Castle. Gardeners' Market with wide selection of interesting plants. Wonderful day out for all the family with lots of places to eat and drink incl picnic places down by the River Usk. Unmissable. Various cafes, PH and restaurants available for refreshments. Not all the gardens are wheelchair accessible.

32 WOODLANDS FARM
Penrhos NP15 2LE. Craig Loane & Charles Horsfield. *3m N of Raglan. At Raglan, turn off A40 towards Mitchel Troy. Almost immed turn L for Tregaer, then Penrhos and follow NGS signs.* Home-made teas at Woodlands Farm. **Combined adm £6, chd free.** **Sun 28 Apr (2-6). Combined with The Old Vicarage, Penrhos.**
Quirky in its design and built to entertain with hidden nooks, paths and water feature that invite you into its 'rooms' within the garden. Hidden Acers, a viewing platform within a modern 'ruin' - all the easier to admire the creation below, the new parterre garden and pavilion and its eco credentials make the experience truly unique and will give first time and returning visitors lots to enjoy. Plant stall at the Old Vicarage.

Gwent County Volunteers

County Organiser
Joanna Kerr, Glebe House, Llanvair Kilgeddin, Abergavenny NP7 9BE, 01873 840422, joanna@amknet.com

County Treasurer
Helen Fergusson-Kelly, Sunnyside, The Hendre, Monmouth NP25 5HQ, 01600 714928, helen_fk@hotmail.com

Assistant County Organiser
Sue Carter, St Pega's, 47 Hereford Road, Monmouth NP25 3HQ, 01600 772074, stpegas47@hotmail.co.uk

GWYNEDD, ANGLESEY & CONWY

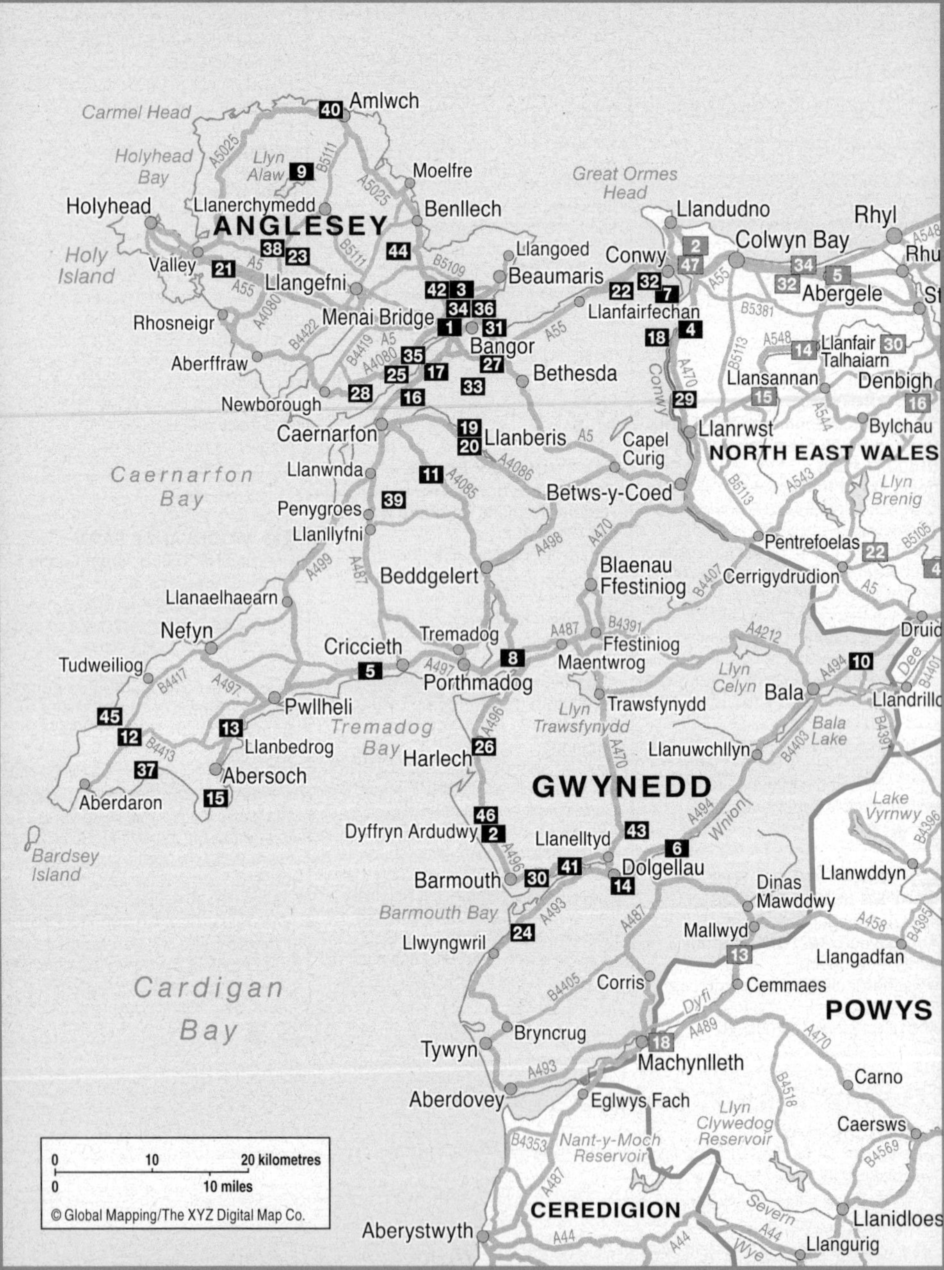

Opening Dates

February

Sunday 10
37 Plas Yn Rhiw

Saturday 16
31 Penrhyn Castle

March

Friday 29
26 Llyn Rhaeadr
35 Plas Newydd Country House & Gardens

Saturday 30
26 Llyn Rhaeadr

Sunday 31
5 Bont Fechan Farm
22 Gwel Yr Ynys
26 Llyn Rhaeadr

April

Monday 1
5 Bont Fechan Farm
26 Llyn Rhaeadr

Sunday 7
8 Bwlch y Fedwen

Wednesday 24
34 Plas Cadnant

Sunday 28
22 Gwel Yr Ynys

May

Saturday 4
43 Ty Capel Ffrwd

Sunday 5
18 Gilfach
22 Gwel Yr Ynys
26 Llyn Rhaeadr
30 Pen y Bryn
41 Tanybryn
43 Ty Capel Ffrwd

Monday 6
26 Llyn Rhaeadr
43 Ty Capel Ffrwd

Saturday 11
14 Craig y Ffynnon
29 Maenan Hall

Sunday 12
5 Bont Fechan Farm
6 Bryn Gwern
14 Craig y Ffynnon
29 Maenan Hall
40 Sunningdale

Saturday 18
13 Coron

Sunday 19
13 Coron

Saturday 25
45 Ty Gwyn, Llangwnadl

Sunday 26
22 Gwel Yr Ynys
26 Llyn Rhaeadr
27 Llys-y-Gwynt
41 Tanybryn
45 Ty Gwyn, Llangwnadl

Monday 27
26 Llyn Rhaeadr

June

Saturday 1
16 Crûg Farm

Saturday 8
9 Cae Newydd
22 Gwel Yr Ynys

Sunday 9
8 Bwlch y Fedwen
9 Cae Newydd
22 Gwel Yr Ynys
32 Pensychnant

National Gardens Weekend

Saturday 15
5 Bont Fechan Farm
7 Bunclody
15 Crowrach Isaf
26 Llyn Rhaeadr
28 Maen Hir

Sunday 16
5 Bont Fechan Farm
7 Bunclody
10 Caerau Gardens
15 Crowrach Isaf
18 Gilfach
19 Glan Llyn
20 Groeslon
26 Llyn Rhaeadr
28 Maen Hir
36 Plas Rhianfa
44 Ty Gwyn, Llanbedrgoch

Sunday 23
42 Treffos School

Saturday 29
25 Llanidan Hall

July

Wednesday 3
23 Gwyndy Bach

Saturday 6
1 Adare
11 Cilfechydd Barn
33 Pentir Gardens

Sunday 7
1 Adare
27 Llys-y-Gwynt
32 Pensychnant

Saturday 13
4 Bodnant Garden
25 Llanidan Hall

Sunday 14
40 Sunningdale

Saturday 20
24 Henddol Wood

Sunday 21
24 Henddol Wood

Thursday 25
39 St John the Baptist & St George

Saturday 27
12 Coed Ty Mawr

Sunday 28
3 Arcady
12 Coed Ty Mawr

August

Sunday 4
6 Bryn Gwern
47 41 Victoria Drive

Sunday 18
18 Gilfach
29 Maenan Hall

Sunday 25
26 Llyn Rhaeadr

Monday 26
26 Llyn Rhaeadr

We are small but full of surprises . . .

February 2014

Sunday 9
37 Plas Yn Rhiw

Saturday 22
31 Penrhyn Castle

Gardens open to the public

4 Bodnant Garden
16 Crûg Farm
24 Henddol Wood
31 Penrhyn Castle
32 Pensychnant
35 Plas Newydd Country House & Gardens
37 Plas Yn Rhiw

By appointment only

2 An Artist's Garden
17 Foxbrush
21 Gwaelod Mawr
38 Rhyd
46 Ty Newydd

Also open by Appointment ☎

The Gardens

ABERCLWYD MANOR
See North East Wales

1 NEW ADARE

Holyhead Road, Menai Bridge LL59 5RH. Frances & John Simpson. *Menai Bridge on the A5 towards Llanfair PG. Travelling W on A55, take exit 8A then A5 to Menai Bridge. Garden on L soon after 30mph limit on entering town. From Menai Bridge town, take A5 towards Llanfair PG. Garden is on R at turn to cemetery*. Home-made teas. **Adm £3.50, chd free. Sat 6, Sun 7 July (2-6).**
A plantswoman's 1/3 of an acre cottage style garden, intensively planted with unusual herbaceous plants and shrubs. In this jewel of a garden there is a pond, gravel garden, shaded area, gazebo, vegetable patch and summer house. Many of the beds are colour themed. Good views of Snowdon and the Menai Straits are weather dependent. We are small but full of surprises. Separate wheelchair access to front and back gardens.

2 AN ARTIST'S GARDEN

Ty Llwyd, Dyffryn Ardudwy LL44 2EP. Karen Hall, 01341 242623, karen.artistsgarden@gmail.com, www.artistsgarden.co.uk. *5m N of Barmouth on A496. From Harlech, drive through village of Dyffryn Ardudwy, after 20mph sign garden is a few yards on R. From Barmouth, garden is after 20mph sign & school on L of rd. Ty Llwyd is a grey painted house & garage with a rusty tin roof*. Home-made teas. **Adm £3, chd free. Visitors welcome by appt May to Sept.**
The garden is 140ft long situated in a thriving village. Slate paths meander through the plantings and there are three ponds. At the bottom of the garden is a textile studio, open for visitors to view. The garden is full of texture and colour, An Artist's Garden. There is a plant sales area.

3 NEW ARCADY

Llansadwrn, Menai Bridge LL59 5SE. Mr James Weisters. *3m N of Menai Bridge. A5025 Amlwch/Benllech exit from Britannia Bridge. Approx 3m turn R to Llansadwrn (1m after Pentraeth Motors). 1m Arcady on L. Parking at house opp*. Home-made teas. **Adm £4, chd free. Sun 28 July (11-5).**
Surrounded by farmland and with views of Snowdon range. Approx 1 acre of quirky, structured garden - originally laid out by the artist Ed Povey - pagoda and meditation garden, laburnum walk, small orchard, lawn, ponds and hidden places. Gravel paths with steps.

A maturing country garden which blends seamlessly into the open landscape . . .

4 ◆ BODNANT GARDEN

Tal-y-Cafn, nr Colwyn Bay LL28 5RE. National Trust, 01492 650460, www.nationaltrust.org.uk. *8m S of Llandudno. From A55 exit at J19. Follow brown signs to Garden. Just off A470 on B rd to Eglwysbach.* **Adm £9.30, chd £4.65. For NGS: Sat 13 July (10-4.30). For other opening times and information, please phone or see garden website.**
Among the finest gardens in the country with rhododendrons, magnolias, camellias and the famous laburnum arch. Summer colours incl roses, water lilies, herbaceous borders and hydrangeas. Superb autumn colours in October. Formal Italianate-style terraces contrast with steeply sided shrub borders and the dell. The garden is steep in places and has many steps. Please ensure motorised wheelchairs have a fully charged battery.
NCH

BODYSGALLEN HALL & SPA
See North East Wales

5 BONT FECHAN FARM

Llanystumdwy LL52 0LS. Mr & Mrs J D Bean, 01766 522604. *2m W of Criccieth. On the A497 to Pwllheli on L of main rd*. Home-made teas. **Adm £2.50, chd free. Sun 31 Mar, Mon 1 Apr, Sun 12 May, Sat 15, Sun 16 June (11-5). Visitors also welcome by appt Apr to July.**
Cottage garden with rockery, fish pond, herbaceous border, steps to river. Large variety of plants. Nicely planted tubs; good vegetable garden and poultry. Rhododendron and azaleas.

6 BRYN GWERN

Llanfachreth, Dolgellau, Gwynedd LL40 2DH. H O & P D Nurse, 01341 450255, antique_pete@btinternet.com. *5m NE of Dolgellau. Do not go to village of Llanfachreth, stay on A494 Bala-Dolgellau rd: 13m from Bala. Take 1st Llanfachreth turn R. From Dolgellau 4m Llanfachreth turn L, follow signs. No coach parking*. Cream teas and home-made cakes. **Adm £3, chd free. Sun 12 May, Sun 4 Aug (10-5). Visitors also welcome by appt.**
Unusual natural garden in 2-acres, planted with paulona tormentosa, clerodendron, pieris, arbutus, magnolias, azaleas, rhododendrons and many other trees and shrubs, bulbs, herbaceous, water and bog plants, clematis, honeysuckle, akebia quinlata. Where ducks, guinea fowl and chickens roam free. Enjoy your cream tea to the fantastic views Cader Idris. Quilting expert - buy or ask advice. Grass paths, steep slopes, but fantastic views from flat area.

BRYN HALEN ISAF
See North East Wales

7 BUNCLODY

Henryd Road, Henryd, Conwy LL32 8YG. Mrs Dawn Humphreys. *1½ m S of Conwy. Cross river on bridge. At mini r'about turn L through*

arch to Gyffin B5106. Take rd R of Style Box (hairdressers), Henryd Rd & follow approx ¾ m to Henryd. Home-made teas. **Adm £3.50, chd free (share to Kidney Research). Sat 15, Sun 16 June (2-6).**
A ½ acre cottage style series of rooms. Pinks and purples incl a silver and white mini woodland, formal circular lawn with box hedging, pretty rambling brook, with bridges and pond. Secret walled garden, bog garden, conservatory. Lovely views. All created from a mud patch 9yrs ago.

8 BWLCH Y FEDWEN

Penrhyndeudraeth LL48 6BT. David & Gillian Surman. *22m N of Dolgellau, 3m E of Porthmadog. Opp Griffin PH, take A4085 along High St to village car park. Walking from there, follow signs to garden approx 150yds*. Home-made teas. **Adm £3.50, chd free. Sun 7 Apr, Sun 9 June (11-4).**
With views towards the Rhinogs and Moelwyns, ½ acre of neglected, rocky hillside has been transformed, providing terraced gardens with inter-twining paths, many steps with handrails, seating and all yr-round interesting plants, a proliferation of spring bulbs, hellebores, roses, clematis and trees incl embothrium, halesia, koelreuteria, camellias, azaleas, magnolias.

9 CAE NEWYDD

Rhosgoch, Anglesey LL66 0BG. Hazel & Nigel Bond, 01407 831354, nigel@cae-newydd.co.uk. *3m SW of Amlwch. Turn L immed after Amlwch Town sign on A5025 from Benllech, follow signs for leisure centre & Lastra Farm. After L turn for Lastra Farm, follow rd for approx 3m, pass through Rhosgoch, keep to main rd, follow signs for Llyn Alaw, ¼ m. Garden/car park on L*. Light refreshments. **Adm £3.50, chd free. Sat 8, Sun 9 June (11-5). Visitors also welcome by appt Apr to Sept.**
A maturing country garden which blends seamlessly into the open landscape with stunning views of Snowdonia and Llyn Alaw. Good variety of shrubs and trees, large wildlife pond, meadow areas, polytunnel, greenhouse, vegetable garden and chicken run. Adjacent sheltered paddock garden. Formal pond and patio area, raised beds. All yr-round interest, Apr for spring bulbs, June for aquilegias, roses etc. Hay meadow best seen in June. Garden area closest to house suitable for wheelchairs.

Craig y Ffynnon

10 CAERAU GARDENS

Sarnau, Bala LL23 7LG. Mr & Mrs Toby Hickish, 7894164273, info@caerau-gardens.co.uk, www.caerau-gardens.co.uk. *3m NE of Bala. From A5 N of Corwen turn L A494 to Bala. Approx 5m turn R into Sarnau, keep R up hill approx 1m. From Bala take A494 NE. After approx 3m turn L into Sarnau, keep R up hill approx 1m. Coaches strictly by appt*. Home-made teas, snacks and cakes. **Adm £3, chd £2.50. Sun 16 June (2-5). Visitors and groups also welcome by appt. Coaches welcome.**
The highest garden in Wales open to the public. Over 3 acres of gardens, stunning views at over 1,000ft. Pets corner. Adventure playground and an excellent reputation for home cooked food. Now open all year. Sunken trampoline, pet's corner, wooden fort, zip wire, croquet lawn. Featured in BBC1 Wales programme - The Seven Ages of Wales. Details on our website. Gravel paths, some steep slopes.

CAEREUNI
See North East Wales

11 CILFECHYDD BARN

Waunfawr, Caernarfon LL54 7AJ. Mr & Mrs Newsham, 01286 650020, newsham.stuart@googlemail.com. *4½ m SE of Caernarfon. On A4085 past Snowdonia Parc Tavern, on R after 150yrds next to Dudley Park Nature Reserve. Postcode not suitable for SatNav. Parking at house if weather good, otherwise at PH & Nature Reserve*. Home-made teas. **Adm £3.50, chd free (share to Freshfield Animal Charity, Caernarfon). Sat 6 July (11-4.30). Visitors also welcome by appt June to Sept.**
Award winning nature garden with stream fed pond full of natural plants. Various interesting garden areas with many roses, both cultivars and species. Polytunnel, fruit gardens incl newly planted 50 tree orchard. Large vegetable plot with pottager. Garden alongside own small holding with free range poultry and pigs etc. Garden at its best late June and July. Limited wheelchair access.

12 COED TY MAWR
Ty Mawr, Bryncroes, Pwllheli LL53 8EH. Nonni & David Goadby, 01758 730359, nonni@goadby.net, www.coed-tymawr.co.uk. *12m W of Pwllheli. Take B4413 Llanbedrog to Aberdaron. 1³/₄ m past Sarn Meyllteyrn Turn R at Penygroeslon sign.* Home-made teas. **Adm £4, chd free. Sat 27, Sun 28 July (10.30-4.30). Visitors also welcome by appt Apr to Sept.**
Outstanding 5-acre woodland garden created from wilderness and situated among some of the most beautiful scenery of Wales. Over 3,000 trees and shrubs incl growing collections of magnolia, rhododendron, hydrangea and cornus. Also large pond, orchard, fernery, vegetable, oriental and sea-view gardens. Plenty of seating. Sit on the raised deck, take in the sea views and enjoy a homemade tea. Grass paths.

'. . . refreshing to find something different from the manicured gardens of today . . .'

13 CORON
Llanbedrog LL53 7NN. Mr & Mrs B M Jones. *3m SW of Pwllheli. Turn R off A499 opp Llanbedrog Village sign, before garage, up private drive.* Cream teas. **Adm £3.50, chd free. Sat 18, Sun 19 May (10.30-5).**
6-acre mature garden featuring Davidia involucrata, overlooking Cardigan Bay. Pathways leading through extensively planted areas with rhododendrons, embothriom, azaleas, camellias, bluebell walks, wooded slopes and rock outcrops providing shelter for tender plants, lakes and bog gardens; orchards, walled vegetable and formal garden.

14 CRAIG Y FFYNNON
Ffordd y Gader, Dolgellau LL40 1RU. Jon & Shân Lea. *Take Tywyn rd from Dolgellau main sq. Park on rd by Penbryn Garage. Walk up rd signed Cader Idris. Garden entrance on L 50yds from junction.* Home-made teas. **Adm £4, chd free (share to Eisteddfod yr Urdd Bro Meirion 2014). Sat 11, Sun 12 May (10-5).**
N-facing 2-acre Victorian garden set out in 1870s. Majority of garden planted with mature specimen trees, rhododendrons and azaleas predominate. More formal herbaceous borders and greenhouse enclosed by box hedges. Wildlife pond; bees and call ducks; unusual shade-loving plants and ferns. '...refreshing to find something different from the manicured gardens of today.' Frances Denby.

15 CROWRACH ISAF
Bwlchtocyn LL53 7BY. Margaret & Graham Cook, 01758 712860, crowrach_isaf@hotmail.com. *1¹/₂ m SW of Abersoch. Follow rd through Abersoch & Sarn Bach, L at sign for Bwlchtocyn for ¹/₂ m until junction and no-through rd - Cim Farm. Turn R, parking 50 metres on R.* Cream teas. **Adm £3, chd free. Sat 15, Sun 16 June (1-5). Visitors also welcome by appt June to Sept.**
2-acre plot incl 1 acre fenced against rabbits, developed from 2000, incl island beds, windbreak hedges, vegetable garden, wild flower area and wide range of geraniums, shrubs and herbaceous perennials. Views over Cardigan Bay and Snowdonia. Grass and gravel paths, some gentle slopes.

16 ◆ CRÛG FARM
Griffiths Grossing, Caernarfon LL55 1TU. Mr & Mrs B Wynn-Jones, 01248 670232, www.crug-farm.co.uk. *2m NE of Caernarfon. ¹/₄ m off main A487 Caernarfon to Bangor rd. Follow signs from r'about.* **Adm £3, chd free. For NGS: Sat 1 June (10-5). For other opening times and information, please phone or see garden website.**
3 acres; grounds to old country house (not open). Gardens filled with choice, unusual collections of plants. Collected by the Wynn-Jones, Gold Medallists and recipients of The President's Award RHS Chelsea Flower Show. National Collection of Paris, Polygonatum and Coriaria. Limited wheelchair access.
NCH

ESGAIR ANGELL
See Powys

17 FOXBRUSH
Felinheli LL56 4JZ. Mr & Mrs B S Osborne, 01248 670463. *3m SW of Bangor. On Bangor to Caernarfon rd, entering village opp Felinheli signpost.* **Adm £3, chd free. Visitors welcome by appt Mar to June. Refreshments available by prior arrangement.**
Fascinating country garden created over 40 yrs, from waste land. Still cared for solely by the same lady. Rare and interesting plant collections incl rhododendrons, ferns, hydrangea, clematis and roses cover a 45ft long pergola. Fan-shaped knot garden, 3 bridges and new plantings replace those lost in the floods of 2004. Wildlife mill pond created 2011 full of amphibians and wild ducks, wildflowers abound. Very relaxed wildlife garden.

18 GILFACH
Rowen LL32 8TS. James & Isoline Greenhalgh, 01492 650216. *4m S of Conwy. At Xrds 100yds E of Rowen S towards Llanrwst, past Rowen School on L; turn up 2nd drive on L.* Home-made teas. **Adm £3, chd free. Suns 5 May, 16 June, 18 Aug (2-5.30). Visitors also welcome by appt May to Aug.**
1-acre country garden on S-facing slope with magnificent views of the R Conwy and mountains; set in 35 acres of farm and woodland. Collection of mature shrubs is added to yearly; woodland garden, herbaceous border and small pool. Spectacular view of the Conwy Valley.

19 NEW GLAN LLYN
Llanberis, Caernarfon LL55 4EL. Mr Bob Stevens. *On A4086, ¹/₂ m from Llanberis village. From A55, leave at J11, at r'about take 1st exit onto A5 (signed Betws-y-Coed). At next r'about take 2nd exit onto A4244 (signed Pentir, Llanberis). At next r'about take 1st exit, (A4244), signed Llanberis. At T-junction turn L onto A4086. On A4086 rd, ¹/₂ m from Llanberis village. Next door to the Gallt-y-Glyn hotel, opp DMM.* **Combined adm £5, chd free. Sun 16 June (11-5). Combined with Groeslon.**
A 3 acre woodland edge garden incl 2 acres of woodland, wildlife ponds, stream, wildflower area, raised sphagnum bog garden, three green roofs, cacti house (almost completed), many unusual trees,

shrubs and herbaceous perennials. The garden is on fairly steep sloping ground, no wheelchair access to the woodland.

20 NEW GROESLON
Caenarfon Road, Llanberis LL55 4EL. Mr Robert Vaughan. *On A4086 ¾ m W of Llanberis. On A4086 travelling W into Llanberis turn R 200metres before Lakeview Hotel.* **Combined adm £5, chd free. Sun 16 June (11-5). Combined with Glan Llyn.**
2 acres comprising of woodland, fish pond, wildlife pond, stream, wildflower areas, many exotic trees and shrubs and a variety of ducks and chickens. Views over Llyn Padarn. Some steep gravel paths.

21 GWAELOD MAWR
Caergeiliog, Anglesey LL65 3YL. John & Tricia Coates, 01407 740080. *6m E of Holyhead. ½ m E of Caergeiliog. From A55 J4. r'about 2nd exit signed Caergeiliog. 300yds, Gwaelod Mawr is 1st house on L.* **Adm £3, chd free. Visitors welcome by appt May to July.**
2½ -acre garden created by owners over 20yrs with lake, large rock outcrops and palm tree area. Spanish style patio and laburnum arch lead to sunken garden and wooden bridge over lily pond with fountain and waterfall. Peaceful Chinese orientated garden offering contemplation. Separate Koi carp pond. Abundant seating throughout. Gravel paths.

22 GWEL YR YNYS
Parc Moel Lus, Penmaenmawr LL34 6DN. Mr Dafydd Lloyd-Borland, 07968 243119, gwelyrynysgarden@btinternet.com, www.gwelyrynys.com. *J16 off A55 Penmaenmawr. Take R corner to main village along Conwy Rd ½ m. At Mountain View Hotel take sharp L into Conwy Old Rd. Take 3rd L, turn up hill to Ysgol Pen Cae. Transport available from here to garden. (June dates only). Other dates: Conwy Rd L at Nat West Bank, 2nd R Merton Park. At top L, immed R into Park Moel Lus. Follow rd to top, rd turns to L & garden is last house on R.* Home-made teas. **Adm £3.50, chd free. Suns 31 Mar, 28 Apr, 5, 26 May (12-2); Sat 8 June (11-4); Sun 9 June (11-3). Visitors also welcome by appt Mar to Sept.**
A ¾ -acre challenging garden developed over the last 7 yrs in an elevated position some 650ft above sea level. The garden is set above the village parallel with Mountain Lane offering fantastic views of Anglesey, Puffin Island and Foel Lus behind. Natural planting incl a very large range of herbaceous plants, shrubs and trees. Chickens enjoy the garden too. Featured on BBC Gardeners' World, also in local press and Daily Post.

Eat home-made teas overlooking the sea on 1916 colonnaded verandah . . .

23 GWYNDY BACH
Tynlon, Llandrygarn LL65 3AJ. Keith & Rosa Andrew, 01407 720651, keithandrew.art@gmail.com. *5m W of Llangefni. From Llangefni take B5109 towards Bodedern, cottage exactly 5m out on L.* Home-made teas. **Adm £3, chd free. Wed 3 July (11-5). Visitors also welcome by appt May to July.**
¾ -acre artist's garden, set amidst rugged Anglesey landscape. Romantically planted in informal intimate rooms with interesting rare plants and shrubs, box and yew topiary, old roses and Japanese garden with large Koi pond. National Collection of Rhapis miniature Japanese palms. Studio attached. Gravel entrance to garden.
NCH

24 ◆ HENDDOL WOOD
Ffordd Henddol, Friog LL38 2RZ. Clive & Jennifer Elliott. *½ m S of Fairbourne. Situated off Dolgellau/Tywyn A493 rd. Enter Friog, after ¼ m park on main rd. Proceed on foot up Ffordd Panteinion for 40 yards then turn immed L following garden signs.* **Adm £3.50, chd free. Sat 20, Sun 21 July (1-5)**
¾ -acre hillside garden with magnificent views of Barmouth Bay. Woodland walk amongst rocky outcrops and native trees. Lower area planted with many shrubs for all seasons, collection of grasses, exotica and riotous colourful herbaceous borders. Unusual artefacts in the woods and borders, fairy glen and original Fairbourne Beach hut. Eat homemade teas overlooking sea on 1916 colonnaded verandah.

25 LLANIDAN HALL
Brynsiencyn LL61 6HJ. Mr J W Beverley (Head Gardener), 07759 305085, beverley.family@btinternet.com. *5m E of Llanfair Pwll. From Llanfair PG (Anglesey) follow A4080 towards Brynsiencyn for 4m. Turn at Groeslon PH. Continue for 1m, garden entrance on R.* Light refreshments. **Adm £3.50, chd free (share to CAFOD). Sat 29 June, Sat 13 July (10-4). Visitors also welcome by appt.**
Walled garden of 1¾ acres. Physic and herb gardens, ornamental vegetable garden, herbaceous borders, water features and many varieties of old roses. Sheep, rabbits and hens to see. Children must be kept under supervision. Llanidan Church will be open for viewing. Hard gravel paths, gentle slopes.

26 LLYN RHAEADR
Parc Bron-y-Graig, Centre of Harlech LL46 2SR. Mr D R Hewitt & Miss J Sharp, 01766 780224. *Centre of Harlech. From A496 take B4573 into Harlech, take turning to main car parks S of town, L past overspill car park, garden 75yds on R.* **Adm £3, chd free (share to WWF UK). Fri 29, Sat 30, Sun 31 Mar, Mon 1 Apr, Suns, Mons 5, 6, 26, 27 May, Sat 15, Sun 16 June, Sun 25, Mon 26 Aug (2-5). Visitors also welcome by appt.**
Hillside garden blending natural wildlife areas with garden plants, shrubs, vegetables and fruit. Small lake with 20 species of waterfowl with gazebos, fish and wildlife ponds, waterfalls, woodland, rockeries, lawns, borders, snowdrops, daffodils, heathers, bluebells, ferns, camellias, azaleas, rhododendrons, wild flowers, views of Tremadog Bay, Lleyn Peninsula. Good paths and seating. Waterfowl.

27 LLYS-Y-GWYNT

Pentir Road, Llandygai, Bangor LL57 4BG. Jennifer Rickards & John Evans, 01248 353863. *3m S of Bangor. 300yds from Llandygai r'about at J11 of A5 & A55, just off A4244. From A5 & A55 follow signs for services (Gwasanaethau) and find 'No Through Road' sign 50yds beyond. Turn R then L. (Sat Nav does not find us due to large postcode area).* Home-made teas. **Adm £3, chd free. Sun 26 May, Sun 7 July (11-4). Visitors and groups also welcome by appt. Coaches permitted.**

Rambling 2-acre garden in harmony with and incl magnificent views of Snowdonia. Bronze Age burial cairn. Exposed site incl wandering paths, levels and planting to create shelter, interest and micro climates and lead to varied 'rooms'. Ponds, waterfall, bridge, N-facing rockery and well organised compost. Local materials and crafts used. Yr-round interest and wildlife. Good family garden.

28 MAEN HIR

Dwyran, Anglesey LL61 6UY. Mr & Mrs K T Evans. *6m SE of Llanfairpwll. From Llanfair P.G (Anglesey) follow A4080 through village Brynsiencyn. Continue on this rd for approx 2m. Maen Hir on R.* Home-made teas. **Adm £3.50, chd free. Sat 15, Sun 16 June (11-5).**

Set in 7 acres incl beautiful walled garden with gazebo, old roses and mixed herbaceous borders replanted 2007. Courtyard, outer garden, woodland walks, greenhouse, potting shed, cutting patch and hay meadow. Maen Hir enjoys magnificent views of Snowdonia range.

29 MAENAN HALL

Maenan, Llanrwst LL26 0UL. The Hon Mr & Mrs Christopher Mclaren, 01492 640441, cmmclaren@gmail.com. *2m N of Llanrwst. On E side of A470, 1/4 m S of Maenan Abbey Hotel.* Home-made teas. **Adm £4, chd free (share to St Davids Hospice). Sat 11, Sun 12 May, Sun 18 Aug (10.30-5.30). Visitors also welcome by appt Apr to Oct.**

Superbly beautiful garden (about 4 hectares) on the slopes of the Conwy Valley, with dramatic views of Snowdonia, set amongst mature hardwoods. Both upper part, with sweeping lawns, ornamental ponds and retaining walls, and bluebell carpeted woodland dell contain copious specimen shrubs and trees, many originating at Bodnant. In spring Magnolias, Rhododendrons, Camellias, Pieris and Cherries amongst many others make a breathtaking display. Upper part of garden accessible but with fairly steep slopes.

Ty Capel Ffrwd

Every garden visit makes a difference

THE OLD RECTORY, LLANFIHANGEL GLYN MYFYR

See North East Wales

30 PEN Y BRYN

Glandwr, Barmouth LL42 1TG. Phil & Jenny Martin. *2m E of Barmouth. On A496 7m W of Dolgellau, 2m E of Barmouth, situated on N side of Mawddach Estuary. Park in or nr layby and walk L up narrow lane.* Cream teas. **Adm £3, chd free (share to Gwynedd Hospice at Home). Sun 5 May (11-5).**

A glorious hillside garden with panoramic views of The Mawddoch Estuary. Woodland walks awash with Bluebells in the spring. Lawns on different levels with vibrant rhododendrons and azaleas, arches of clematis, honeysuckle and roses. Heather filled natural rocks, unusual conifer feature, a rock cannon and a pond for wildlife.

31 ◆ PENRHYN CASTLE

Bangor LL57 4HN. National Trust, 01248 353084, www.nationaltrust.org.uk. *3m E of Bangor. On A5122. Buses from Llandudno, Caernarfon, Betws-y-Coed; alight: Grand Lodge Gate. J11 A55, signed from thereon Sat Nav LL57 4HT.* **Adm £4, chd £1. For NGS: Sat 16 Feb (11-3); Sat 22 Feb 2014. For other opening times and information, please phone or see garden website.**

Large grounds incl Victorian walled garden; fine trees, shrubs, wild garden, good views, snowdrop walks. Gravelled and grassed paths, some steps, exposed tree roots, some surfaces bark and chippings.

32 ◆ PENSYCHNANT

Sychnant Pass, nr Conwy LL32 8BJ. Pensychnant Foundation Wardens Julian Thompson & Anne Mynott, 01492 592595, www.pensychnant.co.uk. *2 1/2 m W of Conwy. Top of Sychnant Pass between Conwy & Penmaenmawr. From Conwy turn L into Upper Gate St by Heddlu/Police; after 2 1/2 m Pensychnant's drive signed on R. From Penmaenmawr, fork R by Mountain View PH; summit of Sychnant Pass after walls, Pensychnant's drive on L.* **Adm £3.50, chd free. For NGS: Sun 9 June, Sun 7 July (11-5). For other opening times and information,**

please phone or see garden website.
Diverse herbaceous 'cottage garden' borders surrounded by mature shrubs, banks of rhododendrons, ancient and Victorian woodlands. 12 acre woodland walks with views of Conwy Mountain and Sychnant. Woodland birds. Picnic tables, archaelogical trail on mountain. A peaceful little gem. Large Victorian gothic house (open) with art exhibition. Partial wheelchair access, please phone for advice.

GROUP OPENING

33 PENTIR GARDENS

Pentir, Bangor LL57 4UY. *Take A4244 from J11 of A55/A5, continue for 3m to Pentir. Turn R signed Caerhun/Vaynol PH, into Pentir Square.* Tea at Bryn Meddyg. **Combined adm £4.50, chd free. Sat 6 July (12-5).**

BRYN MEDDYG
Mr Wyn James

2 RHYD Y GROES
Mr & Mrs IwanThomas

NEW **TAN Y BRYN**
Mrs Liz Battle

TY UCHAF
Miss Belinda Thompson

Ty Uchaf A small densely packed cottage garden containing a wide and varied range of cottage favourites, plus more unusual planting schemes and combinations. It enjoys a romantic-feel, prioritizing colour and texture. A secret gate takes visitors into neighbouring **Bryn Meddyg**, where refreshments are available. A 10 min walk takes you to **Tan y Bryn**, a compartmentalized garden with mature shrubs enveloping a lawned area surrounded by herbaceous planting. The garden also includes veg plot, paddock with stunning views, pond and a dwarf conifer collection. Continue along road to the secluded garden **2 Rhyd y Groes** to again enjoy views of Moel y Ci and Menai Strait. This immaculate garden is divided into a number of 'rooms' with a variety of planted areas, seated areas incl pond and summerhouse. Sculptures dispersed throughout.

On summer days, scented plants infuse the air . . .

34 PLAS CADNANT

Menai Bridge LL59 5NH. Mr A J Tavernor, www.plascadnantgardens.co.uk. *Turn off A545 1/2 m E of Menai Bridge, at Cadnant Bridge, follow drive over cattle grids.* Home-made teas. **Adm £6.50, chd free. For NGS: Wed 24 Apr (12-5).**
Early C19 Picturesque garden that has been undergoing restoration since 1996. Work still ongoing, but much to see incl valley garden with waterfalls, large walled garden (now an ornamental garden with herbaceous planting) and early pit house. Some steps, gravel paths and steep slopes. Local community stalls. Featured on S4C. Limited wheelchair access. Some steps, gravel paths, slopes.

35 ◆ PLAS NEWYDD COUNTRY HOUSE & GARDENS

Llanfairpwll, Anglesey LL61 6DQ. National Trust, 01248 714795, www.nationaltrust.org.uk. *2m S of Llanfairpwll on A4080. A55 J7 & J8 on A4080.* **Adm £7, chd £3.50. For NGS: Fri 29 Mar (10-4.30). For other opening times and information, please phone or see garden website.**
Plas Newydd is a beautiful C18 country house with spectacular panoramic views across the Menai Strait to Snowdonia. Set in beautiful gardens, there are tranquil walks, an Australasian arboretum and a pretty Italianate Terrace Garden. The house is the family home of the Marquess of Anglesey. Some slopes and gravel paths.

36 PLAS RHIANFA

Glyngarth, Beaumaris LL59 5NS. Anna Roberts, 01248 713 656, info@plasrhianfa.com, www.plasrhianfa.com. *Crossing Menai Bridge follow signs for Beaumaris. Once out of Menai Bridge town, Plas Rhianfa is approx 1m on R. Signed on main rd.* Light refreshments. **Adm £5, chd free. Sun 16 June (11-4).**
Work began on the garden in 1851 and was designed by Sir John Hay-Williams. Interesting points incl the Grade II listed aviary, the parterre gardens and tea-room with frontage to the Menai Straits. The garden boasts glorious views over to the Snowdonia mountain range towards Conwy. Members of staff will be on hand to talk about the garden and information sheets will be provided. Garden is on different levels, separated by steps.

37 ◆ PLAS YN RHIW

Rhiw, Pwllheli LL53 8AB. National Trust, 01758 780219, www.nationaltrust.org.uk. *4m E of Aberdaron. 12m from Pwllheli, signed from B4413 to Aberdaron.* **Adm £2, chd £1. For NGS: Sun 10 Feb (11-3); Sun 9 Feb 2014. For other opening times and information, please phone or see garden website.**
Essentially a cottage garden of 3/4 acre laid out around C17 manor house (not open) overlooking Porth Neigwl. Flowering shrubs and trees flourish in compartments framed by formal box hedges and paths. On summer days, scented plants infuse the air. A place of romance and charm. Snowdrops in spring.

38 RHYD

Trefor, Anglesey LL65 4TA. Jeff Hubble, 01407 720320, jeffh43@btinternet.com. *7m W of Llangefni, nr Holyhead. From Bodedern 2 1/4 m along B5109 towards Llangefni, turn L. From A55 take J5 to Llanerchymedd turn L Trefor Xrds, 1st R, 1st house on R.* Light refreshments. **Adm £3.50, chd free. Visitors welcome by appt May to Aug.**
5 acres of gardens, arboretum, meadows and nature reserve. Herbaceous beds, pergolas, ponds, stream, rockery, garden room, decking and fernery. Many species of roses, climbing and standard. Clematis and rhododendron. Wide variety of herbaceous plants especially hosta and primula. Many places to sit and ponder or watch the wildlife.

39 ST JOHN THE BAPTIST & ST GEORGE

Lon Batus, Carmel LL54 7AR. Bishop Abbot Demetrius. *7m SE of Caernarfon. On A487 Porthmadog Rd, at Dinas r'about exit 1st L to Groeslon, turn L at PO for 1½ m. At village centre turn L & L again at Xrds.* Tea. **Adm £2, chd free. Thur 25 July (2-4).**

Holy community in the making under the authority of The Orthodox Catholic and Holy Synod of Milan. This is not a garden in the traditional sense but it and the monastery are a spiritual retreat from the stresses and strains of modern life, surrounded on all sides by space and rural tranquillity. We are privileged to share a glimpse of a more contemplative life. Monastery antique collection.

40 SUNNINGDALE

Bull Bay Road, Bull Bay, Amlwch LL68 9SD. Michael Cross & Gill Boniface, 01407 830753, mikeatbb@aol.com. *1½ m NW of Amlwch. A55 over Britannia Bridge, 2nd turning Amlwch (17m). A5025 through Amlwch. Keep on A5025 past golf course. Trecastell Hotel on L. Garden 5 houses further on. Parking signed. No parking at house.* Home-made teas. **Adm £3, chd £1. Sun 12 May, Sun 14 July (11-4). Visitors also welcome by appt Apr to July.**

A seaside garden. Headland is a wild area with beaches, caves, cliffs, wildflowers and heathers. It has spectacular views with seating to soak up the atmosphere and take in the wild life. Front garden has raised pond and associated planting. The sheltered rear garden is cottage style with raised vegetable beds, a small wild area and gabion seating. Access via steps. Children must be strictly supervised. Overall winner of Amlwch town garden competition.

41 TANYBRYN

Bontddu, Dolgellau LL40 2UD. Mrs Beryl Jones. *From Barmouth to Dogellau on A496 in the village of Bontddu.* Cream teas. **Adm £3, chd free. Sun 5, Sun 26 May (10-5).**

In the village of Bontddu with a view of Cader Idris across the R Mawddach. Approx 1 acre of woodland garden with unusual shrubs, shade loving plants, azaleas, rhododendrons and mixed borders. The Afon Cwmllechen forms the boundary on 2 sides with a small stream running through the garden and small wild-life pond and many wild birds. S4C's Byw yn yr Ardd. Some gravel paths and steep slopes but mostly flat grass.

Spiritual retreat from the stresses and strains of modern life . . .

42 TREFFOS SCHOOL

Llansadwrn, Anglesey LL59 5SD. Stuart and Joyce Humphreys. *2½ m N of Menai Bridge. A5025 Amlwch/Benllech exit from the Britannia Bridge onto Anglesey. Approx 3m turn R towards Llansadwrn. Entrance to Treffos School is 200yds on L.* Cream teas. **Adm £3, chd free. Sun 23 June (12-3).**

7 acres, child-friendly garden, in rural location, surrounding C17 house now run as school. Garden consists of mature woodland, underplanted with spring flowering bulbs and rhododendrons, ancient beech avenue leading down to rockery, herbaceous borders and courtyards. Art and Craft activities for children. Also face painting.

43 TY CAPEL FFRWD

Llanfachreth, nr Dolgellau LL40 2NR. Revs Mary & George Bolt, 01341 422006, georgebolt@talktalk.net. *4m NE of Dolgellau, 18m SW of Bala. From A470 nr Dolgellau take A497 towards Bala. Turn L after 200yds signed Dolgellau. 1st R signed Llanfachreth, 4m. Uphill to village, L at T-junction, past war memorial on L, ½ m. Park nr chapel, walk 30yds downhill to garden. No parking beside cottage. From S via Trawsfynydd, go through Ganllwyd, 1st L signpost Llanfachreth follow signs. Parking along the lane before the chapel.* Home-made teas. **Adm £3, chd free. Sat 4, Sun 5, Mon 6 May (11-5). Visitors also welcome by appt Mar to Sept.**

True cottage garden in Welsh mountains. Azaleas, rhododendrons, acers; large collection of aquilegia. Many different hostas give added strength to spring bulbs and corms. Stream flowing through the garden, 10ft waterfall and on through a small woodland bluebell carpet. For summer visitor's there is a continuous show of colour with herbaceous plants, roses, clematis and lilies, incl cardiocrinum giganteum. Weather permitting the Welsh harp will be played in the garden. From the back gate there is a short circular walk with open views of Cader and Y Garn.

44 TY GWYN, LLANBEDRGOCH

Llanbedrgoch, Anglesey LL76 8NX. Keith & Anna Griffiths. *2m inland W of Red Wharf Bay. A5025 from Menai Bridge through Pentraeth. Turn L to Llanbedrgoch. L at staggered Xrds in village on rd to Talwrn. After 1m turn R up unmade rd of concrete strips. Garden 1m on L at bottom of small dip.* Home-made teas. **Adm £4, chd free. Sun 16 June (12-5).**

Wildish 9-acres incl wild flower meadow, limestone pavement and hazel copses together with landscaped formal lawns and gardens separated into a number of 'green rooms' of different interest incl gazebo and pond, small walled garden, topiary yews and box hedging. Adjacent to several SSSI's, incl Cors Goch, an International Wetlands Nature Reserve.

45 NEW TY GWYN, LLANGWNADL

Llangwnadl, Pwllheli LL53 8NT. Mrs Sue Taylor. *Turn off B4417 between Morfa Nefyn & Aberdaron following signs for Porth Colmon, continue across small Xrds & follow NGS signs. Ty Gwyn is located on L side directly after a white bungalow which is on R bend.* Home-made teas. **Adm £3, chd free. Sat 25, Sun 26 May (10-4).**

Ty Gwyn is a holiday home and shows what can be done with a garden with minimum maintenance. Over ¾ of an acre it consists of a lawned area with small pond, herbaceous borders, pagoda,and small gravel/japanese area leading to a wildlife pond with bridge. Steep drive, wildlife area not suitable for wheelchairs.

46 TY NEWYDD

Dyffryn Ardudwy LL44 2DB. Guy & Margaret Lloyd, 01341 247357, guylloyd@btinternet.com. *5½ m N of Barmouth, 4½ m S of Harlech. A496 Barmouth to Harlech rd, ½ m N of Dyffryn Ardudwy, area sometimes referred to as 'Ty Canol'. At bus shelter & phone box turn down lane towards sea, driveway 30yds on L.* Home-made teas. **Adm £3, chd free. Visitors welcome by appt Feb to Dec.**

3½ -acre maritime garden diversley planted with trees and shrubs to provide yr-round interest through contrasting foliage colours and forms as well as floral displays. Plants incl a number of more tender subjects such as echium, grevillea and pittosporum. Areas devoted to fruit and vegetable growing and the so called Diamond apple tree.

47 NEW 41 VICTORIA DRIVE

Llandudno Junction LL31 9PF. Allan Evans. *Llandudno Junction. A55 from Bangor take J18, then 1st exit to Conwy, A546, straight on at next r'about (Tesco), at next r'about (Daily Post) take 3rd exit, Victoria Dr is 1st L. From Colwyn Bay J18 take 2nd exit. Park on Victoria Drive.* Home-made teas. **Adm £3, chd free. Sun 4 Aug (1-4).**

An interesting small garden, so much to see incl prize winning sweet peas and dahlias being grown in a confined space. A talk on how to grow these prizewinners is given by the garden owner. Several compact borders maximising every bit of the garden, fruit shrubs and fuchsia make it well worth a visit. Greenhouses are used to start plants off during the winter.

Gwaelod Mawr

© Fiona Lea

Gwynedd County Volunteers

County Organisers

North Grace Meirion-Jones, Parc Newydd, Rhosgadfan, Caernarfon LL54 7LF, 01286 831195

South Hilary Nurse, Bryn Gwern, Llanfachreth, Dolgellau LL40 2DH, 01341 450255

County Treasurers

South Michael Bishton, Bronclydwr, Rhoslefain, Tywyn LL36 9LT, 01654 710882, m.bishton@btopenworld.com

North Nigel Bond, Cae Newydd, Rhosgoch, Amlwch, Anglesey LL66 0BG, 01407 831354, nigel@cae-newydd.co.uk

Assistant County Organisers

North Hazel Bond, Cae Newydd, Rhosgoch, Amlwch, Anglesey LL66 0BG, 01407 831354, nigel@cae-newydd.co.uk

North Janet Jones, Coron, Llanbedrog, Pwllheli LL53 7NN, 01758 740296 coron@hotmail.co.uk

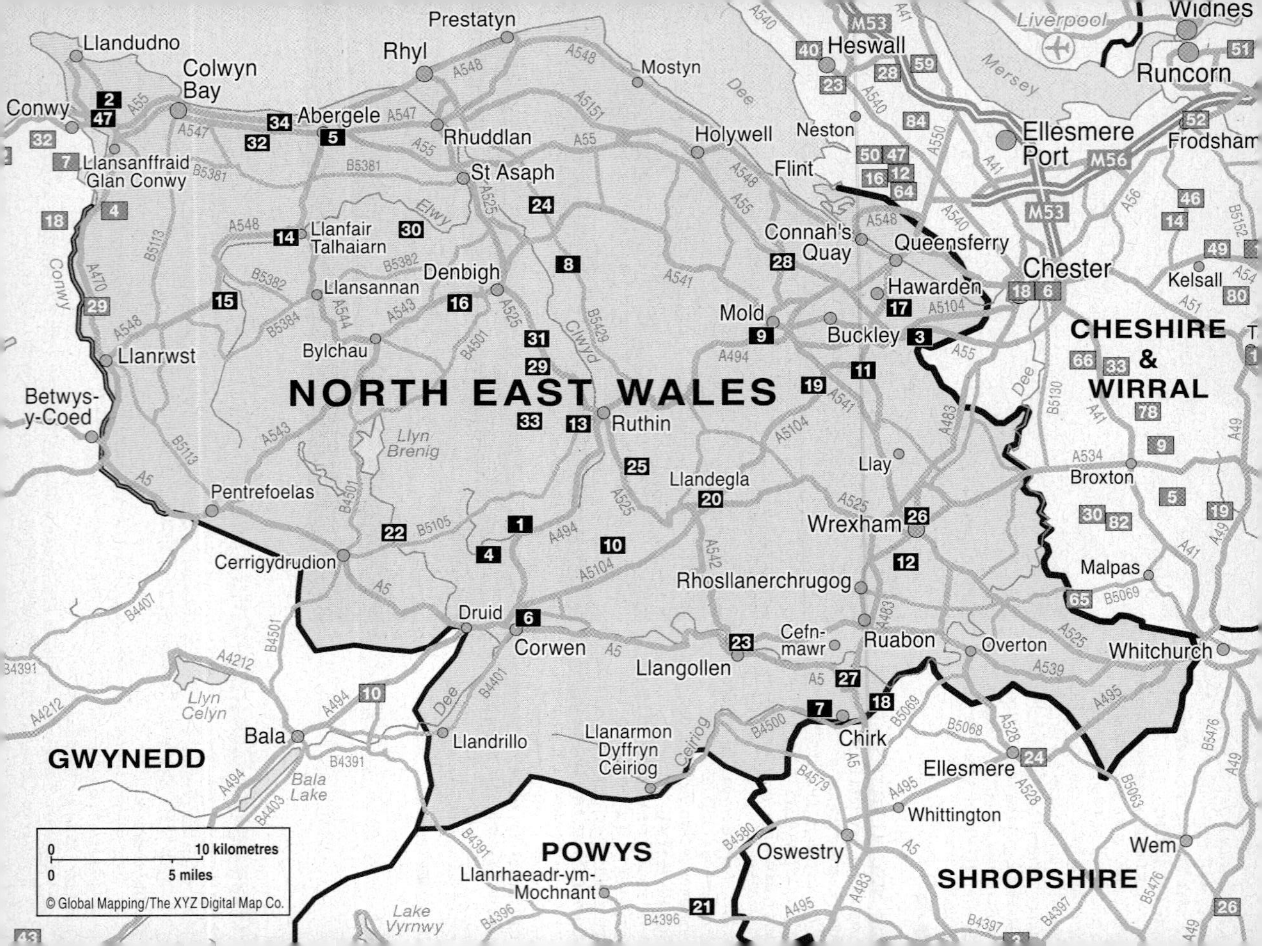
NORTH EAST WALES
CHESHIRE & WIRRAL
SHROPSHIRE
POWYS
GWYNEDD
Llandudno
Colwyn Bay
Conwy
Rhyl
Prestatyn
Abergele
Rhuddlan
St Asaph
Mostyn
Holywell
Flint
Neston
Heswall
Liverpool
Widnes
Runcorn
Ellesmere Port
Frodsham
Chester
Kelsall
Queensferry
Connah's Quay
Hawarden
Buckley
Mold
Llanfair Talhaiarn
Llansannan
Denbigh
Bylchau
Llanrwst
Betwys-y-Coed
Llansanffraid Glan Conwy
Ruthin
Llyn Brenig
Pentrefoelas
Cerrigydrudion
Llandegla
Llay
Wrexham
Rhosllanerchrugog
Ruabon
Cefn-mawr
Druid
Corwen
Llangollen
Overton
Whitchurch
Malpas
Broxton
Chirk
Ellesmere
Whittington
Oswestry
Wem
Llandrillo
Llanarmon Dyffryn Ceiriog
Bala
Bala Lake
Llyn Celyn
Lake Vyrnwy
Llanrhaeadr-ym-Mochnant
Mersey
Dee
Clwyd
Elwy
Conwy
Ceiriog
0 10 kilometres
0 5 miles
© Global Mapping/The XYZ Digital Map Co.

Opening Dates

February

Wednesday 6
1 Aberclwyd Manor

Wednesday 13
1 Aberclwyd Manor
8 Clwydfryn

Wednesday 20
1 Aberclwyd Manor

Wednesday 27
1 Aberclwyd Manor

March

Wednesday 6
1 Aberclwyd Manor

Wednesday 13
1 Aberclwyd Manor
8 Clwydfryn

Wednesday 20
1 Aberclwyd Manor

Sunday 24
17 Hawarden Castle

Wednesday 27
1 Aberclwyd Manor

April

Wednesday 3
1 Aberclwyd Manor

Sunday 7
32 Tudor Cottage

Wednesday 10
1 Aberclwyd Manor
8 Clwydfryn

Wednesday 17
1 Aberclwyd Manor

Tuesday 23
13 Firgrove

Wednesday 24
1 Aberclwyd Manor

Tuesday 30
13 Firgrove

May

Wednesday 1
1 Aberclwyd Manor

Saturday 4
10 Dibleys Nurseries

Sunday 5
10 Dibleys Nurseries
12 Erddig Hall
22 The Old Rectory, Llanfihangel Glyn Myfyr

Monday 6
6 Caereuni
10 Dibleys Nurseries

Tuesday 7
13 Firgrove

Wednesday 8
1 Aberclwyd Manor
8 Clwydfryn

Tuesday 14
13 Firgrove

Wednesday 15
1 Aberclwyd Manor

Saturday 18
28 90 St Peters Park

Tuesday 21
13 Firgrove

Wednesday 22
1 Aberclwyd Manor

Sunday 26
5 33 Bryn Twr and Lynton

Monday 27
6 Caereuni

Tuesday 28
13 Firgrove

Wednesday 29
1 Aberclwyd Manor

June

Tuesday 4
13 Firgrove

Wednesday 5
1 Aberclwyd Manor

Tuesday 11
13 Firgrove

Wednesday 12
1 Aberclwyd Manor
8 Clwydfryn

National Gardens Weekend

Saturday 15
5 33 Bryn Twr and Lynton
12 Erddig Hall
18 Hillside
27 Queen Anne Cottage
29 Stella Maris
31 Tan-y-Parc

Sunday 16
18 Hillside
21 Llangedwyn Hall
27 Queen Anne Cottage
29 Stella Maris
31 Tan-y-Parc

Tuesday 18
13 Firgrove

Wednesday 19
1 Aberclwyd Manor

Saturday 22
7 Chirk Castle

Sunday 23
16 Gwaenynog
25 Penllwyn

Tuesday 25
2 Bodysgallen Hall & Spa
13 Firgrove

Wednesday 26
1 Aberclwyd Manor

Saturday 29
19 Leeswood Green Farm
32 Tudor Cottage

Sunday 30
9 The Cottage Nursing Home
19 Leeswood Green Farm
32 Tudor Cottage

July

Tuesday 2
13 Firgrove

Wednesday 3
1 Aberclwyd Manor

Saturday 6
34 Y Bwthyn

Home-made teas . . . how lovely . . .

Sunday 7
22 The Old Rectory, Llanfihangel Glyn Myfyr
26 Prices Lane Allotments

Tuesday 9
13 Firgrove

Wednesday 10
1 Aberclwyd Manor
8 Clwydfryn

Sunday 14
5 33 Bryn Twr and Lynton

Tuesday 16
13 Firgrove

Wednesday 17
1 Aberclwyd Manor

Tuesday 23
13 Firgrove

Wednesday 24
1 Aberclwyd Manor

Sunday 28
3 Broughton & Bretton Allotments
20 Llandegla Village Gardens

Tuesday 30
13 Firgrove

Wednesday 31
1 Aberclwyd Manor

August

Sunday 4
11 Dove Cottage

Tuesday 6
13 Firgrove

Wednesday 7
1 Aberclwyd Manor

Tuesday 13
13 Firgrove

Wednesday 14
1 Aberclwyd Manor
8 Clwydfryn

Tuesday 20
13 Firgrove

Wednesday 21
1 Aberclwyd Manor

Sunday 25
29 Stella Maris

Monday 26
6 Caereuni
29 Stella Maris

Tuesday 27
13 Firgrove

Wednesday 28
1 Aberclwyd Manor

September

Tuesday 3
13 Firgrove

Wednesday 4
1 Aberclwyd Manor

Tuesday 10
13 Firgrove

Wednesday 11
1 Aberclwyd Manor
8 Clwydfryn

Wednesday 18
1 Aberclwyd Manor

Wednesday 25
1 Aberclwyd Manor

Gardens open to the public

7 Chirk Castle
12 Erddig Hall

By appointment only

4 Bryn Halen Isaf
14 Garthewin
15 Glog Ddu
23 Pear Tree Cottage
24 Pen Y Graig Bach
30 Tal-y-Bryn Farm
33 Tyddyn Bach

Also open by Appointment ☎

1 Aberclwyd Manor
5 33 Bryn Twr and Lynton
8 Clwydfryn
11 Dove Cottage
13 Firgrove
19 Leeswood Green Farm
20 Swn y Gwynt, Llandegla Village Gardens
22 The Old Rectory, Llanfihangel Glyn Myfyr
25 Penllwyn
27 Queen Anne Cottage
28 90 St Peters Park
29 Stella Maris
31 Tan-y-Parc
32 Tudor Cottage

Look out for group openings and really make a day of it . . .

The Gardens

1 ABERCLWYD MANOR

Derwen, Corwen LL21 9SF. Miss Irene Brown & Mr G Sparvoli, 01824 750431, irene662010@live.com. *7m from Ruthin. Travelling on A494 from Ruthin to Corwen. At Bryn S.M service station turn R, follow sign to Derwen. Aberclwyd gates will be seen on L before Derwen.* **Adm £3, chd free. Every Wed 6 Feb to 25 Sept (11-4). Visitors also welcome by appt Feb to Oct.**
A 4 acre garden on a sloping hillside overlooking the Upper Clwyd Valley. The garden has many mature trees underplanted with snowdrops, fritillaries and cyclamen. An Italianate garden of box hedging lies below the house and shrubs, ponds, perennials, roses and an orchard are also to be enjoyed within this cleverly structured area. Spring flowers, snowdrops, helebores etc. Lots of roses in June. Lots of structure and hedges. Garden is advertised in the local press from time to time. Mostly flat with some steps and slopes.

BANK HOUSE
See Cheshire & Wirral

150 BARREL WELL HILL
See Cheshire & Wirral

BODNANT GARDEN
See Gwynedd

2 BODYSGALLEN HALL & SPA

The Royal Welsh Way, nr Llandudno LL30 1RS. The National Trust, 01492 584466, www.bodysgallen.com. *2m from Llandudno. Take A55 to its intersection with A470 (The Royal Welsh Way) towards Llandudno. Proceed 1m, hotel is 1m on R.* **Adm £4, chd free. Tue 25 June (1-5).**
Garden is well known for C17 box-hedged parterre. Stone walls surround lower gardens with rose gardens and herbaceous borders. Outside walled garden is cascade over rocks. Enclosed working fruit and vegetable garden with espalier-trained fruit trees, hedging area for cut flowers with walls covered in wineberry and Chinese gooseberry. Restored Victorian woodland, walks with stunning views of Conwy and Snowdonia. Gravel paths in places and steep slopes.

BRIARFIELD
See Cheshire & Wirral

ALLOTMENTS

3 BROUGHTON & BRETTON ALLOTMENTS

Main Road, Broughton CH4 0NT. Broughton & Bretton Allotments Association, www.broughtonandbrettonallotments.co.uk. *5m W of Chester. On A5104 (signed Penyffordd) in village of Broughton.* Home-made teas at War Memorial Institute. **Adm £3, chd free. Sun 28 July (1-6).**
56 half sized allotment plots used by the local community to grow a mix of vegetables, flowers and soft fruit. Seasonal produce for sale.

Bring a bag for plants – help us give more to charity

4 NEW BRYN HALEN ISAF
Melin-Y-Wig, Corwen LL21 9RD. Ms Karen Williams, 01824 750792, herbwoman47@hotmail.com. *Between Melin-Y-Wig & Bryn SM. From A5 Maerdy turn at The Goat PH signed Betws GG. Continue through Betws GG to Melin-Y-Wig then follow NGS signs up hill. Take 1st R to Bryn Halen continue along lane to car park. A494 from Ruthin turn R after Bryn SM service station & follow rd for 2½ m take 1st turning L.* Tea, vegan biscuits, herb tea and coffee with soya milk. **Adm £3.50, chd free. Visitors welcome by appt** only **Fris 21 June, 5 July (6-8.30), Suns 23 June, 7 July (12-5).**
This is a unique and unusual 4 acre garden of wildlife friendly land incl bog areas, ponds, young woodland and cultivated beds for vegetables, but the emphasis is on growing herbs for medicinal use. The land is cultivated using organic and animal free methods. 45 minute guided talk by a local professional herbalist is incl in the visit. Garden owner featured in The Herbalist.

5 33 BRYN TWR AND LYNTON
Lynton, Highfield Park, Abergele LL22 7AU. Mr & Mrs Colin Knowlson, 01745 832002, apk@slaters.com. *From A55 heading W take slip rd into Abergele town centre. Turn L at 2nd set of T-lights signed Llanfair TH, 3rd rd on L into Bryn Twr garden. No.33 on L.* Home-made teas. **Adm £3.50, chd free. Sun 26 May, Sat 15 June, Sun 14 July (1-5). Visitors also welcome by appt.**
Many changes have been made to the gardens, mixed herbaceous and shrub borders, some trees plus many unusual plants. New areas maturing well. Garage with interesting fire engine cars and memorabilia, newly built greenhouse over water capture system, the surrounding planting coming along nicely. Limited wheelchair access.

BURTON VILLAGE GARDENS
See Cheshire & Wirral

BRIARFIELD
See Cheshire & Wirral

CAERAU GARDENS
See Gwynedd

6 CAEREUNI
Ffordd Ty Cerrig, Godre'r Gaer, nr Corwen LL21 9YA. Mr S Williams, www.plantationcaereunigarden.co.uk. *1m N of Corwen. From A5 Corwen to Bala rd, turn R at T-lights onto A494 to Chester. 1st R after lay-by. House ¼ m on L. From A494 Chester to Corwen rd take 1st L after junction where A5104 from Llandegla joins.* Refreshments at Glandwr Plant Centre. **Adm £3.50, chd £1. Mons 6, 27 May; 26 Aug (2-5).**
Plantsman's collection of rare trees, shrubs, plants, containers of tender plants and topiary set in a quirky themed garden. This 0.3 acre garden incls Japanese smoke water garden, old ruin, Spanish courtyard, Welsh gold mine, Chinese peace garden, Mexican chapel, 1950s petrol garage, woodman's lodge and jungle.

Ride through the garden on a miniature railway . . .

CHESTER CATHEDRAL
See Cheshire & Wirral

7 ◆ CHIRK CASTLE
Chirk, nr Wrexham LL14 5AF. National Trust, 01691 777701, www.nationaltrust.org.uk. *7m S of Wrexham, 2m W of Chirk Village. Follow brown signs from A483 to Chirk Village. 2m W on minor rds.* **Adm £10, chd £5. For NGS: Sat 22 June (10-5). For other opening times and information, please phone or see garden website.**
5½ -acre hilltop garden with good views over Shropshire and Cheshire. Formal garden with outstanding yew topiary. Rose garden, herbaceous borders, more informal further from the building with rare trees and shrubs, pond, thatched hawk house, ha-ha with terrace and pavilion. Newly opened vegetable garden with fruit and cut flowers. Plant Swop - bring your spare plants on the day and swop them.

28 CHRISTCHURCH ROAD
See Cheshire & Wirral

8 CLWYDFRYN
Bodfari LL16 4HU. Keith & Susan Watson, 01745 710232, clwydfryn@btinternet.com. *5m outside Denbigh. Halfway between Bodfari & Llandyrnog on B5429.* **Adm £3.50, chd free. Weds 13 Feb, 13 Mar, 10 Apr, 8 May, 12 June, 10 July, 14 Aug, 11 Sept (11-4). Visitors also welcome by appt Feb to June incl.**
¾ -acre plantswoman's garden, well worth a visit any time of the yr. Collection of epimediums, hellebores and daffodils in spring. Many unusual spring shade loving plants and perennial borders in summer. Grass border, orchard and colourful cottage garden potager. Garden has access up a slope from the parking area to the main garden.

9 THE COTTAGE NURSING HOME
54 Hendy Road, Mold CH7 1QS. Mr & Mrs A G & L I Lanini. *10m W of Chester. From Mold town centre take A494 towards Ruthin. 2nd R into Hafod Park. Straight on to T-junction. Turn R onto Hendy Rd. Garden at junction of Hendy Rd & Clayton Rd.* Cream teas. **Adm £2, chd £1 (share to British Heart Foundation). Sun 30 June (2-5).**
Beautiful garden set in approx 1 acre. Well-established shrubs, herbaceous plants and abundance of colourful window boxes and tubs. Heart-shaped patio, incl water feature and pergola, with natural reclaimed stone walling.

29 DEE PARK ROAD
See Cheshire & Wirral

10 DIBLEYS NURSERIES
Cefn Rhydd, Llanelidan LL15 2LG. Mr & Mrs R Dibley. *7m S of Ruthin. Take A525 to Xrds by Llysfasi Agricultural College. Turn onto B5429 towards Llanelidan. After 1½ m turn L, 1m up lane on L. Brown tourist signs from A525.* Home-made teas. **Adm £3.50, chd free. Sat 4, Sun 5, Mon 6 May (10-5).**
8-acre arboretum with wide selection of rare and unusual trees. There will be a lovely display of rhododendrons, magnolias, cherries and camellias. Ride through the garden on a miniature railway. ¾ acre of glasshouses are open to show a spectacular display of streptocarpus and other house plants. National

Collection of *Streptocarpus*. The nursery has been awarded seven RHS gold medals this year. Limited wheelchair access to glasshouses, uneven ground in arboretum.

NCH

11 DOVE COTTAGE

Rhos Road, Penyffordd, nr Chester CH4 0JR. Chris & Denise Wallis, 01244 547539, dovecottage@supanet.com. *6m SW of Chester. From Chester A55 S exit A550 follow signs for Corwen. Turn L immed opp Penyffordd railway stn. From Wrexham A541 for Mold, R at Pontblyddyn for Chester, turn R immed opp Penyffordd railway stn.* Home-made teas. **Adm £3.50, chd free. Sun 4 Aug (2-5). Visitors also welcome by appt June to Aug.**

Approx 1½-acre garden, shrubs and herbaceous plants set informally around lawns. Established vegetable area, 2 ponds (1 wildlife), summerhouse,and woodland planted area. Gravel paths.

12 ◆ ERDDIG HALL

nr Wrexham LL13 0YT. National Trust, 01978 315150, www.nationaltrust.org.uk. *2m S of Wrexham. Signed from A483/A5125 Oswestry rd; also from A525 Whitchurch rd.* **Adm £7, chd £3.15. For NGS: Sun 5 May, Sat 15 June (11-4.30). For other opening times and information, please phone or see garden website.**

Important, listed Grade I, historic garden. Formal C18 and later Victorian design elements incl pleached lime tree avenues, trained fruit trees, wall plants and climbers, herbaceous borders, roses, herb border, annual bedding, restored glasshouse and vine house. National Collection of Hedera. Free garden tours at set times during the day. Guide dogs are admitted to the property. All areas of the garden are accessible. Gravelled paths, two steps which can be avoided and there are some short sloping sections.

NCH

13 FIRGROVE

Llanfwrog, Ruthin LL15 2LL. Philip & Anna Meadway, 01824 702677, meadway@firgrovecountryhouse.co.uk, www.firgrovecountryhouse.co.uk. *1½m SW of Ruthin. Exit Ruthin on B5105 towards Cerrigydrudion. After church & inn, garden is ½m on the R.* Light refreshments. **Adm £3.50, chd £2. Every Tue 23 Apr to 10 Sept (11.30-3.30). Visitors also welcome by appt Apr to Sept, between 11.30 and 3.30.**

1½-acre mature plantsman's garden that is still developing. A garden for all seasons whose microclimate allows tender and unusual shrubs to thrive. Some underplanted with streptocarpus for the summer. A collection of large exotics for summer containers. Many varieties of camellias, magnolias and clematis. An expanding collection of brugmansia suaveolens, candida and sanguinea.

A garden for all seasons whose microclimate allows tender and unusual shrubs to thrive . . .

14 GARTHEWIN

Llanfair T.H., LL22 8YR. Mr Michael Grime, 01745 720288. *6m S of Abergele & A55. From Abergele take A548 to Llanfair TH & Llanrwst. Entrance to Garthewin 300yds W of Llanfair TH on A548 to Llanrwst. Sat nav misleading.* **Adm £3.50, chd free. Visitors welcome by appt Apr to Oct, no coaches, max 40 visitors.**

Valley garden with ponds and woodland areas. Much of the 8 acres have been reclaimed and redesigned providing a younger garden with a great variety of azaleas, rhododendrons and young trees, all within a framework of mature shrubs and trees.

15 GLOG DDU

Llangernyw, Abergele LL22 8PS. Pamela & Anthony Harris, 01745 860611. *1m S of Llangernyw. Through Llangernyw going S on A548. R into Uwch Afon. L after 1m at grass triangle. Follow rd, past new houses, down narrow lane. Glog Ddu is the house on R at end.* **Adm £3, chd free. Visitors welcome by app mid Feb to mid March. Parking for 12 cars. Not suitable for coaches. Visitors must phone to make arrangements.**

The result of three generations of gardening enthusiasm, a garden inspired by an Edwardian plantsman with a fascinating history. Approx 2-acres consisting of snowdrops rhododendrons, herbaceous borders, rare trees and shrubs, many grown from seed. Planted for yr-round interest with an emphasis on autumn colour. New prairie border. 250 plus different varieties of snowdrops to see early in the season and many hard-to-find snowdrops for sale.

GRAFTON LODGE

See Cheshire & Wirral

16 GWAENYNOG

Denbigh LL16 5NU. Major & Mrs Tom Smith. *1m W of Denbigh. On A543, Lodge on L, ¼m drive.* Cream teas. **Adm £3.50, chd free (share to St James Church, Nantglyn). Sun 23 June (2-5.30).**

2 acres incl the restored walled garden where Beatrix Potter wrote and illustrated the 'Tale of the Flopsy Bunnies'. Also a small exhibition of some of her work. C16 house (not open) visited by Dr Samuel Johnson during his Tour of Wales. Herbaceous borders some recently replanted, espalier fruit trees, rose pergola and vegetable area.

17 HAWARDEN CASTLE

Hawarden CH5 3PB. Sir William & Lady Gladstone. *6m W of Chester. On B5125 just E of Hawarden village. Entrance via farm shop.* **Adm £3, chd £3, (under 2yrs free). Sun 24 Mar (2-5.30).**

Large garden and picturesque ruined castle. Please take care and supervise children. Dogs on short leads only. No wheelchair access to Old Castle.

18 HILLSIDE

Pont-y-Blew, Chirk LL14 5BH. Ferelith & Robert Smith. *2m E of Chirk. Follow B5070 to Chirk. Turn into Collery Rd & follow NGS signs to Pont-y-Blew or follow NGS signs from Halton r'about A483 (McDonalds).* Home-made teas. **Combined adm £4, chd free. Sat 15, Sun 16 June (1-5). Combined with Queen Anne Cottage.**

Country cottage garden in fabulous setting, looking across the lower Ceiriog Valley. C17 half-timbered cottage (not open) in middle of

$^3/_4$ -acre lawned garden with mixed borders, woodland stream, roses, fruit and vegetable gardens. Wild flower bank. Stream and lower garden accessible by steep paths. Limited wheelchair access.

♿ ✿ ☕

INGLEWOOD
See Cheshire & Wirral

19 LEESWOOD GREEN FARM
Leeswood CH7 4SQ. Anne Saxon & John Glenn, 01352 771222, annemsaxon@yahoo.co.uk. *3m SE of Mold. 9m NW of Wrexham. Off A541 W. At Pontblyddyn, from Wrexham, turn L after garage into Dingle Rd. After ½ m at T-junction turn L. Garden after 50yds on R approached by lane.* Home-made teas. **Adm £3.50, chd free. Sat 29, Sun 30 June (12-5). Visitors also welcome by appt Mar to Oct. Limited parking, no coaches.**
Plantswoman's garden surrounding C15 farmhouse in lovely rural location. Many unusual trees, shrubs, perennials and bulbs set around lawns. Ornamental vegetable garden, orchard and paved areas with some unusual features. Meadow with wild flowers and seating to enjoy the vistas. Large plant stall. Gravel area near house. Lawned areas slight incline.

♿ 🐕 ✿ ☕ ☎

GROUP OPENING

20 LLANDEGLA VILLAGE GARDENS
Llandegla LL11 3AP. *10m W of Wrexham. Off A525 at Llandegla Memorial Hall. Parking & minibus from hall. Please park in centre of village because parking is difficult for some gardens.* Cream teas at Llandegla Memorial Hall. **Combined adm £5, chd free. Sun 28 July (2-6).**

ERW LLAN
Mr & Mrs Keith Jackson

GLAN-YR-AFON
Mr & Mrs D C Ion

13 MAES TEG
Phil & Joan Crawshaw

11 MAES TEG
Mr & Mrs L Evans

PLAS YN COED
Fraser & Helen Robertson

SWN Y GWYNT
Phil Clark
Visitors also welcome by appt June to Sept.
01978 790344

TY SIONED
Mr & Mrs Muia

Selection of 7 widely varied gardens in the picturesque village of Llandegla. Plas yn Coed, set in 2 acres, nestling into the hillside with fabulous views. Many herbaceous perennials, shrubs and trees to provide yr-round interest. Ty Sioned is a terraced garden with beautiful panoramic views. The terraces consist of a variety of herbaceous plants and shrubs, You will find Swn y Gwynt a real plantsman's garden. This garden demonstrates the interest which can be developed in a shady garden with a wide variety of plants and shrubs. 11 & 13 Maes Teg demonstrate how much interest can be achieved in a compact space, with colourful herbaceous plants, and shrubs for all-yr colour, water features, yet low maintenance. Erw Llan is a ¼ -acre garden made to attract wildlife. Habitats are provided and plants are grown for birds, butterflies and insects. There is also a well maintained pond to encourage other wildlife. Glan yr Afon has a 1-acre informal country garden with a wide variety of features incl stream, 2 ponds, herbaceous borders, rockery, several ancient trees and vegetable patch.

✿ ☕

Set in beautiful, tranquil, sheltered valley . . .

21 LLANGEDWYN HALL
Llangedwyn, Oswestry SY10 9JW. Mr & Mrs T M Bell. *8m W of Oswestry. On B4396 to Llanrhaeadr-ym-Mochnant about 5m W of Llynclys Xrds.* Home-made teas. **Adm £4, chd free. Sun 16 June (12-5).**
Approx 4-acre formal terraced garden on 3 levels, designed and laid out in late C17 and early C18. Unusual herbaceous plants, sunken rose garden, small water garden, walled kitchen garden and woodland walk.

♿ ✿ ☕

NESS BOTANIC GARDENS
See Cheshire & Wirral

22 THE OLD RECTORY, LLANFIHANGEL GLYN MYFYR
Corwen LL21 9UN. Mr & Mrs E T Hughes, 01490 420568, elwynthomashughes@hotmail.com. *2½ m NE of Cerrigydrudion. From Ruthin take B5105 SW for 12m to Llanfihangel Glyn Myfyr. Turn R just after Crown PH (follow signs). Proceed for ⅓ m, garden on L.* Home-made teas. **Adm £3.50, chd free (share to Cancer Research U.K). Suns 5 May; 7 July (2-5). Visitors also welcome by appt Mar to July.**
Garden of approx 1 acre set in beautiful, tranquil, sheltered valley. A garden for all seasons; hellebores; abundance of spring flowers; mixed borders; water, bog, and gravel gardens; walled garden with old roses, pergola, bower and garden of meditation. Also hardy orchids, gentians, daffodils, rhododendrons and acers. Limited wheelchair access in places.

♿ ✿ ☕ ☎

23 PEAR TREE COTTAGE
Geufron, Llangollen LL20 8DY. Mr & Mrs M Davies, 01978 861704. *½ m N of Llangollen. From Llangollen take A542 towards Ruthin. Turn R immed after Llangollen Pavilion, up Tower Rd, straight at Xrds, up steep hill to Xrd. Turn R down lane to garden. From Horseshoe Pass turn L into Tower Rd just before brown Llangollen Pavilion sign. Parking for 6 cars only, accessible by minibus.* Home-made teas. **Adm £3.50, chd free. Visitors welcome by appt June to July.**
Steeply sloping S-facing cottage garden full of colourful plants and vegetables many propagated by the owners. Wide steps edged with showy pots, lead down to the pond and terrace where the magnificent views can be admired. 2 waterfalls cascade into the natural looking pond. This is an organic garden which attracts many species of wildlife. Steep slopes and steps make this garden unsuitable for the disabled and young children.

✿ ☕ ☎

Bodysgallen Hall & Spa

24 PEN Y GRAIG BACH
Tremeirchion, St Asaph LL17 0UR. Roger Pawling, 01745 710286, rogerpawling@gmail.com. *Approx 3m S of A55 between Tremeirchion & Bodfari in Vale of Clwyd. From Rhuallt junction on A55 follow signs S to Tremeirchion. Continue on B5429 towards Bodfari. Ignore Sat Nav. Take 2nd L at wide verge, up hill, L at fork. After 200 metres turn R at 1st house. Continue up hill to cottage at road's end.* **Adm £2.50, chd free. Visitors welcome by appt Jan to Dec. Please give advance notice.**
Half-acre wildlife-friendly rural cottage garden. Box hedges and fruit trees enclose 5 plots of herbaceous perennials, flowering shrubs, soft fruit and vegetables. Colour throughout the year. 2 acres of paddocks and a pond are managed organically. Beehives. Stunning views from sea to mountains. Organic, wildlife friendly. Two acres. Ornamental garden with all year colour. Wild flower meadows, ponds, fruit trees, and ornamental and native trees.

Wildlife-friendly rural garden with stunning views of sea and mountains . . .

25 NEW PENLLWYN
Penllwyn, Graigfechan, Ruthin LL15 2EU. Malcolm & Ann Ingham, 01824 308157. *4m S of Ruthin. A525 Ruthin to Wrexham Rd at Xrds by Llysfasi College take B5429 to Graigfechan. Drive 2km & park at Three Pigeons Inn. From A494 Ruthin to Mold Rd take B5429 to Graigfechan. After parking turn L & Penllwyn is 5mins walk on R. Hard standing parking by roadside with steps leading to garden gate.* **Adm £3.50, chd free. Sun 23 June (12-4). Visitors also welcome by appt June to Aug.**
1 acre of terraced garden and woodland managed for wildlife with spectacular views over the Vale of Clwyd. Sloping lawns, flower beds, vegetables, chickens, water feature, two small ponds and woodland all accessed by meandering path and steps. Some uneven paths and steep steps. Many and various nest boxes. Bird feeding station and three Vintage Cars.

ALLOTMENTS

26 PRICES LANE ALLOTMENTS
Prices Lane, Wrexham LL11 2NB. Wrexham Allotment & Leisure Gardeners Association. *1m from town centre. From A483, take exit for Wrexham Ind Estate & follow A5152 towards town centre. Allotments signed from there.* **Adm £3, chd free. Sun 7 July (12-6).**
120 plus plots, growing a good variety of flowers, fruit and vegetables. Plots for the disabled and school children. Association shop, selling a wide range of garden requisites and seeds.

27 QUEEN ANNE COTTAGE
Whitehurst Gardens, Chirk LL14 5AS. Michael Kemp, 01691 774003, mikekemp40@yahoo.co.uk. *A5 from Chirk to Llangollen. 50 metres off Whitehurst r'about, turning on R.* **Combined adm £4, chd free. Sat 15, Sun 16 June (1-5). Combined with Hillside. Visitors also welcome by appt Apr to Sept.**
Small woodland cottage garden on two levels set around C17 summerhouse. Selection of unusual trees, shrubs, herbaceous and old roses. New area under development. Some steps.

ROSEWOOD
See Cheshire & Wirral

THE ROWANS
See Cheshire & Wirral

SAIGHTON GRANGE
See Cheshire & Wirral

28 90 ST PETERS PARK
Northop CH7 6YU. Mr P Hunt, 01352 840758, philipbhunt@hotmail.co.uk. *3m N of Mold, 3m S of Flint. Leave A55 at Northop exit J33. Opp cricket ground, turn R. Take 5th turning on R. Garden on R.* Home-made teas. **Adm £3, chd free. Sat 18 May (2-5.30). Visitors also welcome by appt all yr.**
Garden planted by professional botanist and horticulturalist, Custos Hortorum at Chester Cathedral and creator of Cloister Garth, Cheshire Garden of Distinction. A plantsman's garden with exotic and rare species of trees and ornamental plants. Unique garden cruck house with sedum roof, beamed ceilings, stained glass windows and inglenook fireplace. Other interesting timber framed structures. Featured on S4C.

29 STELLA MARIS
Mynydd Llech, Llanrhaeadr, Denbigh LL16 4PW. Mrs J E Moore, 01745 890475, jemoore01@live.com. *3m SE of Denbigh. Take A525 Denbigh to Ruthin rd. After 3m from Denbigh or 4m from Ruthin turn W at Xrds to Mynydd Llech. Garden ½ m on L. Visitors will be asked to exit the garden by a different route which will lead back to A525 just 150 metre closer to Denbigh.* Cream teas. **Adm £3.50, chd free. Sat 15, Sun 16 June, Sun 25, Mon 26 Aug (11.30-5). Visitors also welcome by appt June to Sept. Lane unsuitable for large coaches.**
This 1½ acre garden has been developed over 30yrs and now offers a good collection of specimen trees, interesting shrubs, herbaceous borders, gravel garden and ponds. Areas of late flowering shrubs, herbaceous plants and a new rose garden complement the outstanding views over the Vale of Clwyd. Visitors are welcome to bring a picnic to enjoy in the field. Some lawned slopes and gravel drive.

30 TAL-Y-BRYN FARM
Llannefydd LL16 5DR. Mr & Mrs Gareth Roberts, 01745 540256, llaeth@villagedairy.co.uk, www.village dairy.co.uk. *3m W of Henllan. From Henllan take rd signed Llannefydd. After 2½ m turn R signed Bont Newydd. Garden ½ m on L.* Light refreshments. **Adm £3.50, chd**

free (share to Elderly Committee of Llannefydd). **Visitors welcome by appt Apr to Sept. Tours of the yoghurt dairy may also be booked.**
Medium-sized working farmhouse cottage garden. Ancient farm machinery. Incorporating ancient privy festooned with honeysuckle, clematis and roses. Terraced arches, sunken garden pool and bog garden, fountains and old water pumps. Herb wheels, shrubs and other interesting features. Lovely views of the Clwydian range. Water feature and new rose tunnel.

31 TAN-Y-PARC

Llanrhaeadr, Denbigh LL16 4NL. Mrs Sandra Edwards, 01745 890807, dottycom3_@hotmail.com. *3m S of Denbigh. 5m N of Ruthin. Take A525 from Denbigh or Ruthin. Follow signs at Llanrhaeadr.* Cream teas. **Adm £3, chd free. Sat 15, Sun 16 June (1-5). Visitors also welcome by appt June to Aug.**
Small cottage garden, new planted borders in paddock area, greenhouse and raised vegetable plots, fruit bushes. Rear garden enclosed with beech hedges, 2 large raised beds. Pergola with grape vine. New features in paddock, pond and wild flower area. level grass areas.

32 TUDOR COTTAGE

Isallt Road, Llysfaen, Colwyn Bay LL29 8LJ. Mr & Mrs C Manifold, 01492 518510. *1 1/2 m SE of Old Colwyn. Turn S off A547 between Llandulas & Old Colwyn up Highlands Rd. Go up hill for 1/2 m. Fork R onto Tan-y-Graig Rd. Ignore Sat Nav. Go 3/4 m to Swings. Take Isallt Rd on far R. Go 1/2 m. Garden up unadopted rd on L.* Tea, hot chocolate (April only). **Adm £3.50, chd free. Sun 7 Apr (2-4); Sat 29, Sun 30 June (1-5). Visitors also welcome by appt. Refreshments by prior arrangement.**
3/4 -acre garden on different levels set amongst natural rock faces. Unusual and varied planting featuring cottage, scree, Japanese, shade and bog gardens. Display bedding, an abundance of colourful pots and baskets, together with quirky statues, ponds, bridges and a folly. Lovely views from upper level. Some uneven paths and steep steps. Care required.

33 TYDDYN BACH

Bontuchel, Ruthin LL15 2DG. Mr & Mrs L G Starling, 01824 710248, les.starling@boyns.net. *4m W of Ruthin. B5105 from Ruthin, turn R at Cross Keys PH, on rd to Bontuchel/ Cyffylliog. Go through Bontuchel, without turning, heading towards Cyffylliog. 400yrds (river on R) turn L up narrow steep hill just before chevron signs at next bridge. House 1st on L.* **Adm £3, chd free. Visitors welcome by appt July to Aug.**
Mainly organic, very pretty cottage garden with prolific vegetable garden. Wildlife friendly with hedges and wood pile. Greenhouse packed with plants for both pots and the garden. Small wildlife pond completed in May 2010 and small stumpery completed 2012. Excellent views of surrounding countryside.

34 NEW Y BWTHYN

New Road, Llanddulas, Abergele LL22 8EL. Mr David Roberts & Mr Mark Cooke. *Travelling from Bangor or Rhyl take exit 23 off A55 signed Llanddulas. Through village pass The Valentine Inn (on R) then take 1st R into Beaula Avenue, continue then take 2nd L into New Rd. Go to top of hill & Y Bwthyn is last bungalow on L.* Home-made teas. **Adm £3.50, chd free. Sat 6 July (12-5).**
A garden with meandering paths that leads the eye to explore the varied themes created within the different 'rooms'. From a cottage garden (busy and lush) to a lawned area of tranquility and space. From a shady grove to a watery nook, all within the back drop of the beautiful Llanddulas mountain. An artists garden with roses, clematis, hostas and ferns featured as some of the favourites.

A garden with meandering paths that leads the eye to explore . . .

North East Wales

County Organiser
Jane Moore, Stella Maris, Mynydd Llech, Llanrhaedr, Denbigh LL16 4PW, 01745 890475, jemoore01@live.com

Booklet Coordinator
Roy Hambleton, Greenheys, Cefn Bychan Road, Pantymwyn, Mold GH7 5EN, 01352 740206, royhambleton@btinternet.com

County Treasurers
Elizabeth Sasse, Ty'r Ardd, High Street, Caerwys, Mold CH7 5BB, 01352 720220, Elizabeth.sasse246@btinternet.com
Wendy Sime, Park Cottage, Penley, Wrexham LL13 0LS, 01948 830126, sjsime@hotmail.com

Press & Publicity Officer
Ann Rathbone, Woodfirld House, Station Lane, Hawarden CH5 3EG, 01244 532948, rathbone.ann@gmail.com

Assistant County Organisers
Fiona Bell, Plas Ashpool, Llandyrnog, Denbigh LL16 4HP, 01824 790612, bell_fab@hotmail.com
Ruth Davies, Arfryn, Pentrecelyn, nr Ruthin LL15 2HR, 01978 790475, arfrynpentrecelyn@btinternet.com
Bill & Dawn Jones, Tan y Coed, Llanasa, nr Holywell CH8 9NE, 01745 889919, w.jones844@btinternet.com
Mrs Ann Knowlson, Lynton, Highfield Park, Abergele LL22 7AU, 01745 832002, apk@slaters.com
Ann Rathbone, Woodfield House, Station Lane Hawarden CH5 3EG, 01244 532948, rathbone.ann@gmail.com
Anne Saxon, Leeswood Green Farm, Leeswood, Mold CH7 4SQ, 01352 771222, annemsaxon@yahoo.com
Susan Watson, Clwydfryn, Bodfari, Denbigh LL16 4HU, 01745 710232, clwydfryn@btinternet.com

"Lemon drizzle cake, Victoria sponge ... yummy!"

POWYS

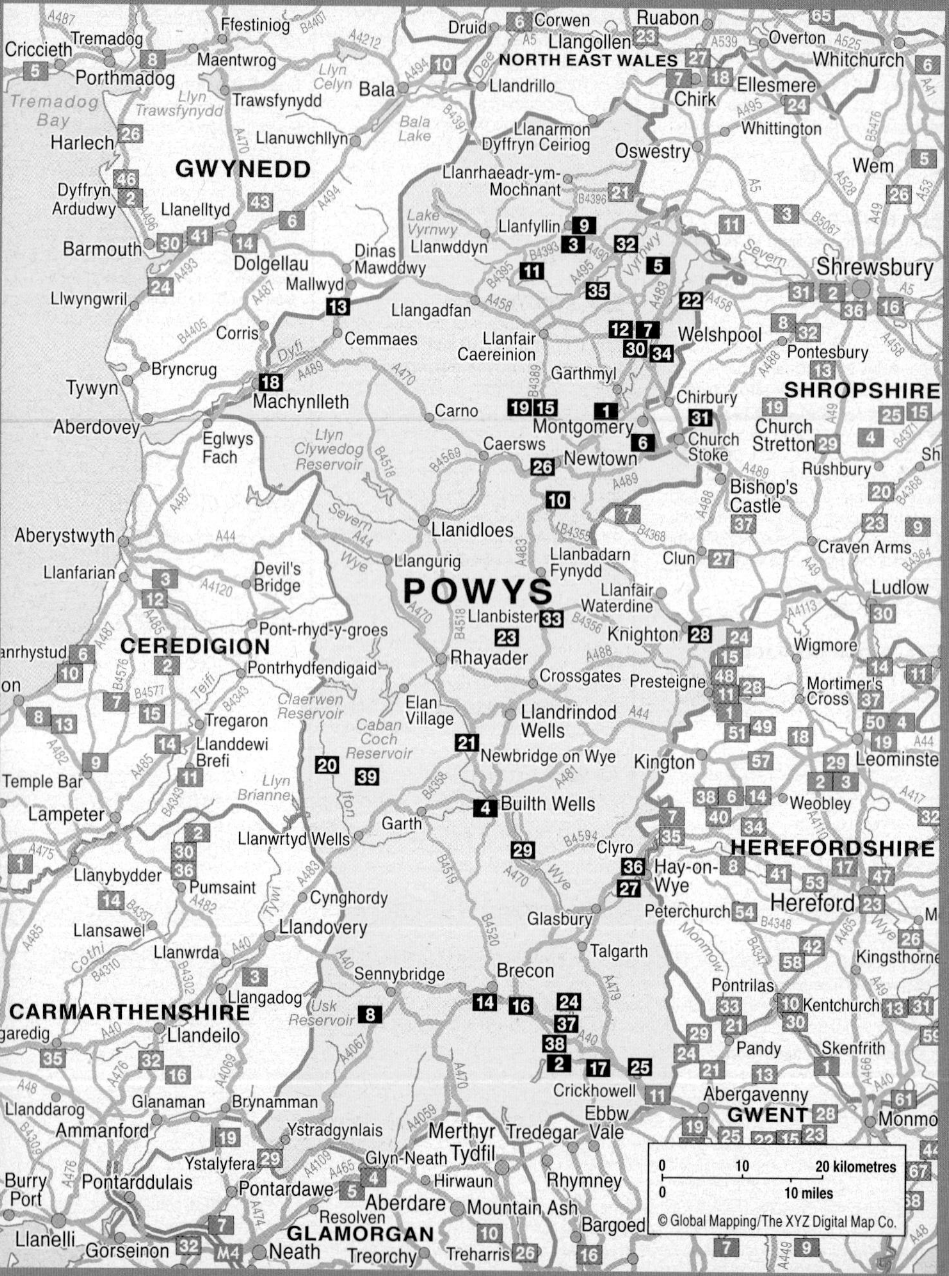

Ffestiniog
Corwen
Ruabon
Tremadog
Criccieth
Porthmadog
Maentwrog
Druid
Llangollen
Overton
Whitchurch
NORTH EAST WALES
Llyn Celyn
Bala
Llandrillo
Ellesmere
Chirk
Tremadog Bay
Llyn Trawsfynydd
Trawsfynydd
Bala Lake
Whittington
Harlech
Llanuwchllyn
Llanarmon Dyffryn Ceiriog
Oswestry
GWYNEDD
Wem
Dyffryn Ardudwy
Llanrhaeadr-ym-Mochnant
Llanelltyd
Lake Vyrnwy
Llanfyllin
Barmouth
Dolgellau
Dinas Mawddwy
Llanwddyn
Vyrnwy
Severn
Shrewsbury
Mallwyd
Llwyngwril
Llangadfan
Corris
Cemmaes
Llanfair Caereinion
Welshpool
Pontesbury
Dyfi
Bryncrug
Garthmyl
Tywyn
Machynlleth
SHROPSHIRE
Carno
Chirbury
Aberdovey
Montgomery
Church Stretton
Eglwys Fach
Llyn Clywedog Reservoir
Caersws
Newtown
Church Stoke
Rushbury
Bishop's Castle
Severn
Aberystwyth
Llanidloes
Wye
Llangurig
Llanbadarn Fynydd
Clun
Craven Arms
Llanfarian
Devil's Bridge
POWYS
Llanfair Waterdine
Ludlow
Llanbister
Pont-rhyd-y-groes
Knighton
anrhystud
CEREDIGION
Rhayader
Wigmore
Pontrhydfendigaid
Crossgates
Presteigne
Mortimer's Cross
on
Teifi
Claerwen Reservoir
Elan Village
Tregaron
Caban Coch Reservoir
Llandrindod Wells
Llanddewi Brefi
Newbridge on Wye
Kington
Leominster
Temple Bar
Llyn Brianne
Builth Wells
Weobley
Lampeter
Garth
Llanwrtyd Wells
Clyro
HEREFORDSHIRE
Hay-on-Wye
Llanybydder
Pumsaint
Tywi
Cynghordy
Hereford
Peterchurch
Glasbury
Llansawel
Llandovery
Monnow
Cothi
Llanwrda
Talgarth
Kingsthorne
Sennybridge
Brecon
Pontrilas
Llangadog
Kentchurch
CARMARTHENSHIRE
Usk Reservoir
garedig
Llandeilo
Pandy
Skenfrith
Crickhowell
Llanddarog
Glanaman
Brynamman
Abergavenny
Ebbw Vale
GWENT
Ammanford
Ystradgynlais
Merthyr Tydfil
Tredegar
Monmo
Glyn-Neath
Ystalyfera
Hirwaun
Rhymney
Burry Port
Pontarddulais
Pontardawe
Aberdare
Mountain Ash
Resolven
Bargoed
Llanelli
Gorseinon
GLAMORGAN
Neath
Treorchy
Treharris
0 10 20 kilometres
0 10 miles
© Global Mapping/The XYZ Digital Map Co.

Opening Dates

March

Sunday 31
22 Maesfron Hall and Gardens
38 Ty Cam

April

Tuesday 2
2 Ashford House

Wednesday 3
18 Grandma's Garden

Tuesday 9
2 Ashford House

Tuesday 16
2 Ashford House

Saturday 20
7 1 Church Bank

Sunday 21
1 Abernant
7 1 Church Bank
38 Ty Cam

Tuesday 23
2 Ashford House

Tuesday 30
2 Ashford House

Enjoy the wonderful views from one of the many seats; your senses will be rewarded . . .

May

Saturday 4
23 Mill Cottage
35 Tan-y-Llyn

Sunday 5
23 Mill Cottage
29 Pontsioni House
35 Tan-y-Llyn
38 Ty Cam

Monday 6
23 Mill Cottage

Tuesday 7
2 Ashford House

Friday 10
12 Dingle Nurseries & Garden

Saturday 11
12 Dingle Nurseries & Garden
31 Priest Weston Gardens

Sunday 12
10 Cwm-Weeg
21 Llysdinam
31 Priest Weston Gardens

Tuesday 14
2 Ashford House

Sunday 19
4 Caer Beris Manor Hotel
10 Cwm-Weeg
17 Gliffaes Country House Hotel

Tuesday 21
2 Ashford House

Saturday 25
23 Mill Cottage

Sunday 26
4 Caer Beris Manor Hotel
10 Cwm-Weeg
20 Llwyn Madoc
38 Ty Cam
39 Tyn y Cwm

Tuesday 28
2 Ashford House

June

Saturday 1
35 Tan-y-Llyn

Sunday 2
10 Cwm-Weeg
19 Gregynog Hall & Garden
29 Pontsioni House
33 The Rock House
35 Tan-y-Llyn

Tuesday 4
2 Ashford House

Saturday 8
31 Priest Weston Gardens

Sunday 9
10 Cwm-Weeg
13 Esgair Angell
14 Ffrwdgrech House
25 The Neuadd
31 Priest Weston Gardens

Tuesday 11
2 Ashford House

National Gardens Weekend

Saturday 15
23 Mill Cottage

Sunday 16
10 Cwm-Weeg
13 Esgair Angell
15 Fraithwen
23 Mill Cottage
26 Newtowns Milford Road Gardens
27 Pen-y-Maes
33 The Rock House
38 Ty Cam

Tuesday 18
2 Ashford House

Friday 21
30 Powis Castle Garden

Saturday 22
5 Cartref

Sunday 23
1 Abernant
5 Cartref
9 Creigle, 8 Penybryn
10 Cwm-Weeg

Tuesday 25
2 Ashford House

Saturday 29
7 1 Church Bank

Sunday 30
7 1 Church Bank
10 Cwm-Weeg
16 Glanusk

July

Tuesday 2
2 Ashford House

Saturday 6
35 Tan-y-Llyn

Sunday 7
10 Cwm-Weeg
35 Tan-y-Llyn

Tuesday 9
2 Ashford House

Saturday 13
32 Rhosddu House

Sunday 14
10 Cwm-Weeg
37 Treberfydd

Tuesday 16
2 Ashford House

Sunday 21
10 Cwm-Weeg
38 Ty Cam

Tuesday 23
2 Ashford House

Saturday 27
31 Priest Weston Gardens

Sunday 28
10 Cwm-Weeg
31 Priest Weston Gardens

Tuesday 30
2 Ashford House

August

Sunday 4
3 Bachie Uchaf
10 Cwm-Weeg
15 Fraithwen

Tuesday 6
2 Ashford House

Sunday 11
8 Crai Gardens
10 Cwm-Weeg
22 Maesfron Hall and Gardens
39 Tyn y Cwm

Tuesday 13
2 Ashford House

Sunday 18
10 Cwm-Weeg
Tuesday 20
2 Ashford House
Sunday 25
10 Cwm-Weeg
38 Ty Cam
Tuesday 27
2 Ashford House

September

Sunday 1
10 Cwm-Weeg
Tuesday 3
2 Ashford House
Tuesday 10
2 Ashford House
Tuesday 17
2 Ashford House
Tuesday 24
2 Ashford House

October

Saturday 12
12 Dingle Nurseries & Garden
Sunday 13
12 Dingle Nurseries & Garden
Thursday 24
17 Gliffaes Country House Hotel

Gardens open to the public

2 Ashford House
12 Dingle Nurseries & Garden
18 Grandma's Garden
19 Gregynog Hall & Garden
30 Powis Castle Garden

By appointment only

6 Castell y Gwynt
11 Cyfie Farm
24 Neuadd
28 Pont Faen House
34 Rowan
36 Tawryn

Also open by Appointment ☎

1 Abernant
5 Cartref
7 1 Church Bank
14 Ffrwdgrech House
15 Fraithwen
21 Llysdinam
23 Mill Cottage
25 The Neuadd
26 Glynderyn, Newtowns Milford Road Gardens
31 Priest Weston Gardens
31 Quarry House, Priest Weston Gardens
31 Ty'n y Bryn, Priest Weston Gardens

Examples of archaic sundials, fossilised wood and stone heads . . .

The Gardens

1 ABERNANT

Garthmyl SY15 6RZ. J A & B M Gleave, 01686 640494, john.gleave@mac.com. *On A483 mid-way between Welshpool & Newtown (both 8m). 1½ m S of Garthmyl. Approached over steep humpback bridge, then straight ahead through gate. No parking for coaches.* Home-made teas. **Adm £3.50, chd free. Sun 21 Apr, Sun 23 June (11-5). Visitors also welcome by appt Apr to July.**

Approx 3 acres incl cherry orchard, roses, knot garden, lavender, box hedging, rockery, pond, shrubs, ornamental trees, raised specimen fern beds in natural setting. Examples of archaic sundials, fossilised wood and stone heads. Additional woodland of 9 acres, pond and stream with borrowed views of the Severn Valley. April - 90 cherry trees blossom, picnics welcome.

2 ◆ ASHFORD HOUSE

Talybont-on-Usk LD3 7YR. Mrs E Anderson, 01874 676271. *6½ m SE of Brecon. Off A40 on B4558. 1m SE of Talybont-on-Usk.* **Adm £3, chd free. For NGS: Every Tue 2 Apr to 24 Sept (2-5). For other opening times and information, please phone.**

1-acre walled garden surrounded by woodland and wild garden approx 4 acres altogether. Mixed shrub and herbaceous borders; meadow garden and pond; alpine house and beds; vegetables. A relaxed plantsman's garden. Weekly openings mean visitors may enjoy a peaceful garden in its everyday state. Wheelchair access to main garden only.

ASHLEY FARM
See Herefordshire

3 NEW BACHIE UCHAF

Bachie Road, Llanfyllin SY22 5NF. Glyn & Glenys Lloyd. *S of Llanfyllin. Going towards Welshpool on A490 turn R onto Bachie Rd after Llanfyllin primary school. Keep straight for 0.8m. Take drive R uphill at cottage on L.* Home-made teas. **Adm £4, chd free. Sun 4 Aug (2-5).**

Inspiring, colourful hillside country garden. Gravel paths meander around extensive planting and over streams cascading down into ponds. Specimen trees, shrubs and veg garden. Enjoy the wonderful views from one of the many seats; your senses will be rewarded.

BRILLEY COURT
See Herefordshire

BRYAN'S GROUND
See Herefordshire

4 CAER BERIS MANOR HOTEL

Builth Wells LD2 3NP. Mr & Mrs Peter & Katharine Smith, www.caerberis.com. *W edge Builth Wells. From Builth Wells town centre take A483 signed Llandovery. Caer Beris Manor is on L as you leave Builth.* Home-made teas. **Adm £5, chd free. Sun 19, Sun 26 May (11-5).**

27 acres of mature parklands planted early C20 by Lord Swansea. Many varied specimen trees forming Arboretum. Large displays of rhododendrons at time of opening. 3 sites of Special Scientific Interest. Concert by Builth Wells Ladies Voice Choir. Sunday lunches. Afternoon teas. Lower parkland can be accessed by car or wheelchair.

5 CARTREF

Sarnau, nr Arddleen, Llanymynech SY22 6QL. Neil & Stella Townsend, 01938 590485, stella@tiscali.co.uk. *8m N of Welshpool. Take A483 from Welshpool towards Oswestry. Turn L after 6m at Arddleen, bear R then turn R towards Sarnau. Turn R after 1m. Continue for approx ½ m. Cartref is on L.* Home-made teas. **Adm £3, chd free. Sat 22, Sun 23 June (10-4). Visitors also welcome by appt.**

1-acre modern cottage garden with an emphasis on attracting wildlife and

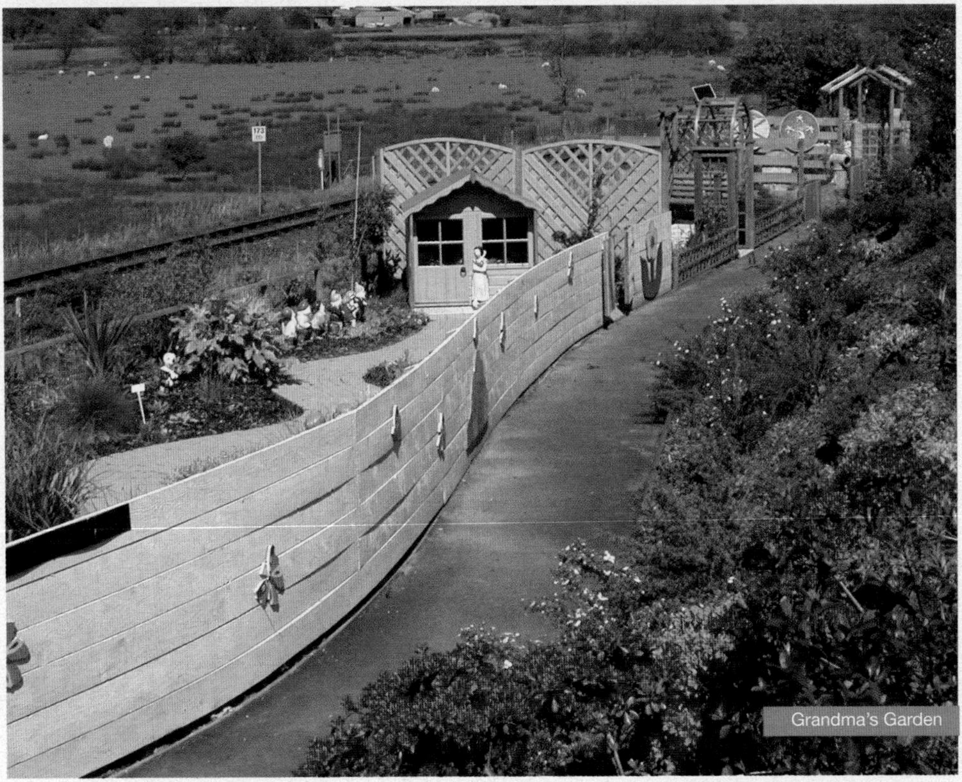

Grandma's Garden

recycling materials. Woodland, ponds, perennial borders and a kitchen garden give yr-round interest. Meandering paths join areas and give unexpected views within the garden. Spring bulbs make the garden particularly pretty in April and May. Dragonfly weekend.

6 CASTELL Y GWYNT

Llandyssil, Montgomery SY15 6HR. John & Jacqui Wynn-Jones, 01686 668569, jacquiwj@btinternet.com. *2m out of Montgomery on the Sarn Rd, 1st R, 1st R.* Home-made teas. **Adm £3.50, chd free. Visitors welcome by appt Apr to Aug.**

1½ -acre garden at 900ft, set within 6 acres of land managed for wildlife. Native woodland corridors with mown rides surround hayfield/wild flower meadow and pool with turf roofed summerhouse. Enclosed kitchen garden with boxed beds of vegetables, fruit and cutting flowers, greenhouse and orchard. Shrubberies, deep mixed borders and more formal areas close to house. Outstanding views of Welsh mountains. Circular path around the whole property which gives unique views of the house, garden and surrounding countryside. Bring good footwear and enjoy the walk.

7 1 CHURCH BANK

Welshpool SY21 7DR. Mel & Heather Parkes, 01938 559112. *Centre of Welshpool. Church Bank leads onto Salop Rd from Church St. Follow one way system & use Main Car Park then short walk - follow signs.* Home-made teas. **Adm £3, chd free. Sat 20, Sun 21 Apr, Sat 29, Sun 30 June (12-5). Visitors also welcome by appt Apr to Sept.**

A jewel in the town, Gothic arch over a zig zag path leads to exotic arbours in the intimate rear garden of an old town house. Sounds of water fill the air and interesting plants fill the space. Exciting alterations for this year, the garden has been enlarged and extensively revised. Enjoy the new garden room.

CLOISTER GARDEN

See Herefordshire

8 NEW CRAI GARDENS

Crai LD3 8YU. *13m SW of Brecon. Turn W off A4067 signed Crai. Village hall is 50yds straight ahead; park here for admission & information about gardens.* Home-made teas in the village hall. **Combined adm £5, chd free. Sun 11 Aug (2-6).**

Eight gardens in the Crai valley which offer a variety of sizes and styles, of planting and hard landscaping.

9 CREIGLE, 8 PENYBRYN

8 Penybryn, High Street, Llanfyllin SY22 5AP. Elaine Watts. *Centre of Llanfyllin. Next door to Seeds Restaurant.* Home-made teas. **Adm £3, chd free. Sun 23 June (2-5).**

A large cottage garden with vegetables and flowers situated in the very centre of a small town.

10 CWM-WEEG
Dolfor, Newtown SY16 4AT. Dr W Schaefer & Mr K D George. *4½ m SE of Newtown. Take A489 E from Newtown for 1½ m, turn R towards Dolfor. After 2m turn L down farm track, signed at entrance.* Home-made teas. **Adm £3.50, chd free. Every Sun 12 May to 1 Sept (2-5).**
2½ -acre garden set within 22 acres of wild flower meadows and bluebell woodland with stream centred around C15 farmhouse (open by prior arrangement). Formal garden in English landscape tradition with vistas, grottos, lawns and extensive borders terraced with stone walls, translates older garden vocabulary into an innovative C21 concept. Featured in BBC Wales, - I own Britain's best Garden. Limited access.

11 CYFIE FARM
Llanfihangel, Llanfyllin SY22 5JE. Group Captain Neil & Mrs Claire Bale, 01691 648451, info@cyfiefarm.co.uk, www.cyfiefarm.co.uk. *6m SE of Lake Vyrnwy. B490 N from Llanfyllin, turn L B4393 after ½ m towards Lake Vyrnwy. After approx 4m, L B4382 signed Llanfihangel/Dolanog. Through Llanfihangel 1½ m towards Dolanog, 1st L, 3rd on L.* Light refreshments. **Adm £3.50, chd free. Visitors welcome by appt. 2 days notice required.**
Beautiful 1-acre hillside garden with spectacular views of Vyrnwy valley and Welsh hills. Linger over the roses or wander through the woodland garden with rhododendrons and bluebell banks. Many places to sit and contemplate the stunning views. New this yr - wild flower meadow. Unusual garden statues. Limited wheelchair access.

12 ◆ DINGLE NURSERIES & GARDEN
Welshpool SY21 9JD. Mr & Mrs D Hamer, 01938 555145, www.dinglenurseries.co.uk. *2m NW of Welshpool. Take A490 towards Llanfyllin & Guilsfield. After 1m turn L at sign for Dingle Nurseries & Garden.* **Adm £3.50, chd free. For NGS: Fri 10, Sat 11 May, Sat 12, Sun 13 Oct (9-5). For other opening times and information, please phone or see garden website.**
RHS recommended 4½ -acre garden on S-facing site, sloping down to lakes surrounded by yr-round interest. Beds mostly colour themed with a huge variety of rare and unusual trees, ornamental shrubs and herbaceous plants. Set in hills of mid Wales this beautiful and well known garden attracts visitors from Britain and abroad. Open all yr except 24 Dec - 2 Jan.

EDGE VILLA
See Shropshire

13 NEW ESGAIR ANGELL
Aberangell, Machynlleth SY20 9QJ. Carole Jones. *In Dovey Forest, Aberangell, just off A470, midway between Dolgellau & Machynlleth. From A470, turn into village, passing Caravans on R, to small Xrds. Carry straight on, through black & white gateposts & into forest, for approx 2m, passing forestry track & gated rd on the L. At the next Xrds, turn L, signed Aberlefenni & drive up steep hill for about 200m. At bungalow on corner, turn R, you will find Esgair Angell slightly further on at end of rd.* Home-made teas and refreshments. **Adm £4, chd free. Sun 9, Sun 16 June (12-5).**
The garden of about 2 acres, sits above the R Angell, within the Dovey Forest and Snowdonia National Park. A crystal-clear lake, which supports an abundance of plant and animal life is surrounded by a small wood, a wildlife meadow, our grand giant oak, vegetable garden and the aviaries that house our families of eagle owls and barn owls. Limited wheelchair access, mainly laid to lawn. Access on gravelled area above the lake, offering extensive views of the garden.

14 FFRWDGRECH HOUSE
Ffrwdgrech, Brecon LD3 8LB. Mr & Mrs Michael Evans, 01874 622519, ffrwdgrech@btinternet.com. *½ m W of Brecon. Enter Brecon from A40 bypass. Take 3rd turning on R, Ffrwdgrech Rd. In ¾ m at oak gate, Lodge on L.* Home-made teas. **Adm £3, chd free. Sun 9 June (2-5). Visitors also welcome by appt Apr to Oct. Refreshments by prior arrangement.**
7-acre Victorian pleasure garden, lake, specimen trees incl fine examples of ginkgo, swamp cyprus, davidia involucrata, subtropical shrubs, rhododendrons and azaleas. Beautiful stream and waterfall, woodland walks. Views of Brecon Beacons. Robert Lugar designed garden, landscape and water features. Award winning woodland. Listed lawns for rare fungi specimens. Bat sanctuary. Limited access.

15 FRAITHWEN
Tregynon SY16 3EW. Sydney Thomas, 01686 650307. *6m N of Newtown. On B4389 mid-way between villages of Bettws Cedewain & Tregynon.* Home-made teas. **Adm £3, chd free. Sun 16 June, Sun 4 Aug (2-6). Visitors also welcome by appt Mar to Sept.**
1½ -acre established garden with herbaceous borders, rockeries and ponds. Planted with rare plants for yr-round interest. Re opening after long absence due to illness. Plants in flower every day of the year. Partial wheelchair access. Some steps, gravel and slopes.

Linger over the roses or wander through the woodland garden . . . .

GLANGRWYNEY COURT
See Gwent

16 GLANUSK
Llanfrynach, Brecon LD3 7UY. Mike & Lorraine Lewis. *1½ m SE of Brecon. Leave A40 signed Llanfrynach, Pencelli. Cross narrow bridge (R Usk), 40 metres on R.* Home-made teas. **Adm £3.50, chd free. Sun 30 June (2-6).**
2-acre garden on the R Usk. Steep bank has prairie and perennial planting criss-crossed with paths. Old orchard incl specimen trees, grass pattern, rose border and small woodland walk leading to stone circle. The formal garden incl borders, boxballs, rose pergola and beech hedge.

17 GLIFFAES COUNTRY HOUSE HOTEL
Gliffaes Rd, Crickhowell NP8 1RH. Mrs N Brabner & Mr & Mrs J C Suter, www.gliffaes.com. *3½ m W of Crickhowell. 1m off A40, 2½ m W of Crickhowell.* Light refreshments (incl soup). Cream teas (May only). **Adm £3, chd £1. Sun 19 May (2-6); Thur 24 Oct (11-4).**
The Gliffaes garden lies in a dream position on a plateau 120ft above the spectacular fast flowing R Usk. It incl breath-taking views of the Brecon Beacons, 33 acres of parkland, lawns, an ornamental pond, spring bulbs, rhododendrons, azaleas, heathers, shrubs, ornamental trees, fine maples.

18 ◆ GRANDMA'S GARDEN
Dolguog Estates, Felingerrig, Machynlleth SY20 8UJ. Diana & Richard Rhodes, 01654 702244, www.plasdolguog.co.uk/grandmasgarden. *1½ m E of Machynlleth. Turn L off A489 Machynlleth to Newtown rd. Follow brown tourist signs to Plas Dolguog Hotel.* **Adm £4, chd £1.50. For NGS: Wed 3 Apr (10.30-4.30). For other opening times and information, please phone or see garden website.**
Inspiration for the senses, unique, fascinating, educational and fun. Strategic seating, continuous new attractions, wildlife abundant, 9 acres of peace. Sculptures, poetry arboretum. Seven sensory gardens, wildlife pond, riverside boardwalk, stone circle, labyrinth. Azaleas and bluebells in May. Children welcome. Open every Sun & Wed (10.30-4.30).

19 ◆ GREGYNOG HALL & GARDEN
Tregynon, Newtown SY16 3PW. Gregynog, 01686 650224, www.gregynog.wales.ac.uk. *5m N of Newtown. From main A483, take turning for Berriew. In Berriew follow sign for Bettws then for Tregynon.* **Adm £3, chd £1 (£2.50 car park fee also payable). For NGS: Sun 2 June (11-4.30). For other opening times and information, please phone or see garden website.**
Grade I listed garden set within 750 acres of Gregynog Estate with fountains, lily lake, and water garden. A mass display of rhododendrons and yew hedge create a spectacular backdrop to the sunken lawns. Printed walks leaflet available. Special events throughout the year. Shop and Courtyard Cafe open for lunches and welsh afternoon teas. Gravel paths in some areas.

Inspiration for the senses, unique, fascinating, educational and fun . . .

HILL HOUSE FARM
See Herefordshire

IVY COTTAGE
See Herefordshire

LLANFOIST VILLAGE GARDENS
See Gwent

LLANGEDWYN HALL
See North East Wales

LLANTHONY AND DISTRICT GARDENS
See Gwent

20 LLWYN MADOC
Beulah, Llanwrtyd Wells LD5 4TU. Patrick & Miranda Bourdillon. *8m W of Builth Wells. On A483 at Beulah take rd towards Abergwesyn for 1m. Drive on R.* Home-made teas. **Adm £3, chd free. Sun 26 May (2-6).**
Terraced garden in attractive wooded valley overlooking newly restored lake; yew hedges; rose garden with pergola; kitchen garden and small orchard; azaleas and rhododendrons.

21 LLYSDINAM
Newbridge-on-Wye LD1 6NB. Sir John & Lady Venables-Llewelyn & Llysdinam Charitable Trust, 01597 861190, elster@f2s.com. *5m SW of Llandrindod Wells. Turn W off A470 at Newbridge-on-Wye; turn R immed after crossing R Wye; entrance up hill.* Home-made teas. **Adm £3, chd free. Sun 12 May (2-6). Visitors also welcome by appt.**
Llysdinam Gardens are among the loveliest in Mid Wales, especially noted for a magnificent display of rhododendrons and azaleas in May. Covering some 6 acres in all, they command sweeping views down the Wye Valley. Successive family members have developed the gardens over the last 150yrs to incl woodland with specimen trees, large herbaceous and shrub borders and a water garden, all of which provide varied and colourful planting throughout the year. The Victorian walled kitchen garden and extensive greenhouses grow a wide variety of vegetables, hothouse fruit, and exotic plants. Gravel paths.

22 MAESFRON HALL AND GARDENS
Trewern, Welshpool SY21 8EA. Dr & Mrs TD Owen, www.maesfron.co.uk. *4m E of Welshpool. On N side of A458 Welshpool to Shrewsbury rd.* Home-made teas. **Adm £4, chd free. Sun 31 Mar, Sun 11 Aug (2-5).**
Georgian house (partly open) built in Italian villa style set in 4 acres of S-facing gardens on lower slopes of Moel-y-Golfa with panoramic views of The Long Mountain. Terraces, walled kitchen garden, tropical garden, restored Victorian conservatories, tower and shell grotto. Woodland and parkland walks with wide variety of trees. Sun 31 March - Annual Grand Easter Egg Hunt in the grounds with over 300 eggs to be found. Sun 11 August a lazy Summer's afternoon with a free glass of Pimms. Some gravel, steps and slopes.

23 MILL COTTAGE
Abbeycwmhir LD1 6PH. Mr & Mrs B D Parfitt, 01597 851935, nkmillcottage@yahoo.co.uk, www.abbeycwmhir.co.uk. *8m N of Llandrindod Wells. Turn L off A483 1m N of Crossgates r'about, then 3½ m on L, signed Abbeycwmhir. Limited parking.* **Adm £3, chd free. Sat 4, Sun 5, Mon 6, Sat 25 May, Sat 15, Sun 16 June (12-6). Visitors also welcome by appt May to Sept. Please phone first.**
⅓ -acre streamside garden in spectacular valley setting on the Glyndwr Way, consisting mainly of mature, rare and unusual trees and shrubs, particularly interesting to the plantsman. Rockery with numerous ericaceous plants and interesting water feature. Beautiful church and Abbey ruins nearby on a national trail - Glydr's Way.

Cwm-Weeg

MONTPELIER COTTAGE
See Herefordshire

24 NEUADD

Llangors, Brecon LD3 7TS. Paul & Kathleen Johnson, 01874 658670, pckmj@tiscali.co.uk. *6m E of Brecon. On B4560 on N edge of village.* **Adm £3, chd free. Visitors welcome by appt May to Sept. Refreshments by arrangement for groups.**

1-acre informal garden set around Victorian Gothic Revival house, designed to blend harmoniously with its rural setting and gardened organically to encourage wildlife. Mixed borders feature shrub roses, interesting perennials, native and cottage garden plants, bulbs, grasses and ferns. A developing woodland garden contains plants tolerant of dry shade. Small vegetable and fruit garden. Mainly grass paths, difficult for wheelchairs if wet.

25 THE NEUADD

Llanbedr, nr Crickhowell NP8 1SP. Robin & Philippa Herbert, 01873 812164. *1m NE of Crickhowell. Leave Crickhowell by Llanbedr Rd. At junction with Great Oak Rd bear L and continue up hill for 0.9m, garden on L. Ample parking.* Home-made teas. **Adm £3.50, chd free. Sun 9 June (2-6). Visitors also welcome by appt June.**

Robin and Philippa Herbert have worked on the restoration of the garden at the Neuadd since 1999 and have planted a wide range of unusual trees and shrubs in the dramatic setting of the Brecon Beacons National Park. One of the major features is the walled garden, which has both traditional and decorative planting of fruit, vegetables and flowers. There is also a woodland walk with ponds, streams and a formal garden with flowering terraces. Decorative walled garden. Owner is a wheelchair user and nearly all garden accessible, however some paths are quite steep.

GROUP OPENING

26 NEWTOWNS MILFORD ROAD GARDENS

Newtown SY16 3HD. *½ m W of Newtown. On B4568 Newtown to Aberhafesp rd. Glynderyn, 1st gate past Dolerw Park Drive. Ty Ffynnon, Milford Park, 1st rd on R past Dolerw Park Drive.* Home-made teas. **Combined adm £4, chd free. Sun 16 June (2-5).**

GLYNDERYN
Janet & Frank Podmore
Visitors also welcome by appt. 01686 626745

TY FFYNNON
Russell & Jackie Morgan

Glynderyn - lovingly restored by plant enthusiast, this 1/4 -acre garden with geometric beds complements the 1965 bungalow. Oblong rose and raised alpine beds, curved pergola for wisterias begin the journey around the garden with views across the valley. Trees, shrubs, small pond, wild flower and vegetable patch create diverse interest. Ty Ffynnon - the garden of over 1/4 acre welcomes you with a great wisteria. Steps and paths lead you up the terraced garden filled with conifers, shrubs ferns and roses with spectacular views across the valley. A secret garden filled with woodland plants is an additional delight. Plants for sale at Glynderyn only.

THE PANT
See Gwent

27 PEN-Y-MAES
Hay-on-Wye HR3 5PP. Shân Egerton. *1m SW of Hay-on-Wye. On B4350 towards Brecon.* Cream teas. **Adm £4, chd free.** **Sun 16 June (2-5).**
2-acre garden incl mixed herbaceous borders; topiary; walled formal kitchen garden; shrub, modern and climbing roses, peony borders, espaliered pears. Fine mulberry. Beautiful dry stone walling and mature trees. Great double view of Black Mountains and the Brecon Beacons. Emphasis on foliage and shape. Artist's garden.

28 PONT FAEN HOUSE
Farrington Lane, Knighton LD7 1LA. Mr John & Mrs Brenda Morgan, 01547 520847. *S of Knighton off Ludlow Rd. W from Ludlow on A4113 into Knighton. 1st L after 20mph sign before school.* Home-made teas. **Adm £3, chd free.** **Visitors welcome by appt Apr to Sept.**
Colourful 1/2 -acre garden, full of flowers, surrounds house on edge of town. Paths through floriferous arches and gazebos lead from shady, ferny corners to deep borders around lawns. Trees incl specimen beech, shrubs, perennials and annuals, fish pond and small vegetable plot. Seats with vistas through garden to hills beyond.

29 PONTSIONI HOUSE
Aberedw, Builth Wells LD2 3SQ. Mr & Mrs Jonathan Reeves. *3m SE of Builth Wells. On B4567 between Erwood Bridge & Aberedw on Radnorshire side of R Wye.* Home-made teas. **Adm £3, chd free.** **Sun 5 May, Sun 2 June (2.30-7).**
With a background of old ruins and steep rocky woodland, this Wye Valley garden has been created mainly over the last 10yrs. Herbaceous and shrub borders, terraces and natural rockery merge with lawns, bluebell and young rhododendron bank. Walks through wildflower meadow along a mile of old railway line with bluebell woods and walks up to the Aberedw Rocks. Spectacular rocky and woody situation. Extensive bluebells. Brecon & Radnor Express.

Walks through wildflower meadow . . .

30 ◆ POWIS CASTLE GARDEN
Welshpool SY21 8RF. National Trust, 01938 551929, www.nationaltrust.org.uk. *1m S of Welshpool. From Welshpool take A490 S towards Newtown. After 3/4 m turn R up lane for 1/4 m.* **Adm £9.60, chd £4.80. For NGS: Fri 21 June (11-5). For other opening times and information, please phone or see garden website.**
Laid out in early C18 with finest remaining examples of Italian terraces in Britain. Richly planted herbaceous borders; enormous yew hedges; lead statuary, large wild flower areas. One of the NT's finest gardens. National Collection of *Laburnum*. Short 'behind the scenes' tours running throughout the day. Step free route around the garden, gravel paths, due to steep slopes only 4-wheeled PMV's are allowed in.

GROUP OPENING

31 NEW PRIEST WESTON GARDENS
Priest Weston, Montgomery SY15 6DF. *Approx 4m E Montgomery. From Churchstoke take unclassified rd signed for Priest Weston, 3m. House will be signed from finger post in Priestweston.* Home-made teas at Quarry House. **Combined adm £3.50, chd free.** **Sat 11, Sun 12 May, Sat 8, Sun 9 June, Sat 27, Sun 28 July (10-5).**

NEW QUARRY HOUSE
Roger & Christine Dixon
Visitors also welcome by appt Apr to Sept.
01938 561397
chris.rog.dixon@hotmail.co.uk

NEW TY'N Y BRYN
Mr & Mrs M Watkins
Visitors also welcome by appt Apr to Sept. Small groups welcome.
01938 561694

Quarry House stands in an elevated position with stunning views south towards the Kerry Ridgeway and west towards the Snowdonia. The garden has evolved over 18yrs into a series of herbaceous borders, accessed by steep zig-zagged grass paths and steps. A lower lawn is bordered by lilac trees Ty'n y Bryn. A path leads up from Quarry House to a large organic vegetable garden then on to a wild flower meadow (harebells, lady's bedstraw) where you may picnic. A path then returns to the garden of Quarry House. These gardens are not suitable for people who are unsure of foot.

32 RHOSDDU HOUSE
Llansantffraid SY22 6TH. Margaret Clennett & Peter Stokes. *3m SSW of Llansantffraid. From Welshpool on A490 after 7m turn R (signed Trefnannau) at a L bend. After 1/2 m take 1st L & continue on a winding lane 1 1/2 m.* **Adm £3.50, chd free.** **Sat 13 July (2-5).**
1-acre informal rural garden with views of the Vrynwy valley. Wildlife pond, mixed island beds, vegetable plot, orchard, young and mature ornamental trees.

33 THE ROCK HOUSE

Llanbister LD1 6TN. Jude Boutle & Sue Cox. *10m N of Llandrindod Wells. From Llandrindod Wells, turn R off A483 at Llanbister onto B4356. Go through village, past school & war memorial on L, up short hill, over cattle grid & turn immed R up track (take care). Park on track & in quarry.* Home-made teas. **Adm £3.50, chd free. Sun 2, Sun 16 June (2-5).**

An acre of informal hillside garden at 1000ft, with sweeping views over Radnorshire Hills, managed using organic principles. The garden features hardy perennials and shrubs, raised beds, a walkway over a bog garden, dry shady border, fish and wildlife ponds, grazed bluebell meadow and a laburnum arch. There will be a children's quiz to keep small people busy in the garden and meadow. On 2nd June (only) come and meet some prickly visitors courtesy of Howey Hedgehog Rescue.

34 ROWAN

Leighton, Welshpool SY21 8HJ. Tinty Griffith, 01938 552197. *2m E of Welshpool. From Welshpool take B4388 (Buttington to Montgomery). At Leighton turn L after school then at church straight ahead between stone pillars. 1st on R, parking in churchyard.* Home-made teas. **Adm £3.50, chd free. Visitors welcome by appt Apr to July.**

1 acre of traditional plantsman's country garden with village church as backdrop. Discrete paths meander around island beds and mixed borders with irises, roses, unusual and rare plants, trees dripping with climbers and a series of planted pools and marshy areas. Lovely views over Montgomeryshire countryside and the borrowed landscape. Gravelled entrance, level grassed areas, some slopes.

STAPLETON CASTLE COURT GARDEN
See Herefordshire

STAUNTON PARK
See Herefordshire

35 TAN-Y-LLYN

Meifod SY22 6YB. Callum Johnston & Brenda Moor, www.tanyllyn-nursery.co.uk. *1m SE of Meifod. From Oswestry on A495 turn L in village, cross R Vyrnwy & climb hill for ½ m. From Welshpool on A490 look for Meifod sign on L just past Groesllwyd.* Home-made teas. **Adm £3, chd free (share to Powys Carers Service). Sat 4, Sun 5 May, Sat 1, Sun 2 June, Sat 6, Sun 7 July (2-5).**

Surrounded by woodland and pasture, Tanyllyn sits in a quiet valley above the Dyffryn Meifod in the old county of Montgomeryshire. The garden grows out of the landscape, and the surroundings are seen though portholes, sculpted hedges and openings in the trees. Exhibitions May: Kevan Hopson June: Michele Coxon July: Liz Hancock.

There will be a children's quiz to keep small people busy in the garden . . .

36 TAWRYN

6 Baskerville Court, Clyro HR3 5SS. Chris & Clive Young, 01497 821939. *1m NW of Hay-on-Wye. Leave A438 Hereford to Brecon rd at Clyro. Baskerville Court is behind church & Baskerville Arms Hotel. Please park in village.* **Adm £3, chd free. Visitors welcome by appt Apr to Oct.**

1-acre steeply-terraced garden on an oriental theme. Come and see the Ghost Dragon and the River of Slate. Lots of new crooked paths and planting. Stunning views of the Black Mountains and Kilvert's Church. Colour all yr. Talks by Chris on NGS and its charities to garden groups, WI etc. Please call for more information. 3 different talks to choose from. Proceeds to NGS.

37 TREBERFYDD

Llangasty, Bwlch, Brecon LD3 7PX. David Raikes, www.treberfydd.com. *6½ m E of Brecon. From Crickhowell take A40 toward Bwlch. Once through villiage of Bwlch, turn R on B4560 towards Llangorse (turning just past Gate Shop). Take 1st L marked for Pennorth. Entrance to Treberfyddd House is approx 2m down lane. From Brecon leave A40 at turning to Pennorth. After 2½ m you will see sign for Llangasty Church. Entrance to R, over cattle grid.* Home-made teas. **Adm £5, chd free. Sun 14 July (1-6).**

Grade 1-listed Victorian Gothic house with 10 acres of grounds designed by W A Nesfield. Magnificent Cedar of Lebanon, avenue of mature Beech, towering Atlantic Cedars, Victorian rockery, herbaceous border and manicured lawns ideal for a picnic. Wonderful views of the Black Mountains. Beacons Nurseries in walled garden. House tours at 2 and 4pm, art exhibition, outdoor sculpture.

38 TY CAM

Talybont on Usk, Brecon, Powys LD3 7JD. Harry & Ceri Chapman. *7m E of Brecon off A40. Located nr centre of village. Look out for the mushrooms.* **Adm £2, chd free. Suns 31 Mar, 21 Apr, 5, 26 May, 16 June, 21 July, 25 Aug (2-6).**

Small garden of secret surprises on 3 levels with steps built on a railway embankment. Attractive features incl patios, decks, pergolas, ponds and waterfalls. Many choice herbaceous plants, trees and shrubs. Small 'menagerie', chickens, aviary birds and a resident rabbit! Woodturning workshop and craft gallery featuring works by local artists. Woodturning workshop and craft gallery.

39 NEW TYN Y CWM

Beulah, Llanwrtyd Wells LD5 4TS. Steve & Christine Carrow. *10m W of Builth Wells. On A483 at Beulah take rd towards Abergwesyn for 2m. Drive drops down to L.* Home-made teas. **Adm £3, chd free. Sun 26 May, Sun 11 Aug (2-5.30). Also opening Llwyn Madoc (Sun 26 May only).**

Garden mainly started 11 years ago, lower garden has spring/woodland area, raised beds mixed with vegetables, fruit trees, fruit and flowers. Perennial borders, summer house gravel paths through rose and clematis pergola. Upper garden, partly sloped, includes bog, winter, water gardens and perennial beds with unusual slate steps. Beautiful views. Property bounded by small rive. Lower garden has wide gravel mainly level paths. Upper garden is grassed with slopes and not suitable for wheelchairs.

UPPER TAN HOUSE
See Herefordshire

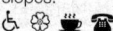

"Lemon drizzle cake, Victoria sponge ... yummy!"

Abernant

Powys County Volunteers

County Organisers

South Sarah Lee, Tredwern, Llandefalle, Brecon LD3 5PP, 01874 754627, sarahlee@berringtons.com
North Christine Scott, Bryn-y-Llidiart, Cefn Coch, Llanrhaeadr ym Mochnant, Oswestry SY10 0BP, 01691 780080, christinemargaretscott@yahoo.com

County Treasurer

North Gwyneth Jackson-Jones, Bryn yr Aur, Delwyn Lane, Llanfyllin SY22 5LB, 01691 648578, g.jackson-jones@tiscali.co.uk
South Edward Gilbertson, Cathedine Hill, Cathadine, Bwlch, Brecon LD3 7SX, 01874 732267, edwardgilbertson@aol.com

Publicity

North Group Captain Neil Bale, Cyfie Farm, Llanfihangel, Llanfyllin SY22 5JE, 01691 648451, info@cyfiefarm.co.uk

Assistant County Organisers

North Penny Davies, Plas Derwen, Llansantffraid, Powys SY22 6SX, 01691 828373, digbydavies@aol.com
South Shân Egerton, Pen-y-Maes, Hay-on-Wye HR3 5PP, 01497 820423, sre@waitrose.com
North Susan See-Paynton, Oerle Hall, Berriew SY21 8QX, 01686 650531, susanakeen@aol.co.uk
South Katherine Smith, Caer Beris Manor, Builth Wells, Powys LD2 3NP, 01982 552601, caerberis@btconnect.com

Early Openings 2014

Plan your garden visiting well ahead – put these dates in your 2014 diary!

Gardens across the country open from early January onwards – before the new Yellow Book is published – with glorious displays of colour including hellebores, aconites, snowdrops and carpets of spring bulbs.

Bedfordshire

Sun 26 January
King's Arms Garden

Buckinghamshire

Sun 23 February
Quainton Gardens

Cornwall

Suns 9, 16, 23 February
Coombegate Cottage

Cumbria

Sun 16 February
Lower Rowell Farm & Cottage
Summerdale House

Devon

Sun 2, Fri 14 February
Cherubeer Gardens

Suns 9, 16 February
Littleham House Cottage

Sat 15, Sun 16 February
1 Feebers Cottage

Essex

Groups welcome by appt at snowdrop time, late January to early March
Byndes Cottage

Sun 9 February
Writtle College

Gloucestershire

Sun 26 January
Lindors Country House

Suns 2, 16 February
Home Farm

Suns 9, 16 February
Kempsford Manor

Suns 16, 23 February
Trench Hill

Sun 23 February
Dr Jenner's House & Garden

Gwynedd

Sun 9 February
Plas Yn Rhiw

Sat 22 February
Penrhyn Castle

Hampshire

Sun 16 February
Bramdean House
The Down House

Fri 21, Sun 23, Mon 24 February
Little Court

Herefordshire

Thurs 6, 13, 20, 27 February
Ivy Croft

Wed 19 February
The Weir

Kent

Sat 8, Sun 9 February
Spring Platt

Sun 16 February
Copton Ash

Suns 16, 23 February
Mere House

Lancashire

Suns 2, 9, 16, 23 February
Weeping Ash

Lincolnshire

Sun 23 February
21 Chapel Street

Norfolk

Tue 28 January
The Mowle

Northamptonshire

Sun 23 February
Jericho

Somerset, Bristol & South Glos

Suns 2, 9 February
Rock House

Sun 9 February
East Lambrook Manor Gardens

Suffolk

Sun 16 February
Gable House

Surrey

Sun 16 February
Gatton Park

Sussex

Tues, Weds, Thurs 11, 12, 13, 18, 19, 20 February.

Fri 7 Mar Special Hellebore Day
Pembury House

Wiltshire

Sats, Suns 8, 9, 15, 16 February
Lacock Abbey Gardens

Sun 23 February
Avon Cottage

Yorkshire

Wed 26 February
Austwick Hall

Pembury House, Sussex

© Leigh Clapp

Accommodation available at NGS Gardens

We feature here a list of NGS gardens offering accommodation, listed by Yellow Book county. You will find contact details in the garden listing.

We are happy to provide this list to help you find accommodation, however please note:

The NGS has no statutory control over the establishments or their methods of operating. The NGS cannot become involved in legal or contractual matters and cannot get involved in seeking financial recompense. All liability for loss, disappointment, negligence or other damage is hereby excluded.

Bedfordshire

Luton Hoo Hotel Golf & Spa

Berkshire

Field Farm Cottage
Littlecote House Hotel
Rookwood Farm House, Stockcross Gardens
Sunningdale Park
Whitehouse Farm Cottage

Buckinghamshire

Danesfield House
Laplands Farm
Magnolia House, Grange Drive Wooburn
Nether Winchendon House
Westend House

Cambridgeshire

Chequer Cottage, Streetly End Gardens
39 Foster Road
Kenilworth Smallholding
Madingley Hall
Pavilion House

Carmarthenshire & Pembrokeshire

Blaenfforest
The Cors
The Crystal Garden
Dyffryn Fernant
Pant-y-fedwen
Picton Castle & Gardens
Rhosygilwen Mansion
Swan Cottage
Talardd
Ty Castell
Upton Castle Gardens

Cornwall

The Barn House
Benallack Barn
Boconnoc
Bonython Manor
Carminowe Valley Garden
Carwinion
Cosawes Barton
Creed House
Glendurgan
Hidden Valley Gardens
Trelissick
Trerice
Trevoole Farm
Trewithen

Cumbria

Askham Hall
Brackenrigg Lodge
Lakeside Hotel & Rocky Bank
Langholme Mill
Matson Ground
Olde Oaks
Rydal Hall
Swarthmoor Hall
Windy Hall

Derbyshire

Brick Kiln Farm
Stone Croft, Barlborough Gardens
Tissington Hall

Devon

Cliffe
Coombe Trenchard
Dartington Hall Gardens
The Downes
Durcombe Water
East Woodlands Farmhouse
Fursdon
Goren Farm
Langtrees
Regency House
The Stannary
Whitstone Bluebells
Whitstone Farm

Dorset

Deans Court
Domineys
Holworth Farmhouse
Marren
Pen Mill Farm
The Secret Garden
Windy Willums

Essex

Chippins
Hedingham Castle
Rookwoods

Glamorgan

Bryn-y-Ddafad
Gileston Manor
Miskin Manor Country Hotel
Slade

Gloucestershire

Barnsley House
Berrys Place Farm
Charingworth Court, Winchcombe Gardens
Kempsford Manor
Lindors Country House
Matara Gardens of Wellbeing
Sudeley Castle Gardens & Exhibitions
Wells Cottage

Gwent

April House, Coed-y-Paen Village Gardens
The Bell at Skenfrith
Brynderi
Castle House
Glangrwyney Court
Penpergwm Lodge

Gwynedd

Caerau Gardens
Coed Ty Mawr
Plas Cadnant
Plas Rhianfa

Hampshire

Ashen Bank, Sway Village Gardens
12 Christchurch Road
Durmast House
The Mill at Gordleton
Tylney Hall Hotel

Herefordshire

Brobury House Gardens
Caves Folly Nurseries
Holme Lacy House Hotel
Kentchurch Court, Kentchurch Gardens
Lawless Hill
Midland Farm
Montpelier Cottage
The Old Rectory, Byford
The Old Rectory, Thruxton
Wellbrook Manor
Wolferlow House

Isle of Wight

Northcourt Garden

Kent

Boldshaves
Canterbury Cathedral Gardens
Cottage Farm
Great Oaks House, Shipbourne Gardens
Hever Castle & Gardens
Mistral, Wye Gardens
Rock Farm
The Secret Gardens of Sandwich at The Salutation
Sissinghurst Castle
Wickham Lodge

Lancashire, Merseyside & Greater Manchester

Little Stubbins
Mill Barn
The Ridges
Sefton Villa, Sefton Park Gardens

Leicestershire & Rutland

The Grange
Hedgehog Hall
Hill Top Farm, Braunston Gardens

Lincolnshire

Goltho House
Hall Farm
Hope House
Marigold Cottage, Sutton on Sea Gardens
Stoke Rochford Hall

London

28 Old Devonshire Road
58A Teignmouth Road
West Lodge Park

Norfolk

Bagthorpe Hall
Blickling Hall Estate
Chaucer Barn
Hindringham Hall
Manor House Farm, Wellingham
The Old Rectory, Ridlington
Severals Grange

North East

Gibside
Loughbrow House
Thornley House
Wallington
Whalton Manor Gardens

North East Wales

Aberclwyd Manor
Bodysgallen Hall & Spa
33 Bryn Twr and Lynton
Dove Cottage
Firgrove
Tal-y-Bryn Farm

Northamptonshire

Dale House, Spratton Gardens

Nottinghamshire

Hodsock Priory Gardens
The Summer House
Thoresby Hall Hotel & Spa

Oxfordshire

Asthall Manor
Broughton Poggs & Filkins Gardens
Buttslade House, Sibford Gower Gardens
Gowers Close, Sibford Gower Gardens
South Newington House
Trinity College

Powys

Caer Beris Manor Hotel
Cyfie Farm
Esgair Angell
Gliffaes Country House Hotel
Grandma's Garden
Gregynog Hall & Garden
Llwyn Madoc
Mill Cottage
Quarry House, Priest Weston Gardens
Treberfydd
Tyn y Cwm

Shropshire

Brownhill House
The Citadel
Edge Villa
Goldstone Hall Gardens
Marehay Farm

Somerset, Bristol & South Gloucestershire

Binham Grange Gardens
Cherry Bolberry Farm
Church Farm House
Cricket House and Gardens
Farndon Thatch
Hangeridge Farmhouse
Harptree Court
Honeyhurst Farm
Self Realization Meditation Healing Centre Garden
Stoberry Garden
Ston Easton Park
Westbrook House

Staffordshire, Birmingham & West Midlands

Colour Mill
Woodbrooke Quaker Study Centre

Suffolk

Bays Farm
Fen House, Pakenham Gardens
The Lucy Redman Garden
Rosemary

Surrey

Coverwood Lakes
Great Fosters
7 Rose Lane

Sussex

Ashdown Park Hotel
Butlers Farmhouse
Copyhold Hollow
Holly House
King John's Lodge
Knellstone House
Lordington House
Newtimber Place
Ocklynge Manor
The Old Farmhouse
Pindars
South Grange
West Dean Gardens

Warwickshire

The Granary
The Limes, Avon Dassett Gardens
Springfield House, Warmington Village Gardens

Wiltshire

Becketts House, Edington Gardens
Broomsgrove Lodge
The Coach House, Dauntsey Gardens
The Mill House
The Pound House
Ridleys Cheer
Stourhead Garden
Wellaway
Whatley Manor

Worcestershire

Brook Farm
Nafford House, Eckington Gardens
Rectory Cottage

Yorkshire

Austwick Hall
Cold Cotes
Daneswell House, Stamford Bridge Gardens
Devonshire Mill
Dowthorpe Hall & Horse Pasture Cottage
Fawley House
Four Gables
Goldsborough Hall
Holly Croft
Low Hall, Dacre Banks & Summerbridge Gardens
Low Sutton
Lower Heugh Cottage Garden
Manor Farm
Millgate House
Oswaldkirk Hall
Ripley Castle Gardens
Rudding Park
Shandy Hall Gardens

Acknowledgements

Each year the NGS receives fantastic support from the community of garden photographers who donate and make available images of gardens for use in The Yellow Book and NGS publicity material. The NGS would like to thank them for their generous donations.

We also thank the garden owners who have kindly submitted images of their gardens.

Unless otherwise stated, photographs are kindly supplied by permission of the garden owner.

The Yellow Book 2013 Production Team: Elna Broe, Linda Ellis, Stephanie Fudge, Rachel Hick, Kali Masure, Elizabeth Milner, Chris Morley, Wendy Morton, Azam Parkar, Hazel Sallis, Jane Sennett, Georgina Waters. With special thanks to our NGS County Volunteers.

Designed by Level Partnership Ltd · Maps designed and produced by Global Mapping © The XYZ Digital Map Co

Data manipulation and image setting by Chat Noir Design, France · Printed in Italy

Published by Constable, an imprint of Constable & Robinson Ltd, 55-56 Russell Square, London WC1B 4HP
www.constablerobinson.com

A catalogue record of this book is available from the British Library.

Typeset in Helvetica Neue font family

The papers used by the NGS are natural recyclable products made from wood grown in sustainable forests.

ISBN 978-1-472106-40-7
ISSN 1365-0572
EAN 9 781905 942008

First published February 2013

If you require this information in alternative formats, please telephone 01483 211535 or email ngs@ngs.org.uk

Garden Visiting Around the World

The National Gardens Scheme is without doubt the largest and oldest of its type in the world but there are others in existence. So if you're heading off on holiday and you're a passionate garden visitor here are the details of other schemes that you can support.

America

GARDEN CONSERVANCY
Publication Open Days Directory
W www.gardenconservancy.org
Visit America's very best rarely seen private gardens. Open Days is a national programme of The Garden Conservancy, a non-profit organisation dedicated to preserving America's gardening heritage.

VIRGINIA'S HISTORIC GARDEN WEEK
21 – 28 April 2013
W www.vagardenweek.org
Tour proceeds fund the restoration and preservation of Virginia's historic gardens.
Every April, visitors are welcomed to more than 250 of Virginia's most beautiful gardens, homes and historic landmarks during "America's Largest Open House". This 8-day statewide event provides visitors a unique opportunity to see unforgettable gardens at the peak of Virginia's springtime colour, as well as beautiful houses sparkling with over 2,000 fabulous flower arrangements created by Garden Club of Virginia members.

Australia

OPEN GARDENS AUSTRALIA
Publication Open Gardens Australia
Contact Richard Barley
E national@opengarden.org.au
W www.opengarden.org.au
Around 600 inspiring gardens drawn from every Australian state and territory including tropical gardens, arid-zone gardens and gardens featuring Australia's unique flora.

Belgium

JARDINS OUVERTS DE BELGIQUE – OPEN TUINEN VAN BELGIË
Publication Catalogue of private Belgian Open Gardens, published annually in March
Contact Dominique Petit-Heymans
E info@jardinsouverts.be
W www.jardinsouverts.be
A non-profit organization founded in 1994. Over 200 remarkable private gardens throughout Belgium open to members. Membership of €25 entitles you to the full-colour yearly agenda, comprising photographs, descriptions, opening dates and access plans of the gardens. Most of the proceeds from entry fees support charities chosen by garden owners.

France

JARDINS ET SANTE
E contact@jardins-sante.org
W www.jardins-sante.org
Founded in 2004, Jardins et Santé is a charitable voluntary association with humanitarian aims. Increasing numbers of gardens open each year across many regions of France. Entry often includes guided tours, exhibitions and concerts. Funds raised from visitor entry fees help finance scientific research in the field of mental illness and also contribute to developing the therapeutic role of the garden, particularly in hospitals and care centres.
Each year the Charity receives appeals from over 50 establishments seeking assistance for the creation of healing gardens. We are happy to be able to contribute towards many of these projects.
Our role as information hub for the growing interest, research and activities in the field of hortitherapy is rapidly gaining momentum. Our most recent Symposium, held under the patronage of the French Ministry of Health, took place in Paris in November 2012. Further details can be found on our website.

Japan

THE N.G.S. JAPAN
Contact Tamie Taniguchi
E tamieta@syd.odn.ne.jp
W www.ngs-jp.org
The N.G.S. Japan was founded in 2001. Most of the proceeds from the entry fees support children's and welfare charities as nominated by owners and Japanese garden conservation. It has run a series of lectures entitled 'Lifestyle & Gardening with Charity' since 2004.

Netherlands

NETHERLANDSE TUINENSTICHTING (DUTCH GARDEN SOCIETY, NTS)
Publication Open Tuinengids, published annually in March.
E info@tuinenstichting.nl
W www.tuinenstichting.nl
Nearly 300 private gardens from all over Holland open on behalf of the Dutch Garden Trust. This is a not-for-profit organisation which was founded in 1980 to protect and restore Dutch gardening heritage consisting of gardens, public parks, urban spaces and cemeteries.

New Zealand

PRIVATE GARDENS OF NEW ZEALAND/ GARDENS TO VISIT
W www.gardenstovisit.co.nz
W www.ruralattractions.co.nz
W www.wineriestovisit.co.nz
The New Zealand websites showcase private gardens of New Zealand which also operate B&Bs and farm stays. In addition some properties can also provide venues for private and corporate hospitality and weddings. Properties may also feature plant, art and sculpture sales, picnics and fishing. Please also check the websites for details of guided, multi-day garden tours.

Scotland

SCOTLAND'S GARDENS
Publication Scotland's Gardens Guide
Contact Paddy Scott
T 0131 226 3714
E info@scotlandsgardens.org
W www.scotlandsgardens.org
Founded in 1931 Scotland's Gardens facilitates the opening of Scotland's finest gardens of all sizes and kinds to the public as a means of raising money for charity. 40% of the funds raised goes to charities nominated by each garden owner whilst 60% net goes to the Scotland's Gardens beneficiaries: Maggie's Cancer Caring Centres, The Queen's Nursing Institute Scotland, The Gardens Fund of The National Trust for Scotland and Perennial.

National Plant Collections

Approximately 70 gardens that open for The National Gardens Scheme are custodians of a National Plant Collection, although this may not always be noted in the garden description. These gardens carry the **NCH** (National Collection Holder) symbol.
The county that appears after the garden name indicates the section of The Yellow Book where the entry can be found.

Plant Heritage 12 Home Farm, Loseley Park, Guildford, Surrey GU3 1HS. Tel: 01483 447540 Website: www.plantheritage.com

ACER (EXCL PALMATUM CVS.), ALNUS, SORBUS
Blagdon
North East

AKEBIA
190 Barnet Road
London

ALNUS & BETULA
Stone Lane Gardens
Devon

ANEMONE NEMOROSA CVS.
Kingston Lacy
Dorset

ANEMONE NEMOROSA, ASTER NOVAE-ANGLIAE, SANGUISORBA
Avondale Nursery
Warwickshire

ARUNCUS & FILIPENDULA
Windy Hall
Cumbria

ASTER (AUTUMN FLOWERING)
The Picton Garden
Herefordshire

ASTILBE AND POLYSTICHUM (FERNS)
Holehird Gardens
Cumbria

ASTILBE, IRIS ENSATA, TULBAGHIA
Marwood Hill
Devon

BRUGMANSIAS
Valducci Flower & Vegetable Gardens
Shropshire

BRUNNERA & OMPHALODES
Hearns House
Oxfordshire

BUDDLEJA & CLEMATIS VITICELLA
Longstock Park
Hampshire

BUXUS
Ickworth House Park & Gardens
Suffolk

CAMELLIA
The Lost Gardens of Heligan
Cornwall

CARPINUS BETULUS CVS.
West Lodge Park
London

CEANOTHUS
Eccleston Square
London

CENTAUREA
Bide-a-Wee Cottage
North East

CENTAUREA AND HELENIUM CVS.
Yew Tree House Garden & Special Perennials Nursery
Cheshire & Wirral

CLEMATIS VITICELLA CVS. AND LAPAGERIA ROSEA (AND NAMED CULTIVARS)
Roseland House
Cornwall

CORIARIA, PARIS, POLYGONATUM
Crûg Farm
Gwynedd & Anglesey

CORNUS
Newby Hall & Gardens
Yorkshire

COTINUS
Bath Priory Hotel
Somerset, Bristol & S Glos

CYCLAMEN (EXCLUDING PERSICUM CVS.)
Higher Cherubeer
Devon

DICENTRA
Boundary Cottage
Yorkshire

DIGITALIS
The Harris Garden
Berkshire

EMBOTHRIUM, EUCRYPHIA, MAGNOLIA SPP., RHODODENDRON FORRESTII
Bodnant Garden
Gwynedd & Anglesey

EUCALYPTUS SPP.
The World Garden at Lullingstone Castle
Kent

EUCALYPTUS, PODOCARPACEAE & ARALIACEAE
Meon Orchard
Hampshire

EUCRYPHIA
Whitstone Farm
Devon

EUONYMUS (DECIDUOUS)
East Bergholt Place - The Place for Plants
Suffolk

EUPHORBIA
University of Oxford Botanic Garden
Oxfordshire

EUPHORBIA (HARDY)
Firvale Allotment Garden
Yorkshire

GALANTHUS
Byndes Cottage
Essex

GEUMS
1 Brickwall Cottages
Kent

GUNNERA
The Mowle
Norfolk

Bromley Hall, Hertfordshire

Bring a bag for plants – help us give more to charity

The Society of Garden Designers

Members of The Society of Garden Designers participating in the NGS in 2013.

FSGD (Fellow of the Society of Garden Designers is awarded to Members of the Society of Garden Designers for exceptional contributions to the Society of Garden Designers or to the profession)

Rosemary Alexander FSGD
Roderick Griffin FSGD
Ian Kitson FSGD
Julie Toll FSGD

MSGD (Member of the Society of Garden Designers is awarded after passing adjudication)

Mhairi Clutson MSGD
Rosemary Coldstream MSGD
Pamela Johnson MSGD
Emma Plunket MSGD
Jilayne Rickards MSGD
Charles Rutherfoord MSGD
Ana Sanchez-Martin MSGD
Tom Stuart-Smith MSGD

Pre-Registered Member (Pre-registered Member is a member working towards gaining Registered Membership)

Selina Botham
Judy Bryant
Fiona Cadwallader
Wendy Cartwright
Virginia von Celsing
Colette Charsley
Anna Dargavel
Dr Sara Gadd
Louise Hardwick
Janette King
Sue Neave
Kate Smart
Helen Thomas
Julia Whiteaway
Susan Young

The Stones & Roses Garden, Lancashire

© Julia Stanley

Garden Index

This index lists gardens alphabetically and gives the Yellow Book county section in which they are to be found.

A

C

Look out for the NGS yellow arrows...

D

E

F

H

N

O

P

T

U

V

W

Y

Z

SOUTHPORT FLOWER SHOW
AUGUST 15–18TH
GARDENING...
...WITH PRIDE
SOUTHPORTFLOWERSHOW.CO.UK

'As good as it gets'
Harden's Guide 2013
SPECTACULAR SURROUNDINGS
A WARM WELCOME
SUPREMELY COMFORTABLE AND STYLISH ROOMS
ONLY TWO HOURS NORTH OF LONDON

deJager
Top Quality, Top Size Bulbs
Flower Bulb Specialists Since 1868
Order direct online at
www.dejager.co.uk
Retail and
Wholesale
Tel: 01622 840229
FOR A FREE CATALOGUE

Dave Ford Tree Care
Complete Arboricultural Service
Tree Surgery with a heart...
Fully Insured
Commercial & Domestic
Free Quotations
Surrey, Sussex...
• Felling
• Pruning
• Stump Removing
• Hedgerow Management
• Planting
• Ongoing Maintenance Programs
T: 01306 611661
www.davefordtreecare.co.uk

Beaulieu's Hidden Gem
FAIRWEATHER'S
GARDEN CENTRE
Fairweather's is a truly inspiring gardening visit. We have been growing plants for over 50 years and are well known for our new introductions.
We offer an outstanding range of home grown plants, including our specialist ranges of Agapanthus, Heuchera and Lavender.
Visit one of our Agapanthus open days to view our fantastic collection on Saturday 20th July and Saturday 3rd August, further details can be found on our website www.fairweathers.co.uk
Also at Fairweather's...
DIG · LEARN · GROW · ENJOY
Patrick's PATCH
Visit Patrick's Patch – our productive vegetable garden where we grow a wide range of vegetables, fruit and cut flowers. Entry by donation!
Steff's Kitchen
Enjoy great home grown cooking in our licenced café.
High Street, Beaulieu, Hampshire, SO42 7YB
Tel: 01590 612307